ALGEBRA 1
TEACHER'S EDITION

Kenneth J. Travers
Professor of
Mathematics Education
University of Illinois
Urbana, Illinois

LeRoy C. Dalton
Mathematics Area
Chairperson
Wauwatosa School District
Wauwatosa, Wisconsin

Katherine P. Layton
Mathematics Teacher
Beverly Hills High School
Beverly Hills, California

Laidlaw Brothers • Publishers
A Division of Doubleday & Company, Inc.
River Forest, Illinois

Sacramento, California • Chamblee, Georgia
Dallas, Texas • Toronto, Canada

CONTENTS OF THE TEACHER'S EDITION

ISBN 0-8445-1839-5

Copyright © 1987 by Laidlaw Brothers, Publishers
A Division of Doubleday & Company, Inc.

Printed in the United States of America
23456789 10 11 12 13 14 15   543210987

A challenging textbook that considers the individual needs of students and teachers

LAIDLAW ALGEBRA 1

LAIDLAW ALGEBRA 1 is a comprehensive course in first-year algebra. This textbook effectively combines fundamentals of algebra with practical applications, providing students with the mathematical tools they need to become productive, successful citizens in our increasingly technological world.

- The content includes traditional algebra topics plus a chapter each on statistics, probability, and trigonometry, as well as additional advanced topics.
- Problem-solving skills and problem-solving strategies are thoroughly developed along with real-world applications, to help students develop algebra concepts and skills within a meaningful context.
- Computer-related activities and materials are included in recognition of the increasing importance of computer technology.
- The program has many provisions for adapting the course to individual needs and interests.

LAIDLAW ALGEBRA 1 leads students through a clear, consistent learning sequence.

The **lesson title** states the topic to be covered.

Important properties and definitions are prominently highlighted to draw attention, and for quick reference.

Clearly labeled **examples** with solutions guide learning.

9.3 Integral Exponents

In Chapter 5, a rule was given for division of powers where a and b are positive integers and $x \neq 0$.

If $a = b$, then $\frac{x^a}{x^b} = 1$.

If $a > b$, then $\frac{x^a}{x^b} = x^{a-b}$.

If $a < b$, then $\frac{x^a}{x^b} = \frac{1}{x^{b-a}}$.

It would be simpler if the rule $\frac{x^a}{x^b} = x^{a-b}$ could be used in all cases—that is, when $a = b$, $a > b$, or $a < b$.

Suppose $\frac{x^a}{x^b} = x^{a-b}$ is used when $a = b$. Then $\frac{x^5}{x^5} = x^{5-5} = x^0$. But you know that $\frac{x^5}{x^5} = 1$. This suggests that x^0 should be defined as 1.

Next consider $\frac{x^a}{x^b} = x^{a-b}$ when $a < b$. Then $\frac{x^2}{x^5} = x^{2-5} = x^{-3}$. But you already know that $\frac{x^2}{x^5} = \frac{1}{x^{5-2}} = \frac{1}{x^3}$. This suggests that x^{-3} should be defined as $\frac{1}{x^3}$.

Therefore, to make the rule $\frac{x^a}{x^b} = x^{a-b}$ true for *all* cases, the following definitions are stated.

Zero Exponent and Negative Integral Exponents	If x is a nonzero real number and b is a positive integer, then $x^0 = 1$, and $x^{-b} = \frac{1}{x^b}$.

EXAMPLES

1 **Rewrite each expression with positive exponents only. Then simplify the result.**

a. $(-6)^{-2} \cdot 4^0$ 　　　　 **b.** $(3a)^{-2}$ 　　　　 **c.** $\frac{x^{-3}}{x^{-5}}$

SOLUTIONS

a. $(-6)^{-2} \cdot 4^0 = \frac{1}{(-6)^2} \cdot 1$

$= \frac{1}{(-6)^2}$

$= \frac{1}{36}$

b. $(3a)^{-2} = \frac{1}{(3a)^2}$

$= \frac{1}{3^2 a^2}$

$= \frac{1}{9a^2}$

c. $\frac{x^{-3}}{x^{-5}} = \frac{\frac{1}{x^3}}{\frac{1}{x^5}}$

$= \frac{1}{x^3} \cdot \frac{x^5}{1}$

$= \frac{x^5}{x^3}$

$= x^{5-3}$

$= x^2$

<table>
<tr><td>Properties of
Integral Exponents</td><td colspan="2">If x and y are nonzero real numbers and a and b are
integers, then</td></tr>
<tr><td></td><td>1. $x^a \cdot x^b = x^{a+b}$</td><td>2. $(xy)^a = x^a y^a$</td></tr>
<tr><td></td><td>3. $\frac{x^a}{x^b} = x^{a-b}$</td><td>4. $\left(\frac{x}{y}\right)^b = \frac{x^b}{y^b}$</td></tr>
</table>

2 Rewrite each expression, using the appropriate property above. Then simplify the result.

a. $(6s)^2 \cdot (6s)^{-5}$

b. $(mn)^{-3}$

c. $\frac{(-4d)^2}{(-4d)^{-3}}$

d. $\left(\frac{8x}{y}\right)^{-2}$

SOLUTIONS

a. $(6s)^2 \cdot (6s)^{-5} = (6s)^{2+(-5)}$
$= (6s)^{-3}$
$= 6^{-3}s^{-3}$
$= \frac{1}{6^3} \cdot \frac{1}{s^3}$
$= \frac{1}{216} \cdot \frac{1}{s^3}$
$= \frac{1}{216s^3}$

b. $(mn)^{-3} = m^{-3}n^{-3}$
$= \frac{1}{m^3} \cdot \frac{1}{n^3}$
$= \frac{1}{m^3 n^3}$

c. $\frac{(-4d)^2}{(-4d)^{-3}} = (-4d)^{2-(-3)}$
$= (-4d)^5$
$= (-4)^5 d^5$
$= -1024d^5$

d. $\left(\frac{8x}{y}\right)^{-2} = \frac{(8x)^{-2}}{y^{-2}}$
$= \frac{8^{-2}x^{-2}}{y^{-2}}$
$= \frac{y^2}{64x^2}$

ORAL EXERCISES

Match each definition or property on the left with the property on the right.

1. $x^0 = 1$

2. $\frac{x^a}{x^b} = x^{a-b}$

3. $x^{-b} = \frac{1}{x^b}$

4. $x^a \cdot x^b = x^{a+b}$

5. $\left(\frac{x}{y}\right)^b = \frac{x^b}{y^b}$

6. $(xy)^a = x^a y^a$

WRITTEN EXERCISES

A. Rewrite each of the following by using the definitions of zero and negative integral exponents:

1. 10^0 **2.** 1^0 **3.** 4^{-2}

4. $(-4)^{-2}$ **5.** 8^0 **6.** $(-8)^0$

7. 9^{-1} **8.** $(-9)^{-1}$ **9.** $10,000^0$

10. $(-12)^0$ **11.** $\left(\frac{a}{b}\right)^{-2}$ **12.** $\left(\frac{3}{4}\right)^{-3}$

Simplify each of the following by using the properties of integral exponents:

13. $(12x)^0$ **14.** $(5x)^{-2}$ **15.** $3^5 \cdot 3^{-2}$

16. $\frac{3^5}{3^2}$ **17.** $(-4)^{-2} \cdot (-4)$ **18.** $(ab)^{-4}$

B. 19. $\frac{(-2)^3}{(-2)^6}$ **20.** $\left(\frac{x}{y}\right)^4$ **21.** $3^{-3} \cdot 3^{-2}$

Rewrite each expression with positive exponents only. Then simplify the result.

22. 6^{-1} **23.** 12^{-1} **24.** a^{-1} **25.** $\left(\frac{1}{3}\right)^{-1}$

26. $\left(\frac{1}{6}\right)^{-1}$ **27.** $\left(\frac{1}{a}\right)^{-1}$ **28.** $\left(\frac{1}{b}\right)^{-1}$ **29.** $\left(\frac{3}{4}\right)^{-1}$

30. $\left(\frac{4}{5}\right)^{-1}$ **31.** $\left(\frac{8}{7}\right)^{-1}$ **32.** $\left(\frac{a}{b}\right)^{-1}$ **33.** $(-5)^{-1}$

34. $(-13)^{-1}$ **35.** $(-a)^{-1}$ **36.** $\left(-\frac{1}{3}\right)^{-1}$ **37.** $\left(-\frac{1}{9}\right)^{-1}$

38. $\left(-\frac{1}{a}\right)^{-1}$ **39.** $\left(-\frac{1}{b}\right)^{-1}$ **40.** $\left(-\frac{3}{4}\right)^{-1}$ **41.** $\left(-\frac{2}{3}\right)^{-1}$

42. $\left(-\frac{a}{b}\right)^{-1}$ **43.** 4^{-3} **44.** 3^{-3} **45.** a^{-3}

46. $(-a)^{-2}$ **47.** $(-b)^{-4}$ **48.** $\frac{1}{x^{-2}}$ **49.** $\frac{1}{y^{-3}}$

Simplify each of the following by using the properties of integral exponents:

50. $(3a)^{-2} \cdot (3a)^{-1}$ **51.** $(4b)^{-1} \cdot (4b)^{-1}$ **52.** $(-5x)^{-2}$

53. $(-2n)^{-3}$ **54.** $\frac{(mn)^{-5}}{(mn)^{-3}}$ **55.** $\frac{(ab)^{-7}}{(ab)^4}$

56. $\left(\frac{3x}{4}\right)^{-2}$ **57.** $\left(\frac{2y}{3}\right)^{-3}$ **58.** $(3ab)^{-2}$

C. 59. $(4xy)^{-3}$ **60.** $\left(\frac{9mn}{4}\right)^0$ **61.** $\left(\frac{7xy}{-3}\right)^0$

62. $\frac{2.4 \times 10^3}{1.2 \times 10^2}$ **63.** $\frac{3.6 \times 10^5}{1.8 \times 10}$ **64.** $\frac{3.9 \times 10^{-6}}{1.3 \times 10^{-8}}$

65. $\frac{6.4 \times 10^{-5}}{1.6 \times 10^{-9}}$ **66.** $\frac{315a^{-3}y^9}{-70a^{-2}y^6}$ **67.** $\frac{156x^{-4}y^9}{-12x^{-6}y^3}$

68. $\frac{52m^3n^{-2}}{4m^{-5}n^4}$ **69.** $\frac{60s^4t^{-4}}{150s^{-4}t^4}$ **70.** $\frac{13x^2y^3z^{-4}}{325x^2y^{-1}}$

Abundant exercises, all covering the lesson topic, assure great flexibility in assigning practice. **Every lesson** has:

Oral Exercises for use in class to review or clarify concepts, or as part of the assignment.

Written Exercises to promote mastery of the lesson topic. Always divided into three groups of increasing difficulty, labeled A, B, and C.

Plus: Cumulative **Mixed Review** is available in the Teacher's Edition margins of every lesson.

Selected Answers in the back of the book provide the answers to all odd-numbered lesson exercises and Chapter Review exercises, to aid study.

The first problem-solving lesson, lesson 1.6, introduces a *5-step method* for solving problems that is used consistently throughout the book. In the *Plan* step, students learn to choose from *strategies* for attacking a problem. In this way LAIDLAW ALGEBRA 1 encourages and guides students in employing an organized, consistent approach to problem solving.

First page of the introductory problem-solving lesson

1.6 Problem Solving—The Five-Step Process

You can use the five steps listed below to help you solve problems.

1. **Understand** the problem. Read carefully to determine what is given and what it is you are to do or to find.

2. **Plan** for solving the problem. Planning can include any of the following **problem-solving strategies:**
   - Make a table.
   - Draw a diagram.
   - Use a formula.
   - Look for a pattern.
   - Write and solve an equation.
   - Use a model.
   - Make a guess and then check the answer.
   - Work backwards.
   - Solve a simpler, but related problem.
   - Use logical reasoning.
   - Use estimation.

   These strategies are introduced throughout the book. Often more than one strategy is used in the same problem. Also, you might use a different set of strategies in solving a given problem than someone else might use.

3. **Solve** the problem. Some problems may require computations at this time; others may require some other method for solving them.

4. **Answer** the problem. The computational result, if there is one, may or may not be the answer to the problem.

5. **Review** the problem. Is there another method you can use to check your answer? Does your answer seem reasonable?

EXAMPLE

Max drew a family tree. He listed himself in the first row, his 2 parents in the second row, and his 4 grandparents in the third row. How many great-great-great-great-great-grandparents did he list in the eighth row?

Understand: *Given:* Max listed himself (1 person) in the first row, his 2 parents in the second row, and his 4 grandparents in the third row.

To find: the number of people listed in the eighth row

Problem-solving lessons throughout LAIDLAW ALGEBRA 1 help students learn to use a variety of strategies to solve increasingly complex problems.

A sample problem-solving lesson (3 pages)

9.9 Problem Solving—Rate Problems

The following formula is used to solve problems involving *rate of work:*

rate of work × time = work completed

$$rt = w$$

EXAMPLES

1 It takes an experienced carpenter 3 days to build a wooden deck on the back house. It takes an apprentice carpenter 4 days to do the same job. How long take them if they work together on the same deck? (Assume that in working tog the carpenters can continue to work at their same rates.)

Understand: *Given:* An experienced carpenter takes 3 days.
An apprentice carpenter takes 4 days.

To find: how many days it will take if they work together

Plan: Since the experienced carpenter can build the deck alone in 3 $\frac{1}{3}$ of the job can be completed in one day. (Rate of work is expressed in terms of the job to be done.) The rate of work apprentice is $\frac{1}{4}$ of the job per day.

Making a Table is a helpful problem-solving strategy that can be here. Let t = time (in days) required for the two carpenters w together to build the deck.

	Rate of work	Time	Work completed	
Experienced carpenter	$\frac{1}{3}$	t	$\frac{t}{3}$	experienced ca part of the job
Apprentice carpenter	$\frac{1}{4}$	t	$\frac{t}{4}$	apprentice carpe part of the job

Solve: $\frac{t}{3} + \frac{t}{4} = 1$ *1 indicates a complete job.*

$$12\left(\frac{t}{3} + \frac{t}{4}\right) = 12 \cdot 1 \quad LCD \text{ is } 12.$$

$$4t + 3t = 12$$
$$7t = 12$$
$$t = 1\frac{5}{7}$$

Answer: The carpenters can complete the deck in $1\frac{5}{7}$ days.

Review: Does it seem reasonable that it will take 2 carpenters worki gether $1\frac{5}{7}$ days to build a deck, if it takes 3 days for one car working alone and 4 days for the other carpenter alo complete the same task?

As you have seen in previous chapters, the following formula is used to solve problems involving *rate of travel:* $rt = d$, where r = rate of travel, t = time, and d = distance traveled.

2 At full throttle, a motorboat traveled 15 miles downstream (with the current) in the same amount of time it took to return 10 miles upstream (against the current). The speed of the boat at full throttle in still water is 30 miles per hour. What is the speed of the current?

Understand: *Given:* The distance traveled is 15 miles downstream and 10 miles upstream in the same amount of time. The rate of travel is 30 miles per hour in still water.

To find: speed of the current

Plan: Since $rt = d$, then $t = \frac{d}{r}$. Let c = rate of current in miles per hour.

	Distance	Rate of travel	Time	
Downstream	15	$30 + c$	$\frac{15}{30 + c}$	*The current increases the rate of travel.*
Upstream	10	$30 - c$	$\frac{10}{30 - c}$	*The current decreases the rate of travel.*

Solve: $\frac{15}{30 + c} = \frac{10}{30 - c}$ *The times are equal.*

$$15(30 - c) = 10(30 + c)$$
$$450 - 15c = 300 + 10c$$
$$150 = 25c$$
$$c = 6$$

Answer: The speed of the current is 6 miles per hour.

Review: Does it seem reasonable that the speed of a river's current is 6 miles per hour when a boat travels 15 miles downstream in the same amount of time it takes to return 10 miles upstream at a constant speed of 30 miles per hour?

ORAL EXERCISES

Use the following problem to answer exercises 1–4:

Edna owns a florist shop. She can arrange the flowers for a wedding in 2 hours. Her helper can do it in 3 hours. How long will it take them if they work together?

1. What is Edna's rate of work? (How much of the job can she do in one hour?)

2. What is her helper's rate of work?

3. If t represents the number of hours it takes them to arrange the flowers together, what expression will represent the work completed by Edna? By her helper?

4. What equation would you use to solve the problem?

The **Problem-Solving Handbook** in the back of the text is a valuable student resource. This section names and describes all the strategies used in the book and gives a sample problem using each. The Handbook also serves as a source of additional problems to solve.

A sample page from
Problem-Solving Handbook

PROBLEM-SOLVING HANDBOOK

The following list of strategies is useful in solving a great variety of problems:
- Make a table.
- Draw a diagram.
- Use a formula.
- Look for a pattern.
- Write and solve an equation.
- Use a model.
- Make a guess and then check the answer.
- Work backwards.
- Solve a simpler but related problem.
- Use logical reasoning.
- Use estimation.

It is important for you to realize that more than one strategy is often used in solving a given problem. It is entirely possible that you might solve a problem by using a different set of strategies than someone else. To help you understand these problem-solving strategies, a brief description of each one is given, as well as a problem that might be solved by using the given strategy. A hint is given as to how you might solve each problem, but the work is left to you.

Make a Table

This strategy is useful in organizing the given information into a more understandable form that makes it easier to find missing or superfluous information or to recognize a pattern.

Example:

A window decorator has the following sweaters and vests for a display: a red long-sleeved sweater, a white vest, a black vest, a black long-sleeved sweater, a blue vest, a

white long-sleeved sweater, and a red vest. The decorator wants to have one long-sleeved sweater and one vest of each of the four colors (red, white, black, and blue). Which colors of sweaters or vests are missing?

HINT: Make a table as follows:

	Red	White	Black	Blue
Sweater	X	X	X	
Vest	X	X	X	X

Draw a Diagram

Often it is helpful to draw a sketch, a geometric figure, a number line, or any other diagram so that the relationships can be visualized more easily and a method for solving the problem will become more apparent.

Examples:

Four people, Lou, Marian, Pete, and Rich, each want to play one game of tennis with each of the other people. How many different pairings are possible?

HINT: One way to solve this problem is to draw a point to stand for each person and then connect the points in as many ways as possible to determine the possible number of pairings. Let *L* stand for Lou, *M* for Marian, *P* for Pete, and *R* for Rich.

Use a Formula

This strategy is useful in situations in which a standard mathematical formula might apply.

Use the following problem to complete the table below and to answer exercise 6.

A fishing boat traveled 25 miles downstream in the same amount of time it took to return 15 miles upstream. If the speed of the boat in still water is 12 miles per hour, what is the speed of the current? Let *c* = the speed of the current.

5.

	Distance	Rate	Time
Downstream			
Upstream			

6. What equation would you use to solve this problem?

WRITTEN EXERCISES

A. Solve each problem.

1. Eduardo and his brother each has his own lawn mower. If it takes Eduardo 2 hours to mow a certain lawn and it takes his brother 3 hours to mow the same lawn, how long will it take them working together?

2. A fence can be painted with a sprayer in 3 hours. It takes 5 hours to paint the fence with a brush. How long will it take to paint the fence, using both the sprayer and the brush?

3. An airplane cruises at 140 miles per hour in still air. At that speed, the plane flew 400 miles with the wind in the same amount of time it took to fly 300 miles back (against the wind). What is the speed of the wind, assuming that it remains constant?

4. Heather and George rented a small boat with an electric motor. The top speed of the boat in still water was 3 miles per hour. At top speed, an 8-mile trip downstream took the same amount of time as a 2-mile trip upstream. What was the rate of the current?

B. 5. At cruising speed, an airplane flew 500 kilometers with the wind in the same amount of time it took to fly 400 kilometers against the wind. If the constant speed of the wind is 20 kilometers per hour, what is the cruising speed of the airplane?

6. A motorboat traveled 90 kilometers downstream in the same amount of time it took to return 40 kilometers upstream. The rate of the current is 5 kilometers per hour. What is the speed of the boat in still water?

7. Two typists working together can type a manuscript in 5 hours. The faster typist can complete the manuscript in 9 hours. How long will it take the slower typist?

8. A swimming pool can be filled in 15 hours, using a small hose. The same pool can be filled in 12 hours, using a larger hose. How long will it take to fill the pool if both hoses are used at the same time?

C. 9. A water-storage tank can be filled by one pipe in 32 minutes and by another pipe in 16 minutes. A third pipe can empty the tank in 24 minutes. How long will it take to fill an empty tank if all three pipes are operating?

10. A railroad tank car can be filled in $6\frac{6}{7}$ hours, using two pipes. If one pipe alone can fill the tank car in 12 hours, how long will it take the other pipe alone to fill it?

An additional optional feature, titled **Challenge,** appears in every chapter and usually poses *non-routine problems* to further broaden problem-solving skills. See pages 50, 73, 111, etc.

CHALLENGE

There are two more books on top of your algebra book than there are beneath it. The pile of books has three times as many books as there are books beneath the algebra book. How many books are on top of your algebra book?

A full-page optional **Computer** feature in every chapter involves students in applying computer skills to topics from the chapter. See pages 25, 63, 99, etc.

Computer Handbook in the back of the text includes background information plus a dictionary of computer commands, to help students when performing the activities.

More Computer Activities are available as blackline masters in the Teacher's Resources or as spirit duplicating masters.

COMPUTER

Can a computer be used to show the solution set of an inequality? The program below, written for an Apple II computer, does just that.

(If your computer is not an Apple, see the Computer Handbook on pages 541–546 for Applesoft commands that must be modified for other computers.)

```
10 HOME: PRINT "                    Y": PRINT
20 FOR I = 1 TO 20: PRINT "                    !": NEXT
25 PRINT: PRINT "                    Y";
30 VTAB 12: HTAB 1: PRINT "X ----------------+--------
   -------- X"
40 REM Y >= 2X + 1 IS INEQUALITY
50 LET BN = 2: REM 1 = "<=", 2 = ">=", 3 = "="
60 FOR Y = - 10 TO 10: FOR X = - 16 TO 16
70 IF (X = (Y + 1) / 2) THEN GOSUB 140
80 ON BN GOTO 90,110: GOTO 120
90 IF (X < (Y + 1) / 2) THEN GOSUB 140: GOTO 120
100 GOTO 120
110 IF (X > (Y + 1) / 2) THEN GOSUB 140
120 NEXT: NEXT
130 GOTO 130
140 IF X < > 0 AND Y < > 0 THEN VTAB Y + 12: HTAB X +
    19: PRINT ".";
150 RETURN
```

EXERCISES

1. What does the variable BN in line 50 do? Make it 1 or 3 or some other number; now what are the results?
2. Change the equations in lines 40, 70, 90, and 110 to plot another inequality. Enter and RUN the program. What are the results?
3. Why does the program need three versions of the equation to plot the solution set?
4. What is the purpose of the testing on line 140 before printing the point?

Calculator is a frequent textbook feature that promotes students' use of calculators in exercises on chapter topics. See pages 17, 39, 148, etc.

For correlated computer courseware see page T13.

CALCULATOR

You can use a calculator to check whether a given ordered pair is a solution of a system of equations.

Example: The solution for Example 2 in Section 8.5 is (−1, 2). This can be checked as follows:

ENTER   DISPLAY

$4x + 5y = 6$

4 [×] 1 [+/−] [=] [M+] 5 [×] 2 [+] [RM] [=]   *6*

$6x − 7y = −20$

6 [×] 1 [+/−] [=] [M+] 7 [+/−] [×] 2 [+] [RM] [=]   *−20*

EXERCISES

Use a calculator to check the following solutions. If a given solution is incorrect, give the correct solution.

1. $3x + y = 10$ (3, 1)
   $2x + y = 7$

2. $x + 3y = 14$ (5, 3)
   $x − 2y = −1$

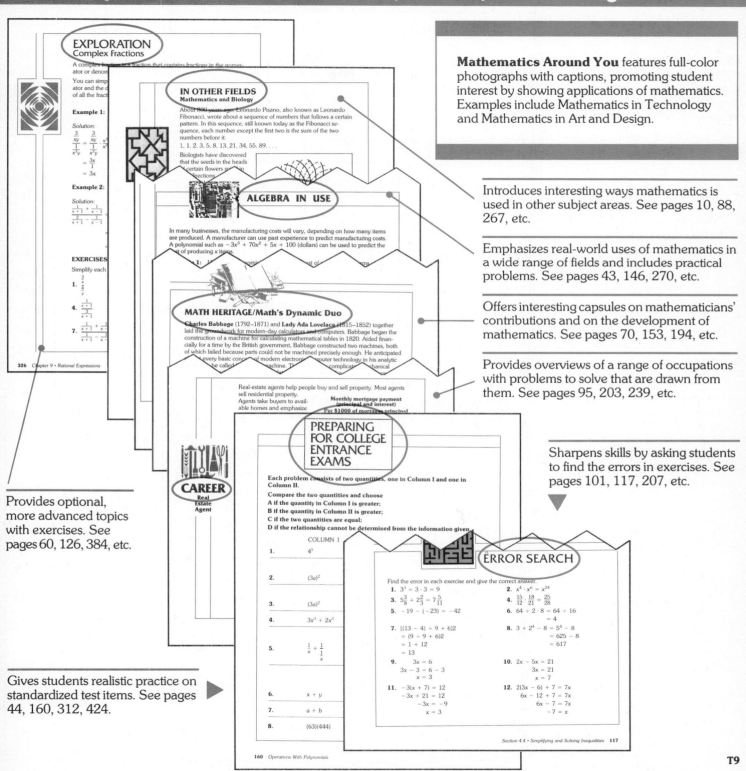

EXPLORATION
Complex Fractions

A complex fraction is a fraction that contains fractions in the numerator or denominator.

You can simplify a complex fraction by ... the ... of all the fractions ...

Example 1:

Solution:

$$\frac{\frac{3}{xy}}{\frac{1}{x^2y}} = \frac{\frac{3}{xy}}{\frac{1}{x^2y}} \cdot \frac{x^2y}{x^2y}$$

$$= \frac{3x}{1}$$

$$= 3x$$

Example 2:

Solution:

$$\frac{\frac{1}{x+1} + \frac{1}{x-1}}{\frac{2}{x+1} - \frac{1}{x-1}}$$

EXERCISES

Simplify each ...

1. $\frac{\frac{3}{x}}{\frac{4}{y}}$

4. $\frac{\frac{1}{x+1}}{\frac{2}{x+1}}$

7. $\frac{\frac{1}{x+1} + \frac{1}{x-1}}{\frac{1}{x+1} - \frac{1}{x-1}}$

326 Chapter 9 • Rational Expressions

IN OTHER FIELDS
Mathematics and Biology

About 800 years ago, Leonardo Pisano, also known as Leonardo Fibonacci, wrote about a sequence of numbers that follows a certain pattern. In this sequence, still known today as the Fibonacci sequence, each number except the first two is the sum of the two numbers before it:

1, 1, 2, 3, 5, 8, 13, 21, 34, 55, 89. . . .

Biologists have discovered that the seeds in the heads of certain flowers ... in ... directions.

ALGEBRA IN USE

In many businesses, the manufacturing costs will vary, depending on how many items are produced. A manufacturer can use past experience to predict manufacturing costs. A polynomial such as $-3x^3 + 70x^2 + 5x + 100$ (dollars) can be used to predict the ... of producing x items.

MATH HERITAGE/Math's Dynamic Duo

Charles Babbage (1792–1871) and **Lady Ada Lovelace** (1815–1852) together laid the groundwork for modern-day calculators and computers. Babbage began the construction of a machine for calculating mathematical tables in 1820. Aided financially for a time by the British government, Babbage constructed two machines, both of which failed because parts could not be machined precisely enough. He anticipated ... every basic concept of modern electronic computer technology in his analytic ... he called ... machine. Th... complicat... mechanical ...

Real-estate agents help people buy and sell property. Most agents sell residential property. Agents take buyers to available homes and emphasize ...

Monthly mortgage payment (principal and interest) Per $1000 of mortgage principal

CAREER
Real Estate Agent

PREPARING FOR COLLEGE ENTRANCE EXAMS

Each problem consists of two quantities, one in Column I and one in Column II.

Compare the two quantities and choose

A if the quantity in Column I is greater;
B if the quantity in Column II is greater;
C if the two quantities are equal;
D if the relationship cannot be determined from the information given.

	COLUMN I
1.	4^5
2.	$(3a)^2$
3.	$(3a)^2$
4.	$3x^4 + 2x^3$
5.	$\frac{1}{x} + \frac{1}{\frac{1}{x}}$
6.	$x + y$
7.	$a + b$
8.	$(63)(444)$

160 Operations With Polynomials

ERROR SEARCH

Find the error in each exercise and give the correct answer.

1. $3^3 = 3 \cdot 3 = 9$
2. $x^4 \cdot x^6 = x^{24}$
3. $5\frac{3}{8} + 2\frac{2}{3} = 7\frac{5}{11}$
4. $\frac{15}{12} - \frac{18}{21} = \frac{25}{28}$
5. $-19 - (-23) = -42$
6. $64 \div 2 \cdot 8 = 64 \div 16$
   $= 4$
7. $[(13 - 4) \div 9 + 6]2$
   $= (9 \div 9 + 6)2$
   $= 1 + 12$
   $= 13$
8. $3 + 2^4 - 8 = 5^4 - 8$
   $= 625 - 8$
   $= 617$
9. $3x = 6$
   $3x - 3 = 6 - 3$
   $x = 3$
10. $2x - 5x = 21$
    $3x = 21$
    $x = 7$
11. $-3(x + 7) = 12$
    $-3x + 21 = 12$
    $-3x = -9$
    $x = 3$
12. $2(3x - 6) + 7 = 7x$
    $6x - 12 + 7 = 7x$
    $6x - 7 = 7x$
    $-7 = x$

Section 4.4 • Simplifying and Solving Inequalities **117**

Mathematics Around You features full-color photographs with captions, promoting student interest by showing applications of mathematics. Examples include Mathematics in Technology and Mathematics in Art and Design.

Introduces interesting ways mathematics is used in other subject areas. See pages 10, 88, 267, etc.

Emphasizes real-world uses of mathematics in a wide range of fields and includes practical problems. See pages 43, 146, 270, etc.

Offers interesting capsules on mathematicians' contributions and on the development of mathematics. See pages 70, 153, 194, etc.

Provides overviews of a range of occupations with problems to solve that are drawn from them. See pages 95, 203, 239, etc.

Sharpens skills by asking students to find the errors in exercises. See pages 101, 117, 207, etc.

Provides optional, more advanced topics with exercises. See pages 60, 126, 384, etc.

Gives students realistic practice on standardized test items. See pages 44, 160, 312, 424.

Continuous Maintenance, Review, and Testing

Skills Maintenance, in every chapter, lets students review skills from preceding chapters or previous courses. See pages 7, 35, 108, etc.

SKILLS MAINTENANCE

Write each of the following as an algebraic expression:

1. the product of a, b, and c
2. five times the sum of a and b
3. the difference of -12 and x
4. the sum of $7a$ and $\frac{b}{9}$

Evaluate if $x = 8$ and $y = -4$.

5. $2xy$
6. $(x + y)(x - y)$
7. xy^2
8. $(2y)^2$
9. $\frac{x^2}{y}$
10. $\frac{6}{x - y}$

Simplify.

11. $2 \cdot 3^2 - 3 \cdot 4 + 5$
12. $(6 - 4)^2 + (3 + 2)^1$
13. $\frac{(4 + 5)^2}{3}$
14. $3(4 -$

Complet

$A = \{1, 2$

17. -3
20. $\{0\}$

Find eac
23. $7 +$
26. -0.

Find each
29. $15 -$
32. -52

Find each
35. $-2($
38. $-0.$

Find each
41. -28
44. $-4.$

Solve ea
47. $a +$
50. $-8x$

Self-Quiz during each chapter gives students a diagnostic tool to check their mastery of the chapter so far. See pages 13, 46, 82, etc.

Find each difference.

7. $21 - 35$
10. $76 - (-109)$
13. $-21 - (-35)$
16. $149 - 76$
19. $-35 - 21$
22. $-115 - (-53)$

B. 25. $(19 - 25) - 16$
27. $19 - (25 - 16)$
29. $(-16 - 53) - (-1$
31. $-16 - [53 - (-18$
33. $0.93 - (-0.5)$
36. $\frac{5}{9} - \frac{2}{9}$
39. $-\frac{1}{7} - \left(-\frac{2}{5}\right)$
42. $-\frac{2}{9} - \left(-\frac{1}{2}\right)$

45. Compare your answe
46. Compare your answe

Write an algebraic expr
47. a number decreased

C. 49. sale price of an item
50. the final cost of an ite
51. Find $x - 3.7$ if $x = 2$
53. Find $507 - x$ if $x =$
55. Find $x - y$ if $x = -$

288 Chap

SELF-QUIZ

Complete.

1. Let $A = \{1, 2, 3\}$ and $B =$

Which symbol, $=$, $<$, or $>$,

2. -6 ● $-\frac{12}{2}$
3.

Complete.

6. $|-3|$ ● $\frac{3}{}$

46 Chapter 2 • Real Numbers

2-page **Chapter Review** at chapter-end includes both a *vocabulary list* and review *exercises,* all keyed to the lessons for further study if needed. See pages 26, 64, 100, etc.

CHAPTER 3 REVIEW

VOCABULARY

addition property of equality (3.2)
division property of equality (3.3)
equation (3.1)
equivalent sentences (3.1)
formula (3.8)
multiplication property of equality (3.3)
open sentence (3.1)
repeating decimal (3.4)
replacement set (3.1)
solution set (3.1)
subtraction property of equality (3.2)
terminating decimal (3.4)

REVIEW EXERCISES

3.1 **Solve. The replacement set is $\{6, 7, 8\}$.**

1. $x + 6 = 13$
2. $9 + y = 15$
3. $13 = a + 5$
4.

3.2 Solve.
7.

3.3 13. $-$
16. $0.$

3.4 Renam
19. $\frac{9}{20}$

Renam
23. $0.$

3.5 Solve
27. $6a$

29. $5x$
31. 42

3.6 33. $6x$
35. $\frac{1}{3}$
37. $\frac{4}{9}r$

Renam
39. $6a$
41. $3r$
43. $4.$

Solve
16. $3x$
19. $9n$
22. $3x$
25. $2(4$

Solve.
28. A h
Cel

29. A s
was

30. Dur
list

102 Cha

CHAPTER 3 TEST

Which term best completes each sentence?

equation   open sentence   equivalent   replacement set   solution set

1. The set of numbers that makes an open sentence true is a(n) _____
2. Open sentences that have the same solution set are said to be _____
3. An algebraic sentence in which two expressions are connected by the symbol $=$ is called a(n) _____

Chapter Test follows the Review and can provide helpful preparation for formal assessment. See pages 28, 66, 102, etc.

CUMULATIVE REVIEW CHAPTERS 1–7

Choose the correct answer.

1. Name the coefficient in $2x^3y^4$.
   A. 3   **B.** 2   **C.** 7   **D.** 4
2. Evaluate $x^2(xy)^3$ if $x = 4$ and $y = -3$.
   A. 288   **B.** 27,648   **C.** -288 **D.** $-27,648$
3. Name the property illustrated by the following: $xy = yx$.
   A. Commutative property of multiplication   **B.** Associative property of multiplication
   C. Distributive property   **D.** Identity property of multiplication
4. Simplify $-(9)^2 - 4 + 2.3(0.8)$.
   A. -83.16 **B.** 80.1   **C.** -81.9 **D.** None of these
5. Give the degree of $3x^2y^4$.
   A. 3   **B.** 2   **C.** 4   **D.** 6
6. Which set describes the set of whole numbers?
   A. $\{1, 2, 3, 4, \ldots\}$ **B.** $\{0, 1, 2, 3, 4, \ldots\}$
   C. $\{\ldots, -3, -2, -1, 0, 1, 2, 3, \ldots\}$ **D.** $\{0, 2, 4, 6, 8, \ldots\}$
7. If $x < 0$, then $|x| =$ _____.
   A. $-x$ **B.** x **C.** 0   **D.** None of these
8. Simplify $-249 + 53$.
   A. 216   **B.** -196 **C.** 302   **D.** -302
9. Simplify $-123 - 78$.
   A. -45 **B.** 201   **C.** 45   **D.** -201
10. Simplify $-18(12)(-15)$.
    A. -231 **B.** -3240 **C.** 3240   **D.** 54
11. Simplify $-\frac{7}{8} \div \frac{13}{16}$.
    A. $-\frac{14}{13}$ **B.** $-\frac{91}{128}$ **C.** $-\frac{13}{14}$ **D.** None of these
12. Solve $0.5 = y + 3.91$.
    A. -3.41 **B.** 3.96   **C.** 4.41   **D.** None of these
13. Solve $-8.05 - x = 15.9$.
    A. 7.85   **B.** 23.95   **C.** -7.85 **D.** -23.95
14. Solve $\frac{3}{8}x = -15$.
    A. 40   **B.** $5\frac{5}{8}$ **C.** $-5\frac{5}{8}$ **D.** -40

Four **Cumulative Reviews** on chapters 1-3, 1-7, 8-11, and 8-15 provide maintenance and are entirely multiple-choice. See pages 103, 247, 395, 521.

The extended margins provide daily teaching help adjacent to the full-size student pages (most answers are overprinted on the pages):

Objective(s) of each lesson.

Teacher's Notes: page references to the Teaching Suggestions in the Manual.

Classroom Examples to assist in development of the lesson topic.

Mixed Review to continuously maintain concepts and skills previously introduced.

OBJECTIVE
Solve problems by using a system of two equations in two variables.

TEACHER'S NOTES
See p. T31.

CLASSROOM EXAMPLE
Susan's class spent $43.20 on 41 flowchart templates and packages of graph paper. The templates cost $0.90 each and the paper cost $1.25 per package. How many of each did the class buy?
Let x = the number of templates.
Let y = the number of packages of paper.
Then $x + y = 41$ and $0.90x + 1.25y = 43.20$.
$90(x + y) = 90(41)$
$100(0.90x + 1.25y) = 100(43.20)$
$90x + 90y = 3690$
$-(90x + 125y = 4320)$
$ -35y = -630$
$ y = 18$
$x + 18 = 41$
$ x = 23$
The class bought 23 templates and 18 packages of graph paper.

MIXED REVIEW
Factor completely.
1. $36x^2 - 9y^2$
   $9(2x - y)(2x + y)$
2. $12p + 48q$ $12(p + 4q)$
3. $8y^2 + 6y - 2$
   $2(4y - 1)(y + 1)$

8.6 | **Problem Solving**

Sometimes a problem that can be solved by using one equation in one variable can be solved more easily by using a system of two equations in two variables.

EXAMPLES

1 The owner of a hobby shop spent $1250 on 9000 miniature cars and trucks. The cars cost $0.13 each and the trucks cost $0.15 each. How many of each did she buy?

Understand: *Given:* $1250 was spent on 9000 items.
Some of the items cost $0.13 and some cost $0.15.
To find: how many of each item the owner bought

Plan: Let c = the number of cars. Let t = the number of trucks.
Then, $c + t = 9000$ and $0.13c + 0.15t = 1250$.

Solve: $13(c + t) = 13(9000)$ $\longrightarrow$ $13c + 13t = 117{,}000$
$100(0.13c + 0.15t) = 100(1250)$ $\longrightarrow$ $-(13c + 15t = 125{,}000)$
Multiplying by 100 clears ${-2t = -8000}$
the equation of decimals. $ t = 4000$
$c + 4000 = 9000$
$ c = 5000$

Answer: The owner bought 5000 cars and 4000 trucks.

ORAL EXERCISES

Translate each problem into a system of equations.

1. A 180-foot length of rope must be cut into two pieces. One piece has to be three times longer than the other. How long will each piece be?

2. Twice the length of a rectangle is equal to five times the width. The perimeter of the rectangle is 77 meters. Find the length and the width.

3. For an experiment, 40 volunteers have to be divided into two groups. One group must have 4 more than 5 times the number of people in the other group. How many people should be in each group?

4. In an algebra class of 28 students, the number of girls is 5 less than twice the number of boys. How many boys and how many girls are in the class?

WRITTEN EXERCISES

A. 1–4. Solve Oral Exercises 1–4.

B. Solve.

5. The measure of one angle is 18 more than twice another. If the angles are supplementary, find the measure of each angle.

6. The length of a rectangle is 3 inches more than the width. The perimeter is 42 inches. Find the length and the width.

7. The perimeter of a rectangle is 14 centimeters. Twice the width is equal to $\frac{1}{3}$ the length. Find the length and the width.   length = 6 cm, width = 1 cm

8. There are sixteen coins in a piggy bank. If the coins are all nickels and dimes and they total $1.05, how many of each are there?   5 dimes, 11 nickels

9. A basketball center made 23 baskets for a total score of 34. How many field goals did the center make? (A field goal is worth two points and a free throw is worth one point.)

10. During a 24-hour period in Alaska, the period of daylight was 18 hours longer than the period of darkness. How long was the period of darkness?

C. 11. A bank clerk gave a customer change for $200. The customer requested that the change be in singles and fives. If the customer received 136 bills, did the customer receive the correct change?

12. The perimeter of an isosceles triangle is 26 inches. The base is 2 inches longer than the length of a side. Find the length of a side of the triangle.

13. A car left a gas station and headed east. A second car left the gas station at the same time and headed west. The second car was traveling 10 kilometers per hour faster than the first car. After 3 hours the cars were 300 kilometers apart. What was the speed of each car?

14. Complementary angles are two angles whose measures have the sum of 90. If two angles are complementary and the measure of one is 16 more than the other, what are the angle measures?

4. $4x^2 + 8xy + 4y^2$
   $4(x + y)^2$

5. $6a(x - y) + b(x - y)$
   $(6a + b)(x - y)$

TEACHER'S RESOURCE MASTERS
Practice Master 34, Part 2
Quiz 15

ASSIGNMENT GUIDE
Minimum
1–9 odd
Regular
5–9
Maximum
8–10, 11–13 odd

PROBLEM-SOLVING STRATEGIES
Use a Formula (2, 6, 7, 12).
Draw a Diagram (2, 6, 7, 12, 13, 14).
Write an Equation (1–14).

Additional Answers
See p. T60.

Page references to all masters in Teacher's Resources.

Assignment Guide of exercises for 3 course levels.

Page references to suggested **Enrichment Activities** in the Manual.

Additional Answers to lesson exercises.

Problem-Solving Strategies that are helpful in certain exercises.

References to the correlated **computer courseware.**

The Teacher's Manual beginning on page T14 includes all these resources:

- **A Daily Lesson Assignment Guide** for 3 suggested course levels.

- A guide to the **supplementary materials.**

- **Performance Objectives** for every lesson.

- **Enrichment Activities** for every chapter, for use as the teacher decides.

ENRICHMENT ACTIVITIES

Enrichment Activity 1

Find the pattern for squaring a 2-digit number whose units digit is 5.

$(75)^2 = 5625$ $(45)^2 = 2025$
$(65)^2 = ?$ $(25)^2 = ?$ $(95)^2 = ?$

Answer $(75)^2 = 5625$
These digits depend on the tens digit of the original number. These digits will always be 25.

Let k represent the tens digit in the original number. In this example, let $k = 7$; then $k + 1 = 8$. The product $k(k + 1)$, or $7(8)$, is to the left of the 25 in the product. The following explanation uses the expanded form of the original number. Let k represent the tens digit in the original number. Then $10k + 5$ is the expanded form of the number.
$(10k + 5)^2 = 100k^2 + 100k + 25$
$= 100k(k + 1) + 25$
Using $(75)^2 = (10k + 5)^2$

legs was 14 more than twice the number of heads. Find the number of cows.

Answer Let $x =$ the number of cows and $y =$ the number of chickens.

Then $x + y =$ the number of heads and $4x + 2y =$ the number of legs.
$4x + 2y - 14 = 2x + 2y$
$2x = 14$
$x = 7$
So, there are 7 cows in the group.

Enrichment Activity 3

Find the missing digits in the division. There is only one solution.

$5\,\overline{)\,1}$ ...

Enricl...

1. Simpl...

Answer

2. Simpl...
 7) +

Answer

3. Write...
 ber of...

Answer

4. Simpl...

Answer

5. In a ...

mentally. Point out that the exercises include factoring techniques from previous sections.

6.7 Point out that in Example 3 students should recognize the perfect-square trinomial after removing the common monomial factor of -1.

6.8 Many students will find that solving quadratic equations by using factoring and the zero product property is a logical extension of solving linear equations. At this point you do not need to identify these equations as quadratic.

6.9 Encourage students to draw a sketch for each problem, if possible.

7·Relations and Functions

Overview This chapter begins with students graphing ordered pairs on a coordinate plane and then graphing two-variable equations. The term *relation* is defined, and different ways to represent a relation are presented. Next the concept of *function* is defined and ways for writing a function rule are shown. Slope is introduced, and students find the slope of a line, using the coordinates of two points on the line. Also students draw the graph of a line, given a point on the line and the slope of the line. The slope-intercept form of a straight line is presented. Students then write equations of lines if for any line they know the slope and the y-intercept, the slope and one point on the line, or two points on the line. The chapter concludes with a problem-solving section involving the concepts of velocity and acceleration, using linear equations.

Teaching Suggestions

7.1 When you introduce the concept of graphing points in a coordinate system, use a grid, not just a sketch of a set of axes. Have students strive for accuracy. Adequate tools include graph paper, a straightedge, and a sharpened pencil. Have students label the axes by placing the numbers adjacent to the lines. Use the basic vocabulary of graphing to help students master correct terminology. Your lesson should include plotting points on the axes as well as identification of the quadrants.

In the C exercises, students may choose any x, and then solve for y. Encourage them to choose both positive and negative values for x. Some equations will not have domains as the entire set of real numbers, for example: $x^2 + y^2 = 4$, $x = y^2$, or $x = |y|$.

7.2 In the graphing of a linear equation, usually only a few solutions are plotted; however, point out that a linear equation has an infinite number of solutions. The graph represents all these solutions. When you demonstrate such a graph, place arrowheads on the endpoints of the segment you draw, and remind students that the graph is infinite. Also, when you plot points for the class, you might occasionally misplot a point to demonstrate that such a mistake will be spotted when you try to connect all the points with a straightedge.

7.3 Stress that all sets of ordered pairs are relations, but only certain sets of ordered pairs are functions. That is, every function is a relation, but not every relation is a function.

Also, some relations have the set of real numbers as both domain and range, for example, $\{(x, y) : x + y = 1\}$. Other relations have finite domains and ranges, for example, $\{(1, 2), (3, 4), (5, 7)\}$.

Another way to check a given set of ordered pairs to see whether or not it is a function is to look at the x values. If any of them are identical, then the relation is not a function. If all the x values are different, then the relation is a function. The vertical-line test serves the same purpose when considering a relation that has already been graphed.

7.4 Notations of the form $f(x) = 3x + 4$, $f:x \to 3x + 4$, and $y = 3x + 4$ are merely three ways of expressing the same rule for the function f.

7.5 Most students find it easy to think of slope as *rise over run*. When finding slope, they should focus on the importance of order, both in the division and the subtractions. Make sure the students do not misinterpret subscripts for exponents.

A useful demonstration would be to start with a linear equation such as $3x + y = 6$, and find four ordered pairs that satisfy the equation. Use these ordered pairs in different combinations to find the slope of the line. Verify that the value of the slope is always the same.

Provide students with practice in identifying slopes by examining graphs of lines. Make sure that you include cases with slopes that are positive, negative, zero, and undefined.

While slope is a concept that is presently being related only to graphs of linear functions, you might mention that in advanced math courses, the slope of curves is discussed by examining the behavior of the graph

- **Chapter Overviews.**

- **Teaching Suggestions** for every lesson.

- **Additional Answers** to text exercises.

Teacher's Resources. A 3-ring binder that gives you all these blackline masters plus dividers to organize them:

Practice for every lesson

Enrichment activities to assign when appropriate

Computer activities

Tests
- Chapter Tests (free-response and multiple-choice versions)
- Quizzes (two on each chapter)
- Cumulative Tests (quarterly and semester tests, two versions of each, all multiple-choice)

Teaching Aids including reproducible tables, grid paper, etc.

Classroom Management tools including Homework Record, Practice Master Record, Quiz and Test Record, Correlation Chart of Teacher's Resources to textbook, and more.

Spirit Duplicating Masters of the Practice, Enrichment, and Computer activities.

Spirit Duplicating Masters of the Tests and Quizzes.

Solutions Manual giving the teacher detailed solutions to all textbook exercises.

Correlated Software for computer-assisted instruction. Entitled *Graphing in the Coordinate Plane,* includes two disks with a Teacher's Manual. Students graph equations and inequalities and write equations from graphs.

OTHER COMPREHENSIVE TEXTBOOKS AVAILABLE

LAIDLAW GEOMETRY

LAIDLAW ALGEBRA 2 WITH TRIGONOMETRY

DAILY LESSON GUIDE

Assignment Guide

Day	Minimum Course		Regular Course		Maximum Course	
1	1.1	1–13 odd, 17–37	1.1	15–41 odd, 43–56	1.1	23–33 odd, 35–56
2	1.2	1–18, 19–61 odd	1.2	1–29 odd, 34–58	1.2	24–29, 34–67
3	1.3	1–12, 13–23 odd	1.3	1–11 odd, 13–24	1.3	16–33
4	1.4	1–59 odd	1.4	31–60	1.4	36–38, 43–69
5	1.5	1–15, 22–27, 29–35 odd	1.5	1–15 odd, 22–38	1.5	18–42
6	1.6	1–10	1.6	3–12	1.6	7–16
7	Chapter Review		Chapter Review		Chapter Review	
8	Chapter Test		Chapter Test		Chapter Test	
9	Problem-Solving Handbook		Problem-Solving Handbook		Problem-Solving Handbook	
10	2.1	1–26, 27–43 odd	2.1	13–46, 47–55 odd	2.1	28–62
11	2.2	1–16, 17–27 odd	2.2	9–30	2.2	15–36
12	2.3	1–16, 17–39 odd	2.3	9–15, 17–39, 44	2.3	17–26, 32–49
13	2.4	5–9, 18–23, 30–48	2.4	11–17 odd, 24–35, 40–51, 61, 65	2.4	31–51, 53–69 odd
14	2.5	1–47 odd	2.5	25–48	2.5	33–56
15	2.6	1–12, 13–21 odd, 29–45	2.6	35–68	2.6	23–61 odd, 63–76
16	2.7	1–13 odd, 19–27 odd, 28–39	2.7	19–42	2.7	19–41 odd, 43–54
17	2.8	1–5 odd, 6–10	2.8	5–12	2.8	7–14
18	2.9	1–18	2.9	9–27	2.9	13–29
19	Chapter Review		Chapter Review		Chapter Review	
20	Chapter Test		Chapter Test		Chapter Test	
21	Problem-Solving Handbook		Problem-Solving Handbook		Problem-Solving Handbook	
22	3.1	1–12, 13–27 odd	3.1	16–35	3.1	13–35 odd, 37–44

Day	Minimum Course		Regular Course		Maximum Course	
23	3.2	1–11 odd, 13–37	3.2	15–35 odd, 36–53	3.2	25–53
24	3.3	1–24, 29–39 odd	3.3	13–42	3.3	23–39 odd, 40–60
25	3.4	1–16, 21–24, 29–32	3.4	13–24, 29–40	3.4	17–24, 29–32, 37–48
26	3.5	1–11 odd, 13–31	3.5	13–39 odd, 41–50	3.5	19–37, 41–52
27	3.6	1–53 odd	3.6	19–51	3.6	13–53 odd, 55–62, 65–68
28	3.7	1–10, 19–36	3.7	11–38	3.7	11–39 odd, 41–53
29	3.8	1–8, 11–17 odd	3.8	11–22	3.8	13–18, 21–26
30	3.9	1–6, 7–13 odd	3.9	7–16	3.9	8–17
31	3.10	1–7 odd, 9–14	3.10	9–18	3.10	9–15 odd, 17–22
32	Chapter Review		Chapter Review		Chapter Review	
33	Chapter Test		Chapter Test		Chapter Test	
34	Problem-Solving Handbook		Problem-Solving Handbook		Problem-Solving Handbook	
35	Cumulative Review		Cumulative Review		Cumulative Review	
36	4.1	1–10, 11–29 odd	4.1	11–30	4.1	11–15 odd, 16–20, 26–37
37	4.2	1–12, 13–21 odd, 31–40	4.2	13–41	4.2	21–50
38	4.3	1–23 odd	4.3	13–24	4.3	21–32
39	4.4	1–11 odd, 17–27 odd	4.4	13–24	4.4	13–27 odd, 29–32
40	4.5	1–14	4.5	9–22	4.5	9–16, 17–27 odd
41	4.6	1–12, 13–33 odd	4.6	13–40	4.6	27–49
42	4.7	1–7 odd, 9–26	4.7	9–30	4.7	21–36
43	4.8	1–17 odd, 25–49 odd	4.8	25–46	4.8	37–54, 67–73 odd
44	4.9	1–5 odd, 10–14	4.9	7–14	4.9	11–18
45	Chapter Review		Chapter Review		Chapter Review	
46	Chapter Test		Chapter Test		Chapter Test	
47	Problem-Solving Handbook		Problem-Solving Handbook		Problem-Solving Handbook	
48	5.1	1–6, 11–31 odd, 33–50, 54, 55	5.1	17–59	5.1	1–12, 33–63

Day	Minimum Course		Regular Course		Maximum Course	
49	5.2	1–15 odd, 17–34	5.2	17–42	5.2	17–27 odd, 29–43, 45–53 odd
50	5.3	1–49 odd	5.3	21–46	5.3	25–36, 41–52
51	5.4	1–9 odd, 15–24	5.4	13–28	5.4	19–34
52	5.5	1–21 odd	5.5	11–22	5.5	13–20, 23–25
53	5.6	1–11 odd, 13–26	5.6	13–32	5.6	13–33 odd, 35–43
54	5.7	1–9 odd, 11–21	5.7	11–26	5.7	11–25 odd, 26–31
55	5.8	1–5, 7	5.8	3–8	5.8	5–10
56	5.9	1–15 odd, 17–20, 26–29	5.9	17–32	5.9	17–29 odd, 31–39
57	5.10	1–11 odd, 13–32	5.10	13–37 odd, 39–51	5.10	21–38, 39–53 odd
58	5.11	1–29 odd	5.11	15–29	5.11	21–30, 31–39 odd
59	Chapter Review		Chapter Review		Chapter Review	
60	Chapter Test		Chapter Test		Chapter Test	
61	Problem-Solving Handbook		Problem-Solving Handbook		Problem-Solving Handbook	
62	6.1	1–31 odd, 33–44	6.1	33–60	6.1	48–75
63	6.2	1–19 odd, 21–38	6.2	21–39, 43–59 odd	6.2	21–45 odd, 46–60
64	6.3	1–21 odd, 23–40, 47	6.3	23–52	6.3	37–60, 61–71 odd
65	6.4	1–15 odd, 17–25, 55–62	6.4	35–53 odd, 59–68, 69–77 odd	6.4	21–45 odd, 55–65 odd, 85–95 odd
66	6.5	1–39 odd	6.5	25–44	6.5	31–43, 49–61 odd
67	6.6	1–15 odd, 17–32	6.6	17–29 odd, 30–46	6.6	23–42, 49–55 odd
68	6.7	1–32	6.7	13–29 odd, 30–52	6.7	23–46, 51–65 odd
69	6.8	1–11 odd, 31–42, 49, 50	6.8	23–42	6.8	39–52, 53–63 odd
70	6.9	1–4	6.9	2–5	6.9	3–6
71	Chapter Review		Chapter Review		Chapter Review	
72	Chapter Test		Chapter Test		Chapter Test	
73	Problem-Solving Handbook		Problem-Solving Handbook		Problem-Solving Handbook	

Day	Minimum Course		Regular Course		Maximum Course	
74	7.1	1–43 odd	7.1	28–49	7.1	31–39, 43–55
75	7.2	1–4, 5–25 odd, 29–31	7.2	5–13 odd, 16–27	7.2	5–21 odd, 29–43 odd
76	7.3	1–39 odd	7.3	7–19 odd, 22–34	7.3	22–35, 41–49 odd
77	7.4	1–35 odd, 40, 42	7.4	25–44	7.4	30–49
78	7.5	1–21 odd	7.5	7–27	7.5	13–31
79	7.6	1–9, 11–29 odd	7.6	10–28	7.6	21–39
80	7.7	1–15 odd, 17–20, 25–28	7.7	17–32	7.7	22–32, 33–41 odd
81	7.8	1–9 odd	7.8	5–9	7.8	7–9, 11, 12
82	Chapter Review		Chapter Review		Chapter Review	
83	Chapter Test		Chapter Test		Chapter Test	
84	Problem-Solving Handbook		Problem-Solving Handbook		Problem-Solving Handbook	
85	Cumulative Review		Cumulative Review		Cumulative Review	
86	Cumulative Review		Cumulative Review		Cumulative Review	
87	8.1	1–15 odd, 23–39 odd	8.1	23–34, 41–47 odd	8.1	29–40, 41, 45, 49, 50
88	8.2	1–11 odd, 13–21, 34–36	8.2	16–31	8.2	13–47 odd
89	8.3	1–11 odd, 16–21	8.3	13–24	8.3	13–23 odd, 25–30
90	8.4	1–11 odd, 16–24	8.4	13–27 odd, 28–30, 33–36	8.4	19–27, 31–36
91	8.5	1–23 odd	8.5	13–24	8.5	18–29
92	8.6	1–9 odd	8.6	5–9	8.6	8–10, 11–13 odd
93	8.7	1–3 odd, 5–8	8.7	5–10	8.7	7–12
94	8.8	1–4, 5–11 odd	8.8	5–12	8.8	7–14
95	8.9	1–5 odd, 7–13	8.9	7–16	8.9	9–18
96	8.10	1–15	8.10	4–18	8.10	7–21
97	8.11	1–5 odd, 7–12	8.11	7–15	8.11	10–18
98	Chapter Review		Chapter Review		Chapter Review	

Day	Minimum Course		Regular Course		Maximum Course	
99	Chapter Test		Chapter Test		Chapter Test	
100	Problem-Solving Handbook		Problem-Solving Handbook		Problem-Solving Handbook	
101	9.1	1–9 odd, 11–19	9.1	11–24	9.1	15–25, 31–35 odd
102	9.2	10–18, 19–49 odd	9.2	25–49	9.2	44–60, 67–73 odd
103	9.3	7–21 odd, 22–38	9.3	22–46	9.3	22–25, 33–55 odd, 62–70
104	9.4	1–9 odd, 21–38	9.4	33–40, 49–58	9.4	11, 12, 17–51 odd, 63–71 odd
105	9.5	7–15 odd, 25–44	9.5	24–48	9.5	21–43 odd, 45–55
106	9.6	1–21 odd	9.6	9–19	9.6	18–28
107	9.7	1–7 odd, 15–20, 31–63 odd, 74–76	9.7	37–75 odd	9.7	61–81
108	9.8	1–9 odd, 17–27	9.8	11–39 odd, 40	9.8	15–29 odd, 33–40
109	9.9	1–7	9.9	3–9	9.9	4–10
110	9.10	1–5 odd, 13–41 odd	9.10	21–38	9.10	25–38, 43–46
111	Chapter Review		Chapter Review		Chapter Review	
112	Chapter Test		Chapter Test		Chapter Test	
113	Problem-Solving Handbook		Problem-Solving Handbook		Problem-Solving Handbook	
114	10.1	5–11 odd, 13–24	10.1	15–28	10.1	17–32
115	10.2	5–15 odd, 27–35	10.2	21–35	10.2	21–39 odd, 41–45
116	10.3	1–9 odd, 13–17	10.3	9–18	10.3	11–20
117	10.4	1–8, 9–27 odd	10.4	1–7 odd, 9–28	10.4	9–30
118	10.5	1–11 odd, 13–20	10.5	7–20	10.5	13–26
119	10.6	1–10	10.6	5–14	10.6	5–13 odd, 14–18
120	Chapter Review		Chapter Review		Chapter Review	
121	Chapter Test		Chapter Test		Chapter Test	
122	Problem-Solving Handbook		Problem-Solving Handbook		Problem-Solving Handbook	
123	11.1	1–15 odd, 17–29	11.1	17–37	11.1	17–39 odd, 41–48

Day	Minimum Course		Regular Course		Maximum Course	
124	11.2	1–15 odd, 25–31	11.2	25–39	11.2	25–35 odd, 36–44
125	11.3	4–19	11.3	13–26	11.3	21–36
126	11.4	9–16, 29–37	11.4	17–33	11.4	17–39 odd, 44–48
127	11.5	1–23 odd, 41–55 odd	11.5	25–63	11.5	47–57, 65–73
128	11.6	1–11 odd, 13–26	11.6	25–44	11.6	34–48, 49–57 odd
129	11.7	1–9 odd, 13–32	11.7	13–39 odd, 41–51	11.7	27–44, 47–53
130	11.8	1–37 odd	11.8	26–43	11.8	35–52
131	11.9	5–24	11.9	7–26	11.9	13–32
132	Chapter Review		Chapter Review		Chapter Review	
133	Chapter Test		Chapter Test		Chapter Test	
134	Problem-Solving Handbook		Problem-Solving Handbook		Problem-Solving Handbook	
135	Cumulative Review		Cumulative Review		Cumulative Review	
136	12.1	1–29 odd	12.1	21–35	12.1	27–36, 43–51 odd
137	12.2	1–29 odd	12.2	24–38	12.2	27–41
138	12.3	1–9 odd, 14–31	12.3	11–33	12.3	17–34, 41–49 odd
139	12.4	1–12, 13–35 odd	12.4	13–36	12.4	19–36, 37–47 odd
140	12.5	1–11 odd, 13–25 odd	12.5	13–25	12.5	22–26, 29–36
141	12.6	1–6	12.6	5–10	12.6	7–12
142	12.7	1–7 odd, 13–29 odd, 30	12.7	17–30	12.7	11–27 odd, 31–39 odd
143	12.8	1–8	12.8	3–10	12.8	5–12
144	Chapter Review		Chapter Review		Chapter Review	
145	Chapter Test		Chapter Test		Chapter Test	
146	Problem-Solving Handbook		Problem-Solving Handbook		Problem-Solving Handbook	
147	13.1	1–4, 10–13	13.1	8–14	13.1	10–15
148	13.2	1–9 odd	13.2	9–13	13.2	11–15
149	13.3	1–6	13.3	5–10	13.3	7–12
150	13.4	1–15 odd	13.4	8–15	13.4	12–16, 19–21

Day	Minimum Course		Regular Course		Maximum Course	
151	13.5	1–15 odd	13.5	12–19	13.5	14–21
152	13.6	3–19 odd, 27	13.6	13–20, 24, 26	13.6	16–21, 28, 36–38
153	Chapter Review		Chapter Review		Chapter Review	
154	Chapter Test		Chapter Test		Chapter Test	
155	Problem-Solving Handbook		Problem-Solving Handbook		Problem-Solving Handbook	
156	14.1	1–17 odd	14.1	9–18	14.1	15–24
157	14.2	1–7 odd, 9–44	14.2	9–18	14.2	13–22
158	14.3	1–8	14.3	3–10	14.3	5–12
159	14.4	7–19 odd, 21–24	14.4	18–28	14.4	22–32
160	14.5	1–5 odd, 7–14	14.5	9–19	14.5	12–22
161	14.6	1–10	14.6	5–14	14.6	7–16
162	Chapter Review		Chapter Review		Chapter Review	
163	Chapter Test		Chapter Test		Chapter Test	
164	Problem-Solving Handbook		Problem-Solving Handbook		Problem-Solving Handbook	
165	15.1	1–9 odd, 24–38	15.1	11–14, 19–22, 27–38	15.1	22–41
166	15.2	1–9 odd, 11–19	15.2	9–22	15.2	11–24
167	15.3	3–10, 13–20	15.3	7–22	15.3	13–28
168	15.4	1–12, 25–30, 43–51, 58–66	15.4	12–24, 31–36, 40–54, 67, 68	15.4	25–33, 40–62, 66–69
169	15.5	4–8, 15–24	15.5	13–27	15.5	16–30
170	15.6	1–7 odd, 9–17	15.6	9–21	15.6	9–22
171	Chapter Review		Chapter Review		Chapter Review	
172	Chapter Test		Chapter Test		Chapter Test	
173	Problem-Solving Handbook		Problem-Solving Handbook		Problem-Solving Handbook	
174	Cumulative Review		Cumulative Review		Cumulative Review	
175	Cumulative Review		Cumulative Review		Cumulative Review	

GUIDE TO TEACHER'S RESOURCES

Use After Section	Practice Master	Quiz or Test	Enrichment Master	Computer Master
1.1	P1, Part 1			
1.2	P1, Part 2			
1.3	P2, Part 1	Quiz 1		
1.4	P2, Part 2			
1.5	P3, Part 1			
1.6	P3, Part 2	Quiz 2		
Ch. 1		T1–T2		
Test		T31–T32	E1–E2	C1
2.1	P4, Part 1			
2.2	P4, Part 2			
2.3	P5, Part 1			
2.4	P5, Part 2			
2.5	P6, Part 1	Quiz 3		
2.6	P6, Part 2			
2.7	P7, Part 1			
2.8	P7, Part 2			
2.9	P8, Part 1	Quiz 4		
Ch. 2		T3–T4		
Test		T33–T34		C2–C3
3.1	P8, Part 2			
3.2	P9, Part 1			
3.3	P9, Part 2			
3.4	P10, Part 1			
3.5	P10, Part 2	Quiz 5		
3.6	P11, Part 1			
3.7	P11, Part 2			
3.8	P12, Part 1			
3.9	P12, Part 2			
3.10	P13, Part 1	Quiz 6		
Ch. 3		T5–T6		
Test		T35–T36	E3	C4
Cum. Rev: Ch. 1–3		T76–T79		
4.1	P13, Part 2			
4.2	P14, Part 1			
4.3	P14, Part 2			
4.4	P15, Part 1	Quiz 7		
4.5	P15, Part 2			
4.6	P16, Part 1			
4.7	P16, Part 2			
4.8	P17, Part 1			
4.9	P17, Part 2	Quiz 8		
Ch. 4		T7–T8		
Test		T37–T38		C5
5.1	P18, Part 1			
5.2	P18, Part 2			
5.3	P19, Part 1			
5.4	P19, Part 2			
5.5	P20, Part 1	Quiz 9		
5.6	P20, Part 2			
5.7	P21, Part 1			
5.8	P21, Part 2			
5.9	P22, Part 1			
5.10	P22, Part 2			
5.11	P23, Part 1	Quiz 10		
Ch. 5		T9–T10		
Test		T39–T40	E4–E7	C6
6.1	P23, Part 2			
6.2	P24, Part 1			
6.3	P24, Part 2			
6.4	P25, Part 1			
6.5	P25, Part 2	Quiz 11		
6.6	P26, Part 1			
6.7	P26, Part 2			
6.8	P27, Part 1			
6.9	P27, Part 2	Quiz 12		
Ch. 6		T11–T12		
Test		T41–T42		C7
7.1	P28, Part 1			
7.2	P28, Part 2			
7.3	P29, Part 1	Quiz 13		
7.4	P29, Part 2			
7.5	P30, Part 1			
7.6	P30, Part 2			
7.7	P31, Part 1			
7.8	P31, Part 2	Quiz 14		

Use After Section	Practice Master	Quiz or Test	Enrichment Master	Computer Master
Ch. 7		T13–T14		
Test		T43–T44	E8	C8
Cum. Rev:				
Ch. 1–7		T80–T87		
8.1	P32, Part 1			
8.2	P32, Part 2			
8.3	P33, Part 1			
8.4	P33, Part 2			
8.5	P34, Part 1			
8.6	P34, Part 2	Quiz 15		
8.7	P35, Part 1			
8.8	P35, Part 2			
8.9	P36, Part 1			
8.10	P36, Part 2			
8.11	P37, Part 1	Quiz 16		
Ch. 8		T15–T16		
Test		T45–T46		C9
9.1	P37, Part 2			
9.2	P38, Part 1			
9.3	P38, Part 2			
9.4	P39, Part 1			
9.5	P39, Part 2	Quiz 17		
9.6	P40, Part 1			
9.7	P40, Part 2			
9.8	P41, Part 1			
9.9	P41, Part 2			
9.10	P42, Part 1	Quiz 18		
Ch. 9		T17–T18		
Test		T47–T48	E9	C10
10.1	P42, Part 2			
10.2	P43, Part 1	Quiz 19		
10.3	P43, Part 2			
10.4	P44, Part 1			
10.5	P44, Part 2			
10.6	P45, Part 1	Quiz 20		
Ch. 10		T19–T20		
Test		T49–T50		C11
11.1	P45, Part 2			
11.2	P46, Part 1			
11.3	P46, Part 2			
11.4	P47, Part 1	Quiz 21		
11.5	P47, Part 2			
11.6	P48, Part 1			
11.7	P48, Part 2			

Use After Section	Practice Master	Quiz or Test	Enrichment Master	Computer Master
11.8	P49, Part 1			
11.9	P49, Part 2	Quiz 22		
Ch. 11		T21–T22		
Test		T51–T52	E10–E12	C12
Cum. Rev:				
Ch. 8–11		T88–T91		
12.1	P50, Part 1			
12.2	P50, Part 2			
12.3	P51, Part 1			
12.4	P51, Part 2			
12.5	P52, Part 1	Quiz 23		
12.6	P52, Part 2			
12.7	P53, Part 1			
12.8	P53, Part 2	Quiz 24		
Ch. 12		T23–T24		
Test		T53–T54	E13–E14	C13
13.1	P54, Part 1			
13.2	P54, Part 2	Quiz 25		
13.3	P55, Part 1			
13.4	P55, Part 2			
13.5	P56, Part 1			
13.6	P56, Part 2	Quiz 26		
Ch. 13		T25–T26		
Test		T55–T56	E15–E16	C14
14.1	P57, Part 1			
14.2	P57, Part 2	Quiz 27		
14.3	P58, Part 1			
14.4	P58, Part 2			
14.5	P59, Part 1			
14.6	P59, Part 2	Quiz 28		
Ch. 14		T27–T28		
Test		T57–T58		C15
15.1	P60, Part 1			
15.2	P60, Part 2	Quiz 29		
15.3	P61, Part 1			
15.4	P61, Part 2			
15.5	P62, Part 1			
15.6	P62, Part 2	Quiz 30		
Ch. 15		T29–T30		
Test		T59–T60		C16
Cum. Rev:				
Ch. 8–15		T92–T99		

TEACHER'S NOTES

1·Introduction to Algebra

Overview This chapter introduces basic concepts that are necessary for the work covered in the remainder of the text. These concepts include writing, evaluating, and simplifying algebraic expressions; evaluating numerical and algebraic expressions that contain exponents; using properties of addition and multiplication to simplify expressions; evaluating expressions by using the order of operations; and using the distributive property to combine like terms. The chapter concludes with a problem-solving section that introduces the five-step process for solving problems (Understand, Plan, Solve, Answer, and Review). This section also lists several problem-solving strategies that will be used throughout the text.

Teaching Suggestions

1.1 Point out that learning algebra is similar to learning a foreign language, except that in algebra English phrases are translated into math symbols.

Have students evaluate expressions that contain parentheses and that involve fractions and decimals.

Review the concept of perimeter, since exercises 40–42 involve this concept. Remind students that they can probably discover the formulas by simply drawing a figure. At this time discuss the difference between linear and square units, the former being used for perimeter and the latter for area.

Notice that in exercises 53 and 56 the parentheses can be in more than one place.

1.2 Have students write each of the following expressions and then compute the value:

1. the sum of 4 and 3 squared $4 + 3^2 = 13$

2. the sum of the squares of 4 and 3 $4^2 + 3^2 = 25$

3. the square of the sum of 4 and 3 $(4 + 3)^2 = 49$

4. the quantity 4 plus 3, squared $(4 + 3)^2 = 49$

5. 4 plus 3, quantity squared $(4 + 3)^2 = 49$

Students should realize that three of these expressions have the same meaning and value.

Students need to be able to distinguish between expressions such as $5x^2$ and $(5x)^2$.

Because exercises 63–65 involve area and volume, point out that square and cubic units are needed for these exercises.

1.3 If students confuse the commutative and associative properties, you might compare the commutative property to a person who *commutes* to and from school or work: the position switches back and forth. To demonstrate the associative property, have three students stand next to one another in a line. First group two students together (*associate* them), and have the third one farther away. Next have the middle student move over toward the third student but remain between the two students. This middle student will now be *associated* with the third student. Association results in a regrouping of elements without the changing of order.

The properties in this section form the basis for almost all algebraic computation that will follow. You will refer to these properties throughout the remainder of the course.

Most of the exercises involve multiplying monomials. Stress that the coefficients are multiplied, while the exponents of common bases are added.

1.4 Students enjoy and usually remember mnemonic devices. The following sentence will help them recall the order of operations: *Please excuse my dear Aunt Sally.*

Please: Do **p**arentheses first,

excuse: **e**xponents come next,

my **d**ear: **m**ultiply and **d**ivide from left to right,

Aunt **S**ally: **a**dd and **s**ubtract from left to right.

Remind students that the order of operations is also a rule *within* any set of grouping symbols. Point out that a fraction bar is a grouping symbol.

Exercises 66–69 help prepare students to multiply binomials.

At this time each student should find out how his or her calculator operates. Generally, a more sophisticated calculator will have the algebraic order of operations built in, but a simpler unit will not.

1.5 There are two concepts in this section that should be emphasized. First, the coefficient of a term such as

y or ab is 1. And second, the concept of combining like terms is used when students add or subtract monomials. Have students compare expressions such as the sum $3x + 5x$ and the product $(3x)(5x)$. A common error that students make when combining like terms is to change the exponent. Stress that an expression such as $3x + 5x^2$ cannot be simplified, while the product $(3x)(5x^2)$ can be written as $15x^3$.

Some students may need a hint in order to do exercise 37. If so, the figure can be split into two rectangles by either a horizontal or a vertical line.

1.6 This section provides a pleasant diversion from the rest of the chapter. The problems in the exercises are not typical math homework problems. Before discussing them with the class, you should work out the solutions. Have students who have worked the exercises correctly explain their solutions. You may find that more than one approach will be explained. Students will then see that there is more than one way to solve a given problem.

2·Real Numbers

Overview This chapter begins with the concepts of sets and subsets and then covers the fact that the set of real numbers has the following subsets: counting numbers, whole numbers, integers, rational numbers, and irrational numbers. Opposites, order, absolute value, and addition of positive and negative numbers are illustrated with the use of a real-number line. Next, rules are presented for addition, subtraction, multiplication, and division. Nonroutine problems are solved by using one of the following strategies: *guess-and-check, logical reasoning, solve a simpler problem,* or *use a table.* Finally, axioms are presented, and reasons for each step in the proof of a rule or theorem are completed by using definitions, axioms, other proven theorems, and logical reasoning.

Teaching Suggestions

2.1 This section introduces basic set ideas that are fundamental to number theory and will be used throughout the text.

A helpful way to define *infinite set* is "A set that has no last element." The null set may create difficulty for some students. $\varnothing$ and $\{\ \}$ are the only valid symbols for this set; $\{\varnothing\}$ is incorrect since it is not empty.

2.2 Graphing numbers on a number line illustrates the order of those numbers. Have students graph a list of random numbers on one number line to establish the uniqueness and order of the numbers.

Point out that a given number may be named in infinitely many ways. For example, show that $\frac{2}{3} = \frac{4}{6}$ by subdividing the number line.

Using the definition of absolute value, you can show how any number and its opposite are the same distance from 0.

You might want to illustrate the density of rational numbers by finding rational numbers between any given two. For example, between the rational numbers $\frac{3}{7}$ and $\frac{4}{7}$ lie $\frac{31}{70}$, $\frac{32}{70}$, and so on.

Point out that $-x$ is read "the opposite of x," since $-x$ does not necessarily denote a negative number.

2.3 and 2.4 Several methods of addition are presented in these sections. Students should understand and practice each method.

When students are adding a positive and a negative number, point out that each number has an opposite effect on the other and the number with the smaller absolute value "cancels" part of the other.

Stress the importance of lining up decimal points.

2.5 Point out that students need to change *every* subtraction problem into an addition problem, with the only thought being "add the opposite."

Addition and subtraction can be contrasted by finding $a + b$ and $a - b$, using different sets of replacements for a and b. Also, for a given a and b, $a - b$ should be contrasted with $b - a$, not only to infer that subtraction is not commutative, but to show that these expressions are opposites, that is, $a - b = -(b - a)$.

In exercises 7–32, students should read the problems out loud, being careful to say "minus" and "negative" when indicated. Students may benefit from circling the minus signs in their written work to help understand the subtraction property.

Some students may need assistance doing exercises 52–56. Suggest that they first insert parentheses around the variable(s) and then replace the variable(s) with the given value(s). This procedure will reduce errors.

2.6 The rules for multiplication are usually applied rather consistently by students. However, when the rules for multiplication are compared with the rules for addition, students often confuse them. Emphasize that the product of two negative numbers is a positive number, while the sum of two negative numbers results in a negative number. When three or more numbers are multiplied, point out that an odd number of negative factors results in a negative answer.

2.7 Division is the inverse of multiplication. Illustrate this by examples such as $\frac{a}{b} = c$, which implies that $cb = a$, when $b \neq 0$.

Students often think of fractions in lowest terms as two numbers. Show that such a number represents a unique point on a number line. Students should place the negative sign for the numerator or the denominator at the center of the fraction.

2.8 If a model has been discovered that fits a problem and has been used successfully, then students should be directed to apply the model, practicing deductive thinking whenever possible. Verbal problems provide a wealth of material for discussion of concepts, principles, and skills. Offer students a choice of problems to do and do not regard any or all of them as absolutely essential.

2.9 When the field properties are introduced, it would be wise to indicate why subtraction and division do not satisfy all of them.

Use numerical examples to show the validity of the distributive property. Point out that evaluating is sometimes easier in the $a(b + c)$ form and at other times easier in the $ab + ac$ form.

3·Equations

Overview In this chapter, students first solve equations by using one of the properties of equality. Then they simplify equations by using the distributive property and solve the equation, using one or more of the properties of equality. With the introduction of repeating decimals, students have a more complete understanding of the set of rational numbers and a better understanding of algebra. Practice in problem solving is developed by the introduction of such strategies as *use a formula* and *write an equation*. The chapter concludes with a problem-solving section involving percents.

Teaching Suggestions

3.1 In this section students are introduced to the algebraic definition of an equation and use such terms as *replacement set, solution set,* and *equivalent equations.*

Remind students to be aware of positive and negative integers when using the replacement sets. By using a given replacement set, students experience solving equations while limiting the realm of possibilities for solutions.

3.2 This section introduces students to the addition property of equality and the subtraction property of equality. Students should begin to understand that equivalent equations occur when the same number is added to or subtracted from each side of the equation. Stress this equivalency. Remind students that when solving an equation, they will isolate the variable on one side of the equal sign and that the variable itself needs to have a coefficient of positive one, though the solution may be positive or negative.

3.3 In this section students use the multiplication and the division properties of equality to solve equations. Some students may need to review multiplicative inverse.

3.4 Repeating decimals may cause difficulty for some students. Encourage students to refer to the examples in order to compute the decimals correctly. Probably the most difficult concept for students to understand is the method used to rename a repeating decimal as a fraction. Have students refer to the examples and remind them that the original equation is multiplied by some power of 10, so that *only* the block of repeating digits is to the right of the decimal point.

3.5 Some students may need extra practice when using the distributive property to combine like terms that involve fractions, especially when a common denominator must be found. To solve many of the exercises, students need to understand that $3x + (-2x) = 10$ is equivalent to $3x - 2x = 10$. Many students may be challenged by exercises 41–52.

3.6 Solving two-step equations allows students to apply the knowledge gained in the previous sections of the chapter.

3.7 This section provides practice with equations. Many of the equations involve the application of the distributive property and some involve the use of fractions and finding the lowest common denominator prior to solving. Students may benefit from a thorough discussion of the steps needed to solve the equations in the exercises.

3.8 All necessary formulas are given. Review the correct terminology for area and volume, such as 24 square feet $= 24$ ft^2 and 12 cubic feet $= 12$ ft^3. Help students develop an understanding of how to interpret a problem and how to choose which formula to use. Then it is just a matter of substituting the given information and solving the equation correctly.

3.9 This section involves the ability of the students to read a problem, to understand what is read, to devise a plan using a variable to represent an unknown number, to write and solve an equation representing the given information, and finally, to check that the answer is correct. The strategy of drawing a diagram, especially when distance, rate, and time are involved, will help students learn to identify the needed information and aid in their understanding of exactly what the problem is asking them to find. The interpretation of the problems may be difficult for some students; however, they should not have trouble solving the equations.

3.10 Problem solving with percents develops students' ability to identify the given information, to choose a variable to represent the unknown, and then to translate that information into an equation. Remind students that they are dealing with a portion of a whole and that multiplication will be a function in the translation of the equation. Point out that when students write an equation, they need to write the percent as a decimal and they should be careful in the placement of the decimal point.

4·Inequalities

Overview In this chapter, students begin by graphing inequalities. Then they solve inequalities by using one of the properties of inequalities. Sentences are translated into inequalities. The concepts of intersection and union of sets are introduced and used to solve compound sentences and sentences involving absolute value. Finally, the chapter concludes with problems involving inequalities.

Teaching Suggestions

4.1 In this section simple inequalities and their graphs are presented. Some students may need to review the definition of real numbers and their position on the number line.

Some students may find an explanation of the comparison property helpful:

For any pair of real numbers, if a is one of the numbers and b is the other, then either $a < b$, $a = b$, or $a > b$. You should also mention that $x < 1$ has the same meaning as $1 > x$. This will be very helpful when students rewrite compound inequalities.

4.2 The addition and subtraction properties of inequality are analogous to those properties used to solve equations.

Remind students to use the check step to determine whether some of the values from the solution set are true for the inequality and to verify the correct shading on the number line.

Exercises 41–50 have the variable on the right side of the inequality. You might want to practice a few of this type with students.

4.3 A common error that students make is to forget to reverse the order of the inequality when they multiply or divide both sides of the inequality by a negative number. You might want to show some false inequalities that result when the order is not changed. For example,

$$-4 < 7$$
$$-2(-4) < -2(7)$$
$$8 < -14 \quad \text{This is false.}$$

4.4 You may find it advantageous to review solving equations with more than one step before beginning this section. Remind students to reverse the order of the inequality when they multiply or divide both sides of the inequality by a negative number.

Examples 3 and 4 are important and should be thoroughly discussed so that students understand what happens when the variable is eliminated.

4.5 In this section students translate sentences into inequalities. You might want to provide additional examples using *at most* and *at least*, such as the following:

There are at most twenty students in this class.

One needs to score at least 59% to pass this test.

These terms will be used in the problem-solving section later in the chapter.

You might want to point out that exercises 27–28 have two unknowns, and that the inequalities will contain two variables.

4.6 In this section, students are introduced to the concepts of intersection and union of sets. Remind students that the intersection or union of sets within the parentheses need to be found first.

Point out that $A \cap \varnothing = \varnothing$ and $A \cup \varnothing = A$.

Suggest that students use a different color to graph each of the three sets described in the C exercises. Then when students have an overlap of at least two colors on the number line, they will have the intersection of these sets.

4.7 In this section a development based on graphing is given for solving compound sentences. Also the following statements may be helpful:

The solution set of an "and" sentence is the *intersection* of the solution set of the simple sentences.

The solution set of an "or" sentence is the *union* of the solution sets of the simple sentences.

Point out that the solution to some conjunctions such as $x < 0$ and $x > 2$ is the empty set.

4.8 Emphasize which sentences involving absolute value are conjunctions and which are disjunctions. Discuss the examples thoroughly.

4.9 Students will solve problems by writing and solving inequalities. Discuss the examples thoroughly. Remind students to be sure to answer the problem. For example, if the solution to an inequality is $x > 4.3$ and x represents the number of people, then the smallest value for x is 5.

5·Operations With Polynomials

Overview This chapter involves operations with polynomials. It begins with a discussion of the degree of a polynomial, then addition of polynomials is presented. Next a discussion of the opposites of polynomials and subtraction of polynomials is presented. The coverage of multiplication of polynomials includes a presentation of the following properties: product of powers, power of a power, and power of a product. The FOIL method is used to multiply two binomials. Solving equations involves simplifying a polynomial expression and solving for the variable. The problem-solving section involves solving uniform-motion problems, using the formula $d = rt$. Division of polynomials begins with a presentation of the rule for division of powers, then division by a monomial, and finally division by a binomial.

Teaching Suggestions

5.1 The concepts of like terms, polynomials in descending order, and polynomials in simplest form are used as students simplify and add polynomials. Review like terms, if necessary.

Use Example 2 to illustrate aligning like terms vertically when students add polynomials. Point out that arranging each polynomial in descending order of powers makes it easier to match up the terms. Mention that ascending order of powers will work just as well, but descending order is more common.

5.2 Subtraction of a polynomial is described as addition of the opposite. However, some students may make errors by not changing the sign of *every* term when finding the opposite of a polynomial.

5.3 This section develops skills in multiplying monomials. Point out to students that the prefix *mono* means "one"; therefore, a monomial is a polynomial with only one term. Have students pay special attention to the examples.

5.4 Since many exercises in this section use the distributive property, review simple examples, such as $-6(2x + 9) = -12x - 54$.

You might want to provide an example in which the monomial is to the right of the polynomial, such as $(7b^2 - 6a)2b$.

5.5 Since students are familiar with the distributive property, the examples illustrate multiplication of one polynomial by another polynomial, using this property. Discuss the examples in both horizontal and vertical form.

5.6 This section stresses the multiplication of two binomials using the FOIL method. The FOIL method is really a double application of the distributive property:
$$(a + b)(c + d) = a(c + d) + b(c + d)$$
$$= ac + ad + bc + bd.$$

5.7 Solving equations involving polynomials is an extension of solving other algebraic equations. Point out to students that these exercises require a step-by-step approach.

5.8 When discussing the examples, point out the table that describes the rate, time, and distance for each problem.

It may be helpful to classify the examples as follows:

Example 1: Opposite directions   The sum of the distances in each direction equals the total distance.

Example 2: Round trip   Distances are equal.

Example 3: Same direction   Distances are equal.

When discussing each oral exercise, have students set up as much of the $rt = d$ table as possible. You might also have students read the written exercises and classify each example as *opposite directions, round trip,* or *same direction.*

5.9 When discussing the division of powers, you may wish to illustrate each as follows:

$$a > b, \frac{x^a}{x^b} \text{ or } \frac{x^6}{x^2} = \frac{x \cdot x \cdot x \cdot x \cdot x \cdot x}{x \cdot x} = x^4$$

$$a < b, \frac{x^a}{x^b} \text{ or } \frac{x^3}{x^5} = \frac{x \cdot x \cdot x}{x \cdot x \cdot x \cdot x \cdot x} = \frac{1}{x^2}$$

$$a = b, \frac{x^a}{x^b} = \frac{x^2}{x^2} = \frac{x \cdot x}{x \cdot x} = 1$$

You may want to mention that $\frac{x^4}{x^7} = \frac{1}{x^3} = x^{-3}$. However, at this point in the book, students will use only positive exponents.

The power of a quotient may cause some difficulty for some students. If necessary, provide examples such as $\left(\frac{-4x^3}{3x}\right)^2$ and remind students to find the power of a product first before dividing.

The C exercises will probably cause difficulty for the average student.

5.10 Remind students to simplify the numerical quotient and to simplify the variables. Many students do well in dividing two monomials, but have difficulty when dividing a binomial or polynomial by a monomial. Many students make the mistake of dividing the denominator, a monomial, into only one term in the numerator, such as

$$\frac{24x + 9x^2y + 3y^2}{3y} = \frac{8x}{y} + 9x^2y + 3y^2.$$

Stress that students should first rewrite each term of the numerator over the denominator and then divide, as follows:

$$\frac{24x}{3y} + \frac{9x^2y}{3y} + \frac{3y^2}{3y} = \frac{8x}{y} + 3x^2 + y.$$

5.11 You may want to review writing a polynomial in descending order and filling in any missing terms, using 0 as a coefficient.

Emphasize the similarity between long division of whole numbers and division of polynomials.

$$
\begin{array}{r}
32 \\
21\overline{)672} \\
63 \\
\hline
42 \\
42 \\
\hline
0
\end{array}
$$

1) divide
2) multiply
3) subtract
4) bring down

$$
\begin{array}{r}
3x + 2 \\
2x + 1\overline{)6x^2 + 7x + 2} \\
6x^2 + 3x \\
\hline
4x + 2 \\
4x + 2 \\
\hline
0
\end{array}
$$

6·Factoring Polynomials

Overview This chapter begins with a discussion of prime factorization, which is then used to find the greatest common factor and the least common multiple of pairs of integers. Then students factor polynomials by removing the greatest common monomial factor, by identifying a polynomial as the difference of two squares or as a perfect-square trinomial, or by finding the binomial factors of trinomials in the form $x^2 + bx + c$ and $ax^2 + bx + c$. Quadratic equations are solved by factoring and by using the zero product property. The chapter concludes with a problem-solving section in which students write an equation and then factor the polynomial within the equation to solve the problem.

Teaching Suggestions

6.1 Begin this section with a review of exponential notation. Some students may prefer to use a factor tree. If so, have them circle each prime number to remind them that that "branch" is finished:

6.2 Review the product of powers property. In this section, students do not need to factor integer coefficients into their prime factors.

6.3 If necessary, present an example such as $x^2 - 9$ before discussing the examples in the text.

Remind students to combine like terms whenever possible in the C exercises.

6.4 Emphasize that students should examine the terms of a trinomial in this order: first term, last term, then middle term. Stress that only if the first and the last terms are squares will students need to examine the middle term.

6.5 Caution students to be careful with positive and negative signs when multiplying to obtain the constant and when adding to obtain the coefficient of the linear term. If necessary, review the rules for addition and the rules for multiplication of positive and negative numbers.

6.6 Emphasize to students that with practice they will be able to factor many of these trinomials mentally. Point out that the exercises include factoring techniques from previous sections.

6.7 Point out that in Example 3 students should recognize the perfect-square trinomial after removing the common monomial factor of -1.

6.8 Many students will find that solving quadratic equations by using factoring and the zero product property is a logical extension of solving linear equations. At this point you do not need to identify these equations as quadratic.

6.9 Encourage students to draw a sketch for each problem, if possible.

7·Relations and Functions

Overview This chapter begins with students graphing ordered pairs on a coordinate plane and then graphing two-variable equations. The term *relation* is defined, and different ways to represent a relation are presented. Next the concept of *function* is defined and ways for writing a function rule are shown. Slope is introduced, and students find the slope of a line, using the coordinates of two points on the line. Also students draw the graph of a line, given a point on the line and the slope of the line. The slope-intercept form of a straight line is presented. Students then write equations of lines if for any line they know the slope and the y-intercept, the slope and one point on the line, or two points on the line. The chapter concludes with a problem-solving section involving the concepts of velocity and acceleration, using linear equations.

Teaching Suggestions

7.1 When you introduce the concept of graphing points in a coordinate system, use a grid, not just a sketch of a set of axes. Have students strive for accuracy. Adequate tools include graph paper, a straight-edge, and a sharpened pencil. Have students label the axes by placing the numbers adjacent to the lines. Use the basic vocabulary of graphing to help students master correct terminology. Your lesson should include plotting points on the axes as well as identification of the quadrants.

In the C exercises, students may choose any x, and then solve for y. Encourage them to choose both positive and negative values for x. Some equations will not have domains as the entire set of real numbers, for example: $x^2 + y^2 = 4$, $x = y^2$, or $x = |y|$.

7.2 In the graphing of a linear equation, usually only a few solutions are plotted; however, point out that a linear equation has an infinite number of solutions. The graph represents all these solutions. When you demonstrate such a graph, place arrowheads on the end-points of the segment you draw, and remind students that the graph is infinite. Also, when you plot points for the class, you might occasionally misplot a point to demonstrate that such a mistake will be spotted when you try to connect all the points with a straightedge.

7.3 Stress that all sets of ordered pairs are relations, but only certain sets of ordered pairs are functions. That is, every function is a relation, but not every relation is a function.

Also, some relations have the set of real numbers as both domain and range, for example, $\{(x, y) : x + y = 1\}$. Other relations have finite domains and ranges, for example, $\{(1, 2), (3, 4), (5, 7)\}$.

Another way to check a given set of ordered pairs to see whether or not it is a function is to look at the x values. If any of them are identical, then the relation is not a function. If all the x values are different, then the relation is a function. The vertical-line test serves the same purpose when considering a relation that has already been graphed.

7.4 Notations of the form $f(x) = 3x + 4$, $f : x \rightarrow 3x + 4$, and $y = 3x + 4$ are merely three ways of expressing the same rule for the function f.

7.5 Most students find it easy to think of slope as *rise over run*. When finding slope, they should focus on the importance of order, both in the division and the subtractions. Make sure the students do not misinterpret subscripts for exponents.

A useful demonstration would be to start with a linear equation such as $3x + y = 6$, and find four ordered pairs that satisfy the equation. Use these ordered pairs in different combinations to find the slope of the line. Verify that the value of the slope is always the same.

Provide students with practice in identifying slopes by examining graphs of lines. Make sure that you include cases with slopes that are positive, negative, zero, and undefined.

While slope is a concept that is presently being related only to graphs of linear functions, you might mention that in advanced math courses, the slope of curves is discussed by examining the behavior of the graph very close to a particular point on it. Calculus students are always fascinated by the importance of the concept of slope.

7.6 The slope-intercept form of a linear equation immediately tells the slope and y-intercept of its graph. These quantities often provide an efficient way of graphing the equation.

It is interesting to note that although the same slope may seem to indicate the presence of two parallel lines, that is not always the case. For example, the equations $3x - 2y = 1$ and $6x - 4y = 2$ will have the same slope when written in $y = mx + b$ form, but the graphs coincide.

Give students lots of practice in graphing lines using the slope and the y-intercept. Common mistakes occur when negative slopes occur.

7.7 This section covers finding the equation of a line when given (1) the slope and the y-intercept, (2) the slope and any point, or (3) any two points on the line. For case (3), point out that students must find the slope first, and that using either one of the two given points will yield the same result for the equation of the line.

You might also teach the point-slope form (see C exercises) and use it in *any* situation where $y = mx + b$ may be used. One advantage of using the point-slope form is that the equation for the line is the end result of simplification.

7.8 For problems involving velocity and acceleration, point out that the easiest approach is to first write the ordered pairs that are given, and then find the slope.

8·Linear Systems

Overview This chapter begins with solving a system of equations by graphing. Then three types of systems—*consistent, consistent and dependent,* and *inconsistent*—are defined. Algebraic techniques for solving a system of equations include using the substitution method, the addition or subtraction method, and multiplication with the addition-subtraction method. These methods are applied in problem solving, motion and mixture problems, and puzzle problems. Then graphing a linear inequality is presented, along with solving a system of inequalities by graphing. Finally, absolute value equations are graphed.

Teaching Suggestions

8.1 Review graphing on the coordinate plane. Have students graph various equations, and review slope, y-intercept, and ordered pairs.

Stress the check of the solution. By checking the ordered pair in each equation, students can determine if the ordered pair is a solution of the system. Point out that the solution makes both equations true at the same time, and it is considered a conjunction, or an "and" sentence.

Before assigning exercises 41–43, you may want to review the formula for finding the area of a triangle and the method for determining the lengths of a segment bounded by intersecting lines.

8.2 Before beginning this section, review the slope-intercept form of an equation. Students should be able to determine the following for a system of equations: the slope of each line, whether the two lines are parallel, and whether the y-intercepts are the same.

Discuss the slope and the y-intercepts of Examples 1 and 2. Emphasize the differences to further explain which systems are consistent and dependent, consistent, or inconsistent. Also stress the number of solutions associated with each type of system. Example 3 discusses the differences among the three types of systems further.

8.3 The substitution method is one approach to solving a system algebraically. Stress solving an equation for one variable if necessary, as in Examples 2 and 3. Have students solve for a positive variable.

Many students need to be reminded that this is a system of equations and values for both variables are needed. Stress that the solution for one variable in one equation can be substituted in either original equation to determine the other variable and that solutions are written as an ordered pair.

Use Example 3 to explain what happens when the variable drops out and a true equation results. Likewise, use Example 4 to explain what happens when a false equation results. Before assigning the C exercises, you will probably need to give an example that has an ordered triple as its solution. For example, $x = 5$, $y = x + 1$, $z = 2x + 4$ has as a solution $(5, 6, 14)$.

8.4 Using the addition or the subtraction method is the second approach given for solving a system of equations. Many students have trouble determining when to add or subtract the equations. Point out that the addition method is used when the coefficients of like terms are additive inverses, as in Example 1. When coefficients of like terms are the same, the subtraction method is used, as in Example 2. Some students need to be reminded that every term in the one equation is to be subtracted from the similar term in the other equation.

You may want to discuss with better students that the addition and the subtraction method need not be used, but with a little work the substitution method is also possible. Stress the importance of finding the solution for both variables.

Before you assign the written exercises, it may help some students if you first go through each exercise and determine what method of solving the system of equations will be used, the addition or the subtraction method.

8.5 Many students find the multiplication with addition and subtraction approach to solving a system of equations the most difficult. Drill and practice are necessary. Some students will make mistakes by not multiplying each term of the equation by the same number, and some will make mistakes with the sign of a term when adding or subtracting the two equations.

Discuss the examples thoroughly. Example 2 is difficult for many students to comprehend. A careful analysis of each equation should stress a search for the least common multiple of the coefficients of a single variable. This will determine what to multiply each equation by. Again remind students to find the solution for each variable and to check their answers.

8.6 Stress the plan of each example when you discuss Examples 1 and 2. Any approach for solving the system of equations can be used: substitution, addition or subtraction, or multiplication with addition and subtraction.

Before assigning the written exercises, you may need to review the following: perimeter of a rectangle, coin problems, isosceles triangles, and distance problems.

8.7 Before beginning this section, it would be helpful to review Section 5.8, in which uniform-motion problems had one equation and one unknown. Remind students to plan for the solution and to draw a diagram if necessary.

Discuss Example 1 thoroughly and remind students to solve for both variables.

Example 2 is a mixture problem with more than one component. Stress the importance of the table. Once this step is completed, many students find the rest of the process easy. Point out that the approach used to solve the system of equations in this example is not the only one to use. You may want to do the same example using the substitution method.

In Example 3 you will find a mixture problem using percents. Review the conversion of a percent to a decimal.

The Oral Exercises stress the planning step. For exercise 5, you may need to remind students to convert minutes to a fraction of an hour.

8.8 Before discussing Example 2, explain that a two-digit number can be written as $10t + u$. For example, 36 can be written as $3(10) + 6$.

Help students translate each problem in the Oral Exercises. Before assigning the C exercises, you may want to explain how to write a two-place decimal. For example, if the sum of the digits of a two-place decimal is 7, let t = tenths digit and let h = hundredths digit, then $t + h = 7$. Remind students to multiply the tenths digit by 0.1 and the hundredths digit by 0.01.

8.9 Point out that to graph a linear inequality, students need to use the terms *boundary line* and *half plane*. Since the graph of a linear inequality can be a half plane, or a half plane and a boundary line, have students determine when each of the above will occur.

Many students may have difficulty determining which half plane to shade. After students have graphed the line, have them choose a point in the half plane where they think it should be shaded and then substitute the coordinates of this point in the original inequality. If the statement is true, then that part of the graph should be shaded.

Point out that an inequality should be in slope-intercept form before it is graphed. Example 3 reviews the graph of a single variable on the coordinate plane as well as changing the coefficient of a variable in an inequality from negative to positive.

Before assigning exercises 16–18, review how to write an equation and an inequality from its graph.

8.10 This section is an extension of the previous section and involves a system of inequalities. The solution of this system is the intersection of two half planes.

Students should use two different-colored pencils to help them identify the intersection of the half planes.

Point out that Example 3 has no solution because there is no intersection of the half planes.

8.11 This section shows students how to graph absolute value equations on the coordinate plane. First review the meaning of absolute value and the graph of equations such as $x = 3$ on a number line.

Many students will find this section difficult. Demonstrate how to graph on the coordinate plane equations that involve one variable, such as $|y| = 3$. Students should see that there are two solutions, $y = 3$ and $y = -3$, both horizontal lines.

Discuss the examples thoroughly. Ask students if they see any similarities between the graphs of Examples 2 and 4 and of Examples 3 and 5.

In the C exercises, students graph absolute value inequalities. Before assigning these exercises, you may want to give some additional examples, such as $|x| \leq 4$ and $|y| \geq 3$.

9·Rational Expressions

Overview This chapter extends the concepts of rational numbers to rational expressions. It begins by defining a rational expression and by showing a procedure to find equivalent rational expressions. Next students find the simplest form of a rational expression by factoring the numerator and the denominator and then using the greatest common factor of the numerator and the denominator. Properties of integral exponents are presented, and students multiply and divide rational expressions. Finding the least common denominator of rational expressions precedes the sections in which students add and subtract rational expressions. Then students solve equations with rational expressions. The chapter has a problem-solving section involving rates of work and rates of travel. Finally, students are given formulas that involve more than one variable, and they solve the formula for a specified variable.

Teaching Suggestions

9.1 Students need to have an understanding of rational numbers in order to understand rational expressions. Provide more examples if necessary to remind students of the types of expressions that are *not* polynomials, such as expressions with variables appearing under a radical sign. Stress that the denominator of a rational expression cannot be 0, and that certain values of the replacement set may have to be excluded. Students need to factor polynomials, in order to find

these values, and to find equivalent rational expressions.

9.2 For students to simplify a rational expression, they must first factor the polynomials of the rational expression completely, and then identify the greatest common factor of the numerator and the denominator. Stress the importance of first factoring to find the greatest common factor, and then simplifying.

9.3 Students should become well-acquainted with the properties of integral exponents. These properties are important in simplifying rational expressions.

9.4 Rational expressions are multiplied in a manner similar to that of multiplying rational numbers. Again, students must have good skills in factoring in order to express the products in simplest form.

9.5 Rational expressions are divided in a manner similar to that of dividing rational numbers. The "flip-and-multiply" (FAM) method, in which the divisor is inverted and the factors are multiplied, is used to change division problems to multiplication problems. All previous techniques learned for multiplication of rational expressions can then be used.

9.6 In order to add or subtract rational expressions that have different denominators, students should be encouraged to find the least common denominator. Of course any common denominator is sufficient when adding or subtracting rational expressions, but it is usually simpler to use the least common denominator.

9.7 Rational expressions are added or subtracted in a manner similar to that of adding or subtracting rational numbers. Remind students to always check the result and to be sure that it is in simplest form. In some cases a problem can be made easier by simplifying the rational expressions before adding or subtracting them.

9.8 In this section students solve equations with rational expressions by adding, subtracting, multiplying, dividing, and simplifying rational expressions. If students have any difficulties with these topics, review those concepts. When solving an equation with rational expressions, students must remember to multiply all terms of the equation by the least common denominator. They must also remember to eliminate any extraneous roots that occur. Point out that cross multiplication can be used as a shortcut when each side of the equation is a fraction. Students should check their answers.

9.9 Discuss the steps of each example. Emphasize that by making a table, students can organize the given and the needed information.

9.10 Formulas are general facts, rules, or principles that are usually expressed as mathematical equations. They often involve rational expressions with more than one variable and sometimes it is convenient to solve such equations for one of the variables. In this section, students are given formulas used in different fields. Any background information that you can provide on the formulas, such as what the variables represent, physical laws used in deriving the formulas, or the derivations of the formulas, will help students understand the meanings of the formulas.

10·Variation Functions

Overview This chapter introduces variation functions with the concept of direct variation in the form of $y = kx$. Next ratios and proportions are presented and used to solve direct-variation problems. Proportions are also used to solve percent problems. Then the concept of inverse variation is introduced in the form of $xy = k$ (or $y = \frac{k}{x}$). Proportions are used to solve problems involving inverse variation. The chapter concludes with a problem-solving section including direct and inverse variations.

Teaching Suggestions

10.1 To introduce the concept of direct variation, present several sets of ordered pairs that belong to direct variation functions and have students guess the equation. Or give a relation and have students provide sets of ordered pairs. After sketching the graphs of several direct variation functions, discuss the properties of their graphs.

Emphasize that in a direct variation function when $k > 0$, if x increases, then y increases. If $k < 0$, then as $|x|$ increases, $|y|$ increases. In most application problems, k is positive. Students may also observe that the ratio of y to x is constant, which is developed in the next section.

Discuss what the constant of variation represents in the examples. Students often write different equations when the relationship is not stated, as in exercises 23 and 24. If $y = kx$, then $x = (\frac{1}{k})y$. Exercises 31 and 32 involve a change of units. The constant of proportionality depends on the units used.

10.2 Point out that the condition $x_1 \neq 0$ and $x_2 \neq 0$ are necessary because if either value is zero, then the ratio is undefined. If $\frac{y_1}{x_1} = \frac{y_2}{x_2}$ then $x_2 y_1 = x_1 y_2$ because the product of the means equals the product of the extremes. This results from using the multiplication property of equality, and multiplying each side by $x_1 x_2$.

$$\frac{y_1}{x_1} = \frac{y_2}{x_2}$$

$$(x_1 x_2)\left(\frac{y_1}{x_1}\right) = (x_1 x_2)\left(\frac{y_2}{x_2}\right)$$

$$x_2 y_1 = x_1 y_2$$

Before assigning the exercises, discuss the properties of fractions. In exercise 8, mention that division of fractions is needed. In exercises 23–32 students must use parentheses when writing the product of the means equal to the product of the extremes. Point out that fractions may be reduced before multiplying. In exercises 43–45, the numerator and the denominator of the fractions should be factored first, the domain stated, and the fraction reduced before solving the proportion.

10.3 This section presents percents using proportions. One advantage to this method is that all percent problems are solved using the same proportion:

$$\frac{\text{part}}{\text{whole}} = \frac{\text{percent amount}}{100}.$$

Students should be encouraged to look at different ways to solve problems. If a 30% reduction is given in price, the new price can be calculated by computing 30% of the original price and then subtracting from the original price. However, computing 70% of the original price yields the same result.

In exercise 12 some students may need the hint to use the relationship

$$\% \text{ of profit} = \frac{\text{selling price} - \text{buying price}}{\text{buying price}}.$$

10.4 Students usually find indirect variation more difficult than direct variation. The section might be introduced by discussing some inverse relationships that should be familiar to students, such as, the more people who share the cost of a gift, the less each individual pays; the faster one drives, the less time it takes to reach a given destination; the farther one sits from a lamp, the less illumination one receives. In each of these relationships, as one variable increases, the other decreases.

Both forms of the definition $y = \frac{k}{x}$, $x \neq 0$ and $xy = k$ should be used. The latter indicates that the product of x and y is a constant in inverse variation.

In the Oral Exercises, point out that students need to verify that each inverse variation can be written in the form $y = \frac{k}{x}$. Exercises 1–16 are easily solved using the definition $xy = k$. In exercises 21, 22, and 27 the inverse relationship is not explicitly stated, and students may not realize that *same area* and *same distance* are denoting constants.

In the C exercises the one variable is defined to vary inversely as the square of the other. You might want to expand on the question in exercise 30 and ask questions of the form, If y varies inversely as x^2, what is the change in y when x is doubled? Tripled? Halved?

10.5 The proportions for inverse variation are derived from the definition of an inverse variation function. An important step of the proof shows that $x_1 y_1 = x_2 y_2$. When students write a proportion for an inverse variation, have them check their work by verifying that $x_1 y_1 = x_2 y_2$. Other proportions are equivalent to $\frac{x_1}{x_2} = \frac{y_2}{y_1}$, such as $\frac{x_1}{y_2} = \frac{x_2}{y_1}$.

In exercises 13–20 students should write a general proportion, substitute the given values, and then solve, using a calculator when appropriate. Encourage students to check the reasonableness of their answers and to keep in mind that in an inverse variation with $k > 0$, an increase in one variable causes a decrease in the value of the other variable.

10.6 Some of the exercises may need discussion. In exercises 4 and 14, the relationship of the variables is not stated as direct or inverse variation. In exercise 9, the area of the carpet must be calculated and used in the proportion. In exercise 15, students must use the equation

$$\text{percent of increase} = \frac{\text{new salary} - \text{old salary}}{\text{old salary}}.$$

11·Radicals

Overview This chapter begins with the definition of square root and introduces the terms and notation associated with radicals. Students then use the *divide-and-average* method to approximate irrational square roots. The Pythagorean theorem is used to find the length of the hypotenuse of a right triangle. Radicals are then multiplied, divided, simplified, added, and subtracted. Radical equations are solved. Finally, students use the distance formula to find the distance between two points on the coordinate plane.

Teaching Suggestions

11.1 This section defines *square roots, radical sign,* and *radicand.* It is important for students to understand that if $a \geq 0$, then $\sqrt{a}$ represents a positive number and $-\sqrt{a}$ represents a negative number. Write several rational numbers without signs on the board, such as 8, $\frac{1}{2}$, 3.25. Students will probably agree that each of these rational numbers represents a positive number and that to indicate a negative number, the negative sign must be written. Point out that the same convention is true for radicals.

Use the graph of $y = x^2$ to emphasize that a positive real number has two square roots. Given a positive y, there are two values of x such that $x^2 = y$. If $y = 0$, then $x = 0$, and if $y < 0$, then there is no real x for which $x^2 = y$. Students will learn in advanced algebra that negative numbers have square roots in the set of complex numbers.

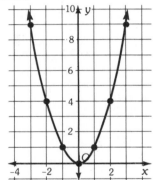

11.2 Before beginning this section, review the structure of the real number system and the distinguishing characteristics of each of the subsets: rationals, irrationals, integers, whole numbers, and natural numbers. Rational numbers have a repeating decimal representation. Irrational numbers have a nonrepeating decimal representation. Give students a list of numbers such as -18, $\frac{4}{3}$, -7, 0.46, $0.101001000 \ldots$, 16, and 0 and have them list all the subsets to which each number belongs.

Students should be able to locate the approximate value of an irrational square root between two consecutive perfect-square integers. To introduce the topic of approximation, ask students the following: Which is larger, $\sqrt{87}$ or 9? $-\sqrt{15}$ or -4? $\sqrt{0.64}$ or 0.8? $\sqrt{475}$ or 20?

For the average student, it is sufficient to use the divide-and-average method to find an approximation correct to the tenths place. Most students will use a calculator to approximate square roots.

11.3 Students should learn the Pythagorean theorem as it is stated in words. Give students an opportunity to state the relationship for various right triangles in which the legs and the hypotenuse are represented by letters other than a, b, and c.

In Example 2, since the variables stand for the sides of a triangle, only the positive square root is a sensible answer. Demonstrate the construction of a length equal to $\sqrt{2}$. Point out that a length equal to $\sqrt{3}$ can be constructed by using a right triangle with legs $\sqrt{2}$ and 1. This is a good time to distinguish between irrational numbers and their rational approximations.

Exercise 35 requires students to find the leg of a triangle, given the hypotenuse and the other leg.

Students may be curious about the name *Pythagorean theorem*. Pythagoras was born about 580 B.C. and lived on the island of Samos. Pythagoras and his students studied mathematics, astronomy, and philosophy. In addition to discovering the Pythagorean theorem, they discovered irrational numbers. Students could be assigned to give a brief report on Pythagoras. Information can be found in an encyclopedia or a book about the history of mathematics. Students may recall that Pythagoras was mentioned in the Math Heritage feature in Chapter 2.

11.4 This section is the first of several that present the procedures for performing operations on square roots and simplification rules. Before assigning exercises 31–40, review the property of division of powers for simplifying expressions in the form $\frac{x^a}{x^b}$. In the C exercises, exercises of the form $(a\sqrt{x})(b\sqrt{x})$ are given. Using the associative and commutative properties of multiplication, show that this product is equal to (ab) $(\sqrt{x} \cdot \sqrt{x})$ or abx. In exercises 47 and 48, a counterexample will show that the statement is false.

11.5 Students have difficulty simplifying radicals containing variables because they do not understand when to use absolute value. Present some examples to students and ask them to tell the conditions for

which the radicand is positive and whether the radical represents a positive or a negative number. For example, in the expression $\sqrt{3x}$, x must be positive and $\sqrt{3x}$ stands for a positive number. However, in the expression $\sqrt{2x^2}$, x may be positive or negative, but $\sqrt{2x^2}$ still represents a positive number. $x\sqrt{2}$ is not positive if x is negative. Therefore, the correct simplification is $|x|\sqrt{2}$.

Review with students that x^2, x^4, and x^6 are positive, but x^3, x^5, and x^7 are positive or negative, depending on the value of x.

Students need to review the multiplication properties of exponents before completing exercises 49–61. Since $(x^3)^2 = x^3 \cdot x^3 = x^6$, x^3 is a square root of x^6. Encourage students to look for shortcuts when simplifying radicals. For example, $\sqrt{5} \cdot \sqrt{10}$ can be rewritten $\sqrt{5} \cdot \sqrt{5 \cdot 2}$, and then simplified to $5\sqrt{2}$. In exercises 53 and 54, the negative numbers are squared first, thus the radicand is positive.

11.6 Students may have trouble adding and subtracting radicals correctly if they have not completely simplified the terms. It is a good idea to review the fact that $\sqrt{3} = 1 \cdot \sqrt{3}$ and $-\sqrt{3} = -1 \cdot \sqrt{3}$. Students often consider the implied coefficient to be 0. Students may need to practice additional examples that include square roots of fractions before you assign the exercises.

11.7 This final section on radical operations reviews the special product patterns $(a + b)^2$, $(a - b)^2$, and $(a + b)(a - b)$. As an introduction to the section, have students complete some examples of these forms without radicals. Students should be able to multiply a binomial by its conjugate without writing the middle terms. In exercises 41, 53, and 54, the numerator and denominator of the fractions contain a common factor. Several examples of this type will review correct simplification of fractions.

11.8 Extraneous solutions occur when solving radical equations because the squaring process is not reversible. If $a = b$, then $a^2 = b^2$, but the converse is not true. If $a^2 = b^2$, then $a = b$ or $a = -b$. The following might be used to show students why the extraneous root occurs in Example 3. If $\sqrt{x + 5} = x + 3$, then $x + 3 \geq 0$ in order for $\sqrt{x + 5}$ to represent a nonnegative number. Therefore, $x \geq -3$ and the solution $x = -4$ does not satisfy this condition.

Factorable quadratic equations occur in the solutions

to the exercises, beginning with exercise 27. The students will need to review the zero product property in order to solve these problems. In exercises 51 and 52, students should combine like radical terms before squaring.

Exploration All students should be introduced to radicals other than square roots. Before beginning this feature, have students make a chart of values for the functions $y = x^3$ and $y = x^4$, using both negative and positive values of x. Students should become familiar with the cubes and fourth powers of 2, 3, 4, and 5 to aid in the simplification of higher-order radicals. You may want to have students use the factored form of the numbers. For example, $\sqrt[4]{162} = \sqrt[4]{3^4} \cdot 2$.

11.9 This section on the distance formula provides application problems and demonstrates a relationship between algebra and geometry. In the derivation of the distance formula it is stated that $|a - b|^2 = (a - b)^2$. You might show examples when $a - b$ is positive and then examples when $a - b$ is negative. The proof would be as follows: If $a - b \geq 0$, then $|a - b| = a - b$ and $|a - b|^2 = (a - b)^2$. If $a - b < 0$, then $|a - b| = b - a$, but $(b - a)^2 = (a - b)^2$.

In Example 2, y represents a coordinate of a point, not a distance, so both positive and negative values are solutions to the problem. Have students verify that the distances are equal. In exercise 17, radicals must be subtracted and squared in order to find the distance. In exercise 31, if the three points lie on a circle, the distance from each point to the center must be the same.

Other problems of a geometric nature could be used in this section. Students could be asked to determine if a triangle is isosceles or equilateral by finding the length of the three sides.

12•Quadratic Equations

Overview In this chapter, students learn to solve quadratic equations by factoring, by using the square-root property, by completing the square so that one side of the equation is a perfect-square trinomial, or by using the quadratic formula. Then the discriminant is used to determine the nature of the roots of a quadratic equation. Next students solve problems by writing and solving quadratic equations. The concept of quadratic function is introduced and graphed as a parabola. Finally, students use quadratic functions to solve problems.

Teaching Suggestions

12.1 Introduce the section with a review of factoring. Include polynomials that have common monomial factors, binomials that are the difference of two squares, and trinomials. Remind students to look for a common monomial factor as the first step in the factoring process.

Students usually find it easier to factor if the leading coefficient is positive. The factoring is difficult in exercises 22, 26, and 33 because the coefficients are large and have many factors. In exercises 37–42, students are given the roots of an equation and asked to write the equation. These problems require the students to reverse the process of the previous exercises. Students often forget to set the trinomial equal to zero to form an equation.

The C exercises contain third degree equations that have x as a common factor.

12.2 Students will be familiar with the square-root property from the previous chapter. This section prepares students for the method of completing the square and the quadratic formula. In expressing the answers to some problems, students will need to use their knowledge of simplifying square roots, including square roots of decimals. A short review of square root simplification with examples like $\sqrt{0.81}$ and $\sqrt{1.44}$ will help students to completely simplify the answers to the exercises.

In the C exercises the left side of each equation is a perfect-square trinomial. These exercises could be used to introduce the next section on completing the square.

12.3 Introduce the section by presenting some perfect-square trinomials. Have students factor them. Review the general form $a^2x^2 + 2abx + b^2$. Emphasize that the first step of the process of completing the square is to change the coefficient of x^2 to 1 so that the trinomial is in the form $x^2 + 2bx + b^2$. Point out that if the first two terms are given, then the number to be added to make a perfect-square trinomial is the square of one-half the coefficient of the linear term. Have students practice several examples where the coefficient of x is odd or is a fraction before beginning the problem set.

The method of solving by completing the square is presented so that students can follow the derivation of the quadratic formula in the next section. Exercise 50 is a derivation of the quadratic formula.

12.4 It may help students to follow the derivation of the quadratic formula from the standard form of the equation by using an exercise from the previous section in a parallel development. Students should not be expected to learn the derivation. Point out in the statement of the quadratic formula that the equation must be in standard form, and discuss the restriction that $b^2 - 4ac \geq 0$. In exercise 14, there are no real solutions, and students should write the answer to the exercise as *no real solution*.

Students will probably have trouble simplifying answers such as $\dfrac{4 \pm 2\sqrt{3}}{16} = \dfrac{2(2 \pm \sqrt{3})}{2 \cdot 8} = \dfrac{2 \pm \sqrt{3}}{8}$, and finding the value of $b^2 - 4ac$ when a, b, or c is irrational.

12.5 This section provides an opportunity for students to discover some relationships between the discriminant of a quadratic equation and the numbers that are the roots. Use examples from previous assignments and present them in chart form such as the following:

Equation	Value of $b^2 - 4ac$	Roots	Description of Roots

Using this chart, students should discover how the discriminant can be used to determine the nature of the roots.

In the Oral Exercises, it is assumed that a, b, and c are rational. This section provides a good opportunity for students to use calculators.

12.6 Students will probably find that problems that are solved by a quadratic equation are difficult. Discuss the examples with the class. In Example 3, have students fill in the steps between $\dfrac{36}{5-c} - 2 = \dfrac{42}{5+c}$ and $c^2 + 39c - 40 = 0$.

$$\frac{36}{5-c} - 2 = \frac{42}{5+c}$$
$$(5-c)(5+c)\left[\frac{36}{5-c} - 2\right] = \left[\frac{42}{5+c}\right](5-c)(5+c)$$
$$36(5+c) - 2(5-c)(5+c) = 42(5-c)$$
$$180 + 36c - 2(25 - c^2) = 210 - 42c$$
$$180 + 36c - 50 + 2c^2 = 210 - 42c$$
$$2c^2 + 78c - 80 = 0$$
$$c^2 + 39c - 40 = 0$$

Before discussing Example 4, provide some problems related to work and rates, such as the following: If it takes Sue 2 hours to stuff envelopes, how much of the job will she do in an hour? $\left(\frac{1}{2}\right)$ If it takes Joe 3 hours to do the same job, what part of the job will he complete in an hour? $\left(\frac{1}{3}\right)$ If they work together for an hour, what part of the job will be done? $\left(\frac{1}{2} + \frac{1}{3}, \text{ or } \frac{5}{6}\right)$ Then the question, How long should they work together to complete the job? can lead to an equation.

12.7 Introduce this section on quadratic functions with a review of the definition of a function. Provide examples of linear and constant functions that were studied previously.

In Example 2, discuss the order of operations when evaluating $-2x^2 + 3$.

Stress that, when graphing a quadratic function, students should find the vertex and the y-intercept. Encourage them to use the axis of symmetry to find another point with the same y-coordinate as the intercept. Discuss questions such as the following:

If the equation of the axis of symmetry is $x = 2$, and the y-intercept $= 3$, name another point on the graph. $(4, 3)$

If the points $(-2, 4)$ and $(3, 4)$ are points on a parabola, what is the equation of the axis of symmetry? $\left(x = \frac{1}{2}\right)$

12.8 Discuss why the graph of the function shown in Example 1 has a maximum value and what that value is. Students should see from the graph that a given value for height may be attained at two different time values. In most of the exercises the students are asked to find the minimum or maximum function value and the x value at which it occurs.

13·Statistics

Overview In this chapter, students learn to organize data by using a stem-and-leaf display and by using a frequency distribution. Students use graphs to help them interpret information about data. Measures of central tendency (mode, median, and mean) and measures of variation (range, variance, and standard deviation) are used to describe certain characteristics of a set of data.

Teaching Suggestions

You may want to let students use calculators in some sections.

13.1 Students should find that a stem-and-leaf display is a fast and easy way to organize raw data.

In Example 2, point out that it is not necessary to list the stem 28, since it has no leaves. However, the 28 would have to be listed when the data are used to make a graph. The graph would be distorted in shape if the stem 28 were omitted.

In Example 3, emphasize that the numbers for the group on the left are read in reverse order. That is, 4 | 6 is the number 64.

You may want to point out that stem-and-leaf displays are useful because individual numbers are readily obtainable. In the next section, students may find that making a grouped frequency distribution is a faster way of organizing data, but once a number has been assigned to an interval, its actual value is no longer obtainable from the table.

13.2 Students may already be familiar with the fence tally method. Point out that the tally marks are grouped by fives for easier counting.

Many scientists and researchers used grouped frequency distributions. They usually must determine what intervals will be used with the data that have been collected. The smallest number of intervals used is usually 6, or there would not be enough differentiation of the scores. The largest number of intervals is usually 20, or the work done with the scores could become too cumbersome. The difference between the smallest and the largest number of an interval must be the same for each interval. That is, each interval must be of the same "length." (An exception is when an open-ended interval is used, such as the "65 and over.") Finally, a score cannot belong to more than one interval. That is, intervals such as 5–10, 10–15, 15–20, and so on, should not be used.

13.3 Point out that bar charts can be used when the data are not numbers. However, the histogram and the frequency polygon are more often used for data that are numbers.

13.4 Point out to students that the mode is the only measure of central tendency that can be used with data that are not numbers.

The median is the measure of central tendency usually used when extreme numbers are not an important consideration. For example, a median is more often used to describe the average cost of a house or to describe the average income of a group of people.

The mean is preferred as the measure of central tendency when *every* number is considered important. A student's grade average is usually the mean of all the scores. Sports, such as football and bowling, use the mean to describe different averages.

13.5 You might mention that sometimes statisticians write the range as the indicated difference between the smallest number and the greatest number from the set of data. In Example 1, the range for Test Form A would be written as 78–86 and the range for Test Form B would be written as 30–100.

Point out that the variance and standard deviation are used in conjunction with the mean of a set of data. That is, the variance or the standard deviation would not be used to describe the spread of the data if the mode or the median was used to represent the set of data.

Calculator Some students will find this calculator feature useful as a time saver when computing standard deviations. You may want to use this feature as a part of the lesson. If a calculator does not have memory keys, it can still save time on arithmetic computations.

13.6 Emphasize that quartiles are used to describe the spread of the data when the median is the measure of central tendency used to represent the data.

Make sure students understand that Q_2 should not be included in the data when finding Q_1 and Q_3 when Q_2 is the average of two numbers. On the other hand, Q_2 must be included when finding both Q_1 and Q_3 if Q_2 is one of the numbers of the set of data.

The box-and-whisker plot is another type of graph, showing pictorially how the data are spread in relation to the quartiles and the extreme values of the data.

14·Probability

Overview This chapter on probability begins with ways to present the sample space for a situation by making a list, a table, or a tree diagram. The fundamental counting principle and the concepts of permutations and combinations are introduced as ways to count the outcomes in a sample space. The section on experimental probability involves experiments with chance in which the ratio of the number of specific outcomes to the total number of times the experiment is performed is considered. Then theoretical probability is presented, in which the sample space consists of equally likely outcomes, mutually exclusive events, events that are not mutually exclusive, and finally, successive independent events and successive dependent events.

Teaching Suggestions

14.1 Emphasize the relationship between outcomes and sample space. Using a tree diagram will help students to understand the fundamental counting principle. In Example 3, if they can actually see that there are four possible photographs that can be used with each book-cover color, then they will realize that by multiplying the number of colors by the number of photographs, they will obtain the number of possible outcomes.

14.2 Students will probably have little difficulty with permutations. However, when combinations are introduced, they may become confused. Consequently, for each exercise, have students first determine whether or not the order of arrangement is important. Then they should find it fairly easy to apply the principle of permutations and combinations.

14.3 You may want to review percent before beginning this section.

Emphasize that a sample space consists of all possible outcomes, while an event consists of only some outcomes. When students toss a coin, record telephone numbers, and count letters in the written exercises, they will understand the concepts better.

14.4 In this section, students determine the probability of an event occurring without actually performing the experiment.

Students should understand that the probability of an event that is certain to occur is always 1, while the probability of an event that is certain not to occur is always 0. Often it is easier to find the probability of an event not occurring if the probability that the event will occur is found and then subtracted from 1. For example, show that the solution to Example 7 can also be found as follows:

$$p(1) + p(2) + p(4) + p(5) + p(6)$$
$$= \frac{1}{6} + \frac{1}{6} + \frac{1}{6} + \frac{1}{6} + \frac{1}{6} = \frac{5}{6}$$

Similarly, in Example 8, point out to students that an alternative solution is p(queen) $\times$ p(red card) = $\frac{4}{52} \times \frac{1}{2} = \frac{2}{52} = \frac{1}{26}$.

14.5 Students may have some difficulty determining what constitutes mutually exclusive events. Stress that students need to define A, B, and A $\cap$ B, and then find p(A), p(B), and p(A $\cap$ B), when using the addition rule for mutually exclusive events or the addition rule for events not mutually exclusive.

14.6 In this section, students consider events that are successive and independent, and ten events that are successive and dependent. Review the fundamental counting principle from Section 14.1 and show that the multiplication rule is essentially the same principle.

15·Right-Triangle Trigonometry

Overview This chapter begins with the classification of angles according to their measurements and the classification of triangles according to the measurements of their angles. Then the terms that relate to the sides and the angles of a right triangle are introduced. Next the corresponding angles and the corresponding sides of similar triangles are presented and the trigonometric ratios of the acute angles of a right triangle are introduced. A trigonometric table is then used to find the sine, the cosine, and the tangent of a given angle or to find the measurement of an angle, given the trigonometric decimal approximation. Right triangles are solved. Finally the chapter concludes with a problem-solving section involving trigonometric concepts.

Teaching Suggestions

15.1 Students are introduced to some basic geometric definitions, such as the naming of a ray, an angle, a triangle, and types of angles and triangles. Stress the importance of these definitions, which are used in the written exercises. When discussing the naming of a ray, have students also name the following:

$$\overset{\longleftarrow}{\underset{R \qquad\qquad T}{\bullet\qquad\qquad\bullet}} \qquad (\overrightarrow{TR})$$

Parts of a right triangle and the Pythagorean theorem are mentioned in this section. Have students review these concepts, if necessary. In the C exercises, students are asked to determine if the numbers given could represent lengths of the sides of a right triangle. You may want to do an example comparable to these if you assign these exercises.

15.2 The importance of similar triangles is stressed. Students will need practice in setting up the proportions. Remind them to be consistent when they compare the corresponding parts of two triangles.

15.3 Before discussing the trigonometric ratios of sine, cosine, and tangent, you may want to review simplifying a ratio. Students will be asked to use the Pythagorean theorem to determine the length of a missing side before applying the trigonometric ratio. Ask students if they can see the relationship between the sine of one acute angle and the cosine of its complement. Discuss the relationship between the tangents of two acute angles.

Before assigning the C exercises, you may want to do an example such as the following:
If sin A is $\frac{3}{5}$, what is cos A?

15.4 Students will familiarize themselves with a trigonometric table by finding the sine, cosine, and tangent of an angle. In Example 3, students learn what to do if the sine, cosine, or tangent is not specifically listed in the table.

15.5 In this section, students learn how to use trigonometric ratios to find the measures of sides and angles in a right triangle. Discuss the examples thoroughly. Point out that students should always use the function that involves the simplest calculation. Example 3 in volves the Pythagorean theorem and then the trigonometric ratios. You may want to decide whether or not these calculations are to be done by using a calculator.

15.6 In this section, students determine distances from one object to another through the use of the trigonometric ratios. The angle of elevation and the angle of depression are used in the exercises. Stress the importance of making a correct diagram.

Computer The BASIC commands SIN and COS assume that the given angles are measured in *radians,* not in degrees. The program converts the value you input for S (in degrees) to a value in radians that BASIC can properly interpret. Line 40 contains a STEP statement that converts to radians (S degrees = S * PI / 180 radians) in a FOR loop that runs from 1° to 360°. The triangles drawn, therefore, appear as if the computer worked in degrees. To see this, you can use "70,45" and "70,15" as input values for the program. The results will be triangles with their terminal sides spaced 45° and 15° apart, respectively, on the screen.

ENRICHMENT ACTIVITIES

Enrichment Activity 1

Find the pattern for squaring a 2-digit number whose units digit is 5.

$(75)^2 = 5625$ $(45)^2 = 2025$
$(65)^2 = ?$ $(25)^2 = ?$ $(95)^2 = ?$

Answer $(75)^2 = \underset{\smile}{5625}$

These digits depend ↑ ↑ These digits will
on the tens digit of ⎤ ⎣ always be 25.
the original number.⎦

Let k represent the tens digit in the original number. In this example, let $k = 7$; then $k + 1 = 8$. The product $k(k + 1)$, or $7(8)$, is to the left of the 25 in the product.

The following explanation uses the expanded form of the original number. Let k represent the tens digit in the original number. Then $10k + 5$ is the expanded form of the number.

$$(10k + 5)^2 = 100k^2 + 100k + 25$$
$$= 100k(k + 1) + 25$$

Using $(75)^2 = (10k + 5)^2$
$$= (10 \cdot 7 + 5)^2$$
$$= 100(7)(7 + 1) + 25$$
$$= 100 (56) + 25$$
$$= 5625$$

Enrichment Activity 2

1. Simplify $\dfrac{(12)(\frac{1}{4})}{(18)(\frac{1}{3})} \div \dfrac{(16)(\frac{1}{2})}{(\frac{1}{5})(25)}$.

Answer $\dfrac{5}{16}$

2. Simplify $6 + 7[4(3a + 2b + 6) + 3(4b + 6a - 7) + 2]$.

Answer $210a + 140b + 41$

3. Write an algebraic expression describing the number of feet in y yards, f feet, and i inches.

Answer $3y + f + \dfrac{i}{12}$

4. Simplify $5x + y + 3.5z - 1\frac{1}{6}z + 2\frac{1}{2}x + 3\frac{1}{2}y$.

Answer $7\frac{1}{2}x + 4\frac{1}{2}y + 2\frac{1}{3}z$

5. In a group of cows and chickens, the number of legs was 14 more than twice the number of heads. Find the number of cows.

Answer Let $x =$ the number of cows and $y =$ the number of chickens.

Then $x + y =$ the number of heads and $4x + 2y =$ the number of legs.

$$4x + 2y - 14 = 2x + 2y$$
$$2x = 14$$
$$x = 7$$

So, there are 7 cows in the group.

Enrichment Activity 3

Find the missing digits in the division. There is only one solution.

Answer $50\overline{)1900}$ with quotient 38

Enrichment Activity 4

Consider the properties in Section 1.3. Investigate each property with respect to subtraction and division. Decide which, if any, hold for subtraction or division.

Answer Let a, b, and c be any numbers.

	Subtraction	Division
Commutative property	$a - b \neq b - a$	$a \div b \neq b \div a$
Associative property	$(a - b) - c \neq$ $a - (b - c)$	$(a \div b) \div c \neq$ $a \div (b \div c)$
Identity property	$a - 0 \neq 0 - a \neq a$	$a \div 1 \neq 1 \div a \neq a$
Distributive property of division over subtraction	$a \div (b - c) \neq a \div b - a \div c$ or $(b - c) \div a = b \div a - c \div a$	
Substitution property	If $a = b$, then a may be substituted for b.	

The distributive property holds in only one of the two cases, and the substitution property holds for subtraction and division.

Enrichment Activity 5

A man bought an item on sale at Store A for 10% off. Later he noticed that the same item was on sale at Store B for 20% off. When he returned to Store A, the manager gave him a refund of 10% of what he had paid. What percent of the original price did he lose by this double discount method?

Answer Let x be the original price. Let y be the sale price at 20% off. Let z be the price at 10% off the sale price, which is 10% off the original price.

Then $y = (1 - 0.2)x = 0.8x$
$z = (1 - 0.1)(1 - 0.1)x = 0.9(0.9)x = 0.81x$
$z - y = 0.81x - 0.8x = 0.01x$
He lost 1% of the original price.

Variation Suppose Store A gave 20% off and then 20% off the sale price and Store B gave 40% off. How much more did Store A charge than Store B?

Answer In the same manner as the previous answer,
$z - y = 0.64x - 0.6x$
$\qquad = 0.04x$
Store A charged 4% more than Store B.

Enrichment Activity 6

A rope is placed over the top of a fence, with the same length on both sides. The rope weighs $\frac{1}{3}$ pound per foot. On one end of the rope, a monkey hangs holding a banana, and on the other end is a weight weighing the same as the monkey. The banana weighs 2 ounces per inch. The length of the rope in feet is equal to the age of the monkey, and the monkey's weight in ounces is equal to the monkey's mother's age. Together, the ages of the monkey and his mother total 30 years. The weight of the banana plus $\frac{1}{2}$ the weight of the monkey is $\frac{1}{4}$ as much as the sum of the weights of the monkey and the rope, with all weights in the same units. The monkey's mother is $\frac{1}{2}$ as old as the monkey will be when it is 3 times as old as the mother was when she was $\frac{1}{2}$ as old as the monkey will be when it is twice as old as it is now. How long is the banana?

Answer Let monkey's age be a a_m; monkey's

mother's age, $a_{mm} = \frac{3}{2}a_m$. Let x be rope length in feet; weight of rope, $w = \frac{16x}{3}$ oz. Let y be banana length in feet; weight is 24 oz/ft.

Since $a_m + a_{mm} = 30$, $a_m = 12$ years. and $a_{mm} = 18$ years. $24y + \frac{1}{2}(18) = \frac{1}{4}(18 + 64)$, from which y, the length of banana, is $5\frac{3}{4}$ inches.

Enrichment Activity 7

Each letter represents one of the ten decimal digits and each letter is a different digit. Decode the letters.

$$\begin{array}{r} S\ E\ N\ D \\ +\ M\ O\ R\ E \\ \hline M\ O\ N\ E\ Y \end{array}$$

Answer

$$\begin{array}{r} 9\ 5\ 6\ 7 \\ +\ \ 1\ 0\ 8\ 5 \\ \hline 1\ 0\ 6\ 5\ 2 \end{array}$$

M must be 1. S must then be 9, or 8 if 1 is carried from the hundreds place.

Enrichment Activity 8

On a 50-question test, each correct answer scores $+5$ points and each incorrect answer scores -2 points. How many answers are correct if a student scores 166? 117? What is the least number of correct answers needed so that the score is positive? Find a rule to do these problems.

Answer Use the guess-and-check strategy. Start by assuming that if there are 25 correct answers, then there are 25 incorrect answers. So the resulting score is $25(5) + 25(-2) = 75$. Inductively, it can be seen that each additional correct answer results in $+7$ points, $+5$ for being correct and $-(-2)$ for one less incorrect. A score of 166 is 91 points more than 75, and $91 = 7 \cdot 13$. Thus, there are 13 more correct answers, or $13 + 25 = 38$ correct answers. A score of 117 results from 31 correct answers. At least 15 answers must be correct so that the score is positive.

Let $x =$ the number of correct answers; then the rule is $5x - 2(50 - x) =$ the given score.

Enrichment Activity 9

The base of an isosceles triangle is 12 cm less than twice one of the equal sides. The perimeter is 64 cm. Find the length of each side.

Answer Let x = length of each equal side; then $2x - 12$ = length of base.

$$\text{Perimeter} = x + x + (2x - 12) = 64$$
$$4x - 12 = 64$$
$$4x = 76$$
$$x = 19$$

$$2x - 12 = 2(19) - 12$$
$$= 26$$

So the lengths of the three sides are 19 cm, 19 cm, and 26 cm.

Enrichment Activity 10

What number decreased by $\frac{3}{5}$ of itself equals 26?

Answer Let x = the number.

$$x - \frac{3}{5}x = 26$$
$$\frac{2}{5}x = 26$$
$$\frac{5}{2} \cdot \frac{2}{5}x = \frac{5}{2} \cdot 26$$
$$x = 65$$

Enrichment Activity 11

Solve each problem.

1. If 18 is added to a number and that sum is multiplied by 2, then the product is more than 90. What numbers are possible?

Answer Let n = possible numbers.

$$2(n + 18) > 90$$
$$n + 18 > 45$$
$$n > 27$$

Any number greater than 27 is possible.

2. Dan is paid twice as much per hour as Peter. If Dan works 8 hours and Peter works 5 hours, together they earn less than $84. How much does Peter earn per hour?

Answer Let x = Peter's hourly wage.

$$5x + 8(2x) < 84$$
$$5x + 16x < 84$$
$$21x < 84$$
$$x < 4$$

Peter earns less than $4 per hour.

3. A package of paper towels containing 280 sheets costs $1.19. At what price would a roll containing 200 sheets have a lower price per sheet?

Answer Let x = lower price.

$$\frac{1.19}{280} > \frac{x}{200}$$
$$238 > 280x$$
$$0.85 > x$$

A package of 200 sheets costing $0.84 or less has a lower price per sheet.

4. A TV repairer charges $24 for the first hour of labor and $18 for each additional hour or part of an hour. How many hours could the repairer work to have the bill be at most $132?

Answer Let x = number of hours worked.

$$24 + 18(x - 1) \le 132$$
$$24 + 18x - 18 \le 132$$
$$18x \le 126$$
$$x \le 7$$

The repairer could work at most 7 hours.

Enrichment Activity 12

Many banks offer more than one checking-account plan. When choosing a plan, you want to determine which plan will be more economical for you.

Consider the following two plans:

Plan A	Plan B
$600 minimum balance	$3 per month basic fee
No further fees	10¢ per check written

Plan A appears to offer free checking, but the $600 could earn interest in a savings account if it were not required to maintain the minimum balance. The interest that could be earned is actually the cost of Plan A.

Suppose the $600 required for Plan A could earn 6% annual interest in a savings account. Would Plan A cost less than Plan B for a person who writes an average of seven checks each month? Consider the cost of each plan over a year. In one year, $600 at 6% interest would have earned $36. To compare this to the cost of Plan B for one year, write an inequality:

Plan A　　　　Plan B

$$(600)(0.06) \overset{?}{<} 12[3 + 0.10(7)]$$
$$36 \overset{?}{<} 12(3.70)$$
$$36 < 44.40$$

Plan A does cost less for a person who writes an average of seven checks per month.

EXERCISES In the following exercises, the interest rate is 6% and the charge per check is 10¢.

1. Write an inequality and determine if Plan A, as described above, costs less when an average of two checks per month are written.

2. At another bank, a minimum balance of $400 is required for Plan A. The basic fee under Plan B is $1 per month.

   a. Does this bank's Plan A cost less when an average of eight checks are written per month?

   b. Does this bank's Plan A cost less when an average of fifteen checks are written per month?

   c. For what number of checks per month is Plan A more economical than Plan B?

Answers

1. $(600)(0.06) \overset{?}{<} 12[3 + 0.10(2)]$
   $$36 < 38.40$$
   Plan A costs less.

2. a. for 8 checks
   $$(400)(0.06) \overset{?}{<} 12[1 + 0.10(8)]$$
   $$24 < 21.60 \quad \text{This is false.}$$
   Plan A costs more than Plan B.

   b. for 15 checks
   $$(400)(0.06) \overset{?}{<} 12[1 + 0.10(15)]$$
   $$24 < 30$$
   Plan A costs less than Plan B.

   c. Let x = number of checks per month.
   $$(400)(0.06) < 12(1 + 0.10x)$$
   $$24 < 12 + 1.2x$$
   $$12 < 1.2x$$
   $$10 < x \quad \text{or} \quad x > 10$$
   So Plan A costs less when the number of checks is at least 11.

Enrichment Activity 13

You can find $(59)^2$ by rewriting 59 as $(50 + 9)^2$.
Since $(a + b)^2 = a^2 + 2ab + b^2$,
Then $(50 + 9)^2 = 50^2 + 2(50 \cdot 9) + 9^2$
$$= 2500 + 900 + 81$$
$$= 3481$$
So $(59)^2 = 3481$
Study this shortcut.

Write $(59)^2$ as

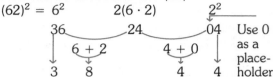

Add the digits from right to left as shown.

Now use the shortcut to find $(62)^2$.

$(62)^2 = 6^2 \qquad 2(6 \cdot 2) \qquad 2^2$

36 $\qquad$ 24 $\qquad$ 04 $\quad$ Use 0

$6 + 2 \qquad 4 + 0 \qquad$ as a place-

3 $\quad$ 8 $\qquad$ 4 $\qquad$ 4 $\quad$ holder.

EXERCISES Use the shortcut.

1. $(87)^2$ 2. $(51)^2$ 3. $(34)^2$ 4. $(49)^2$ 5. $(63)^2$

Answers

1. 7569 2. 2601 3. 1156 4. 2401 5. 3969

Enrichment Activity 14

What do you do if the exponents are negative? An important rule to know: For every nonzero number b and every positive number n, $b^{-n} = \dfrac{1}{b^n}$.

Examples:

1. $\dfrac{b^3}{b^7} = b^{3-7} = b^{-4}$ 2. $(b^2)^{-3} = b^{-6}$

3. $\dfrac{1}{a^2b} = a^{-2}b^{-1}$ or $(a^2b)^{-1}$

4. $\dfrac{a^{-5}b^2}{a^3b^4} = a^{-5-3}b^{2-4} = a^{-8}b^{-2}$

EXERCISES Simplify each expression so that each denominator is 1.

1. $\dfrac{a^{-3}b^2}{a^5b^{-3}}$ 2. $\dfrac{x^{-5}s^3}{x\,s^{-4}}$ 3. $\dfrac{4a^{-3}bc^{-2}}{a^{-1}b^{-1}c}$ 4. $\dfrac{2r^{-1}}{sr^{-2}}$

5. $\dfrac{6ab^{-2}}{a^{-1}b}$ 6. $\dfrac{rs^3t^{-1}}{(rs)^2t^3}$ 7. $\dfrac{(ab)^3c}{ab^2c^2}$ 8. $\dfrac{(2s)^2t^{-3}}{s^3t^{-1}}$

9. $\dfrac{(x^2y^{-1})^2}{y^3}$ 10. $\dfrac{(mn)^2}{(m^2n^{-1})^2}$

Answers

1. $a^{-8}b^5$ 2. $x^{-6}s^7$ 3. $4a^{-2}b^2c^{-3}$ 4. $2s^{-1}r$
5. $6a^2b^{-3}$ 6. $r^{-1}st^{-4}$ 7. a^2bc^{-1} 8. $4s^{-1}t^{-2}$
9. x^4y^{-5} 10. $m^{-2}n^4$

Enrichment Activity 15

A mathematician named Goldbach had two theories about prime numbers. These theories are called *Goldbach's Guess.*

The first theory states that every even number greater than or equal to 6 may be written as the sum of two odd prime numbers. For example, $8 = 3 + 5$; $12 = 5 + 7$; $20 = 13 + 7$ or $20 = 3 + 17$.

Can you find two odd prime numbers whose sum is 10? 16? 24? 30?

The second theory states that an odd number greater than or equal to 9 may be written as the sum of three odd prime numbers. For example, $11 = 3 + 3 + 5$; $15 = 5 + 5 + 5$ or $15 = 3 + 5 + 7$.

Can you find three odd prime numbers whose sum is 13? 17? 25? 33? Why doesn't this theory work for 5, 7, or 3? Why doesn't this theory work for an even number?

Answers $10 = 3 + 7$ or $5 + 5$
$16 = 3 + 13$ or $5 + 11$
$24 = 5 + 19$ or $7 + 17$ or $11 + 13$
$30 = 7 + 23$ or $11 + 19$ or $13 + 17$
$13 = 3 + 3 + 7$ or $3 + 5 + 5$
$17 = 3 + 3 + 11$ or $3 + 7 + 7$ or $5 + 5 + 7$
$25 = 3 + 3 + 19$ or $3 + 5 + 17$ or $3 + 11 + 11$
$33 = 3 + 7 + 23$ or $3 + 11 + 19$ or $3 + 13 + 17$
The theory does not work for 3, 5, or 7 because 1 is not a prime number. It does not work for an even number because the sum of three odd numbers will always be an odd number.

Enrichment Activity 16

There is a theory that states that the square of the sum of any two numbers can never be less than four times the product of the two numbers. That is, if a and b are the two numbers, then $(a + b)^2 \geq 4ab$.

1. Let $a = 2$ and let $b = 3$. Substitute these values and check the theory.
2. Let $a = 4$ and let $b = 8$. Substitute these values and check the theory.
3. Let $a = 4$ and let $b = -8$. Substitute these values and check the theory.
4. What if $a = b$?

Answers

1. $(a + b)^2 \geq 4ab$

$(2 + 3)^2 \overset{?}{\geq} 4 \cdot 2 \cdot 3$

$5^2 \overset{?}{\geq} 24$

$25 \geq 24$ ✔

2. $(a + b)^2 \geq 4ab$

$(4 + 8)^2 \overset{?}{\geq} 4 \cdot 4 \cdot 8$

$(12)^2 \overset{?}{\geq} 128$

$144 \geq 128$ ✔

3. $(a + b)^2 \geq 4ab$

$[4 + (-8)]^2 \overset{?}{\geq} 4 \cdot 4(-8)$

$(-4)^2 \overset{?}{\geq} -128$

$16 \geq -128$ ✔

4. $(a + b)^2 = (a + a)^2$
$= (2a)^2$
$= 4 \cdot a \cdot a$
$= 4ab$ ✔

Enrichment Activity 17

Without graphing, tell whether each line would intersect the shaded region shown in 1 point, 0 points, or infinitely many points.

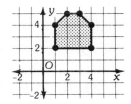

1. $y = 1$ **2.** $y = x - 2$ **3.** $x = 1$
4. $y + x = 3$ **5.** $y = x + 2$ **6.** $y = 3$
7. $y + x = 8$ **8.** $y = x + 2$ **9.** $y = 2$
10. $y = x + 8$ **11.** $x = 2$ **12.** $y = 4x$

Answers

1. 0 points   **2.** infinitely many points
3. infinitely many points   **4.** infinitely many points
5. infinitely many points   **6.** infinitely many points
7. 1 point   **8.** 1 point
9. infinitely many points   **10.** infinitely many points
11. 0 points   **12.** 1 point

Enrichment Activity 18

Each set of ordered pairs lists three vertices of a rectangle. Determine the coordinates of the fourth vertex.

1. $\left(-\frac{1}{2}, -1\right), (-5, -7), (-5, -1)$
2. $(1, -2.5), (-3, -3), (1, -3)$
3. $(-3, -3), (-4, 4), (0, 0)$
4. $(0, 0), (2, 4), (2, -1)$

Answers

1. $\left(-\frac{1}{2}, -7\right)$ **2.** $(-3, -2.5)$ **3.** $(-7, 1)$ **4.** $(4, 3)$

Enrichment Activity 19

Show that the equation of the line having x-intercept $(a, 0)$ and y-intercept $(0, b)$ is $\frac{x}{a} + \frac{y}{b} = 1$.

Answer

$$y = mx + b$$
$$0 = m(a) + b$$
$$am = -b$$
$$m = -\frac{b}{a}$$
$$y = -\frac{b}{a}x + b$$
$$y = b\left(-\frac{x}{a} + 1\right)$$
$$\frac{y}{b} = \frac{-x}{a} + 1$$
$$\frac{x}{a} + \frac{y}{b} = 1$$

Enrichment Activity 20

Simplify the following for each $f(x)$: $\frac{1}{h}[f(x + h) - f(x)]$:

1. $f(x) = 2x + 1$ **2.** $f(x) = x^2 + 7x$
3. $f(x) = x^2$ **4.** $f(x) = -3x + 5$
5. $f(x) = x^2 - 6x + 4$ **6.** $f(x) = x^3$

Answers

1. 2   **2.** $2x + h + 7$ **3.** $2x + h$
4. -3 **5.** $2x + h - 6$ **6.** $3x^2 + 3xh + h^2$

Enrichment Activity 21

Graphs of quadratic equations such as $y = ax^2 + bx + c$ are always cup-shaped or curved. These curves are called parabolas. Some parabolas are thin and others are flat, but they all have the same general shape.

To graph a quadratic equation, choose some numbers for x and compute the corresponding values for y. In some cases you may first want to choose some values for y and then compute x.

Example: Graph $y = -2x^2 + 1$.

x	y
0	1
1	-1
-1	-1
2	-7
-2	-7

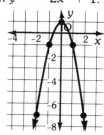

Graph the following quadratic equations:

1. $y = 2x^2$ **2.** $y = x^2 - 1$ **3.** $y = -x^2$
4. $y^2 = x$ **5.** $y^2 + 1 = x$ **6.** $y = -x^2 + 2x$

7. $y = \frac{1}{2}x^2$ **8.** $y = x^2 + 2x + 1$

Answers

1. $y = 2x^2$

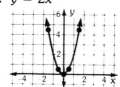

2. $y = x^2 - 1$

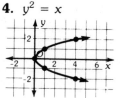

3. $y = -x^2$

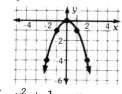

4. $y^2 = x$

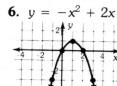

5. $y^2 + 1 = x$

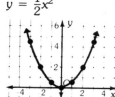

6. $y = -x^2 + 2x$

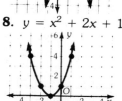

7. $y = \frac{1}{2}x^2$

8. $y = x^2 + 2x + 1$

Enrichment Activity 22

You can use determinants to solve a system of equations. The determinant in both denominators is formed from the coefficients of x and y. In the numerator for the value of x, the coefficients of x are replaced by the constants. Likewise, in the numerator for the values of y, the coefficients of y are replaced by the constants.

You can find the general solution of the system by using determinants. The solution can be written as follows:

$$Ax + By = C$$
$$Dx + Ey = F$$

$$x = \frac{CE - BF}{AE - BD} = \frac{\begin{vmatrix} C & B \\ F & E \end{vmatrix}}{\begin{vmatrix} A & B \\ D & E \end{vmatrix}}; \quad y = \frac{AF - CD}{AE - BD} = \frac{\begin{vmatrix} A & C \\ D & F \end{vmatrix}}{\begin{vmatrix} A & B \\ D & E \end{vmatrix}}$$

Example: Use determinants to solve the system.

$3x - y = 11$
$5x + 7y = 1$

$$x = \frac{\begin{vmatrix} 11 & -1 \\ 1 & 7 \end{vmatrix}}{\begin{vmatrix} 3 & -1 \\ 5 & 7 \end{vmatrix}} = \frac{77 - (-1)}{21 - (-5)} = \frac{78}{26} = 3$$

$$y = \frac{\begin{vmatrix} 3 & 11 \\ 5 & 1 \end{vmatrix}}{\begin{vmatrix} 3 & -1 \\ 5 & 7 \end{vmatrix}} = \frac{3 - 55}{21 - (-5)} = \frac{-52}{26} = -2$$

So $(x, y) = (3, -2)$.

Solve each system of equations by using determinants.

1. $3x + 2y = 1$
   $2x - 3y = 18$
2. $x + y = 1$
   $x - y = 5$
3. $2x + y = -5$
   $2x + 3y = 10$
4. $2x - 5y = 1$
   $4x + 2y = 14$

Answers

1. $(3, -4)$ 2. $(3, -2)$ 3. $\left(-\frac{25}{4}, \frac{15}{2}\right)$ 4. $(3, 1)$

Enrichment Activity 23

Here is a convincing argument that $2 = 1$.

$a = b$	Given
$a \cdot a = a \cdot b$	Multiply both sides by a.
$a^2 = ab$	Subtract b^2 from both
$a^2 - b^2 = ab - b^2$	sides.
$(a - b)(a + b) = b(a - b)$	Factor.
$\frac{(a - b)(a + b)}{a - b} = \frac{b(a - b)}{a - b}$	Divide both sides by $(a - b)$.
$a + b = b$	
$b + b = b$	Substitute b for a.
$2b = b$	
$\frac{2b}{b} = \frac{b}{b}$	Divide both sides by b.
$2 = 1$	

Does this argument convince you that $2 = 1$? Where does the argument break down?

Answer This argument had better not convince you that $2 = 1$. The argument breaks down when you divide both sides by $(a - b)$, since it is given that $a = b$, $a - b = 0$ and division by 0 is not allowed.

Enrichment Activity 24

Solve, using scientific notation.

1. Guy, an astrophysicist at one of the national laboratories, wants to find how many seconds it takes for a radio signal to reach the sun from the earth. He knows the sun is 147,000,000 kilometers from the earth and the radio signal travels at a speed of 300,000 kilometers per second. How many seconds does it take?

2. Joanne, an astronomy professor at a university, wants to find how many seconds it takes for light from the sun to reach Mercury. She knows Mercury is 46,700,000 kilometers from the sun and light travels at a speed of 300,000 kilometers per second. How many seconds does it take?

3. Kathy, a meteorologist for the National Weather Service, wants to know the volume of a droplet of water in a fog. She knows that the formula for the volume of a sphere is $V = \frac{4}{3}\pi r^3$ and that the radius of the droplet is 0.00273 centimeter. What is its volume?

4. Pat, a student of quantum physics, wants to know how many atoms there are in a thin square of gold foil. He knows the diameter of a gold atom is about 0.00000000025 meter. The foil measures 1 centimeter on each side and is 0.000001 meter thick. How many gold atoms are there?

Answers

1. 490 sec
2. 156 sec
3. 8.52×10^{-8} cm^3
4. 1.22×10^{19}

Enrichment Activity 25

The following criteria can be used to determine whether an integer is divisible by one of the divisors listed.

Divisor	Criteria of Divisibility
2	The last digit is 0, 2, 4, 6, or 8.
3	The sum of the digits is divisible by 3.
4	The integer named by the last two digits is divisible by 4.
5	The last digit is 0 or 5.
7	Group the digits by threes from the right, mark them alternately positive and negative, and total them. The sum is divisible by 7.
9	The sum of the digits is divisible by 9.
10	The last digit is 0.
11	Mark the digits alternately positive and negative from the right, and total the signed digits. The sum is divisible by 11.
13	Use the same procedure as for 7. The sum is divisible by 13.

1. Is 9,876,543 divisible by 3?
2. Is 21,987,654 divisible by 3?
3. Is 2,468,642 divisible by 4?
4. Is 22,446,688 divisible by 4?
5. Is 789,987 divisible by 7?
6. Is 987,987 divisible by 7?
7. Is 123,456,789 divisible by 9?
8. Is 12,345,678,910 divisible by 9?
9. Is 11,111,111 divisible by 11?
10. Is 111,111,111 divisible by 11?
11. Is 10,987,654,321 divisible by 13?
12. Is 1,917,151,314 divisible by 13?

Answers
1. yes 2. yes 3. no 4. yes 5. no 6. yes
7. yes 8. no 9. yes 10. no 11. no 12. yes

Enrichment Activity 26

Kermit the convict broke out of the state penitentiary. His absence was not noticed until a half hour later, when Willy and Wally the wardens and Benny the bloodhound started chasing after him. Willy and Wally could run only 4 miles per hour, but Benny could run 12 miles per hour. Kermit could run only 3 miles per hour. Benny runs up to Kermit and then back to Willy and Wally, and so on back and forth until Willy and Wally catch Kermit. How far does Benny the bloodhound run all together?

Answer   Let $x =$ the time (in hours) it takes for Willy and Wally to catch Kermit.

$$3\left(\tfrac{1}{2}\right) + 3x = 4x$$

$$x = \frac{3}{2}$$

$$\tfrac{3}{2}(12) = 18 \text{ mi}$$

Enrichment Activity 27

A formula used in the field of nutrition to predict the weight of an average adult after being on a diet for a certain number of days is

$$D = \frac{1}{c}\left[C + (cW - C)\left(\frac{3500 - c}{3500}\right)^{t}\right]$$

where $c =$ calories per pound for constant weight
$C =$ number of calories consumed daily
$W =$ initial weight
$t =$ time in days
$D =$ weight after t days

Use this formula to solve the following problems:
1. Otto is on a 2000-calorie diet. Otto requires 16 calories per pound of body weight per day to maintain his current body weight. He now weighs 350 pounds. What will Otto weigh in 90 days?
2. Helga's doctor recommended that she go on a 1500-calorie diet. She now weighs 200 pounds and requires 19 calories per pound of body weight per day to maintain her present body weight. What will Helga weigh in 30 days?

Answers
1. 274 pounds   2. 182 pounds

Enrichment Activity 28

The following formula is used to determine the monthly payment for a given loan:

$$m = \frac{P\left(\frac{r}{12}\right)\left(1 + \frac{r}{12}\right)^{n}}{\left(1 + \frac{r}{12}\right)^{n} - 1}$$

where $P =$ amount borrowed
$r =$ annual interest rate
$n =$ number of months to repay loan
$m =$ monthly payment

The total interest can then be determined. Use this formula to solve the following problems:
1. Paul and Betsy borrowed $90,000 to buy a house. The annual rate of interest is 10% and the loan must be paid back over a period of 360 months. What is their monthly payment? What is the total interest that they will pay?
2. Brian borrowed $8000 to buy a new car. The annual rate of interest is 8% and the loan must be paid back over a period of 48 months. What is Brian's monthly payment? What is the total interest that Brian will pay?

Answers
1. $789.81; $194,333.19   2. $195.30; $1374.56

Enrichment Activity 29

1. Two commonly used temperature scales, Fahrenheit and Celsius, can be compared by using ratios. 0°C corresponds to 32°F and 100°C corresponds to 212°F, so the ratio of the change in Celsius degrees to the change in Fahrenheit degrees is $\frac{100}{180}$ or $\frac{5}{9}$. A change of 27° on the Fahrenheit scale would correspond to a change of 15° Celsius. $\frac{5}{9} = \frac{\text{change in C}}{27}$.

When the temperature drops from 18°C to −2°C, how many degrees Fahrenheit does it drop?

2. Consider temperature scales, A, B, and C. The charts below indicate corresponding temperatures.

A	B		B	C
12	32		20	54
36	48		32	81

If the temperature drops 12 degrees on scale A, how many degrees does it drop on scale C?

3. You know that to convert a Fahrenheit temperature to a Celsius temperature, the formula $C = \frac{5}{9}(F - 32)$ is used. Write equations to change "A" temperatures to "B" temperatures and "B" temperatures to "C" temperatures. Using these two relationships, derive an equation to convert "A" temperatures to "C" temperatures.

Answers

1. a drop of 20°C $\frac{5}{9} = \frac{20}{F}$

$$F = \frac{9}{5} \cdot 20 = 36$$

2. a drop of 12°A   a drop of 8°B

$\frac{B}{A} = \frac{16}{24} = \frac{2}{3}$ $\frac{C}{B} = \frac{27}{12} = \frac{9}{4}$

$\frac{2}{3} = \frac{B}{12}$ $\frac{9}{4} = \frac{C}{8}$

A change of 12°A = 8°B. A change of 8°B = 18°C.

Alternately: $\frac{C}{A} = \left(\frac{B}{C}\right)\left(\frac{B}{A}\right)$

$\frac{C}{A} = \left(\frac{9}{4}\right)\left(\frac{2}{3}\right) = \frac{3}{2}$

$\frac{3}{2} = \frac{C}{12}$ $C = 18$

3. Equations $B = \frac{2}{3}A + 24$

$$C = \frac{9}{4}B + 9$$

Substitute the expression for B into the second equation to derive $C = \left(\frac{3}{2}\right)A + 63$.

Enrichment Activity 30

A sequence is a listing of numbers in a definite order. 1, 3, 5, 7 is a sequence and is different from the sequence 7, 5, 3, 1. The elements of a sequence are called terms, and a sequence may have an infinite number of terms. A geometric sequence is a sequence in which the ratio of each term to the preceding one is constant. For example, 2, 4, 8, 16 is a geo-

metric sequence, since $\frac{4}{2} = \frac{8}{4} = \frac{16}{8} = \frac{32}{16}$. The ratio of the terms is 2.

Which of the following are geometric sequences? For those that are, give the constant ratio.

1. 81, 27, 9, 3, 1   2. 1, −1, 1, −1
3. 1, 4, 9, 16, 25   4. 5, 1, $\frac{1}{5}$, $\frac{1}{25}$

Give the next three terms of each geometric sequence.

5. $\frac{2}{3}$, $\frac{1}{3}$ 6. 5, 15   7. 9, 12   8. 1, −2

9. In a geometric sequence the first term is 4 and the third term is 25. What is the second term? (There are two answers.)

10. The first term of a geometric sequence is 6 and the fifth term is 96. What are the second, third, and fourth terms? (There are two sets of answers.)

Answers

1. Yes, $r = \frac{1}{3}$ 2. Yes, $r = -1$ 3. No

4. Yes, $r = \frac{1}{5}$ 5. $\frac{1}{6}$, $\frac{1}{12}$, $\frac{1}{24}$ 6. 45, 135, 405

7. 16, $\frac{64}{3}$, $\frac{256}{9}$ 8. 4, −8, 16   9. 10 or −10

10. 12, 24, 48 or −12, 24, −48 Students may be given the hint to first consider a 3-term geometric sequence in which the first term is 6 and the third term is 96.

Enrichment Activity 31

In an isosceles right triangle, the lengths of the two legs are equal.

1. If the legs have length 3, what is the length of the hypotenuse?
2. Find the length of the hypotenuse, **a.** When the legs have length 4. **b.** When the legs have length 8. **c.** When the legs have length $\sqrt{2}$.
3. Prove that if the length of a leg of an isosceles right triangle is x, then the length of the hypotenuse is $x\sqrt{2}$.
4. Find the length of the legs of an isosceles right triangle **a.** When the hypotenuse is $5\sqrt{2}$. **b.** When the hypotenuse is $8\sqrt{2}$. **c.** When the hypotenuse is 12. **d.** When the hypotenuse is 7.
5. Find the perimeter of an isosceles right triangle that has a hypotenuse with length 6.

Answers

1. $3\sqrt{2}$ 2. **a.** $4\sqrt{2}$ **b.** $8\sqrt{2}$ **c.** 2

3. $x^2 + x^2 = c^2$
$2x^2 = 2^2$
$x\sqrt{2} = c$

4. a. 5 **b.** 8 **c.** $6\sqrt{2}$ **d.** $\frac{7}{2}\sqrt{2}$ **5.** $6 + 6\sqrt{2}$

Enrichment Activity 32

Positive integers a, b, and c that satisfy the Pythagorean theorem are called Pythagorean triples. Below are three formulas for generating these triples.

	Leg	Leg	Hypotenuse
n odd number ≥ 3	n	$\frac{n^2 - 1}{2}$	$\frac{n^2 + 1}{2}$
m even number ≥ 4	m	$\frac{m^2}{4} - 1$	$\frac{m^2}{4} + 1$
m and n integers $m > n$	$2mn$	$m^2 - n^2$	$m^2 + n^2$

1. Find the first 5 triples for each formula.
2. Show that each formula satisfies the Pythagorean theorem.
3. Show that the only right triangle in which the sides are consecutive integers is the 3, 4, 5 triangle.

Answers   **1.** 3, 4, 5   4, 3, 5   4, 3, 5
     5, 12, 13   6, 8, 10   6, 8, 10
     7, 24, 25   8, 15, 17   12, 5, 13
     9, 40, 41   10, 24, 26   8, 15, 17
     11, 60, 61   12. 35, 37   16, 12, 20

2. $n^2 + \left(\frac{n^2 - 1}{2}\right)^2$ $m^2 + \left(\frac{m^2}{4} - 1\right)^2$

$= n^2 + \frac{n^4 - 2n^2 + 1}{4}$ $= m^2 + \frac{m^4}{16} - \frac{m}{2} + 1$

$= \frac{n^4 + 2n^2 + 1}{4}$ $= \frac{m^4}{16} + \frac{m^2}{2} + 1$

$= \left(\frac{n^2 + 1}{2}\right)^2$ $= \left(\frac{m^2}{4} + 1\right)^2$

$(2mn)^2 + (m^2 - n^2)^2 = 4m^2n^2 + m^4 - 2m^2n^2 + n^4$
$= m^4 + 2m^2n^2 + n^4$
$= (m^2 + n^2)^2$

3. $x^2 + (x + 1)^2 = (x + 2)^2$
$x^2 + x^2 + 2x + 1 = x^2 + 4x + 4$
$2x^2 + 2x + 1 = x^2 + 4x + 4$
$x^2 - 2x - 3 = 0$
$(x - 3)(x + 1) = 0$
$x = 3$ or $x = -1$

Enrichment Activity 33

From the graph of $y = x^2 - 4x + 3$, determine the following:

1. For what values of x is $x^2 - 4x + 3 < 0$?
2. For what values of x is $x^2 - 4x + 3 \geq 0$?

Graph a quadratic function to solve the following:
3. $x^2 - x - 6 \leq 0$ **4.** $x^2 - 6x + 8 > 0$
5. $x^2 - 2x + 1 < 0$ **6.** $x^2 - 4x + 4 \geq 0$
7. $x^2 - 4x + 1 < 0$
8. Use graphs to show that the solution sets of $-x^2 - 3x + 10 > 0$ and $x^2 + 3x - 10 \leq 0$ are the same.

Answers
1. $x : 1 < x < 3$ **2.** $x \leq 1$ or $x \geq 3$
3. $-2 \leq x \leq 3$ **4.** $x < 2$ or $x > 4$
5. $\varnothing$ **6.** all reals   **7.** $2 - \sqrt{3} < x < 2 + \sqrt{3}$
8.

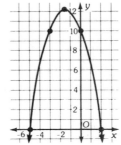 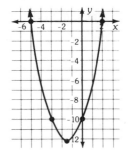

$y = -x^2 - 3x - 10$ $y = x^2 + 3x - 10$
$-5 \leq x \leq 2$ $-5 \leq x \leq 2$

Enrichment Activity 34

A circle with its center at (0, 0) and radius r has the equation $x^2 + y^2 = r^2$. The equation can be derived from the distance formula.

$\sqrt{(x - 0)^2 + (y - 0)^2} = r$
$x^2 + y^2 = r^2$

1. Write the equations of circles with their center at (0, 0) and the following radii:
     a. 4   **b.** 1   **c.** $\sqrt{3}$ **d.** $\frac{1}{2}$

2. The system of equations $\begin{matrix} x^2 + y^2 = 25 \\ y = x + 1 \end{matrix}$ represents the intersection of a circle with its center at (0, 0) and a line. Graph the circle and the line on the same coordinate plane.

3. Find the intersection of the system algebraically by substituting the expression for y in the equation of the circle.
$$x^2 + (x + 1)^2 = 25$$
Then solve the resulting quadratic equation for x, and find the points of intersection.

4. A circle and a line do not always intersect in two points. Draw sketches of other possibilities.

5. Suppose the quadratic equation has a negative discriminant. In how many points do the line and the circle intersect?

6. Solve the following systems:
   a. $x^2 + y^2 = 16$
   $y - x = -4$
   b. $x^2 + y^2 = 36$
   $y = x + 9$
   c. $x^2 + y^2 = 20$
   $x - 2y = 10$

7. A circle of radius $2\sqrt{5}$ has its center at (0, 0). Find the points of intersection of the circle and the line containing the points $(-1, 7)$ and $(3, 3)$.

Answers
1. **a.** $x^2 + y^2 = 16$ 2.
   b. $x^2 + y^2 = 1$
   c. $x^2 + y^2 = 3$
   d. $x^2 + y^2 = \frac{1}{4}$

3. $(-4, -3), (3, 4)$ 4.

5. none   6. **a.** $(4, 0)\ (0, -4)$ **b.** $\emptyset$ **c.** $(2, -4)$
7. $(4, 2)\ (2, 4)$

Enrichment Activity 35

Scores can be tallied by using the box tally method. In the box tally method,
| = 1, Γ = 2, Π = 3, □ = 4,
⊠ = 5, ⊠| = 6, ⊠|| = 7, and so on.
Use this method to do exercises 5–12 on pages 437–438.

Enrichment Activity 36

Circle graphs are often used to convey statistical information. Find examples of circle graphs in newspapers and magazines, and bring the examples to class. Be prepared to discuss the topic of each graph, and know which components are the most important and which are the least important.

Enrichment Activity 37

The Birthday Problem
Perform the following experiment with the students in one class: Ask each student to give the month and the day of his or her birthday. If your class consists of 23 students or more, the probability of at least two birthdays falling on the same month and day is about 0.5. After performing the experiment, show students that the probability of at least two people having the same birthday can be found by using complementary events—that is,

the probability of at least 2 with the same birthday = 1 − the probability of no 2 having the same birthday.

The probability that no 2 students have the same birthday is $\frac{365}{365} \times \frac{364}{365} \times \frac{363}{365} \times \ldots \times \frac{365 - n + 1}{365}$. Each denominator is the total number of days possible in a year (assuming no leap year). Each numerator is the number of days each successive student has to choose from without duplicating a birthday already given. Have students compute the probability of at least two birthdays being the same for the number of students in the class.

Enrichment Activity 38

Gregor Mendel (1822–1884) is credited with using probability in the study of the transmission of dominant and recessive characteristics in heredity. Mendel found that when he crossed a purebred pea plant having a dominant characteristic (D) with a purebred pea plant having a recessive characteristic (r), a plant with the dominant characteristic resulted.

	r	r
D	Dr	Dr
D	Dr	Dr

However, when two plants from this generation (the Dr plants) were crossed, the offspring had the following characteristics:

	D	r
D	DD	Dr
r	rD	rr

1. How many types of offspring are there in the new generation?
2. How many plants in the new generation have the dominant characteristic?
3. How many plants have the recessive characteristic?
4. What is the probability of a plant's having the dominant characteristic?
5. What is the probability of a plant's having the recessive characteristic?

Answers

1. 3   **2.** 3   **3.** 1   **4.** $\frac{3}{4}$ **5.** $\frac{1}{4}$

Enrichment Activity 39

1. A boy who is 120 cm tall casts a shadow 48 cm long at the same time that a light pole casts a shadow 120 cm long. How high is the light pole?
2. A girl who is 5 feet tall casts a shadow 15 inches long. At the same time, a flagpole 8 feet tall casts a shadow. Find the length of the flagpole's shadow. (Use the same unit of measurement.)
3. A department store escalator is 80 feet long. If it rises 30 feet vertically, find the angle it makes with the floor.
4. Radar has detected a jet at a horizontal distance of 22 miles from the control tower. The angle of elevation from the tower to the jet is 15. How high is the plane above the ground to the nearest mile?
5. A 100-m tall cable television tower casts a 70-m shadow. A nearby telephone pole casts a 14-m shadow. Find the height of the telephone pole.
6. A water-skier jumped from point C on the ramp to point B on the water. If $m\angle C = 90$, $b = 130$ ft and $m\angle A = 40$, how long was the jump?
7. A helicopter is 213 m above a level, straight highway. The angle of depression from the helicopter to an accident at point A on the highway ahead is 17. Measured along the ground, how far is the helicopter from the accident?

Answers

1. 300 cm   **2.** 24 inches   **3.** 22°
4. 6 miles   **5.** 20 m   **6.** 109 ft   **7.** 696 m

Enrichment Activity 40

Make a picture on the coordinate plane by connecting these ordered pairs.

Start

1) $(-5, 2)$	17) $(5, -5)$	32) $(3, 0)$
2) $(-4, 1.8)$	18) $(6, -5)$	33) $(2, 0)$
3) $(-3, 1.5)$	19) $(7, -5)$	34) $(1, 0)$
4) $(-2, 1)$	20) $(7.5, -4)$	35) $(0, 0)$
5) $(-2, 0)$	21) $(8, -3)$	36) $(0, 1)$
6) $(-3, -1)$	22) $(8, -2)$	37) $(1, 2)$
7) $(-4, -2)$	23) $(9, -1)$	38) $(1, 3)$
8) $(-4, -3)$	24) $(9, 0)$	39) $(1, 4)$
9) $(-3, -4)$	25) $(9, 1)$	40) $(0, 5)$
10) $(-2, -5)$	26) $(8, 0.3)$	41) $(-1, 5)$
11) $(-1, -5)$	27) $(7.5, 0)$	42) $(-2, 5)$
12) $(0, -5)$	28) $(7, 0)$	43) $(-3, 4)$
13) $(1, -5)$	29) $(6, 0)$	44) $(-3, 3)$
14) $(2, -5)$	30) $(5, 0)$	45) $(-4, 2.5)$
15) $(3, -5)$	31) $(4, 0)$	46) $(-5, 2)$
16) $(4, -5)$		

Answer

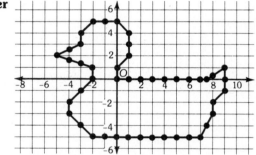

Enrichment Activity 41

1. Use 5 books of different sizes.
2. Stack them in one pile with the largest on the bottom and the smallest on the top.
3. Move all the books from Stack 1 to either Stack 2 or Stack 3.

Stack 1   Stack 2   Stack 3

4. Moves are subject to the following rules:
   a. You may not put a larger book on a smaller one.
   b. You may move only one book at a time.
5. Count the number of steps it takes.
6. Try again. See if you can beat your first try.

PERFORMANCE OBJECTIVES

Chapter 1

The student can do the following:

1.1 Write English phrases as algebraic expressions.

Simplify numerical expressions.

Evaluate algebraic expressions that have parentheses or fraction bars.

Determine the number of terms in an expression.

1.2 Identify coefficients, factors, and variables in terms.

Write products, using exponents.

Use natural-number exponents to simplify numerical expressions.

Use natural-number exponents to evaluate algebraic expressions.

1.3 Identify and use properties of addition and multiplication.

Multiply factors that involve powers.

1.4 Evaluate expressions, using the order of operations.

1.5 Classify a polynomial as a monomial, a binomial, or a trinomial.

Determine the degree of a monomial.

Identify like terms.

Use the distributive property to simplify polynomials.

1.6 Solve problems, emphasizing *draw a diagram* and *look for a pattern*.

Chapter 2

The student can do the following:

2.1 Identify the meaning of set symbols.

Recognize whether or not one set is a subset of another set.

Use the following methods to describe sets: complete listing, partial listing, and set-builder notation.

2.2 Use a number line to give the opposite of any integer.

Use a number line to compare rational numbers.

Give the absolute value of any real number.

2.3 Find the sum of two or more integers, using a number line if necessary.

2.4 Find the sum of two or more real numbers by using the absolute values of the numbers.

Find the sum of two real numbers with different signs by using the additive inverse property.

2.5 Find the difference of any two real numbers by using the subtraction property.

2.6 Find the product of two or more real numbers.

2.7 Find the quotient of any two real numbers.

2.8 Solve nonroutine problems by using the following strategies: *guess-and-check, logical reasoning, solve a simpler problem,* and *use a table*.

2.9 Identify the axiom or theorem illustrated by a sentence.

Give the reason for each statement in a proof.

Chapter 3

The student can do the following:

3.1 Find the solution set of an open sentence by replacing the variable with each number of a given replacement set.

3.2 Solve an equation by using the addition property of equality or the subtraction property of equality.

3.3 Solve an equation by using the multiplication property of equality or the division property of equality.

3.4 Write a rational number as either a repeating decimal or a terminating decimal.

Rename a terminating decimal as a fraction.

Rename a repeating decimal as a fraction.

3.5 Solve an equation by using the distributive property to simplify before using the multiplication property of equality or the division property of equality.

3.6   Solve an equation by using the addition or the subtraction property of equality and then the multiplication or the division property of equality.

3.7   Solve an equation by using the distributive property, the addition or subtraction property, and the multiplication or the division property of equality.

3.8   Solve a problem by using a formula, substituting given values into the formula, and then solving for the unknown variable in the formula.

3.9   Solve a problem by writing and solving an equation.

3.10   Solve a percent problem by writing and solving an equation.

Chapter 4

The student can do the following:

4.1   Graph inequalities.

4.2   Solve an inequality by using the addition property of inequality or the subtraction property of inequality.

4.3   Solve an inequality by using the multiplication property of inequality or the division property of inequality.

4.4   Solve an inequality by using the addition or the subtraction property of inequality and then the multiplication or the division property of inequality.

4.5   Translate sentences, using $<$, $>$, $\leq$, or $\geq$.

4.6   Find the union of sets.
Find the intersection of sets.

4.7   Solve disjunctions.
Solve conjunctions.

4.8   Solve a sentence involving absolute value.

4.9   Solve a problem by writing and solving an inequality.

Chapter 5

The student can do the following:
5.1   Find the sum of two polynomials by using the vertical or the horizontal method.

5.2   Find the opposite of a polynomial.
Find the difference of two polynomials.

5.3   Find the product of two monomials by using the following: product of powers, power of a power, and power of a product.

5.4   Find the product of a polynomial and a monomial.

5.5   Find the product of two polynomials.

5.6   Find the product of polynomials by using the FOIL method or the special products patterns.

5.7   Solve equations involving polynomials.

5.8   Solve uniform motion problems by using the formula $d = rt$.

5.9   Simplify expressions by using the properties for division of powers and for the power of a quotient.

5.10   Simplify the quotient of two monomials.
Simplify the quotient of a polynomial divided by a monomial.

5.11   Simplify the quotient of a polynomial divided by a binomial.

Chapter 6

The student can do the following:
6.1   Factor an integer as a product of prime numbers and write the result in exponential form.
Find the GCF of two numbers.
Find the LCM of two numbers.

6.2   Factor a polynomial by removing a common monomial or binomial factor.

6.3   Factor a polynomial that is the difference of two squares.

6.4   Factor a polynomial that is a perfect-square trinomial.

6.5   Factor a polynomial of the form $x^2 + bx + c$.

6.6   Factor a polynomial of the form $ax^2 + bx + c$.

6.7   Change a polynomial by grouping terms, rearranging terms, and/or removing a common monomial factor before factoring completely.

6.8   Solve an equation by using the zero product property and factoring.

6.9   Solve a problem by writing and factoring an equation.

Chapter 7

The student can do the following:

7.1 Graph ordered pairs of real numbers on a coordinate plane.

7.2 Graph a linear equation in two variables by solving the equation for y and making a table of at least three solutions.

Write a linear equation in two variables in standard form.

7.3 Identify the domain and the range of a relation.

Given a relation in a table, describe the relation as a set of ordered pairs and by a mapping.

Given a relation that is described by a set of ordered pairs, graph the relation and tell whether it is a function.

Using a given domain, list the ordered pairs in a relation described by an open sentence. Then determine whether the relation is a function.

7.4 Use the mapping notation or the f of x notation to write a rule that defines a function.

Given the domain value, find the range value of a function that is described by the f of x notation.

Determine whether an equation describes a linear function.

7.5 Find the slope of a line, using the coordinates of two points on the line.

Draw the graph of a line, given a point on the line and the slope of the line.

7.6 Write a linear equation in slope-intercept form and give the slope and the y-intercept.

Draw the graph of a line, given the y-intercept and the slope.

Given a pair of equations of lines, determine if the lines are parallel.

7.7 Write the equation of a line, given the slope and the y-intercept of the line.

Write the equation of a line, given the slope of the line and the coordinates of any point on the line.

Write the equation of a line, given the coordinates of two points on the line.

7.8 Solve a problem by writing and solving a linear equation.

Chapter 8

The student can do the following:

8.1 Solve a system of linear equations by graphing.

8.2 For a system of linear equations, change both equations to slope-intercept form and tell if the solution set is empty, contains exactly one ordered pair, or contains many ordered pairs. Then graph the system and give the solution set.

8.3 Solve a system of linear equations by using the substitution method.

Solve a system of linear equations by using the substitution method where first one of the equations must be solved for one of its variables.

8.4 Solve a system of linear equations by using the addition or the subtraction method.

8.5 Solve a system of linear equations by using multiplication with the addition-subtraction method.

8.6 Solve problems by using a system of two equations in two variables.

8.7 Solve motion and mixture problems by using a system of linear equations.

8.8 Solve puzzle problems by using a system of linear equations.

8.9 Graph linear inequalities.

8.10 Graph a system of linear inequalities.

8.11 Graph absolute value equations.

Chapter 9

The student can do the following:

9.1 Find an equivalent rational expression for a given rational expression. Tell what values must be excluded from the replacement set so that the denominator of a rational expression will not equal 0.

9.2 Change a rational expression to simplest form.

9.3 Simplify an expression by using the properties of integral exponents.

9.4 Multiply rational expressions.

9.5 Divide rational expressions.

9.6 Find the LCD of rational expressions.

9.7 Add rational expressions.

Subtract rational expressions.

9.8 Solve equations containing rational expressions.

9.9 Solve rate problems.

9.10 Solve an equation or a formula for a specified variable.

Chapter 10

The student can do the following:

10.1 Determine if an equation describes a direct variation.

Write the equation of a direct variation that is described by words.

Solve a problem by using the direct-variation method.

10.2 Solve a proportion that contains a variable.

Solve a direct-variation problem by using a proportion.

10.3 Solve a percent problem by using the proportion

$$\frac{part}{whole} = \frac{percent\ amount}{100}.$$

10.4 Determine if an equation describes an inverse variation.

Write the equation of an inverse variation that is described by words.

Solve a problem by using the inverse-variation method.

10.5 Solve an inverse-variation problem by using a proportion.

10.6 Solve a problem that involves direct variation or inverse variation by using a proportion.

Chapter 11

The student can do the following:

11.1 Find the positive and negative square roots of a rational number that is a perfect square.

11.2 Approximate the square root of a rational number that is not a perfect square, using the *divide-and-average* method.

11.3 Use the *Table of Squares and Square Roots* to find an approximate value.

Use the Pythagorean theorem to find the length of the hypotenuse of a right triangle.

11.4 Multiply and divide radicals.

11.5 Simplify radical expressions.

11.6 Add and subtract radicals.

11.7 Multiply binomials containing radicals.

11.8 Solve radical equations.

11.9 Apply the distance formula.

Chapter 12

The student can do the following:

12.1 Solve a quadratic equation by factoring and using the zero product property.

Given the roots of a quadratic equation, find the equation.

12.2 By using the square root property for equations, solve equations that can be expressed in the form $x^2 = a$ or $(x + y)^2 = a$.

12.3 Solve a quadratic equation by completing the square.

12.4 Solve a quadratic equation by using the quadratic formula.

12.5 Find the value of the discriminant of a quadratic equation.

Then tell if the roots are real and equal, if they are rational and not equal, if they are irrational and unequal, or if there are no real-number roots.

12.6 Use quadratic equations to solve word problems.

12.7 Tell whether or not an equation describes a quadratic function.

Graph a quadratic function.

12.8 Find the real-number roots, if any, for a quadratic equation by graphing.

Solve maximum-minimum problems by graphing quadratic functions.

Chapter 13

The student can do the following:

13.1 Make stem-and-leaf displays.

Make and use two-sided stem-and-leaf displays.

13.2 Make a frequency distribution and a grouped frequency distribution.

13.3 Use a bar chart, histogram, or frequency polygon to describe data.

13.4 Find the mode(s), if any, of a set of data.
Find the median of a set of data.
Find the mean of a set of data.

13.5 Find the range of a set of data.
Find the variance and the standard deviation of a set of data.

13.6 Find the quartiles for a set of data.
Find the interquartile range and the semi-interquartile range for a set of data. Make and use box-and-whisker plots.

Chapter 14

The student can do the following:

14.1 Determine the sample space of a given situation by making a list, a table, or a tree diagram.
Use the fundamental counting principle to determine how many outcomes are possible for a given situation.

14.2 Find factorials.
Find a permutation of k objects chosen from a set of n objects.
Find a combination of k objects chosen from a set of n objects.

14.3 Find the experimental probability of an event, and express it as a fraction, a decimal, or a percent.

14.4 Find the theoretical probability of an event.
Find the probability of an event certain to happen or certain not to happen.
Find the probability of the complement of an event.
Make predictions, using probability.

14.5 Find the probability of "A or B" for A and B mutually exclusive and not mutually exclusive.

14.6 Find the probability of successive events, for A and B independent events or dependent events.

Chapter 15

The student can do the following:

15.1 Find the measure of the complement of an acute angle.
Find the measure of the supplement of an angle.
Find the measure of the third angle of a triangle, given the measures of the other two angles.

15.2 Solve proportions involving similar triangles.

15.3 Find the sine, cosine, and tangent of the acute angles of a right triangle.

15.4 Use a trigonometric table to find the required information.

15.5 Solve a right triangle.

15.6 Use trigonometry in problem solving.

CHAPTER 4

Written Exercises   Page 107

16.
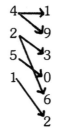

18.

20.

22.

24.

26.

28.

30.

32. is not less than   **34.** is not greater than nor equal to

Written Exercises   Pages 128–129

25. $n = 17$ or $n = -1$ **26.** $z = 3$ or $z = -9$
27. $m = 3.4$ or $m = -3.4$
28. $n = 1.7$ or $n = -1.7$
29. $f = 3.2$ or $f = -3.2$
30. $g = 27.3$ or $g = -27.3$
31. $c > 2$ or $c < -8$ **32.** $d > 7$ or $d < 3$
33. $3 < x < 7$ **34.** $3 < y < 11$
35. $-5.6 < n < 9.6$ **36.** $-10.5 < m < -3.5$
37. $-3 < m < 3$ **38.** $n < 2.4$ or $n < -2.4$
39. $-32.4 \le w \le 32.4$ **40.** $t \ge 9.3$ or $t \le -9.3$
41. $-3.1 < v < 3.1$ **42.** $y \ge 2.05$ or $y \le -2.05$
43. $-3 < y < 3$ **44.** $-20 < t < 20$
45. $m \ge 10$ or $m \le -10$ **46.** $-10 \le u \le 10$
47. $b > 30$ or $b < -30$ **48.** $\frac{2}{5} \le c \le \frac{6}{5}$
49. $e > \frac{2}{3}$ or $e < -2$ **50.** $g = \frac{13}{10}$ or $g = \frac{1}{2}$
51. $-1 < r < \frac{2}{3}$ **52.** $t \ge 8.5$ or $t \le -0.7$
53. $w = 11.3$ or $w = 6.5$ **54.** $-4.3 < s < 1.9$

55. $-3 < w < 6$ **56.** $x \ge 1$ or $x < -\frac{4}{3}$
57. $t = \frac{12}{5}$ or $t = -2$ **58.** $-2 \le y \le \frac{5}{2}$
59. $b > 3$ or $b < -4$ **60.** $c = \frac{11}{3}$ or $c = -3$
61. $v \ge \frac{8}{5}$ or $v \le -2$ **62.** $f = \frac{16}{7}$ or $f = -2$
63. $-\frac{7}{2} \le v \le \frac{5}{2}$ **64.** $d = 4$ or $d = -\frac{8}{3}$
65. $-\frac{5}{2} < h < 2$ **66.** $m > 1$ or $m < -\frac{7}{3}$

CHAPTER 7

Written Exercises   Page 217

42.   **44.**   **46.**
 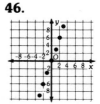

Written Exercises   Pages 220–221

18. (a) {(4, 1), (4, 9),   **20.** (a) {(−1, 3), (2, 4),
(2, 3), (5, 0),   (3, 3), (4, 6),
(2, 6), (1,2)}   (5, 3), (6, 4)}

(b) D   R   (b) D   R

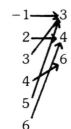 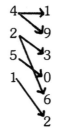

no   yes

22. yes   **24.** no   **26.** yes

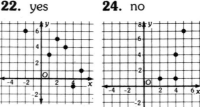 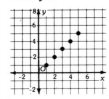

28. {(0, 1), (1, 3), (2, 5), (3, 7), (4, 9)}; yes

30. {(0, 0), (1, 1), (2, 2), (3, 3), (4, 4)}; yes

32. {(0, -4), (1, -3), (2, -2), (3, -1), (4, 0)}; yes

34. {(0, 0), (1, -1), (2, -2), (3, -3), (4, -4)}; yes

36. {(0, 2), (1, 2), (2, 2), (3, 2), (4, 2)}; yes

38. {(0, 0), (1, -1), (2, -2), (3, -3), (4, -4)}; yes

Chapter 7 Test   Page 246

14.

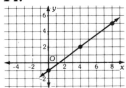

CHAPTER 8

Written Exercises   Page 254

20.

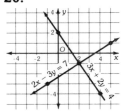

22.

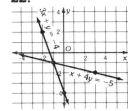

24.

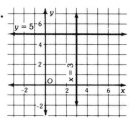

26.

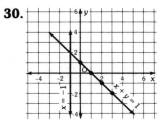

28.

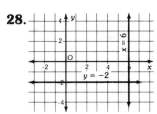

30.

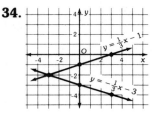

32.

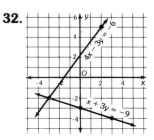

34.

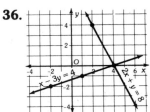

36.

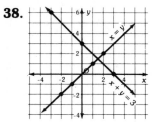

38.

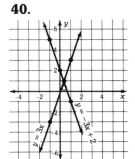

40.

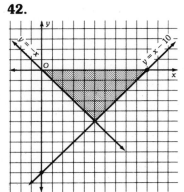

42.

44.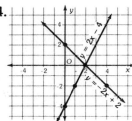

46.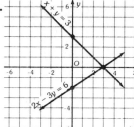

48.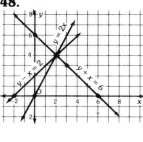

50. 2 hours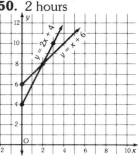

Written Exercises   Page 256

8.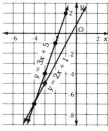

14.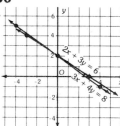

16.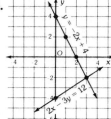

18.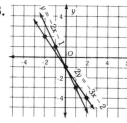

22.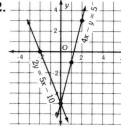

26.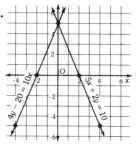

32.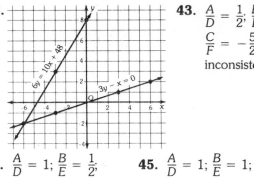

43. $\dfrac{A}{D} = \dfrac{1}{2}$; $\dfrac{B}{E} = \dfrac{1}{2}$;
$\dfrac{C}{F} = -\dfrac{5}{2}$
inconsistent

44. $\dfrac{A}{D} = 1$; $\dfrac{B}{E} = \dfrac{1}{2}$;
$\dfrac{C}{F} = 1$
consistent

45. $\dfrac{A}{D} = 1$; $\dfrac{B}{E} = 1$;
$\dfrac{C}{F} = 1$
consistent and
dependent

46. $\dfrac{A}{D} = \dfrac{1}{2}$; $\dfrac{B}{E} = \dfrac{1}{2}$;
$\dfrac{C}{F} = \dfrac{3}{5}$
inconsistent

47. $\dfrac{A}{D} = 1$; $\dfrac{B}{E} = 1$;
$\dfrac{C}{F} = 1$
consistent and
dependent

48. $\dfrac{A}{D} = \dfrac{1}{5}$; $\dfrac{B}{E} = \dfrac{1}{5}$; $\dfrac{C}{F} = \dfrac{15}{61}$
inconsistent

Oral Exercises   Page 269

1. $x + y = 180$
$x = 3y$

2. $2l = 5w$
$2(l + w) = 77$

3. $x + y = 40$
$y = 5x + 4$

4. $x + y = 28$
$y = 2x - 5$

Written Exercises   Page 269

1. 135 ft, 45 ft **2.** 27.5 m, 11 m
3. 6 people, 34 people **4.** 11 boys, 17 girls
5. 54, 126 **6.** 12 in., 9 in. **9.** 11 field goals
10. 3 hours **11.** yes; 120 singles, 16 fives
12. 8 inches **13.** 45 km/h, 55 km/h **14.** 37, 53

Algebra In Use   Page 271

1. (75, $400) **2.** (100, $650) **3.** (75, $650)

Written Exercises   Page 281

10.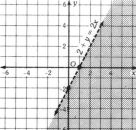

12.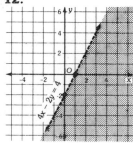

14.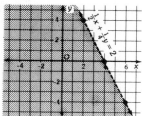

16. $y \le 3$

17. $y \ge -x + 1$

18. $y > -\dfrac{2}{3}x + 2$

20. (1, 1), (2, 1), (3, 1),
(1, 2), (2, 2), (3, 2),
(1, 3), (2, 3), (1, 4),
(2, 4), (1, 5), (1, 6)

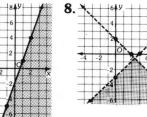

Written Exercises   Page 285

4.

6.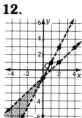

8.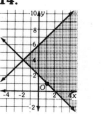

10.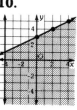

12.

14.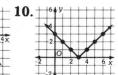

16.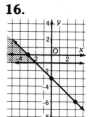

18.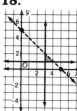

20.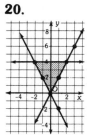

Self-Quiz   Page 285

1.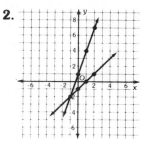

2.

3.

Written Exercises   Page 287

2.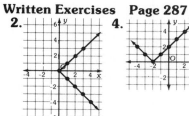

4.

6.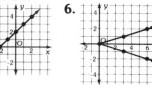

8.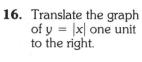

10.

12.

14.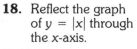

16. Translate the graph of $y = |x|$ one unit to the right.

17. Translate the graph of $y = |x|$ one unit up.

18. Reflect the graph of $y = |x|$ through the x-axis.

Chapter 8 Review   Pages 290–291

42.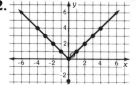

44.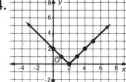

Chapter 8 Test   Page 292

20. 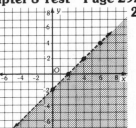   **21.**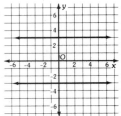

22. 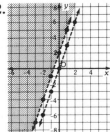   **23.**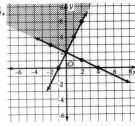

24. 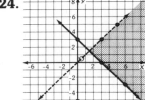   **25.**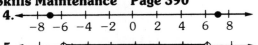

26. 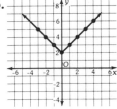   **27.**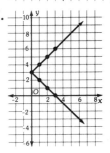

CHAPTER 9

Oral Exercises   Page 311
5. $(y - 3)(y - 2)(y - 1)$ **6.** $(a + 6)^2(a - 4)$
Written Exercises   Page 311
14. $(x - 3)(x + 2)(x - 2)$ **15.** $(y + 6)^2(y - 3)$
17. $(x - 2)(x + 1)(x + 2)$
20. $(n - 3)(n - 2)(n - 1)$
21. $-6(m + 3)(m - 3)$
22. $3(x - 2)^2(x + 3)(x - 9)$

23. $(y + 2)(y - 2)(y - 3)$
24. $-4(x + 5)(x - 5)$
25. $3(x + 5y)(x - 5y)$
26. $12(y + 4)(y - 2)(y + 3)$
27. $(3n - 1)(n - 4)(2n + 3)$
28. $(a - 1)^2(a + 1)$

CHAPTER 11
Written Exercises   Page 371
25. $\sqrt{2x + 6}$ **26.** $\sqrt{15 - 3y}$ **40.** $\sqrt{2xy}$
43. $3s^3t^3$ **47.** no **48.** ·no

Written Exercises   Page 377
25. $\sqrt{2}$ **26.** $2\sqrt{2}$ **27.** $8\sqrt{5}$ **28.** $4\sqrt{7}$
29. $14\sqrt{10}$ **30.** $9\sqrt{10}$ **31.** $2\sqrt{7} - 5\sqrt{2}$
32. $\sqrt{6} + 2\sqrt{3}$ **33.** $13\sqrt{7} - 3\sqrt{2}$
34. $14\sqrt{3} + 10\sqrt{6}$ **36.** $14\sqrt{2b}$
39. $11y\sqrt{3y}$ **40.** $8y\sqrt{5y}$ **42.** $7x^2\sqrt{3}$ **45.** $\dfrac{5\sqrt{6}}{2}$
46. $\dfrac{16\sqrt{10}}{5}$ **47.** $\dfrac{34\sqrt{7}}{7}$ **48.** $\dfrac{29\sqrt{6}}{6}$
56. $x^4\sqrt{x} + x^3\sqrt{x} - x^2\sqrt{x}$

Skills Maintenance   Page 390

4. ◄─────────────────────►
       -8 -6 -4 -2 0 2 4 6 8

5. ◄─────────────────────►
       -8 -6 -4 -2 0 2 4 6 8

6. $x > 4$ or $x < -8$
       ◄─────────────────────►
       -10 -8 -6 -4 -2 0 2 4 6

CHAPTER 12
Oral Exercises   Page 412
  3. no real roots
  4. real, unequal, rational
  5. real, unequal, irrational
  6. real, equal, rational
  7. real, unequal, rational
  8. real unequal, irrational
  9. no real roots
 10. real, unequal, irrational
 11. real, unequal, rational

Written Exercises   Page 412
 10. 225 **11.** 0 **12.** −16 **13.** −8; no real roots
 14. 52; real, unequal, irrational
 15. 0; real, equal, rational
 16. 289; real, unequal, rational
 17. 1764; real, unequal, rational
 18. 65; real, unequal, irrational
 19. 21; real, unequal, irrational

20. 169; real, unequal, rational
21. 121; real, unequal, rational
22. 29; real, unequal, irrational
23. $-\frac{3}{4}$; no real roots
24. 0; real, equal, rational
25. 0; real, equal, rational
26. -12; no real roots **27.** $-1.035, -3.863$
28. $-3.170, -10.098$ **29.** no real roots
30. $1.395, -2.151$ **31.** $2.9565, -0.5075$
32. $-1.0705, -2.8025$
33. real, unequal, may   **34.** real, equal, may be
be rational or ir-   rational or irrational
rational, depending
on the value of b
35. no real roots   **36.** real, unequal, may
be rational or
irrational

Written Exercises   Page 420

32. (a) $x = -4$
(b) $(-4, -28)$
(c) $-0.3, -7.7$
(d) 4

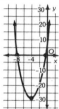

34. (a) $x = -\frac{1}{6}$
(b) $\left(-\frac{1}{6}, -\frac{47}{12}\right)$
(c) no x-intercepts
(d) -4

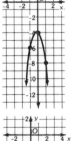

36. (a) $x = \frac{1}{2}$
(b) $\left(\frac{1}{2}, -\frac{7}{4}\right)$
(c) no x-intercepts
(d) -2

38.   **40.**

CHAPTER 13
Written Exercises   Page 435

15.

1	2, 3, 4, 5,
·	8, 9, 9
2	3, 3, 4, 4, 6,
·	6, 6, 6, 7, 7
3	0, 1, 2, 4,
·	5, 8, 8
4	0, 0, 2, 2, 4,
·	7, 7, 7, 8, 9
5	1, 2, 2, 2, 3,
·	4, 6, 6, 6, 7
6	2, 4, 7,
·	7, 7, 9
7	0, 3, 3, 3,
·	5, 6, 6
8	1, 1, 2, 3, 7,
·	7, 8, 8, 9
9	0, 0, 1,
·	3, 3, 8

16.

1	1, 2, 2, 3,
·	4, 4, 7
2	1, 2, 6, 7,
·	7, 8, 8, 9
3	0, 7,
·	7, 9
4	1, 2, 2, 2, 6, 6,
·	7, 7, 7, 7, 7, 8
5	0, 1, 1, 2,
·	3, 3, 6, 7
6	2, 3, 4, 4,
·	4, 7, 9
7	0, 1, 1, 2, 2, 2,
·	4, 5, 5, 6, 7, 7
8	0, 0, 5, 6, 7,
·	8, 8, 9, 9, 9
9	0, 2, 2, 2, 2,
·	3, 4, 7, 8

Written Exercises   Pages 437–438

6.

Color	Frequency
red	3
green	5
white	4
blue	11
yellow	3
Total	26

7.

Score	Frequency
59	4
60	1
61	1
62	2
63	1
64	1
65	2
66	2
67	3
68	2
69	1
70	1
Total	21

8.

Number	Frequency
5	1
$5\frac{1}{2}$	2
6	6
$6\frac{1}{2}$	3
7	2
$7\frac{1}{2}$	4
8	1
$8\frac{1}{2}$	1
9	2
$9\frac{1}{2}$	2
Total	24

9.

Interval	Frequency
1–10	3
11–20	5
21–30	4
31–40	5
41–50	5
51–60	6
Total	28

10.

Interval	Frequency
0.6–1.0	8
1.1–1.5	4
1.6–2.0	4
2.1–2.5	4
2.6–3.0	6
3.1–3.5	2
Total	28

11.

Interval	Frequency
101–110	2
111–120	4
121–130	4
131–140	5
141–150	5
151–160	1
161–170	7
Total	28

12.

Interval	Frequency
11–20	6
21–30	5
31–40	3
41–50	1
51–60	5
61–70	4
Total	24

13.

Number	Frequency	Cumulative frequency
12	7	7
13	5	12
14	4	16
18	2	18
20	1	19
25	5	24

14.

Number	Frequency	Cumulative frequency
50	7	7
60	3	10
70	7	17
80	2	19
90	3	22
100	2	24

15.

Interval	Frequency	Cumulative frequency
1–5	7	7
6–10	4	11
11–15	9	20
16–20	8	28
21–25	5	33
26–30	7	40

16.

Interval	Frequency	Cumulative frequency
101–200	5	5
201–300	7	12
301–400	8	20
401–500	6	26
501–600	7	33
601–700	6	39

CHAPTER 14

Written Exercises   Page 468

16.

First number   Second number   Outcome

17.

Coin		Die 1	2	3	4	5	6
	H	(H, 1)	(H, 2)	(H, 3)	(H, 4)	(H, 5)	(H, 6)
	T	(T, 1)	(T, 2)	(T, 3)	(T, 4)	(T, 5)	(T, 6)

18.

First die		Second die 1	2	3	4
	1	(1, 1)	(1, 2)	(1, 3)	(1, 4)
	2	(2, 1)	(2, 2)	(2, 3)	(2, 4)
	3	(3, 1)	(3, 2)	(3, 3)	(3, 4)
	4	(4, 1)	(4, 2)	(4, 3)	(4, 4)

23. ABC, ABD, ABE, ACD, ACE, ADE, BCD, BCE, BDE, CDE

24. 1, 2, 3; 1, 2, 4; 1, 2, 5; 1, 2, 6; 1, 3, 4; 1, 3, 5; 1, 3, 6; 1, 4, 5; 1, 4, 6; 1, 5, 6; 2, 3, 4; 2, 3, 5; 2, 3, 6; 2, 4, 5; 2, 4, 6; 2, 5, 6; 3, 4, 5; 3, 4, 6; 3, 5, 6; 4, 5, 6

ALGEBRA 1

Kenneth J. Travers
Professor of
Mathematics Education
University of Illinois
Urbana, Illinois

LeRoy C. Dalton
Mathematics Area
Chairperson
Wauwatosa School District
Wauwatosa, Wisconsin

Katherine P. Layton
Mathematics Teacher
Beverly Hills High School
Beverly Hills, California

Laidlaw Brothers • Publishers
A Division of Doubleday & Company, Inc.
River Forest, Illinois

Sacramento, California • Chamblee, Georgia
Dallas, Texas • Toronto, Canada

Editorial Acknowledgments

Editorial Manager Max V. Lyles / Senior Editor Mary Fraser /
Editors Cecilia Laspisa, Robert C. Mudd, Janet Kapche Razionale,
Kathryn Domovich Wroblewski / Production Manager Kathleen Kasper /
Production Editor Anthony Giometti / Photo Researcher William A. Cassin /
Manager, Art and Design Gloria J. Muczynski / Artist Paul Hazelrigg
Designer Lynne C. Miller/Miller & Seper
Full-color insert designed by Lynne C. Miller and Victor F. Seper, Jr./Miller & Seper

Educator/Reviewers

Gerald T. Cowles Oak Park and River Forest High School; Oak Park, Illinois
Arthur C. Dotterweich School Board of Manatee County; Bradenton, Florida
Ruth Ellen Doane, S.P. Our Lady of the Westside Catholic School; Chicago, Illinois
Donna Gabanski Homewood-Flossmoor High School; Flossmoor, Illinois
Robert Gyles Community School District 4; New York, New York
George Levine Nyack Public Schools; Nyack, New York
Norma Lewis Sycamore Junior High School; Cincinnati, Ohio
Deborah Neuman Oak Park and River Forest High School; Oak Park, Illinois
Steven Reinhart Chippewa Falls Area Middle School; Chippewa Falls, Wisconsin

Cover Photograph

E.B Weill/ © The Image Bank

Photo Credits

H. Abernathy/H. Armstrong Roberts, p. D (bottom); Peter Arnold, Inc., p. 361; Art Resource, p. O (right); Royce Bair & Associates, p. 209; Beech Aircraft Corp., p. 95; The Bettmann Archive, p. 194; Biological Photo Service, p. 24; Camerique, pp. 1, 173, 202, B, I (bottom), K (top right); D. Cavagnaro/DRK Photo, p. 267; Click/Chicago Ltd., pp. 29, 431, 491; Ed Cooper Photo, pp. N–O (background); FBI/U.S. Dept. of Justice, p. 43; Rollin Geppert, p. 293; Grant Heilman, p. 105; Gerald Holly/Corn's Photo Service, p. 389; Wolfgang Hoyt/Esto Photographics Inc., pp. M, P; Michael J. Hruby/Laidlaw Brothers, p. 203; Jeff Jacobson/Archive Pictures Inc., p. J; Phillip MacMillan James/Click/Chicago Ltd., p. G; Ralph Krubner/H. Armstrong Roberts, p. O (left); Karl Kummels/Shostal Associates, p. N; Dennis Mansell, p. 6; Joseph Martin/Scala/Art Resource, p. H; Richard Megna/Fundamental Photographs, p. A; M. Messenger, p. 272; J.T. Miller/The Stock Market, p. K (bottom); Alfred Pasieka/Taurus, p. I (top); Photri, p. 351; Olivier Rebbot/Boston, p. E; H. Armstrong Roberts, pp. 67, 137, 239, 251, 335, 354, 397, 478, L (both); Shostal Associates, p. D (top); Clyde H. Smith/Peter Arnold, Inc., p. F Valan Photos, p. 465; Fred Whitehead/Animals, Animals, p. C; John Zoiner/Peter Arnold, Inc., p. K (top left).

ISBN 0-8445-1838-7

Copyright © 1987 by Laidlaw Brothers, Publishers

A Division of Doubleday & Company, Inc.

Printed in the United States of America

23456789 10 11 12 13 14 15   543210987

CONTENTS

1   Introduction to Algebra

2   Real Numbers

7 Relations and Functions

8 Linear Systems

15	Right-Triangle Trigonometry

CHAPTER 1

Introduction to Algebra

How many seconds are in one year? (Use
1 year = 365 days.)   31,536,000 seconds

1

OBJECTIVES

Write English phrases as algebraic expressions.

Simplify numerical expressions.

Evaluate algebraic expressions that have parentheses or fraction bars.

Determine the number of terms in an expression.

TEACHER'S NOTES

See p. T23.

CLASSROOM EXAMPLES

1. Write each as an algebraic expression.
   a. the sum of y and 7
      $y + 7$
   b. the difference of 11 and k $11 - k$
   c. the product of r and s rs
   d. the quotient of y and 6
      $\frac{y}{6}$ or $y \div 6$

2. Simplify $5(8 - 2)$.   30

3. Evaluate $\frac{x}{5+y}$ if $x = 3$ and $y = 7$. $\frac{1}{4}$

4. Evaluate $\frac{5+a}{10-b}$ if $a = 3$ and $b = 2$.   1

MIXED REVIEW

Perform the indicated operation.

1. $5\frac{3}{8} + 2\frac{1}{4}$ $7\frac{5}{8}$

2. $7.2 - 1.83$ 5.37

3. $15.30 \div 0.05$ 306

4. $\frac{1}{5} \times \frac{3}{7}$ $\frac{3}{35}$

5. $46.2 \div 60$ 0.77

1.1   Algebraic Expressions and Variables

Why learn algebra? One reason is that algebra provides a systematic way of solving certain types of problems. Algebra is a precise language for expressing relationships between quantities.

Last year Park High School won three more football games than Case High School won.

Notice that you do not know how many games Case High School won. Therefore, you could let x represent this unknown quantity. Then $x + 3$ is an **algebraic expression** representing the number of games won by Park High School. The letter x is called a **variable.**

EXAMPLES

1   **Write each as an algebraic expression.**

   a.   the sum of m and 5   **b.**   the difference of 12 and y

   c.   the product of x and y **d.**   the quotient of a number and 3

   SOLUTIONS

   a. $m + 5$ **b.** $12 - y$

   c. xy or $x \cdot y$ or $x(y)$ **d.** $\frac{n}{3}$ or $n \div 3$

A **numerical expression,** such as $3 + 5$, is the name for a number. The number named by an expression is the **value** of the expression. The value of $3 + 5$ is 8. When you replace an expression with the simplest or most common name, you have **simplified** the expression.

2   **Simplify $6(4 - 2)$.**

   SOLUTION

   $6(4 - 2) = 6(2)$ *Simplify what is in the parentheses first.*

            $= 12$

The value of an algebraic expression depends on the value of the variable. To **evaluate** $n + 5$ when $n = 12$, replace n with 12. $12 + 5 = 17$.

3   **Evaluate $\frac{a}{6+b}$ if $a = 3$ and $b = 12$.**

   SOLUTION

   $\dfrac{a}{6 + b} = \dfrac{3}{6 + 12}$ *Simplify what is under the fraction bar first.*

         $= \dfrac{3}{18}$

         $= \dfrac{1}{6}$

A **term** is a number, a variable, or an indicated product or quotient. The expression $2b - \frac{2.5}{3} + n - 6$ has four terms: $2b$, $\frac{2.5}{3}$, n, and 6.

Parentheses are often used to group expressions. In a fraction such as $\frac{4 + c}{8 - d}$, the bar is used as a grouping symbol as well as a division symbol.

| **4** | **Evaluate $\frac{4 + c}{8 - d}$ if $c = 2$ and $d = 5$.** |

SOLUTION

$$\frac{4 + c}{8 - d} = \frac{4 + 2}{8 - 5}$$

$$= \frac{6}{3} \quad \text{Simplify what is above the fraction bar.}$$
$$\quad\quad \text{Simplify what is below the fraction bar.}$$

$$= 2$$

TEACHER'S RESOURCE MASTERS

Practice Master 1, Part 1

ASSIGNMENT GUIDE

Minimum
1–13 odd, 17–37

Regular
15–41 odd, 43–56

Maximum
23–33 odd, 35–56

ORAL EXERCISES

Read each expression.

1. $9 + 3$ **2.** $5 \cdot 8$ **3.** $12 - a$ **4.** $\frac{15}{a}$

Simplify each expression.

5. $(8 + 20) - 3$ 25 **6.** $8 + (20 - 3)$ 25 **7.** $12 - (4 \cdot 3)$ 0

8. $(12 - 4) \cdot 3$ 24 **9.** $\frac{1 + 7}{4}$ 2 **10.** $\frac{15 - 5}{2}$ 5

Evaluate each expression if $a = 6$ and $b = 5$.

11. $a + b$ 11 **12.** $a(2 + b)$ 42 **13.** $\frac{ab}{2}$ 15 **14.** $\frac{17 - b}{a}$ 2

How many terms does each expression have?

15. $a + 2 - b + c$ 4 **16.** $7a + \frac{1}{2}a - 15$ 3

17. $2(6) - n$ 2 **18.** $\frac{24(7) + 1}{n}$ 1

ADDITIONAL ANSWERS

Oral Exercises
1. the sum of 9 and 3
2. the product of 5 and 8
3. the difference of 12 and a
4. the quotient of 15 and a

WRITTEN EXERCISES

A. Write each of the following as an algebraic expression:

1. the sum of a and b $a + b$

2. the product of x and $2y$ $x(2y)$

3. r divided by s $\frac{r}{s}$

4. the product of x, y, and z xyz

5. the sum of six times x and y $6x + y$

6. six times the sum of x and y $6(x + y)$

7. the product of a and 5 $a(5)$

8. the sum of $3x$ and $\frac{y}{8}$ $3x + \frac{y}{8}$

Simplify each of the following:

9. $(11 - 9) + 4$ 6 **10.** $(15 \cdot 5) - 7$ 68 **11.** $68 - (32 \div 4)$ 60

12. $24 \div (6 + 2)$ 3 **13.** $(6 \cdot 2) \cdot 3$ 36 **14.** $(8 \cdot 3) \div 6$ 4

B. **15.** $\dfrac{4.2(3)}{6}$ 2.1 **16.** $\left(\dfrac{2}{3} \div \dfrac{1}{4}\right) \cdot 5$ $13\frac{1}{3}$ **17.** $\dfrac{5}{8} - \left(\dfrac{1}{4} \div \dfrac{1}{2}\right)$ $\frac{1}{8}$

18. $18.3 - (6 + 0.2)$ 12.1 **19.** $(9 + 6)(42 \div 7)$ 90 **20.** $(6 + 2)(5 + 8)$ 104

Evaluate if $x = 2$, $y = 3$, and $z = 5.6$.

21. $12 - z$ 6.4 **22.** $10(x)$ 20 **23.** xyz 33.6 **24.** $z - y$ 2.6

25. $\dfrac{z - x}{y}$ 1.2 **26.** $\dfrac{27}{y}$ 9 **27.** $4(y + 7)$ 40 **28.** $(xz) + y$ 14.2

Evaluate if $a = 1$, $b = 2$, $c = \frac{1}{2}$, and $x = 5$.

29. bc 1 **30.** $x(b + c)$ $12\frac{1}{2}$ **31.** $(b + a)(c + x)$ $16\frac{1}{2}$

32. $(4b) - (x - a)$ 4 **33.** $8(x + b)$ 56 **34.** $\dfrac{a + b}{x + a}$ $\frac{1}{2}$

In each of the following expressions, x stands for the smaller of two numbers and y stands for the larger number. Write each expression.

35. the difference of y and x $y - x$

36. six less than the smaller number $x - 6$

37. two more than the larger number $y + 2$

38. seven more than the sum of the two numbers $(x + y) + 7$

39. one less than the product of the numbers $xy - 1$

Expressions for the perimeter of some geometric figures are given below. Find each perimeter.

rectangle   square   regular pentagon

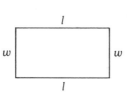

$P = 2(l + w)$ $P = 4s$ $P = 5h$

40. square; $s = 132$ cm 528 cm

41. rectangle; $l = 20$ mm, $w = 13$ mm 66 mm

42. regular pentagon; $h = 15$ in. 75 in.

Write each of the following as an algebraic expression:

43. If a equals the speed in miles per hour, what is the speed in miles per minute?

44. If m equals the weight in ounces, what is the weight in pounds? $\frac{m}{16}$ pounds

45. If Karen is y years old and Joan is 5 years older than Karen, what is Joan's age? $y + 5$ years

46. If the length of a rectangle is l and the width is 5 meters less than one half the length, what is the width? $w = \frac{1}{2}l - 5$

Written Exercises
43. $\frac{a}{60}$ miles per minute

C. 47. If Rosa had c calories for breakfast, twice as many calories for lunch as breakfast, and k calories for dinner, what was the total number of calories for the day? $c + 2c + k$ cal

48. If p equals the price in cents, what is the price in dollars? $\frac{p}{100}$ dollars

Insert parentheses to form a true statement.

49. $8 \cdot 2 - 2 = 0$ $8 \cdot (2 - 2) = 0$

50. $5 - 4 \cdot 6 = 6$ $(5 - 4) \cdot 6 = 6$

51. $15 - 5 - 3 = 13$ $15 - (5 - 3) = 13$

52. $24 \div 6 \cdot 4 = 16$ $(24 \div 6) \cdot 4 = 16$

53. $3 \cdot 8 \div 4 = 6$ $3 \cdot (8 \div 4) = 6$

54. $14 - 4 \div 2 = 5$ $(14 - 4) \div 2 = 5$

55. $13 + 8 \div 3 = 7$ $(13 + 8) \div 3 = 7$

56. $12 \cdot 4 \div 2 = 24$ $12 \cdot (4 \div 2) = 24$

MATH HERITAGE/Signs of the Times

For centuries, mathematicians have saved time and effort by substituting symbols for words. Among the most commonly used are the operation symbols $+$, $-$, $\times$, and $\div$. However, they did not always look this way. In fact, no one is quite certain just how they did evolve, but here are some possible explanations.

$+$ The **addition** sign may originally have been the first letter of the Italian word *più*, which means *plus*. Most probably, though, it is a shorthand form of the Latin word *et*, which means *and*, a word frequently used to indicate addition.

$-$ The **subtraction** sign may have derived from a bar that traders in medieval times used to mark the difference in the weight of a receptacle from the weight of the merchandise. It is also possible that the subtraction sign is a shorthand form of the Latin abbreviation $\overline{m}$ for *minus*.

$\times$ This symbol, based on a figure known as St. Andrew's Cross, is only one of the ways to indicate **multiplication**. The German mathematician Leibniz refused to use it because it was too easily confused with the variable x. He preferred and made popular the raised dot ($\cdot$) and the cap symbol ($\cap$).

$\div$ The **division** symbol as it is known today first appeared in print in 1659 and has long been used in continental Europe to indicate subtraction. Although in the 18th century the mathematician Gallimard used the reverse capital D (Π) for division, this symbol never became popular. It is possible that the present symbol derived from the bar separating the numerator from the denominator of a fraction.

CALCULATOR

The calculator features in this book will show you how a calculator can be used with various topics. Calculators can range in abilities from those that perform only arithmetic operations to those that can be programmed like computers.

The calculator features are written with the assumption that your calculator has certain capabilities. If your calculator does not have these capabilities, or if it has more capabilities than are shown, you may have to make adjustments from the steps shown in the examples.

Your calculator should have the following capabilities:
1. Accepts and displays an 8-digit number.
2. Can perform addition $+$, subtraction $-$, multiplication $\times$ and division $\div$.
3. Can find square roots $\sqrt{}$.
4. Can repeatedly multiply or divide by a constant number.
5. Can handle negative numbers in both input and output.
6. Has a floating decimal point.
7. Has a memory in which numbers can be added $\boxed{M+}$ or subtracted $\boxed{M-}$, and the memory key can be cleared $\boxed{CM}$ without clearing the display $\boxed{C}$.
8. Uses algebraic logic. That is, you would enter "number, operation, number, equals" instead of "number, enter, number, operation."

You should already know how to do arithmetic with your calculator. You should also know how to do the following:

		ENTER	DISPLAY
1.	Square a number.	3 $\times$ 3 $=$ or 3 $\times$ $=$	*9.*
2.	Find the cube of a number.	5 $\times$ 5 $\times$ 5 $=$ or 5 $\times$ $=$ $=$	*125.*
3.	Enter negative numbers.	$-$ 3 $=$ or 3 $-$ $=$ or 3 $+/-$	*3.⁻ or ⁻3.*
4.	Find the reciprocal of a number.	1 $\div$ 8 $=$ or 8 $\div$ $=$	*0.125*

SKILLS MAINTENANCE

Add.

1. $\frac{3}{5} + \frac{2}{3}$ $1\frac{4}{15}$

2. $8.6 + 2.39$ 10.99

3. $6\frac{3}{4} + 2\frac{1}{2}$ $9\frac{1}{4}$

4. $9.63 + 11.89$ 21.52

5. $0.409 + 0.3284$ 0.7374

6. $7\frac{1}{3} + 8\frac{5}{6}$ $16\frac{1}{6}$

7. $10\frac{2}{5} + 7\frac{3}{4}$ $18\frac{3}{20}$

8. $18.4 + 20.36$ 38.76

9. $\frac{3}{8} + \frac{5}{12}$ $\frac{19}{24}$

10. $17.8 + 24.86$ 42.66

11. $4.3 + 0.972$ 5.272

12. $\frac{7}{12} + \frac{3}{16}$ $\frac{37}{48}$

13. $4\frac{3}{8} + 2\frac{11}{12}$ $7\frac{7}{24}$

14. $3\frac{1}{6} + 2\frac{5}{8}$ $5\frac{19}{24}$

15. $15.06 + 11.923$ 26.983

Subtract.

16. $\frac{7}{8} - \frac{3}{4}$ $\frac{1}{8}$

17. $2.36 - 1.409$ 0.951

18. $10\frac{2}{3} - 7\frac{9}{10}$ $2\frac{23}{30}$

19. $18.603 - 4.39$ 14.213

20. $27.6 - 15.029$ 12.571

21. $\frac{9}{10} - \frac{5}{6}$ $\frac{1}{15}$

22. $4\frac{3}{8} - 2\frac{2}{3}$ $1\frac{17}{24}$

23. $5.6 - 3.804$ 1.796

24. $15\frac{3}{5} - 8\frac{7}{8}$ $6\frac{29}{40}$

25. $3.8 - 2.04$ 1.76

26. $311 - 10.84$ 300.16

27. $6\frac{7}{10} - 3\frac{4}{15}$ $3\frac{13}{30}$

28. $18.06 - 13.79$ 4.27

29. $\frac{15}{16} - \frac{1}{3}$ $\frac{29}{48}$

30. $12 - 8\frac{7}{10}$ $3\frac{3}{10}$

Multiply.

31. 4.3×2.06 8.858

32. 18.3×9.4 172.02

33. $\frac{1}{2} \times \frac{2}{3}$ $\frac{1}{3}$

34. $\frac{4}{5} \times \frac{7}{8}$ $\frac{7}{10}$

35. 2.03×8.12 16.4836

36. $2\frac{2}{3} \times 6$ 16

37. 3.09×20 61.8

38. $4\frac{5}{6} \times \frac{3}{4}$ $3\frac{5}{8}$

39. $9\frac{1}{2} \times 3\frac{1}{5}$ $30\frac{2}{5}$

40. 17.89×2.3 41.147

41. $3\frac{1}{3} \times 1\frac{4}{5}$ 6

42. 3.009×300 902.7

43. 60×0.01 0.6

44. $\frac{2}{3} \times 8\frac{1}{2}$ $5\frac{2}{3}$

45. 0.7×0.056 0.0392

Divide.

46. $4.8 \div 1.2$ 4

47. $12.6 \div 0.06$ 210

48. $\frac{2}{3} \div \frac{2}{5}$ $1\frac{2}{3}$

49. $3\frac{1}{4} \div 2\frac{1}{8}$ $1\frac{9}{17}$

50. $30.6 \div 3.6$ 8.5

51. $211.5 \div 50$ 4.23

52. $1200 \div 0.5$ 2400

53. $86 \div 0.04$ 2150

54. $\frac{1}{2} \div \frac{7}{8}$ $\frac{4}{7}$

55. $6\frac{3}{10} \div \frac{7}{8}$ $7\frac{1}{5}$

56. $4\frac{2}{3} \div 1\frac{1}{2}$ $3\frac{1}{9}$

57. $8.7 \div 30$ 0.29

58. $15.6 \div 2.4$ 6.5

59. $0.012 \div 0.002$ 6

60. $\frac{3}{4} \div 1\frac{1}{2}$ $\frac{1}{2}$

1.2 Factors, Coefficients, and Exponents

In multiplication expressions, the numbers being multiplied are called **factors.** When one or more of the factors are variables, the factors can be written without a multiplication sign.

factors   factors   factors
↓ ↓   ↓↓   ↓↓
$3(6)$ $4a$ ab

When a variable or a product of variables is multiplied by a number, the number is called the **numerical coefficient** or simply the **coefficient.** The coefficient of $4a$ is 4. The coefficient of n is 1, because $n = 1 \cdot n$. Repeated multiplication by the same factor is sometimes expressed as a **power.** The **base** is the factor, and the **exponent** tells how many times to use the base as a factor.

exponent
$$4^3 = 4 \cdot 4 \cdot 4$$
base

read: *"the third power of 4"* or *"4 to the third power"*

Expression	Meaning	Read
4^2	$4 \cdot 4$	four squared
x or x^1	x	x or x to the first power
$(3x)^3$	$3x \cdot 3x \cdot 3x$	the quantity $3x$ cubed
$3x^3$	$3 \cdot x \cdot x \cdot x$	the product of 3 and x cubed
$4 + x^2$	$4 + x \cdot x$	the sum of 4 and x squared
$(x + 4)^2$	$(x + 4)(x + 4)$	the quantity $x + 4$ squared
6^4	$6 \cdot 6 \cdot 6 \cdot 6$	6 to the fourth power

TEACHER'S NOTES

See p. T23.

CLASSROOM EXAMPLES

1. Find each value.
   a. 4^3 64
   b. $(3.1)^2$ 9.61
   c. $\left(\frac{2}{3}\right)^2$ $\frac{4}{9}$

2. Evaluate if $x = 4$ and $y = 1.2$.
   a. $(3x)^2$ 144
   b. $2y^2$ 2.88
   c. x^2y 19.2

MIXED REVIEW

Perform the indicated operation.

1. $4\frac{2}{3} \div 1\frac{1}{6}$ 4
2. $\frac{3}{4} + 1\frac{5}{6}$ $2\frac{7}{12}$
3. $\frac{4}{5} - \frac{1}{2}$ $\frac{3}{10}$
4. What percent of 20 is 4? 20
5. $(46.1)(2.9)$ 133.69
6. Simplify $(8 \cdot 3) \div 4$. 6

TEACHER'S RESOURCE MASTERS

Practice Master 1, Part 2

EXAMPLES

1   **Find each value.**

  a. 6^3 **b.** $(4.2)^2$ **c.** $\left(\frac{3}{4}\right)^2$

SOLUTIONS

a. $6^3 = 6 \cdot 6 \cdot 6$
$= 216$

b. $(4.2)^2 = 4.2(4.2)$
$= 17.64$

c. $\left(\frac{3}{4}\right)^2 = \frac{3}{4}\left(\frac{3}{4}\right)$
$= \frac{9}{16}$

2   **Evaluate if $m = 3$ and $n = 2.5$.**

  a. $(2m)^2$ **b.** $2n^2$ **c.** m^3n

SOLUTIONS

a. $(2m)^2 = (2 \cdot 3)^2$
$= 6^2$
$= 36$

b. $2n^2 = 2(2.5)^2$
$= 2(6.25)$
$= 12.5$

c. $m^3n = 3^3 \cdot 2.5$
$= 27(2.5)$
$= 67.5$

ASSIGNMENT GUIDE

Minimum
1–18, 19–61 odd

Regular
1–29 odd, 34–58

Maximum
24–29, 34–67

ORAL EXERCISES

Name the factors in each product.

1. $5(6)$ 5; 6   **2.** $3a$ 3; a   **3.** ab a; b   **4.** $\frac{1}{2}b$ $\frac{1}{2}$; b

5. abc a; b; c   **6.** $4ab$ 4; a; b   **7.** $8(a + 1)$ **8.** $(a + b)(a - b)$

Name the coefficient for each.

9. $4y$ 4   **10.** $6abc$ 6   **11.** $16p^2q^2$ 16   **12.** $\frac{1}{4}s^2$ $\frac{1}{4}$

13. a^2 1   **14.** $8p^2xy^3$ 8   **15.** $\frac{12}{5}x^2$ $\frac{12}{5}$ **16.** $\frac{9}{7}m^2np$ $\frac{9}{7}$

Name the exponent and the base for each.

17. 5^2 2; 5   **18.** x^3 3; x   **19.** m^5 5; m   **20.** $(2x)^2$ 2; 2x   **21.** $(x + y)^4$

WRITTEN EXERCISES

A. **Write each product, using exponents.**

1. $5 \cdot 5 \cdot 5$ 5^3 **2.** $a \cdot a \cdot a \cdot a \cdot a$ a^5 **3.** $5x(5x)$ $(5x)^2$

4. $a \cdot a \cdot y \cdot y \cdot y$ a^2y^3 **5.** $3 \cdot b \cdot b \cdot b$ $3b^3$ **6.** $(3 + m)(3 + m)$

Find each value.

7. 5^2 25   **8.** 2^3 8   **9.** 2^5 32   **10.** $4(3^2)$ 36

11. 7^2 49   **12.** 10^1 10   **13.** 10^2 100   **14.** 10^3 1000

15. 10^4 10,000   **16.** 10^5 100,000   **17.** 10^6 1,000,000   **18.** 10^7

B. **Evaluate if $a = 4$ and $b = 2$.**

19. $3a$ 12   **20.** ab^2 16   **21.** $4ab$ 32   **22.** $6(a + 1)$ 30   **23.** $(a + b)^2$ 36

24. b^3 8   **25.** $3a^2$ 48   **26.** $(3b)^2$ 36   **27.** b^4a^2 256   **28.** $(a + b)^3$

29. $\frac{a^3}{2}$ 32   **30.** $\frac{b^2}{a}$ 1   **31.** $(ab)^2$ 64   **32.** $\left(\frac{a}{b}\right)^2$ 4   **33.** $(a + b)^4$

Evaluate if $m = 2$ and $n = 5$.

34. $\frac{m^3n}{10}$ 4   **35.** n^2m 50   **36.** $(m + n)^2$ 49   **37.** n^2m^3 200

38. $\frac{n^2}{m^3}$ $\frac{25}{8}$ **39.** $m(n^2)$ 50   **40.** $(mn)^2$ 100   **41.** m^n 32

42. $3n^2$ 75   **43.** $(3n)^2$ 225   **44.** 3^n 243   **45.** $3(m^3)$ 24

46. $\frac{m^3}{n}$ $\frac{8}{5}$ **47.** $\frac{6^2}{n - m}$ 12   **48.** $\frac{12}{4n^2}$ $\frac{3}{25}$ **49.** $\frac{n - m}{n^3}$ $\frac{3}{125}$

Find each value.

50. $(3.5)^2$ 12.25   **51.** $(0.2)^3$ 0.008   **52.** $\left(\frac{1}{4}\right)^2$ $\frac{1}{16}$ **53.** $\left(\frac{1}{3}\right)^3$ $\frac{1}{27}$

ADDITIONAL ANSWERS

Oral Exercises
7. 8; $(a + 1)$
8. $(a + b)$; $(a - b)$
21. 4; $(x + y)$

Written Exercises
6. $(3 + m)^2$
18. 10,000,000
28. 216
33. 1296

54. $(11.2 + 0.8)^2$ **55.** $\left(\frac{1}{4} + \frac{3}{4}\right)^6$ 1   **56.** $(1.5 \cdot 0.2)^2$ **57.** $\left(\frac{2}{3} \cdot \frac{1}{6}\right)^2$ $\frac{1}{81}$

58. $\left(\frac{3}{5} + \frac{9}{10}\right)^3$ $\frac{27}{8}$ **59.** $(0.2 - 0.04)^3$ **60.** $\frac{1.2^3}{2.4}$ 0.72   **61.** $\frac{8.4 - 2.4}{2^4}$ 0.375

62. Use $(I^2)R$ to find the wattage of an electrical circuit if $I = 8$ amperes and $R = 0.2$ ohms.   12.8 watts

C. 63. Use $h(w^2)$ to find the volume in cubic centimeters of a square prism if $h = 5.3$ centimeters and $w = 3.9$ centimeters.   80.613 cubic centimeters

Use with exercise 63.

5.3 cm

3.9 cm

3.9 cm

64. Use $\pi(R^2 - r^2)$ to find the area of the top of a washer in square inches if $R = 4$ inches and $r = 2$ inches. Use 3.14 for π. (HINT: Find R^2 and r^2 first.)   37.68 square inches

Use with exercise 64.

Washer

65. Use $2\pi^2 r^2 R$ to find the volume of a torus (a doughnut-shaped surface) in cubic centimeters if $r = 1.5$ centimeters and $R = 4$ centimeters. Use 3.14 for π.

66. If $5^4 = 625$, how would you find the value of 5^5?

67. What would you multiply the value of x^5 by to get x^6? x

68. Write $b^7 \cdot b^4$, using only one exponent. b^{11}

Use with exercise 65.

IN OTHER FIELDS
Mathematics and Health

Health experts have done much research on the effects of sun on the skin. Generally, the length of time you can stay in the sun without burning depends upon your skin type. If you have fair skin, 15 minutes is considered safe. People with medium skin can stay out for 20 minutes without protection. Twenty-five minutes is the limit for those with olive or dark skin.

To permit all people to stay in the sun longer, products called sunscreens have been developed. Sunscreens are usually numbered from 2 to 15, with the lower-numbered types providing the least protection and the higher-numbered types providing the most protection. These numbers are referred to as the SPF, Sun Protection Factor.

To find how long you can stay in the sun without getting sunburned, multiply the amount of time you can spend in the sun unprotected times the SPF of the sunscreen. The product is the amount of time you can spend in the sun with a sunscreen. For example, if you have medium skin and use a sunscreen with an SPF of 6, you can stay out 6 times as long, or 2 hours, because $20 \times 6 = 120$ minutes.

1.3	Properties

The following properties may be used to simplify expressions:

Let a, b, and c be any numbers.	Addition	Multiplication
Commutative property	$a + b = b + a$	$ab = ba$
Associative property	$(a + b) + c = a + (b + c)$	$(ab)c = a(bc)$
Identity property	$a + 0 = 0 + a = a$	$a \cdot 1 = 1 \cdot a = a$

Distributive property of multiplication over addition	$a(b + c) = ab + ac$ or $(b + c)a = ba + ca$
Substitution property	If $a = b$, then a may be substituted for b.

EXAMPLES

1 **Simplify $\frac{1}{3}t(12)$.**

SOLUTION

$\frac{1}{3}t(12) = 12\left(\frac{1}{3}t\right)$ *Commutative property of multiplication*

$= \left(12 \cdot \frac{1}{3}\right)t$ *Associative property of multiplication*

$= 4t$ *Substitution property*

Notice that the result is the product of the numerical factors times the variable (or variables).

2 **Simplify $(2.5x)(0.3y)$.**

SOLUTION

$(2.5x)(0.3y) = 0.75xy$ *Multiply the coefficients.*

Using the properties can make some computations easier.

3 **Simplify $17 + (83 + 37)$.**

SOLUTION

$17 + (83 + 37) = (17 + 83) + 37$

$= 100 + 37$

$= 137$

OBJECTIVES

Identify and use properties of addition and multiplication.

Multiply factors that involve powers.

TEACHER'S NOTES

See p. T23.

CLASSROOM EXAMPLES

1. Simplify $\frac{1}{4}a(20)$. $5a$
2. Simplify $(1.4x)(0.2y)$. $0.28xy$
3. Simplify $43 + (16 + 52)$. 111
4. Simplify $(8 + 16) + (30 + 12)$. 66
5. Find $2^2(2^3)$ and 2^5. 32
6. Simplify $(6x^2y)(3x^4)$. $18x^6y$
7. Simplify $(8x^3)\left(\frac{1}{4}x\right)$. $2x^4$

MIXED REVIEW

1. $(3x)^3$ $27x^3$
2. $\left(\frac{1}{3}\right)^2$ $\frac{1}{9}$
3. 40% of 800 320
4. 39.1×2.4 93.84
5. Evaluate $\frac{8 + a}{14 - b}$ if $a = 2$ and $b = 4$. 1
6. $4\frac{1}{2} + 6\frac{2}{3}$ $11\frac{1}{6}$

TEACHER'S RESOURCE
MASTERS
Practice Master 2, Part 1
Quiz 1

ASSIGNMENT GUIDE
Minimum
1–12, 13–23 odd
Regular
1–11 odd, 13–24
Maximum
16–33

4   **Simplify $(13 + 19) + (27 + 31)$.**

SOLUTION

$$\begin{aligned}
(13 + 19) + (27 + 31) &= 13 + (19 + 27) + 31 \\
&= 13 + (27 + 19) + 31 \\
&= (13 + 27) + (19 + 31) \\
&= 40 + 50 \\
&= 90
\end{aligned}$$

5   **Find $2^3(2^2)$ and 2^5.**

SOLUTION

$$\begin{aligned}
2^3(2^2) &= (2 \cdot 2 \cdot 2)(2 \cdot 2) \\
&= 8(4) \\
&= 32
\end{aligned}$$

$$\begin{aligned}
2^5 &= 2 \cdot 2 \cdot 2 \cdot 2 \cdot 2 \\
&= 32
\end{aligned}$$

Notice that $2^3(2^2) = 2^5$.

Multiplication of Powers	**In multiplying powers, if the bases are the same, then** $x^m \cdot x^n = x^{m+n}$.

6   **Simplify $(8x^2y)(2x^3)$.**

SOLUTION

$$\begin{aligned}
(8x^2y)(2x^3) &= (8 \cdot 2)x^{2+3}y \quad \textit{Multiply the coefficients. Add the exponents of x.} \\
&= 16x^5y
\end{aligned}$$

7   **Simplify $(2x^3)\left(\frac{1}{2}x\right)$.**

SOLUTION

$$\begin{aligned}
(2x^3)\left(\tfrac{1}{2}x\right) &= \left(2 \cdot \tfrac{1}{2}\right)x^{3+1} \quad x = x^1 \\
&= x^4
\end{aligned}$$

ORAL EXERCISES

Name the property illustrated.

1. $4 + 5 = 5 + 4$ Comm. prop. of add.

2. $3 + (5 + m) = (3 + 5) + m$ Assoc. prop. of add.

3. $12(6 + 2) = 12(6) + 12(2)$ Dist. prop.

4. $xy = yx$ Comm. prop. of mult.

5. $2(3x) = (2 \cdot 3)x$ Assoc. prop. of mult.

6. $(x + y)z = xz + yz$ Dist. prop.

Name the property that justifies each step.

7. $60 + (112 + 40) = 60 + (40 + 112)$ Comm. prop. of add.
           $= (60 + 40) + 112$ Assoc. prop. of add.

8. $7(6 + 1) = 7 \cdot 6 + 7 \cdot 1$ Dist. prop.
        $= 7 \cdot 6 + 7$ Ident. prop. of mult.

Is each true or false? If false, give the correct answer.

9. $2(5x) = (2 \cdot 5)x$ true   **10.** $x^2 \cdot x^3 = x^6$ false; x^5 **11.** $3x^2(4x^3) = 7x^5$
                                                                         false; $12x^5$

WRITTEN EXERCISES

A. Simplify. Use the properties to make the computations easier.

1. $6 \cdot 4 \cdot 5 \cdot 25$ 3000   **2.** $8 + 13 + 2 + 7$ 30   **3.** $32 + 17 + 8$ 57

4. $20 \cdot 23 \cdot 5$ 2300   **5.** $8(12) + 2(12)$ 120   **6.** $8(24)\left(\frac{1}{8}\right)$ 24

Simplify.

7. $13(2a)$ 26a **8.** $4(8a)(6)$ 192a **9.** $2a(7)(3)$ 42a

10. $6xy\left(\frac{1}{3}\right)$ 2xy **11.** $9ab\left(\frac{1}{3}\right)$ 3ab **12.** $8y(y)$ 8y^2

B. 13. $5a^3(2a^2)$ 10a^5 **14.** $4m^5(3m)$ 12m^6 **15.** $2x(4x^3)$ 8x^4

16. $7a^2b(11a^2b^4)$ 77a^4b^5 **17.** $3x^2y(10x^3y^2)$ 30x^5y^3 **18.** $5rs(2s^2r)$ 10r^2s^3

19. $2x^2(3x^2)$ 6x^4 **20.** $2.4xy(4.3x^2)$ 10.32x^3y **21.** $1.3abc(5a^2b^2)$
                                                                             6.5a^3b^3c

Is each expression equivalent to $24m^5n^6$? Answer yes or no.

22. $24n^6m^5$ **23.** $12m^3n(2m^2n^5)$ **24.** $4mn(6m^4n^5)$

C. Determine the missing factor for each.

25. $9 \cdot \underline{}\!\!\!{}^{2n^2} = 18n^2$ **26.** $3y \cdot \underline{}\!\!\!{}^{5y^2} = 15y^3$

27. $0.2rs \cdot \underline{}\!\!\!{}^{0.7r^2s^3} = 0.14r^3s^4$ **28.** $3y \cdot \underline{}\!\!\!{}^{0.5y^2} = 1.5y^3$

29. Use the properties to prove $3x + 6x = 9x$.

Simplify.

30. $(3x)^2$ 9x^2 **31.** $(xy)^2$ x^2y^2 **32.** $(2x^2)^2$ 4x^4 **33.** $(xy)^n(2x^2)$ $2x^{n+2}y^n$

ADDITIONAL ANSWERS

Written Exercises

22. yes

23. yes

24. yes

29. $3x + 6x = 9x$
      $(3 + 6)x = 9x$
          $(9)x = 9x$

SELF-QUIZ

Match each word with its description.

a. the 6 in $6x$ **b.** the 2 in $5x^2$ **c.** $5x^2$ in $5x^2 + 6x$ **d.** the x in $6x$

1. exponent   b.   **2.** term   c.   **3.** coefficient   a.   **4.** variable   d.

Simplify.

5. $24 - (6 + 8)$ 10   **6.** 2^4 16   **7.** $5x(7)$ 35x **8.** $\frac{1}{4}x(6x)$ $\frac{3}{2}x^2$

Evaluate if $a = 4$ and $b = 5$.

9. $\frac{3a}{b}$ $\frac{12}{5}$ **10.** $2b^2$ 50   **11.** $(b - 1)(2 + a)$ 24

TEACHER'S NOTES

See p. T23.

CLASSROOM EXAMPLES

1. Simplify $6 \cdot 2 \div 3 - 1$. 3

2. Simplify $80 - 2^2 \cdot 3 + (6 - 2)$. 72

3. Simplify $64 - \dfrac{(12 - 3)^2}{3}$. 37

4. Evaluate $a^2 + 3a - 5 + a$ if $a = 4$. 27

5. Simplify $[2(7 - 5) + 3]4 + 8$. 36

6. Simplify $\{[16 - (12 - 8) \div 2] \div 7 + 5\}2$. 14

MIXED REVIEW

1. $(4y^3)(2xy^2)$ $8xy^5$

2. $(5y)^3$ $125y^3$

3. $(5.1x)(0.04xy)$ $0.204x^2y$

4. 3^3 27

5. Simplify $78 - 2^3 \cdot 8 + (3 - 1)$. 16

TEACHER'S RESOURCE MASTERS

Practice Master 2, Part 2

1.4 Order of Operations

More than one value can be obtained for the following numerical expression unless an agreement is made to follow a certain **order of operations:**

$3 + 4 \cdot 2$ $3 + 4 \cdot 2$

   $7 \cdot 2$ $3 + 8$

    14   11

The following order of operations should be used when simplifying an expression:

1. Perform operations within parentheses or other grouping symbols.

2. Evaluate powers.

3. Perform multiplication and division from left to right.

4. Perform addition and subtraction from left to right.

If the above order of operations is followed, the value of the expression $3 + 4 \cdot 2$ is 11.

EXAMPLES

1   **Simplify $2 \cdot 5 + 8 \div 4 - 1$.**

SOLUTION

$$\begin{aligned}
2 \cdot 5 + 8 \div 4 - 1 &= 10 + 8 \div 4 - 1 \\
&= 10 + 2 - 1 \\
&= 12 - 1 \\
&= 11
\end{aligned}$$

2   **Simplify $112 - 3^2 \cdot 6 + (8 - 3)$.**

SOLUTION

$$\begin{aligned}
112 - 3^2 \cdot 6 + (8 - 3) &= 112 - 3^2 \cdot 6 + 5 \\
&= 112 - 9 \cdot 6 + 5 \\
&= 112 - 54 + 5 \\
&= 58 + 5 \\
&= 63
\end{aligned}$$

3   **Simplify $32 - \dfrac{(7 - 5)^3}{2}$.**

SOLUTION

$$\begin{aligned}
32 - \frac{(7 - 5)^3}{2} &= 32 - \frac{2^3}{2} \\
&= 32 - \frac{8}{2} \\
&= 32 - 4 \\
&= 28
\end{aligned}$$

4   **Evaluate $a^2 + 2a - 6 + a$ if $a = 5$.**

SOLUTION

$$
\begin{aligned}
a^2 + 2a - 6 + a &= 5^2 + 2(5) - 6 + 5 \\
&= 25 + 2(5) - 6 + 5 \\
&= 25 + 10 - 6 + 5 \\
&= 35 - 6 + 5 \\
&= 29 + 5 \\
&= 34
\end{aligned}
$$

ASSIGNMENT GUIDE

Minimum
1–59 odd

Regular
31–60

Maximum
36–38, 43–69

Nested grouping symbols are grouping symbols within other grouping symbols. Expressions within nested grouping symbols should be evaluated starting with the innermost pair of grouping symbols.

Nested grouping symbols include the following: ( ), [ ], and { }.

5   **Simplify $[3(9 - 2) + 2]5 + 17$.**

SOLUTION

$$
\begin{aligned}
[3(9 - 2) + 2]5 + 17 &= [3(7) + 2]5 + 17 \\
&= [21 + 2]5 + 17 \\
&= [23]5 + 17 \\
&= 115 + 17 \\
&= 132
\end{aligned}
$$

6   **Simplify $\{[21 - (19 - 4) \div 3] \div 4 + 1\}3$.**

SOLUTION

$$
\begin{aligned}
\{[21 - (19 - 4) \div 3] \div 4 + 1\}3 &= \{[21 - 15 \div 3] \div 4 + 1\}3 \\
&= \{[21 - 5] \div 4 + 1\}3 \\
&= \{16 \div 4 + 1\}3 \\
&= \{4 + 1\}3 \\
&= 5(3) \\
&= 15
\end{aligned}
$$

ORAL EXERCISES

What is the first step in evaluating each expression?

1. $12 - \underline{9 \div 3}$

2. $\underline{(12 - 9)} \div 3$

3. $\underline{12 \cdot 9} \div 3$

4. $\underline{12 - 9} + 3$

5. $20 - \underline{18 \div 3} + 3$

6. $6[18 \div \underline{(3 + 3)}]$

7. $\dfrac{3}{4} \div \underline{\left(\dfrac{1}{2} + \dfrac{1}{6}\right)}$

8. $2.6 + \underline{5 \cdot 9.8}$

9. $\underline{144 \div 12} \div 2$

WRITTEN EXERCISES

A. 1–9. Simplify each expression in Oral Exercises 1–9.

Simplify.

10. $32 \div 2 - 16 \div 2$ 8
11. $6 \div 6 + 2^3$ 9
12. $(9 + 4 + 2) \div 5 - 2$ 1

13. $\frac{3^3}{9 - 2}$ $\frac{27}{7}$
14. $3 \cdot 2^3 - 4 \cdot 2 + 1$ 17
15. $(17 - 9)6 \div (8 + 4)$ 4

16. $3^4 \div (8 + 1)$ 9
17. $\frac{(3 + 1)^4}{2} + 9 \div 3$ 131
18. $(8 - 1)^2 + 4$ 53

19. $1.6 \div 4 + 1$ 1.4
20. $\frac{(3 + 5)^2}{2}$ 32
21. $3.1 + 4.2 \div 2$ 5.2

Evaluate if $a = 2$ and $b = 6$.

22. $5a + 2b$ 22
23. $2a + \frac{42}{b}$ 11
24. $a^2 + b^2$ 40

25. $10 + 5a - b$ 14
26. $3b^2 + 2a$ 112
27. $b^2 - 2b + 5$ 29

28. $\frac{ab}{3} + \frac{b}{a}$ 7
29. $a(2b - 3)$ 18
30. $\frac{b^2}{3} + 4a$ 20

B. Simplify.

31. $5(5 - 1) \div (6 - 2)$ 5
32. $(2 + 1)(3 - 1) \div [6 - (7 - 4)]$ 2

33. $(6 - 4) \div 2 + 8 \div (4 - 2) + 1$ 6
34. $4 \cdot 3^3 - 2 \cdot 3^2 - 3 \cdot 4 + 6$ 84

35. $2^5 \div 2^2 \div 2^3 \div 2$ 0.5
36. $12^2 - 5 \cdot 2.4 \cdot 3$ 108

37. $\frac{10^2 - 2^4}{10 + 2^2}$ 6
38. $4 - \left(\frac{5 - 4}{3}\right)^2 + \frac{8}{9}$ $4\frac{7}{9}$

39. $\{12 - (9 - 3) + 4\}3$ 30
40. $(17 - 5) \div (2 + 1) \cdot (14 \div 2)$ 28

41. $\frac{3}{8} \div \left(\frac{1}{2} + \frac{3}{4}\right)$ $\frac{3}{10}$
42. $\left[\frac{2}{3} + \left(1 \div \frac{3}{4}\right)\right]\frac{1}{4}$ $\frac{1}{2}$

43. $\{[(3 + 18) \div 7] + 4\} \cdot \left(\frac{20 + 15}{7} + 1\right)$ 42

44. $\left\{4 + \left[\frac{10 - 4}{2} - 1\right] \cdot 3\right\} \div (8 - 6)$ 5

Evaluate if $x = 3$, $y = 5$, $z = 2$, and $s = 4$.

45. $s^2 + s$ 20
46. $2s + xs^2$ 56
47. $s^x + sx$ 76
48. $x^2 - 2x + 12$ 15

49. $y^4 + 4y - 11$
50. $s^2y + sy^2$ 180
51. $\frac{z^2 + 2x + 1}{s^2 + 4}$ $\frac{11}{20}$
52. $\frac{y^2 - z^3}{s^3 + 2}$ $\frac{17}{66}$

53. $\frac{xyz}{s}$ $\frac{15}{2}$
54. $\frac{x + y + s}{z}$ 6
55. $\frac{7x - y}{s^2}$ 1
56. $\frac{(x + y)^2}{s}$ 16

57. $2y^2 - 3x^2$ 23
58. $\frac{5s^3}{2x^2}$ $\frac{160}{9}$
59. $z^4 - s^2$ 0
60. $\frac{z^4}{s}$ 4

C. Insert grouping symbols in each exercise to form a true statement.

61. $12 + 4^2 \cdot 24 - 18 \div 3 = 44$ $12 + 4^2 \cdot [(24 - 18) \div 3] = 44$

62. $3 \cdot 6 + 2 \cdot 9 + 3 = 42$ $3 \cdot 6 + 2 \cdot (9 + 3) = 42$

63. $24 + 2^2 - 3 - 2 \cdot 6 = 670$ $(24 + 2)^2 - (3 - 2) \cdot 6 = 670$

64. $3^4 - 6 + 4 \cdot 2 + 5 = 11$ $3^4 - (6 + 4) \cdot (2 + 5) = 11$

65. $3 + 4^2 - 6 + 1 \cdot 8 - 3 = 14$ $(3 + 4)^2 - (6 + 1) \cdot (8 - 3) = 14$

Is the expression on the left equal to the expression on the right? Let $a = 5$ and $b = 2$.

66. $a^2 - b^2$; $(a + b)(a - b)$ yes

67. $(a + 2)(b + 4)$; $(a + 2)b + (a + 2)4$ yes

68. $(a + b)^2$; $a^2 + 2ab + b^2$ yes

69. $(a - b)^2$; $a^2 - 2ab + b^2$ yes

CALCULATOR

Enter the following into your calculator:

ENTER   DISPLAY

2 $\boxed{+}$ 3 $\boxed{\times}$ 4 $\boxed{=}$ $20.$ or $24.$?

Was your result 20 or 14? If your result was 20, your calculator performs the operations as you enter them. If your result was 14, your calculator was programmed to use the order of operations. Make sure you make the entries into your calculator so that your result will agree with the order of operations.

You can use a calculator to evaluate expressions.

Example: Let $x = 2$ and $y = 5$. Evaluate $x^2 - 7xy + 3y^2$.

ENTER   DISPLAY

2 $\boxed{\times}$ 2 $\boxed{M+}$ 7 $\boxed{\times}$ 2 $\boxed{\times}$ 5 $\boxed{M-}$ 3 $\boxed{\times}$ 5 $\boxed{\times}$ 5 $\boxed{M+}$ $\boxed{RM}$ $20.$

Notice how each term of the expression is evaluated and then added or subtracted in the memory. (On some calculators, $\boxed{=}$ may have to be pressed before $\boxed{M+}$ or $\boxed{M-}$.)

EXERCISES

Use a calculator to do the following:

1. Find $3.4 + 5.6 \times 9.8$.   58.28

2. Find $2 + 8 \div 2$.   6

3. Let $x = 4$ and $y = 0.2$. Evaluate the expression above.   10.52

4. Do exercises 27–34 in Section 1.4.

Classify a polynomial as a monomial, a binomial, or a trinomial.

Determine the degree of a monomial.

Identify like terms.

Use the distributive property to simplify polynomials.

See p. T23.

CLASSROOM EXAMPLES

1. Simplify $5y + 12y$. $17y$
2. Simplify $8x^3y^2 + 12x^3y^2 + 5x^3y^2$. $25x^3y^2$
3. Simplify $9xy + xy$. $10xy$

MIXED REVIEW

1. Simplify $56 - \dfrac{(9-2)^2}{7}$. 49
2. Evaluate $\dfrac{m^2n}{m}$ if $m = 3$ and $n = 2$. 6
3. Simplify $[3(8-2) + 6]2 + 3$. 51
4. Evaluate 8^3. 512
5. Simplify $(5x^2y)(2x^3y)$. $10x^5y^2$
6. Simplify $(30xy^2)(\frac{1}{2}x)$. $15x^2y^2$

TEACHER'S RESOURCE MASTERS

Practice Master 3, Part 1

1.5 | Polynomials

A **monomial** is a term that is a number (called a **constant**), a variable, or a product of a constant and one or more than one variable.

Term	Monomial?	
6	yes	
$\frac{x}{3}$	yes	$\frac{x}{3} = \frac{1}{3} \cdot x$
$5xy$	yes	
$4\sqrt{x}$	no	The x is under a radical symbol.
$\frac{4}{x}$	no	The x is in the denominator.
$5x^2$	yes	
$2x + 3$	no	This is a sum of 2 terms.

The **degree** of a monomial is the sum of the exponents of the variables. The degree of a nonzero constant is 0.

Monomial	Degree
17	0
x or x^1	1
ab	2
$4m^2n^3$	5
$\sqrt{4}xy^2$	3
$3^2x^3y^4$	7

A **polynomial** is a monomial or the sum (or difference) of monomials. Polynomials are classified by the number of terms in them.

Monomials (one term)	Binomials (two terms)	Trinomials (three terms)
$\frac{1}{2}x$	$x - 5$	$x^2 - 6x + 5$
5	$2y + 15$	$y + 2y^2 + 7y^3$
$6x^2$	$3m^2 - m$	$7z + 6yz^2 - 1$
ab	$5x^4 - xy$	$m^4 - 13n^2 - 2$

Like terms are terms that differ only in their coefficients.

Terms	Like terms?	
4, 2	yes	Both are constant terms.
$3x, 6y$	no	The variables are different.
$2m, 5m$	yes	
$6x^3y, 6x^2y$	no	The exponents of x are different.
$3ab^2c, 8ab^2c$	yes	

The distributive property is used to combine like terms when simplifying polynomials.

18   *Chapter 1 • Introduction to Algebra*

You may want to introduce this topic using **Algebra Tiles.** They are a physical model for teaching algebraic concepts and are available from Cuisenaire Co. of America, Inc., 12 Church Street, New Rochelle, NY 10802.

EXAMPLES

ASSIGNMENT GUIDE

Minimum
1–15, 22–27, 29–35 odd

Regular
1–15 odd, 22–38

Maximum
18–42

1 **Simplify $6a + 15a$.**

SOLUTION $6a + 15a = (6 + 15)a$ *Distributive property*

$\qquad\qquad\qquad = 21a$ *Substitution property*

2 **Simplify $24x^2y + 5x^2y + 2x^2y$.**

SOLUTION $24x^2y + 5x^2y + 2x^2y = (24 + 5)x^2y + 2x^2y$

$\qquad\qquad\qquad\qquad\qquad = 29x^2y + 2x^2y$

$\qquad\qquad\qquad\qquad\qquad = (29 + 2)x^2y$

$\qquad\qquad\qquad\qquad\qquad = 31x^2y$

3 **Simplify $6mn + mn$.**

SOLUTION $6mn + mn = 6mn + 1mn$ *Identity property of multiplication*

$\qquad\qquad\qquad = (6 + 1)mn$

$\qquad\qquad\qquad = 7mn$

ORAL EXERCISES

Tell whether the given expression is a monomial. If the expression is a monomial that has a variable or variables, give its coefficient.

1. $\frac{2}{3}$ yes

2. $6a$ yes; 6

3. $\sqrt{x}$ no

4. $x \cdot 3$ yes; 3

5. $\frac{5x}{4}$ yes; $\frac{5}{4}$

6. $\sqrt{4b}$ no

7. $\frac{1}{2}t$ yes; $\frac{1}{2}$

8. $3x + 4$ no

9. $\frac{3}{x}$ no

10. xy yes; 1

11. $\sqrt{2}$ yes

12. $\frac{3}{2}xy$ yes; $\frac{3}{2}$

WRITTEN EXERCISES

A. Classify each polynomial as a monomial, a binomial, or a trinomial.

1. $6x^2 - 4$ binomial

2. $a^3 + 2b^2 - 4$ trinomial

3. $13m^2$ monomial

4. $m^2 - 2 + 3m^2$ trinomial

5. $4x^2y - 3x^2y$ binomial

6. $x^3 + 6x^3y + 8x^3$ trinomial

Are the monomials like terms?

7. $4m^2n, 7m^2n$ yes

8. $16st^2, 5st^2$ yes

9. $8mn^2, 12m^2n$ no

10. $12st^2, 24s^2t$ no

11. $9, 16$ yes

12. $3xyz, xyz$ yes

13. $5mn^2p^2, \frac{1}{2}mn^2p^2$ yes

14. $3xy, 0.4yx$ yes

15. $10y^4, 10y^2$ no

B. Copy and replace the ?'s to make pairs of like terms.

16. $3x^2y; 3x^?y$ 2

17. $9a^3b^2; \underline{\ ?\ }a^3b^2$ any number but 0

18. $0.2a$; 4 <u>?</u> a

19. x^3y^5; $2x^?y^?$ 3; 5

20. $a^2b^2c^3$; $a^?b^?c^?$ 2; 2; 3

21. m^5; <u>?</u> m^5 any number but 0

Simplify.

22. $15c + 10c$ $25c$

23. $8g + 13g$ $21g$

24. $x + 8x$ $9x$

25. $19g + g$ $20g$

26. $6x^2 + 5x^2$ $11x^2$

27. $7y^2 + 3y^2$ $10y^2$

28. $14r^3 + 12r^3 + 6r^3$ $32r^3$

29. $11s^4 + 9s^4 + 5s^4$ $25s^4$

30. $12rs^2 + rs^2 + rs + 5rs$ $13rs^2 + 6rs$

31. $20a^2b + 15a^2b + ab + 15ab$
$35a^2b + 16ab$

32. $5x^2yz + 3x^2yz + 2x^2yz$ $10x^2yz$

33. $8(x + x)$ $16x$

34. $14(a^2 + a^2)$ $28a^2$

35. $7(x^2y + 2x^2y)$ $21x^2y$

C. **Write and simplify a polynomial for the area of each figure. The angles shown are right angles.**

36.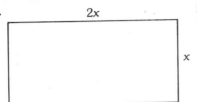

37.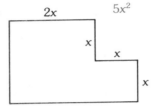

Simplify. Use the idea of like terms to make the computation easier.

38. $3 \cdot 57 + 5 \cdot 57 + 2 \cdot 57$ 570

39. $27 \cdot 50 + 27 \cdot 30 + 27 \cdot 20$ 2700

40. Write a monomial in two variables that has a degree of 3. 40–42. Answers will vary.

41. Write a binomial so that each term has a degree of 1.

42. Write a binomial in one variable so that one term has a degree of 1 and the other has a degree of 2.

CHALLENGE

Andrew paid $2 to enter a flea market. He spent half the money he had left while there. It cost him $1 to leave (parking). After repeating this spending pattern two more times, he went home with $1. How much money did he have to begin with? $36

EXPLORATION
Venn Diagrams

A useful tool for solving certain types of problems is the *Venn diagram*. A Venn diagram uses circles (or any simple closed curves) inside a rectangle to represent relationships among groups of people or objects. Often these groups are referred to as **sets.**

Example: There are 25 freshmen who have seen *Star Gazers, Part I,* 36 who have seen *Star Gazers, Part II,* and 17 who have seen both movies. How many freshmen saw one movie, but did not see both?

Solution: The rectangle represents all freshmen.

Circle A represents those who saw *Part I.*

Circle B represents those who saw *Part II.*

The overlap represents those who saw both.

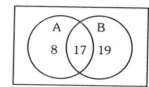

Therefore, there are $36 - 17 = 19$ freshmen who did not see *Part I* and $25 - 17 = 8$ freshmen who did not see *Part II*. A total of $19 + 8 = 27$ freshmen saw one movie but did not see both.

EXERCISES

Use the following information to complete the diagram and answer the questions.

There are 128 students taking biology.

There are 100 students taking Spanish.

There are 80 students taking art.

There are 30 students taking biology and Spanish.

There are 40 students taking Spanish and art.

There are 28 students taking biology and art.

There are 10 students taking all three subjects.

A—students taking biology
B—students taking Spanish
C—students taking art

1. How many students are taking biology and Spanish, but not art? 20

2. How many students are taking biology and art, but not Spanish? 18

3. How many students are taking art, but not biology or Spanish? 22

4. How many students are taking at least one of the three courses? 220

OBJECTIVE

Solve problems, emphasizing *draw a diagram* and *look for a pattern*.

TEACHER'S NOTES

See p. T24.

CLASSROOM EXAMPLE

Karen sat alone in the first row of the school auditorium. Two of her friends sat in the second row with four friends in the third row. How many friends did Karen have in the tenth row? 512

MIXED REVIEW

1. Evaluate mn^2 if $m = 4$ and $n = 5$. 100

2. Simplify $(1.6x)(0.8xy)$.
   $1.28x^2y$

3. Simplify $3 \cdot 8 + 6 \div 2 - 3$. 24

4. Simplify $6(r^2s^3 + 5r^2s^3)$.
   $36r^2s^3$

5. Simplify $(9 - 3)^2 + 5$.
   41

6. Evaluate $c^2 + 4c - 10$ if $c = 3$. 11

TEACHER'S RESOURCE MASTERS

Practice Master 3, Part 2

Quiz 2

You can use the five steps listed below to help you solve problems.

1. **Understand** the problem. Read carefully to determine what is given and what it is you are to do or to find.

2. **Plan** for solving the problem. Planning can include any of the following **problem-solving strategies:**
   - Make a table.
   - Draw a diagram.
   - Use a formula.
   - Look for a pattern.
   - Write and solve an equation.
   - Use a model.
   - Make a guess and then check the answer.
   - Work backwards.
   - Solve a simpler, but related problem.
   - Use logical reasoning.
   - Use estimation.

   These strategies are introduced throughout the book. Often more than one strategy is used in the same problem. Also, you might use a different set of strategies in solving a given problem than someone else might use.

3. **Solve** the problem. Some problems may require computations at this time; others may require some other method for solving them.

4. **Answer** the problem. The computational result, if there is one, may or may not be the answer to the problem.

5. **Review** the problem. Is there another method you can use to check your answer? Does your answer seem reasonable?

EXAMPLE

Max drew a family tree. He listed himself in the first row, his 2 parents in the second row, and his 4 grandparents in the third row. How many great-great-great-great-great-grandparents did he list in the eighth row?

Understand: *Given:* Max listed himself (1 person) in the first row, his 2 parents in the second row, and his 4 grandparents in the third row.

To find: the number of people listed in the eighth row

Plan: **Draw a diagram** of a family tree and **look for a pattern.** Sometimes it helps to write an expression for the pattern.

ASSIGNMENT GUIDE
Minimum
1–10

Regular
3–12

Maximum
7–16

Max Lewis

Alice Miles (mother) — William Lewis (father)

Sara Dobbs (grandmother) — John Miles (grandfather) — Julia Sanders (grandmother) — Samuel Lewis (grandfather)

The pattern shown is 1, 2, 4, . . . According to this pattern, the number doubles with the generation shown in each row. This pattern can be shown with the expression 2^{n-1}. To find the number of people in the eighth row, find 2^{8-1}.

Solve: $2^{8-1} = 2^7 = 128$

Answer: Max listed 128 great-great-great-great-great-grandparents in the eighth row.

Review: Continue the doubling pattern for eight terms: 1, 2, 4, 8, 16, 32, 64, 128. The answer checks.

ORAL EXERCISES

Match each pattern with an expression where 1, 2, 3, . . . are used as replacements for n. Then give the next three terms for each pattern.

1. 2, 4, 6, . . .   d; 8, 10, 12

2. 5, 10, 15, . . .   h; 20, 25, 30

3. 7, 13, 19, . . .   a; 25, 31, 37

4. 6, 10, 14, . . .   f; 18, 22, 26

5. 1, 4, 9, . . .   c; 16, 25, 36

6. 7, 13, 23, . . .   j; 37, 55, 77

7. 2, 5, 10, 17, . . .   b; 26, 37, 50

8. 2, 6, 12, 20, . . .   i; 30, 42, 56

9. 5, 11, 29, 83, . . .   e; 245, 731, 2189

10. 3, 5, 9, 17, . . .   g; 33, 65, 129

a. $6n + 1$

b. $n^2 + 1$

c. n^2

d. $2n$

e. $3^n + 2$

f. $4n + 2$

g. $2^n + 1$

h. $5n$

i. $n^2 + n$

j. $2n^2 + 5$

WRITTEN EXERCISES

A. 1. What is the seventh even number?   14   **2.** What is the tenth odd number?   19

3. What is the sum of the first ten odd numbers?   100

4. What is the sum of the first ten even numbers?   110

B. **5.** These are the first four triangular numbers. What is the tenth triangular number? 55

1 •   3 ••   6 •••   10 ••••

6. These are the first four square numbers. What is the eighth square number? 64

1 •   4 ••   9 •••   16 ••••

7. These are rectangular numbers. If you continue the pattern, what will the seventh rectangular number be? 56

2 ••   6 •••   12 ••••   20 •••••

8. These are the first four pentagonal numbers. What is the sixth pentagonal number? 51

1 •   5 ••   12 •••   22 ••••

9. Big Wally sells used cars. The first week he sold one car. After that, every week he sold 2 more cars than he sold the week before. How many cars had he sold at the end of 15 weeks? 225 cars

10. Sue was paid $1 for her first day of work. Every day after that her salary doubled. How much money had she made after 14 days? $16,383

11. A culture of bacteria has 30 cells. Each cell divides to form 2 cells once every half hour. How many cells are there after 5 hours? 30,720 cells

12. A square table has seating for 4 people. Two square tables that share a side have seating for 6. How many seats are available if 8 tables are placed in a line?

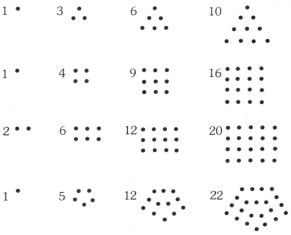

C. **13.** There are 7 people in a room. Each person shakes hands with each of the other people in the room. How many handshakes are there in all?

21 handshakes

14. An ant is climbing out of a well at a rate of 1 foot per hour. At the end of each hour it falls $\frac{1}{2}$ foot back down the well. How many hours will it take to climb out of a 20-foot well? 39 hours

15. The sum of the angles of a triangle is 180°. What is the sum of the angles of an octagon? 1080°

16. Radioactive carbon, ^{14}C, is often used to date fossils. ^{14}C decays with a half-life of 5600 years. This means that after 5600 years, half the quantity decays and half remains. If a fossil insect is found in rock that has only $\frac{1}{4}$ the usual amount of ^{14}C, how old is the fossil?

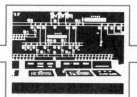

COMPUTER

Is there a three-digit number such that the sum of the cubes of each of its digits equals the original number itself? It would be very difficult to answer this question without the help of a computer.

Problem

Let A = the hundreds digit
Let B = the tens digit
Let C = the ones digit

Is there a number such that $A^3 + B^3 + C^3 = ABC$?

The ones digit can be any integer between 0 and 9.
The tens digit can be any integer between 0 and 9.
The hundreds digit can be any integer between 1 and 9.

Program

```
10 FOR A = 1 TO 9
20 FOR B = 0 TO 9
30 FOR C = 0 TO 9
40 IF (A * A * A + B * B * B + C * C * C) = (100 * A + 10
   * B + C) THEN PRINT A;B;C
50 NEXT C
60 NEXT B
70 NEXT A
80 END
```

EXERCISES

1. Pretend that you are the computer. What is the first number that you would check?

2. How is the value of the three-digit number represented in the program?

3. RUN the program. What is the printout?

4. Modify this program to answer this question: Is there a four-digit number such that the sum of each of its digits raised to the fourth power equals the original number?

ANSWERS

1. 100

2. 100 * A + 10 * B + C

3. 153, 370, 371, 407

4. Change line 40 to the following:
   40 IF (A * A * A * A +
   B * B * B * B + C *
   C * C * C + D * D *
   D * D) = (1000 * A
   + 100 * B + 10 * C
   + D) THEN PRINT A;
   B; C; D

   and insert the following:
   35 FOR D = 0 TO 9 and
   45 NEXT D
   Prints: 1634, 8208, 9474

CHAPTER 1 REVIEW

VOCABULARY

algebraic expression (1.1)
associative property (1.3)
base (1.2)
binomial (1.5)
coefficient (1.2)
commutative property (1.3)
constant (1.5)
degree (1.5)
distributive property (1.3)
evaluate (1.1)

exponent (1.2)
expression (1.1)
factor (1.2)
identity property (1.3)
like terms (1.5)
monomial (1.5)
multiplication of powers (1.3)
nested grouping symbols (1.4)
numerical expression (1.1)
order of operations (1.4)

polynomial (1.5)
powers (1.2)
problem-solving
  strategies (1.6)
simplified (1.1)
substitution property (1.3)
term (1.5)
trinomial (1.5)
value (1.1)
variable (1.1)

REVIEW EXERCISES

1.1   **Simplify.**

1. $(6 + 5) \cdot 10$ 110

2. $(3 \cdot 4) - 2$ 10

3. $\dfrac{12}{8 - 4}$ 3

4. $37 + (26 - 11)$ 52

5. $12 \cdot (6 - 4)$ 24

6. $\left(\dfrac{3 + 9}{4}\right) - 2$ 1

Evaluate if $a = 3$ and $b = 5$.

7. $6 \cdot a$ 18

8. $a \cdot b$ 15

9. $\left(\dfrac{25}{b}\right) - a$ 2

10. $\dfrac{b}{a \cdot a}$ $\dfrac{5}{9}$

11. $6(b + a)$ 48

12. $\dfrac{b \cdot b}{b - a}$ $\dfrac{25}{2}$

Write an algebraic expression for each.

13. two less than a number x $x - 2$

14. If m equals the weight in pounds, what is the weight in ounces? $16m$

15. the product of two numbers, m and x mx

16. three more than twice a number m $2m + 3$

1.2   **Find each value.**

17. 4^2 16

18. $\left(\dfrac{1}{3}\right)^2$ $\dfrac{1}{9}$

19. $(0.8 + 2.3)^2$ 9.61

20. 5^3 125

21. $(2.4)^3$ 13.824

22. $2(3^4)$ 162

Evaluate if $x = 2$ and $y = 4.2$.

23. $4y$ 16.8

24. yx^3 33.6

25. $(x + y)^2$ 38.44

26. $(3y)^2$ 158.76

27. $3^2(y^2)$ 158.76

28. $\dfrac{y^2}{x^3}$ 2.205

29. $\dfrac{y^2}{x}$ 8.82   **30.** $(y - x)^2$ 4.84   **31.** $4x^2$ 16

1.3   Simplify.

32. $3^3 \cdot 3^2$ 243   **33.** $a^4 \cdot a$ a^5 **34.** $3s(4s)$ $12s^2$

35. $m^2 \cdot 3n$ $3m^2n$ **36.** $b^3(3b^5)$ $3b^8$ **37.** $\frac{1}{4}r^2s(12rs^3)$ $3r^3s^4$

38. $3b(2a^2b^4)$ $6a^2b^5$ **39.** $2^4a^3(a^{11})$ $16a^{14}$ **40.** $18m\left(\frac{1}{3}m^2\right)$ $6m^3$

41. $2r^2s(3rs^4)$ $6r^3s^5$ **42.** $m^3 \cdot m^5$ m^8 **43.** $3n^2\left(\frac{1}{9}n^{10}\right)$ $\frac{1}{3}n^{12}$

44. $2r(3r^2)(6r)$ $36r^4$ **45.** $3s(s^4)\left(\frac{2}{3}s^3\right)$ $2s^8$ **46.** $8q\left(\frac{1}{4}q^3\right)$ $2q^4$

1.4   Simplify.

47. $24 \div 2 - 2 \cdot 3$ 6   **48.** $2(4 - 3) + 7$ 9

49. $4(1 + \frac{1}{4}) - 3$ 2   **50.** $16 \div 2 \cdot 4$ 32

51. $2.3(3.6 - 1.5)$ 4.83   **52.** $2 \cdot 3 + 8 \cdot 5^2$ 206

53. $(3 \cdot 4 + 9) \div [15 \div (3 + 2)]$ 7   **54.** $7\{2 + 3[5 - (9 - 7)]\}$ 77

Evaluate if $m = 2$ and $n = 3$.

55. $m + 12 - m^2$ 10   **56.** $3m^2 + 2n$ 18   **57.** $20 - m^3 \div 4 + 6$

58. $3m^2 - 2m + 1$ 9   **59.** $5m^2 - n^2$ 11   **60.** $18 \div n^2$ 2

1.5   Simplify.

61. $12a + a$ $13a$ **62.** $6x^2 + 5x^2$ $11x^2$ **63.** $14x^2y + 3x^2y$

64. $2rs + 6r^2s^2 + 3rs$ $5rs + 6r^2s^2$ **65.** $9m + 8m^2 + 2m^2 + 3m$

66. $3a + 5a + 6a + 4a^2$ $14a + 4a^2$ **67.** $2x^2y + 3x^2y + 6xy^2$

1.6   Solve.

68.

What is the total number of squares in the figure? 14

69.

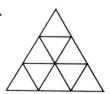

What is the total number of triangles in the figure? 13

TEACHER'S RESOURCE
MASTERS

Chapter 1 Test

Multiple-Choice Test

PROBLEM–SOLVING
HANDBOOK

p. 528

CHAPTER 1 TEST

Translate each phrase to an algebraic expression.

1. a number m decreased by 18 $m - 18$

2. the cost in cents if d is the cost in dollars $100d$

Simplify.

3. $8 + (9 - 3)$ 14

4. $(15 - 2) \cdot 3$ 39

5. 3^4 81

6. $\left(\frac{2}{3}\right)^2$ $\frac{4}{9}$

7. $(3 + 5)^2$ 64

8. $4x(3xy)$ $12x^2y$

9. $6a^2b(2ab^2)$ $12a^3b^3$

10. $76 - (30 + 9)$ 37

11. $20 - 2^4 + 3 \cdot 4$ 16

12. $96 - (3 + 2) \cdot 12$ 36

13. $3x^2y + 2x^2y$ $5x^2y$

14. $3x + 7x$ $10x$

Evaluate if $x = 3$, $y = 5$, and $z = 1$.

15. $6(x + 1)$ 24

16. xy 15

17. $\frac{x + z}{y}$ $\frac{4}{5}$

18. y^2 25

19. $(4y)^2$ 400

20. $\frac{z^2}{(y - x)^2}$ $\frac{1}{4}$

Tell how many terms each expression has.

21. $x + y$ 2

22. $2x + 3 - \frac{3y}{2}$ 3

23. $5xy^2$ 1

Identify the coefficient in each term.

24. $3xy$ 3

25. $\frac{1}{5}x$ $\frac{1}{5}$

26. z 1

Write each product, using exponents.

27. $2 \cdot x \cdot x$ $2x^2$

28. $m \cdot m \cdot m$ m^3

29. $(x + b)(x + b)$

Which property is illustrated?

30. $(ab)c = a(bc)$

31. $6 + 0 = 6$

32. $x + y = y + x$

Classify each polynomial as a monomial, a binomial, or a trinomial.

33. $x^2 + 2x - 9$ trinomial

34. $3m^2$ monomial

35. $2y + 8$ binomial

Give the degree of each monomial.

36. $4x^2$ 2

37. 3^2m^8 8

38. $3xy^3$ 4

Are the pairs of monomials like terms?

39. $8ab$, $9ab$ yes

40. $2x$, $3y$ no

41. ab^2, $3ab^2$ yes

Solve.

42. These are the first four hexagonal numbers. What is the fifth hexagonal number? 45

1   6   15   28

CHAPTER 2

Real Numbers

There were 17 coins taken from a parking meter. The total value of the coins was $3.05. All of the coins were either dimes or quarters. How many of each coin were taken from the parking meter? 9 quarters, 8 dimes

Identify the meaning of set symbols.

Recognize whether or not one set is a subset of another set.

Use the following methods to describe sets: complete listing, partial listing, and set-builder notation.

TEACHER'S NOTES

See p. T24.

CLASSROOM EXAMPLE

If $N = \{x|x$ is a counting number$\}$ and $R = 1, 3, 5, 7, 9, \ldots\}$, is $R \subset N$?   yes

MIXED REVIEW

1. Find the value of 5^4.   625
2. Simplify $35 - 2^2 + 3 \cdot 4$.
   43
3. Simplify $8x^3y + 6x^3y + x^3y$. $15x^3y$
4. Evaluate $4^2(y^2)$ if $y = 3$.
   144
5. Simplify $[16 - (9 - 3) + 2]3 + 6$.   42
6. Simplify $(9pq)(3p^3q^2)$.
   $27\,p^4q^3$

2.1 | Sets and Subsets

A **set** is a collection of objects, called **elements** or **members** of the set. In algebra, one often deals with sets of numbers, but sets can also consist of other things, such as words, letters, people, or geometric figures. Sets are usually described in one of three ways:

Complete listing $S = \{1, 2, 3, 4, 5, 6, 7, 8, 9, 10, 11, 12\}$
Partial listing $S = \{1, 2, 3, \ldots, 12\}$
Set-builder notation $S = \{x|x$ is a counting number less than or equal to 12$\}$

The set-builder notation above is read as "the set of all x such that x is a counting number less than or equal to 12."

Often a capital letter is used to name a set. The braces { } mean "the set whose elements or members are." In the partial-listing method, the three dots indicate that the pattern is continued as shown by the first few numbers.

If *every* element of set S is also an element of another set, T, then S is a **subset** of T. We can use the following notation to tell whether or not an element belongs to a given set and whether or not one set is a subset of another.

Notation	Meaning
$3 \in S$	3 is an element of set S.
$15 \notin S$	15 is not an element of set S.
$\{3\} \subset S$	The set consisting of 3 is a subset of set S.
$\{15\} \not\subset S$	The set consisting of 15 is not a subset of set S.

In a **finite set,** a count of the elements will end. Set S above is an example of a finite set. Some sets, however, are **infinite sets.** If you tried to count the elements in the set, the count would continue without end.

One example of an infinite set is the set of **counting** (or **natural**) **numbers,** $\{1, 2, 3, 4, \ldots\}$. The set of **whole numbers** includes all of the counting numbers, as well as the number 0.

NOTE: A set is a subset of itself. Why?

EXAMPLE

If $N = \{x|x$ **is a counting number**$\}$ **and** $T = \{2, 4, 6, 8, 10, \ldots\}$ **or** $T = \{x|x$ **is an even counting number**$\}$, **is** T **a subset of** N?

SOLUTION   Since all of the elements of T are also in N, $T \subset N$.

The set of counting numbers is a subset of the set of whole numbers. The set of **integers** is another set often used in algebra. The integers are the following:

$\{\ldots, -3, -2, -1, 0, 1, 2, 3, \ldots\}$

Notice that the pattern continues in each direction.

The set of counting numbers and the set of whole numbers are subsets of the set of integers. The set of integers is a subset of another set, the set of **rational numbers.**

> **A rational number is a number that can be expressed in the form $\frac{a}{b}$, where a and b are both integers and $b \neq 0$.**

The following are examples of rational numbers:

$$\frac{3}{4} \qquad -\frac{5}{2}\left(-\frac{5}{2} = \frac{-5}{2}\right) \qquad 5\left(5 = \frac{5}{1}\right) \qquad 0\left(0 = \frac{0}{1}\right) \qquad 1.4\left(1.4 = \frac{7}{5}\right)$$

If a number cannot be expressed in the form $\frac{a}{b}$, where a and b are integers and $b \neq 0$, then the number is called an **irrational number.** Some examples are $\sqrt{2}$, $\sqrt{3}$, and π. Irrational numbers will be discussed in a later chapter.

Together, the set of rational numbers and the set of irrational numbers make up the set of **real numbers.**

The **empty set** (or **null set**) is another important set in algebra. As the name suggests, the empty set contains *no* elements. The empty set can be shown by two symbols: $\varnothing$ or $\{\ \}$ The empty set is considered to be a subset of *every* set.

ORAL EXERCISES

Choose the best answer.

1. The set of (natural, whole) numbers includes all of the counting numbers and 0.

2. A count of the number of elements in a(n) (finite, infinite) set will end. The count of the elements would continue without end in a(n) (finite, infinite) set.

Use the following sets for exercises 3–10. Tell if each statement is true or false.

$A = \{1, 2\} \qquad B = \{\ \} \qquad C = \{1, 2, 3, 4, 5\} \qquad D = \{-3, -2, -1, 0, 1, 2, 3\} \qquad E = \{0\}$

3. $1 \in A$ T

4. $\{1, 2\} \in C$ F

5. $\{1, 2\} \subset C$ T

6. $E \in D$ F

7. $B \subset A$ T

8. $E \not\subset B$ T

9. $5 \notin D$ T

10. $\{1\} \not\subset A$ F

WRITTEN EXERCISES

A. Use the sets below with exercises 1–12. Complete each statement, using $\in$, $\notin$, $\subset$, or $\not\subset$.

$A = \left\{\frac{1}{2}, 1, \frac{3}{2}\right\} \qquad B = \{\ \} \qquad C = \{1, 2, 3, 4, 5\}$

$D = \{0\} \qquad E = \left\{0, \frac{1}{2}, 1, \frac{3}{2}\right\} \qquad F = \{-1, 0, 1, 2, 3, 4, 5\}$

1. $1 \underline{\quad \in \quad} A$

2. $5 \underline{\quad \notin \quad} B$

3. $A \underline{\quad \subset \quad} E$

4. $D \underline{\quad \subset \quad} E$

5. $\left\{\frac{1}{2}\right\} \underline{\quad \not\subset \quad} F$

6. $-1 \underline{\quad \notin \quad} A$

7. $0 \underline{\quad \notin \quad} B$

8. $B \underline{\quad \subset \quad} A$

9. $C \underline{\quad \subset \quad} F$

10. $\{0\} \underline{\quad \not\subset \quad} B$

11. $\frac{3}{2} \underline{\quad \in \quad} E$

12. $D \underline{\quad \not\subset \quad} A$

TEACHER'S RESOURCE MASTERS

Practice Master 4, Part 1

ASSIGNMENT GUIDE

Minimum
1–26, 27–43 odd

Regular
13–46, 47–55 odd

Maximum
28–62

ADDITIONAL ANSWERS

Written Exercises

21. $\{0, 1, 2, 3, 4, 5, 6, 7, 8, 9, 10, 11, 12, 13, 14\}$
    $\{0, 1, 2, \ldots, 14\}$

22. $\{x \mid x$ is an even counting number less than or equal to $20\}$
    $\{2, 4, 6, \ldots, 20\}$

23. $\{x \mid x$ is an integer greater than -5 and less than $5\}$
    $\{-4, -3, -2, -1, 0, 1, 2, 3, 4\}$

24. $\{x \mid x$ is an integer greater than -11 and less than $1\}$
    $\{-10, -9, -8, \ldots, 0\}$

25. {x|x is an odd counting number less than or equal to 11}
{1, 3, 5, 7, 9, 11}

26. {1, 2, 3, 4, 5, 6, 7, 8, 9, 10, 11, 12, 13, 14, 15, 16, 17, 18, 19}
{1, 2, 3, ... , 19}

27. finite

28. finite

29. finite

30. infinite

35. {0, 1, 2, 3, 4, 5, 6}

36. {−2, −1, 0, 1, 2, 3, 4, 5}

37. {1, 3, 5}

38. {0, 2, 4, 6, 8}

39. {10, 20, 30, 40, 50, 60, 70, 80, 90}

40. {−3, −2, −1, 0, 1, 2, 3}

44. {−3, −2, −1, ...}

47. whole, integer, rational, real

48. counting, whole, integer, rational, real

49. rational, real

50. integer, rational, real

51. real

52. rational, real

53. counting, whole, integer, rational, real

54. counting, whole, integer, rational, real

55. rational, real

56. real

57. rational, real

58. rational, real

59. rational, real

60. rational, real

61. rational, real

62. real

B. Use the sets for exercises 1–12 to complete exercises 13–20. Some exercises have more than one correct answer. List all correct answers.

13. $\frac{1}{2} \in$ ___A, E___

14. $B \subset$ ___A, B, C, D, E, F___

15. $C \subset$ ___C, F___

16. $0 \in$ ___D, E, F___

17. $1 \notin$ ___B, D___

18. $F \not\subset$ ___A, B, C, D, E___

19. $4 \notin$ ___A, B, D, E___

20. $A \subset$ ___A, E___

Write each set by using two other methods for describing the set.

21. {x|x is a whole number less than 15}

22. {2, 4, 6, 8, 10, 12, 14, 16, 18, 20}

23. {−4, −3, −2, ... , 4}

24. {−10, −9, −8, −7, −6, −5, −4, −3, −2, −1, 0}

25. {1, 3, 5, ... , 11}

26. {x|x is a counting number less than or equal to 19}

Is each set finite or infinite?

27. {all metersticks in your classroom}

28. {all metersticks in your school}

29. {all metersticks in your state}

30. {0, 3, 6, 9, 12, ...}

31. {0, 3, 6, 9, ... , 21} finite

32. {x|x is a whole number greater than 5} infinite

33. {x|x is a counting number less than 10} finite

34. {x|x is an integer less than 1} infinite

Describe each set by a complete listing.

35. whole numbers less than 7

36. integers from −2 through 5

37. odd counting numbers less than 6

38. even whole numbers less than 9

39. counting numbers less than 100 that are multiples of 10

40. integers greater than −4 and less than or equal to 3

Describe each set by a partial listing.

41. all whole numbers {0, 1, 2, 3, ...}

42. all counting numbers {1, 2, 3, 4, ...}

43. integers less than 3 {..., 0, 1, 2}

44. integers greater than −4

45. whole numbers greater than 8 {9, 10, 11, ...}

46. counting numbers that are multiples of 10 {10, 20, 30, ...}

C. Each number below belongs to which set or sets of numbers? Choose from _real_, _rational_, _integer_, _whole_, or _counting_. List all correct answers.

47. 0

48. 5

49. $\frac{1}{2}$

50. −3

51. $\sqrt{2}$

52. $-1\frac{2}{3}$

53. 1

54. 2000

55. 2.3

56. π

57. 0.01

58. $-\frac{10}{7}$

59. −6.7

60. $1\frac{7}{9}$

61. −0.4

62. $\sqrt{3}$

2.2 Using a Number Line

A tire gauge is used to measure the number of pounds of air pressure per square inch in a tire. The scale used to read the air pressure in a tire is part of a **real-number line.**

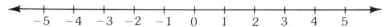

Integers are shown on the number line above. Positive numbers are to the right of 0, and negative numbers are to the left of 0. Zero is neither positive nor negative.

The integers divide the number line into segments that are one unit long. From -3 to -2 or from 3 to 4 is one unit.

Sets of numbers are *graphed* on a number line by locating *points* with the proper *coordinates*.

EXAMPLES

1 **Graph the set of whole numbers.**

SOLUTION

point

coordinate

The number is the coordinate of the point.
The point is the graph of the number.

Every real number can be represented on the number line. The rational numbers 1, $-\frac{3}{2}$, and $\frac{13}{4}$ are shown on the number line below.

To graph rational numbers, you can subdivide the unit segment into appropriate parts.

2 **Graph the set $\left\{-\frac{1}{5}, \frac{3}{5}, \frac{8}{5}, \frac{11}{5}\right\}$.**

SOLUTION Subdivide the unit segments into fifths.

OBJECTIVES

Use a number line to give the opposite of any integer.

Use a number line to compare rational numbers.

Give the absolute value of any real number.

TEACHER'S NOTES

See p. T24.

CLASSROOM EXAMPLES

1. Graph the set of whole numbers.

2. Graph the set $\left\{-\frac{1}{3}, \frac{2}{3}, \frac{5}{3}, \frac{10}{3}\right\}$.

3. Give the opposite of -4 and the opposite of $\frac{9}{2}$.
   The opposite of -4 is 4.
   The opposite of $\frac{9}{2}$ is $-\frac{9}{2}$.

4. Graph $-3, -2, 3,$ and 5.

5. Give the following:
   $\left|\frac{15}{4}\right|$ $|0|$ $|-5|$ $-|8|$
   $\left|\frac{15}{4}\right| = \frac{15}{4}$ $|0| = 0$
   $|-5| = 5$ $-|8| = -8$

Two numbers corresponding to points that are the *same distance* but in *opposite directions* from the 0-point are called **opposites**. Zero is said to be its own opposite.

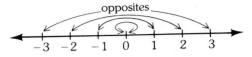

Note that positive integers do not need the $+$ sign.

| **3** | **Give the opposite of -3 and the opposite of $\frac{7}{2}$.** |

SOLUTION   The opposite of -3 is 3. The opposite of $\frac{7}{2}$ is $-\frac{7}{2}$.

NOTE: The set of integers can be described as the set of whole numbers and their opposites.

On a number line, the greater number is graphed to the right of the lesser number. The lesser number is graphed to the left of the greater number.

| **4** | **Graph -4, -1, 2, and 4.** |

SOLUTION

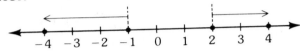

"negative 4 **is less than** negative 1."   "4 **is greater than** 2"

The **absolute value** of a number x, represented by $|x|$, is its distance from 0 on the number line without considering direction. The absolute value of 0 is 0. So,

$|x| = x$ if $x = 0$ or if $x > 0$

$|x| = -x$ if $x < 0$

(read: "the opposite of x")

| **5** | **Give the following:** $\left|\frac{17}{4}\right|$ $|0|$ $|-3|$ $-|9|$ |

SOLUTION

$$\left|\frac{17}{4}\right| = \frac{17}{4} \qquad |0| = 0 \qquad |-3| = -(-3) = 3 \qquad -|9| = -9$$

ORAL EXERCISES

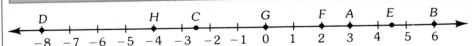

Give the coordinate of each point.

1. A 3   **2.** B 6   **3.** H -4 **4.** D -8

Tell which point has the given coordinate.

5. $-2\frac{1}{2}$ C   **6.** 2 F   **7.** $4\frac{1}{2}$ E   **8.** -4 H

34   *Chapter 2 • Real Numbers*

You may want to introduce this topic using **Algebra Tiles.** They are a physical model for teaching algebraic concepts and are available from Cuisenaire Co. of America, Inc., 12 Church Street, New Rochelle, NY 10802.

WRITTEN EXERCISES

A. For exercises 1–8, refer to a number line if necessary to decide which symbol, =, <, or >, should replace each ●.

1. 8 ● -9 $>$ **2.** 14 ● -15 $>$ **3.** -11 ● -9 $<$ **4.** 0 ● -1 $>$

5. $-\frac{3}{4}$ ● -1 $>$ **6.** $1\frac{1}{2}$ ● $1\frac{1}{4}$ $>$ **7.** 0 ● $\frac{0}{8}$ $=$ **8.** 0.8 ● 1 $<$

9. The absolute value of a positive number or 0 is (the number itself, its opposite).

10. The absolute value of a negative number is (the number itself, its opposite).

B. Graph each of the following sets of numbers on a number line. If necessary, use a number line with unit segments subdivided into fractional parts.

11. $-6, -4, -2, 0, 2, 4, 6$ **12.** $1, -2, 3, -4, 5$

13. $-4, -3, 6, 2, 0$ **14.** $0, 4, 7, -1, -5$

15. $-2, -\frac{4}{3}, -\frac{2}{3}, 0, \frac{2}{3}, \frac{4}{3}, 2$ **16.** $-1\frac{1}{5}, -\frac{4}{5}, -\frac{2}{5}, 0, \frac{2}{5}, \frac{4}{5}, 1\frac{1}{5}, 1\frac{3}{5}$

Complete.

17. $|5| = \underline{\ 5\ }$ **18.** $\left|\frac{4}{5}\right| = \underline{\ \frac{4}{5}\ }$ **19.** $|-5| = \underline{\ 5\ }$ **20.** $\left|\frac{8}{9}\right| = \underline{\ \frac{8}{9}\ }$

21. $|0| = \underline{\ 0\ }$ **22.** $|\underline{\ 0\ }| = 0$ **23.** $|-5.76| = \underline{\ 5.76\ }$ **24.** $|5.76| = \underline{\ 5.76\ }$

25. $-|7| = \underline{\ -7\ }$ **26.** $-\left|1\frac{1}{5}\right| = \underline{\ -1\frac{1}{5}\ }$ **27.** $-|-6| = \underline{\ -6\ }$ **28.** $-\left|-\frac{4}{5}\right| = \underline{\ -\frac{4}{5}\ }$

C. 29. Find $-x$ if $x = 3$. -3 **30.** Find $-x$ if $x = -5$. 5

31. Find $-(-x)$ if $x = 4$. 4 **32.** Find $-(-x)$ if $x = -5$. -5

33. Find $|-x|$ if $x = 2.7$. 2.7 **34.** Find $-|-x|$ if $x = -3$. -3

35. Find $-|-x|$ if $x = 5$. -5 **36.** Find $-|-(-x)|$ if $x = -2$. -2

ADDITIONAL ANSWERS

Written Exercises

For the odd-numbered solutions, see *Answers to Selected Exercises*, p. 568.

12.

14.

16.

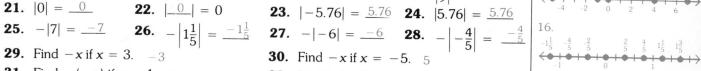

SKILLS MAINTENANCE

Evaluate the following if $x = 4$ and $y = 6$:

1. xy 24 **2.** $\frac{8}{y-x}$ 4 **3.** $xy - x$ 20 **4.** $5x - y$ 14

Simplify.

5. $(10 \cdot 4) - 15$ 25 **6.** $56 - (45 - 9)$ 20 **7.** $\frac{36}{8-2}$ 6 **8.** $\frac{5}{6} - \left(\frac{2}{3} - \frac{1}{3}\right)$ $\frac{1}{2}$

Find each value.

9. 2^6 64 **10.** 10^5 $100{,}000$ **11.** $2(5^2)$ 50 **12.** $\left(\frac{2}{3}\right)^2$ $\frac{4}{9}$

Simplify.

13. $20a + 3a$ $23a$ **14.** $6x^3 + 5x^3 + x^3$ $12x^3$ **15.** $15x^2y + 9x^2y$ $24x^2y$

MATH HERITAGE/The Name Lives On

The contributions of some mathematicians have been so significant that their discoveries still bear their names.

Pythagoras (580 B.C.–?) formulated the *Pythagorean theorem,* which states that the square of the length of the hypotenuse of a right triangle is equal to the sum of the squares of the lengths of the other two sides.

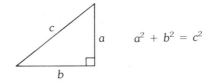

$$a^2 + b^2 = c^2$$

Edmund Halley (1656–1742) calculated the orbit of a comet in 1682 and predicted that it would return in 1758. The comet appeared on Christmas Day of that year and is still referred to as *Halley's Comet.*

Christian Doppler (1803–1853) first described the *Doppler effect,* which is the apparent change in the frequency of sound, light, or radio waves caused by motion. An example is the increase and the decrease in the pitch, or the frequency, of the sound waves from a train's whistle as the train passes an observer.

Johann Elert Bode (1747–1826) devised a series of numbers, referred to as *Bode's law,* which closely approximate the relative distances of the planets from the sun.

August Ferdinand Möbius (1790–1868) is best known for the *Möbius strip,* a one-sided surface obtained by giving a half twist to one end of a strip of paper and then joining the ends. The resulting strip has but one edge and one surface.

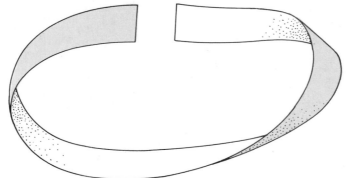

George Boole (1815–1864) developed *Boolean algebra,* a system of expressing logical statements symbolically. Once expressed in this way, the statements can be written and proved in a manner similar to that used in ordinary algebra.

2.3 | Addition on the Number Line

A number line can be used to show addition of positive and negative numbers. A positive number can be represented by a move in the positive direction, and a negative number can be represented by a move in the negative direction.

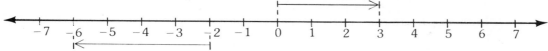

A move of 3 units in the positive direction.

A move of 4 units in the negative direction.

EXAMPLES

1 | **Add 4 + 3.**

SOLUTION

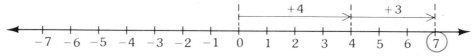

Start at 0.
Move 4 units to the right.
Move 3 more units to the right.
So 4 + 3 = 7.

2 | **Add −4 + (−3).**

SOLUTION

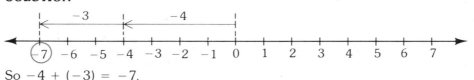

So −4 + (−3) = −7.

3 | **Add 4 + (−3).**

SOLUTION

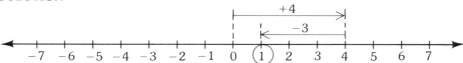

Start at 0.
Move 4 units to the right.
Then move 3 units to the left.
So 4 + (−3) = 1.

OBJECTIVE

Find the sum of two or more integers, using a number line if necessary.

TEACHER'S NOTES

See p. T24.

CLASSROOM EXAMPLES
1. Add 6 + 2.

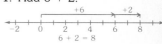

6 + 2 = 8

2. Add −5 + (−2).

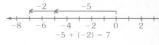

−5 + (−2) = 7

3. Add 3 + (−2).

3 + (−2) = 1

4. Add −5 + 2.

−5 + 2 = −3

5. Add 3 and (−3).

3 + (−3) = 0

6. Add −2 + 5 + (−1) + (−6).

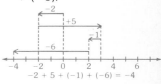

−2 + 5 + (−1) + (−6) = −4

1. Graph $\left\{-\frac{2}{3}, -\frac{1}{3}, 1, \frac{5}{3}\right\}$.

2. Given: $A = \{1, 2, 3, 4, 5\}$
   $B = \{\ \}$
   $C = \{1, 3, 5\}$
   $D = \{1, 2, 4, 6\}$

   Label the following true or false.

   a. $C \subset A$ T

   b. $B \subset D$ T

   c. $5 \notin C$ F

   d. $\{1, 3\} \not\subset C$ F

3. Evaluate $252 - \dfrac{14^2}{4}$.   203

4. Simplify.

   a. $[5 + (6 - 4)2]4 - 3$ 33

   b. $14x^3y^2 + x^3y^2 + 8x^3y^2$
     $23x^3y^2$

5. Give the following.

   a. $-|-8|$ -8

   b. $\left|\frac{3}{8}\right|$ $\frac{3}{8}$

   c. $|0|$ 0

   d. $|6|$ 6

---

4   **Add $-4 + 3$.**

SOLUTION

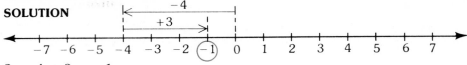

So $-4 + 3 = -1$.

The sum of a number and its opposite is 0.

5   **Add $5 + (-5)$.**

SOLUTION

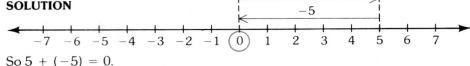

So $5 + (-5) = 0$.

You can add more than two numbers on a number line.

6   **Add $-4 + 8 + (-3) + (-2)$.**

SOLUTION

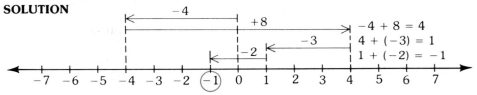

$-4 + 8 = 4$
$4 + (-3) = 1$
$1 + (-2) = -1$

So $-4 + 8 + (-3) + (-2) = -1$.

ORAL EXERCISES

What two numbers are being added on each number line?

1. 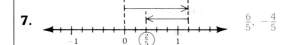 $5, -2$

2. $-2, 5$

3. $-2, -5$

4. $-7, 9$

5. $-\frac{3}{3}, \frac{2}{3}$

6. $1.2, -1.9$

7. $\frac{6}{5}, -\frac{4}{5}$

8. $-0.9, 1.8$

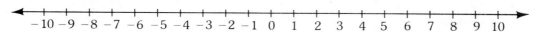

A. Find each sum by referring to the number line below.

$$\longleftarrow \overset{\hspace{0.2em}\text{|}}{\underset{-10}{}}\,\overset{\text{|}}{\underset{-9}{}}\,\overset{\text{|}}{\underset{-8}{}}\,\overset{\text{|}}{\underset{-7}{}}\,\overset{\text{|}}{\underset{-6}{}}\,\overset{\text{|}}{\underset{-5}{}}\,\overset{\text{|}}{\underset{-4}{}}\,\overset{\text{|}}{\underset{-3}{}}\,\overset{\text{|}}{\underset{-2}{}}\,\overset{\text{|}}{\underset{-1}{}}\,\overset{\text{|}}{\underset{0}{}}\,\overset{\text{|}}{\underset{1}{}}\,\overset{\text{|}}{\underset{2}{}}\,\overset{\text{|}}{\underset{3}{}}\,\overset{\text{|}}{\underset{4}{}}\,\overset{\text{|}}{\underset{5}{}}\,\overset{\text{|}}{\underset{6}{}}\,\overset{\text{|}}{\underset{7}{}}\,\overset{\text{|}}{\underset{8}{}}\,\overset{\text{|}}{\underset{9}{}}\,\overset{\text{|}}{\underset{10}{}}\longrightarrow$$

1. $2 + 4$ 6
2. $-5 + 3$ -2
3. $-2 + (-4)$ -6
4. $-5 + (-3)$ -8
5. $-4 + 6$ 2
6. $4 + (-5)$ -1
7. $-4 + (-2)$ -6
8. $-3 + (-5)$ -8
9. $-4 + 9$ 5
10. $2 + (-4)$ -2
11. $6 + (-10)$ -4
12. $-10 + 8$ -2
13. $4 + (-4)$ 0
14. $3 + (-3)$ 0
15. $-6 + 6$ 0
16. $-7 + 7$ 0

B. Find each sum. (Use a number line if necessary.)

17. $2 + (-6) + 4$ 0
18. $8 + (-3) + 4$ 9
19. $2 + (-5 + 6)$ 3
20. $5 + (-8 + 4)$ 1
21. $(-3 + 7) + (-5)$ -1
22. $(-7 + 6) + (-2)$ -3
23. $-3 + 7 + (-2) + (-8)$ -6
24. $-4 + (-3) + 5 + (-2)$ -4
25. $10 + (-5) + 20 + (-22)$ 3
26. $-13 + 7 + (-6) + 13$ 1
27. $0.8 + 0.7$ 1.5
28. $0.36 + 0.95$ 1.31
29. $0.46 + 0.9$ 1.36
30. $-0.16 + 0.12$ -0.04
31. $0.3 + (-0.24)$ 0.06
32. $-0.6 + (-0.32)$
33. $0.63 + (-0.5)$ 0.13
34. $-0.2 + 0.46$ 0.26
35. $-0.4 + 0.65$ 0.25
36. $\frac{2}{5} + \left(-\frac{2}{5}\right)$ 0
37. $-\frac{3}{7} + \frac{5}{7}$ $\frac{2}{7}$
38. $\frac{4}{5} + \frac{3}{5}$ $\frac{7}{5}$
39. $-\frac{4}{5} + \left(-\frac{1}{5}\right)$ -1

C.
40. $2.16 + (-5.8)$ -3.64
41. $-0.29 + 6.1$ 5.81
42. $-0.5 + 4$ 3.5
43. $-0.269 + (-0.9)$
44. $6 + (-0.519)$ 5.481
45. $-4.1 + 8.65$ 4.55
46. $-\frac{4}{5} + \left(-\frac{1}{2}\right)$ $-1\frac{3}{10}$
47. $\frac{4}{5} + \left(-\frac{1}{4}\right)$ $\frac{11}{20}$
48. $-\frac{4}{5} + \frac{1}{2}$ $-\frac{3}{10}$
49. $-\frac{7}{8} + \frac{4}{9}$ $-\frac{31}{72}$

ADDITIONAL ANSWERS

Written Exercises

32. -0.92

43. -1.169

CALCULATOR

Your calculator can be used to perform operations with negative numbers. Many calculators have a change-sign key $\boxed{\pm}$. To find the sum $-8 + (-10)$ on such a calculator,

ENTER   DISPLAY

$8 \boxed{\pm} \boxed{+} 10 \boxed{\pm} \boxed{=}$ $18.\text{-}$

How would you find the sum by using your calculator if it does not have a change-sign key?

EXERCISES

Do Written Exercises 1–26 by using a calculator.

Find the sum of two or more real numbers by using the absolute values of the numbers.

Find the sum of two real numbers with different signs by using the additive inverse property.

TEACHER'S NOTES

See p. T24.

CLASSROOM EXAMPLES

1. Find the sum of 4 and 5, using absolute value.
$$4 + 5 = |4| + |5| = 9$$

2. Find the sum of -4 and -6, using absolute value.
$$-4 + (-6) = -(|-4| + |-6|) = -(4 + 6) = -10$$

3. Find the sum of 12 and -8, using absolute value.
$$12 + (-8) = |12| - |-8| = 12 - 8 = 4$$

4. Find the sum of 10 and -12, using absolute value.
$$10 + (-12) = -(|-12| - |10|) = -(12 - 10) = -2$$

5. Find the sum of 13 and -5, using the additive inverse property.
Rename 13 as 8 plus the opposite of -5.
$$13 = 8 + -(-5)$$
$$13 + (-5) = (8 + 5) + (-5)$$
$$= 8 + [5 + (-5)]$$
$$= 8 + 0$$
$$= 8$$

2.4 | Addition, Using Absolute Value

You have learned how to add numbers such as the following by using a number line.

$$3 + 2 = 5$$

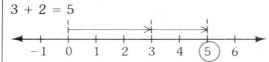

$$-4 + (-1) = -5$$

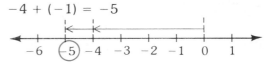

$$6 + (-3) = 3$$

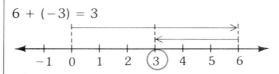

$$2 + (-6) = -4$$

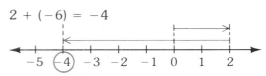

The following rules are to be used to find the sum of two positive numbers and the sum of two negative numbers:

Rule I — **If x and y are both positive, then $x + y = |x| + |y|$.**

Rule II — **If x and y are both negative, then $x + y = -(|x| + |y|)$.**

EXAMPLES

1 **Find the sum of 6 and 8, using absolute value.**
SOLUTION $6 + 8 = |6| + |8| = 14$

2 **Find the sum of -6 and -8, using absolute value.**
SOLUTION $-6 + (-8) = -(|-6| + |-8|) = -(6 + 8) = -14$

The following rules apply when adding a positive and a negative number:

Rule III — **If x is a positive number and y is a negative number, and if $|x| > |y|$, then $x + y = |x| - |y|$.**

Rule IV — **If x is a positive number and y is a negative number, and if $|y| > |x|$, then $x + y = -(|y| - |x|)$.**

3 **Find the sum of 16 and -13, using absolute value.**
SOLUTION $16 + (-13) = |16| - |-13| = 16 - 13 = 3$

4 **Find the sum of 12 and -17, using absolute value.**
SOLUTION $12 + (-17) = -(|-17| - |12|) = -(17 - 12) = -5$

You may want to introduce this topic using **Algebra Tiles.** They are a physical model for teaching algebraic concepts and are available from Cuisenaire Co. of America, Inc., 12 Church Street, New Rochelle, NY 10802.

The examples below show another method that can be used to add numbers when one is positive and the other is negative. These examples make use of the fact that the sum of a number and its opposite is 0. The number and its opposite are called **additive inverses**.

Additive Inverse Property	$x + (-x) = 0$

5   **Find the sum of 15 and -7, using the additive inverse property.**

SOLUTION

Rename 15 as 8 plus the opposite of -7.

$$
\begin{aligned}
15 + (-7) &= (8 + 7) + (-7) && \text{Addition fact} \\
&= 8 + [7 + (-7)] && \text{Associative property of addition} \\
&= 8 + 0 && \text{Additive inverse property} \\
&= 8 && \text{Identity property of addition}
\end{aligned}
$$

6   **Find the sum of 18 and -24, using the additive inverse property.**

SOLUTION

Rename -24 as -6 plus the opposite of 18.

$$
\begin{aligned}
18 + (-24) &= 18 + [-18 + (-6)] && \text{Addition fact} \\
&= [18 + (-18)] + (-6) && \text{Associative property of addition} \\
&= 0 + (-6) && \text{Additive inverse property} \\
&= -6 && \text{Identity property of addition}
\end{aligned}
$$

ORAL EXERCISES

Find each sum.

1. $7 + 19$ 26   **2.** $-21 + 16$ -5 **3.** $19 + (-8)$ 11   **4.** $-17 + 16$ -1

5. $7 + (-19)$ -12 **6.** $-8 + (-5)$ -13 **7.** $-19 + (-8)$ -27 **8.** $-7 + (-6)$ -13

WRITTEN EXERCISES

A. **For each of these additions, tell which property or rule of addition was used in each step.**

$15 + (-8)$
$= (7 + 8) + (-8)$ **1.** _____
$= 7 + [8 + (-8)]$ **2.** _____
$= 7 + 0$ **3.** _____
$= 7$ **4.** _____

$-27 + 19$
$= [-19 + (-8)] + 19$ **5.** _____
$= [-8 + (-19)] + 19$ **6.** _____
$= -8 + (-19 + 19)$ **7.** _____
$= -8 + 0$ **8.** _____
$= -8$ **9.** _____

6. Find the sum of 12 and -29, using the additive inverse property.

Rename -29 as -17 plus the opposite of 12.

$$
\begin{aligned}
-29 &= -12 + (-17) \\
12 + (-29) &= 12 [-12 \\
&\quad + (-17)] \\
&= [12 + (-12)] \\
&\quad + (-17) \\
&= 0 + (-17) \\
&= -17
\end{aligned}
$$

MIXED REVIEW

1. Simplify $16 + 4 \div 2 - 12 \div 3$.   14

2. Evaluate 1.5^3.   3.375

3. Add $(-0.8) + (-0.56)$. -1.36

4. Illustrate the associative property of multiplication.   Answers may vary.

5. Evaluate $\dfrac{a^2 b}{a}$ if $a = 4$ and $b = 1.6$.   6.4

6. Add $\left(\frac{3}{8}\right) + \left(-\frac{1}{3}\right)$. $\frac{1}{24}$

TEACHER'S RESOURCE MASTERS

Practice Master 5, Part 2

ASSIGNMENT GUIDE

Minimum
5–9, 18–23, 30–48

Regular
11–17 odd, 24–35, 40–51, 61, 65

Maximum
31–51, 53–69 odd

$26 + (-8) + (-34)$
$= 26 + [-8 + (-34)]$ **10.** _____
$= 26 + [-(|-8| + |-34|)]$ **11.** _____
$= 26 + [-(8 + 34)]$ **12.** _____
$= 26 + (-42)$ **13.** _____
$= 26 + [-26 + (-16)]$ **14.** _____
$= [26 + (-26)] + (-16)$ **15.** _____
$= 0 + (-16)$ **16.** _____
$= -16$ **17.** _____

$9 + 23 + (-18)$
$= (9 + 23) + (-18)$ **18.** _____
$= 32 + (-18)$ **19.** _____
$= (14 + 18) + (-18)$ **20.** _____
$= 14 + [18 + (-18)]$ **21.** _____
$= 14 + 0$ **22.** _____
$= 14$ **23.** _____

B. Find each sum, using absolute value.

24. $-18 + 27$ 9   **25.** $27 + (-33)$ −6   **26.** $-23 + 16$ −7

27. $-82 + 73$ −9   **28.** $-90 + (-64)$ −154   **29.** $-22 + (-34)$ −56

30. $87 + 48$ 135   **31.** $98 + 87$ 185   **32.** $-237 + 42$ −195

33. $464 + (-38)$ 426   **34.** $-791 + (-47)$ −838   **35.** $-829 + (-59)$ −888

36. $-64 + 41 + (-104)$ −127   **37.** $-64 + 84 + 104$ 124

38. $52 + (-112) + 164$ 104   **39.** $52 + (-411) + (-164)$ −523

40. $0.5 + 0.37$ 0.87   **41.** $-0.92 + (-0.6)$ −1.52   **42.** $-0.12 + 0.23$ 0.11

43. $11.7 + (-3.4)$ 8.3   **44.** $-3.1 + (-5.3)$ −8.4   **45.** $-8.3 + 2.47$ −5.83

46. $\frac{2}{7} + \frac{3}{7}$ $\frac{5}{7}$ **47.** $-\frac{2}{7} + \left(-\frac{3}{7}\right)$ $-\frac{5}{7}$ **48.** $-\frac{2}{7} + \frac{1}{2}$ $\frac{3}{14}$

49. $\frac{3}{4} + \left(-\frac{2}{3}\right)$ $\frac{1}{12}$ **50.** $-\frac{3}{8} + \frac{1}{3}$ $-\frac{1}{24}$ **51.** $-\frac{1}{2} + \frac{1}{6}$ $-\frac{1}{3}$

C. Each exercise consists of two quantities, one in Column I and one in Column II. Compare the two quantities and decide which of the following is true:

a. The quantity in Column I is the greater.

b. The quantity in Column II is the greater.

c. The two quantities are equal.

d. The relationship cannot be determined because not enough information has been given.

     Column I   *Column II*

52. $82(19) + 4(32)$ $87(12) + 3(46)$ a

53. $5(2 + 3 + 7)$ $10 + 5(3) + 35$ c

54. $3x + 4y$ if $x = 2$ $5x + y$ if $x = 3$ d

55. $6(8) + 3$ $\frac{96}{3} + 24$ b

56. $-3 + (-7) + 15 + (-9)$ $-4 + 23 + (-9) + (-1)$ b

57. $6(9) - x + (-40)$ $27(10) - 3x + 10$ d

58. $3(2x + 1)$ if $x = 4$ $6x + 3$ if $x = 4$ c

59. $59(6) + \frac{12}{4}$ $54(7) + \frac{15}{5}$ b

Find each sum.

60. Find $-31 + x$ if $x = -16$. $\quad -47$

61. Find $56 + (-y)$ if $y = 83$. $\quad -27$

62. Find $-23 + x$ if $x = 8$. $\quad -15$

63. Find $72 + y$ if $y = -36$. $\quad 36$

64. Find $x + (-16)$ if $x = -27$. $\quad -43$

65. Find $-y + x$ if $y = -23$ and $x = -14$.

66. $349 + (-726) + (-426) + (-1009)$

67. $-648 + 88 + (-98) + 352 \quad -306$

68. $-3.8 + (-1.5) + 8.9 + 8.2 \quad 11.8$

69. $\frac{1}{2} + \left(-\frac{3}{8}\right) + \left(-\frac{1}{4}\right) + \left(-\frac{2}{3}\right) \quad -\frac{19}{24}$

ALGEBRA IN USE

Your fingerprints are unique! Yet, for purposes of identification, each person's fingerprints belong to one of 1024 groups. These groups help increase the speed of the identification process, since people in the other 1023 groups can be eliminated.

At the beginning of the identification process, a fingerprint is classified as one of the following:

Arch
Ridges
enter
on one
side of
the finger
and leave on the other side.

Loop
Ridges
enter on
one side of
the finger
and loop
around
to leave on the same side.

Whorl
Ridges
appear to be circular in shape.

When all ten fingerprints are available, a person can be assigned one of 1024 fractions. The fraction is found by assigning a loop and an arch a value of 0 and a whorl a value of 1, then evaluating the following expression:

$$\frac{\left(16 \times \begin{smallmatrix}\text{right}\\\text{index}\end{smallmatrix}\right) + \left(8 \times \begin{smallmatrix}\text{right}\\\text{ring}\end{smallmatrix}\right) + \left(4 \times \begin{smallmatrix}\text{left}\\\text{thumb}\end{smallmatrix}\right) + \left(2 \times \begin{smallmatrix}\text{left}\\\text{middle}\end{smallmatrix}\right) + \left(1 \times \begin{smallmatrix}\text{left}\\\text{little}\end{smallmatrix}\right) + 1}{\left(16 \times \begin{smallmatrix}\text{right}\\\text{thumb}\end{smallmatrix}\right) + \left(8 \times \begin{smallmatrix}\text{right}\\\text{middle}\end{smallmatrix}\right) + \left(4 \times \begin{smallmatrix}\text{right}\\\text{little}\end{smallmatrix}\right) + \left(2 \times \begin{smallmatrix}\text{left}\\\text{index}\end{smallmatrix}\right) + \left(1 \times \begin{smallmatrix}\text{left}\\\text{ring}\end{smallmatrix}\right) + 1}$$

Example: A person has a whorl on the right index, left middle, right little, and left ring fingers. The person has a loop or an arch on the other fingers. Find the fraction that will identify this person's group.

Solution: $\dfrac{16 \times 1 + 8 \times 0 + 4 \times 0 + 2 \times 1 + 1 \times 0 + 1}{16 \times 0 + 8 \times 0 + 4 \times 1 + 2 \times 0 + 1 \times 1 + 1} = \dfrac{16 + 2 + 1}{4 + 1 + 1} = \dfrac{19}{6}$

EXERCISE

Find the fraction that will identify your own fingerprint group.

Find the next number in the sequence.

1. 1, 3, 5, 7, 9, . . . 11

2. 3, 6, 9, 12, 15, . . . 18

3. 4, 4, 9, 9, 14, . . . 14

4. 1, 2, 4, 8, 16, . . . 32

5. $-2, -4, -6, -8, -10, . . .$ -12

6. $3, 1, -1, -3, -5, . . .$ -7

7. 1, 10, 100, 1000, 10,000, . . . 100,000

8. $1\frac{1}{2}, 3, 4\frac{1}{2}, 6, 7\frac{1}{2}, . . .$ 9

9. 2.1, 2.4, 2.7, 3, 3.3, . . . 3.6

10. $-2.5, -3, -3.5, -4, -4.5, . . .$ -5

11. $-7, -4, -1, 2, 5, . . .$ 8

12. 13, 12, 10, 7, 3, . . . -2

13. $-5, -4, -2, 1, 5, . . .$ 10

14. $\frac{1}{10}, \frac{1}{5}, \frac{3}{10}, \frac{2}{5}, \frac{1}{2}, . . .$ $\frac{3}{5}$

15. $\frac{1}{4}, \frac{1}{2}, \frac{3}{4}, 1, 1\frac{1}{4}, . . .$ $1\frac{1}{2}$

16. 5, 3, 5, 6, 5, 9, . . . 5

17. 24, 3, 12, 3, 6, . . . 3

18. 9, 16, 25, 36, 49, . . . 64

19. $0, -5, 0, -10, 0, -15 . . .$ 0

20. 4, 1, 8, 1, 12, . . . 1

21. 8, 9, 12, 13, 16, . . . 17

22. $5, 3, 2, 0, -1, . . .$ -3

23. 2.9, 2.5, 2.1, 1.7, 1.3, . . . 0.9

24. 2, 7, 17, 37, 77, . . . 157

25. 1.75, 3.5, 7, 14, 28, . . . 56

26. $-1, -3.5, -6, -8.5, -11, . . .$ -13.5

27. 4, 4, 8, 8, 12, 12, . . . 16

28. 2, 4, 3, 9, 4, . . . 16

29. 1, 3, 6, 10, 15, 21, . . . 28

30. $\frac{9}{4}, \frac{6}{4}, \frac{3}{4}, 0, -\frac{3}{4}, . . .$ $-\frac{6}{4}$

31. 3, 9, 4, 10, 5, 11, . . . 6

32. 4, 2, 8, 0, 12, -2, . . . 16

33. 12, 22, 33, 45, 58, . . . 72

34. $-4, -9, -15, -22, -30, . . .$ -39

35. $-49, -36, -25, -16, . . .$ -9

36. 26, 35, 46, 59, 74, . . . 91

37. $-9, -3, 3, 9, 15, . . .$ 21

38. 10, 4, 15, 4, 20, 4, . . . 25

39. $24\frac{1}{4}, 18\frac{1}{4}, 12\frac{1}{4}, 6\frac{1}{4}, . . .$ $\frac{1}{4}$

40. 0.1, 0.3, 0.9, 2.7, . . . 8.1

41. $8, 8\frac{1}{2}, 8, 8\frac{1}{4}, . . .$ 8

42. $-3, -6, -12, -24, . . .$ -48

43. $7\frac{4}{9}, 8\frac{5}{9}, 9\frac{6}{9}, 10\frac{7}{9}, . . .$ $11\frac{8}{9}$

44. 7, 3, 7, 6, 7, 9, 7, . . . 12

45. 3, 6, 18, 21, 63, . . . 66

46. 2, 8, 3, 27, 4, 64, . . . 5

47. 16, 256, 15, 225, 14, 196, 13, . . . 169

48. 5376, 1344, 336, 84, . . . 21

2.5 | Subtraction

OBJECTIVE

Find the difference of any two real numbers by using the subtraction property.

You know that when two numbers are additive inverses, their sum is zero. Additive inverses are useful in subtraction of real numbers. Notice the following pattern:

additive inverses

$27 - 12 = 15$ $\qquad$ $27 + (-12) = 15$

same result

$41 - 19 = 22$ $\qquad$ $41 + (-19) = 22$

same result

These examples suggest a rule for subtraction.

Subtraction Property	**For all real numbers a and b, $a - b = a + (-b)$.**

EXAMPLES

1 **Subtract $7 - 9$.**
SOLUTION
$7 - 9 = 7 + (-9)$
$\qquad = -2$

2 **Subtract $-7 - 9$.**
SOLUTION
$-7 - 9 = -7 + (-9)$
$\qquad = -16$

3 **Subtract $7 - (-9)$.**
SOLUTION
$7 - (-9) = 7 + [-(-9)]$
$\qquad = 7 + 9$
$\qquad = 16$

4 **Subtract $-7 - (-9)$.**
SOLUTION
$-7 - (-9) = -7 + [-(-9)]$
$\qquad = -7 + 9$
$\qquad = 2$

ORAL EXERCISES

Complete each sentence.

1. $7 - 2 = 7 + \underline{-2}$

2. $-7 - 2 = -7 + \underline{-2}$

3. $7 - (-2) = 7 + \underline{2}$

4. $-7 - (-2) = -7 + \underline{2}$

5. $-2 - \underline{7} = -2 + (-7)$

6. $0 - 3 = 0 + \underline{-3}$

7. $5 - \underline{9} = 5 + (-9)$

8. $0 - (-3) = 0 + \underline{3}$

9. $5 - \underline{-9} = 5 + 9$

WRITTEN EXERCISES

A. Use the subtraction property to express each difference as a sum.

1. $20 - 9$

2. $4 - 11$

3. $-8 - 13$

4. $34 - (-29)$

5. $48 - (-31)$

6. $-29 - (-17)$

TEACHER'S NOTES
See p. T24.

CLASSROOM EXAMPLES
1. Subtract $6 - 11$.
$\quad 6 - 11 = 6 + (-11)$
$\qquad = -5$
2. Subtract $-8 - 12$.
$\quad -8 - 12 = -8 + (-12)$
$\qquad = -20$
3. Subtract $6 - (-13)$.
$\quad 6 - (-13) = 6 + [-(-13)]$
$\qquad = 6 + 13$
$\qquad = 19$
4. Subtract $-12 - (-15)$.
$\quad -12 - (-15) = -12 +$
$\qquad [-(-15)]$
$\qquad = -12 + 15$
$\qquad = 3$

MIXED REVIEW
1. Find $-16 + x$ if $x = -14$.
$\quad -30$
2. Evaluate $314 - \dfrac{3^4}{3} \cdot$ 287
3. Simplify $5 \cdot 3 + 9 - 8 \div 2$.
$\quad 20$
4. Add $(-1.92) + (8.3)$.
$\quad 6.38$
5. Evaluate $\dfrac{c^3}{d - 3}$ if $c = 5$
and $d = 7$. 31.25

ASSIGNMENT GUIDE

Minimum
1-47 odd

Regular
25-48

Maximum
33-56

ADDITIONAL ANSWERS

Written Exercises

1. $20 + (-9)$

2. $4 + (-11)$

3. $-8 + (-13)$

4. $34 + [-(-29)]$

5. $48 + [-(-31)]$

6. $-29 + [-(-17)]$

Find each difference.

7. $21 - 35$ $\quad -14$ **8.** $76 - 129$ $\quad -53$ **9.** $21 - (-35)$ $\quad 56$

10. $76 - (-109)$ $\quad 185$ **11.** $-21 - 45$ $\quad -66$ **12.** $-73 - 109$ $\quad -182$

13. $-21 - (-35)$ $\quad 14$ **14.** $-76 - (-109)$ $\quad 33$ **15.** $35 - 21$ $\quad 14$

16. $149 - 76$ $\quad 73$ **17.** $35 - (-21)$ $\quad 56$ **18.** $109 - (-126)$ $\quad 235$

19. $-35 - 21$ $\quad -56$ **20.** $-109 - 76$ $\quad -185$ **21.** $-35 - (-21)$ $\quad -14$

22. $-115 - (-53)$ $\quad -62$ **23.** $511 - 482$ $\quad 29$ **24.** $-2478 - (-2478)$ $\quad 0$

B. 25. $(19 - 25) - 16$ $\quad -22$ **26.** $[-71 - (-54)] - (-38)$ $\quad 21$

27. $19 - (25 - 16)$ $\quad 10$ **28.** $-71 - [-54 - (-38)]$ $\quad -55$

29. $(-16 - 53) - (-18)$ $\quad -51$ **30.** $[210 - (-49)] - 67$ $\quad 192$

31. $-16 - [53 - (-18)]$ $\quad -87$ **32.** $21 - (-49 - 63)$ $\quad 133$

33. $0.93 - (-0.5)$ $\quad 1.43$ **34.** $-1.7 - (-2.64)$ $\quad 0.94$ **35.** $0.29 - 0.238$ $\quad 0.052$

36. $\dfrac{5}{9} - \dfrac{2}{9}$ $\quad \frac{1}{3}$ **37.** $\dfrac{3}{7} - \left(-\dfrac{5}{7}\right)$ $\quad \frac{8}{7}$ **38.** $\dfrac{3}{5} - \left(-\dfrac{2}{5}\right)$ $\quad 1$

39. $-\dfrac{1}{7} - \left(-\dfrac{2}{5}\right)$ $\quad \frac{9}{35}$ **40.** $\dfrac{1}{2} - \dfrac{3}{5}$ $\quad -\frac{1}{10}$ **41.** $\dfrac{2}{3} - \dfrac{1}{9}$ $\quad \frac{5}{9}$

42. $-\dfrac{2}{9} - \left(-\dfrac{1}{2}\right)$ $\quad \frac{5}{18}$ **43.** $\dfrac{1}{5} - \left(-\dfrac{1}{12}\right)$ $\quad \frac{17}{60}$ **44.** $-\dfrac{1}{8} - \left(-\dfrac{1}{3}\right)$ $\quad \frac{5}{24}$

45. Compare your answers for exercises 7 and 15. Is subtraction commutative?   no

46. Compare your answer for exercises 25 and 27. Is subtraction associative?   no

Write an algebraic expression for each of the following:

47. a number decreased by -12 $w - (-12)$ **48.** the sum of a number x and -3.6

$\qquad\qquad\qquad\qquad\qquad\qquad\qquad\qquad\qquad x + (-3.6)$

C. 49. sale price of an item that is reduced 25% $c - 0.25c$

50. the final cost of an item that is increased 10% $c + 0.1c$

51. Find $x - 3.7$ if $x = 2.4$. -1.3 **52.** Find $8.32 - y$ if $y = 9.6$. -1.28

53. Find $507 - x$ if $x = -408$. 915 **54.** Find $y - (-451)$ if $y = -297$. 154

55. Find $x - y$ if $x = -47$ and $y = 83$.   **56.** Find $x - y$ if $x = 3.4$ and $y = -8.09$.

$\qquad\qquad\qquad\qquad\qquad -130$ $\qquad\qquad\qquad\qquad\qquad 11.49$

SELF-QUIZ

Complete.

1. Let $A = \{1, 2, 3\}$ and $B = \{2, 3, 4, 5, 6\}$. $4 \notin$ ___A___

Which symbol, $=$, $<$, or $>$, should replace each ●?

2. -6 ● $-\dfrac{12}{2}$ $=$ **3.** 4 ● 3.9 $>$ **4.** $\dfrac{1}{3}$ ● $\dfrac{2}{3}$ $<$ **5.** 2.0 ● 2.01 $<$

Complete.

6. $|-3| =$ ___3___   **7.** $\left|\dfrac{8}{9}\right| =$ ___$\frac{8}{9}$___

Give the opposite of each rational number.

8. -8.9 8.9

9. 0 0

10. $\frac{7}{8}$ $-\frac{7}{8}$

Find each sum. Refer to a number line if necessary.

11. $-4 + 15$ 11

12. $19 + (-8)$ 11

13. $-3 + (-5)$ -8

Find each sum.

14. $15.1 + 8.2$ 23.3

15. $-41 + 27$ -14

16. $-16 + 23$ 7

17. $-\frac{1}{4} + \left(-1\frac{1}{2}\right)$ $-1\frac{3}{4}$

Find each difference.

18. $8.9 - 2.04$ 6.86

19. $-\frac{3}{4} - \frac{2}{3}$ $-1\frac{5}{12}$

20. $4 - (-92)$ 96

21. $-6 - (-18)$ 12

IN OTHER FIELDS
Mathematics and Literature

Alice's Adventures in Wonderland, written by Lewis Carroll, is recognized by almost everyone as a classic in children's literature. What many are surprised to learn is that Carroll was a professor of mathematics at Oxford, whose real name was Charles Lutwidge Dodgson. Dodgson used his real name only when writing on mathematical topics and his pen name when writing children's literature.

One of the unique qualities of *Alice's Adventures in Wonderland* is its appeal to children and adults as well. For decades, mathematicians and logicians have tried to look beyond what appears to be children's nonsense and to find a logical meaning in much of it. Some believe that *Alice's Adventures in Wonderland* is full of symbolic logic, a topic on which Carroll often wrote as a mathematician. An example of this can be found in the story when Alice says, "Let me see: four times five is twelve, and four times six is thirteen and four times seven is—oh dear! I shall never get to twenty at that rate!"

Mathematicians propose different explanations for this passage, such as the use of bases other than base 10. Perhaps the simplest explanation is that the multiplication table traditionally stops at 12. If you continue the nonsense progression, $4 \times 6 = 13$, $4 \times 7 = 14$, $4 \times 8 = 15$, and so on, you will end with $4 \times 12 = 19$, which is one short of 20. So Alice's fear that she will never get to twenty may be well-founded.

CLASSROOM EXAMPLES

1. Multiply $-26(2)$.
   $-26(2) = -52$

2. Multiply $-56\left(-\frac{1}{4}\right) = 14$.
   $-56\left(-\frac{1}{4}\right) = 14$

3. Multiply $(-2)^3(-5)^2$.
   $(-2)^3(-5)^2 = (4)(-2)(-5)$
   $ (-5)$
   $ = 4(-2)(25)$
   $ = (-8)(25)$
   $ = -200$

4. Multiply $-5(6)(-2)(-3)$.
   $-5(6)(-2)(-3)$
   $= -1(5)(6)(-1)(2)(-1)(3)$
   $= (-1)(-1)(-1)(5)(6)(2)(3)$
   $= -1(1)(30)(6)$
   $= -180$

MIXED REVIEW

1. Subtract $(18 - 46) - 15$.
   -43

2. Add $[14 + (-28)] + (-36)$. $\quad -50$

3. Simplify $9x^4y^3 + 2x^4y^3 + 3x^4y^3$. $\quad 14x^4y^3$

4. Find the next number in the series 1, 4, 8, 13, 19, 26, ... $\quad 34$

5. Evaluate $(-32x^3y^2)\left(-\frac{1}{4}x^2y\right)$. $\quad 8x^5y^3$

2.6 Multiplication

Multiplication of two positive numbers is already a familiar process. You can think of multiplication as repeated addition.

$3 + 3 + 3 + 3 = 12$ or $4(3) = 12$

Look at the following pattern to see what happens when a positive number and a negative number are multiplied. Note that the first factor remains the same and the product decreases by 4 as the second factor decreases by 1.

$4(2) = 8$
$4(1) = 4$
$4(0) = 0$
$4(-1) = -4$
$4(-2) = -8$

From the pattern above you can see that a positive number times a negative number is a negative number. Since multiplication is commutative, $4(-2) = -2(4) = -8$. Use a pattern similar to the first one to find a rule for multiplying two negative numbers.

$-4(2) = -8$
$-4(1) = -4$
$-4(0) = 0$ *The product increases by 4 each time.*
$-4(-1) = 4$
$-4(-2) = 8$

The product of two negative numbers is a positive number.

EXAMPLES

1 **Multiply $-16(3)$.**

SOLUTION

$-16(3) = -48$

2 **Multiply $-104\left(-\frac{1}{2}\right)$.**

SOLUTION

$-104\left(-\frac{1}{2}\right) = 52$

3 **Multiply $(-3)^3(-4)^2$.**

SOLUTION

$(-3)^3(-4)^2 = (-3)(-3)(-3)(-4)(-4)$
$ = 9(-3)(16)$
$ = -27(16)$
$ = -432$

In the multiplication of real numbers, as in addition, absolute values may be used.

Rule I	**To multiply two positive or two negative real numbers, find the product of their absolute values. The product is positive.**

Rule II	To multiply one positive real number and one negative real number, find the product of their absolute values. The product is negative.

TEACHER'S RESOURCE MASTERS

Practice Master 6, Part 2

ASSIGNMENT GUIDE

Minimum
1–12, 13–21 odd, 29–45

Regular
35–68

Maximum
23–61 odd, 63–76

The following property can be useful when more than two factors are multiplied.

Multiplication Property of -1	For every real number a, $-a = -1(a)$.

4   **Multiply $-3(2)(-6)(-4)$.**

SOLUTION

$$-3(2)(-6)(-4) = -1(3)(2)(-1)(6)(-1)(4)$$
$$= -1(-1)(-1)(3)(2)(6)(4) \quad \text{\textit{Use the commutative and associative}}$$
$$= -1(1)(6)(24) \quad\quad\quad\quad\quad \text{\textit{properties of multiplication.}}$$
$$= -1 \cdot 144$$
$$= -144$$

ORAL EXERCISES

Express each sum as a product by telling what number should replace the ?.

1. $7 + 7 + 7 = 3(?)$ 7

2. $-8 + (-8) + (-8) + (-8) = ?(-8)$ 4

3. $-5 + (-5) = 2(?)$ -5

4. $12 + 12 + 12 = ?(12)$ 3

5. What is the sign of the product of an odd number of negative factors if no factor is zero?   negative

6. What is the sign of the product of an even number of negative factors if no factor is zero?   positive

WRITTEN EXERCISES

A. Find each product.

1. $5(31)$ 155   **2.** $14(6)$ 84   **3.** $4(-15)$ -60 **4.** $23(-8)$ -184

5. $-4(602)$ -2408 **6.** $-5(73)$ -365 **7.** $-8(-94)$ 752   **8.** $-5(-13)$ 65

9. $12(10)$ 120   **10.** $6(12)$ 72   **11.** $10(-17)$ -170 **12.** $-17(10)$ -170

13. $-1(-1)$ 1   **14.** $-1(-1)(-1)$ -1

15. $-1(-1)(-1)(-1)$ 1   **16.** $-12(-1)(3)(-1)$ -36

17. $2(1)(3)(-2)(-4)$ 48   **18.** $-1(-2)(3)(-1)(-8)(-4)$ -192

B. 19. $2\left(\frac{1}{2}\right)$ 1   **20.** $\frac{1}{9}(9)$ 1   **21.** $-4\left(-\frac{1}{4}\right)$ 1   **22.** $-\frac{1}{17}(-17)$ 1

23. $18(-74)$ -1332 **24.** $-27(89)$ **25.** $-12(-64)$ 768   **26.** $-36(-12)$
                         -2403 432

27. $\left[4\left(-\frac{4}{5}\right)\right]\left(-\frac{2}{3}\right)$ $2\frac{2}{15}$ **28.** $[6(-2)](-4)$ 48 **29.** $4\left[\left(-\frac{4}{5}\right)\left(-\frac{2}{3}\right)\right]$ $2\frac{2}{15}$

30. $6[(-2)(-4)]$ 48 **31.** $[(-8)(-14)](-26)$ -2912 **32.** $[(-7)(-5)](-3)$ -105

33. $-8[(-14)(-26)]$ -2912 **34.** $-7[(-5)(-53)]$ -1855 **35.** $-8(0)(11)(-74)$ 0

36. $-7(12)(0)(-47)$ 0 **37.** $-1(14)(-2)(-4)$ -112 **38.** $15(-2)(-1)(-6)$ -180

39. $-5(-4)(-7)(-3)(-11)$ **40.** $-13(-3)(-2)(-9)(-4)$ **41.** $-24(12)\left(\frac{2}{3}\right)$ -192

42. $-13(34)\left(\frac{1}{2}\right)$ -221 **43.** $25(-14)\left(\frac{4}{5}\right)$ -280 **44.** $36(-8)(0.65)$ -187.2

45. $-124(-74)(-0.3)$ **46.** $-236(-58)(8.1)$ **47.** $-345(89)$ $-30,705$

48. $-747(29)$ $-21,663$ **49.** $\frac{3}{5}\left(-\frac{2}{7}\right)$ $-\frac{6}{35}$ **50.** $\frac{3}{5}\left(-\frac{4}{11}\right)$ $-\frac{12}{55}$

51. $-\frac{2}{7}\left(\frac{4}{7}\right)$ $-\frac{8}{49}$ **52.** $-\frac{4}{9}\left(\frac{5}{9}\right)$ $-\frac{20}{81}$ **53.** $0.7(-0.8)(2.6)$ -1.456

54. $-0.4(0.9)(1.8)$ -0.648 **55.** $-0.6(-0.7)(-2.3)$ **56.** $0.45(-0.12)$ -0.054

57. $-0.16(-0.16)$ 0.0256 **58.** $-1.5(-1.25)$ 1.875 **59.** $2.6(3.5)(1.8)$ 16.38

60. $(-5)^2(-2)^3$ -200 **61.** $1.3^2(-1)^5$ -1.69 **62.** $\left(-\frac{2}{5}\right)^2\left(\frac{5}{6}\right)$ $\frac{2}{15}$

Write an algebraic expression for each of the following:

63. the product of a number n and -4.6 **64.** the product of x and the sum of 2 and -8

65. the product of two consecutive integers $n(n + 1)$ where n is an integer   **66.** the product of two consecutive odd integers $n(n + 2)$ where n is an odd integer

C. Use the rules for order of operations to evaluate each expression.

67. $71 - [(-3)(-2)]^2$ 35 **68.** $[12(53) + (-31)(19)](-3)$ -141

69. $-42 + (67)(12) - 8(15)$ 642 **70.** $3[-7 + (21)(5)]$ 294

71. $3x^2$ if $x = -8$ 192 **72.** $5x + 2xy$ if $x = -3$ and $y = 9$ -69

73. $(x - 2)(-5)$ if $x = -8$ 50 **74.** $4^3(x - y)$ if $x = -3$ and $y = -7$ 256

75. $5x^2y$ if $x = -16$ and $y = -4$ -5120 **76.** $3x^2 - 9y^2$ if $x = 15$ and $y = -4$ 531

CHALLENGE

Find the missing digits if each digit from 0 to 9 appears exactly one time.

$\square\,0\,2 \times 3\,\square = \square\,5\,\square\,\square\,\square$

2.7 | Division

You can check the result of a division exercise by multiplying the quotient by the divisor.

dividend   divisor   quotient   **CHECK**

$$28 \div 7 = 4 \qquad 4 \times 7 = 28$$

TEACHER'S NOTES

See p. T25.

Accordingly, using your knowledge of multiplication, you can determine the value of n in each of the following:

$36 \div 12 = n$	$n \times 12 = 36$	So $n = 3$.
$-36 \div (-12) = n$	$n \times (-12) = -36$	So $n = 3$.
$36 \div (-12) = n$	$n \times (-12) = 36$	So $n = -3$.
$-36 \div 12 = n$	$n \times 12 = -36$	So $n = -3$.

Notice that in the first two cases, the dividend and the divisor are both positive or both negative. In the last two cases, one number is positive and one is negative.

These cases suggest the following rules:

CLASSROOM EXAMPLES

1. Divide 64 by 16.
   $64 \div 16 = 4$

2. Divide -72 by -8.
   $-72 \div (-8) = 9$

3. Divide 96 by -12.
   $96 \div (-12) = -8$

4. Divide -63 by 9.
   $-63 \div 9 = -7$

5. Divide $\frac{6}{7}$ by $-\frac{1}{3}$.
   $\frac{6}{7} \div -\frac{1}{3} = \frac{6}{7} \cdot \frac{-3}{1} = \frac{-18}{7}$
   $= -2\frac{4}{7}$

6. Divide $-2\frac{1}{5}$ by $\frac{3}{10}$.
   $-2\frac{1}{5} \div \frac{3}{10} = -\frac{11}{5} \cdot \frac{10}{3}$
   $= \frac{-22}{3} = -7\frac{1}{3}$

Rule I — **To divide two real numbers that are both positive or both negative, find the quotient of their absolute values. The quotient is positive.**

Rule II — **To divide one positive real number and one negative real number, find the quotient of their absolute values. The quotient is negative.**

EXAMPLES

1 | **Divide 75 by 3.**

SOLUTION

$75 \div 3 = 25$

2 | **Divide -42 by -7.**

SOLUTION

$-42 \div (-7) = 6$

3 | **Divide 100 by -10.**

SOLUTION

$100 \div (-10) = -10$

4 | **Divide -30 by 6.**

SOLUTION

$-30 \div 6 = -5$

Consider $-2 \div 3$ and $2 \div (-3)$. Expressing each quotient as a fraction results in $-2 \div 3 = \frac{-2}{3}$ and $2 \div (-3) = \frac{2}{-3}$.

According to the rules for division, each quotient is negative. Therefore, $\frac{-2}{3} = \frac{2}{-3} = -\frac{2}{3}$. Now consider $-2 \div (-3)$. According to the rules for division, the quotient is positive. Therefore, $-2 \div (-3) = \frac{-2}{-3} = \frac{2}{3}$.

Rational numbers expressed in the form $\frac{a}{b}$ or $-\frac{a}{b}$, where a and b are positive, are said to be written in **standard form**.

1. Perform the indicated operation.

   a. 6^3 216

   b. $(3.5x)(-2.4x^3y)$
   $-8.4x^4y$

   c. $(6-9)-(15-3)$ -15

   d. $(108x^3y)\left(-\frac{1}{4}x^2y\right)$
   $-27x^5y^2$

2. Simplify.

   a. $2^4 \div 2$ 8

   b. $(3+4)(6-1) \div [5-(6-3)]$ 17.5

3. Evaluate $b^4 - b$ if $b = -3$.   84

4. Simplify $8y^2 + 12y^2 + y^2$.
   $21y^2$

5. Find the difference.
   $-1620 - (-1620)$ 0

TEACHER'S RESOURCE MASTERS

Practice Master 7, Part 1

ASSIGNMENT GUIDE

Minimum
1–13 odd, 19–27 odd, 28–39

Regular
19–42

Maximum
19–41 odd, 43–54

You have had experience with the division of rational numbers. The same procedures apply when negative numbers are involved. The examples below make use of the fact that the quotient of two numbers can be determined by multiplying the dividend by the *reciprocal* of the divisor.

That is, $\dfrac{2}{3} \div \dfrac{5}{7} = \dfrac{\frac{2}{3}}{\frac{5}{7}} = \dfrac{\frac{2}{3} \cdot \frac{7}{5}}{\frac{5}{7} \cdot \frac{7}{5}}$

$= \dfrac{\frac{2}{3} \cdot \frac{7}{5}}{1}$

$= \dfrac{14}{15}$

Multiplicative Inverse	For each nonzero a, there is exactly one real number $\frac{1}{a}$, called the reciprocal or the multiplicative inverse of a, such that $a\left(\frac{1}{a}\right) = \frac{1}{a}(a) = 1$.

5 **Divide $\frac{5}{9}$ by $-\frac{1}{4}$.**

SOLUTION

$\dfrac{5}{9} \div \left(-\dfrac{1}{4}\right) = \dfrac{5}{9} \times \left(-\dfrac{4}{1}\right)$

$= -\dfrac{20}{9}$, or $-2\dfrac{2}{9}$

6 **Divide $-1\frac{1}{3}$ by $\frac{3}{4}$.**

SOLUTION

$-1\dfrac{1}{3} \div \dfrac{3}{4} = -\dfrac{4}{3} \div \dfrac{3}{4}$

$= -\dfrac{4}{3} \times \dfrac{4}{3} = -\dfrac{16}{9}$,

or $-1\dfrac{7}{9}$

ORAL EXERCISES

What number should replace n in each case?

1. $-32 \div 8 = n$ because $n \times 8 = -32$. -4 **2.** $72 \div 8 = n$ because $n \times 8 = 72$.   9

3. $-48 \div (-6) = n$ because $n \times (-6) = -48$.   8

Express each of the following as a fraction in standard form:

4. $\dfrac{-1}{2}$ $-\frac{1}{2}$ **5.** $\dfrac{-5}{-6}$ $\frac{5}{6}$ **6.** $-\left(\dfrac{-3}{-2}\right)$ $-\frac{3}{2}$

Give the multiplicative inverse of each rational number.

7. 5 $\frac{1}{5}$ **8.** $-\dfrac{4}{5}$ $-\frac{5}{4}$ **9.** $\dfrac{4}{5}$ $\frac{5}{4}$ **10.** $-3\dfrac{1}{4}$ $-\frac{4}{13}$ **11.** $-\dfrac{5}{2}$ $-\frac{2}{5}$ **12.** $-2\dfrac{1}{8}$ $-\frac{8}{17}$

WRITTEN EXERCISES

A. What number should replace each question mark?

1. $\dfrac{1}{3} \div \dfrac{2}{5} = \dfrac{1}{3} \times ?$ $\frac{5}{2}$ **2.** $\dfrac{2}{5} \div \left(-\dfrac{1}{4}\right) = \dfrac{2}{5} \times ?$ -4 **3.** $\dfrac{3}{8} \div \left(-\dfrac{4}{7}\right) = \dfrac{3}{8} \times ?$ $-\frac{7}{4}$

4. $-\dfrac{2}{7} \div \dfrac{3}{10} = -\dfrac{2}{7} \times ?$ $\frac{10}{3}$ **5.** $\dfrac{8}{5} \div \left(-\dfrac{10}{3}\right) = \dfrac{8}{5} \times ?$ $-\frac{3}{10}$ **6.** $-\dfrac{7}{8} \div \left(-\dfrac{7}{4}\right) = -\dfrac{7}{8} \times ?$
$-\frac{4}{7}$

Find each quotient.

7. $-108 \div 3$ **8.** $-108 \div (-3)$ **9.** $108 \div 3$ **10.** $108 \div (-3)$

11. $-345 \div (-5)$ **12.** $345 \div 5$ **13.** $345 \div (-5)$ **14.** $-345 \div 5$

15. $405 \div 9$ **16.** $-405 \div (-9)$ **17.** $-405 \div 9$ **18.** $405 \div (-9)$

B. 19. $2.5 \div (-0.5)$ -5 **20.** $-0.32 \div 0.08$ -4 **21.** $-0.045 \div 0.05$ -0.9

22. $14.4 \div 1.2$ 12 **23.** $-1.19 \div 0.17$ -7 **24.** $-17.5 \div 0.35$ -50

25. $22.8 \div 0.57$ 40 **26.** $4.5 \div (-2.5)$ -1.8 **27.** $-2.79 \div 3.1$ -0.9

28. $2.99 \div (-2.3)$ -1.3 **29.** $-75 \div 0.25$ -300 **30.** $-92 \div (-0.23)$ 400

31. $\frac{2}{5} \div \frac{1}{3}$ $1\frac{1}{5}$ **32.** $\frac{6}{25} \div 1\frac{1}{4}$ $\frac{24}{125}$ **33.** $-\frac{4}{7} \div \left(-3\frac{1}{2}\right)$ $\frac{8}{49}$

34. $-\frac{7}{16} \div \frac{1}{2}$ $-\frac{7}{8}$ **35.** $-\frac{6}{7} \div \frac{3}{5}$ $-1\frac{3}{7}$ **36.** $\frac{11}{24} \div \frac{11}{12}$ $\frac{1}{2}$

37. $-\frac{4}{35} \div \left(-1\frac{5}{7}\right)$ $\frac{1}{15}$ **38.** $\frac{7}{34} \div \left(-2\frac{5}{8}\right)$ $-\frac{4}{51}$ **39.** $-\frac{20}{21} \div \frac{5}{7}$ $-1\frac{1}{3}$

40. $-\frac{10}{11} \div \left(-\frac{2}{3}\right)$ $1\frac{4}{11}$ **41.** $3\frac{3}{5} \div \frac{3}{10}$ 12 **42.** $-\frac{13}{40} \div \left(-5\frac{1}{5}\right)$ $\frac{1}{16}$

C. Use the order of operations to evaluate each expression.

43. $-4[27 + 108 \div (-9)]$ -60 **44.** $5 + (-9)^2 \div 3 - (-2)(6)$ 44

45. $21 + (-8)(4) \div (-16)$ 23 **46.** $-55 \div (-11)(-7) \div 5^2$ $-1\frac{2}{5}$

47. $-4\{(18 - 12) \div [6 - (-2)]\}$ -3 **48.** $34 \div (-17) + (-24) \div (-2)^3$ 1

49. $54 \div 27 \div (-3)$ $-\frac{2}{3}$ **50.** $54 \div [27 \div (-3)]$ -6

Choose the letter of the correct answer.

51. $(97 - 105 \div 3)2 - 42(6)$

    a. $-15,000$ b. $\underline{-128}$
    c. -118 d. -308

52. $15^2 \div 3(-5) - (-32) \div \frac{1}{8}$

    e. $\underline{241}$ f. 261
    g. -341 h. -119

53. $19 + [-3(4)^2 \div (-2)] - [5 - (-2)^3]4$

    a. $\underline{-9}$ b. -105
    c. 55 d. -57

54. $6 \div (-1) + [2(3)]^2 - 8[3 + 2(-4)]$

    e. -58 f. 52
    g. $\underline{70}$ h. 59

CHALLENGE

Which is greater—2^{100} or 3^{75}? 3^{75}

Solve nonroutine problems using the following strategies: *guess-and-check, logical reasoning, solve a simpler problem,* and *use a table.*

TEACHER'S NOTES

See p. T25.

CLASSROOM EXAMPLES

1. Given: the numbers −8, −6, −4, −2, 0, 2, 4, 6, and 8. Find where each number should be placed so that the sum of each row, each column, and each diagonal is the same.

6	−4	−2
−8	0	8
2	4	−6

Answers may vary.

2. Given: the expression $(-4)^{12}$. Find the units digit of the value of the expression.

	Units digit
$(-4)^1$	4
$(-4)^2$	6
$(-4)^3$	4
$(-4)^4$	6

Pattern indicates the units digit of the number represented by $(-4)^{12}$ is 6.

2.8 Problem Solving

EXAMPLES

1 $A = \{-4, -3, -2, -1, 0, 1, 2, 3, 4\}$. Place the members of set A in the square so that the sum of each row, each column, and each diagonal is the same.

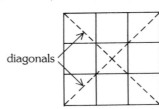

diagonals

Understand: *Given:*   the numbers $-4, -3, -2, -1, 0, 1, 2, 3,$ and 4

  To find: where each number should be placed so that the sum of each row, each column, and each diagonal is the same

Plan: Use the **guess-and-check** strategy to place the numbers in the squares. Although any guess is acceptable, it is possible to reduce the number of tries by using **logical reasoning.** For example, if you put all positive numbers in one row and all negative numbers in another row, the sums cannot be equal. Why?

Solve: Make a guess. One guess is shown below.

−4	1	4
2	0	−1
−3	−2	3

Check the guess: Are the sums of the rows, the columns, and the diagonals the same? No, but they are close. Use this fact to make your next guess.

Answer: The numbers can be placed as follows:

3	−2	−1
−4	0	4
1	2	−3

There are other possible arrangements. Can you find them?

Review: Read the problem again. Does your answer satisfy the conditions of the problem?

2 What is the units digit of the number represented by $(-8)^{92}$?

Understand: *Given:* the expression $(-8)^{92}$

To find: the units digit of the value of the expression

Plan: Sometimes the size of the numbers involved makes it difficult to determine how to solve a problem. In such cases, you can **solve a simpler problem**—that is, one in which the numbers are smaller or one that requires fewer steps.

Solve: *Use a table* to list the units digits of the powers of -8, starting with the exponent 1.

Expression	Exponent	Units digit of the number represented by the expression
$(-8)^1$	1	8
$(-8)^2$	2	4
$(-8)^3$	3	2
$(-8)^4$	4	6
$(-8)^5$	5	8
$(-8)^6$	6	4
$(-8)^7$	7	2
$(-8)^8$	8	6

Find a pattern in the last column. Every fourth units digit is 6. The exponents in the expressions whose values have a units digit of 6 are all multiples of 4. Therefore, since the exponent in the expression $(-8)^{92}$ is a multiple of 4, the units digit of the expression's value should be 6.

Answer: The units digit of the number represented by $(-8)^{92}$ is 6.

Review: Does it seem reasonable that a pattern found in the first 8 powers will apply when the exponent is 92?

ORAL EXERCISES

1–5. Identify the five problem-solving strategies used in the two example problems.

WRITTEN EXERCISES

A. Solve.

1. What is the next number in the sequence $\frac{1}{4}, \frac{7}{12}, \frac{11}{12}, 1\frac{1}{4}$? $1\frac{7}{12}$

2. How many $2\frac{5}{8}$-foot boards can be cut from a board that is $15\frac{3}{4}$ feet long? 6

MIXED REVIEW

1. Evaluate $\left|-\frac{5}{6}\right|$. $\frac{5}{6}$

2. What is the opposite of -0.8? 0.8

3. Find the product $\frac{5}{6}\left(\frac{30}{8}\right)$. $3\frac{1}{8}$

4. Sue's checkbook balance is $112. She wrote a check for $163. Determine Sue's current balance. $-$51

5. Simplify $108 - \frac{6^3}{2^2}$. 54

6. $\left(-\frac{16}{50}\right) \div \frac{8}{12}$ $\frac{12}{25}$

TEACHER'S RESOURCE MASTERS

Practice Master 7, Part 2

ASSIGNMENT GUIDE

Minimum
1–5 odd, 6–10

Regular
5–12

Maximum
7–14

ADDITIONAL ANSWERS

Oral Exercises

1–5. Guess-and-check, logical reasoning, solve a simpler problem, use a table, and find a pattern.

PROBLEM–SOLVING
STRATEGIES

Solve a Simpler Problem
(7, 9).

Use a Diagram (2, 4, 5, 12).

Use Logical Reasoning (6, 8,
10, 13).

Guess-and-Check (3, 5).

Look for a Pattern (1, 3, 11,
14).

3. Mrs. Zeedyk has three children. When asked how old her children are, she answers as follows: "Babs is 9 years older than Debbie, and Jack is 7 years younger than Babs. The sum of their ages is 20 years." How old is Debbie?

5. Mr. Moussad has bought 20 fruit trees. He wants to plant the same number of trees on each side of his orchard, which is square. How many trees will he plant on each side? 6 trees

4. A ball is dropped from a height of 64 inches. Each time it hits the ground, the ball bounces back $\frac{3}{4}$ of its previous height. What is the total distance the ball will have traveled when it hits the ground for the fourth time?

6. Evelyn sent some postcards and some letters to 19 of her friends. The postage for a postcard was $0.14, and the postage for a letter was $0.22. She did not send both a postcard and a letter to the same friend. If she spent $3.78 for postage, how many postcards and how many letters did Evelyn send?

B. **7.** The number 15 can be written as the sum of three whole-number addends such that adding 2 to one addend, subtracting 2 from another addend, and multiplying the third addend by 2 will yield the same result. What are the three addends? 4, 8, 3

9. The sum of 9 numbers is 2759. If each of the 9 numbers is increased by 10, what is the sum of the new numbers?

8. Find a number such that when you multiply the number by itself, the product is between 2.95 and 3.05. typical
answer: 1.73

10. Write 10,000,000 as the product of two whole numbers that do not end in zero.

11. If the following arrangement of numbers were continued, in which column would 88 be placed? Column B

A	B	C	D	E
	2	3	4	5
9	8	7	6	
	10	11	12	13
17	16	15	14	
	18	19	20	21
25	24	23	22	
	26	27	28	29

12. A farmer has a square field, each side of which is 800 meters long. In the center of the field is an unusable square region, each side of which is 400 meters long. The farmer has divided the land that can be used into four rectangular sections, all the same size and shape. What is the length and the width of each section? 600 m long, 200 m wide

C. **13.** Find two fractions that satisfy these conditions: (1) The numerator of the first fraction is greater than its denominator. (2) The numerator of the second fraction is less than its denominator. (3) The fractions are equivalent. typical answer: any fraction with a positive numerator and a negative denominator and an equivalent fraction with a negative numerator and a positive denominator

14. Place the following numbers in a magic square so that the sum of each row, each column, and each diagonal is the same: $\frac{1}{12}$, $\frac{1}{6}$, $\frac{1}{4}$, $\frac{1}{3}$, $\frac{5}{12}$, $\frac{1}{2}$, $\frac{7}{12}$, $\frac{2}{3}$, $\frac{3}{4}$

$\frac{1}{2}$	$\frac{1}{12}$	$\frac{2}{3}$
$\frac{7}{12}$	$\frac{5}{12}$	$\frac{1}{4}$
$\frac{1}{6}$	$\frac{3}{4}$	$\frac{1}{3}$

2.9 | Proofs in Algebra

Some of the following 12 properties of real numbers have already been discussed in Chapter 1 and Chapter 2.

Let a, b, and c be any real numbers.	Addition	Multiplication
Closure property	$a + b$ is a real number.	ab is a real number.
Commutative property	$a + b = b + a$	$ab = ba$
Associative property	$(a + b) + c = a + (b + c)$	$(ab)c = a(bc)$
Identity property	$a + 0 = 0 + a = a$	$a \cdot 1 = 1 \cdot a = a$
Inverse property	$a + (-a) = -a + a = 0$	$a\left(\frac{1}{a}\right) = \frac{1}{a}(a) = 1$

Distributive property of multiplication over addition	$a(b + c) = ab + ac$ or $(b + c)a = ba + ca$
Substitution property	If $a = b$, then a may be substituted for b.

These properties are **axioms.** An axiom is a statement that is assumed to be true. A **theorem** is a statement that is shown to be true by using definitions, axioms, theorems that have already been proved, and logical reasoning. The chain of reasoning by which a theorem is shown to be true is known as a **proof.**

EXAMPLES

CLASSROOM EXAMPLES
1. Given: the real number 4
   Prove: $0 \cdot 4 = 0$
   PROOF
   $0 \cdot 4$
   $= 0 \cdot 4 + 0$
      Ident. prop. of add.
   $= 0 \cdot 4 + [4 + (-4)]$
      Inv. prop. of add.
   $= (0 \cdot 4 + 4) + (-4)$
      Assoc. prop. of add.
   $= (0 \cdot 4 + 1 \cdot 4) + (-4)$
      Ident. prop. of mult.
   $= (0 + 1)4 + (-4)$
      Dist. prop.
   $= 1 \cdot 4 + (-4)$
      Ident. prop. of add.
   $= 4 + (-4)$
      Ident. prop. of mult.
   $= 0$
      Inv. prop. of add.

Prove that for every real number a, $0 \cdot a = 0$. This theorem is called the *multiplication property of 0*.

PROOF

$0 \cdot a = 0 \cdot a + 0$	*Identity property of addition*
$= 0 \cdot a + [a + (-a)]$	*Inverse property of addition*
$= (0 \cdot a + a) + (-a)$	*Associative property of addition*
$= (0 \cdot a + 1 \cdot a) + (-a)$	*Identity property of multiplication*
$= (0 + 1)a + (-a)$	*Distributive property of multiplication over addition*
$= 1 \cdot a + (-a)$	*Identity property of addition*
$= a + (-a)$	*Identity property of multiplication*
$= 0$	*Inverse property of addition*

2. Given: the real number 6
Prove: $-1 \cdot 6 = -6$

PROOF

$-1 \cdot 6$

$= -1 \cdot 6 + 0$
Ident. prop. of add.

$= -1 \cdot 6 + [6 + (-6)]$
Inv. prop. of add.

$= (-1 \cdot 6 + 6) + (-6)$
Assoc. prop. of add.

$= (-1 \cdot 6 + 1 \cdot 6)$
$\quad + (-6)$
Ident. prop. of mult.

$= (-1 + 1)6 + (-6)$
Dist. prop.

$= 0 \cdot 6 + (-6)$
Inv. prop. of add.

$= 0 + (-6)$
Mult. prop. of zero

$= -6$
Ident. prop. of add.

3. Given: the real numbers
8 and 10
Prove: $\frac{8}{10} = 8 \cdot \frac{1}{10}$

PROOF

$\frac{8}{10} = (8 \div 10) \cdot 1$
Ident. prop. of mult.

$= (8 \div 10) \cdot \left(10 \cdot \frac{1}{10}\right)$
Inv. prop. of mult.

$= [(8 \div 10) \cdot 10] \cdot \frac{1}{10}$
Assoc. prop. of mult.

$= 8 \cdot \frac{1}{10}$
Def. of div.

MIXED REVIEW

1. Perform the indicated
   operation.
   a. $5 + (-0.286)$ 4.714
   b. $(-14)(-6)$ 84
   c. $(-5.6) \div (0.7)$ -8
   d. $[(-15)-(-23)]$
      $- (-18)$ 26

The *multiplication property of* -1 was first presented in Section 2.6. Now it can be proved as a theorem.

2   **Prove that for every real number a, $-1 \cdot a = -a$.**

PROOF

$-1 \cdot a = -1 \cdot a + 0$	*Identity property of addition*
$= -1 \cdot a + [a + (-a)]$	*Inverse property of addition*
$= (-1 \cdot a + a) + (-a)$	*Associative property of addition*
$= (-1 \cdot a + 1 \cdot a) + (-a)$	*Identity property of multiplication*
$= (-1 + 1)a + (-a)$	*Distributive property*
$= 0 \cdot a + (-a)$	*Inverse property of addition*
$= 0 + (-a)$	*Multiplication property of 0*
$= -a$	*Identity property of addition*

You can use the following definitions in completing some proofs:

> **Subtraction is the inverse operation of addition. That is, $(m - n) + n = m$.**
>
> **Division is the inverse operation of multiplication. That is, $(m \div n) \cdot n = m$, where $n \neq 0$.**

3   **Prove that for any real numbers m and n, where $n \neq 0$, $m \div n = m \cdot \frac{1}{n}$.**

PROOF

$m \div n = (m \div n) \cdot 1$	*Identity property of multiplication*
$= (m \div n) \cdot \left(n \cdot \frac{1}{n}\right)$	*Inverse property of multiplication*
$= [(m \div n) \cdot n] \cdot \frac{1}{n}$	*Associative property of multiplication*
$= m \cdot \frac{1}{n}$	*Definition of division*

ORAL EXERCISES

Complete.

1. A(n) __axiom__ is a statement that is assumed to be true.

2. A(n) __theorem__ is a statement that is shown to be true.

3. A __proof__ is the chain of logical reasoning used to show that a theorem is true.

4. The inverse operation of addition is __subtraction__.

5. The inverse operation of multiplication is __division__.

WRITTEN EXERCISES

A. Name the properties illustrated.

1. $x(y + z) = xy + xz$

2. $m(n + 1) = m(1 + n)$

3. $a + b = 1(a + b)$

4. $m + (n + 1) = (m + n) + 1$

5. $x + 0 = x + (-y + y)$

6. $0(m + n) = 0$

7. $a(bc) = (bc)a$

8. $-(a + b) + (a + b) = 0$

B. Give a reason for each step in the proof. Variables stand for real numbers.

Prove: $a - b = a + (-b)$

PROOF (This is a proof of the *subtraction property* on page 45.)

$a - b = (a - b) + 0$ **9.** Identity property of addition

$= (a - b) + [b + (-b)]$ **10.** Inverse property of addition

$= [(a - b) + b] + (-b)$ **11.** Associative property of addition

$= a + (-b)$ **12.** Definition of Subtraction

Use the definition of multiplication of real numbers in the next proof.

Multiplication of Real Numbers	**For all real numbers a, b, c, and d, where $b \neq 0$ and $d \neq 0$,** $\frac{a}{b} \cdot \frac{c}{d} = \frac{ac}{bd}$.

Prove: $\frac{ab}{ac} = \frac{b}{c}$, where $a \neq 0$ and $c \neq 0$

PROOF

$\frac{ab}{ac} = \frac{a}{a} \cdot \frac{b}{c}$ **13.** Definition of multiplication

$= a \cdot \frac{1}{a} \cdot \frac{b}{c}$ *Theorem as proved in Example 3*

$= 1 \cdot \frac{b}{c}$ **14.** Inverse property of multiplication

$= \frac{b}{c}$ **15.** Identity property of multiplication

Complete each proof by giving a reason for each step.

Prove: $a + (b - c) = (a + b) - c$

PROOF

$a + (b - c) = a + [b + (-c)]$ **16.** Subtraction property

$= (a + b) + (-c)$ **17.** Associative property of addition

$= (a + b) - c$ **18.** Subtraction property

Prove: $(-a) + (-b) = -(a + b)$

PROOF

$(-a) + (-b) = (-1a) + (-1b)$ **19.** Multiplication property of -1

$= -1(a + b)$ **20.** Distributive property

$= -(a + b)$ **21.** Multiplication property of -1

---

2. Simplify each of the following.

  a. $5x^3y^2(-8x^2y)$
     $-40x^5y^3$

  b. $4 \cdot 3 + 5 \cdot 3^2$ 57

3. Evaluate each of the following if $x = 2$, $y = 3$, and $z = 4$.

  a. $\frac{5y^2}{z}$ 11.25

  b. $\left(\frac{x}{y}\right)^2$ $\frac{4}{9}$

4. Find each value.

  a. $3(2^3)$ 24

  b. $(1.6)^3$ 4.096

5. Graph each of the following sets on the number line.

  a. $\{-3, -2, -1, 0, 1\}$

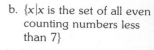

  b. $\{x \mid x$ is the set of all even counting numbers less than 7$\}$

TEACHER'S RESOURCE MASTERS

Practice Master 8, Part 1

Quiz 4

ASSIGNMENT GUIDE

Minimum
1–18

Regular
9–27

Maximum
13–29

Prove: $a(b - c) = ab - ac$

PROOF

$$a(b - c) = a[b + (-c)]$$
$$= ab + a(-c)$$
$$= ab + a(-1c)$$
$$= ab + [a(-1)]c$$
$$= ab + (-ac)$$
$$= ab - ac$$

22. Subtraction property

23. Distributive property

24. Multiplication property of -1

25. Associative property of multiplication

26. Multiplication property of -1

27. Subtraction property

C. Three more properties (or axioms) that you can use to prove theorems are as follows:

Reflexive Property	For every real number a, $a = a$.
Symmetric Property	For all real numbers a and b, if $a = b$, then $b = a$.
Transitive Property	For all real numbers a, b, and c, if $a = b$ and $b = c$, then $a = c$.

Example:

Prove: If $a = b$, then $a + c = b + c$.

PROOF

$a + c = a + c$ Reflexive property

$a = b$ Given

$a + c = b + c$ Substitution property

28. *Prove:* If $a = b$, then $ac = bc$.

29. *Prove:* If $a = b$, then $a - c = b - c$.

EXPLORATION
Field Axioms and Clock Arithmetic

A set S, together with two operations, is a **field** if the first 11 properties listed in Section 2.9 (the closure, associative, commutative, identity, and inverse properties of addition and of multiplication and the distributive property of multiplication over addition) are true for all numbers of the set.

Continued on next page.

Clock arithmetic can be used to illustrate whether a set S is a field or not. On a 12-hour clock, the 12 is replaced with a 0.

Notice that S is a *finite set* with $S = \{0, 1, 2, 3, 4, 5, 6, 7, 8, 9, 10, 11\}$. If it is 10 o'clock now, in 3 hours it will be 1 o'clock. So $10 + 3 = 1$ in clock arithmetic.

Addition on a Clock	If a sum is greater than or equal to 12, subtract the largest multiple of 12 possible.

Example 1: Find $11 + 10$.

Solution: $11 + 10 = 21$
 $21 - 12 = 9$

So $11 + 10 = 9$.

Multiplication on a Clock	If a product is greater than or equal to 12, subtract the largest multiple of 12 possible.

Example 2: Find 8×7.

Solution: $8 \times 7 = 56$
 $56 - 48 = 8$

So $8 \times 7 = 8$.

In order for S to be a field, all 11 properties must be tested.

Closure property of addition:

Is $a + b \in S$? Yes. The sum of any two numbers in S is also in S. For example, $10 + 11 = 9$, and $9 \in S$. Every possible addition fact would have to be tested in order to prove this.

Closure property of multiplication:

Is $ab \in S$? Yes. The product of any two numbers in S is also in S. For example, $8 \times 7 = 8$, and $8 \in S$. (Every possible multiplication fact would have to be tested.)

Continued on next page.

Associative property of addition:

Is $a + (b + c) = (a + b) + c$? Yes. Test a few cases. (Remember that *every* possible case would have to be tested.)

Associative property of multiplication:

Is $a(bc) = (ab)c$? Yes. Test a few cases.

Commutative property of addition:

Is $a + b = b + a$? Yes. Test a few cases.

Commutative property of multiplication:

Is $ab = ba$? Yes. Test a few cases.

Identity property of addition:

Is $a + 0 = 0 + a = a$? Yes. The identity element for addition in the set S is 0.

Identity property of multiplication:

Is $a \cdot 1 = 1 \cdot a = a$? Yes. The identity element for multiplication in the set S is 1.

Inverse property of addition:

For each a in S, is there an element b such that $a + b = b + a = 0$? Yes. For example, 2 is the additive inverse of 10 because $10 + 2 = 2 + 10 = 0$. Find the additive inverse of each element of S.

Inverse property of multiplication:

For each a in S, is there an element b such that $ab = ba = 1$? No. The numbers 2, 4, 6, 8, and 10 do not have multiplicative inverses. You do not have to test the element 0.

Distributive property:

Is $a(b + c) = ab + ac$? Yes. Test a few cases.

Since S does not contain a multiplicative inverse for *every* element of S, S is not a field.

EXERCISE

Use the clock at the right and test all 11 properties to see if $S = \{0, 1, 2\}$ is a field. (NOTE: For a sum or a product greater than or equal to 3, subtract the largest possible multiple of 3.)

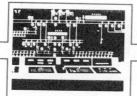

COMPUTER

TEACHER'S RESOURCE MASTERS

Computer Master 2

A computer does not interpret numbers in the exact same way that people do. What is wrong with the output of the program below?

```
10 FOR X = 1 TO 2
20 READ A, B, C
30 IF C = A - B THEN GOTO 50
40 PRINT A; " MINUS "; B; " DOES NOT EQUAL "; C: GOTO 60
50 PRINT A; " MINUS "; B; " EQUALS "; C
60 NEXT X
70 END
80 DATA 4,2,2,,.56,,.45,,.11
```

EXERCISES

1. Why does it seem that the computer is making a mathematical error? When you perform the same two operations in your head, how are the computer's answer and your answer different?

2. Computers seem to make certain types of errors because of the way computers handle "floating point," or decimal, constants. Think of a way to "fix" this program. (HINT: There are at least two ways: using the ABS function or using division.)

3. Type the following and then press RETURN:
FOR I = 1 TO 40: ? 2 ^ I: NEXT
Analyze the result. After the computer prints the first 29 integers, what happens?

4. Write a print statement for an 18-digit number with a decimal point between the ninth and tenth digits. What is the result? Now write a print statement for an 18-digit number with a decimal point before the ninth digit and another that prints the decimal point after the tenth digit. Keep experimenting with multiplication print statements, and analyze the way computers handle the answers.

ENRICHMENT

See Activities 5–8,
p. T42.

CHAPTER 2 REVIEW

VOCABULARY

absolute value (2.2)
additive inverse (2.4)
additive inverse property
  (2.4)
axiom (2.9)
complete listing (2.1)
coordinate (2.2)
counting (natural) numbers
  (2.1)
element (member) (2.1)
empty (null) set (2.1)
finite set (2.1)

graph (2.2)
infinite set (2.1)
integers (2.1)
irrational numbers (2.1)
multiplication property
  of −1 (2.6)
multiplication property
  of 0 (2.9)
multiplicative inverse
  (reciprocal) (2.7)
opposites (2.2)
partial listing (2.1)

proof (2.9)
rational numbers (2.1)
real-number line (2.2)
real numbers (2.1)
set (2.1)
set-builder notation (2.1)
standard form of rational
  numbers (2.7)
subset (2.1)
subtraction property (2.5)
whole numbers (2.1)

REVIEW EXERCISES

2.1 Use the sets below for exercises 1–8. Complete each statement, using $\in$, $\notin$, or $\subset$.

$D = \{1, 3, 8\}$ $E = \{\ \}$ $F = \{1, 2, 3, \ldots, 10\}$

1. $D \underline{\ \subset\ } F$ **2.** $E \underline{\ \subset\ } F$ **3.** $3 \underline{\ \in\ } D$ **4.** $10 \underline{\ \notin\ } D$

5. $D \underline{\ \subset\ } D$ **6.** $8 \underline{\ \notin\ } E$ **7.** $1 \underline{\ \in\ } F$ **8.** $C \underline{\ \notin\ } F$

2.2 Which symbol, $=$, $<$, or $>$, should replace each ●?

9. $6.0 \bullet \frac{6}{1}$ $=$ **10.** $5 \bullet 5.01$ $<$ **11.** $7.09 \bullet 70.9$ $<$ **12.** $3\frac{3}{5} \bullet \frac{4}{5}$ $>$

13. $0.7 \bullet 0.07$ $>$ **14.** $61.3 \bullet 6.13$ $>$ **15.** $\frac{13}{1} \bullet 13$ $=$ **16.** $4\frac{8}{9} \bullet 4\frac{5}{9}$ $>$

2.3 Evaluate.

17. $|6|$ 6 **18.** $|0|$ 0 **19.** $|-4|$ 4 **20.** $\left|\frac{8}{3}\right|$ $\frac{8}{3}$

21. $|-1.6|$ 1.6 **22.** $\left|2\frac{3}{4}\right|$ $2\frac{3}{4}$ **23.** $\left|-\frac{5}{6}\right|$ $\frac{5}{6}$ **24.** $|3.19|$ 3.19

2.4 What is the opposite of each number?

25. 4 -4 **26.** -8 8 **27.** 0 0 **28.** -0.2 0.2

Find each sum by referring to a number line.

29. $-8 + 6$ -2 **30.** $7 + (-9)$ -2 **31.** $-14 + 9$ -5 **32.** $-3 + (-8)$

33. $7 + 9$ 16 **34.** $-5 + (-2)$ -7 **35.** $-23 + 10$ -13 **36.** $15 + (-10)$

Find each sum.

37. $-81 + 64$ -17 **38.** $157 + 243$ 400 **39.** $74 + (-93)$ -19

ADDITIONAL ANSWERS

32. -11

36. 5

40. $-18 + (-43)$ -61 **41.** $0.2 + 8.91$ 9.11 **42.** $-3.1 + 2.4$ -0.7

43. $6.7 + (-9.8)$ -3.1 **44.** $-0.3 + (-0.46)$ -0.76 **45.** $\frac{2}{3} + \frac{2}{3}$ $1\frac{1}{3}$

46. $-\frac{4}{5} + \frac{1}{5}$ $-\frac{3}{5}$ **47.** $-\frac{4}{5} + \left(-\frac{1}{3}\right)$ $-1\frac{2}{15}$ **48.** $-\frac{7}{7} + \frac{1}{6}$ $-\frac{5}{6}$

49. $65 + (-43) + 7$ 29 **50.** $-9.6 + 7.8 + (-1.2)$ **51.** $\frac{1}{2} + \left(-\frac{1}{3}\right) + \frac{5}{6}$ 1

2.5 **Find each difference.** -3

52. $18 - 6$ 12 **53.** $14 - 81$ -67 **54.** $18 - (-23)$ 41

55. $-26 - (-4)$ -22 **56.** $-6 - 27$ -33 **57.** $4.6 - 1.83$ 2.77

58. $-2.6 - 3.9$ -6.5 **59.** $2.6 - (-8.7)$ 11.3 **60.** $-1.09 - (-8.2)$

61. $\frac{3}{4} - \left(-\frac{1}{2}\right)$ $1\frac{1}{4}$ **62.** $-\frac{2}{5} - \left(-\frac{9}{10}\right)$ $\frac{1}{2}$ **63.** $-\frac{5}{6} - \frac{1}{3}$ $-1\frac{1}{6}$

64. $-1\frac{1}{4} - 2\frac{1}{12}$ $-3\frac{1}{3}$ **65.** $2\frac{1}{6} - \left(-4\frac{1}{4}\right)$ $6\frac{5}{12}$ **66.** $1\frac{1}{2} - 3\frac{3}{4}$ $-2\frac{1}{4}$

2.6 **Find each product.**

67. $19(40)$ 760 **68.** $-32(-45)$ 1440 **69.** $17(-26)$ -442

70. $-37(19)$ -703 **71.** $2.4(8.6)$ 20.64 **72.** $-3.1(41.6)$

73. $5.0(-9.6)$ -48 **74.** $-20.1(-5.4)$ 108.54 **75.** $\frac{3}{4}\left(\frac{16}{21}\right)$ $\frac{4}{7}$

76. $-\frac{2}{3}\left(\frac{15}{16}\right)$ $-\frac{5}{8}$ **77.** $-\frac{4}{7}\left(-\frac{21}{20}\right)$ $\frac{3}{5}$ **78.** $\frac{5}{6}\left(-\frac{3}{20}\right)$ $-\frac{1}{8}$

79. $-2^3(3^4)$ -648 **80.** $(-3)^2(2^4)$ 144 **81.** $\left(-\frac{1}{2}\right)^2(4)^2$ 4

82. $-\frac{1}{3}(-9)^2$ -27 **83.** $\left(\frac{1}{4}\right)^2(8)^2$ 4 **84.** $\frac{1}{9}(-3)^2$ 1

2.7 **Find each quotient.**

85. $-54 \div 3$ -18 **86.** $96 \div (-4)$ -24 **87.** $-69 \div (-23)$ 3

88. $102 \div 6$ 17 **89.** $\frac{11}{2} \div \frac{121}{4}$ $\frac{2}{11}$ **90.** $-\frac{15}{7} \div \frac{5}{14}$ -6

91. $-\frac{2}{3} \div \left(-\frac{8}{9}\right)$ $\frac{3}{4}$ **92.** $\frac{6}{7} \div \frac{18}{35}$ $1\frac{2}{3}$ **93.** $17.01 \div 2.7$ 6.3

94. $32.4 \div (-0.6)$ -54 **95.** $-21 \div 4.2$ -5 **96.** $-297.85 \div (-3.7)$

2.8 **Solve.** 80.5

97. In a card game, Todd went in the hole 45 points on the first hand. On the next hand, he scored 34 points. What was his total score then? -11

98. Find two numbers whose sum is 23 and whose product is -50. $-2, 25$

2.9 **99.** Name the theorem that states that for every real number a, $-1 \cdot a = -a$.

100. Name the axiom that states that for all real numbers a and b, $a + b = b + a$.
commutative property of addition

60. 7.11
72. -128.96
99. Mult. prop. of -1

CHAPTER 2 TEST

Use the sets below for exercises 1–8. Complete each sentence, using $\in$, $\notin$, or $\subset$.

$W = \{0\}$ $X = \{0, 1, 2, 3, 4\}$ $Y = \{0, 2, 4\}$ $Z = \{5\}$

1. $0 \underline{\in} X$

2. $Y \underline{\subset} X$

3. $0 \underline{\notin} Z$

4. $4 \underline{\in} Y$

5. $W \underline{\subset} Y$

6. $4 \underline{\notin} Z$

7. $2 \underline{\in} Y$

8. $Z \underline{\subset} Z$

Which symbol, $=$, $<$, or $>$, should replace each ●?

9. $-3 ● -2.99$ $<$

10. $3.0 ● \frac{6}{2}$ $=$

11. $25 ● 14.99$ $>$

12. What is the absolute value of -4? 4

13. What is the opposite of $\frac{2}{3}$? $-\frac{2}{3}$

Find each sum by referring to a number line.

14. $6 + 12$ 18

15. $-6 + 18$ 12

16. $6 + (-15)$ -9

17. $-4 + (-7)$ -11

18. $-12 + 12$ 0

19. $-8 + (-7)$ -15

Find each sum.

20. $28 + 97$ 125

21. $-4.3 + 16.04$ 11.74

22. $-\frac{2}{3} + \left(-\frac{7}{10}\right)$ $-1\frac{11}{30}$

23. $14 + (-8.09)$ 5.91

24. $-\frac{3}{4} + \frac{5}{6}$ $\frac{1}{12}$

25. $\frac{1}{9} + \left(-\frac{2}{3}\right)$ $-\frac{5}{9}$

Find each difference.

26. $-23 - (-97)$ 74

27. $14.6 - 19.04$ -4.44

28. $\frac{4}{5} - \frac{1}{3}$ $\frac{7}{15}$

29. $-92 - 106$ -198

30. $\frac{7}{8} - \left(-\frac{1}{4}\right)$ $1\frac{1}{8}$

31. $-7.5 - (-8)$ 0.5

Find each product.

32. $92(-13)$ -1196

33. $-\frac{4}{5}\left(-\frac{15}{32}\right)$ $\frac{3}{8}$

34. $406(89)$ $36,134$

35. $-3.2(8.06)$ -25.792

36. $\frac{6}{7}\left(-\frac{14}{24}\right)$ $-\frac{1}{2}$

37. $-6.1(-0.4)$ 2.44

Find each quotient.

38. $-840 \div (-30)$ 28

39. $74 \div \left(-\frac{2}{5}\right)$ -185

40. $-20.4 \div (-0.51)$ 40

41. $368 \div 16$ 23

42. $-\frac{8}{9} \div \left(-\frac{2}{3}\right)$ $1\frac{1}{3}$

43. $1.035 \div (-2.3)$ -0.45

Solve.

44. If the value of an investment was $2350 but has dropped $20 a day for the last 8 days, what is the value now? $2190

45. Name the theorem that states that for every real number a, $0 \cdot a = 0$. multiplication property of 0

CHAPTER 3

Equations

How long will it take a cyclist to travel 10 kilometers if he averages 40 kilometers per hour? $\frac{1}{4}$ hour

OBJECTIVE

Find the solution set of an open sentence by replacing the variable with each number of a given replacement set.

TEACHER'S NOTES

See p. T25.

CLASSROOM EXAMPLES

1. Find the solution set of $2x + 3 = 13$. The replacement set is $\{-2, 5, 6\}$.

$$2x + 3 = 13$$
$$2(-2) + 3 \overset{?}{=} 13$$
$$-4 + 3 \neq 13$$

$$2x + 3 = 13$$
$$2(5) + 3 \overset{?}{=} 13$$
$$10 + 3 = 13$$

$$2x + 3 = 13$$
$$2(6) + 3 \overset{?}{=} 13$$
$$12 + 3 \neq 13$$

The solution set of $2x + 3 = 13$ is $\{5\}$.

2. Find the solution set of $y(3 + y) = 10$. The replacement set is $\{0, 2, 5\}$.

$$y(3 + y) = 10$$
$$0(3 + 0) \overset{?}{=} 10$$
$$0 \neq 10$$

$$y(3 + y) = 10$$
$$2(3 + 2) \overset{?}{=} 10$$
$$10 = 10$$

$$y(3 + y) = 10$$
$$5(3 + 5) \overset{?}{=} 10$$
$$40 \neq 10$$

The solution set of $y(3 + y) = 10 = \{2\}$.

3.1	Sets and Equations

An **equation** is an algebraic sentence in which two expressions are connected by the symbol $=$. Equations that contain one or more than one variable are called **open sentences.** When replacement is made for the variable (or variables), the result is true or false.

The given set of numbers from which you choose a replacement for a variable is called the **replacement set.** The set of numbers from the replacement set that makes the open sentence true is called the **solution set.** Open sentences that have the same solution set are said to be **equivalent.**

EXAMPLES

1   **Find the solution set of $3x + 5 = 17$. The replacement set is $\{-3, 2, 4\}$.**

SOLUTION   Replace x with -3, then 2, then 4.

$$3x + 5 = 17$$
$$3(-3) + 5 \overset{?}{=} 17$$
$$-9 + 5 \overset{?}{=} 17$$
$$-4 \neq 17$$
$$-4 = 17 \text{ is false.}$$

$$3x + 5 = 17$$
$$3 \cdot 2 + 5 \overset{?}{=} 17$$
$$6 + 5 \overset{?}{=} 17$$
$$11 \neq 17$$
$$11 = 17 \text{ is false.}$$

$$3x + 5 = 17$$
$$3 \cdot 4 + 5 \overset{?}{=} 17$$
$$12 + 5 \overset{?}{=} 17$$
$$17 = 17$$
$$17 = 17 \text{ is true.}$$

Only the replacement of x with 4 in the equation makes the sentence true. The solution set of $3x + 5 = 17$ is $\{4\}$.

2   **Find the solution set of $x(2 + x) = 24$. The replacement set is $\{3, 4, 5\}$.**

SOLUTION   If the same variable is used more than once in an equation, replace it with the same number each time. Replace *both* x's in the equation with 3, then 4, then 5.

$$x(2 + x) = 24$$
$$3(2 + 3) \overset{?}{=} 24$$
$$3 \cdot 5 \overset{?}{=} 24$$
$$15 \neq 24$$
$$15 = 24 \text{ is false.}$$

$$x(2 + x) = 24$$
$$4(2 + 4) \overset{?}{=} 24$$
$$4 \cdot 6 \overset{?}{=} 24$$
$$24 = 24$$
$$24 = 24 \text{ is true.}$$

$$x(2 + x) = 24$$
$$5(2 + 5) \overset{?}{=} 24$$
$$5 \cdot 7 \overset{?}{=} 24$$
$$35 \neq 24$$
$$35 = 24 \text{ is false.}$$

The solution set of $x(2 + x) = 24$ is $\{4\}$.

Sometimes a solution set contains more than one number.

3   **Find the solution set of $x^2 = 9$. The replacement set is $\{-3, -2, 2, 3\}$.**

SOLUTION

$$x^2 = 9$$
$$x \cdot x = 9$$
$$-3(-3) \overset{?}{=} 9$$
$$9 = 9$$
$$9 = 9 \text{ is true.}$$

$$x^2 = 9$$
$$x \cdot x = 9$$
$$-2(-2) \overset{?}{=} 9$$
$$4 \neq 9$$
$$4 = 9 \text{ is false.}$$

$$x^2 = 9$$
$$x \cdot x = 9$$
$$2 \cdot 2 \overset{?}{=} 9$$
$$4 \neq 9$$
$$4 = 9 \text{ is false.}$$

$$x^2 = 9$$
$$x \cdot x = 9$$
$$3 \cdot 3 \overset{?}{=} 9$$
$$9 = 9$$
$$9 = 9 \text{ is true.}$$

Recall that x^2 means $x \cdot x$ and that the product of two negative integers is positive. So there are actually two integers from the replacement set that can replace x and make the sentence true. The solution set of $x^2 = 9$ is $\{-3, 3\}$.

Complete each sentence.

1. A(n) _____equation_____ is an algebraic sentence in which two expressions are connected by the symbol $=$.

2. The _____replacement set_____ is a given set of numbers from which you choose a replacement for a variable.

3. The set of numbers that makes an open sentence true is called the _____solution set_____.

4. Open sentences that have the same solution set are said to be _____equivalent_____.

A. **Find the solution set of each equation if the replacement set is $\{2, 4, 6\}$.**

1. $x + 6 = 12$ $\{6\}$

2. $12 = a + 8$ $\{4\}$

3. $16 = b + 14$ $\{2\}$

Find the solution set of each equation if the replacement set is $\{8, 10, 12\}$.

4. $18 = y + 10$ $\{8\}$

5. $31 = a + 19$ $\{12\}$

6. $x + 15 = 25$ $\{10\}$

Find the solution set of each equation if the replacement set is $\{14, 16, 18\}$.

7. $y + 14 = 28$ $\{14\}$

8. $27 = y + 11$ $\{16\}$

9. $a + 28 = 42$ $\{14\}$

Find the solution set of each equation if the replacement set is $\{-7, -5, -3\}$. The solution set may be the empty set.

Examples: $x + 4 = 1$ $\{-3\}$ $5 + y = 7$ $\{ \ \}$

10. $y + 9 = 16$ $\{ \ \}$

11. $x + 10 = 7$ $\{-3\}$

12. $13 = a + 10$ $\{ \ \}$

B. **Find the solution set of each equation if the replacement set is $\{1, 5, 9\}$.**

13. $20 = b + 19$ $\{1\}$

14. $x + 5 = 10$ $\{5\}$

15. $30 = a + 25$ $\{5\}$

Find the solution set of each equation if the replacement set is $\{-10, -5, 5\}$.

16. $110 = x + 100$ $\{ \ \}$

17. $y^2 = 100$ $\{-10\}$

18. $x + x = 10$ $\{5\}$

19. $b + 49 = 54$ $\{5\}$

20. $x^2 = 25$ $\{-5, 5\}$

21. $24 + y = 14$ $\{-10\}$

Find the solution set of each equation if the replacement set is $\{15, 20, 25\}$.

22. $x + 13 = 28$ $\{15\}$

23. $y + 32 = 57$ $\{25\}$

24. $a + 34 = 54$ $\{20\}$

25. $38 = y + 23$ $\{15\}$

26. $a^2 = 400$ $\{20\}$

27. $b^2 = 225$ $\{15\}$

---

3. Find the solution set of $x^2 = 16$. The replacement set is $\{-4, -2, 2, 4\}$.

$x^2 = 16$
$(-4)^2 \stackrel{?}{=} 16$
$16 = 16$
$x^2 = 16$
$(-2)^2 \stackrel{?}{=} 16$
$4 \neq 16$
$x^2 = 16$
$(2)^2 \stackrel{?}{=} 16$
$4 \neq 16$
$x^2 = 16$
$(4)^2 \stackrel{?}{=} 16$
$16 = 16$

The solution set of $x^2 = 16$ is $\{-4, 4\}$.

MIXED REVIEW

1. Illustrate the symmetric property.   Answers may vary.

2. Simplify $2^3 a^5(a^{12})$. $8a^{17}$

3. Complete.
   a. $\left|-\frac{3}{5}\right|$ $\frac{3}{5}$
   b. $-|-9|$ -9

4. Simplify $(9 + 3)(72 \div 8)$. 108

5. Evaluate if $a = 3$ and $b = 4$. $\frac{a^3 b}{12}$ 9

TEACHER'S RESOURCE MASTERS

Practice Master 8, Part 2

ASSIGNMENT GUIDE

Minimum
1–12, 13–27 odd

Regular
16–35

Maximum
13–35 odd, 37–44

Find the solution set of each equation if the replacement set is $\{x \mid x$ is an integer and $x > 0$ and $x < 6\}$.

28. $x(x + 6) = 27$ $\{3\}$

29. $y(y + 9) = 70$ $\{5\}$

30. $a(8 + a) = 48$ $\{4\}$

31. $b(12 + b) = 28$ $\{2\}$

32. $x(x - 3) = 10$ $\{5\}$

33. $y(y - 4) = 0$ $\{4\}$

34. $x^2 = 1$ $\{1\}$

35. $y^2 + 20 = 24$ $\{2\}$

36. $a^2 + 9 = 18$ $\{3\}$

C. Find the solution set of each equation if the replacement set is $\{-13, -12, -11, -10, -9, 9, 10, 11, 12, 13\}$.

37. $a^2 + 5 = 405$ $\{\ \}$

38. $x^2 - 1 = 120$ $\{-11, 11\}$

39. $b^2 - 10 = 134$ $\{-12, 12\}$

40. $y^2 + y = 110$ $\{10\}$

41. $a^2 + a = 90$ $\{-10\}$

42. $b^2 + b^2 = 162$ $\{-9, 9\}$

43. $x(x + x) = 338$ $\{-13, 13\}$

44. $x(x - x) = 0$ $\{-13, -12, -11, -10, -9, 9, 10, 11, 12, 13\}$

MATH HERITAGE/Contributions, Please!

The **googol** is the contribution of a nine-year-old boy to the field of mathematics. The nephew of American mathematician Edward Kasner suggested that this term be used to name 10^{100}, or 1 followed by 100 zeros. An even larger number than the googol is the **googolplex,** which is 10 to the googol power, or 10 multiplied by itself a googol number of times.

The Romans contributed the symbol ∞ , which they used to denote the number 1000, but it wasn't until the 17th century that the mathematician John Wallis used the symbol to stand for **infinity.**

The Greeks contributed a letter from their alphabet, π (pi), to the field of mathematics to represent the ratio of the circumference of a circle to its diameter. Just about everyone else contributed to the establishment of the numerical value of π. The ancient Chinese, the Hebrews, and the Babylonians all considered the value of π to be exactly 3. By 1500 B.C., the Egyptians had determined the value more accurately to be 3.16. The astronomer Ptolemy later calculated it to be 3.1416. By the year 1720, the Japanese mathematician Matsunaga had determined the value of π to 50 decimal places. Mathematicians today realize that an exact decimal value for π is impossible or, at best, π in the sky.

3.2	Solving Equations, Using Addition or Subtraction

OBJECTIVE

Solve an equation by using the addition property of equality or the subtraction property of equality.

If two students each have $100 in a savings account, then they have an equal amount of money.

$100 = $100

If the same amount is then deposited into each account, the students still have an equal amount of money.

$100 + $50 = $100 + $50

If the same number is added to each side of an equation, the result will be an equation equivalent to the original equation.

Addition Property of Equality	**If *a*, *b*, and *c* are any real numbers and *a* = *b*, then *a* + *c* = *b* + *c*.**

EXAMPLES

 Solve $x + 15 = 7$. The replacement set is the set of integers.

SOLUTION

$$x + 15 = 7$$
$$x + 15 + (-15) = 7 + (-15) \quad \text{Add } -15 \text{ to each side.}$$
$$x + 0 = -8$$
$$x = -8$$

The solution set of $x + 15 = 7$ is $\{-8\}$. When you solve an equation, you usually write the solution without set notation—for example, $x = -8$.

CHECK

Replace x in the original equation with -8.

$$x + 15 = 7$$
$$-8 + 15 \stackrel{?}{=} 7$$
$$7 = 7 \quad \text{✓} \quad \text{True}$$

TEACHER'S NOTES
See p. T25.

CLASSROOM EXAMPLES

1. Solve $y + 8 = 12$. The replacement set is the set of integers.
$$y + 8 = 12$$
$$y + 8 + (-8) = 12 + (-8)$$
$$y + 0 = 4$$
$$y = 4$$

2. Solve $k - 4\frac{1}{2} = 16$. The replacement set is the set of rational numbers.
$$k - 4\frac{1}{2} = 16$$
$$k - 4\frac{1}{2} + 4\frac{1}{2} = 16 + 4\frac{1}{2}$$
$$k = 20\frac{1}{2}$$

3. Solve $p + 12 = 9$. The replacement set is the set of rational numbers.
$$p + 12 = 9$$
$$p + 12 - 12 = 9 - 12$$
$$p = -3$$

MIXED REVIEW

1. Find the solution set of $y^2 = 25$. The replacement set is $\{-5, -3, 3, 5\}$. $\{-5, 5\}$

| 2 | **Solve $y - 3\frac{1}{2} = 11$. The replacement set is the set of rational numbers.** |

SOLUTION

$$y - 3\tfrac{1}{2} = 11$$

$$y - 3\tfrac{1}{2} + 3\tfrac{1}{2} = 11 + 3\tfrac{1}{2} \quad \text{Add } 3\tfrac{1}{2} \text{ to each side.}$$

$$y = 14\tfrac{1}{2}$$

CHECK

$$y - 3\tfrac{1}{2} = 11$$

$$14\tfrac{1}{2} - 3\tfrac{1}{2} \stackrel{?}{=} 11$$

$$11 = 11 \quad \text{✔ True}$$

If the same number is subtracted from each side of an equation, the result will be an equation equivalent to the original equation.

| **Subtraction Property of Equality** | **If a, b, and c are any real numbers and $a = b$, then $a - c = b - c$.** |

| 3 | **Solve $n + 10 = 7$. The replacement set is the set of rational numbers.** |

SOLUTION

$$n + 10 = 7$$

$$n + 10 - 10 = 7 - 10 \quad \text{Subtract 10 from each side.}$$

$$n = -3$$

CHECK

$$n + 10 = 7$$

$$-3 + 10 \stackrel{?}{=} 7$$

$$7 = 7 \quad \text{✔ True}$$

Notice that in Example 3 above, the same solution would result if -10 were added to each side. *Adding -10 gives the same result as subtracting 10.*

ORAL EXERCISES

State the number that you would add to or subtract from both sides of the equation in order to solve the equation.

1. $x + 6 = 9$ Subtract 6.

2. $y + 8 = 15$ Subtract 8.

3. $a + 12 = 12$

4. $s + (-3) = 1$ Add 3.

5. $x - 9 = 5$ Add 9.

6. $6 = a + 4$ Subtract 4.

7. $-3 = y + (-4)$ Add 4.

8. $10 = s - 15$ Add 15.

9. $8 + x = 19$

10. $-6 + a = 7$ Add 6.

11. $15 = x + 8$ Subtract 8.

12. $24 = -7 + y$ Add 7.

A. 1–12. Solve each equation in Oral Exercises. Check. The replacement set is the set of integers.

B. Solve each equation. Check. The replacement set is the set of rational numbers.

13. $-5 + a = 0$ 5

14. $n + 10 = 25$ 15

15. $a + 42 = 13$ −29

16. $s + 18 = 5$ −13

17. $y + (-25) = 31$ 56

18. $c + (-36) = 17$ 53

19. $x - 15 = 7$ 22

20. $n - 18 = 20$ 38

21. $a + 3.4 = 21$ 17.6

22. $s + 3.8 = 45$ 41.2

23. $16 + x = 32$ 16

24. $9 + y = 31$ 22

25. $153 = s - 78$ 231

26. $412 = a - 309$ 721

27. $0.3 = x + 2.46$

28. $4.7 = y + 6.39$ −1.69

29. $s - 0.69 = -2.13$

30. $a - 0.18 = -0.47$

31. $16.4 = t - 8.7$ 25.1

32. $51.4 = u - 30.9$ 82.3

33. $16.7 = x + 23.4$

34. $x + \dfrac{1}{3} = \dfrac{7}{3}$ 2

35. $s + \dfrac{1}{8} = \dfrac{5}{8}$ $\frac{1}{2}$

36. $y - \dfrac{2}{5} = \dfrac{13}{5}$ 3

37. $u - \dfrac{1}{9} = \dfrac{5}{9}$ $\frac{2}{3}$

38. $\dfrac{3}{4} = x + \dfrac{1}{2}$ $\frac{1}{4}$

39. $\dfrac{1}{4} = y + \dfrac{1}{8}$ $\frac{1}{8}$

40. $v - \dfrac{1}{6} = \dfrac{1}{3}$ $\frac{1}{2}$

41. $s - \dfrac{5}{12} = \dfrac{1}{6}$ $\frac{7}{12}$

42. $\dfrac{1}{3} = x + \dfrac{5}{9}$ $-\frac{2}{9}$

C. 43. $7 - a = -4$ 11

44. $-10 = 15 - x$ 25

45. $3 - s = 5$ −2

46. $7 = 4 - y$ −3

47. $8.64 - x = -4.9$ 13.54

48. $-5.16 = 12.3 - a$

49. $1.3 - y = 6.8$ −5.5

50. $9.32 = 7.26 - c$ −2.06

51. $\dfrac{7}{8} - x = -\dfrac{3}{8}$ $1\frac{1}{4}$

52. $\dfrac{2}{9} = \dfrac{7}{9} - s$ $\frac{5}{9}$

53. $\dfrac{1}{6} - a = \dfrac{3}{4}$ $-\frac{7}{12}$

54. $\dfrac{9}{10} = \dfrac{1}{5} - y$ $-\frac{7}{10}$

CHALLENGE

Find the pattern. $\dfrac{2}{9} = 0.\overline{2}$

$\dfrac{7}{9} = 0.\overline{7}$

$\dfrac{49}{99} = 0.\overline{49}$

$? = 0.\overline{426}$ $\frac{426}{999}$

$? = 0.\overline{2235}$ $\frac{2235}{9999}$

$? = 0.\overline{31779}$ $\frac{31779}{99999}$

OBJECTIVE

Solve an equation by using the multiplication property of equality or the division property of equality.

CLASSROOM EXAMPLES

1. Solve $4y = -76$.

$$4y = -76$$
$$\tfrac{1}{4}(4y) = \tfrac{1}{4}(-76)$$
$$\left(\tfrac{1}{4} \cdot 4\right)y = -19$$
$$y = -19$$

2. Solve $\tfrac{1}{5}y = 12$.

$$\tfrac{1}{5}y = 12$$
$$5\left(\tfrac{1}{5}\right)y = 5(12)$$
$$y = 60$$

3. Solve $\tfrac{x}{3} = 12$.

$$\tfrac{x}{3} = 12$$
$$3\left(\tfrac{x}{3}\right) = 3(12)$$
$$x = 36$$

4. Solve $3x = -15$.

$$3x = -15$$
$$\tfrac{3x}{3} = -\tfrac{15}{3}$$
$$x = -5$$

MIXED REVIEW

1. Perform the indicated operation.
   a. $[-18 - (-3) \div (-5)$ 3
   b. $-64 \div 0.08$ -800
   c. $\left(-\tfrac{5}{6}\right) - \left(-\tfrac{1}{4}\right)$ $-\tfrac{7}{12}$
2. Solve $y - 15 = -38$.
   -23

3.3 Solving Equations, Using Multiplication or Division

If each side of an equation is multiplied by the same nonzero number, the result will be an equation equivalent to the original equation.

Multiplication Property of Equality	If a, b, and c are any real numbers and $a = b$, then $ca = cb$.

From now on, assume that the replacement set is the set of real numbers. Exceptions that are not obvious will be noted.

EXAMPLES

1 **Solve $5x = -45$.**

SOLUTION

$$5x = -45$$
$$\tfrac{1}{5}(5x) = \tfrac{1}{5}(-45) \quad \text{Multiply each side by the reciprocal (multiplicative inverse) of 5.}$$
$$\left(\tfrac{1}{5} \cdot 5\right)x = -9 \quad \text{Associative property of multiplication}$$
$$x = -9$$

CHECK

Replace x in the original equation with -9.
$$5x = -45$$
$$5(-9) \stackrel{?}{=} -45$$
$$-45 = -45 \ \blacktriangleright$$

2 **Solve $\tfrac{1}{3}x = 6$.**

SOLUTION

$$\tfrac{1}{3}x = 6$$
$$3\left(\tfrac{1}{3}x\right) = 3(6) \quad \text{Multiply each side by the reciprocal (multiplicative inverse) of } \tfrac{1}{3}.$$
$$x = 18$$

CHECK

$$\tfrac{1}{3}x = 6$$
$$\tfrac{1}{3}(18) \stackrel{?}{=} 6$$
$$6 = 6 \ \blacktriangleright$$

Solve $\frac{a}{5} = 10$.

SOLUTION

$$\frac{a}{5} = 10$$

$$5\left(\frac{a}{5}\right) = 5(10) \qquad \text{Multiply each side by the reciprocal (multiplicative inverse) of } \frac{1}{5} \text{ because } \frac{a}{5} \text{ means } \frac{1}{5}(a).$$

$$a = 50$$

CHECK

$$\frac{a}{5} = 10$$

$$\frac{50}{5} \overset{?}{=} 10$$

$$10 = 10 \ \vee$$

Some equations are more easily solved if the division property of equality is used instead of the multiplication property of equality.

Division Property of Equality	If a, b, and c are any real numbers, and $a = b$ and $c \neq 0$, then $\frac{a}{c} = \frac{b}{c}$.

4

Solve $5x = -45$.

SOLUTION

$$5x = -45$$

$$\frac{5x}{5} = \frac{-45}{5} \qquad \text{Divide each side by 5.}$$

$$x = -9$$

Compare this equation and its solution to the equation and the solution shown in Example 1.

ORAL EXERCISES

Give the reciprocal (multiplicative inverse) of each number.

1. $\frac{2}{3}$ $\frac{3}{2}$ **2.** $\frac{3}{2}$ $\frac{2}{3}$ **3.** $-\frac{2}{3}$ $-\frac{3}{2}$

4. $-\frac{3}{2}$ $-\frac{2}{3}$ **5.** $\frac{1}{2}$ 2 **6.** $-\frac{1}{2}$ -2

7. 2 $\frac{1}{2}$ **8.** -2 $-\frac{1}{2}$ **9.** -13 $-\frac{1}{13}$

To solve each equation, tell (a) the number each side should be *multiplied* by and (b) the number each side should be *divided* by. Then solve each equation.

10. $3x = 21$ $\frac{1}{3}; 3; 7$ **11.** $-4y = -20$ $-\frac{1}{4}; -4; 5$ **12.** $15 = 5a$ $\frac{1}{5}; 5; 3$

13. $-6b = 18$ $-\frac{1}{6}; -6; -3$ **14.** $-24 = 8m$ $\frac{1}{8}; 8; -3$ **15.** $-15x = -60$

16. $20y = -80$ $\frac{1}{20}; 20; -4$ **17.** $-50 = 75a$ $\frac{1}{75}; 75; -\frac{2}{3}$ **18.** $-25 = -100b$

3. Find the solution set of $x(3 + x) = 18$. The replacement set is $\{-1, 2, 4, 5\}$.
$\{\ \}$

4. Simplify $4.6 + 8 \cdot 4^2$.
132.6

5. Find the next number in the series $\{1, 6, 13, 22, 33, \ldots\}$.   46

TEACHER'S RESOURCE MASTERS

Practice Master 9, Part 2

ASSIGNMENT GUIDE

Minimum
1–24, 29–39 odd

Regular
13–42

Maximum
23–39 odd, 40–60

ADDITIONAL ANSWERS

Oral Exercises
15. $-\frac{1}{15}; -15; 4$
18. $-\frac{1}{100}; -100; \frac{1}{4}$

A. Solve each equation. Check.

1. $8y = 32$ 4
2. $12x = 108$ 9
3. $-7a = -42$ 6
4. $-b = 45$ -45
5. $-6 = -x$ 6
6. $13 = -y$ -13
7. $\frac{1}{3}m = 6$ 18
8. $-\frac{1}{4}n = 12$ -48
9. $9 = \frac{1}{3}y$ 27
10. $-16 = -\frac{1}{8}x$ 128
11. $5x = -60$ -12
12. $-7y = 35$ -5

B.
13. $13a = 91$ 7
14. $8s = -136$ -17
15. $-8x = 824$ -103
16. $12y = -84$ -7
17. $-9s = -108$ 12
18. $-15a = -75$ 5
19. $144 = -12a$ -12
20. $-132 = -11s$ 12
21. $1.2x = 24$ 20
22. $0.8y = 3.2$ 4
23. $-0.13s = 0.104$ -0.8
24. $0.25a = -0.15$ -0.6
25. $14 = 2.8x$ 5
26. $1.46 = 7.3y$ 0.2
27. $\frac{1}{2}a = 1$ 2
28. $\frac{1}{3}s = 39$ 117
29. $\frac{3}{4}y = -6$ -8
30. $-\frac{5}{6}x = 15$ -18
31. $-12 = \frac{2}{3}a$ -18
32. $-5 = -\frac{1}{4}s$ 20
33. $\frac{x}{3} = 12$ 36
34. $\frac{y}{4} = 4$ 16
35. $-\frac{a}{2} = 8$ -16
36. $\frac{s}{3} = -6$ -18
37. $10 = \frac{x}{9}$ 90
38. $-18 = \frac{y}{2}$ -36
39. $\frac{2}{3} = 5a$ $\frac{2}{15}$

C.
40. $\frac{s}{2.4} = 0.2$ 0.48
41. $\frac{x}{6} = \frac{2}{3}$ 4
42. $-\frac{2}{3}y = 1\frac{1}{9}$ $-1\frac{2}{3}$
43. $-\frac{2}{9}a = -\frac{4}{3}$ 6
44. $\frac{4}{5} = \frac{2}{15}s$ 6
45. $-\frac{x}{2} = 1\frac{1}{4}$ $-2\frac{1}{2}$
46. $-\frac{y}{3} = 1\frac{2}{3}$ -5
47. $\frac{a}{3} = \frac{5}{9}$ $1\frac{2}{3}$
48. $-\frac{30}{9} = \frac{5s}{3}$ -2
49. $\frac{x}{7} = -\frac{7}{2}$ $-24\frac{1}{2}$
50. $\frac{5}{6} = -\frac{1}{12}c$ -10
51. $-0.25x = -6$ 24
52. $-0.75t = -9$ 12
53. $\frac{x}{8} = -\frac{9}{4}$ -18
54. $-\frac{s}{5} = -\frac{7}{12}$ $2\frac{11}{12}$

55. Corn muffins cost six for $1.92. How much is one muffin? $0.32

56. A pizza that cost $7.60 was cut into 8 wedges. How much is one piece worth?

57. Gina paid $5.52 to have a roll of film with 24 exposures developed. How much did each print cost? $0.23

58. Vince paid $31.50 for a weekly commuter train ticket. He used the ticket for 10 rides. How much did each ride cost?

59. Greg needs an average of 92 on five math tests to get an A on his report card. His average on the first four tests is 90. What grade must he get on the fifth test to raise his average to 92?   100

60. In a stock-car race, Alfreda averaged 118.5 miles per hour for the first five laps. She wants to average 120 miles per hour for the first six laps. What must her average rate of speed be for the sixth lap?   127.5 miles per hour

3.4 Repeating Decimals

Rational numbers have been defined in Chapter 2 as any numbers that can be expressed in the form $\frac{a}{b}$, where a and b are integers and b is not zero. Every rational number, therefore, can be renamed as a decimal by dividing a by b.

EXAMPLES

1 **Rename $\frac{2}{3}$ as a decimal.**

SOLUTION

$$\frac{2}{3} \rightarrow 3)\overline{2.000\ldots} \quad \begin{array}{r} 0.666\ldots \\ \hline \underline{1\,8} \\ 20 \\ \underline{18} \\ 20 \\ \underline{18} \\ 2 \end{array}$$

$$\frac{2}{3} = 0.666\ldots = 0.\overline{6}$$

2 **Rename $-\frac{3}{11}$ as a decimal.**

SOLUTION

$$\left|-\frac{3}{11}\right| \rightarrow 11)\overline{3.0000\ldots} \quad \begin{array}{r} 0.2727\ldots \\ \hline \underline{2\,2} \\ 80 \\ \underline{77} \\ 30 \\ \underline{22} \\ 80 \\ \underline{77} \\ 3 \end{array}$$

$$-\frac{3}{11} = -0.\overline{27}$$

A bar is used to indicate which digit or digits repeat. $0.\overline{6}$ and $-0.\overline{27}$ are called **repeating decimals.**

3 **Rename $\frac{5}{6}$ as a decimal.**

SOLUTION

$$\frac{5}{6} \rightarrow 6)\overline{5.000\ldots} \quad \begin{array}{r} 0.833\ldots \\ \hline \underline{4\,8} \\ 20 \\ \underline{18} \\ 20 \\ \underline{18} \\ 2 \end{array}$$

$$\frac{5}{6} = 0.8\overline{3}$$

Notice that the bar is only over the 3, because 3 is the only digit that repeats.

4 **Rename $-\frac{5}{8}$ as a decimal.**

SOLUTION

$$\left|-\frac{5}{8}\right| \rightarrow 8)\overline{5.000\ldots} \quad \begin{array}{r} 0.625000\ldots \\ \hline \underline{4\,8} \\ 20 \\ \underline{16} \\ 40 \\ \underline{40} \\ 0 \end{array}$$

$$-\frac{5}{8} = -0.625\overline{0} = -0.625$$

If the only repeating digit is 0, the result is also called a **terminating decimal** and is usually written without the $\overline{0}$.

Every rational number $\frac{a}{b}$ can be renamed as a repeating decimal, and every repeating decimal names a rational number.

OBJECTIVES

Write a rational number as either a repeating decimal or a terminating decimal.

Rename a terminating decimal as a fraction.

Rename a repeating decimal as a fraction.

TEACHER'S NOTES

See p. T25.

CLASSROOM EXAMPLES

1. Rename $\frac{1}{3}$ as a decimal.
$$3)\overline{1.000\ldots} \quad 0.\overline{3}$$

2. Rename $-\frac{1}{9}$ as a decimal.
$$\left|-\frac{1}{9}\right| 9)\overline{1.000\ldots} \quad -0.\overline{1}$$

3. Rename $\frac{1}{6}$ as a decimal.
$$6)\overline{1.000\ldots} \quad 0.1\overline{6}$$

4. Rename $-\frac{3}{8}$ as a decimal.
$$\left|-\frac{3}{8}\right| 8)\overline{3.000\ldots} \quad -0.375$$

5. Rename each decimal as a fraction.
   a. 0.6
   $$0.6 = \frac{6}{10} = \frac{3}{5}$$
   b. -0.52
   $$-0.52 = -\frac{52}{100} = -\frac{13}{25}$$
   c. 0.375
   $$0.375 = \frac{375}{1000} = \frac{3}{8}$$

6. Rename $0.\overline{53}$ as a fraction.
$$\begin{array}{r} 100x = 53.\overline{53} \\ 1x = 0.\overline{53} \\ \hline 99x = 53 \\ x = \frac{53}{99} \end{array}$$

7. Rename $0.\overline{127}$ as a fraction.

$$1000x = 127.\overline{127}$$
$$1x = 0.\overline{127}$$
$$\overline{}$$
$$999x = 127$$
$$x = \frac{127}{999}$$

8. Rename $0.7\overline{32}$ as a fraction.

$$1000x = 732.\overline{32}$$
$$10x = 7.\overline{32}$$
$$\overline{}$$
$$990x = 725$$
$$x = \frac{725}{990} = \frac{145}{198}$$

MIXED REVIEW

1. Solve each equation. Check.
   a. $\frac{y}{6} = \frac{4}{7}$ $3\frac{3}{7}$
   b. $-24a = -168$ 7
   c. $14c + 82 = 165$ $5\frac{13}{14}$
   d. $20x - 53 = 403$ $22\frac{4}{5}$

2. Illustrate the following properties.
   a. distributive property
   b. identity property of addition
   c. transitive property.
   Answers may vary.

3. Simplify $\frac{5 \cdot 8 \cdot 6}{11}$. $3\frac{1}{11}$

4. Perform the indicated operation.
   a. $\frac{3}{8}\left(-\frac{1}{3}\right)$ $-\frac{1}{8}$
   b. $16 - (-20 - 4)$ 40

5. Evaluate if $a = 2$ and $b = 4$.
   a. $\frac{a^2}{b^2}$ $\frac{1}{4}$
   b. $\frac{b^2}{a^2}$ 4

To rename a terminating decimal as a fraction, first express the decimal as a fraction in which the denominator is a power of ten, and then express the fraction in simplest form.

5   **Rename each decimal as a fraction.**
   a. 0.8   **b.** -0.45 **c.** 0.625

SOLUTIONS

a. $0.8 = \frac{8}{10} = \frac{4}{5}$ **b.** $-0.45 = -\frac{45}{100} = -\frac{9}{20}$ **c.** $0.625 = \frac{625}{1000} = \frac{5}{8}$

To rename a repeating decimal as a fraction, use the method shown below.

6   **Rename $0.\overline{45}$ as a fraction.**

SOLUTION

Step 1:   Let $x = 0.4545\ldots$

Step 2:   Multiply *both* sides of the equation by 10^n, so that the block of repeating digits (in this example, 45) is *in front of* the decimal point. The exponent n will be the number of digits in the block of repeating digits (in this example, $n = 2$).

$$10^2 = 100 \qquad 100 \cdot x = 100 \cdot 0.4545\ldots$$
$$100x = 45.\overline{45}$$

Step 3:   Subtract the original equation from the result of Step 2.

$$100x = 45.\overline{45}$$
$$-1x = 0.\overline{45}$$
$$\overline{}$$
$$99x = 45$$

Step 4:   Solve the equation resulting from Step 3.

$$99x = 45$$
$$x = \frac{45}{99} = \frac{5}{11}$$

$$0.\overline{45} = \frac{5}{11}$$

7   **Rename $0.\overline{375}$ as a fraction.**

SOLUTION

Let $x = 0.\dot{3}75375\ldots$

$$1000x = 375.\overline{375}$$
$$-1x = 0.\overline{375}$$
$$\overline{}$$
$$999x = 375$$
$$x = \frac{375}{999} = \frac{125}{333}$$

To rename a repeating decimal as a fraction when only some of the digits after the decimal point repeat, you change *Step 3* above. The original equation is multiplied by some power of 10, so that only the block of repeating digits is *after* the decimal point.

8	**Rename $0.5\overline{38}$ as a fraction.**

SOLUTION

Let $x = 0.5\overline{38}$

$1000x = 538.\overline{38}$

$-\quad 10x = \quad\ 5.\overline{38}$

$990x = 533$

$x = \dfrac{533}{990}$

TEACHER'S RESOURCE MASTERS

Practice Master 1, Part 1

ASSIGNMENT GUIDE

Minimum
1–16, 21–24, 29–32

Regular
13–24, 29–40

Maximum
17–24, 29–32, 37–48

ORAL EXERCISES

Tell which digit or digits repeat for each of the following decimals.

1. $0.666\ldots$ 6
2. $0.1666\ldots$ 6
3. $0.8333\ldots$ 3

4. $5.6363\ldots$ 63
5. $21.1818\ldots$ 18
6. $19.43939\ldots$ 39

7. $2.357357\ldots$ 357
8. $6.340909\ldots$ 09
9. $0.714285714285\ldots$ 714285

WRITTEN EXERCISES

A. Rename each rational number as a terminating or a repeating decimal. If the answer is not a terminating decimal, use a bar to indicate which digits repeat.

1. $\dfrac{2}{3}$ $0.\overline{6}$
2. $\dfrac{3}{4}$ 0.75
3. $-\dfrac{3}{5}$ -0.6
4. $\dfrac{7}{8}$ 0.875

5. $\dfrac{9}{10}$ 0.9
6. $\dfrac{1}{3}$ $0.\overline{3}$
7. $-\dfrac{27}{100}$ -0.27
8. $3\dfrac{1}{5}$ 3.2

9. $6\dfrac{2}{3}$ $6.\overline{6}$
10. $-\dfrac{1}{4}$ -0.25
11. $\dfrac{1}{2}$ 0.5
12. $-6\dfrac{2}{5}$ -6.4

B. 13. $\dfrac{4}{9}$ $0.\overline{4}$
14. $\dfrac{5}{8}$ 0.625
15. $\dfrac{2}{11}$ $0.\overline{18}$
16. $\dfrac{9}{20}$ 0.45

17. $\dfrac{11}{3}$ $3.\overline{6}$
18. $\dfrac{4}{11}$ $0.\overline{36}$
19. $\dfrac{19}{9}$ $2.\overline{1}$
20. $\dfrac{25}{3}$ $8.\overline{3}$

21. $\dfrac{27}{32}$ 0.84375
22. $-\dfrac{82}{75}$ $-1.09\overline{3}$
23. $\dfrac{1}{7}$ $0.\overline{142857}$
24. $-\dfrac{3}{7}$ $-0.\overline{428571}$

Rename each decimal as a fraction in simplest form.

25. 0.3 $\dfrac{3}{10}$
26. 0.78 $\dfrac{39}{50}$
27. 0.375 $\dfrac{3}{8}$
28. $0.\overline{7}$ $\dfrac{7}{9}$

29. $0.\overline{2}$ $\dfrac{2}{9}$
30. $0.\overline{63}$ $\dfrac{7}{11}$
31. $0.\overline{18}$ $\dfrac{2}{11}$
32. $3.1\overline{6}$ $3\dfrac{1}{6}$

33. $4.8\overline{3}$ $4\dfrac{5}{6}$
34. $-5.\overline{47}$ $-5\dfrac{47}{99}$
35. $0.\overline{186}$ $\dfrac{62}{333}$
36. $-0.\overline{262}$ $-\dfrac{262}{999}$

C. 37. $0.\overline{296}$ $\dfrac{8}{27}$
38. $-0.1\overline{27}$ $-\dfrac{7}{55}$
39. $-5.1\overline{3}$ $-5\dfrac{2}{15}$
40. $6.25\overline{4}$ $6\dfrac{14}{55}$

41. $-1.3\overline{78}$ $-1\dfrac{25}{66}$
42. $0.70\overline{4}$ $\dfrac{317}{450}$
43. $0.82\overline{8}$ $\dfrac{373}{450}$
44. $-0.13\overline{8}$ $-\dfrac{5}{36}$

45. $0.21\overline{6}$ $\dfrac{13}{60}$
46. $0.340\overline{9}$ $\dfrac{15}{44}$
47. $0.\overline{142857}$ $\dfrac{1}{7}$
48. $0.\overline{428571}$ $\dfrac{3}{7}$

Solve an equation by using the distributive property to simplify before using the multiplication property of equality or the division property of equality.

TEACHER'S NOTES
See p. T25.

CLASSROOM EXAMPLES

1. Solve $4x + 8x = 36$.

$$4x + 8x = 36$$
$$(4 + 8)x = 36$$
$$12x = 36$$
$$\frac{12x}{12} = \frac{36}{12}$$
$$x = 3$$

2. Solve $8x + (-3)x = 45$.

$$8x + (-3)x = 45$$
$$[8 + (-3)]x = 45$$
$$5x = 45$$
$$\frac{5x}{5} = \frac{45}{5}$$
$$x = 9$$

3. Solve $x - 4x = 18$.

$$x - 4x = 18$$
$$1x + (-4)x = 18$$
$$-3x = 18$$
$$\frac{-3x}{-3} = \frac{18}{-3}$$
$$x = -6$$

MIXED REVIEW

1. Perform the indicated operation.
   a. $-20 - (-18 - 2)$ 0
   b. $-\frac{3}{8} + \frac{1}{5}$ $-\frac{7}{40}$
   c. $0.56 \div (-0.8)$ -0.7
   d. $(3x^3y)(-4x^3y)$
      $-12x^6y^2$

3.5	# Using the Distributive Property

The distributive property can be used to derive an equation of the type $ax = c$ from an equation of the type $bx + dx = c$.

EXAMPLES

1   **Solve $7x + 3x = 20$.**

SOLUTION

$$7x + 3x = 20$$
$$(7 + 3)x = 20 \quad \text{Use the distributive property to combine like terms.}$$
$$10x = 20$$
$$\frac{10x}{10} = \frac{20}{10} \quad \text{Divide each side by 10.}$$
$$x = 2$$

CHECK

$$7x + 3x = 20$$
$$7 \cdot 2 + 3 \cdot 2 \stackrel{?}{=} 20$$
$$14 + 6 \stackrel{?}{=} 20$$
$$20 = 20 \quad ✔$$

2   **Solve $12x + (-5)x = 14$.**

SOLUTION

$$12x + (-5)x = 14$$
$$[12 + (-5)]x = 14 \quad \text{Use the distributive property to combine like terms.}$$
$$7x = 14$$
$$\frac{7x}{7} = \frac{14}{7} \quad \text{Divide each side by 7.}$$
$$x = 2$$

Remember to check.

3   **Solve $y - 6y = 20$.**

SOLUTION

$$y - 6y = 20$$
$$(1)y + (-6)y = 20 \quad \text{Use the distributive property to combine like terms.}$$
$$-5y = 20$$
$$\frac{-5y}{-5} = \frac{20}{-5} \quad \text{Divide each side by } -5.$$
$$y = -4$$

Remember to check.

Apply the distributive property to combine like terms.

1. $3x + 2x$ $5x$　　　　**2.** $3x + (-2)x$ x　　　　**3.** $3x - 2x$ x

4. $2x + (-2)x$ 0　　　**5.** $2x - 3x$ $-x$　　　**6.** $2x + 4x$ $6x$

7. $2x + x$ $3x$　　　　**8.** $2x - 7x$ $-5x$　　　**9.** $2x - x$ x

A. Solve each equation. Check.

1. $6x + 3x = 18$ 2　　**2.** $5a + 6a = 22$ 2　　**3.** $15 = 4y + y$ 3

4. $-2y + (-5y) = -21$　　**5.** $14 = 6s + s$ 2　　**6.** $-12 = -3x + (-3x)$

7. $32 = 8a + (-4a)$ 8　　**8.** $-5x + (-7x) = -12$ 1　　**9.** $-15 = -3y + (-2y)$

10. $x + 4x = 25$ 5　　**11.** $24 = 5y + y$ 4　　**12.** $4x + 6x = 25$ $2\frac{1}{2}$

B. 13. $24 = 5y + 3y$ 3　　**14.** $-21 = -4s + (-3s)$ 3 **15.** $-6x + (-2x) = -32$

16. $5y + (-4y) = 2$ 2　　**17.** $-3a + 7a = 36$ 9　　**18.** $42 = 12y + (-5y)$

19. $0.6x + 0.3x = 3.6$ 4　　**20.** $1.2y + 0.6y = 5.4$ 3　　**21.** $0.5s + 2.1s = 0.52$

22. $-0.4a + (-0.2a) = -0.18$ 0.3　　**23.** $-4.3x + (-1.5x) = -5.8$ 1

24. $0.9y + (-0.5y) = 2$ 5　　　**25.** $1.2s + (-0.7s) = 1.5$ 3

26. $\frac{1}{2}x + \frac{3}{2}x = 8$ 4　　**27.** $\frac{1}{3}y + \frac{5}{3}y = 12$ 6　　**28.** $\frac{1}{2}a + \frac{2}{3}a = 21$ 18

29. $\frac{1}{5}s + \frac{3}{4}s = 38$ 40　　**30.** $\frac{1}{4}x + \frac{2}{3}x = 22$ 24　　**31.** $\frac{1}{3}y + \frac{1}{2}y = 15$ 18

32. $14a - 8a = 48$ 8　　**33.** $9x - 6x = 15$ 5　　**34.** $4y - y = 27$ 9

35. $4s - 7s = 18$ -6　　**36.** $16 = 7x - 11x$ -4　　**37.** $y - 6y = -30$ 6

38. $-5a - (-7a) = 10$ 5　　**39.** $-16 = -11s - 5s$ 1　　**40.** $3x - (-2x) = -25$

-5

C. 41. $-2\frac{1}{2}x + \left(-1\frac{1}{3}x\right) = 7$ $-1\frac{19}{23}$　　**42.** $1\frac{3}{4}y + 2\frac{1}{2}y = 9$ $2\frac{2}{17}$

43. $-3\frac{1}{2}a - \left(-2\frac{1}{2}a\right) = 15$ -15　　**44.** $5a - 3\frac{1}{4}a = 7$ 4

45. $-6\frac{1}{4}x + 9\frac{3}{4}x = 14$ 4　　**46.** $-2\frac{2}{3}y - 5\frac{5}{6}y = 4\frac{1}{4}$ $-\frac{1}{2}$

47. $-3.6s + (-0.8s) = 0.88$ -0.2　　**48.** $-0.7x - 2.4x = -31$ 10

Solve for x. Let a, b, c, and d be any nonzero rational number where $a \neq c$ and $b \neq d$. Let x be any rational number.

49. $ax = b$ $x = \frac{b}{a}$　　　　　**50.** $cx = d$ $x = \frac{d}{c}$

51. $ax - cx = d$ $x = \frac{d}{a - c}$　　　**52.** $bx + dx = c$ $x = \frac{c}{b + d}$

---

2. Graph the set $\{-3, -2, 1, 2, 3\}$ on the number line.

3. Evaluate if $a = -6$ and $b = 2$.

   a. $4^2(a^2)(b)$ 1152

   b. $\left(\frac{b}{a}\right)^2$ $\frac{1}{9}$

4. Simplify $(16x^3y)\left(-\frac{1}{8}xy^3\right)$.

   $-2x^4y^4$

5. Simplify $\frac{3^2 \cdot 2^2}{8}$. $4\frac{1}{2}$

TEACHER'S RESOURCE MASTERS

Practice Master 1, Part 2

Quiz 5

ASSIGNMENT GUIDE

Minimum
1–11 Odd, 13–31

Regular
13–39 odd, 41–50

Maximum
19–37, 41–52

ADDITIONAL ANSWERS

Written Exercises

   4. 3

   6. 2

   9. 3

   15. 4

   18. 6

   21. 0.2

SELF-QUIZ

Find the solution set of each equation if the replacement set is $\{-4, -1, 2\}$.

1. $x + 5 = 4$ −1

2. $y + (-3) = -7$ −4

Solve each equation. Check.

3. $-7 + c = -10$

4. $a - 4 = -3$ 1

5. $7x = 28$ 4

6. $\frac{z}{3} = -5$

7. $\frac{-3b}{4} = 15$ −20

8. $-\frac{a}{7} = -2$ 14

9. $-7x + 4x = 21$

10. $10y - y = 36$

Rename each rational number as a terminating or a repeating decimal. If the answer is not a terminating decimal, use a bar to indicate which digits repeat.

11. $\frac{7}{8}$ 0.875

12. $\frac{5}{9}$ $0.\overline{5}$

13. $\frac{8}{11}$ $0.\overline{72}$

14. $\frac{5}{6}$ $0.8\overline{3}$

Rename each decimal as a fraction in simplest form.

15. 0.4 $\frac{2}{5}$

16. 2.16 $2\frac{4}{25}$

17. $1.\overline{3}$ $1\frac{1}{3}$

18. $0.\overline{27}$ $\frac{3}{11}$

SKILLS MAINTENANCE

Evaluate if $x = -2$, $y = 3$, and $z = 4.8$.

1. $15 - x$ 17

2. $x - 5$ −7

3. $y - 10$ −7

4. $4x$ −8

5. $-8xy$ 48

6. $-3(z - 6)$ 3.6

7. $x^2 + x$ 2

8. $y^2x - yx^2$ −30

9. $z^2 - 2z$ 13.44

10. $3(x + y)$ 3

11. $x(5 - y)$ −4

12. $10(z - x)$ 68

Write each of the following as an algebraic expression:

13. the product of m and n mn

14. the difference of x and y $x - y$

15. four times the sum of s and t $4(s + t)$

16. d divided by r $\frac{d}{r}$

Name the property illustrated.

17. $c + d = d + c$ Comm. prop. of add.

18. $b(cd) = (bc)d$ Assoc. prop. of mult.

19. $(x + y)z = xz + yz$ Dist. prop.

20. $ab = ba$ Comm. prop. of mult.

Use the sets below for exercises 21–24. Complete each statement, using $\in$, $\notin$, $\subset$, or $\not\subset$.

$A = \{0, 1, 2, 3\}$ $\quad B = \{0, 2, 4\}$ $\quad C = \{1, 3\}$ $\quad D = \{\ \}$

21. C $\underline{\ \subset\ }$ A

22. 0 $\underline{\ \notin\ }$ C

23. 2 $\underline{\ \in\ }$ B

24. D $\underline{\ \subset\ }$ A

Which symbol, $=$, $<$, or $>$, should replace each ●?

25. 2.3 ● −4.9 $>$

26. $-5\frac{7}{8}$ ● $-6\frac{1}{2}$ $>$

27. 8.01 ●80.1 $<$

28. 426 ● 451 $<$

Complete.

29. $|-7| = \underline{\ \ 7\ \ }$

30. $|15| = \underline{\ \ 15\ \ }$

31. $-\left|\frac{7}{8}\right| = \underline{\ -\frac{7}{8}\ }$

32. $-\left|-1\frac{2}{3}\right| = \underline{\ -1\frac{2}{3}\ }$

3.6 | Solving Two-Step Equations

OBJECTIVE

Solve an equation by using the addition or the subtraction property of equality and then the multiplication or the division property of equality.

Sometimes more than one property of equality must be used to solve an equation. First use the addition or the subtraction property of equality, then use the multiplication or the division property of equality.

TEACHER'S NOTES

See p. T25.

EXAMPLES

1 **Solve $4x + 6 = 22$.**

SOLUTION $4x + 6 = 22$

$4x + 6 - 6 = 22 - 6$ *Subtract 6 from each side.*

$4x = 16$

$\dfrac{4x}{4} = \dfrac{16}{4}$ *Divide each side by 4.*

$x = 4$

CHECK $4x + 6 = 22$

$4 \cdot 4 + 6 \stackrel{?}{=} 22$

$16 + 6 \stackrel{?}{=} 22$

$22 = 22$ ✔

2 **Solve $-8 + \frac{3n}{5} = 13$.**

SOLUTION $-8 + \dfrac{3n}{5} = 13$

$-8 + \dfrac{3n}{5} + 8 = 13 + 8$ *Add 8 to each side.*

$\dfrac{3n}{5} = 21$

$\dfrac{5}{3}\left(\dfrac{3n}{5}\right) = \dfrac{5}{3}(21)$ *Multiply each side by the reciprocal of $\frac{3}{5}$.*

$n = 35$

Remember to check.

When there is a variable on each side of an equation, choose either variable term and add its opposite to each side. No matter which side of the equation you start with, the solution will be the same.

3 **Solve $5x + 6 = -3x + 22$.**

SOLUTION $5x + 6 = -3x + 22$

$3x + 5x + 6 = 3x + (-3x) + 22$ *Add 3x to each side.*

$8x + 6 = 22$

$8x + 6 - 6 = 22 - 6$ *Subtract 6 from each side.*

$8x = 16$

$\dfrac{8x}{8} = \dfrac{16}{8}$ *Divide each side by 8.*

$x = 2$

Remember to check.

CLASSROOM EXAMPLES

1. Solve $3y + 8 = 35$.

$3y + 8 = 35$

$3y + 8 - 8 = 35 - 8$

$3y = 27$

$\dfrac{3y}{3} = \dfrac{27}{3}$

$y = 9$

2. Solve $-6 + \frac{2n}{4} = 18$.

$-6 + \dfrac{2n}{4} = 18$

$-6 + \dfrac{2n}{4} + 6 = 18 + 6$

$\dfrac{2n}{4} = 24$

$\dfrac{4}{2}\left(\dfrac{2n}{4}\right) = \dfrac{4}{2}(24)$

$n = 48$

3. Solve $4y + 12 = -2y + 30$.

$4y + 12 = -2y + 30$

$2y + 4y + 12 = 2y + (-2y) + 30$

$6y + 12 = 30$

$6y + 12 - 12 = 30 - 12$

$6y = 18$

$\dfrac{6y}{6} = \dfrac{18}{6}$

$y = 3$

1. Find the solution set of $c^2 = 36$. The replacement set is $\{-6, -2, 2, 6\}$. $\{-6, 6\}$

2. Graph on the number line $\{x | x$ is the set of odd counting numbers$\}$.

3. Evaluate if $d = 3$, $e = -4$ and $f = -2$. $(de) + f$
   -14

4. Simplify $3(4xy^3 + 2xy^3)$.
   $18xy^3$

5. Solve each equation.
   a. $3a = -24$ -8
   b. $\frac{2a}{3} = -14$ -21

TEACHER'S RESOURCE MASTERS

Practice Master 11, Part 1

ASSIGNMENT GUIDE

Minimum
1–53 odd

Regular
19–51

Maximum
13–53 odd, 55–62, 65–68

ORAL EXERCISES

Compare each pair of equations and tell whether they are equivalent.

1. $3x + 6 = 18$; $3x = 12$ yes
2. $2x - 5 = 7$; $2x = 12$ yes
3. $4x - 6 = 14$; $4x = 8$ no
4. $6x + 8 = 20$; $6x = 12$ yes
5. $3x + 2 = 14$; $x = 4$ yes
6. $2x - 6 = 4$; $x = 1$ no
7. $6x + 16 = -2x$; $8x = 16$ no
8. $4x + 14 = -3x$; $7x = -14$ yes
9. $6 - 3x = 6x - 3$; $x = 1$ yes
10. $9 - 2x = 9x - 2$; $x = -1$ no

WRITTEN EXERCISES

A. Tell how each equation was derived from the equation above.

1. $6x + 3 = 2x - 5$
   $4x + 3 = -5$ Subt. $2x$.
   $4x = -8$ Subt. 3.
   $x = -2$ Div. by 4.

2. $y - 12 = -9y + 18$
   $10y - 12 = 18$ Add $9y$.
   $10y = 30$ Add 12.
   $y = 3$ Div. by 10.

3. $-3a + 4 = 2a - 6$
   $-5a + 4 = -6$ Subt. $2a$.
   $-5a = -10$ Subt. 4.
   $a = 2$ Div. by -5.

4. $9s - 4 = 8 + 6s$
   $3s - 4 = 8$ Subt. $6s$.
   $3s = 12$ Add 4.
   $s = 4$ Div. by 3.

5. $8x - 6 = 5x + 9$
   $3x - 6 = 9$ Subt. $5x$.
   $3x = 15$ Add 6.
   $x = 5$ Div. by 3.

6. $x - 16 = 7x + 2$
   $-16 = 6x + 2$ Subt. x.
   $-18 = 6x$ Subt. 2.
   $-3 = x$ Div. by 6.

7. $10 - 2a = -a + 16$
   $10 - a = 16$ Add a.
   $-a = 6$ Subt. 10.
   $a = -6$ Div. by -1.

8. $14 + (-3y) = -5y + 20$
   $14 + 2y = 20$ Add $5y$.
   $2y = 6$ Subt. 14.
   $y = 3$ Div. by 2.

9. $-9 + 6s = 5 - s$
   $-9 + 7s = 5$ Add s.
   $7s = 14$ Add 9.
   $s = 2$ Div. by 7.

10. $-4x - 3 = x - 8$
    $-3 = 5x - 8$ Add $4x$.
    $5 = 5x$ Add 8.
    $1 = x$ Div. by 5.

11. $x + 9 = 30 - 2x$
    $3x + 9 = 30$ Add $2x$.
    $3x = 21$ Subt. 9.
    $x = 7$ Div. by 3.

12. $7x + 8 = 5x - 12$
    $2x + 8 = -12$ Subt. $5x$.
    $2x = -20$ Subt. 8.
    $x = -10$ Div. by 2.

B. Solve each equation. Check.

13. $4x + 1 = 17$ $\quad 4$

14. $3y + 2 = 23$ $\quad 7$

15. $5s - 2 = 3$ $\quad 1$

16. $2a - 3 = 5$ $\quad 4$

17. $-6x + 4 = 16$ $\quad -2$

18. $-5y + 7 = 27$ $\quad -4$

19. $3 - 5s = 0$ $\quad \frac{3}{5}$

20. $12a - 10 = 26$ $\quad 3$

21. $10x - 9 = 11$ $\quad 2$

22. $\frac{1}{3}y - 2 = 5$ $\quad 21$

23. $\frac{1}{4}a - 1 = 3$ $\quad 16$

24. $5 - 6x = 0$ $\quad \frac{5}{6}$

25. $-15 = 3s - 9$ $\quad -2$

26. $-4 = 2x - 10$ $\quad 3$

27. $3y + 0.8 = y$ $\quad -0.4$

28. $5a + 0.9 = 2a$ $\quad -0.3$

29. $\frac{1}{7}s + \frac{2}{7} = -\frac{5}{7}$ $\quad -7$

30. $-\frac{1}{4} = \frac{1}{4}x + \frac{3}{4}$ $\quad -4$

31. $-3a = 11 - 2a$ $\quad -11$

32. $-4s = 13 - 3s$ $\quad -13$

33. $4y - 7 = -3y$ $\quad 1$

34. $3x - 9 = -6x$ $\quad 1$

35. $\frac{2}{3}a - 2 = 4$ $\quad 9$

36. $\frac{3}{4}s - 4 = 8$ $\quad 16$

37. $\frac{5}{2}x + 12 = 2$ $\quad -4$

38. $\frac{7}{2}y - 4 = 10$ $\quad 4$

39. $-5 + \frac{4a}{3} = 7$ $\quad 9$

40. $2s + 7 = -s + 9$ $\quad \frac{2}{3}$

41. $2x + 5 = -2x + 8$ $\quad \frac{3}{4}$

42. $4x - 6 = 3x - 4$ $\quad 2$

43. $3x - 4 = 2x - 6$ $\quad -2$

44. $7y + 5 = 5y - 7$ $\quad -6$

45. $4a - 3 = a + 6$ $\quad 3$

46. $6x - 2 = x + 13$ $\quad 3$

47. $17 - 2s = 2 + s$ $\quad 5$

48. $3 - y = 6y + 24$

49. $-4 + a = -6a - 11$

50. $12x - 6 = 8x + 10$ $\quad 4$

51. $7 - 6y = -4y - 5$

52. $-3 - 6s = -8 - 2s$

53. $\frac{2}{5}a - 2 = \frac{1}{5}a + 4$ $\quad 30$

54. $\frac{1}{3}x - \frac{5}{3} = -\frac{2}{3}x + \frac{1}{3}$

C.

55. $\frac{3}{4}y + 8 = \frac{1}{2}y + 4$ $\quad -16$

56. $-\frac{5}{6}s - \frac{1}{6} = -\frac{1}{3}s + \frac{11}{6}$ $\quad -4$

57. $\frac{2}{7}y - \frac{5}{7}y = \frac{3}{7}y + 1$ $\quad -1\frac{1}{6}$

58. $\frac{3}{8}a + \frac{7}{8}a = \frac{5}{8}a + 3$ $\quad 4\frac{4}{5}$

59. $-4(2a - 5) = -4a + 10$ $\quad 2\frac{1}{2}$

60. $3(4x - 2) = 4x - (2x - 14)$ $\quad 2$

61. $5(6x + 5) = -12x - 7$ $\quad -\frac{16}{21}$

62. $-3(8y - 7) = 15 - (4y + 4)$ $\quad \frac{1}{2}$

Solve each equation for x. Let a, b, c, and d be any nonzero rational number where $a \neq c$ and $b \neq -d$. Let x be any rational number.

63. $x + a = c$ $\quad x = c - a$

64. $ax + b = c$ $\quad x = \frac{c - b}{a}$

65. $ax + b = cx + d$ $\quad x = \frac{d - b}{a - c}$

66. $ax - b = c + b$ $\quad x = \frac{c + 2b}{a}$

67. Three of the Great Lakes—Erie, Michigan, and Superior—cover a combined area of 63,910 square miles. The area of Lake Erie is 12,390 square miles less than the area of Lake Michigan. The combined area of Lake Erie and Lake Michigan is 510 square miles more than the area of Lake Superior. What is the area of each lake?

68. In a local election, Candidate A received 25% more voters than Candidate B. Candidate B received 8% more than twice the percent of votes that Candidate C received. Candidate A received 3% more than 5 times the percent of votes that Candidate C received. What percent of the votes did each candidate receive? A: 53%; B: 28%; C: 10%

OBJECTIVE

Solve an equation by using the distributive property, the addition or the subtraction property, and the multiplication or the division property of equality.

3.7 | Practice With Equations

In the following example, the equation is first simplified, using the distributive property, and then solved, using the subtraction and the division properties of equality.

EXAMPLES

CLASSROOM EXAMPLES

1. Solve
$3y + 8y + 4y + 5 = 50$.
$3y + 8y + 4y + 5 = 50$
$(3 + 8 + 4)y + 5 = 50$
$15y + 5 = 50$
$15y + 5 - 5 = 50$
$\qquad\qquad\qquad -5$
$15y = 45$
$\frac{15y}{15} = \frac{45}{15}$
$y = 3$

2. Solve $4(3y + 6) = 60$.
Method I
$4(3y + 6) = 60$
$12y + 24 = 60$
$12y + 24 - 24 = 60 - 24$
$12y = 36$
$\frac{12y}{12} = \frac{36}{12}$
$y = 3$

Method II
$4(3y + 6) = 60$
$\frac{4(3y + 6)}{4} = \frac{60}{4}$
$3y + 6 = 15$
$3y + 6 - 6 = 15 - 6$
$3y = 9$
$\frac{3y}{3} = \frac{9}{3}$
$y = 3$

1 | **Solve $4x + 3x + 2x + 6 = 24$.**

SOLUTION

$4x + 3x + 2x + 6 = 24$
$(4 + 3 + 2)x + 6 = 24$ *Use the distributive property to combine like terms.*
$9x + 6 = 24$
$9x + 6 - 6 = 24 - 6$ *Subtract 6 from each side.*
$9x = 18$
$\frac{9x}{9} = \frac{18}{9}$ *Divide each side by 9.*
$x = 2$

CHECK

$4x \quad + 3x \quad + 2x \quad + 6 = 24$
$4(2) + 3(2) + 2(2) + 6 \overset{?}{=} 24$
$8 + 6 + 4 + 6 \overset{?}{=} 24$
$24 = 24$ ✔

2 | **Solve $3(2x + 4) = 42$.**

SOLUTION

Note that in Method I, 3 is eliminated by using the distributive property. In Method II, 3 is eliminated by division.

Method I
$3(2x + 4) = 42$
$6x + 12 = 42$
$6x + 12 - 12 = 42 - 12$
$6x = 30$
$\frac{6x}{6} = \frac{30}{6}$
$x = 5$

CHECK
$3(2x + 4) = 42$
$3(2 \cdot 5 + 4) \overset{?}{=} 42$
$3(10 + 4) \overset{?}{=} 42$
$42 = 42$ ✔

Method II
$3(2x + 4) = 42$
$\frac{3(2x + 4)}{3} = \frac{42}{3}$
$2x + 4 = 14$
$2x + 4 - 4 = 14 - 4$
$2x = 10$
$\frac{2x}{2} = \frac{10}{2}$
$x = 5$

Tell whether the equations in each pair are equivalent.

1. $3(2x + 1) = 9$; $6x + 3 = 9$ yes

2. $2(4x + 3) = 22$; $4x + 3 = 11$ yes

3. $3x - 6x + 9x - 8 = 10$; $18x - 8 = 10$

4. $8x - 5 = 2x + 7$; $6x = 12$ yes

5. $3x - 4 = -2x + 11$; $5x = 7$ no

6. $3(x + 4) - 2x = 14$; $3x + 4 - 2x = 14$

7. $4(x + 3) = x + 15$; $4x + 12 = x + 15$

8. $5(x + 2) = 4(x - 2)$; $5x + 2 = 4x - 2$

WRITTEN EXERCISES

A. Solve each equation. Check.

1. $7y - 6 = 4y + 9$ 5

2. $2(3x + 4) = 20$ 2

3. $4(a + 2) - 3a = 17$ 9

4. $3(s + 2) = s + 8$ 1

5. $4(x + 3) = 2(x - 2)$ -8

6. $2x - 5x + 13x + 6 = 36$ 3

7. $y + 3y + 5y + 4 = 22$ 2

8. $4a + a + 3a + 10 = 34$ 3

9. $10s + 2s + 3s + 4 = 34$ 2

10. $5x - 8x + 10x - 10 = 11$ 3

B. 11. $4x + 2 = 14$ 3

12. $3y + 5 = 17$ 4

13. $a - 4 = 6$ 10

14. $3s + 5 = 2s + 1$ -4

15. $2x + 8 = x + 3$ -5

16. $5y - 3 = y + 13$ 4

17. $\frac{1}{4}a - \frac{3}{4}a - 3 = 9$ -24

18. $-\frac{1}{5}x + \frac{3}{5}x + 2 = 3$ $2\frac{1}{2}$

19. $-3(2y - 5) = -3y$ 5

20. $-2(3a - 4) = -4a$ 4

21. $-2s + 6s - 5s = 14$ -14

22. $3x - 8x + 2x = 18$ -6

23. $1.2y = 7.2 + 0.8y$ 18

24. $7.3a = -16.5 + 1.3a$ -2.75

25. $6(-3x + 4) = -10x + 8$ 2

26. $4(-2y + 5) = -4y + 4$ 4

27. $7 - (5a + 5) = -a$ $\frac{1}{2}$

28. $8 - (7s + 5) = -s$ $\frac{1}{2}$

29. $2x = 12x - (7x - 15)$ -5

30. $3y = 9y - (3y - 18)$ -6

31. $-(17a - 43) = 6a - 26$ 3

32. $-(18x - 21) = 7x - 29$ 2

33. $2(y - 4) - 3(y - 1) = 4$ -9

34. $3(x - 3) - 2(x + 1) = 5$ 16

35. $5(4s - 2) = 2(2s - 1)$ $\frac{1}{2}$

36. $2(5a - 2) = 3(3a + 4)$ 16

37. $5y + 1 = 4(y - 2)$ -9

38. $3x + 4 = 2(x - 2)$ -8

39. $3(2y + 4) = 5(3y + 6)$ -2

40. $4(3a - 6) = 2(4a + 8)$ 10

C. 41. $\frac{3}{8}x + \frac{1}{4}x + \frac{1}{2}x - 6 = 30$ 32

42. $\frac{1}{2}y + \frac{5}{6}y + \frac{2}{3}y + 4 = 12$ 4

43. $4.9y - 3.2y + 5.3y - 4.2 = 16.8$ 3

44. $2.1(2x + 0.8) + 3.36 = 0.6(1.3x - 3)$

45. $\frac{3}{4}(8a - 12) + \frac{1}{2} = \frac{1}{3}(9a + 6)$ $3\frac{1}{2}$

46. $0.5(2a - 3.2) + 4 = 1.2(0.3a + 4)$

MIXED REVIEW

1. Solve each equation.
   a. $3a + 15 = -2a - 18$
      $-6\frac{3}{5}$
   b. $63 = 6x + x$ 9
   c. $3y - (-2y) = -24$ -4
   d. $\frac{2}{3}y + \frac{1}{3}y = -54$ -54

2. Rename $0.\overline{043}$ as a fraction. $\frac{43}{999}$

3. Rename 0.18 as a fraction. $\frac{9}{50}$

4. Name the property illustrated.
   a. $a(bc) = (ab)c$ Assoc. prop. of mult.
   b. $ab = ba$ Comm. prop. of mult.

5. Complete.
   a. $-\left|\frac{5}{6}\right|$ $-\frac{5}{6}$
   b. $-\left|-3\frac{1}{2}\right|$ $-3\frac{1}{2}$

TEACHER'S RESOURCE MASTERS

Practice Master 11, Part 2

ASSIGNMENT GUIDE

Minimum
1–10, 19–36

Regular
11–38

Maximum
11–39 odd, 41–53

ADDITIONAL ANSWERS

Oral Exercises

3. no

6. no

7. yes

(continued on next page)

Solve each equation for x. Assume that no replacements are allowed for variables that will make a denominator 0.

47. $a(x + b) = c$ $\quad x = \frac{c}{a} - b$

48. $ax + bx + cx + d = e$ $\quad x = \frac{e - d}{a + b + c}$

49. $a(x + b) = c(x + d)$ $\quad x = \frac{cd - ab}{a - c}$

50. $ax - bx = c(x + d)$ $\quad x = \frac{cd}{a - b - c}$

51. Consecutive positive integers are integers in counting order, such as 1, 2, 3, 4. Find two consecutive positive integers such that 3 times the first integer plus 5 times the second integer is equal to 197.   24 and 25

52. Find 3 consecutive odd integers such that the sum of the first and twice the second is 73.

53. Six times a number decreased by 3 more than 4 times the number is 357. What is the number?   180

IN OTHER FIELDS
Mathematics and Athletics

Most high-school athletic teams require a student to have a physical examination before participation is allowed. This is to safeguard the health of the student because the vigorous exercise usually required in most sports can make existing health problems worse.

The heart is a muscle that pumps blood to the rest of the body. If a person is fit, the heart will pump more blood with each beat, but the heart won't pump as often as it will in a person who is not fit. To avoid overtaxing the heart, you can determine how fast your heart should beat per minute while you are exercising.

1. Subtract your age from 220. This will provide your *maximum* heart rate.

2. While resting, count your pulse for 10 seconds, then multiply by 6. This will provide your *resting* heart rate.

To figure out how fast your heart should beat during exercise, use your answers to numbers 1 and 2 above.

3. Subtract your resting heart rate from your maximum heart rate.

4. Find 75% of the difference.

5. Add your answer to your resting heart rate.

While exercising, check your pulse. If it is higher than your answer to number 5, slow down. If it is lower, exercise a little harder or faster.

3.8 Problem Solving—Formulas

OBJECTIVE

Solve a problem by using a formula, substituting given values into the formula, and then solving for the unknown variable in this formula.

A **formula** is an equation that states a rule. Often formulas are helpful in solving problems. **Using a formula** is one of several problem-solving strategies. In this lesson you will use this strategy to solve each problem. Some common formulas follow:

$d = rt$ Distance = rate · time

$A = bh$ Area of a rectangle = base · height

$V = \frac{1}{3}\pi r^2 h$ Volume of a cone = $\frac{1}{3}$(3.14)(radius squared)(height). Use 3.14 as an approximation for π.

$P = 2(l + w)$ Perimeter of a rectangle = 2(length + width)

$I = prt$ Interest = principal · annual rate · time in years

$C = np$ Cost = number of items · price per item

When you solve problems, you can use any formula that is helpful.

TEACHER'S NOTES

See p. T25.

EXAMPLE

Juanita borrowed $5000 from a bank to help pay her college expenses. She paid the loan back after 2 years, and the interest amounted to $1300. What annual rate of interest did the bank charge Juanita? Use the formula $I = prt$; interest = principal · annual rate expressed as a decimal · time in years.

Understand: *Given:*   The principal (amount borrowed) was $5000.
                    The interest was $1300.
                    The time (in years) was 2 years.
                    The formula is $I = prt$.

             To find: the annual rate of interest

Plan: Substitute 1300 for I, 5000 for p, and 2 for t in the formula.

$$I = prt$$
$$1300 = 5000 \cdot r \cdot 2$$

Solve: $1300 = 5000 \cdot r \cdot 2$
$$1300 = 10{,}000r$$
$$\frac{1{,}300}{10{,}000} = \frac{10{,}000r}{10{,}000}$$
$$0.13 = r$$

Since rate of interest is usually expressed as a percent, change 0.13 to 13%.

Answer: The bank charged Juanita 13% annual interest.

Review: Substitute 0.13 for r in the formula.

$$I = prt$$
$$1300 \stackrel{?}{=} 5000(0.13)(2)$$
$$1300 = 1300 \quad ✔$$

CLASSROOM EXAMPLE

Roger borrowed $3000 from the bank. He repaid the loan during a period of four years. If he paid $1080 interest, determine the annual rate of interest charged by the bank.

$1080 = 3000 \cdot r \cdot 4$
$1080 = 12{,}000r$
$\frac{1080}{12{,}000} = \frac{12{,}000r}{12{,}000}$
$0.09 = r$
$0.09 = 9\%$

MIXED REVIEW

1. Find three consecutive even numbers whose sum is 84.   26, 28, 30

2. Solve $2(3y + 5) = 42$. $5\frac{1}{3}$

3. Simplify $\{[6(5 - 8) + 2]3\} - 6$. -54

4. Solve $x - 4\frac{1}{2} = -18$. $-13\frac{1}{2}$

5. Karen paid $228 for a monthly train ticket. She used the ticket for 19 rides. Determine the cost per ride.　$12

6. Evaluate if $a = -3$ and $b = 1.5$. $a^2(b)$　13.5

TEACHER'S RESOURCE MASTERS

Practice Master 12, Part 1

ASSIGNMENT GUIDE

Minimum
1–8, 11–17 odd

Regular
11–22

Maximum
13–18, 21–26

ADDITIONAL ANSWERS

Oral Exercises

1. $V = 10(9)(8)$

2. $P = 2(15 + 12)$

3. $A = 23(16)$

4. $d = 55(4)$

5. $P = 4(12)$

6. $A = \left(13\frac{1}{2}\right)^2$

7. $C = 3.14(3)$

8. $A = 3.14(5^2)$

9. $1.29 = 6p$

10. $I = 2000(0.12)(1.5)$

ORAL EXERCISES

Name the equation you would use to solve each problem. Use the given formula.

1. If a toolshed is 10 feet long, 9 feet wide, and 8 feet high, what is the volume? Use $V = lwh$; Volume = length · width · height.

2. What is the distance around a rectangular picture frame that is 15 inches long and 12 inches wide? Use $P = 2(l + w)$; Perimeter = 2(length + width).

3. A rectangular floor is 23 feet long and 16 feet wide. What is the area of the floor? Use $A = lw$; Area = length · width.

4. How far will a motorist travel if he averages 55 miles per hour for 4 hours? Use $d = rt$; distance = rate · time.

5. What is the distance around a square flowerbed that is 12 meters on one side? Use $P = 4s$; Perimeter = 4 · side.

6. What is the floor area of a square room $13\frac{1}{2}$ feet on one side? Use $A = s^2$; Area = side squared.

7. What is the distance around a circular rug that is 3 meters in diameter? Use $C = \pi d$; Circumference = 3.14 · diameter.

8. What is the area of a circular pond that has a radius of 5 meters? Use $A = \pi r^2$; Area = 3.14 · radius squared.

9. What is the price per item if 6 items cost $1.29? Use $C = np$; Cost = number of items · price per item.

10. What is the interest due on a loan of $2000 at 12% for $1\frac{1}{2}$ years? Use $I = prt$; Interest = principal · rate · time.

WRITTEN EXERCISES

A. Use the formulas given for each geometric figure to find the required quantity. Use 3.14 for π.

P = perimeter　　A = area　　C = circumference　　S = surface area　　V = volume

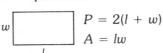

$P = 2(l + w)$
$A = lw$

$P = a + b + c$
$A = \frac{1}{2}bh$

$C = 2\pi r$
$A = \pi r^2$

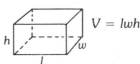

$V = lwh$

$S = 2\pi r^2 + 2\pi rh$
$V = \pi r^2 h$

$S = 4\pi r^2$
$V = \frac{4}{3}\pi r^3$

1. perimeter of a rectangle if $l = 12$ feet and $w = 8$ feet　40 ft

2. area of a triangle if $b = 14$ inches and $h = 8$ inches　56 in²

3. circumference of a circle if $r = 10$ feet　62.8 ft

4. area of a rectangle if $l = 25$ meters and $w = 13$ meters　325 m²

5. perimeter of a triangle if $a = 10$ inches, $b = 15$ inches, and $c = 12$ inches　37 in.

6. volume of a rectangular solid if $l = 15$ inches, $w = 12$ inches, and $h = 10$ inches　1800 in³

7. area of a circle if $r = 8$ cm　200.96 cm²

8. surface area of a cylinder if $r = 8$ feet and $h = 20$ feet　1406.72 ft²

9. volume of a cylinder if $r = 6$ feet and $h = 10$ feet   1130.4 ft³

10. volume of a sphere if $r = 9$ inches   3052.08 in³

B. Decide which of the following formulas is the correct one to use for each problem and use that formula to solve the problem.

$I = prt$	Interest = principal · annual rate · time in years
$d = rt$	Distance = rate (how fast) · time (how long)
$A = \frac{1}{2}bh$	Area of a triangle $= \frac{1}{2} \cdot$ base · height
$C = np$	Cost = number of items · price per item
$C = \frac{5}{9}(F - 32)$	Celsius temperature $= \frac{5}{9}$(Fahrenheit temperature $- 32$)

11. On a bicycle tour, Chang and Estella traveled 82.5 miles. If the tour lasted $7\frac{1}{2}$ hours with 2 hours allowed for rest stops, what was the average rate of speed? $d = rt$; 15 mi/h

12. A service-station owner bought a box of auto parts for $214.80. If each part cost $8.95, how many parts were in the box? $C = np$; 24 parts

13. Manuel planted a garden in the shape of a triangle with a base of 12 feet and a height of 8 feet. Find the area of the garden. $A = \frac{1}{2}bh$; 48 ft²

14. The interest on Rosita's loan amounts to $1320. What is the principal if the rate is 12% and she pays it back in 2 years? $I = prt$; $5500

15. For exercise 14, what would the interest be if Rosita pays back the loan in one year? $I = prt$; $660

16. What is the temperature in Celsius if a thermometer reads 77° Fahrenheit? $C = \frac{5}{9}(F - 32)$; 25°C

17. If a triangular piece of glass has an area of 150 in² and the height measures 15 inches, how long is the base?

18. How long will it take a marathon runner to travel $26\frac{1}{4}$ miles if the runner averages $7\frac{1}{2}$ miles per hour? $d = rt$; $3\frac{1}{2}$ hours

19. A class purchased 12 pizzas for a party. If the total cost of the pizzas was $107.40, what was the average price per pizza? $C = np$; $8.95

20. If the temperature is 15° Celsius on a given day, what is the number of degrees Fahrenheit? $C = \frac{5}{9}(F - 32)$; 59°F

Written Exercises
17. $A = \frac{1}{2}bh$; 20 inches

PROBLEM–SOLVING STRATEGIES

Use a Formula (1–26).

C. Solve.

21. In the formula $A = \frac{1}{2}h(a + b)$,   6
$A = 66$, $a = 10$, and $b = 12$. Find h.

22. In the formula $A = p + prt$, $A = 155$, $r = 10$, and $t = 3$. Find p.   5

23. In the formula $V = \frac{1}{3}\pi r^2 h$, $V = 628$ and $r = 10$. Find h.   6

24. In the formula $W = \frac{1}{2}mv^2$, $W = 9$ and $v = 3$. Find m.   2

25. It is 220 miles from Skunk Hollow to Fedora. It takes Mario 4 hours to drive from one to the other, and it takes Pamela $5\frac{1}{2}$ hours to drive the same distance. If both Mario and Pamela want to arrive at the same time, how many miles head start must Pamela have? Use the formula $d = rt$.
60 mi

26. The longest side of a triangle is twice the length of the shortest side. The third side is 4 feet less than the longest side. The perimeter of the triangle is 41 feet. What are the lengths of the sides? Use the formula $P = a + b + c$.   9 ft, 18 ft, 14 ft

1. Suzanne sold 64 tickets to the charity auction. She sold 16 more than twice the number of tickets Bill sold. How many did Bill sell?

   Let x = number of tickets Bill sold.

   $$2x + 16 = 64$$
   $$2x + 16 - 16 = 64 - 16$$
   $$2x = 48$$
   $$x = 24$$

   Bill sold 24 tickets.

2. A bus left Orlando heading to Atlanta, a distance of 420 miles, at an average speed of 60 miles per hour. At the same time, a bus departs Atlanta bound for Orlando at an average speed of 45 miles per hour. If they follow the same route, after how many hours did they pass?

   $$60t + 45t = 420$$
   $$105t = 420$$
   $$\frac{105t}{105} = \frac{420}{105}$$
   $$t = 4$$

   The buses pass each other in 4 hours.

3.9 | Problem Solving—Writing Equations

Another problem-solving strategy is **writing an equation.** First, choose a variable to represent one of the unknown numbers. Then, if possible, represent each remaining unknown number with an expression involving the same variable. Finally, decide how the given and the unknown numbers are related and write an equation to represent the relationship.

EXAMPLES

1 Joyce sold 17 tickets to a benefit baseball game. This was 5 more than 3 times the number of tickets that Robert sold. How many tickets did Robert sell?

Understand: *Given:*   Joyce sold 17 tickets.

   17 is 5 more than 3 times the number Robert sold.

   To find: how many tickets Robert sold

Plan: Let x = the number of tickets Robert sold.

   Write an equation based on the information given.

   $$3x + 5 = 17$$

Solve:
$$3x + 5 = 17$$
$$3x + 5 - 5 = 17 - 5$$
$$3x = 12$$
$$\frac{3x}{3} = \frac{12}{3}$$
$$x = 4$$

Answer: Robert sold 4 tickets.

Review: Are the 17 tickets that Joyce sold 5 more than 3 times the 4 tickets that Robert sold?

2 A twin-engine airplane flew from Houston to Memphis, a distance of 550 miles, and averaged 130 miles per hour. A single-engine airplane flew from Memphis to Houston and averaged 90 miles per hour. If both airplanes left at the same time and flew the same route, after how many hours did they pass?

Understand: *Given:*   The distance from Houston to Memphis is 550 miles.

   The twin-engine plane (Plane A) averaged 130 miles per hour.

   The single-engine plane (Plane B) averaged 90 miles per hour.

   The planes left at the same time and flew the same route.

   To find: After how many hours did the planes pass each other?

Plan: There are three problem-solving strategies that will help you find the solution to the problem.

1. *Draw a diagram.* Sometimes a sketch will help you understand a problem more clearly because you can actually picture the situation.

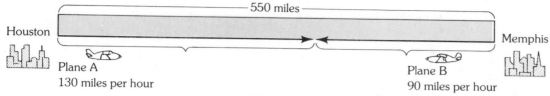

Houston

Plane A
130 miles per hour

— 550 miles —

Plane B
90 miles per hour

Memphis

2. *Use the formula d = rt* (distance = rate · time). Let t = the number of hours that each plane traveled until the planes passed each other.

Express the distance traveled by Plane A to where the planes passed as $130t$. Similarly, express Plane B's distance as $90t$. Since the planes left at the same time and flew the same route toward each other, then the total distance traveled was 550 miles.

3. *Write an equation.* $130t + 90t = 550$

Solve:
$$130t + 90t = 550$$
$$220t = 550$$
$$\frac{220t}{220} = \frac{550}{220}$$
$$t = 2\frac{1}{2}$$

Answer: The planes passed each other in $2\frac{1}{2}$ hours.

Review: Will $2\frac{1}{2}$ hours of flying at 90 miles per hour and $2\frac{1}{2}$ hours of flying at 130 miles per hour result in a total distance of 550 miles?

MIXED REVIEW

1. Solve each equation.
   a. $4y + 3 = -2y + 9$ 1
   b. $\frac{8n}{3} = 112$ 42

2. Given: $3080 principal
          3 years
          8% interest rate
   Determine: interest charged
   $739.20

3. Simplify $(-8.2)^3$.
   -551.368

4. Illustrate the transitive property.   Answers will vary

5. Evaluate $5^3 \cdot 2 + 6^3 \cdot 2$.
   682

TEACHER'S RESOURCE MASTERS

Practice Master 12, Part 2

ASSIGNMENT GUIDE

Minimum
1–6, 7–13 odd

Regular
7–16

Maximum
8–17

ADDITIONAL ANSWERS

Oral Exercises

1. Let s = a certain number.
   $6s = 42$

2. Let x = a number.
   $x + (-5) = -23$

3. Let a = Ho's age.
   $2a + 5 = 17$

4. Let l = Ernestine's weight.
   $3l - 8 = 187$

ORAL EXERCISES

For each problem tell (a) which unknown quantity you would represent by a variable and (b) the equation you would use to solve the problem.

1. If 6 times a certain number is 42, what is the number?

2. The sum of a number and -5 is -23. What is the number?

3. Yolanda is twice Ho's age plus 5 years. Yolanda is 17 years old. How old is Ho?

4. Clyde weighs 3 times as much as Ernestine, less 8 pounds. Clyde weighs 187 pounds. How much does Ernestine weigh?

5. A father is 5 more than 8 times his daughter's age. If the father is 29 years old, how old is his daughter?

6. One number is 6 more than 5 times another, and their sum is 48. Find the numbers.

5. Let y = the daughter's age.
$8y + 5 = 29$

6. Let n = one number.
$n + 5n + 6 = 48$

A. Choose the correct equation for each problem. Solve.

1. A certain number is 4 less than 3 times another, and their sum is 16. Find the numbers.   b; 5 and 11

   a. $a + (3a + 4) = 16$
   b. $a + (3a - 4) = 16$
   c. $a + 3(a + 4) = 16$

2. The sum of twice a certain number and 5 more than that number is 14. Find the number.   a; 3

   a. $2x + (x + 5) = 14$
   b. $2x + (x - 5) = 14$
   c. $x + 2(x + 5) = 14$

3. A rectangular movie screen is to have a perimeter of 140 feet. If the length is to be 30 feet more than the width, what must the width be?   c; 20 feet

   a. $w + (w + 30) = 140$
   b. $2w + (2w + 30) = 140$
   c. $2w + 2(w + 30) = 140$

4. Two cyclists ride toward each other from points 54 miles apart. One cyclist is traveling 15 miles per hour. The other is traveling 12 miles per hour. In how many hours will the two cyclists meet if they do not stop?   a; 2 hours

   a. $15t + 12t = 54$
   b. $15t - 12t = 54$
   c. $15t + 54 = 12t$

Solve.

5. Barb paid $25 down on a set of weights that cost $120. If she paid the balance in 5 equal installments, how much would each installment be? $19

6. If Bev deposits $253 into her checking account, she will have a total of $514.25. How much money is in Bev's account? $261.25

B.
7. Jean Paul bought a pair of skis on sale. He then sold them for $225, which was twice as much as he paid for them, less $70. How much did he pay for the skis on sale? $147.50

8. In an election, there are 96,000 registered voters. This is 6 times the number of people who actually voted. How many people actually voted?   16,000 people

9. Wally is 3 times older than Debbie, minus 2 years. Wally is 43 years old. How old is Debbie?   15 years

10. A baseball team won 12 out of 15 games. What percent of the games did the baseball team win?   80%

11. A soccer team played 12 games and won 5 times as many games as it lost. How many games did the soccer team win?   10 games

12. Juanita bought a radio for $99. If she paid $39 down and will pay $15 each month, in how many months will the radio be paid for?   4 months

13. John drove to school and back in 45 minutes. It took him 3 minutes less to drive back than it did to drive to school. How long did it take John to drive to school?   24 minutes

14. If a car travels 40 miles per hour for half of the time and 50 miles per hour for the other half of the time, how long would it take for the car to travel 270 miles?   6 hours

C. 15. The formula for finding the area of a trapezoid is $A = \frac{1}{2}h(a + b)$, where h is the height and $a + b$ is the sum of the two bases. A trapezoid has an area of 54 square feet and a height of 6 feet. If the longer base is 3 more than twice the length of the shorter base, what is the length of each base? 5 feet, 13 feet

16. A garden is 20 feet longer than twice its width. If the perimeter measures 220 feet, find the length and the width of the garden. 80 feet long, 30 feet wide

17. The combined record speed of a one-engine, a two-engine, and a four-engine gasoline-powered airplane is 794 miles per hour. The record speed of the four-engine plane is twice that of the one-engine plane. The record speed of the two-engine plane is 86 miles per hour less than that of the four-engine plane. The combined record speed of the one-engine and the two-engine plane is 90 miles per hour more than the record speed of the four-engine plane. What is the record speed of each type of airplane?

CAREER
Landscape Architect

Landscape architects appreciate nature and use creativity and artistic talent to design the landscaping for outdoor areas. They plan the arrangement of plants, walkways, and natural features. Often they prepare drawings of a site, showing existing and proposed features. Also, they must estimate the costs involved for the purchase of vegetation and for building materials used to construct such things as terraces, benches, and fountains.

Suppose a landscape architect is estimating how much it will cost to sod a rectangular lawn 60 feet by 50 feet. At $4 per square yard, how much should be estimated for sodding the lawn?

Suppose a landscape architect has designed a walkway to enclose a circular flowerbed that has a diameter of 25 feet. Plants will be spaced every 6 inches around the outside of the flowerbed. At $0.79 per plant, how much will be estimated for these plants?

CLASSROOM EXAMPLES

1. A refrigerator is purchased for a cost of $840. The down payment is 30% of the purchase price. Determine the amount of down payment.

$x = 0.30(840)$

$x = \$252$

2. On a quiz, Lucille answered 4 questions out of 10. What percent of the questions were answered?

$10y = 4$

$\frac{10y}{10} = \frac{4}{10}$

$y = \frac{4}{10} = \frac{40}{100} = 40\%$

3. Mrs. Bucek bought chaise lounges and paid 25% off the list price. The discount was $98. Determine the list price.

$98 = 0.25x$

$\frac{98}{0.25} = \frac{0.25x}{0.25}$

$\$392 = x$

MIXED REVIEW

1. Complete.
   a. $|-10|$ 10
   b. $-|12|$ -12

3.10 Problem Solving With Percents

You can solve a percent problem by writing an equation and then solving it.

EXAMPLES

1 The Meyers bought a chair for $380 and made a down payment of 25% of the purchase price. How much was the down payment?

Understand: *Given:* The chair cost $380.
The Meyers made a down payment of 25% of the purchase price.

To find: How much was the down payment?

Plan: Let x = the amount of the down payment.
Translate *What number is 25% of 380?* into an equation.
$x = 0.25(380)$ *Write 25% as a decimal.*

Solve: Solve the equation. $x = 0.25(380)$
$x = 95$

Answer: The down payment was $95.

Review: Does it seem reasonable that $95 is 25% of $380?

2 A basketball player made 6 free throws out of 10 attempts. What percent of the attempts did the basketball player make?

Understand: *Given:* A basketball player made 6 free throws out of 10 attempts.

To find: What percent of the attempts were made?

Plan: Let y = the percent of the attempts made.
Translate *What percent of 10 is 6?* into an equation.
$y(10) = 6$

Solve: Solve the equation. $10y = 6$
$\frac{10y}{10} = \frac{6}{10}$
$y = \frac{6}{10} = \frac{60}{100} = 60\%$ *Write $\frac{6}{10}$ as a percent.*

Answer: The basketball player made 60% of the free-throw attempts.

Review: Does it seem reasonable that 60% of 10 is 6?

3 Andy bought stereo speakers and paid 30% off the list price. The discount was $78. What was the list price?

Understand: *Given:* Andy bought speakers for 30% off the list price.
The discount was $78.

To find: What was the list price?

Plan: Let n = the list price.
Translate *78 is 30% of what number?* into an equation.
$78 = 0.30n$

Solve: Solve the equation.
$$78 = 0.3n$$
$$\frac{78}{0.3} = \frac{0.3n}{0.3}$$
$$260 = n$$

Answer: The list price of the speakers was $260.

Review: Does it seem reasonable that 78 is 30% of 260?

2. Simplify $4^3x^3(x^{12})$.　$64x^{15}$
3. Find the value $4^3(4^2)$.
　1024
4. Solve each equation.
　a. $y - 3.6 = 3y$
　　$- 12.8$　4.6
　b. $3(y + 6) = 42$　8
5. Find the difference.
　a. $35 - (-18 - 3)$　56
　b. $-16 - (-14 + 9)$　-11

TEACHER'S RESOURCE MASTERS

Practice Master 13, Part 1
Quiz 6

ASSIGNMENT GUIDE
Minimum
1–7 odd, 9–14
Regular
9–18
Maximum
9–15 odd, 17–22

ADDITIONAL ANSWERS
Oral Exercises
22. $x = 0.15(40)$
24. $15 = 0.75x$
26. $360x = 270$
28. $x = 0.70(85)$

ORAL EXERCISES

Change each percent to a decimal.

1. 7%　0.07
2. 15%　0.15
3. 1.5%　0.015
4. 29%　0.29
5. 70%　0.7
6. 410%　4.1
7. 33.75%　0.3375
8. 0.9%　0.009

Change each fraction to a percent.

9. $\frac{1}{2}$　50%
10. $\frac{3}{4}$　75%
11. $\frac{8}{100}$　8%
12. $\frac{21}{50}$　42%
13. $\frac{9}{10}$　90%
14. $\frac{42}{100}$　42%
15. $\frac{15}{10}$　150%
16. $\frac{108}{1000}$　10.8%

Choose a variable and translate each sentence into an equation.

17. What number is 9% of 800?　$x = 0.09(800)$
18. What percent of 96 is 72?　$96x = 72$
19. 12 is 60% of what number?　$12 = 0.6x$
20. What percent of 120 is 54?　$120x = 54$
21. 36 is 20% of what number?　$36 = 0.2x$
22. What number is 15% of 40?
23. What percent of 40 is 30?　$40x = 30$
24. 15 = 75% of what number?
25. What number is 40% of 70?　$x = 0.4(70)$
26. What percent of 360 is 270?
27. What percent of 110 is 88?　$110x = 88$
28. What number is 70% of 85?
29. 36 = 60% of what number?　$36 = 0.6x$
30. What percent of 40 is 70?　$40x = 70$

WRITTEN EXERCISES

A. Solve.

1. An employee received a 9% pay increase. If his hourly wage increased by $0.72, how much was he earning per hour before the pay raise?　$8

2. A community's fund-raising campaign has collected $41,000. Its goal is $50,000. What percent of its goal has been reached?　82%

3. Medical insurance will pay 80% of the doctor's surgery fee. If the doctor's fee is $1500, how much will insurance pay? How much will the patient pay? $1200; $300

4. One auto insurance company gives a 10% discount on insurance for a second car. If the insurance premium on a second car is $185 before the discount, what is the premium after the discount?

5. A real-estate salesperson received 6% commission for selling a house. The commission was $5100. What was the selling price? $85,000

6. During a TV broadcast lasting 60 minutes, commercials are scheduled for 12 minutes. What percent of the time is commercials? 20%

7. Chris scored 68 correct out of 85 items on a test. What percent of the items were correct? 80%

8. The interest on an auto loan for one year is $495. If $5500 is the amount borrowed, what is the interest rate? 9%

B. 9. One store offers a 20% discount on merchandise to its employees. How much less will an employee pay for a $750 refrigerator? $150

10. A bank pays 11% per year in interest on a 1-year certificate. How much interest is earned on $2000? $220

11. The Scanlons purchased a house and made a down payment of 20% of the purchase price. If the down payment was $19,000, what was the purchase price? $95,000

12. The regular fare of an airline ticket is $160. During certain times of the day, the airline offers a 40% discount off the regular ticket price. How much is the discount? $64

13. A video recorder costs $650 plus $45.50 in sales tax. What percent is the sales tax rate? 7%

14. The selling price of a washing machine was $495 plus 6% sales tax. How much did the customer pay? $524.70

15. One credit-card company charges a finance charge of 1.8% per month on any unpaid balance. What is the monthly finance charge on $450? $8.10

16. On a chapter test 15% of the algebra students got A's. If 12 students got A's, how many students took the test? 80 students

C. 17. Electric rates are 50% higher during the summer months. If the nonsummer rate is $0.07 per kwh (kilowatt-hour), what is the summer rate per kwh? $0.105

18. Oranges cost $0.59 per pound in season. The cost of oranges is 66% higher out of season. How much do oranges cost per pound out of season? Round your answer to the nearest cent. $0.98

19. Playing time for a football game is 60 minutes. A television broadcast of the game took $2\frac{1}{2}$ hours. The broadcast included playing time, time-outs, halftime, and commercials. What percent of the broadcast was the playing time? 40%

20. The reduced price of an item is $60. The original price was $75. By how much did the price of the item decrease? What was the percent of decrease? $15; 20%

21. The monthly rent for an apartment went from $390 to $429. What is the increase in rent? What is the percent of increase? $39; 10%

22. A homeowner's annual real-estate taxes went from $1050 to $1134. What is the increase in taxes? What is the percent of increase? $84; 8%

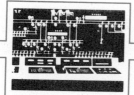

COMPUTER

Quick, what is the fractional number equivalent of the decimal number 0.9872?

Given enough time, you could find the answer, providing your arithmetic is correct. Study this program. Will it convert 0.9872 to a fraction?

```
10 PRINT: PRINT "INPUT ANY 4-DIGIT DECIMAL NUMBER"
20 PRINT "OR PRESS RETURN TO END"
30 PRINT "START WITH '0.':";: INPUT DE$
40 IF DE$ = "" THEN END
50 IF LEFT$ (DE$,2) < > "0." OR LEN (DE$) > 6 THEN 30
60 NU$ = RIGHT$ (DE$, LEN (DE$) - 2)
70 N% = VAL (NU$): D% = 10 ^ LEN (NU$)
80 REM NOW REDUCE FRACTION
90 X = 1
100 X = X + 1: IF (N% / X) = INT (N% / X) AND (D% / X) =
    INT (D% / X) THEN LET N% = N% / X: D% = D% / X: GOTO
    90
110 IF X < N% THEN 100
120 PRINT DE$;" = ";N%;" / ";D%
130 GOTO 10
```

EXERCISES

1. Describe what the computer is doing in lines 90 to 110 by drawing a flow chart.

2. What is the purpose of LEN in line 70?

3. Do you think this program will convert, with mathematical accuracy, any four-digit decimal number to its fractional number equivalent?

4. If you have a computer available, enter the program and RUN it. Was your answer to the third question correct?

5. Why does this program need to use numeric variables of the integer type (N%, D%)? Remove the % symbols from these variables and see what happens.

ANSWERS

1. See Complete Solutions Manual.

2. LEN indicates how big D%, the denominator, is to be, based on how long the decimal input is.

3. Answers will vary.

4. Answers will vary; the program performs as desired.

5. Without "%" the program does not perform integer division, and N / D is not reduced to lowest terms.

TEACHER'S RESOURCE
MASTERS

Enrichment Master 3

ENRICHMENT

See Activities 9–10,
p. T42.

ADDITIONAL ANSWERS
12. 3.14

CHAPTER 3 REVIEW

VOCABULARY

addition property
of equality (3.2)

division property
of equality (3.3)

equation (3.1)

equivalent sentences (3.1)

formula (3.8)

multiplication property
of equality (3.3)

open sentence (3.1)

repeating decimal (3.4)

replacement set (3.1)

solution set (3.1)

subtraction property
of equality (3.2)

terminating decimal (3.4)

REVIEW EXERCISES

3.1 **Solve. The replacement set is {6, 7, 8}.**

1. $x + 6 = 13$ 7

2. $9 + y = 15$ 6

3. $13 = a + 5$ 8

4. $16 = 8 + b$ 8

5. $m + m = 12$ 6

6. $n^2 = 36$ 6

3.2 **Solve. Check. The replacement set is the set of rational numbers.**

7. $-8 + a = 2$ 10

8. $b + (-6) = 12$ 18

9. $m - 13 = 4$ 17

10. $\frac{7}{9} - n = \frac{2}{9}$ $\frac{5}{9}$

11. $y - \frac{3}{4} = \frac{5}{6}$ $1\frac{7}{12}$

12. $10.8 + x = 13.94$

3.3 **13.** $-9y = 108$ -12

14. $-90 = -15x$ 6

15. $3.4n = 0.544$ 0.16

16. $0.23m = -0.184$ -0.8

17. $\frac{a}{4} = 8$ 32

18. $\frac{b}{12} = 12$ 144

3.4 **Rename each rational number as a terminating or as a repeating decimal.**

19. $\frac{9}{20}$ 0.45

20. $\frac{2}{3}$ $0.\overline{6}$

21. $\frac{1}{6}$ $0.1\overline{6}$

22. $\frac{7}{11}$ $0.\overline{63}$

Rename each decimal as a fraction in simplest form.

23. 0.8 $\frac{4}{5}$

24. 0.625 $\frac{5}{8}$

25. $0.\overline{27}$ $\frac{3}{11}$

26. $2.8\overline{3}$ $2\frac{5}{6}$

3.5 **Solve each equation. Check.**

27. $6a + a = 56$ 8

28. $-2b + (-3b) = 40$ -8

29. $5x - 9x = 36$ -9

30. $\frac{1}{6}y + \frac{2}{3}y = 15$ 18

31. $42 = \frac{3}{4}n + \frac{1}{8}n$ 48

32. $0.4m + 0.9m = 6.5$ 5

3.6 **33.** $6x + 9 = 45$ 6

34. $8y - 6 = 74$ 10

35. $-9a + 6 = 51$ -5

36. $\frac{3}{4}b - 8 = 1$ 12

37. $\frac{4}{9}m - \frac{5}{9} = -\frac{7}{27}$ $\frac{2}{3}$

38. $0.8n + 0.27 = 0.59$ 0.4

3.7 **39.** $6a + 9 = 57$ 8

40. $8b - 6 = 90$ 12

41. $3n + 4 = n + 16$ 6

42. $4x - 7 = 2x + 23$ 15

43. $4.95 = 4.5 + 0.9m$ 0.5

44. $-\frac{2}{7}y + \frac{5}{7}y - 2 = 28$ 70

3.8 **Solve.**

45. If the interest on a $5000 loan for one year is $800, what is the rate of interest? Use the formula $I = prt$.   16%

3.9 **For the following problems, (*a*) write an equation and (*b*) use that equation to solve the problem.**

46. A certain number is 4 less than 6 times another, and their sum is 45. Find the two numbers. $x + 6x - 4 = 45$; 7 and 38

3.10 **Solve.**

47. During a special sale, customers were given 20% off the ticketed price on any purchase. One customer had $35 deducted from the total bill. What was the total before the discount? $175

ERROR SEARCH

Find the error in each exercise and give the correct answer.

1. $5x - 3 = 18$
$5x = 18 - 3$
$5x = 15$
$x = \frac{15}{5}$
$x = 3$

2. $3b + 4 = 6$
$\frac{3b}{3} + 4 = \frac{6}{3}$
$b + 4 = 2$
$b = 2 - 4$
$b = -2$

3. $2(4a + 3) = 47$
$8a + 3 = 47$
$8a = 47 - 3$
$a = 44$
$a = \frac{44}{8}$
$a = 5\frac{1}{2}$

4. $3(9x - 2) = 12$
$9x - 2 = 4$
$9x = 6$
$x = \frac{2}{3}$

ERROR SEARCH
1. $5x - 3 = 18$
$5x = 18 + 3$
$5x = 21$
$x = \frac{21}{5}$
$x = 4\frac{1}{5}$

2. $3b + 4 = 6$
$3b = 6 - 4$
$3b = 2$
$b = \frac{2}{3}$

3. $2(4a + 3) = 47$
$8a + 6 = 47$
$8a = 47 - 6$
$8a = 41$
$a = \frac{41}{8}$
$a = 5\frac{1}{8}$

4. $3(9x - 2) = 12$
$9x - 2 = 4$
$9x = 6$
$x = \frac{2}{3}$

CHAPTER 3 TEST

Which term best completes each sentence?

equation   open sentence   equivalent   replacement set   solution set

1. The set of numbers that makes an open sentence true is a(n) ___solution set___.

2. Open sentences that have the same solution set are said to be ___equivalent___.

3. An algebraic sentence in which two expressions are connected by the symbol $=$ is called a(n) ___equation___.

Solve. The replacement set is the set of rational numbers.

4. $-5 + x = 6$ 11

5. $y - \frac{1}{4} = \frac{3}{8}$ $\frac{5}{8}$

6. $0.7 + a = 1.8$ 1.1

Solve. Check.

7. $8t = 36$ $4\frac{1}{2}$

8. $\frac{a}{4} = -12$ -48

9. $-\frac{5}{8}r = -140$ 224

Rename each rational number as a repeating decimal.

10. $\frac{1}{3}$ $0.\overline{3}$

11. $\frac{5}{6}$ $0.8\overline{3}$

12. $\frac{9}{11}$ $0.\overline{81}$

Rename as a fraction in simplest form.

13. 0.6 $\frac{3}{5}$

14. 0.875 $\frac{7}{8}$

15. $0.1\overline{6}$ $\frac{1}{6}$

Solve. Check.

16. $3x - 7x = 24$ -6

17. $-0.6y - 1.2y = 3.6$ -2

18. $\frac{1}{6}a + \frac{3}{4}a = 33$ 36

19. $9n - 23 = 85$ 12

20. $\frac{2}{3}m - \frac{1}{2} = \frac{5}{6}$ 2

21. $0.12b + 1.6 = 16$ 120

22. $3x + 8 = 5x - 6$ 7

23. $\frac{1}{3}y - \frac{3}{4} = \frac{5}{6}y + \frac{3}{8}$ $-2\frac{1}{4}$

24. $0.4a + 2 = 1.1a - 6.4$ 12

25. $2(4x + 3) = 30$ 3

26. $2y - 3y + 7y + 2\frac{1}{2} = 5$ $\frac{5}{12}$

27. $9 - (2a + 6) = -9$ 6

Solve.

28. A hot-water heater is set at 140° Fahrenheit. What is the temperature setting in degrees Celsius? Use the formula $C = \frac{5}{9}(F - 32)$.   60°C

29. A sandwich and a glass of milk cost $3.75. If the sandwich cost four times the milk, what was the price of each item? $3 for the sandwich, $0.75 for the milk

30. During a clearance sale, last year's model of an appliance was reduced 40% from its original list price. If the list price was $795, how much was it marked down? $318

CUMULATIVE REVIEW: CHAPTERS 1–3

Choose the correct answer.

1. Evaluate $3x + 5$ if $x = 4$. C
   - **A.** 12
   - **B.** 27
   - **C.** 17
   - **D.** 32

2. Evaluate $(2x)^3$ if $x = 5$. D
   - **A.** 30
   - **B.** 40
   - **C.** 250
   - **D.** 1000

3. Name the property illustrated by the following: $(5 + 6) + 3 = 5 + (6 + 3)$. B
   - **A.** Commutative property of addition
   - **B.** Associative property of addition
   - **C.** Distributive property
   - **D.** Identity property of addition

4. Simplify $[3(7 - 2)] \div (9 - 6)$. B
   - **A.** 2
   - **B.** 5
   - **C.** 6
   - **D.** 7

5. Simplify $3x^2 + 7x^2$. B
   - **A.** 10
   - **B.** $10x^2$
   - **C.** $10x$
   - **D.** $10x^4$

6. Write an algebraic expression for *the next odd number after an odd number* x.   D
   - **A.** 1
   - **B.** x
   - **C.** $x + 1$
   - **D.** $x + 2$

7. If $A = \{1, 2\}$, then 2 _____ A. A
   - **A.** $\in$
   - **B.** $\notin$
   - **C.** $\subset$
   - **D.** None of these

8. What is the absolute value of -3? C
   - **A.** -3
   - **B.** 0
   - **C.** 3
   - **D.** None of these

9. Refer to the number line to find the sum of -3 and 8. B

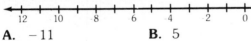

   - **A.** -11
   - **B.** 5
   - **C.** -5
   - **D.** 11

10. Simplify $-23 + (-17)$. A
    - **A.** -40
    - **B.** -6
    - **C.** 6
    - **D.** 40

11. Simplify $35 - (-18)$. D
    - **A.** -53
    - **B.** -17
    - **C.** 17
    - **D.** 53

12. Simplify $-5(6)(-18)$. D
    - **A.** 60
    - **B.** -48
    - **C.** -18
    - **D.** 540

13. Simplify $0.23 \div (-9.2)$. B
    - **A.** -40
    - **B.** -0.025
    - **C.** 0.025
    - **D.** 40

14. Simplify $4m^5 (3m)$. C
    - **A.** $7m^5$
    - **B.** $12m^5$
    - **C.** $12m^6$
    - **D.** $7m^6$

15. Give the degree of the monomial x^3y^4. A
    A. 7   **B.** 4   **C.** 12   **D.** 3

16. Find the solution set of $x + 15 = 27$ if the replacement set is {10, 12, 14, 16}. B
    A. {10}   **B.** {12}   **C.** {14}   **D.** {16}

17. Solve $n - 22 = 13$. D
    A. -35 **B.** -9 **C.** 9   **D.** 35

18. Solve $7x = 84$. A
    A. 12   **B.** 77   **C.** 91   **D.** 588

19. Rename $\frac{7}{8}$ as a terminating or a repeating decimal. A
    A. 0.875   **B.** 7.7   **C.** 8.7   **D.** $1.\overline{142857}$

20. Solve $-4x + 12x = 56$. C
    A. 3.5   **B.** 4   **C.** 7   **D.** 40

21. Solve $5x + 3 = 38$. B
    A. 4.6   **B.** 7   **C.** 8.2   **D.** 10.6

22. Solve $8y - 6 = 5y + 3$. C
    A. -10 **B.** -3 **C.** 3   **D.** 10

23. Solve $n + 16 = 3$. B
    A. -19 **B.** -13 **C.** 13   **D.** 19

24. Solve $9x - 15 = 3$. D
    A. -2 **B.** -1 **C.** 1   **D.** 2

25. Using the formula $I = prt$, find the amount of interest paid on $2000 borrowed for 3 years at 14% per year. B
    A. $280   **B.** $840   **C.** $2280   **D.** $84

26. Find three consecutive integers whose sum is 51. C
    A. 15, 17, 19   **B.** 13, 17, 21   **C.** 16, 17, 18   **D.** None of these

27. Find the length of a rectangle whose length is 4 feet greater than its width and whose perimeter is 48 feet. B
    A. 10 feet   **B.** 14 feet   **C.** 20 feet   **D.** 28 feet

28. Name the property illustrated by the following: $a(b + c) = ab + ac$. C
    A. Commutative property of multiplication   **B.** Associative property of multiplication
    C. Distributive property   **D.** Identity property of multiplication

29. Simplify $291 - 4^2 \cdot 3 + (3 + 6)$. D
    A. 834   **B.** 99   **C.** 234   **D.** 252

30. Evaluate $x(3y - 2)$ if $x = 3$ and $y = 4$. A
    A. 30   **B.** -28 **C.** -38 **D.** -42

CHAPTER 4

Inequalities

The wingspan of an owl is from 1.8 to 2 times the height of the owl. What is the height of an owl with a wingspan of 90 cm?   45 to 50 cm

CLASSROOM EXAMPLES

Given: $x < 7$.

A solution is any real number less than 7.

Given: $x > 4$.

A solution is any real number greater than 4.

Given: $x \leq 5$.

A solution is any real number less than or equal to 5.

Given: $x \geq 6$.

A solution is any real number greater than or equal to 6.

Given: $x \neq 9$.

A solution is any real number not equal to 9.

MIXED REVIEW

1. Perform the indicated operation.
   a. $(-8)(13)$ -104
   b. $-\frac{13}{18} \div -\frac{1}{2}$ $1\frac{4}{9}$
   c. $46 + (-38)$ 8
   d. $15 - (-18 - 56)$ 89

2. Simplify $(-38 \cdot 3) - 5$.
   -119

3. Complete.
   a. $-|-36|$ -36
   b. $\left|\frac{5}{6}\right|$ $\frac{5}{6}$

4. Evaluate if $f = 4$ and $g = -3$. $(f + g)^3$ 1

5. Find each value.
   a. $\left(\frac{1}{6}\right)^3$ $\frac{1}{216}$
   b. $(1.1)^3$ 1.331

4.1	Order and Graphing

An **inequality** is a mathematical sentence containing $<$, $>$, $\leq$, $\geq$, or $\neq$. All of the following are inequalities:

$$-2 < 1 \qquad 5 > -3 \qquad -4 \leq 1 \qquad 4 \geq 3 \qquad 0 \neq -3$$

An inequality that contains $<$, $>$, $\leq$, or $\geq$, tells you about the **order** of numbers on a number line.

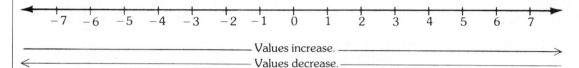

When an inequality involves a variable, the solution set can be graphed on a number line. The replacement set is the set of real numbers.

$x < 3$ is read "x is less than 3." Any real number *less than* 3 is a solution.

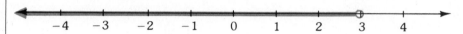

$x > 3$ is read "x is greater than 3." Any real number *greater than* 3 is a solution.

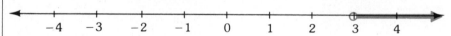

$x \leq 3$ is read "x is less than or equal to 3." Any real number *less than or equal to* 3 is a solution.

$x \geq 3$ is read "x is greater than or equal to 3." Any real number *greater than or equal to* 3 is a solution.

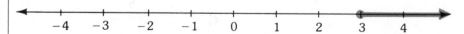

$x \neq 3$ is read "x is not equal to 3." Any real number *not equal to* 3 is a solution.

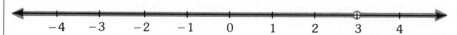

A solid dot ● on a graph indicates that the particular point is part of the solution set. A small circle ○ indicates that the particular point is not part of the solution set. A solid arrowhead ➡ (or ⬅) indicates that the solution set continues indefinitely in the positive (or negative) direction.

State which symbol, $<$ or $>$, you would use to make each sentence true.

1. $2 \bullet 5$ $<$ **2.** $-1 \bullet -8$ $>$ **3.** $-3 \bullet 0$ $<$ **4.** $5 \bullet -7$ $>$

5. $-9 \bullet -6$ $<$ **6.** $1.6 \bullet -2.3$ $>$ **7.** $-\frac{3}{4} \bullet -\frac{11}{4}$ $>$ **8.** $\frac{3}{8} \bullet \frac{7}{8}$ $<$

State the inequality for each graph, using the variable x.

9.

10.

11.

12.
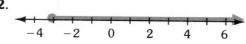

13.
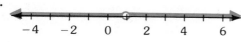

14.

15.
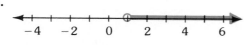

16.

WRITTEN EXERCISES

A. Graph the solution set of each inequality.

1. $x < 2$ **2.** $y < -1$ **3.** $m > -3$ **4.** $n > 3$ **5.** $s \geq -5$

6. $r \geq -1$ **7.** $x \leq 4$ **8.** $y \leq -2$ **9.** $m \neq 0$ **10.** $n \neq 1$

B. 11. $s \geq -4\frac{1}{2}$ **12.** $r \leq -1$ **13.** $x < \frac{1}{2}$ **14.** $y < -\frac{3}{4}$ **15.** $m > -1.5$

16. $n > 3.5$ **17.** $s \leq 2\frac{1}{4}$ **18.** $r \leq 1\frac{3}{4}$ **19.** $x \neq \frac{9}{2}$ **20.** $y \geq -\frac{7}{3}$

21. $m \geq \frac{5}{3}$ **22.** $x \neq \frac{4}{3}$ **23.** $t \leq -\frac{1}{2}$ **24.** $v > 2\frac{1}{4}$ **25.** $w \neq \frac{4}{5}$

26. $q > -0.4$ **27.** $y \leq -3\frac{2}{3}$ **28.** $x \neq \frac{11}{3}$ **29.** $y \geq \frac{13}{3}$ **30.** $x < -\frac{5}{2}$

C. The symbol $\neq$ means "is not equal to." What do you think each of the following symbols means?

31. $\not>$ **32.** $\not<$ **33.** $\not\leq$ **34.** $\not\geq$

Match each sentence in exercises 35–38 to an equivalent sentence in a–d.

a. $x < 2$ **b.** $x \leq 2$ **c.** $x > 2$ **d.** $x \geq 2$

35. $x \not> 2$ b.   **36.** $x \not< 2$ d.   **37.** $x \not\leq 2$ c.   **38.** $x \not\geq 2$ a.

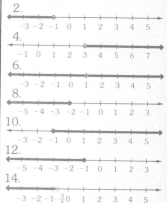

SKILLS MAINTENANCE

Simplify.

1. $3 \cdot 9 + 4$ 31

2. $36 \div 2 + 4$ 22

3. $5 \cdot (7 + 3)$ 50

4. $63 \div (6 + 3) \cdot 7$ 49

5. $3 \cdot 4^2 \div (6 \div 3)$ 24

6. $\frac{15 - 3}{3} + 2(8 + 1)$ 22

Evaluate if $m = 9$ and $n = 4$.

7. $3mn$ 108

8. $\frac{2m}{n}$ $4\frac{1}{2}$

9. $n(m + n)$ 52

10. $m \div 3 + 2 \cdot n$ 11

11. $m^2 n^3$ 5184

12. $(m + n)^2$ 169

Simplify.

13. $7x^2 y + 5x^2 y$ $12x^2 y$

14. $15x + 3x + 4y + y$ $18x + 5y$

15. $x^2 + x + 3x^2 + 4x$ $4x^2 + 5x$

16. $mn + m^2 n + 31mn$ $m^2 n + 32mn$

17. $3.5x(5x^4)$ $17.5x^5$

18. $4y^2(6y^4)$ $24y^6$

19. $\frac{2}{3}m^2 n\left(\frac{9}{10}m^2 n^6\right)$ $\frac{3}{5}m^4 n^7$

20. $\frac{1}{4}vw(10v^2)$ $\frac{5}{2}v^3 w$

21. $15(-23)$ -345

22. $14 + (-18)$ -4

23. $19 - (-13)$ 32

24. $-105 \div (-3)$ 35

25. $206 \div (-2)$ -103

26. $-19(-23)$ 437

27. $-13 - (-24)$ 11

28. $-16 + 47$ 31

Solve.

29. $x - 4 = 8$ 12

30. $y + 5 = -8$ -13

31. $12t = 36$ 3

32. $\frac{v}{8} = -4$ -32

33. $\frac{2w}{9} = 8$ 36

34. $3r + 6 = r - 5$ $-5\frac{1}{2}$

35. $3(y - 4) = y + 2$ 7

36. $m + 3m = 39 - 3$ 9

37. $-3b = b + 8$ -2

38. $q + 7 = 9 - q$ 1

39. $\frac{8c}{3} - 1 = 7$ 3

40. $-\frac{5}{9}d = \frac{1}{3}$ $-\frac{3}{5}$

Write each as an algebraic expression.

41. seven more than a number v $v + 7$

42. the quotient of 108 and a number q $\frac{108}{q}$

43. the product of two numbers, m and n mn

44. four less than a number u $u - 4$

45. three less than twice a number c $2c - 3$

46. the product of 8 and the sum of 3 and a number f $8(3 + f)$

<table>
<tr><td>

4.2

</td><td>

Solving Inequalities, Using Addition or Subtraction

</td></tr>
</table>

In Chapter 3 you found the solutions to some equations by adding the same number to each side of an equation. You used the *addition property of equality*.

There is a similar property of inequality. You can use the **addition property of inequality** to add the same number to each side of an inequality.

Addition Property of Inequality	**Let a, b, and c be any real numbers.** **If $a < b$, then $a + c < b + c$.** **If $a > b$, then $a + c > b + c$.**

EXAMPLES

1	**Solve $x - 3 < -1$. Graph the solution set. The replacement set is the set of real numbers.**

SOLUTION

$$x - 3 < -1$$
$$x - 3 + 3 < -1 + 3 \quad \text{Add 3 to each side.}$$
$$x < 2$$

CHECK

Since the solution set is an infinite set, you cannot check every solution. Try a few values, using the graph to help you choose appropriate values to check.

Try -5. $\quad -5 - 3 \overset{?}{<} -1$ $\qquad\qquad$ Try -7. $\quad -7 - 3 \overset{?}{<} -1$
$\qquad\qquad -8 < -1$ ✔ $\qquad\qquad\qquad\qquad -10 < -1$ ✔

Remember that the replacement set for each variable is the set of real numbers. Exceptions that are not obvious will be noted.

You found the solutions to some equations by subtracting the same number from each side of an equation. You used the *subtraction property of equality*. You can use the **subtraction property of inequality** to subtract the same number from each side of an inequality.

Subtraction Property of Inequality	**Let a, b, and c be any real numbers.** **If $a < b$, then $a - c < b - c$.** **If $a > b$, then $a - c > b - c$.**

OBJECTIVE

Solve an inequality by using the addition property of inequality or the subtraction property of inequality.

TEACHER'S NOTES

See p. T26.

CLASSROOM EXAMPLES

1. Solve $x - 5 < -3$. Graph the solution set. The replacement set is the set of real numbers.
$$x - 5 < -3$$
$$x - 5 + 5 < -3 + 5$$
$$x < 2$$

2. Solve $x + 6 \geq -4$. Graph the solution set.
$$x + 6 \geq -4$$
$$x + 6 - 6 \geq -4 - 6$$
$$x \geq -10$$

3. Solve $x + 3.9 \leq 4.3$.
$$x + 3.9 \leq 4.3$$
$$x + 3.9 + (-3.9)$$
$$\qquad \leq 4.3 + (-3.9)$$
$$x \leq 0.4$$

MIXED REVIEW

1. Simplify $\frac{16 - 4}{2} + 3(8 + 2)$. 36
2. Solve $\frac{8c}{2} - 3 = 12$. $3\frac{3}{4}$
3. Simplify $\left(-\frac{1}{4}x^3y^4\right)(-36x^2y)$. $9x^5y^5$
4. Evaluate $\frac{16}{2a^2}$ if $a = -2$. 2
5. Complete $|0|$. 0

ASSIGNMENT GUIDE

Minimum
1–12, 13–21 odd, 31–40

Regular
13–41

Maximum
21–50

ADDITIONAL ANSWERS

Written Exercises

For the odd-numbered solutions, see *Answers to Selected Exercises*, p. 571.

2.

4.

6.

---

2 Solve $x + 5 \geq -2$. Graph the solution set.

SOLUTION

$$x + 5 \geq -2$$
$$x + 5 - 5 \geq -2 - 5 \quad \text{Subtract 5 from each side.}$$
$$x \geq -7$$

CHECK

Try 4. $\quad 4 + 5 \overset{?}{\geq} -2$
$$9 \geq -2 \quad \checkmark$$

You can use either addition or subtraction to solve some inequalities.

3 Solve $x + 4.1 \leq 5.6$.

SOLUTIONS

$$x + 4.1 \leq 5.6 \qquad\qquad x + 4.1 \leq 5.6$$
$$x + 4.1 + (-4.1) \leq 5.6 + (-4.1) \qquad x + 4.1 - 4.1 \leq 5.6 - 4.1$$
$$x \leq 1.5 \qquad\qquad x \leq 1.5 \quad \text{Remember to check.}$$

ORAL EXERCISES

State which symbol, $<$ or $>$, you would use to make each sentence true.

1. If $11 > 8$, then $11 + 9 \; \bullet \; 8 + 9$. $>$

2. If $15 < 24$, then $15 + (-7) \; \bullet \; 24 + (-7)$. $<$

3. If $x + 4 > 6$, then $x + 4 - 4 \; \bullet \; 6 - 4$. $>$

4. If $s - 5 > 7$, then $s - 5 + 5 \; \bullet \; 7 + 5$. $>$

Solve.

5. $x - 3 > 2 \quad x > 5$

6. $y - 5 < -8 \quad y < -3$

7. $z + 1 \geq 4 \quad z \geq 3$

8. $r - 7 \leq 6 \quad r \leq 13$

9. $s + 2 \geq -3 \quad s \geq -5$

10. $t - 3 < 7 \quad t < 10$

11. $s + 3 < 4 \quad s < 1$

12. $t - 1 > -3 \quad t > -2$

13. $v - 2 \leq -3 \quad v \leq -1$

14. $x + 4 \geq 2 \quad x \geq -2$

15. $y + 5 \geq -4 \quad y \geq -9$

16. $z + 10 < -2 \quad z < -12$

WRITTEN EXERCISES

A. Solve each inequality. Graph the solution set.

1. $x + 7 > 12 \quad x > 5$

2. $y + 8 > 14 \quad y > 6$

3. $z - 3 < -4 \quad z < -1$

4. $w - 7 < -9 \quad w < -2$

5. $q + 4 \geq -3 \quad q \geq -7$

6. $n + 2 \leq -6 \quad n \leq -8$

7. $m - 8 < 8$ $m < 16$ **8.** $s - 4 \geq 5$ $s \geq 9$ **9.** $t - 7 < -11$ $t < -4$

10. $v + 7 > -4$ $v > -11$ **11.** $z + 9 \leq 6$ $z \leq -3$ **12.** $x - 3 < 5$ $x < 8$

B. Solve each inequality.

13. $n - 1.6 < 3.1$ $n < 4.7$ **14.** $m + 6.2 > 4.5$ $m > -1.7$ **15.** $x - \frac{1}{4} \leq \frac{11}{4}$ $x \leq 3$

16. $s + \frac{7}{8} \geq \frac{13}{8}$ $s \geq \frac{3}{4}$ **17.** $t - \frac{7}{3} > 8$ $t > 10\frac{1}{3}$ **18.** $v + 9 < \frac{21}{2}$ $v < 1\frac{1}{2}$

19. $z - 4.3 > 12.9$ $z > 17.2$ **20.** $r + 2.81 \leq 11.5$ $r \leq 8.69$ **21.** $q - 0.9 \geq 8$ $q \geq 8.9$

22. $1.75 + x < 7.3$ $x < 5.55$ **23.** $2.6 + y > 1.9$ $y > -0.7$ **24.** $8.1 + s \leq 6.5$

$s \leq -1.6$

25. $w + 8.9 \leq 6.3$ $w \leq -2.6$ **26.** $q - 15.67 > 19.024$ $q > 34.694$

27. $x - 4\frac{2}{3} < 8\frac{1}{6}$ $x < 12\frac{5}{6}$ **28.** $y + 16\frac{1}{5} \geq 4\frac{2}{3}$ $y \geq -11\frac{8}{15}$

29. $q - (-8.6) \geq 9.403$ $q \geq 0.803$ **30.** $t + (-0.072) < -9.63$ $t < -9.558$

31. $b - 11\frac{1}{4} > -4\frac{1}{6}$ $b > 7\frac{1}{12}$ **32.** $d + \left(-15\frac{3}{10}\right) \leq -18\frac{2}{3}$ $d \leq -3\frac{11}{30}$

33. $r - \left(-3\frac{2}{5}\right) < -8\frac{1}{4}$ $r < -11\frac{13}{20}$ **34.** $e + 15\frac{1}{9} \geq 10\frac{1}{6}$ $e \geq -4\frac{17}{18}$

35. $3.06 + g \geq -9.305$ $g \geq -12.365$ **36.** $-0.01 + h < 16.037$ $h < 16.047$

37. $-18\frac{2}{3} + i \leq -3\frac{5}{6}$ $i \leq 14\frac{5}{6}$ **38.** $5\frac{3}{8} + m > -2\frac{1}{6}$ $m > -7\frac{13}{24}$

39. $n + 0.0003 > 9.807$ $n > 9.8067$ **40.** $p - 8\frac{7}{12} \geq -3\frac{2}{5}$ $p \geq 5\frac{11}{60}$

C. Solve each inequality. (NOTE: If $a < x$, then $x > a$.)

41. $4.8 \geq t + 9.1$ $t \leq -4.3$ **42.** $11.7 > 5.9 + r$ $r < 5.8$

43. $10.3 < 9.4 + m$ $m > 0.9$ **44.** $10x > 9(x + 2)$ $x > 18$

45. $4(3y + 5) > 2y$ $y > -2$ **46.** $4(3s + 3) > 11s + 2$ $s > -10$

47. $3(3x + 4) < 8x$ $x < -12$ **48.** $2(4y + 7) < 7y$ $y < -14$

49. $-3(6t + 2) > -19t - 1$ $t > 5$ **50.** $-2(3w - 4) \leq -7w + 4$ $w \leq -4$

8.

10.

12.

CHALLENGE

In a survey, 236 of the 350 people interviewed like mushrooms on pizza, 187 like green peppers, and 75 like both toppings. How many of the people interviewed don't like either topping?   2

OBJECTIVE

Solve an inequality by using the multiplication property of inequality or the division property of inequality.

TEACHER'S NOTES

See p. T26.

1. Multiply each side of $-3 < 8$ by 3.
$$-3 < 8$$
$$3(-3) < 3(8)$$
$$-9 < 24$$

2. Divide each side of $-4 < 8$ by 2.
$$-4 < 8$$
$$\frac{-4}{2} < \frac{8}{2}$$
$$-2 < 4$$

3. Multiply each side of $-3 < 8$ by -3.
$$-3 < 8$$
$$-3(-3) > -3(8)$$
$$9 > -24$$

4. Divide each side of $-4 < 8$ by -2.
$$-4 < 8$$
$$\frac{-4}{-2} > \frac{8}{-2}$$
$$2 > -4$$

5. Solve $\frac{x}{3} > 2$. Graph the solution set.
$$\frac{x}{3} > 2$$
$$3\left(\frac{x}{3}\right) > 3(2)$$
$$x > 6$$

4.3 Solving Inequalities, Using Multiplication or Division

In Chapter 3 you found the solution to some equations by multiplying or dividing each side of the equation by the same number. You used the *multiplication property of equality* or the *division property of equality*.

There are similar properties of inequality. You can use the **multiplication property of inequality** to multiply each side of an inequality by the same nonzero number. Or you can use the **division property of inequality** to divide each side of the inequality by the same nonzero number. If you multiply or divide by a *positive* number, the order of the inequality *remains the same*. If you multiply or divide by a *negative* number, the order of the inequality *reverses*.

EXAMPLES

1   **Multiply each side of $-4 < 6$ by 2.**

SOLUTION
$$-4 < 6$$
$$2(-4) \; ? \; 2(6)$$
$$-8 < 12$$

2   **Divide each side of $-4 < 6$ by 2.**

SOLUTION
$$-4 < 6$$
$$\frac{-4}{2} \; ? \; \frac{6}{2}$$
$$-2 < 3$$

3   **Multiply each side of $-4 < 6$ by -2.**

SOLUTION
$$-4 < 6$$
$$-2(-4) \; ? \; -2(6)$$
$$8 > -12$$

4   **Divide each side of $-4 < 6$ by -2.**

SOLUTION
$$-4 < 6$$
$$\frac{-4}{-2} \; ? \; \frac{6}{-2}$$
$$2 > -3$$

Multiplication Property of Inequality	Let a, b, and c be any real numbers, and $c > 0$. If $a < b$, then $ac < bc$. If $a > b$, then $ac > bc$. Let a, b, and c be any real numbers, and $c < 0$. If $a < b$, then $ac > bc$. If $a > b$, then $ac < bc$.

Division Property of Inequality	Let a, b, and c be any real numbers, and $c > 0$. If $a < b$, then $\frac{a}{c} < \frac{b}{c}$. If $a > b$, then $\frac{a}{c} > \frac{b}{c}$. Let a, b, and c be any real numbers, and $c < 0$. If $a < b$, then $\frac{a}{c} > \frac{b}{c}$. If $a > b$, then $\frac{a}{c} < \frac{b}{c}$.

5 Solve $\frac{x}{2} > 1$. Graph the solution set.

SOLUTION

$$\frac{x}{2} > 1$$

$$2\left(\frac{x}{2}\right) > 2(1) \quad \textit{Multiply each side by 2.}$$

$$x > 2$$

CHECK

Try 3. $\quad \frac{3}{2} \overset{?}{>} 1$

$$\frac{3}{2} > 1 \quad \text{✔}$$

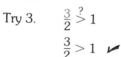

6 Solve $-4x < 8$. Graph the solution set.

SOLUTION

$$-4x < 8$$

$$\frac{-4x}{-4} > \frac{8}{-4} \quad \textit{Divide each side by } -4, \textit{ and reverse the order of the inequality.}$$

$$x > -2$$

CHECK

Try -1. $\quad -4(-1) \overset{?}{<} 8$

$$4 < 8 \quad \text{✔}$$

7 Solve $\frac{3}{4}x \geq -8$.

SOLUTION

$$\frac{3}{4}x \geq -8$$

$$\frac{4}{3}\left(\frac{3}{4}x\right) \geq \frac{4}{3}(-8) \quad \textit{Multiply each side by the multiplicative inverse of } \frac{3}{4}.$$

$$x \geq -\frac{32}{3} \quad \textit{Remember to check.}$$

You can use multiplication or division to solve some inequalities.

8 Solve $5x - 8x < 12$.

SOLUTIONS

$$5x - 8x < 12 \qquad \text{or} \qquad 5x - 8x < 12$$

$$-3x < 12 \qquad\qquad\qquad -3x < 12 \qquad \textit{Combine like terms.}$$

$$\frac{-3x}{-3} > \frac{12}{-3} \qquad\qquad -\frac{1}{3}(-3x) > -\frac{1}{3}(12)$$

$$x > -4 \qquad\qquad\qquad x > -4 \qquad \textit{Remember to check.}$$

6. Solve $-2x < 6$. Graph the solution set.

$$-2x < 6$$
$$\frac{-2x}{-2} > \frac{6}{-2}$$
$$x > -3$$

7. Solve $\frac{2}{3}x \geq -4$.

$$\frac{2}{3}x \geq -4$$
$$\frac{3}{2}\left(\frac{2}{3}x\right) \geq \frac{3}{2}(-4)$$
$$x \geq -6$$

8. Solve $4x - 7x < 15$.

$$4x - 7x < 15$$
$$-3x < 15$$
$$\frac{-3x}{-3} > \frac{15}{-3}$$
$$x > -5$$

MIXED REVIEW

1. Simplify $\frac{8 + 3(2)}{7}$. 2

2. Simplify $\left\{4 + \left[\frac{12 - 3}{3} + 2\right]3\right\}$. 19

3. Solve $\frac{8y}{4} - 12 = -36$.
   -12

4. Solve $-5b = b + 32$. $5\frac{1}{3}$

5. Find each difference.
   a. $\frac{1}{8} - \left(-\frac{1}{5}\right)$ $\frac{13}{40}$
   b. $[-18 - (-12 - 14)]$ 8

TEACHER'S RESOURCE MASTERS

Practice Master 14, Part 2

ASSIGNMENT GUIDE

Minimum
1–23 odd

Regular
13–24

Maximum
21–32

ORAL EXERCISES

State which symbol, $<$ or $>$, you would use to make each sentence true.

1. If $5 < 7$, then $5(2)$ ● $7(2)$. $<$

2. If $-8 < -2$, then $-8(-3)$ ● $-2(-3)$. $>$

3. If $-4 < 5$, then $\frac{-4}{-2}$ ● $\frac{5}{-2}$. $>$

4. If $-3 > -12$, then $\frac{-3}{4}$ ● $\frac{-12}{4}$. $>$

Solve.

5. $\frac{n}{5} < 3$ $n < 15$

6. $-8s > 16$

7. $\frac{m}{-4} > -2$ $m < 8$

8. $-2t \leq 8$

9. $\frac{s}{-2} < 10$ $s > -20$

10. $9w < -18$

11. $6r < 12$ $r < 2$

12. $\frac{x}{-3} \leq 4$

13. $10v \geq -10$ $v \geq -1$

14. $\frac{z}{8} \geq 5$ $z \geq 40$

15. $-8s > -24$

16. $\frac{t}{6} > -1$

WRITTEN EXERCISES

A. Solve each inequality.

1. $\frac{x}{4} < -1$ $x < -4$

2. $7y \leq -21$ $y \leq -3$

3. $\frac{-2z}{3} > 4$ $z < -6$

4. $\frac{3m}{4} \geq -5$ $m \geq -\frac{20}{3}$

5. $\frac{t}{-3} < -2$ $t > 6$

6. $-4v > 9$ $v < -\frac{9}{4}$

7. $-6n \leq 6$ $n \geq -1$

8. $\frac{2w}{5} > -2$ $w > -5$

9. $\frac{v}{2} \leq 3$ $v \leq 6$

10. $\frac{s}{3} < 4$ $s < 12$

11. $\frac{6z}{5} \geq 3$ $z \geq \frac{5}{2}$

12. $-5r < 12$ $r > -\frac{12}{5}$

B. Solve each inequality. Graph the solution set.

13. $-a > 0$ $a < 0$

14. $-b < 0$ $b > 0$

15. $-\frac{5}{9}c < -\frac{5}{9}$ $c > 1$

16. $3y > -3$ $y > -1$

17. $4x + 10x > 16$ $x > \frac{8}{7}$

18. $9s + 3s > 30$ $s > \frac{5}{2}$

19. $\frac{2}{3}t + \frac{1}{3}t < -8$ $t < -8$

20. $-\frac{5}{8}r + \frac{3}{8}r < -12$ $r > 48$

21. $x - \frac{x}{2} > 11$ $x > 22$

22. $t - \frac{3t}{4} > -2$ $t > -8$

23. $-6.4s + 3s > 1.7$ $s < -0.5$

24. $-18r - 8.7r < 13.35$ $r > -0.5$

C. a and b represent real numbers. Describe the real numbers represented by c so that the inequality is true.

25. $ac < bc$, when $a > 0$ and $b < 0$. $c < 0$

26. $ac < bc$, when $a < 0$ and $b > 0$. $c > 0$

27. $\frac{a}{c} < \frac{b}{c}$, when $a > 0$ and $b < 0$. $c < 0$

28. $\frac{a}{c} > \frac{b}{c}$, when $a < 0$ and $b > 0$. $c < 0$

29. $ac > bc$, when $a > 0$ and $b < 0$. $c > 0$

30. $ac > bc$, when $a < 0$ and $b > 0$. $c < 0$

31. $\frac{a}{c} < \frac{b}{c}$, when $a < 0$ and $b > 0$. $c > 0$

32. $\frac{a}{c} > \frac{b}{c}$, when $a > 0$ and $b < 0$. $c > 0$

4.4 | Simplifying and Solving Inequalities

Solving an inequality may require using more than one property.

EXAMPLES

1 **Solve $6 + \frac{7}{10}x - x > 9$.**

SOLUTION

$$6 + \frac{7}{10}x - x > 9$$

$$6 + \frac{7}{10}x - \frac{10}{10}x > 9$$

$$6 - \frac{3}{10}x > 9 \qquad \text{\textit{Combine like terms.}}$$

$$6 + (-6) - \frac{3}{10}x > 9 + (-6) \qquad \text{\textit{Add -6 to each side.}}$$

$$-\frac{3}{10}x > 3$$

$$-\frac{10}{3}\left(-\frac{3}{10}x\right) < \left(-\frac{10}{3}\right) \cdot 3 \qquad \text{\textit{Multiply each side by the multiplicative inverse of $-\frac{3}{10}$,}}$$
$$\text{\textit{and reverse the order of the inequality.}}$$

$$x < -10 \qquad \text{\textit{Remember to check.}}$$

2 **Solve $5x + 9 \geq 4 - 3x$.**

SOLUTION

$$5x + 9 \geq 4 - 3x$$
$$5x + 3x + 9 \geq 4 - 3x + 3x \qquad \text{\textit{Add $3x$ to each side to isolate the variable on the left}}$$
$$\text{\textit{side.}}$$

$$8x + 9 \geq 4$$

$$8x + 9 + (-9) \geq 4 + (-9) \qquad \text{\textit{Add -9 to each side.}}$$

$$8x \geq -5$$

$$\frac{8x}{8} \geq \frac{-5}{8} \qquad \text{\textit{Divide each side by 8.}}$$

$$x \geq -\frac{5}{8} \qquad \text{\textit{Remember to check.}}$$

Sometimes the solution set is the set of all real numbers or the empty set.

3 **Solve $2x - 4 < 2x + 5$.**

SOLUTION

$$2x - 4 < 2x + 5$$
$$2x - 2x - 4 < 2x - 2x + 5$$
$$-4 < 5$$

This is a true statement. Therefore, the solution set is the set of all real numbers.

OBJECTIVE

Solve an inequality by using the addition or the subtraction property of inequality and then the multiplication or the division property of inequality.

TEACHER'S NOTES

See p. T26.

CLASSROOM EXAMPLES

1. Solve $3 + \frac{3}{5}x - x > 7$.
$$3 + \frac{3}{5}x - x > 7$$
$$3 + \frac{3}{5}x - \frac{5}{5}x > 7$$
$$3 - \frac{2}{5}x > 7$$
$$3 + (-3) - \frac{2}{5}x > 7 + (-3)$$
$$-\frac{2}{5}x > 4$$
$$-\frac{5}{2}\left(-\frac{2}{5}x\right) < -\frac{5}{2}(4)$$
$$\frac{8}{6} - \frac{5}{2}\left(-\frac{2}{5}x\right) < -\frac{5}{2}(4)$$
$$x < -10$$

2. Solve $4x + 6 \geq 1 - 3x$.
$$4x + 6 \geq 1 - 3x$$
$$4x + 3x + 6 \geq 1 - 3x$$
$$\qquad\qquad + 3x$$
$$7x + 6 \geq 1$$
$$7x + 6 + (-6) \geq 1 + (-6)$$
$$7x \geq -5$$
$$\frac{7x}{7} \geq \frac{-5}{7}$$
$$x \geq -\frac{5}{7}$$

3. Solve $3x - 5 < 3x + 8$.
$$3x - 5 < 3x + 8$$
$$3x - 3x - 5 < 3x - 3x$$
$$\qquad\qquad + 8$$
$$-5 < 8 \quad \text{TRUE}$$
Solution set is set of all real numbers.

4. Solve $3x - 8 \geq 5x - 2x + 5$.

$$3x - 8 \geq 5x - 2x + 5$$
$$3x - 8 \geq 3x + 5$$
$$3x - 3x - 8 \geq 3x - 3x + 5$$
$$-8 \geq 5 \quad \text{FALSE}$$

Solution set is empty.

MIXED REVIEW

1. Simplify $[(3)(-8)](-6)$.
   114
2. Simplify $-5.6 \div -0.14$.
   40
3. Simplify $3^2 x^5 (x^{10})$. $\quad 9x^{15}$
4. Evaluate $\frac{s^2}{t^2}$ if $s = 6$ and $t = -3$. $\quad 4$
5. Solve $\frac{y}{7} = -8$. $\quad -56$

TEACHER'S RESOURCE MASTERS

Practice Master 15, Part 1

Quiz 7

ASSIGNMENT GUIDE

Minimum
1–11 odd, 17–27 odd

Regular
13–24

Maximum
13–27 odd, 29–32

ADDITIONAL ANSWERS

Oral Exercises

1. subtracting 7 from both sides; dividing both sides by 3

2. adding 10 to both sides; dividing both sides by 9

3. subtracting 4 from both sides; dividing both sides by -6

4 Solve $4x - 5 \geq 7x - 3x + 2$.

SOLUTION

$$4x - 5 \geq 7x - 3x + 2$$
$$4x - 5 \geq 4x + 2$$
$$4x - 4x - 5 \geq 4x - 4x + 2$$
$$-5 \geq 2$$

This is a false statement. Therefore, the solution set is empty.

ORAL EXERCISES

Tell how each inequality was derived from the inequality above it.

1. $3x + 7 > 4$
$3x > -3$
$x > -1$

2. $9y - 10 < -8$
$9y < 2$
$y < \frac{2}{9}$

3. $-6s + 4 < 17$
$-6s < 13$
$s > -\frac{13}{6}$

4. $-35 - t < 15$
$-t < 50$
$t > -50$

5. $\frac{r}{2} - 3 > 7$
$\frac{r}{2} > 10$
$r > 20$

6. $\frac{2}{3}m + 5 < 3$
$\frac{2}{3}m < -2$
$m < -3$

7. $-\frac{5}{4}v - 8 > 17$
$-\frac{5}{4}v > 25$
$v < -20$

8. $7x - 5 > 2x + 20$
$5x - 5 > 20$
$5x > 25$
$x > 5$

9. $-2y + 3 < 8y - 7$
$-10y + 3 < -7$
$-10y < -10$
$y > 1$

10. $2a - 2 + 4a < -4$
$6a - 2 < -4$
$6a < -2$
$a < -\frac{1}{3}$

11. $8b > 7 - 8b + 5$
$8b > 12 - 8b$
$16b > 12$
$b > \frac{3}{4}$

12. $1 + 3s > 6 + 4s$
$1 - s > 6$
$-s > 5$
$s < -5$

WRITTEN EXERCISES

A. Solve each inequality.

1. $3 - 2t < 7 \quad t > -2$

2. $5 - 6g < 21 \quad g > -\frac{8}{3}$

3. $2s - 15 > 6 \quad s > \frac{21}{2}$

4. $3r - 12 > 9 \quad r > 7$

5. $5y - 8 < -7 \quad y < \frac{1}{5}$

6. $3x - 7 < -11$ $\quad x < -\frac{4}{3}$

7. $5m - 2 > 0 \quad m > \frac{2}{5}$

8. $6n - 11 > 0 \quad n > \frac{11}{6}$

9. $-6x + 8 > -3$ $\quad x < \frac{11}{6}$

10. $5 - 9t > -2 \quad t < \frac{7}{9}$

11. $-\frac{2}{3}m - 1 > 5 \quad m < -9$

12. $-\frac{3}{5}n - 3 > 6$

B. **13.** $\frac{1}{3}x > \frac{4}{3}x$ $x < 0$ **14.** $\frac{1}{4}y > \frac{5}{4}y$ $y < 0$

15. $6m - 3 < -5m$ $m < \frac{3}{11}$ **16.** $7n - 5 < -2n$ $n < \frac{5}{9}$

17. $5m + 16 - 8m > 4$ $m < 4$ **18.** $12n - 7 + 8n > 23$ $n > \frac{3}{2}$

19. $6p < -19 + 7p - 3$ $p > 22$ **20.** $3q < -15 + 2q + 4$ $q < -11$

21. $-\frac{1}{2}q > 3 - \frac{3}{4}q - 7$ $q > -16$ **22.** $\frac{5}{6}r > 5 - \frac{2}{3}r$ $r > \frac{10}{3}$

23. $\frac{2}{5}r - 6 > \frac{4}{5}r + 8$ $r < -35$ **24.** $\frac{1}{8}s - 2 > \frac{3}{8}s + 10$ $s < -48$

25. $-2t + 8 < 11 - 2t$ all real nos.   **26.** $7 - 6y < 12 + 3y - 9y$ all real nos.

27. $3x + 5 > 5x + 8 - 2x$ $\varnothing$ **28.** $4 + 5r - 7 < 5r - 9$ $\varnothing$

C. **29.** $-1.3 - 1.7r < -1.1 - 1.2r$ $r > -0.4$ **30.** $-1.9s - 1.4 < -1.2s - 1.12$

31. $2(6z - 5) < -14$ $z < -\frac{1}{3}$ **32.** $3(2w + 4) < 6$ $w < -1$ $s > -0.4$

33. $7(r + 3) < -8r - 9$ $r < -2$ **34.** $3(s - 8) < 13s + 16$ $s > -4$

ERROR SEARCH

Find the error in each exercise and give the correct answer.

1. $3^3 = 3 \cdot 3 = 9$ 27   **2.** $x^4 \cdot x^6 = x^{24}$ x^{10}

3. $5\frac{3}{8} + 2\frac{2}{3} = 7\frac{5}{11}$ $8\frac{1}{24}$ **4.** $\frac{15}{12} \cdot \frac{18}{21} = \frac{25}{28}$ $1\frac{1}{14}$

5. $-19 - (-23) = -42$ 4   **6.** $64 \div 2 \cdot 8 = 64 \div 16$
     $= 4$ 256

7. $[(13 - 4) \div 9 + 6]2$ **8.** $3 + 2^4 - 8 = 5^4 - 8$
   $= (9 \div 9 + 6)2$ $= 625 - 8$
   $= 1 + 12$ $= 617$ 11
   $= 13$ 14

9. $3x = 6$ **10.** $2x - 5x = 21$
   $3x - 3 = 6 - 3$ $3x = 21$
      $x = 3$ 2 $x = 7$ -7

11. $-3(x + 7) = 12$ **12.** $2(3x - 6) + 7 = 7x$
   $-3x + 21 = 12$ $6x - 12 + 7 = 7x$
     $-3x = -9$ $6x - 7 = 7x$
      $x = 3$ -11 $-7 = x$ -5

4. adding 35 to both sides; multiplying both sides by -1

5. adding 3 to both sides; multiplying both sides by 2

6. subtracting 5 from both sides; multiplying both sides by $\frac{3}{2}$

7. adding 8 to both sides; multiplying both sides by $-\frac{4}{5}$

8. subtracting $2x$ from both sides; adding 5 to both sides; dividing both sides by 5

9. subtracting $8y$ from both sides; subtracting 3 from both sides; dividing both sides by -10.

10. adding like terms on left side; adding 2 to both sides; dividing both sides by 6

11. adding like terms on right side; adding $8b$ to both sides; dividing both sides by 16

12. subtracting $4s$ from both sides; subtracting 1 from both sides; multiplying both sides by -1

Written Exercises
12. $n < -15$

TEACHER'S NOTES

See p. T26.

CLASSROOM EXAMPLES

Translate each sentence to an inequality.

a. 8 is greater than y. $8 > y$ or
   $y < 8$

b. Three times a number is greater than -3.
   $3n > -3$

c. A number is at most 5.
   $n \leq 5$

d. A number is no less than 9.
   $n \geq 9$

MIXED REVIEW

1. $3(2^3)$ 24

2. $3 + (-0.56)$ 2.44

3. $(-6.08) \div (-3.2)$ 1.9

4. $(8 + 6) \div (24 \div 12)$ 7

5. $6 \cdot 3 + 4 \cdot 2^2$ 34

TEACHER'S RESOURCE MASTERS

Practice Master 15, Part 2

ASSIGNMENT GUIDE

Minimum
1–14

Regular
9–22

Maximum
9–16, 17–27 odd

4.5 | Writing Inequalities

Many problems in algebra may involve inequalities. In order to solve such problems, you need to know how to write them, using one of the inequality symbols $>$, $<$, $\geq$, or $\leq$.

Meaning of inequality	*Inequality*
x is less than 7.	$x < 7$
x is greater than 2.	$x > 2$
x is at most 5.	$x \leq 5$
x is no more than 5.	
x is at least 9.	$x \geq 9$
x is no less than 9.	

EXAMPLE

Translate each sentence to an inequality. When necessary, choose a variable before translating.

a. 9 is greater than x.

b. Four times a number is greater than -6.

c. A number is at most 6.

d. A number is no less than 8.

SOLUTIONS

a. $9 > x$ or $x < 9$.

b. Let z = the number. Then $4z > -6$.

c. Let s = the number. Then $s \leq 6$.

d. Let t = the number. Then $t \geq 8$.

ORAL EXERCISES

Translate each sentence, using $<$, $>$, $\leq$, or $\geq$.

1. 5 is greater than x. $5 > x$ or $x < 5$

2. 7 is less than y. $7 < y$ or $y > 7$

3. $y - 2$ is less than 3. $y - 2 < 3$

4. $2m$ is greater than 6. $2m > 6$

5. $6s$ is no more than 18. $6s \leq 18$

6. $p + 3$ is at least 15. $p + 3 \geq 15$

WRITTEN EXERCISES

A. Choose a variable and then write each sentence, using $<$, $>$, $\leq$, or $\geq$.

1. Three times a number is greater than 12. $3m > 12$

2. Twice a number is less than -20. $2w < -20$

3. Three times a number is less than the number increased by 12. $3v < v + 12$

4. One half of a number is greater than the number plus 17. $\frac{1}{2}a > a + 17$

5. A number is at most 7. $z \leq 7$

6. A number is at least -6. $s \geq -6$

7. Four times a number is at most $\frac{2}{3}$. $4t \leq \frac{2}{3}$

8. Three fourths of a number is at least -3. $\frac{3}{4}x \geq -3$

B. **9.** Seven less than twice a number is greater than the number increased by 3. $2n - 7 > n + 3$

10. Nineteen more than the product of 3 and a number is less than the number increased by 2. $3y + 19 < y + 2$

11. The sum of a number and 12 is more than 3 times the number.

12. The sum of a number and 15 is more than 4 times the number.

13. Twenty less than a number is no less than 48. $d - 20 \geq 48$

14. Fifteen more than a number is no more than 32. $b + 15 \leq 32$

15. A number is multiplied by 6, then 8 is added to the result, and the total is at least 50. $6t + 8 \geq 50$

16. A number is multiplied by 5, then 4 is subtracted from the product, and the result is at most 25. $5v - 4 \leq 25$

C. **17.** U.S. senators must be at least 30 years old. $s \geq 30$

18. Members of the House of Representatives must be no less than 25 years old.

19. Round-trip airfare is no more than $378. $r \leq 378$

20. In 1938, the rate of pay was no less than $0.25 per hour. $r \geq 0.25$

21. By 1981, the rate of pay was at least $3.35 per hour. $r \geq 3.35$

22. Roger's test average is at least 92. $a \geq 92$

23. Marie's bowling average is no more than 146. $a \leq 146$

24. The time of the red traffic signal is at most 2 minutes. $t \leq 2$

25. The delivery charge is at least $18. $c \geq 18$

26. The state's driving age is no younger than 16 years old. $d \geq 16$

27. The circumference of any circle is more than 3 times the diameter. $c > 3d$

28. The perimeter of a rectangle is at least 4 times the length of its shorter side. $p \geq 4s$

SELF-QUIZ

Graph the solution set of each inequality.

1. $x \leq 3$ **2.** $y > -2$ **3.** $v \neq 5$

Solve each inequality.

4. $s - 5 \geq 3$ $s \geq 8$

5. $m + 8 < 4$ $m < -4$

6. $\frac{t}{4} < 2$ $t < 8$

7. $-8y > 6$ $y < -\frac{3}{4}$

8. $\frac{4c}{5} \geq -1$ $c \geq -1\frac{1}{4}$

9. $-\frac{v}{3} \leq -2$ $v \geq 6$

10. $2r - 3 < 9$ $r < 6$

11. $5 - \frac{3a}{4} \geq 11$ $a \leq -8$

12. $5t - 2t > -15$ $t > -5$

13. $6s - 2 \leq 8s + 10$ $s \geq -6$

Choose a variable and then write each sentence, using $<$, $>$, $\leq$, or $\geq$.

14. Four times a number is less than 9. $4n < 9$

15. Six more than twice a number is less than the number increased by 10. $2x + 6 < x + 10$

TEACHER'S NOTES

See p. T26.

CLASSROOM EXAMPLES

1.

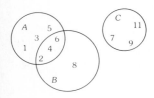

Use the diagram to find each intersection or union.

a. $A \cap B$ {2, 4, 6}

b. $(A \cap B) \cup C$ {2, 4, 6, 7, 9, 11}

c. $A \cap C$ ∅

d. $(A \cap C) \cup B$ {2, 4, 6, 8}

2. Use the given sets to find each intersection or union.
$A = \{6, 8, 10, 12\}$
$B = \{8, 12, 16\}$
$C = \{16\}$

a. $A \cup B$ {6, 8, 10, 12, 16}

b. $(A \cup B) \cap C$ {16}

c. $A \cap C$ ∅

d. $(A \cap C) \cup B$ {8, 12, 16}

MIXED REVIEW

1. Solve each equation.

a. $s - 3.5 = -14.8$ -11.3

b. $\frac{x}{5} + 15 = 38$ 115

| 4.6 | Intersection and Union of Sets |

$A = \{1, 2, 3, 4\}$ $B = \{2, 4, 6, 8\}$ $C = \{5, 7, 9\}$

The **intersection** of two sets is a set consisting of those elements that are *common to both sets*. The intersection of A and B is {2, 4}, or $A \cap B = \{2, 4\}$. The diagram below is shaded to show the intersection of A and B.

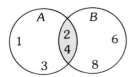

The diagram below shows that there are no elements that are common to sets A and C. The intersection of A and C is the empty set, or $A \cap C = \varnothing$.

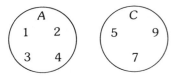

The **union** of two sets is a set consisting of all the elements that *belong to either set or to both sets*. The union of A and B is {1, 2, 3, 4, 6, 8}, or $A \cup B = \{1, 2, 3, 4, 6, 8\}$. The diagram below is shaded to show the union of A and B.

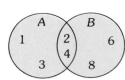

EXAMPLES

| 1 | **Use the diagram to find each intersection or union in the examples.**

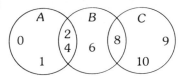

a. $A \cap B$

c. $A \cap C$

b. $(A \cap B) \cup C$

d. $(A \cap C) \cup B$

SOLUTIONS

a. $A \cap B = \{2, 4\}$

c. $A \cap C = \varnothing$

b. $(A \cap B) \cup C = \{2, 4, 8, 9, 10\}$

d. $(A \cap C) \cup B = \{2, 4, 6, 8\}$

2	**Use the given sets to find each intersection or union.**

$A = \{1, 2, 3, 4\}$ $B = \{2, 4, 6\}$ $C = \{5, 6\}$

a. $A \cup B$ **b.** $(A \cup B) \cap C$

c. $A \cap C$ **d.** $(A \cap C) \cup B$

SOLUTION

a. $A \cup B = \{1, 2, 3, 4, 6\}$ **b.** $(A \cup B) \cap C = \{6\}$

c. $A \cap C = \varnothing$ **d.** $(A \cap C) \cup B = \{2, 4, 6\}$, or B

ORAL EXERCISES

Find the intersection of the sets.

1. $\{1, 2\} \cap \{2, 3\}$ $\{2\}$ **2.** $\{2, 3\} \cap \{1, 2\}$ $\{2\}$

3. $\{2, 3\} \cap \{1, 2, 3, 4\}$ $\{2, 3\}$ **4.** $\{1, 2, 3, 4\} \cap \{2, 3\}$ $\{2, 3\}$

Find the union of the sets.

5. $\{1, 3\} \cup \{2, 4\}$ $\{1, 2, 3, 4\}$ **6.** $\{2, 4\} \cup \{1, 3\}$ $\{1, 2, 3, 4\}$

7. $\{2, 4\} \cup \{1, 2, 3, 4\}$ $\{1, 2, 3, 4\}$ **8.** $\{1, 2, 3, 4\} \cup \{2, 4\}$ $\{1, 2, 3, 4\}$

WRITTEN EXERCISES

A. Find the intersection and the union of the sets.

1. $\{3, 6, 9, 12\}, \{4, 8, 12, 16\}$ **2.** $\{4, 8, 12, 16\}, \{2, 4, 6\}$

3. $\{-4, -2, 0\}, \{-2, 0, 2\}$ **4.** $\{1, 2, 3, 4\}, \{1, 3\}$

5. $\{-2, -1, 0, 1, 2\}, \{-1, 0, 1\}$ **6.** $\{5, 10, 15, 20\}, \{8, 10, 12\}$

7. $\{2, 3, 5, 7, 11\}, \{1, 3, 5, 7, 9\}$ **8.** $\{-3, -2, -1\}, \{-6, -5, -4\}$

9. $\{1, 2, 3, \ldots\}, \{2, 4, 6, \ldots\}$ **10.** $\{3, 6, 9, \ldots\}, \{1, 2, 3, \ldots\}$

11. $\{1, 3, 5, \ldots\}, \{2, 4, 6, \ldots\}$ **12.** $\{-2, -1, 0, \ldots\}, \{1, 2, 3, \ldots\}$

B. Use the given sets to find each union or intersection.

$A = \{-8, -6, -4\}$ $B = \{-8, -4, 6\}$ $C = \{4, 6, 8\}$ $D = \{-6, 4, 8\}$

13. $A \cap B$ $\{-8, -4\}$ **14.** $B \cap C$ $\{6\}$ **15.** $C \cap D$ $\{4, 8\}$

16. $B \cap D$ $\varnothing$ **17.** $(A \cap B) \cup C$ **18.** $(B \cap C) \cup D$

19. $(C \cap D) \cup A$ **20.** $(B \cap D) \cup C$ C **21.** $C \cup D$ $\{-6, 4, 6, 8\}$

22. $A \cup B$ $\{-8, -6, -4, 6\}$ **23.** $A \cup C$ **24.** $A \cup D$

Use the given sets to find each union or intersection.

$E = \{-3\}$ $G = \{-9, -7, -5, -3\}$ $I = \{\text{integers}\}$ $F = \varnothing$

$H = \{-7, -5, 5, 7, 9, 11\}$

25. $E \cap F$ F **26.** $F \cap H$ F **27.** $E \cup G$ G **28.** $E \cup I$ I

2. Simplify $-15(-18 - 6)$
  360

3. Complete.
  a. $-|-12|$ -12
  b. $|-8|$ 8

4. Simplify $8x^3y^2 + 5x^3y^2 + 12x^3y^2$. $25x^3y^2$

5. Solve $8x + 3 \geq 19$. $x \geq 2$

TEACHER'S RESOURCE MASTERS

Practice Master 16, Part 1

ASSIGNMENT GUIDE

Minimum
1–12, 13–33 odd

Regular
13–40

Maximum
27–49

ADDITIONAL ANSWERS

Written Exercises

1. $\{12\}$; $\{3, 4, 6, 8, 9, 12, 16\}$

2. $\{4\}$; $\{2, 4, 6, 8, 12, 16\}$

3. $\{-2, 0\}$; $\{-4, -2, 0, 2\}$

4. $\{1, 3\}$; $\{1, 2, 3, 4\}$

5. $\{-1, 0, 1\}$; $\{-2, -1, 0, 1, 2\}$

6. $\{10\}$; $\{5, 8, 10, 12, 15, 20\}$

7. $\{3, 5, 7\}$; $\{1, 2, 3, 5, 7, 9, 11\}$

8. $\varnothing$; $\{-6, -5, -4, -3, -2, -1\}$

9. $\{2, 4, 6, \ldots\}$; $\{1, 2, 3, \ldots\}$

(continued on next page)

29. $G \cap H$ {−7, −5}   **30.** $F \cup G$ G   **31.** $F \cup H$ H   **32.** $I \cup G$ I

33. $H \cup I$ I   **34.** $F \cap I$ F   **35.** $G \cap I$ G   **36.** $G \cup H$

37. $E \cap I$ E   **38.** $E \cap G$ E   **39.** $F \cup I$ I   **40.** $E \cup F$ E

C. Use the given sets to describe each intersection or union. Then graph the intersection or union on a number line.

J = {real numbers greater than −3}

K = {real numbers less than or equal to 5}

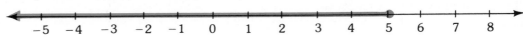

L = {real numbers greater than or equal to −4}

41. $J \cup K$ all real nos.   **42.** $J \cup L$ L   **43.** $J \cap K$ $-3 < x \le 5$

44. $J \cap L$ J   **45.** $K \cup L$ all real nos.   **46.** $K \cap L$ $-4 \le x \le 5$

47. $(K \cup L) \cap J$ J   **48.** $K \cup (L \cap J)$ **49.** $(K \cap L) \cap J$ $-3 < x \le 5$

MATH HERITAGE/The Origin of < and >

Thomas Harriot (1560–1621), an English mathematician, is acknowledged to be the first to use < and >, the commonly used symbols for "is less than" and "is greater than."

In 1585, Harriot was sent by Sir Walter Raleigh to survey and map the territory now known as North Carolina. Accompanying Harriot on this excursion was Captain John White, who made sketches of the people they encountered.

Upon returning to England, Harriot published a book about his experiences in the New World, which included the sketches made by Captain White. Among White's drawings appeared the symbol ⋉, which he had noticed on the shoulder blade of an Indian chief. Many people believe Harriot merely modified this Indian symbol so that it became what is known today as < and >.

4.7 | Solving Compound Sentences

OBJECTIVES

Solve disjunctions.
Solve conjunctions.

TEACHER'S NOTES

See p. T27.

A compound sentence is formed when two sentences are combined with the word **and** or the word **or.**

When *and* is used to combine two sentences, the resulting sentence is called a **conjunction.** The inequalities $x > -1$ and $x < 3$ can be combined as $-1 < x < 3$, which is read as "x is greater than -1 and less than 3." Study the graph of the conjunction $-1 < x < 3$ below.

Notice that only those points that belong to *both* the graph $-1 < x$ and the graph $x < 3$ are in the graph of the conjunction. So, $-1 < x < 3$ means that x is between -1 and 3. The solution set of a conjunction is the *intersection* of the solution sets of the sentences in the conjunction.

$-1 < x$

$x < 3$

$-1 < x < 3$

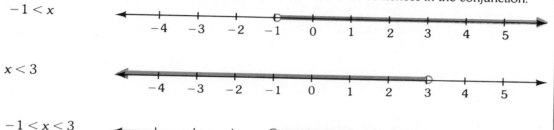

CLASSROOM EXAMPLES

1. Solve the conjunction $2y > y - 3$ and $3y + 2 < 5$. Graph the solution set.

$$2y > y - 3$$
$$2y - y > y - y - 3$$
$$y > -3$$
and
$$3y + 2 < 5$$
$$3y + 2 - 2 < 5 - 2$$
$$3y < 3$$
$$\frac{3y}{3} < \frac{3}{3}$$
$$y < 1$$
$$-3 < y < 1$$

When *or* is used to combine two sentences, the resulting sentence is called a **disjunction.** Study the graph of the disjunction $x < -2$ or $x > 1$ below.

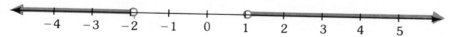

Notice that those points that belong to *either* the graph $x < -2$ or the graph $x > 1$ are in the graph of the disjunction. The solution set of a disjunction is the *union* of the solution sets of the sentences in the disjunction.

$x < -2$

$x > 1$

$x < -2$ or $x > 1$

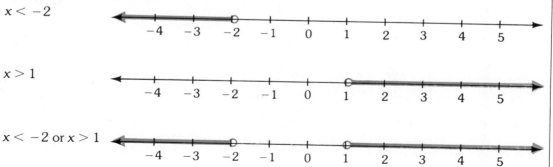

2. Solve the disjunction $2x + 4 > -2$ or $3x < x + 2$. Graph the solution set.

$$2x + 4 > -2$$
$$2x + 4 - 4 > -2 - 4$$
$$2x > -6$$
$$\frac{2x}{2} > \frac{-6}{2}$$
$$x > -3$$
or
$$3x < x + 2$$
$$3x - x < x - x + 2$$
$$2x < 2$$
$$\frac{2x}{2} < \frac{2}{2}$$
$$x < 1$$
$$x > -3 \quad \text{or} \quad x < 1$$

MIXED REVIEW

1. $A = \{1, 2, 3, 4, 5, 6\}$
   $B = \{1, 2, 4\}$ $C = \{7, 9\}$
   Indicate the set.
   a. $A \cup B$ A
   b. $A \cap C$ $\emptyset$

2. Solve $3x - 4 = 2x + 15$.
   19

3. Evaluate $\frac{y}{x \cdot x}$ if $y = -20$
   and $x = -2$. -5

4. $(-32xy^2)\left(-\frac{1}{8}x^3y\right)$ $4x^4y^3$

5. $\{10 - \frac{12 - 4}{-1} + 5\}$ 23

TEACHER'S RESOURCE
MASTERS

Practice Master 16, Part 2

ASSIGNMENT GUIDE

Minimum
1–7 odd, 9–26

Regular
9–30

Maximum
21–36

ADDITIONAL ANSWERS

Oral Exercises

1. e.

2. f.

3. b.

4. d.

5. a.

6. c.

The inequality symbol $\leq$ is a combination of the symbols $<$ and $=$. When an inequality and an equation are combined, a disjunction is formed.

$x \leq 2$ means $x < 2$ or $x = 2$. Similarly, $y \geq 1$ means $y > 1$ or $y = 1$.

EXAMPLES

1   **Solve the conjunction $3y > y - 4$ and $4y + 1 < 5$. Graph the solution set.**

SOLUTION

$$3y > y - 4 \qquad \text{and} \qquad 4y + 1 < 5$$
$$3y - y > y - y - 4 \qquad\qquad 4y + 1 - 1 < 5 - 1$$
$$2y > -4 \qquad\qquad\qquad 4y < 4$$
$$\frac{2y}{2} > \frac{-4}{2} \qquad\qquad\qquad \frac{4y}{4} < \frac{4}{4}$$
$$y > -2 \qquad\qquad\qquad y < 1$$

$$-2 < y < 1$$

2   **Solve the disjunction $3x + 5 > -1$ or $2x < x + 3$. Graph the solution set.**

SOLUTION

$$3x + 5 > -1 \qquad \text{or} \qquad 2x < x + 3$$
$$3x + 5 - 5 > -1 - 5 \qquad\qquad 2x - x < x - x + 3$$
$$3x > -6 \qquad\qquad\qquad x < 3$$
$$\frac{3x}{3} > \frac{-6}{3}$$
$$x > -2$$

$$x > -2 \text{ or } x < 3$$

Notice that the solution set is the set of all real numbers. The graph of the solution set is the entire number line.

ORAL EXERCISES

Match each graph with one of the inequalities.

1.

a. $x \leq -1$

2.
$\qquad$ **b.** $y < 1$ or $y > 3$

3.
$\qquad$ **c.** $-2 < x < 2$

4.
$\qquad$ **d.** $m > 1$ or $m < 3$

5.
$\qquad$ **e.** $x \geq -3$

6.
$\qquad$ **f.** $x > 2$ and $x < 0$

Written Exercises
For the odd-numbered solutions, see *Answers to Selected Exercises*, p. 572.

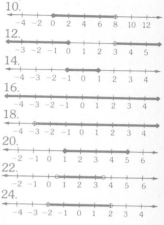

10.

12.

14.

16.

18.

20.

22.

24.

26. $b < -0.3$ or $b > 0.8$

28. all real numbers

30. $d < 4$

32.

34. all real numbers

36. $y > \dfrac{3}{4}$ or $y = -\dfrac{3}{4}$

WRITTEN EXERCISES

A. Write the conjunction without using the word *and*.

1. $x < 7$ and $3 > x$ $\quad x < 3$

2. $y < 9$ and $-2 > y$ $\quad y < -2$

3. $-3 < s$ and $s < 5$ $\quad -3 < s < 5$

4. $-4 < z$ and $z < 12$ $\quad -4 < z < 12$

5. $t > -1$ and $5 > t$ $\quad -1 < t < 5$

6. $v > -3$ and $3 > v$ $\quad -3 < v < 3$

7. $8 > m$ and $0 < m$ $\quad 0 < m < 8$

8. $4 > n$ and $-3 < n$ $\quad -3 < n < 4$

B. Graph each conjunction or disjunction.

9. $-2 < x < 7$ **10.** $0 \leq m < 8$ **11.** $0 < r \leq 6$ **12.** $e > 3$ or $e \leq 0$

13. $t < -5$ or $t > 0$ **14.** $-1 \leq n \leq 1$ **15.** $-4 \leq z \leq 4$ **16.** $x < 1$ or $x > -3$

17. $y < 4$ or $y > 0$ **18.** $x > -3$ or $x > 0$ **19.** $x \geq 2$ or $x > 4$ **20.** $x \geq 1$ and $x \leq 5$

Solve each conjunction or disjunction. Graph the solution set.

21. $2x > 7$ and $3x < 15$ $\quad 3\frac{1}{2} < x < 5$

22. $10y > 5$ and $4y < 14$ $\quad \frac{1}{2} < y < 3\frac{1}{2}$

23. $z + 1 < 6$ and $z + 5 > 8$ $\quad 3 < z < 5$

24. $w - 7 < -5$ and $w + 3 > 1$ $\quad -2 < w < 2$

25. $-5a > 2.5$ or $3a > 1.5$

26. $7b < -2.1$ or $-2b < -1.6$

27. $10j < 50$ or $30j > 90$

28. $0.1k < 2$ or $0.4k > -8$

29. $7 > 3c - 2$ or $c > 3c - 1$

30. $5 > 3d - 4$ or $d > 2d - 4$

C. 31. $2.6e < -5.2$ or $e + 1 = -1$

32. $-\frac{1}{3}f + \frac{2}{5} > \frac{7}{5}$ or $\frac{3}{2}f = -\frac{9}{2}$ $\quad f \leq -3$

33. $2n - \frac{5}{8} > \frac{11}{8}$ or $-3n - \frac{5}{7} > -\frac{26}{7}$

34. $4.1n + 1.8 > -6.4$ or $3n - 7 < -9$

35. $-14x - 1 > \frac{25}{3}$ or $9x = 13x + \frac{8}{3}$

36. $8y - \frac{1}{2} > \frac{11}{2}$ or $16y + 21 = 9$

EXPLORATION
Boolean Algebra and Symbolic Logic

Boolean algebra was developed by George Boole (1815–1864). It is an algebra that deals with a set of elements that are not necessarily numbers and with the operations on the set. Boolean algebra is often used with symbolic logic.

The variables p and q represent statements. Symbolic logic uses operations and rules to determine a **truth value.** The truth value will depend upon the values (true or false) of p and q and upon the operation used. The following table shows some of the operations used in symbolic logic:

Operation	Read	Symbol	
Conjunction	p and q	$p \wedge q$	Notice the similarity
Disjunction	p or q	$p \vee q$	to $\cap$ and $\cup$.
Negation	not p	$\sim p$	

The truth values for each operation are shown in the following tables:

Conjunction

p	q	$p \wedge q$
T	T	T
T	F	F
F	T	F
F	F	F

Disjunction

p	q	$p \vee q$
T	T	T
T	F	T
F	T	T
F	F	F

Negation

p	$\sim p$
T	F
F	T

Example: Let p be the statement $2 < 4$ and q be the statement $5 > 6$. Find each truth value.

a. $p \wedge q$ **b.** $p \vee q$ **c.** $p \wedge \sim q$

Solutions: Statement p is true and statement q is false. Therefore, you can refer to the tables above to determine each truth value.

a. When p is true and q is false, $p \wedge q$ is false.

b. When p is true and q is false, $p \vee q$ is true.

c. When q is false, $\sim q$ is true. When p is true and $\sim q$ is true, $p \wedge \sim q$ is true.

EXERCISES

Let p be the statement $-2 > -4$ and let q be the statement $3 > 1$. Find each truth value.

1. $p \wedge q$ T   **2.** $p \vee q$ T   **3.** $\sim p \vee q$ T   **4.** $\sim p \wedge q$ F

5. $p \vee \sim q$ T   **6.** $p \wedge \sim q$ F   **7.** $\sim p \wedge \sim q$ F   **8.** $\sim p \vee \sim q$ F

4.8 | Sentences Involving Absolute Value

Remember that the **absolute value** of a number is the distance between the point for that number and the 0 point on the number line.

$|x| = 3$ x is 3 units from 0.

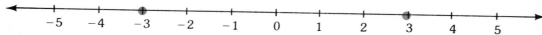

Therefore, $|x| = 3$ means $x = -3$ or $x = 3$.

$|x| < 3$ x is less than 3 units from 0.

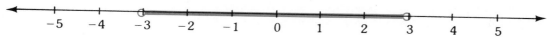

Therefore, $|x| < 3$ means $x > -3$ **and** $x < 3$. In other words, $-3 < x < 3$.

$|x| > 3$ x is more than 3 units from 0.

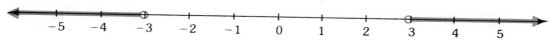

Therefore, $|x| > 3$ means $x < -3$ **or** $x > 3$.

$|x| \le 3$ x is less than 3 units from 0 or x is 3 units from 0.

Therefore, $|x| \le 3$ means $x \ge -3$ and $x \le 3$. In other words, $-3 \le x \le 3$.

$|x| \ge 3$ x is more than 3 units from 0 or x is 3 units from 0.

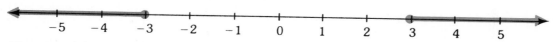

Therefore, $|x| \ge 3$ means $x \le -3$ or $x \ge 3$.

You can use these explanations to solve and graph more-complicated sentences involving absolute value.

EXAMPLES

1 | **Solve $|a + 7| = 4$. Graph the solution set.**

SOLUTION

$|a + 7| = 4$ means $a + 7 = 4$ or $a + 7 = -4$

$$
\begin{array}{lll}
a + 7 = 4 & \quad\text{or}\quad & a + 7 = -4 \\
a + 7 - 7 = 4 - 7 & & a + 7 - 7 = -4 - 7 \\
\qquad a = -3 & & \qquad a = -11
\end{array}
$$

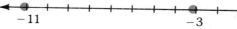

OBJECTIVE

Solve a sentence involving absolute value.

TEACHER'S NOTES

See p. T27.

CLASSROOM EXAMPLES

1. Solve $|a + 8| = 6$.
   Graph the solution set.
   $$a + 8 = 6$$
   $$a + 8 - 8 = 6 - 8$$
   $$a = -2$$
   or
   $$a + 8 = -6$$
   $$a + 8 - 8 = -6 - 8$$
   $$a = -14$$

2. Solve $|b + 4| < 6$.
   Graph the solution set.
   $$-6 < b + 4$$
   $$-6 - 4 < b + 4 - 4$$
   $$-10 < b$$
   and
   $$b + 4 < 6$$
   $$b + 4 - 4 < 6 - 4$$
   $$b < 2$$
   $$-10 < b < 2$$

3. Solve $|x - 3| \ge 5$.
   Graph the solution set.
   $$x - 3 \ge 5$$
   $$x - 3 + 3 \ge 5 + 3$$
   $$x \ge 8$$
   or
   $$x - 3 \le -5$$
   $$x - 3 + 3 \le -5 + 3$$
   $$x \le -2$$

4. Solve $|3y - 4| > 8$.
Graph the solution set.

$$3y - 4 > 8$$
$$3y - 4 + 4 > 8 + 4$$
$$3y > 12$$
$$\frac{3y}{3} > \frac{12}{3}$$
$$y > 4$$

or

$$3y - 4 < -8$$
$$3y - 4 + 4 < -8 + 4$$
$$3y < -4$$
$$\frac{3y}{3} < \frac{-4}{3}$$
$$y < -\frac{4}{3}$$

MIXED REVIEW

1. Find the value of $\left(\frac{1}{7}\right)^3$.
$\frac{1}{343}$

2. Solve $y + 9 = 8 - y$. $-\frac{1}{2}$

3. Solve the inequality
$4m - 6 > 3$. $m > \frac{9}{4}$

4. Find the solution set of $x^2 = 64$. The replacement set $= \{-8, 4, 4, 8\}$. $\{-8, 8\}$

5. Express $\frac{5}{6}$ as a decimal.
0.83

TEACHER'S RESOURCE MASTERS

Practice Master 17, Part 1

ASSIGNMENT GUIDE

Minimum
1–17 odd, 25–49 odd

Regular
25–46

Maximum
37–54, 67–73 odd

---

2 | **Solve $|b + 3| < 4$. Graph the solution set.**

SOLUTION $|b + 3| < 4$ means $-4 < b + 3 < 4$

$$-4 < b + 3 \qquad \text{and} \qquad b + 3 < 4$$
$$-4 - 3 < b + 3 - 3 \qquad\qquad b + 3 - 3 < 4 - 3$$
$$-7 < b \qquad\qquad\qquad b < 1$$

$$-7 < b < 1$$

3 | **Solve $|c - 7| \geq 4$. Graph the solution set.**

SOLUTION $|c - 7| \geq 4$ means $c - 7 \geq 4$ or $c - 7 \leq -4$

$$c - 7 \geq 4 \qquad \text{or} \qquad c - 7 \leq -4$$
$$c - 7 + 7 \geq 4 + 7 \qquad\qquad c - 7 + 7 \leq -4 + 7$$
$$c \geq 11 \qquad\qquad\qquad c \leq 3$$

4 | **Solve $|2y - 3| > 7$. Graph the solution set.**

SOLUTION $|2y - 3| > 7$ means $2y - 3 > 7$ or $2y - 3 < -7$

$$2y - 3 > 7 \qquad \text{or} \qquad 2y - 3 < -7$$
$$2y - 3 + 3 > 7 + 3 \qquad\qquad 2y - 3 + 3 < -7 + 3$$
$$2y > 10 \qquad\qquad\qquad 2y < -4$$
$$\frac{2y}{2} > \frac{10}{2} \qquad\qquad\qquad \frac{2y}{2} < \frac{-4}{2}$$
$$y > 5 \qquad\qquad\qquad y < -2$$

ORAL EXERCISES

Translate each open sentence into an equivalent compound sentence.

1. $|x| = 7$ **2.** $|y| = 6$ **3.** $|x| \leq 3$ **4.** $|x| < 5$

5. $|t| < 8$ **6.** $|x| > 7$ **7.** $|y| \leq 9$ **8.** $|n| \geq 9$

WRITTEN EXERCISES

A. Solve. Graph the solution set.

1. $|x| = 4$ $4, -4$ **2.** $|y| = 2$ $2, -2$ **3.** $|s| < 5$ $-5 < s < 5$

4. $|t| < 3$ $-3 < t < 3$
7. $|p| \geq 4$
10. $|w| \leq 2$ $-2 \leq w \leq 2$
13. $|r| = 7$ $7, -7$
16. $|x| = 3$ $3, -3$

5. $|m| > 7$
8. $|q| \geq 3$
11. $|z| > 3$
14. $|s| < 6$ $-6 < s < 6$
17. $|y| \geq 7$

6. $|n| > 1$
9. $|v| \leq 4$ $-4 \leq v \leq 4$
12. $|s| < 8$ $-8 < s < 8$
15. $|m| \geq 2$
18. $|t| \leq 6$ $-6 \leq t \leq 6$

19. $|x - 3| = 2$
22. $|n - 5| < 2$

20. $|p - 2| = 7$
23. $|x + 3| > 1$

21. $|m + 7| < 3$
24. $|y + 6| > 1$

B. Solve.

25. $|n - 8| = 9$
28. $|2n| = 3.4$
31. $|c + 3| > 5$
34. $|y - 7| < 4$
37. $\left|\dfrac{m}{3}\right| < 1$
40. $\left|\dfrac{t}{3}\right| \geq 3.1$
43. $|2.1y| < 6.3$
46. $\left|\dfrac{9}{10}u\right| \leq 9$
49. $\left|e + \dfrac{2}{3}\right| > \dfrac{4}{3}$
52. $|t - 3.9| \geq 4.6$
55. $|2w - 3| < 9$
58. $|4y - 1| \leq 9$
61. $|5v + 1| \geq 9$
64. $|3d - 2| = 10$

26. $|z + 3| = 6$
29. $\left|\dfrac{f}{2}\right| = 1.6$
32. $|d - 5| > 2$
35. $|n - 2| < 7.6$
38. $\left|\dfrac{n}{1.2}\right| > 2$
41. $|3v| < 9.3$
44. $\left|\dfrac{3}{4}t\right| < 15$
47. $\left|\dfrac{4}{5}b\right| > 24$
50. $\left|g - \dfrac{9}{10}\right| = \dfrac{2}{5}$
53. $|w - 8.9| = 2.4$
56. $\left|3x + \dfrac{1}{2}\right| \geq \dfrac{7}{2}$
59. $|2b + 1| > 7$
62. $|7f - 1| = 15$
65. $|4h + 1| < 9$

27. $|2m| = 6.8$
30. $\left|\dfrac{g}{3}\right| = 9.1$
33. $|x - 5| < 2$
36. $|m + 7| < 3.5$
39. $\left|\dfrac{w}{8.1}\right| \leq 4$
42. $|4y| \geq 8.2$
45. $\left|\dfrac{4}{5}m\right| \geq 8$
48. $\left|c - \dfrac{4}{5}\right| \leq \dfrac{2}{5}$
51. $\left|r + \dfrac{1}{6}\right| < \dfrac{5}{6}$
54. $|s + 1.2| < 3.1$
57. $|5t - 1| = 11$
60. $|3c - 1| = 10$
63. $|2v + 1| \leq 6$
66. $|3m + 2| > 5$

C. 67. $\left|3t - \dfrac{1}{2}\right| < \dfrac{7}{2}$ $-1 < t < \dfrac{4}{3}$
69. $|3p - 6| < 7$ $-\dfrac{1}{3} < p < \dfrac{13}{3}$
71. $|4 - d| \leq 7$ $-3 \leq d \leq 11$
73. $|x| > 0$ $x \neq 0$

68. $|4r - 2| < 8$ $-\dfrac{3}{2} < r < \dfrac{5}{2}$
70. $|6 - c| \geq 2$ $c \geq 8$ or $c \leq 4$
72. $|x| \geq 0$ all real numbers
74. $|x| < 0$ $\varnothing$

CLASSROOM EXAMPLES

1. Kelly has $630 in an account. If she deposits $15 each week into the account, how many weeks will it take to have more than $910 in the account?

Let x = number of deposits.

$$15x + 630 > 910$$
$$15x > 280$$
$$\frac{15x}{15} > \frac{280}{15}$$
$$x > 18.6 \text{ weeks}$$

at least 19 weeks

2. Roberta rents a trailer for 3 days. She pays $60 per day and $0.22 per mile. She estimates the total cost at between $310 and $370. How many miles will the trailer travel?

Let x = number of miles trailer will travel.

$$0.22x + 3(60) \geq 310$$
$$0.22x + 180 \geq 310$$
$$0.22x + 180 - 180 \geq 310 - 180$$
$$0.22x \geq 130$$
$$\frac{0.22x}{0.22} \geq \frac{130}{0.22}$$
$$x \geq 590.90$$

and

$$0.22x + 3(60) \leq 370$$
$$0.22x + 180 \leq 370$$
$$0.22x + 180 - 180 \leq 370 - 180$$
$$0.22x \leq 190$$
$$\frac{0.22x}{0.22} \leq \frac{190}{0.22}$$
$$x \leq 863.63$$

$$590.90 \leq x \leq 863.63$$

4.9 Problem Solving

EXAMPLES

1 Pat has $564 in her account at the credit union. Each payday she deposits $25 into the account. How many deposits must she make to have more than $850 in the account?

Understand: *Given:* The account has $564.
She makes deposits of $25 each.
She wants to have more than $850 in the account.

To find: the number of deposits she must make

Plan: Let x = the number of deposits.

Write an inequality, using this variable and the given facts.

total amount of deposits to be made	+	the current balance	>	total amount wanted

$$25x + 564 > 850$$

Solve:
$$25x + 564 > 850$$
$$25x + 564 + (-564) > 850 + (-564)$$
$$25x > 286$$
$$\frac{25x}{25} > \frac{286}{25}$$
$$x > 11\frac{11}{25}$$

Answer: In this case the variable represents some number of deposits of $25 each. Therefore, the answer needs to be a positive integer. It does not make sense for the answer to be a fractional number. Pat must make at least 12 deposits to have more than $850 in the account.

Review: Try 12. If Pat makes 12 deposits of $25 each, added to the $564 she already has, will she have more than $850 in her account?

2 Mike plans to rent a truck for 2 days. He must pay $55 per day and $0.20 per mile. He estimates that the total cost will be at least $230 and no more than $270. How many miles does he plan to drive the truck?

Understand: *Given:* The truck is rented for two days at $55 per day.
He is charged $0.20 per mile driven.
He will spend at least $230.
He will spend no more than $270.

To find: the number of miles he will drive the truck

Plan: Let x = the number of miles he will drive the truck.
The cost depends on how many miles the truck is driven.

$$\text{cost} = \frac{\text{charge}}{\text{per mile}} \cdot \frac{\text{miles}}{\text{driven}} + \frac{\text{days}}{\text{rented}} \cdot \frac{\text{charge}}{\text{per day}}$$

$$= 0.2x + 2(55)$$

He estimates the cost will be at least $230.
So, $0.2x + 2(55) \geq 230$.
Also, he estimates the cost will be at most $270.
So, $0.2x + 2(55) \leq 270$.

Solve: Solve both inequalities.

$$0.2x + 2(55) \geq 230 \quad \text{and} \quad 0.2x + 2(55) \leq 270$$
$$0.2x + 110 \geq 230 \qquad\qquad 0.2x + 110 \leq 270$$
$$0.2x + 110 - 110 \geq 230 - 110 \quad 0.2x + 110 - 110 \leq 270 - 110$$
$$0.2x \geq 120 \qquad\qquad\qquad 0.2x \leq 160$$
$$\frac{0.2x}{0.2} \geq \frac{120}{0.2} \qquad\qquad\qquad \frac{0.2x}{0.2} \leq \frac{160}{0.2}$$
$$x \geq 600 \qquad\qquad\qquad x \leq 800$$
$$600 \leq x \leq 800$$

Answer: Mike will drive the truck at least 600 miles and no more than 800 miles.

Review: If Mike drives the truck at least 600 miles and pays $0.20 per mile in addition to paying $55 per day for 2 days, will he have to pay at least $230?

If Mike drives the truck no more than 800 miles and pays $0.20 per mile in addition to paying $55 per day for 2 days, will he pay no more than $270?

ORAL EXERCISES

Tell what is given and what you must find in each problem. Do not solve.

1. The fuel gauge in Mrs. Figueroa's car does not work, but she knows that if she drives less than 250 miles after filling the tank, she won't run out of gas. If she has driven 137 miles since last filling the tank, how much farther can she drive before filling the tank again?

2. Mr. Santos knows that he can write checks totaling less than $300 and still maintain the required minimum balance in his checking account. If he writes a check for $129, how much will be available in the account?

3. The yield from 25 acres of wheat was more than 1000 bushels. What was the yield per acre?

4. A store makes a profit of $4 on each blank videotape it sells. How many blank tapes must be sold to make a profit of at least $200?

MIXED REVIEW

1. Find the solution set of $y^2 = 8$. The replacement set is $\{-9, -2, 2, 9\}$. $\varnothing$

2. Find the quotient of $-\frac{14}{15} \div -\frac{1}{3}$. $2\frac{4}{5}$

3. Illustrate the inverse property of addition.   Answers may vary.

4. Simplify $4 \cdot 3 + 4 \cdot 3^2$.   48

5. Convert $0.1\overline{28}$ to a fraction. $\frac{127}{990}$

TEACHER'S RESOURCE MASTERS

Practice Master 17, Part 2
Quiz 8

ASSIGNMENT GUIDE

Minimum
1–5 odd, 10–14

Regular
7–14

Maximum
11–18

ADDITIONAL ANSWERS

Oral Exercises
1. Given: less than 250 miles; driven 137 miles
   Find: How much farther can she drive?

2. Given: less than $300 check for $129
   Find: money in account

3. Given: more than 1000 bushels from 25 acres
   Find: yield per acre

(continued on next page)

4. **Given:** profit of $4 per blank videotape; profit of at least $200
   Find: How many tapes must be sold?

5. **Given:** $30 to spend; film developing costs $8; film costs $4 a roll
   Find: How many rolls of film can be purchased?

6. **Given:** parts stamped at 25 per minute
   Find: minutes necessary to stamp between 1000 and 1500 parts

Written Exercises
1. less than 113 miles
2. $170
3. more than 40 bushels
4. 50 tapes
5. no more than 5 rolls of film
6. between 40 and 60 minutes
8. 19 hours
10. 5 hours
11. at least 72 copies
12. between 22 and 35 miles per gallon
15. between 1.67 and 3.67
16. between $160,000 and $280,000

PROBLEM-SOLVING STRATEGIES

Use Logical Reasoning (7, 9, 11, 13, 16, 17).

Write an Inequality (7, 8, 9, 10, 12, 14, 15, 16, 17, 18).

Use a Diagram (14, 15, 18).

Guess and Check (8, 10, 13).

5. Jessica has at most $30 to spend at the camera store. If she must pay $8 to have film developed, how many rolls of film at $4 each can she buy?

6. A machine can stamp metal parts at a rate of 25 per minute. How many minutes will it take the machine to stamp between 1000 and 1500 parts?

WRITTEN EXERCISES

A. 1–6. Solve each problem in oral exercises 1–6 by using inequalities.

B. 7. Anne has $881 in her savings account. If she deposits $55 each week, what is the smallest number of weeks before she will have more than $1200 in the account? 6 weeks

9. A hamburger costs $1.45 and a glass of milk costs $0.90. If you want to buy one glass of milk, how many hamburgers can you also buy and still spend less than $5.50? 3 hamburgers

11. To cover expenses, the school newspaper staff must sell at least 850 copies of each issue. If there are 778 prepaid subscriptions, how many additional copies must be sold?

13. A car wash will pay you $3.55 an hour for working part-time. How many full hours must you work to earn at least $25.00 a week? 8 hours

C. 15. The length of a rectangle is twice its width. If the perimeter is between 10 meters and 22 meters, what are the possible values of the width (to the nearest hundredth meter)?

17. In a certain income tax bracket, taxpayers pay between $1380 and $2260 in federal tax. If the tax is computed as $1380 plus 22% of the taxable income over $11,200, what is the taxable income for the taxpayer in this tax bracket? $11,200 \le t \le 15,200$

8. At a fruit and vegetable stand, you can earn $4.50 an hour for working after school and on Saturday. What is the smallest number of full hours you can work and earn more than $85 a week?

10. A parking garage charges 75¢ for the first hour (or part of an hour) and 50¢ for each additional hour (or part of an hour). What is the greatest number of hours you could park a car in the garage and still spend less than $3.00?

12. An auto manufacturer made several tests to see how far a particular model could travel on 10 gallons of gas. If the results were all between 220 and 350 miles, how many miles per gallon did that model get?

14. A calculator manufacturer prices its calculators at 2 times the manufacturing cost plus $2.50 per calculator. If the company wants to make a calculator that sells for at most $9.98, what must the manufacturing cost of the calculator be? $3.74 at most

16. A salesperson is paid $16,000 a year plus 5% of the amount of sales made. What must the sales amount to if the salesperson's annual income is to be between $24,000 and $30,000?

18. To make a profit, a factory must produce 3 times as many TVs as video recorders. The number of TVs must exceed the number of video recorders by more than 5200. How many video recorders should be produced? more than 2600

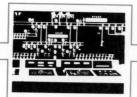

COMPUTER

TEACHER'S RESOURCE MASTERS

Computer Master 4

Can a computer be used to show the solution set of an inequality? The program below, written for an Apple II computer, does just that.

(If your computer is not an Apple, see the Computer Handbook on pages 541–546 for Applesoft commands that must be modified for other computers.)

```
 10 HOME: PRINT "                          Y": PRINT
 20 FOR I = 1 TO 20: PRINT "                        !": NEXT
 25 PRINT: PRINT "                    Y";
 30 VTAB 12: HTAB 1: PRINT "X ----------------+--------
    ------- X"
 40 REM Y >= 2X + 1 IS INEQUALITY
 50 LET BN = 2: REM 1 = "<=", 2 = ">=", 3 = "="
 60 FOR Y = - 10 TO 10: FOR X = - 16 TO 16
 70 IF (X = (Y + 1) / 2) THEN GOSUB 140
 80 ON BN GOTO 90,110: GOTO 120
 90 IF (X < (Y + 1) / 2) THEN GOSUB 140: GOTO 120
100 GOTO 120
110 IF (X > (Y + 1) / 2) THEN GOSUB 140
120 NEXT: NEXT
130 GOTO 130
140 IF X < > 0 AND Y < > 0 THEN VTAB Y + 12: HTAB X +
    19: PRINT ".";
150 RETURN
```

EXERCISES

1. What does the variable BN in line 50 do? Make it 1 or 3 or some other number; now what are the results?

2. Change the equations in lines 40, 70, 90, and 110 to plot another inequality. Enter and RUN the program. What are the results?

3. Why does the program need three versions of the equation to plot the solution set?

4. What is the purpose of the testing on line 140 before printing the point?

CHAPTER 4 REVIEW

VOCABULARY

absolute value (4.8)

addition property of inequality (4.2)

conjunction (4.7)

disjunction (4.7)

division property of inequality (4.3)

inequality (4.1)

intersection (4.6)

multiplication property of inequality (4.3)

order (4.1)

subtraction property of inequality (4.2)

union (4.6)

REVIEW EXERCISES

4.1 **Graph the solution set of each inequality.**

1. $x \geq 3$ **2.** $y < -2$ **3.** $r \neq 0$ **4.** $s > -4$ **5.** $t \leq 5$

4.2, **Solve each inequality.**

4.3,

4.4

6. $n + 4 > -2$ $n > -6$

7. $4 + m \leq 3$ $m \leq -1$

8. $-x < 1$ $x > -1$

9. $4z \geq -8$ $z \geq -2$

10. $\dfrac{9x}{10} > 3$ $x > \dfrac{10}{3}$

11. $-5a + a \leq -2$ $a \geq \dfrac{1}{2}$

12. $8s + 3 > -2s + 8$ $s > 0.5$

13. $3c + 7 - 4c \geq 10$ $c \leq -3$

14. $2x + 3 < 2x + 5$ all real numbers

15. $7y - 3 > -y + 8y + 2$ $\varnothing$

4.5 **Choose a variable and then write each sentence, using $<$, $>$, $\leq$, or $\geq$.**

16. Twice a number is no less than 14. $2n \geq 14$

17. Three times a number is at most 11. $3m \leq 11$

18. One more than four times a number is at least 36. $4x + 1 \geq 36$

19. Six less than a number is no more than 18. $y - 6 \leq 18$

4.6 **Find the intersection and the union of the sets.**

20. $\{0, 2, 4, 6, 8\}, \{1, 2, 3, 4, 5, 6\}$ $\{2, 4, 6\}; \{0, 1, 2, 3, 4, 5, 6, 8\}$

21. $\{0, 5, 10, 15\}, \{0, 10, 20\}$ $\{0, 10\}; \{0, 5, 10, 15, 20\}$

22. $\{1, 3, 5\}, \{1, 2, 3, 4, 5\}$ $\{1, 3, 5\}; \{1, 2, 3, 4, 5\}$

23. $\{3, 7, -8\}, \varnothing$ $\varnothing; \{3, 7, -8\}$

24. $\{2, 7, 9, 12\}, \{1, 6, 8\}$ $\varnothing; \{1, 2, 6, 7, 8, 9, 12\}$

25. $\{-3, -2, -1, 0\}, \{0, 1, 2, 3\}$ $\{0\}; \{-3, -2, -1, 0, 1, 2, 3\}$

Use the given sets to find each union or intersection.

$A = \{-1, 0, 1\}$ $B = \{-3, -1, 1, 3\}$ $C = \{-2, 2\}$

26. $A \cap B$ $\{-1, 1\}$

27. $A \cup C$ $\{-2, -1, 0, 1, 2\}$

28. $(A \cup B) \cap C$ $\varnothing$

29. $(B \cup C) \cap A$ $\{-1, 1\}$

30. $(A \cap B) \cup C$ $\{-2, -1, 1, 2\}$

31. $(A \cup C) \cap B$ $\{-1, 1\}$

32. $(A \cap B) \cap C$ $\varnothing$

33. $(A \cup B) \cup C$
$\{-3, -2, -1, 0, 1, 2, 3\}$

4.7 **Write each conjunction without using the word _and_.**

34. $x < 5$ and $0 > x$ $x < 0$

35. $t > 5$ and $t < 12$ $5 < t < 12$

36. $-\dfrac{3}{2} \le r$ and $r \le \dfrac{7}{2}$ $-\dfrac{3}{2} \le r \le \dfrac{7}{2}$

37. $-3 < b$ and $b > 5$ $b > 5$

Graph each conjunction or disjunction.

38. $-3 < x < 4$

39. $-4 \le x < 1$

40. $s \le 3$ or $s > 5\dfrac{1}{2}$

41. $t < -1$ or $t \ge 1$

Solve each conjunction or disjunction.

42. $x - 1 > -\dfrac{1}{2}$ and $x + 1 < 3$ $\dfrac{1}{2} < x < 2$

43. $m + 1 > 5$ and $m - 2 > -2$ $m > 4$

44. $w + \dfrac{1}{4} < -\dfrac{3}{4}$ or $w - 1 > \dfrac{3}{4}$

45. $2t + 1 > 5$ or $t - 8 < 7$

46. $v - 8 > 1$ and $2v + 1 < 21$ $9 < v < 10$

47. $5b - 3 \ge 7$ and $2b - 3 \le 17$

48. $2f + \dfrac{3}{4} \ge -\dfrac{5}{4}$ or $3f - 2 \le -11$

49. $3g - 1 > 8$ or $5g + 1 = 16$ $g \ge 3$

4.8 **Solve. Graph the solution set.**

50. $|v| = 4$ $4, -4$

51. $|w| < 7$ $-7 < w < 7$

52. $|d| \ge 8$ $d \ge 8$ or $d \le -8$

53. $|r - 2| < 4$ $-2 < r < 6$

54. $|a + 3| \ge 2$ $a \ge -1$ or $a \le -5$

55. $|d - 3| > 0$ $d \ne 3$

56. $|2t| < 8.6$ $-4.3 < t < 4.3$

57. $|3c| \ge 19.2$ $c \ge 6.4$ or $c \le -6.4$

58. $\left|\dfrac{c}{9}\right| = 1$ $9, -9$

59. $\left|\dfrac{f}{1.4}\right| < 3$ $-4.2 < f < 4.2$

60. $\left|2v - \dfrac{1}{2}\right| \le \dfrac{7}{2}$ $-\dfrac{3}{2} \le v \le 2$

61. $|2d + 3| > 9$ $d > 3$ or $d < -6$

62. $\left|f + \dfrac{4}{5}\right| \ge \dfrac{3}{5}$ $f \ge -\dfrac{1}{5}$ or $f \le -\dfrac{7}{5}$

63. $\left|2g - \dfrac{1}{3}\right| < \dfrac{2}{3}$ $-\dfrac{1}{6} < g < \dfrac{1}{2}$

4.9 **Solve.**

64. Diane plans to spend no more than $95 for skirts and blouses. She bought two blouses at $21.50 each. How much can she spend on skirts?

65. The credit limit on a charge account is $1150. If $362 is already charged to the account, how much credit is available? $788

66. Allison's scores on three tests were 79, 84, and 92. What can the lowest score on her next test be in order for her to have an average of at least 86? 89

67. Vincent's bowling scores were 111, 120, and 135. What must he score on the next game in order to maintain his average of 128? 146

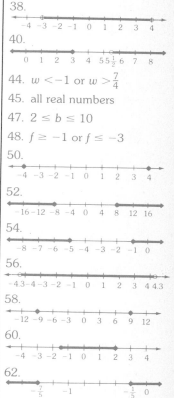

38.

40.

44. $w < -1$ or $w > \dfrac{7}{4}$

45. all real numbers

47. $2 \le b \le 10$

48. $f \ge -1$ or $f \le -3$

50.

52.

54.

56.

58.

60.

62.

64. $52

TEACHER'S RESOURCE
MASTERS

Chapter 4 Test

Multiple-Choice Test

PROBLEM–SOLVING
HANDBOOK

p. 53

ADDITIONAL ANSWERS

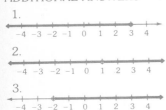

CHAPTER 4 TEST

Graph the solution set of each inequality.

1. $s \le 3$

2. $t \ne 1$

3. $x > -2$

Solve each inequality.

4. $a - 2 \le 0$ $a \le 2$

5. $b - 3 > -4$ $b > -1$

6. $f - 1.2 < 8.6$ $f < 9.8$

7. $r + 4 \ge -3$ $r \ge -7$

8. $h + \frac{3}{4} < \frac{1}{4}$ $h < -\frac{1}{2}$

9. $m + 2.6 > 1.6$ $m > -1$

10. $\frac{x}{3} \le 9$ $x \le 27$

11. $\frac{m}{-2} \ge -8$ $m \le 16$

12. $\frac{3y}{4} < -4$ $y < -\frac{16}{3}$

13. $3v > -9$ $v > -3$

14. $-2w \le 18$ $w \ge -9$

15. $5m \ge 15$ $m \ge 3$

16. $3r + 8 < 14$ $r < 2$

17. $6z + 9 \ge 4z + 3$ $z \ge -3$ **18.** $2x - 3 < 2(x - 4)$

$\varnothing$

Choose a variable and then write each sentence, using $<$, $>$, $\le$, or $\ge$.

19. Five times a number is at most 21. $5n \le 21$

20. Nine less than a number is greater than 12. $x - 9 > 12$

21. One more than twice a number is less than 10. $2y + 1 < 10$

Use the given sets to find each union or intersection.

$R = \{-4, -3, -2, -1\}$ $S = \{-4, -2, 2, 4\}$ $T = \{0, 1, 2, 3\}$

22. $R \cup S$

23. $R \cup T$

24. $R \cap S$ $\{-4, -2\}$

25. $R \cap T$ $\varnothing$

26. $(S \cup T) \cap R$ $\{-4, -2\}$

27. $(S \cap T) \cup R$

Solve each conjunction or disjunction.

28. $6v > 36$ and $\frac{3v}{5} < 6$ $6 < v < 10$

29. $\frac{x}{3} + 3 < -2$ or $4x - 2 > 10$

30. $3y + 6 < 18$ and $2y - 3 > 1$ $2 < y < 4$ **31.** $3m - 7 < 11$ or $2m + 6 = 18$ $m \le 6$

Solve.

32. $|r| > 7$ $r > 7$ or $r < -7$

33. $|3f| \le 12$ $-4 \le f \le 4$

34. $|x + 5| = 5$ $0, -10$

35. Robert plans to spend no more than \$17 on a cassette tape and some packages of batteries. If he buys a tape at \$9.75, how many packages of batteries at \$2.39 each can he buy?
3 packages

CHAPTER 5

Operations with Polynomials

Tanya and Steve drove to the beach at 40 mi/h. The return trip took 10 minutes longer at 30 mi/h. How long did it take to drive to the beach? $\frac{1}{2}$ hour

OBJECTIVE

Find the sum of two poly-
nomials by using the vertical
or the horizontal method.

CLASSROOM EXAMPLES

1. Arrange the terms of each
   polynomial so that the
   powers of the variable x
   are in descending order.

   a. $6x + 14x^2 - 3$
      $14x^2 + 6x - 3$

   b. $4xy^3 + 3x^2y^2 + 5x^5y$
      $- 7$ $5x^5y + 3x^2y^2$
      $+ 4xy^3 - 7$

   c. $-6x^3y + 4x^2y - 2xy$
      $+ 3$ $-6x^3y + 4x^2y$
      $- 2xy + 3$

2. Simplify the sum of $4x^2$
   $+ 3x$ and $9x^2 - 6x - 3$.

   $4x^2 + 3x$
   $\underline{+9x^2 - 6x - 3}$
   $13x^2 - 3x - 3$

MIXED REVIEW

Perform the indicated operation.

1. $58 - (-24)$ 82

2. $[3(-9)](-4)$ 108

3. $4 + (-0.14)$ 3.86

4. $1.52 \div (-0.08)$ -19

5. $\frac{3}{8}\left(-\frac{1}{4}\right)$ $-\frac{3}{32}$

TEACHER'S RESOURCE
MASTERS

Practice Master 18, Part 1

5.1 | Adding Polynomials

The **degree of a polynomial** is determined by the term that has the greatest degree. A polynomial is usually written in *simplest form* so that the powers of one of its variables are in
descending order.

Polynomial	Degree	Descending order for x
$\sqrt{13}x^3$	3	$\sqrt{13}x^3$
$12 - x$	1	$-x + 12$
$x^2 + 4x^4 + 6 + 2x$	4	$4x^4 + x^2 + 2x + 6$
$-4 + x^2$	2	$x^2 - 4$
$5xy^3 + 6x^2y^2$	4	$6x^2y^2 + 5xy^3$

EXAMPLES

1   **Arrange the terms of each polynomial so that the powers of the variable x
are in descending order.**

   a. $7x + 3x^2 - 5 + 8x^3$

   b. $6xy^3 + 5x^2y^2 + 4x^3y + 7$

   c. $-9x^2y + 3x^4y^3 - 6xy^2 + 8$

SOLUTIONS

   a. $8x^3 + 3x^2 + 7x - 5$

   b. $4x^3y + 5x^2y^2 + 6xy^3 + 7$

   c. $3x^4y^3 - 9x^2y - 6xy^2 + 8$

To add polynomials, group like terms and use the distributive property to combine like terms.
Write the sum in simplest form.

2   **Simplify the sum of $5x^2 + 6x$ and $8x^2 - 3x - 2$.**

   SOLUTION

$$(5x^2 + 6x) + (8x^2 - 3x - 2) \qquad \text{or}$$
$$= 5x^2 + 8x^2 + 6x - 3x - 2$$
$$= (5 + 8)x^2 + (6 - 3)x - 2$$
$$= 13x^2 + 3x - 2$$

$$\begin{array}{r} 5x^2 + 6x \\ +\ 8x^2 - 3x - 2 \\ \hline 13x^2 + 3x - 2 \end{array}$$

ORAL EXERCISES

**Name the term of each polynomial that has the greatest degree. Tell what the degree
of the polynomial is.**

1. $3x + x^3$ $x^3, 3$

2. $10p^2 + 8$ $10p^2, 2$

3. $x - 6x^3$ $6x^3, 3$

4. $2q^4 + 5q$ $2q^4, 4$

5. $12r + r^2 - 3$ $r^2, 2$

6. $6a^2b^3 + 5b^4$ $6a^2b^3, 5$

You may want to introduce this topic using **Algebra Tiles.** They are a physical model for teaching algebraic concepts
and are available from Cuisenaire Co. of America, Inc., 12 Church Street, New Rochelle, NY 10802.

7. $10y - y^4 + 8y^2$ $y^4, 4$

8. $3x^2y - x^4$ $x^4, 4$

9. $y^3 + xy^2 + x^4$ $x^4, 4$

10. $st^3 + s^2t + s^3$ $st^3, 4$

11. $-3ab^3 + 4a^2b^3$ $4a^2b^3, 5$

12. $8x^2y - 12xy^2 - x^4$ $x^4, 4$

Tell if the terms in each pair are like terms.

13. $3x^3, -3y^3$ no

14. $7xy^2, -3xy^2$ yes

15. $7y, \frac{9}{10}y$ yes

16. $7a, 6b$ no

17. $4r^2s, -3r^2s$ yes

18. c^2d^2, cd^2 no

WRITTEN EXERCISES

A. Arrange the terms of the polynomials so that the powers of the variable are in descending order.

1. $x - 3x^2 + x^3$ $x^3 - 3x^2 + x$

2. $9 - y^4 + 5y$ $-y^4 + 5y + 9$

3. $10t^2 + t^3 + 8t$ $t^3 + 10t^2 + 8t$

4. $7 - 3n + n^2$ $n^2 - 3n + 7$

5. $x^2 - 2x + 2x^3 - 5$

6. $3y + 8y^2 - 9 - 7y^3$

7. $4t + 9 + 8t^2 - 7t^3$

8. $2s + 3s^2 + 7 - 4s^3$

9. $-m^2 + 2m^3 + 8m^4 - 7m$

10. $10 + q^2 + 3q - 4q^3$

Simplify each sum.

11. $(2x + 3) + (3x - 8)$ $5x - 5$

12. $(6t - 3) + (5t + 2)$ $11t - 1$

13. $(5y + 9) + (6y - 11)$ $11y - 2$

14. $(11z + 7) + (4z + 14)$ $15z + 21$

15. $(4a - 5) + (3a + 6)$ $7a + 1$

16. $(5b + 7) + (3b - 4)$ $8b + 3$

17. $(12x + 2) + (9x - 5)$ $21x - 3$

18. $(2z + 3) + (z - 5)$ $3z - 2$

19. $(3y - 8) + (2y + 7)$ $5y - 1$

20. $(7n + 3) + (n + 6)$ $8n + 9$

21. $(x^2 - 2x + 3) + (x^2 - 7x + 7)$

22. $(y^2 - 3y + 9) + (y^2 - 12y + 2)$

23. $(2x - 2y + 3z) + (5x - 6y - 12z)$

24. $(4a - 6b + 2c) + (3a + 2b - 4c)$

25. $(r^2 - 2rs - 4) + (s^2 + 5rs + 8)$

26. $(2w^2 - 5tw - 3) + (t^2 + 6tw + 5)$

27. $(3x^2 - 2x + 3) + (x^2 - 7x + 7)$

28. $(y^2 - 3y + 9) + (2y^2 - 12y + 2)$

29. $(9p + 5q + 9r) + (9p - 2q + 4r)$

30. $(9u + 7v - 6w) + (7u - 8v + 12w)$

31. $(3x^2 + 5xy - 7y^2) + (6x^2 - 7xy + 6y^2)$

32. $(4m^2 - 3mn + 5n^2) + (2m^2 + 6mn - 7n^2)$

B. 33. $(5a - 2b + 3c) + (6a + 4b - 8c)$

34. $(2r + 8s + t) + (5r + 7s + 6t)$

35. $(4p - 2q - r) + (-7p + 2q + 4r)$

36. $(4x - 3y - 2z) + (-4x + 6y - 2z)$

37. $(3a + 2b + 4c) + (4a - 3b - 6c)$

38. $(6r - 7s - 2t) + (-5r + 7s + 2t)$

39. $(9vw - 6vw^2 - 5vw^3) + (-8vw + 9vw^2 - 11vw^3)$ $vw + 3vw^2 - 16vw^3$

40. $(3ab + 12ab^2 - 7ab^3) + (2ab + 4ab^2 - 7ab^3)$ $5ab + 16ab^2 - 14ab^3$

41. $(4m - 9n - 6p + 5q) + (7m + 9n - 6p - 5q)$ $11m - 12p$

ASSIGNMENT GUIDE

Minimum
1–6, 11–31 odd, 33–50, 54–55

Regular
17–59

Maximum
1–12, 33–63

ADDITIONAL ANSWERS

Written Exercises

5. $2x^3 + x^2 - 2x - 5$

6. $-7y^3 + 8y^2 + 3y - 9$

7. $-7t^3 + 8t^2 + 4t + 9$

8. $-4s^3 + 3s^2 + 2s + 7$

9. $8m^4 + 2m^3 - m^2 - 7m$

10. $-4q^3 + q^2 + 3q + 10$

21. $2x^2 - 9x + 10$

22. $2y^2 - 15y + 11$

23. $7x - 8y - 9z$

24. $7a - 4b - 2c$

25. $r^2 + 3rs + s^2 + 4$

26. $t^2 + tw + 2w^2 + 2$

27. $4x^2 - 9x + 10$

28. $3y^2 - 15y + 11$

29. $18p + 3q + 13r$

30. $16u - v + 6w$

31. $9x^2 - 2xy - y^2$

32. $6m^2 + 3mn - 2n^2$

33. $11a + 2b - 5c$

34. $7r + 15s + 7t$

35. $-3p + 3r$

36. $3y - 4z$

37. $7a - b - 2c$

38. r

42. $(x^2 + 2xy + 3y^2) + (2x^2 - 2xy - 5y^2)$ $3x^2 - 2y^2$

43. $(4a^2 - 2ab - 3b^2) + (-8a^2 + 5ab - 2b^2)$ $-4a^2 + 3ab - 5b^2$

44. $(10b^2 - 5a^2 - 8ab) + (10ab - 7a^2 - 8b^2)$ $2b^2 - 2ab + 12a^2$

45. $(x^2 - 2xy + y^2) + (4x^2 - 4xy - y^2)$ $5x^2 - 6xy$

46. $(r + 2s) + (3s - 4r) + (5r - 7s)$ $2r - 2s$

47. $(2a + 3b) + (-2a - 4b) + (-4a + 5b)$ $-4a + 4b$

48. $(2p^2 + 3q) + (-p^2 - 2q) + (3p^2 - 4q)$ $4p^2 - 3q$

49. $(-m^2 + 3m) + (-2m^2 + 4m) + (-3m^2 - 8m)$ $-6m^2 - m$

50. $(z - z^2) + (-3z - 8z^2) + (6z^2 - 5z)$ $-3z^2 - 7z$

51. $(-u - y) + (4u - 3y) + (8u + 4y)$ $11u$

52. $(3xy + 4xy^2 + 7xy^3) + (-3xy + 4xy^2 - 7xy^3)$ $8xy^2$

53. $(9ab - 2ab^2 - 5ab^3) + (-9ab + 4ab^2 + 5ab^3)$ $2ab^2$

54. $(8xy - 7x^2y + 2x^3y) + (2xy - 5x^2y + 9x^3y)$ $11x^3y - 12x^2y + 10xy$

55. $(3xy + 12xy^2 - 7xy^3) + (2xy + 4xy^2 - 7xy^3)$ $5xy + 16xy^2 - 14xy^3$

C. 56. $(6xy - 5x^2y + 3x^3y) + (2xy - 5x^2y + 4x^3y) + (-5xy + 9x^2y + 2x^3y)$

57. $(xy + 10xy^2 - 5xy^3) + (-2xy + 3xy^2 + xy^3) + (6xy - 8xy^2 + 4xy^3)$

58. $(2s^2t - 3st^2 - st) + (4st - 3st^2 + s^2t) + (-st^2 + 3s^2t - 2st)$

59. $(st^3 + 3st^2 + 4s^2t) + (st^2 - 3s^2t - st^3) + (-s^2t + 2st^2 + 2st^3)$

60. $(3p^2 + 2pq + 2q^2) + (4pq - 3q^2 - 2p^2) + (-q^2 - 3pq + p^2)$

61. $(-rs - r^2 + s^2) + (3r^2 - 3rs - 2s^2) + (4s^2 - 4rs + 3r^2)$

62. $(a^2b + b^2 - 3a^2) + (4a^2b + 14a^2 + 9b^2) + (-5a^2 - 6b^2 - 4a^2b)$

63. $(cd^2 + 4c^2d + 3c^3d) + (9c^2d^2 + 6cd^2 + 3cd^3) + (8cd + 5c^2d^2 + 5c^2d)$

56. $9x^3y - x^2y + 3xy$

57. $5xy + 5xy^2$

58. $6s^2t + st - 7st^2$

59. $6st^2 + 2st^3$

60. $2p^2 + 3pq - 2q^2$

61. $5r^2 - 8rs + 3s^2$

62. $6a^2 + a^2b + 4b^2$

63. $3c^3d + 9c^2d + 14c^2d^2$
    $+ 7cd^2 + 3cd^3 + 8cd$

CHALLENGE

CHALLENGE

3 and 2 or 1 and 4

Find at least one pair of positive integers the difference of whose squares is five times their difference.

5.2 | Subtracting Polynomials

In Chapter 2, you learned that the subtraction property, $x - y = x + (-y)$, is useful in subtracting real numbers. For example, $12 - (-5) = 12 + [-(-5)] = 12 + 5$.

This same property can be used in subtraction of polynomials. That is, to subtract one polynomial from another, you can *add* the opposite of the polynomial being subtracted to the other polynomial. In order to do this, you need to use the following procedure.

Opposite of a Polynomial	To find the opposite (additive inverse) of a polynomial, you must change each term of the polynomial to its opposite.

Polynomial	Opposite
$-4x$	$-(-4x)$ or $4x$
$x^2 + 9$	$-(x^2 + 9)$ or $-x^2 - 9$
$x^3 - 3x^2 + 2$	$-(x^3 - 3x^2 + 2)$ or $-x^3 + 3x^2 - 2$

In each subtraction problem below, the problem is first changed to an addition problem involving the opposite of a polynomial.

EXAMPLES

1 **Subtract $4x - 11$ from $7x + 3$.**

SOLUTION

$$(7x + 3) - (4x - 11) = (7x + 3) + (-4x + 11) \quad \text{Add the opposite of } 4x - 11.$$
$$= 7x + 3 + (-4x) + 11$$
$$= 7x + (-4x) + 3 + 11$$
$$= [7 + (-4)]x + 14 \quad \text{Use the distributive property.}$$
$$= 3x + 14$$

2 **Simplify $(6x^2 + 8x - 5) - (2x^2 + 3x - 4)$.**

SOLUTION

$$(6x^2 + 8x - 5) - (2x^2 + 3x - 4)$$
$$= (6x^2 + 8x - 5) + (-2x^2 - 3x + 4) \quad \text{Add the opposite of } 2x^2 + 3x - 4.$$
$$= 6x^2 + 8x - 5 - 2x^2 - 3x + 4$$
$$= 6x^2 - 2x^2 + 8x - 3x - 5 + 4$$
$$= (6 - 2)x^2 + (8 - 3)x - 1$$
$$= 4x^2 + 5x - 1$$

OBJECTIVES

Find the opposite of a polynomial.

Find the difference of two polynomials.

TEACHER'S NOTES

See p. T27.

CLASSROOM EXAMPLES

1. Subtract $3x - 9$ from $6x + 3$.

$(6x + 3) - (3x - 9)$
$= (6x + 3) + (-3x + 9)$
$= 6x + 3 + (-3x) + 9$
$= 6x + (-3x) + 3 + 9$
$= [6 + (-3)]x + 12$
$= 3x + 12$

2. Simplify $(4x^2 + 3x - 9) - (6x^2 + 5x - 3)$.

$(4x^2 + 3x - 9) - (6x^2 + 5x - 3)$
$= 4x^2 + 3x - 9 + (-6x^2 - 5x + 3)$
$= 4x^2 + 3x - 9 - 6x^2 - 5x + 3$
$= 4x^2 - 6x^2 + 3x - 5x - 9 + 3$
$= (4 - 6)x^2 + (3 - 5)x - 6$
$= -2x^2 - 2x - 6$

MIXED REVIEW

Find each sum.

1. $(6x^3y + 4x^2y - 5) + (-3x^2y - 5x^3y + 2)$ $x^3y + x^2y - 3$
2. $(3xy^2 - 5) + (2xy^2 + 3x^3y + 5)$ $3x^3y + 5xy^2$
3. $-\frac{4}{5} + \left(-\frac{1}{9}\right)$ $-\frac{41}{45}$
4. $-18 + (-10.35)$ -28.35
5. $0.56 + (-1.8)$ -1.24

You may want to introduce this topic using **Algebra Tiles**. They are a physical model for teaching algebraic concepts and are available from Cuisenaire Co. of America, Inc., 12 Church Street, New Rochelle, NY 10802.

TEACHER'S RESOURCE MASTERS

Practice Master 18, Part 2

ADDITIONAL ANSWERS

Oral Exercises
6. $-b^3 + 2b - 4$

Written Exercises
17. $x - y - 2$
18. $2s + t - 5$
19. $7y - z + 1$
20. $7w + 9t - 12$
21. $-5a - b + 3$
22. $c - 2$
23. $a + ab - 4b$
24. $-4s - st + t$
25. $12x - xy + y$
26. $15p - 3pq$
27. $3x^2 + 12x$
28. $3y^2 + 12y$
29. $-10x + 14$
30. $-9y + 22$
31. $-9x - 7$
32. $17y - 11$
33. $-4x^2 - 16x + 9$
34. $-3p^2 - 9p - 13$
35. $5x^2 - 15x + 5$
36. $11p^2 + 2p - 18$
37. $4x^2y^2 \div 11xy$

ORAL EXERCISES

Name the opposite of each polynomial.

1. $4x$ $-4x$
2. $-5y$ $5y$
3. $8x^2 + 3$ $-8x^2 - 3$
4. $-9t^2 + 7$ $9t^2 - 7$
5. $-5r - 9$ $5r + 9$
6. $b^3 - 2b + 4$
7. $-x + 1$ $x - 1$
8. $-s - 3$ $s + 3$
9. $z^2 - 3wz - 2w^2$ $-z^2 + 3wz + 2w^2$
10. $5m^3 + 3m - 8$ $-5m^3 - 3m + 8$

WRITTEN EXERCISES

A. Simplify each difference.

1. $(3r - 10) - (8r + 3)$ $-5r - 13$
2. $(5s + 8) - (-2s - 4)$ $7s + 12$
3. $(-4t - 6) - (2t + 5)$ $-6t - 11$
4. $(15y + 2) - (11y - 8)$ $4y + 10$
5. $(-8m - 7) - (2m - 4)$ $-10m - 3$
6. $(-7z + 9) - (5z + 2)$ $-12z + 7$
7. $(10x - 3) - (13x + 8)$ $-3x - 11$
8. $(14y + 4) - (18y - 3)$ $-4y + 7$
9. $(-9s - 5) - (-4s - 10)$ $-5s + 5$
10. $(11t - 12) - (20t + 12)$ $-9t - 24$
11. $(14r + 3) - (12r + 3)$ $2r$
12. $(20z + 5) - (20z - 5)$ 10
13. $(8b - 1.8) - (3b - 1.5)$ $5b - 0.3$
14. $(12a - 3.2) - (7a - 2.8)$ $5a - 0.4$
15. $(10c + 8.1) - (-5c - 4.7)$ $15c + 12.8$
16. $(5y - 6) - (7y + 3.8)$ $-2y - 9.8$

B. 17. $(3x + 2 + y) - (2x + 4 + 2y)$
18. $(8s + 3t + 1) - (6s + 2t + 6)$
19. $(9y - 4z - 3) - (2y - 3z - 4)$
20. $(10w + 3t - 4) - (3w - 6t + 8)$
21. $(a + 3b + 9) - (6a + 4b + 6)$
22. $(2c + 9d + 1) - (c + 9d + 3)$
23. $(5a + 8ab + 3b) - (4a + 7ab + 7b)$
24. $(8s + 3st + 4t) - (12s + 4st + 3t)$
25. $(9x - 6xy - 2y) - (-3x - 5xy - 3y)$
26. $(7p - 5pq - q) - (-8p - 2pq - q)$
27. $(9x^2 + 5x) - (6x^2 - 7x)$
28. $(12y^2 + 4y) - (9y^2 - 8y)$
29. $(x^2 - 5x + 7) - (x^2 + 5x - 7)$
30. $(y^2 - 2y + 11) - (y^2 + 7y - 11)$
31. $(x^2 - 11x + 4) - (x^2 - 2x + 11)$
32. $(y^2 + 10y - 13) - (y^2 - 7y - 2)$
33. $(4x^2 - 14x + 2) - (8x^2 + 2x - 7)$
34. $(6p^2 - 12p - 6) - (9p^2 - 3p + 7)$
35. $(5x^2 + 7) - (15x + 2)$
36. $(11p^2 - 11) - (-2p + 7)$
37. $(5x^2y^2 + 6xy - 1) - (x^2y^2 - 5xy - 1)$
38. $(0.2t^2 - 0.7t) - (0.4t^2 + 0.8t)$
39. $(8x^2 - 4x + 3) - (7x - 11)$
40. $(12y^2 + 9y - 13) - (11y - 21)$
41. $(13p - 13) - (-18p^2 + 13p - 7)$
42. $(12m - 10) - (2m^2 + 12m - 12)$
43. $(15n - 3) - (6n^2 - 15n - 6)$
44. $(21s - 2) - (8s^2 - 4s + 9)$

C. Simplify each expression.

45. $(5x^2t^2 - 6xt + 17) - (11x^2t^2 + 4xt - 6)$
46. $(x^2 - 2x) - (x - 5) + (x^2 + 3x - 4)$ $2x^2 + 1$
47. $(m^2 - 8m) + (6m - 2) - (m^2 - 2m + 2)$ -4

48. $(s^2 - 3s - 9) - (3s^2 + 3s - 6) + (-5s^2 - 2s + 5)$ $-7s^2 - 8s + 2$

49. $(3x^2 - 4x + 5) - (2x^2 + 2x - 7) + (x^2 - x + 4)$ $2x^2 - 7x + 16$

50. From the sum of $2x + 5y$ and $-3x - 4y$, subtract $x - y$. $-2x + 2y$

51. From the sum of $3x^2 + 8x$ and $4x^2 - 7x$, subtract $8x^2 + x$. $-x^2$

52. Subtract $m^2 - 2m + 2$ from the sum of $m^2 - 8m$ and $6m - 2$. -4

53. Subtract the sum of $3x^2 - 4y^2$ and $2x^2 + 5y^2$ from the difference of $5x^2 - 10y^2$ and $2x^2 - y^2$. $-2x^2 - 10y^2$

54. Subtract the sum of $2x^2 + xy - y^2$ and $3x^2 + 4xy + y^2$ from the difference of $x^2 - 2xy + y^2$ and $x^2 + 4xy + y^2$. $-5x^2 - 11xy$

38. $-0.2t^2 - 1.5t$

39. $8x^2 - 11x + 14$

40. $12y^2 - 2y + 8$

41. $18p^2 - 6$

42. $-2m^2 + 2$

43. $-6m^2 + 30n + 3$

44. $-8s^2 + 25s - 11$

45. $-6x^2t^2 - 10xt + 23$

EXPLORATION
Polygonal Numbers

A series of numbers can be represented by
$x_n = n + \frac{1}{2}(m - 2)(n^2 - n)$ for $n = 1$, $n = 2$, $n = 3$, and so on.

If $m = 3$, these numbers are **triangular numbers**.

Triangular number	Dot representation

$x_1 = 1 + \frac{1}{2}(3 - 2)(1^2 - 1)$

$\quad = 1 + \frac{1}{2}(1)(0)$

$\quad = 1$ 1 •

$x_2 = 2 + \frac{1}{2}(3 - 2)(2^2 - 2)$

$\quad = 2 + \frac{1}{2}(1)(2)$

$\quad = 3$ 3

$x_3 = 3 + \frac{1}{2}(3 - 2)(3^2 - 3)$

$\quad = 3 + \frac{1}{2}(1)(6)$

$\quad = 6$ 6

The pattern can be continued to give more triangular numbers.

EXERCISES

1. If $m = 4$, the numbers are **square numbers.** Find the first four square numbers.

2. If $m = 5$, the numbers are **pentagonal numbers.** Find the first four pentagonal numbers.

EXPLORATION
EXERCISES
1. 1, 4, 9, 16
2. 1, 5, 12, 22

OBJECTIVE

Find the product of two monomials by using the following: product of powers, power of a power, and power of a product.

CLASSROOM EXAMPLES

1. Multiply $4x$ and $3y$. $\quad 4x \cdot 3y = 4 \cdot 3 \cdot x \cdot y = 12xy$

2. Multiply $x^3 \cdot x^4$. $\quad x^3 \cdot x^4 = x^{3+4} = x^7$

3. Multiply $-5y^3$ and $3y^2$. $\quad -5y^3 \cdot 3y^2 = -5 \cdot 3 \cdot y^{3+2} = -15y^5$

4. Find the third power of y^4. $\quad (y^4)^3 = y^{4 \cdot 3} = y^{12}$

5. Find the square of ab. $\quad (ab)^2 = a^2 \cdot b^2 = a^2b^2$

6. Find $(2x)^2$. $\quad (2x)^2 = 2^2 \cdot x^2 = 4x^2$

7. Find $(3a^2)^3$. $\quad (3a^2)^3 = 3^3 \cdot (a^2)^3 = 3^3 \cdot a^{2 \cdot 3} = 27a^6$

5.3 | Multiplying Monomials

To multiply a monomial by a monomial, multiply the coefficients of each term and the variables of each term.

EXAMPLES

1   **Multiply $3x$ and $2y$.**

SOLUTION
$$3x \cdot 2y = 3 \cdot 2 \cdot x \cdot y = 6xy$$

The following properties are used to multiply monomials that contain exponents.

Product of Powers	**Let x be any real number, and let a and b be any positive integers. Then $x^a \cdot x^b = x^{a+b}$.**

2   **Multiply x^2 and x^3.**

SOLUTION
$$x^2 \cdot x^3 = x^{2+3} = x^5$$
Think: $\quad x^2 \cdot x^3 = (x \cdot x)(x \cdot x \cdot x) = x^5$

3   **Multiply $-2y^3$ and $4y^2$.**

SOLUTION
$$-2y^3 \cdot 4y^2 = -2 \cdot 4 \cdot y^{3+2} = -8y^5$$

Power of a Power	**Let x be any real number, and let a and b be any positive integers. Then $(x^a)^b = x^{ab}$.**

4   **Find the third power of x^4.**

SOLUTION
$$(x^4)^3 = x^{4 \cdot 3} = x^{12}$$
Think: $\quad (x^4)^3 = (x \cdot x \cdot x \cdot x)(x \cdot x \cdot x \cdot x)(x \cdot x \cdot x \cdot x) = x^{12}$

Power of a Product	**Let x and y be any real numbers, and let a be any positive integer. Then $(xy)^a = x^a y^a$.**

5   **Find the square of xy.**

SOLUTION
$$(xy)^2 = x^2 \cdot y^2 = x^2y^2$$
Think: $\quad (xy)^2 = (xy)(xy) = x^2y^2$

6   **Find $(3x)^2$**

SOLUTION
$$(3x)^2 = 3^2 \cdot x^2 = 9x^2$$

7   Find $(5a^2)^3$.

SOLUTION

$(5a^2)^3 = 5^3 \cdot (a^2)^3 = 5^3 \cdot a^{2 \cdot 3} = 125a^6$

ORAL EXERCISES

True or false?

1. $3(5x) = (3 \cdot 5)x$ true   **2.** $3(5n) = 8n$ false   **3.** $x^2 \cdot x^5 = x^{10}$ false

4. $x^2 \cdot x^4 = x^6$ true   **5.** $(y^2)^3 = y^5$ false   **6.** $(2m)^3 = 6m^3$ false

7. $(3n^2)(n^3) = 3n^6$ false   **8.** $(2x^2)(x^4) = 2x^6$ true   **9.** $(x^3)^4 = x^{12}$ true

Find each product.

10. $(3x^2)(4x^3)$ $12x^5$ **11.** $(9st)(-2)$ $-18st$ **12.** $(-16)\left(-\frac{1}{4}t\right)$ $4t$ **13.** $(3a)(-4b)$

14. $(6r^2)(4r)$ $24r^3$ **15.** $(2m^2)(3m^3)$ $6m^5$ **16.** $(2x^2)^3$ $8x^6$ $-12ab$ **17.** $(x^3y)^2$ x^6y^2

WRITTEN EXERCISES

A. Find each product.

1. $(-21)\left(\frac{1}{3}n\right)$ **2.** $(-8)\left(\frac{1}{4}r\right)$ $-2r$ **3.** $(12ab)\left(\frac{1}{3}\right)$ $4ab$ **4.** $(18de)\left(\frac{1}{3}\right)$ $6de$

5. $(-5a)(-3b)$ **6.** $(-8m)(-2n)$ **7.** $(2.1m)(3m)$ $6.3m^2$ **8.** $(1.3n)(4n)$ $5.2n^2$

9. $(7t^2)(3t^3)$ $21t^5$ **10.** $(6w^4)(3w)$ $18w^5$ **11.** $(x^3)(x^2)$ x^5 **12.** $(y^2)(y^4)$ y^6

13. $(a^3)^2$ a^6 **14.** $(2b^2)^3$ $8b^6$ **15.** $(12x)^2$ $144x^2$ **16.** $(10y^2)^3$ $1000y^6$

17. $(2z)^3$ $8z^3$ **18.** $(4v)^2$ $16v^2$ **19.** $(7x^4)^2$ $49x^8$ **20.** $(5c^3)^3$ $125c^9$

B. 21. $(7s^4t)(14s^2t^4)$ $98s^6t^5$ **22.** $(13a^3b)(8a^2b^3)$ $104a^5b^4$

23. $(14m^4)\left(-\frac{1}{2}m^3\right)$ $-7m^7$ **24.** $(12s^3)\left(-\frac{1}{6}s^5\right)$ $-2s^8$

25. $(4n^5)(-3s^3)$ $-12n^5s^3$ **26.** $(-9m^2)(-2t^4)$ $18m^2t^4$

27. $(0.5rs)(-3sr^2)$ $-1.5r^3s^2$ **28.** $(0.2ad)(-8d^2a)$ $-1.6a^2d^3$

29. $(-2s)^3$ $-8s^3$ **30.** $(-3r)^2$ $9r^2$

31. $(3^2x^3)^3$ $729x^9$ **32.** $(5^3x)^2$ $15{,}625x^2$

33. $(xy)^3y^4$ x^3y^7 **34.** $(rs)^5r^3$ r^8s^5

35. $a^4(da)$ da^5 **36.** $(x^2y^3)(x^3y^2)$ x^5y^5

37. $(w^4t^3)(w^2t^3)$ w^6t^6 **38.** $(2p)^4(2p)^3$ $128p^7$

39. $(5b)^3(2b)^4$ $2000b^7$ **40.** $(4r)^2(3r)^3$ $432r^5$

MIXED REVIEW

Perform the indicated operation.

1. $(6x^3y + 2xy + 5)$
   $- (-8x^3y + 2xy - 3)$
     $14x^3y + 8$

2. $(-14x^3y^2)\left(-\frac{1}{7}xy\right)$ $2x^4y^3$

3. $-7.2 \div (-0.08)$ 90

4. $(5x^3y + 8xy - 4) + (2x^3y$
   $+ 8xy + 9)$ $7x^3y + 16xy$
     $+ 5$

5. $(5x^3y)(-2x^3y)$ $-10x^6y^2$

TEACHER'S RESOURCE MASTERS

Practice Master 19, Part 1

ASSIGNMENT GUIDE

Minimum
1–49 odd

Regular
21–46

Maximum
25–36, 41–52

ADDITIONAL ANSWERS

Written Exercises

1. $-7n$

5. $15ab$

6. $16mn$

C. 41. $s^7 \cdot s^2 \cdot s^3$ s^{12}

42. $x^3 \cdot x^6 \cdot x$ x^{10}

43. $y^7 \cdot (-y^6) \cdot y$ $-y^{14}$

44. $-t^4 \cdot t^3 \cdot t^2$ $-t^9$

45. $(xyz)^2(xyz)^3$ $x^5y^5z^5$

46. $(rst)^6(rst)^2$ $r^8s^8t^8$

47. $(-s)(-4s)^3(2s)^2$ $256s^6$

48. $(-2r)^4(3r)^3(-1)$ $-432r^7$

49. $(-0.4x^2y)(-x^2y^3)(-5y^4)$ $-2x^4y^8$

50. $(-2a^3cd^2)(-acd)^3(0.8a^2b)$ $1.6a^8c^4d^5b$

Simplify each expression. Each exponent is a positive integer.

51. $3^x \cdot 3^{2x+4}$ 3^{3x+4}

52. $4^y \cdot 4^{y-3}$ 4^{2y-3}

ALGEBRA IN USE

In many businesses, the manufacturing costs will vary, depending on how many items are produced. A manufacturer can use past experience to predict manufacturing costs. A polynomial such as $-3x^3 + 70x^2 + 5x + 100$ (dollars) can be used to predict the cost of producing x items.

Example 1:   Using the polynomial above, find the cost of producing 10 items.

Solution: $-3(10)^3 + 70(10)^2 + 5(10) + 100 = -3000 + 7000 + 50 + 100$
$$= 4150$$

To find the average cost per item, divide the polynomial by x (the number of items).

Example 2:   Use the polynomial $-3x^3 + 70x^2 + 5x + 100$ to represent the cost of producing x items. What is the average cost per item for producing 10 items? For producing 20 items?

Solution: $\dfrac{-3x^3 + 70x^2 + 5x + 100}{x} = \underbrace{-3x^2 + 70x + 5 + \dfrac{100}{x}}$

expression representing the average cost per item

$x = 10$: $-3(10)^2 + 70(10) + 5 + \dfrac{100}{10} = \$415$

$x = 20$: $-3(20)^2 + 70(20) + 5 + \dfrac{100}{20} = \$210$

EXERCISES

Use the polynomial $-2x^3 + 50x^2 + 30x + 1000$ (dollars) to represent the cost of producing x items. Find the average cost per item.

1. $x = 10$ $\$430$

2. $x = 20$ $\$280$

3. $x = 4$ $\$448$

4. $x = 25$ $\$70$

5. $x = 5$ $\$430$

6. $x = 8$ $\$427$

5.4 | Multiplying a Polynomial by a Monomial

OBJECTIVE

Find the product of a polynomial and a monomial.

TEACHER'S NOTES

See p. T27.

To multiply a polynomial by a monomial, multiply each term of the polynomial by the monomial.

EXAMPLES

1 **Multiply 3s and 4s + 7.**

SOLUTION

$3s(4s + 7) = 3s \cdot 4s + 3s \cdot 7$ *Use the distributive property.*
$\qquad\qquad = 12s^2 + 21s$

2 **Multiply 4y and 7y − 3.**

SOLUTION

$4y(7y - 3) = 4y \cdot [7y + (-3)]$ *Use the subtraction property.*
$\qquad\qquad = 4y \cdot 7y + 4y \cdot (-3)$ *Use the distributive property.*
$\qquad\qquad = 28y^2 + (-12y)$
$\qquad\qquad = 28y^2 - 12y$

SHORTCUT

$4y(7y - 3) = 4y \cdot 7y - 4y \cdot 3$
$\qquad\qquad = 28y^2 - 12y$

3 **Multiply −4y and 5y² + 6y − 2.**

SOLUTION

$(-4y)(5y^2 + 6y - 2) = (-4y)(5y^2) + (-4y)(6y) - (-4y)(2)$
$\qquad\qquad\qquad\qquad = -20y^3 - 24y^2 + 8y$

CLASSROOM EXAMPLES

1. Multiply 4x and 5x + 6.
   $4x(5x + 6)$
   $= 4x \cdot 5x + 4x \cdot 6$
   $= 20x^2 + 24x$

2. Multiply 5y and 3y − 2.
   $5y(3y - 2)$
   $= 5y \cdot 3y + 5y \cdot (-2)$
   $= 15y^2 - (-10y)$
   $= 15y^2 - 10y$

3. Multiply −2y and $3y^2$ + 8y − 5.
   $-2y(3y^2 + 8y - 5)$
   $= (-2y)(3y^2) + (-2y)(8y)$
   $\quad + (-2y)(-5)$
   $= -6y^3 + (-16y^2) + (10y)$
   $= -6y^3 - 16y^2 + 10y$

MIXED REVIEW

Simplify.
1. $(9 + 3) \div (18 \div 3)$ 2
2. $4(x^2y + 5x^2y)$ $24x^2y$
3. $5 \cdot 2 + 3 \cdot 2^3$ 34

Evaluate if $a = -3$ and $b = 4$.
4. $\dfrac{b^3}{a}$ $-21\frac{1}{3}$
5. $(a + b)^3$ 1

TEACHER'S RESOURCE MASTERS

Practice Master 19, Part 2

ORAL EXERCISES

True or false?

1. $2x(x^2 - 4x) = 2x^3 - 8x$ false

2. $3t(t^2 + 2t) = 3t^2 + 6t$ false

3. $a^2(a + 5b) = a^3 + 5ab$ false

4. $5b(b - a^2) = 5b^2 - 5a^2b$ true

Find each product.

5. $5a(2a - 4b)$ $10a^2 - 20ab$

6. $(7x + 5y)(2x)$ $14x^2 + 10xy$

7. $3x(4x + 5y)$ $12x^2 + 15xy$

8. $(4b - 3a)(5a)$ $20ab - 15a^2$

You may want to introduce this topic using **Algebra Tiles**. They are a physical model for teaching algebraic concepts and are available from Cuisenaire Co. of America, Inc., 12 Church Street, New Rochelle, NY 10802.

ASSIGNMENT GUIDE

Minimum
1–9 odd, 15–24

Regular
13–28

Maximum
19–34

ADDITIONAL ANSWERS

Written Exercises

1. $14x^2y^2 + 56xy$

2. $4mn + 6n^2$

3. $18rs - 12s^2$

4. $-35x^2y^2 - 43xy$

5. $15x^3 - 10x^2 + 15x$

6. $16y^3 + 24y^2 - 12y$

7. $24m^3n^3 + 20m^2n^2$

8. $21a^3b^3 - 27a^2b^2$

9. $12x^3 - 18x^2 + 12x$

10. $16y^3 + 20y^2 - 28y$

11. $2c^2$

12. $-12d^3 - 20d$

19. $6a^3b + 14a^2b^2 - 12ab^3$

20. $30m^4n - 10m^3n + 15m^2n$

21. $-33t^3 - 18t^2w - 36tw^2$

22. $-65s^2t^2 - 10st^3 - 5t^4$

23. $-x^6 + x^5 - x^4 + 2x^3$

24. $3y^6 + 2y^5 + y^4 - y^3$

25. $-6x^2y - 4xy - 5txy$

26. $-20b^3 - 8b^2x - 10x^2b$
    $- bx^2$

29. $6c^3 - 10c^2 - 3c$

WRITTEN EXERCISES

A. Find each product.

1. $7xy(2xy + 8)$

2. $2n(2m + 3n)$

3. $3s(6r - 4s)$

4. $(7xy + 9)(-5xy)$

5. $5x(3x^2 - 2x + 3)$

6. $(4y^2 + 6y - 3)4y$

7. $4mn(6m^2n^2 + 5mn)$

8. $3ab(7a^2b^2 - 9ab)$

9. $6x(2x^2 - 3x + 2)$

10. $(4y^2 + 5y - 7)4y$

11. $2c(4c - 3c)$

12. $4d(-3d^2 - 5)$

B.

13. $-5(3a^2 + 8)$ $-15a^2 - 40$

14. $x(4x^2y - 3y^2)$ $4x^3y - 3xy^2$

15. $8b(b^3 - 2b)$ $8b^4 - 16b^2$

16. $-3a^2(a^3 + 3a)$ $-3a^5 - 9a^3$

17. $2d^4(-4d^3 - 11d^2)$ $-8d^7 - 22d^6$

18. $5q^2r(4qr^2 + q^2r^2)$ $20q^3r^3 + 5q^4r^3$

19. $2ab(3a^2 + 7ab - 6b^2)$

20. $(6m^3 - 2m^2 + 3m)5mn$

21. $-3t(11t^2 + 6tw + 12w^2)$

22. $(13s^2 + 2st + t^2)(-5t^2)$

23. $-x^3(x^3 - x^2 + x - 2)$

24. $(3y^3 + 2y^2 + y - 1)y^3$

C.

25. $2xy(1 - 4t - 3x) - 3x(2y - yt)$

26. $(4b^2 + 3bx + 2x^2)(-5b) + x(7b^2 - bx)$

27. $3st(2t^2 - 4s) - 3st(t^2 - 4s)$ $3st^3$

28. $8b(b^2 - 3a) - 4a(3a - 6b)$ $8b^3 - 12a^2$

29. $4c^3 - c[3 - 2c(c - 5)]$

30. $7d^2 - d[4d - 3d(2d - 1)]$ $6d^3$

Simplify each expression. (Each base is a real number, and each exponent is a positive integer.)

31. $a^2(a^{x+1} + a^y)$ $a^{x+3} + a^{y+2}$

32. $x^n(2x^n - 4x)$ $2x^{2n} - 4x^{n+1}$

33. $x^{a+1}(x^a + x)$ $x^{2a+1} + x^{a+2}$

34. $b^{2n}(b^{2n} - 1)$ $b^{4n} - b^{2n}$

CALCULATOR

When you are using a calculator to find the power of a number or the power of powers, you need to enter the base one time.

Example 1:   Find 4^3.

ENTER

DISPLAY

⊙ 4 ⊗ ⊜ ⊜   *64.*

$4^3 = 64$

Example 2:   Find $(4^3)^2$.

ENTER

DISPLAY

⊙ 4 ⊗ ⊜ ⊜ ⊗ ⊜   *4096.*

$(4^3)^2 = 4096$

5.5 | Multiplying Polynomials

You can use the distributive property to multiply one polynomial by another.

OBJECTIVE

Find the product of two polynomials.

TEACHER'S NOTES
See p. T27.

EXAMPLES

1 | **Multiply $3s - 2t$ and $2s + 6t$.**

SOLUTION

$(3s - 2t)(2s + 6t)$

$= (3s - 2t)2s + (3s - 2t)6t$ *Use the distributive property to multiply each term of $2s + 6t$ by $3s - 2t$.*

$= 3s \cdot 2s - 2t \cdot 2s + 3s \cdot 6t - 2t \cdot 6t$ *Use the distributive property two more times.*

$= 6s^2 - 4st + 18st - 12t^2$

$= 6s^2 + 14st - 12t^2$

or

$$\begin{array}{r} 3s - 2t \\ (\times)\ \ 2s + 6t \\ \hline 6s^2 - \quad 4st \\ (+)\ \ \underline{\quad\quad 18st - 12t^2} \\ 6s^2 + 14st - 12t^2 \end{array}$$

2 | **Multiply $x + 3$ and $x^2 + 2x + 4$.**

SOLUTION

$(x + 3)(x^2 + 2x + 4)$

$= (x + 3)x^2 + (x + 3)2x + (x + 3)4$

$= x \cdot x^2 + 3x^2 + x \cdot 2x + 3 \cdot 2x + 4x + 12$

$= x^3 + 3x^2 + 2x^2 + 6x + 4x + 12$

$= x^3 + 5x^2 + 10x + 12$

or

$$\begin{array}{r} x^2 + 2x + 4 \\ (\times)\ \ \underline{\qquad\quad x + 3} \\ x^3 + 2x^2 + \quad 4x \\ (+)\ \ \underline{\qquad 3x^2 + \quad 6x + 12} \\ x^3 + 5x^2 + 10x + 12 \end{array}$$

To multiply two polynomials, multiply each term of one polynomial by each term of the other polynomial.

CLASSROOM EXAMPLES

1. Multiply $3x - 2y$ and $5x + 4y$.

$$\begin{array}{r} 3x - 2y \\ (\times)\ \ 5x + 4y \\ \hline 15x^2 - 10xy \\ (+)\ \ \underline{\quad\quad 12xy - 8y^2} \\ 15x^2 + 2xy - 8y^2 \end{array}$$

2. Multiply $x + 4$ and $x^2 + 3x + 5$.

$$\begin{array}{r} x^2 + 3x + 5 \\ (\times)\ \ \underline{\qquad\quad x + 4} \\ x^3 + 3x^2 + 5x \\ (+)\ \ \underline{\qquad 4x^2 + 12x + 20} \\ x^3 + 7x^2 + 17x + 20 \end{array}$$

MIXED REVIEW

1. Evaluate $x^2 - y^2$ if $x = -2$ and $y = 3$. -5

2. Complete.
   a. $\left|-\frac{5}{11}\right|$ $\frac{5}{11}$
   b. $-\left|\frac{5}{6}\right|$ $-\frac{5}{6}$

3. Simplify $(-5x^3y)(2xy)$. $-10x^4y^2$

4. Find the solution set of $y^2 = 121$. The replacement set is $\{-11, -4, 4, 11\}$. $\{-11, 11\}$

5. Express $\frac{45}{72}$ as a decimal. 0.625

ORAL EXERCISES

Complete.

1. $(x - 2y)(2x + 3y) = (x - 2y) \underline{\quad 2x \quad} + (x - 2y) \underline{\quad 3y \quad}$

2. $(a + b)(a - 7b) = (a + b) \underline{\quad a \quad} + (a + b) \underline{\quad (-7b) \quad}$

3. $(2m - 3)(4m - 5) = (2m - 3) \underline{\quad 4m \quad} + (2m - 3) \underline{\quad (-5) \quad}$

You may want to introduce this topic using **Algebra Tiles**. They are a physical model for teaching algebraic concepts and are available from Cuisenaire Co. of America, Inc., 12 Church Street, New Rochelle, NY 10802.

ASSIGNMENT GUIDE

Minimum
1–21 0dd

Regular
11–22

Maximum
13–20, 23–25

ADDITIONAL ANSWERS

Written Exercises

11. $2x^3 + 19x^2 + 37x + 14$

12. $6x^3 + 11x^2 - 2x - 8$

13. $2a^3 + 11a^2 + 24a + 18$

14. $3y^3 + 26y^2 + 4y - 8$

15. $9t^3 + 15t^2 + 7t + 1$

16. $4x^3 + 28x^2 + 65x^2 + 50$

17. $4a^3 - 39a^2 + 90a + 25$

18. $6b^3 - 59b^2 + 140b$
      $+ 25$

19. $8x^3 - 28x^2 + 30x - 9$

20. $27x^3 - 54x^2 + 32$

21. $3x^2 - 6xy - 7x + 3y^2$
      $+ 7y + 4$

22. $5b^2 - 10bc - 7b + 5c^2$
      $+ 7c + 2$

4. $(8r - 5s)(2r + 3s) = (8r - 5s)\ \underline{\quad 2r \quad} + (8r - 5s)\ \underline{\quad 3s \quad}$

5. $(x + 2)(x^2 - 1) = \underline{\quad (x + 2) \quad} x^2 + \underline{\quad (x + 2) \quad} (-1)$

6. $(3y - 5)(y^2 + 5) = \underline{\quad (3y - 5) \quad} y^2 + \underline{\quad (3y - 5) \quad} 5$

7. $(5y - 7)(5y + 7) = \underline{\quad (5y - 7) \quad} 5y + \underline{\quad (5y - 7) \quad} 7$

8. $(x + 7)(x - 8) = \underline{\quad (x + 7) \quad} x + \underline{\quad (x + 7) \quad} (-8)$

WRITTEN EXERCISES

A. Find each product.

1. $(x + 4)(x + 3)$ $x^2 + 7x + 12$

2. $(y + 2)(y + 4)$ $y^2 + 6y + 8$

3. $(s + 7)(s - 2)$ $s^2 + 5s - 14$

4. $(b - 6)(b + 6)$ $b^2 - 36$

5. $(3c - 5)(c + 3)$ $3c^2 + 4c - 15$

6. $(8d + 4)(d - 6)$ $8d^2 - 44d - 24$

7. $(n - 7)(4n - 5)$ $4n^2 - 33n + 35$

8. $(t + 4)(5t - 3)$ $5t^2 + 17t - 12$

9. $(x^2 + 3)(x - 4)$ $x^3 - 4x^2 + 3x - 12$

10. $(z^2 - 5)(z - 6)$ $z^3 - 6z^2 - 5z + 30$

B. 11. $(x + 7)(2x^2 + 5x + 2)$

12. $(3x + 4)(2x^2 + x - 2)$

13. $(2a + 3)(a^2 + 4a + 6)$

14. $(3y + 2)(y^2 + 8y - 4)$

15. $(3t + 1)(3t^2 + 4t + 1)$

16. $(2x + 5)(2x^2 + 9x + 10)$

17. $(a - 5)(4a^2 - 19a - 5)$

18. $(b - 5)(6b^2 - 29b - 5)$

19. $(2x - 3)(4x^2 - 8x + 3)$

20. $(3x - 4)(9x^2 - 6x - 8)$

21. $(3x - 3y - 4)(x - y - 1)$

22. $(5b - 5c - 2)(b - c - 1)$

C. 23. $(3b^a + 1)(b^a - 2)$ $3b^{2a} - 5b^a - 2$

24. $(a^x + 1)(a^x - 1)$ $a^{2x} - 1$

25. $(y^c + 3)(y^c - 3)$ $y^{2c} - 9$

26. $(x^b + y^a)(x^b - y^a)$ $x^{2b} - y^{2a}$

SKILLS MAINTENANCE

Give the additive inverse of each polynomial.

1. $3x$ $-3x$

2. $(-4a)$ $4a$

3. $2x - 6$ $-2x + 6$

Evaluate each polynomial if $a = -3$, $b = 5$, and $c = 4$.

4. $-3b^2$ -75

5. $a^2 - 2$ 7

6. $bc + 2a^2$ 38

Simplify each sum.

7. $(3x + 2) + (4x - 7)$ $7x - 5$

8. $(x^2 - 7x + 7) + (x^2 - 2x + 3)$ $2x^2 - 9x + 10$

Simplify each difference.

9. $(3a - 11) - (7a + 2)$ $-4a - 13$

10. $(x^2 - 5x + 7) - (x^2 + 5x - 7)$ $-10x + 14$

Find each product.

11. $(5x - 4)(-5x)$ $-25x^2 + 20x$

12. $(4y^2 + 5y - 7)4y$ $16y^3 + 20y^2 - 28y$

5.6 | Special Products

There is a shortcut for finding the product of two binomials.

Multiply the **F**irst terms.

Multiply the **O**utside terms.

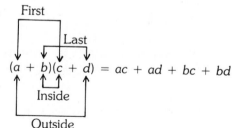

Multiply the **I**nside terms.

Multiply the **L**ast terms.

This shortcut is sometimes called the **FOIL** method.

EXAMPLE

Use the FOIL method to multiply $x + 2$ and $x + 4$.

$$\begin{array}{cccc} \text{F} & \text{O} & \text{I} & \text{L} \\ \downarrow & \downarrow & \downarrow & \downarrow \end{array}$$

SOLUTION: $(x + 2)(x + 4) = x \cdot x + 4x + 2x + 2 \cdot 4$

$= x^2 + 6x + 8$

Study the special products of the binomials below.

Square of a sum

$(a + b)^2 = (a + b)(a + b) = a^2 + 2ab + b^2$

Square of a difference

$(a - b)^2 = (a - b)(a - b) = a^2 - 2ab + b^2$

Product of the sum and difference of two numbers

$(a + b)(a - b) = a^2 - b^2$

ORAL EXERCISES

Complete by using the FOIL method.

1. $(x + 5)(x + 7) = x^2 + 7x + 5x + \underline{\ 35\ }$

2. $(y - 3)(y - 7) = y^2 - \underline{\ 7y\ } - 3y + 21$

3. $(z + 5)(z + 4) = \underline{\ z^2\ } + 4z + 5z + 20$

4. $(a - 2)(a + 3) = a^2 + 3a - \underline{\ 2a\ } - 6$

OBJECTIVE

Find the product of polynomials by using the FOIL method or the special products patterns.

TEACHER'S NOTES

See p. T27.

CLASSROOM EXAMPLE

Use the FOIL method to multiply $x + 5$ and $x + 7$.

$(x + 5)(x + 7)$

$= x \cdot x + 7x + 5x + 5 \cdot 7$

$= x^2 + 12x + 35$

MIXED REVIEW

Perform the indicated operation.

1. $(3x^3)^2$ $9x^6$

2. $(5x^2 + 3x - 5) + (12x^2 + 6x + 8)$ $17x^2 + 9x + 3$

3. $6(5x^2 + 2x - 4)$ $30x^2 + 12x - 24$

4. $4(4^2)$ 64

5. $(6x^2 - 5x + 14) - (3x^2 + 9x + 10)$ $3x^2 - 14x + 4$

TEACHER'S RESOURCE MASTERS

Practice Master 20, Part 2

ASSIGNMENT GUIDE

Minimum
1–11 odd, 13–26

Regular
13–32

Maximum
13–33 odd, 35–43

ADDITIONAL ANSWERS

Written Exercises

1. $x^2 + 5x + 6$

2. $y^2 - 6y + 5$

3. $z^2 + 10z + 24$

4. $a^2 - 2a - 35$

5. $2s^2 - 13s + 21$

6. $10t^2 - 22t - 24$

7. $m^2 - 25$

8. $s^2 - 36$

9. $r^2 - 2r + 1$

10. $t^2 + 6t + 9$

11. $49 + 14y + y^2$ or $y^2 + 14y + 49$

12. $25 - x^2$ or $-x^2 + 25$

14. $15m^2 + 22mn + 8n$

22. $20m^2 - 22mn + 6n^2$

23. $x^2 - 12x + 36$

24. $y^2 - 16y + 64$

25. $64s^2 + 144s + 81$

26. $a^2 - 121$

27. $b^2 - 225$

28. $100 - c^2$ or $-c^2 + 100$

29. $49 - 14d + d^2$ or $d^2 - 14d + 49$

30. $169 + 26r + r^2$ or $r^2 + 26r + 169$

31. $9p^5 + 24p^4 + 16p^3$

32. $16q^4 - 64q^3 + 64q^2$

33. $4x^2 - 12xy + 9y^2$

34. $9m^2 + 24mn + 16n^2$

---

5. $(2 + k)(3 + k) = 6 + 2k + 3k + \underline{k^2}$

6. $(a + 4)(a - 5) = \underline{a^2} - 5a + 4a - \underline{20}$

7. $(2x + 3)(x + 5) = 2x^2 + \underline{10x} + \underline{3x} + 15$

8. $(2y + 3)(3y - 2) = \underline{6y^2} - \underline{4y} + 9y - 6$

9. $(4x - 5)(x - 4) = \underline{4x^2} - 16x - 5x + \underline{20}$

10. $(3a - 4)(5a + 1) = 15a^2 + \underline{3a} - 20a - \underline{4}$

Match the factors in Column A with their products in Column B.

Column A

11. $(x + 3)^2$ b

12. $(x + 3)(x - 3)$ d

13. $(3x + 2)^2$ a

14. $(3x - 2)^2$ e

15. $(x - 3)^2$ f

16. $(3x + 2)(3x - 2)$ c

Column B

a. $9x^2 + 12x + 4$

b. $x^2 + 6x + 9$

c. $9x^2 - 4$

d. $x^2 - 9$

e. $9x^2 - 12x + 4$

f. $x^2 - 6x + 9$

WRITTEN EXERCISES

A. Find each product.

1. $(x + 2)(x + 3)$

2. $(y - 5)(y - 1)$

3. $(z + 4)(z + 6)$

4. $(a - 7)(a + 5)$

5. $(2s - 7)(s - 3)$

6. $(5t + 4)(2t - 6)$

7. $(m - 5)(m + 5)$

8. $(s + 6)(s - 6)$

9. $(r - 1)^2$

10. $(t + 3)^2$

11. $(7 + y)^2$

12. $(5 - x)(5 + x)$

B.

13. $(3t + 2s)(2t + 4s)$ $6t^2 + 16st + 8s^2$

14. $(5m + 4n)(3m + 2n)$

15. $(5 - 7x)(7 - 5x)$ $35 - 74x + 35x^2$

16. $(3 - 10x)(5 - 2x)$ $15 - 56x + 20x^2$

17. $(3xy + 4)(4xy - 5)$ $12x^2y^2 + xy - 20$

18. $(2xy - 3)(5xy + 6)$ $10x^2y^2 - 3xy - 18$

19. $(5t - 3)(8t + 9)$ $40t^2 + 21t - 27$

20. $(3x + 5)(5x - 3)$ $15x^2 + 16x - 15$

21. $(7y + 4)(4y - 7)$ $28y^2 - 33y - 28$

22. $(5m - 3n)(4m - 2n)$

23. $(x - 6)^2$

24. $(y - 8)^2$

25. $(8s + 9)^2$

26. $(a + 11)(a - 11)$

27. $(b + 15)(b - 15)$

28. $(10 - c)(10 + c)$

29. $(7 - d)^2$

30. $(13 + r)^2$

31. $p^3(3p + 4)^2$

32. $q^2(4q - 8)^2$

33. $(2x - 3y)^2$

34. $(3m + 4n)^2$

C.

35. $(2x^a + 1)(x^a - 2)$ $2x^{2a} - 3x^a - 2$

36. $(3y^b + 2)(2y^b + 3)$ $6y^{2b} + 13y^b + 6$

37. $(y^b - 4)(3y^b - 2)$ $3y^{2b} - 14y^b + 8$

38. $(x^n + 1)(x^n - 1)$ $x^{2n} - 1$

39. $(y^{2a} + 2)(y^{2a} - 2)$ $y^{4a} - 4$

40. $(x^a + y^b)(x^a - y^b)$ $x^{2a} - y^{2b}$

41. $(s^m + t^n)^2$ $\quad s^{2m} + 2s^m t^n + t^{2n}$

42. $(w^a - z^b)^2$ $\quad w^{2a} - 2w^a z^b + z^{2b}$

43. $(y^a + z^b)(y^a - z^b)$ $\quad y^{2a} - z^{2b}$

SELF-QUIZ

Simplify.

1. $(3x^2 + 2x + 3) + (x^2 - 3x + 7)$

2. $(y^2 - 3y + 6) + (5y^2 - 2y - 8)$

3. $(4a^2 + 3a + 5) - (a^2 - 5a + 3)$

4. $(-c^2 + 9c - 7) - (4c^2 - 7c + 7)$

Find each product.

5. $(4n^2)(5n^3)$ $\quad 20n^5$

6. $(x^2 y)^3$ $\quad x^6 y^3$

7. $3z(2z^2 - 3z + 4)$ $\quad 6z^3 - 9z^2 + 12z$

8. $(a + 3)(a^2 + 4a + 2)$ $\quad a^3 + 7a^2 + 14a + 6$

9. $(3t - 5)(2t + 3)$ $\quad 6t^2 - t - 15$

10. $(x + y)^2$ $\quad x^2 + 2xy + y^2$

11. $(2x + 3)(2x - 3)$ $\quad 4x^2 - 9$

12. $(r + 3)(2r - 5)$ $\quad 2r^2 + r - 15$

SELF-QUIZ

1. $4x^2 - x + 10$

2. $6y^2 - 5y - 2$

3. $3a^2 + 8a + 2$

4. $-5c^2 + 16c - 14$

MATH HERITAGE/Math's Dynamic Duo

Charles Babbage (1792–1871) and **Lady Ada Lovelace** (1815–1852) together laid the groundwork for modern-day calculators and computers. Babbage began the construction of a machine for calculating mathematical tables in 1820. Aided financially for a time by the British government, Babbage constructed two machines, both of which failed because parts could not be machined precisely enough. He anticipated almost every basic concept of modern electronic computer technology in his analytic engine, as he called his second machine. This was a very complicated mechanical device designed to store and manipulate numbers in much the same way as present-day computers.

Lady Lovelace's contribution is evident in more than one way. Besides giving constant encouragement to Babbage, she created the binary number system, a feat that many feel entitles her to be referred to as the first programmer. Not only did she translate Babbage's notes into French, but she added significantly to them. Such accomplishments in mathematics were most unusual for a woman in the 19th century. Incidentally, she was the daughter of Lord Byron.

When an equation involves polynomials, clear the equation of parentheses first, combine like terms, and then solve for the variable.

EXAMPLES

CLASSROOM EXAMPLES

1. Solve $(2x - 4) + (x + 3) = 14$.

$$(2x - 4) + (x + 3) = 14$$
$$2x + x - 4 + 3 = 14$$
$$3x - 1 = 14$$
$$3x = 15$$
$$x = 5$$

2. Solve $[(3y)^2 + 5] - (y^2 - y) = 8y^2$.

$$[(3y)^2 + 5] - (y^2 - y) = 8y^2$$
$$(9y^2 + 5) - y^2 + y = 8y^2$$
$$9y^2 - y^2 + y + 5 = 8y^2$$
$$8y^2 + y + 5 = 8y^2$$
$$y + 5 = 0$$
$$y = -5$$

3. Solve $3x(4x - 5) - (11x^2 - 2) = (x + 2)^2$.

$$3x(4x - 5) - (11x^2 - 2) = (x + 2)^2$$
$$12x^2 - 15x - 11x^2 + 2 = x^2 + 4x + 4$$
$$12x^2 - 11x^2 - 15x + 2 = x^2 + 4x + 4$$
$$x^2 - 15x + 2 = x^2 + 4x + 4$$
$$-15x + 2 = 4x + 4$$
$$-19x = 2$$
$$x = -\frac{2}{19}$$

1 **Solve $(3x - 5) + (x + 8) = 11$.**

SOLUTION
$$(3x - 5) + (x + 8) = 11$$
$$3x + x - 5 + 8 = 11$$
$$4x + 3 = 11$$
$$4x = 8$$
$$x = 2$$

CHECK $(3x - 5) + (x + 8) = 11$

$(3 \cdot 2 - 5) + (2 + 8) \stackrel{?}{=} 11$ *Substitute 2 for x in the equation.*

$(6 - 5) + 10 \stackrel{?}{=} 11$

$1 + 10 \stackrel{?}{=} 11$

$11 = 11$ ✔

2 **Solve $[(2y)^2 + 8] - (y^2 - y) = 3y^2$.**

SOLUTION $[(2y)^2 + 8] - (y^2 - y) = 3y^2$
$$(4y^2 + 8) - y^2 + y = 3y^2$$
$$4y^2 - y^2 + y + 8 = 3y^2$$
$$3y^2 + y + 8 = 3y^2$$
$$y + 8 = 0 \quad \text{Add } -3y^2 \text{ to each side.}$$
$$y = -8$$

Remember to check.

3 **Solve $2x(3x - 2) - (5x^2 - 4) = (x + 3)^2$.**

SOLUTION $2x(3x - 2) - (5x^2 - 4) = (x + 3)^2$
$$6x^2 - 4x - 5x^2 + 4 = x^2 + 6x + 9 \quad \text{Multiply first.}$$
$$6x^2 - 5x^2 - 4x + 4 = x^2 + 6x + 9$$
$$x^2 - 4x + 4 = x^2 + 6x + 9 \quad \text{Combine like terms.}$$
$$-4x + 4 = 6x + 9 \quad \text{Add } -x^2 \text{ to each side.}$$
$$-10x = 5$$
$$x = -\frac{1}{2}$$

Remember to check.

Solve.

1. $2x + 1 = 7$ 3

2. $4y - 3 = 9$ 3

3. $3z + 4z + 2 = 16$ 2

4. $5z + z + 4 = 10$ 1

5. $a + 3a - 5 = 3$ 2

6. $m^2 + 2m = m^2 - 8$ −4

7. $n(n + 2) = n^2 + 4$ 2

8. $3s - s^2 = 15 - s^2$ 5

9. $t^2 + 10 = t(t + 2)$ 5

10. $4x + 3 = 5x - 2$ 5

WRITTEN EXERCISES

A. Solve.

1. $(4y - 3) - (8y + 6) = 19$ −7

2. $(9 - 5t) - (t - 7) = 40$ −4

3. $(x^2 - 4x + 10) - (x^2 - 2x + 12) = 30$ **4.** $(s^2 + 7s + 9) - (s^2 + 5s - 7) = 8$ −4

5. $3(x - 5) = x + 7$ 11

6. $4(x + 3) = x - 9$ −7

7. $3(2y + 5) - 3y = 2(y + 5) - 3(2y - 4)$ **8.** $(s - 5)(s + 1)^2 = s(s + 1)(s - 4)$ −1

9. $(x + 2)(x + 3) = x(x + 4) + 7$ 1

10. $(y + 7)(y + 3) = 21 + y(y + 1)$ 0

B. 11. $(r - 3)^2 - (2r - 1)^2 = 3(2 - r^2)$ 1

12. $(5x + 2)(6x - 3) = 15x(2x - 3) + 15$

13. $(4z - 1)(3z + 5) = 2(2z + 3)(3z - 1)$

14. $(4x + 3)^2 - (x + 6)^2 = 3(5x^2 - 1)$ 2

15. $(x - 6)^2 + 2(x - 1)^2 = 3x(x - 8) + 6$

16. $(x + 2)(x - 2) - (x - 1)^2 = 0$ $\frac{5}{2}$

17. $(x - 4)(x + 4) - (x + 3)^2 = 0$ $-\frac{25}{6}$

18. $(2x + 5)(7x - 3) = 14(x^2 + 1)$ 1

19. $6(5y^2 - 1) = (5y - 4)(6y + 7)$ 2

20. $(x - 4)^2 = (x + 2)^2$ 1

21. $(x + 3)^2 = (x - 5)^2$ 1

22. $(t + 3)(2t - 9) = (t + 2)(2t - 1)$ $-\frac{25}{6}$

23. $(4x + 5)(3x + 1) = (2x + 3)(6x + 1) + 15$ −13

24. $(2a - 1)(4a + 3) = 12 + (8a + 5)(a - 1)$ 2

25. $(3b + 2)(4b - 1) + 24 = (6b - 2)(2b - 1)$ $\frac{-4}{3}$

C. 26. $(2x - 3)(2x + 3) - 12x = (2x - 3)^2$ ∅

27. $(x^2 - 1)(x - 3) = (x - 1)(x^2 - 2x - 3)$ all real numbers

Solve for x.

28. $(a - b)x = 3(a - b), a \neq b$ 3

29. $(a + b)x = n(a + b), a \neq -b$ n

30. $\frac{3abx}{4} = c, a \neq 0, b \neq 0$ $\frac{4c}{3ab}$

31. $2(x - a) = (a + 2)^2 - a^2$ $3a + 2$

32. $\frac{abx}{a} = c, a \neq 0, b \neq 0$ $\frac{c}{b}$

MIXED REVIEW

1. Solve $\frac{10v}{2} - 6 = 19$.   5

2. Solve $3y = y + 16$.   8

3. Express $0.\overline{13}$ as a fraction. $\frac{13}{99}$

4. Illustrate the distributive property of multiplication over addition.   Answers may vary.

5. Find the value.
   a. $\left(\frac{1}{9}\right)^3$ $\frac{1}{729}$
   b. $(1.4)^2$ 1.96

TEACHER'S RESOURCE MASTERS

Practice Master 21, Part 1

ASSIGNMENT GUIDE

Minimum
1–9 odd, 11–21

Regular
11–26

Maximum
11–25 odd, 26–31

ADDITIONAL ANSWERS

Written Exercises
   3. −16
   7. 1
   12. $\frac{1}{2}$
   13. $-\frac{1}{3}$
   15. −4

OBJECTIVE

Solve uniform motion problems by using the formula $d = rt$.

TEACHER'S NOTES

See p. T27.

CLASSROOM EXAMPLES

1. Ron and Sam started from the same point at the same time and drove in opposite directions. Ron drove 20 mi/h faster than Sam. After four hours, they were 392 miles apart. Find the rate of each.

   Let r = Sam's rate.
   Then $r + 20$ = Ron's rate.

	Rate	Time	Distance
Sam	r	4	$4r$
Ron	$r + 20$	4	$4(r + 20)$

   $4r + 4(r + 20) = 392$
   $4r + 4r + 80 = 392$
   $8r + 80 = 392$
   $8r = 312$
   $r = 39$

   Answer: Sam's rate was 39 mi/h and Ron's rate was 59 mi/h.

2. Barbara traveled on roller skates at 12 mi/h until she lost one wheel. She then walked back to the starting point at 2 mi/h. If she walked for 3 hours longer than her skating time, how long did the whole trip take?

5.8 | Problem Solving

In Chapter 3, you solved some problems, using the formula $d = rt$ (d = distance, r = rate, and t = time). In this lesson you will be solving *uniform-motion problems*, using the formula $d = rt$ when the rate is a uniform (constant) speed that is traveled for a given length of time.

Two strategies that will help you solve uniform-motion problems are (1) drawing a diagram to help you understand the facts and (2) making a table to organize the given data.

EXAMPLES

1 Chris and Leslie started from the same point at the same time and drove in opposite directions. Chris drove 10 mi/h (miles per hour) faster than Leslie. After two hours, they were 200 miles apart. Find the rate of each.

Understand: *Given:* Chris drove 10 mi/h faster than Leslie.
They drove from the same point for 2 hours in opposite directions.
After 2 hours they were 200 miles apart.

To find: each person's rate

Plan: Draw a diagram.

The total distance traveled was 200 miles.

Use the formula $d = rt$.

Let r = Leslie's rate.

Then $r + 10$ = Chris's rate.

Make a table with the given data.

	Rate	Time	Distance
Leslie	r	2	$2r$
Chris	$r + 10$	2	$2(r + 10)$

Write an equation, using the fact that the total distance driven was 200 miles.

$2r + 2(r + 10) = 200$

Solve: Solve for r:
$$2r + 2(r + 10) = 200$$
$$2r + 2r + 20 = 200$$
$$4r + 20 = 200$$
$$4r = 180$$
$$r = 45$$

Answer: Leslie's rate was 45 mi/h and Chris's rate was 55 mi/h.

Review: Does it seem reasonable that if each person drove for 2 hours, Leslie at 45 mi/h and Chris at 55 mi/h, they would be 200 miles apart?

---

2 Jack rode his bike at 15 mi/h until it got a flat tire. He then walked with the bike back to the starting point at 3 mi/h. If he walked for 2 hours longer than he rode, how long did the whole trip take?

Understand: *Given:* Jack rode his bike at 15 mi/h.
He walked his bike at 3 mi/h.
He walked 2 hours longer than he rode.

To find: how long the whole trip took

Plan: Draw a diagram.

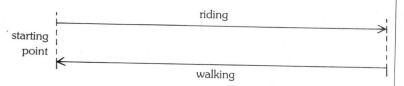

This round-trip has equal riding and walking distances.
Let t = time riding the bike.
Then $t + 2$ = time walking with the bike.
Make a table with the given data.

	Rate	Time	Distance
Riding	15	t	$15t$
Walking	3	$t + 2$	$3(t + 2)$

Write an equation, using the fact that the riding and the walking distances are equal.
$$15t = 3(t + 2)$$

Solve: Solve for t:
$$15t = 3(t + 2)$$
$$15t = 3t + 6$$
$$12t = 6$$
$$t = \frac{1}{2}$$

Answer: Jack rode the bike for $\frac{1}{2}$ hour and walked with the bike for $2\frac{1}{2}$ hours. So the whole trip took 3 hours.

Review: Does it seem reasonable that if Jack rode his bike at 15 mi/h for $\frac{1}{2}$ hour, he would have to walk his bike at 3 mi/h for $2\frac{1}{2}$ hours to get back to where he started from?

Let t = the time Barbara skated.
Then $t + 3$ = the time she walked.

	Rate	Time	Distance
Skating	12	t	$12t$
Walking	2	$t + 3$	$2(t + 3)$

$$12t = 2(t + 3)$$
$$12t = 2t + 6$$
$$10t = 6$$
$$t = \frac{3}{5}$$

Answer: Barbara skated for $\frac{3}{5}$ hour and walked for $3\frac{3}{5}$ hours. The whole trip took $4\frac{1}{5}$ hours.

3. Terry started running at 3 mi/h. Twenty minutes later, Jeremy started roller-skating from the same place along the same route at 6 mi/h. How long did it take Jeremy to catch up with Terry?

Let t = the time Jeremy skated.
Then $t + \frac{1}{3}$ = the time Terry ran.

	Rate	Time	Distance
Jeremy	6	t	$6t$
Terry	3	$t + \frac{1}{3}$	$3\left(t + \frac{1}{3}\right)$

$$6t = 3\left(t + \frac{1}{3}\right)$$
$$6t = 3t + 1$$
$$3t = 1$$
$$t = \frac{1}{3}$$

Answer: It took Jeremy $\frac{1}{3}$ hour (or 20 minutes) to catch up with Terry.

3   Kate started running at 6 mi/h. Ten minutes later, Mike started roller-skating from the same place along the same route at 10 mi/h. How long did it take Mike to catch up with Kate?

Understand: *Given:*   Kate ran a certain distance at 6 mi/h. Mike roller-skated the same distance at 10 mi/h.
Mike started 10 minutes after Kate.

To find: how long it took Mike to catch up with Kate

Plan: Draw a diagram.

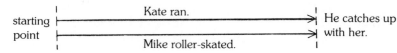

Let $t = $ time Mike roller-skated.

Then $t + \dfrac{1}{6} = $ time Kate ran.

10 minutes $= \dfrac{1}{6}$ hour

Make a table with the given data.

	Rate	Time	Distance
Mike roller-skated	10	t	$10t$
Kate ran	6	$t + \dfrac{1}{6}$	$6\left(t + \dfrac{1}{6}\right)$

Write an equation, using the fact that the distance ran and the distance roller-skated are equal.

$$10t = 6\left(t + \frac{1}{6}\right)$$

Solve: Solve for t:
$$10t = 6\left(t + \frac{1}{6}\right)$$
$$10t = 6t + 1$$
$$4t = 1$$
$$t = \frac{1}{4}$$

Answer: It took Mike $\dfrac{1}{4}$ hour (or 15 minutes) to catch up with Kate.

Review: Does it seem reasonable that Mike would catch up by roller-skating for 15 minutes at 10 mi/h if Kate started 10 minutes earlier from the same place and ran at 6 mi/h?

ORAL EXERCISES

Solve.

1. Nick drove 10 km/h faster than Pat. Let $r = $ Pat's rate. Describe Nick's rate, using r. $r + 10$

2. Jessica rode her bike for 2 hours longer than Matthew. Let $t = $ Jessica's time riding. Describe Matthew's time, using t.

3. Two trains left the same station at the same time, traveling in opposite directions. Train A traveled 25 mi/h faster than train B. Let r = train B's rate. Describe train A's rate, using r. $r + 25$

4. For t hours two trucks traveled in opposite directions from the same rest area. Driver A drove at 55 mi/h and driver B drove at 45 mi/h. Describe each truck's distance, using t. $A = 55t$, $B = 45t$

5. During road construction it takes an hour longer than usual to travel between two towns. Let t = normal traveling time. Describe the traveling time during road construction, using t. $t + 1$

6. Boat A takes 45 minutes longer than boat B to travel between two harbors. Let t = boat A's traveling time. Describe boat B's traveling time, using t. $t - 45$

WRITTEN EXERCISES

A. Solve.

1. Two trains traveled in opposite directions from the same station for 4 hours. One train traveled 24 km/h faster than the other train. How fast did each train travel if the total distance was 864 km?

2. The Huber family drove to the beach at 55 mi/h. The return trip took $\frac{3}{4}$ hour longer, driving at 40 mi/h through road construction. How long did it take to drive to the beach? 2 hours

3. Gail rode her bike at 15 km/h on a bicycle path. Carol started 1 hour later from the same place along the same path. Carol caught up with Gail by riding at 20 km/h. How long did it take Carol to catch up with Gail? 3 hours

4. Two planes left at the same time and flew in opposite directions from the airport. One plane traveled at 500 mi/h and the other plane traveled at 450 mi/h. In how many hours were the planes 3325 miles apart? $3\frac{1}{2}$ hours

B. 5. Joyce and Al paddled a canoe down the river at 4 mi/h. 45 minutes later Nate traveled down the river in a motorboat at 10 mi/h from the same point. How long did it take Nate to pass them?

6. Suzanne walked to the shopping center at 3 mi/h. The return trip on the bus took 30 minutes less traveling time. If the bus averaged 12 mi/h, how long did the bus ride take? 10 minutes

7. Two groups of hikers that were 15 miles apart on a hiking trail began hiking toward each other at the same time. The slower group traveled $2\frac{1}{2}$ mi/h and the faster group traveled $3\frac{1}{2}$ mi/h. How long did it take them to meet on the trail?

8. A camper and a car left the same point, driving in opposite directions. The camper averaged 10 km/h less than the car. After 2 hours they were 320 km apart. What was the rate of each vehicle? 85 km/h, 75 km/h

C. 9. Sherry began cross-country skiing at 8 km/h at 1:00 P.M. If Bill left from the same place 15 minutes later and skied at 12 km/h, at what time did he pass Sherry? 1:45 P.M.

10. Going to the airport from the hotel, a taxi traveled at 45 km/h. Returning from the airport to the hotel, the taxi traveled at 60 km/h. If the return trip took 5 minutes less, how long did each trip take?

Written Exercises
1. 96 km/h; 120 km/h
5. 30 minutes
7. $2\frac{1}{2}$ hours
10. 20 minutes; 15 minutes

PROBLEM–SOLVING STRATEGIES

Use a Diagram (1–10).
Use a Formula (1–10).
Write an Equation (1–10).
Make a Table (1–10).

Each problem consists of two quantities, one in **Column I** and one in **Column II**.

Compare the two quantities and choose
A if the quantity in Column I is greater;
B if the quantity in Column II is greater;
C if the two quantities are equal;
D if the relationship cannot be determined from the information given.

	COLUMN I	COLUMN II	
1.	4^5	5^4	A
	$a = 2$		
2.	$(3a)^2$	$3^2 a^2$	C
	$a = 2$		
3.	$(3a)^2$	$3a^2$	A
4.	$3x^3 + 2x^3$	$5x^3$	C
	$x \neq 0$		
5.	$\dfrac{1}{x} + \dfrac{1}{\frac{1}{x}}$	$\dfrac{1}{x^2}$	D
	$x < 0$ and $y < 0$		
6.	$x + y$	$x - y$	B
7.	$a + b$	$a - b$	D
8.	$(63)(444)$	$(7)(222)(3)(9)$	B

9.	$(-11)(144)(-11)$	$(-12)(121)(-12)$	C

	$x - 3 = 5$		
10.	$3x - 7$	$x^2 - 49$	A

	$a = b$		
11.	$a(a - b)$	1	B

	$r + s + t = x$		
12.	$r + s$	$x - t$	C

	$0.4x = 1.6y$		
	$x > 0$		
	$y > 0$		
13.	x	y	A

	$c > 0$		
	$d > 0$		
14.	$\dfrac{c + d}{c}$	$1 + \dfrac{d}{c}$	C

	$a > b$		
	$b > c$		
15.	c	a	B

	$49 < x < 63$		
16.	x	50	D

	$-3x + 4 < 13$		
17.	x	-3	A

	$x \neq 0$		
	$y \neq 0$		
	$\dfrac{1}{x} < \dfrac{1}{y}$		
18.	x	y	A

19.	The distance covered in 15 minutes at the average rate of 36 mi/h	The distance covered in 20 minutes at the average rate of 30 mi/h	B

20.	$x^2 - y^2$	$(x + y)(x - y)$	C

OBJECTIVE

Simplify expressions by using the properties for division of powers and for the power of a quotient.

CLASSROOM EXAMPLES

1. Simplify $\frac{3^4}{3^2}$.

$$\frac{3^4}{3^2} = 3^{4-2} = 3^2 = 9$$

2. Simplify $\frac{(-3)^5}{(-3)^8}$.

$$\frac{(-3)^5}{(-3)^8} = \frac{1}{(-3)^{8-5}} = \frac{1}{(-3)^3}$$
$$= \frac{1}{-27} = -\frac{1}{27}$$

3. Simplify $\frac{x^3y^2z}{xy^3z}$. $\quad \frac{x^3y^2z}{xy^3z}$

$$= \frac{x^3 \cdot y^2 \cdot z}{x \cdot y^3 \cdot z} = \frac{x^3}{x} \cdot \frac{y^2}{y^3} \cdot \frac{z}{z}$$
$$= x^{3-1} \cdot \frac{1}{y^{3-2}} \cdot 1 = \frac{x^2}{y}$$

4. Simplify $\frac{de^2f^3}{de^3f}$.

$$\frac{de^2f^3}{de^3f} = \frac{d}{d} \cdot \frac{e^2}{e^3} \cdot \frac{f^3}{f}$$
$$= 1 \cdot \frac{1}{e^{3-2}} \cdot f^{3-1} = \frac{f^2}{e}$$

5. Simplify $\left(\frac{-4x}{3}\right)^3$. $\quad \left(\frac{-4x}{3}\right)^3$

$$= \frac{(-4x)^3}{3^3} = \frac{(-4)^3x^3}{3^3}$$
$$= -\frac{64x^3}{27}$$

5.9 | Quotients of Powers

Quotients involving powers that have the same base can be simplified, as shown in the following examples:

$$\frac{3^2}{3^2} = 1 \qquad\qquad \frac{3^6}{3^2} = \frac{3^2 \cdot 3^4}{3^2} = 3^4 \qquad\qquad \frac{3^2}{3^6} = \frac{3^2}{3^2 \cdot 3^4} = \frac{1}{3^4}$$

These examples suggest the rule for division of powers.

Division of Powers	**Let x be any nonzero real number, and let a and b be any positive integers.**
	If $a = b$, then $\dfrac{x^a}{x^b} = 1$.
	If $a > b$, then $\dfrac{x^a}{x^b} = x^{a-b}$.
	If $a < b$, then $\dfrac{x^a}{x^b} = \dfrac{1}{x^{b-a}}$.

EXAMPLES

1   **Simplify $\frac{4^{10}}{4^8}$.**

SOLUTION $\dfrac{4^{10}}{4^8} = 4^{10-8} = 4^2 = 16$.

2   **Simplify $\frac{(-5)^4}{(-5)^7}$.**

SOLUTION $\dfrac{(-5)^4}{(-5)^7} = \dfrac{1}{(-5)^{7-4}} = \dfrac{1}{(-5)^3} = \dfrac{1}{-125} = -\dfrac{1}{125}$

3   **Simplify $\frac{tx^4y^3}{t^3xy^3}$.**

NOTE: If a, b, c, and d are any real numbers, $b \neq 0$, and $d \neq 0$, then $\dfrac{ac}{bd} = \dfrac{a}{b} \cdot \dfrac{c}{d}$

SOLUTION $\dfrac{tx^4y^3}{t^3xy^3} = \dfrac{t \cdot x^4 \cdot y^3}{t^3 \cdot x \cdot y^3} = \dfrac{t}{t^3} \cdot \dfrac{x^4}{x} \cdot \dfrac{y^3}{y^3} = \dfrac{1}{t^{3-1}} \cdot x^{4-1} \cdot 1 = \dfrac{x^3}{t^2}$

4   **Simplify $\frac{rs^5t^2}{rs^3t^6}$.**

SOLUTION $\dfrac{rs^5t^2}{rs^3t^6} = \dfrac{r}{r} \cdot \dfrac{s^5}{s^3} \cdot \dfrac{t^2}{t^6} = 1 \cdot s^{5-3} \cdot \dfrac{1}{t^{6-2}} = \dfrac{s^2}{t^4}$

Study the following example: $\left(\dfrac{3}{5}\right)^2 = \dfrac{3}{5} \cdot \dfrac{3}{5} = \dfrac{3^2}{5^2}$

This example suggests the following property for the power of a quotient.

Power of a Quotient	Let x and y be any real numbers where $y \neq 0$, and let a be any positive integer. $$\left(\frac{x}{y}\right)^a = \frac{x^a}{y^a}$$

5 **Simplify** $\left(\dfrac{-2x}{3}\right)^3$.

SOLUTION

$$\left(\frac{-2x}{3}\right)^3 = \frac{(-2x)^3}{3^3} = \frac{(-2)^3 x^3}{3^3} = \frac{-8x^3}{27}$$

1. $5x(3x^2 + 2x - 5)$ $15x^3 + 10x^2 - 25x$

2. $(-6x^2 + 5x - 10) - (3x^2 + 4x - 5)$ $-9x^2 + x - 5$

3. $(3x^2y)(5x^2y + 5x)$ $15x^4y^2 + 15x^3y$

4. $(12y^3 + 8y^2 - 5y - 12) + (5y^2 - 8)$ $12y^3 + 13y^2 - 5y - 20$

5. $(3x - 5)^2$ $9x^2 - 30x + 25$

6. $(2x - 5)(2x + 5)$ $4x^2 - 25$

ORAL EXERCISES

Simplify each expression.

1. $\dfrac{a^6}{a^4}$ a^2

2. $\left(\dfrac{3}{5}\right)^3$ $\dfrac{27}{125}$

3. $\dfrac{2^3}{2^5}$ $\dfrac{1}{4}$

4. $\dfrac{(3x)^5}{(3x)^2}$ $27x^3$

5. $(2x)^5$ $32x^5$

6. $\dfrac{r^8}{r^3}$ r^5

7. $\dfrac{s^7}{s^4}$ s^3

8. $\dfrac{t^9}{t^{12}}$ $\dfrac{1}{t^3}$

9. $\dfrac{u^3}{u^8}$ $\dfrac{1}{u^5}$

10. $\dfrac{3c^2}{c}$ $3c$

WRITTEN EXERCISES

A. Simplify each expression.

1. $\dfrac{10^{12}}{10^9}$ 1000

2. $\dfrac{(-3)^6}{(-3)^9}$ $-\dfrac{1}{27}$

3. $\dfrac{(-2)^5}{(-2)^7}$ $\dfrac{1}{4}$

4. $\dfrac{10^6}{10^4}$ 100

5. $\dfrac{(-7)^5}{(-7)^5}$ 1

6. $\dfrac{(-5)^4}{(-5)^4}$ 1

7. $\left(\dfrac{1}{2}\right)^3$ $\dfrac{1}{8}$

8. $\left(\dfrac{-5}{t}\right)^6$ $\dfrac{15625}{t^6}$

9. $\left(\dfrac{r}{-w}\right)^7$ $-\dfrac{r^7}{w^7}$

10. $\dfrac{x^5}{x^3}$ x^2

11. $\dfrac{(-5)^5}{(-5)^2}$ -125

12. $\dfrac{(-4)^6}{(-4)^3}$ -64

13. $\dfrac{(0.4)^3}{0.4}$ 0.16

14. $\dfrac{(xy)^8}{(xy)^6}$ x^2y^2

15. $\dfrac{(ab)^9}{(ab)^7}$ a^2b^2

16. $\dfrac{(xy)^3}{(xy)^7}$ $\dfrac{1}{x^4y^4}$

B. 17. $\dfrac{r^8s^{12}}{r^4s^5}$ r^4s^7

18. $\dfrac{a^7b^{12}}{a^4b^9}$ a^3b^3

19. $\dfrac{m^3n^8}{m^7n^{10}}$ $\dfrac{1}{m^4n^2}$

20. $\dfrac{t^2u^6}{t^5u^{11}}$ $\dfrac{1}{t^3u^5}$

21. $\dfrac{x^{10}y^4}{x^6y^8}$ $\dfrac{x^4}{y^4}$

22. $\dfrac{z^6w^7}{z^9w^2}$ $\dfrac{w^5}{z^3}$

23. $\dfrac{(2p)^7}{(2p)^3}$ $16p^4$

24. $\dfrac{(3r)^8}{(3r)^4}$ $81r^4$

25. $\left(\dfrac{2x}{3y}\right)^3$ $\dfrac{8x^3}{27y^3}$

26. $\left(\dfrac{3r}{2s}\right)^4$ $\dfrac{81r^4}{16s^4}$

27. $\dfrac{2ab(6a^2b^3)}{-12a^3b^3}$ $-b$

28. $\dfrac{4xy^2(-8xy^3)}{16x^2y^2}$ $-2y^3$

29. $\dfrac{(2mn^2)^2(-6m^3n)}{(2m^2n^2)^2}$ $-6mn$

30. $\dfrac{(6xy)^2(-18x^3y)}{3x^2y^3}$ $-216x^3$

C. 31. $\dfrac{x^ay^2z}{x^ayz}$ y

32. $\dfrac{x^{3a}}{x^{2a}}$ x^a

33. $\dfrac{x^ay^2}{x^b}$ $x^{a-b}y^2$

34. $\dfrac{x^ay^b}{x^cy^8}$ $x^{a-c}y^{b-8}$

35. $\dfrac{a^{3m-2n}b^3}{a^{2m+2n}b^2}$ $a^{m-4n}b$

36. $\dfrac{-24m^2(m-n)^7}{6m^3(m-n)^6}$

37. $\dfrac{12x^2(x-y)^6}{-4x^4(x-y)^5}$ $\dfrac{-3(x-y)}{x^2}$

38. $\dfrac{r^{5a}s^{3b}t^{2c}}{r^{2a}s^bt^c}$ $r^{3a}s^{2b}t^c$

39. $\dfrac{x^{4d}y^{4e}z^{2f}}{x^{2d}y^{3e}z^f}$ $x^{2d}y^ez^f$

TEACHER'S RESOURCE MASTERS

Practice Master 22, Part 1

ASSIGNMENT GUIDE

Minimum
1–15 odd, 17–20, 26–29

Regular
17–32

Maximum
17–29 odd, 31–39

ADDITIONAL ANSWERS

Written Exercises
36. $-\dfrac{4(m-n)}{m}$

Simplify the quotient of two monomials.

Simplify the quotient of a polynomial divided by a monomial.

TEACHER'S NOTES

See p. T28.

CLASSROOM EXAMPLES

1. Simplify $\dfrac{16x^4y}{24x^2y}$.

$$\dfrac{16x^4y}{24x^2y} = \dfrac{\overset{2}{\cancel{16}}}{\underset{3}{\cancel{24}}} \cdot x^{4-2} \cdot \dfrac{y}{y}$$

$$= \dfrac{2x^2}{3}$$

2. Simplify $\dfrac{32a^5b^2}{50a^3b}$.

$$\dfrac{32a^5b^2}{50a^3b^4} = \dfrac{\overset{16}{\cancel{32}}}{\underset{25}{\cancel{50}}} \cdot$$

$$\dfrac{a^{5-3}}{b^{4-2}} = \dfrac{16a^2}{25b^2}$$

3. Divide $26x^2 + 8x$ by $2x$.

$$\dfrac{26x^2 + 8x}{2x} = \dfrac{26x^2}{2x} + \dfrac{8x}{2x}$$

$$= 13x + 4$$

4. Divide $36x^3y + 16x^2y - 8xy^2$ by $4xy$.

$$\dfrac{36x^3y + 16x^2y - 8xy^2}{4xy} =$$

$$\dfrac{36x^3y}{4xy} + \dfrac{16x^2y}{4xy} - \dfrac{8xy^2}{4xy}$$

$$= 9x^2 + 4x - 2y$$

MIXED REVIEW

1. Find the solution set of $x^2 = 81$. $\{-9, 9\}$

2. Find the value of $(2.7)^3$.   19.683

5.10 | Dividing by Monomials

To divide a monomial by a monomial, simplify the numerical quotient and simplify the variables.

EXAMPLES

1 **Simplify** $\dfrac{12x^5y}{30x^2y}$.

SOLUTION

$$\dfrac{12x^5y}{30x^2y} = \dfrac{\overset{2}{\cancel{12}}}{\underset{5}{\cancel{30}}} \cdot x^{5-2} \cdot \dfrac{y}{y} = \dfrac{2x^3}{5}$$

2 **Simplify** $\dfrac{48s^4t}{56s^3t^5}$.

SOLUTION

$$\dfrac{48s^4t}{56s^3t^5} = \dfrac{\overset{6}{\cancel{48}}}{\underset{7}{\cancel{56}}} \cdot \dfrac{s^{4\ 3}}{t^{5\ 1}} = \dfrac{6s}{7t^4}$$

To divide a polynomial by a monomial, divide each term of the polynomial by the monomial.

3 **Divide** $10x^2 + 6x$ **by** $2x$.

SOLUTION

$$\dfrac{10x^2 + 6x}{2x} = \dfrac{10x^2}{2x} + \dfrac{6x}{2x}$$

$$= 5x + 3$$

4 **Divide** $24x^3y + 16x^2y^2 - 12xy^3$ **by** $4xy$.

SOLUTION

$$\dfrac{24x^3y + 16x^2y^2 - 12xy^3}{4xy} = \dfrac{24x^3y}{4xy} + \dfrac{16x^2y^2}{4xy} - \dfrac{12xy^3}{4xy}$$

$$= 6x^2 + 4xy - 3y^2$$

ORAL EXERCISES

Simplify each quotient.

1. $\dfrac{4x}{2x}$ 2

2. $\dfrac{8y}{4}$ 2y

3. $\dfrac{10a}{5}$ 2a

4. $\dfrac{6c}{3c}$ 2

5. $\dfrac{-7}{14d}$ $-\dfrac{1}{2d}$

6. $\dfrac{3t + 6}{3}$ $t + 2$

7. $\dfrac{7z - 14}{7}$ $z - 2$

8. $\dfrac{3x^2 - 6x}{3x}$ $x - 2$

9. $\dfrac{8m^2 + 4m}{4m}$ $2m + 1$

10. $\dfrac{10n^2 + 2n}{2n}$ $5n + 1$

A. Simplify each quotient.

1. $\dfrac{12x^5}{x^2}$ $12x^3$

2. $\dfrac{-s^3}{5s^6}$ $-\dfrac{1}{5s^3}$

3. $\dfrac{t^2}{-3t^5}$ $-\dfrac{1}{3t^3}$

4. $\dfrac{9w^4}{18w^4}$ $\dfrac{1}{2}$

5. $\dfrac{-8x^4}{-5x^3}$ $\dfrac{8}{5}x$

6. $\dfrac{12x^2 - 2x}{2x}$

7. $\dfrac{13y^2 - 11y}{y}$

8. $\dfrac{19z^3 - 6z^2}{z^2}$

9. $\dfrac{8b - 16b^2}{8b}$

10. $\dfrac{22a - 11a^3}{11a}$

11. $\dfrac{24x^2 + 12x}{6x}$

12. $\dfrac{32c^3 - 16c^2}{8c^2}$

B. 13. $\dfrac{21xy^2}{7xy}$ $3y$

14. $\dfrac{21m^2n}{7mn}$ $3m$

15. $\dfrac{-2.8x^5}{7x^5}$ -0.4

16. $\dfrac{3.2y^7}{-8y^3}$ $-0.4y^4$

17. $\dfrac{-33z^5}{-11z^7}$ $\dfrac{3}{z^2}$

18. $\dfrac{-42a^3}{-6a^8}$ $\dfrac{7}{a^5}$

19. $\dfrac{52x^2y^2}{13xy}$ $4xy$

20. $\dfrac{26r^2s^2}{13rs}$ $2rs$

21. $\dfrac{19w^3v^2}{-3.8w^2v}$ $-5wv$

22. $\dfrac{-17a^4b^2}{3.4a^3b}$ $-5ab$

23. $\dfrac{28x^4 + 42x^3 - 14x^2}{7x^2}$ $4x^2 + 6x - 2$

24. $\dfrac{32s^4 - 40s^3 - 16s^2}{8s^2}$ $4s^2 - 5s - 2$

25. $\dfrac{-36x^2 - 12x + 30}{-6}$ $6x^2 + 2x - 5$

26. $\dfrac{-64x^2 - 16x + 40}{-8}$ $8x^2 + 2x - 5$

27. $\dfrac{22t^2 - 33t - 9}{11}$ $2t^2 - 3t - \dfrac{9}{11}$

28. $\dfrac{24b^2 - 36b - 11}{12}$ $2b^2 - 3b - \dfrac{11}{12}$

29. $\dfrac{17x^3 - 34x^2}{-17x^2}$ $-x + 2$

30. $\dfrac{19c^3 - 38c^2}{-19c^2}$ $-c + 2$

31. $\dfrac{48r^5 - 32r^4}{8r^3}$ $6r^2 - 4r$

32. $\dfrac{56m^7 - 35m^5}{7m^4}$ $8m^3 - 5m$

33. $\dfrac{x^3 + 7x^2 - 3x + 2}{x}$ $x^2 + 7x - 3 + \dfrac{2}{x}$

34. $\dfrac{y^3 - 5y^2 + 2y + 3}{y}$ $y^2 - 5y + 2 + \dfrac{3}{y}$

35. $\dfrac{6a^2b^2 - 9ab}{3ab}$ $2ab - 3$

36. $\dfrac{12m^2n^2 - 18mn}{3mn}$ $4mn - 6$

37. $\dfrac{-10z^3 - 15z^2 + 5z}{-5z}$ $2z^2 + 3z - 1$

38. $\dfrac{-12y^3 + 18y^2 - 6y}{-6y}$ $2y^2 - 3y + 1$

C. Simplify each expression.

39. $\left(\dfrac{st}{2}\right)^3 \cdot \left(\dfrac{4}{st}\right)^2$ $2st$

40. $\left(\dfrac{3}{xy}\right)^2 \cdot \left(\dfrac{xy}{6}\right)^2$ $\dfrac{1}{4}$

41. $\left(\dfrac{3ab}{4}\right)^2 \cdot \left(\dfrac{2}{ab}\right)^3$ $\dfrac{9}{2ab}$

42. $\dfrac{17b^9}{b^7} + \dfrac{20b^7}{5b^6} - \dfrac{8b}{2}$ $17b^2$

43. $\dfrac{-3x^4}{2x^2} + \dfrac{7x^5}{8x^4} - \dfrac{17x}{x}$ $-\dfrac{3}{2}x^2 + \dfrac{7}{8}x - 17$

44. $(18ax^3 + 6ax^2 - 12ax) \div (6ax)$

45. $(16by^3 + 12by^2 - 8by) \div (-4by)$

46. $(6x^3y^3 - 9x^2y^2 + xy - 1) \div (3xy)$

47. $(4a^3b^2c - 8a^2bc^3 + ab^3c^4) \div (4abc)$

48. $(21st^4 + 15s^2t^3 - 9s^3t^2) \div 3st^2$

49. $\dfrac{6y^a}{2y^a}$ 3

50. $\dfrac{4x^{2b}}{6x^b}$ $\dfrac{2}{3}x^b$

51. $\dfrac{-3y^c}{4y^{2c}}$ $-\dfrac{3}{4y^c}$

52. $\dfrac{-5x^{4m}}{2x^{3m}}$ $-\dfrac{5}{2}x^m$

53. $\dfrac{12z^{2a}}{-4z^{4a}}$ $\dfrac{-3}{z^{2a}}$

54. $\dfrac{18x^{3a}}{-9x^{6a}}$ $-\dfrac{2}{x^{3a}}$

---

3. Simplify $6t^2(-5t^2 + 8t)$.
   $-30t^4 + 48t^3$

4. Simplify $(9 + 3)[72 \div (-8)]$. -108

5. Solve $4(x + 5) = 3(x - 4)$. -32

TEACHER'S RESOURCE MASTERS

Practice Master 22, Part 2

ASSIGNMENT GUIDE

Minimum
1–11 odd, 13–32

Regular
13–37 odd, 39–51

Maximum
21–38, 39–53 odd

ADDITIONAL ANSWERS

Written Exercises

6. $6x - 1$

7. $13y - 11$

8. $19z - 6$

9. $1 - 2b$

10. $2 - a^2$

11. $4x + 2$

12. $4c - 2$

44. $3x^2 + x - 2$

45. $-4y^2 - 3y + 2$

46. $2x^2y^2 - 3xy + \dfrac{1}{3} - \dfrac{1}{3xy}$

47. $a^2b - 2ac^2 + \dfrac{b^2c^3}{4}$

48. $7t^2 + 5st - 3s^2$

OBJECTIVE

Simplify the quotient of a polynomial divided by a binomial.

TEACHER'S NOTES

See p. T28.

CLASSROOM EXAMPLES

1. Divide $11x - 35 + 6x^2$ by $2x + 7$.

$$\begin{array}{r} 3x \quad - \quad 5 \\ 2x + 7 \overline{)6x^2 + 11x - 35} \\ \underline{6x^2 + 21x} \\ -10x - 35 \\ \underline{-10x - 35} \\ 0 \end{array}$$

2. Divide $x^3 + 7x^2 + 15x + 12$ by $x + 2$.

$$\begin{array}{r} x^2 + 5x \quad + \quad 5 \quad + \frac{2}{x+2} \\ x + 2 \overline{)x^3 + 7x^2 + 15x + 12} \\ \underline{x^3 + 2x^2} \\ 5x^2 + 15x \\ \underline{5x^2 + 10x} \\ 5x + 12 \\ \underline{5x + 10} \\ 2 \end{array}$$

5.11 Dividing Polynomials

Dividing a polynomial by a binomial is similar to long division of whole numbers.

Long division   *Algebra*

$31 \overline{)685}$ $2x + 1 \overline{)6x^2 + 7x + 5}$

$$\begin{array}{r} 2 \\ 31 \overline{)685} \\ \underline{62} \\ 6 \end{array}$$ $$\begin{array}{r} 3x \\ 2x + 1 \overline{)6x^2 + 7x + 5} \\ \underline{6x^2 + 3x} \\ 4x \end{array}$$

1. *Divide $6x^2$ by $2x$. Write the quotient above the x^2 term.*
2. *Multiply $(2x + 1)$ by $3x$.*
3. *Subtract $(6x^2 + 3x)$ from $(6x^2 + 7x)$.*

$$\begin{array}{r} 22 \\ 31 \overline{)685} \\ \underline{62} \\ 65 \\ \underline{62} \\ 3 \end{array}$$ $$\begin{array}{r} 3x + 2 \\ 2x + 1 \overline{)6x^2 + 7x + 5} \\ \underline{6x^2 + 3x} \\ 4x + 5 \\ \underline{4x + 2} \\ 3 \end{array}$$

4. *Bring down the next term. Divide $4x$ by $2x$. Write the quotient above the x term.*
5. *Multiply $(2x + 1)$ by 2.*
6. *Subtract $(4x + 2)$ from $(4x + 5)$.*

CHECK

(Quotient)(Divisor) + Remainder = Dividend

$(22)(31) + 3 = 682 + 3$ $(3x + 2)(2x + 1) + 3 = (6x^2 + 3x + 4x + 2) + 3$

$\qquad\qquad = 685$ ✔ $\qquad\qquad\qquad\qquad = 6x^2 + 7x \times 5$ ✔

When you divide polynomials, always arrange the terms in each polynomial so that the powers of the variable are in descending order.

EXAMPLES

1   **Divide $-6x - 9 + 8x^2$ by $4x + 3$.**

SOLUTION

$$\begin{array}{r} 2x - 3 \\ 4x + 3 \overline{)8x^2 - 6x - 9} \\ \underline{8x^2 + 6x} \\ -12x - 9 \\ \underline{-12x - 9} \\ 0 \end{array}$$

Multiply $(4x + 3)$ by $2x$.
Subtract. Bring down -9.
Multiply $(4x + 3)$ by -3.
Subtract.

So $\dfrac{8x^2 - 6x - 9}{4x + 3} = 2x - 3$.

CHECK

$(2x - 3)(4x + 3) = 8x^2 + 6x - 12x - 9$

$\qquad\qquad\qquad = 8x^2 - 6x - 9$ ✔

Since the remainder is 0, the divisor and the quotient are factors of the dividend.

If the division has a remainder, then the result can be written as a **mixed expression.** A mixed expression is the sum or difference of a polynomial and a rational expression, for example, $x^2 + 6x - 3 + \frac{7}{x - 5}$.

You may want to introduce this topic using **Algebra Tiles.** They are a physical model for teaching algebraic concepts and are available from Cuisenaire Co. of America, Inc., 12 Church Street, New Rochelle, NY 10802.

2 | **Divide $x^3 + 1$ by $x - 2$.**

SOLUTION

First insert "missing" terms with 0 coefficients so that the dividend has the powers of x in descending order. Then divide.

$$
\begin{array}{r}
x^2 + 2x + 4 \\
x - 2 \overline{)x^3 + 0x^2 + 0x + 1}
\end{array}
$$

$$
\begin{array}{rl}
\underline{x^3 - 2x^2} & \text{Multiply } (x - 2) \text{ by } x^2. \\
2x^2 + 0x & \text{Subtract. Bring down } 0x. \\
\underline{2x^2 - 4x} & \text{Multiply } (x - 2) \text{ by } 2x. \\
4x + 1 & \text{Subtract. Bring down } 1. \\
\underline{4x - 8} & \text{Multiply } (x - 2) \text{ by } 4. \\
9 & \text{Subtract.}
\end{array}
$$

So $(x^3 + 1) \div (x - 2) = x^2 + 2x + 4 + \dfrac{9}{x - 2}$.

CHECK

$(x^2 + 2x + 4)(x - 2) + 9 = x^3 - 2x^2 + 2x^2 - 4x + 4x - 8 + 9$
$$= x^3 + 1 \ ✔$$

ORAL EXERCISES

Arrange the terms of each polynomial so that the powers of x are in descending order.

1. $5 + 7x^2 + 3x$ $\quad 7x^2 + 3x + 5$

2. $2x + x^2 + 3$ $\quad x^2 + 2x + 3$

3. $8 + x^2 - 2x$ $\quad x^2 - 2x + 8$

4. $2x^3 + 4 - x$ $\quad 2x^3 - x + 4$

5. $-2x^3 + x^4 + 5$ $\quad x^4 - 2x^3 + 5$

6. $-8 + x^3$ $\quad x^3 - 8$

7. $x^2 - 7 + 9x$ $\quad x^2 + 9x - 7$

8. $3x^2 + 8x + x^3 + 5$ $\quad x^3 + 3x^2 + 8x + 5$

Name the "missing" term or terms that need 0 coefficients.

9. $12 + x^2$ $\quad x$

10. $4k^2 - 32$ $\quad k$

11. $x^3 + 4x^2 + 9$ $\quad x$

12. $3x + 10 + 2x^3$ $\quad x^2$

13. $x^4 + 3x^2 + 6$ $\quad x^3, x$

14. $x^3 + 9x^4 + 7$ $\quad x^2, x$

15. $10 + 5x^3 + 6x^4$ $\quad x^2, x$

16. $4x^3 + 8$ $\quad x^2, x$

WRITTEN EXERCISES

A. Divide.

1. $x + 1 \overline{)x^2 + 2x + 1}$ $\quad x + 1$

2. $y + 2 \overline{)y^2 + 4y + 4}$ $\quad y + 2$

3. $z + 2 \overline{)z^2 + 5z + 6}$ $\quad z + 3$

4. $m + 4 \overline{)m^2 + 5m + 4}$ $\quad m + 1$

MIXED REVIEW

Solve each equation.

1. $p + 9(p - 8) = p - 9$
$\quad p = 7$

2. $y - 6 = -24$ $\quad y = -18$

3. $\frac{z}{4} = -8$ $\quad z = -32$

4. $-3b = b + 14$ $\quad b = -\frac{7}{2}$

5. $2(y + 6) = 3(y - 8)$
$\quad y = 36$

TEACHER'S RESOURCE MASTERS

Practice Master 23, Part 1

Quiz 10

ASSIGNMENT GUIDE

Minimum
1–29 odd

Regular
15–29

Maximum
21–30, 31–39 odd

5. $x - 3\overline{)x^2 - x - 6}$ $x + 2$

6. $y - 5\overline{)y^2 - 2y - 15}$ $y + 3$

7. $x - 4\overline{)x^2 - 7x + 12}$ $x - 3$

8. $y - 2\overline{)y^2 - 5y + 6}$ $y - 3$

9. $(-55x + 28 + 25x^2) \div (5x - 4)$

10. $(-84x + 36 + 24x^2) \div (8x - 4)$

11. $(-24a^2 - 35 + 58a) \div (-6a + 7)$

12. $(-16b^2 - 55 + 98b) \div (-8b + 5)$

13. $\dfrac{4x^3 + 5x - 9}{2x - 3}$ $2x^2 + 3x + 7 + \frac{12}{2x - 3}$

14. $\dfrac{9x^3 + 5x - 8}{3x - 2}$ $3x^2 + 2x + 3 + - \frac{2}{3x - 2}$

B. 15. $\dfrac{27y^2 - 24y + 8}{9y - 2}$ $3y - 2 + \frac{4}{9y - 2}$

16. $\dfrac{25r^2 - 20r + 11}{5r + 2}$ $5r - 6 + \frac{23}{5r + 2}$

17. $\dfrac{48m^2 + 8m + 7}{12m - 1}$ $4m + 1 + \frac{8}{12m - 1}$

18. $\dfrac{63y^2 + 3y + 10}{-7y + 2}$ $-9y - 3 + \frac{16}{-7y + 2}$

19. $(6x^3 - 35x^2 + 4) \div (6x + 1)$

20. $(4x^3 + 17x^2 + 3) \div (4x + 1)$

21. $(2x^3 + 9x^2 + 5x - 9) \div (x + 3)$

22. $(3x^3 + 8x^2 + x - 7) \div (x + 2)$

23. $(-57 + 20t^2 - 21t) \div (-4t + 9)$

24. $(-70 + 24s^2 - 38s) \div (-4s + 11)$

25. $(10w^2 - 18 + 23w) \div (2w + 3)$

26. $(16 + 3y - 10y^2) \div (5y + 1)$

27. $\dfrac{x^3 + 3x^2 + 3x + 1}{x + 1}$ $x^2 + 2x + 1$

28. $\dfrac{x^3 - 3x^2 - x + 3}{x - 1}$ $x^2 - 2x - 3$

29. $\dfrac{4x^3 + 12x^2 + 11x + 3}{2x + 3}$ $2x^2 + 3x + 1$

30. $\dfrac{9x^3 - 12x^2 + x + 2}{3x - 2}$ $3x^2 - 2x - 1$

C. **The second polynomial is a factor of the first. Divide to find the other factor of the first polynomial.**

31. $x^3 + 8; x + 2$ $(x + 2)(x^2 - 2x + 4)$

32. $x^3 - 8; x - 2$ $(x - 2)(x^2 + 2x + 4)$

33. $x^3 - 1; x - 1$ $(x - 1)(x^2 + x + 1)$

34. $x^3 + 1; x + 1$ $(x + 1)(x^2 - x + 1)$

35. $8x^3 + 1; 2x + 1$ $(2x + 1)(4x^2 - 2x + 1)$ **36.** $27x^3 - 8; 3x - 2$

37. $x^4 - 5x^2 + 6; x^2 - 2$ $(x^2 - 2)(x^2 - 3)$ **38.** $x^4 - 6x^2 + 8; x^2 - 2$

39. A sand-yacht racer has been experimenting with sails that measure x feet along the base and $2x + 4$ feet in height. Now the racer wants to change the sails so that they have the same area but measure $x + 2$ feet along the base. What height should be used? (The sails are triangular.) $2x$ ft

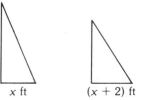

x ft $(x + 2)$ ft

40. Find the volume of the aquarium. Then find how many fish it can hold if each fish requires $x + 5$ cubic inches of space. $2x^2 - 10x$ fish

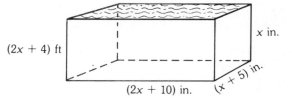

$(2x + 4)$ ft x in. $(2x + 10)$ in. $(x + 5)$ in.

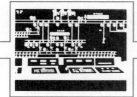

COMPUTER

The sums of any column, row, or diagonal in an algebraic magic square are the same. Without a computer, it would be very time-consuming to find a value for X that would make the algebraic magic square on the right work. The following program uses one method for solving this algebraic magic square:

An Algebraic Magic Square

X + 2	3(X − 7)	X(X − 7)
X − 3	X − 1	X + 1
$X^2 − 5X − 18$	X + 3	2(X − 6)

```
10 REM  ----------
20 REM : G : H : I :
30 REM  ----------
40 REM : J : K : L :
50 REM  ----------
60 REM : M : N : O :
70 REM  ----------
80 FOR X = - 100 TO 100: REM CHECK POSSIBLE VALUES
   FOR X
90 LET G = X + 2: LET H = 3 * (X - 7)
100 LET I = X * (X - 7): LET J = X - 3
110 LET K = X - 1: LET L = X + 1
120 LET M = X * X - 5 * X - 18: LET N = X + 3
130 LET O = 2 * (X - 6)
140 REM NOW TEST THESE VALUES IN THE MAGIC SQUARE
150 IF G + H + I < > M + K + I THEN 210
200 PRINT "ONE POSSIBLE SOLUTION FOR X IS ";X
210 NEXT X: END
```

EXERCISES

1. Enter and RUN this program. What value or values for X did the computer output?

2. Add the necessary line(s) so that the program prints only *one* solution.

3. Modify the equations for G, H, I, J, K, L, M, N, and O to generate your own magic square. Does it have a solution?

ANSWERS

1. X = 0, 8

2. Add the following:
   155 IF G + H + I <> J + K + L THEN 210
   160 IF G + H + I <> M + N + O THEN 210
   165 IF G + H + I <> I + L + O THEN 210
   170 IF G + H + I <> G + K + O THEN 210
   180 IF G + H + I <> G + J + M THEN 210
   190 IF G + H + I <> H + K + N THEN 210
   Solution: X = 8

3. Answers will vary with student's response.

ENRICHMENT

See Activities 13–14
p. T44.

ADDITIONAL ANSWERS

3. $6a^2 + 5a - 15$

19. $12x^2y^2 + xy - 20$

20. $12y^3 - 23y^2 + 16y - 4$

26. 8

CHAPTER 5 REVIEW

VOCABULARY

degree of a polynomial (5.1)

division of powers (5.9)

FOIL method (5.6)

mixed expression (5.11)

opposite of a polynomial (5.2)

power of a power (5.3)

power of a product (5.3)

power of a quotient (5.9)

product of powers (5.3)

REVIEW EXERCISES

5.1   **Simplify each sum.**

1. $(3x + 2) + (4x - 7)$ $7x - 5$

2. $(6y - 3) + (5y + 2)$ $11y - 1$

3. $(5a - 4) + (6a^2 - 11)$

4. $(3n^2 - 9m^2) + (-3n^2 - 9m^2)$
$-18m^2$

5.2   **Simplify each difference.**

5. $(3x - 11) - (7x + 2)$ $-4x - 13$

6. $(-6y + 7) - (6y + 3)$ $-12y + 4$

7. $(x - 2y) - (3x - 7y)$ $-2x + 5y$

8. $(x^2 - 5x + 7) - (x^2 + 5x - 7)$
$-10x + 14$

5.3   **Find each product.**

9. $(16xy)\left(\frac{1}{2}\right)$ $8xy$

10. $(10a^2)^2$ $100a^4$

11. $(6x^3)(-2y^5)$ $-12x^3y^5$

12. $(-4m^2)(-3n^4)$ $12m^2n^4$

5.4   **Find each product.**

13. $3m(4m - 7)$ $12m^2 - 21m$

14. $2a(2b + 3a)$ $4ab + 6a^2$

15. $y(2y^2z - 3z^2)$ $2y^3z - 3yz^2$

16. $3x^4(-4x^3 - 9x^2)$ $-12x^7 - 27x^6$

5.5   **Find each product.**

17. $(a + 5)(a + 2)$ $a^2 + 7a + 10$

18. $(x - 4)(x + 4)$ $x^2 - 16$

19. $(3xy + 4)(4xy - 5)$

20. $(3y - 2)(4y^2 - 5y + 2)$

5.6   **Find each product, using the FOIL method.**

21. $(m + 1)(m - 1)$ $m^2 - 1$

22. $(a + c)(a - c)$ $a^2 - c^2$

23. $(4 + y)(3 + y)$ $12 + 7y + y^2$

24. $(3x + 5)(5x - 3)$
$15x^2 + 16x - 15$

5.7   **Solve.**

25. $(5x + 2) - (3x + 4) = 14$ 8

26. $(y^2 - 3y + 9) - (y^2 - 4y + 7) = 10$

27. $(2x - 1)(2x + 3) = 4x^2 + 9$ 3

28. $(x - 3)^2 - (2x - 1)^2 = 3(2 - x^2)$
1

5.8   **Solve.**

29. Alicia and Saul started from the same point at the same time and drove in opposite directions. Alicia drove 15 mi/h faster than Saul. After three hours, they were 285 miles apart. Find the rate of each.

30. Wally ran at 6 mi/h, then walked back to his starting point at 3 mi/h. If he walked for 2 hours longer than he ran, how long did the whole trip take?   6 hours

5.9 **Simplify each expression.**

31. $\dfrac{x^6}{x^2}$ x^4

32. $\dfrac{(-7)^4}{(-7)^3}$ -7

33. $\dfrac{a^7b^{10}}{a^3b^6}$ a^4b^4

34. $\left(\dfrac{-3n}{4}\right)^2$ $\dfrac{9n^2}{16}$

5.10 **Simplify each quotient.**

35. $\dfrac{8a^4}{a^2}$ $8a^2$

36. $\dfrac{6x^8}{18x^8}$ $\dfrac{1}{3}$

37. $\dfrac{24a^2b}{8ab}$ $3a$

38. $\dfrac{-35x^4}{-7x^6}$ $\dfrac{5}{x^2}$

5.11 **Divide.**

39. $(6x^2 - 4x - 2) \div (3x + 1)$ $2x - 2$

40. $(12x^2 + x - 1) \div (4x - 1)$ $3x + 1$

41. $(6x^2 - 2x - 8) \div (2x + 2)$ $3x - 4$

42. $(-6x + 8x^2 - 9) \div (4x + 3)$ $2x - 3$

ERROR SEARCH

Find the error in each exercise and give the correct answer.

1. $(y + 7z)(y - 2z) = y^2 - 2yz + 7yz - 14z^2$
$$= y^2 - 9yz - 14z^2 \quad y^2 + 5yz - 14z^2$$

2. $x(x - 3)(x - 7) = x(x^2 - 7x - 3x + 21)$
$$= x(x^2 - 10x + 21)$$
$$= x^3 - 10x^2 + 21 \quad x^3 - 10x^2 + 21x$$

3. $(6x^2 + 3x) + (2x^2 - x + 4) = 6x^2 + 2x^2 + 3x + x + 4$
$$= (6 + 2)x^2 + (3 + 1)x + 4$$
$$= 8x^2 + 4x + 4$$

4. $(5x - 7) - (11x + 4) = [5x + (-7)] + [-(11x + 4)]$
$$= [5x + (-7)] + [-11x + (-4)]$$
$$= [5x + (-11x)] + [-7 + (-4)]$$
$$= [5 + (-11)]x + [-7 + (-4)]$$
$$= -16x + (-11) \quad -6x + (-11)$$
$$= -16x - 11 \quad -6x - 11$$

5. $(3x - 5y)(2x + 6y) = (3x - 5y)(2x) + (3x - 5y)(6y)$
$$= (3x \cdot 2x - 5y \cdot 2x) + (3x \cdot 6y - 5y \cdot 6y)$$
$$= 6x - 10xy + 18xy - 30y^2 \quad 6x^2 - 10xy + 18xy - 30y^2$$
$$= 6x + (-10 + 18)xy - 30y^2 \quad 6x^2 + (-10 + 18)xy - 30y^2$$
$$= 6x + 8xy - 30y^2 \quad 6x^2 + 8xy - 30y^2$$

ERROR SEARCH
3. $8x^2 + 2x + 4$

TEACHER'S RESOURCE
MASTERS

Chapter 5 Test

Multiple–Choice Test

PROBLEM-SOLVING
HANDBOOK

p. 531

ADDITIONAL ANSWERS

8. $8a^3b + 12a^2b^2 - 20ab^3$

10. $m^3 + 2m^2 - m + 6$

15. 15 minutes $\left(\frac{1}{4}\ \text{hour}\right)$

CHAPTER 5 TEST

Simplify each sum.

1. $(5y + 9) + (6y - 11)$ $11y - 2$

2. $(-3n^2 + n) + (6n^2 - 2n)$ $3n^2 - n$

Simplify each difference.

3. $(17x + 2) - (12x - 9)$ $5x + 11$

4. $(9x^2 + 5x) - (6x^2 - 7x)$ $3x^2 + 12x$

Find each product.

5. $(2a^2)(8a^3)$ $16a^5$

6. $(4x^2y)(8x^4y^2)$ $32x^6y^3$

7. $(6xy + 8)(-4xy)$ $-24x^2y^2 - 32xy$

8. $4ab(2a^2 + 3ab - 5b^2)$

9. $(2s - 7)(2s + 7)$ $4s^2 - 49$

10. $(m + 3)(m^2 - m + 2)$

Find each product, using the FOIL method.

11. $(y + 7)(y - 3)$ $y^2 + 4y - 21$

12. $(mn + 4)(mn - 4)$ $m^2n^2 - 16$

Solve.

13. $3(x + 2) = x - 4$ -5

14. $(y + 3)(y + 2) = y(y + 3) + 8$ 1

15. Laura started walking at 4 mi/h. Fifteen minutes later, Todd started running from the same place along the same route at 8 mi/h. How long did it take Todd to catch up with Laura?

16. Alex and Bernice started from the same point at the same time and drove in opposite directions. Alex drove 5 miles per hour faster than Bernice. After 3 hours, they were 255 miles apart. Find the rate of each. 45 mi/h, 40 mi/h

Simplify each expression.

17. $\dfrac{(-3)^2}{(-3)^5}$ $-\dfrac{1}{27}$

18. $\dfrac{xy^5z^2}{xy^3z^6}$ $\dfrac{y^2}{z^4}$

Simplify each quotient.

19. $\dfrac{18a^2 - 2a}{2a}$ $9a - 1$

20. $\dfrac{-48x^3}{-12x^5}$ $\dfrac{4}{x^2}$

Divide.

21. $(3x^2 - x - 2) \div (x - 1)$ $3x + 2$

22. $(6x^2 + 2x - 20) \div (2x + 4)$ $3x - 5$

CHAPTER 6

Factoring Polynomials

An architect enlarged a square window-opening by 2 meters on one side and 3 meters on the other side. If the area of the enlarged window is 20 square meters, what is the length of a side of the original opening?   2 meters

OBJECTIVES

Factor an integer as a product of prime numbers and write the result in exponential form.

Find the GCF of two numbers.

Find the LCM of two numbers.

TEACHER'S NOTES

See p. T28.

CLASSROOM EXAMPLES

1. Factor 72 as a product of prime numbers.

$72 = 8 \cdot 9$
$= 2 \cdot 4 \cdot 3 \cdot 3$
$= 2 \cdot 2 \cdot 2 \cdot 3 \cdot 3$
$= 2^3 \cdot 3^2$

2. Factor -164 as the product of prime numbers.

$-164 = -1 \cdot 164$
$= -1 \cdot 2 \cdot 82$
$= -1 \cdot 2 \cdot 2 \cdot 41$
$= -1 \cdot 2^2 \cdot 41$

3. Find the GCF of 140 and 200.

$140 = 2 \cdot 70$
$= 2 \cdot 2 \cdot 35$
$= 2 \cdot 2 \cdot 5 \cdot 7$
$200 = 2 \cdot 100$
$= 2 \cdot 2 \cdot 50$
$= 2 \cdot 2 \cdot 2 \cdot 25$
$= 2 \cdot 2 \cdot 2 \cdot 5 \cdot 5$
$GCF = 2 \cdot 2 \cdot 5$
$= 20$

4. Find the LCM of 140 and 200.

$140 = 2 \cdot 2 \cdot 5 \cdot 7$
$200 = 2 \cdot 2 \cdot 2 \cdot 5 \cdot 5$
$LCM = 2 \cdot 2 \cdot 2 \cdot 5 \cdot 5 \cdot 7$
$= 1400$

6.1 | Prime Factors

A number is factored when it is expressed as the product of two or more integers. Some numbers can be factored as the product of different pairs of positive integers. For example, $18 = 1 \cdot 18$, $18 = 2 \cdot 9$, and $18 = 3 \cdot 6$.

The number 11, however, can be factored *only* as $11 = 1 \cdot 11$. Because 11 has no other positive-integer factors (called *integral* factors) besides 1 and itself, 11 is said to be a **prime number.** The first ten prime numbers are 2, 3, 5, 7, 11, 13, 17, 19, 23, and 29.

A *prime number* is any integer greater than 1 that has only two positive integral factors, 1 and itself. Numbers that are not prime are called **composite numbers.** Every composite number can be expressed as a product of prime-number factors.

EXAMPLES

1 | **Factor 90 as a product of prime numbers.**

SOLUTION Start with any pair of factors and proceed as below. Stop when all of the factors are prime.

$90 = 2 \cdot 45$ or $90 = 9 \cdot 10$
$= 2 \cdot 3 \cdot 15$ $= 3 \cdot 3 \cdot 10$
$= 2 \cdot 3 \cdot 3 \cdot 5$ $= 3 \cdot 3 \cdot 2 \cdot 5$
$= 2 \cdot 3^2 \cdot 5$ *Write the prime factors* $= 3^2 \cdot 2 \cdot 5$
        in exponential form.

Note that the same prime factors appear in both solutions. Only the order in which they are listed is different. This illustrates the following property of positive integers:

Unique Factoring Property	**The prime factorization of any composite positive integer into a product of primes is unique (one, and only one, way), except for the order of the factors.**

To find the prime factorization of a negative number, express the number as the product of -1 and its prime factors.

2 | **Factor -180 as a product of prime numbers.**

SOLUTION $-180 = -1 \cdot 180$ *First factor -180 as $-1 \cdot 180$.*
$= -1 \cdot 2 \cdot 90$ *Then factor 180.*
$= -1 \cdot 2 \cdot 2 \cdot 45$
$= -1 \cdot 2 \cdot 2 \cdot 3 \cdot 15$
$= -1 \cdot 2 \cdot 2 \cdot 3 \cdot 3 \cdot 5$
$= -1 \cdot 2^2 \cdot 3^2 \cdot 5$

Finding the *greatest common factor* (GCF) of two numbers is made easier by completely factoring the two numbers.

MIXED REVIEW

Perform the indicated operation.

1. $(-5m^2)(-6m^3)$ $30m^5$
2. $6a(-3a^3 + 8a^2)$ $-18a^4 + 48a^3$
3. $x(3x^3y - 5z)$ $3x^4y - 5xz$
4. $(5a^2 + 16) + (4a^2 - 8)$ $9a^2 + 8$
5. $(-12a^3 + 8a^2 - 5)$ $- (8a^3 + 8a^2 + 8)$ $- 20a^3 - 13$

| 3 | **Find the GCF of 360 and 540.** |

SOLUTION   First completely factor the two numbers.

$360 = 2 \cdot 180$

$\quad\ = 2 \cdot 2 \cdot 90$

$\quad\ = 2 \cdot 2 \cdot 2 \cdot 45$

$\quad\ = 2 \cdot 2 \cdot 2 \cdot 3 \cdot 15$

$\quad\ = 2 \cdot 2 \cdot 2 \cdot 3 \cdot 3 \cdot 5$

$540 = 2 \cdot 270$

$\quad\ = 2 \cdot 2 \cdot 135$

$\quad\ = 2 \cdot 2 \cdot 3 \cdot 45$

$\quad\ = 2 \cdot 2 \cdot 3 \cdot 3 \cdot 15$

$\quad\ = 2 \cdot 2 \cdot 3 \cdot 3 \cdot 3 \cdot 5$

Next group the common prime factors.

$360 = 2 \cdot 2 \cdot 2 \cdot 3 \cdot 3 \cdot 5$

$540 = 2 \cdot 2 \cdot 3 \cdot 3 \cdot 3 \cdot 5$

Then multiply the *common* prime factors to find the GCF.

$2 \cdot 2 \cdot 3 \cdot 3 \cdot 5 = 180$

$GCF = 180$

TEACHER'S RESOURCE MASTERS

Practice Master 23, Part 2

It is also possible to find the *least common multiple* (LCM) of two numbers by completely factoring the two numbers.

ASSIGNMENT GUIDE

Minimum
1–31 odd, 33–44

Regular
33–60

Maximum
48–75

| 4 | **Find the LCM of 360 and 540.** |

SOLUTION   First completely factor the two numbers, and then group the common prime factors.

$360 = 2 \cdot 2 \cdot 2 \cdot 3 \cdot 3 \cdot 5$

$540 = 2 \cdot 2 \cdot 3 \cdot 3 \cdot 3 \cdot 5$

Multiply the common prime factors *and* the remaining prime factors to find the LCM.

$2 \cdot 2 \cdot 3 \cdot 3 \cdot 5 \cdot 2 \cdot 3 = 1080$

common prime   remaining
factors   prime factors

$LCM = 1080$

ORAL EXERCISES

Identify each integer as prime or composite.

1. 7   P
2. 12   C
3. 19   P
4. 17   P
5. 51   C
6. 29   P
7. 54   C
8. 31   P
9. 67   P
10. 91   C
11. 5   P
12. 33   C
13. 15   C
14. 13   P
15. 41   P
16. 53   P

ADDITIONAL ANSWERS

Written Exercises

8. $-1 \cdot 2 \cdot 3 \cdot 5$

12. $-1 \cdot 2^2 \cdot 5^2$

16. $-1 \cdot 2 \cdot 3 \cdot 5^2$

WRITTEN EXERCISES

A. Give the prime factorization of each integer. Express the result in exponential form.

1. 8 2^3
2. -10 $-1 \cdot 2 \cdot 5$
3. 12 $2^2 \cdot 3$
4. -25 $-1 \cdot 5^2$

5. 18 $2 \cdot 3^2$
6. -64 $-1 \cdot 2^6$
7. 36 $2^2 \cdot 3^2$
8. -30

9. -32 $-1 \cdot 2^5$
10. 81 3^4
11. 24 $2^3 \cdot 3$
12. -100

13. 75 $3 \cdot 5^2$
14. 105 $3 \cdot 5 \cdot 7$
15. 125 5^3
16. -150

17. 48 $2^4 \cdot 3$
18. 135 $3^3 \cdot 5$
19. 42 $2 \cdot 3 \cdot 7$
20. 245 $5 \cdot 7^2$

21. 72 $2^3 \cdot 3^2$
22. 128 2^7
23. -144 $-1 \cdot 2^4 \cdot 3^2$
24. 200 $2^3 \cdot 5^2$

25. 250 $2 \cdot 5^3$
26. 192 $2^6 \cdot 3$
27. 210 $2 \cdot 3 \cdot 5 \cdot 7$
28. 216 $2^3 \cdot 3^3$

29. 224 $2^5 \cdot 7$
30. -169 $-1 \cdot 13^2$
31. 625 5^4
32. -121 $-1 \cdot 11^2$

B. Find the greatest common factor of each pair of integers.

33. 20, 36 4
34. 32, 48 16
35. 18, 45 9
36. 42, 63 21

37. 54, 81 27
38. 60, 75 15
39. 24, 40 8
40. 42, 56 14

41. 27, 72 9
42. 54, 63 9
43. 36, 48 12
44. 75, 100 25

45. 60, 150 30
46. 72, 144 72
47. 50, 125 25
48. 42, 350 14

49. 168, 600 24
50. 216, 144 72
51. 169, 338 169
52. 187, 391 17

Find the least common multiple of each pair of integers.

53. 20, 40 40
54. 30, 36 180
55. 45, 54 270
56. 27, 36 108

57. 32, 48 96
58. 50, 75 150
59. 42, 56 168
60. 18, 24 72

C. 61. 45, 63 315
62. 27, 72 216
63. 100, 150 300
64. 50, 125 250

65. 144, 300 3600
66. 169, 338 338
67. 121, 363 363
68. 168, 224 672

69. 216, 350 37,800
70. 600, 750 3000
71. 187, 221 2431
72. 377, 455 13,195

73. Cartons 24 inches tall are being stacked next to cartons 36 inches tall. What is the shortest height at which the stacks will be the same height? 72 inches

74. A bakery wants to sell breadsticks in two sizes of boxes—one to hold 36 breadsticks and the other to hold 24 breadsticks. The breadsticks will also be packaged in cellophane bags inside each box. In order to use the same size bags in each box and as few bags as possible, how many breadsticks should each bag hold? 12 bread sticks

75. When two musical notes are played at the same time, they produce harmony. For any two pairs of notes, you can determine which pair produces the closest harmony by finding the GCF of their frequencies. The greater the GCF, the closer the harmony. A, C, and C sharp have frequencies of 220, 264, and 275. Which pair of these notes harmonizes best? A and C sharp

CALCULATOR

Large numbers can be factored by using a calculator to factor out primes in order. First determine if the number is even. If it is, divide by 2. If the result is even, divide by 2 again. When you obtain a result that is not even, try 3, the next larger prime number. Keep dividing by 3 until you obtain a result that is not divisible by 3. Then try 5, the next larger prime number, and so on. When you obtain a result that is a prime number, you can stop. The method is shown in the following example.

Example: Completely factor 4914.

Keep track of each dividend and each prime factor on paper.

	DISPLAY	PAPER	
		dividend	factor

Since 4914 is even, divide 4914 by 2.
4914 ÷ 2 = 2457 4914   2

Divide by 3. (Why not 2?)
÷ 3 = 819 2457   3

Divide by 3 again.
÷ 3 = 273 819   3

Divide by 3 again.
÷ 3 = 91 273   3

Divide by 3 again.
÷ 3 = 30.333333 91

91 is not divisible by 3.
Try 5. (Why not 4?)
91 ÷ 5 = 18.2

91 is not divisible by 5.
Try 7. (Why not 6?)
91 ÷ 7 = 13 7

Why stop now?
$4914 = 2 \cdot 3^3 \cdot 7 \cdot 13$ ←

Check 2 × 3 × 3 × 3 × 7 × 13 4914

EXERCISES

Completely factor each number by using a calculator.

1. 720   **2.** 12,600   **3.** 15,125   **4.** 27,300

CALCULATOR EXERCISES
1. $2^4 \cdot 3^2 \cdot 5$
2. $2^3 \cdot 3^2 \cdot 5^2 \cdot 7$
3. $5^3 \cdot 11^2$
4. $2^2 \cdot 3 \cdot 5^2 \cdot 7 \cdot 13$

OBJECTIVE

Factor a polynomial by removing a common monomial
or binomial factor.

TEACHER'S NOTES

See p. T28.

CLASSROOM EXAMPLES

1. Factor each polynomial by
   removing the greatest
   common monomial factor.
   a. $14x + 7$
   $14x + 7 = 7 \cdot 2x + 7 \cdot 1$
   $\quad\quad = 7(2x + 1)$

   b. $8y^2 + 2y$
   $8y^2 + 2y$
   $= 2y \cdot 4y + 2y \cdot 1$
   $= 2y(4y + 1)$

   c. $12x^3 + 6x^2 - 2x$
   $12x^3 + 6x^2 - 2x$
   $= 2x \cdot 6x^2 + 2x \cdot 3x$
   $\quad - 2x \cdot 1$
   $= 2x(6x^2 + 3x - 1)$

   d. $15x^3 - 5x^2$
   $5x^3 - 5x^2$
   $= 5x^2 \cdot 3x - 5x^2 \cdot 1$
   $= 5x^2(3x - 1)$

2. Factor over the integers
   $x(r + s) + y(r + s)$.
   $x(r + s) + y(r + s)$
   $= (r + s)(x + y)$

3. Factor $ac + cd + fa + df$
   over the integers.
   $ac + cd + fa + df$
   $= c(a + d) + f(a + d)$
   $= (a + d)(c + f)$

6.2 | Monomial Factors

You have already used the distributive property to find products. That is,
$$a(b + c) = ab + ac.$$

By reversing the process, you can *factor* a polynomial.
$$ab + ac = a(b + c)$$

In factoring a polynomial, you rewrite a sum as a product. In the examples that follow, this type of factoring is called **removing the greatest common monomial factor.**

EXAMPLES

1   **Factor each polynomial by removing the greatest common monomial factor.**

   a. $12x + 6$ **b.** $5y^2 + 3y$ **c.** $2x^3 + 4x^2 - 2x$ **d.** $12x^3 - 8x^2$

SOLUTIONS

  a. $12x + 6 = 6 \cdot 2x + 6 \cdot 1$ *The greatest common monomial factor is 6.*
$$= 6(2x + 1)$$

     CHECK $6(2x + 1) = 6 \cdot 2x + 6 \cdot 1$
$$= 12x + 6 \ \checkmark$$

  b. $5y^2 + 3y = y \cdot 5y + y \cdot 3$ *The greatest common monomial factor is y.*
$$= y(5y + 3)$$

     CHECK $y(5y + 3) = y \cdot 5y + y \cdot 3$
$$= 5y^2 + 3y \ \checkmark$$

  c. $2x^3 + 4x^2 - 2x = 2x \cdot x^2 + 2x \cdot 2x - 2x \cdot 1$ *The greatest common monomial*
$$= 2x(x^2 + 2x - 1) \quad\quad \textit{factor is 2x.}$$

     CHECK $2x(x^2 + 2x - 1) = 2x \cdot x^2 + 2x \cdot 2x - 2x \cdot 1$
$$= 2x^3 + 4x^2 - 2x \ \checkmark$$

  d. $12x^3 - 8x^2 = 4x^2 \cdot 3x - 4x^2 \cdot 2$ *The greatest common monomial factor is $4x^2$.*
$$= 4x^2(3x - 2) \quad\quad \textit{Note that 4 is not factored into prime factors.}$$

     CHECK $4x^2(3x - 2) = 4x^2 \cdot 3x - 4x^2 \cdot 2$
$$= 12x^3 - 8x^2 \ \checkmark$$

A polynomial is completely factored over the integers when no more variable factors can be removed from the polynomial factor and no more integral factors can be removed except 1 and -1. Such a polynomial is called a **prime polynomial** with respect to the integers.

The following polynomials are prime polynomials:

$3a + 5b$

$2y - 7x$

$3m + 4n^2 - 5p^2$

Some polynomials have a common binomial factor that can be removed as if it were a monomial factor.

| **2** | **Factor over the integers $x(a + b) + y(a + b)$.** |

SOLUTION Remove the common binomial factor $(a + b)$ as if it were a monomial factor.

$x(a + b) + y(a + b) = (a + b)(x + y)$ *The common factor is $(a + b)$.*

| **3** | **Factor $ax + xy + by + ab$ over the integers.** |

SOLUTION

Method I
$$ax + xy + by + ab = (ax + ab) + (xy + by)$$
$$= a(x + b) + y(x + b) \quad \textit{The common factor}$$
$$= (x + b)(a + y) \quad \textit{is $(x + b)$.}$$

Method II
$$ax + xy + by + ab = (ax + xy) + (ab + by)$$
$$= x(a + y) + b(a + y) \quad \textit{The common factor}$$
$$= (a + y)(x + b) \quad \textit{is $(a + y)$.}$$

In this book, we will shorten the instruction "factor over the integers" to "factor completely."

ORAL EXERCISES

Which of the following are prime polynomials?

1. $3x + 6$ no

2. $y - 5y$ no

3. $8 - 4a$ no

4. $a - b$ yes

5. $2a - 8b$ no

6. $x + 3x$ no

7. $2x + 3y$ yes

8. $4x^2 + \frac{1}{4}$ yes

WRITTEN EXERCISES

A. Complete.

1. $3x + 3y = \underline{\ 3\ }(x + y)$

2. $5(a + b) = 5\underline{\ a\ } + 5b$

3. $mn + n^2 = n(\underline{\ m\ } + \underline{\ n\ })$

4. $5a^2 - 5a = \underline{\ 5a\ }(a - 1)$

5. $6x^3 + 3xy^2 = \underline{\ 3x\ }(2x^2 + y^2)$

6. $a^3b - b = b(\underline{\ a^3 - 1\ })$

7. $mn + np + n^2 = \underline{\ n\ }(m + p + n)$

8. $-3xy + 9yz - 6xz = -3(\underline{\hspace{2cm}})$
$$xy - 3yz + 2xz$$

Name the common monomial factor.

9. $6a - 18$ 6

10. $12 + 4x$ 4

11. $4y^2 + 24$ 4

12. $3n^2 - 6$ 3

13. $9x - 9$ 9

14. $2x^2 + 4x + 8$ 2

15. $10a - 15b$ 5

16. $5y^2 + 15y$ 5y

17. $3a^2 - 6a - 9$ 3

18. $25x + 5$ 5

19. $32y^2 - 8y$ 8y

20. $24x^2 - 18x + 6$ 6

MIXED REVIEW

Give the prime factorization.

1. 410 $2 \cdot 5 \cdot 41$

2. 300 $s^2 \cdot 3 \cdot 5^2$

3. 779 $19 \cdot 41$

4. Find the least common multiple of 72 and 60. 360

5. Find the greatest common factor of 72 and 60. 12

TEACHER'S RESOURCE MASTERS

Practice Master 24, Part 1

ASSIGNMENT GUIDE

Minimum
1–19 odd, 21–38

Regular
21–39, 43–59 odd

Maximum
21–45 odd, 46–60

B. Factor completely.

21. $4x + 8$ $4(x + 2)$

22. $18y - 3$ $3(6y - 1)$

23. $6a + 24$ $6(a + 4)$

24. $20b - 5$ $5(4b - 1)$

25. $3x + 12$ $3(x + 4)$

26. $8y - 16$ $8(y - 2)$

27. $2a - 10b$ $2(a - 5b)$

28. $4x - 12y$ $4(x - 3y)$

29. $9s + 72$ $9(s + 8)$

30. $5a^2 + 2a$ $a(5a + 2)$

31. $6x^2 + 7x$ $x(6x + 7)$

32. $2a - 8b$ $2(a - 4b)$

33. $3x - 15y$ $3(x - 5y)$

34. $xy^2 + y^2$ $y^2(x + 1)$

35. $ab^2 + 3b^2$ $b^2(a + 3)$

36. $m^2n + m$ $m(mn + 1)$

37. $xy^2 + y$ $y(xy + 1)$

38. $3a^3 - 2a^2$ $a^2(3a - 2)$

39. $8a^4 - 4a^3 + 2a^2$ $2a^2(4a^2 - 2a + 1)$

40. $4y^5 + 16y^4 - 12y^3$ $4y^3(y^2 + 4y - 3)$

41. $5b^3 + 10b^2 + 15b$ $5b(b^2 + 2b + 3)$

42. $2x^3 - 4x^2 + 8x$ $2x(x^2 - 2x + 4)$

C. 43. $32x^3y - 24x^2y + 8xy$

44. $36a^3b - 27a^2b + 18ab$

45. $9m^3n + 3m^2n + 6mn$

46. $18x^3y - 36x^2y - 6xy$

ADDITIONAL ANSWERS

Written Exercises

43. $8xy(4x^2 - 3x + 1)$

44. $9ab(4a^2 - 3a + 2)$

45. $3mn(3m^2 + m + 2)$

46. $6xy(3x^2 - 6x - 1)$

Factor completely, if possible. Write *prime* if the polynomial cannot be factored over the integers.

47. $x(m + n) + y(m + n)$ $(m + n)(x + y)$

48. $4m + n$ prime

49. $a(b - c) + d(b - c)$ $(b - c)(a + d)$

50. $8a^2 - 5b^2$ prime

51. $2(a + b) - c(a + b)$ $(a + b)(2 - c)$

52. $x(a - b) - y(a - b)$ $(a - b)(x - y)$

53. $(ab + bc) + (da + dc)$ $(a + c)(b + d)$

54. $9a^2 + 8ab + 13b^2$ prime

55. $(mn - mp) + (nr - rp)$ $(n - p)(m + r)$

56. $9ab + a^2 + 2b^2$ prime

57. $mx + xy + ny + mn$ $(x + n)(m + y)$

58. $as + st + bt + ab$ $(s + b)(t + a)$

59. $8x - 12 - 10ax + 15a$

$(4 - 5a)(2x - 3)$

60. $2ax^2 + bx^2 + 2ay^2 + by^2$

$(x^2 + y^2)(2a + b)$

CHALLENGE

Each container holds two marbles. The marbles are either blue (B) or green (G). One container holds two blue marbles, one holds two green marbles, and one holds a blue marble and a green marble. None of the labels on the containers are correct. From which container can you draw only one marble and then correctly label all three containers?   BG

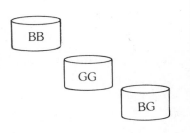

6.3 | Difference of Two Squares

OBJECTIVE

Factor a polynomial that is the difference of two squares.

TEACHER'S NOTES

See p. T28.

Recall from Chapter 5 that the product of $(a + b)(a - b)$ was expressed as the binomial $a^2 - b^2$. This occurred by using the FOIL method.

$$(a + b)(a - b) = a^2 \underbrace{- ab + ab} - b^2$$
$$= a^2 + \quad 0 \quad - b^2$$
$$= a^2 - b^2$$

So, $(a + b)(a - b) = a^2 - b^2$.

$$\begin{array}{ccc} \text{the sum of} & \times & \text{the difference} & = & \text{the difference} \\ \text{two numbers} & & \text{of the numbers} & & \text{of the squares} \end{array}$$

$$(3y + 2)(3y - 2) = 9y^2 \underbrace{- 6y + 6y} - 4$$
$$= 9y^2 + \quad 0 \quad - 4$$
$$= 9y^2 - 4$$

To factor the difference of the squares of two expressions, reverse the above steps.

$$a^2 - b^2 = a^2 + \quad 0 \quad - b^2$$
$$= a^2 \overbrace{- ab + ab} - b^2$$
$$= (a^2 - ab) + (ab - b^2)$$
$$= a(a - b) + b(a - b)$$
$$= (a + b)(a - b)$$

CLASSROOM EXAMPLES

1. Factor $9x^2 - 64y^2$.

   $9x^2 - 64y^2$
   $= 3^2x^2 - 8^2y^2$
   $= (3x)^2 - (8y)^2$
   $= (3x + 8y)(3x - 8y)$

2. Find the difference of the squares of 40 and 20.

   $40^2 - 20^2$
   $= (40 + 20)(40 - 20)$
   $= 60 \cdot 20$
   $= 1200$

3. Factor $8x^2 - 8y^2$.

   $8x^2 - 8y^2$
   $= 8(x^2 - y^2)$
   $= 8(x + y)(x - y)$

4. By what factor can you multiply each binomial so that the product will be the difference of two squares?

   a. $9 + b$
      $(9 + b)(9 - b)$
      $= 81 - b^2$
   b. $6x - 5y^2$
      $(6x - 5y^2)(6x + 5y^2)$
      $= 36x^2 - 25y^4$
   c. $4m - 2n$
      $(4m - 2n)(4m + 2n)$
      $= 16m^2 - 4n^2$

EXAMPLES

1   **Factor $9x^2 - 16y^2$.**

SOLUTION

$$\begin{aligned} 9x^2 - 16y^2 &= 3^2x^2 - 4^2y^2 && \text{Express each coefficient as a square.} \\ &= (3x)^2 - (4y)^2 && \text{Power of a product} \\ &= (3x + 4y)(3x - 4y) && \text{Factor the difference of two squares.} \end{aligned}$$

CHECK

$$\begin{aligned} (3x + 4y)(3x - 4y) &= 9x^2 - 12xy + 12xy - 16y^2 \\ &= 9x^2 - 16y^2 \end{aligned}$$

2   **Find the difference of the squares of 50 and 30.**

SOLUTION

$$\begin{aligned} 50^2 - 30^2 &= (50 + 30)(50 - 30) \\ &= 80 \cdot 20 \\ &= 1600 \end{aligned}$$

1. Find the value of $\left(-\frac{1}{8}\right)^4$.

$\frac{1}{4096}$

2. Solve $\frac{3x}{4} = 24$. 32

3. Multiply $(6x^3 + 5)$
   $(4x^3 - 12)$. $24x^6 - 52x^3$
   $- 60$

4. Evaluate $\frac{3x}{-5b}$ if $x = 7$ and
   $b = 2$. $-\frac{21}{10}$

5. Simplify $\{4(x + 5) - 4\}$
   $- 3x$. $x + 16$

TEACHER'S RESOURCE
MASTERS

Practice Master 24, Part 2

ASSIGNMENT GUIDE

Minimum
1–21 odd, 23–40, 47

Regular
23–52

Maximum
37–60, 61–71 odd

Sometimes a difference of two squares may result if a common monomial factor is removed from a polynomial.

3 | **Factor $6x^2 - 6y^2$.**

SOLUTION

$6x^2 - 6y^2 = 6(\underbrace{x^2 - y^2}_{\text{difference of two squares}})$

$= 6(x + y)(x - y)$

Sometimes it is helpful to multiply a given expression by a factor that will give a difference of two squares as a product.

4 | **By what factor can you multiply each binomial so that the product will be the difference of two squares?**

a. $8 + a$ **b.** $5x - 3y^2$ **c.** $6m - 7n$

SOLUTIONS

a. $\underbrace{(8 + a)}_{\text{given factor}}(8 - a) = \underbrace{64 - a^2}_{\text{product (difference of two squares)}}$

b. $\underbrace{(5x - 3y^2)}_{\text{given factor}}(5x + 3y^2) = \underbrace{25x^2 - 9y^4}_{\text{product (difference of two squares)}}$

c. $\underbrace{(6m - 7n)}_{\text{given factor}}(6m + 7n) = \underbrace{36m^2 - 49n^2}_{\text{product (difference of two squares)}}$

ORAL EXERCISES

By what factor can you multiply the given binomial so that the product is the difference of two squares?

1. $a - b$ $a + b$ **2.** $x + y$ $x - y$ **3.** $3x - 8$ $3x + 8$ **4.** $4a + b$ $4a - b$

5. $2x + 5y$ $2x - 5y$ **6.** $9a - 4b$ $9a + 4b$ **7.** $m^2 + 1$ $m^2 - 1$ **8.** $n^2 - 1$ $n^2 + 1$

WRITTEN EXERCISES

A. Factor completely.

1. $a^2 - b^2$ $(a + b)(a - b)$ **2.** $r^2 - s^2$ $(r + s)(r - s)$

3. $9 - m^2$ $(3 + m)(3 - m)$ **4.** $4 - n^2$ $(2 + n)(2 - n)$

5. $16a^2 - 9$ $(4a + 3)(4a - 3)$ **6.** $25x^2 - 64$ $(5x + 8)(5x - 8)$

7. $4y^2 - 16z^2$ $4(y + 2z)(y - 2z)$ **8.** $3t^2 - 75z^2$ $3(t + 5z)(t - 5z)$

9. $36m^2 - 49n^2$ $(6m + 7n)(6m - 7n)$ **10.** $9a^2 - 100b^2$ $(3a + 10b)(3a - 10b)$

11. $16a^2b^2 - 81$ $(4ab + 9)(4ab - 9)$ **12.** $49x^2y^2 - 64$ $(7xy + 8)(7xy - 8)$

By what can you multiply the given binomial so that the product is the difference of two squares? Then give the product.

13. $m - n$ $(m + n); m^2 - n^2$

14. $s + t$ $(s - t); s^2 - t^2$

15. $7 - a$ $(7 + a); 49 - a^2$

16. $8 + b$ $(8 - b); 64 - b^2$

17. $2x - 7$ $(2x + 7); 4x^2 - 49$

18. $3x + y$ $(3x - y); 9x^2 - y^2$

19. $4a + 9b$ $(4a - 9b); 16a^2 - 81b^2$

20. $5m - 2n$ $(5m + 2n); 25m^2 - 4n^2$

21. $a^2 + 3$ $(a^2 - 3); a^4 - 9$

22. $b^2 - 5$ $(b^2 + 5); b^4 - 25$

B. Factor completely.

23. $81 - x^2$ $(9 + x)(9 - x)$

24. $36 - y^2$ $(6 + y)(6 - y)$

25. $a^2 - 16b^2$ $(a + 4b)(a - 4b)$

26. $m^2 - 25n^2$ $(m + 5n)(m - 5n)$

27. $x^2 - y^2$ $(x + y)(x - y)$

28. $a^2 - b^2$ $(a + b)(a - b)$

29. $64 - 49a^2$ $(8 + 7a)(8 - 7a)$

30. $144 - 9s^2$ $9(4 + s)(4 - s)$

31. $81x^2 - 25y^2$ $(9x + 5y)(9x - 5y)$

32. $16a^2 - 4b^2$ $4(2a + b)(2a - b)$

33. $4 - 4b^2$ $4(1 + b)(1 - b)$

34. $7 - 7x^2$ $7(1 + x)(1 - x)$

35. $4y^2 - 36$ $4(y + 3)(y - 3)$

36. $5a^2 - 45$ $5(a + 3)(a - 3)$

37. $7m^2n^2 - 7$ $7(mn + 1)(mn - 1)$

38. $5x^2 - 125y^2$ $5(x + 5y)(x - 5y)$

39. $11a^2b^2 - 99$ $11(ab + 3)(ab - 3)$

40. $6 - 24m^2n^2$ $6(1 + 2mn)(1 - 2mn)$

41. $5 - 45x^2y^2$ $5(1 + 3xy)(1 - 3xy)$

42. $8x^2 - 18y^2$ $2(2x + 3y)(2x - 3y)$

43. $2a^2 - 18b^2$ $2(a + 3b)(a - 3b)$

44. $m^2 - m^2n^2$ $m^2(1 + n)(1 - n)$

45. $a^2 - a^2b^2$ $a^2(1 + b)(1 - b)$

46. $11x^2y^2 - 44z^2$ $11(xy + 2z)(xy - 2z)$

47. $6m^2n^2 - 54m^2p^2$ $6m^2(n + 3p)(n - 3p)$

48. $7x^2y^2 - 63x^2z^2$ $7x^2(y + 3z)(y - 3z)$

Find the difference of the squares by factoring.

49. $12^2 - 8^2$ 80

50. $13^2 - 5^2$ 144

51. $75^2 - 25^2$ 5000

52. $145^2 - 5^2$ $21{,}000$

53. $21^2 - 1$ 440

54. $32^2 - 2^2$ 1020

55. $23^2 - 9$ 520

56. $64 - 16$ 48

57. $25 - 9$ 16

58. $81 - 36$ 45

59. $7^2 - 8^2$ -15

60. $5^2 - 6^2$ -11

C. Factor each of the following:

Example: $(a + b)^2 - (c + d)^2 = [(a + b) + (c + d)][(a + b) - (c + d)]$
$$= (a + b + c + d)(a + b - c - d)$$

61. $(x + y)^2 - (m + n)^2$

62. $(a - b)^2 - (c - d)^2$

63. $(m - n)^2 - (x + y)^2$

64. $(x - 3y)^2 - (a - 5b)^2$

65. $(a^2 + 1)^2 - (b^2 + 3)^2$

66. $(m^2 - 2)^2 - (n^2 + 4)^2$

67. $(x^2 + y^2)^2 - (a^2 + b^2)^2$

68. $(2ab - 5)^2 - (8ab + 3)^2$

69. $x^4 - y^4$

70. $16 - y^4$

71. $m^4 - 81n^4$

72. $81c^4 - 1$

Factor a polynomial that is a perfect-square trinomial.

TEACHER'S NOTES

See p. T28.

CLASSROOM EXAMPLES

1. Write as trinomials.

a. $(x + 4)^2$

$(x + 4)^2$
$= x^2 + 8x + 16$

b. $(3x + 5)^2$

$(3x + 5)^2$
$= 9x^2 + 30x + 25$

c. $(4x - 3y)^2$

$(4x - 3y)^2$
$= 16x^2 - 24xy + 9y^2$

d. $(6y^2 - z^3)^2$

$(6y^2 - z^3)^2$
$= 36y^4 - 12y^2z^3 + z^6$

2. Is $x^2 + 16x + 64$ a perfect-square trinomial?   Yes

3. Is $4x^2 + 10xy + 81y^2$ a perfect-square trinomial?

No

MIXED REVIEW

Factor completely.

1. $(x + y)^2 - (a + b)^2$
$(x + y + a + b)(x + y - a - b)$

2. $9x^2 - 9y^2$ $9(x - y)(x + y)$

3. $11a^2b - 77$ $11(a^2b - 7)$

4. $4x^2 - 36y^2$
$4(x - 3y)(x + 3y)$

5. $16 - y^2$ $(4 - y)(4 + y)$

6.4   Perfect-Square Trinomials

Recall from Chapter 5 that the square of a binomial results in a **perfect-square trinomial.** This is illustrated by using the FOIL method.

$(a + b)^2 = (a + b)(a + b)$
$\qquad = a^2 + ab + ba + b^2$
$\qquad = a^2 + 2ab + b^2$

— square of the first term
— twice the product of the two terms
— square of the second term

If the binomial to be squared is $(a - b)$, the sign of the middle term in the trinomial will be negative.

$(a - b)^2 = (a - b)(a - b)$
$\qquad = a^2 - ab - ba + b^2$
$\qquad = a^2 - 2ab + b^2$

The following will help you identify perfect-square trinomials:

$(a + b)^2 = a^2 + 2ab + b^2$
$(a - b)^2 = a^2 - 2ab + b^2$

EXAMPLES

1   **Write as trinomials.**

a. $(a + 5)^2$ **b.** $(2x + 3)^2$ **c.** $(3s - 2t)^2$ **d.** $(4y^2 - z^3)^2$

SOLUTIONS

a. $(a + 5)^2 = (a + 5)(a + 5)$
$\qquad\qquad = a^2 + \underbrace{10a}_{} + 25$

twice the product of the two terms

b. $(2x + 3)^2 = (2x + 3)(2x + 3)$
$\qquad\qquad = 4x^2 + \underbrace{12x}_{} + 9$

twice the product of the two terms

c. $(3s - 2t)^2 = (3s - 2t)(3s - 2t)$
$\qquad\qquad = 9s^2 - \underbrace{12st}_{} + 4t^2$

twice the product of the two terms

d. $(4y^2 - z^3)^2 = (4y^2 - z^3)(4y^2 - z^3)$
$\qquad\qquad = 16y^4 - \underbrace{8y^2z^3}_{} + z^6$

twice the product of the two terms

To determine if a trinomial is a perfect-square trinomial, reverse the steps in Example 1.

2   **Is $a^2 + 10a + 25$ a perfect-square trinomial?**

SOLUTION   Ask the following questions:
1. Is the first term a square? Yes, because it is a^2.
2. Is the last term a square? Yes, because $25 = 5^2$.
3. Is the middle term twice the product of a and 5? Yes, because $10a = 2 \cdot a \cdot 5$.

If the answer to each of the three questions is yes, then the trinomial is a perfect-square trinomial. You can also check the answer.

$$\text{CHECK}\quad a^2 + 10a + 25 = a^2 + 2 \cdot a \cdot 5 + 5^2$$
$$= a^2 + 10a + 5^2$$
$$= (a + 5)^2 \;\checkmark$$

3   **Is $4x^2 + 20xy + 36y^2$ a perfect-square trinomial?**

SOLUTION

1. Is the first term a square? Yes, because $4x^2 = (2x)^2$.
2. Is the last term a square? Yes, because $36y^2 = (6y)^2$.
3. Is the middle term twice the product of $2x$ and $6y$? No, because $20xy \neq 2 \cdot 2x \cdot 6y$.

$4x^2 + 20xy + 36y^2$ is not a perfect-square trinomial.

ORAL EXERCISES

Complete.

1. $x^2 + 2x + 1 = (x + \underline{\;1\;})^2$

2. $a^2 - 8a + 16 = (\underline{\;a\;} - 4)^2$

3. $y^2 - 6y + 9 = (y - \underline{\;3\;})^2$

4. $b^2 + 4b + 4 = (\underline{\;b\;} + 2)^2$

5. $(a + 7)^2 = a^2 + 14a + \underline{\;49\;}$

6. $(b - 4)^2 = b^2 - \underline{\;8b\;} + 16$

7. $(3x + 1)^2 = 9x^2 + \underline{\;6x\;} + 1$

8. $(5y - 2)^2 = \underline{\;25y^2\;} - 20y + 4$

9. $(x^2 + 4)^2 = x^4 + 8x^2 + \underline{\;16\;}$

10. $(2 - 5x)^2 = \underline{\;4\;} - 20x + 25x^2$

WRITTEN EXERCISES

A. Express the square of each binomial as a perfect-square trinomial.

1. $(x + 3)^2$ $x^2 + 6x + 9$

2. $(y - 2)^2$ $y^2 - 4y + 4$

3. $(a - 5)^2$ $a^2 - 10a + 25$

4. $(b + 8)^2$ $b^2 + 16b + 64$

5. $(2x + 3)^2$ $4x^2 + 12x + 9$

6. $(2y + 7)^2$ $4y^2 + 28y + 49$

7. $(4m - 6)^2$ $16m^2 - 48m + 36$

8. $(5a - 2)^2$ $25a^2 - 20a + 4$

9. $(2x + 3y)^2$ $4x^2 + 12xy + 9y^2$

10. $(9a - 6b)^2$ $81a^2 - 108ab + 36b^2$

TEACHER'S RESOURCE MASTERS

Practice Master 25, Part 1

ASSIGNMENT GUIDE

Minimum
1–15 odd, 17–25, 55–62

Regular
35–53 odd, 59–68, 69–77 odd

Maximum
21–45 odd, 55–65 odd, 85–95 odd

11. $(4m + 8n)^2$ $16m^2 + 64mn + 64n^2$

12. $(2x - 9y)^2$ $4x^2 - 36xy + 81y^2$

13. $(xy - 3)^2$ $x^2y^2 - 6xy + 9$

14. $(a^2 + 3)^2$ $a^4 + 6a^2 + 9$

15. $(y^2 - 5)^2$ $y^4 - 10y^2 + 25$

16. $(3m^2 - n^2)^2$ $9m^4 - 6m^2n^2 + n^4$

B. Determine whether each expression is a perfect-square trinomial. If it is, factor it. If it is not, write *no*.

17. $x^2 + 2x + 1$ $(x + 1)^2$

18. $y^2 - 4y + 4$ $(y - 2)^2$

19. $z^2 - 8a + 8$ no

20. $m^2 - 2m + 1$ $(m - 1)^2$

21. $n^2 + 6n + 9$ $(n + 3)^2$

22. $b^2 + 12b + 24$ no

23. $x^2 - 18x + 81$ $(x - 9)^2$

24. $4a^2 + 4a + 1$ $(2a + 1)^2$

25. $y - 7y + 49$ no

26. $25m^2 - 60m + 36$ $(5m - 6)^2$

27. $x^2 - 2xy + y^2$ $(x - y)^2$

28. $9a^2 - 6a + 1$ $(3a - 1)^2$

29. $y^2 - 20y + 20$ no

30. $4m^2 - 4mn + n^2$ $(2m - n)^2$

31. $36a^2 + 12ab + b^2$ $(6a + b)^2$

32. $16m^2 - 24mn + 9n^2$ $(4m - 3n)^2$

33. $25x^2 - 30xy + 9y^2$ $(5x - 3y)^2$

34. $5x^2 + 10xy + 12y^2$ no

35. $16a^2 - 8ab + b^2$ $(4a - b)^2$

36. $x^2 + 18x + 81$ $(x + 9)^2$

37. $7a^2 + 14ab + 14b^2$ no

38. $25m^2 - 10mn + n^2$ $(5m - n)^2$

39. $a^2 + 20a + 100$ $(a + 10)^2$

40. $a^2 - 2ab + b^2$ $(a - b)^2$

41. $x^2y^2 - 4xy + 4$ $(xy - 2)^2$

42. $m^2n^2 + 16mn + 64$ $(mn + 8)^2$

43. $5a^2 + 6a + 25$ no

44. $81 - 18x + x^2$ $(9 - x)^2$

45. $25 - 20m + 4m^2$ $(5 - 2m)^2$

46. $49 - 14y + y^2$ $(7 - y)^2$

47. $a^2 + a + 1$ no

48. $4x^2 + 8x + 9$ no

49. $1 - 14m + 49m^2$ $(1 - 7m)^2$

50. $16a^2 - 40ab + 25b^2$ $(4a - 5b)^2$

51. $1 - 12n + 36n^2$ $(1 - 6n)^2$

52. $y^2 - y + 1$ no

53. $25x^2 - 60xy + 36y^2$ $(5x - 6y)^2$

54. $16a^2 - 72ab + 81b^2$ $(4a - 9b)^2$

Factor completely.

55. $a^2 - 9$ $(a + 3)(a - 3)$

56. $b^2 - 4$ $(b + 2)(b - 2)$

57. $9x^2 + 12x + 4$ $(3x + 2)^2$

58. $2y^2 + 4y + 12$ $2(y^2 + 2y + 6)$

59. $2a^2 + 16a + 4$ $2(a^2 + 8a + 2)$

60. $4m^2 + 12m + 9$ $(2m + 3)^2$

61. $16y^2 - 81$ $(4y + 9)(4y - 9)$

62. $25x^2 - 36$ $(5x + 6)(5x - 6)$

63. $5a^2 + 5a + 30$ $5(a^2 + a + 6)$

64. $3m^2 + 6m + 15$ $3(m^2 + 2m + 5)$

65. $4n^2 - 36$ $4(n + 3)(n - 3)$

66. $36y^2 - 16$ $4(3y + 2)(3y - 2)$

67. $64a^2 - 16a + 1$ $(8a - 1)^2$

68. $144x^2 - 24x + 1$ $(12x - 1)^2$

Adding a term to a given expression to form a perfect-square trinomial is called completing the square. Complete the square, then factor.

Examples: a. $x^2 + 6x + \underline{\hspace{1cm}} = x^2 + 2 \cdot x \cdot 3 + \underline{3^2} = (x + 3)^2$

b. $4a^2 - 12ab + \underline{\hspace{1cm}} = (2a)^2 - 2 \cdot 2a \cdot 3b + \underline{(3b)^2} = (2a - 3b)^2$

69. $a^2 + 8a + \underline{\hspace{1cm}}$ 4^2; $(a + 4)^2$

70. $b^2 - 2b + \underline{\hspace{1cm}}$ 1^2; $(b - 1)^2$

71. $y^2 - 10y + \underline{\hspace{1cm}}$ 5^2; $(y - 5)^2$

72. $x^2 + 6x + \underline{\hspace{1cm}}$ 3^2; $(x + 3)^2$

73. $m^2 - 12m + \underline{\hspace{1cm}}$ 6^2; $(m - 6)^2$

74. $n^2 + 4n + \underline{\hspace{1cm}}$ 2^2; $(n + 2)^2$

75. $16a^2 + 8ab + \underline{\hspace{1cm}}$ b^2; $(4a + b)^2$

76. $4x^2 - 4xy + \underline{\hspace{1cm}}$ y^2; $(2x - y)^2$

77. $25m^2 - 40mn + \underline{\hspace{1cm}}$

78. $9m^2 - 24mn + \underline{\hspace{1cm}}$

79. $25a^2 + 20ab + \underline{\hspace{1cm}}$ $(2b)^2$; $(5a + 2b)^2$

80. $4x^2 + 12xy + \underline{\hspace{1cm}}$ $(3y)^2$; $(2x + 3y)^2$

81. $16x^2 + \underline{\hspace{1cm}} + 9b^2$ $24xb$; $(4x + 3b)^2$

82. $25a^2 - \underline{\hspace{1cm}} + 4c^2$ $20ac$; $(5a - 2c)^2$

83. $\underline{\hspace{1cm}} - 30xy + 25y^2$ $(3x)^2$; $(3x - 5y)^2$

84. $\underline{\hspace{1cm}} + 84st + 49t^2$ $(6s)^2$; $(6s + 7t)^2$

C. Factor the following perfect-square trinomials over the rational numbers:

Examples: a. $x^2 + x + \frac{1}{4} = x^2 + 2 \cdot x \cdot \frac{1}{2} + \left(\frac{1}{2}\right)^2 = \left(x + \frac{1}{2}\right)^2$

b. $y^2 - 1.6y + 0.64 = y^2 - 2 \cdot y \cdot 0.8 + (0.8)^2 = (y - 0.8)^2$

85. $x^2 + \frac{1}{2}x + \frac{1}{16}$ $\left(x + \frac{1}{4}\right)^2$

86. $y^2 - y + \frac{1}{4}$ $\left(y - \frac{1}{2}\right)^2$

87. $\frac{1}{4}a^2 + \frac{2}{3}a + \frac{4}{9}$ $\left(\frac{1}{2}a + \frac{2}{3}\right)^2$

88. $\frac{1}{9}m^2 - \frac{1}{2}m + \frac{9}{16}$ $\left(\frac{1}{3}m - \frac{3}{4}\right)^2$

89. $x^2 + 1.4x + 0.49$ $(x + 0.7)^2$

90. $y^2 - 0.6y + 0.09$ $(y - 0.3)^2$

91. $0.04a^2 + 0.12a + 0.09$ $(0.2a + 0.3)^2$

92. $10.24b^2 - 9.6b + 2.25$ $(3.2b - 1.5)^2$

93. $0.16c^2 - 0.24cd + 0.09d^2$

94. $1.21x^2 - 2.64xy + 1.44y^2$

95. The area of a square is $9s^2 - 12s + 4$. How long is each side? $3s - 2$

SELF-QUIZ

Find the greatest common factor of each pair of integers.

1. 24, 40 8

2. 36, 54 18

3. 15, 60 15

Find the least common multiple of each pair of integers.

4. 24, 9 72

5. 20, 25 100

6. 10, 25 50

Factor completely.

7. $24x + 6$ $6(4x + 1)$

8. $5a - 15b$ $5(a - 3b)$

9. $x^2y + x$ $x(xy + 1)$

10. $a^2 - 81$ $(a + 9)(a - 9)$

11. $16x^2 - 25$ $(4x + 5)(4x - 5)$

12. $5y^2 - 80$ $5(y + 4)(y - 4)$

13. $c^2 - 2c + 1$ $(c - 1)^2$

14. $y^2 + 14y + 49$ $(y + 7)^2$

15. $4a^2 - 12a + 9$ $(2a - 3)^2$

TEACHER'S NOTES

See p. T28.

CLASSROOM EXAMPLES

1. Factor $x^2 + 7x + 10$ completely.
   $x^2 + 7x + 10 = (x + 2)(x + 5)$

2. Factor $y^2 - 11y + 18$ completely.
   $y^2 - 11y + 18 = (y - 2)(y - 9)$

3. Factor $p^2 - 6p - 16$ completely.
   $p^2 - 6p - 16 = (p + 2)(p - 8)$

4. Factor $p^2 + 6p - 16$ completely.
   $p^2 + 6p - 16 = (p - 2)(p + 8)$

MIXED REVIEW

Perform the indicated operation.

1. $(x^2 - y)(x^2 + y)$
   $x^4 - y^2$

2. $(a^2 + 12a + 27) \div (a + 9)$ $a + 3$

3. $(y + 6)(y - 12)$ $y^2 - 6y - 72$

4. $(y^2 + 3y + 8) - (y^2 - 3y - 5)$ $6y + 13$

5. $(3y^3 + 5y^2 - 6) + (2y^3 + 8y^2 + 3)$ $5y^3 + 13y^2 - 3$

6.5 Trinomials: $x^2 + bx + c$

In the trinomial $x^2 + bx + c$, the second-degree term is often called the **quadratic term,** bx is called the **linear term,** and c is called the **constant.**

If $(x + 3)(x + 4) = x^2 + 7x + 12$, then $x^2 + 7x + 12$ can be factored as $(x + 3)(x + 4)$. Notice that the coefficient of the linear term is 7, and 7 is equal to $3 + 4$, while the constant, 12, is equal to $3 \cdot 4$. Also, 3 and 4 appear as terms in each binomial factor.

So to factor a trinomial of the form $x^2 + bx + c$, you need to find two numbers whose sum is b and whose product is c.

EXAMPLES

1   **Factor $x^2 + 11x + 30$ completely.**

SOLUTION

1. The constant c is positive, so the two numbers are either both positive or both negative. Since the coefficient b is also positive, the two numbers are both positive.
   $$x^2 + 11x + 30 = (x + ?)(x + ?)$$

2. List pairs of positive integers whose product is 30 and select the pair that has a sum of 11.

1	30
2	15
3	10
5	6

3. Check your selection.
   $$(x + 5)(x + 6) = x^2 + 6x + 5x + 30$$
   $$= x^2 + 11x + 30$$

2   **Factor $y^2 - 15y + 54$ completely.**

SOLUTION

1. The constant c is positive and the coefficient b is negative. So both numbers must be negative.
   $$y^2 - 15y + 54 = (y \quad)(y \quad)$$

2. List pairs of negative integers whose product is 54 and select the pair that has a sum of -15.

-1	-54
-2	-27
-3	-18
-6	-9

3. Check your selection.
   $$(y - 6)(y - 9) = y^2 - 9y - 6y + 54$$
   $$= y^2 - 15y + 54$$

You may want to introduce this topic using **Algebra Tiles.** They are a physical model for teaching algebraic concepts and are available from Cuisenaire Co. of America, Inc., 12 Church Street, New Rochelle, NY 10802.

3   **Factor $a^2 - 3a - 28$ completely.**

SOLUTION

1. The constant c is negative, so one of the two numbers is negative and the other is positive. Since the coefficient b is negative, the negative number must have the greater absolute value.

$$a^2 - 3a - 28 = (a \quad)(a \quad)$$

2. List pairs of numbers whose product is -28 and select the pair that has a sum of -3.

$$\begin{array}{rr} 1 & -28 \\ 2 & -14 \\ 4 & -7 \end{array}$$

3. Check your selection.

$$(a + 4)(a - 7) = a^2 - 7a + 4a - 28$$
$$= a^2 - 3a - 28$$

4   **Factor $a^2 + 3a - 28$ completely.**

SOLUTION

1. The constant c is negative and the coefficient b is positive. So one number is negative and the other is positive. The positive number must have the greater absolute value.

$$a^2 + 3a - 28 = (a \quad)(a \quad)$$

2. List pairs of numbers whose product is -28 and select the pair that has a sum of 3.

$$\begin{array}{rr} -1 & 28 \\ -2 & 14 \\ -4 & 7 \end{array}$$

3. Check your selection.

$$(a - 4)(a + 7) = a^2 + 7a - 4a - 28$$
$$= a^2 + 3a - 28$$

TEACHER'S RESOURCE MASTERS

Practice Master 25, Part 2

Quiz 11

ASSIGNMENT GUIDE

Minimum
1–39 odd

Regular
25–44

Maximum
31–43, 49–61 odd

ORAL EXERCISES

For each trinomial, give two numbers, the product of which is equal to the constant and the sum of which is equal to the coefficient of the linear term.

1. $x^2 + 5x + 6$ $2, 3$

2. $y^2 - 12y + 35$ $-5, -7$

3. $a^2 - 10a - 24$ $2, -12$

4. $b^2 + 7b + 12$ $3, 4$

5. $m^2 + 5m - 24$ $-3, 8$

6. $n^2 - 9n + 18$ $-3, -6$

7. $x^2 + 4x - 21$ $-3, 7$

8. $y^2 + 15y + 56$ $7, 8$

9. $a^2 - 4a - 21$ $3, -7$

10. $b^2 + 7b - 60$ $-5, 12$

WRITTEN EXERCISES

A. Factor completely.

1. $a^2 + 6a + 8$ $(a + 2)(a + 4)$

2. $x^2 + 4x + 3$ $(x + 3)(x + 1)$

3. $y^2 + 7y + 12$ $(y + 3)(y + 4)$

4. $b^2 + 7b + 6$ $(b + 6)(b + 1)$

5. $m^2 + 10m + 21$ $(m + 3)(m + 7)$

6. $n^2 + 3n - 4$ $(n + 4)(n - 1)$

7. $a^2 + 3a - 10$ $(a + 5)(a - 2)$

8. $b^2 + 7b - 8$ $(b + 8)(b - 1)$

9. $x^2 + 2x - 8$ $(x + 4)(x - 2)$

10. $y^2 + 6y - 27$ $(y + 9)(y - 3)$

11. $m^2 + m - 42$ $(m + 7)(m - 6)$

12. $n^2 - 8n + 7$ $(n - 7)(n - 1)$

13. $a^2 + 6a + 5$ $(a + 5)(a + 1)$

14. $b^2 - 11b + 18$ $(b - 9)(b - 2)$

15. $x^2 - 9x + 14$ $(x - 7)(x - 2)$

16. $y^2 - 5y + 6$ $(y - 3)(y - 2)$

17. $m^2 - 6m + 5$ $(m - 5)(m - 1)$

18. $n^2 - 13n + 36$ $(n - 9)(n - 4)$

19. $a^2 - 9a + 18$ $(a - 6)(a - 3)$

20. $b^2 - b - 6$ $(b - 3)(b + 2)$

B.

21. $x^2 - 2x - 8$ $(x - 4)(x + 2)$

22. $y^2 - 5y - 14$ $(y - 7)(y + 2)$

23. $m^2 - m - 72$ $(m - 9)(m + 8)$

24. $n^2 + 5n - 24$ $(n + 8)(n - 3)$

25. $a^2 + 4a - 32$ $(a + 8)(a - 4)$

26. $b^2 - 10b + 21$ $(b - 7)(b - 3)$

27. $x^2 + 9x + 20$ $(x + 5)(x + 4)$

28. $y^2 + 12y + 20$ $(y + 10)(y + 2)$

29. $m^2 - 6m + 8$ $(m - 4)(m - 2)$

30. $n^2 - 14n - 15$ $(n - 15)(n + 1)$

31. $a^2 - 8a + 15$ $(a - 5)(a - 3)$

32. $b^2 + 6b + 8$ $(b + 4)(b + 2)$

33. $x^2 + 10x + 16$ $(x + 8)(x + 2)$

34. $y^2 - 11y + 28$ $(y - 7)(y - 4)$

35. $m^2 - 13m + 22$ $(m - 11)(m - 2)$

36. $n^2 + 14n + 48$ $(n + 8)(n + 6)$

37. $x^2 + 8xy + 12y^2$ $(x + 6y)(x + 2y)$

38. $a^2 - 11ab - 60b^2$ $(a - 15b)(a + 4b)$

39. $m^2 - 7mn + 10n^2$ $(m - 5n)(m - 2n)$

40. $x^2 + 8xy + 15y^2$ $(x + 3y)(x + 5y)$

41. $x^2 - xy - 12y^2$ $(x + 3y)(x - 4y)$

42. $a^2 + ab - 30b^2$ $(a + 6b)(a - 5b)$

43. $a^2 - 14ab + 48b^2$ $(a - 8b)(a - 6b)$

44. $c^2 + 10cd + 16d^2$ $(c + 2d)(c + 8d)$

45. $x^2 + 12xz - 45z^2$ $(x + 15z)(x - 3z)$

46. $s^2 - 15st + 54t^2$ $(s - 9t)(s - 6t)$

47. $s^2 + 3st - 70t^2$ $(s + 10t)(s - 7t)$

48. $c^2 + 17cd + 60d^2$ $(c + 5d)(c + 12d)$

C.

49. $a^4 - 64b^2$ $(a^2 + 8b)(a^2 - 8b)$

50. $a^4 - 11a^2 + 30$ $(a^2 - 6)(a^2 - 5)$

51. $m^4 - 11m^2 + 18$

52. $(2a - b)^2 - 2(2a - b) - 15$

53. $(m - n)^2 + 7(m - n) + 12$

54. $(x + y)^2 - 4(x + y) - 12$

55. $(4x - y)^2 - 3(4x - y) - 10$

56. $(a + b)^2 + 3(a + b) + 2$

57. $5x^2 + 20x + 15$ $5(x + 3)(x + 1)$

58. $3y^2 + 15y + 12$ $3(y + 4)(y + 1)$

59. $5s^2 + 10s - 240$ $5(s + 8)(s - 6)$

60. $7t^2 + 14t - 245$ $7(t + 7)(t - 5)$

61. $3x^2 - 33xy + 90y^2$ $3(x - 6y)(x - 5y)$

62. $5a^2 + 65ab + 200b^2$ $5(a + 8b)(a + 5b)$

6.6 | Trinomials: $ax^2 + bx + c$

OBJECTIVE

Factor a polynomial of the form $ax^2 + bx + c$.

TEACHER'S NOTES

See p. T28.

In Section 6.5, the trinomials were of the form $x^2 + bx + c$. Some trinomials of the form $ax^2 + bx + c$, in which the coefficient of the quadratic term is not 1, can also be factored.

EXAMPLES

1 **Factor $2x^2 + 9x + 10$ completely.**

SOLUTION

1. The only factors of the quadratic term are $2x \cdot x$.

2. The constant c is positive, and the coefficient b is positive. So both numbers are positive.
$$2x^2 + 9x + 10 = (2x + \quad)(x + \quad)$$

3. List pairs of positive numbers whose product is 10.
   1   10
   2   5

4. List the possible binomial factors and the linear term that results from each.
Binomial factors	Linear term
$(2x + 1)(x + 10)$	$21x$
$(2x + 10)(x + 1)$	$12x$
$(2x + 2)(x + 5)$	$12x$
$(2x + 5)(x + 2)$	$9x$ ← the linear term of the trinomial

5. Check the binomial factors.
$$(2x + 5)(x + 2) = 2x^2 + 4x + 5x + 10$$
$$= 2x^2 + 9x + 10$$

2 **Factor $8x^2 - 35x + 12$ completely.**

SOLUTION

1. The factors of the quadratic term can be $x \cdot 8x$ or $2x \cdot 4x$.
$$8x^2 - 35x + 12 \stackrel{?}{=} (x \quad)(8x \quad)$$
   or
$$8x^2 - 35x + 12 \stackrel{?}{=} (2x \quad)(4x \quad)$$

2. The constant c is positive, and the coefficient b is negative. So both numbers must be negative.

3. List pairs of negative integers whose product is 12.
   -1 -12
   -2 -6
   -3 -4

CLASSROOM EXAMPLES

1. Factor $2x^2 + 17x + 35$ completely.
   $2x^2 + 17x + 35$
   $= (2x + 7)(x + 5)$

2. Factor $6x^2 - 19x + 15$ completely.
   $6x^2 - 19x + 15$
   $= (2x - 3)(3x - 5)$

3. Factor $3x^2 - x - 30$ completely.
   $3x^2 - x - 30$
   $= (3x - 10)(x + 3)$

MIXED REVIEW

1. Simplify $4(x - 3) - 6x + 5$. $-2x - 7$

2. Convert $0.\overline{203}$ to a fraction. $\frac{203}{999}$

3. Convert 0.58 to a fraction. $\frac{29}{50}$

4. Solve $4(y + 3) = 6(y - 2)$. $y = 12$

5. Evaluate $\frac{x - y}{y}$ if $x = 3$ and $y = -1$. -4

ASSIGNMENT GUIDE

Minimum
1–15 odd, 17–32

Regular
17–29 odd, 30–46

Maximum
23–42, 49–55 odd

4. List the possible binomial factors and the linear term that results from each.

Binomial factors	*Linear term*
$(x - 1)(8x - 12)$	$-20x$
$(x - 12)(8x - 1)$	$-97x$
$(x - 2)(8x - 6)$	$-22x$
$(x - 6)(8x - 2)$	$-50x$
$(x - 3)(8x - 4)$	$-28x$
$(x - 4)(8x - 3)$	$-35x \leftarrow$ *the linear term of the trinomial*

Since the correct binomial factors have been found, there is no need to list the possible binomial factors and the linear term for $(2x\quad)(4x\quad)$.

5. Check the binomial factors.
$$(x - 4)(8x - 3) = 8x^2 - 3x - 32x + 12$$
$$= 8x^2 - 35x + 12$$

---

3 **Factor $2x^2 - 3x - 14$ completely.**

SOLUTION

1. The only factors of the quadratic term are $2x \cdot x$.

2. The constant c is negative, so only one of the two numbers is negative.

3. List pairs of numbers whose product is -14.

1	-14
14	-1
2	-7
7	-2

4. List the possible binomial factors and the linear term that results from each.

Binomial factors	*Linear term*
$(2x + 1)(x - 14)$	$-27x$
$(2x + 14)(x - 1)$	$12x$
$(2x + 2)(x - 7)$	$-12x$
$(2x + 7)(x - 2)$	$3x$
$(x + 1)(2x - 14)$	$-12x$
$(x + 14)(2x - 1)$	$27x$
$(x + 2)(2x - 7)$	$-3x \leftarrow$ *the linear term of the trinomial*

5. Check the binomial factors.
$$(x + 2)(2x - 7) = 2x^2 - 7x + 4x - 14$$
$$= 2x^2 - 3x - 14$$

With experience, you can find correct binomial factors without actually considering every possibility.

Find the missing binomial factor.

1. $12x^2 + 17x + 6 = (3x + 2)\underline{\quad(4x + 3)\quad}$

2. $3y^2 + 10y - 8 = (3y - 2)\underline{\quad(y + 4)\quad}$

3. $6a^2 - 43a + 72 = (2a - 9)\underline{\quad(3a - 8)\quad}$

4. $2n^2 - 5n - 3 = (2n + 1)\underline{\quad(n - 3)\quad}$

5. $6m^2 + 7m - 20 = (3m - 4)\underline{\quad(2m + 5)\quad}$

6. $6b^2 + 23b + 20 = (2b + 5)\underline{\quad(3b + 4)\quad}$

7. $2y^2 + 7y + 6 = (2y + 3)\underline{\quad(y + 2)\quad}$

8. $6x^2 + 7x + 2 = (3x + 2)\underline{\quad(2x + 1)\quad}$

9. $3a^2 - 7a - 6 = (3a + 2)\underline{\quad(a - 3)\quad}$

10. $4y^2 - 8y + 3 = (2y - 3)\underline{\quad(2y - 1)\quad}$

WRITTEN EXERCISES

A. Factor completely.

1. $3b^2 + 5b + 2 \quad (3b + 2)(b + 1)$

2. $y^2 + y - 72 \quad (y + 9)(y - 8)$

3. $5b^2 + 9b - 2 \quad (5b - 1)(b + 2)$

4. $2n^2 + 13n - 7 \quad (2n - 1)(n + 7)$

5. $5y^2 + 2y - 7 \quad (5y + 7)(y - 1)$

6. $2y^2 + 3y + 1 \quad (2y + 1)(y + 1)$

7. $3b^2 + 4b + 1 \quad (3b + 1)(b + 1)$

8. $5n^2 + 6n + 1 \quad (5n + 1)(n + 1)$

9. $2b^2 + 5b + 3 \quad (2b + 3)(b + 1)$

10. $2y^2 + 7y + 5 \quad (2y + 5)(y + 1)$

11. $2n^2 - 7n + 5 \quad (2n - 5)(n - 1)$

12. $3y^2 + 4y - 7 \quad (3y + 7)(y - 1)$

13. $3b^2 - 8b + 5 \quad (3b - 5)(b - 1)$

14. $3x^2 - 10x - 25 \quad (3x + 5)(x - 5)$

15. $2b^2 + 9b + 10 \quad (2b + 5)(b + 2)$

16. $2m^2 - 13m + 15 \quad (2m - 3)(m - 5)$

B. 17. $3a^2 - 11a - 4 \quad (3a + 1)(a - 4)$

18. $5x^2 + 9x - 18 \quad (5x - 6)(x + 3)$

19. $3x^2 + 11x + 10 \quad (3x + 5)(x + 2)$

20. $2m^2 - 5m + 3 \quad (2m - 3)(m - 1)$

21. $3x^2 - 10x + 7 \quad (3x - 7)(x - 1)$

22. $5a^2 - 16a + 3 \quad (5a - 1)(a - 3)$

23. $2n^2 - 9n + 10 \quad (2n - 5)(n - 2)$

24. $y^2 - 4y - 32 \quad (y - 8)(y + 4)$

25. $2a^2 - 7a + 6 \quad (2a - 3)(a - 2)$

26. $3m^2 - 11m + 6 \quad (3m - 2)(m - 3)$

27. $8x^2 - 2x - 1 \quad (4x + 1)(2x - 1)$

28. $7y^2 - 23y + 6 \quad (7y - 2)(y - 3)$

29. $4m^2 - 12m + 5 \quad (2m - 5)(2m - 1)$

30. $8n^2 + 18n - 5 \quad (2n + 5)(4n - 1)$

31. $9a^2 + 3a - 2 \quad (3a + 2)(3a - 1)$

32. $15m^2 - m - 2 \quad (5m - 2)(3m + 1)$

33. $9x^2 + 9x - 4 \quad (3x + 4)(3x - 1)$

34. $4a^2 + 13a - 35 \quad (4a - 7)(a + 5)$

35. $6a^2 + a - 12 \quad (3a - 4)(2a + 3)$

36. $18m^2 + 21m - 4 \quad (6m - 1)(3m + 4)$

37. $14x^2 - 13x - 12 \quad (2x - 3)(7x + 4)$

38. $4a^2 - 4a - 35 \quad (2a + 5)(2a - 7)$

39. $6a^2 - 17a + 12 \quad (3a - 4)(2a - 3)$

40. $21x^2 + 5x - 6 \quad (3x + 2)(7x - 3)$

41. $9m^2 + 6m - 8 \quad (3m - 2)(3m + 4)$

42. $40b^2 + b - 6 \quad (8b - 3)(5b + 2)$

43. $12a^2 - 29ab + 14b^2$

44. $18a^2 - 57ab + 35b^2 \quad (6a - 5b)(3a - 7b)$

45. $14m^2 - 57mn - 27n^2$

46. $40x^2 + 39xy - 40y^2 \quad (8x - 5y)(5x + 8y)$

47. $16a^2 + 56ab + 49b^2 \quad (4a + 7b)^2$

48. $64x^2 + 112xy + 49y^2 \quad (8x + 7y)^2$

ADDITIONAL ANSWERS

Written Exercises

43. $(4a - 7b)(3a - 2b)$

45. $(2m - 9n)(7m + 3n)$

54. $(5x - 5y - 2)(x - y - 1)$

C. 49. $9b^2 - 36b + 36$ $9(b - 2)^2$

50. $5a^2 + 30a + 45$ $5(a + 3)^2$

51. $4x^2 + 16x + 16$ $4(x + 2)^2$

52. $a^4 - 9a^2$ $a^2(a + 3)(a - 3)$

53. $4x^4 - 25x^2$ $x^2(2x + 5)(2x - 5)$

54. $5(x - y)^2 - 7(x - y) + 2$

55. $6n^2 - 18n + 12$ $6(n - 2)(n - 1)$

56. $24a^2 + 78a - 21$ $3(4a - 1)(2a + 7)$

MATH HERITAGE/Strange but True

Nicholas Saunderson (1682–1739) was a professor of mathematics at Cambridge. King George II made him a doctor of laws, and he eventually became a fellow of the Royal Society. Saunderson authored two works, *Algebra* and *Method of Fluxions*, and he did much to promote the philosophy of Newton among the mathematicians of his time. What's so strange about all of this? Saunderson was totally blinded by smallpox at the age of one.

Évariste Galois (1811–1832), the "teenage mathematician," was responsible for our modern theory of algebraic equations of higher degree. Even though he made his mark as one of the most original mathematicians who ever lived, Galois was constantly failing exams and fighting with his teachers, most of whom did not recognize his genius. In the space of only three or four years, Galois managed to be imprisoned twice, once for his political views and once for threatening the life of the king of France.

When challenged to a duel at the age of twenty, Galois seemed to know that he would lose, so he spent the entire night before the duel writing out his mathematical theories. He died the day after the duel, after having been shot through the stomach.

Charles Dodgson (1832–1898) was not only a mathematician but also the foremost children's photographer of his time. He is best known, however, for the children's stories he wrote, in which symbolic logic abounds. His most famous story is *Alice's Adventures in Wonderland*, written under the pen name Lewis Carroll.

6.7 | Factoring Techniques

OBJECTIVE
Change a polynomial by grouping terms, rearranging terms, and/or removing a common monomial factor before factoring completely.

Unless a polynomial is prime, it can be factored. Use the following steps to factor a polynomial completely, as the product of prime polynomials:

1. Find the greatest monomial factor and then factor the remaining polynomial, if possible.
$$3x^3 + 21x^2 + 36x = 3x(x^2 + 7x + 12) = 3x(x + 3)(x + 4)$$

2. Determine if the polynomial is the difference of two squares.
$$18y^3 - 32x^2y = 2y(9y^2 - 16x^2) = 2y(3y + 4x)(3y - 4x)$$

3. If the polynomial is a trinomial, determine if it is a perfect square.
$$4x^2 + 24xy + 36y^2 = 4(x^2 + 6xy + 9y^2) = 4[x^2 + 2 \cdot x \cdot 3y + (3y)^2] = 4(x + 3y)^2$$

4. If the trinomial is not a perfect square, determine if it is of the form $x^2 + bx + c$ or of the form $ax^2 + bx + c$ and determine if it can be factored.
$$x^2 + 15x + 54 = (x + 6)(x + 9)$$
$$8a^2 - 35a + 12 = (a - 4)(8a - 3)$$

A polynomial may not always appear to be factorable. You may therefore have to change the polynomial to a type that you can recognize by doing one of the following:

Group the terms.　Rearrange the terms.　Remove the greatest common monomial factor.

TEACHER'S NOTES
See p. T29.

CLASSROOM EXAMPLES
1. Factor $2r^2 - 2s^2 + ar^2 - as^2$.
$$2r^2 - 2s^2 + ar^2 - as^2$$
$$= (2r^2 - 2s^2) + (ar^2 - as^2)$$
$$= 2(r^2 - s^2) + a(r^2 - s^2)$$
$$= (2 + a)(r^2 - s^2)$$
$$= (2 + a)(r + s)(r - s)$$

2. Factor $10y + y^2 + 21$.
$$10y + y^2 + 21$$
$$= y^2 + 10y + 21$$
$$= (y + 7)(y + 3)$$

3. Factor $-x^2 - 10x - 25$.
$$-x^2 - 10x - 25$$
$$= -1(x^2 + 10x + 25)$$
$$= -1(x + 5)^2$$

EXAMPLES

1　**Factor $2x^2 - 2y^2 + ax^2 - ay^2$.**

SOLUTION

$2x^2 - 2y^2 + ax^2 - ay^2$

$= (2x^2 - 2y^2) + (ax^2 - ay^2)$　*Group the terms having a common monomial factor.*

$= 2(x^2 - y^2) + a(x^2 - y^2)$　*Remove the greatest common monomial factors.*

$= (2 + a)(x^2 - y^2)$　*Apply the distributive property.*

$= (2 + a)(x + y)(x - y)$　*Factor the difference of two squares.*

2　**Factor $4n + n^2 + 3$.**

SOLUTION

$4n + n^2 + 3 = n^2 + 4n + 3$　*Rearrange the terms as a trinomial of the form $x^2 + bx + c$.*

$= (n + 3)(n + 1)$　*Factor the trinomial.*

3　**Factor $-x^2 - 6x - 9$.**

SOLUTION

$-x^2 - 6x - 9 = -1(x^2 + 6x + 9)$　*Remove the common monomial factor of -1.*

$= -1(x + 3)^2$　*Factor the perfect-square trinomial.*

MIXED REVIEW
1. Illustrate the commutative property of multiplication.　Answers may vary.

Simplify each of the following.
2. $\frac{4 \cdot 6(2)}{3}$　16
3. $5 \cdot 2 + 5 \cdot 3^2$　55
4. $3^3 a^2(a^4)$　$27a^6$
5. $15(x^2y - 3xy^2)$　$15x^2y - 45xy^2$

ASSIGNMENT GUIDE

Minimum
1–32

Regular
13–29 odd, 30–52

Maximum
23–46, 51–65 odd

ADDITIONAL ANSWERS

Oral Exercises

6. a

9. a

Written Exercises

33. $(y + 4)(y - 4)(y + 1)(y - 1)$

47. $(a + 10)(a - 10)(b + 2)$

48. $(a + 2b)(a - 2b)(a + 2)$

49. $(m + 4)(m - 4)(n + p)$

50. $(x + z)(2y + z - x)$

ORAL EXERCISES

Tell which technique you would use first to factor each expression.

a. Group the terms.　　**b.** Rearrange the terms.　　**c.** Remove a common monomial factor.

1. $3a + a^2 + 2$　b

2. $3x^2 - 12$　c

3. $y^3 + y^2 - y - 1$　a

4. $3b^3 - 12b$　c

5. $9 + m^2 - 6m$　b

6. $mx^2 - my^2 + nx^2 - ny^2$

7. $2n + n^2 - 24$　b

8. $-x^2 + 8x - 16$　c

9. $2x^2 - 2y^2 + 5x^2 - 5y^2$

WRITTEN EXERCISES

A.　Factor completely.

1. $6a^2 - 21a - 12$　$3(2a + 1)(a - 4)$

2. $2b^2 + 10b - 28$　$2(b + 7)(b - 2)$

3. $2n^2 + 10n + 8$　$2(n + 4)(n + 1)$

4. $4m^2 + 26m - 14$　$2(2m - 1)(m + 7)$

5. $5n^2 + 20n - 60$　$5(n - 2)(n + 6)$

6. $-x^2 - 14x - 13$　$-1(x + 13)(x + 1)$

7. $64a^2 - 1$　$(8a + 1)(8a - 1)$

8. $12y^2 - 10y - 12$　$2(3y + 2)(2y - 3)$

9. $-2b + 1 + b^2$　$(b - 1)^2$

10. $18x^2 + 21x - 9$　$3(3x - 1)(2x + 3)$

11. $3n^2 - 3n$　$3n(n - 1)$

12. $3y^2 + 15y + 18$　$3(y + 3)(y + 2)$

B.　13. $-3x + x^2 - 18$　$(x - 6)(x + 3)$

14. $2a^3 - 20a^2 + 18a$　$2a(a - 9)(a - 1)$

15. $6y^3 - 3y^2 - 30y$　$3y(2y - 5)(y + 2)$

16. $12m^2 + 33m - 9$　$3(4m - 1)(m + 3)$

17. $8a^3 + 2a^2 - 6a$　$2a(4a - 3)(a + 1)$

18. $3n^3 - 27n$　$3n(n + 3)(n - 3)$

19. $3a^2 + 6a - 24$　$3(a + 4)(a - 2)$

20. $6x^3 + 3x^2 - 3x$　$3x(2x - 1)(x + 1)$

21. $4y^2 - 24y + 20$　$4(y - 5)(y - 1)$

22. $2b^2 + 12b - 80$　$2(b + 10)(b - 4)$

23. $3m^3 - 33m^2 + 84m$　$3m(m - 7)(m - 4)$

24. $4a^2 - 32a + 60$　$4(a - 3)(a - 5)$

25. $2n^2 + 14n + 24$　$2(n + 3)(n + 4)$

26. $a^4 - b^4$　$(a^2 + b^2)(a + b)(a - b)$

27. $(m - 7)^2 - 4$　$(m - 5)(m - 9)$

28. $5a^2 - 45$　$5(a + 3)(a - 3)$

29. $3x^4 - 24x^2 + 48$　$3(x + 2)^2(x - 2)^2$

30. $3y^2 + 8y + 4$　$(3y + 2)(y + 2)$

31. $b^2 - 6b + 9$　$(b - 3)^2$

32. $16 - (x + 4)^2$　$-x(x + 8)$

33. $y^4 - 17y^2 + 16$

34. $6x^2 - 15x^3$　$3x^2(2 - 5x)$

35. $3a^2 + a - 2$　$(3a - 2)(a + 1)$

36. $(b - 2)^2 - 9$　$(b + 1)(b - 5)$

37. $m^4 + 8m^2 - 9$　$(m^2 + 9)(m + 1)(m - 1)$

38. $2n^2 - 5n + 3$　$(2n - 3)(n - 1)$

39. $y^2 - 12y - 28$　$(y - 14)(y + 2)$

40. $a^4 + 6a^2 - 7$　$(a^2 + 7)(a + 1)(a - 1)$

41. $b^4 - 6b^2 - 16$　$(b^2 - 8)(b^2 + 2)$

42. $5x^2 - 80$　$5(x + 4)(x - 4)$

43. $y^3 - y$　$y(y + 1)(y - 1)$

44. $49m^2 + 70m + 25$　$(7m + 5)^2$

45. $1 - 9n^2$　$(1 + 3n)(1 - 3n)$

46. $2 - 2x^2$　$2(1 + x)(1 - x)$

47. $a^2b + 2a^2 - 100b - 200$

48. $a^3 - 4ab^2 + 2a^2 - 8b^2$

49. $m^2n + m^2p - 16n - 16p$

50. $2xy + 2yz + z^2 - x^2$

C. **51.** $\frac{1}{2}x^2 - 2x + 2$ $\frac{1}{2}(x - 2)^2$

52. $(2m + 3)^2 - (m - 1)^2$

53. $a^2 - 10a + 25 - b^2$

54. $\frac{1}{3}b^2 + 4b - 15$ $\frac{1}{3}(b + 15)(b - 3)$

55. $\frac{1}{2}y^2 + \frac{5}{2}y + 2$ $\frac{1}{2}(y + 4)(y + 1)$

56. $x^3 - x^2 - 4x + 4$ $(x + 2)(x - 2)(x - 1)$

57. $(4m^2 - 12m + 9) - m^4$

58. $n^3 + n^2 - n - 1$ $(n + 1)^2(n - 1)$

59. $(a + b)^2 - (a - b)^2$ $4ab$

60. $x^2 - (y^2 - 6y + 9)$

61. $c^2d^2 - 4c^2 + b^2d^2 - 4b^2$

62. $8x^3 + 4x^2 - 2x - 1$ $(2x + 1)^2(2x - 1)$

63. $x^2 - 2xy + y^2 - 9$

64. $4a^2 - 12a + 9 - a^4$

65. $x^4 - 10x^2 + 9$

66. $16t^8 - 8t^4 + 1$ $(2t^2 + 1)^2(2t^2 - 1)^2$

52. $(3m + 2)(m + 4)$

53. $(a - 5 + b)(a - 5 - b)$

57. $-(m^2 - 2m + 3)(m + 3)(m - 1)$

60. $(x + y - 3)(x - y + 3)$

61. $(b^2 + c^2)(d + 2)(d - 2)$

63. $(x - y + 3)(x - y - 3)$

64. $-(a^2 - 2a + 3)(a + 3)(a - 1)$

65. $(x + 3)(x - 3)(x + 1)(x - 1)$

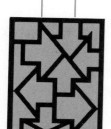

IN OTHER FIELDS
Mathematics and Art

Mathematics is sometimes considered to be highly structured and lacking in opportunities for creativity. Many people consider art to be just the opposite. However, the best practical mathematicians of the fifteenth century were the Renaissance painters, such as Leon Battista Alberti. These artists considered themselves the most learned mathematicians of that era. Alberti, in fact, wrote that the first requirement of the painter was to study geometry.

In an attempt to represent the feeling of space in their paintings, the fifteenth-century artists developed what is known as a system of perspectivity. The formulation of this system, in turn, led to a breakthrough in mathematics—the discovery of projective geometry. Desargues's theorem, fundamental to the study of projective geometry, was formulated by its discoverer in an effort to assist in the education of artists.

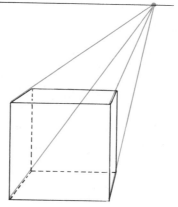

For two thousand years, people believed that euclidean geometry was the only geometry. The questions raised by the Renaissance painters regarding perspective, which euclidean geometry could not answer, led to the development of non-euclidean geometries. One of these, Riemannian geometry, later enabled Einstein to formulate his theory of relativity.

OBJECTIVE

Solve an equation by using the zero product property and factoring.

TEACHER'S NOTES

See p. T29.

CLASSROOM EXAMPLES

1. Solve $y^2 - 64 = 0$.
$$y^2 - 64 = 0$$
$$(y + 8)(y - 8) = 0$$
$$y + 8 = 0 \text{ or } y - 8 = 0$$
$$y = -8 \qquad y = 8$$
The equation $y^2 - 64 = 0$ has two solutions, -8 and 8.

2. Solve $y^2 + 8y = 0$ by factoring.
$$y^2 + 8y = 0$$
$$y(y + 8) = 0$$
$$y = 0 \text{ or } y + 8 = 0$$
$$y = -8$$
The equation $y^2 + 8y = 0$ has two solutions, 0 and -8.

3. Solve $y^2 - 13y = -40$.
$$y^2 - 13y = -40$$
$$y^2 - 13y + 40 = 0$$
$$(y - 5)(y - 8) = 0$$
$$y - 5 = 0 \text{ or } y - 8 = 0$$
$$y = 5 \qquad y = 8$$
The equation $y^2 - 13y = -40$ has two solutions, 5 and 8.

6.8 Zero Product Property

Equations can sometimes be solved by factoring. To do this, apply the **zero product property**.

Zero Product Property	If a and b are real numbers and $ab = 0$, then $a = 0$ or $b = 0$, or both a and $b = 0$.

EXAMPLES

1   **Solve $x^2 - 9 = 0$.**

SOLUTION
$$x^2 - 9 = 0$$
$$(x + 3)(x - 3) = 0 \qquad \text{Factor } x^2 - 9.$$
$$x + 3 = 0 \text{ or } x - 3 = 0 \quad \text{Zero product property}$$
$$x = -3 \qquad\qquad x = 3$$

The equation $x^2 - 9 = 0$ has two solutions, -3 and 3.

CHECK   Replace x with -3. Replace x with 3.
$$x^2 - 9 = 0$$
$$(-3)^2 - 9 \stackrel{?}{=} 0$$
$$0 = 0 ✔$$
$$x^2 - 9 = 0$$
$$3^2 - 9 \stackrel{?}{=} 0$$
$$0 = 0 ✔$$

2   **Solve $x^2 + 6x = 0$ by factoring.**

SOLUTION
$$x^2 + 6x = 0$$
$$x(x + 6) = 0 \qquad \text{Factor } x^2 + 6x.$$
$$x = 0 \text{ or } x + 6 = 0 \quad \text{Zero product property}$$
$$x = -6$$

The equation $x^2 + 6x = 0$ has two solutions, 0 and -6.

CHECK
$$x^2 + 6x = 0$$
$$0^2 + 6(0) \stackrel{?}{=} 0$$
$$0 = 0 ✔$$
$$x^2 + 6x = 0$$
$$(-6)^2 + 6(-6) \stackrel{?}{=} 0$$
$$0 = 0 ✔$$

3 Solve $x^2 - 7x = -10$.

SOLUTION $x^2 - 7x = -10$

$x^2 - 7x + 10 = 0$ *Derive an equation in which one side is 0.*

$(x - 2)(x - 5) = 0$ *Factor $x^2 - 7x + 10$.*

$x - 2 = 0$ or $x - 5 = 0$ *Zero product property*

$x = 2$ $x = 5$

The equation $x^2 - 7x = -10$ has two solutions, 2 and 5.

CHECK $x^2 - 7x = -10$

$2^2 - 7(2) + 10 \stackrel{?}{=} 0$

$4 - 14 + 10 \stackrel{?}{=} 0$

$0 = 0$ ✔

$x^2 - 7x = -10$

$5^2 - 7(5) + 10 \stackrel{?}{=} 0$

$25 - 35 + 10 \stackrel{?}{=} 0$

$0 = 0$ ✔

MIXED REVIEW

Perform the indicated operation.

1. $6x^3y(-4xy + 8y)$
   $-24x^4y^2 + 48x^3y^2$

2. $(5x^3 + 3x + 5) + (4x^2 + 5x - 7)$ $5x^3 + 4x^2 + 8x - 2$

3. $(5x^3)^2$ $25x^6$

4. $(y^2 + 3y - 40) \div (y + 8)$ $y - 5$

5. $(6y^2 - 5)(6y^2 + 5)$ $36y^4 - 25$

TEACHER'S RESOURCE MASTERS

Practice Master 27, Part 1

ASSIGNMENT GUIDE

Minimum
1–11 odd, 31–42, 49, 50

Regular
23–42

Maximum
39–52, 53–63 odd

ORAL EXERCISES

Find the missing solution for each equation.

1. $x(x + 2) = 0$; $x = 0$ or $x = \underline{-2}$

2. $y(y - 3) = 0$; $y = 3$ or $y = \underline{0}$

3. $(a + 4)(a + 5) = 0$; $a = -4$ or $a = \underline{-5}$

4. $m^2 - 4 = 0$; $m = -2$ or $m = \underline{2}$

5. $n^2 - 2n - 24 = 0$; $n = -4$ or $n = \underline{6}$

6. $a^2 + 2a - 3 = 0$; $a = 1$ or $a = \underline{-3}$

7. $y^2 = 8y$; $y = 0$ or $y = \underline{8}$

8. $4x^2 = 36$; $x = -3$ or $x = \underline{3}$

9. $x^2 = 9$; $x = 3$ or $x = \underline{-3}$

10. $y^2 = 16$; $y = -4$ or $y = \underline{4}$

11. $a^2 + a - 6 = 0$; $a = 2$ or $a = \underline{-3}$

12. $b^2 - 5b + 6 = 0$; $b = 3$ or $b = \underline{2}$

WRITTEN EXERCISES

A. Solve.

1. $x^2 - 5x + 6 = 0$ $2, 3$

2. $n^2 - 4n = 0$ $0, 4$

3. $a^2 = 100$ $-10, 10$

4. $b^2 + 7b + 10 = 0$ $-5, -2$

5. $m^2 - 5m - 6 = 0$ $-1, 6$

6. $n^2 + 3n = 0$ -3

7. $x^2 - 3x - 10 = 0$ $-2, 5$

8. $y^2 + y - 6 = 0$ $2, -3$

9. $a^2 + 7a = 0$ $-7, 0$

10. $b^2 - b - 56 = 0$ $-7, 8$

11. $m^2 - 8m - 9 = 0$ $-1, 9$

12. $n^2 - 4n - 12 = 0$ $-2, 6$

13. $x^2 - 36 = 0$ $-6, 6$

14. $y^2 - 8y - 33 = 0$ $11, -3$

15. $3a^2 = 75$ $-5, 5$

16. $4b^2 - 8b = 0$ $2, 0$

17. $m^2 = 4m + 12$ $-2, 6$ **18.** $n^2 = 6n - 9$ 3

19. $x^2 = -7x - 10$ $-5, -2$ **20.** $y^2 + 4y + 4 = 0$ -2

21. $(a + 5)(a - 5) = 0$ $5, -5$ **22.** $5a^2 + 3a - 2 = 0$ $\frac{2}{5}, -1$

B. 23. $9m^2 - 36m = 0$ $0, 4$ **24.** $n^2 - 16 = 0$ $4, -4$

25. $x^2 + 4x + 3 = 0$ $-1, -3$ **26.** $3y^2 - 2 = y^2 + 6$ $-2, 2$

27. $a^2 = 7a$ $0, 7$ **28.** $b^2 + 5b + 4 = 0$ $-4, -1$

29. $m^2 - 6m + 9 = 0$ 3 **30.** $n^2 - 5n + 6 = 0$ $2, 3$

31. $x^2 + x - 12 = 0$ $-4, 3$ **32.** $y^2 - 8y + 16 = 0$ 4

33. $b^2 + 7b = -12$ $-4, -3$ **34.** $a^2 - 8a = 0$ $0, 8$

35. $x^2 + 12x = 0$ $0, -12$ **36.** $y^2 - 7y = -10$ $2, 5$

37. $m^2 = 3 - 2m$ $-3, 1$ **38.** $7n^2 - 28n = 0$ $0, 4$

39. $a^2 + 16 = 8a$ 4 **40.** $b^2 + 25 = 10b$ 5

41. $2y^2 - 4y = 48$ $-4, 6$ **42.** $5x^2 + 10x = 40$ $-4, 2$

43. $3x^2 - 14x + 11 = 0$ $3\frac{2}{3}, 1$ **44.** $5y^2 = 3y + 2$ $-\frac{2}{5}, 1$

45. $6m^2 + 11m = -4$ $-1\frac{1}{3}, -\frac{1}{2}$ **46.** $2n^2 - 17n + 21 = 0$ $1\frac{1}{2}, 7$

47. $6x^2 + x = 15$ $-1\frac{2}{3}, 1\frac{1}{2}$ **48.** $24y^2 + 26y - 63 = 0$ $-2\frac{1}{4}, 1\frac{1}{6}$

49. $10a^2 - 11a + 3 = 0$ $\frac{3}{5}, \frac{1}{2}$ **50.** $5b^2 + 12b + 7 = 0$ $-1\frac{2}{5}, -1$

51. $15m^2 = 13m + 20$ $-\frac{4}{5}, 1\frac{2}{3}$ **52.** $3n^2 + 7n = 0$ $-2\frac{1}{3}, 0$

C. 53. $(x + 2)^2 - 5(x + 2) = 6$ $4, -3$ **54.** $(y - 1)^2 - 5(y - 1) + 6 = 0$ $3, 4$

55. $(a + 3)^2 - (a + 3) - 12 = 0$ $1, -6$ **56.** $b^3 - 13b^2 + 36b = 0$ $0, 4, 9$

57. $3n^3 + 2n^2 = n$ $-1, 0, \frac{1}{3}$ **58.** $m^3 + m^2 = 4m + 4$ $-2, -1, 2$

59. $3a^5 = 27a^3$ $-3, 0, 3$ **60.** $b^3 - 2b^2 = 15b$ $-3, 0, 5$

61. $(9x^2 - 1) - (4x^2 - 1) = 45$ **62.** $6y^2 + 5y - 4 - 3(y^2 + y - 2) = 18$

63. $(x - 5)(x + 5) - (x - 5)^2 = 10(x - 5)$ **64.** $(2x - 3)(x + 4) = (2x + 1)(x + 2)$

CHALLENGE

Prove that the product of any four consecutive positive integers plus 1 is always a perfect square.

6.9 | Problem Solving

You have seen that factoring can sometimes be used to find the solution set of an equation. It is often advantageous to solve problems by writing an equation and then factoring a polynomial within the equation to find the answer.

EXAMPLE

If a rectangular patio is to have an area of 80 square feet and the length of the patio is to be 6 feet less than twice the width, what must the width be? What will the length be?

Understand: *Given:* The patio is rectangular in shape.
The area of the patio is to be 80 square feet.
The length of the patio is to be 6 feet less than twice the width.

To find: the length and the width of the patio

Plan: Let w = the width of the patio in feet.
Then $2w - 6$ = the length of the patio in feet.
The formula for finding the area of a rectangle is $A = l \cdot w$.
Thus, the equation to be used is $80 = (2w - 6) \cdot w$.

Solve:
$80 = (2w - 6)w$
$80 = 2w^2 - 6w$
$40 = w^2 - 3w$ *Divide both sides by 2.*
$0 = w^2 - 3w - 40$ *Derive an equation in which one side is 0.*
$0 = (w - 8)(w + 5)$ *Factor $w^2 - 3w - 40$.*
$w = 8$ or $w = -5$

Answer: A rectangle cannot be -5 feet wide, so it must be 8 feet wide. Its length is $2w - 6$, or 10 feet.

Check: Is the length (10 feet) 6 feet less than twice the width (8 feet)? Is 80 square feet the area of a rectangle with a length of 10 feet and a width of 8 feet?

ORAL EXERCISES

Tell the equation you would use to solve each problem.

1. The length of a rectangular pier is 5 times its width. The area of the pier is 45 square feet. Find the length and the width. $45 = 5w \cdot w$

2. The rectangular floor of a room has an area of 140 square feet. The length is 6 feet less than twice the width. Find the length and the width. $140 = (2w - 6)w$

3. The area of a rectangular floor is 260 square feet. The length of the floor is 4 feet less than 3 times the width. Find the length and the width. $260 = (3w - 4)w$

5. The length of a rectangular deck is 2 meters greater than its width. If the area of the deck is 35 square meters, what are the length and the width?

4. The length of a corridor is 5 feet less than 5 times the width. If the area of the corridor is 60 square feet, what are the length and the width? $60 = (5w - 5)w$

6. The width of a rectangular vegetable garden is 3 meters less than its length. The area of the garden is 70 square meters. Find the length and the width.

WRITTEN EXERCISES

A. Solve.

1. Marion wants to build a rectangular patio, using concrete tiles that measure 1 foot square. There are 120 such tiles. If the length of the patio is to be 8 feet less than twice the width, what must the length and the width of the patio be?

2. Loretta's house has a square patio. She wants to enlarge it by 5 feet on one side and by 2 feet on the other side. If the area of the enlarged patio will be 130 square feet, what is the length of a side of the original patio?   8 feet

B. 3. One year, Josef put in a rectangular garden, with its length 5 feet more than its width. The next year, he increased the length by 3 feet and decreased the width by 2 feet. If the area of the second garden was 119 square feet, was the second garden larger or smaller than the first?

4. A photograph is 7 inches long and 5 inches wide. It is surrounded by a border of uniform width. If the area of the border alone is 64 square inches, what is the border's width?   2 inches

C. 5. Paul owns a boat that is $15\frac{1}{2}$ feet long. He wants to store it in a shed that has a floor in the shape of a rectangle. The area of the floor is 176 square feet. If the length of the floor is 5 feet greater than the width, will the boat fit in the shed?   yes

6. Jeanette asked her math teacher how old she was. Her math teacher replied, "If 10 times my age in 15 years is subtracted from the square of my present age, the result is 149." How old is Jeanette's math teacher?   23 years old

CAREER
Photographer

Photographers use cameras and film to take photographs of people, places, and events. They may own several cameras and lenses. Some photographers develop and print their own photographs.

Before taking a photograph, photographers adjust parts of their cameras to control the flow of light onto the film. The *shutter speed setting* controls the length of time that the shutter remains open. Each setting either almost doubles or halves the exposure time of an adjacent setting. Notice that the shutter settings allow light exposure from 1/1000 sec to 2 sec.

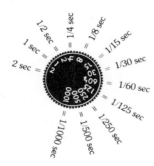

The *aperture* controls the size of the opening through which light enters the camera onto the film. The size of an aperture is measured by f-stops. Each next higher f-stop decreases the light flow by half. Similarly, each next lower f-stop doubles the light flow. Notice that the smallest f-stop has the largest aperture.

NOTE: The smaller the number, the larger the aperture.

Suppose a photographer wants to double the exposure. The shutter is set at 125 and the f-stop is set at 16. How can the camera setting be changed?

Suppose a photographer wants to decrease the exposure by half. The shutter is set at 250 and the f-stop is set at 8. How can the camera setting be changed?

CAREER

Set the shutter at 60 or set the f-stop at 11.

Set the shutter at 500 or set the f-stop at 11.

SKILLS MAINTENANCE

Solve each equation.

1. $-7 + x = 9$ 16

2. $y - 5 = -11$ -6

3. $a + 35 = -19$ -54

4. $23 + b = 34$ 11

5. $13s = 78$ 6

6. $\frac{t}{9} = \frac{2}{3}$ 6

7. $-18 = -4r$ 4.5

8. $2.1x = 31.5$ 15

9. $\frac{9}{10}b = 45$ 50

10. $-6x - 3x = 27$ -3

11. $\frac{3}{10}x + \frac{9}{10}x = 6$ 5

12. $a + 3a = 14$ $3\frac{1}{2}$

13. $\frac{2}{3}x - 8 = 4$ 18

14. $8 - 9x = 20$ $-1\frac{1}{3}$

15. $4 - y = 5y - 20$ 4

Rename each rational number as a terminating decimal or a repeating decimal, using a bar to indicate which digits repeat.

16. $\frac{7}{20}$ 0.35

17. $\frac{6}{11}$ $0.\overline{54}$

18. $\frac{8}{9}$ $0.\overline{8}$

19. $\frac{11}{12}$ $0.91\overline{6}$

20. $-\frac{2}{3}$ $-0.\overline{6}$

21. $-\frac{5}{6}$ $-0.8\overline{3}$

22. $\frac{13}{25}$ 0.52

23. $\frac{17}{10}$ 1.7

Solve each inequality.

24. $x + 8 > -5$ $x > -13$

25. $y - 7 \leq 0$ $y \leq 7$

26. $\frac{a}{3} < \frac{3}{4}$ $a < \frac{9}{4}$

27. $\frac{4b}{5} \geq -12$ $b \geq -15$

28. $-6r > 3$ $r < -\frac{1}{2}$

29. $-5t \leq -20$ $t \geq 4$

Solve each conjunction or disjunction. Graph the solution set.

30. $3x < 6$ or $5x > 25$ $x < 2$ or $x > 5$

31. $4y \geq 4$ and $3y \leq 9$ $1 \leq y \leq 3$

32. $-4b > 2$ and $-b < 4$ $-4 < b < -\frac{1}{2}$

33. $-3t > 3$ or $-2t < -4$ $t < -1$ or $t > 2$

Multiply.

34. $x(x + 5)$ $x^2 + 5x$

35. $-4a(a - 1)$ $-4a^2 + 4a$

36. $a(a - b + c)$ $a^2 - ab + ac$

37. $-r(st - rt)$ $-rst + r^2t$

38. $(x + 6)(x - 6)$ $x^2 - 36$

39. $(2y + 3)(2y - 3)$ $4y^2 - 9$

40. $(8 + a)(8 - a)$ $64 - a^2$

41. $(3b + 2)(3b - 2)$ $9b^2 - 4$

42. $(3b + 4)(2b - 3)$ $6b^2 - b - 12$

43. $(y - 3z)(y - 5z)$ $y^2 - 8yz + 15z^2$

44. $(7 - x)(5 + x)$ $35 + 2x - x^2$

45. $(6 + x)(8 - 3x)$ $48 - 10x - 3x^2$

Solve.

46. A television set costs $595 plus $35.70 in sales tax. Find the sales-tax rate. 6%

47. A bookstore employee is allowed 30% off the list price of any book purchase. How much does the employee pay for a $21 book? $14.70

48. An employee received an 8% pay raise. Before the raise, her monthly salary was $1900. What is her monthly salary after the raise? $2052

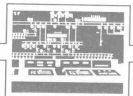

COMPUTER

What are the prime factors, if any, of 49,105? What about 31,063? Or an even larger number, like 7,932,156? Identifying prime numbers or prime factors of nonprime numbers can be an enormous task without the help of a computer. In fact, mathematicians today are using mainframe computers in a search for the largest prime number.

Enter the following program. Then RUN it.

```
10 REM PRIME FACTORIZATION
20 DIM PR(25)
30 LET A = 0
40 INPUT "ENTER A NUMBER: ";N: IF N = 2 THEN 80
50 LET X = 2
60 IF N / X = INT (N / X) THEN PR(A) = X: A = A + 1: N =
   N / X: GOTO 50
70 LET X = X + 1: IF X < = SQR(N) THEN 60
80 IF A = 0 THEN PRINT "THERE ARE NO FACTORS FOR ";N:
   PRINT: GOTO 30
90 PRINT "PRIME FACTORS ARE ";: FOR I = 0 TO (A - 1):
   PRINT PR(I);" * ";: NEXT I: PRINT N: PRINT: GOTO 30
```

EXERCISES

1. Analyze the program, in particular, lines 50, 60, and 70. How does the computer store each prime factor as it is found?

2. This program identifies prime factors. Write another program, based on this program, that identifies prime numbers.

CHAPTER 6 REVIEW

VOCABULARY

composite number (6.1)

constant (6.5)

linear term (6.5)

perfect-square trinomial (6.4)

prime number (6.1)

prime polynomial (6.2)

quadratic term (6.5)

removing the greatest common monomial factor (6.2)

unique factoring property (6.1)

zero product property (6.8)

REVIEW EXERCISES

6.1   **Give the prime factorization of each integer. Express the result in exponential form.**

     1. 108 $2^2 \cdot 3^3$ **2.** -130 $-1 \cdot 2 \cdot 5 \cdot 13$ **3.** 225 $3^2 \cdot 5^2$

     Find the greatest common factor of each pair of integers.

     4. $75, 45$ 15 **5.** $42, 56$ 14 **6.** $60, 210$ 30

     Find the least common multiple of each pair of integers.

     7. $16, 20$ 80 **8.** $50, 125$ 250 **9.** $15, 35$ 105

6.2   **Name the greatest common monomial factor.**

     10. $15x + 20$ 5 **11.** $18x^2 - 4x$ $2x$ **12.** $2y^2 + 4y - 8$ 2

     Name the common binomial factor.

     13. $a(x + y) + b(x + y)$ $(x + y)$ **14.** $(c + d)r - (c + d)s$ $(c + d)$

     Factor completely.

                                                      $2a^2(2a - 3)$

     15. $6a^2 + 2$ $2(3a^2 + 1)$ **16.** $2x - 6y$ $2(x - 3y)$ **17.** $4a^3 - 6a^2$

6.3   **18.** $x^2 - y^2$ $(x + y)(x - y)$ **19.** $9a^2 - 16$ $(3a + 4)(3a - 4)$

     20. $4x^2 - 25y^2$ $(2x + 5y)(2x - 5y)$ **21.** $36s^2 - 49t^2$ $(6s + 7t)(6s - 7t)$

6.4   **22.** $a^2 - 12a + 36$ $(a - 6)^2$ **23.** $c^2 + 6cd + 9d^2$ $(c + 3d)^2$

     24. $4x^2 - 20x + 25$ $(2x - 5)^2$ **25.** $16s^2 + 40st + 25t^2$ $(4s + 5t)^2$

6.5   **26.** $x^2 - 14x + 13$ $(x - 13)(x - 1)$ **27.** $y^2 + 5y + 6$ $(y + 3)(y + 2)$

     28. $a^2 + 4a - 32$ $(a + 8)(a - 4)$ **29.** $c^2 - 6c - 16$ $(c - 8)(c + 2)$

6.6   **30.** $2x^2 - 3x - 2$ $(2x + 1)(x - 2)$ **31.** $5d^2 + 3d - 2$ $(5d - 2)(d + 1)$

     32. $3a^2 - 8a + 4$ $(3a - 2)(a - 2)$ **33.** $8x^2 - 14x - 15$ $(2x - 5)(4x + 3)$

6.7   **34.** $6t^2 - 12t + 6$ $6(t - 1)^2$ **35.** $a^2b - 3ab - 4b$ $b(a - 4)(a + 1)$

     36. $x^3 - 8x^2 - 20x$ $x(x + 2)(x - 10)$ **37.** $8b^2 - 32$ $8(b + 2)(b - 2)$

     38. $a^4 - b^4$ $(a^2 + b^2)(a + b)(a - b)$ **39.** $2z^2 - 8z + 8$ $2(z - 2)^2$

6.8 **Solve.**

40. $x^2 - 6x = 0$ 0, 6

41. $y^2 + 12y + 36 = 0$ -6

42. $a^2 - 25 = 0$ $-5, 5$

43. $2t^2 - 10t = 12$ $-1, 6$

44. $n^2 - 14n = -49$ 7

45. $5x^2 = 3x + 2$ $-\frac{2}{5}, 1$

6.9 **46.** The length of a rectangular driveway is 1 meter more than 3 times its width. If its area is 80 square meters, what are the length and the width of the driveway?

47. A picture is 18 inches long and 12 inches wide. It is surrounded by a border of uniform width that has an area of 99 square inches. What is the width of the border? $1\frac{1}{2}$ inches

ERROR SEARCH

Find the error in each exercise and give the correct answer.

1.
$$x^2 - 2x = 8$$
$$x^2 - 2x - 8 = 0$$
$$(x + 4)(x - 2) = 0$$
$$x + 4 = 0 \text{ or } x - 2 = 0$$
$$x = -4 \qquad x = 2$$

2.
$$b^2 + 4 = 5b$$
$$b^2 + 5b + 4 = 0$$
$$(b + 4)(b + 1) = 0$$
$$b + 4 = 0 \text{ or } b + 1 = 0$$
$$b = -4 \qquad b = -1$$

3. $7a^3 - a^3 - a^2 - 2a = 0$
$$a(6a^2 - a - 2) = 0$$
$$a(3a - 2)(2a - 1) = 0$$
$$a = 0 \text{ or } 3a - 2 = 0 \text{ or } 2a - 1 = 0$$
$$3a = 2 \qquad 2a = 1$$
$$a = \frac{2}{3} \qquad a = \frac{1}{2}$$

4.
$$9(x^2 + x) = 4$$
$$9x^2 + 9x = 4$$
$$9x^2 + 9x - 4 = 0$$
$$(3x + 1)(3x - 4) = 0$$
$$3x + 1 = 0 \text{ or } 3x - 4 = 0$$
$$3x = -1 \qquad 3x = 4$$
$$x = -\frac{1}{3} \qquad x = \frac{4}{3}$$

TEACHER'S RESOURCE
MASTERS

Chapter 6 Test

Multiple-Choice Test

PROBLEM–SOLVING
HANDBOOK

p. 532

ADDITIONAL ANSWERS

12. $x + y$

30. $-1\frac{1}{2}, 1\frac{1}{4}$

CHAPTER 6 TEST

Give the prime factorization of each integer. Express the result in exponential form.

1. 165 $3 \cdot 5 \cdot 11$ **2.** 270 $2 \cdot 3^3 \cdot 5$ **3.** 360 $2^3 \cdot 3^2 \cdot 5$

Find the greatest common factor of each pair of integers.

4. 36, 96 12   **5.** 48, 150 6   **6.** 140, 84 28

Find the least common multiple of each pair of integers.

7. 24, 40 120   **8.** 12, 30 60   **9.** 5, 18 90

Name the common factor.

10. $5xy - 20xz$ $5x$ **11.** $12ab + 18bc$ $6b$ **12.** $a(x + y) + b(x + y)$

Factor completely.

13. $x^2 - b^2$ $(x + b)(x - b)$ **14.** $y^2 - 25$ $(y + 5)(y - 5)$

15. $4x^2 - y^2$ $(2x + y)(2x - y)$ **16.** $c^2 + 8c + 16$ $(c + 4)^2$

17. $9a^2 + 30a + 25$ $(3a + 5)^2$ **18.** $36s^2 - 60st + 25t^2$ $(6s - 5t)^2$

19. $s^2 + 8s + 15$ $(s + 3)(s + 5)$ **20.** $x^2 - 7x + 6$ $(x - 6)(x - 1)$

21. $t^2 - t - 12$ $(t - 4)(t + 3)$ **22.** $2a^2 - 17a + 21$ $(2a - 3)(a - 7)$

23. $3b^2 - 13b + 14$ $(3b - 7)(b - 2)$ **24.** $6x^2 - 13x + 6$ $(2x - 3)(3x - 2)$

25. $5pq^2 - 20p$ $5p(q + 2)(q - 2)$ **26.** $2y^2 - 8y + 8$ $2(y - 2)^2$

27. $t^4 - 3t^2 + 2$ $(t^2 - 2)(t + 1)(t - 1)$

Solve.

28. $4t^2 - 16t = 0$ 0, 4   **29.** $x^2 - 11x + 18 = 0$ 2, 9 **30.** $8a^2 + 2a - 15 = 0$

31. The length of a rectangle is 4 centimeters more than three times its width, and its area is 64 square centimeters. Find the length and the width of the rectangle. 4 cm wide, 16 cm long

32. A block of 96 theater seats was reserved. The number of seats in each row was 4 less than the number of rows. Find the number of rows and the number of seats in each row. 12 rows, 8 seats in each row

CHAPTER 7

Relations and Functions

A skier's velocity at 1 second is 5 meters per second and at 3 seconds is 10 meters per second. What is the skier's velocity at 4 seconds? (Assume the skier is accelerating at a constant rate.)   12.5 meters per second

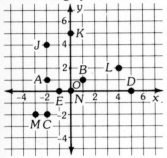

a. Name the ordered pair for each point: A, B, C, D, E.

Point	Ordered pair
A	(−2, 1)
B	(1, 1)
C	(−2, −2)
D	(5, 0)
E	(−1, 0)

b. Name the point for each ordered pair: (−2, 4), (0, 5), (4, 2), (−3, −2), (0, 0).

Ordered pair	Point
(−2, 4)	J
(0, 5)	K
(4, 2)	L
(−3, −2)	M
(0, 0)	N

7.1 Ordered Pairs and the Coordinate Plane

On a digital clock, 10:12 and 12:10 represent different times. The order in which the numbers are listed is important.

In algebra, any pair of numbers may be represented by using the variables x and y. The pair of numbers may be written as (x, y). Such a pair of numbers is called an **ordered pair.** The first number is called the **x-coordinate** or **abscissa.** The second number is called the **y-coordinate** or **ordinate.**

As was shown in Chapter 2, any real number can be graphed on a number line. Any ordered pair of real numbers can be graphed in a plane by using two perpendicular real-number lines that intersect at their 0-points.

The horizontal number line is called the **x-axis.** The *positive* direction is to the *right,* and the *negative* direction is to the *left.* The vertical number line is called the **y-axis.** The *positive* direction is *up,* and the *negative* direction is *down.* The 0-point on both number lines is called the **origin.** It is labeled O or $(0, 0)$.

Together, the x-axis and the y-axis are called the **axes.** The axes determine a plane, called the **coordinate plane.**

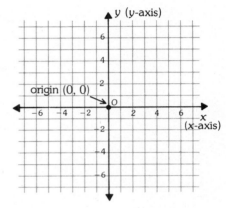

The **graph** of an ordered pair (x, y) is a *point* on the coordinate plane. The numbers in an ordered pair are called the **coordinates** of the point they locate.

EXAMPLES

| 1 | Graph (2, 6) and (6, 2). |

SOLUTION

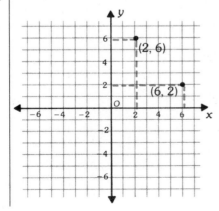

Since (2, 6) means $x = 2$ and $y = 6$, locate by going 2 units to the right, then 6 units up. Since (6, 2) means $x = 6$ and $y = 2$, locate by going 6 units to the right, then 2 units up.

2 | Use the graph at the right.

a. Name the ordered pair for each point:
A, J, D, G, E.

b. Name the point for each ordered pair:
$(-4, 3)$, $(0, -3)$, $(-4, -3)$, $(0, 0)$, $(-4, 0)$.

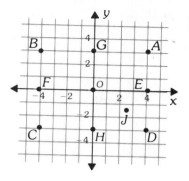

MIXED REVIEW

Restate each decimal as a fraction.

1. $0.\overline{53}$ $\frac{53}{99}$

2. $0.1\overline{48}$ $\frac{147}{990}$

3. Solve $5x - 12 = 3(x + 4)$.   12

4. Evaluate $\frac{12s^2}{t}$ if $s = 4$ and $t = -4$. -48

5. Complete. $|-25| =$ 25

TEACHER'S RESOURCE MASTERS

Practice Master 28, Part 1

ASSIGNMENT GUIDE

Minimum
1–43 odd

Regular
28–49

Maximum
31–39, 43–55

SOLUTIONS

a.
Point	Ordered pair
A	$(4, 3)$
J	$\left(2\frac{1}{2}, -1\frac{1}{2}\right)$
D	$(4, -3)$
G	$(0, 3)$
E	$(4, 0)$

b.
Ordered pair	Point
$(-4, 3)$	B
$(0, -3)$	H
$(-4, -3)$	C
$(0, 0)$	O
$(-4, 0)$	F

The axes separate the coordinate plane into four **quadrants,** numbered as shown. Points on the axes are in none of the quadrants.

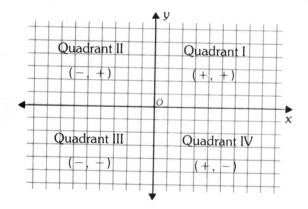

ORAL EXERCISES

In which quadrant or on which axis will (x, y) be graphed if

1. $x > 0$ and $y > 0$?   first

2. $x < 0$ and $y < 0$?   third

3. $x > 0$ and $y < 0$?   fourth

4. $x < 0$ and $y > 0$?   second

5. $x = 0$?   y-axis

6. $y = 0$?   x-axis

28.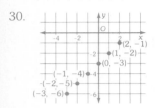

30.

32.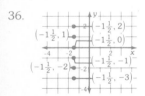

34.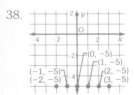

36.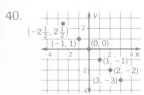

38.

40.

Complete.

7. The point that is on both of the axes is called the _____origin_____.

8. The x-axis and the y-axis determine the _____coordinate_____ plane.

9. The first coordinate of an ordered pair is called the _____x-coordinate_____ or the _____abscissa_____.

10. The second coordinate of an ordered pair is called the _____y-coordinate_____ or the _____ordinate_____.

WRITTEN EXERCISES

A. Name the point for each ordered pair.

1. (3, 4) *A*	**2.** (−1, 5) *F*
3. (0, 2) *C*	**4.** (2, 0) *H*
5. (1, −3) *G*	**6.** (4, 3) *B*
7. (−6, −1) *K*	**8.** (−2, −4) *I*
9. (0, 0) *O*	**10.** (0, −3) *L*
11. (−3, 0) *J*	**12.** (3, −3) *D*

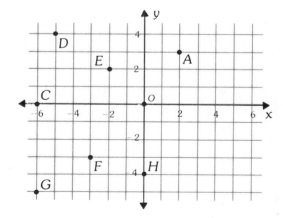

Name the ordered pair for each point.

13. *A* (2, 3)	**14.** *O* (0, 0)
15. *C* (−6, 0)	**16.** *D* (−5, 4)
17. *E* (−2, 2)	**18.** *F* (−3, −3)
19. *G* (−6, −5)	**20.** *H* (0, −4)

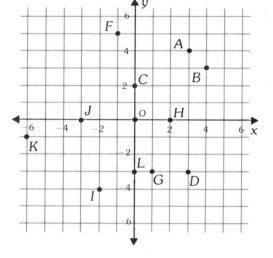

B. Which points from exercises 13–20 are

21. in Quadrant I? *A*

22. in Quadrant II? *D, E*

23. in Quadrant III? *F, G*

24. in Quadrant IV? none

25. on the x-axis? *O, C*

26. on the y-axis? *O, H*

27. on both axes? *O*

Graph the sets of ordered pairs, using separate axes for each exercise.

28. {(0, 2), (0, 1), (0, 0), (0, −1), (0, −2), (0, −3)}

29. {(1, 2), (2, 4), (3, 6), (4, 8), (5, 10), (6, 12)}

30. {(2, −1), (1, −2), (0, −3), (−1, −4), (−2, −5), (−3, −6)}

31. {(−3, 2), (−3, 1), (−3, 0), (−3, −1), (−3, −2), (−3, −3)}

32. {(3, 0), (2, 0), (1, 0), (0, 0), (−1, 0), (−2, 0)}

33. {(0, 2), (1, 1), (2, 0), (3, −1), (4, −2), (5, −3)}

34. {(−4, 5), (−2, 4), (0, 3), (2, 2), (4, 1), (6, 0)}

35. {(8, −9), (6, −6), (4, −3), (2, 0), (−2, 3), (−4, 6)}

36. $\left\{\left(-1\frac{1}{2}, 2\right), \left(-1\frac{1}{2}, 1\right), \left(-1\frac{1}{2}, 0\right), \left(-1\frac{1}{2}, -1\right), \left(-1\frac{1}{2}, -2\right), \left(-1\frac{1}{2}, -3\right)\right\}$

37. $\left\{\left(2, \frac{1}{2}\right), \left(1, \frac{1}{2}\right), \left(0, \frac{1}{2}\right), \left(-1, \frac{1}{2}\right), \left(-2, \frac{1}{2}\right), \left(-3, \frac{1}{2}\right)\right\}$

38. {(3, −5), (2, −5), (1, −5), (0, −5), (−1, −5), (−2, −5)}

39. $\left\{(3, 3), (2, 2), (1, 1), (0, 0), (−1, −1), \left(-2\frac{1}{2}, -2\frac{1}{2}\right)\right\}$

40. $\left\{(3, −3), (2, −2), (1, −1), (0, 0), (−1, 1), \left(-2\frac{1}{2}, 2\frac{1}{2}\right)\right\}$

Refer to your graphs from exercises 28–40 to answer exercises 41–42.

41. If a point is on the y-axis, what is its x-coordinate? 0

42. If a point is on the x-axis, what is its y-coordinate? 0

C. For each of the following exercises, find five ordered pairs such that when the *x* value and the *y* value are substituted into the equation, a true statement is formed. Graph these ordered pairs.

43. $y = x$

44. $y = -x$

45. $y = x + 1$

46. $y = x - 1$

47. $y = -x + 1$

48. $y = -x - 1$

49. $y = 2x + 1$

50. $y = 3x - 2$

51. $y = -2x + 3$

52. $y = -\frac{1}{2}x + 4$

53. $y = \frac{1}{2}x + 4$

54. $y = \frac{1}{2}x$

55. In exercises 43–54, what seems to be true if you were to connect the points for the ordered pairs of each graph? The points form a straight line.

44.

46.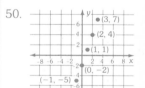

48.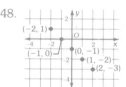

50.

52.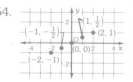

54.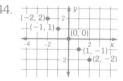

OBJECTIVES

Graph a linear equation in two variables by solving the equation for y and making a table of at least three solutions.

Write a linear equation in two variables in standard form.

TEACHER'S NOTES

See p. T29.

CLASSROOM EXAMPLES

1. Graph $2x - y = 4$.

   Solve for y.

   $2x - y = 4$

   $-y = -2x + 4$

   $y = 2x - 4$

   Make a table.

   $y = 2x - 4$

Let x =	Then y =
-1	$2(-1) - 4 = -6$
0	$2(0) - 4 = -4$
2	$2(2) - 4 = 0$

   Graph.

   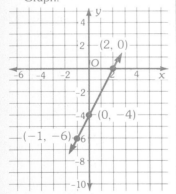

2. Write the equation
   $2x - y = 6 + x - 3y$
   in standard form.

   $2x - y = 6 + x - 3y$

   $2x - y - x + 3y$
   $= 6 + x - 3y - x + 3y$

   $x + 2y = 6$

7.2	Graphing Two-Variable Equations

Open sentences that contain two variables have solutions that are ordered pairs of numbers. Since ordered pairs can be graphed in the coordinate plane, you can graph equations containing two variables.

EXAMPLES

1 **Graph $3x - y = 6$.**

SOLUTION

To find an ordered pair that will make this open sentence a true statement, let x be any real number. Then solve the resulting equation for the corresponding value of y.

Let $x = 1$. Substitute this value in the equation $3x - y = 6$.

$3x - y = 6$

$3(1) - y = 6$

$3 - y = 6$

$-y = 3$

$y = -3$

So one solution is $(1, -3)$.

A more convenient way to find solutions is to first solve the equation for y.

$3x - y = 6$

$-y = -3x + 6$

$y = 3x - 6$

Next use several values for x and find the corresponding values for y, and make a table showing the ordered pairs.

$y = 3x - 6$

Let x =	Then y =	Ordered pair
0	$3(0) - 6 = -6$	$(0, -6)$
1	$3(1) - 6 = -3$	$(1, -3)$
$1\frac{1}{2}$	$3\left(1\frac{1}{2}\right) - 6 = -1\frac{1}{2}$	$\left(1\frac{1}{2}, -1\frac{1}{2}\right)$
2	$3(2) - 6 = 0$	$(2, 0)$
$2\frac{1}{2}$	$3\left(2\frac{1}{2}\right) - 6 = 1\frac{1}{2}$	$\left(2\frac{1}{2}, 1\frac{1}{2}\right)$
3	$3(3) - 6 = 3$	$(3, 3)$
4	$3(4) - 6 = 6$	$(4, 6)$
-1	$3(-1) - 6 = -9$	$(-1, -9)$

Then graph the ordered pairs in the table.

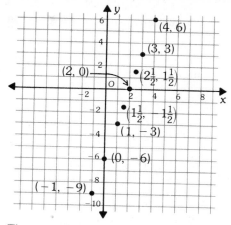

The variable x can be replaced by any real number. All points representing the solutions of $3x - y = 6$ lie on the same straight line. So the graph of $3x - y = 6$ is shown below.

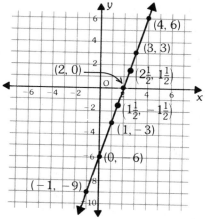

A **linear equation in two variables** is an equation whose graph in the coordinate plane is a straight line.

Any linear equation in two variables can be written in the form $ax + by = c$, where a, b, and c are real numbers, a and b are not both zero, and x and y are variables. The equation $ax + by = c$ is called the **standard form** of a linear equation. Notice that each term is a first-degree monomial or a constant.

| 2 | **Write the equation $3x - y = 7 + x - 4y$ in standard form.** |

SOLUTION $3x - y = 7 + x - 4y$

$$3x - y - x + 4y = 7 + x - 4y - x + 4y$$
$$2x + 3y = 7$$

So $a = 2$, $b = 3$, and $c = 7$.

So $a = 1$, $b = 2$, and $c = 6$.

3. Graph $2x + 3y = 6$.
   Solve for y.
   $$2x + 3y = 6$$
   $$3y = -2x + 6$$
   $$y = -\tfrac{2}{3}x + 2$$
   Make a table.
   $y = -\tfrac{2}{3}x + 2$

Let $x =$	Then $y =$
-1	$-\tfrac{2}{3}(-1) + 2$ $= 2\tfrac{2}{3}$
0	$-\tfrac{2}{3}(0) + 2$ $= 2$
1	$-\tfrac{2}{3}(1) + 2$ $= 1\tfrac{1}{3}$

   Graph.

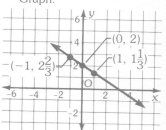

MIXED REVIEW

Perform the indicated operation.

1. $(6y^2 + 5y - 3) + (-8y^2 - 4y - 8)$ $-2y^2 + y - 11$

2. $(5y^2 - 6) - (4y^2 + 3y + 10)$ $y^2 - 3y - 16$

3. $5x^2(-3y^2)$ $-15x^2y^2$

4. $\dfrac{16x^3y}{-4xy^3}$ $-\dfrac{4x^2}{y^2}$

5. $(x^2 + 2xy + y^2) \div (x + y)$ $(x + y)$

TEACHER'S RESOURCE MASTERS

Practice Master 28, Part 2

COMPUTER SOFTWARE

Graphing Linear Equations and Inequalities

ASSIGNMENT GUIDE

Minimum
1–4, 5–25 odd, 29–31

Regular
5–13 odd, 16–27

Maximum
5–21 odd, 29–43 odd

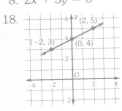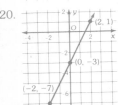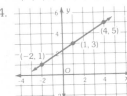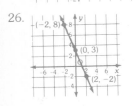
Two points determine a unique straight line. So in order to graph a linear equation, you need to find two solutions of the equation. But it is a good idea to graph at least three points as a check. If all the points do not lie on the same line, you have made an error.

3 | **Graph $2x + 3y = 7$.**

SOLUTION

Solve for y.

$$2x + 3y = 7$$
$$3y = -2x + 7$$
$$y = -\frac{2}{3}x + \frac{7}{3}$$

Make a table.

$$y = -\frac{2}{3}x + \frac{7}{3}$$

Let $x =$	Then $y =$
-1	$-\frac{2}{3}(-1) + \frac{7}{3} = 3$
0	$-\frac{2}{3}(0) + \frac{7}{3} = \frac{7}{3}$
2	$-\frac{2}{3}(2) + \frac{7}{3} = 1$

Graph.

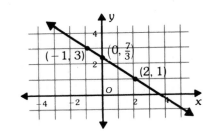

ORAL EXERCISES

Complete.

1. An equation whose graph in the coordinate plane is a straight line is called a ___linear equation___.

2. If an open sentence contains two variables, then each solution is ___an ordered pair___.

3. The graph of an ordered pair is a ___point___.

4. To graph a linear equation in two variables, it is enough to graph ___2___ solutions. But you should graph at least ___3___ as a check.

5. In a linear equation, each term is a ___first-degree___ monomial or a constant.

A. Complete each table.

1. $y = -3x + 4$

Let x =	Then y =
-2	$-3(-2) + 4 = 10$
0	$-3(0) + 4 = 4$
2	$-3(2) + 4 = -2$

2. $y = 2x - 5$

Let x =	Then y =
-3	$2(-3) - 5 = -11$
0	$2(0) - 5 = -5$
3	$2(3) - 5 = 1$

3. $y = \frac{1}{2}x + 1$

Let x =	Then y =
-2	$\frac{1}{2}(-2) + 1 = 0$
0	$\frac{1}{2}(0) + 1 = 1$
2	$\frac{1}{2}(2) + 1 = 2$

4. $y = -\frac{2}{3}x + \frac{5}{3}$

Let x =	Then y =
-2	$-\frac{2}{3}(-2) + \frac{5}{3} = 3$
1	$-\frac{2}{3}(1) + \frac{5}{3} = 1$
4	$-\frac{2}{3}(4) + \frac{5}{3} = -1$

B. Write each equation in standard form.

5. $3x = -2y + 8$ $3x + 2y = 8$

6. $2y + x = 3x - 4$ $-2x + 2y = -4$

7. $x - y + 6 = 10$ $x - y = 4$

8. $5x - y + 2 = 3x - 6y + 8$

9. $x + y = 2 + x$ $0x + y = 2$ or $y = 2$

10. $x - 1 = 3y + 4x$ $-3x - 3y = 1$

11. $7x - 3x + y = 2 - 4y$ $4x + 5y = 2$

12. $x + 3 = 0$ $x + 0y = -3$ or $x = -3$

13. $y - 9 = 7$ $y = 16$

14. $5x + 2y = 2y - 8$ $5x = -8$

15. $12 - x = y - x$ $y = 12$

16. $\frac{1}{2}x - \frac{1}{4}y = -x + 1$ $\frac{3}{2}x - \frac{1}{4}y = 1$

Find three solutions for each equation. Then draw the graph of the equation.

17. $y = 3x - 5$

18. $y = \frac{1}{2}x + 4$

19. $y = -x + 1$

20. $y = 2x - 3$

21. $y = 4x$

22. $y = -\frac{3}{4}x + \frac{1}{4}$

23. $y = \frac{1}{2}x - \frac{1}{2}$

24. $y = \frac{2}{3}x + \frac{7}{3}$

25. $y = 3x - 2$

26. $y = -\frac{5}{2}x + 3$

27. $y = -2x - 3$

28. $y = -3x + \frac{3}{2}$

C.
29. $2x - 3y = 8$

30. $3x + 2y = 5$

31. $4x - y = 7$

32. $2x + 5y = 10$

33. $-3x + 4y = 8$

34. $-5x - y = 6$

35. $3x - 2y = 6$

36. $2x + 3y = 4$

37. $4x + 4y = -6$

Graph seven solutions for each of the following:

38. $y = x^2$

39. $y = |x|$

40. $y = -|x|$

41. $y = -x^2$

42. $y = x^2 + 1$

43. $y = x^2 - 1$

44. $y = x^3 - 12$

45. $y = \frac{12}{x}$

46. $y = 3x$

28.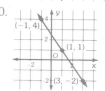

30.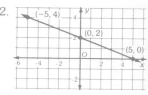

32.

34.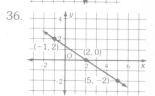

36.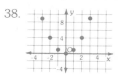

38.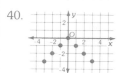

40.

Additional Answers
See p. T58.

OBJECTIVES

Identify the domain and the range of a relation.

Given a relation in a table, describe the relation as a set of ordered pairs and by a mapping.

Given a relation that is described by a set of ordered pairs, graph the relation and tell whether it is a function.

Using a given domain, list the ordered pairs in a relation described by an open sentence. Then determine whether the relation is a function.

TEACHER'S NOTES

See p. T29.

CLASSROOM EXAMPLES

1. Use four ways to represent the ordered pairs (1, 2), (2, 3), (3, 4), (4, 5) as a relation.

   List: {(1, 2), (2, 3), (3, 4), (4, 5)}

   Table:

x	y
1	2
2	3
3	4
4	5

   Mapping: *Domain   Range*

   1 ⟶ 2
   2 ⟶ 3
   3 ⟶ 4
   4 ⟶ 5

   Graph:

   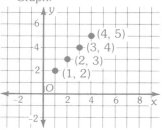

7.3 | Relations and Functions

A **relation** is any set of ordered pairs. A relation can be represented in *several ways.*

One way is to actually *list* the ordered pairs in the set. For example, the set {(1, 6), (3, 6), (3, 8)} is a relation. In a relation, the set of first elements (or *x*-coordinates) of the ordered pairs is called the **domain (D).** The set of second elements (or *y*-coordinates) is called the **range (R).** For the relation above, the domain is {1, 3} and the range is {6, 8}. Notice that the element 3 is listed only once in the domain and that the element 6 is listed only once in the range.

A second way to represent a relation is in the form of a *table.*
This table represents the relation {(1, 2), (2, 4), (3, 6)}.

x	y
1	2
2	4
3	6

A third way to represent a relation is with a *mapping.*
This mapping represents the relation {(3, 0), (9, 1), (9, 2)}.

Domain   Range

3 ⟶ 0
9 ⟶ 1
  ⟶ 2

A fourth way to represent a relation is by *graphing.*
This graph represents the relation {(1, 3), (2, 3), (1, 7), (−3, 2)}.

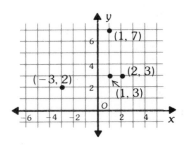

Some relations can also be represented by an open sentence in two variables. Recall that an open sentence in two variables has solutions that are ordered pairs. $y = 3x + 1$ represents a relation. If a replacement set is not specified for *x*, it is assumed to be all real numbers.

A *function* is a special relation.

Definition of Function	**A function is a relation in which each element in the domain is paired with exactly one element in the range.**

{(1, 3), (2, 3), (3, 4)}

This relation is a function.

Each *x* value is paired with exactly one *y* value.

{(1, 3), (1, 4), (3, 4)}

This relation is not a function.

The *x* value of 1 is paired with two *y* values, 3 and 4.

A simple method called the **vertical-line test** can help you determine when a relation is a function. If you can draw a vertical line at any place on the graph and it crosses more than one point of the graph, the relation is *not* a function. If a vertical line never crosses more than one point, the relation *is* a function.

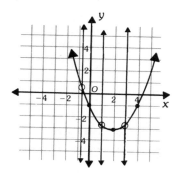

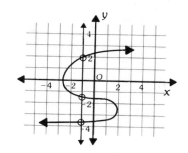

Vertical lines cross at only one point. The graph *does* represent a function.

A vertical line crosses the graph at more than one point. The graph does *not* represent a function.

ORAL EXERCISES

For each relation, state the domain and the range. Tell whether or not the relation is a function.

1. {(1, 8), (2, −3), (4, 3), (−6, 7)}

2. {(−1, 3), (−1, 2), (−1, 6)}

3. {(4, −2), (15, −2), (8, 6)}

4. {(0, 1), (−1, 1), (−1, 2), (0, 2)}

Name the ordered pairs of the mapping.

5.
```
  D      R
 −1 ──→ 5
  3 ──→ 6
  8 ←─→ 18
  2 ╲  21
      ╲→ 4
```

6.
```
  D      R
  4 ──→ 1
  2 ──→ 3
  5 ──→ 0
  4 ──→ 9
```

WRITTEN EXERCISES

A. For each relation, state the domain and the range.

1. {(3, 0), (−3, 2), (1, 6), (2, 6)}

2. $\left\{\left(\frac{4}{5}, 1\right), \left(-\frac{1}{5}, 1\right), \left(\frac{2}{5}, 2\right), \left(\frac{2}{5}, 3\right)\right\}$

3. {(0.8, 2), (1.2, 3), (1.5, 3), (2.3, 6), (2.8, 9)}

4. {(−1, 0), (−6, 1), (−5, 2), (−5, 3), (−4, 4), (−4, 5)}

5. {(1, 1), (−1, 1), (2, 2), (−2, 2), (3, 3), (−3, 3), (4, 4), (−4, 4)}

6. {(1, −1), (1, 1), (4, 2), (4, −2), (9, 3), (9, −3), (16, 4), (−16, −4)}

2. State whether or not each of the following relations is a function.

  a. {(2, 3), (3, 4), (4, 5)}
    This relation is a function.

  b. {(2, 3), (4, 3), (4, 5)}
    This relation is not a function.

MIXED REVIEW

State the property that each of the following equations illustrates.

1. $7x + 4y = 4y + 7x$
  Comm. prop. of add.

2. $mn - \frac{1}{mn} = 1$
  Inv. prop. of mult.

3. $(2a + 11b) + 7c = 2a + (11b + 7c)$
  Assoc. prop. of add.

4. $6x(11y + 5z) = 66xy + 30xz$
  Dist. prop. of mult. over add.

5. $4r^8s^6t^7 \cdot 1 = 4r^8s^6t^7$
  Ident. prop. of mult.

TEACHER'S RESOURCE MASTERS

Practice Master 29, Part 1

Quiz 13

ASSIGNMENT GUIDE

Minimum
1–39 odd

Regular
7–19 odd, 22–34

Maximum
22–35, 41–49 odd

Use the vertical-line test to determine if each relation is a function.

7.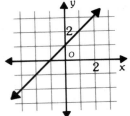

8.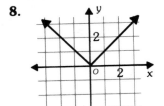

9.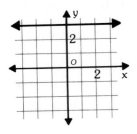

10.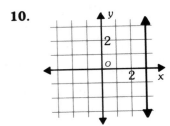

11.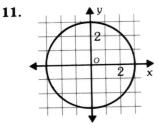

12.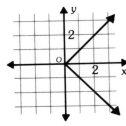

Each table below describes a relation. Describe the relation (*a*) as a set of ordered pairs, and (*b*) by a mapping. Then tell whether or not the relation is a function.

13.
x	y
2	3
8	9
16	17
64	65
128	129

14.
x	y
2	1
2	2
3	5
6	5
7	6

15.
x	y
4	7
4	8
4	9
5	2
5	3

16.
x	y
0	1
2	3
4	5
6	7
8	9
10	11

17.
x	y
1	2
2	4
3	6
4	8
5	10
6	12

18.
x	y
4	1
4	9
2	3
5	0
2	6
1	2

19.
x	y
0	1
0	2
1	1
1	3
3	6
4	7

20.
x	y
−1	3
2	4
3	3
4	6
5	3
6	4

21.
x	y
3	5
4	5
6	6
7	8
8	7
5	1

B. **Graph each relation. Tell whether or not each relation is also a function.**

22. $\{(1, 3), (-2, 6), (3, 4), (5, 1), (2, 5), (4, -1)\}$

23. $\{(1, 6), (2, 6), (3, 4), (5, -1)\}$

24. $\{(4, 1), (4, 4), (2, 1), (2, -3), (5, 7)\}$

25. $\{(3, -5), (-5, 3), (4, 2), (4, -2), (-2, 4), (2, -4)\}$

26. $\{(1, 1), (2, 2), (3, 3), (4, 4), (5, 5)\}$

27. $\{(4, 3), (5, 3), (6, 3), (7, 3), (8, 3)\}$

Let the domain for the following relations be $\{0, 1, 2, 3, 4\}$. List the ordered pairs in each relation. Then graph the relation. Is each relation a function?

28. $y = 2x + 1$ **29.** $y = 5x$ **30.** $y = |x|$

31. $y = \frac{1}{2}x$ **32.** $y = x - 4$ **33.** $y = |x - 1|$

34. $y = -x$ **35.** $y = -2x + 1$ **36.** $y = 2$

37. $y = x^2$ **38.** $y = -|x|$ **39.** $y = |-x|$

C. **Find the value of n so that the relation is *not* a function. The replacement set for n is the set of real numbers.**

Example: Let the relation be $\{(2n + 1, 4), (3n - 5, 7)\}$.

The relation will not be a function if the two x-coordinates are the same number and the y-coordinates are different. So find the value of n that *will* result in the same x-coordinate. In this case,

$$2n + 1 = 3n - 5$$
$$2n + 1 + 5 - 2n = 3n - 5 + 5 - 2n$$
$$6 = n.$$

The relation will not be a function when $n = 6$.

40. $\{(2n + 1, 4), (6n - 7, 5)\}$ $n = 2$ **41.** $\{(4n + 1, 8), (2n + 5, 9)\}$ $n = 2$

42. $\{(5n + 6, 3), (2n - 9, 4)\}$ $n = -5$ **43.** $\{(-2n + 1, -4), (-6n + 8, 0)\}$ $n = \frac{7}{4}$

44. $\{(-5n + 6, -9), (2n - 3, 15)\}$ $n = \frac{9}{7}$ **45.** $\left\{\left(\frac{4}{5}n + 3, 11\right), \left(\frac{1}{10}n - 1, -3\right)\right\}$ $n = -\frac{40}{7}$

46. $\{(n^2 + 4n + 4, 3), (n^2 - 4n + 4, -1)\}$ $n = 0$

47. $\{(n^2 + 3n + 2, -1), (n^2 + 5n + 6, 6)\}$ $n = -2$

48. $\{(n^2 - 3n + 1, 8), (n^2 + 2n, 4)\}$ $n = \frac{1}{5}$

49. $\{(4n^2 - n + 8, 0), (4n^2 + n - 1, 16)\}$ $n = \frac{9}{2}$

(b) D   *R*
2 ⟶ 3
8 ⟶ 9
16 ⟶17
64 ⟶ 65
128⟶129

yes

14. *(a)* $\{(2, 1), (2, 2), (3, 5),$
$(6, 5), (7, 6)\}$

(b) D   *R*

2   1
3   2
6   5
7 ⟶ 6

no

15. *(a)* $\{(4, 7), (4, 8), (4, 9),$
$(5, 2), (5, 3)\}$

(b) D   *R*
4   7
5   8
  9
  2
  3

no

16. *(a)* $\{(0, 1), (2, 3), (4, 5),$
$(6, 7), (8, 9), (10, 11)\}$

(b) D   *R*
0 ⟶ 1
2 ⟶ 3
4 ⟶ 5
6 ⟶ 7
8 ⟶ 9
10⟶11

yes

For the odd-numbered solutions, see *Answers To Selected Exercises*, p. 578.

Additional Answers
See p. T58.

EXPLORATION

Exercises

1. not prime

2. $37 = 1^2 + 6^2$

3. $41 = 4^2 + 5^2$

4. 3 + 11 or 7 + 7

5. 3 + 13 or 5 + 11

6. 7 + 11 or 5 + 13

7. 3 + 3 + 7 or 3 + 5 + 5

8. 3 + 5 + 7 or 5 + 5 + 5

9. 2 + 2 + 13 or 3 + 7 + 7 or 3 + 3 + 11 or 5 + 5 + 7

10. The divisors of 496 are 1, 2, 4, 8, 16, 31, 62, 124, and 248. 1 + 2 + 4 + 8 + 16 + 31 + 62 + 124 + 248 = 496

EXPLORATION
Elementary Number Theory

Much of elementary number theory involves the set of counting (natural) numbers. Mathematicians have studied many properties of numbers that deal with prime numbers.

One theorem states that a prime number in the form $4n + 1$ can be written as the sum of two square numbers in only one way.

n	$4n + 1$	
1	5	$5 = 1^2 + 2^2$
2	9	not prime
3	13	$13 = 2^2 + 3^2$
4	17	$17 = 1^2 + 4^2$

A **conjecture** is a statement that has not been proved to be true or to be false. One conjecture says that an even number greater than 4 can be expressed as a sum of two odd prime numbers.

$$6 = 3 + 3 \qquad 8 = 3 + 5 \qquad 10 = 3 + 7 \qquad 12 = 5 + 7$$

Another conjecture says that an odd number greater than 5 can be expressed as the sum of three prime numbers.

$$7 = 2 + 2 + 3 \qquad 9 = 3 + 3 + 3 \qquad 11 = 2 + 2 + 7$$

A **perfect number** is a number that is equal to the sum of its divisors, excluding the number itself.

$$6 = \underbrace{1 + 2 + 3}_{\text{divisors of 6}} \qquad 28 = \underbrace{1 + 2 + 4 + 7 + 14}_{\text{divisors of 28}}$$

EXERCISES

Use each given number as the value of n in the expression $4n + 1$ and write any resulting prime number as the sum of two square numbers.

1. 8   **2.** 9   **3.** 10

Express each number as the sum of two odd prime numbers.

4. 14   **5.** 16   **6.** 18

Express each number as the sum of three prime numbers.

7. 13   **8.** 15   **9.** 17

10. Show that 496 is a perfect number.

Functions and Functional Notation

OBJECTIVES

Use the mapping notation or the f of x notation to write a rule that defines a function.

Given the domain value, find the range value of a function that is described by the f of x notation.

Determine whether an equation describes a linear function.

From the definition of a function, you know that each element in the domain is paired with exactly one element in the range. The pairing is done through a *rule* that associates elements in the domain with elements in the range.

A rule that defines a function can be written using different notations. Two notations are the **mapping notation** and the **f of x notation**.

$f = \{(2, 4), (5, 7), (3, 9)\}$

mapping notation	f of x notation
$f{:}x \rightarrow y$	$f(x) = y$
$f{:}2 \rightarrow 4$	$f(2) = 4$
$f{:}5 \rightarrow 7$	$f(5) = 7$
$f{:}3 \rightarrow 9$	$f(3) = 9$

The notation $f{:}x \rightarrow y$ is read "f maps x to y." The notation $f(x) = y$ is read "f of x equals y." The notation is also read as "f at x equals y." The notation does *not* mean "f times x."

Letters other than f can be used to name a function. Other letters commonly used are g, h, F, G, and H.

Rules for functions can be illustrated by a *function machine*. An input value for x is entered into the function machine. The function machine performs the operations indicated by the rule and then gives the output value (or y value).

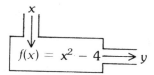

For the input $x = 3$, the function machine squares 3 and then subtracts 4 from this result, giving the output value 5.

TEACHER'S NOTES
See p. T29.

CLASSROOM EXAMPLES

1. What is the output value for $x = 2$? For $x = 3$? For $x = -2$?
   $f{:}x \rightarrow x^2 + 5$
   $f(x) = x^2 + 5$
   $f(2) = 2^2 + 5 = 9$
   $f(3) = 3^2 + 5 = 14$
   $f(-2) = (-2)^2 + 5 = 9$

2. Is the equation $3x - 4y = 12$ a linear function?
   $3x - 4y = 12$
   $\qquad -4y = -3x + 12$
   $\qquad\quad y = \frac{3}{4}x - 3$
   $3x - 4y = 12$ is a linear function, with $m = \frac{3}{4}$, and $b = -3$.

3. Graph $y = 1$.

x	y
0	1
1	1
2	1

EXAMPLES

1   **What is the output value for $x = 1$? For $x = -2$? For $x = 6$?**

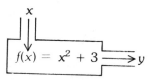

SOLUTION

$f(x) = x^2 + 3$
$f(1) = 1^2 + 3 = 4$
$f(-2) = (-2)^2 + 3 = 7$
$f(6) = 6^2 + 3 = 39$

The value of $f(x)$ is called the **functional value** or the **range value**.

MIXED REVIEW

Evaluate if $k = 7$ and $m = -3$.

1. $\frac{k + m}{m}$ $-\frac{4}{3}$

2. $5^2 (m^2)$ 225

3. $\frac{m^2}{km}$ $-\frac{3}{7}$

4. $(k + m)^3$ 64

5. $k - m$ 10

TEACHER'S RESOURCE
MASTERS

Practice Master 29, Part 2

ASSIGNMENT GUIDE

Minimum
1–35 odd, 40, 42

Regular
25–44

Maximum
30–49

ADDITIONAL ANSWERS

Oral Exercises

2. Add 1 to the value of x.

3. Multiply the value of x by 2, then add 4 to the result.

A **linear function** is any set of ordered pairs (x, y) that is the solution set of the equation $y = mx + b$, where m and b are real numbers. Each value for x results in exactly one value for y.

---

2   **Is the equation $5x - 6y = 15$ a linear function?**

SOLUTION

Try to write the given equation in the form $y = mx + b$. If you can, then the equation is a linear function.

$$5x - 6y = 15$$
$$-6y = -5x + 15$$
$$y = \frac{5}{6}x + \left(-\frac{5}{2}\right)$$

So the equation $5x - 6y = 15$ is a linear function, with $m = \frac{5}{6}$, and $b = -\frac{5}{2}$.

When $m = 0$ in the equation $y = mx + b$, the equation is equivalent to $y = b$. In this case, the equation represents a **constant function.** The graph is a horizontal line, since every element in the domain is paired with the same element in the range.

---

3   **Graph $y = 3$.**

SOLUTION

x	y
-2	3
0	3
2	3

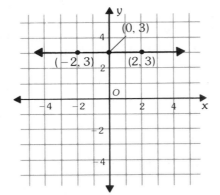

ORAL EXERCISES

Complete.

1. A ___rule___ associates elements in the domain of a function with elements in the range.

Describe what the function machine will do to an input value. Then find the output value if the input value is $x = 3$.

2. x

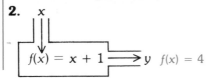

$f(x) = x + 1 \longrightarrow y$ $f(x) = 4$

3. x

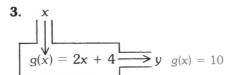

$g(x) = 2x + 4 \longrightarrow y$ $g(x) = 10$

4. x

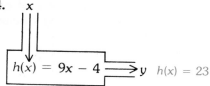

$h(x) = 9x - 4 \Rightarrow y$ $h(x) = 23$

5. x

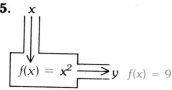

$f(x) = x^2 \Rightarrow y$ $f(x) = 9$

6. x

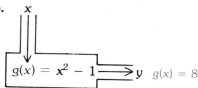

$g(x) = x^2 - 1 \Rightarrow y$ $g(x) = 8$

7. x

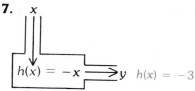

$h(x) = -x \Rightarrow y$ $h(x) = -3$

8. x

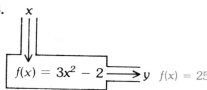

$f(x) = 3x^2 - 2 \Rightarrow y$ $f(x) = 25$

9. x

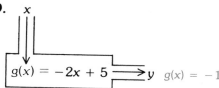

$g(x) = -2x + 5 \Rightarrow y$ $g(x) = -1$

4. Multiply the value of x by 9, then subtract 4 from the result.

5. Square the value of x.

6. Square the value of x, then subtract 1 from the result.

7. Find the opposite of the value of x.

8. Square the value of x, multiply that number by 3, then subtract 2 from the result.

9. Multiply the value of x by -2, then add 5 to the result.

WRITTEN EXERCISES

A. Write each rule in the form of an equation.

1. $f{:}x \rightarrow 3x + 4$ $y = 3x + 4$

2. $h{:}x \rightarrow x$ $y = x$

3. $g{:}x \rightarrow -2x + 1$ $y = -2x + 1$

4. $h{:}x \rightarrow x^2 - 2x + 1$ $y = x^2 - 2x + 1$

5. $g{:}x \rightarrow x + 1$ $y = x + 1$

6. $f{:}x \rightarrow \frac{1}{2}x^3$ $y = \frac{1}{2}x^3$

Write each rule or equation in the $f(x)$ notation.

7. $f{:}x \rightarrow -\frac{1}{7}x + 4$ $f(x) = -\frac{1}{7}x + 4$

8. $y = 2x + 3$ $f(x) = 2x + 3$

9. $g{:}x \rightarrow 5x - \frac{3}{4}$ $g(x) = 5x - \frac{3}{4}$

10. $h{:}x \rightarrow x^2 - x + 4$ $h(x) = x^2 - x + 4$

11. $y = \frac{1}{2}x + \frac{1}{4}$ $f(x) = \frac{1}{2}x + \frac{1}{4}$

12. $y = 0.1x^2 - 4$ $f(x) = 0.1x^2 - 4$

B. Find each functional value as indicated if $g(x) = 3x - 5$.

13. $g(0)$ -5

14. $g(1)$ -2

15. $g(-3)$ -14

16. $g\left(\frac{1}{2}\right)$ $-\frac{7}{2}$

17. $g\left(\frac{1}{3}\right)$ -4

18. $g\left(-\frac{1}{3}\right)$ -6

Find each functional value as indicated if $h(x) = x^2 - x$.

19. $h(-2)$ 6

20. $h(0)$ 0

21. $h(2)$ 2

22. $h(1)$ 0

23. $h(3)$ 6

24. $h(-3)$ 12

SELF-QUIZ

Written Exercises

27. yes; $m = 0$; $b = 3$

34. yes; $m = 0$; $b = -5$

37. yes; $m = -2$; $b = -1$

46. $x^2 + 2xh + h^2 + x + h$
    $- 1$

47. $x^2 + 2xh + h^2 + 3x$
    $+ 3h - 4$

48. $-x^2 - 2xh - h^2 + 4x$
    $+ 4h - 1$

49. $x^2 + 2xh + h^2 - 3x$
    $- 3h + 2$

Determine whether each of the following equations is a linear function. If an equation is a linear function, specify the value of m and of b. If it is not linear, write "not a linear function."

25. $4x + 5y = 20$ yes; $m = -\frac{4}{5}$; $b = 4$

26. $x^2 - y = 4$ not a linear function

27. $3y + 2x = 9 + 2x$

28. $x - 3y = 6$ yes; $m = \frac{1}{3}$; $b = -2$

29. $x^3 = y$ not a linear function

30. $2x = 3y - 15$ yes; $m = \frac{2}{3}$; $b = 5$

31. $\frac{1}{2}x + \frac{1}{4}y = 1$ yes; $m = -2$; $b = 4$

32. $5x = 20$ not a linear function

33. $2x + \frac{2}{3}y = 8$ yes; $m = -3$; $b = 12$

34. $3(x - 1) = 3x + y + 2$

35. $x^2 - \frac{3}{4}y = 6$ not a linear function

36. $x = 4(y + 2)$ yes; $m = \frac{1}{4}$; $b = -2$

37. $y = 2y - x + 3x + 1$

38. $y = \frac{4x - 1}{2}$ yes; $m = 2$; $b = -\frac{1}{2}$

39. Which of the equations from exercises 25–38 is a constant function? 27; 34

C. Find $f(x + h)$ for each exercise below.

Example: $f(x) = 2x + 1$
$$f(x + h) = 2(x + h) + 1$$
$$= 2x + 2h + 1$$

40. $f(x) = 3x - 4$ $3x + 3h - 4$

41. $f(x) = \frac{1}{2}x - 5$ $\frac{1}{2}x + \frac{1}{2}h - 5$

42. $f(x) = 3(x + 1)$ $3x + 3h + 3$

43. $f(x) = x^2$ $x^2 + 2xh + h^2$

44. $f(x) = -x^2$ $-x^2 - 2xh - h^2$

45. $f(x) = x^2 + x$ $x^2 + 2xh + h^2 + x + h$

46. $f(x) = x^2 + x - 1$

47. $f(x) = x^2 + 3x - 4$

48. $f(x) = -x^2 + 4x - 1$

49. $f(x) = x^2 - 3x + 2$

SELF-QUIZ

1.
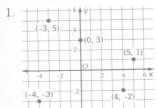

2.
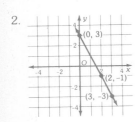

4.
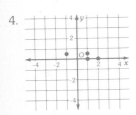

SELF-QUIZ

1. Graph the set of ordered pairs on the same set of axes.
   $\{(-3, 5), (4, -2), (5, 1), (0, 3), (-4, -3)\}$

2. Find at least three solutions for $y = -2x + 3$. Then draw the graph.

3. State the domain and the range for the relation.
   $\left\{\left(1, \frac{1}{2}\right), \left(-1, \frac{1}{2}\right), (1, 0), (2, 0)\right\}$ $D = \{-1, 1, 2\}$ $R = \left\{0, \frac{1}{2}\right\}$

4. Graph the relation in exercise 3. Is the relation a function? no

5. Find $f(2)$ if $f(x) = 3x - 2$. $f(2) = 4$

7.5 | Slope

OBJECTIVES

Find the slope of a line using the coordinates of two points on the line.

Draw the graph of a line, given a point on the line and the slope of the line.

When you push a cart up a ramp, the steeper the ramp is, the more work it is to push the cart. When you talk about steepness, you are talking about **slope**.

The slope of a line through points A and B is the ratio of the vertical change to the horizontal change from point A to point B, providing that the horizontal change is not 0.

3 ft vertical change

7 ft

horizontal change

The cart would go through a vertical change of 3 feet for a horizontal change of 7 feet.

EXAMPLES

1 Find the slope of the line shown.

SOLUTION

$$\text{slope} = \frac{\text{vertical change}}{\text{horizontal change}} = \frac{3}{5}$$

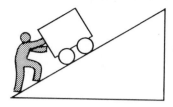

2 Find the slope of the line shown.

SOLUTION

$$\text{slope} = \frac{6}{-4}$$
$$= \frac{3}{-2}$$
$$= -\frac{3}{2}$$

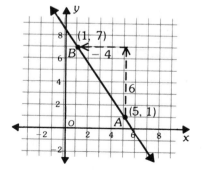

TEACHER'S NOTES

See p. T29.

CLASSROOM EXAMPLES

1. Find the slope of the line shown.

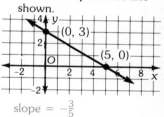

$$\text{slope} = \frac{2}{2}$$
$$= 1$$

2. Find the slope of the line shown.

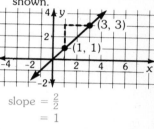

$$\text{slope} = -\frac{3}{5}$$

3. Find the slope of the line shown.

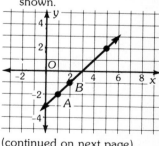

(continued on next page)

from A to B: slope $= m$
$= \frac{1}{1} = 1$

from B to C: slope $= m$
$= \frac{3}{3} = 1$

from C to A: slope $= m$
$= \frac{4}{4} = 1$

4. Find the slope of the line with points at $(2, 5)$ and $(1, -4)$.
$m = \frac{-4 - 5}{1 - 2}$
$= \frac{-9}{-1}$
$= 9$

5. Find the slope of the line $y = 2$.

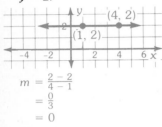

$m = \frac{2 - 2}{4 - 1}$
$= \frac{0}{3}$
$= 0$

6. Find the slope of the line $x = 2$.

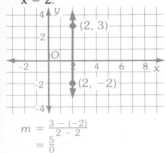

$m = \frac{3 - (-2)}{2 - 2}$
$= \frac{5}{0}$
But division by 0 is undefined.

Usually the letter m represents slope. If you know more than two points that are on a line, you can use any two of them to find the slope of the line.

3   **Find the slope of the line shown.**

SOLUTION

from A to B: slope $= m = \frac{8}{6} = \frac{4}{3}$

from B to C: slope $= m = \frac{4}{3}$

from C to A: slope $= m = \frac{-12}{-9} = \frac{4}{3}$

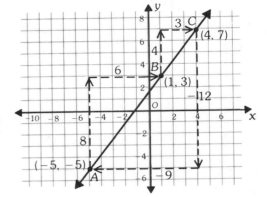

Notice in the examples that lines having a *positive slope* slant *upward to the right*, and that lines having a *negative slope* slant *downward to the right*.

Slope Formula	For a line with points (x_1, y_1) and (x_2, y_2), the slope is $\frac{y_2 - y_1}{x_2 - x_1}$ (if $x_2 - x_1 \neq 0$).

NOTE: The 1 and the 2 are called *subscripts*. x_1 is read "x sub 1." Subscripts are used to distinguish between different x values and different y values.

The ratio $\frac{y_2 - y_1}{x_2 - x_1}$ results in the same value for the slope as the ratio $\frac{y_1 - y_2}{x_1 - x_2}$.

4   **Find the slope of the line with points at $(3, 7)$ and $(1, -5)$.**

SOLUTION $m = \frac{y_2 - y_1}{x_2 - x_1}$

$= \frac{-5 - 7}{1 - 3}$

$= \frac{-12}{-2}$

$= 6$

$m = \frac{y_1 - y_2}{x_1 - x_2}$

$= \frac{7 - (-5)}{3 - 1}$

$= \frac{12}{2}$

$= 6$

5   **Find the slope of the line $y = 3$.**

SOLUTION $m = \frac{y_2 - y_1}{x_2 - x_1}$

$= \frac{3 - 3}{4 - 1}$

$= \frac{0}{3}$

$= 0$

A **horizontal line** has slope 0.

6   **Find the slope of the line $x = 3$.**

SOLUTION $m = \dfrac{y_2 - y_1}{x_2 - x_1}$

$$= \dfrac{4 - (-1)}{3 - 3}$$

$$= \dfrac{5}{0}$$

But division by 0 is undefined. **A vertical line** has a slope that is undefined.

You can graph a line if you know a point on the line and the slope of the line.

7   **Graph the line that passes through $(-1, 3)$ and has slope $-\dfrac{5}{2}$.**

SOLUTION

Graph the point $(-1, 3)$.
Go down 5 units, then right 2 units.
You could also go up 5 units, then left 2 units.

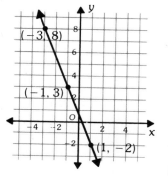

ORAL EXERCISES

Classify the slope of each line as positive, negative, zero, or undefined.

1.   positive

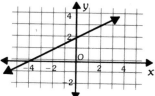

2.   undefined

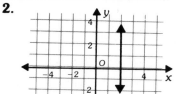

3.   negative

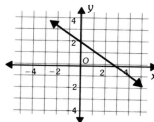

4.   zero

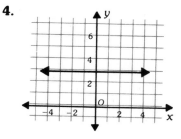

Complete.

5. The slope of a line is the ratio of the _____vertical_____ change to the _____horizontal_____ change, providing that the _____horizontal_____ change is not zero.

7. Graph the line that passes through $(-2, 4)$ and has slope $-\dfrac{7}{2}$.

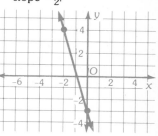

MIXED REVIEW

1. Simplify $12 \cdot (8 - 13)$.
   60

2. Find the quotient of $-\dfrac{12}{17}$ and $\dfrac{5}{34}$. $-\dfrac{24}{5}$

3. Subtract $(6x^2 + 5x + 9)$ from $(-9x^2 - 8x - 3)$.
    $-15x^2 - 13x - 12$

4. Solve $5p - 16 = 3p + 48$.   32

5. Evaluate $-|-35|$. -35

TEACHER'S RESOURCE MASTERS

Practice Master 30, Part 1

COMPUTER SOFTWARE

Graphing Linear Equations and Inequalities

ASSIGNMENT GUIDE

Minimum
1–21 odd

Regular
7–27

Maximum
13–31

Find the slope of each line.

6. 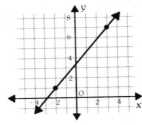 $m = \frac{6}{5}$

7. 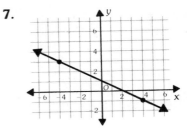 $m = -\frac{1}{2}$

8. 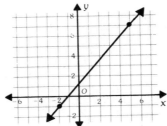 $m = \frac{8}{7}$

9. 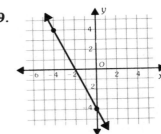 $m = -2$

14.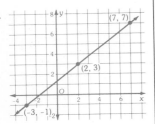

16.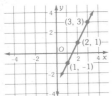

18.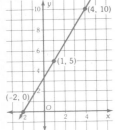

20.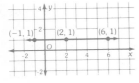

WRITTEN EXERCISES

A. Find the slope of the line containing these points. If the slope is undefined, write undefined.

1. (1, 4) and (3, 8) 2

2. (3, −1) and (−2, 3) $-\frac{4}{5}$

3. (11, 4) and (8, 7) −1

4. (−5, 3) and (2, 3) 0

5. (8, 6) and (8, −1) undefined

6. $\left(3\frac{1}{2}, 4\right)$ and $\left(5\frac{1}{2}, -1\right)$ $-\frac{5}{2}$

7. (7, 5) and (7, −2) undefined

8. (3, −2) and (−4, −6) $\frac{4}{7}$

9. (3, −8) and (4, −2) 6

10. (6, −1) and (−6, 1) $-\frac{1}{6}$

11. (−3, −5) and (−6, 10) −5

12. (2, −1) and (5, −1) 0

B. Draw the graph of the line, given a point on the line and the slope of the line.

13. (1, 3); $m = \frac{3}{4}$

14. (2, 1); $m = 2$

15. (1, 4); $m = -\frac{1}{2}$

16. (2, 3); $m = \frac{4}{5}$

17. (−1, −3); $m = -\frac{2}{3}$

18. (1, 5); $m = \frac{5}{3}$

19. (−2, 4); $m = -\frac{7}{3}$

20. (6, 1); $m = 0$

21. (1, 4); m is undefined.

Without graphing, determine if the three points lie on the same straight line.

22. (1, 4), (4, 6), (7, 8) yes

23. (8, 5), (6, 8), (10, 2) yes

24. (−8, −2), (−5, 3), (2, 8) no

25. (−1, 10), (3, 4), (7, −4) no

26. (2, 7), (−6, 7), (5, 7) yes

27. (5, 8), (2, 7), (−1, 6) yes

C. Find the slope of each side of the following figures:

28.

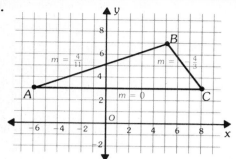

29.

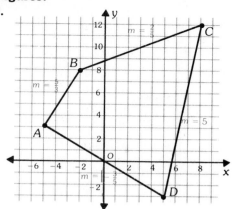

30.

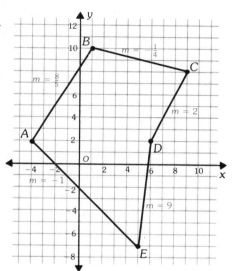

31.

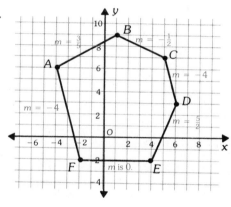

Find the missing coordinate so that the line containing the two points has the given slope.

Example: $(2, 3)$, $(5, y)$; $m = 3$

$$\frac{y - 3}{5 - 2} = 3$$

$$\frac{y - 3}{3} = 3$$

$$y - 3 = 9$$

$$y = 12$$

32. $(-1, -3)$, $(3, y)$; $m = -4$ $\quad -19$

33. $(1, 7)$, $(-2, y)$; $m = \frac{2}{3}$ $\quad 5$

34. $(4, -1)$, $(1, y)$; $m = -6$ $\quad 17$

35. $(-5, 10)$, $(-3, y)$; $m = 2$ $\quad 14$

36. $(4, -3)$, $(2, y)$; $m = -\frac{1}{3}$ $\quad -\frac{7}{3}$

37. $(-1, 3)$, $(2, y)$; $m = \frac{5}{2}$ $\quad \frac{21}{2}$

Write a linear equation in slope-intercept form and give the slope and the y-intercept.

Draw the graph of a line, given the y-intercept and the slope.

Given a pair of equations of lines, determine if the lines are parallel.

TEACHER'S NOTES

See p. T30.

CLASSROOM EXAMPLES

1. What is the slope of the line for $y = \frac{3}{4}x + 12$?

$y = \frac{3}{4}x + 12$

Let x =	Then y =
4	15
8	18

$m = \frac{18 - 15}{8 - 4} = \frac{3}{4}$

2. Find the y-intercept of the line for $y = \frac{3}{4}x + 5$. Graph the line.

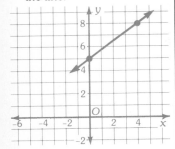

3. Find the slope and the y-intercept of the line for $2x - 3y = 6$.

$2x - 3y = 6$

$-3y = -2x + 6$

$y = \frac{2}{3}x + (-2)$

So $m = \frac{2}{3}$ and $b = -2$.

7.6 | Slope-Intercept Form

In Section 7.4, you saw that a linear equation in the form $y = mx + b$, $m \neq 0$, is a linear function. You can find the slope of a linear function by finding and using two points on the graph.

EXAMPLES

1 **What is the slope of the line for $y = \frac{2}{3}x + 5$?**

SOLUTION

First find two points on the line and then find the slope, using these two points.

$y = \frac{2}{3}x + 5$

Let x =	Then y =
3	7
6	9

$m = \frac{y_2 - y_1}{x_2 - x_1}$

$= \frac{9 - 7}{6 - 3}$

$= \frac{2}{3}$

Notice that $\frac{2}{3}$ is the coefficient of x in the equation $y = \frac{2}{3}x + 5$. The m in the equation $y = mx + b$ is the same m used to represent the slope. So m, the slope, is $\frac{2}{3}$. Thus, if the linear equation is written in standard form, you can solve the equation for y to find the slope of the line.

In the equation $y = mx + b$, b is the value of the **y-intercept.** The y-intercept of a line is the y-coordinate when $x = 0$ in $y = mx + b$. The line intersects the y-axis at the point $(0, b)$.

2 **Find the y-intercept of the line for $y = \frac{4}{3}x + 4$. Graph the line.**

SOLUTION

The line is in the form $y = mx + b$. So the y-intercept is 4.

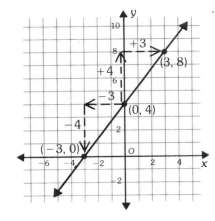

<table>
<tr><td>

Slope-Intercept Form

</td><td>

The equation $y = mx + b$ is called the slope-intercept form of a straight line, where m is the slope and b is the y-intercept.

</td></tr>
</table>

3 Find the slope and the y-intercept of the line for $6x - 7y = 10$.

SOLUTION Write the equation in slope-intercept form, $y = mx + b$.

$6x - 7y = 10$

$-7y = -6x + 10$

$y = \frac{6}{7}x - \frac{10}{7}$ or $y = \frac{6}{7}x + \left(-\frac{10}{7}\right)$

So $m = \frac{6}{7}$ and $b = -\frac{10}{7}$.

Two distinct lines are **parallel** if their slopes are equal or if both slopes are undefined.

4 Are the lines for $2x + 3y = 6$ and $4x + 6y = 24$ parallel?

SOLUTION Write each equation in slope-intercept form.

$2x + 3y = 6$ $4x + 6y = 24$

$3y = -2x + 6$ $6y = -4x + 24$

$y = -\frac{2}{3}x + 2$ $y = -\frac{2}{3}x + 4$

$m = -\frac{2}{3}$ $m = -\frac{2}{3}$

So the lines for $2x + 3y = 6$ and $4x + 6y = 24$ are parallel. Notice that the y-intercepts have different values.

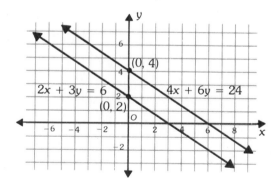

4. Are the lines for $3x + 4y = 12$ and $6x + 8y = 24$ parallel?

$3x + 4y = 12$

$4y = -3x + 12$

$y = -\frac{3}{4}x + 3$

$m = -\frac{3}{4}$

$6x + 8y = 24$

$8y = -6x + 24$

$y = -\frac{3}{4}x + 3$

$m = -\frac{3}{4}$

So the lines for $3x + 4y = 12$ and $6x + 8y = 24$ are parallel.

MIXED REVIEW

Perform the indicated operation.

1. $16 - (-46 - 24)$ 86
2. $\frac{1}{5} - \left(-\frac{4}{5}\right)$ 1
3. $\frac{1}{5} + \left(\frac{4}{5}\right)$ 1
4. $6 + (-0.58)$ 5.42
5. $(-3)\left(\frac{5}{6}\right)$ $-\frac{5}{2}$

TEACHER'S RESOURCE MASTERS

Practice Master 30, Part 2

COMPUTER SOFTWARE

Graphing Linear Equations and Inequalities

ORAL EXERCISES

1. In the equation $y = mx + b$, the letter __m__ represents the slope of the line.

2. In the equation $y = mx + b$, the letter __b__ represents the y-intercept.

ASSIGNMENT GUIDE

Minimum
1–9, 11–29 odd

Regular
10–28

Maximum
21–39

ADDITIONAL ANSWERS

Written Exercises

For the odd-numbered solutions see *Answers To Selected Exercises*, p. 581.

18.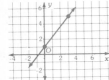

20.

22.

30.

32.

3. The equation $y = mx + b$ is called the _____slope-intercept_____ form of a line.

4. To find the slope and the y-intercept of a line whose equation is written in standard form, you can solve the equation for __y__.

5. For the y-intercept, the x-coordinate has a value of __0__.

6. Two lines are parallel if their slopes are _____equal_____ or if both slopes are ____undefined____.

WRITTEN EXERCISES

A. Find the slope and the y-intercept for each.

1. $y = 4x + 7$ 4; 7

2. $y = -\frac{2}{3}x + 6$ $-\frac{2}{3}$; 6

3. $y = \frac{5}{2}x - 11$ $\frac{5}{2}$; -11

4. $y = -\frac{7}{5}x + \frac{4}{5}$ $-\frac{7}{5}$; $\frac{4}{5}$

5. $y = -11x + 17$ -11; 17

6. $y = 2x$ 2; 0

7. $y = x - 3$ 1; -3

8. $y = -\frac{1}{4}x - \frac{11}{2}$ $-\frac{1}{4}$; $-\frac{11}{2}$

9. $y = -\frac{11}{5}x$ $-\frac{11}{5}$; 0

B. Write each equation in slope-intercept form. Then give the slope and the y-intercept.

10. $2x + 3y = 9$ $y = -\frac{2}{3}x + 3$; $-\frac{2}{3}$; 3

11. $x - 3y = 5$ $y = \frac{1}{3}x - \frac{5}{3}$; $\frac{1}{3}$; $-\frac{5}{3}$

12. $3x - 5y = 11$ $y = \frac{3}{5}x - \frac{11}{5}$; $\frac{3}{5}$; $-\frac{11}{5}$

13. $4x + y = 5$ $y = -4x + 5$; -4; 5

14. $-x + y = 4$ $y = x + 4$; 1; 4

15. $-3x + 2y = -7$ $y = \frac{3}{2}x - \frac{7}{2}$; $\frac{3}{2}$; $-\frac{7}{2}$

16. $3x - 2y = -8$ $y = \frac{3}{2}x + 4$; $\frac{3}{2}$; 4

17. $3y + 6 = 0$ $y = -2$; 0; -2

Graph the line for each equation, using the y-intercept and the slope.

18. $y = \frac{4}{3}x + 1$

19. $y = -\frac{3}{2}x + 2$

20. $y = 2$

21. $y = -2x + 2$

22. $y = \frac{5}{2}x - 3$

23. $y = -\frac{4}{7}x + 2$

Given the pair of equations of lines, determine if the lines are parallel.

24. $x - y = 4$
    $3x - 3y = 10$ yes

25. $4x + 5y = 8$
    $8x + 10y = 20$ yes

26. $3x - 2y = 4$
    $6x - 6y = 12$ no

27. $7x - y = 4$
    $x - 7y = 8$ no

28. $3x + 2y = 10$
    $-6x - 4y = -4$ yes

29. $3x - 2y = 15$
    $-6x + 5y = -30$ no

C. Given the following information, graph each line:

30. The y-intercept is 3 and the line is parallel to $y = \frac{1}{3}x + 5$.

31. The y-intercept is -2 and the line is parallel to $2x - 3y = 8$.

32. The line passes through the point with coordinates $(1, 3)$ and is parallel to $y = -x + 8$.

33. The line passes through the point with coordinates $(-2, 4)$ and is parallel to $3x - y = 7$.

Two lines are **perpendicular** (intersect to form a right angle) if $m_1 \cdot m_2 = -1$. Here m_1 represents the slope of one of the lines, and m_2 represents the slope of the other line. Thus, one slope is the negative reciprocal of the other.

Determine if the following pairs of lines are parallel or perpendicular.

34. $3x - 4y = 12$
$4x + 3y = 12$ perpendicular

35. $2x + 5y = 10$
$2x + 5y = -10$ parallel

36. $x + 3y = 6$
$3x + 9y = 12$ parallel

37. $4x - y = 4$
$\frac{1}{2}x + 2y = 6$ perpendicular

38. $2x + 3y = 6$
$2x = -3y$ parallel

39. $4x = 5y$
$10x + 8y = 15$ perpendicular

SKILLS MAINTENANCE

Write each of the following as an algebraic expression:

1. the product of $2a$ and b $2ab$

2. the sum of $\frac{7}{8}x$ and $\frac{3}{4}y$ $\frac{7}{8}x + \frac{3}{4}y$

3. four times the sum of c and d $4(c + d)$

4. ten more than s $s + 10$

Evaluate if $x = 4$ and $y = 3$.

5. $\frac{x}{y^2}$ $\frac{4}{9}$

6. $(x^2)y^2$ 144

7. $(x^3y)^2$ $36{,}864$

Name the property illustrated.

8. $x(y + z) = xy + xz$ Dist. prop.

9. $(ab)c = a(bc)$ Assoc. prop. of mult.

10. $x + y = y + x$ Comm. prop. of add.

11. $cd = dc$ Comm. prop. of mult.

Solve.

12. $x - 14 = 23$ 37

13. $y + 8.4 = 19.3$ 10.9

14. $12a = 86$ $\frac{43}{6}$

15. $\frac{3}{4}s - 10 = 11$ 28

16. $18 = t + 3t$ $\frac{9}{2}$

17. $2.3r + (-4.9r) = 13$ -5

Solve each inequality. Graph the solution set.

18. $3.5 + x > 6$ $x > 2.5$

19. $b - 8 < -3$ $b < 5$

20. $\frac{a}{5} \le -\frac{3}{5}$ $a \le -3$

21. $-3c + 5 \ge 17$ $c \le -4$

Choose a variable and then write each sentence, using $<$, $>$, $\le$, or $\ge$.

22. A number is greater than -15. $n > -15$

23. Three times a number is less than 24.

24. A number is at least 10. $n \ge 10$

25. Two-thirds of a number is at most -5.

Graph each conjunction or disjunction.

26. $-4 < x < 1$

27. $2 \le y < 7$

28. $a > 12$ or $a < 6$

Solve.

29. $|r + 3| = 12$ $r = 9$ or $r = -15$

30. $|n - 8| < 5$ $3 < n < 13$

SKILLS MAINTENANCE

18.

19.

20.

21.

23. $3n < 24$

25. $\frac{2}{3}x \le -5$

26.

27.

28.

Write the equation of a line, given the slope and the y-intercept of the line.

Write the equation of a line, given the slope of the line and the coordinates of any point on the line.

Write the equation of a line, given the coordinates of two points on the line.

TEACHER'S NOTES

See p. T30.

CLASSROOM EXAMPLES

1. Write the equation of the line that has slope $-\frac{3}{4}$ and y-intercept 8.
   $y = mx + b$
   $y = -\frac{3}{4}x + 8$

2. Write the equation of the line that has slope 8 and passes through the point with coordinates $(2, -4)$.
   $y = mx + b$
   $y = 8x + b$
   $-4 = 8(2) + b$
   $-4 = 16 + b$
   $-20 = b$
   The equation of the line is $y = 8x - 20$.

3. Write the equation of the line that passes through the points with coordinates $P(4, -2)$ and $Q(6, 1)$.
   $m = \frac{1 - (-2)}{6 - 4} = \frac{3}{2}$

7.7 | Writing Equations of Lines

The equation of a line can be found if any one of the following three situations is known:
- the slope and the y-intercept of the line
- the slope of the line and the coordinates of any point on the line
- the coordinates of two points on the line

EXAMPLES

1 **Write the equation of the line that has slope $-\frac{5}{2}$ and y-intercept 4.**

SOLUTION

Since $m = -\frac{5}{2}$ and $b = 4$, use the slope-intercept form of a linear equation and substitute these values.

$y = mx + b$

$y = -\frac{5}{2}x + 4$

2 **Write the equation of the line that has slope 6 and passes through the point with coordinates $(1, -2)$.**

SOLUTION

Since $m = 6$, use the slope-intercept form of a linear equation and substitute this value.

$y = mx + b$

$y = 6x + b$

You do *not* know the value of b. However, you know that the point with coordinates $(1, -2)$ is on the line. So $(1, -2)$ satisfies the equation $y = 6x + b$. Substitute these values for x and for y and solve for b.

$y = 6x + b$

$-2 = 6(1) + b$

$-2 = 6 + b$

$-8 = b$

The equation of the line is $y = 6x - 8$.

3 **Write the equation of the line that passes through the points with coordinates $P(1, 6)$ and $Q(3, -4)$.**

SOLUTION

Use the two given points to find the slope of the line.

$m = \frac{y_2 - y_1}{x_2 - x_1} = \frac{-4 - 6}{3 - 1} = -\frac{10}{2} = -5$

Then use *either* of the two points and proceed as in the previous example to solve for b.

For point $P(1, 6)$
$$y = -5x + b$$
$$6 = -5(1) + b$$
$$6 = -5 + b$$
$$11 = b$$

For point $Q(3, -4)$
$$y = -5x + b$$
$$-4 = -5(3) + b$$
$$-4 = -15 + b$$
$$11 = b$$

Regardless of which point you choose, the value for b is the same.
The equation of the line is $y = -5x + 11$.

ORAL EXERCISES

Find the equation of each line.

	Slope	y-intercept	
1.	$-\frac{1}{2}$	3	$y = -\frac{1}{2}x + 3$
3.	$-\frac{4}{5}$	6	$y = -\frac{4}{5}x + 6$
5.	$\frac{7}{3}$	8	$y = \frac{7}{3}x + 8$
7.	$-\frac{2}{5}$	$-\frac{1}{5}$	$y = -\frac{2}{5}x - \frac{1}{5}$
9.	-4	0	$y = -4x$

	Slope	Point	
2.	2	$(1, 2)$	$y = 2x$
4.	1	$(-1, 1)$	$y = x + 2$
6.	-1	$(0, 4)$	$y = -x + 4$
8.	-2	$(0, -1)$	$y = -2x - 1$
10.	3	$(1, 0)$	$y = 3x - 3$

WRITTEN EXERCISES

A. Write the equation of each line in slope-intercept form.

	Slope	y-intercept	
1.	4	2	$y = 4x + 2$
3.	-1	3	$y = -x + 3$
5.	0	-6	$y = -6$
7.	$\frac{1}{2}$	$-\frac{2}{3}$	$y = \frac{1}{2}x - \frac{2}{3}$

	Slope	y-intercept	
2.	$\frac{1}{4}$	-7	$y = \frac{1}{4}x - 7$
4.	-5	$\frac{1}{4}$	$y = -5x + \frac{1}{4}$
6.	0	$-\frac{2}{3}$	$y = -\frac{2}{3}$
8.	$\frac{7}{2}$	-4	$y = \frac{7}{2}x - 4$

	Slope	Point	
9.	2	$(1, 3)$	$y = 2x + 1$
11.	$\frac{1}{2}$	$(2, 7)$	$y = \frac{1}{2}x + 6$
13.	-3	$(1, 1)$	$y = -3x + 4$
15.	$-\frac{1}{4}$	$(2, 1)$	$y = -\frac{1}{4}x + \frac{3}{2}$

	Slope	Point	
10.	-2	$(3, -1)$	$y = -2x + 5$
12.	$\frac{1}{4}$	$(0, 4)$	$y = \frac{1}{4}x + 4$
14.	$\frac{3}{2}$	$(6, 1)$	$y = \frac{3}{2}x - 8$
16.	0	$(3, 5)$	$y = 5$

For point $P(4, -2)$
$$y = \frac{3}{2}x + b$$
$$-2 = \frac{3}{2}(4) + b$$
$$-2 = 6 + b$$
$$-8 = b$$

For point $Q(6, 1)$
$$y = \frac{3}{2}x + b$$
$$1 = \frac{3}{2}(6) + b$$
$$1 = 9 + b$$
$$-8 = b$$

The equation of the line is $y = \frac{3}{2}x - 8$.

MIXED REVIEW

1. Graph $\{-2, 0, 4, 6\}$ on a number line.

2. Solve $\frac{4y}{2} - 8 = 36$ 22

3. Find the value of $(-6.1)^2$.   37.21

4. Factor completely. $5x^2 - 10xy + 5y^2$ $5(x - y)^2$

5. Simplify. $3^2a^4(a^5)$ $9a^9$

TEACHER'S RESOURCE MASTERS

Practice Master 31, Part 1

ASSIGNMENT GUIDE

Minimum
1–15 odd, 17–20, 25–28

Regular
17–32

Maximum
22–32, 33–41 odd

	Point	Point			Point	Point	

B. 17. (4, 3) | (1, 7) $y = -\frac{4}{3}x + \frac{25}{3}$ **18.** (5, 9) | (2, 6) $y = x + 4$

19. (1, 4) | (3, 9) $y = \frac{5}{2}x + \frac{3}{2}$ **20.** (5, 0) | (0, 3) $y = -\frac{3}{5}x + 3$

21. (7, 1) | (10, −3) $y = -\frac{4}{3}x + \frac{31}{3}$ **22.** (6, −1) | (2, 3) $y = -x + 5$

23. (4, 2) | (3, 2) $y = 2$ **24.** (3, −1) | (10, −1) $y = -1$

After writing each equation in slope-intercept form, change the equation to standard form.

25. slope = 2; y-intercept = 3   **26.** slope = $-\frac{3}{2}$; y-intercept = 1

27. slope = $\frac{1}{4}$; point on line = (1, −1)   **28.** slope = −3; point on line = (2, 7)

29. slope = $\frac{8}{5}$; point on line = (−1, 0)   **30.** two points are (1, 7), (−3, 4)

31. two points are (8, 3), (10, −5)   **32.** two points are (−3, −2), (2, −6)

C. If a line has slope m and (x_1, y_1) is a point on the line, then $y - y_1 = m(x - x_1)$ is the **point-slope form** for a straight line. (Let (x, y) be any other point on the line, $m = \frac{y - y_1}{x - x_1}$, and $x - x_1 \neq 0$. Multiply both sides of the equation by $x - x_1$ to get the point-slope form.)
Use the point-slope form to write the equation of each line. Then change each equation to slope-intercept form.

	Slope	Point			Slope	Point	

33. 2 | (3, 7) $y = 2x + 1$ **34.** $\frac{3}{4}$ | (−1, 2) $y = \frac{3}{4}x + \frac{11}{4}$

35. −4 | (2, −3) $y = -4x + 5$ **36.** $-\frac{7}{3}$ | (1, 1) $y = -\frac{7}{3}x + \frac{10}{3}$

37. 6 | $\left(\frac{1}{3}, -\frac{2}{3}\right)$ $y = 6x - \frac{8}{3}$ **38.** 1 | $\left(\frac{1}{4}, \frac{3}{4}\right)$ $y = x + \frac{1}{2}$

39. $\frac{1}{2}$ | $\left(-\frac{1}{6}, -\frac{5}{6}\right)$ $y = \frac{1}{2}x - \frac{3}{4}$ **40.** $-\frac{4}{9}$ | $\left(\frac{1}{2}, \frac{1}{2}\right)$ $y = -\frac{4}{9}x + \frac{13}{18}$

Write the equations of the lines that contain the sides of these figures. Find one equation for each side.

41.

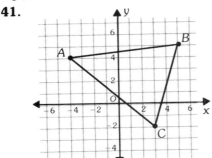

42.

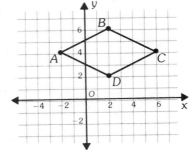

CAREER
Civil Engineer

Civil engineers plan, design, and supervise the construction of roads, tunnels, airports, bridges, harbors, buildings, and water-supply and sewage systems. They need to have creativity, an analytical mind, a capacity for detail, as well as an interest in mathematics and science.

Suppose a civil engineer designed a highway with embankments on either side. The drawing shows the width of the highway, the slopes of the embankments, and the depth of each embankment from the roadway to the base of the embankment. Find x and y.

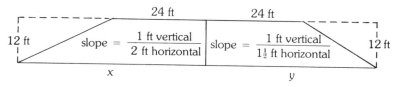

Suppose a civil engineer needs to calculate the number of gallons in a 1-foot section of pipe that is 6 inches in diameter. The formula that is used to calculate the number of gallons in 1 foot of pipe is $G = 0.0408d^2$ (gallons = 0.0408 · square of pipe diameter in inches). Calculate the number of gallons in the pipe.

CAREER
$x = 48$ feet; $y = 42$ feet
$G = 1.4688$ gal

CLASSROOM EXAMPLE

A bus is traveling at a constant velocity of 10 meters per second. The bus then accelerates at a constant rate for 8 seconds until it has a velocity of 20 meters per second. What is the linear equation that describes the bus' velocity during acceleration?

Let (0, 10) represent the time and the velocity at the beginning of acceleration.

Let (0, 20) represent the time and the velocity at the end of acceleration.

$m = \frac{20 - 10}{8 - 0} = \frac{10}{8} = \frac{5}{4}$

$y = \frac{5}{4}x + b$

$10 = b$

$y = \frac{5}{4}x + 10$

7.8 | Problem Solving

Velocity (speed) can be described by the linear equation $y = mx + b$, where x represents the time (in some unit), y represents the velocity (distance per unit of time), and the slope m represents the acceleration. **Acceleration** is the rate of increase of velocity per unit of time. When the velocity is constant, the graph is a horizontal line with slope 0. When the velocity increases because there is a constant rate of acceleration, the graph is a line with positive slope. On the graphs below, (0, b) represents the point where the velocity is first measured.

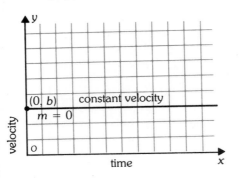

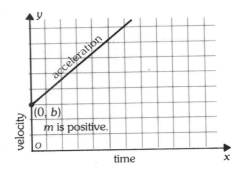

EXAMPLE

A car is traveling at a constant velocity of 15 meters per second. The car then accelerates at a constant rate for 5 seconds until it has a velocity of 30 meters per second. What is the linear equation that describes the car's velocity during acceleration?

Understand: *Given:* The initial velocity is 15 m/sec.
The final velocity is 30 m/sec.
The time of acceleration is 5 seconds.

To find: the linear equation that describes the car's velocity during acceleration

Plan: Let (0, 15) represent the time and the velocity at the beginning of acceleration.

Let (5, 30) represent the time and the velocity at the end of acceleration.

Use the two ordered pairs to find the slope of the line. Then find the y-intercept.

Solve: To find m: $m = \frac{y_2 - y_1}{x_2 - x_1} = \frac{30 - 15}{5 - 0} = \frac{15}{5} = 3$

$y = mx + b$, so $y = 3x + b$.

To find b: One ordered pair is (0, 15). Since $x = 0$, the y-intercept is 15.

Answer: The linear equation that describes the car's velocity is $y = 3x + 15$.

Review: Use the other ordered pair to see if the resulting statement is true.

$$y = 3x + 15$$
$$30 \overset{?}{=} 3(5) + 15$$
$$30 \overset{?}{=} 15 + 15$$
$$30 = 30 \quad \checkmark$$

ORAL EXERCISES

1. In the Example, what did the variable x represent?   time

2. In the Example, what did the variable y represent?   velocity

3. What had to be true about the rate of acceleration in order for the velocity to be described by a linear equation?   constant rate

4. If the y-intercept had not been given, how could you have found the value of b?   Substitute the values of any ordered pair and m into $y = mx + b$ and then solve for b.

WRITTEN EXERCISES

A. **In exercises 1–6, assume that each car is accelerating at a constant rate. Write the linear equation that describes each car's velocity.**

1. The car's velocity at 0 seconds is 10 meters per second and at 3 seconds is 25 meters per second. $y = 5x + 10$

2. The car's velocity at 0 seconds is 12 meters per second and at 4 seconds is 36 meters per second. $y = 6x + 12$

B. 3. The car's velocity at 2 seconds is 20 meters per second and at 4 seconds is 30 meters per second. $y = 5x + 10$

4. The car's velocity at 3 seconds is 15 meters per second and at 6 seconds is 30 meters per second. $y = 5x$

5. The car's velocity at 0 seconds is 30 meters per second and at 3 seconds is 15 meters per second. $y = -5x + 30$

6. The car's velocity at 2 seconds is 35 meters per second and at 5 seconds is 8 meters per second. $y = -9x + 53$

Solve.

7. The car's velocity at 0 seconds is 10 meters per second and at 3 seconds is 25 meters per second. What is the car's velocity at 4 seconds?

8. The car's velocity at 1 second is 35 meters per second and at 3 seconds is 25 meters per second. What is the car's velocity at 4 seconds?

9. The car's velocity at 1 second is 15 meters per second and at 4 seconds is 30 meters per second. What is the car's velocity at 7 seconds?

10. The car's velocity at 2 seconds is 50 meters per second and at 4 seconds is 30 meters per second. What is the car's velocity at 6 seconds?

MIXED REVIEW

Simplify.

1. $\frac{18 - 4}{7} + 3(7 + 2)$ 29

2. $-83 + 16$ -67

3. $5(x^2y + xy^2)$ $5x^2y + 5xy^2$

4. $(9 + 3)(54 \div 9)$ 72

5. $\frac{6 - 5(2)}{-2}$ 2

TEACHER'S RESOURCE MASTERS

Practice Master 31, Part 2

Quiz 14

ASSIGNMENT GUIDE

Minimum
1–9 odd

Regular
5–9

Maximum
7–9, 11, 12

ADDITIONAL ANSWERS

Written Exercises

7. 30 meters per second

8. 20 meters per second

9. 45 meters per second

10. 10 meters per second

C. When water at a certain temperature is added to water at a different temperature, you can use linear equations to find the temperature of the mixture. The equations are based on the fact that heat = mass × change in temperature.

Example: 200 grams of water at 75°C is added to 150 grams of water at 40°C. What is the temperature of the mixture?

Let x = the temperature of the mixture.

Since the water is mixed together, the heat lost by the warmer water is equal to the heat gained by the cooler water.

For the warmer water, y = the amount of heat lost.

y = mass × the change in temperature

y = mass × (initial temperature − final temperature)

$y = 200(75 - x)$

For the cooler water, y = the amount of heat gained.

y = mass × the change in temperature

y = mass × (final temperature − initial temperature)

$y = 150(x - 40)$

$$200(75 - x) = 150(x - 40)$$
$$15{,}000 - 200x = 150x - 6000$$
$$21{,}000 = 350x$$
$$x = 60$$

The temperature of the warmer and cooler water mixed together is 60°C.

Find the final temperature when the two amounts of water are added together.

11. 150 grams of water at 75°C is added to 200 grams of water at 40°C.   55°C

12. 100 grams of water at 90°C is added to 25 grams of water at 70°C.   86°C

13. 175 grams of water at 50°C is added to 250 grams of water at 20°C.   about 32°C

14. 350 grams of water at 85°C is added to 30 grams of water at 20°C.   about 80°C

CHALLENGE

$x^2 - x = (x - 1)^2 + (x - 1)$

Proof: $x^2 - x = x^2 - x$
$- 2x + 2x + 1 - 1$
$= (x^2 - 2x + 1) + (-x + 2x$
$- 1)$
$= (x - 1)^2 + (x - 1)$

CHALLENGE

What is the pattern? Prove it. $5^2 - 5 = 4^2 + 4$
$7^2 - 7 = 6^2 + 6$

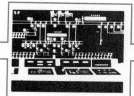

COMPUTER

TEACHER'S RESOURCE MASTERS

Computer Master 7

Are computers really intelligent? The question cannot be answered categorically yet. What can be stated categorically, however, is that research now being conducted in artificial intelligence (AI) is among the most intriguing research of our time.

What can be done to make a computer seem to think on its own? The program below demonstrates some of the possibilities. Enter the program. When you RUN it, enter the names of five objects and their X and Y coordinates on an imaginary grid.

```
10  SX = 0: SY = 0: DIM PS(5,1),NA$(5): GOSUB 130: I = 1
20  PRINT: PRINT "I AM AT ";SX;"X, ";SY;"Y ON THE GRID,"
30  X = PS(I,0) - SX: Y = PS(I,1) - SY
40  PRINT "LET ME SEE NOW , , ,": GOSUB 120
50  D$ = "EAST": IF X < 0 THEN D$ = "WEST"
60  PRINT "I'M MOVING ";ABS (X);" UNITS ";D$;",":
    GOSUB 120
70  D$ = "NORTH": IF Y < 0 THEN D$ = "SOUTH"
80  PRINT "NOW I'M GOING ";ABS (Y);" UNITS ";D$;",":
    GOSUB 120
90  PRINT "I FOUND THE ";NA$(I);"!"
100 SX = SX + X: SY = SY + Y: I = I + 1: IF I < 6 THEN 20
110 PRINT "I'M FINISHED!": END
120 PRINT: FOR T = 1 TO 2000: NEXT T: RETURN
130 FOR I = 1 TO 5
140 PRINT "NAME OF OBJECT ";I;: INPUT NA$(I)
150 INPUT "ITS COORDINATES ON GRID (X,Y)? ";
    PS(I,0),PS(I,1)
160 NEXT I: RETURN
```

EXERCISES

1. How does the program determine how to arrive at the next object?

2. Modify the program to print out the slope of the computer's move from object to object.

ANSWERS

1. The program subtracts the x-coordinate of the second object from that of the first object, and then subtracts the y-coordinates. Depending upon whether the differences are positive or negative, the location moves north or south, then east or west.

2. Add the following:
   ```
   85 PRINT "THAT GIVES
      A SLOPE OF ";:
      IF X = 0 THEN
      PRINT
      "*UNDEFINED*":
      GOSUB 120: GOTO
      90
   87 PRINT (Y/X);
      "....": GOSUB 120
   ```

ENRICHMENT

See Activities 17–20,
p. T45.

ADDITIONAL ANSWERS
For the odd-numbered solutions, see *Answers To Selected Exercises*, p. 581.

2.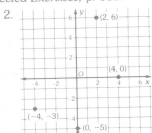

8.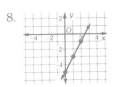

10.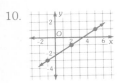

12. domain = {1, 2, 3, 8, 0, −9}   range = {3, −4, 7, −1}   yes

13. domain = {3, 5, 0} range = {2, 5, −1, 0} no

14. domain = {−1, 2, 0, −4} range = {−9, 8, 6, 7} yes

CHAPTER 7 REVIEW

VOCABULARY

abscissa (7.1)

acceleration (7.8)

axes (7.1)

constant function (7.4)

coordinate plane (7.1)

coordinates (7.1)

domain (7.3)

ƒ of x notation (7.4)

function (7.3)

functional value (7.4)

horizontal line (7.5)

linear equation in two
  variables (7.2)

linear function (7.4)

mapping notation (7.4)

ordered pair (7.1)

ordinate (7.1)

origin (7.1)

parallel (7.6)

perpendicular (7.6)

point-slope form (7.7)

quadrant (7.1)

range (7.3)

range value (7.4)

relation (7.3)

slope (7.5)

slope formula (7.5)

slope-intercept form (7.6)

standard form (7.2)

velocity (7.8)

vertical line (7.5)

vertical-line test (7.3)

x-axis (7.1)

x-coordinate (7.1)

y-axis (7.1)

y-coordinate (7.1)

y-intercept (7.6)

REVIEW EXERCISES

7.1   **Graph the sets of ordered pairs, using separate axes for each exercise.**

  1. {(1, −4), (2, 3), (5, −2), (0, 3), (−6, 0)}

  2. {(−4, −3), (0, −5), (2, 6), (4, 0)}

  3. {(4, 4), (0, 0), (−3, −5), (−4, −4)}

In which quadrant or on which axis is each of the following points?

  4. (8, −3)   fourth

  6. (−2, −1)   third

  5. (0, 5)   y-axis

  7. (−6, 7)   second

7.2   **Find at least three solutions for each equation, then draw the graph of the equation.**

  8. $y = 2x − 5$

  10. $2x − 3y = 7$

  9. $y = −3x + 4$

  11. $3x + 2y = −4$

7.3   **For each relation, state the domain and the range. Tell whether or not each relation is a function.**

  12. {(1, 3), (2, 3), (3, 3), (8, −4), (0, 7), (−9, −1)}

  13. {(3, 2), (5, 2), (3, 5), (5, −1), (0, 0)}

  14. {(−1, −9), (2, 8), (0, 6), (−4, 7)}

Let the domain for the following relations be $\{-3, -1, 0, 1, 3\}$. List the ordered pairs in each relation.

15. $y = 2x - 8$ **16.** $y = x + 6$ **17.** $y = \frac{1}{3}x - 1$

7.4 Find $f(3)$ for each of the functions.

18. $f(x) = 2x - 8$ -2 **19.** $f(x) = \frac{2}{3}x + 4$ 6 **20.** $f(x) = x^2 - 2x + 1$ 4

Determine whether each of the following is a linear function.

21. $3x - 2y = 7$ yes   **22.** $x^2 - y = 4$ no   **23.** $2x + y = 3x - 4y + 8$ yes

7.5 Find the slope of the line containing the points whose coordinates are given.

24. $(-2, 5)$ and $(3, 1)$ $-\frac{4}{5}$ **25.** $(4, -1)$ and $(7, 8)$ 3

Draw the graph of the line, given coordinates of a point on the line and the slope of the line.

26. $(2, -5)$; $m = \frac{5}{2}$ **27.** $(8, 3)$; $m = 14$

7.6 Write each equation in slope-intercept form. Then give the slope and the y-intercept.

28. $2x - y = 8$ $y = 2x - 8$; 2; -8 **29.** $3x + 4y = 10$

$y = -\frac{3}{4}x + \frac{5}{2}$; $-\frac{3}{4}$, $\frac{5}{2}$

30. $-x + 3y = 5$ $y = \frac{1}{3}x + \frac{5}{3}$; $\frac{1}{3}$, $\frac{5}{3}$

7.7 Write each equation for the given line in slope-intercept form.

31. The coordinates of two points on the line are $(1, 5)$ and $(6, -3)$.

32. The slope is $-\frac{3}{2}$ and the coordinates of a point on the line are $(-1, 6)$.

33. The slope is $\frac{10}{7}$ and the y-intercept is 4. $y = \frac{10}{7}x + 4$

34. The slope is -8 and the y-intercept is -3. $y = -8x - 3$

7.8 **35.** A car is traveling at a constant velocity of 12 meters per second, and accelerates for 3 seconds until it has a velocity of 27 meters per second. (Assume that the car is accelerating at a constant rate.) Write the linear equation that describes the car's velocity. $y = 5x + 12$

36. The car's velocity at 1 second is 15 meters per second and at 4 seconds is 30 meters per second. What is the car's velocity at 6 seconds? (Assume that the car is accelerating at a constant rate.) 40 meters per second

15. $\{(-3, -14), (-1, -10), (0, -8), (1, -6), (3, -2)\}$

16. $\{(-3, 3), (-1, 5), (0, 6), (1, 7), (3, 9)\}$

17. $\{(-3, -2), (-1, -\frac{4}{3}), (0, -1), (1, -\frac{2}{3}), (3, 0)\}$

26.

31. $y = -\frac{8}{5}x + \frac{33}{5}$

32. $y = -\frac{3}{2}x + \frac{9}{2}$

TEACHER'S RESOURCE
MASTERS

Chapter 7 Test

Multiple-Choice Test

PROBLEM-SOLVING
HANDBOOK

p. 533

ADDITIONAL ANSWERS

1.

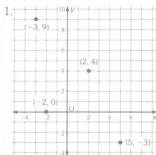

3.

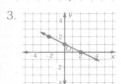

5. domain = $\{-1, 2, 3, 4\}$
   range = $\{0, -1, 7, 4\}$
   no

6. (b)   D   R
       4 ⟶ 9
       2 ⟶ 1
       0 ⟶ 3
           8

7. $\{(-2, -2), (4, 1), (6, 2)\}$

8. $y = -3x - 2$

12.

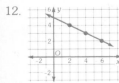

Additional Answers
See p. T59.

CHAPTER 7 TEST

1. Graph the set of ordered pairs. $\{(-3, 9), (2, 4), (5, -3), (-2, 0)\}$

2. In which quadrant is the point with coordinates $(3, -8)$?   fourth

3. Find at least three solutions for $y = -\frac{1}{2}x + 1$. Then draw the graph.

4. Write $4x - 2y + 3 = x + 5y - 4$ in standard form. $3x - 7y = -7$

5. State the domain and the range of this set of ordered pairs. Tell whether or not the relation is also a function. $\{(-1, 0), (2, -1), (3, 7), (4, 7), (2, 4)\}$

6. Describe the relation shown in the table as (a) a set of ordered pairs, and (b) by a mapping.   (a) $\{(4, 9), (4, 1), (2, 3), (0, 8)\}$

x	y
4	9
4	1
2	3
0	8

7. Let the domain be $\{-2, 4, 6\}$. List the ordered pairs in the relation $y = \frac{1}{2}x - 1$.

8. Write the rule in the form of an equation that defines the function $f:x \rightarrow -3x - 2$.

9. Find $f(-2)$ if $f(x) = -3x + 4$.   10

10. Is $3x - 5y + 8 = -2x + 4$ a linear function?   yes

11. Find the slope of the line containing the points with coordinates $(2, -3)$ and $(8, 7)$. $\frac{5}{3}$

12. Draw the graph of the line that passes through the point with coordinates $(2, 4)$ and has slope $-\frac{1}{2}$.

13. A line has the equation $3x - 5y = 10$. Write this equation in slope-intercept form. Then give the slope of the line and its y-intercept. $y = \frac{3}{5}x - 2; \frac{3}{5}; -2$

14. Graph the line for the equation $y = \frac{3}{4}x - 1$, using the y-intercept and the slope.

15. Given the pair of equations $\frac{15}{2}x - \frac{5}{2}y = 15$ and $-9x + 3y = 15$, determine if the lines are parallel.   yes

16. Write the equation of the line that has slope -4 and y-intercept $\frac{3}{2}$. $y = -4x + \frac{3}{2}$

17. A line has a slope of 2. The point with coordinates $(-2, -9)$ is on this line. Express the linear equation in slope-intercept form. $y = 2x - 5$

18. Write the equation of the line that passes through the points with coordinates $P(4, 1)$ and $Q(2, 3)$. $y = -x + 5$

19. A car's velocity at 1 second is 8 meters per second, and at 2 seconds is 12 meters per second. Write the linear equation that describes the car's velocity during acceleration. (Assume the car is accelerating at a constant rate.) $y = 4x + 4$

Mathematics Around You

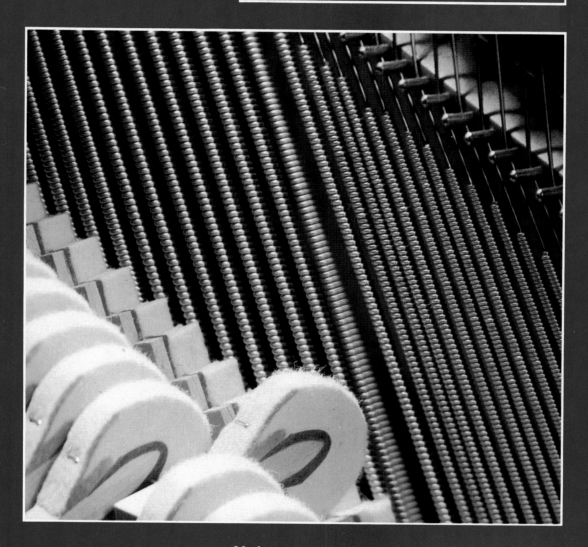

Mathematics is involved in more areas than you might expect. In this photograph, the vibrating string of a piano is shown. In the feature on page 351, there is a more detailed description of the relationship between mathematics and music.

Mathematics in Nature

A honeycomb consists of a series of interlocking hexagons.

This delicate spiderweb illustrates another geometric design occurring in nature. Note the angles formed by strands radiating from a central point.

C

D

Upper left: The quartz crystal shown in this photograph is called amethyst. If you look closely, you will find hexagonal patterns.

Lower left: Sunflowers have an interesting relationship to a sequence of numbers called the Fibonacci sequence. In the feature on page 267, you will find a more detailed description of this relationship.

Below: These starfish are another example of geometric shapes occurring in nature.

This highly magnified photograph of a snowflake illustrates the fact that every snowflake has six sides.

F

Mathematics in Art and Design

This modern sculpture by Philip MacMillan James makes use of simple geometric shapes to produce an unusual design.

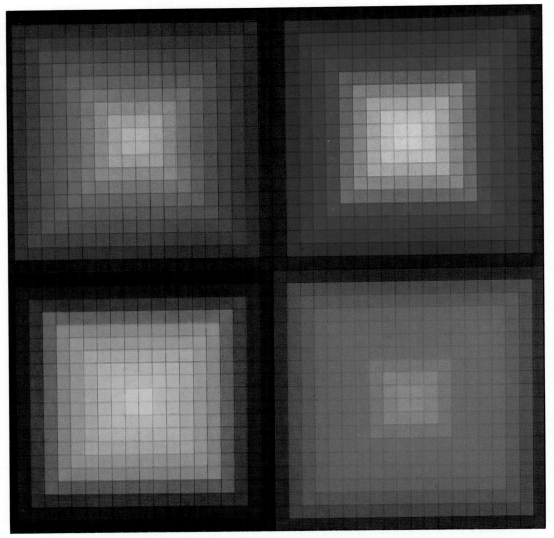

Above: The paintings of Victor Vasarely are often very mathematical in nature. This painting, called "Arcturus II," was painted in 1966 and appears in the Joseph H. Hirshhorn Museum in Washington, D.C.

Upper right: With the use of modern computers, many interesting designs such as the one shown here can be created.

Lower right: The figure shown here is called a hypercube. Note the smaller cube within the larger cube. This figure has applications to four-dimensional space.

H

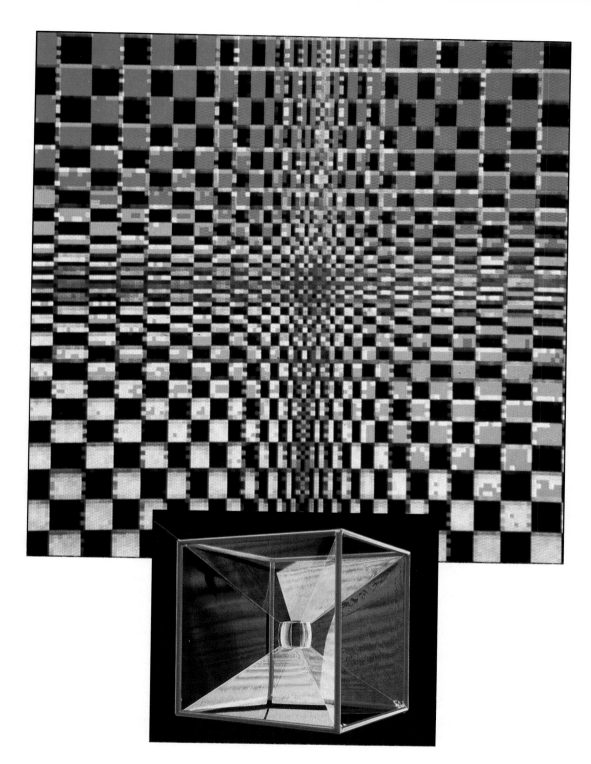

I

Mathematics in Technology

Below: This photograph of a typical industrial setting shows a variety of geometric shapes.

Upper left: This photo of the control room of a coal-fired power plant shows the highly sophisticated equipment that is used to monitor the plant. Notice the computers in use. Nowadays computers are used in almost every type of industry.

Upper right: Without the use of mathematics, the National Aeronautics and Space Administration would never be able to launch spacecraft such as the one in this photograph.

Lower right: The steel girders in this photograph illustrate the recurring use of triangles. Triangles are used frequently in bridges, frameworks of buildings, and so on, because the triangle is a rigid figure.

Background photo: The Great Temple of Amun in Karnak, Egypt, is shown here. Notice the variety of mathematical shapes. **Above:** The Neptune Temple in Paestum, Italy, employs several mathematical shapes in its classic design.

Mathematics in Architecture

The National Commercial Bank in Jedda, Saudi Arabia, is in the shape of a triangular prism.

Background photo: Note the variety of mathematical shapes in this modern building. **Left:** The Congress Building in Brasília, Brazil, is another example of striking architecture that involves a variety of mathematical shapes. **Above:** This ancient mosque is in Isfahan, Iran. Note the variety of shapes in the design. **Right:** This photograph shows the interior of Alvarado Square in Albuquerque, New Mexico.

This modern building illustrates the use of various mathematical figures.

CUMULATIVE REVIEW CHAPTERS 1–7

Choose the correct answer.

1. Name the coefficient in $2x^3y^4$. B
   - **A.** 3
   - **B.** 2
   - **C.** 7
   - **D.** 4

2. Evaluate $x^2(xy)^3$ if $x = 4$ and $y = -3$. D
   - **A.** 288
   - **B.** 27,648
   - **C.** -288
   - **D.** $-27,648$

3. Name the property illustrated by the following: $xy = yx$. A
   - **A.** Commutative property of multiplication
   - **B.** Associative property of multiplication
   - **C.** Distributive property
   - **D.** Identity property of multiplication

4. Simplify $-(9)^2 - 4 + 2.3(0.8)$. A
   - **A.** -83.16
   - **B.** 80.1
   - **C.** -81.9
   - **D.** None of these

5. Give the degree of $3x^2y^4$. D
   - **A.** 3
   - **B.** 2
   - **C.** 4
   - **D.** 6

6. Which set describes the set of whole numbers? B
   - **A.** $\{1, 2, 3, 4, \ldots\}$
   - **B.** $\{0, 1, 2, 3, 4, \ldots\}$
   - **C.** $\{\ldots, -3, -2, -1, 0, 1, 2, 3, \ldots\}$
   - **D.** $\{0, 2, 4, 6, 8, \ldots\}$

7. If $x < 0$, then $|x| = $ _____. A
   - **A.** $-x$
   - **B.** x
   - **C.** 0
   - **D.** None of these

8. Simplify $-249 + 53$. B
   - **A.** 216
   - **B.** -196
   - **C.** 302
   - **D.** -302

9. Simplify $-123 - 78$. D
   - **A.** -45
   - **B.** 201
   - **C.** 45
   - **D.** -201

10. Simplify $-18(12)(-15)$. C
    - **A.** -231
    - **B.** -3240
    - **C.** 3240
    - **D.** 54

11. Simplify $-\frac{7}{8} \div \frac{13}{16}$. A
    - **A.** $-\frac{14}{13}$
    - **B.** $-\frac{91}{128}$
    - **C.** $-\frac{13}{14}$
    - **D.** None of these

12. Solve $0.5 = y + 3.91$. A
    - **A.** -3.41
    - **B.** 3.96
    - **C.** 4.41
    - **D.** None of these

13. Solve $-8.05 - x = 15.9$. D
    - **A.** 7.85
    - **B.** 23.95
    - **C.** -7.85
    - **D.** -23.95

14. Solve $\frac{3}{8}x = -15$. D
    - **A.** 40
    - **B.** $5\frac{5}{8}$
    - **C.** $-5\frac{5}{8}$
    - **D.** -40

15. Solve $-42 = \frac{x}{3}$. D

    A. 126   **B.** -14 **C.** 14   **D.** -126

16. Solve $11y - 9y = 30$ D

    A. 2   **B.** -2 **C.** -15 **D.** 15

17. Solve $4y + 9 = 51$. A

    A. $10\frac{1}{2}$ **B.** 168   **C.** 15   **D.** None of these

18. Rename $\frac{5}{6}$ as a terminating or a repeating decimal. B

    A. $0.8\overline{3}$ **B.** $0.8\overline{3}$ **C.** 0.8   **D.** 0.83

19. Which graph represents $x \le 5$? D

    A. 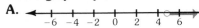   **B.**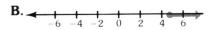

    C. 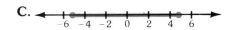   **D.**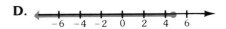

20. Solve $x - 2.1 < 3.6$. B

    A. $x > 1.5$ **B.** $x < 5.7$ **C.** $x < 1.5$ **D.** $x > 5.7$

21. Solve $-3x > 2$. B

    A. $x > -\frac{2}{3}$ **B.** $x < -\frac{2}{3}$ **C.** $x < \frac{2}{3}$ **D.** $x > \frac{2}{3}$

22. Solve $\frac{5}{8}x \ge -10$. B

    A. $x \le 16$ **B.** $x \ge -16$ **C.** $x \ge 16$ **D.** $x \le -16$

23. Solve $4x - 12 < 8$. A

    A. $x < 5$ **B.** $x < -1$ **C.** $x < 80$ **D.** $x < 20$

24. Translate the following into an inequality: *The sum of a number and 10 is greater than three times the number.* D

    A. $10 > 3x$ **B.** $10x > 3x$ **C.** $10 + x \ge 3x$ **D.** $x + 10 > 3x$

25. Find the intersection of $\{0, 1, 2, 3\}$ and $\{0, 3, 6\}$. C

    A. $\{0, 1, 2, 3, 6\}$ **B.** $\{ \ \}$ **C.** $\{0, 3\}$ **D.** $\{1, 2, 6\}$

26. Graph the solution set of the following conjunction: $4x > x + 3$ and $2x + 3 < 5$. D

    A.   **B.**   **C.**   **D.** None of these

27. Graph the solution set of the following disjunction: $2x + 1 > -3$ or $3x < 4x - 3$. A

    A.   **B.**   **C.**   **D.** None of these

28. Solve $|r - 5| > 2$. Graph the solution set. A

A.  **B.** **C.** **D.** None of these

29. If 3 times an integer is decreased by 5, the result is between -11 and 25. What is the integer? C

A. $-2 \leq x \leq 10$ 　　　**B.** $\{-2, -1, 0, 1, 2, 3, 4, 5, 6, 7, 8, 9, 10\}$

C. $\{-1, 0, 1, 2, 3, 4, 5, 6, 7, 8, 9\}$ 　　　　　　　　　**D.** $-2 < x < 10$

30. Simplify $(2x^2 - 5xy + 3) + (x^2 + 4xy + 5)$. B

A. $3x^2 + 9xy + 8$ 　　**B.** $3x^2 - xy + 8$ 　　**C.** $3x^2 + xy + 8$ 　　**D.** $2x^2 - 5xy + 5$

31. Simplify $(10x - 4xy - 2y) - (-3x + 5xy + 8y)$. A

A. $13x - 9xy - 10y$ 　　**B.** $7x - xy - 6y$ 　　**C.** $7x - 9xy - 10y$ **D.** $13x - xy - 6y$

32. Simplify $(3x^2)^3$. D

A. $9x^5$ 　　　　　**B.** $9x^6$ 　　　　　**C.** $27x^5$ 　　　　　**D.** $27x^6$

33. Simplify $(-8m^2)(2m)^2$. C

A. $16m^4$ 　　　　**B.** $-16m^4$ 　　　　**C.** $-32m^4$ 　　　　**D.** $-32m^2$

34. Simplify $-3x(5x^2 + 6xy + 9y^2)$. A

A. $-15x^3 - 18x^2y - 27xy^2$ 　　　　**B.** $15x^3 + 18x^2y + 27xy^2$

C. $-15x^2 - 18xy - 27y^2$ 　　　　　**D.** $2x^3 + 3x^2y + 6xy^2$

35. Simplify $(2a - 6)(a + 5)$. B

A. $2a^2 + 16a + 30$ 　　**B.** $2a^2 + 4a - 30$ 　　**C.** $2a^2 - a - 1$ 　　**D.** $2a^2 - 4a + 30$

36. Simplify $(x - 4)^2$. D

A. $x^2 - 8x + 8$ 　　**B.** $x^2 + 16$ 　　**C.** $x^2 + 8x + 16$ 　　**D.** $x^2 - 8x + 16$

37. Solve $2(3x + 5) - 3x = 2(x + 4) - 3(2x + 6)$. B

A. 4 　　　　**B.** $-\dfrac{20}{7}$ 　　　　**C.** 0 　　　　**D.** $-\dfrac{16}{7}$

38. Simplify $\dfrac{x^6 y^8}{x^2 y^4}$. D

A. $x^3 y^2$ 　　　　**B.** $x^8 y^{12}$ 　　　　**C.** $x^{12} y^{32}$ 　　　　**D.** $x^4 y^4$

39. Simplify $\dfrac{-40x^3}{5x^7}$. B

A. $8x^4$ 　　　　**B.** $-\dfrac{8}{x^4}$ 　　　　**C.** $-8x^4$ 　　　　**D.** $\dfrac{8}{x^4}$

40. Give the prime factorization of 200. B

A. $2^2 \cdot 5^3$ 　　　　**B.** $2^3 \cdot 5^2$ 　　　　**C.** $2 \cdot 10^2$ 　　　　**D.** None of these

41. Find the greatest common factor of 168 and 528. B

A. 3696 　　　　**B.** 24 　　　　**C.** 154 　　　　**D.** 6

42. Find the least common multiple of 32 and 24. D

A. 768 　　　　**B.** 8 　　　　**C.** 2 　　　　**D.** 96

43. Name the common monomial factor of $3x^2 + 6x + 9$. B

A. x **B.** 3   **C.** $3x$ **D.** 1

44. Factor $4x^2 - y^2$. A

A. $(2x + y)(2x - y)$ **B.** $(4x + y)(x - y)$ **C.** $(2x + y)^2$ **D.** $(2x - y)^2$

45. Factor $9x^2 + 6x + 1$. D

A. $(3x - 1)^2$ **B.** $(3x + 1)(3x - 1)$ **C.** $(9x + 1)^2$ **D.** $(3x + 1)^2$

46. Factor $x^2 - 6x + 5$. C

A. $(x + 3)(x + 2)$ **B.** $(x + 5)(x + 1)$ **C.** $(x - 5)(x - 1)$ **D.** $(x - 3)(x + 2)$

47. Factor $5x^2 + 14x - 3$. A

A. $(5x - 1)(x + 3)$ **B.** $(5x + 3)(x - 1)$ **C.** $(5x + 1)(x - 3)$ **D.** $(x + 1)(x - 3)$

48. Factor $4y^2 - 16y - 20$. C

A. $(4y - 5)(y + 4)$ **B.** $4(y^2 - 4y - 5)$ **C.** $4(y + 1)(y - 5)$ **D.** None of these

49. Solve $x^2 = 15 - 2x$. B

A. $-3, 5$ **B.** $3, -5$ **C.** $-3, -5$ **D.** $3, 5$

50. In which quadrant is $x < 0$ and $y > 0$? B

A. 1st   **B.** 2nd   **C.** 3rd   **D.** 4th

51. Write $12 - 3y = 7x - 4x + y$ in standard form. C

A. $3x + 4y - 12 = 0$ **B.** $4y = -3x + 12$ **C.** $3x + 4y = 12$ **D.** $y = -\frac{3}{4}x + 3$

52. What is the domain of the relation $\{(-1, 0), (-6, 1), (-5, 2), (-5, 3)\}$? A

A. $\{-6, -5, -1\}$ **B.** $\{0, 1, 2, 3\}$

C. $\{-6, -5, -1, 0, 2, 3\}$ **D.** None of these

53. Find $g(-2)$ if $g(x) = 3x^2 + 4$. B

A. 24   **B.** 16   **C.** -8 **D.** -2

54. Find the slope of the line containing points with the coordinates $(4, 1)$ and $(-8, 1)$. B

A. undefined   **B.** 0   **C.** $\frac{1}{3}$ **D.** -3

55. Find the slope of the line containing points with the coordinates $(0, 4)$ and $(2, 6)$. C

A. undefined   **B.** 0   **C.** 1   **D.** -1

56. Write $3x - 2y = 5$ in slope-intercept form. D

A. $3x - 2y - 5 = 0$ **B.** $-2y = 3x + 5$ **C.** $3x = 2y + 5$ **D.** $y = \frac{3}{2}x - \frac{5}{2}$

57. Write the equation of the line that has slope $-\frac{3}{4}$ and y-intercept 8. A

A. $y = -\frac{3}{4}x + 8$ **B.** $-\frac{3}{4}y + x = 8$ **C.** $x = -\frac{3}{4y} + 8$ **D.** $-\frac{3}{4}x + y = 8$

58. Write the equation of the line that passes through the points with coordinates $(4, 9)$ and $(5, 0)$. C

A. $y = -9x + 5$ **B.** $y = -\frac{x}{9} + 9\frac{4}{9}$ **C.** $y = -9x + 45$ **D.** $y = -\frac{1}{9}x + \frac{5}{9}$

CHAPTER 8

Linear Systems

The spiral of this shell is based on the Fibonacci sequence, described on page 267. Give the 20th term of this sequence.

6765

251

CLASSROOM EXAMPLES

1. Solve by graphing.

$2x + 3y = 6$

$4x - 3y = 12$

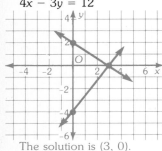

The solution is (3, 0).

2. Solve by graphing.

$y = 3x + 4$

$y = 4x + 3$

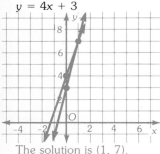

The solution is (1, 7).

MIXED REVIEW

Find each value.

1. $5(3)^2$ 45

2. $(-6.3)^3$ -250.047

3. $\left(\frac{1}{9}\right)^4$ $\frac{1}{6561}$

4. $4 + 3(5)^2$ 79

5. $3(-4) + 6(-2)^2$ 12

8.1 | Graphing Systems

The linear equations $x + y = 6$ and $2x - y = 6$ are graphed at the right. Notice that the graphs of these two equations intersect at the point $(4, 2)$. So $(4, 2)$ is a solution of *both* equations. The equations $x + y = 6$ and $2x - y = 6$ are said to form a **system of equations.** The solutions of a system of equations are the ordered pairs that satisfy both equations in the system. Therefore, $(4, 2)$ is a solution of the system.

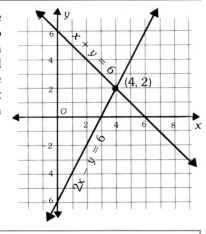

EXAMPLES

1 **Solve by graphing.** $x + 2y = 2$

$3x - 2y = -10$

SOLUTION

1. Graph both equations on the same set of axes.

2. Determine the point of intersection. $(-2, 2)$

3. Check the solution in *both* equations.

$x + 2y = 2$	$3x - 2y = -10$
$-2 + 2(2) \overset{?}{=} 2$	$3(-2) - 2(2) \overset{?}{=} -10$
$-2 + 4 \overset{?}{=} 2$	$-6 - 4 \overset{?}{=} -10$
$2 = 2$ ✔	$-10 = -10$ ✔

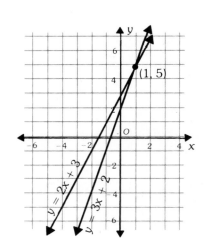

2 **Solve by graphing.** $y = 2x + 3$

$y = 3x + 2$

SOLUTION

As shown on the graph, the solution is $(1, 5)$.

CHECK

$y = 2x + 3$	$y = 3x + 2$
$5 \overset{?}{=} 2(1) + 3$	$5 \overset{?}{=} 3(1) + 2$
$5 = 5$ ✔	$5 = 5$ ✔

For each pair of lines, tell the coordinates of the point of intersection.

1. lines a and b $\quad(-5, -1)$
2. lines b and c $\quad(4, -4)$
3. lines c and d $\quad(0, 4)$
4. lines a and c $\quad(1, 2)$
5. lines b and d $\quad(-2, -2)$
6. lines a and d $\quad(-1, 1)$

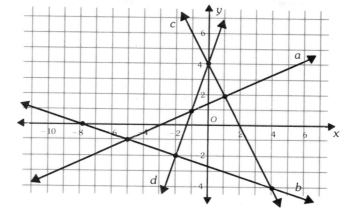

Determine whether or not the given ordered pair is a solution of the system.

7. $x - y = -1$
   $x + y = -1$ $\quad(0, 1)$ no

8. $x - y = 2$
   $x + y = 4$ $\quad(1, 2)$ no

9. $y = x + 2$
   $y = 2x$ $\quad(2, 4)$ yes

10. $x + y = 1$
    $x = 2$ $\quad(2, 1)$ no

WRITTEN EXERCISES

A. Tell whether each statement is true or false.

1. $2x - y = 1$ means $2x - y = 1$ or $x + y = 2$. false
   $x + y = 2$

2. $2x - 3y = 6$ means $2x - 3y = 6$ and $x + 3y = -3$. true
   $x + 3y = -3$

3. $2x - y = 10$ means $2x - y = 10$ and $x + 2y = -5$. true
   $x + 2y = -5$

4. $3x + y = 3$ means $3x + y = 3$ or $x - 4y = 1$. false
   $x - 4y = 1$

Solve each system by graphing and check your solutions.

5. $x + y = 0$
   $x - y = 0$ $\quad(0, 0)$

6. $x + y = 2$
   $x - y = 2$ $\quad(2, 0)$

7. $y = x + 1$
   $y = -x + 1$ $\quad(0, 1)$

8. $y = x + 5$
   $y = -4x$ $\quad(-1, 4)$

9. $x + y = 1$
   $x = 3$ $\quad(3, -2)$

10. $2x - y = 1$
    $x + y = 2$ $\quad(1, 1)$

TEACHER'S RESOURCE MASTERS

Practice Master 32, Part 1

COMPUTER SOFTWARE

Graphing Linear Equations and Inequalities

ASSIGNMENT GUIDE

Minimum
1–15 odd, 23–39 odd

Regular
23–34, 41–47 odd

Maximum
29–40, 41, 45, 49, 50

ADDITIONAL ANSWERS

Written Exercises

For the odd-numbered solutions, see *Answers to Selected Exercises*, p. 582.

6.
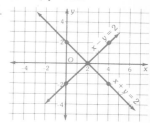

8.
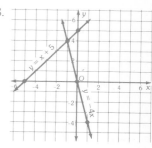

(continued on next page)

10.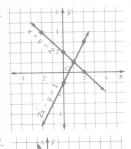

11. $x = 3$
    $y = 5$ $(3, 5)$

12. $2x + y = 4$
    $y = 2$ $(1, 2)$

13. $x = 3$
    $2x + 3y = 0$ $(3, -2)$

14. $y = -1$
    $2x + 2y = 2$ $(2, -1)$

15. $x + 4y = 8$
    $x = -4$ $(-4, 3)$

16. $2x - 3y = 0$
    $2x + 3y = 0$ $(0, 0)$

17. $x - y = 9$
    $2x + y = 6$ $(5, -4)$

18. $3x + y = 6$
    $x - 2y = 2$ $(2, 0)$

19. $x + y = 2$
    $2y - x = 10$ $(-2, 4)$

20. $3x + 2y = 4$
    $2x - 3y = 7$ $(2, -1)$

21. $2x - y = 10$
    $x + 2y = -5$ $(3, -4)$

22. $3x + y = -4$
    $x + 4y = -5$
    $(-1, -1)$

12.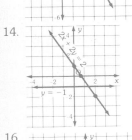

B. 23. $2x - y = -5$
    $x + y = 2$ $(-1, 3)$

24. $x = 3$
    $y = 5$ $(3, 5)$

25. $y = 3x - 2$
    $y = -2x + 3$ $(1, 1)$

26. $3x - 2y = -4$
    $x + 2y = -4$ $(-2, -1)$

27. $y - x = 1$
    $2x + y = 4$ $(1, 2)$

28. $x = 6$
    $y = -2$ $(6, -2)$

29. $2x + y = 4$
    $2x - 3y = 12$ $(3, -2)$

30. $x + y = 1$
    $x = -1$ $(-1, 2)$

-31. $y = \frac{1}{2}$
    $x = -\frac{1}{4}$ $\left(-\frac{1}{4}, \frac{1}{2}\right)$

14.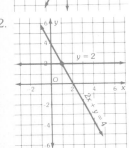

32. $4x - 3y = -6$
    $x + 3y = -9$ $(-3, -2)$

33. $3x + 2y = 7$
    $x - 4y = -7$ $(1, 2)$

34. $y = \frac{1}{3}x - 1$
    $y = -\frac{1}{3}x - 3$
    $(-3, -2)$

35. $2x - 4y = 4$
    $5x + 12y = 10$ $(2, 0)$

36. $2x + y = 8$
    $x - 3y = 4$ $(4, 0)$

37. $8x + 3y = -16$
    $7y - 12x = 24$
    $(-2, 0)$

38. $x + y = 3$
    $x = y$ $\left(\frac{3}{2}, \frac{3}{2}\right)$

39. $y = -x$
    $x - y = 3$ $\left(\frac{3}{2}, -\frac{3}{2}\right)$

40. $y = 3x$
    $y = -3x + 2$ $\left(\frac{1}{3}, 1\right)$

16.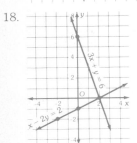

C. Find the area of the triangle whose vertices are formed by the intersection of the lines of the given system of equations.

41. $x + y = 4$
    $y = x$
    the y-axis 4

42. $y = -x$
    $y = x - 10$
    the x-axis 25

43. $2x + y = 5$
    $y = x - 4$
    $y = 5$ 27

Solve by graphing. Use fractions to estimate the coordinates when necessary.

44. $y = 2x - 4$
    $y = -2x + 2$ $\left(\frac{3}{2}, -1\right)$

45. $8x = 7$
    $5y = 2$ $\left(\frac{7}{8}, \frac{2}{5}\right)$

46. $x + y = 3$
    $2x - 3y = 6$ $(3, 0)$

Solve by graphing.

47. $y = x - 2$
    $x = 4$
    $y = 2$ $(4, 2)$

48. $y + x = 6$
    $y - x = 2$
    $y = 2x$ $(2, 4)$

49. $x + 2y = 8$
    $2x - 3y = 2$
    $11x + y = 46$ $(4, 2)$

18.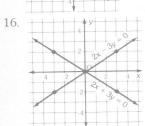

Additional Answers
See p. T59.

Write and graph a system to answer the problem.

50. The cost of renting a rug cleaner from one store is $4, plus $2 an hour. Another store rents cleaners for $6, plus $1 an hour. When are the total rental costs the same?

8.2 | Types of Systems

So far, the graphs of the systems have intersected in one point, and the system had one solution. Such a system is called **consistent**. Not all systems have one solution. Some systems have no solution or an infinite number of solutions.

EXAMPLES

1 **Solve by graphing.** $y + x = 3$
$y + x = -2$

SOLUTION

The graphs are *parallel lines*—the lines do not intersect. Since the lines have no point in common, the system has no solution. Such a system is called **inconsistent**.

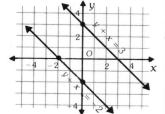

2 **Solve by graphing.** $x - 2y = 2$
$3x - 6y = 6$

SOLUTION

The graphs are the same line. The system has an infinite number of solutions. Such a system is called **consistent and dependent**.

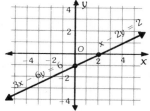

To determine, without graphing, if a system is consistent, consistent and dependent, or inconsistent, write the equations of the system in slope-intercept form.

1. The system is consistent if the lines for the equations have different slopes.
2. The system is consistent and dependent if the lines for the equations have the same slope and y-intercept.
3. The system is inconsistent if the lines for the equations have the same slope but different y-intercepts.

3 **Determine whether each system is consistent, consistent and dependent, or inconsistent.**

a. $x + 3y = -9$
$4x - 3y = -6$

b. $y = -x + 3$
$2y = -2x + 6$

c. $y = 3x + 5$
$2y = 6x + 4$

SOLUTIONS

a. $y = -\frac{1}{3}x - 3$

$y = \frac{4}{3}x + 2$

different ⎯⏌ different
consistent

b. $y = -x + 3$

$y = -x + 3$

same ⎯⏌ same
consistent and dependent

c. $y = 3x + 5$

$y = 3x + 2$

same ⎯⏌ different
inconsistent

OBJECTIVE

For a system of linear equations, change both equations to slope-intercept form and tell if the solution set is empty, contains exactly one ordered pair, or contains many ordered pairs. Then graph the system and give the solution set.

TEACHER'S NOTES

See p. T30.

CLASSROOM EXAMPLES

1. Solve by graphing.

$y + x = 4$

$y + x = -4$

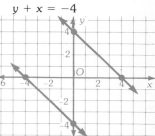

The graphs are parallel lines. The system has no solution.

2. Solve by graphing.

$x - y = 2$

$2x - 2y = 4$

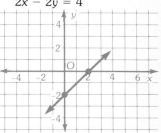

The graphs are the same line. The system has an infinite number of solutions.

3. Determine whether each system is consistent, consistent and dependent, or inconsistent.

a. $x + 2y = -6$
$3x + 5y = 15$
$y = -\frac{1}{2}x - 3$
$y = -\frac{3}{5}x + 3$
consistent

b. $y = -x + 2$
$3y = -3x + 6$
$y = -x + 2$
$y = -x + 2$
consistent and dependent

c. $y = 2x + 4$
$2y = 4x + 7$
$y = 2x + 4$
$y = 2x + \frac{1}{2}$
inconsistent

MIXED REVIEW

Perform the indicated operation.

1. $(6x + 5)(3x - 4)$
$18x^2 - 9x - 20$

2. $6a^2b(8a^3b^2 - 6ab)$
$48a^5b^3 - 36a^3b^2$

3. $(2a - b)^2$
$4a^2 - 4ab + b^2$

4. $(3x + 6)(3x - 6)$
$9x^2 - 36$

5. $(x + y)^2$ $x^2 + 2xy + y^2$

TEACHER'S RESOURCE MASTERS

Practice Master 32, Part 2

ORAL EXERCISES

True or false?

1. An inconsistent system has an infinite number of solutions.   false

2. Every system has at least one solution.   false

3. A consistent and dependent system has only one solution.   false

4. A consistent system has no solution.   false

Without graphing, determine if the system is (a) consistent, (b) consistent and dependent, or (c) inconsistent. Then state how many solutions, if any, it has.

5. $y = 2x - 5$ consistent and
$y = 2x - 5$ dependent; infinite

6. $y = 2x - 5$ consistent; one
$y = -2x - 5$

7. $y = 2x + 5$ inconsistent; none
$y = 2x - 5$

8. $y = -x + 3$ consistent; one
$y = x + 3$

9. $y = -3x + 4$ inconsistent; none
$y = -3x$

10. $y = \frac{1}{2}x - 2$ consistent and dependent; infinite
$y = \frac{1}{2}x - 2$

WRITTEN EXERCISES

A. Determine whether each system has one solution, no solution, or an infinite number of solutions. If the system has only one solution, solve by graphing.

1. $y = x + 4$
$y = -x + 2$ $(-1, 3)$

2. $y = 2x + 3$
$y = 3x + 2$ $(1, 5)$

3. $y = x - 6$
$2y = -2x - 4$ $(2, -4)$

4. $-y = x - 4$
$y - x = -2$ $(3, 1)$

5. $x - 2y = 6$
$4y = 2x - 12$ infinite

6. $x + y = 2$
$x - y = 4$ $(3, -1)$

7. $y = 3x - 5$
$y = 3x + 2$ none

8. $y = 3x + 5$
$y = 2x + 1$ $(-4, -7)$

9. $y = x - 5$
$y = x - 5$ infinite

10. $y = 5x + 3$
$y = 5x - 3$ none

11. $x + y = 4$
$x - y = 2$ $(3, 1)$

12. $y = -x + 3$
$y = -x + 2$ none

B. 13. $y = \frac{1}{3}x - \frac{4}{3}$
$y = \frac{1}{3}x - \frac{4}{3}$ infinite

14. $2x + 3y = 6$
$3x + 4y = 8$ $(0, 2)$

15. $x - y = 6$
$2x - 2y = 4$ none

16. $y = -2x + 4$
$2x - 3y = 12$ $(3, -2)$

17. $y + 2 = 3x$
$8x - 2y = -2$

18. $2y = -3x - 2$
$y = -2x - 1$ $(0, -1)$

19. $y = \frac{1}{4}x - 2$
$y = \frac{1}{2}x - 2$ $(0, -2)$

20. $2x + y = -3$
$2y + 6 = -4x$ infinite

21. $2x - 5y = 10$
$4x = 10y + 30$ none

22. $4x - y = 5$
$2y = -5x - 10$ $(0, -5)$

23. $3x + 4y = 6$
$2x - y = -7$ $(-2, 3)$

24. $5y - 2 = 2x$
$4x = 10y - 4$ infinite

25. $3y - 2 = 4x$
$12x - 9y = 1$ none

26. $5x + 2y = 10$
$4y - 20 = 10x$ $(0, 5)$

27. $3y + 5 = x$
$3x = 9y + 15$ infinite

28. $x - 18 = 6y$
$3y + 9 = \frac{1}{2}x$ infinite

29. $2x - 3y = 3$
$x - 2y = -2$ $(12, 7)$

30. $2y = 3x$
$2y - 3x = 8$ none

31. $y = 2x + 2$
$y = 4x - 2$ $(2, 6)$

32. $3y - x = 0$
$6y = 10x + 48$ $(-6, -2)$

33. $4y + 3x = 0$
$2y - 3x = 18$ $(-4, 3)$

Find the value of m that makes each system inconsistent.

34. $y = mx + 2$
$y = 4x - 2$ 4

35. $5x + 10y = 6$
$y = mx + 4$ $-\frac{1}{2}$

36. $y = 3x - 7$
$mx - y = 9$ 3

37. $y = mx + 3$
$y = 4x - 2$ 4

38. $y = \frac{1}{4}x - 5$
$y = mx + 2$ $\frac{1}{4}$

39. $3x - 4y = 8$
$y = mx + 1$ $\frac{3}{4}$

C. Find the value of b that makes each system consistent and dependent.

40. $y = 4x + 3$
$y = 4x - b$ -3

41. $y = \frac{1}{4}x - 5$
$y = \frac{1}{4}x - b$ 5

42. $y = \frac{3}{4}x + b$
$3x - 4y = 8$ -2

The systems are in the form $Ax + By + C = 0$ and $Dx + Ey + F = 0$. Write three ratios $\left(\frac{A}{D}, \frac{B}{E}, \text{and } \frac{C}{F}\right)$ for each system. Then determine if the system is consistent, consistent and dependent, or inconsistent. If the system is consistent, then $\frac{A}{D} \neq \frac{B}{E}$. If the system is consistent and dependent, then $\frac{A}{D} = \frac{B}{E} = \frac{C}{F}$. If the system is inconsistent, then $\frac{A}{D} = \frac{B}{E} \neq \frac{C}{F}$.

43. $-3x + y + 5 = 0$
$-6x + 2y - 2 = 0$

44. $x - 2y - 4 = 0$
$x - 4y - 4 = 0$

45. $-x + 3y + 4 = 0$
$-x + 3y + 4 = 0$

46. $x + y - 3 = 0$
$2x + 2y - 5 = 0$

47. $\frac{1}{3}x - y - \frac{4}{3} = 0$
$\frac{1}{3}x - y - \frac{4}{3} = 0$

48. $2x + 5y = 15$
$10x + 25y = 61$

CHALLENGE

There are two more books on top of your algebra book than there are beneath it. The pile of books has three times as many books as there are books beneath the algebra book. How many books are on top of your algebra book?   5 books

COMPUTER SOFTWARE

Graphing Linear Equations and Inequalities

ASSIGNMENT GUIDE

Minimum
1–11 odd, 13–21, 34–36

Regular
16–31

Maximum
13–47 odd

ADDITIONAL ANSWERS

Written Exercises

For the odd-numbered solutions, see *Answers to Selected Exercises*, p. 584.

2.
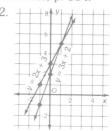

4.
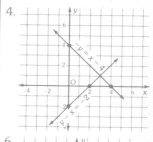

6.
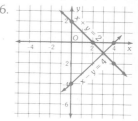

Additional Answers
See p. T60.

OBJECTIVES

Solve a system of linear equations by using the substitution method.

Solve a system of linear equations by using the substitution method where first one of the equations must be solved for one of its variables.

TEACHER'S NOTES

See p. T30.

CLASSROOM EXAMPLES

1. Solve by the substitution method. $x = 3y$
$$4x - y = 11$$

$$4x - y = 11$$
$$4(3y) - y = 11$$
$$12y - y = 11$$
$$11y = 11$$
$$y = 1$$

$$x = 3y$$
$$x = 3(1)$$
$$x = 3$$
The solution is (3, 1).

2. Solve by the substitution method. $2a - 3b = 6$
$$a - 2b = 3$$

$$a - 2b = 3$$
$$a = 3 + 2b$$
$$2(3 + 2b) - 3b = 6$$
$$6 + 4b - 3b = 6$$
$$b = 0$$

$$a = 3 + 2b$$
$$a = 3 + 2(0)$$
$$a = 3$$
The solution is (3, 0).

8.3 | Substitution Method

It is often easier, faster, and more accurate to solve a system algebraically, rather than by graphing. One type of algebraic approach is called the **substitution method.**

EXAMPLES

1 **Solve by the substitution method.** $x = 2y$
$$2x - y = 3$$

SOLUTION
Since $x = 2y$, substitute $2y$ for x in the second equation and solve for y.

$$2x - y = 3$$
$$2(2y) - y = 3$$
$$4y - y = 3$$
$$3y = 3$$
$$y = 1$$

The solution is (2, 1).

CHECK $x = 2y$
$$2 \overset{?}{=} 2(1)$$
$$2 = 2 \ \checkmark$$

Replace y with 1 in either of the equations and solve for x.

$x = 2y$	or	$2x - y = 3$
$x = 2(1)$		$2x - 1 = 3$
$x = 2$		$2x = 4$
		$x = 2$

$$2x - y = 3$$
$$2(2) \quad 1 \overset{?}{=} 3$$
$$4 - 1 \overset{?}{=} 3$$
$$3 = 3 \ \checkmark$$

2 **Solve by the substitution method.** $3a - 5b = 8$
$$a - 3b = 2$$

SOLUTION   In order for the substitution method to be used, one of the equations must be solved for a variable. In the second equation, the coefficient of a is 1. Therefore, it would be easy to solve the second equation for a.

$$a - 3b = 2$$
$$a = 2 + 3b$$

Substitute $2 + 3b$ for a in the first equation and solve for b.

$$3a - 5b = 8$$
$$3(2 + 3b) - 5b = 8$$
$$6 + 9b - 5b = 8$$
$$4b = 2$$
$$b = \frac{1}{2}$$

Solve for a.
$$a = 2 + 3b$$
$$a = 2 + 3\left(\frac{1}{2}\right)$$
$$a = 3\frac{1}{2}$$

The solution is $\left(3\frac{1}{2}, \frac{1}{2}\right)$.   NOTE: *The values in the ordered pair are written in the alphabetical order of the variables.*

The check is left to you.

3 | **Solve by the substitution method.** $-x = -2y - 4$
$$-2x + 4y = -8$$

SOLUTION

$-x = -2y - 4$ *Solve the first equation for x.*

$x = 2y + 4$

$-2x + 4y = -8$

$-2(2y + 4) + 4y = -8$ *Substitute and solve for y.*

$-4y - 8 + 4y = -8$

$-8 = -8$

If you attempt to solve a system and a true equation such as $-8 = -8$ results, then the system is consistent and dependent. The graph for each equation is the same line. Any ordered pair that satisfies one equation will satisfy the other.

CHECK

Find a few solutions to one of the equations and determine if these solutions are also solutions to the other equation.

4 | **Solve by the substitution method.** $x - \frac{1}{2}y = 4$
$$2x - y = 3$$

SOLUTION

$x - \frac{1}{2}y = 4$

$x = 4 + \frac{1}{2}y$ *Solve the first equation for x.*

$2x - y = 3$

$2\left(4 + \frac{1}{2}y\right) - y = 3$ *Substitute and solve for y.*

$8 + y - y = 3$

$8 \neq 3$

If you attempt to solve a system and a false equation such as $8 = 3$ results, then the system is inconsistent. The graph for the system is a pair of parallel lines. No ordered pair will satisfy both equations.

CHECK

Write both equations in slope-intercept form to verify that the system is inconsistent.

3. Solve by the substitution method. $-x = -3y - 6$
$$-2x + 6y = -12$$

$-x = -3y - 6$

$x = 3y + 6$

$-2x + 6y = -12$

$-2(3y + 6) + 6y = -12$

$-6y - 12 + 6y = -12$

$-12 = -12$

The system is consistent and dependent. Any ordered pair that satisfies one equation will satisfy the other.

4. Solve by the substitution method. $x - \frac{1}{4}y = 8$
$$4x - y = 3$$

$x - \frac{1}{4}y = 8$

$x = 8 + \frac{1}{4}y$

$4x - y = 3$

$4(8 + \frac{1}{4}y) - y = 3$

$32 + y - y = 3$

$32 \neq 3$

The system is inconsistent. No ordered pair will satisfy both equations.

MIXED REVIEW

Find $f(5)$ for each relation.

1. $f(x) = 3x - 8$ 7
2. $f(x) = \frac{2}{5}x + 6$ 8

Solve.

3. $3b = 2b - 8$ -8
4. $\frac{5d}{2} + 3 = 12$ $\frac{18}{5}$
5. $6x - 5 = 2x + 12$ $\frac{17}{4}$

ORAL EXERCISES

Determine the solution of each system.

1. $y = 5$
$x + y = 8$ $(3, 5)$

2. $x = 4$
$x = y - 2$ $(4, 6)$

3. $2x - y = 6$
$y = 4$ $(5, 4)$

ASSIGNMENT GUIDE

Minimum
1–11 odd, 16–21

Regular
13–24

Maximum
13–23 odd, 25–30

ADDITIONAL ANSWERS

Written Exercises
4. $(-3, -2)$
22. $(-0.4, 2)$
26. $(10, 5, 16)$
28. $(5, -3, 2)$

4. $y = -x$
$y - x = 4$ $(-2, 2)$

5. $y = x$
$x - 3y = 2$ $(-1, -1)$

6. $x = 2y$
$x + 3y = 10$ $(4, 2)$

Complete.

7. Solve. $2x - y = 6$
$x + 3y = 17$

$x + 3y = 17$ $\longrightarrow$ $2\underline{(-3y + 17)} - y = 6$ $\longrightarrow$ $x = 17 - 3\underline{(4)}$
$x = \underline{-3y + 17}$ $ y = 4$ $ x = 5$

WRITTEN EXERCISES

A. **Determine whether each system has one solution, no solution, or an infinite number of solutions. If the system has only one solution, solve by substitution.**

1. $x = 3$
$2y + x = 3$ $(3, 0)$

2. $d = 2$
$3c - 2d = -4$ $(0, 2)$

3. $a = 2$
$b = 3a + 6$ $(2, 12)$

4. $m = -3$
$n + 2m = -8$

5. $x + y = 3$
$x = y + 1$ $(2, 1)$

6. $x - 2y = 0$
$x = y$ $(0, 0)$

7. $y + 2x = 2$
$3x - 4y = 3$ $(1, 0)$

8. $2m + n = 1$
$m - n = 8$ $(3, -5)$

9. $s + 7t = 20$
$s - t = 4$ $(6, 2)$

10. $m = -3$
$n + 3 = 2m$ $(-3, -9)$

11. $x + 3y = -4$
$y = -x$ $(2, -2)$

12. $y = -x + 3$
$2y + 2x = 4$ none

B. **13.** $4y + 3x = 0$
$2y - 3x = 18$ $(-4, 3)$

14. $4x + 3y = 5$
$2x - y = -5$ $(-1, 3)$

15. $v = 2 - u$
$u - v = 0$ $(1, 1)$

16. $g = 5 - 5f$
$f + g = -3$ $(2, -5)$

17. $y = 3x - 7$
$3x - y = 7$ infinite

18. $4a + 3b = 1$
$4a + b = -5$ $(-2, 3)$

19. $5p + 7q = 1$
$4p - 2q = 16$ $(3, -2)$

20. $3c + 6d = -9$
$d = c - 1$ $\left(-\frac{1}{3}, -\frac{4}{3}\right)$

21. $x = 2y$
$\frac{1}{4}x + \frac{1}{2}y = 10$ $(20, 10)$

22. $3a + 2b = 2.8$
$0.6b - 2a = 2$

23. $2x + y = 1$
$3x - 6y = -1$ $\left(\frac{1}{3}, \frac{1}{3}\right)$

24. $\frac{1}{2}x - \frac{1}{4}y = 2$
$3x + 2y = 5$ $(3, -2)$

C. **Use the substitution method to solve each system. Express the results as an ordered triple (x, y, z).**

25. $y = 2$
$x = y + 6$
$z = x - 2y$ $(8, 2, 4)$

26. $x = 2y$
$x - y = 5$
$3z - x + y = 11$

27. $x + y = 12$
$2x + 3y = 29$
$x - z + 2y = 14$
$(7, 5, 3)$

28. $x = 2y + 11$
$y = -3$
$x - 2y - 3z = 5$

29. $x = y + 1$
$z = 2y$
$x + y + z = 9$ $(3, 2, 4)$

30. $x = 2z - 9$
$y = z - 1$ $(-1, 3, 4)$
$2x + 3y - z = 3$

CHALLENGE

For each exercise, determine the answer and then put the answer in the box of square A that corresponds to the exercise number. To check your answers, the sum of each row, each column, and each diagonal should be the same. Evaluate each of the following expressions when $a = -1$, $b = -2$, and $c = 3$.

1. ab^2
2. $c(a - b)$
3. $ac - b + a$
4. $a - b^2 + 2c$
5. $-b^2 + c$
6. $abc - c^2$
7. $a + b + c$
8. $-a + bc$
9. $c - (a - b)$

square A

1	2	3
-4	3	-2
4	**5**	**6**
1	-1	-3
7	**8**	**9**
0	-5	2

For each exercise, determine the answer and then put the answer in the box of square B that corresponds to the exercise number. To check your answers, the sum of each row, each column, and each diagonal should be the same. $\triangle XYZ$ is similar to $\triangle ABC$, which means that the corresponding sides are proportional. For example, $\frac{XZ}{AC} = \frac{XY}{AB}$.

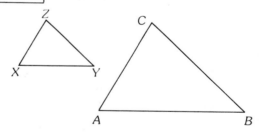

10. Find XY if $YZ = 9$, $BC = 18$, and $AB = 26$.
11. Find XZ if $XY = 4$, $AC = 12$, and $AB = 8$.
12. Find XY if $XZ = 6$, $AC = 18$, and $AB = 33$.
13. Find YZ if $XZ = 6$, $AC = 9$, and $BC = 12$.
14. Find AC if $XZ = 1$, $XY = 2.68$, and $AB = 26.8$.
15. Find BC if $XY = 8$, $YZ = 5$, and $AB = 19.2$.
16. Find BC if $YZ = 4$, $XY = 8$, and $AB = 18$.
17. Find AC if $XZ = 5$, $XY = 6$, and $AB = 16.8$.
18. Find AB if $YZ = 4$, $XY = 3.5$, and $BC = 8$.

square B

10	11	12
13	6	11
13	**14**	**15**
8	10	12
16	**17**	**18**
9	14	7

OBJECTIVE

Solve a system of linear equations by using the addition or the subtraction method.

CLASSROOM EXAMPLES

1. Solve. $3x + 4y = 12$
$2x - 4y = 8$

$3x + 4y = 12$
$\underline{+2x - 4y = 8}$
$5x + 0 = 20$
$5x = 20$
$x = 4$

$3x + 4y = 12$
$3(4) + 4y = 12$
$12 + 4y = 12$
$4y = 0$
$y = 0$
The solution is $(4, 0)$.

2. Solve. $3r - 4s = 12$
$3r - 6s = 10$

$3r - 4s = 12$
$\underline{-(3r - 6s = 10)}$
$0 + 2s = 2$
$2s = 2$
$s = 1$

$3r - 4s = 12$
$3r - 4(1) = 12$
$3r - 4 = 12$
$3r = 16$
$r = \frac{16}{3}$
The solution is $\left(\frac{16}{3}, 1\right)$.

8.4 | Addition or Subtraction Method

The **addition method** and the **subtraction method** are algebraic techniques for solving a system of equations. The addition method is useful when the coefficients of like terms in a system are additive inverses.

EXAMPLES

1 Solve. $4x + 7y = 6$
$\underbrace{3x - 7y}_{\text{additive inverse}} = 29$

SOLUTION Add like terms to obtain one equation in one variable.

$4x + 7y = 6$
$\underline{+3x - 7y = 29}$
$7x + 0 = 35$ $\quad$ *Solve for x.*
$7x = 35$
$x = 5$

Replace x with 5 in either equation and solve for y.

$4x + 7y = 6$ $\qquad\qquad$ $3x - 7y = 29$
$4(5) + 7y = 6$ $\quad$ or $\quad$ $3(5) - 7y = 29$
$20 + 7y = 6$ $\qquad\qquad$ $15 - 7y = 29$
$7y = -14$ $\qquad\qquad$ $-7y = 14$
$y = -2$ $\qquad\qquad\quad$ $y = -2$

The solution is $(5, -2)$.

CHECK $\qquad$ $4x + 7y = 6$ $\qquad\qquad\qquad$ $3x - 7y = 29$
$4(5) + 7(-2) \stackrel{?}{=} 6$ $\qquad$ $3(5) - 7(-2) \stackrel{?}{=} 29$
$20 + (-14) \stackrel{?}{=} 6$ $\qquad\qquad$ $15 + 14 \stackrel{?}{=} 29$
$6 = 6$ ✔ $\qquad\qquad\qquad$ $29 = 29$ ✔

Use the subtraction method when a term, other than a constant, in one equation is the same as a term in the other equation.

2 Solve. $2c - 6d = -3$
$\underbrace{2c}_{\text{same term}} - 9d = -4$

SOLUTION $\qquad$ $2c - 6d = -3$
$\underline{-(2c - 9d = -4)}$ $\quad$ *Subtract.*
$0 + 3d = 1$ $\qquad$ *Solve for d.*
$3d = 1$
$d = \frac{1}{3}$

Replace d with $\frac{1}{3}$ and solve for c.

$$2c - 6d = -3 \qquad\qquad 2c - 9d = -4$$

$$2c - 6\left(\tfrac{1}{3}\right) = -3 \quad \text{or} \quad 2c - 9\left(\tfrac{1}{3}\right) = -4$$

$$2c - 2 = -3 \qquad\qquad 2c - 3 = -4$$

$$2c = -1 \qquad\qquad 2c = -1$$

$$c = -\tfrac{1}{2} \qquad\qquad c = -\tfrac{1}{2}$$

The solution is $\left(-\frac{1}{2}, \frac{1}{3}\right)$. The check is left to you.

---

3   **Solve.** $3a = 11 - b$
                     $2a = b - 1$

SOLUTION   Rearrange the equations so that the addition method can be used.

$$
\begin{array}{rl}
3a + b = 11 & \\
+2a - b = -1 & \\
\hline
5a = 10 &
\end{array}
\quad \text{or} \quad
\begin{array}{rl}
3a = 11 - b & \\
+2a = -1 + b & \\
\hline
5a = 10 &
\end{array}
$$

$$a = 2 \qquad\qquad\qquad a = 2$$

$$3a = 11 - b \qquad\qquad 2a = b - 1$$

$$3(2) = 11 - b \qquad\qquad 2(2) = b - 1$$

$$6 = 11 - b \qquad\qquad 4 = b - 1$$

$$b = 5 \qquad\qquad\qquad b = 5$$

The solution is (2, 5). The check is left to you.

ORAL EXERCISES

Tell the equation that results from adding the equations in each system.

1. $a + b = -6$
     $a - b = -6$ $2a = -12$

2. $2x - y = 4$
     $x + y = 2$ $3x = 6$

3. $4p + q = -5$
     $-4p + 4q = 20$
                   $5q = 15$

Tell the equation that results from subtracting the second equation from the first.

4. $x + 2y = 6$
     $x - 3y = 1$ $5y = 5$

5. $2m + n = 4$
     $m + n = 4$ $m = 0$

6. $c + 3d = 4$
     $-6c + 3d = 3$ $7c = 1$

WRITTEN EXERCISES

A. Determine whether each system has one solution, no solution, or an infinite number of solutions. If the system has only one solution, solve by the addition or the subtraction method.

1. $2x - y = 5$
     $2x + y = 3$ $(2, -1)$

2. $x + 2y = 8$
     $-x + y = 1$ $(2, 3)$

3. $3x - 2y = -4$
     $x - 2y = -4$ $(0, 2)$

---

3. Solve. $3a = 10 - b$
                $a = b - 2$

$$
\begin{array}{rl}
3a + b = 10 & \\
+ \; a - b = -2 & \\
\hline
4a = 8 &
\end{array}
$$

$$a = 2$$

$$3a = 10 - b$$

$$3(2) = 10 - b$$

$$6 = 10 - b$$

$$b = 4$$

The solution is (2, 4).

MIXED REVIEW

1. Solve the system of equations.
   $3x + y = 9$
   $x - y = 3$ $(3, 0)$

2. Find the sum.
   $0.46 + (-5.83)$ -5.37

3. Illustrate the inverse property of multiplication.   Answers may vary.

4. Rewrite $0.\overline{407}$ as a fraction. $\frac{407}{999}$

5. Add. $(6x^2 + 5x + 3)$
   $+ (-8x^2 - 7x - 9)$
   $-2x^2 - 2x - 6$

TEACHER'S RESOURCE MASTERS

Practice Master 33, Part 2

ASSIGNMENT GUIDE

Minimum
1–11 odd, 16–24

Regular
13–27 odd, 28–30, 33–36

Maximum
19–27, 31–36

4. $5x + 3y = 6$
$3x + 3y = 2$ $\left(2, -\frac{4}{3}\right)$

5. $4x + 2y = 0$
$x - 2y = 15$ $(3, -6)$

6. $2a + b = 5$
$5a - b = 9$ $(2, 1)$

7. $3g - 4h = -6$
$3g - 3h = -15$ $(14, -9)$

8. $4x - 3y = 7$
$x - 3y = 1$ $\left(2, \frac{1}{3}\right)$

9. $2m - 6n = 8$
$-2m - 7n = 5$
$(1, -1)$

10. $-8p - q = 5$
$8p + q = -5$ infinite

11. $8t - 3x = -7$
$-8t - 3x = -7$ $\left(0, \frac{7}{3}\right)$

12. $x - 2y = 7$
$2x + 2y = 8$ $(5, -1)$

B. 13. $2x - 2y = 2$
$2x + 2y = 10$ $(3, 2)$

14. $2c - 3d = 12$
$4c + 3d = 24$ $(6, 0)$

15. $-x + 2y = 7$
$2x + 2y = 8$ $(5, -1)$

16. $-7x - 4y = -20$
$6x - 4y = -20$ $(0, 5)$

17. $2x - y = 3$
$2x + y = -1$ $\left(\frac{1}{2}, -2\right)$

18. $-2x + 3y = 3$
$3x + 3y = 18$ $(3, 3)$

19. $2a - 2b = -6$
$3a + 2b = 16$ $(2, 5)$

20. $-2x + y = 4$
$2x + 3y = 8$ $\left(-\frac{1}{2}, 3\right)$

21. $2x + 2y = 10$
$6x - 2y = 6$ $(2, 3)$

22. $x + 2y = 5$
$4x - 2y = 20$ $(5, 0)$

23. $-2s + 2t = 4$
$6s - 2t = 20$ $(6, 8)$

24. $x + y = 3$
$-x + 3y = 2$ $\left(\frac{7}{4}, \frac{5}{4}\right)$

25. $-2q - 9r = -2$
$-2q - 9r = -4$ none

26. $-9v - 3w = -7$
$-6v - 3w = -1$ $\left(2, -\frac{11}{3}\right)$

27. $2x + 2y = 10$
$2x + 2y = 10$ infinite

28. $4x - 2y = -1$
$-4x + 4y = -4$

29. $x + \frac{2}{3}y = 6$
$-x - \frac{1}{6}y = -3$ $(2, 6)$

30. $5x + 0.5y = 2$
$2x + 0.5y = 0.5$
$(0.5, -1)$

ADDITIONAL ANSWERS

Written Exercises

28. $\left(-\frac{3}{2}, -\frac{5}{2}\right)$

31. $(3.2, 4)$

32. $(6, 1)$

33. $\left(-\frac{7}{5}, \frac{4}{25}\right)$

C. 31. $-0.2x - 0.14y = -1.2$
$0.2x + 0.22y = 1.52$

32. $\frac{1}{4}x - \frac{1}{2}y = 1$
$\frac{3}{4}x + \frac{1}{2}y = 5$

33. $x + 5y - 4x = 5$
$y + 7x + 4y = -9$

34. $-\frac{1}{5}r + \frac{4}{5}s = 1$
$\frac{1}{5}r - \frac{4}{5}s = -4$ none

35. $-1.6u - 1.25v = -1.7$
$7.4u - 1.25v = -6.2$
$(-0.5, 2)$

36. $-3.8x - 4.4y = -8.2$
$6.1y - 3.8x = 2.3$ $(1,1)$

CHALLENGE

Jessica and Matthew are siblings. Matthew has as many brothers as sisters and Jessica has twice as many brothers as sisters. How many children are in the family? 7 children

OBJECTIVE

Solve a system of linear equations by using multiplication with the addition-subtraction method.

8.5	# Multiplication With the Addition-Subtraction Method

EXAMPLES

1 **Solve.** $2x + 3y = 6$
$x + 2y = 5$

SOLUTION

In this example, adding or subtracting the equations will not eliminate a variable. However, if both sides of the second equation were multiplied by -2 (or both sides of the first equation were multiplied by $-\frac{1}{2}$), then the x could be eliminated by addition. Remember, multiplying both sides of an equation by the same nonzero number produces an equivalent equation.

$-2(x + 2y) = -2(5)$ *Multiply the second equation by -2.*
$-2x - 4y = -10$

Replace the second equation in the system with its equivalent equation and solve the resulting system.

$$\begin{array}{r} 2x + 3y = 6 \\ + -2x - 4y = -10 \\ \hline -y = -4 \\ y = 4 \end{array}$$

The solution is $(-3, 4)$.

CHECK

$$\begin{array}{r} 2x + 3y = 6 \\ 2(-3) + 3(4) \overset{?}{=} 6 \\ 6 = 6 \end{array} \checkmark$$

$$\begin{array}{r} 2x + 3y = 6 \\ 2x + 3(4) = 6 \\ 2x = -6 \\ x = -3 \end{array}$$

$$\begin{array}{r} x + 2y = 5 \\ -3 + 2(4) \overset{?}{=} 5 \\ 5 = 5 \end{array} \checkmark$$

CLASSROOM EXAMPLES

1. Solve. $2x + 4y = 8$
$x + 6y = 6$

$-2(x + 6y) = -2(6)$
$-2x - 12y = -12$
$2x + 4y = 8$

$$\begin{array}{r} 2x + 4y = 8 \\ + -2x - 12y = -12 \\ \hline -8y = -4 \\ y = \frac{1}{2} \end{array}$$

$2x + 4y = 8$
$2x + 4(\frac{1}{2}) = 8$
$2x = 6$
$x = 3$
The solution is $(3, \frac{1}{2})$.

2. Solve. $2x + 3y = 8$
$3x - 6y = 12$

$3(2x + 3y) = 3(8)$
$2(3x - 6y) = 2(12)$
$6x + 9y = 24$
$-(6x - 12y = 24)$

$$\begin{array}{r} 21y = 0 \\ y = 0 \end{array}$$

$2x + 3y = 8$
$2x + 3(0) = 8$
$2x = 8$
$x = 4$
The solution is $(4, 0)$.

2 **Solve.** $4x + 5y = 6$
$6x - 7y = -20$

SOLUTION

Notice that the coefficients of the x-terms in both equations are factors of 12. Therefore, the x could be eliminated by subtraction if both sides of the first equation were multiplied by 3 and both sides of the second equation were multiplied by 2.

$$\begin{array}{l} 3(4x + 5y) = 3(6) \longrightarrow 12x + 15y = 18 \\ 2(6x - 7y) = 2(-20) \longrightarrow -(12x - 14y = -40) \\ \hline \qquad\qquad\qquad\qquad\qquad 29y = 58 \\ \qquad\qquad\qquad\qquad\qquad\quad y = 2 \end{array}$$

$4x + 5y = 6$
$4x + 5(2) = 6$
$4x + 10 = 6$
$4x = -4$
$x = -1$

The solution is $(-1, 2)$.

The check is left to you.

ORAL EXERCISES

To solve the system,

(a) which equation(s) would you multiply?

(b) by what number(s) would you multiply each equation?

(c) would you then add or subtract the equations?

1. $x + 3y = 12$ first;
$4x - 2y = 8$ -4; add

2. $2x + 3y = 2$ second;
$3x - y = 14$ 3; add

3. $5x - 2y = 10$
$3x - y = 3$

4. $x - 2y = -1$ first;
$-3x - y = -4$ 3; add

5. $4a + 2b = -2$ second; 2;
$2a - 3b = 1$ subtract

6. $2c + 3d = 2$
$3c + 4d = 4$

WRITTEN EXERCISES

A. Determine whether each system has one solution, no solution, or an infinite number of solutions. If the system has only one solution, solve by multiplication with the addition-subtraction method.

1. $3x + 3y = 12$
$x - y = 4$ $(4, 0)$

2. $2a - 2b = 2$
$a + b = 5$ $(3, 2)$

3. $2x - 3y = 12$
$4x - 2y = 24$ $(6, 0)$

4. $2x - 5y = 12$
$3x + y = 1$ $(1, -2)$

5. $3x + 2y = 8$
$2x + y = 1$ $(-6, 13)$

6. $2c + 3d = 12$
$4c - d = 10$ $(3, 2)$

7. $x - 5y = 0$
$2x - 3y = 7$ $(5, 1)$

8. $2x - y = 6$
$x + 3y = 17$ $(5, 4)$

9. $2x + y = 3$
$4x + 2y = 6$ infinite

10. $2c - 7d = 3$
$5c - 4d = -6$

11. $2a - 3b = 22$
$4a + b = 2$ $(2, -6)$

12. $5x - 2y = 11$
$3x + 5y = 19$ $(3, 2)$

B. 13. $5a - 2b = 8$
$2a + 7b = 11$ $(2, 1)$

14. $3c + 2d = 2$
$c - 4d = 3$ $\left(1, -\frac{1}{2}\right)$

15. $3x + y = 4$
$6x - 2y = 16$ $(2, -2)$

16. $3x + 2y = 1$
$2x - 3y = 5$ $(1, -1)$

17. $3x + 3y = 5$
$2x - 5y = 1$ $\left(\frac{4}{3}, \frac{1}{3}\right)$

18. $2a + 4b = 1$
$3a - 3b = 6$ $\left(\frac{3}{2}, -\frac{1}{2}\right)$

19. $\frac{1}{2}x + \frac{1}{2}y = 3$
$\frac{1}{4}x - y = 4$ $(8, -2)$

20. $3a + 4b = 4$
$\frac{1}{2}a - b = 0$ $\left(\frac{4}{5}, \frac{2}{5}\right)$

21. $2c + 3d = 3$
$3c - 5d = 2$ $\left(\frac{21}{19}, \frac{5}{19}\right)$

22. $0.4a - 0.5b = 1$
$0.4a + b = -2$ $(0, -2)$

23. $1.6x + 0.4y = 1$
$0.4x - 0.1y = 1$

24. $3.2x + 7.3y = 0$
$x = -3.5y$ $(0, 0)$

C. 25. $2x - y = 4$
$0.2x + 0.3y = 1$

26. $7x = 2y + 6$
$6 = 5x - y$ $(2, 4)$

27. $10 = y - 2x$
$2y = 5 - x$ $(-3, 4)$

28. $2(2x - 3y) = -2$
$8x - 3y + 6 = -30 - 7y + 3y$

29. $5x - 2(y - x) = 3x + 12$
$5x + 29 - 6 = 2x + 5$

IN OTHER FIELDS
Mathematics and Biology

About 800 years ago, Leonardo Pisano, also known as Leonardo Fibonacci, wrote about a sequence of numbers that follows a certain pattern. In this sequence, still known today as the Fibonacci sequence, each number except the first two is the sum of the two numbers before it:

1, 1, 2, 3, 5, 8, 13, 21, 34, 55, 89, . . .

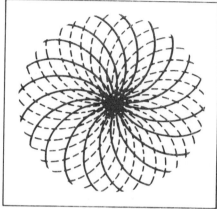

Biologists have discovered that the seeds in the heads of certain flowers spiral in two directions, clockwise and counterclockwise, as shown in the illustration at the right. If you count the number of spirals in a certain kind of sunflower, you will notice that 21 spirals go in one direction and 34 go in the other direction. This ratio is expressed as 21:34. In some varieties, the ratio may be 34:55. Notice that the numbers in both ratios are next to each other in the Fibonacci sequence.

Pinecones also have two sets of spirals. Their centers, however, number 8 spirals in one direction and 13 in the other. These two numbers also appear next to each other in the Fibonacci sequence.

If you count the spirals in a pineapple, the ratio may be either 5:8 or 8:13. Notice the location of these numbers in the Fibonacci sequence. Other plants use the same counting system.

OBJECTIVE

Solve problems by using a system of two equations in two variables.

8.6 Problem Solving

Sometimes a problem that can be solved by using one equation in one variable can be solved more easily by using a system of two equations in two variables.

EXAMPLES

1 The owner of a hobby shop spent $1250 on 9000 miniature cars and trucks. The cars cost $0.13 each and the trucks cost $0.15 each. How many of each did she buy?

Understand: *Given:* $1250 was spent on 9000 items.
Some of the items cost $0.13 and some cost $0.15.

To find: how many of each item the owner bought

Plan: Let c = the number of cars. Let t = the number of trucks.
Then, $c + t = 9000$ and $0.13c + 0.15t = 1250$.

Solve: $13(c + t) = 13(9000) \longrightarrow \qquad 13c + 13t = 117{,}000$

$100(0.13c + 0.15t) = 100(1250) \longrightarrow \underline{-(13c + 15t = 125{,}000)}$

Multiplying by 100 clears $\qquad\qquad\qquad -2t = -8000$
the equation of decimals. $\qquad\qquad\qquad\qquad t = 4000$

$c + 4000 = 9000$

$\qquad c = 5000$

Answer: The owner bought 5000 cars and 4000 trucks.

Review: Does 0.13 times 5000 plus 0.15 times 4000 equal 1250?

Systems can be used to solve many different problems involving geometry.

2 Supplementary angles are two angles whose measures have the sum of 180. If two angles are supplementary and the measure of one is three times the measure of the other, find the measure of each angle.

Understand: *Given:* two supplementary angles, the measure of one angle is 3 times the measure of the other

To find: the measures of the angles

Plan: Let g = one angle measure. Let h = the other angle measure.
Then $g + h = 180$ and $g = 3h$.

Solve: $g + h = 180 \qquad g + h = 180$

$\qquad\qquad g = 3h \qquad 3h + h = 180$ Substitute 3h for g.

$\qquad\qquad\qquad\qquad\qquad 4h = 180$

$\qquad\qquad\qquad\qquad\qquad\quad h = 45$

$g = 3h$

$g = 3(45)$

$g = 135$

Answer: The measure of one angle is 45. The measure of the other is 135.

Review: Does $45 + 135 = 180$? Does $135 = 3(45)$?

ORAL EXERCISES

Translate each problem into a system of equations.

1. A 180-foot length of rope must be cut into two pieces. One piece has to be three times longer than the other. How long will each piece be?

2. Twice the length of a rectangle is equal to five times the width. The perimeter of the rectangle is 77 meters. Find the length and the width.

3. For an experiment, 40 volunteers have to be divided into two groups. One group must have 4 more than 5 times the number of people in the other group. How many people should be in each group?

4. In an algebra class of 28 students, the number of girls is 5 less than twice the number of boys. How many boys and how many girls are in the class?

WRITTEN EXERCISES

A. 1–4. Solve Oral Exercises 1–4.

B. Solve.

5. The measure of one angle is 18 more than twice another. If the angles are supplementary, find the measure of each angle.

6. The length of a rectangle is 3 inches more than the width. The perimeter is 42 inches. Find the length and the width.

7. The perimeter of a rectangle is 14 centimeters. Twice the width is equal to $\frac{1}{3}$ the length. Find the length and the width. length = 6 cm, width = 1 cm

8. There are sixteen coins in a piggy bank. If the coins are all nickels and dimes and they total $1.05, how many of each are there? 5 dimes, 11 nickels

9. A basketball center made 23 baskets for a total score of 34. How many field goals did the center make? (A field goal is worth two points and a free throw is worth one point.)

10. During a 24-hour period in Alaska, the period of daylight was 18 hours longer than the period of darkness. How long was the period of darkness?

C. 11. A bank clerk gave a customer change for $200. The customer requested that the change be in singles and fives. If the customer received 136 bills, did the customer receive the correct change?

12. The perimeter of an isosceles triangle is 26 inches. The base is 2 inches longer than the length of a side. Find the length of a side of the triangle.

13. A car left a gas station and headed east. A second car left the gas station at the same time and headed west. The second car was traveling 10 kilometers per hour faster than the first car. After 3 hours the cars were 300 kilometers apart. What was the speed of each car?

14. Complementary angles are two angles whose measures have the sum of 90. If two angles are complementary and the measure of one is 16 more than the other, what are the angle measures?

4. $4x^2 + 8xy + 4y^2$
   $4(x + y)^2$

5. $6a(x - y) + b(x - y)$
   $(6a + b)(x - y)$

TEACHER'S RESOURCE MASTERS

Practice Master 34, Part 2

Quiz 15

ASSIGNMENT GUIDE

Minimum
1–9 odd

Regular
5–9

Maximum
8–10, 11–13 odd

PROBLEM–SOLVING STRATEGIES

Use a Formula (2, 6, 7, 12).

Draw a Diagram (2, 6, 7, 12, 13, 14).

Write an Equation (1–14).

Additional Answers
See p. T60.

ALGEBRA IN USE

Suppose that you are interested in joining a health club. You have decided to choose one of two clubs, Club A or Club B.

Club A charges $240 per year. There is no extra charge to use any of the equipment. Club B charges $180 per year, but there is an extra fee of $5 per session to work out on one machine that you know you would like to use. Which club should you join? (You can assume that all other features of the clubs are approximately the same.)

Break-even analysis can help you answer the question. Break-even analysis involves solving a system of equations, then basing the answer to the problem on the point of intersection of the graphs of each equation.

Represent the cost (C) of each club as a linear equation. Let x represent the number of times you might use the one machine at Club B.

Club A: $C = 240$ Club B: $C = 180 + 5x$ Graph: C

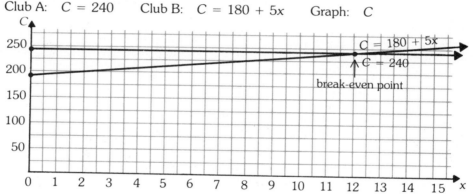

The **break-even point** is the point of intersection of these two lines. This is the point where the cost of each club is the same.

Solve for the point of intersection.

$240 = 180 + 5x$ *Use substitution.*

$60 = 5x$

$x = 12$

So if you use the one machine at Club B 12 times, the cost for the year is the same for Club B as it is for Club A ($240). If you expect to use the one machine fewer than 12 times a year, Club B is the better choice. The cost for the year is less than that for Club A. If you expect to use the one machine more than 12 times a year, Club A is the better choice. The initial fee at Club A is more, but the extra cost at Club B will make Club B's total cost greater.

EXERCISES

Find the break-even point for each.

		Initial fee	*Cost per visit*
1.	Club A	$400	$0
	Club B	$250	$2
2.	Club A	$350	$3
	Club B	$450	$2
3.	Club A	$500	$2
	Club B	$275	$5

MATH HERITAGE/Emmy Noether

Emmy Noether (1882–1935), whose innovations in higher algebra gained her recognition as the most creative abstract algebraist of modern times, was born in Germany. Her father was a university professor of mathematics who played an important role in the development of the theory of algebraic functions.

At the age of 31, she began to lecture on mathematics, occasionally substituting for her father at Erlangen University. Finally, in 1919, after years of unsuccessful attempts to overcome the objections of some faculty members who wished to exclude women lecturers from the university, she won formal admission as an academic lecturer.

When the Nazis came to power in Germany, Noether, along with many other scholars from the universities, was dismissed. Even though she had by this time achieved great status as a mathematician, to the Nazis this was outweighed by the fact that she was a female intellectual, Jewish, and a liberal.

To escape the madness that had overcome her fatherland, Noether emigrated to the United States where she became a mathematics professor at Bryn Mawr College. Her contribution to the field of mathematics was cut short after only one and a half years in the United States. She died suddenly after an apparently successful operation.

OBJECTIVE

Solve motion and mixture problems by using a system of linear equations.

TEACHER'S NOTES

See p. T31.

CLASSROOM EXAMPLES

1. Kevin paddled his canoe 5 kilometers upstream in 30 minutes. The return trip took 12 minutes. Determine the speed of the canoe in still water and the speed of the current.

Let x = still-water speed of canoe.

Let y = speed of the current.

	r	t	d
Down	$x + y$	$\frac{1}{5}$ or 0.2	5
Up	$x - y$	$\frac{1}{2}$ or 0.5	5

$r \cdot t = d$

$(x + y)0.2 = 5$
$(x - y)0.5 = 5$
$0.2x + 0.2y = 5$
$0.5x - 0.5y = 5$
$5(0.2x + 0.2y) = 5(5)$
$2(0.5x - 0.5y) = 2(5)$

$\begin{aligned} x + y &= 25 \\ + x - y &= 10 \\ \hline 2x &= 35 \end{aligned}$

$x = 17.5$

$0.2(17.5) + 0.2y = 5$
$3.5 + 0.2y = 5$
$0.2y = 1.5$
$y = 7.5$

8.7 | Motion and Mixture Problems

In Section 5.8 uniform-motion problems were solved by using one equation in one unknown. In this section, uniform-motion problems are solved by using a system of equations.

The speed of a boat is affected by the speed and the direction of the current, just as the speed of a plane is affected by the speed and the direction of the wind. To solve problems involving uniform-motion, a table is helpful for determining equations to use in the system.

EXAMPLES

1 During practice rowing sessions, a collegiate rowing team rowed 3 kilometers upstream (against the current) in 12 minutes. It took 6 minutes to row the 3 kilometers downstream (with the current). What is the speed in *kilometers per hour* of the scull (boat) in still water, and what is the speed of the current?

Understand: *Given:* It took 12 minutes rowing against the current to row 3 kilometers and it took 6 minutes rowing with the current to row 3 kilometers.

To find: the speed of the current and the still-water speed of the scull

Plan: Let x = still-water speed of scull (km/h). Let y = speed of the current (km/h).

Set up a table by using the formula $r \cdot t = d$. Express time in hours.

	Rate	Time	Distance	$r \cdot t = d$
Downstream	$x + y$	$\frac{1}{10}$ or 0.1	3	$(x + y)0.1 = 3$
Upstream	$x - y$	$\frac{1}{5}$ or 0.2	3	$(x - y)0.2 = 3$

Use the table to write a system.

$(x + y)0.1 = 3 \longrightarrow 0.1x + 0.1y = 3$
$(x - y)0.2 = 3 \longrightarrow 0.2x - 0.2y = 3$

Solve:

$$2(0.1x + 0.1y) = 2(3)$$
$$0.2x + 0.2y = 6$$
$$\underline{+\,0.2x - 0.2y = 3}$$
$$0.4x \qquad\quad = 9$$
$$x = 22.5$$

$$0.1(22.5) + 0.1y = 3$$
$$2.25 + 0.1y = 3$$
$$0.1y = 0.75$$
$$y = 7.5$$

Answer: The speed of the scull in still water is 22.5 kilometers per hour. The speed of the current is 7.5 kilometers per hour.

Review: How fast is the scull moving downstream? $22.5 + 7.5 = 30$ km/h. At 30 km/h, how long would it take to go 3 kilometers? $\frac{1}{10}$ of an hour or 6 minutes. Does this agree with the information in the problem?

In mixture problems, two or more components are combined to produce a mixture with a certain value. A table is useful to determine the *amount* of each component and the *value* of each component.

2 A 2-pound box of rice that is a mixture of white rice and wild rice sells for $1.80 per pound. White rice sells for $0.75 per pound and wild rice sells for $2.25 per pound. How much of each type of rice was used to make the mixture?

Understand: *Given:* White rice costs $0.75 per pound. Wild rice costs $2.25 per pound. The two-pound mixture costs $1.80 per pound.

To find: the amount of each ingredient in the mixture

Plan: Let x = the amount of white rice in the mixture. Let y = the amount of wild rice in the mixture.

	White rice	Wild rice	Mixture
Amount	x	y	2
Value	$0.75x$	$2.25y$	$1.80(2)$

Use the table to write two equations for the problem.

$$x + y = 2 \longrightarrow x + y = 2$$
$$0.75x + 2.25y = 1.80(2) \longrightarrow 0.75x + 2.25y = 3.6$$

Solve:

$$75(x + y) = 75(2) \longrightarrow 75x + 75y = 150$$
$$100(0.75x + 2.25y) = 100(3.6) \longrightarrow \underline{-(75x + 225y = 360)} \; \text{Subtract.}$$
$$-150y = -210$$
$$y = 1.4$$

$$x + 1.4 = 2$$
$$x = 0.6$$

Answer: The mixture consists of 0.6 pound of white rice and 1.4 pounds of wild rice.

Review: The check is left to you.

The speed of the canoe in still water is 17.5 kilometers per hour. The speed of the current is 7.5 kilometers per hour.

2. A five-pound mixture of pasta noodles sells for $1.20 per pound. Small noodles sell for $0.80 per pound and large noodles sell for $1.60 per pound. How much of each type of noodle was used to make the mixture?

Let x = the amount of small noodles in the mixture. Let y = the amount of large noodles in the mixture.

	Sml	Lrg	Mix
Amt	x	y	5
Val	$0.8x$	$1.6y$	$1.20(5)$

$$x + y = 5$$
$$0.8x + 1.6y = 1.20(5)$$
$$x + y = 5$$
$$0.8x + 1.6y = 6$$
$$80(x + y) = 80(5)$$
$$100(0.8x + 1.6y) = 100(6)$$
$$80x + 80y = 400$$
$$\underline{-(80x + 160y = 600)}$$
$$-80y = -200$$
$$y = 2.5$$

$$x + 2.5 = 5$$
$$x = 2.5$$

The mixture consists of 2.5 pounds of small noodles and 2.5 pounds of large noodles.

3. How much of a 12% saline solution should be mixed with a 20% saline solution to obtain 100 ounces of a 16% saline solution?

Let x = the amount of the 12% solution. Let y = the amount of the 20% solution.

	12%	20%	Mix
Amt of sol	x	y	100
Salt in sol	$0.12x$	$0.2y$	0.16 $\times 100$

$x + y = 100$
$0.12x + 0.2y = 0.16(100)$
$x + y = 100$
$0.12x + 0.2y = 16$
$12(x + y) = 12(100)$
$100(0.12x + 0.2y) = 100(16)$

$\quad 12x + 12y = 1200$
$\underline{-(12x + 20y = 1600)}$
$\quad\quad -8y = -400$
$\quad\quad\quad\; y = 50$

$x + 50 = 100$
$\quad\;\; x = 50$

50 ounces of the 12% saline solution should be mixed with 50 ounces of the 20% saline solution.

MIXED REVIEW
1. Simplify. $\dfrac{48x^4y^5}{16x^2y^7} \;\; \dfrac{3x^2}{y^2}$
2. Find the product of $(-8x^3y^2)$ and $(-13xy^4)$.
   $104x^4y^6$
3. Complete.
   a. $-|-6|$ $\;-6$
   b. $|-8|$ $\;8$
4. Find the difference of $\frac{1}{6} - \left(-\frac{1}{3}\right)$. $\;\frac{1}{2}$
5. Give a partial listing of the set of whole numbers greater than 7.
   $\{8, 9, 10, \ldots\}$

Sometimes mixture problems involve the strength or percentage of the components.

3   How much of a 10% saline solution should a nurse mix with an 18% saline solution to obtain 128 ounces of a 15% saline solution?

Understand: *Given:*   One solution is 10% saline. The other solution is 18% saline. A total of 128 ounces is needed.

To find: how much of each solution should be mixed

Plan: Let r = the amount of the 10% solution. Let s = the amount of the 18% solution.

	10% solution	18% solution	Mixture
Amount of solution	r	s	128
Salt in solution	$0.10r$	$0.18s$	$0.15(128)$

$r + s = 128 \longrightarrow r + s = 128$
$0.10r + 0.18s = 0.15(128) \rightarrow 0.10r + 0.18s = 19.2$

Solve: $10(r + s) = 10(128) \longrightarrow 10r + 10s = 1280$
$100(0.10r + 0.18s) = 100(19.2) \rightarrow \underline{10r + 18s = 1920}$ *Subtract.*
$\quad\quad\quad\quad\quad\quad\quad\quad\quad\quad\quad\quad -8s = -640$
$\quad\quad\quad\quad\quad\quad\quad\quad\quad\quad\quad\quad\quad\; s = 80$

$r + 80 = 128$
$\quad\;\; r = 48$

Answer: The nurse should mix 48 ounces of the 10% saline solution with 80 ounces of the 18% saline solution.

Review: The check is left to you.

ORAL EXERCISES

Complete each table.

1. A small airplane flies 600 kilometers in 5 hours against the wind. Returning with the wind requires only 4 hours. Find the speed of the plane in still air and the speed of the wind.

	Rate	Time	Distance	$r \cdot t = d$
Against the wind	$x - y$	5	600	$(x - y)5 = 600$
With the wind	$x + y$	4	600	$(x + y)4 = 600$

2. A lab technician needs to make 1000 grams of a 42% alcohol solution. The technician has some 40% alcohol solution and some 46% alcohol solution. How much of each must be used?

	40% solution	46% solution	Mixture
Amount	r	s	1000
Alcohol in solution	$0.40r$	$0.46s$	$0.42(1000)$

3. It takes a boat with a battery-powered outboard motor $\frac{1}{2}$ hour to go 2 kilometers downstream. It takes 1 hour for the boat to go the same distance upstream. What is the speed of the boat and the speed of the current?

	Rate	Time	Distance	$r \cdot t = d$
Downstream	$x + y$	0.5	2	$(x + y)0.5 = 2$
Upstream	$x - y$	1	2	$(x - y)1 = 2$

4. A company wants to make a blend of teas worth $3 a pound. The company has tea worth $2.70 a pound and tea worth $3.60 a pound. How much of each must be used to make 60 pounds of blended tea?

	$2.70-per-lb tea	$3.60-per-lb tea	$3-per-lb tea
Amount	x	y	60
Value	2.70x	3.60y	3(60)

WRITTEN EXERCISES

A. 1–4. Solve Oral Exercises 1–4.

B. Solve.

5. Melinda rented a bicycle and rode 5 kilometers with the wind in 15 minutes. Returning against the wind took 20 minutes. What is the speed of the wind and the average speed of the bike?

6. A soil analysis indicated that a lawn needed fertilizer that was 21% nitrogen. A landscaper had some fertilizer that was 10% nitrogen and some that was 30% nitrogen. How much of each kind of fertilizer is needed to make 60 pounds of 21% nitrogen fertilizer?

7. How many pounds of a 90%-germination-rate bluegrass seed must be mixed with an 80%-germination-rate bluegrass seed to produce 2 pounds of an 87%-germination-rate bluegrass seed?

8. When flying with the wind, a passenger plane cruises 2240 kilometers in 3 hours. When flying against the wind, the plane cruises the same distance in 4 hours. Find the speed of the plane in still air and the speed of the wind.

9. Skim milk is 0.1% fat. Whole milk is 3.5% fat. How much skim milk and how much whole milk are needed to make 8 gallons of 2% milk? $3\frac{9}{17}$ gal, $4\frac{8}{17}$ gal

10. A swamp buggy goes 18 kilometers downstream in 4 hours. It goes the same distance upstream in 6 hours. Find the speed of the swamp buggy in still water and the speed of the current.

C. 11. One alloy (mixture of metals) is 20% copper and another alloy is 50% copper. How much of each alloy should be used to make 100 grams of an alloy that is 45% copper?

12. A jeep traveled 200 kilometers in 5 hours. If the jeep averaged 25 kilometers per hour on back roads and 50 kilometers per hour on paved roads, how much of the trip was on back roads?

TEACHER'S RESOURCE MASTERS

Practice Master 35, Part 1

ASSIGNMENT GUIDE

Minimum
1–3 odd, 5–8

Regular
5–10

Maximum
7–12

ADDITIONAL ANSWERS

Written Exercises
1. 135 km/h, 15 km/h
2. 333.33 g, 666.67 g
3. 3 km/h, 1 km/h
4. 40 lb, 20 lb
5. 2.5 km/h, 17.5 km/h
6. 27 lb, 33 lb
7. $1\frac{2}{5}$ lb, $\frac{3}{5}$ lb
8. 653.33 km/h, 93.34 km/h
10. 3.75 km/h, 0.75 km/h
11. 16.67 g, 83.33 g
12. 2 hours

PROBLEM–SOLVING STRATEGIES

Make a Table (5–12).

Write an Equation (1–12).

Draw a Diagram (5, 8, 10, 12).

OBJECTIVE

Solve puzzle problems by using a system of linear equations.

TEACHER'S NOTES

See p. T31.

See p. T31.

CLASSROOM EXAMPLES

1. Ken is four and a half years older than Betsy. Three times Ken's age added to six times Betsy's age is 36. How old are Ken and Betsy?

   Let x = Ken's age. Let y = Betsy's age. Then $x = y + 4\frac{1}{2}$ and $3x + 6y = 36$.

   $x = y + 4\frac{1}{2}$ $x - y = 4\frac{1}{2}$

   $-3(x - y) = -3\left(4\frac{1}{2}\right)$

   $3x + 6y = 36$

   $-3x + 3y = -13\frac{1}{2}$
   $+3x + 6y = 36$
   _____
   $9y = 22\frac{1}{2}$
   $y = 2\frac{1}{2}$

   $x - 2\frac{1}{2} = 4\frac{1}{2}$
   $x = 7$

   Ken is 7 years old and Betsy is $2\frac{1}{2}$ years old.

2. The sum of the digits of a two-digit number is 14. If the digits are interchanged, the new number formed is 18 greater than the original number. Find the original number.

   Let t = the tens digit of the original number.

   Let u = the unit digit of the original number.

8.8 Puzzle Problems

Many problems that would be difficult to solve by using a *guess-and-check method* are easy to solve by using a system of equations.

EXAMPLES

1 Anita is five and a quarter years older than Juan. Six times Anita's age added to five times Juan's age is 301. How old are Anita and Juan?

Understand: *Given:* Anita's age is Juan's age plus $5\frac{1}{4}$ years.
Six times Anita's age plus five times Juan's age equals 301.

To find: Anita's age and Juan's age

Plan: Let a = Anita's age. Let j = Juan's age. Then $a = j + 5\frac{1}{4}$ and $6a + 5j = 301$.

Solve: $a = j + 5\frac{1}{4}$ $a - j = 5\frac{1}{4}$

$-6(a - j) = -6\left(5\frac{1}{4}\right) \longrightarrow -6a + 6j = -31\frac{1}{2}$

$6a + 5j = 301 \longrightarrow \underline{+ \quad 6a + 5j = \quad 301}$

$11j = \quad 269\frac{1}{2}$

$j = 24\frac{1}{2}$

$a - 24\frac{1}{2} = 5\frac{1}{4}$

$a = 29\frac{3}{4}$

Answer: Anita is $29\frac{3}{4}$ years old and Juan is $24\frac{1}{2}$ years old.

Review: Is Anita $5\frac{1}{4}$ years older than Juan if she is $29\frac{3}{4}$ years old and he is $24\frac{1}{2}$ years old? Does $6\left(29\frac{3}{4}\right) + 5\left(24\frac{1}{2}\right) = 301$?

Any number can be written in *expanded notation*. For example, 24 is equal to $2(10) + 4$. In general, a two-digit number can be written as $10t + u$ where t represents the digit in the tens place and u represents the digit in the units place.

2 The sum of the digits of a two-digit number is 12. If the digits are interchanged, the new number formed is 36 greater than the original number. Find the original number.

Understand: *Given:* The sum of the digits of a two-digit number is 12. By interchanging the digits a new number is formed that is 36 more than the original number.

To find: the original number

Plan: Let $t =$ the tens digit of the original number. Let $u =$ the units digit of the original number. Then, $10t + u$ represents the original number and $10u + t$ represents the new number.

Solve:

$$t + u = 12 \longrightarrow t + u = 12$$
$$10u + t = (10t + u) + 36 \longrightarrow 9u - 9t = 36$$
$$t + u = 12 \longrightarrow u + t = 12$$
$$\tfrac{1}{9}(9u - 9t) = \tfrac{1}{9}(36) \longrightarrow \underline{u - t = 4}$$
$$2u = 16$$
$$u = 8$$

$$t + 8 = 12$$
$$t = 4$$

Answer: The original number is $10(4) + 8$, or 48.

Review: Does $4 + 8 = 12$? Does $84 = 48 + 36$?

Then $10t + u$ represents the original number and $10u + t$ represents the new number.

$$t + u = 14$$
$$10u + t = (10t + u) + 18$$
$$t + u = 14$$
$$9u - 9t = 18$$
$$t + u = 14$$
$$\tfrac{1}{9}(9u - 9t) = \tfrac{1}{9}(18)$$
$$u + t = 14$$
$$\underline{u - t = 2}$$
$$2u = 16$$
$$u = 8$$
$$t + 8 = 14$$
$$t = 6$$

The original number is $10(6) + 8$, or 68.

ORAL EXERCISES

Translate each problem into a system of two equations.

1. The sum of two numbers is 12 and their difference is 4. Find the numbers.

2. Ling Su is 5 years older than Betty. The sum of their ages is 27. How old are Ling Su and Betty?

3. The tens digit of a two-digit number is 4 greater than the units digit. The sum of the digits is 10. Find the number.

4. The sum of two numbers is 170. One number is 4 times the other. Find the numbers. $a + b = 170$ $a = 4b$

WRITTEN EXERCISES

A. 1–4. Solve Oral Exercises 1–4.

B. Solve.

5. One number is 5 more than another, and their sum is 27. Find the numbers. 16, 11

6. The sum of a number and twice another number is 16. The second number is 4 less than the first. Find the numbers.

7. Find two numbers whose sum is 33, if the difference of three times the larger and twice the smaller is 29. 19, 14

8. Five times the smaller of two numbers is 4 more than the larger number. The sum of twice the smaller number and three times the larger is 27. Find the numbers.

9. The units digit of a number is 2 more than the tens digit. What is the number if it equals 4 times the sum of its two digits? 24

10. Three times Ravi's age is 6 more than twice Anna's age. The sum of their ages is 32. How old are Ravi and Anna?

MIXED REVIEW
Solve.
1. $3x + 7 = 4x - 8$ 15
2. $y + 9 = -28 - y$ $-\frac{37}{2}$ or $-18\frac{1}{2}$
3. $q - 9 = -q - 10$ $-\frac{1}{2}$
Find each product.
4. $\frac{3}{5}\left(-\frac{4}{7}\right)$ $-\frac{12}{35}$
5. $[5(3)](-8)$ -120

TEACHER'S RESOURCE MASTERS
Practice Master 35, Part 2

ASSIGNMENT GUIDE
Minimum
1–4, 5–11 odd
Regular
5–12
Maximum
7–14
(continued on next page)

11. A number is 6 greater than 5 times its unit digit. The units digit of the two-digit number is twice the tens digit. Find the number. 36

C. 13. The sum of the digits of a two-place decimal is 9. When the digits are interchanged, the new decimal formed is 0.27 greater than the original decimal. What is the original decimal? 0.36

12. The tens digit of a two-digit number is 3 greater than the units digit. Eight times the sum of the digits is 1 less than the number. Find the number. 41

14. Find a way to represent the difference between a three-digit number and the number named by reversing the order of the digits. Show that the difference is always divisible by 99.

CAREER

Real Estate Agent

Real-estate agents help people buy and sell property. Most agents sell residential property. Agents take buyers to available homes and emphasize various selling features of each home. Agents also obtain listings, or agreements, from homeowners who wish to sell their homes. When a home is sold, the seller pays a commission to the listing agent and to the buyer's agent. Each commission is a percent of the selling price.

Suppose a real-estate agent estimates the monthly mortgage payment for a home buyer. The monthly payment is determined by the principal amount borrowed, the mortgage interest rate, and the length of the mortgage loan. Find the principal amount borrowed if the buyer makes a down payment of 20% of the $85,000 selling price. Then use the table to find the monthly mortgage payment for a 12% mortgage rate and a 30-year loan. $68,000; $699.72

Monthly mortgage payment
(principal and interest)
Per $1000 of mortgage principal

Mortgage rate	20-year loan	25-year loan	30-year loan
11%	$10.33	$ 9.81	$ 9.53
$11\frac{1}{4}$	10.50	9.99	9.72
$11\frac{1}{2}$	10.67	10.17	9.91
$11\frac{3}{4}$	10.84	10.35	10.10
12	11.02	10.54	10.29
$12\frac{1}{4}$	11.19	10.72	10.46
$12\frac{1}{2}$	11.37	10.91	10.68
$12\frac{3}{4}$	11.54	11.10	10.87
13	11.72	11.28	11.07
$13\frac{1}{4}$	11.90	11.47	11.26
$13\frac{1}{2}$	12.08	11.66	11.46
$13\frac{3}{4}$	12.26	11.85	11.66
14	12.44	12.04	11.85
$14\frac{1}{4}$	12.62	12.23	12.05
$14\frac{1}{2}$	12.80	12.43	12.25
$14\frac{3}{4}$	12.99	12.62	12.45
15	13.17	12.81	12.65
$15\frac{1}{2}$	13.54	13.20	13.05
16	13.92	13.59	13.45
$16\frac{1}{2}$	14.29	13.99	13.86
17	14.67	14.38	14.26

CHALLENGE

CHALLENGE
1. 12 ft
5. a. 974 + 61 or 971 + 64 or 961 + 74 or 964 + 71 = 1035
   b. 149 + 67 or 147 + 69 or 167 + 49 or 169 + 47 = 216
   c. 976 − 14 = 962
   d. 146 − 97 = 49
   e. 941(76) = 71,516
   f. 479(16) = 7664

1. A large log is being moved by rolling it on cylinders. If the circumference of each cylinder is 6 feet, how far will the log move for each revolution of the cylinders?

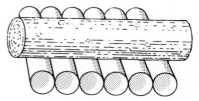

2. 1 melon + 1 banana balance $3\frac{1}{2}$ pears.   2 bananas + 3 pears balance 3 melons.

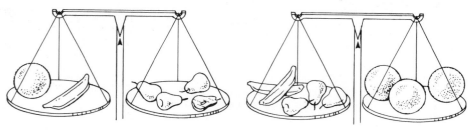

How many pears are needed to balance 1 melon?   2 pears

3. The figure at the right represents 160% of a given area. Shade 50% of the given area.

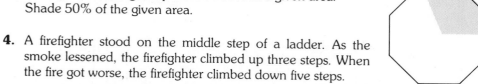

4. A firefighter stood on the middle step of a ladder. As the smoke lessened, the firefighter climbed up three steps. When the fire got worse, the firefighter climbed down five steps.

   Later, the firefighter climbed up the last six steps and was at the top of the ladder. How many steps were in the ladder?   9 steps

5. Use the digits 1, 4, 6, 7, and 9 to form a three-digit and a two-digit number that will give the following:

   a. the largest sum possible
   b. the smallest sum possible
   c. the largest difference possible
   d. the smallest difference possible
   e. the largest product possible
   f. the smallest product possible

CLASSROOM EXAMPLES

1. Graph $y \geq x - 2$.

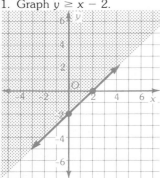

2. Graph $y + x < -3$.

$y < -x - 3$

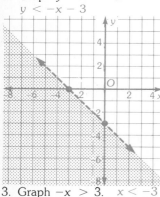

3. Graph $-x > 3$. $x < -3$

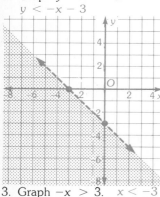

8.9 | Graphing Inequalities

The graph of a linear equation separates the coordinate plane into three sets of points: the points on the line; the points in the region above, or to the left of the line; and the points below, or to the right of the line. The line is called the **boundary line** and the regions are called **half planes.** The graph of a linear inequality can be a half plane or a half plane and a boundary line.

EXAMPLES

1 | **Graph $y \geq x - 1$.**

SOLUTION

Determine the boundary line by graphing $y = x - 1$. If a vertical line is drawn through any point on the boundary line, the y-coordinates of the points above the boundary line will be greater than the y-coordinate of the point on the boundary line. Therefore, the half plane above the boundary line is the graph of $y \geq x - 1$. Shade the half plane above the boundary line.

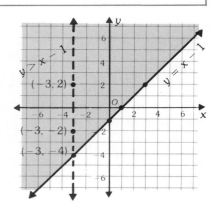

CHECK

To be sure that the correct half plane is shaded, pick a point not on the boundary line and check the coordinates of that point in the inequality.

Check $y \geq x - 1$ for $(0, 0)$.   NOTE: *The point $(0, 0)$ is usually the easiest point to check.*

$$0 \overset{?}{\geq} 0 - 1$$
$$0 \geq -1 \; \blacktriangleright$$

This statement is true, so the correct half plane has been shaded.

2 | **Graph $y + x < -1$.**

SOLUTION

Solve for y. $y < -x + (-1)$.

Draw the boundary line. Since the boundary line is not part of the graph of the inequality, draw it as a dashed line. Shade the appropriate half plane.

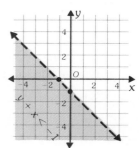

CHECK

Check $y + x < -1$ for $(0, 0)$.

$$0 + 0 \overset{?}{<} -1$$
$$0 < -1$$

This inequality is false. So the correct half plane has been shaded.

3 | **Graph** $-x > 1$.

SOLUTION

Solve for x. $x < -1$

Remember to change the direction of the inequality sign.
Graph the boundary line.
Shade the appropriate half plane. The coordinates of the points to the left of the boundary line satisfy $x < -1$.
Check a point.

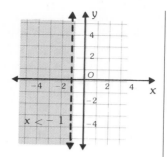

ORAL EXERCISES

Determine which, if any, of the given points are solutions of the inequality.

1. $x \le 4$ (−1, 5), (0, 0), (1, 5), (5, 5)

2. $y > -1$ (−1, −5), (−2, 0), (3, −4)

3. $x + y < 6$ (−1, −5), (0, 0), (1, 5), (5, 5)

4. $y \le 3x - 2$ (−4, −15), (0, 0), (0, −2)

Tell the equation of the boundary line; whether the line should be solid or dashed; and whether the shaded half plane will be above, below, to the right, or to the left of the boundary line.

5. $y \ge x + 2$

6. $y < 4$

7. $y \le x$

8. $y > -x - 2$

9. $y > -2x$

10. $y \le \frac{1}{2}x + 1$

WRITTEN EXERCISES

A. Graph.

1. $y \ge x$

2. $x > -2$

3. $y < 4$

4. $y > x + 3$

5. $y < 2x$

6. $4y - 8 \ge 0$

B. **7.** $y - x > 3$

8. $y > -x$

9. $x + y < 5$

10. $2 + y < 2x$

11. $2x - y < 0$

12. $4x - 2y > 4$

13. $-2x - 2y \ge 4$

14. $\frac{1}{2}x + \frac{1}{4}y < 2$

15. $2y - x + 2 > 0$

Write an inequality for each graph.

16.

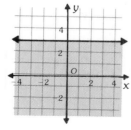

17.

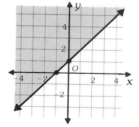

18.

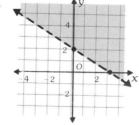

MIXED REVIEW

Restate each decimal in fractional form.
1. 0.74 $\frac{37}{50}$
2. $0.2\overline{08}$ $\frac{103}{495}$
3. $0.\overline{61}$ $\frac{61}{99}$

Perform the indicated operation.
4. $(-14x^3 + 3x^2 - 5x + 6) - (3x^3 + 3x^2 + 2x - 9)$ $-17x^3 - 7x + 15$

5. $(2x^2 + 4x - 30) \div (x + 5)$ $2x - 6$

TEACHER'S RESOURCE MASTERS

Practice Master 36, Part 1

COMPUTER SOFTWARE

Graphing Linear Equations and Inequalities

ASSIGNMENT GUIDE

Minimum
1–5 odd, 7–13

Regular
7–16

Maximum
9–18

ADDITIONAL ANSWERS

Oral Exercises

5. $y = x + 2$; solid; above

6. $y = 4$; dashed; below

7. $y = x$; solid; below

8. $y = -x - 2$; dashed; above

9. $y = -2x$; dashed; above

10. $y = \frac{1}{2}x + 1$; solid; below

(continued on next page)

Written Exercises

For the odd-numbered solutions, see *Answers to Selected Exercises*, p. 586.

2.

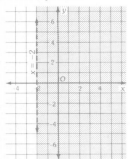

4.

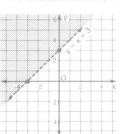

6.

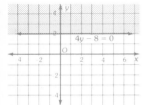

8.

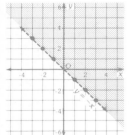

Additional Answers
See p. T60.

C. Solve each problem by graphing. HINT: The solutions are whole numbers.

19. One type of sticker costs $1 and another type costs $3. What combinations of stickers can you get if you want to spend less than $9 and you want at least one of each kind?

20. Posters sell for $4 and decals sell for $2. What combinations of posters and decals can you buy if you want to spend $16 or less and you want to buy at least one of each?

EXPLORATION
Linear Programming

Linear programming is a method for solving problems in which the goal is to find a maximum value or a minimum value of a function. The problems often involve production and profit.

Example: A company produces both electric clocks and battery clocks. The profit of each type of clock is $6 and $10, respectively. To meet demands, the company must produce at least 500 electric clocks and 750 battery clocks each week. The company can produce no more than 3000 clocks per week. How many of each type of clock should be produced to maximize profits?

Solution: Let x = the number of electric clocks produced.
Let y = the number of battery clocks produced.
Then $6x + 10y$ = the total weekly profit.

The restrictions, called **constraints,** on production are as follows:
$x \geq 500 \qquad y \geq 750 \qquad x + y \leq 3000$

A theorem states that the maximum value (or minimum value) of the profit will be found at one of the vertices of the region formed by graphing the system of inequalities of the restrictions.

Find the vertices:

A: Use $x = 500$ and $y = 750$.
     Then $A = (500, 750)$.

B: Use $y = 750$ and $x + y = 3000$.
     $x = 3000 - y$
       $= 3000 - 750$
       $= 2250$
     Then $B = (2250, 750)$.

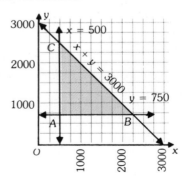

Continued on next page

C: Use $x = 500$ and $x + y = 3000$.
$$y = 3000 - x$$
$$= 3000 - 500$$
$$= 2500$$
Then $C = (500, 2500)$.

Substitute the ordered pairs for the vertices into $6x + 10y$ to determine which vertex will yield the maximum profit.

A: $6(500) + 10(750) = 3000 + 7500 = 10,500$
B: $6(2250) + 10(750) = 13,500 + 7500 = 21,000$
C: $6(500) + 10(2500) = 3000 + 25,000 = 28,000$

To make a maximum profit, the company should produce 500 electric clocks and 2500 battery clocks.

EXERCISES

1. What is the maximum value of the expression $8x + 12y$, given the restrictions shown by the graph? 72

2. What is the minimum value of the expression $2x + 3y$, given the restrictions shown by the graph? 4

3. A sofa manufacturer makes two types of sofa frames, both of which require time on two machines. The first type of frame requires 4 minutes on one machine and 3 minutes on the other. The second type of frame requires 5 minutes on one machine and 6 minutes on the other. Each machine can be used a maximum of 180 minutes a day. The profit on the first type of sofa frame is $8; the profit on the second type of sofa frame is $12. In order to make a maximum profit, how many of each type of frame should be made each day? 20

Use with exercise 1.

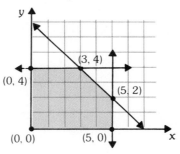

Use with exercise 2.

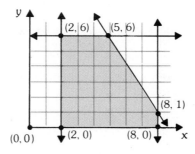

3.

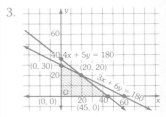

1. Solve. $y \le 3$
$\qquad x \ge 4$

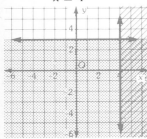

2. Solve. $y > -\frac{1}{2}x + 3$
$\qquad y > 2x + 2$

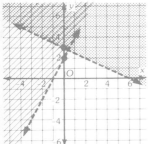

3. Solve. $-3y + 6x < -3$
$\qquad y < 2x + 1$

Solve $-3y + 6x < -3$ for y. $y > 2x + 1$

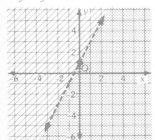

The system has no solution.

| 8.10 | Systems of Inequalities |

To find the solution set of a system of inequalities, graph each inequality on the same set of axes. The graph of the solution set is the intersection of the two half planes.

EXAMPLES

| 1 | **Solve.** $y \le 2$ |
| | $\qquad x \ge 3$ |

SOLUTION Graph the boundary line $y = 2$ and shade the appropriate half plane. Then graph the boundary line $x = 3$ and shade the appropriate half plane. The graph of the solution set is the double-shaded region shown in the diagram.

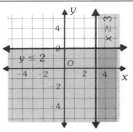

| 2 | **Solve.** $y > -\frac{1}{2}x + 2$ |
| | $\qquad y > 3x - 3$ |

SOLUTION Graph each inequality.

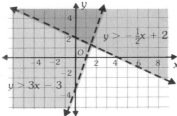

| 3 | **Solve.** $-2y + 6x < -4$ |
| | $\qquad y < 3x + 2$ |

SOLUTION

Solve the first equation for y. $y > 3x + 2$

Graph each inequality. The system has no solution.

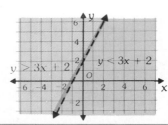

ORAL EXERCISES

Match each system with its graph.

1. $x \ge 2$
$\quad y \le 2$

2. $y \le -x + 4$
$\quad y \le x$

3. $y \le x + 2$
$\quad y \ge -x + 4$

4. $x \le 2$
$\quad y \ge 2$

a.

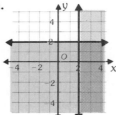

b.

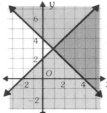

c.

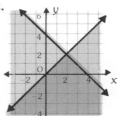

d.

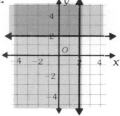

WRITTEN EXERCISES

A. Graph.

1. $x > y$
$y < 4$

2. $x > 3$
$y < 6$

3. $y < -2$
$x < -3$

4. $x \geq -2$
$y \leq 3$

5. $y \geq 2x$
$y \geq -1$

6. $y \leq 3x - 2$
$x \geq -3$

B. 7. $y > -x + 2$
$y > x - 2$

8. $x + y < 2$
$x - y > 3$

9. $y - 3 \leq 0$
$x + 2y \geq 4$

10. $x + 4 \geq 0$
$x - 2y \geq -6$

11. $y \leq -x + 3$
$x \geq 1$

12. $y < x - 1$
$y > 2x - 1$

13. $x - y < 4$
$x + y > 3$

14. $-x + y \leq 6$
$x + y \geq 2$

15. $5x - 2y < 6$
$y > -x + 1$

16. $-y - x \geq 3$
$y \geq -1$

17. $-2x + y \leq 2$
$3x + 2y \leq 4$

18. $x \geq 3$
$y \geq 1$
$x + y < 5$

C. 19. $y > -2$
$x + y < 5$
$x - y > 5$

20. $y - 2x \geq 0$
$y \geq -2x$
$4 \geq y$

21. $x \geq -1$
$x \leq 4$
$y < -x + 5$
$y > -x - 1$

MIXED REVIEW

Find $f(4)$ for each relation.
1. $f(x) = 5x - 2$ 18
2. $f(x) = \frac{3}{8}x + 5$ $6\frac{1}{2}$
3. $f(x) = 3x + 4$ 16
4. Simplify $3[5(a - 2) + 6a]$. $33a - 30$
5. Give the prime factorization of 140.
$2^2 \cdot 5 \cdot 7$

TEACHER'S RESOURCE MASTERS

Practice Master 36, Part 2

COMPUTER SOFTWARE

Graphing Linear Equations and Inequalities

ASSIGNMENT GUIDE

Minimum
1–15
Regular
4–18
Maximum
7–21

SELF-QUIZ

Solve by graphing.

1. $-3x + y = 5$
$-2x + y = 4$ $(-1, 2)$

2. $y = 3x + 1$
$y = x - 1$ $(-1, -2)$

3. $x + 2y = 4$
$x - y = 1$ $(2, 1)$

Without graphing, determine if the system is consistent, consistent and dependent, or inconsistent. Then state how many solutions, if any, it will have.

4. $y = 4x - 2$
$y = -x - 3$ consistent; 1

5. $y = x - 1$
$-2x + y = 1$ consistent; 1

6. $x - y = 1$
$2y = 2x - 2$
consistent and dependent; infinite

Solve by substitution.

7. $x = y$
$x - y = 4$ none

8. $x - y = 6$
$y = 3x$ $(-3, -9)$

9. $n = 7 - m$
$m - n = 3$ $(5, 2)$

Solve.

10. $6x + y = -20$
$3x - 2y = 10$ $(-2, -8)$

11. $x - y = 2$
$-x + 2y = 5$ $(9, 7)$

12. $2x - 3y = 5$
$3x - 4y = 9$ $(7, 3)$

ADDITIONAL ANSWERS

Oral Exercises
1. a
2. c
3. b
4. d

Written Exercises
For the odd-numbered solutions, see *Answers to Selected Exercises*, p. 587.
2.

Additional Answers
See p. T60.

1. Graph $|x| + 2 = y$. Graph the system.
$y = x + 2$ for $x \geq 0$
$y = -x + 2$ for $x < 0$

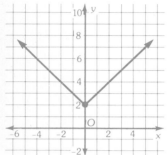

2. Graph $|y + 2| = x$.
Graph the system.
$x = y + 2$ for $y \geq -2$
$x = -(y + 2)$ for $y < -2$

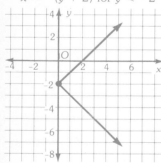

8.11 | Graphing Absolute-Value Equations

The graph of $|x| = 2$ on a number line consists of two points, the coordinates of which are 2 and -2.

EXAMPLES

1 **Graph $|x| = 2$.**

SOLUTION To graph $|x| = 2$, you have to graph the system $x = 2$, because $|x| = 2$ means $x = 2$ or
$$x = -2$$
$x = -2$. In the coordinate plane, the graph of $|x| = 2$ is two parallel lines.

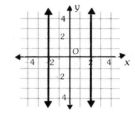

2 **Graph $|x| = y$.**

SOLUTION In this equation, the value of y cannot be negative. If x is a positive number, then $y = x$. If $x = 0$, then $y = 0$. If x is a negative number, then y has to equal the opposite of x. So to graph $|x| = y$, you must graph the system below.

$y = x$ for $x \geq 0$
$y = -x$ for $x < 0$

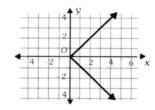

3 **Graph $|y| = x$.**

SOLUTION Because the value of x cannot be negative, graph the following system:

$x = y$ for $y \geq 0$
$x = -y$ for $y < 0$

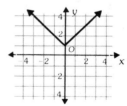

4 **Graph $|x| + 1 = y$.**

SOLUTION Graph $y = x + 1$ for $x \geq 0$.
Graph $y = -x + 1$ for $x < 0$.

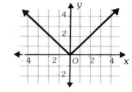

5 **Graph $|y + 1| = x$.**

SOLUTION When $y < -1$, then $y + 1$ will be a negative number.
So graph the system $x = y + 1$ for $y \geq -1$
$$x = -(y + 1) \text{ for } y < -1.$$

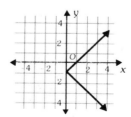

Complete.

1. $|y| = 3$ means $y = 3$ or $y =$ ___-3___.

2. $|y| = x$ means $y = x$ for $y \geq 0$ or $y = -x$ for ___$y < 0$___.

3. $x = |y| + 1$ means $x = y + 1$ for ___$y \geq 0$___ or $x =$ ___$-y + 1$___ for $y < 0$.

4. $y = |x + 1|$ means $y =$ ___$x + 1$___ for ___$x \geq -1$___ or $y =$ ___$-(x + 1)$___ for ___$x < -1$___.

WRITTEN EXERCISES

A. Graph.

   1. $|y| = 4$ **2.** $|y| = x$ **3.** $x = |y| + 2$

   4. $y = |x + 2|$ **5.** $y = |2x|$ **6.** $x = |3y|$

B. **7.** $x = |y| - 3$ **8.** $y = -|x|$ **9.** $x = 2 \cdot |y|$

   10. $y = |x - 3|$ **11.** $y = |x| - 1$ **12.** $y = -2 \cdot |x|$

C. **13.** $|x| \leq 2$ **14.** $|y| \geq 1$ **15.** $y \geq |x + 3|$

The graph of $y = |x + 1|$ can be obtained by shifting or translating the graph of $y = |x|$ one unit to the left. Tell how each graph can be obtained from the graph of $y = |x|$.

   16. $y = |x - 1|$ **17.** $y = |x| + 1$ **18.** $y = -|x|$

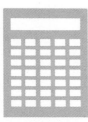

CALCULATOR

You can use a calculator to check whether a given ordered pair is a solution of a system of equations.

Example: The solution for Example 2 in Section 8.5 is $(-1, 2)$. This can be checked as follows:

ENTER   DISPLAY

$4x + 5y = 6$

4 ⊠ 1 ⊞ ⊟ M+ 5 ⊠ 2 ⊞ RM ⊟

$6x - 7y = -20$

6 ⊠ 1 ⊞ ⊟ M+ 7 ⊞ ⊠ 2 ⊞ RM ⊟

EXERCISES

Use a calculator to check the following solutions. If a given solution is incorrect, give the correct solution.

   1. $3x + y = 10$ $(3, 1)$ **2.** $x + 3y = 14$ $(5, 3)$
   $2x + y = 7$ correct $x - 2y = -1$ correct

MIXED REVIEW

Graph each of the following sets of numbers on a number line.

1. $\{x \mid x$ is an even whole number between 3 and 14$\}$

2. $\{x \mid x$ is a counting number less than 5$\}$

3. Solve $3(y + 5) = 37$. $\frac{22}{3}$ or $7\frac{1}{3}$

4. Simplify $\dfrac{-40y^3z^2}{-8y^4z^5}$. $\dfrac{5}{yz^3}$

5. Evaluate $(-8)^3$. -512

TEACHER'S RESOURCE MASTERS

Practice Master 37, Part 1

Quiz 16

COMPUTER SOFTWARE

Graphing Linear Equations and Inequalities

ASSIGNMENT GUIDE

Minimum
1–5 odd, 7–12

Regular
7–15

Maximum
10–18

ADDITIONAL ANSWERS

Written Exercises

For the odd-numbered solutions, see *Answers to Selected Exercises*, p. 587.

Additional Answers
See p. T61.

SKILLS MAINTENANCE

Write each of the following as an algebraic expression:

1. the product of a, b, and c abc

2. five times the sum of a and b $5(a + b)$

3. the difference of -12 and x $-12 - x$

4. the sum of $7a$ and $\frac{b}{9}$ $7a + \frac{b}{9}$

Evaluate if $x = 8$ and $y = -4$.

5. $2xy$ -64

6. $(x + y)(x - y)$ 48

7. xy^2 128

8. $(2y)^2$ 64

9. $\frac{x^2}{y}$ -16

10. $\frac{6}{x - y}$ $\frac{1}{2}$

Simplify.

11. $2 \cdot 3^2 - 3 \cdot 4 + 5$ 11

12. $(6 - 4)^2 + (3 + 2)^3$ 129

13. $\frac{(4 + 5)^2}{3}$ 27

14. $3(4 - 1) \div (5 - 2)$ 3

15. $(7 - 5) \div 2 + 4 \div 2 + 1$ 4

16. $\frac{5^2 - 3^3}{5 + 3^2}$ $-\frac{1}{7}$

Complete each statement using $\in$, $\notin$, $\subset$, or $\not\subset$.

$A = \{1, 2, 3, 4, 5, 6\}$ $B = \{\ \}$ $C = \{-3, -2, -1, 0, 1, 2, 3\}$ $D = \{2, 4, 6\}$

17. $-3 \underline{\ \in\ } C$

18. $B \underline{\ \subset\ } D$

19. $4 \underline{\ \in\ } A$

20. $\{0\} \underline{\ \subset\ } C$

21. $-2 \underline{\ \notin\ } A$

22. $\{5\} \underline{\ \not\subset\ } D$

SKILLS MAINTENANCE
24. -5

Find each sum.

23. $7 + (-4) + 3$ 6

24. $-4 + 6 + (-5) + (-2)$

25. $4 + (-6 + 3)$ 1

26. $-0.15 + 0.2$ 0.05

27. $-0.3 + (-0.7)$ -1

28. $\frac{3}{4} + \left(-\frac{1}{2}\right)$ $\frac{1}{4}$

Find each difference.

29. $15 - 37$ -22

30. $31 - (-12)$ 43

31. $-28 - 45$ -73

32. $-52 - (-46)$ -6

33. $(17 - 42) - 34$ -59

34. $-30 - (62 - 57)$ -35

Find each product.

35. $-2(-2)(-2)$ -8

36. $5(-6)(-4)$ 120

37. $-4(5)(-2)(-3)2$ -240

38. $-0.42(0.6)$ -0.252

39. $\frac{3}{5}\left(-\frac{10}{21}\right)$ $-\frac{2}{7}$

40. $-\frac{4}{9}\left(-\frac{3}{16}\right)$ $\frac{1}{12}$

Find each quotient.

41. $-282 \div 6$ -47

42. $-408 \div (-8)$ 51

43. $324 \div (-9)$ -36

44. $-4.38 \div 0.06$ -73

45. $1\frac{1}{3} \div \left(-\frac{2}{3}\right)$ -2

46. $-2\frac{2}{3} \div \left(-3\frac{1}{3}\right)$ $\frac{4}{5}$

Solve each equation. The replacement set is the set of rational numbers.

47. $a + (-23) = 12$ 35

48. $-62 - b = -75$ 13

49. $0.4 = x + 16.8$ -16.4

50. $-8x = 72$ -9

51. $-4x = -64$ 16

52. $-17x = -272$ 16

288   *Chapter 8 • Linear Systems*

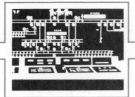

COMPUTER

The more organization given to handling a task, the more efficiently the task can be done. Programming—particularly of large and complex problems—is simplified by a sound organization. The program below, which is incomplete, illustrates the method of "top-down" programming.

Problem: to solve a system of equations expressed as $Ax + By = C$

$$Dx + Ey = F$$

The following equations apply: $x = \dfrac{CE - BF}{AE - DB}$ $y = \dfrac{AF - CD}{AE - DB}$

```
10 REM FIRST INPUT A,B,C,D,E AND F
20 GOSUB 200
30 REM NEXT, CALCULATE DENOMINATOR
40 GOSUB 300
50 IF DENOM = 0 THEN GOSUB 500: GOTO 100
60 REM FINALLY, COMPUTE AND PRINT THE VALUES OF
   X AND Y
70 GOSUB 400
100 INPUT "PRESS RETURN TO CONTINUE OR ANY OTHER KEY TO
    END ";A$
110 IF A$ = "" THEN GOTO 10
120 END: REM END OF UPPER-LEVEL CODE
200 REM GET INPUTS OF A,B,C,D,E AND F
290 RETURN
300 REM CALCULATE DENOMINATOR
390 RETURN
400 REM COMPUTE AND PRINT X AND Y
490 RETURN
500 REM DENOMINATOR = 0, EQUATION CANNOT BE SOLVED
590 RETURN
```

EXERCISES

1. What do lines 10 through 70 do?

2. Complete the program by writing the missing subroutines.

3. Study this example of the technique of *top-down* programming. Is it easier to understand than some other BASIC programs in this book?

2.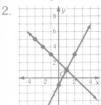

4.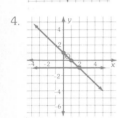

6.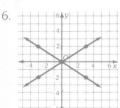

8.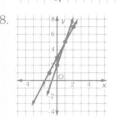

10.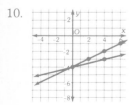

CHAPTER 8 REVIEW

VOCABULARY

addition method (8.4)

boundary line (8.9)

consistent and dependent
   system (8.2)

consistent system (8.2)

half plane (8.9)

inconsistent system (8.2)

ordered triple (8.3)

substitution method (8.3)

subtraction method (8.4)

system of equations (8.1)

REVIEW EXERCISES

8.1   **Solve each system by graphing.**

1. $2x + y = 4$
    $y = 2$ (1, 2)

2. $x + y = 2$
    $2x - y = 1$ (1, 1)

3. $x + 4y = 8$
    $x = -4$ (−4, 3)

4. $y = -1$
    $2x + 2y = 2$ (2, −1)

5. $x = 3$
    $2x + 3y = 0$ (3, −2)

6. $2x - 3y = 0$
    $2x + 3y = 0$ (0, 0)

8.2   **Tell if each system is (a) consistent, (b) inconsistent, or (c) consistent and
dependent. If consistent, solve by graphing.**

7. $y = 3x - 5$
    $y = 3x + 2$ b

8. $y = 2x + 3$
    $y = 3x + 2$ a, (1, 5)

9. $y = x - 5$
    $y = x - 5$ c

10. $y = \frac{1}{2}x - 4$
    $y = \frac{1}{4}x - 4$ a, (0, −4)

11. $y = \frac{1}{3}x - \frac{4}{3}$
    $y = \frac{1}{3}x - \frac{4}{3}$ c

12. $y = 5x + 3$
    $y = 5x - 3$ b

8.3   **Solve each system by the substitution method.**

13. $2b + a = 3$
    $a = 3$ (3, 0)

14. $x = 3 - y$
    $x + 1 = 3y$ (2, 1)

15. $a = 3b - 7$
    $b - a = 3$ (−1, 2)

16. $y = 3x - 16$
    $3y + x = -8$ (4, −4)

17. $x = 8 - 4y$
    $2x - y = 7$ (4, 1)

18. $x = 2y$
    $2x - y = 3$ (2, 1)

8.4   **Solve each system by the addition or the subtraction method.**

19. $3x + y = 4$
    $-3x + 6y = 3$ (1, 1)

20. $4a + b = -5$
    $-4a + 4b = 20$ (−2, 3)

21. $2x + 2y = 24$
    $2x - 2y = -4$ (5, 7)

22. $2x + 2y = 10$
    $6x - 2y = 6$ (2, 3)

23. $x + 2y = 5$
    $4x - 2y = 20$ (5, 0)

24. $2a - 2b = -6$
    $3a + 2b = 16$ (2, 5)

8.5   **Solve each system by multiplication with the addition-subtraction method.**

25. $2x + y = 12$
    $3x + y = 17$ (5, 2)

26. $x + 3y = 9$
    $x + 2y = 7$ (3, 2)

27. $2m - 2n = 10$
    $2m - 4n = 2$ (9, 4)

28. $2x - 3y = -3$
    $3x - 3y = 18$ (21, 15)

29. $3x + 2y = 8$
    $2x + y = 1$ (−6, 13)

30. $2a - 5b = 12$
    $2a - 3b = 12$ (6, 0)

8.6   **Use a system of equations to solve each problem.**

31. A telephone wire 340 meters long must be cut into two pieces. One piece must be 3 times longer than the other. How long will each piece be?   255 m, 85 m

32. The length of a rectangular desk is 22 centimeters less than twice the width. The perimeter of the desk is 106 centimeters. Find the length and the width.

8.7   **33.** A boat traveled 60 miles with the current in 1 hour. The boat took 1.2 hours to make the return trip against the current. What is the speed of the boat in still water and what is the speed of the current?   55 mi/h, 5 mi/h

34. Raisins that sell for $2.60 a pound are to be mixed with nuts that sell for $1.80 a pound to make a 5-pound mixture. How many pounds of raisins and how many pounds of nuts are to be mixed if the mixture sells for $2.10 a pound?

8.8   **35.** Three times Chris's age is 26 more than twice Leslie's age. The sum of their ages is 32. Find their ages.   18, 14

8.9   **Graph.**

36. $x \geq -5$ **37.** $y < 2x - 3$ **38.** $2y - x \geq 4$

8.10   **39.** $y > 2$ **40.** $y \leq x$ **41.** $x + 2y < 6$
         $x \leq 3$ $y - x \leq 6$ $x - 3y > 3$

8.11   **42.** $|x| = y$ **43.** $|y| = x + 1$ **44.** $|x - 2| = y$

ERROR SEARCH

Find the error in each exercise and give the correct answer.

1. $2.3 - x = 7.5$
        $x = 7.5 - 2.3$
        $x = 5.2$

2. $x - 4.9 = 8.5$
        $x = 8.5 - 4.9$
        $x = 3.6$

3. $-14x = 70$
        $\dfrac{14x}{14} = \dfrac{70}{14}$
        $x = 5$

4. $-27 = -2x + 7x$
        $-27 = 9x$
        $\dfrac{-27}{9} = \dfrac{9x}{9}$
        $-3 = x$

32. 28 cm, 25 cm

34. 1.875 lb, 3.125 lb

36.

38.

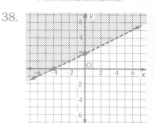

40.

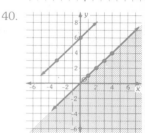

Additional Answers
See p. T61.

ERROR SEARCH

1. $2.3 - x = 7.5$
       $-x = 7.5 - 2.3$
       $-x = 5.2$
       $x = -5.2$

2. $x - 4.9 = 8.5$
       $x = 8.5 + 4.9$
       $x = 13.4$

3. $-14x = 70$
       $\dfrac{-14x}{-14} = \dfrac{70}{-14}$
       $x = -5$

4. $-27 = -2x + 7x$
       $-27 = 5x$
       $\dfrac{-27}{5} = \dfrac{5x}{5}$
       $-5\frac{2}{5} = x$

ADDITIONAL ANSWERS

1. The graphs intersect in one point.

2. The lines are parallel.

3. The graphs are the same line.

4.
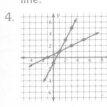

5.
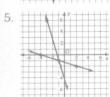

6.
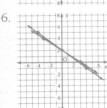

15. $(-2, 5)$

19.
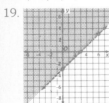

Additional Answers
See p. T62.

CHAPTER 8 TEST

Tell how the graphs of the equations are related if the system is

1. consistent.   **2.** consistent and dependent.   **3.** inconsistent.

Solve by graphing.

4. $2x = y + 1$
$3x - 6y = -3$ $(1, 1)$

5. $7x + 2y = -9$
$x + 3y = -4$ $(-1, -1)$

6. $2x + 3y = 6$
$3x + 4y = 8$ $(0, 2)$

Solve by the substitution method.

7. $5x + 2y = -16$
$x - 4y = 10$ $(-2, -3)$

8. $3x - 2y = 4$
$3x + 4y = 10$ $(2, 1)$

9. $2x + y = 10$
$3x - y = 15$ $(5, 0)$

Solve by the addition or the subtraction method.

10. $x - y = 4$
$x + y = 2$ $(3, -1)$

11. $y = 3x + 6$
$2y = -3x + 3$ $(-1, 3)$

12. $x + 3y = 9$
$-x + 2y = 6$ $(0, 3)$

Solve by multiplication with the addition-subtraction method.

13. $3x + y = 10$
$2x + y = 7$ $(3, 1)$

14. $7a - 5b = -2$
$-8a - b = 9$ $(-1, -1)$

15. $4m + 3n = 7$
$4m + 4n = 12$

Use a system to solve each problem.

16. The sum of the digits of a two-digit number is 11. If the digits are interchanged, the new number formed is 45 greater than the original number. What is the original number? 38

17. A group of 40 volunteers has to be divided into two groups. One group is 4 more than 5 times the other. How many volunteers are in each group? 6, 34

18. An airplane flying with the wind cruises 2240 kilometers in 7 hours. When it is flying against the wind, the plane cruises the same distance in 8 hours. Find the speed of the plane in still air and the speed of the wind. 300 km/h, 20 km/h

Graph.

19. $y > x - 3$

20. $x - y > 2$

21. $4x - y < 5$

22. $y > 3x$
$y > 3x + 2$

23. $x + 2y \geq 4$
$2x - y \leq -2$

24. $y < x$
$y \geq 3 - x$

25. $|y| = 3$

26. $|x| = y - 2$

27. $|y - 3| = x$

CHAPTER 9

Rational Expressions

Rhonda rents rafts. She can put all the rafts away at the end of a day in 30 minutes. Her helper can do it in 50 minutes. How long will it take them if they work together? $18\frac{3}{4}$ minutes

TEACHER'S NOTES

See p. T32.

CLASSROOM EXAMPLES

1. Tell whether or not each expression is a rational expression.
   a. $\frac{3}{8}$ yes
   b. $4x + 1$ yes
   c. $x^2 + 5x + 6$ yes
   d. $\frac{\sqrt{y}}{y + 3}$ no

2. Which values must be excluded from the replacement set of each variable so that the denominator will not equal zero?
   a. $\frac{7}{x}$ 0
   b. $\frac{y^2 + 8y + 15}{y + 6}$ −6
   c. $\frac{4y^2 + 4y}{y^2 - y}$ 0, 1

3. Replace each ? with the correct equivalent rational expression.
   a. $\frac{5}{8} = \frac{5}{8} \cdot 1$
      $= \frac{5}{8} \cdot \frac{2}{2}$
      $= ? \quad \frac{10}{16}$
   b. $\frac{y + 5}{y^3} = \frac{y + 5}{y^3} \cdot 1$
      $= \frac{y + 5}{y^3} \cdot \frac{y + 5}{y + 5}$
      $= ?$
      $\frac{y^2 + 10y + 25}{y^4 + 5y^3}$

9.1 Rational Expressions

In Chapter 2, a rational number was defined as a number that can be expressed in the form $\frac{a}{b}$, where a and b are both integers and $b \neq 0$.

A **rational expression** is an expression that can be written in the form $\frac{N}{D}$, where N and D are both polynomials and $D \neq 0$.

Expression	Rational expression?	
$\frac{4}{5}$	yes	4 and 5 are polynomials (constants).
$2x + 1$	yes	$2x + 1 = \frac{2x + 1}{1}$
$\frac{x^2 - 7x + 6}{x + 4}$	yes	
$\frac{\sqrt{x}}{x + 3}$	no	$\sqrt{x}$ is not a polynomial.

When D is *not* a nonzero constant, certain values of the replacement set for the variable must be excluded so that the denominator cannot be 0.

Rational expression	Excluded value(s)	
$\frac{5}{x}$	0	
$\frac{n^2 + 5n + 6}{n + 3}$	−3	
$\frac{2y^2 + 2y}{y^2 - y}$	0, 1	$y^2 - y = y(y - 1)$. Use the zero-product property.

Given a rational number, you can find an **equivalent rational number** by multiplying by 1.

$$\frac{3}{5} = \frac{3}{5} \cdot 1 \qquad\qquad \frac{3}{5} = \frac{3}{5} \cdot 1$$
$$= \frac{3}{5} \cdot \frac{4}{4} \qquad\qquad = \frac{3}{5} \cdot \frac{9}{9}$$
$$= \frac{12}{20} \qquad\qquad = \frac{27}{45}$$

So, $\frac{3}{5} = \frac{12}{20} = \frac{27}{45}$.

A similar technique can be used to find **equivalent rational expressions** for a given rational expression.

$$\frac{x + 2}{x^3} = \frac{x + 2}{x^3} \cdot 1 \qquad \frac{x + 2}{x^3} = \frac{x + 2}{x^3} \cdot 1 \qquad \frac{x + 2}{x^3} = \frac{x + 2}{x^3} \cdot 1$$
$$= \frac{x + 2}{x^3} \cdot \frac{2}{2} \qquad = \frac{x + 2}{x^3} \cdot \frac{x}{x} \qquad = \frac{x + 2}{x^3} \cdot \frac{x + 2}{x + 2}$$
$$= \frac{2x + 4}{2x^3} \qquad = \frac{x^2 + 2x}{x^4} \qquad = \frac{x^2 + 4x + 4}{x^4 + 2x^3}$$

ORAL EXERCISES

Tell whether or not each expression is a rational expression.

1. 3 yes

2. $\frac{2x + 4}{0}$ no

3. $\frac{5y - 4}{y^2}$ yes

4. $6 \div (2x + 1)$ yes

5. $5v^2 + 7v - 3$ yes

6. $3\sqrt{x} + 2x^2$ no

WRITTEN EXERCISES

A. Replace each ? with the correct equivalent rational expression.

1. $\dfrac{5}{6} = \dfrac{5}{6} \cdot 1$

$= \dfrac{5}{6} \cdot \dfrac{7}{7}$

$= ?$ $\dfrac{35}{42}$

2. $\dfrac{10}{13} = \dfrac{10}{13} \cdot 1$

$= \dfrac{10}{13} \cdot \dfrac{12}{12}$

$= ?$ $\dfrac{120}{156}$

3. $\dfrac{3}{x} = \dfrac{3}{x} \cdot 1$

$= \dfrac{3}{x} \cdot \dfrac{4}{4}$

$= ?$ $\dfrac{12}{4x}$

4. $\dfrac{y}{-3} = \dfrac{y}{-3} \cdot 1$

$= \dfrac{y}{-3} \cdot \dfrac{-1}{-1}$

$= ?$ $\dfrac{-y}{3}$

5. $\dfrac{-2n}{-7} = \dfrac{-2n}{-7} \cdot 1$

$= \dfrac{-2n}{-7} \cdot \dfrac{3}{3}$

$= ?$ $\dfrac{-6n}{-21}$

6. $\dfrac{x}{y} = \dfrac{x}{y} \cdot 1$

$= \dfrac{x}{y} \cdot \dfrac{x}{x}$

$= ?$ $\dfrac{x^2}{xy}$

7. $\dfrac{n}{3} = \dfrac{n}{3} \cdot 1$

$= \dfrac{n}{3} \cdot \dfrac{n+3}{n+3}$

$= ?$ $\dfrac{n^2 + 3n}{3n + 9}$

8. $\dfrac{4}{a} = \dfrac{4}{a} \cdot 1$

$= \dfrac{4}{a} \cdot \dfrac{a-2}{a-2}$

$= ?$ $\dfrac{4a - 8}{a^2 - 2a}$

9. $\dfrac{x+3}{x-1} = \dfrac{x+3}{x-1} \cdot 1$

$= \dfrac{x+3}{x-1} \cdot \dfrac{x+2}{x+2}$

$= ?$ $\dfrac{x^2 + 5x + 6}{x^2 + x - 2}$

10. $\dfrac{y-5}{y+2} = \dfrac{y-5}{y+2} \cdot 1$

$= \dfrac{y-5}{y+2} \cdot \dfrac{y+5}{y+5}$

$= ?$ $\dfrac{y^2 - 25}{y^2 + 7y + 10}$

B. Replace each ? so that the equation names an equivalent rational expression.

11. $\dfrac{4}{5} = \dfrac{?}{30}$ 24

12. $\dfrac{4}{5} = \dfrac{?}{35}$ 28

13. $\dfrac{4}{5} = \dfrac{12}{?}$ 15

14. $\dfrac{4}{5} = \dfrac{20}{?}$ 25

15. $\dfrac{4}{5} = \dfrac{?}{45}$ 36

16. $\dfrac{4}{5} = \dfrac{32}{?}$ 40

17. $\dfrac{8}{x} = \dfrac{32}{?}$ 4x

18. $\dfrac{8}{x} = \dfrac{?}{-x}$ −8

19. $\dfrac{a}{-4} = \dfrac{?}{4}$ −a

20. $\dfrac{-3b}{-4} = \dfrac{3b}{?}$ 4

21. $\dfrac{m}{n} = \dfrac{m^2}{?}$ mn

22. $\dfrac{x-3}{x^2} = \dfrac{x^2 - 3x}{?}$?

23. $\dfrac{a}{4} = \dfrac{?}{4a + 12}$ $a^2 + 3a$

24. $\dfrac{5}{b} = \dfrac{?}{b^2 - 3b}$ $5b - 15$

25. $\dfrac{x+4}{x-2} = \dfrac{?}{x^2 - x - 2}$ $x^2 + 5x + 4$

26. $\dfrac{2a}{3b} = \dfrac{?}{21ab^3}$ $14a^2 b^2$

Which values must be excluded from the replacement set of each variable so that the denominator will not equal zero?

27. $\dfrac{6}{x}$ 0

28. $\dfrac{3a + 2}{2a}$ 0

29. $\dfrac{4y}{y - 1}$ 1

30. $\dfrac{n}{n^2 - 9}$ 3, −3

C. 31. $\dfrac{3n + 5}{n(n - 1)}$ 0, 1

32. $\dfrac{x + 2}{x^2 + x}$ 0, −1

33. $\dfrac{y}{(y - 1)(y + 3)}$ 1, −3

34. $\dfrac{8}{x^2 - 5x + 6}$ 2, 3

35. $\dfrac{5a - a^2}{a^2 - 6a + 5}$ 1, 5

36. $\dfrac{y^2 + 5y + 6}{y^2 + 6y + 8}$ −4, −2

---

4. Replace each ? so that the equation names an equivalent rational expression.

a. $\dfrac{5}{8} = \dfrac{?}{32}$ 20

b. $\dfrac{y + 2}{y^3} = \dfrac{?}{3y^3}$ $3y + 6$

c. $\dfrac{z + 4}{z^3} = \dfrac{z^2 + 4z}{?}$ z^4

MIXED REVIEW

1. Find the slope of a line with points $(3, -5)$ and $(8, 2)$. $\dfrac{7}{5}$

2. Simplify $-5(3x^2 y - 9xy)$. $-15x^2 y + 45xy$

3. Find $f(3)$ if $f(x) = 2x - 7$. -1

4. Write $y = 4x + 6$ in standard form. $-4x + y = 6$

5. Find the sum of $(16y^2 - 5)$ and $(-4y^2 + 9)$. $12y^2 + 4$

TEACHER'S RESOURCE MASTERS

Practice Master 37, Part 2

ASSIGNMENT GUIDE

Minimum
1–9 odd, 11–19

Regular
11–24

Maximum
15–25, 31–35 odd

ADDITIONAL ANSWERS

Written Exercises

22. x^3

TEACHER'S NOTES

See p. T32.

CLASSROOM EXAMPLES

1. Change $\frac{32}{48}$ to simplest form.

$$\frac{32}{48} = \frac{2 \cdot 2 \cdot 2 \cdot 2 \cdot 2}{2 \cdot 2 \cdot 2 \cdot 2 \cdot 3}$$
$$= \frac{(2 \cdot 2 \cdot 2 \cdot 2) \cdot 2}{(2 \cdot 2 \cdot 2 \cdot 2) \cdot 3}$$
$$= \frac{2 \cdot 2 \cdot 2 \cdot 2}{2 \cdot 2 \cdot 2 \cdot 2} \cdot \frac{2}{3}$$
$$= 1 \cdot \frac{2}{3}$$
$$= \frac{2}{3}$$

2. Change $\frac{2x^2 + 4xy}{4x^2 - 2xy}$ to simplest form.

$$\frac{2x^2 + 4xy}{4x^2 - 2xy} = \frac{2x(x + 2y)}{2x(2x - y)}$$
$$= \frac{2x}{2x} \cdot \frac{x + 2y}{2x - y}$$
$$= 1 \cdot \frac{x + 2y}{2x - y}$$
$$= \frac{x + 2y}{2x - y}$$

3. Change $\frac{x^2 + 11x + 18}{x^2 - 81}$ to simplest form.

$$\frac{x^2 + 11x + 18}{x^2 - 81} = \frac{(x + 9)(x + 2)}{(x + 9)(x - 9)}$$
$$= \frac{x + 9}{x + 9} \cdot \frac{x + 2}{x - 9}$$
$$= 1 \cdot \frac{x + 2}{x - 9}$$
$$= \frac{x + 2}{x - 9}$$

4. Change $\frac{6x^2 + 72x + 210}{8x^2 + 40x - 112}$ to simplest form.

$$\frac{6x^2 + 72x + 210}{8x^2 + 40x - 112}$$
$$= \frac{6(x^2 + 12x + 35)}{8(x^2 + 5x - 14)}$$
$$= \frac{2 \cdot 3(x + 5)(x + 7)}{2 \cdot 2 \cdot 2(x + 7)(x - 2)}$$
$$= \frac{2 \cdot (x + 7)}{2 \cdot (x + 7)} \cdot \frac{3 \cdot (x + 5)}{2 \cdot 2 \cdot (x - 2)}$$
$$= 1 \cdot \frac{3(x + 5)}{4(x - 2)}$$
$$= \frac{3(x + 5)}{4(x - 2)}$$

9.2	Simplifying Rational Expressions

A rational expression is in **simplest form** when the numerator and the denominator have no common factors other than 1. To simplify a rational expression, first factor the numerator and the denominator. Then identify the **greatest common factor (GCF)** of the numerator and the denominator.

EXAMPLES

1   Change $\frac{18}{24}$ to simplest form.

SOLUTION

$$\frac{18}{24} = \frac{2 \cdot 3 \cdot 3}{2 \cdot 2 \cdot 2 \cdot 3} \qquad \text{Completely factor numerator and denominator.}$$

$$= \frac{(2 \cdot 3) \cdot 3}{(2 \cdot 3) \cdot 2 \cdot 2} \qquad \text{Group common factors to find GCF.}$$

$$= \frac{2 \cdot 3}{2 \cdot 3} \cdot \frac{3}{4} \qquad \text{GCF is } 2 \cdot 3.$$

$$= 1 \cdot \frac{3}{4} \qquad \frac{2 \cdot 3}{2 \cdot 3} = 1$$

$$= \frac{3}{4} \qquad \text{simplest form}$$

2   Change $\frac{a^2 + ab}{a^2 - ab}$ to simplest form.

SOLUTION

$$\frac{a^2 + ab}{a^2 - ab} = \frac{a(a + b)}{a(a - b)} \qquad \text{Completely factor numerator and denominator.}$$

$$= \frac{a}{a} \cdot \frac{a + b}{a - b} \qquad \text{GCF is } a.$$

$$= 1 \cdot \frac{a + b}{a - b} \qquad \frac{a}{a} = 1$$

$$= \frac{a + b}{a - b} \qquad \text{simplest form}$$

3   Change $\frac{x^2 + 7x + 12}{x^2 - 16}$ to simplest form.

SOLUTION

$$\frac{x^2 + 7x + 12}{x^2 - 16} = \frac{(x + 4)(x + 3)}{(x + 4)(x - 4)}$$

$$= \frac{x + 4}{x + 4} \cdot \frac{x + 3}{x - 4} \qquad \text{GCF is } x + 4.$$

$$= 1 \cdot \frac{x + 3}{x - 4}$$

$$= \frac{x + 3}{x - 4}$$

4 | Change $\dfrac{12n^2 + 12n - 144}{16n^2 - 32n - 48}$ to simplest form.

SOLUTION

$$\dfrac{12n^2 + 12n - 144}{16n^2 - 32n - 48} = \dfrac{12(n^2 + n - 12)}{16(n^2 - 2n - 3)}$$

$$= \dfrac{2 \cdot 2 \cdot 3 \cdot (n + 4)(n - 3)}{2 \cdot 2 \cdot 2 \cdot 2 \cdot (n - 3)(n + 1)}$$

$$= \dfrac{2 \cdot 2 \cdot (n - 3)}{2 \cdot 2 \cdot (n - 3)} \cdot \dfrac{3 \cdot (n + 4)}{2 \cdot 2 \cdot (n + 1)} \quad \text{GCF is } 2 \cdot 2 \cdot (n - 3).$$

$$= 1 \cdot \dfrac{3(n + 4)}{4(n + 1)}$$

$$= \dfrac{3(n + 4)}{4(n + 1)} \qquad \begin{array}{l}\textit{It is common practice to leave}\\ \textit{polynomials in factored form.}\end{array}$$

When simplifying rational expressions, you will sometimes notice factors in the numerator and the denominator that are opposites of each other.

5 | Change $\dfrac{x^2 - 3x}{9 - x^2}$ to simplest form.

SOLUTION

$$\dfrac{x^2 - 3x}{9 - x^2} = \dfrac{x(x - 3)}{(3 - x)(3 + x)} \qquad (x - 3) \text{ and } (3 - x) \text{ are opposites.}$$

$$= \dfrac{x(x - 3)}{-(x - 3)(x + 3)} \qquad 3 - x = -(x - 3)$$

$$= \dfrac{x - 3}{x - 3} \cdot \dfrac{x}{-(x + 3)} \qquad \text{GCF is } x - 3.$$

$$= 1 \cdot \dfrac{x}{-(x + 3)}$$

$$= \dfrac{x}{-(x + 3)} \quad \text{or} \quad -\dfrac{x}{x + 3} \quad \textit{simplest form}$$

NOTE: Although $\dfrac{x}{-(x + 3)}$ may also be written $\dfrac{-x}{x + 3}$ or $\dfrac{x}{-x - 3}$, the form used in this book will be $-\dfrac{x}{x + 3}$.

ORAL EXERCISES

Tell the greatest common factor of the numerator and the denominator of each rational expression.

1. $\dfrac{8}{12}$ 4

2. $\dfrac{12}{36}$ 12

3. $\dfrac{n^2}{3n}$ n

4. $\dfrac{8mn^3}{2m^2n^2}$ $2mn^2$

5. $\dfrac{16xy^3z^2}{4x^2yz^3}$ $4xyz^2$

6. $\dfrac{2q^3m^2}{7qn^3}$ q

7. $\dfrac{3(a - b)^3}{9(a - b)}$ $3(a - b)$

8. $\dfrac{12(x + 2y)^3}{4(x + 2y)^2}$ $4(x + 2y)^2$

9. $\dfrac{(x + y)(x - y)}{(x + y)^2}$ $x + y$

10. $\dfrac{4x}{8xy}$ $4x$

11. $\dfrac{3a^2b^3}{9a^2b^2}$ $3a^2b^2$

12. $\dfrac{5(m + 4)}{6(m + 4)}$ $m + 4$

13. $\dfrac{3(x - 5)}{(x - 5)^2}$ $x - 5$

14. $\dfrac{(y - 2)^3}{7(y - 2)^2}$ $(y - 2)^2$

15. $\dfrac{(a + 4)(a + 5)}{(a - 4)(a + 4)}$ $a + 4$

16. $\dfrac{(b - 3)(b + 2)}{(b + 4)(b - 3)}$ $b - 3$

17. $\dfrac{y + 2}{y^2 - 4}$ $y + 2$

18. $\dfrac{x - 1}{x^2 - 1}$ $x - 1$

5. Change $\dfrac{y^2 - 5y}{25 - y^2}$ to simplest form.

$$\dfrac{y^2 - 5y}{25 - y^2} = \dfrac{y(y - 5)}{(5 - y)(5 + y)}$$

$$= \dfrac{y(y - 5)}{-(y - 5)(y + 5)}$$

$$= \dfrac{y - 5}{y - 5} \cdot \dfrac{y}{-(y + 5)}$$

$$= 1 \cdot \dfrac{y}{-(y + 5)}$$

$$= \dfrac{y}{-(y + 5)} \text{ or } -\dfrac{y}{y + 5}$$

MIXED REVIEW

1. Find the y-intercept of the line for $y = \dfrac{2}{5}x - 8$. -8

2. State the domain of the relation $\{(-8, -10), (11, -11), (-6, 4), (-9, -5)\}$.
$\{-8, 11, -6, -9\}$

3. Find the product of $(6xy^2)$ and $(-xy^2)$. $-6x^2y^4$

4. Illustrate the inverse property of multiplication.
Answers may vary.

5. Find the difference of $(12x^3y - 8xy)$ and $(-15x^3y + 8xy)$. $27x^3y - 16xy$

TEACHER'S RESOURCE MASTERS

Practice Master 38, Part 1

ASSIGNMENT GUIDE

Minimum
10–18, 19–49 odd

Regular
25–49

Maximum
44–60, 67–73 odd

WRITTEN EXERCISES

A. 1–18. Change each rational expression in Oral Exercises to simplest form.

B. Change each rational expression to simplest form.

19. $\dfrac{12x}{8(x+1)}$ $\quad \frac{3x}{2(x+1)}$

20. $\dfrac{y-2}{y^2-4}$ $\quad \frac{1}{y+2}$

21. $\dfrac{n+4}{n^2-16}$ $\quad \frac{1}{n-4}$

22. $\dfrac{6n-12}{8n-16}$ $\quad \frac{3}{4}$

23. $\dfrac{y-2}{2-y}$ $\quad -1$

24. $\dfrac{x^2-6x+9}{x^2-9}$ $\quad \frac{x-3}{x+3}$

25. $\dfrac{2x^2-18}{9-x^2}$ $\quad -2$

26. $\dfrac{y^2-y-2}{y^2-4}$ $\quad \frac{y+1}{y+2}$

27. $\dfrac{v^2-3v}{v^2-2v-3}$ $\quad \frac{v}{v+1}$

28. $\dfrac{b^2-3b}{-b^2+2b+3}$ $\quad -\frac{b}{b+1}$

29. $\dfrac{m^3+m^2n}{m^2+mn}$ $\quad m$

30. $\dfrac{r^2-3r}{3-r}$ $\quad -r$

31. $\dfrac{6n+18}{n^2+6n+9}$ $\quad \frac{6}{n+3}$

32. $\dfrac{y^2+5y+6}{y^2-9}$ $\quad \frac{y+2}{y-3}$

33. $\dfrac{a^3-16a}{16-a^2}$ $\quad -a$

34. $\dfrac{a^2+4a+4}{a^2-4}$ $\quad \frac{a+2}{a-2}$

35. $\dfrac{5n-10}{n^2-4n+4}$ $\quad \frac{5}{n-2}$

36. $\dfrac{4x^2-16}{12x-24}$ $\quad \frac{x+2}{3}$

37. $\dfrac{(x-1)^2}{1-x^2}$ $\quad -\frac{x-1}{x+1}$

38. $\dfrac{a^2+6a+8}{a^2+8a+16}$ $\quad \frac{a+2}{a+4}$

39. $\dfrac{x^2+x-6}{x^2+5x+6}$ $\quad \frac{x-2}{x+2}$

40. $\dfrac{n^2-7n+10}{n^2-4n+4}$ $\quad \frac{n-5}{n-2}$

41. $\dfrac{x^2-9x+20}{x^2-7x+10}$ $\quad \frac{x-4}{x-2}$

42. $\dfrac{y^2-4y-12}{y^2-4}$ $\quad \frac{y-6}{y-2}$

43. $\dfrac{a^2-5a-6}{a^2-36}$ $\quad \frac{a+1}{a+6}$

44. $\dfrac{(5x-y)^3}{(y-5x)^3}$ $\quad -1$

45. $\dfrac{x^2-2x+1}{x^2-3x+2}$ $\quad \frac{x-1}{x-2}$

46. $\dfrac{h^2+8h+7}{h^2+6h-7}$ $\quad \frac{h+1}{h-1}$

47. $\dfrac{2k^2+7k+3}{k^2+2k-3}$ $\quad \frac{2k+1}{k-1}$

48. $\dfrac{3y^2-y-2}{6y^2+7y+2}$ $\quad \frac{y-1}{2y+1}$

49. $\dfrac{2m^2+9m+4}{2m^2+m}$ $\quad \frac{m+4}{m}$

50. $\dfrac{t^2-3t}{t^2-7t+12}$ $\quad \frac{t}{t-4}$

51. $\dfrac{4w+4y}{w^2+2wy+y^2}$ $\quad \frac{4}{w+y}$

52. $\dfrac{3t^2-6t}{t^2-t-2}$ $\quad \frac{3t}{t+1}$

53. $\dfrac{s^2-4s+3}{s^2+s-12}$ $\quad \frac{s-1}{s+4}$

54. $\dfrac{2x^2-5x+3}{x^2+3x-4}$ $\quad \frac{2x-3}{x+4}$

55. $\dfrac{a^2-5a+6}{-a^2+5a-6}$ $\quad -1$

56. $\dfrac{q^2+5q-14}{q^2+8q+7}$ $\quad \frac{q-2}{q+1}$

57. $\dfrac{m^2-7m-8}{m^2-10m+16}$ $\quad \frac{m+1}{m-2}$

58. $\dfrac{2n^2-5n-3}{3n^2-10n+3}$ $\quad \frac{2n+1}{3n-1}$

59. $\dfrac{3d^2+10d-8}{2d^2+11d+12}$ $\quad \frac{3d-2}{2d+3}$

60. $\dfrac{2f^2-5f-3}{4f^2-1}$ $\quad \frac{f-3}{2f-1}$

C. 61. $\dfrac{3n^2-27}{18-9n+n^2}$ $\quad \frac{3(n+3)}{n-6}$

62. $\dfrac{n^2+n-2}{4-n^2}$ $\quad -\frac{n-1}{n-2}$

63. $\dfrac{6a^2+42a+72}{2a^2+12a+18}$ $\quad \frac{3(a+4)}{a+3}$

64. $\dfrac{(m+n)^2(m-n)}{m^2-n^2}$ $\quad m+n$

65. $\dfrac{2x^2-2}{12+8x-4x^2}$ $\quad -\frac{x-1}{2(x-3)}$

66. $\dfrac{x^2-y^2}{3y+3x}$ $\quad \frac{x-y}{3}$

67. $\dfrac{n+4+n^3+4n^2}{n^3-7n^2+n-7}$ $\quad \frac{n+4}{n-7}$

68. $\dfrac{10a^2+3a-18}{14a^2+15a-9}$ $\quad \frac{5a-6}{7a-3}$

69. $\dfrac{12x^2+x-6}{12x^2-17x+6}$ $\quad \frac{4x+3}{4x-3}$

70. $\dfrac{6x^2-x-12}{6x^2-15x+9}$ $\quad \frac{3x+4}{3(x-1)}$

71. $\dfrac{(a+b)^2+(a+b)-2}{a+b+2}$ $\quad a+b-1$

72. $\dfrac{a-b}{(b-a)^3}$ $\quad -\frac{1}{(b-a)^2}$

73. $\dfrac{144x^2+36x-378}{60x^2-60x-45}$ $\quad \frac{6(4x+7)}{5(2x+1)}$

74. $\dfrac{336y^2-28y-168}{192y^2-80y-48}$ $\quad \frac{7(3y+2)}{4(3y+1)}$

Integral Exponents

OBJECTIVE

Simplify an expression by using the properties of integral exponents.

In Chapter 5, a rule was given for division of powers where a and b are positive integers and $x \neq 0$.

If $a = b$, then $\frac{x^a}{x^b} = 1$.

If $a > b$, then $\frac{x^a}{x^b} = x^{a-b}$.

If $a < b$, then $\frac{x^a}{x^b} = \frac{1}{x^{b-a}}$.

It would be simpler if the rule $\frac{x^a}{x^b} = x^{a-b}$ could be used in all cases—that is, when $a = b$, $a > b$, or $a < b$.

Suppose $\frac{x^a}{x^b} = x^{a-b}$ is used when $a = b$. Then $\frac{x^5}{x^5} = x^{5-5} = x^0$. But you know that $\frac{x^5}{x^5} = 1$. This suggests that x^0 should be defined as 1.

Next consider $\frac{x^a}{x^b} = x^{a-b}$ when $a < b$. Then $\frac{x^2}{x^5} = x^{2-5} = x^{-3}$. But you already know that $\frac{x^2}{x^5} = \frac{1}{x^{5-2}} = \frac{1}{x^3}$. This suggests that x^{-3} should be defined as $\frac{1}{x^3}$.

Therefore, to make the rule $\frac{x^a}{x^b} = x^{a-b}$ true for *all* cases, the following definitions are stated.

Zero Exponent and Negative Integral Exponents	**If x is a nonzero real number and b is a positive integer, then** $$x^0 = 1, \text{ and}$$ $$x^{-b} = \frac{1}{x^b}.$$

CLASSROOM EXAMPLES

1. Rewrite each expression with positive exponents only. Then simplify the result.

a. $(-4)^{-3} \cdot 5^0$

$(-4)^{-3} \cdot 5^0 = \frac{1}{(-4)^3} \cdot 1$

$= \frac{1}{(-4)^3}$

$= -\frac{1}{64}$

b. $(5a)^{-2}$

$(5a)^{-2} = \frac{1}{(5a)^2}$

$= \frac{1}{5^2 a^2}$

$= \frac{1}{25a^2}$

c. $\frac{y^{-5}}{y^{-7}}$

$\frac{y^{-5}}{y^{-7}} = \frac{\frac{1}{y^5}}{\frac{1}{y^7}}$

$= \frac{1}{y^5} \cdot \frac{y^7}{1}$

$= \frac{y^7}{y^5}$

$= y^{7-5}$

$= y^2$

EXAMPLES

1   **Rewrite each expression with positive exponents only. Then simplify the result.**

a. $(-6)^{-2} \cdot 4^0$ **b.** $(3a)^{-2}$ **c.** $\frac{x^{-3}}{x^{-5}}$

SOLUTIONS

a. $(-6)^{-2} \cdot 4^0 = \frac{1}{(-6)^2} \cdot 1$

$= \frac{1}{(-6)^2}$

$= \frac{1}{36}$

b. $(3a)^{-2} = \frac{1}{(3a)^2}$

$= \frac{1}{3^2 a^2}$

$= \frac{1}{9a^2}$

c. $\frac{x^{-3}}{x^{-5}} = \frac{\frac{1}{x^3}}{\frac{1}{x^5}}$

$= \frac{1}{x^3} \cdot \frac{x^5}{1}$

$= \frac{x^5}{x^3}$

$= x^{5-3}$

$= x^2$

2. Rewrite each expression, using the appropriate property. Then simplify the result.

a. $(5s)^2 \cdot (5s)^{-4}$

$(5s)^2 \cdot (5s)^{-4}$

$= (5s)^{2+(-4)}$

$= (5s)^{-2}$

$= 5^{-2}s^{-2}$

$= \dfrac{1}{5^2} \cdot \dfrac{1}{s^2}$

$= \dfrac{1}{25} \cdot \dfrac{1}{s^2}$

$= \dfrac{1}{25s^2}$

b. $(xy)^{-4}$

$(xy)^{-4} = x^{-4}y^{-4}$

$= \dfrac{1}{x^4} \cdot \dfrac{1}{y^4}$

$= \dfrac{1}{x^4y^4}$

c. $\dfrac{(-5d)^2}{(-5d)^{-3}}$

$\dfrac{(-5d)^2}{(-5d)^{-3}} = (-5d)^{2-(-3)}$

$= (-5d)^5$

$= (-5)^5 \cdot d^5$

$= -3125d^5$

d. $\left(\dfrac{6x}{y}\right)^{-2}$

$\left(\dfrac{6x}{y}\right)^{-2} = \dfrac{(6x)^{-2}}{y^{-2}}$

$= \dfrac{6^{-2}x^{-2}}{y^{-2}}$

$= \dfrac{y^2}{6^2x^2}$

$= \dfrac{y^2}{36x^2}$

Properties of Integral Exponents

If x and y are nonzero real numbers and a and b are integers, then

1. $x^a \cdot x^b = x^{a+b}$ **2.** $(xy)^a = x^ay^a$

3. $\dfrac{x^a}{x^b} = x^{a-b}$ **4.** $\left(\dfrac{x}{y}\right)^b = \dfrac{x^b}{y^b}$

---

2 **Rewrite each expression, using the appropriate property above. Then simplify the result.**

a. $(6s)^2 \cdot (6s)^{-5}$

b. $(mn)^{-3}$

c. $\dfrac{(-4d)^2}{(-4d)^{-3}}$

d. $\left(\dfrac{8x}{y}\right)^{-2}$

SOLUTIONS

a. $(6s)^2 \cdot (6s)^{-5} = (6s)^{2+(-5)}$

$= (6s)^{-3}$

$= 6^{-3}s^{-3}$

$= \dfrac{1}{6^3} \cdot \dfrac{1}{s^3}$

$= \dfrac{1}{216} \cdot \dfrac{1}{s^3}$

$= \dfrac{1}{216s^3}$

b. $(mn)^{-3} = m^{-3}n^{-3}$

$= \dfrac{1}{m^3} \cdot \dfrac{1}{n^3}$

$= \dfrac{1}{m^3n^3}$

c. $\dfrac{(-4d)^2}{(-4d)^{-3}} = (-4d)^{2-(-3)}$

$= (-4d)^5$

$= (-4)^5 \cdot d^5$

$= -1024d^5$

d. $\left(\dfrac{8x}{y}\right)^{-2} = \dfrac{(8x)^{-2}}{y^{-2}}$

$= \dfrac{8^{-2}x^{-2}}{y^{-2}}$

$= \dfrac{y^2}{8^2x^2}$

$= \dfrac{y^2}{64x^2}$

ORAL EXERCISES

Match each definition or property on the left with the corresponding expression on the right.

1. $x^0 = 1$ d

2. $\dfrac{x^a}{x^b} = x^{a-b}$ a

3. $x^{-b} = \dfrac{1}{x^b}$ e

4. $x^a \cdot x^b = x^{a+b}$ b

5. $\left(\dfrac{x}{y}\right)^b = \dfrac{x^b}{y^b}$ f

6. $(xy)^a = x^ay^a$ c

a. $\dfrac{3^5}{3^3} = 9$

b. $2^4 \cdot 2^3 = 128$

c. $(3 \cdot 4)^2 = 144$

d. $100^0 = 1$

e. $9^{-2} = \dfrac{1}{81}$

f. $\left(\dfrac{2}{3}\right)^4 = \dfrac{16}{81}$

MIXED REVIEW

A. Rewrite each of the following by using the definitions of zero and negative integral exponents:

1. 10^0 1

2. 1^0 1

3. 4^{-2} $\frac{1}{16}$

4. $(-4)^{-2}$ $\frac{1}{16}$

5. 8^0 1

6. $(-8)^0$ 1

7. 9^{-1} $\frac{1}{9}$

8. $(-9)^{-1}$ $-\frac{1}{9}$

9. $10,000^0$ 1

10. $(-12)^0$ 1

11. $\left(\frac{a}{b}\right)^{-2}$ $\frac{b^2}{a^2}$

12. $\left(\frac{3}{4}\right)^{-3}$ $\frac{64}{27}$

Simplify each of the following by using the properties of integral exponents:

13. $(12x)^0$ 1

14. $(5x)^{-2}$ $\frac{1}{25x^2}$

15. $3^5 \cdot 3^{-2}$ 27

16. $\frac{3^5}{3^2}$ 27

17. $(-4)^{-2} \cdot (-4)$ $-\frac{1}{4}$

18. $(ab)^{-4}$ $\frac{1}{a^4 b^4}$

B. 19. $\frac{(-2)^3}{(-2)^6}$ $-\frac{1}{8}$

20. $\left(\frac{x}{y}\right)^4$ $\frac{x^4}{y^4}$

21. $3^{-3} \cdot 3^{-2}$ $\frac{1}{243}$

Rewrite each expression with positive exponents only. Then simplify the result.

22. 6^{-1} $\frac{1}{6}$

23. 12^{-1} $\frac{1}{12}$

24. a^{-1} $\frac{1}{a}$

25. $\left(\frac{1}{3}\right)^{-1}$ 3

26. $\left(\frac{1}{6}\right)^{-1}$ 6

27. $\left(\frac{1}{a}\right)^{-1}$ a

28. $\left(\frac{1}{b}\right)^{-1}$ b

29. $\left(\frac{3}{4}\right)^{-1}$ $\frac{4}{3}$

30. $\left(\frac{4}{5}\right)^{-1}$ $\frac{5}{4}$

31. $\left(\frac{8}{7}\right)^{-1}$ $\frac{7}{8}$

32. $\left(\frac{a}{b}\right)^{-1}$ $\frac{b}{a}$

33. $(-5)^{-1}$ $-\frac{1}{5}$

34. $(-13)^{-1}$ $-\frac{1}{13}$

35. $(-a)^{-1}$ $-\frac{1}{a}$

36. $\left(-\frac{1}{3}\right)^{-1}$ -3

37. $\left(-\frac{1}{9}\right)^{-1}$ -9

38. $\left(-\frac{1}{a}\right)^{-1}$ $-a$

39. $\left(-\frac{1}{b}\right)^{-1}$ $-b$

40. $\left(-\frac{3}{4}\right)^{-1}$ $-\frac{4}{3}$

41. $\left(-\frac{2}{3}\right)^{-1}$ $-\frac{3}{2}$

42. $\left(-\frac{a}{b}\right)^{-1}$ $-\frac{b}{a}$

43. 4^{-3} $\frac{1}{64}$

44. 3^{-3} $\frac{1}{27}$

45. a^{-3} $\frac{1}{a^3}$

46. $(-a)^{-2}$ $\frac{1}{a^2}$

47. $(-b)^{-4}$ $\frac{1}{b^4}$

48. $\frac{1}{x^{-2}}$ x^2

49. $\frac{1}{y^{-3}}$ y^3

Simplify each of the following by using the properties of integral exponents:

50. $(3a)^{-2} \cdot (3a)^{-1}$ $\frac{1}{27a^3}$

51. $(4b)^{-1} \cdot (4b)^{-1}$ $\frac{1}{16b^2}$

52. $(-5x)^{-2}$ $\frac{1}{25x^2}$

53. $(-2n)^{-3}$ $-\frac{1}{8n^3}$

54. $\frac{(mn)^{-5}}{(mn)^{-3}}$ $\frac{1}{m^2 n^2}$

55. $\frac{(ab)^{-7}}{(ab)^4}$ $\frac{1}{a^{11} b^{11}}$

56. $\left(\frac{3x}{4}\right)^{-2}$ $\frac{16}{9x^2}$

57. $\left(\frac{2y}{3}\right)^{-3}$ $\frac{27}{8y^3}$

58. $(3ab)^{-2}$ $\frac{1}{9a^2 b^2}$

C. 59. $(4xy)^{-3}$ $\frac{1}{64x^3 y^3}$

60. $\left(\frac{9mn}{4}\right)^0$ 1

61. $\left(\frac{7xy}{-3}\right)^0$ 1

62. $\frac{2.4 \times 10^3}{1.2 \times 10^2}$ 20

63. $\frac{3.6 \times 10^5}{1.8 \times 10}$ $20,000$

64. $\frac{3.9 \times 10^{-6}}{1.3 \times 10^{-8}}$ 300

65. $\frac{6.4 \times 10^{-5}}{1.6 \times 10^{-9}}$ $40,000$

66. $\frac{315a^{-3}y^9}{-70a^{-2}y^6}$ $-\frac{9y^3}{2a}$

67. $\frac{156x^{-4}y^9}{-12x^{-6}y^3}$ $-13x^2 y^6$

68. $\frac{52m^3 n^{-2}}{4m^{-5}n^4}$ $\frac{13m^8}{n^6}$

69. $\frac{60s^4 t^{-4}}{150s^{-4} t^4}$ $\frac{2s^8}{5t^8}$

70. $\frac{13x^2 y^3 z^{-4}}{325x^2 y^{-1}}$ $\frac{y^4}{25z^4}$

MIXED REVIEW

1. Change $\frac{x^2 - 6x}{x^2 - 8x + 12}$ to simplest form. $\frac{x}{x - 2}$

2. Rewrite $5x + 3y = 10$ in slope-intercept form.
$y = -\frac{5}{3}x + \frac{10}{3}$

3. Find the quotient of $(x^2 + 7x + 10)$ and $(x + 2)$.
$(x + 5)$

4. Evaluate $(6.3)^3$. 250.047

5. Multiply $(2x + 9)(2x - 5)$. $4x + 8x - 45$

TEACHER'S RESOURCE MASTERS

Practice Master 38, Part 2

ASSIGNMENT GUIDE

Minimum
7–21 odd, 22–38

Regular
22–46

Maximum
22–25, 33–55 odd, 62–70

EXPLORATION

Exercises

1. 6.8×10^7

2. 1.948×10^2

3. 1×10^5

4. 4.6×10^{-1}

5. 3.937×10^{-8}

8. 2×10^{-4}; 6×10^{-6}

EXPLORATION
Scientific Notation

Sometimes scientists need to write very large or very small numbers. A light-year (the distance light travels in one year), for example, is 5,880,000,000,000 miles. A picosecond, by contrast, is only 0.000000000001 second.

A uniform but shorter method of expressing such numbers, which utilizes powers of ten, is called **scientific notation**. A number is expressed in scientific notation when it is written as the product of a number (n) and some power of 10, where $1 \le n < 10$.

Example 1: Express 5,880,000,000,000 in scientific notation.

Solution: Count the number of places that the decimal point must be moved so that $1 \le n < 10$.

5,880,000,000,000, $= 5.88 \times 10^{12}$

12 places

*The exponent is the same as the number of places the decimal point was moved. It is **positive** because the original number is greater than 10.*

Example 2: Express 0.000000000001 in scientific notation.

Solution: Count the number of places that the decimal point must be moved so that $1 \le n < 10$.

0.000000000001, $= 1 \times 10^{-12}$

12 places

*The exponent is **negative** because the original number is less than 1.*

EXERCISES

Express each number in scientific notation.

1. 68,000,000   **2.** 194.8   **3.** 100,000   **4.** 0.46

Express each measurement in scientific notation.

5. A nanometer in the metric system equals 0,00000003937 inch.

6. There are more than 3,500,000,000 United States one-dollar bills in circulation. 3.5×10^9

7. A mole is a base unit in the metric system. It contains 602 257 000 000 000 000 000 000 atoms, molecules, ions, or radicals. 6.02257×10^{23}

8. The most powerful optical microscope cannot distinguish objects smaller than 0.0002 mm. An ultramicroscope can be used to view objects as small as 0.000006 mm.

To find the product of two rational numbers, you find the product of the numerators and the product of the denominators and express the result in simplest form. Rational expressions are multiplied in a similar manner.

| Multiplication of Rational Expressions | If $\frac{A}{B}$ and $\frac{C}{D}$ are rational expressions, then $\frac{A}{B} \cdot \frac{C}{D} = \frac{AC}{BD}$. |

OBJECTIVE
Multiply rational expressions.

TEACHER'S NOTES
See p. T32.

EXAMPLES

1 **Multiply $\frac{3}{5} \cdot \frac{20}{21}$ and express the product in simplest form.**

SOLUTION

$$\frac{3}{5} \cdot \frac{20}{21} = \frac{3 \cdot 20}{5 \cdot 21}$$

$$= \frac{3 \cdot 2^2 \cdot 5}{5 \cdot 3 \cdot 7}$$

$$= \frac{(3 \cdot 5) \cdot 2^2}{(3 \cdot 5) \cdot 7}$$

$$= 1 \cdot \frac{2^2}{7}$$

$$= \frac{4}{7}$$

SHORTCUT

$$\frac{3}{5} \cdot \frac{20}{21} = \frac{3 \cdot 20}{5 \cdot 21}$$

$$= \frac{\overset{1}{\cancel{3}} \cdot \overset{4}{\cancel{20}}}{\underset{1}{\cancel{5}} \cdot \underset{7}{\cancel{21}}}$$

$$= \frac{1 \cdot 4}{1 \cdot 7}$$

$$= \frac{4}{7}$$

2 **Multiply $\frac{2a^3}{b^3} \cdot \frac{3b^2}{2}$ and express the product in simplest form.**

SOLUTION

$$\frac{2a^3}{b^3} \cdot \frac{3b^2}{2} = \frac{(2a^3)(3b^2)}{(b^3)(2)}$$

$$= \frac{(2b^2)(3a^3)}{(2b^2)(b)}$$

$$= 1 \cdot \frac{3a^3}{b}$$

$$= \frac{3a^3}{b}$$

SHORTCUT

$$\frac{2a^3}{b^3} \cdot \frac{3b^2}{2} = \frac{2a^3 \cdot 3b^2}{b^3 \cdot 2}$$

$$= \frac{\overset{1}{\cancel{2}}a^3 \cdot 3\overset{1}{\cancel{b^2}}}{\underset{b}{\cancel{b^3}} \cdot \underset{1}{\cancel{2}}}$$

$$= \frac{a^3 \cdot 3}{b \cdot 1}$$

$$= \frac{3a^3}{b}$$

3 **Multiply $\frac{n+3}{4n+2} \cdot \frac{4n+2}{n-3}$ and express the product in simplest form.**

SOLUTION

$$\frac{n+3}{4n+2} \cdot \frac{4n+2}{n-3} = \frac{(n+3)(4n+2)}{(4n+2)(n-3)}$$

$$= \frac{(4n+2)(n+3)}{(4n+2)(n-3)}$$

$$= 1 \cdot \frac{n+3}{n-3}$$

$$= \frac{n+3}{n-3}$$

SHORTCUT

$$\frac{n+3}{4n+2} \cdot \frac{4n+2}{n-3} = \frac{(n+3)(4n+2)}{(4n+2)(n-3)}$$

$$= \frac{(n+3)\overset{1}{\cancel{(4n+2)}}}{\underset{1}{\cancel{(4n+2)}}(n-3)}$$

$$= \frac{(n+3) \cdot 1}{1 \cdot (n-3)}$$

$$= \frac{n+3}{n-3}$$

CLASSROOM EXAMPLES
1. Multiply $\frac{4}{5} \cdot \frac{35}{42}$ and express the product in simplest form.

$$\frac{4}{5} \cdot \frac{35}{42}$$

$$= \frac{4 \cdot 35}{5 \cdot 42}$$

$$= \frac{2^2 \cdot 5 \cdot 7}{5 \cdot 2 \cdot 3 \cdot 7}$$

$$= \frac{(2 \cdot 5 \cdot 7) \cdot 2}{(2 \cdot 5 \cdot 7) \cdot 3}$$

$$= 1 \cdot \frac{2}{3}$$

$$= \frac{2}{3}$$

2. Multiply $\frac{4a^3}{b^3} \cdot \frac{5b^2}{4}$ and express the product in simplest form.

$$\frac{4a^3}{b^3} \cdot \frac{5b^2}{4}$$

$$= \frac{(4a^3)(5b^2)}{(b^3)(4)}$$

$$= \frac{(4b^2)(5a^3)}{(4b^2)(b)}$$

$$= 1 \cdot \frac{5a^3}{b}$$

$$= \frac{5a^3}{b}$$

3. Multiply $\frac{x+5}{3n+4} \cdot \frac{3n+4}{x-5}$ and express the product in simplest form.

$\frac{x+5}{3n+4} \cdot \frac{3n+4}{x-5}$

$= \frac{(x+5)(3n+4)}{(3n+4)(x-5)}$

$= \frac{(3n+4)(x+5)}{(3n+4)(x-5)}$

$= 1 \cdot \frac{x+5}{x-5}$

$= \frac{x+5}{x-5}$

4. Multiply $\frac{6x-6y}{x-y}$

$\cdot \frac{x-2y}{x^2-2xy+y^2}$ and express the product in simplest form.

$\frac{6x-6y}{x-y} \cdot \frac{x-2y}{x^2-2xy+y^2}$

$= \frac{(6x-6y)(x-2y)}{(x-y)(x^2-2xy+y^2)}$

$= \frac{6(x-y)(x-2y)}{(x-y)(x-y)(x-y)}$

$= \frac{(x-y)(x-2y) \cdot 6}{(x-y)(x-y)(x-y)}$

$= 1 \cdot \frac{6(x-2y)}{(x-y)(x-y)}$

$= \frac{6(x-2y)}{(x-y)^2}$

---

4 **Multiply** $\frac{5x+5y}{x-y} \cdot \frac{x+2y}{x^2+2xy+y^2}$ **and express the product in simplest form.**

SOLUTION

$\frac{5x+5y}{x-y} \cdot \frac{x+2y}{x^2+2xy+y^2} = \frac{(5x+5y)(x+2y)}{(x-y)(x^2+2xy+y^2)}$

$= \frac{5(x+y)(x+2y)}{(x-y)(x+y)(x+y)}$

$= \frac{(x+y)(x+2y) \cdot 5}{(x+y)(x-y)(x+y)}$

$= 1 \cdot \frac{5(x+2y)}{(x-y)(x+y)}$

$= \frac{5(x+2y)}{(x-y)(x+y)}$

5 **Multiply** $\frac{y^2+y-6}{y^2-y-2} \cdot \frac{y^2-6y-7}{y^2+7y+12}$ **and express the product in simplest form.**

SOLUTION

$\frac{y^2+y-6}{y^2-y-2} \cdot \frac{y^2-6y-7}{y^2+7y+12} = \frac{(y^2+y-6)(y^2-6y-7)}{(y^2-y-2)(y^2+7y+12)}$

$= \frac{(y+3)(y-2)(y-7)(y+1)}{(y-2)(y+1)(y+4)(y+3)}$

$= \frac{(y+3)(y-2)(y+1)(y-7)}{(y+3)(y-2)(y+1)(y+4)}$

$= 1 \cdot \frac{y-7}{y+4}$

$= \frac{y-7}{y+4}$

ORAL EXERCISES

Find each product.

1. $\frac{a}{b} \cdot \frac{3}{4}$ $\frac{3a}{4b}$

2. $\frac{x}{y} \cdot \frac{2}{3}$ $\frac{2x}{3y}$

3. $\frac{x^2}{2} \cdot \frac{x^3}{3}$ $\frac{x^5}{6}$

4. $\frac{m}{2} \cdot \frac{m}{2}$ $\frac{m^2}{4}$

5. $\frac{3x}{2} \cdot \frac{1}{x}$ $\frac{3}{2}$

6. $\frac{1}{a} \cdot \frac{a}{b}$ $\frac{1}{b}$

7. $\frac{x}{y} \cdot \frac{x}{y}$ $\frac{x^2}{y^2}$

8. $\frac{x}{y} \cdot \frac{y}{x}$ 1

9. $\frac{a}{b^2} \cdot \frac{b}{a^2}$ $\frac{1}{ab}$

WRITTEN EXERCISES

A. Find each product and express it in simplest form.

1. $\frac{4}{x} \cdot \frac{x^2}{4}$ x

2. $\frac{3a}{b} \cdot \frac{c}{3a}$ $\frac{c}{b}$

3. $\frac{a-1}{3a+1} \cdot \frac{3a+1}{a+1}$ $\frac{a-1}{a+1}$

4. $\frac{x}{x-7} \cdot \frac{x-7}{7}$ $\frac{x}{7}$

5. $\frac{3a}{b^2} \cdot \frac{4b^3}{3a^2}$ $\frac{4b}{a}$

6. $\frac{xy}{mn} \cdot \frac{m}{x^3y^2}$ $\frac{1}{nx^2y}$

7. $\dfrac{mn^2}{3} \cdot \dfrac{s}{mnt}$ $\dfrac{ns}{3t}$

8. $\dfrac{ab^2}{x^3y} \cdot \dfrac{x^2}{b^3}$ $\dfrac{a}{bxy}$

9. $\dfrac{xy^2}{x^2y} \cdot \dfrac{xz^2}{y^2z}$ $\dfrac{z}{y}$

10. $\dfrac{x}{y} \cdot \dfrac{a}{b} \cdot \dfrac{xm}{yn} \cdot \dfrac{n^2}{m^2}$ $\dfrac{anx^2}{bmy^2}$

B. 11. $\dfrac{x+4}{x-4} \cdot \dfrac{1}{x+4}$ $\dfrac{1}{x-4}$

12. $\dfrac{3a}{16b} \cdot \dfrac{4b^2}{6a}$ $\dfrac{b}{8}$

13. $\dfrac{4xy^2}{3x} \cdot \dfrac{9x^2}{8x^2y}$ $\dfrac{3y}{2}$

14. $\dfrac{7a^2}{b} \cdot \dfrac{3b}{2a}$ $\dfrac{21a}{2}$

15. $\dfrac{20m^2n^3}{8m} \cdot \dfrac{12mn^2}{5n^3}$ $6m^2n^2$

16. $\dfrac{8x^3y}{3x^2} \cdot \dfrac{9y}{4x^2}$ $\dfrac{6y^2}{x}$

17. $\dfrac{15s^4t}{4s^2} \cdot \dfrac{3t^2}{5st}$ $\dfrac{9st^2}{4}$

18. $\dfrac{3a-3}{4} \cdot \dfrac{8}{a-1}$ 6

19. $\dfrac{m-5}{8} \cdot \dfrac{16}{m-5}$ 2

20. $\dfrac{16}{y-2} \cdot \dfrac{y^2-4}{20}$ $\dfrac{4(y+2)}{5}$

21. $\dfrac{x^2-9}{4} \cdot \dfrac{8}{x+3}$ $2(x-3)$

22. $\dfrac{a^2-4a}{a+2} \cdot \dfrac{a^2-4}{8-2a}$ $-\dfrac{a(a-2)}{2}$

23. $\dfrac{3x-3y}{10xy} \cdot \dfrac{20x^2y^2}{x^2-y^2}$ $\dfrac{6xy}{x+y}$

24. $\dfrac{m^2+5m}{m^2-16} \cdot \dfrac{m^2-4m}{m^2-25}$ $\dfrac{m^2}{(m+4)(m-5)}$

25. $\dfrac{5a}{3a-12} \cdot \dfrac{20-5a}{15a^2}$ $-\dfrac{5}{9a}$

26. $\dfrac{4x+16}{3x^2} \cdot \dfrac{9x}{5x+20}$ $\dfrac{12}{5x}$

27. $\dfrac{8y+24}{2y-6} \cdot \dfrac{3y-9}{4y+12}$ 3

28. $\dfrac{a^2+2a+1}{8a} \cdot \dfrac{2a}{a+1}$ $\dfrac{a+1}{4}$

29. $\dfrac{16x+8}{x^2-2x+1} \cdot \dfrac{x-1}{2x+1}$ $\dfrac{8}{x-1}$

30. $\dfrac{3a^2}{4a+12} \cdot \dfrac{6a-6}{12a^3}$ $\dfrac{3(a-1)}{8a(a+3)}$

31. $\dfrac{2b-2c}{10bc} \cdot \dfrac{5bc}{3b-3c}$ $\dfrac{1}{3}$

32. $\dfrac{2qr^2}{q^2+2qr} \cdot \dfrac{3qr+6r^2}{2q^3r^4}$ $\dfrac{3}{q^3r}$

33. $\dfrac{5x+5y}{3x^2y} \cdot \dfrac{xy^3}{15x+15y}$ $\dfrac{y^2}{9x}$

34. $\dfrac{4vr^4}{10v+15r} \cdot \dfrac{30v+45r}{6v^2r}$ $\dfrac{2r^3}{v}$

35. $\dfrac{x^2-16}{2x+8} \cdot \dfrac{x+4}{x^2+8x+16}$ $\dfrac{x-4}{2(x+4)}$

36. $\dfrac{2y-8}{y^2-16} \cdot \dfrac{y^2+6y+9}{(y+3)^2}$ $\dfrac{2}{y+4}$

37. $\dfrac{a-5}{a+2} \cdot \dfrac{a^2-4}{2-a}$ $-(a-5)$

38. $\dfrac{m^2-16}{m+4} \cdot \dfrac{m-2}{4-m}$ $-(m-2)$

39. $\dfrac{n^2+6n+5}{n-3} \cdot \dfrac{5n-15}{n^2+4n-5}$ $\dfrac{5(n+1)}{n-1}$

40. $\dfrac{y^2-y-6}{y+3} \cdot \dfrac{y^2+3y}{3y-9}$ $\dfrac{y(y+2)}{3}$

41. $\dfrac{m^2-3m-18}{m^2-m-2} \cdot \dfrac{3m+3}{m^2-2m-15}$

42. $\dfrac{n^2-2n-3}{n^2-9} \cdot \dfrac{n^2+4n+3}{n^2-1}$ $\dfrac{n+1}{n-1}$

43. $\dfrac{a^2+5a+6}{a-1} \cdot \dfrac{a^2-1}{a+3}$ $(a+2)(a+1)$

44. $\dfrac{4m^2-9n^2}{6m^2-9mn} \cdot \dfrac{6mn}{4mn+6n^2}$ 1

45. $\dfrac{x^2-4}{5-x} \cdot \dfrac{x-5}{2-x}$ $x+2$

46. $\dfrac{a-5}{a+5} \cdot \dfrac{a^2-25}{5-a}$ $-(a-5)$

47. $\dfrac{m^2-m-6}{m+4} \cdot \dfrac{m+4}{m^2+2m}$ $\dfrac{m-3}{m}$

48. $\dfrac{t^2+t-6}{t-7} \cdot \dfrac{t^2-7t}{2-t}$ $-t(t+3)$

49. $\dfrac{2b^2+11b+5}{b^2+2b-15} \cdot \dfrac{b^2+b-12}{2b^2+b}$ $\dfrac{b+4}{b}$

50. $\dfrac{d^2-4d+4}{d^2+3d} \cdot \dfrac{d^2+2d-3}{d^2-4}$

51. $\dfrac{m^2+2mn+n^2}{m^2+3m+2} \cdot \dfrac{m+2}{m^2+mn}$ $\dfrac{m+n}{m(m+1)}$

52. $\dfrac{2x^2-x-1}{x^2+2x-3} \cdot \dfrac{x^2+7x+12}{2x^2-13x-7}$ $\dfrac{x+4}{x-7}$

53. $\dfrac{2t^2-5t-3}{3t^2-7t-6} \cdot \dfrac{3t^2-10t-8}{-2t^2+7t+4}$ -1

54. $\dfrac{c^2+3c}{c^2+4c-12} \cdot \dfrac{c^2+2c-24}{c^2-4c}$ $\dfrac{c+3}{c-2}$

MIXED REVIEW

Perform the indicated operation.

1. $-|36|$ -36

2. $6y(5x^2y - 2xy)$ $30x^2y^2 - 12xy^2$

3. $(10x^2 - 3xy + 5y^2) + (-12x^2 - 4xy - 3y^2)$ $-2x^2 - 7xy + 2y^2$

4. $(6y^2 - 8y) - (10y^2 - 8y)$ $-4y^2$

5. $-6 + (0.52)$ -5.48

TEACHER'S RESOURCE MASTERS

Practice Master 39, Part 1

ASSIGNMENT GUIDE

Minimum
1–9 odd, 21–38

Regular
33–40, 49–58

Maximum
11, 12, 17–51 odd, 63–71 odd

ADDITIONAL ANSWERS

Written Exercises

41. $\dfrac{3(m-6)}{(m-2)(m-5)}$

50. $\dfrac{(d-2)(d-1)}{d(d+2)}$

55. $\dfrac{2e^2 - 7e - 4}{e^2 - 3e - 4} \cdot \dfrac{e^2 + 2e - 15}{2e^2 - 5e - 3}$ $\dfrac{e+5}{e+1}$

56. $\dfrac{6g^2 + 7g + 2}{4g^2 - 1} \cdot \dfrac{2g^2 - g}{3g^2 - 16g - 12}$ $\dfrac{g}{g-6}$

57. $\dfrac{12y^2 + 5y - 2}{5y^2 + 3y} \cdot \dfrac{10y^2 + 21y + 9}{6y^2 + 13y + 6}$

58. $\dfrac{x^2 - 3x}{x^2 + 7x} \cdot \dfrac{x^2 + 10x + 21}{18 - 2x^2}$ $-\dfrac{1}{2}$

59. $\dfrac{z^2 + 5z - 24}{z^2 - 3z} \cdot \dfrac{z^2 - 3z - 4}{z^2 + 8z}$

60. $\dfrac{b^2 + 6b - 27}{b^2 + 12b + 32} \cdot \dfrac{b^2 + 7b - 8}{b^2 - 4b + 3}$ $\dfrac{b+9}{b+4}$

61. $\dfrac{v^2 - 4v - 21}{3v^2 + 6v} \cdot \dfrac{v^2 + 8v}{v^2 + 11v + 24}$

62. $\dfrac{5x^2 - 25x}{x^2 + 4x - 12} \cdot \dfrac{x^2 + 7x + 6}{3x^2 - 15x}$ $\dfrac{5(x+1)}{3(x-2)}$

C. 63. $\dfrac{a-b}{a+b} \cdot \dfrac{a^2 - b^2}{a+b} \cdot \dfrac{a^2 + 2ab + b^2}{a^2 - 2ab + b^2}$

64. $\dfrac{y^2 - y - 2}{y+1} \cdot \dfrac{y^2 - y - 2}{y+1} \cdot \dfrac{y^2 - 1}{y-2}$

65. $\dfrac{n^2 - 5n + 6}{6n^2 - 17n + 5} \cdot \dfrac{6n^2 + 7n - 3}{2n^2 - 7n + 3} \cdot \dfrac{2n^2 - 7n + 5}{n^2 - 3n + 2}$ $\dfrac{2n+3}{2n-1}$

66. $\dfrac{y}{y-5} \cdot \dfrac{y^2 - 6y + 5}{y^2 - 1} \cdot \dfrac{y^2 - 4y - 5}{y^2 - 5y}$ 1

67. $\dfrac{4x^2 - 16x + 15}{2x^2 + 3x + 1} \cdot \dfrac{4x^2 - 1}{4x^2 - 20x + 25} \cdot \dfrac{x^2 - 6x - 7}{2x^2 - 17x + 21}$ $\dfrac{2x-1}{2x-5}$

68. $\dfrac{a-2}{4a-7} \cdot \dfrac{3a^2 - a - 14}{2a^2 - 14} \cdot \dfrac{4a^2}{a^2 - 4} \cdot \dfrac{4a^2 + a - 14}{6ab - 14b}$ $\dfrac{a^2(a+2)}{b(a^2 - 7)}$

69. $\dfrac{n^2 - 5n + 4}{m^2 - n^2} \cdot \dfrac{m^2 - 2mn + n^2}{n-1}$ $\dfrac{(n-4)(m-n)}{m+n}$

70. $\dfrac{4-b}{b^2} \cdot \dfrac{b^2 - 16}{b^2 - 4b} \cdot \dfrac{4b^3}{16 - b^2}$ 4

71. $\dfrac{a^2 + 7a + 12}{a^2 + 2a - 8} \cdot \dfrac{a^2 + 3a - 10}{a^2 + 8a + 15}$ 1

72. $\dfrac{x}{(x+z)^2 - y^2} \cdot \dfrac{(x-y)^2 - z^2}{xy - y^2 - yz} \cdot \dfrac{(x+y)^2 - z^2}{x^2 + xy - xz}$ $\dfrac{1}{y}$

SELF-QUIZ

Replace each ? so that the equation names an equivalent rational expression.

1. $\dfrac{3}{x+2} = \dfrac{?}{2x+4}$ 6

2. $\dfrac{m+5}{m-1} \cdot \dfrac{?}{m^2 + 4m - 5}$ $m^2 + 10m + 25$

Which values must be excluded from the replacement set of each variable so that the denominator will not equal zero?

3. $\dfrac{3}{x+4}$ -4

4. $\dfrac{3x^2 - 5x + 1}{2x^2 + 5x - 3}$ $\dfrac{1}{2}, -3$

Change each rational expression to simplest form.

5. $\dfrac{15x + 45}{5x + 15}$ 3

6. $\dfrac{2x^2 + x - 3}{2x^2 + 11x + 12}$ $\dfrac{x-1}{x+4}$

Simplify each of the following by using the properties of integral exponents.

7. $\left(\dfrac{2m}{3}\right)^{-2}$ $\dfrac{9}{4m^2}$

8. $\dfrac{x^{-5}}{x^{-8}}$ x^3

9. $\left(\dfrac{5x^2}{2}\right)^0$ 1

Find each product and express it in simplest form.

10. $\dfrac{3b}{b+4} \cdot \dfrac{b+4}{9}$ $\dfrac{b}{3}$

11. $\dfrac{x^2 + 2x - 3}{x^2 + 4x - 5} \cdot \dfrac{x^2 - 3x - 4}{x^2 + 4x + 3}$ $\dfrac{x-4}{x+5}$

9.5 | Dividing Rational Expressions

The rule for dividing rational expressions is very similar to the rule for dividing rational numbers.

Division of Rational Expressions	If $\frac{A}{B}$ and $\frac{C}{D}$ are rational expressions and $C \neq 0$, then $\frac{A}{B} \div \frac{C}{D} = \frac{A}{B} \cdot \frac{D}{C} = \frac{AD}{BC}$.

EXAMPLES

1 **Find the quotient $\frac{2}{3} \div \frac{12}{15}$ and express it in simplest form.**

SOLUTION

$$\frac{2}{3} \div \frac{12}{15} = \frac{2}{3} \cdot \frac{15}{12}$$

$$= \frac{2 \cdot 3 \cdot 5}{3 \cdot 2 \cdot 2 \cdot 3}$$

$$= 1 \cdot \frac{5}{6}$$

$$= \frac{5}{6}$$

2 **Find the quotient $\frac{a}{a-b} \div \frac{b}{a-b}$ and express it in simplest form.**

SOLUTION

$$\frac{a}{a-b} \div \frac{b}{a-b} = \frac{a}{a-b} \cdot \frac{a-b}{b}$$

$$= \frac{(a-b) \cdot a}{(a-b) \cdot b}$$

$$= 1 \cdot \frac{a}{b}$$

$$= \frac{a}{b}$$

3 **Find the quotient $\frac{x^2 - 6x + 9}{4x - 12} \div (x - 3)$ and express it in simplest form.**

SOLUTION

$$\frac{x^2 - 6x + 9}{4x - 12} \div (x - 3) = \frac{x^2 - 6x + 9}{4x - 12} \cdot \frac{1}{x - 3}$$

$$= \frac{(x-3)(x-3) \cdot 1}{4(x-3)(x-3)}$$

$$= \frac{(x-3)^2 \cdot 1}{(x-3)^2 \cdot 4}$$

$$= 1 \cdot \frac{1}{4}$$

$$= \frac{1}{4}$$

OBJECTIVE

Divide rational expressions.

TEACHER'S NOTES

See p. T32.

CLASSROOM EXAMPLES

1. Find the quotient $\frac{2}{3} \div \frac{16}{27}$ and express it in simplest form.

$$\frac{2}{3} \div \frac{16}{27}$$

$$= \frac{2}{3} \cdot \frac{27}{16}$$

$$= \frac{2 \cdot 3 \cdot 3 \cdot 3}{3 \cdot 2 \cdot 2 \cdot 2 \cdot 2}$$

$$= 1 \cdot \frac{9}{8}$$

$$= \frac{9}{8}$$

2. Find the quotient $\frac{x}{x+y} \div \frac{y}{x+y}$ and express it in simplest form.

$$\frac{x}{x+y} \div \frac{y}{x+y}$$

$$= \frac{x}{x+y} \cdot \frac{x+y}{y}$$

$$= \frac{(x+y)x}{(x+y)y}$$

$$= 1 \cdot \frac{x}{y}$$

$$= \frac{x}{y}$$

3. Find the quotient $\frac{x^2 + 7x + 12}{2x + 6} \div (x + 4)$ and express it in simplest form.

$$\frac{x^2 + 7x + 12}{2x + 6} \div (x + 4)$$

$$= \frac{x^2 + 7x + 12}{2x + 6} \cdot \frac{1}{x + 4}$$

$$= \frac{(x+4)(x+3) \cdot 1}{2(x+3)(x+4)}$$

$$= \frac{(x+4)(x+3) \cdot 1}{(x+4)(x+3) \cdot 2}$$

$$= 1 \cdot \frac{1}{2}$$

$$= \frac{1}{2}$$

ORAL EXERCISES

Tell which rational expression should be used to complete each exercise.

1. $\dfrac{7}{8} \div \dfrac{5}{6} = \dfrac{7}{8} \cdot$ _____ $\dfrac{6}{5}$

2. $\dfrac{x^2}{y^2z} \div \dfrac{xy^2}{x} = \dfrac{x^2}{y^2z} \cdot$ _____ $\dfrac{x}{xy^2}$

3. $\dfrac{a^2 - ab}{a - b} \div \dfrac{1}{a} = \dfrac{a^2 - ab}{a - b} \cdot$ _____ $\dfrac{a}{1}$

4. $\dfrac{m + n}{m} \div \dfrac{m^2}{n} = \dfrac{m + n}{m} \cdot$ _____ $\dfrac{n}{m^2}$

5. $\dfrac{x - 2}{x^2 - 5x + 6} \div \dfrac{x^2 - 9}{x^2 - 3x} = \dfrac{x - 2}{x^2 - 5x + 6} \cdot$ _____ $\dfrac{x^2 - 3x}{x^2 - 9}$

6. $\dfrac{a^2 - b^2}{a + b} \div \dfrac{a + b}{a - b} = \dfrac{a^2 - b^2}{a + b} \cdot$ _____ $\dfrac{a - b}{a + b}$

7. $\dfrac{5b}{9ac^3} \div \dfrac{15b^3}{18a^2c^3} = \dfrac{5b}{9ac^3} \cdot$ _____ $\dfrac{18a^2c^3}{15b^3}$

8. $\dfrac{n^2 + 5n - 6}{3n - 6} \div (n + 1) = \dfrac{n^2 + 5n - 6}{3n - 6} \cdot$ _____ $\dfrac{1}{n + 1}$

WRITTEN EXERCISES

A. Find each quotient and express it in simplest form.

1. $\dfrac{5}{6} \div \dfrac{1}{6}$ 5

2. $\dfrac{a}{3} \div \dfrac{a}{6}$ 2

3. $\dfrac{8}{x} \div \dfrac{8}{y}$ $\dfrac{y}{x}$

4. $\dfrac{3}{m} \div \dfrac{4}{m}$ $\dfrac{3}{4}$

5. $\dfrac{n}{5} \div \dfrac{n}{m}$ $\dfrac{m}{5}$

6. $\dfrac{ab}{2} \div \dfrac{ab}{3}$ $\dfrac{3}{2}$

7. $\dfrac{x + 5}{x} \div \dfrac{x + 5}{5}$ $\dfrac{5}{x}$

8. $\dfrac{n}{n - 3} \div \dfrac{4}{n - 3}$ $\dfrac{n}{4}$

9. $\dfrac{ad}{bc} \div \dfrac{a}{b}$ $\dfrac{d}{c}$

10. $\dfrac{xy}{ab} \div \dfrac{xy}{bc}$ $\dfrac{c}{a}$

11. $\dfrac{1}{n} \div \dfrac{n}{m}$ $\dfrac{m}{n^2}$

12. $\dfrac{x}{y} \div \dfrac{z}{y}$ $\dfrac{x}{z}$

13. $\dfrac{1}{m} \div \dfrac{1}{n}$ $\dfrac{n}{m}$

14. $\dfrac{a}{b} \div \dfrac{b}{c}$ $\dfrac{ac}{b^2}$

15. $\dfrac{3}{2x} \div 9$ $\dfrac{1}{6x}$

16. $\dfrac{x^2y}{x} \div \dfrac{x}{y^2}$ y^3

B.

17. $\dfrac{a - 3}{a + 5} \div \dfrac{a + 1}{a + 5}$ $\dfrac{a - 3}{a + 1}$

18. $\dfrac{b + 4}{b - 3} \div \dfrac{b + 4}{b - 2}$ $\dfrac{b - 2}{b - 3}$

19. $\dfrac{n^2 - 9}{n} \div \dfrac{n + 3}{n}$ $n - 3$

20. $\dfrac{m - 3}{m} \div \dfrac{m^2 - 3m}{m}$ $\dfrac{1}{m}$

21. $\dfrac{x^2 - 9}{x^2 - 16} \div \dfrac{x - 3}{x - 4}$ $\dfrac{x + 3}{x + 4}$

22. $\dfrac{y^2 - 36}{y^2 - 49} \div \dfrac{y + 6}{y + 7}$ $\dfrac{y - 6}{y - 7}$

23. $\dfrac{n^2 - 25}{n^2 + 5n} \div \dfrac{n - 5}{1}$ $\dfrac{1}{n}$

24. $\dfrac{a^2 - 64}{a^2 - 8a} \div \dfrac{a + 8}{1}$ $\dfrac{1}{a}$

25. $\dfrac{9mn^2}{8st^2} \div \dfrac{3n^2}{2st}$ $\dfrac{3m}{4t}$

26. $\dfrac{5a}{12bc^2} \div \dfrac{15a}{18b^2c^2}$ $\dfrac{b}{2}$

27. $\dfrac{x - 9}{10} \div \dfrac{9 - x}{5}$ $-\dfrac{1}{2}$

28. $\dfrac{xy}{x - 3} \div \dfrac{4x}{3 - x}$ $-\dfrac{y}{4}$

29. $\dfrac{4x - 16}{3x} \div (3x - 12)$ $\dfrac{4}{9x}$

30. $\dfrac{5x - 25}{2x} \div (4x - 20)$ $\dfrac{5}{8x}$

31. $\dfrac{6a - 27}{4a} \div (4a - 18)$ $\dfrac{3}{8a}$

32. $\dfrac{y^2 - 2y + 1}{y + 1} \div (y - 1)$ $\dfrac{y - 1}{y + 1}$

33. $\dfrac{a^2 - 6a + 9}{a + 3} \div (a - 3)$ $\dfrac{a - 3}{a + 3}$

34. $\dfrac{n^2 - 4}{n - 2} \div \dfrac{n^2 - 4n + 4}{3n - 6}$ $\dfrac{3(n + 2)}{n - 2}$

35. $\dfrac{y^2 - y - 12}{y^2 - 9} \div \dfrac{3y - 12}{y + 3}$ $\quad\frac{y + 3}{3(y - 3)}$

36. $\dfrac{a^2 - 2a - 15}{a^2 - 9} \div \dfrac{2a - 10}{a + 3}$ $\quad\frac{a + 3}{2(a - 3)}$

37. $\dfrac{n^2 - 6n + 9}{n - 3} \div \dfrac{n^2 - 9}{n + 3}$ $\quad 1$

38. $\dfrac{10x^2}{x^2 + 3x} \div \dfrac{2x}{x^2 + 10x + 21}$ $\quad 5(x + 7)$

39. $\dfrac{m - 5}{m^2 + 3m - 10} \div \dfrac{5m - 25}{m^2 - 2m}$ $\quad\frac{m}{5(m + 5)}$

40. $\dfrac{x^2 + 2x}{4x - 5} \div \dfrac{2x^2 + 4x}{16x - 20}$ $\quad 2$

41. $\dfrac{x^2 - 2x - 3}{x^2 - 10x + 21} \div \dfrac{x^2 - x - 2}{x^2 - 3x - 28}$ $\quad\frac{x + 4}{x - 2}$

42. $\dfrac{t^2 + t - 12}{t^2 + t - 2} \div \dfrac{t^2 + 2t - 8}{t^2 - 4}$ $\quad\frac{t - 3}{t - 1}$

43. $\dfrac{2y^2 + y - 6}{y^2 - 4y - 12} \div \dfrac{3y^2 + 22y + 7}{y^2 + y - 42}$ $\quad\frac{2y - 3}{3y + 1}$

44. $\dfrac{2m^2 + 3m - 5}{m^2 + 3m - 4} \div \dfrac{3m^2 - 10m + 8}{m^2 + 2m - 8}$ $\quad\frac{2m + 5}{3m - 4}$

C. 45. $\dfrac{a^2 - b^2}{a^2} \cdot \dfrac{a + b}{a - b} \div \dfrac{a^2 - b^2}{ba}$ $\quad\frac{b(a + b)}{a(a - b)}$

46. $\dfrac{x + 3}{x^2 + x - 2} \div \dfrac{x^2 - 9}{3 - x}$

47. $\dfrac{mn - ms - m^2}{mns} \cdot \dfrac{m^2 n^2 s^3}{mn - ms} \div m^3$

48. $\dfrac{y^2 - 3y}{9 - y^2} \div \dfrac{y}{3 + y}$ $\quad -1$

49. $\dfrac{x^2 - 2xy + y^2}{xy} \cdot \dfrac{x + y}{x - y} \div \dfrac{x^2 - y^2}{x^2}$ $\quad\frac{x}{y}$

50. $\dfrac{a^3 b^3}{a^3 - ab^2} \div \dfrac{abc}{a - b} \cdot \dfrac{ab + bc}{ab}$

51. $\dfrac{m}{m - n} \div \dfrac{(m + n)^2}{m^4 - n^4} \cdot \dfrac{m + n}{m^2 + n^2}$ $\quad m$

52. $\dfrac{48x^2 - 75}{80x^2 - 68x - 40} \div \dfrac{48x^2 + 132x + 90}{50x^2 + 145x + 50}$ $\quad\frac{5(2x + 5)}{8(2x + 3)}$

53. $\dfrac{a^2 - 2a}{a^2 - 3a - 4} \cdot \dfrac{a^2 - 25}{a^2 - 4a - 5} \div \dfrac{a^2 + 5a}{5a^2 + 10a + 5}$ $\quad\frac{5(a - 2)}{a - 4}$

54. $\dfrac{x^3 + 5x^2 - 5x - 25}{2x^2 - 9x + 9} \div \dfrac{x^2 + 10x + 25}{12 - 14x + 4x^2} \cdot \dfrac{x + 5}{x^2 - 4x + 4}$ $\quad\frac{2(x^2 - 5)}{(x - 3)(x - 2)}$

55. $\dfrac{n^2 + 6n - 7}{6n^2 - 7n - 20} \cdot \dfrac{2n^2 + n - 15}{n^2 + 2n - 3} \div \dfrac{n^2 + 5n - 14}{3n^2 - 2n - 8}$ $\quad 1$

CHALLENGE

Kim purchased two candles, each from a different store. The one from the first store was guaranteed to burn for 6 hours. The one from the second store was guaranteed to burn for 4 hours. The candles were exactly the same length. Kim lit both candles at the same time. Some time later, she noticed that one candle was exactly twice as long as the other. How long had the two candles been burning? $\quad$ 3 hours

TEACHER'S NOTES

See p. T32.

CLASSROOM EXAMPLES

1. Find the LCD of $\frac{1}{12}$ and $\frac{1}{15}$.

$12 = 2 \cdot 2 \cdot 3 = 2^2 \cdot 3$

$15 = 3 \cdot 5$

The prime factors are 2, 3, and 5.

$2^2 \cdot 3 \cdot 5 = 4 \cdot 3 \cdot 5$

$= 60$

The LCD of $\frac{1}{12}$ and $\frac{1}{15}$ = 60.

2. Find the LCD of $\frac{8}{10xy}$ and $\frac{1}{4x^2}$.

$10xy = 2 \cdot 5 \cdot x \cdot y$

$4x^2 = 2^2 \cdot x^2$

The prime factors are 2, 5, x, and y.

$2^2 \cdot 5 \cdot x^2 \cdot y = 4 \cdot 5 \cdot x^2 \cdot y$

The LCD of $\frac{8}{10xy}$ and $\frac{1}{4x^2}$ is $20x^2y$.

3. Find the LCD of rational expressions with denominators of $4x - 20$ and $6x - 30$.

$4x - 20 = 4(x - 5) = 2^2 \cdot (x - 5)$

$6x - 30 = 6(x - 5) = 2 \cdot 3 \cdot (x - 5)$

The prime factors are 2, 3, and $x - 5$.

$2^2 \cdot 3 \cdot (x - 5)$

$= 4 \cdot 3 \cdot (x - 5)$

$= 12(x - 5)$

The LCD is $12(x - 5)$.

9.6 | Least Common Denominators

When rational expressions that have different denominators are to be added or subtracted, it is necessary to change those expressions to equivalent expressions having a common denominator. In such instances, it is usually convenient to use the **least common denominator (LCD)**, which is the **least common multiple** of the denominators.

To find the LCD of rational expressions, use the following steps:

1. Completely factor each denominator.
2. Write each prime factor with the greatest exponent used in any one denominator.
3. Multiply these factors.

EXAMPLES

1 **Find the LCD of $\frac{1}{24}$ and $\frac{1}{36}$.**

SOLUTION $24 = 2 \cdot 2 \cdot 2 \cdot 3 = 2^3 \cdot 3$ *Completely factor 24 and 36.*

$36 = 2 \cdot 2 \cdot 3 \cdot 3 = 2^2 \cdot 3^2$

The prime factors are 2 and 3.

$2^3 \cdot 3^2$ *Write each prime factor with the greatest exponent.*

$2^3 \cdot 3^2 = 8 \cdot 9$ *Multiply.*

$= 72$

The LCD of $\frac{1}{24}$ and $\frac{1}{36}$ is 72.

2 **Find the LCD of $\frac{5}{6ab}$ and $\frac{1}{9a^2}$.**

SOLUTION $6ab = 2 \cdot 3 \cdot a \cdot b$

$9a^2 = 3^2 \cdot a^2$

The prime factors are 2, 3, a, and b.

$2 \cdot 3^2 \cdot a^2 \cdot b = 2 \cdot 9 \cdot a^2 \cdot b$

$= 18a^2b$

The LCD of $\frac{5}{6ab}$ and $\frac{1}{9a^2}$ is $18a^2b$.

3 **Find the LCD of rational expressions with denominators of $9x - 18$ and $6x - 12$.**

SOLUTION $9x - 18 = 9(x - 2) = 3^2 \cdot (x - 2)$

$6x - 12 = 6(x - 2) = 2 \cdot 3 \cdot (x - 2)$

The prime factors are 2, 3, and $x - 2$.

$2 \cdot 3^2 \cdot (x - 2) = 2 \cdot 9 \cdot (x - 2)$

$= 18(x - 2)$

The LCD is $18(x - 2)$.

Find the LCD of rational expressions with denominators of $x^2 - y^2$ and $x^2 + 2xy + y^2$.

SOLUTION

$$x^2 - y^2 = (x - y)(x + y)$$
$$x^2 + 2xy + y^2 = (x + y)^2$$

The prime factors are $x - y$ and $x + y$.

$(x - y)(x + y)^2$

The LCD is $(x - y)(x + y)^2$. *It is common practice to leave the LCD in factored form.*

ORAL EXERCISES

Give the LCD of rational expressions having the following denominators. Each denominator has been factored.

1. $6x^2 = 2 \cdot 3 \cdot x^2$
$12y = 2^2 \cdot 3 \cdot y$ $12x^2y$

2. $4ab^2 = 2^2 \cdot a \cdot b^2$
$6a^2b = 2 \cdot 3 \cdot a^2 \cdot b$ $12a^2b^2$

3. $m^2 - n^2 = (m + n)(m - n)$
$m - n = m - n$ $(m + n)(m - n)$

4. $x^2 - 4 = (x + 2)(x - 2)$
$(x + 2)^2 = (x + 2)^2$ $(x - 2)(x + 2)^2$

5. $y^2 - 5y + 6 = (y - 3)(y - 2)$
$y^2 - 4y + 3 = (y - 3)(y - 1)$

6. $a^2 + 12a + 36 = (a + 6)^2$
$a^2 + 2a - 24 = (a + 6)(a - 4)$

WRITTEN EXERCISES

A. Give the LCD of each pair of rational expressions.

1. $\frac{5}{12}, \frac{7}{30}$ 60

2. $\frac{1}{36}, \frac{7}{45}$ 180

3. $\frac{13}{24}, \frac{7}{54}$ 216

4. $\frac{52}{105}, \frac{23}{210}$ 210

5. $\frac{1}{6b}, \frac{4}{9b}$ 18b

6. $\frac{7}{18n^2}, \frac{4}{9n^2}$ 18n^2

7. $\frac{1}{3x}, \frac{2}{x^2}$ 3x^2

8. $\frac{5}{6ab}, \frac{4}{9a^2}$ 18a^2b

B. Give the LCD of rational expressions having the following denominators:

9. $2a - 6b, 4a - 12b$ $4(a - 3b)$

10. $a^2b, 2b^4$ $2a^2b^4$

11. $6a^2 - 9, 10a^2 - 15$ $15(2a^2 - 3)$

12. $3a + 3b, a + b$ $3(a + b)$

13. $x^2 - 9, (x + 3)^2$ $(x - 3)(x + 3)^2$

14. $x^2 - x - 6, x^2 - 5x + 6$

15. $y^2 + 12y + 36, y^2 + 3y - 18$

16. $a^2 - 3a, a^2 + 2a$ $a(a - 3)(a + 2)$

17. $x^2 - x - 2, x^2 - 4$

18. $9 - n^2, n + 3$ $-(n + 3)(n - 3)$

19. $2(a - b), 4(b - a)$ $-4(a - b)$

20. $n^2 - 5n + 6, n^2 - 4n + 3$

21. $3m^2 - 27, 2m + 6, 3 - m$

22. $x - 9, 3x^2 + 3x - 18, x^2 - 4x + 4$

C. 23. $y^2 - 4, y^2 - 5y + 6, y^2 - y - 6$

24. $4x^2 - 100, x + 5, 5 - x$

25. $x^2 - 25y^2, 3x - 15y$

26. $y^2 + 2y - 8, 3y^2 + 21y + 36, 4y + 12$

27. $3n^2 - 13n + 4, 2n^2 - 5n - 12$

28. $a^2 - 2a + 1, a + 1, a - 1$

4. Find the LCD of rational expressions with denominators of $a^2 - b^2$ and $a^2 - 2ab + b^2$.

$a^2 - b^2 = (a - b)(a + b)$
$a^2 - 2ab + b^2 = (a - b)^2$

The prime factors are $a - b$ and $a + b$.

$(a - b)^2(a + b)$

The LCD is $(a - b)^2(a + b)$.

MIXED REVIEW

1. Divide $\frac{3xy^3}{2x}$ by $\frac{9x^2y}{6x^2}$ and express in simplest form.
y^2

2. Simplify $\frac{6 + 5(-4)}{-7}$.   2

3. Find the product of 9 and -12. -108

4. Illustrate the associative property of addition.   Answers may vary.

5. State the range of the relation $\{(4, -3), (7, -8), (-3, -10), (9, -3)\}$.
$\{-3, -8, -10\}$

TEACHER'S RESOURCE MASTERS

Practice Master 40, Part 1

ASSIGNMENT GUIDE

Minimum
1–21 odd

Regular
9–19

Maximum
18–28

Additional Answers
See p. T62.

PREPARING FOR COLLEGE ENTRANCE EXAMS

A relationship exists between figure I and figure II. The same or a similar relationship exists between figure III and one of the figures *a* through *e*. Choose the figure that expresses this similarity.

	I	II	III		a	b	c	d	e

1.

2.

3.

4.

5.

6.

7.

8.

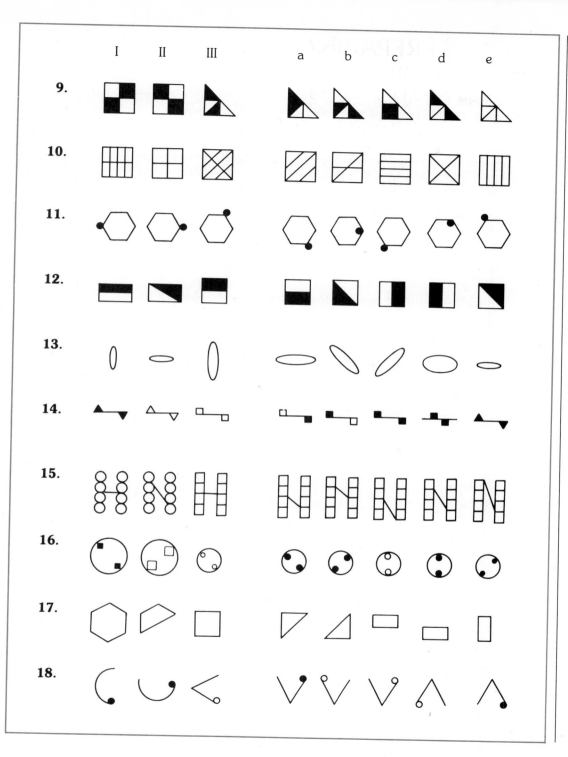

	I	II	III	a	b	c	d	e

CLASSROOM EXAMPLES

1. Add $\frac{4y + 8}{y + 3} + \frac{y + 7}{y + 3}$ and express the sum in simplest form.

$$\frac{4y + 8}{y + 3} + \frac{y + 7}{y + 3}$$
$$= \frac{(4y + 8) + (y + 7)}{y + 3}$$
$$= \frac{5y + 15}{y + 3}$$
$$= \frac{(y + 3) \cdot 5}{(y + 3) \cdot 1}$$
$$= 1 \cdot \frac{5}{1}$$
$$= 5$$

2. Subtract $\frac{y^2 + 4y}{y - 6} - \frac{y^2 + 24}{y - 6}$ and express the difference in simplest form.

$$\frac{y^2 + 4y}{y - 6} - \frac{y^2 + 24}{y - 6}$$
$$= \frac{(y^2 + 4y) - (y^2 + 24)}{y - 6}$$
$$= \frac{4y - 24}{y - 6}$$
$$= \frac{(y - 6) \cdot 4}{(y - 6) \cdot 1}$$
$$= 1 \cdot \frac{4}{1}$$
$$= 4$$

3. Add $\frac{3}{7a^2} + \frac{5}{14a}$ and express the sum in simplest form.

9.7 | Addition and Subtraction of Rational Expressions

Rational expressions are added or subtracted in much the same way as rational numbers. If the denominators are the same, you add or subtract the numerators and write the result over the common denominator. Then when necessary, you express the answer in simplest form.

Addition and Subtraction of Rational Expressions	If $\frac{A}{C}$ and $\frac{B}{C}$ are rational expressions, then $\frac{A}{C} + \frac{B}{C} = \frac{A + B}{C}$ and $\frac{A}{C} - \frac{B}{C} = \frac{A - B}{C}$.

EXAMPLES

1   Add $\frac{3x + 2}{x + 2} + \frac{x + 6}{x + 2}$ and express the sum in simplest form.

SOLUTION

$$\frac{3x + 2}{x + 2} + \frac{x + 6}{x + 2} = \frac{(3x + 2) + (x + 6)}{x + 2}$$
$$= \frac{4x + 8}{x + 2} \qquad \text{the sum}$$
$$= \frac{(x + 2) \cdot 4}{(x + 2) \cdot 1} \qquad \text{GCF is } x + 2.$$
$$= 1 \cdot \frac{4}{1}$$
$$= 4 \qquad \text{simplest form}$$

2   Subtract $\frac{x^2 + 2x}{x - 4} - \frac{x^2 + 8}{x - 4}$ and express the difference in simplest form.

SOLUTION

$$\frac{x^2 + 2x}{x - 4} - \frac{x^2 + 8}{x - 4} = \frac{(x^2 + 2x) - (x^2 + 8)}{x - 4}$$
$$= \frac{2x - 8}{x - 4} \qquad \text{the difference}$$
$$= \frac{(x - 4) \cdot 2}{(x - 4) \cdot 1} \qquad \text{GCF is } x - 4.$$
$$= 1 \cdot \frac{2}{1}$$
$$= 2 \qquad \text{simplest form}$$

To add or subtract rational expressions with *different* denominators, use the following steps:

1. Determine the LCD of the rational expressions.
2. Change the rational expressions to equivalent expressions with the LCD as the denominator.
3. Add or subtract.
4. Express the answer in simplest form.

3   Add $\dfrac{2}{5a^2} + \dfrac{7}{15a}$ and express the sum in **simplest form.**

SOLUTION

$$\dfrac{2}{5a^2} + \dfrac{7}{15a} = \dfrac{2}{5 \cdot a^2} + \dfrac{7}{3 \cdot 5 \cdot a} \qquad \textit{LCD is } 3 \cdot 5 \cdot a^2.$$

$$= \dfrac{2 \cdot 3}{5 \cdot a^2 \cdot 3} + \dfrac{7 \cdot a}{3 \cdot 5 \cdot a \cdot a} \qquad \textit{For each rational expression, multiply the numerator and the denominator by those factors that are in the LCD but not in the denominator.}$$

$$= \dfrac{6}{3 \cdot 5 \cdot a^2} + \dfrac{7a}{3 \cdot 5 \cdot a^2}$$

$$= \dfrac{6 + 7a}{3 \cdot 5 \cdot a^2}$$

$$= \dfrac{7a + 6}{15a^2}$$

4   Subtract $\dfrac{7x + 4}{3x + 9} - \dfrac{2x}{x + 3}$ and express the difference in **simplest form.**

SOLUTION

$$\dfrac{7x + 4}{3x + 9} - \dfrac{2x}{x + 3} = \dfrac{7x + 4}{3(x + 3)} - \dfrac{2x}{x + 3} \qquad \textit{LCD is } 3(x + 3).$$

$$= \dfrac{7x + 4}{3(x + 3)} - \dfrac{3(2x)}{3(x + 3)}$$

$$= \dfrac{7x + 4 - 6x}{3(x + 3)}$$

$$= \dfrac{x + 4}{3(x + 3)}$$

5   Add $\dfrac{x - 3}{x + 2} + \dfrac{3x + 2}{x^2 + 3x + 2}$ and express the sum in **simplest form.**

SOLUTION

$$\dfrac{x - 3}{x + 2} + \dfrac{3x + 2}{x^2 + 3x + 2} = \dfrac{x - 3}{x + 2} + \dfrac{3x + 2}{(x + 2)(x + 1)}$$

$$= \dfrac{(x - 3)(x + 1)}{(x + 2)(x + 1)} + \dfrac{3x + 2}{(x + 2)(x + 1)}$$

$$= \dfrac{x^2 - 2x - 3}{(x + 2)(x + 1)} + \dfrac{3x + 2}{(x + 2)(x + 1)}$$

$$= \dfrac{x^2 + x - 1}{(x + 2)(x + 1)}$$

ORAL EXERCISES

Tell the numerator of each sum or difference.

1. $\dfrac{4}{9} + \dfrac{1}{9} = \dfrac{?}{9}$ 5

2. $\dfrac{6}{7} - \dfrac{3}{7} = \dfrac{?}{7}$ 3

3. $\dfrac{3}{a} + \dfrac{4}{a} = \dfrac{?}{a}$ 7

4. $\dfrac{5x}{9} - \dfrac{x}{9} = \dfrac{?}{9}$ 4x

5. $\dfrac{2a}{6b} - \dfrac{a}{6b} = \dfrac{?}{6b}$ a

6. $\dfrac{n + 4}{n} + \dfrac{3}{n} = \dfrac{?}{n}$ n + 7

7. $\dfrac{y + 2}{2y} + \dfrac{y + 4}{2y} = \dfrac{2y + 6}{2y} = \dfrac{?}{y}$ y + 3

8. $\dfrac{x}{x^2 - 1} - \dfrac{1}{x^2 - 1} = \dfrac{x - 1}{x^2 - 1} = \dfrac{?}{x + 1}$ 1

$$\dfrac{3}{7a^2} + \dfrac{5}{14a}$$

$$= \dfrac{3}{7a^2} + \dfrac{5}{2 \cdot 7 \cdot a}$$

$$= \dfrac{3 \cdot 2}{7 \cdot a^2 \cdot 2} + \dfrac{5 \cdot a}{2 \cdot 7 \cdot a \cdot a}$$

$$= \dfrac{6}{2 \cdot 7 \cdot a^2} + \dfrac{5a}{2 \cdot 7 \cdot a^2}$$

$$= \dfrac{6 + 5a}{2 \cdot 7 \cdot a^2}$$

$$= \dfrac{5a + 6}{14a^2}$$

4. Subtract $\dfrac{13x + 2}{2x - 10} - \dfrac{5x}{x - 5}$ and express the difference in simplest form.

$$\dfrac{13x + 2}{2x - 10} - \dfrac{5x}{x - 5}$$

$$= \dfrac{13x + 2}{2(x - 5)} - \dfrac{5x}{x - 5}$$

$$= \dfrac{13x + 2}{2(x - 5)} - \dfrac{2(5x)}{2(x - 5)}$$

$$= \dfrac{13x + 2 - 10x}{2(x - 5)}$$

$$= \dfrac{3x + 2}{2(x - 5)}$$

5. Add $\dfrac{y - 4}{y + 3} + \dfrac{5y + 3}{y^2 + 7y + 12}$ and express the sum in simplest form.

$$\dfrac{y - 4}{y + 3} + \dfrac{5y + 3}{y^2 + 7y + 12}$$

$$= \dfrac{y - 4}{y + 3} + \dfrac{5y + 3}{(y + 4)(y + 3)}$$

$$= \dfrac{(y - 4)(y + 4)}{(y + 3)(y + 4)}$$

$$+ \dfrac{5y + 3}{(y + 4)(y + 3)}$$

$$= \dfrac{y^2 - 16}{(y + 4)(y + 3)}$$

$$+ \dfrac{5y + 3}{(y + 4)(y + 3)}$$

$$= \dfrac{y^2 + 5y - 13}{(y + 4)(y + 3)}$$

MIXED REVIEW

1. Give the prime factorization of 155.   5 · 31

WRITTEN EXERCISES

A. Add or subtract and express each answer in simplest form.

1. $\frac{3}{8} + \frac{1}{8}$ $\frac{1}{2}$ **2.** $\frac{7}{9} - \frac{4}{9}$ $\frac{1}{3}$

3. $\frac{4}{a} + \frac{3}{a}$ $\frac{7}{a}$ **4.** $\frac{2a}{3} - \frac{a}{3}$ $\frac{a}{3}$

5. $\frac{3a}{10} + \frac{2a}{10}$ $\frac{a}{2}$ **6.** $\frac{2x}{3y} - \frac{x}{3y}$ $\frac{x}{3y}$

7. $\frac{3n}{mn} - \frac{3n}{mn}$ 0 **8.** $\frac{a + 4}{a} + \frac{2}{a}$ $\frac{a + 6}{a}$

9. $\frac{x + 5}{3x} + \frac{x + 7}{3x}$ $\frac{2x + 12}{3x}$ **10.** $\frac{3n}{2} + \frac{n + 9}{2}$ $\frac{4n + 9}{2}$

11. $\frac{11a}{4} + \frac{3b - 5}{4}$ $\frac{11a + 3b - 5}{4}$ **12.** $\frac{2x + 6}{7} + \frac{3x - 9}{7}$ $\frac{5x - 3}{7}$

13. $\frac{17y}{6} + \frac{3y + 4}{6}$ $\frac{10y + 2}{3}$ **14.** $\frac{2n - 3}{2} - \frac{6n + 5}{2}$ $-2(n + 2)$

Change each pair of rational expressions to equivalent rational expressions with the LCD as the denominator.

15. $\frac{4}{5x}$, $\frac{3}{10x^2}$ $\frac{8x}{10x^2}$, $\frac{3}{10x^2}$ **16.** $\frac{2x}{3y}$, $\frac{5x}{7z}$ $\frac{14xz}{21yz}$, $\frac{15xy}{21yz}$

17. $\frac{5}{x + 1}$, $\frac{3}{x - 2}$ **18.** $\frac{2}{x - 3}$, $\frac{4}{3x}$ $\frac{6x}{3x(x - 3)}$, $\frac{4x - 12}{3x(x - 3)}$

19. $\frac{3}{2x + 1}$, $\frac{4}{5x - 3}$ **20.** $\frac{x}{2x + 5}$, $\frac{3}{2x + 1}$

21. $\frac{3}{7x}$, $\frac{x}{x + 5}$ $\frac{3x + 15}{7x(x + 5)}$, $\frac{7x^2}{7x(x + 5)}$ **22.** $\frac{y}{5 - y}$, $\frac{3}{y - 5}$ $-\frac{y}{y - 5}$, $\frac{3}{y - 5}$

23. $\frac{2}{m - 3}$, $\frac{m}{3 - m}$ $\frac{2}{m - 3}$, $-\frac{m}{m - 3}$ **24.** $\frac{n}{n - 7}$, $\frac{4}{n + 1}$

25. $\frac{2x + 3}{x - 4}$, $\frac{x - 3}{2x + 1}$ **26.** $\frac{3x - 1}{x + 5}$, $\frac{2x - 3}{2x + 1}$

B. Add or subtract and express each answer in simplest form.

27. $\frac{x^2}{3} + \frac{x^2}{5}$ $\frac{8x^2}{15}$ **28.** $\frac{2a}{3} + \frac{5b}{2}$ $\frac{4a + 15b}{6}$

29. $\frac{x^2y}{3} + \frac{xy^2}{4}$ $\frac{4x^2y + 3xy^2}{12}$ **30.** $\frac{3n - 5}{4} + \frac{5n - 3}{3}$ $\frac{29n - 27}{12}$

31. $\frac{4}{6a} - \frac{3}{5a}$ $\frac{1}{15a}$ **32.** $\frac{6x}{5y} + \frac{5a}{6b}$ $\frac{36bx + 25ay}{30by}$

33. $\frac{n + 1}{2n} + \frac{2}{n}$ $\frac{n + 5}{2n}$ **34.** $\frac{x + y}{y} - \frac{x - y}{x}$ $\frac{x^2 + y^2}{xy}$

35. $\frac{2a - 1}{a} - \frac{a + 3}{3a}$ $\frac{5a - 6}{3a}$ **36.** $\frac{x - 3}{2x} + \frac{x - 2}{3x}$ $\frac{5x - 13}{6x}$

37. $\frac{a - 1}{3} - \frac{a + 2}{6}$ $\frac{a - 4}{6}$ **38.** $\frac{5}{b + 2} + \frac{3}{b - 2}$ $\frac{4(2b - 1)}{(b + 2)(b - 2)}$

39. $\frac{n - 3}{6} - \frac{n - 1}{10}$ $\frac{n - 6}{15}$ **40.** $\frac{3}{x + 4} - \frac{2}{x - 4}$ $\frac{x - 20}{(x + 4)(x - 4)}$

41. $\dfrac{3b}{(b-3)^2} - \dfrac{2}{b-3}$ $\quad \dfrac{b+6}{(b-3)^2}$

42. $\dfrac{3}{a+2} + \dfrac{7}{a+5}$ $\quad \dfrac{10a+29}{(a+2)(a+5)}$

43. $\dfrac{4x}{x^2-16} - \dfrac{2}{x+4}$ $\quad \dfrac{2}{x-4}$

44. $\dfrac{2m}{m-n} - \dfrac{3n}{m+n}$ $\quad \dfrac{2m^2-mn+3n^2}{(m+n)(m-n)}$

45. $\dfrac{2}{y+3} + \dfrac{y}{(y+3)^2}$ $\quad \dfrac{3(y+2)}{(y+3)^2}$

46. $\dfrac{2a-3}{2a} + \dfrac{a-4}{3a}$ $\quad \dfrac{8a-17}{6a}$

47. $\dfrac{3}{a-4} + \dfrac{7}{a^2-8a+16}$ $\quad \dfrac{3a-5}{(a-4)^2}$

48. $\dfrac{5m+n}{m} - \dfrac{3m-4n}{m^2}$ $\quad$

49. $\dfrac{m}{2m+2n} - \dfrac{n}{3m+3n}$ $\quad \dfrac{3m-2n}{6(m+n)}$

50. $\dfrac{x}{x+1} - \dfrac{3}{x^2+2x+1}$ $\quad \dfrac{x^2+x-3}{(x+1)^2}$

51. $\dfrac{4x}{6x-2y} + \dfrac{3y}{9x-3y}$ $\quad \dfrac{2x+y}{3x-y}$

52. $\dfrac{-12}{y^2-4} + \dfrac{3}{y-2}$ $\quad \dfrac{3}{y+2}$

53. $\dfrac{3}{1} + \dfrac{2}{n-5}$ $\quad \dfrac{3n-13}{n-5}$

54. $\dfrac{4}{1} - \dfrac{5}{a-2}$ $\quad \dfrac{4a-13}{a-2}$

55. $\dfrac{a-2}{a+3} - \dfrac{a-3}{a+5}$ $\quad \dfrac{3a-1}{(a+3)(a+5)}$

56. $\dfrac{4n}{2n+6} - \dfrac{n-1}{n+3}$ $\quad \dfrac{n+1}{n+3}$

57. $x - \dfrac{3x}{x-2}$ $\quad \dfrac{x(x-5)}{x-2}$

58. $n - \dfrac{6n}{n-7}$ $\quad \dfrac{n(n-13)}{n-7}$

59. $\dfrac{3a}{2b-3} - \dfrac{2a}{3b-2}$ $\quad \dfrac{5ab}{(2b-3)(3b-2)}$

60. $\dfrac{3x+2}{3x+6} - \dfrac{x-2}{x^2-4}$ $\quad \dfrac{3x-1}{3(x+2)}$

61. $\dfrac{a}{a^2-9} - \dfrac{1}{2a-6}$ $\quad \dfrac{1}{2(a+3)}$

62. $\dfrac{m-n}{m+n} + \dfrac{4mn}{m^2-n^2}$ $\quad \dfrac{m+n}{m-n}$

63. $\dfrac{3a}{a+b} + \dfrac{2b}{a-b}$ $\quad \dfrac{3a^2-ab+2b^2}{(a+b)(a-b)}$

64. $\dfrac{6}{2x+6} - \dfrac{1}{3x-3}$ $\quad \dfrac{4(2x-3)}{3(x-1)(x+3)}$

65. $\dfrac{5}{3x+6} + \dfrac{x}{x^2-x}$ $\quad \dfrac{8x+1}{3(x+2)(x-1)}$

66. $\dfrac{2x-3}{x+4} - \dfrac{x+7}{x-3}$ $\quad \dfrac{x^2-20x-19}{(x+4)(x-3)}$

67. $\dfrac{m}{1-2m} + \dfrac{4}{2m-1}$ $\quad \dfrac{m-4}{1-2m}$

68. $\dfrac{1}{4y^2-1} + \dfrac{2}{4y-2}$ $\quad \dfrac{2(y+1)}{(2y-1)(2y+1)}$

69. $\dfrac{2}{6z-2} + \dfrac{z}{9z^2-1}$ $\quad \dfrac{4z+1}{(3z-1)(3z+1)}$

70. $\dfrac{3}{x^2-9} + \dfrac{1}{x+3}$ $\quad \dfrac{x}{(x-3)(x+3)}$

71. $\dfrac{10}{v^2-2v+1} - \dfrac{1}{2-2v}$ $\quad \dfrac{v+19}{2(v-1)^2}$

72. $\dfrac{3y}{16-y^2} + \dfrac{1}{4+y}$ $\quad \dfrac{2(y+2)}{(4-y)(4+y)}$

73. $\dfrac{3}{r^2-r-2} - \dfrac{3}{r^2+2r+1}$

74. $\dfrac{q}{q^2-16} - \dfrac{q+1}{q^2+5q+4}$ $\quad \dfrac{4}{(q-4)(q+4)}$

75. $\dfrac{3}{y^2-9} - \dfrac{1}{y^2+4y+3}$ $\quad \dfrac{2}{(y-3)(y+1)}$

76. $\dfrac{5}{x^2-3x-4} - \dfrac{2}{x^2-1}$ $\quad \dfrac{3}{(x-4)(x-1)}$

C. 77. $\dfrac{13}{a} - \dfrac{11}{b} + \dfrac{7}{c}$ $\quad \dfrac{13bc-11ac+7ab}{abc}$

78. $\dfrac{5x-2y}{-x} + \dfrac{4x+3y}{-3x^2} + \dfrac{x-y}{x}$

79. $\dfrac{y+2}{y^2+5y+6} - \dfrac{2+y}{4-y^2} + \dfrac{2-y}{y^2+y-6}$

80. $\dfrac{4}{a-2} + \dfrac{3}{2-a} - \dfrac{2}{a^2-4}$

81. $\dfrac{b+1}{(b-1)^2} + \dfrac{2-2b}{(b-1)^3} + \dfrac{1}{b-1}$ $\quad \dfrac{2}{b-1}$

82. $\dfrac{x-3}{2x+6} - \dfrac{x+3}{3x-9} - \dfrac{5x^2+27}{6x^2-54}$

83. $\dfrac{5}{3n-3} + \dfrac{n}{2n+2} - \dfrac{3n^2}{n^2-1}$

84. $\dfrac{z^2}{x^2-y^2} + \dfrac{z}{(x-y)^2}$

85. $\dfrac{5}{m^2-2m+1} + \dfrac{3}{m+1} - \dfrac{4}{m-1}$

86. $\dfrac{a-6b}{2a^2-5ab+2b^2} - \dfrac{7}{a+2b}$

---

48. $\dfrac{5m^2+mn-3m+4n}{m^2}$

73. $\dfrac{9}{(r-2)(r+1)^2}$

78. $-\dfrac{12x^2-3xy+4x+3y}{3x^2}$

79. $\dfrac{1}{y-2}$

80. $\dfrac{a}{(a+2)(a-2)}$

82. $-\dfrac{2x^2+15x+9}{3(x+3)(x-3)}$

83. $\dfrac{-15n^2+7n+10}{6(n+1)(n-1)}$

84. $\dfrac{xz^2-yz^2+xz+yz}{(x+y)(x-y)^2}$

85. $-\dfrac{(m+4)(m-3)}{(m-1)^2(m+1)}$

86. $-\dfrac{13a^2-31ab+26b^2}{(2a-b)(a-2b)(a+2b)}$

CALCULATOR

You can use a calculator to check computations with rational expressions.

Example: Multiply $\dfrac{x^2 - 2x - 3}{x^2 - 3x} \cdot \dfrac{x^2 + 2x}{x^2 - 4}$.

Solution: $\dfrac{x + 1}{x - 2}$

Check: Choose any value for x so that no denominator will equal 0. Say, let $x = 4$. Notice that it is necessary to record some displays on paper for later use in the calculation.

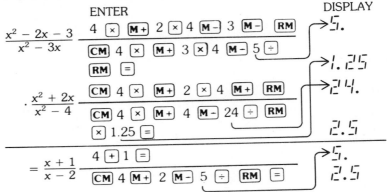

EXERCISES

Use a calculator to check each answer.

1. $\dfrac{x^2 - x - 6}{x^2 + 3x + 2} \cdot \dfrac{x^2 + 3x - 28}{x^2 + 4x - 21} = \dfrac{x - 4}{x + 1}$ correct

2. $\dfrac{x + 1}{x - 2} - \dfrac{x - 1}{x + 3} = \dfrac{6x + 1}{(x - 2)(x + 3)}$ wrong

3. $\dfrac{x^2 + x - 2}{x^2 - 9} \div \dfrac{x^2 - 4}{x^2 + 5x + 6} = \dfrac{x - 1}{x - 3}$ wrong

4. $\dfrac{4}{x + 3} + \dfrac{7}{2x + 1} = \dfrac{5(3x + 5)}{(x + 3)(2x + 1)}$ correct

5. $\dfrac{x}{x + 1} - \dfrac{2}{x + 3} = \dfrac{(x + 2)(x - 1)}{(x + 1)(x + 3)}$ correct

6. $\dfrac{x^2 + x}{x^2 - 9} \div \dfrac{x^2 - 2x}{x^2 + x - 6} = \dfrac{x}{x - 3}$ wrong

7. $\dfrac{5}{2x + 1} + \dfrac{2}{x - 1} = \dfrac{3x - 1}{(2x + 1)(x - 1)}$ wrong

8. $\dfrac{x^2 - x - 12}{x^2 - 5x + 4} \cdot \dfrac{x^2 + 5x - 6}{x^2 + 8x + 12} = \dfrac{x + 3}{x + 2}$ correct

9. $\dfrac{x + 3}{x - 1} + \dfrac{x + 1}{2x + 1} = \dfrac{(3x + 1)(x + 2)}{(x - 1)(2x + 1)}$ correct

Rational Expressions in Equations

Equations with rational expressions can be solved by multiplying *each side* of the equation by the LCD of the rational expressions. Then you solve the resulting equation.

EXAMPLES

1   **Solve** $\frac{x}{2} + \frac{2x}{3} = 7$.

SOLUTION $\frac{x}{2} + \frac{2x}{3} = 7$

$$6\left(\frac{x}{2} + \frac{2x}{3}\right) = 6 \cdot 7 \quad \textit{LCD is 6.}$$

$$6\left(\frac{x}{2}\right) + 6\left(\frac{2x}{3}\right) = 6 \cdot 7 \quad \textit{Use the distributive property.}$$

$$3x + 4x = 42$$
$$7x = 42$$
$$x = 6$$

CHECK $\frac{x}{2} + \frac{2x}{3} = 7$

$$\frac{6}{2} + \frac{2(6)}{3} \stackrel{?}{=} 7$$

$$3 + \frac{12}{3} \stackrel{?}{=} 7$$

$$3 + 4 \stackrel{?}{=} 7$$

$$7 = 7 \; \text{✔}$$

2   **Solve** $3 + \frac{x}{x-2} = \frac{6}{x-2}$.

SOLUTION $3 + \frac{x}{x-2} = \frac{6}{x-2}$ *NOTE:* $x \neq 2$

$$(x-2)\left(3 + \frac{x}{x-2}\right) = (x-2)\left(\frac{6}{x-2}\right) \quad \textit{LCD is } x-2.$$

$$(x-2)3 + (x-2)\left(\frac{x}{x-2}\right) = (x-2)\left(\frac{6}{x-2}\right)$$

$$3(x-2) + x = 6$$
$$3x - 6 + x = 6$$
$$4x = 12$$
$$x = 3$$

CHECK $3 + \frac{x}{x-2} = \frac{6}{x-2}$

$$3 + \frac{3}{3-2} \stackrel{?}{=} \frac{6}{3-2}$$

$$3 + 3 \stackrel{?}{=} 6$$

$$6 = 6 \; \text{✔}$$

CLASSROOM EXAMPLES

1. Solve $\frac{y}{3} + \frac{3y}{4} = 13$.

$$\frac{y}{3} + \frac{3}{4}y = 13$$
$$12\left(\frac{y}{3} + \frac{3}{4}y\right) = 12 \cdot 13$$
$$12\left(\frac{y}{3}\right) + 12\left(\frac{3y}{4}\right) = 12 \cdot 13$$
$$4y + 9y = 156$$
$$13y = 156$$
$$y = 12$$

2. Solve $5 + \frac{y}{y-3} = \frac{9}{y-3}$.

$$5 + \frac{y}{y-3} = \frac{9}{y-3}$$
$$(y-3)\left(5 + \frac{y}{y-3}\right)$$
$$= (y-3)\left(\frac{9}{y-3}\right)$$
$$(y-3)5 + (y-3)\left(\frac{y}{y-3}\right)$$
$$= (y-3)\left(\frac{9}{y-3}\right)$$
$$5(y-3) + y = 9$$
$$5y - 15 + y = 9$$
$$6y = 24$$
$$y = 4$$

3. Solve $\frac{5}{y-2} = \frac{4}{y+5}$.

$$\frac{5}{y-2} = \frac{4}{y+5}$$
$$(y-2)(y+5)\left(\frac{5}{y-2}\right)$$
$$= (y-2)(y+5)\left(\frac{4}{y+5}\right)$$
$$(y+5)5 = (y-2)4$$
$$5y + 25 = 4y - 8$$
$$y = -33$$

4. Solve $\frac{y}{y-2} + 4 = \frac{7}{y-2}$.

$$\frac{y}{y-2} + 4 = \frac{7}{y-2}$$

$$(y-2)\left(\frac{y}{y-2} + 4\right)$$

$$= (y-2)\left(\frac{7}{y-2}\right)$$

$$y + (y-2)4 = 7$$

$$y + 4y - 8 = 7$$

$$5y = 15$$

$$y = 3$$

MIXED REVIEW

Evaluate if $x = 4$ and $y = 0$.

1. $x^2 y$ 0

2. $\frac{3x}{y}$ undefined

3. $\frac{4y^2}{x}$ 0

4. $5x^2$ 80

5. $-3y$ 0

TEACHER'S RESOURCE MASTERS

Practice Master 41, Part 1

---

3   **Solve** $\frac{7}{x+3} = \frac{5}{x-1}$.

SOLUTION $\frac{7}{x+3} = \frac{5}{x-1}$ NOTE: $x \neq -3, 1$

$$(x+3)(x-1)\left(\frac{7}{x+3}\right) = (x+3)(x-1)\left(\frac{5}{x-1}\right)$$

$$(x-1)7 = (x+3)5$$

$$7x - 7 = 5x + 15$$

$$2x = 22$$

$$x = 11$$

SHORTCUT

When each side of the equation is a fraction, cross multiply and skip the second step.

$$\frac{7}{x+3} \diagdown\!\!\!\!\diagup \frac{5}{x-1}$$

The two products, $7(x-1)$ and $5(x+3)$, are the same as those in the third step of the detailed solution.

CHECK $\frac{7}{x+3} = \frac{5}{x-1}$

$$\frac{7}{11+3} \overset{?}{=} \frac{5}{11-1}$$

$$\frac{7}{14} \overset{?}{=} \frac{5}{10}$$

$$\frac{1}{2} = \frac{1}{2} \; ✔$$

Sometimes the solution that is found for an equation is only an *apparent* solution. Such a "solution" is called an **extraneous root.** In solving equations with rational expressions, you often multiply each side of the equation by an expression containing the variable. This procedure can introduce an extraneous root.

4   **Solve** $\frac{x}{x-5} + 3 = \frac{5}{x-5}$.

SOLUTION $\frac{x}{x-5} + 3 = \frac{5}{x-5}$ NOTE: $x \neq 5$

$$(x-5)\left(\frac{x}{x-5} + 3\right) = (x-5)\left(\frac{5}{x-5}\right)$$

$$x + (x-5)3 = 5$$

$$x + 3x - 15 = 5$$

$$4x = 20$$

$$x = 5$$

CHECK $\frac{x}{x-5} + 3 = \frac{5}{x-5}$

$$\frac{5}{5-5} + 3 \overset{?}{=} \frac{5}{5-5}$$

$$\frac{5}{0} + 3 \overset{?}{=} \frac{5}{0}$$ *Since division by 0 is not defined, 5 is not a solution. The solution set is $\varnothing$.*

Identify the LCD in each equation.

1. $\dfrac{5}{3y} = \dfrac{1}{3}$ $3y$

2. $\dfrac{1}{3} + \dfrac{1}{x} = \dfrac{4}{3}$ $3x$

3. $\dfrac{a}{2} - \dfrac{a}{3} = 4$ 6

4. $\dfrac{2}{3x} = \dfrac{1}{6}$ $6x$

5. $\dfrac{3}{m} - \dfrac{2}{3m} = \dfrac{14}{3}$ $3m$

6. $\dfrac{6}{x} = \dfrac{4}{x-1}$ $x(x-1)$

7. $\dfrac{3}{2} = \dfrac{y}{y+2}$ $2(y+2)$

8. $\dfrac{5}{a} = \dfrac{7}{a-4}$ $a(a-4)$

9. $\dfrac{n}{2n+4} = \dfrac{1}{n+2}$ $2(n+2)$

10. $\dfrac{x-2}{x+3} = \dfrac{3}{8}$ $8(x+3)$

WRITTEN EXERCISES

A. 1–10. Solve each equation in Oral Exercises and check the solution.

B. Solve each equation and check the solution.

11. $\dfrac{x}{5} - \dfrac{x}{3} = 2$ -15

12. $\dfrac{y}{3} - \dfrac{y}{4} = 3$ 36

13. $\dfrac{4}{x-4} - \dfrac{x}{x-4} - 2 = 0$ $\varnothing$

14. $\dfrac{-a}{a-3} + \dfrac{a}{a-3} - 5 = 0$ $\varnothing$

15. $\dfrac{1+b}{3-b} = \dfrac{3}{5}$ $\frac{1}{2}$

16. $\dfrac{5}{8x-1} = \dfrac{2}{3x}$ 2

17. $\dfrac{2}{y+3} = \dfrac{5}{y}$ -5

18. $\dfrac{a+5}{a-3} + \dfrac{4}{a-3} = 5$ 6

19. $\dfrac{3}{2x} - \dfrac{1}{3} = \dfrac{5}{6x}$ 2

20. $\dfrac{4}{n+4} = \dfrac{2}{n+5}$ -6

21. $\dfrac{5}{x-3} = \dfrac{3}{x-4}$ $5\frac{1}{2}$

22. $\dfrac{n-2}{n+2} = \dfrac{n+1}{n-2}$ $\frac{2}{7}$

23. $\dfrac{x-2}{x+2} = \dfrac{x-4}{x+4}$ 0

24. $\dfrac{n-2}{n-5} = \dfrac{n+3}{n+5}$ -1

25. $\dfrac{1-n}{1+n} - 1 = \dfrac{2}{1+n}$ $\varnothing$

26. $\dfrac{8}{a-3} - 3 = \dfrac{2-3a}{a+3}$ 19

27. $\dfrac{3}{x-1} - 2 = \dfrac{5-2x}{x+1}$ $2\frac{1}{2}$

28. $\dfrac{3y}{y-2} - 3 = \dfrac{4}{y+2}$ -10

29. $\dfrac{2x}{x-4} - \dfrac{4}{x+5} = 2$ -14

30. $\dfrac{y-1}{y+1} - \dfrac{2y}{y-1} = -1$ 0

31. $\dfrac{x}{10} + \dfrac{1}{x-1} = \dfrac{x+1}{2x-2}$ 5

32. $\dfrac{y}{y-3} + 2 = \dfrac{3}{y-3}$ $\varnothing$

C. 33. $\dfrac{2a+1}{a-1} - \dfrac{3a}{a+2} = \dfrac{-a^2-2}{a^2+a-2}$ $-\frac{1}{2}$

34. $\dfrac{7n^2+8}{3n^2-4n} - 2 = \dfrac{n}{3n-4}$ -1

35. $\dfrac{x}{x-2} = \dfrac{x+3}{x+2} - \dfrac{x}{x^2-4}$ -3

36. $\dfrac{3y^2-10}{2y^2-5y} - 1 = \dfrac{y}{2y-5}$ 2

37. $\dfrac{2(x-3)}{9x^2-1} = \dfrac{2x}{9x^2-15x+4}$ $\frac{6}{7}$

38. $\dfrac{2a^2}{1-a^2} = \dfrac{a}{a-1} - \dfrac{a}{a+1}$ 0

39. $\dfrac{1}{n} - \dfrac{2}{1-n} = \dfrac{8}{n^2-n}$ 3

40. $\dfrac{y}{y+1} - \dfrac{y+1}{y-4} = \dfrac{5}{y^2-3y-4}$ $\varnothing$

ASSIGNMENT GUIDE
Minimum
1–9 odd, 17–27
Regular
11–39 odd, 40
Maximum
15–29 odd, 33–40

ADDITIONAL ANSWERS
Written Exercises
1. 5
2. 1
3. 24
4. 4
5. $\frac{1}{2}$
6. 3
7. -6
8. -10
9. 2
10. 5

ALGEBRA IN USE

To find the location of a fault in a telephone or telegraph wire, a repair crew might use the formula $\dfrac{x}{2\ell - x} = \dfrac{r_1}{r_2}$.

The wire known to be faulty is connected at point B to a wire known to be good.

At point A, the good wire and the faulty wire are connected with testing equipment that gives two readings—the values for r_1 and r_2. These readings are resistances to a current sent through the wires by the testing equipment and are given in units called **ohms.** Let ℓ be the distance between A and B.

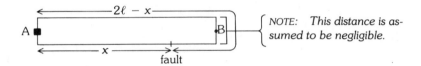

NOTE: *This distance is assumed to be negligible.*

Example: Suppose $r_1 = 500$ ohms, $r_2 = 1000$ ohms, and $\ell = 50$ miles. Find the distance from A to the fault.

Solution:

$$\frac{x}{2\ell - x} = \frac{r_1}{r_2}$$

$$\frac{x}{2 \cdot 50 - x} = \frac{500}{1000}$$

$$x = 33.3 \text{ miles}$$

EXERCISES

1. Find the distance from A to the fault if $r_1 = 250$ ohms, $r_2 = 750$ ohms, and $\ell = 55$ miles. 27.5 miles

2. Find the distance from A to the fault if $r_1 = 500$ ohms, $r_2 = 750$ ohms, and $\ell = 100$ miles. 80 miles

3. Find the distance from A to the fault if $r_1 = 100$ ohms, $r_2 = 200$ ohms, and $\ell = 20$ kilometers. 13.3 kilometers

4. Find the distance from A to the fault if $r_1 = 150$ ohms, $r_2 = 450$ ohms, and $\ell = 12$ kilometers. 6 kilometers

Problem Solving—Rate Problems

OBJECTIVE

Solve rate problems.

TEACHER'S NOTES

See p. T33.

The following formula is used to solve problems involving *rate of work*:

rate of work × time = work completed

$$rt = w$$

EXAMPLES

1   It takes an experienced carpenter 3 days to build a wooden deck on the back of a house. It takes an apprentice carpenter 4 days to do the same job. How long will it take them if they work together on the same deck? (Assume that in working together, the carpenters can continue to work at their same rates.)

Understand: *Given:*   An experienced carpenter takes 3 days.
     An apprentice carpenter takes 4 days.

   To find: how many days it will take if they work together

Plan: Since the experienced carpenter can build the deck alone in 3 days, $\frac{1}{3}$ of the job can be completed in one day. (Rate of work is often expressed in terms of the job to be done.) The rate of work of the apprentice is $\frac{1}{4}$ of the job per day.

Making a Table is a helpful problem-solving strategy that can be used here. Let t = time (in days) required for the two carpenters working together to build the deck.

	Rate of work	Time	Work completed	
Experienced carpenter	$\frac{1}{3}$	t	$\frac{t}{3}$	experienced carpenter's part of the job
Apprentice carpenter	$\frac{1}{4}$	t	$\frac{t}{4}$	apprentice carpenter's part of the job

Solve: $\frac{t}{3} + \frac{t}{4} = 1$ *1 indicates a complete job.*

$$12\left(\frac{t}{3} + \frac{t}{4}\right) = 12 \cdot 1 \text{ LCD is 12.}$$

$$4t + 3t = 12$$

$$7t = 12$$

$$t = 1\frac{5}{7}$$

Answer: The carpenters can complete the deck in $1\frac{5}{7}$ days.

Review: Does it seem reasonable that it will take 2 carpenters working together $1\frac{5}{7}$ days to build a deck, if it takes 3 days for one carpenter working alone and 4 days for the other carpenter working alone to complete the same task?

CLASSROOM EXAMPLES

1. It takes an experienced bricklayer 2 days to build a fireplace. It takes an apprentice bricklayer 3 days to do the same job. How long will it take them if they work together on the same fireplace?

Let t = time (in days) required for the two bricklayers working together to build the fireplace.

	r	t	w
Experienced bricklayer	$\frac{1}{2}$	t	$\frac{t}{2}$
Apprentice bricklayer	$\frac{1}{3}$	t	$\frac{t}{3}$

$$\frac{t}{2} + \frac{t}{3} = 1$$

$$6\left(\frac{t}{2} + \frac{t}{3}\right) = 6 \cdot 1$$

$$3t + 2t = 6$$

$$5t = 6$$

$$t = 1\frac{1}{5}$$

The bricklayers can complete the fireplace in $1\frac{1}{5}$ days.

2. A paddleboat traveled 12 miles downstream (with the current) in the same amount of time it took to return 8 miles upstream (against the current). The speed of the boat in still water is 20 miles per hour. What is the speed of the current?

Let c = rate of current in miles per hour.

	D	r	t
Down-stream	12	$20+c$	$\frac{12}{20+c}$
Up-stream	8	$20-c$	$\frac{8}{20-c}$

$$\frac{12}{20+c} = \frac{8}{20-c}$$
$$12(20 - c) = 8(20 + c)$$
$$240 - 12c = 160 + 8c$$
$$80 = 20c$$
$$c = 4$$

The speed of the current is 4 miles per hour.

MIXED REVIEW

1. Add $\frac{6x+5}{y-2} + \frac{2x-7}{y-2}$ and express in simplest form.
$\frac{2(4x-1)}{y-2}$

2. Find the LCD of $\frac{5}{6xy^2}$ and $\frac{1}{4x^2y}$. $12x^2y^2$

3. Simplify $5 \cdot 2 + 8 \cdot 2^2$.
42

As you have seen in previous chapters, the following formula is used to solve problems involving *rate of travel:* $rt = d$, where r = rate of travel, t = time, and d = distance traveled.

| **2** |

At full throttle, a motorboat traveled 15 miles downstream (with the current) in the same amount of time it took to return 10 miles upstream (against the current). The speed of the boat at full throttle in still water is 30 miles per hour. What is the speed of the current?

Understand: *Given:* The distance traveled is 15 miles downstream and 10 miles upstream in the same amount of time. The rate of travel is 30 miles per hour in still water.

To find: speed of the current

Plan: Since $rt = d$, then $t = \frac{d}{r}$. Let c = rate of current in miles per hour.

	Distance	Rate of travel	Time	
Downstream	15	$30 + c$	$\frac{15}{30+c}$	*The current increases the rate of travel.*
Upstream	10	$30 - c$	$\frac{10}{30-c}$	*The current decreases the rate of travel.*

Solve: $\frac{15}{30+c} = \frac{10}{30-c}$ *The times are equal.*
$$15(30 - c) = 10(30 + c)$$
$$450 - 15c = 300 + 10c$$
$$150 = 25c$$
$$c = 6$$

Answer: The speed of the current is 6 miles per hour.

Review: Does it seem reasonable that the speed of a river's current is 6 miles per hour when a boat travels 15 miles downstream in the same amount of time it takes to return 10 miles upstream at a constant speed of 30 miles per hour?

ORAL EXERCISES

Use the following problem to answer exercises 1–4:

Edna owns a florist shop. She can arrange the flowers for a wedding in 2 hours. Her helper can do it in 3 hours. How long will it take them if they work together?

1. What is Edna's rate of work? (How much of the job can she do in one hour?) $\frac{1}{2}$

2. What is her helper's rate of work? $\frac{1}{3}$

3. If t represents the number of hours it takes them to arrange the flowers together, what expression will represent the work completed by Edna? By her helper? $\frac{t}{2}; \frac{t}{3}$

4. What equation would you use to solve the problem? $\frac{t}{2} + \frac{t}{3} = 1$

Use the following problem to complete the table below and to answer exercise 6.

A fishing boat traveled 25 miles downstream in the same amount of time it took to return 15 miles upstream. If the speed of the boat in still water is 12 miles per hour, what is the speed of the current? Let c = the speed of the current.

5.

	Distance	Rate	Time
Downstream	25	$12 + c$	$\dfrac{25}{12 + c}$
Upstream	15	$12 - c$	$\dfrac{15}{12 - c}$

6. What equation would you use to solve this problem? $\dfrac{25}{12 + c} = \dfrac{15}{12 - c}$

WRITTEN EXERCISES

A. Solve each problem.

1. Eduardo and his brother each has his own lawn mower. If it takes Eduardo 2 hours to mow a certain lawn and it takes his brother 3 hours to mow the same lawn, how long will it take them working together? $1\frac{1}{5}$ h

2. A fence can be painted with a sprayer in 3 hours. It takes 5 hours to paint the fence with a brush. How long will it take to paint the fence, using both the sprayer and the brush? $1\frac{7}{8}$ h

3. An airplane cruises at 140 miles per hour in still air. At that speed, the plane flew 400 miles with the wind in the same amount of time it took to fly 300 miles back (against the wind). What is the speed of the wind, assuming that it remains constant? 20 mi/h

4. Heather and George rented a small boat with an electric motor. The top speed of the boat in still water was 3 miles per hour. At top speed, an 8-mile trip downstream took the same amount of time as a 2-mile trip upstream. What was the rate of the current?

B. 5. At cruising speed, an airplane flew 500 kilometers with the wind in the same amount of time it took to fly 400 kilometers against the wind. If the constant speed of the wind is 20 kilometers per hour, what is the cruising speed of the airplane? 180 km/h

6. A motorboat traveled 90 kilometers downstream in the same amount of time it took to return 40 kilometers upstream. The rate of the current is 5 kilometers per hour. What is the speed of the boat in still water? 13 km/h

7. Two typists working together can type a manuscript in 5 hours. The faster typist can complete the manuscript in 9 hours. How long will it take the slower typist? $11\frac{1}{4}$ h

8. A swimming pool can be filled in 15 hours, using a small hose. The same pool can be filled in 12 hours, using a larger hose. How long will it take to fill the pool if both hoses are used at the same time?

C. 9. A water-storage tank can be filled by one pipe in 32 minutes and by another pipe in 16 minutes. A third pipe can empty the tank in 24 minutes. How long will it take to fill an empty tank if all three pipes are operating? $19\frac{1}{5}$ min

10. A railroad tank car can be filled in $6\frac{6}{7}$ hours, using two pipes. If one pipe alone can fill the tank car in 12 hours, how long will it take the other pipe alone to fill it? 16 h

4. Find the slope of the line with points $(5, -2)$ and $(10, 6)$. $\frac{8}{5}$

5. Simplify $\dfrac{\frac{2x + 6}{4x^2 + 24x + 36}}{\frac{1}{2(x + 3)}}$.

TEACHER'S RESOURCE MASTERS

Practice Master 41, Part 2

ASSIGNMENT GUIDE

Minimum
1–7

Regular
3–9

Maximum
4–10

ADDITIONAL ANSWERS

Written Exercises

4. 1.8 mi/h

8. $6\frac{2}{3}$ h

PROBLEM-SOLVING STRATEGIES

Make a Table (1–10).

Draw a Diagram (3–6).

Write an Equation (1–10).

EXPLORATION
Complex Fractions

A complex fraction is a fraction that contains fractions in the numerator or denominator or both.

You can simplify a complex fraction by multiplying both the numerator and the denominator by the least common denominator (LCD) of all the fractions in the complex fraction.

Example 1: Simplify $\dfrac{\frac{3}{xy}}{\frac{1}{x^2 y}}$.

Solution:

$$\frac{\frac{3}{xy}}{\frac{1}{x^2 y}} = \frac{\frac{3}{xy}}{\frac{1}{x^2 y}} \cdot \frac{x^2 y}{x^2 y} \quad LCD \ of \ \frac{3}{xy} \ and \ \frac{1}{x^2 y} \ is \ x^2 y.$$

$$= \frac{3x}{1}$$

$$= 3x$$

Example 2: Simplify $\dfrac{\frac{1}{x+1} + \frac{1}{x-1}}{\frac{2}{x+1} - \frac{1}{x-1}}$.

Solution:

$$\frac{\frac{1}{x+1} + \frac{1}{x-1}}{\frac{2}{x+1} - \frac{1}{x-1}} = \frac{\frac{1}{x+1} + \frac{1}{x-1}}{\frac{2}{x+1} - \frac{1}{x-1}} \cdot \frac{(x+1)(x-1)}{(x+1)(x-1)} \quad LCD \ of \ \frac{1}{x+1}, \frac{1}{x-1},$$
$$and \ \frac{2}{x+1} \ is \ (x+1)(x-1).$$

$$= \frac{1(x-1) + 1(x+1)}{2(x-1) - 1(x+1)}$$

$$= \frac{2x}{x-3}$$

EXERCISES

Simplify each complex fraction.

1. $\dfrac{\frac{3}{x}}{\frac{4}{y}}$ $\dfrac{3y}{4x}$

2. $\dfrac{\frac{2}{3x}}{\frac{4}{x}}$ $\dfrac{1}{6}$

3. $\dfrac{\frac{7}{y}}{\frac{5}{y^2}}$ $\dfrac{7y}{5}$

4. $\dfrac{\frac{1}{x+1}}{\frac{3}{x+1}}$ $\dfrac{1}{3}$

5. $\dfrac{\frac{9}{a+1}}{\frac{4}{a-1}}$ $\dfrac{9(a-1)}{4(a+1)}$

6. $\dfrac{\frac{2x}{x+1}}{\frac{x}{x-1}}$ $\dfrac{2(x-1)}{x+1}$

7. $\dfrac{\frac{1}{x+1} + \frac{1}{x-1}}{\frac{1}{x+1} - \frac{1}{x-1}}$ $-x$

8. $\dfrac{\frac{3}{y+2} - \frac{2}{y-2}}{\frac{1}{y+2} - \frac{3}{y-2}}$ $-\dfrac{y-10}{2(y+4)}$

9.10 Using Formulas

OBJECTIVE

Solve an equation or a formula for a specified variable.

TEACHER'S NOTES

See p. T33.

Some equations contain rational expressions with more than one variable. Sometimes it is convenient to solve such an equation for one of the variables.

EXAMPLES

1   **Solve $\frac{3}{4y} - 2 = \frac{2}{3x}$ for x.**

SOLUTION

$$\frac{3}{4y} - 2 = \frac{2}{3x}$$

$$12xy\left(\frac{3}{4y} - 2\right) = 12xy\left(\frac{2}{3x}\right) \quad \text{LCD is } 12xy.$$

$$12xy\left(\frac{3}{4y}\right) - 12xy(2) = 12xy\left(\frac{2}{3x}\right)$$

$$9x - 24xy = 8y$$

$$x(9 - 24y) = 8y \qquad \textit{Use the distributive property to remove}$$
$$\textit{the desired variable from two terms.}$$

$$x = \frac{8y}{9 - 24y}$$

Formulas are equations that often involve rational expressions with more than one variable.

2   **Solve $I = \frac{E}{r + R}$ for R. (This formula is used to solve electricity problems.)**

SOLUTION

$$I = \frac{E}{r + R}$$

$$\frac{I}{1} = \frac{E}{r + R}$$

$$I(r + R) = 1 \cdot E \quad \textit{Cross multiply.}$$

$$Ir + IR = E \qquad \textit{Use the distributive property to remove a desired}$$
$$\textit{variable from parentheses indicating a product.}$$

$$IR = E - Ir$$

$$R = \frac{E - Ir}{I}$$

CLASSROOM EXAMPLES

1. Solve $\frac{2}{3x} + 2 = \frac{3}{4y}$ for y.
$$\frac{2}{3x} + 2 = \frac{3}{4y}$$
$$12xy\left(\frac{2}{3x} + 2\right) = 12xy\left(\frac{3}{4y}\right)$$
$$12xy\left(\frac{2}{3x}\right) + 12xy(2) = 12xy\left(\frac{3}{4y}\right)$$
$$8y + 24xy = 9x$$
$$y(8 + 24x) = 9x$$
$$y = \frac{9x}{8 + 24x}$$

2. Solve $I = \frac{E}{r + R}$ for r.
$$I = \frac{E}{r + R}$$
$$\frac{I}{1} = \frac{E}{r + R}$$
$$I(r + R) = 1 \cdot E$$
$$Ir + IR = E$$
$$Ir = E - IR$$
$$r = \frac{E - IR}{I}$$

MIXED REVIEW

Perform the indicated operation.
1. $3x^2y(-8xy)$ $-24x^3y^2$
2. $3^2a^4(a^5)$ $9a^9$
3. $(6x^2 + 9xy + y^2)$
   $+ (6x^2 - 9xy + y^2)$
   $12x^2 + 2y^2$ or
   $2(6x^2 + y^2)$
4. $\dfrac{x^{-5}}{x^{-8}}$ x^3
5. $(-15 \cdot 2) - 5$ -35

ORAL EXERCISES

Tell the LCD for each equation.

1. $\frac{3}{x} + \frac{2}{y} = 4$ xy

2. $\frac{2}{3m} + \frac{3}{4n} = 6$ $12mn$

3. $\frac{2}{5a} - 3 = \frac{7}{10b}$ $10ab$

4. $\frac{3}{2x} - 4 = \frac{1}{3y}$ $6xy$

5. $\frac{1}{4m} + \frac{5}{6n} = 8$ $12mn$

6. $\frac{3y + 5}{y - 1} = \frac{2}{x}$ $x(y - 1)$

ASSIGNMENT GUIDE

Minimum
1–5 odd, 13–41 odd

Regular
21–38

Maximum
25–38, 43–46

ADDITIONAL ANSWERS

Written Exercises

30. $\frac{RD - NL}{N}$

32. $d + 1.3P$

34. $\frac{v^2 - u^2}{2s}$

35. $\frac{24C}{R(n + 1)}$

36. $\frac{fv}{v - f}$

37. $\frac{1.732}{T - S}$

38. $\frac{Rr_2}{r_2 - R}$

39. $\frac{1000kw}{E}$

40. $\frac{72W(72D)}{N}$

WRITTEN EXERCISES

A. Solve each equation for x.

1. $\frac{5}{x} + \frac{3}{y} = 4$ $\quad \frac{5y}{4y - 3}$

2. $\frac{1}{2x} - 3 = \frac{2}{3y}$ $\quad \frac{3y}{2(2 + 9y)}$

3. $\frac{1}{3x} + \frac{3}{4y} = 5$ $\quad \frac{4y}{3(20y - 3)}$

4. $3x - 4 = \frac{5}{6y}$ $\quad \frac{24y + 5}{18y}$

5. $\frac{3x - 4}{x} = \frac{3}{y}$ $\quad \frac{4y}{3(y - 1)}$

6. $\frac{3y + 7}{y - 1} = \frac{4}{x}$ $\quad \frac{4(y - 1)}{3y + 7}$

B. Solve each equation for y.

7. $\frac{2y - 5}{y + 3} = \frac{6}{x}$ $\quad \frac{5x + 18}{2(x - 3)}$

8. $\frac{5x + 3}{x} = \frac{2}{y}$ $\quad \frac{2x}{5x + 3}$

9. $\frac{1}{3x} + \frac{3}{4y} = 5$ $\quad \frac{9x}{4(15x - 1)}$

10. $\frac{1}{2x} - 3 = \frac{2}{3y}$ $\quad \frac{4x}{3(1 - 6x)}$

11. $\frac{5}{x} + \frac{3}{y} = 4$ $\quad \frac{3x}{4x - 5}$

12. $3x - 4 = \frac{5}{6y}$ $\quad \frac{5}{6(3x - 4)}$

13. $\frac{3y + 7}{y - 1} = \frac{4}{x}$ $\quad \frac{7x + 4}{4 - 3x}$

14. $\frac{3x - 4}{x} = \frac{3}{y}$ $\quad \frac{3x}{3x - 4}$

15. $\frac{7x + 3}{x} = \frac{5}{y}$ $\quad \frac{5x}{7x + 3}$

16. $\frac{5y - 2}{y + 2} = \frac{9}{x}$ $\quad \frac{2(x + 9)}{5x - 9}$

Solve each formula for the variable indicated.

17. $A = \frac{1}{2}bh$; for h $\quad \frac{2A}{b}$

18. $A = \frac{1}{2}h(b_1 + b_2)$; for b_1 $\quad \frac{2A - hb_2}{h}$

19. $S = \frac{n}{2}(a + t)$; for t $\quad \frac{2S - na}{n}$

20. $S = \frac{a}{1 - r}$; for r $\quad \frac{S - a}{S}$

21. $P = 2(\ell + w)$; for w $\quad \frac{P - 2\ell}{2}$

22. $v = at + s$; for t $\quad \frac{v - s}{a}$

23. $I = Prt$; for t $\quad \frac{I}{Pr}$

24. $w = \frac{11(h - 40)}{2}$; for h $\quad \frac{2w + 440}{11}$

25. $C = \frac{5(F - 32)}{9}$; for F $\quad \frac{9C + 160}{5}$

26. $S = 2\pi r^2 + 2\pi rh$; for h $\quad \frac{S - 2\pi r^2}{2\pi r}$

27. $V = \frac{1}{3}Bh$; for h $\quad \frac{3v}{B}$

28. $u = f \cdot \frac{k(k + 1)}{n(n + 1)}$; for f $\quad \frac{un(n + 1)}{k(k + 1)}$

Solve each formula for the variable indicated. The field in which the formula is used is listed within the parentheses.

29. $R = \frac{KL}{D^2}$; for L (electricity) $\quad \frac{RD^2}{K}$

30. $N = \frac{RD}{T + L}$; for T (printing)

31. $H = \frac{Nd^3}{80}$; for N (mechanics) $\quad \frac{80H}{d^3}$

32. $d = D - 1.3P$; for D (mechanics)

33. $F = \frac{Wv^2}{gr}$; for W (physics) $\quad \frac{Fgr}{v^2}$

34. $v^2 = u^2 + 2as$; for a (physics)

35. $R = \frac{24C}{b(n + 1)}$; for b (business)

36. $\frac{1}{f} = \frac{1}{u} + \frac{1}{v}$; for u (photography)

37. $S = T - \frac{1.732}{N}$; for N (mechanics)

38. $\frac{1}{R} = \frac{1}{r_1} + \frac{1}{r_2}$; for r_1 (electricity)

39. $kw = \frac{EI}{1000}$; for I (electricity)

40. $N = \frac{72W(72D)}{E}$; for E (printing)

41. $C = \frac{\pi b^2 s}{4c}$; for s (mechanics) $\quad \frac{4Cc}{\pi b^2}$

42. $H = \frac{D^2N}{2.5}$; for N (mechanics) $\quad \frac{2.5H}{D^2}$

C. A winch may be used to lift a boat out of the water onto a trailer. A winch is an example of a simple machine called a wheel and axle.

A winch permits a heavy load to be pulled or lifted with much less force than is needed for pulling or lifting the load directly. The advantage of using a winch can be seen by using the formula below.

wheel

winch

axle

$\dfrac{L}{F} = \dfrac{R}{r}$ Let F = force, L = load, R = radius of the wheel, and r = radius of the axle.

Example: If the radius of the wheel is 12 inches and the radius of the axle is 2 inches, how many pounds of force will be needed to lift a boat weighing 2400 pounds?

$$\dfrac{L}{F} = \dfrac{R}{r}$$

$$\dfrac{2400}{F} = \dfrac{12}{2}$$

$$12F = 2(2400)$$

$$F = 400 \text{ pounds of force}$$

Solve each problem.

43. A boat weighting 1200 pounds is to be pulled onto a trailer, using a winch. If the radius of the wheel is 3 inches and the radius of the axle is $\frac{1}{4}$ inch, how many pounds of force will be needed to lift the boat up from the water?   100 pounds

44. A boat hoist is an example of a wheel and axle used to lift boats out of the water. If the radius of the axle is $1\frac{1}{2}$ inches and 250 pounds of force can lift a 3000-pound boat, what is the radius of the wheel?   18 inches

45. If the radius of the wheel is 10 inches and the radius of the axle is 1 inch, a force of 200 pounds will lift a boat weighing how many pounds?

2000 pounds

46. A boat hoist whose wheel has a radius of 20 inches can lift a 2100-pound boat, using a force of $156\frac{1}{4}$ pounds. What is the radius of the axle?

$1\frac{41}{84}$ inches

CHALLENGE

Find the number that is less than 50 by the same amount that 4 times the number is greater than 50.   20

SKILLS MAINTENANCE

Perform the indicated operation.

1. $38(-92)$ $\ -3496$

2. $17{,}340 \div (-85)$ $\ -204$

3. $536.8 + (-92.76)$ $\ 444.04$

4. $-340.6 - (-18.74)$ $\ -321.86$

Simplify.

5. $3[(11-2) \cdot 6 + 4] \div 87$ $\ 2$

6. $24 \div (5+3) \cdot 27$ $\ 81$

Solve.

7. $3x + 5 = 8x - 15$ $\ 4$

8. $-2y + 5 = 3(y-1)$ $\ 1\frac{3}{5}$

9. $3(x+1) \le 7x - 5$ $\ x \ge 2$

10. $5(9-m) > 6m + 4$ $\ m < 3\frac{8}{11}$

11. $|x-3| < 7$ $\ -4 < x < 10$

12. $\left|\frac{x}{3}\right| \ge 2$ $\ x \ge 6 \text{ or } x \le -6$

SKILLS MAINTENANCE

13. $4a - 3a + 11$

14. $5x^2 - 12x + 13$

32. $y = -2x$

34. $y = 3x - 1$

Perform the indicated operation.

13. $(3a^2 + 2a + 4) + (a^2 - 5a + 7)$

14. $(8x^2 - 7x + 4) - (3x^2 + 5x - 9)$

15. $(5c + 1)(2c - 7)$ $\ 10c^2 - 33c - 7$

16. $(6y^2 - 13y - 8) \div (2y + 1)$ $\ 3y - 8$

Factor.

17. $8m + 2mn$ $\ 2m(4 + n)$

18. $x^2y^3 + xy^2$ $\ xy^2(xy + 1)$

19. $t^2 - 36$ $\ (t + 6)(t - 6)$

20. $3v^2 - 12$ $\ 3(v + 2)(v - 2)$

21. $a^2 + 4ab + 4b^2$ $\ (a + 2b)(a + 2b)$

22. $4c^2 - 12cd + 9d^2$ $\ (2c - 3d)(2c - 3d)$

23. $2m^2 + 5m - 12$ $\ (2m - 3)(m + 4)$

24. $10y^2 - 13y - 3$ $\ (5y + 1)(2y - 3)$

Solve by factoring and using the zero-product property.

25. $2x^2 - 7x - 15 = 0$ $\ -1\frac{1}{2}, 5$

26. $6s^2 - 7s - 3 = 0$ $\ -\frac{1}{3}, 1\frac{1}{2}$

27. $2h^2 - h - 15 = 0$ $\ -2\frac{1}{2}, 3$

28. $2k^2 + 9k - 18 = 0$ $\ -6, 1\frac{1}{2}$

Find the slope of the line that contains these points:

29. $(2, -3)$ and $(4, 7)$ $\ 5$

30. $(8, 5)$ and $(10, -3)$ $\ -4$

Write the equation in slope-intercept form for each line.

31. The line has slope $\frac{3}{2}$ and y-intercept 2.
$y = \frac{3}{2}x + 2$

32. The line has slope -2 and passes through the point $(1, -2)$.

33. The line passes through points $(1, 3)$ and $(2, 8)$. $\ y = 5x - 2$

34. The line is parallel to $y = 3x - 8$ and passes through the point $(2, 5)$.

Solve each system of equations.

35. $2x - 5y = 1$
$5x + 2y = 17$ $\ (3, 1)$

36. $3x + y = -1$
$2x - y = -4$ $\ (-1, 2)$

37. $2x + 3y = 29$
$-x + 2y = 10$ $\ (4, 7)$

38. $3x - 2y = -7$
$-x + 3y = 0$ $\ (-3, -1)$

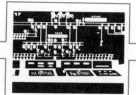

COMPUTER

The program below deals with percent problems. It is in the form of a stock-market investment game, in which the "investor," starting with $100, is asked to invest money. The program has the stock market go up or down randomly, resulting in a percentage of gain or loss of money for the investor.

```
10 MNY = 100: NW = 1: REM MONEY AND WEEK NUMBER
20 PRINT "WEEK ";NW;",  YOU HAVE $";MNY;","
30 PRINT "HOW MUCH DO YOU WANT TO INVEST"
40 INPUT "THIS WEEK (IN DOLLARS)? ";WI
50 IF WI > MNY OR WI < = 0 THEN PRINT "YOU CAN'T PLAY
   THAT AMOUNT!": GOTO 30
60 MNY = MNY - WI
70 FOR PAUSE = 1 TO 80: PRINT ".";: FOR T = 1 TO 50:
   NEXT T: NEXT PAUSE: PRINT
80 SM = INT (51 * RND (1) - 25)
90 MA$ = "UP":GA$ = "GAINED": IF SM < 0 THEN MA$ =
   "DOWN": GA$ = "LOST"
100 IF SM = 0 THEN PRINT "THE MARKET WAS ROCK-STEADY
    THIS WEEK,": GOTO 140
110 PRINT "THE MARKET THIS WEEK WAS ";MA$;","
120 PRINT "YOU HAVE ";GA$;" "; ABS (SM);"% OF"
130 PRINT "YOUR INVESTMENT.": PRINT
140 WI = WI + (WI * SM / 100): MNY = MNY + WI
150 NW = NW + 1: IF MNY > 0 THEN 20
160 PRINT "THAT'S IT, YOU ARE BROKE!": END
```

EXERCISES

1. Enter the program and RUN it at least twice. Did you finish with more or less than your original $100?

2. Is there any way that you can "rig" the program so that the probability of the stock market's going up, rather than down, is increased? Try it.

3. What is the program doing on lines 60, 80, 140, and 150?

ANSWERS

1. Answers will vary.

2. One example: Change line 80 to SM = INT(51 * RND(1) + 25). You can't lose!

3. Line 60: subtracting the week's investment;
   line 80: computing the percent gain or loss;
   line 140: computing the total weekly gain or loss, and resetting starting amount;
   line 150: moving up a week and halting if you are broke

TEACHER'S RESOURCE
MASTERS

Enrichment Master 8

ENRICHMENT

See Activities 23–28
p. T47.

CHAPTER 9 REVIEW

VOCABULARY

equivalent rational
  expressions (9.1)

extraneous root (9.8)

greatest common factor (9.2)

integral exponents (9.3)

least common denominator
  (9.6)

least common multiple (9.6)

negative integral exponent
  (9.3)

rational expression (9.1)

simplest form (9.2)

zero exponent (9.3)

REVIEW EXERCISES

9.1   **Replace each ? so that the equation names an equivalent rational expression.**

1. $\dfrac{5}{8} = \dfrac{?}{56}$ 35

2. $\dfrac{a^2}{b} = \dfrac{?}{ab^2}$ a^3b

3. $\dfrac{3}{x + 1} = \dfrac{?}{x^2 + 3x + 2}$ $3x + 6$

4. $\dfrac{3 - x}{4x} = \dfrac{3x - x^2}{?}$ $4x^2$

5. $\dfrac{b}{3} = \dfrac{b^2 + 4b}{?}$ $3b + 12$

6. $\dfrac{x - 1}{x + 1} = \dfrac{?}{x^2 - 3x - 4}$ $x^2 - 5x + 4$

Which values must be excluded from the replacement set of each variable so that the denominator will not equal zero?

7. $\dfrac{a + 3}{a}$ 0

8. $\dfrac{3}{b + 1}$ -1

9. $\dfrac{m}{m - 6}$ 6

10. $\dfrac{2}{(x + 1)(x - 3)}$ $-1, 3$

11. $\dfrac{x + 2}{x^2 - 7x + 6}$ $1, 6$

12. $\dfrac{3}{2m^2 - m - 1}$ $-\frac{1}{2}, 1$

9.2   **Change each rational expression to simplest form.**

13. $\dfrac{15}{40}$ $\frac{3}{8}$

14. $\dfrac{3m^2n}{9m}$ $\frac{mn}{3}$

15. $\dfrac{(2x + 3)(x - 4)}{(x + 7)(2x + 3)}$ $\frac{x - 4}{x + 7}$

16. $\dfrac{6a^2 + 7a - 3}{4a^2 + 8a + 3}$ $\frac{3a - 1}{2a + 3}$

17. $\dfrac{2s^2 - 13s - 24}{s^2 - 3s - 40}$ $\frac{2s + 3}{s + 5}$

18. $\dfrac{v + 3}{v^2 - 9}$ $\frac{1}{v - 3}$

9.3   **Simplify each of the following by using the properties of integral exponents:**

19. $8^{-3} \cdot 8^5$ 64

20. 7^0 1

21. $\left(\dfrac{a}{b}\right)^{-2}$ $\frac{b^2}{a^2}$

22. $(-3r)^{-3}$ $-\dfrac{1}{27r^3}$

23. $\dfrac{1}{m^{-4}}$ m^4

24. $\dfrac{2^{-3}}{2^{-8}}$ 32

9.4   **Find each product and express it in simplest form.**

25. $\dfrac{r^2s^4}{xy} \cdot \dfrac{x^2y^4}{rs^3}$ $rsxy^3$

26. $\dfrac{m + 1}{2m - 3} \cdot \dfrac{2m - 3}{m + 4}$ $\frac{m + 1}{m + 4}$

27. $\dfrac{4}{x - y} \cdot \dfrac{x^2 - y^2}{16}$ $\frac{x + y}{4}$

28. $\dfrac{9t^2 - 4}{8} \cdot \dfrac{16}{3t + 2}$ $2(3t - 2)$

29. $\dfrac{x^2 - 3x - 4}{x^2 + x - 6} \cdot \dfrac{x^2 + 2x - 3}{x^2 - 4x - 5}$

30. $\dfrac{9 - x^2}{x^2 + x - 2} \cdot \dfrac{x^2 + x - 2}{x^2 - 2x - 3}$ $-\frac{x + 3}{x + 1}$

ADDITIONAL ANSWERS
29. $\frac{(x - 4)(x - 1)}{(x - 5)(x - 2)}$

31. $\dfrac{b^2 + 2b - 3}{b^2 + 7b + 12} \cdot \dfrac{b^2 - 5b - 36}{b^2 + 5b - 6}$

32. $\dfrac{m^2 + 3m}{m^2 - m - 2} \cdot \dfrac{m^2 - 2m - 3}{m^2 + m - 12}$

31. $\dfrac{b - 9}{b + 6}$

32. $\dfrac{m(m + 3)}{(m - 2)(m + 4)}$

9.5 Find each quotient and express it in simplest form.

33. $\dfrac{xy}{5} \div \dfrac{x^2y^2}{15}$ $\dfrac{3}{xy}$

34. $\dfrac{a^2b^3}{cd^4} \div \dfrac{ab^4}{c^3d^2}$ $\dfrac{ac^2}{bd^2}$

35. $\dfrac{m + 3}{m - 1} \div \dfrac{m + 3}{m + 2}$ $\dfrac{m + 2}{m - 1}$

36. $\dfrac{y^2 - 3y + 2}{y + 4} \div (y - 2)$ $\dfrac{y - 1}{y + 4}$

37. $\dfrac{n^2 - 25}{n + 2} \div \dfrac{n + 5}{n + 2}$ $n - 5$

38. $\dfrac{3x^2 + 2x - 1}{3x - 3} \div \dfrac{x + 1}{x - 1}$ $\dfrac{3x - 1}{3}$

39. $\dfrac{t^2 + 3t}{t^2 + t - 6} \div \dfrac{t^2 + 3t + 2}{t^2 - t - 2}$ $\dfrac{t}{t + 2}$

40. $\dfrac{x^2 - x - 6}{x^2 - 16} \div \dfrac{x^2 + 3x + 2}{x^2 + 4x + 3}$

40. $\dfrac{x^2 - 9}{x^2 - 16}$

9.6 Give the LCD of rational expressions having the following denominators:

41. $18, 27a$ $54a$

42. $3x^2, 9x$ $9x^2$

43. $4x, x - 2$ $4x(x - 2)$

44. $x^2 - 4x + 4, x^2 - 4$
$(x - 2)^2(x + 2)$

9.7 Add or subtract and express each answer in simplest form.

45. $\dfrac{3}{5x} + \dfrac{2}{5x}$ $\dfrac{1}{x}$

46. $\dfrac{3}{a + 2} - \dfrac{1}{a + 2}$ $\dfrac{2}{a + 2}$

47. $\dfrac{b + 3}{b - 2} + \dfrac{2b - 6}{b - 2}$ $\dfrac{3(b - 1)}{b - 2}$

48. $\dfrac{c + 3}{c - 3} + \dfrac{2c - 2}{c^2 - 9}$ $\dfrac{(c + 7)(c + 1)}{(c - 3)(c + 3)}$

49. $\dfrac{4y}{2 - y} - \dfrac{-3}{y - 2}$ $\dfrac{-4y - 3}{y - 2}$

50. $\dfrac{x - 2}{x^2 + 5x + 6} - \dfrac{x + 1}{x^2 + 6x + 9}$

50. $-\dfrac{2(x + 4)}{(x + 2)(x + 3)^2}$

51. $\dfrac{3}{x + 2} + \dfrac{5}{2x + 4}$ $\dfrac{11}{2(x + 2)}$

52. $\dfrac{2v}{v - 1} - \dfrac{3v}{2v - 1}$ $\dfrac{v(v + 1)}{(v - 1)(2v - 1)}$

9.8 Solve each equation and check the solution.

53. $\dfrac{x + 4}{x - 2} = \dfrac{x + 5}{x - 3}$ -1

54. $\dfrac{1 + m}{3 - m} = \dfrac{3}{5}$ $\dfrac{1}{2}$

55. $\dfrac{7}{y} = \dfrac{2}{y + 5}$ -7

56. $\dfrac{t^2 - 4}{t + 3} = 2 - \dfrac{t - 2}{t + 3}$ 4

57. $\dfrac{3q - 1}{2q + 4} = \dfrac{4}{5}$ 3

58. $\dfrac{2f - 3}{f} + \dfrac{3}{f} - 1 = 0$ $\varnothing$

9.9 Solve.

59. One pump can fill a tank in 6 hours. Another pump can fill the tank in 8 hours. How long would it take both pumps to fill the tank? $3\frac{3}{7}$ h

60. A boat can travel 70 kilometers downstream in the same amount of time that it can travel 50 kilometers upstream. The speed of the boat in still water is 30 kilometers per hour. What is the speed of the current? 5 km/h

9.10 Solve for the indicated variable.

61. $\dfrac{3 - x}{5 + x} = \dfrac{2}{y}$; for x $\dfrac{3y - 10}{y + 2}$

62. $\dfrac{5 - x}{2 + x} = \dfrac{7}{y}$; for y $\dfrac{7(2 + x)}{5 - x}$

63. $v = a + gt$; for a $v - gt$

64. $f = ma$; for a $\dfrac{f}{m}$

65. $v = lwh$; for w $\dfrac{v}{lh}$

66. $b = a(n - 1)d$; for n $\dfrac{b + ad}{ad}$

TEACHER'S RESOURCE
MASTERS

Chapter 9 Test

Multiple-Choice Test

PROBLEM-SOLVING
HANDBOOK

p. 535

CHAPTER 9 TEST

Replace each ? so that the equation names an equivalent rational expression.

1. $\dfrac{2}{3x - 1} = \dfrac{6}{?}$ $9x - 3$

2. $\dfrac{3m + 4}{m + 1} = \dfrac{?}{m^2 + 5m + 4}$ $3m^2 + 16m + 16$

Which values must be excluded from the replacement set of each variable so that the denominator will not equal zero?

3. $\dfrac{x}{5x^2}$ 0

4. $\dfrac{2x + 1}{x^2 - 1}$ $1, -1$

Change each rational expression to simplest form.

5. $\dfrac{m^2 + mn}{m^2 - n^2}$ $\dfrac{m}{m - n}$

6. $\dfrac{y^2 - 4y}{16 - y^2}$ $-\dfrac{y}{y + 4}$

Simplify each of the following by using the properties of integral exponents:

7. $\left(\dfrac{8m^2n^3y^5}{x^8}\right)^0$ 1

8. $\left(\dfrac{1}{2m}\right)^{-3}$ $8m^3$

9. $\dfrac{y^8}{y^{-3}}$ y^{11}

Find each product and express it in simplest form.

10. $\dfrac{2}{a + b} \cdot \dfrac{a^2 - b^2}{b}$ $\dfrac{2(a - b)}{b}$

11. $\dfrac{x^2 + 2xy + y^2}{x + y} \cdot \dfrac{x^2}{x + y}$ x^2

Find each quotient and express it in simplest form.

12. $\dfrac{c + d}{8} \div \dfrac{c + d}{4}$ $\dfrac{1}{2}$

13. $\dfrac{m^2 + 3m + 2}{m^2 - 2m - 3} \div \dfrac{2m + 8}{m - 3}$ $\dfrac{m + 2}{2(m + 4)}$

Give the LCD of rational expressions having the following denominators:

14. $2r^2, 5rs$ $10r^2s$

15. $x + 3, 2x - 10$ $2(x + 3)(x - 5)$

Add or subtract and express each answer in simplest form.

16. $\dfrac{5}{v^2w} + \dfrac{2}{vw^2}$ $\dfrac{5w + 2v}{v^2w^2}$

17. $\dfrac{x}{x + 3} - \dfrac{2}{x - 1}$ $\dfrac{x^2 - 3x - 6}{(x + 3)(x - 1)}$

Solve each equation and check the solution.

18. $\dfrac{x - 3}{x + 3} = \dfrac{x + 3}{x + 5}$ -6

19. $\dfrac{2}{f - 2} = \dfrac{6f - 10}{f - 2}$ $\varnothing$

Solve.

20. Ikreda can swim 100 meters downstream in the same amount of time that she can swim 80 meters upstream. The speed of the current is 5 meters per minute. How fast could Ikreda swim in still water?   45 m/min

Solve for the indicated variable.

21. $f = ma$; for m $\dfrac{f}{a}$

22. $A = 2\pi r(r + h)$; for h $\dfrac{A - 2\pi r^2}{2\pi r}$

CHAPTER 10

Variation Functions

A carpenter earns $261 for a job that takes 12 hours to complete. If the labor cost of the job varies directly as the number of hours it takes to complete the job, how much will a carpenter earn for a 32-hour job? $704

OBJECTIVES

Determine if an equation describes a direct variation.

Write the equation of a direct variation that is described by words.

Solve a problem by using the direct-variation method.

TEACHER'S NOTES

See p. T33.

CLASSROOM EXAMPLES

1. Barbara traveled 450 miles in her car on 18 gallons of gasoline. If the number of gallons g of gasoline used varies directly as the number of miles m traveled, how many gallons will Barbara's car need in order to travel 700 miles?

Solve for k, then for g.

$g = km$

$18 = k \cdot 450$

$k = \frac{18}{450} = \frac{1}{25}$

$g = \frac{1}{25} \cdot 700$

$g = 28$

Barbara's car will need 28 gallons of gasoline to travel 700 miles.

2. Steven worked 8 hours and earned $28. If the amount of money m earned is directly proportional to the number of hours h worked, how much will Steven earn for working 13 hours?

10.1 Direct Variation

Raul sold 3 raffle tickets for 1 dollar. The table below shows the relation between the number of tickets t and the cost c in dollars.

Cost in dollars (c)	Number of tickets (t)
1	3
2	6
3	9
4	12

From the table, you can see that $t = 3c$. The relation between t and c can then be graphed. Notice that a different-sized unit is used on each axis.

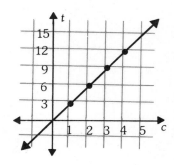

As shown on the graph, the relation described by the equation $t = 3c$ is a function. A linear function is defined by an equation of the form $y = mx + b$, when $m \neq 0$. If $b = 0$, the function is called a **direct variation**.

> A direct variation is a linear function defined by an equation of the form $y = kx$, when $k \neq 0$.

In the direct variation $t = 3c$, t is said to *vary directly* as c, or t is said to be *directly proportional* to c. The number 3 is called the *constant of variation* or the *constant of proportionality*.

EXAMPLES

1 **On a recent trip, Chris traveled 288 miles in his car on 16 gallons of gasoline. If the number of gallons g of gasoline used varies directly as the number of miles m traveled, how many gallons will Chris's car need in order to travel 720 miles?**

SOLUTION

Solve for k, then for g.

$g = km$	*Write a direct-variation equation.*
$16 = k \cdot 288$	*Substitute for g and m.*
$k = \frac{16}{288} = \frac{1}{18}$	*Solve for k.*
$g = \frac{1}{18} \cdot 720$	*Substitute for k and m.*
$g = 40$	*Solve for g.*

Chris's car will need 40 gallons of gasoline to travel 720 miles.

2   Lynn worked 4 hours and earned $15. If the amount of money m earned is directly proportional to the number of hours h worked, how much will Lynn earn for working 9 hours?

SOLUTION

$m = kh$ *Write a direct-variation equation.*

$15 = k \cdot 4$ *Substitute for m and h.*

$k = \dfrac{15}{4} = 3.75$ *Solve for k.*

$m = 3.75 \cdot 9$ *Substitute for k and h.*

$m = 33.75$ *Solve for m.*

Lynn will earn $33.75 for working 9 hours.

$m = kh$
$28 = k \cdot 8$
$k = \dfrac{28}{8} = 3.5$
$m = 3.5 \cdot 13$
$m = 45.5$
Steven will earn $45.50 for working 13 hours.

ORAL EXERCISES

Tell whether each equation describes a direct variation. If it does, state the constant of variation.

1. $y = 8x$ yes; 8

2. $6x = y$ yes; 6

3. $y = 5$ no

4. $y = \frac{1}{3}x$ yes; $\frac{1}{3}$

5. $\frac{y}{x} = 4$ yes; 4

6. $y = \frac{12}{x}$ no

7. $y + 3x = 0$ yes; -3

8. $xy + 4 = y$ no

9. $\frac{x}{6} = y$ yes; $\frac{1}{6}$

10. $y = \frac{16}{x}$ no

11. $\frac{x}{y} = \frac{3}{4}$ yes; $\frac{4}{3}$

12. $2x - 3y = 6$ no

WRITTEN EXERCISES

A. Find the constant of variation k. Let y vary directly as x.

1. If $x = 7$ when $y = 3$, then $k = $ _____. $\frac{3}{7}$

2. If $x = 2$ when $y = 3$, then $k = $ _____. $\frac{3}{2}$

3. If $x = -4$ when $y = 8$, then $k = $ _____. -2

4. If $x = 1$ when $y = -7$, then $k = $ _____. -7

5. If $x = 72$ when $y = 12$, then $k = $ _____. $\frac{1}{6}$

6. If $x = -2$ when $y = -10$, then $k = $ _____.   5

7. If $x = 13$ when $y = 195$, then $k = $ _____.   15

8. If $x = 8$ when $y = -184$, then $k = $ _____. -23

Let y vary directly as x.

9. If $y = 6$ when $x = 4$, find y when $x = 10$.   15

10. If $y = 10$ when $x = 2$, find y when $x = -2$. -10

11. If $x = -3$ when $y = -2$, find x when $y = -4$. -6

12. If $x = 4$ when $y = -3$, find x when $y = 0$.   0

MIXED REVIEW

Simplify.

1. $-104 + 89$ -15

2. $\frac{14 - 2}{2} + 3(7 + 1)$ 30

3. $(6 + 4)(54 \div 9)$ 60

4. $2^3 a^5 (a^8)$ $8a^{13}$

5. $\left[7 + \left(\frac{15 - 3}{4} + 4\right)\right] \div (28 \div 4)$ 2

TEACHER'S RESOURCE MASTERS

Practice Master 42, Part 2

ASSIGNMENT GUIDE

Minimum
5–11 odd, 13–24

Regular
15–28

Maximum
17–32

B. Give the direct-variation equation for each of the following:

13. The total cost c of repair work completed at $12 an hour varies directly as the time t in hours. $c = 12t$

14. When a car travels at a constant rate of 55 miles per hour, the distance d in miles is directly proportional to the time t in hours. $d = 55t$

15. When a typist types 60 words per minute, the number of words n varies directly as the time t spent typing.

16. The total cost c of items selling for $2.50 each is directly proportional to the number i of items. $c = 2.5i$

Use your answers from exercises 13–16 to find the following:

17. c, if $t = 8$ hours $96

18. d, if $t = 4$ hours   220 miles

19. t, if $n = 2700$ words   45 minutes

20. i, if $c = 37.50 15 items

Solve each problem by using the direct-variation method.

21. Ernestine drove 12,000 miles last year and spent $950 on gas and maintenance. If the cost of gas and maintenance varies directly as the number of miles driven, what would the cost of driving 9000 miles be? $712.50

22. The amount of gas used by a car varies directly as the distance traveled. If a car uses 16 gallons of gas to travel 336 miles, how many gallons of gas will be used on a trip of 840 miles?

23. A salesperson earns a $3000 commission on a sale of $150,000. At the same rate, what will the salesperson's commission be on a sale of $90,000?

24. A certain kind of carpeting costs $18.50 per square yard. At the same rate per square yard, how much carpeting will $425.50 buy?   23 square yards

25. Lisa earned $170 for 40 hours of work. If the amount Lisa earns varies directly as the number of hours worked, how much will she earn for 65 hours of work? $276.25

26. The amount of sales tax is directly proportional to the cost of a boat. If the tax on a boat costing $13,000 is $650, what will the tax be on a boat costing $11,500? $575

27. A carpenter earns $50 for a job that takes 4 hours to complete. If the labor cost of the job varies directly as the number of hours it takes to complete the job, how much will the carpenter earn for a 7-hour job? $87.50

28. The weight of an object on the moon is directly proportional to its weight on the earth. If an astronaut who weighs 156 pounds on the earth weighs 26 pounds on the moon, how much would Renaldo weigh on the moon if he weighs 192 pounds on the earth?   32 pounds

29. On a map, $1\frac{1}{2}$ inches represents 50 miles. How many miles will $4\frac{1}{2}$ inches represent?   150 miles

30. There are 140 calories in $3\frac{1}{2}$ cups of cooked broccoli. How many calories are in one cup?

C. 31. In the troy system of weights, $1\frac{1}{2}$ pounds of gold is equivalent to 8640 grains. If the weight of gold in pounds varies directly as its weight in grains, how many grains is 2 ounces of gold?

32. The weight of a brass pipe is directly proportional to its length. If a 2.4-meter length of this pipe weighs 3.6 kilograms, what will a 750-centimeter length of this pipe weigh?   11.25 kg

10.2 | Ratio and Proportion

You know that $y = kx$ describes a direct variation. If the two ordered pairs (x_1, y_1) and (x_2, y_2) are solutions of $y = kx$ when $x_1 \neq 0$ and $x_2 \neq 0$, then

$$y_1 = kx_1 \text{ and } y_2 = kx_2.$$

From these equations you can find the **ratios** (quotients) $\frac{y_1}{x_1}$ and $\frac{y_2}{x_2}$.

$$\frac{y_1}{x_1} = k \text{ and } \frac{y_2}{x_2} = k$$

Since each ratio equals k, the ratios themselves are equal.

$$\frac{y_1}{x_1} = \frac{y_2}{x_2}$$

An equation that states that two ratios are equal is called a **proportion.** For example, the ratios $\frac{3}{5}$ and $\frac{6}{10}$ are equal, and $\frac{3}{5} = \frac{6}{10}$ is a proportion. Notice that $3(10) = 5(6)$.

In the proportion below, y_1 and x_2 are the **extremes,** and x_1 and y_2 are the **means.** In a proportion, the product of the extremes is equal to the product of the means.

extremes ↘   ↙ means
$$\frac{y_1}{x_1} = \frac{y_2}{x_2}$$
means ↗   ↖ extremes

Proportions are useful in solving direct-variation problems. The problems in Examples 1 and 2 in Section 10.1 can be solved by using a proportion.

EXAMPLES

| 1 | **If Chris traveled 288 miles in his car on 16 gallons of gasoline, how many gallons will Chris's car need to travel 720 miles?** |

SOLUTION

Use the ratio $\dfrac{16 \text{ gallons used}}{288 \text{ miles traveled}}$.

Let $x =$ the number of gallons needed to travel 720 miles. Write the proportion.

$$\frac{\text{gallons of gasoline used}}{\text{number of miles traveled}} = \frac{x \text{ gallons}}{\text{number of miles to be traveled}}$$

Substitute the numbers given in the problem and rewrite the proportion.

$$\frac{16}{288} = \frac{x}{720}$$

$16 \cdot 720 = 288 \cdot x$ *Product of extremes equals product of means.*

$$x = \frac{16 \cdot 720}{288}$$

$$x = 40$$

Chris's car needs 40 gallons of gasoline to travel 720 miles.

CHECK

Does 40 gallons seem to be a reasonable amount of gasoline needed to travel 720 miles if a car can travel 288 miles on 16 gallons?

OBJECTIVES

Solve a proportion that contains a variable.

Solve a direct-variation problem by using a proportion.

TEACHER'S NOTES

See p. T33.

CLASSROOM EXAMPLES

1. If Barbara traveled 450 miles in her car on 18 gallons of gasoline, how many gallons will Barbara's car need to travel 700 miles?

   Let $x =$ the number of gallons needed to travel 700 miles.

   $$\frac{18}{450} = \frac{x}{700}$$
   $$18 \cdot 700 = 450 \cdot x$$
   $$x = \frac{18 \cdot 700}{450}$$
   $$x = 28$$

   Barbara's car needs 28 gallons of gasoline to travel 700 miles.

2. If Steven worked 8 hours and earned $28, how much will he earn if he works 13 hours?

   Let $x =$ amount earned in 13 hours.

   $$\frac{8}{28} = \frac{13}{x}$$
   $$8 \cdot x = 13 \cdot 28$$
   $$x = \frac{13 \cdot 28}{8}$$
   $$x = 45.50$$

   Steven will earn $45.50 for working 13 hours.

1. $-9st^2(-8s^2t^2 + 5t)$
   $72s^3t^4 - 45st^3$

2. $(3x^2 - 7x - 40) \div$
   $(x - 5)$ $3x + 8$

3. $(16r^2 + 12rs + 8s^2)$
   $+ (-9r^2 - 6rs - 3s^2)$
   $7r^2 + 6rs + 5s^2$

4. $(42xy^2 + 6xy - 5)$
   $- (30xy^2 - 6xy + 8)$
   $12xy^2 + 12xy - 13$

5. 62% of 430   266.6

TEACHER'S RESOURCE
MASTERS

Practice Master 43, Part 1

Quiz 19

ASSIGNMENT GUIDE

Minimum
5–15 odd, 27–35

Regular
21–35

Maximum
21–39 odd, 41–45

ADDITIONAL ANSWERS

Oral Exercises

3. means y_1 and x_2
   extremes x_1 and y_2

6. means 60 and 75
   extremes 25 and 180

---

2 **If Lynn worked 4 hours and earned \$15, how much will she earn if she works 9 hours?**

SOLUTION

Let x = amount earned in 9 hours.

$\dfrac{4}{15} = \dfrac{9}{x}$ *Write the proportion.*

$4 \cdot x = 9 \cdot 15$ *Product of extremes equals product of means.*

$x = \dfrac{9 \cdot 15}{4}$

$x = 33.75$

Lynn will earn \$33.75 for working 9 hours.

CHECK

Does \$33.75 seem to be a reasonable amount of pay for 9 hours of work if the pay for 4 hours of work is \$15?

ORAL EXERCISES

Name the means and the extremes for each proportion.

1. $\dfrac{a}{b} = \dfrac{c}{d}$ means b and c extremes a and d

2. $\dfrac{2}{3} = \dfrac{8}{12}$ means 3 and 8   extremes 2 and 12

3. $\dfrac{x_1}{y_1} = \dfrac{x_2}{y_2}$

4. $\dfrac{5}{2} = \dfrac{15}{6}$ means 2 and 15   extremes 5 and 6

5. $\dfrac{18}{24} = \dfrac{3}{4}$ means 24 and 3   extremes 18 and 4

6. $\dfrac{25}{60} = \dfrac{75}{180}$

The ordered pairs below belong to a direct variation. Give a proportion for each.

7. (4, 3); (12, 9) $\dfrac{3}{4} = \dfrac{9}{12}$

8. (2, 1); (8, 4) $\dfrac{1}{2} = \dfrac{4}{8}$

9. (3, 5); (12, 20) $\dfrac{5}{3} = \dfrac{20}{12}$

10. (4, 9); (20, 45) $\dfrac{9}{4} = \dfrac{45}{20}$

11. (−5, 3); (−20, 12) $\dfrac{3}{-5} = \dfrac{12}{-20}$

12. (9, −4); (36, −16) $\dfrac{-4}{9} = \dfrac{-16}{36}$

WRITTEN EXERCISES

A. Given that (x_1, y_1) and (x_2, y_2) are ordered pairs of the same direct variation, complete each exercise below.

1. $x_1 = 9, y_1 = 17$
   $x_2 = 36, y_2 = ?$ 68

2. $x_1 = 18, y_1 = ?$
   $x_2 = 54, y_2 = 33$ 11

3. $x_1 = 19, y_1 = 53$
   $x_2 = ?, y_2 = 265$ 95

4. $x_1 = ?, y_1 = 41$
   $x_2 = 156, y_2 = 246$ 26

5. $x_1 = 105, y_1 = 216$
   $x_2 = 210, y_2 = ?$ 432

6. $x_1 = 4.8, y_1 = ?$
   $x_2 = 2.4, y_2 = 1$ 2

7. $x_1 = 3.75, y_1 = 5$
   $x_2 = ?, y_2 = 9$ 6.75

8. $x_1 = ?, y_1 = \dfrac{1}{8}$
   $x_2 = \dfrac{2}{3}, y_2 = \dfrac{1}{2}$ $\frac{1}{6}$

Solve each proportion.

9. $\frac{2}{3} = \frac{x}{18}$ 12

10. $\frac{3}{4} = \frac{36}{y}$ 48

11. $\frac{1}{6} = \frac{-2}{n}$ -12

12. $\frac{2}{7} = \frac{-6}{m}$ -21

13. $\frac{4}{3} = \frac{9}{a}$ $\frac{27}{4}$

14. $\frac{5}{6} = \frac{3}{x}$ $\frac{18}{5}$

15. $\frac{y}{16} = \frac{3}{12}$ 4

16. $\frac{4}{a} = \frac{3}{15}$ 20

17. $\frac{n}{16} = \frac{45}{48}$ 15

18. $\frac{4}{m} = \frac{5}{30}$ 24

19. $\frac{6}{5} = \frac{x}{105}$ 126

20. $\frac{4}{3} = \frac{13}{x}$ $\frac{39}{4}$

B. 21. $\frac{12}{3x} = \frac{10}{3}$ $\frac{6}{5}$

22. $\frac{4}{3y} = \frac{8}{3}$ $\frac{1}{2}$

23. $\frac{8}{a + 1} = \frac{4}{1}$ 1

24. $\frac{n + 2}{3} = \frac{2n}{4}$ 4

25. $\frac{6}{x + 1} = 2$ 2

26. $\frac{9}{y + 1} = 3$ 2

27. $\frac{n + 3}{5} = \frac{2n}{7}$ 7

28. $\frac{-3}{x - 5} = \frac{4}{x + 2}$ 2

29. $\frac{2}{a - 6} = \frac{-4}{a + 3}$ 3

30. $\frac{-4}{2x - 7} = \frac{-3}{3x + 5}$ $-\frac{41}{6}$

31. $\frac{-5}{2n + 7} = \frac{-2}{3n - 4}$ $\frac{34}{11}$

32. $\frac{4}{3y + 2} = \frac{5}{4y - 3}$ 22

Solve each problem by using a proportion.

33. A worker's wages vary directly as the number of hours worked. If $34 is earned for 8 hours of work, how much is earned for 40 hours of work? $170

34. A car used 11 gallons of gasoline to go 253 miles. At that rate, how much gasoline would the car use to go 368 miles? 16 gallons

35. A bus driver travels 172 kilometers in 2 hours. If the distance traveled at a constant rate is directly proportional to the length of time spent traveling, how far will the driver travel in 3 hours?
258 km

36. A recipe for biscuits calls for $\frac{1}{2}$ teaspoon of baking powder and for $\frac{3}{4}$ cup of flour. If the recipe must be increased to include 3 cups of flour, how many teaspoons of baking powder will be required? 2 teaspoons

37. A mixture for outboard-motor fuel calls for 16 ounces of oil for *every* 5 gallons of gasoline. How many ounces of oil should be mixed with $7\frac{1}{2}$ gallons of gasoline? 24 oz

38. There are 16.2 grams of protein in 3 cups of cooked oatmeal. How many grams of protein are there in 4 cups of cooked oatmeal? 21.6 g

39. On a map, 3 centimeters represents 80 kilometers. How many kilometers does 9.6 centimeters represent? 256 km

40. Two cyclists ride their bicycles 4.8 kilometers in $\frac{1}{2}$ hour. At this rate, how far would they travel in $3\frac{1}{2}$ hours?

Written Exercises
40. 33.6 km
41. 1.18 m and 2.36 m

C. 41. A board 3.54 meters long is to be cut into two pieces having lengths in the ratio 1 to 2. Find the length of each piece. (HINT: Let x and $3.54 - x$ equal the lengths of the two pieces.)

42. Two numbers are in a 2 to 3 ratio. The sum of the numbers is 60. Find the two numbers. 24, 36

Solve for x.

43. $\frac{x^2 - 4}{x^2 - x - 6} = \frac{3}{4}$ -1

44. $\frac{x^2 - 9}{x^2 - 8x + 15} = \frac{1}{3}$ -7

45. $\frac{x^2 - 9}{x^2 - x - 6} = \frac{7}{6}$ 4

Proportions and Percents

OBJECTIVE

Solve a percent problem by using the proportion $\frac{\text{part}}{\text{whole}} = \frac{\text{percent amount}}{100}$.

TEACHER'S NOTES

See p. T33.

In Chapter 3, you saw how percent problems can be solved by using an equation. Another method of solving percent problems involves the use of the general proportion $\frac{\text{part}}{\text{whole}} = \frac{\text{percent amount}}{100}$.

EXAMPLES

| 1 | **What number is 72% of 50?** |

SOLUTION

Substitute the numbers given for the means and the extremes of the general proportion. Let x represent the unknown quantity (the part).

$$\frac{x}{50} = \frac{72}{100} \quad \textit{Set up the proportion.}$$

$100x = 3600$ *Cross multiply.*

$x = 36$ *Divide.*

72% of 50 is 36.

| 2 | **72 is what percent of 160?** |

SOLUTION

Substitute the numbers given for the means and the extremes of the general proportion. Let x represent the unknown quantity (the percent amount).

$$\frac{72}{160} = \frac{x}{100}$$

$160x = 7200$

$x = 45$

72 is 45% of 160.

| 3 | **72 is 36% of what number?** |

SOLUTION

Substitute the numbers given for the means and the extremes of the general proportion. Let x represent the unknown quantity (the whole).

$$\frac{72}{x} = \frac{36}{100}$$

$36x = 7200$

$x = 200$

72 is 36% of 200.

NOTE: When possible, you might want to reduce one of the ratios before cross multiplying.

TEACHER'S RESOURCE MASTERS

Practice Master 43, Part 2

Tell what proportion you would use to solve each problem.

1. What number is 75% of 12? $\frac{x}{12} = \frac{75}{100}$

2. 9 is what percent of 45? $\frac{9}{45} = \frac{x}{100}$

3. 15 is 25% of what number? $\frac{15}{x} = \frac{25}{100}$

4. 4 is what percent of 40? $\frac{4}{40} = \frac{x}{100}$

5. What number is 90% of 40? $\frac{x}{40} = \frac{90}{100}$

6. 12 is 60% of what number? $\frac{12}{x} = \frac{60}{100}$

7. 6 is what percent of 15? $\frac{6}{15} = \frac{x}{100}$

8. 34 is 50% of what number? $\frac{34}{x} = \frac{50}{100}$

9. 28 is what percent of 35? $\frac{28}{35} = \frac{x}{100}$

10. 6 is 3% of what number? $\frac{6}{x} = \frac{3}{100}$

ASSIGNMENT GUIDE

Minimum
1–9 odd, 13–17

Regular
9–18

Maximum
11–20

WRITTEN EXERCISES

A. 1–10. Solve each percent problem in Oral Exercises, using a proportion.

B. Solve by using a proportion.

11. One kind of wallpaper is on sale for 25% off the suggested retail price. The retail price of an order is $259. What is the sale price of the order? $194.25

12. Bill had purchased shares of stock for $52.25 each and then sold them for $62.70. What was the percent of profit? 20%

13. In an election, 3500 votes were cast in a certain city precinct. Of these, 70 votes were disallowed because of spoiled ballots. What percent of the votes cast was disallowed? 2%

14. When Emerald received her monthly credit-card statement, it showed a minimum payment due of $13.95, which was 31% of her balance. What was her balance before the payment was made?

15. Bernice sells machinery. Her salary is $350 per month plus 2% of her sales that exceed $500,000 for a given month. What is her salary for a month in which she sells $650,000 worth of machinery? $3350

16. In a high-school survey, 16% of the students said that they drove to school each day. If 332 students drove to school each day, what was the total enrollment of the school? 2075 students

17. Pedro's net pay for one month was $830. For the same month, his expenses were $350 for rent, $84.30 for his car, $135 for food, and $78.10 for utilities. Pedro's monthly expenses were what percent of his net pay? 78%

18. David won the state lottery. His prize was 3.5 million dollars, of which he had to pay 30% in taxes. If he invested 45% of his money after taxes, what amount did he not invest? $1,347,500

C. 19. Twelve students from a certain high school won awards at an elocution contest. This was $16\frac{2}{3}$% of those who competed in the contest. How many students competed in the contest? 72 students

20. If a company must pay a city tax amounting to 0.3% of each employee's gross pay, how much annual tax must a company that employs 125 people with an average gross income of $900 per week pay? $17,550

ADDITIONAL ANSWERS

Written Exercises

1. 9

2. 20%

3. 60

4. 10%

5. 36

6. 20

7. 40%

8. 68

9. 80%

10. 200

14. $45.00

SELF-QUIZ

Find the constant of variation k. Let y vary directly as x.

1. If $x = -3$ when $y = 5$, then $k = $ _____. $-\frac{5}{3}$

2. If $x = 12$ when $y = -7$, then $k = $ _____. $-\frac{7}{12}$

3. If $x = -8$ when $y = -11$, then $k = $ _____. $\frac{11}{8}$

Let y vary directly as x.

4. If $y = 8$ when $x = 5$, find y when $x = 15$. 24

5. If $y = -6$ when $x = 7$, find y when $x = 84$. -72

6. If $x = -4$ when $y = -3$, find x when $y = -15$. -20

Solve each proportion.

7. $\frac{7}{8} = \frac{16}{a}$ $\frac{128}{7}$

8. $\frac{a+3}{16} = \frac{a}{10}$ 5

9. $\frac{n}{3} = \frac{2n-1}{5}$ 3

10. $\frac{2x+1}{18} = \frac{4x-3}{21}$ $\frac{5}{2}$

Solve by using a proportion.

11. 52 is what percent of 65? 80%

12. 65 is 65% of what number? 100

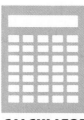

CALCULATOR

You can use the memory keys $\boxed{\text{M+}}$ and $\boxed{\text{RM}}$ to check whether a relation is an example of direct variation.

Example: Given the relation {(2, 6), (3, 9), (4, 12)}, determine whether the relation is an example of a direct variation.

Using the first ordered pair (2, 6), store the quotient $\frac{y}{x}$ in the memory of the calculator. If the relation is a direct variation, then $\frac{y}{x} = k$, where k is a constant for each ordered pair (x, y). So $y = kx$. Then check each ordered pair, using the equation $y = kx$.

	ENTER	DISPLAY	
Use (2, 6).	$6 \boxed{\div} 2 \boxed{=} \boxed{\text{M+}}$	$\exists$	This is the constant value k.
Check (3, 9).	$\boxed{\text{C}} 3 \boxed{\times} \boxed{\text{RM}} \boxed{=}$	$\mathsf{5}$	Each display should agree with each value of y.
Check (4, 12).	$\boxed{\text{C}} 4 \boxed{\times} \boxed{\text{RM}} \boxed{=}$	$\mathsf{12}$	

EXERCISES

Determine whether each relation is a direct variation.

1. {(3.2, 16), (5, 25), (7.9, 39.25)}

2. {(3.4, 15.3), (5.8, 26.1), (6.7, 30.15)}

3. {(2, 5), (1.25, 3.125), (2.5, 6.25)}

CALCULATOR

Exercises

1. not a direct variation

2. is a direct variation

3. is a direct variation

<table>
<tr><td>10.4</td><td>## Inverse Variation</td></tr>
</table>

OBJECTIVES

Determine if an equation describes an inverse variation.

Write the equation of an inverse variation that is described by words.

Solve a problem by using the inverse-variation method.

Louise bought a can of paint that will cover 30 square meters. If she is to paint a rectangular region with an area of 30 square meters, what are some possible lengths and widths of the area she is to paint?

You know that the formula for finding the area of a rectangle is $A = \ell w$ (Area = length × width). So possible solutions are listed in the table below.

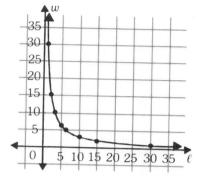

ℓ	1	2	3	5	6	10	15	30
w	30	15	10	6	5	3	2	1

The relation between ℓ and w can be graphed as follows:

The relation above can be expressed by the equation $\ell w = 30$. As the length ℓ becomes larger, the width w becomes smaller, and vice versa. This is an example of an **inverse variation**.

> **An inverse variation is a function defined by an equation of the form $xy = k$ or $y = \frac{k}{x}$ when $x \neq 0$ and k is a nonzero real-number constant.**

Since $y = \frac{k}{x}$ can be written as $y = k \cdot \frac{1}{x}$, y is directly proportional to $\frac{1}{x}$, which is the multiplicative inverse of x. In the inverse variation $y = \frac{k}{x}$, y varies inversely as x, or y is said to be *inversely proportional* to x.

The variable k is called the *constant of variation* or the *constant of proportionality*.

EXAMPLE

The number n of days needed to build a garage varies inversely as the number c of carpenters working. If it takes 12 days for 2 carpenters to build a garage, how many carpenters are needed to complete the job in 4 days?

SOLUTION

Solve for k, then for c.

$n = \dfrac{k}{c}$ *Write an inverse-variation equation.*

$12 = \dfrac{k}{2}$ *Substitute for n and c.*

$k = 12 \cdot 2 = 24$ *Solve for k.*

$4 = \dfrac{24}{c}$ *Substitute for k and n.*

$c = \dfrac{24}{4} = 6$ *Solve for c.*

It will take 6 carpenters to build the garage in 4 days.

TEACHER'S NOTES

See p. T33.

CLASSROOM EXAMPLE

The number n of days needed to build a room addition varies inversely as the number c of carpenters working. If it takes 15 days for 3 carpenters to build the addition, how many carpenters are needed to complete the job in 9 days?

Solve for k, then for c.

$n = \frac{k}{c}$

$15 = \frac{k}{3}$

$k = 15 \cdot 3 = 45$

$9 = \frac{45}{c}$

$c = \frac{45}{9} = 5$

It will take 5 carpenters to build the addition in 9 days.

Evaluate.

1. 16% of 420. 67.2

2. 30 is what percent of 150? 20%

3. 3 is 15% of what number? 20

4. What is 42% of 800? 336

5. What is 116% of 40? 46.4

TEACHER'S RESOURCE MASTERS

Practice Master 44, Part 1

ASSIGNMENT GUIDE

Minimum
1–8, 9–27 odd

Regular
1–7 odd, 9–28

Maximum
9–30

ADDITIONAL ANSWERS

Written Exercises

17. 2.4 h

ORAL EXERCISES

Tell whether each equation is an example of inverse variation.

1. $xy = 3$ yes

2. $y = 3x$ no

3. $\frac{y}{x} = 3$ no

4. $\frac{3}{x} = y$ yes

5. $xy = \frac{1}{3}$ yes

6. $\frac{x}{y} = \frac{1}{3}$ no

7. $y = \frac{1}{x}$ yes

8. $6 = \frac{y}{2x}$ no

9. $y = \frac{14}{3x}$ yes

10. $\frac{y}{3x} = 8$ no

11. $y = \frac{1}{3} \cdot \frac{1}{x}$ yes

12. $\frac{x}{5} = \frac{3}{y}$ yes

13. $xy = \frac{5}{8}$ yes

14. $\frac{x}{2} = \frac{7}{y}$ yes

15. $3y = \frac{6}{x}$ yes

WRITTEN EXERCISES

A. Find the constant of variation k if y varies inversely as x.

1. $y = 4$ when $x = 2$ 8

2. $y = 5$ when $x = 3$ 15

3. $y = 12$ when $x = 9$ 108

4. $y = 2.5$ when $x = 3$ 7.5

5. $y = \frac{9}{4}$ when $x = \frac{2}{3}$ $\frac{3}{2}$

6. $y = 1\frac{2}{3}$ when $x = \frac{3}{5}$ 1

7. $y = 2\frac{1}{4}$ when $x = \frac{3}{4}$ $1\frac{9}{16}$

8. $y = 1.75$ when $x = 0.6$ 1.05

For each of the following y varies inversely as x:

9. If $x = 8$ when $y = 9$, find x when $y = 18$. 4

10. If $x = 2$ when $y = 10$, find y when $x = 4$. 5

11. If $x = 3$ when $y = 12$, find y when $x = 6$. 6

12. If $x = 50$ when $y = 4$, find x when $y = 40$. 5

13. If $x = 2.1$ when $y = 1.1$, find y when $x = 1.1$. 2.1

14. If $x = 0.40$ when $y = 100$, find y when $x = 1.6$. 25

15. If $x = 1.25$ when $y = 4$, find x when $y = 8$. 0.625

16. If $x = 2.9$ when $y = 3$, find x when $y = 1.74$. 5

B. Solve each problem.

17. The time required to reach a destination varies inversely as the rate of travel. If Sylvia drives from her home to the beach at 30 miles per hour, it takes her 4 hours. If she drives at 50 miles per hour, how long will the trip to the beach take?

18. An electrical current varies inversely as the resistance. If the resistance in a certain electrical circuit is 12 ohms and the current is 15 amps, find the current when the resistance is 4 ohms. 45 amps

19. For a seesaw to balance, the distance of the person on each end from the balance point must vary inversely as the person's weight. Angela weighs 90 pounds and her brother weighs 180 pounds. How far from the balance point must Angela be to balance her brother, who is 3 feet from that point on the other side? 6 feet

20. When the tension on a wire is kept constant, the number of vibrations per second varies inversely as the length of the wire. A wire 200 centimeters long vibrates 520 times per second. How long should a wire be so that it will vibrate 320 times per second? 325 cm

21. A rectangle is 36 inches long and 14 inches wide. Another rectangle of equal area is 42 inches long. Find the width of the second rectangle. 12 inches

22. It takes 6 hours for a train to travel a certain distance at the rate of 50 miles per hour. If the train travels the same distance in 4 hours, what is its speed?

22. 75 mi/h

29. 5 lumens

23. The mass of an object varies inversely as its distance from a given point. Debbie has a mass of 24 kilograms and sits 2 meters from the center of a seesaw to balance her sister, who sits 1.5 meters from the center. What is her sister's mass? 32 kilograms

24. Three friends need to pay $100 each to purchase a tent. The cost per person varies inversely as the number of people sharing the cost. How many people would have to equally share the cost of the same tent to make the cost $60 per person? 5 people

25. For a high-school assembly, the number of chairs arranged in a column varies inversely as the distance between them. When the chairs are spaced 20 inches apart, 32 chairs will fit in a column. If the chairs are spaced 16 inches apart, how many chairs will fit in a column? 40 chairs

26. The number of days it takes to wire a building varies inversely as the number of electricians working on it. It takes 14 days for 2 electricians to wire the building. If the job has to be finished in 4 days, how many electricians are needed? 7 electricians

27. A triangle is 20 centimeters long and 10 centimeters high. Another triangle of equal area is 16 centimeters long. Find the height of the second triangle. 12.5 centimeters

28. The number of square tiles on a wall varies inversely as the area covered by the tiles. It takes 168 tiles, each with an area of 16 square inches, to cover the wall. How many tiles with an area of 4 square inches would it take to cover the same wall? 672 tiles

C. 29. The intensity I of a light varies inversely as the square of the distance d from the light. If a lamp bulb 2 feet from a book gives 20 lumens of illumination per square foot on the surface of the book, how many lumens does each square foot of the book receive when the book is held 4 feet from the bulb?

30. How far from a light should an object be placed to receive 4 times as much intensity as it received when it was 2 feet from the light? 1 foot

OBJECTIVE

Solve an inverse-variation problem by using a proportion.

TEACHER'S NOTES

See p. T34.

CLASSROOM EXAMPLE

If it takes 10 days for 3 carpenters to build a shed, how many carpenters are needed to complete the job in 6 days?

$$\frac{d_1}{d_2} = \frac{c_2}{c_1}$$

$$\frac{10}{6} = \frac{c_2}{3}$$

$$6c_2 = 10 \cdot 3$$

$$c_2 = \frac{30}{6}$$

$$c_2 = 5$$

Five carpenters are needed to build a shed in 6 days.

MIXED REVIEW

1. Solve $\frac{8x + 3}{x - 2} - 4 = \frac{5x + 9}{x - 2}$.
   0

2. Solve $3b - 15 = b + 37$. 26

3. Find the y-intercept of the line for $y = -5x + 14$.
   14

4. State the domain and range of the relation $\{(-8, 5), (-4, -10), (-12, -6), (-12, 5)\}$. $\{-8, -4, -12\}; \{5, -10, -6\}$

5. Simplify $-5x^3y(-8xy^2 + 4)$. $40x^4y^3 - 20x^3y$ or $20x^3y(2xy^2 - 1)$

10.5 | Inverse Variation and Proportions

In Section 10.2, you used proportions to solve problems involving direct variation. Proportions can also be used to solve problems involving inverse variation.

If two ordered pairs (x_1, y_1) and (x_2, y_2) are solutions of $y = \frac{k}{x}$, then $y_1 = \frac{k}{x_1}$ and $y_2 = \frac{k}{x_2}$.

From these ratios you can write the equations $x_1y_1 = k$ and $x_2y_2 = k$.

Since both x_1y_1 and x_2y_2 are equal to k, you can write $x_1y_1 = x_2y_2$.

Multiply both sides of this equation by $\frac{1}{x_2y_1}$.

$$x_1y_1\left(\frac{1}{x_2y_1}\right) = x_2y_2\left(\frac{1}{x_2y_1}\right)$$

$$\frac{x_1}{x_2} = \frac{y_2}{y_1}$$

extremes ⟶   ⟵ means

$$\frac{x_1}{x_2} = \frac{y_2}{y_1}$$

means ⟶   ⟵ extremes

EXAMPLE

If it takes 12 days for 2 carpenters to build a garage, how many carpenters are needed to complete the job in 4 days?

SOLUTION   Recall that in the example in Section 10.4, you were told that "the number n of days needed to build a garage varies inversely as the number c of carpenters working." Let c_1 and d_1 represent the number of carpenters and the number of days for one case. Let c_2 and d_2 represent the number of carpenters and the number of days for the other case. Then, according to the formula $\frac{x_1}{x_2} = \frac{y_2}{y_1}$ derived above, you can write the proportion $\frac{d_1}{d_2} = \frac{c_2}{c_1}$.

$$\frac{d_1}{d_2} = \frac{c_2}{c_1}$$

$$\frac{12}{4} = \frac{c_2}{2}$$

$$4c_2 = 12 \cdot 2 \quad \textit{Product of means equals product of extremes.}$$

$$c_2 = \frac{24}{4}$$

$$c_2 = 6$$

Six carpenters are needed to build a garage in 4 days.

CHECK   Does it seem reasonable that a job that takes 2 carpenters 12 days to complete will take 6 carpenters 4 days to complete?

The two ordered pairs in each exercise belong to an inverse variation. Give a proportion for each.

1. (1, 12); (4, 3)

2. (5, 6); (3, 10) $\frac{5}{3} = \frac{10}{6}$

3. (8, 3); (4, 6) $\frac{8}{4} = \frac{6}{3}$

4. $\left(\frac{1}{3}, 15\right)$; (5, 1)

5. (1, 3); $\left(12, \frac{1}{4}\right)$

6. (8, 2); (4, 4) $\frac{8}{4} = \frac{4}{2}$

7. (27, 2); (6, 9)

8. (7, 6); (21, 2) $\frac{7}{21} = \frac{2}{6}$

9. (6, 8); (24, 2) $\frac{6}{24} = \frac{2}{8}$

10. (2, 18); (12, 3)

11. (5, 8); (4, 10) $\frac{5}{4} = \frac{10}{8}$

12. $\left(\frac{1}{3}, 3\right)$; $\left(\frac{1}{2}, 2\right)$ $\frac{\frac{1}{3}}{\frac{1}{2}} = \frac{2}{3}$

ASSIGNMENT GUIDE

Minimum
1–11 odd, 13–20

Regular
7–20

Maximum
13–26

WRITTEN EXERCISES

ADDITIONAL ANSWERS

Oral Exercises
1. $\frac{1}{4} = \frac{3}{12}$
4. $\frac{\frac{1}{3}}{5} = \frac{1}{15}$
5. $\frac{1}{12} = \frac{\frac{1}{4}}{3}$
7. $\frac{27}{6} = \frac{9}{2}$
10. $\frac{2}{12} = \frac{3}{18}$

Written Exercises
13. 180 strides

A. In each table below, *y* is inversely proportional to *x*. Solve for the given letter.

1.
x	1	2	3	
y	18	a	6	9

2.
x	2	3	4	
y	6	4	b	3

3.
x	5	10	30	
y	a	6	2	12

4.
x	8	4	12	
y	3	6	b	2

5.
x	4	6	2	
y	9	a	18	6

6.
x	6	10	15	
y	b	3	2	5

7.
x	12	a	16	
y	4	6	3	8

8.
x	25	10	b	
y	2	5	8	6.25

9.
x	$1\frac{1}{2}$	3	a	
y	4	2	8	$\frac{3}{4}$

10.
x	2	8	a	
y	36	9	16	4.5

11.
x	8	10	25	
y	$12\frac{1}{2}$	10	b	4

12.
x	a	9	15	
y	$7\frac{1}{2}$	10	6	12

B. Solve each problem by using a proportion.

13. The number of strides required to walk a given distance is inversely proportional to the length of each stride. The length of Tim's stride is 3 feet. Each of Sheryl's strides measures 2 feet. If it takes Tim 120 strides to walk a certain distance, how many strides will it take Sheryl to walk the same distance?

14. The time required to audit the books of a small business is inversely proportional to the number of auditors employed. If 2 auditors can complete the audit in 3 days, how many days will 4 auditors require? $1\frac{1}{2}$ days

15. The number of days required to paint a house varies inversely as the number of painters hired. If it takes 2 painters 8 days to paint the house, how many days will it take if 4 painters are hired?
4 days

16. The number of revolutions made by a wheel rolling over a given distance varies inversely as the wheel's circumference. If a wheel with a circumference of 20 inches makes 100 turns in going a certain distance, how many turns will be made by a wheel with a circumference of 25 inches? 80 turns

18. 5 people

19. 100 plants

17. The number of square tiles on a floor is inversely proportional to the area of each tile. If it takes 150 tiles with an area of 1 square foot each to cover a floor, how many tiles with an area of $\frac{1}{2}$ square foot would it take to cover the floor? 300 tiles

18. A renter's share of the rent for an apartment is inversely proportional to the number of people sharing the cost. Three people sharing an apartment pay $150 each per month. How many people would be needed so that each would pay $90 per month?

19. The number of plants used to fill a row of given length in a garden varies inversely as the distance between each plant. If 75 plants are used to fill a row with the plants 20 centimeters apart, how many plants are used to fill the row with the plants 15 centimeters apart?

20. If 2 toothed gears mesh so that one can turn the other, the speeds of the gears vary inversely as the number of teeth in the gears. One gear has 16 teeth and a speed of 150 revolutions per minute. If the other gear has 50 teeth, what is its speed? 48 revolutions per minute

C. 21. Let y vary directly as x and vary inversely as w. If $y = 3$ when $x = 8$ and $w = 24$, find y when $x = 12$ and $w = 18$. (HINT: This is called a **combined variation** and can be expressed by the equation $y = \frac{k}{w}x$.) 6

22. Let y vary directly as x and vary directly as w. If $y = 21$ when $x = 9$ and $w = 7$, find y when $x = \frac{3}{4}$ and $w = 12$. (HINT: This is called a **joint variation** and can be expressed by the equation $y = kxw$.) 3

23. Let a be directly proportional to b and inversely proportional to c. If $a = 0.6$ when $b = 0.4$ and $c = 0.12$, find a when $b = 0.21$ and $c = 0.54$. 0.07

24. Let a be directly proportional to b and directly proportional to c. If $a = \frac{2}{3}$ when $b = \frac{3}{4}$ and $c = \frac{1}{2}$, find a when $b = \frac{3}{8}$ and $c = \frac{1}{4}$. $\frac{1}{6}$

25. Let a be directly proportional to b and inversely proportional to c. If $a = \frac{1}{2}$ when $b = \frac{3}{4}$ and $c = \frac{2}{3}$, find a when $b = \frac{7}{8}$ and $c = \frac{7}{9}$. $\frac{1}{2}$

26. Let a be directly proportional to b and directly proportional to c. If $a = 7.5$ when $b = 3$ and $c = 5$, find a when $b = 5.5$ and $c = 9.1$. 25.025

CHALLENGE

A large carton of yogurt has a diameter that is twice as large as that of a small carton. The large carton is also $1\frac{1}{2}$ times as high as the small carton. If the small carton is sold for $0.65, what should be the price of the large carton, assuming that both are sold at the same price per ounce? (Also assume that both cartons are cylindrical.) $3.90

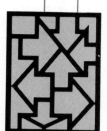

IN OTHER FIELDS
Mathematics and Music

Pythagoras is credited with being the first to apply mathematics to a musical scale. Using two vibrating strings of equal diameter and tension, he noted the relationship between musical harmony and whole numbers. He observed that when the lengths of the strings were in the ratio of 1:2, the strings differed in pitch by one octave. When the ratio was 2:3, the result was an interval of a fifth. An interval of a fourth resulted when the string lengths were in the ratio of 3:4.

You can achieve the same results when using a single string if you apply pressure at the point shown in the illustration below. Starting with any string and the note it sounds, you can go down the scale by increasing the length of the string according to simple fractions expressed as the ratios of whole numbers.

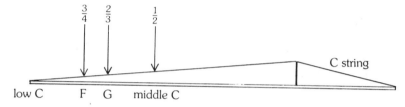

The illustration shows that musical intervals are governed by ratios of whole numbers. The length of the C string is reduced to $\frac{3}{4}$, $\frac{2}{3}$, and $\frac{1}{2}$ by pressing down on the C string at the points indicated. The resulting notes are F, G, and middle C.

Pythagoras further noted that when played at the same time, strings whose lengths were in the ratios 1:2, 2:3, and 3:4 produced consonant tones—that is, tones that are pleasant to listen to.

Pythagoras extended his observations concerning the relationship between musical harmony and whole numbers to include all harmony and all nature.

OBJECTIVE

Solve a problem that involves direct variation or inverse variation by using a proportion.

TEACHER'S NOTES

See p. T34.

CLASSROOM EXAMPLES

1. The safe following distance for 2 cars traveling 30 miles per hour is 54 feet. If the safe distance between 2 cars is directly proportional to the speed of the 2 cars, what would the safe following distance be for 2 cars traveling 55 miles per hour?

Let y_1 and y_2 represent the speeds and let x_1 and x_2 represent the distances.

$$\frac{y_1}{x_1} = \frac{y_2}{x_2}$$
$$\frac{30}{54} = \frac{55}{x_2}$$
$$54 \cdot 55 = 30 \cdot x_2$$
$$2970 = 30x_2$$
$$x_2 = 99$$

The safe following distance for 2 cars traveling 55 miles per hour is 99 feet.

2. If it takes 6 hours to travel a certain distance at the rate of 24 miles per hour, how long would it take to travel the same distance at the rate of 32 miles per hour? The time needed to travel varies inversely as the rate of travel.

Let x_1 and x_2 equal the times. Let y_1 and y_2 equal the rates of speed.

10.6 Problem Solving

EXAMPLES

1 According to the American Automobile Association, the safe following distance for 2 cars traveling 20 miles per hour is 36 feet. If the safe distance between 2 cars is directly proportional to the speed of the 2 cars, what would the safe following distance be for 2 cars traveling 50 miles per hour?

Understand: *Given:* The safe following distance for 2 cars traveling 20 miles per hour is 36 feet.

The safe distance between 2 cars is directly proportional to their speed.

To find: the safe following distance between 2 cars traveling 50 miles per hour

Plan: Let y_1 and y_2 represent the speeds and let x_1 and x_2 represent the distances. Since the safe distance between 2 cars is directly proportional to their speed, use the proportion $\frac{y_1}{x_1} = \frac{y_2}{x_2}$ and solve for x_2.

Solve:
$$\frac{20}{36} = \frac{50}{x_2}$$
$$36 \cdot 50 = 20 \cdot x_2$$
$$1800 = 20x_2$$
$$x_2 = 90$$

Answer: The safe following distance for 2 cars traveling 50 miles per hour is 90 feet.

Review: If 2 cars traveling 20 miles per hour should maintain a safe following distance of 36 feet, does it seem reasonable that 2 cars traveling 50 miles per hour should maintain a safe following distance of 90 feet?

2 If it takes 8 hours to travel a certain distance at the rate of 36 miles per hour, how long would it take to travel the same distance at the rate of 48 miles per hour? The time needed to travel varies inversely as the rate of travel.

Understand: *Given:* It takes 8 hours to travel a certain distance at the rate of 36 miles per hour.

The time varies inversely as the rate of travel.

To find: how long it would take to travel the same distance at the rate of 48 miles per hour

Plan: Let x_1 and x_2 equal the times. Let y_1 and y_2 equal the rates of speed. Since the time varies inversely as the rate of travel, use the proportion $\frac{x_1}{x_2} = \frac{y_2}{y_1}$ and solve for x_2.

Solve:
$$\frac{8}{x_2} = \frac{48}{36}$$
$$48 \cdot x_2 = 8 \cdot 36$$
$$48x_2 = 288$$
$$x_2 = 6$$

Answer: It would take 6 hours to cover the distance at the rate of 48 miles per hour.

Review: If it takes 8 hours to cover a distance at a rate of 36 miles per hour, does it seem reasonable that the same distance can be covered in 6 hours at 48 miles per hour?

$$\frac{x_1}{x_2} = \frac{y_2}{y_1}$$
$$\frac{6}{x_2} = \frac{32}{24}$$
$$32 \cdot x_2 = 6 \cdot 24$$
$$32x_2 = 144$$
$$x_2 = 4.5$$

It would take 4.5 hours to cover the distance at the rate of 32 miles per hour.

MIXED REVIEW
1. Evaluate $\frac{x + y + z}{y}$ if $x = -2$, $y = 3$, and $z = 0$.
$\frac{1}{3}$

2. Find the value of $5(5^2)$.
125

3. Find the product of $(-12x^3y^2)$ and $(-6x^2y^5)$.
$72x^5y^7$

4. 39 is what percent of 60?
65%

5. 12 is 25% of what number? 48

TEACHER'S RESOURCE MASTERS

Practice Master 45, Part 1

Quiz 20

ASSIGNMENT GUIDE

Minimum
1–10

Regular
5–14

Maximum
5–13 odd, 14–18

ORAL EXERCISES

Tell whether each equation defines a direct variation or an inverse variation.

1. $y = \frac{4}{x}$ inverse

2. $\frac{y}{x} = 7$ direct

3. $xy = 12$ inverse

4. $y - 3x = 0$ direct

5. $3x - y = 0$ direct

6. $x = \frac{1}{y}$ inverse

7. $kxy = 1$ inverse

8. $x_1y_1 = x_2y_2$ inverse

9. $\frac{x_1}{y_1} = \frac{x_2}{y_2}$ direct

WRITTEN EXERCISES

A. Solve each problem.

1. The weight of an object on the moon varies directly as its weight on the earth. A person who weighs 180 pounds on the earth weighs 30 pounds on the moon. How much would Manuela weigh on the moon if she weighs 138 pounds on the earth?   23 pounds

2. Cecilia bought dinner for Bob and left a 15% tip for the person who waited on them. If the amount of the tip is determined by the amount of the bill, which was $34.68, how much was the tip that Cecilia left? (Round your answer to the nearest cent.) $5.20

3. The labor costs for an automobile repair are directly proportional to the number of hours a mechanic works on a car. If the cost for 3 hours of work is $87, what will the labor cost be for 7 hours? $203

4. Juanita won the election for vice president of the senior class by a 6 to 5 margin. The losing candidate received 330 votes. How many votes did Juanita receive?   396 votes

B. **5.** The number of days needed to finish repairing a street is inversely proportional to the number of persons working. If it takes 12 days for two persons to repair the street, how many persons are needed to complete the work in 4 days?   6 persons

6. The amount of oatmeal required in a recipe for cookies is directly proportional to the amount of flour required. If the recipe calls for 3 measuring cups of oatmeal and 1 measuring cup of flour, how many cups of oatmeal should be used with $1\frac{1}{2}$ cups of flour? $4\frac{1}{2}$ cups

7. The area of a triangle remains constant while the length of the base varies. If the altitude is 6 feet when the base is 10 feet, find the altitude when the base is 20 feet. (Use $\frac{1}{2}bh = A$.)   3 feet

8. The number of inches that a spring will stretch varies directly as the weight causing it to stretch. If a spring stretches 5 inches under a weight of $4\frac{1}{2}$ pounds, how many inches will it stretch under a weight of 9 pounds?   10 inches

9. The cost of cleaning a carpet is directly proportional to the area of the carpet. The cost of cleaning a carpet that measures 12 feet by 9 feet is $21.60. At the same rate, how much will it cost to clean a carpet that measures 18 feet by 10 feet? $36

10. Unemployment in a certain state for the month of October rose 0.4% from the previous month. If this amounted to 2589 persons who were newly unemployed in October, how many persons were unemployed in September?

11. The current in an electrical circuit varies inversely as the resistance. When the resistance in a certain circuit is 12 ohms, the current is 30 amps. Find the current when the resistance is 18 ohms.   20 amps

12. When the tension on a wire is kept constant, the number of vibrations per second varies inversely as the length of the wire. A wire 400 centimeters long vibrates 160 times per second. How long should a wire be so that it will vibrate 240 times per second? (Round your answer to the nearest centimeter.)

ADDITIONAL ANSWERS

Written Exercises

10. 647,250 persons

12. 267 cm

13. A rectangular flower bed is to have a given area. When the length is 9 meters, the width is 5.5 meters. What is the length when the width is 6 meters?

14. Andrew walked for $1\frac{1}{2}$ hours at 3 miles per hour. How long would the return trip take if he walked at $2\frac{1}{2}$ miles per hour?   1 hour 48 minutes

13. 8.25 m

PROBLEM-SOLVING
STRATEGIES

Use Logical Reasoning
(2, 4, 6, 9, 10).

Write an Equation (1–12).

C. 15. Ho earned $11,975 a year. After receiving his promotion, his annual salary increased to $14,370 a year. This reflected an increase of what percent?   20%

16. Part of the closing costs for a mortgage loan is the points. Each point is 1% of the loan amount. If a mortgage loan for $71,820 is made, what amount of the closing costs will $3\frac{1}{2}$ points be? $2513.70

A **power function** is a function defined by an equation of the form $y = kx^2$ when k is a nonzero constant.

If (x_1, y_1) and (x_2, y_2) are ordered pairs of the same quadratic direct variation and neither pair is $(0, 0)$, then $\frac{y_1}{x_1^2} = \frac{y_2}{x_2^2}$ and y varies directly as x^2.

Example: Given that y varies directly as the *square* of x and that $y = 4$ when $x = 2$, find the value of y when $x = 8$.

$y = kx^2$

$4 = k \cdot 2^2$

$k = \dfrac{4}{2^2}$

$y = 1 \cdot 8^2$

$y = 64$

17. The distance required for a vehicle to come to a complete stop varies directly as the square of the speed of the vehicle. If the stopping distance for a vehicle traveling 16 kilometers per hour is 7 meters, what is the stopping distance for a vehicle traveling 48 kilometers per hour?   63 meters

18. The volume of a sphere varies directly as the cube of the radius. If the volume of a sphere with a radius of 5 centimeters is 125 times that of another sphere, what is the radius of the second sphere?   1 centimeter

CAREER
Veterinarian

Veterinarians diagnose and treat diseased or injured animals. They perform surgery and prescribe medicine and vaccines. They treat animals in hospitals and clinics or on farms and ranches.

Suppose a veterinarian has prescribed medication for a 50-pound dog. This medication will be given in four doses each day at a rate of 10 mg per pound per day. How much should each dose contain?

Suppose a veterinarian has diagnosed an 84-pound animal as 10% dehydrated. The animal should have 30% of its weight in fluids. How much fluid should be replaced?   125 mg; 2.52 lb

SKILLS MAINTENANCE

Solve.

1. $(8x + 3)(2x - 3) = (4x - 3)^2$ 3

2. $4(3y^2 - 2) = (6y - 1)(2y + 3)$ $-\frac{5}{16}$

3. $(x + 2)^2 = (x - 3)^2$ $\frac{1}{2}$

4. $(2y - 1)^2 = (3y - 2)^2 - 5y^2$ $\frac{3}{8}$

Find the slope of the line containing these points.

5. $(2, -3)$ and $(-4, 1)$ $-\frac{2}{3}$

6. $(5, 0)$ and $(5, -8)$ undefined

7. $(-8, 3)$ and $(4, 3)$ 0

8. $(-7, -2)$ and $(-5, 9)$ $\frac{11}{2}$

Write each equation in slope-intercept form. Then give the slope and the y-intercept.

9. $3x + 2y = 8$ $y = -\frac{3}{2}x + 4;\ -\frac{3}{2};\ 4$

10. $-5x - y = 10$

Write the equation of the line in slope-intercept form.

11. slope $= -2$; y-intercept $= 2$

12. slope $= \frac{3}{4}$; point on the line $= (4, -1)$

13. two points are $(5, 0)$ and $(0, 6)$

14. slope $= 8$; y-intercept $= -1$

Which values must be excluded from the replacement set of each variable so that the denominator will not equal zero?

15. $\dfrac{5x}{12(x + 2)}$ -2

16. $\dfrac{7(x - 3)}{7x}$ 0

17. $\dfrac{2x - 5}{8x - 3}$ $\frac{3}{8}$

18. $\dfrac{a - 3}{a^2 + a - 6}$ $2, -3$

19. $\dfrac{b + 4}{b^2 + 2b - 3}$ $1, -3$

20. $\dfrac{y^2 + 6y + 9}{y^2 + 7y + 12}$ $-3, -4$

Change each rational expression to simplest form.

21. $\dfrac{x^2 + x - 6}{x^2 + 6x + 9}$ $\frac{x - 2}{x + 3}$

22. $\dfrac{y^2 - 25}{y^2 - 4y - 5}$ $\frac{y + 5}{y + 1}$

23. $-\dfrac{-2n - 6}{n^2 - 2n - 15}$ $\frac{2}{n - 5}$

Find each product and express it in simplest form.

24. $\dfrac{x^2 - 6x}{x - 6} \cdot \dfrac{x + 3}{x}$ $x + 3$

25. $\dfrac{a^2 - 2a - 24}{a^2 - a - 30} \cdot \dfrac{a + 5}{a^2 - 16}$ $\frac{1}{a - 4}$

26. $\dfrac{x^2 - 3x - 10}{(x - 2)^2} \cdot \dfrac{x - 2}{x - 5}$ $\frac{x + 2}{x - 2}$

27. $\dfrac{5a + 5b}{a^2 - b^2} \cdot \dfrac{a^2 - ab}{(a + b)^2}$ $\frac{5a}{(a + b)^2}$

Find each quotient and express it in simplest form.

28. $\dfrac{x^2 + 2x + 1}{5x} \div (x + 1)$ $\frac{x + 1}{5x}$

29. $\dfrac{x^2 - y^2}{a^2 - b^2} \div \dfrac{x + y}{a + b}$ $\frac{x - y}{a - b}$

30. $\dfrac{x^2 - 64}{(x + 8)^2} \div \dfrac{3x - 24}{2x + 16}$ $\frac{2}{3}$

31. $\dfrac{x + y}{x - y} \div \dfrac{4x - 4y}{3x^2 - 3y^2}$ $\frac{3(x + y)^2}{4(x - y)}$

Add or subtract and express each answer in simplest form.

32. $\dfrac{4}{x + 3} + \dfrac{6}{x - 3}$ $\frac{2(5x + 3)}{(x - 3)(x + 3)}$

33. $\dfrac{2}{x + 4} + \dfrac{3}{x + 3}$ $\frac{5x + 18}{(x + 4)(x + 3)}$

34. $\dfrac{1}{2y^2} + \dfrac{7}{12z^2}$ $\frac{6z^2 + 7y^2}{12y^2z^2}$

35. $\dfrac{4x}{y^2} - \dfrac{3x}{y}$ $\frac{4x - 3xy}{y^2}$

Solve each equation and check the solution.

36. $\dfrac{2}{x + 3} = \dfrac{5}{x}$ -5

37. $\dfrac{x}{x - 3} + 4 = \dfrac{3}{x - 3}$ $\varnothing$

10. $y = -5x - 10;\ -5;\ -10$
11. $y = -2x + 2$
12. $y = \frac{3}{4}x - 4$
13. $y = -\frac{6}{5}x + 6$
14. $y = 8x - 1$

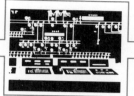

COMPUTER

Assume you have bought an amount of roofing material that will cover a gazebo you plan to build in your backyard. You are not sure of the dimensions you want for the gazebo, but you know you want it to be rectangular. Since you already have the roofing material, the area of your gazebo is established. Now, you want to know all the options available for the gazebo's dimensions so you can make a choice.

The program below first asks you to input an area of a rectangle, and then it lists all the possible dimensions. The program does this much more quickly, and probably more accurately, than you could do it without a computer.

```
10 REM VARIATIONS ON LENGTH & WIDTH WITH CONSTANT AREA
20 PRINT: PRINT
30 INPUT "ENTER CONSTANT AREA OF RECTANGLE? ";AREA
40 FOR LNGTH = 1 TO AREA
50 WIDTH = AREA / LNGTH: IF WIDTH = INT (AREA / LNGTH)
   THEN GOSUB 100
60 NEXT LNGTH
70 PRINT "NUMBER OF POSSIBLE RECTANGLES WITH"
80 PRINT "INTEGER SIDES IS ";AMT
90 END
100 PRINT "LENGTH = ";LNGTH;", WIDTH = ";WIDTH
110 AMT = AMT + 1
120 RETURN
```

EXERCISES

1. Enter and RUN the program. Do you notice any pattern? What is it?

2. Enter prime numbers for the constant area. What results do you get?

3. Modify the program so that it prints all the possible dimensions for a constant *volume* (v = lwh).

CHAPTER 10 REVIEW

VOCABULARY

direct variation (10.1)   inverse variation (10.4)   proportion (10.2)

extremes (10.2)   means (10.2)   ratio (10.2)

REVIEW EXERCISES

10.1 **Find the constant of variation k. Let y vary directly as x.**

 1. If $x = 9$ when $y = 4$, then $k =$ _____ $\frac{4}{9}$.

 2. If $x = -5$ when $y = 3$, then $k =$ _____ $-\frac{3}{5}$.

 3. If $x = 6$ when $y = -12$, then $k =$ _____ -2.

 4. If $x = -11$ when $y = -143$, then $k =$ _____ 13.

 Let y vary directly as x.

 5. If $y = 3$ when $x = 8$, find y when $x = 48$. 18

 6. If $y = -7$ when $x = 4$, find y when $x = 28$. -49

 7. If $x = 6$ when $y = -5$, find x when $y = -45$. 54

 8. If $x = -9$ when $y = -2$, find x when $y = -6$. -27

 Solve.

 9. A car requires 12 gallons of gasoline to travel 300 miles. If the number of gallons g of gasoline used varies directly as the number of miles m traveled, how many gallons are required for a trip of 750 miles? 30 gallons

10.2 **Given that (x_1, y_1) and (x_2, y_2) are ordered pairs of the same direct variation, complete each exercise below.**

 10. $x_1 = 3, y_1 = ?$ **11.** $x_1 = ?, y_1 = 64$

  $x_2 = 7, y_2 = 42$ 18 $x_2 = 32, y_2 = 256$ 8

 12. $x_1 = 17, y_1 = 38$ **13.** $x_1 = 3.6, y_1 = ?$

  $x_2 = 85, y_2 = ?$ 190 $x_2 = 1.2, y_2 = 1$ 3

 Solve each proportion.

 14. $\frac{4}{3} = \frac{5}{x}$ $\frac{15}{4}$ **15.** $\frac{1}{8} = \frac{-2}{n}$ -16 **16.** $\frac{8}{3x} = \frac{16}{3}$ $\frac{1}{2}$

 17. $\frac{a + 3}{5} = \frac{2a}{7}$ 7 **18.** $\frac{-3}{m - 5} = \frac{4}{m + 2}$ 2 **19.** $\frac{-5}{2n - 7} = \frac{-2}{3n + 5}$

 20. If a recipe that calls for $\frac{1}{3}$ teaspoon of salt and for $\frac{2}{3}$ cup of flour is increased to include 2 cups of flour, how many teaspoons of salt are required? 1 teaspoon

10.3 **Solve by using a proportion.**

 21. 24 is what percent of 32? 75%   **22.** 14 is 40% of what number? 35

23. What number is 56% of 125?   70

24. 24 is what percent of 80?   30%

25. 15 is 60% of what number?   25

26. What number is 38% of 300?   114

27. All but 15% of Frances' salary goes into her savings account. If Frances' salary is $650, what amount goes into savings? $552.50

28. Of the first 80 days of the school year, Bobby Joe was present 76 days. What percent of the days was he in attendance?   95%

29. To pay for her car insurance, Laura earned $108. This was 48% of the total premium. What was the amount of the premium? $225

10.4   **For each equation, tell whether it describes a direct or an inverse variation.**

30. $y = 8x$ direct

31. $\frac{y}{x} = 6$ direct

32. $\frac{6}{x} = y$ inverse

33. $xy = 14$ inverse

34. $8 = \frac{y}{4x}$ direct

35. $y = \frac{12}{5x}$ inverse

For each of the following, y varies inversely as x:

36. If $x = 3$ when $y = 12$, find x when $y = 9$.   4

37. If $x = 5$ when $y = 35$, find x when $y = 7$.   25

38. If $x = 12$ when $y = 48$, find y when $x = 16$.   36

39. If $x = 3.1$ when $y = 2.2$, find y when $x = 2.2$.   3.1

10.5   **In each table below, y is inversely proportional to x. Solve for the given letter.**

40.

x	1	2	3
y	12	a	4

6

41.

x	8	b	12
y	3	6	2

4

42.

x	5	10	35
y	c	7	2

14

43.

x	h	33	22
y	6	2	3

11

10.6   **Solve.**

44. The weight of an object on the moon varies directly as its weight on earth. A person who weighs 240 pounds on earth weighs 40 pounds on the moon. How much would Estella weigh on the moon if she weighs 144 pounds on earth?   24 pounds

45. The number of seats on a single ski-lift cable is inversely proportional to the space between them. When they are 10 meters apart, the lift will hold 32 seats. What amount of space must be between the seats if the operator wants to install 40 seats on the cable?   8 meters

46. At the beginning of a trip, Wally had $260. At the end of the trip he had $117 left. The amount he had left is what percent of the amount he had at the beginning?   45%

TEACHER'S RESOURCE
MASTERS

Chapter 10 Test

Multiple-Choice Test

PROBLEM–SOLVING
HANDBOOK

p. 536

ADDITIONAL ANSWERS

3. 62.5 mi

CHAPTER 10 TEST

Give the direct-variation equation for each of the following:

1. At a constant rate of 30 kilometers per hour, the distance d in kilometers varies directly as the time t in hours. $d = 30t$

2. The total salary s earned at $10 an hour varies directly as the number h of hours worked. $s = 10h$

Solve each problem by using the direct-variation method.

3. On a map, 2 inches represents 25 miles. How many miles does 5 inches represent?

4. The amount of sales tax varies directly as the cost of a new car. If the tax on a car costing $14,500 is $797.50, what will the tax be on a car costing $16,000? $880

Solve each proportion.

5. $\frac{4}{7} = \frac{32}{n}$ 56

6. $\frac{1}{7} = \frac{-3}{a}$ -21

7. $\frac{12}{3x} = \frac{10}{3}$ $\frac{6}{5}$

8. $\frac{m + 2}{3} = \frac{2m}{4}$ 4

9. $\frac{2}{x - 6} = \frac{-4}{x + 3}$ 3

10. $\frac{-6}{2y + 11} = \frac{-2}{3y - 4}$ $\frac{23}{7}$

Solve each of the following by using a proportion:

11. What number is 75% of 48? 36

12. 8 is what percent of 50? 16%

13. 225 is 36% of what number? 625

14. What number is 4% of 75? 3

15. 15 is what percent of 250? 6%

16. 360 is 48% of what number? 750

Find the constant of variation k if y varies inversely as x.

17. $y = 8$ when $x = 2$ 16

18. $y = 7$ when $x = 5$ 35

19. $y = 1.5$ when $x = 4$ 6

20. $y = \frac{8}{3}$ when $x = \frac{3}{4}$ 2

Solve each problem by using a proportion.

21. The rate r of travel over a given distance varies inversely as the time t of travel. At 45 miles per hour, it takes 3 hours to travel a certain distance. How long will it take to travel this distance at 30 miles per hour? $4\frac{1}{2}$ hours

22. The number of revolutions made by a wheel rolling over a given distance varies inversely as the wheel's circumference. A wheel with a circumference of 50 inches makes 40 turns in going a certain distance. How many turns will be made by a wheel with a circumference of 10 inches? 200

23. Reaction distance is the distance that a car travels during the time it takes a driver to react and apply the brakes. Reaction distance varies directly as the speed of the car. At 20 miles per hour, the reaction distance is 22 feet. What is the reaction distance at 50 miles per hour? 55 feet

CHAPTER 11

Radicals

A 50-meter cable extends from the top of
a tower to a point 30 meters from the
base of the tower. How tall is the tower?
40 meters

OBJECTIVE

Find the positive and negative square roots of a rational number that is a perfect square.

TEACHER'S NOTES

See p. T34.

CLASSROOM EXAMPLES

Find each square root.

a. $\sqrt{81}$ $\sqrt{81} = 9$

b. $\sqrt{\frac{49}{121}}$ $\sqrt{\frac{49}{121}} = \frac{7}{11}$

c. $-\sqrt{81}$ $-\sqrt{81} = -9$

d. $-\sqrt{\frac{49}{121}}$ $-\sqrt{\frac{49}{121}} = -\frac{7}{11}$

e. $\pm\sqrt{121}$ $\pm\sqrt{121} = \pm 11$

f. $\pm\sqrt{\frac{1}{16}}$ $\pm\sqrt{\frac{1}{16}} = \pm\frac{1}{4}$

MIXED REVIEW

Factor completely.

1. $4x^2 + 3x - 1$
   $(4x - 1)(x + 1)$

2. $8r + 32s$ $8(r + 4s)$

3. $r^2 - s^2$ $(r - s)(r + s)$

4. $x^2 + 2xy + y^2$ $(x + y)^2$

5. $30s + 45t$ $15(2s + 3t)$

TEACHER'S RESOURCE MASTERS

Practice Master 45, Part 2

11.1 Square Roots

To square a number, you multiply it by itself. For example, the square of 5 is $5 \cdot 5$. The square of -5 is $(-5)(-5)$. That is, $5^2 = 25$ and $(-5)^2 = 25$.

The inverse of squaring a number is finding the **square root** of a number. To find the square root of 25, you must find two *equal* factors whose product is 25. Since 5 times 5 is 25, one square root of 25 is 5. Also, -5 times -5 is 25. So another square root of 25 is -5.

Definition of Square Root	If $x^2 = y$, then x is a square root of y.

The symbol $\sqrt{}$ is a **radical sign** and is used to indicate a square root. An expression like $\sqrt{25}$ is a **radical**, and the number 25 under the radical sign is the **radicand.**

Notice that 25 has two square roots, 5 and -5. Every positive real number has a positive square root and a negative square root. 0 has only one square root, 0. Negative real numbers do not have real-number square roots.

To indicate the **positive** (or **principal**) **square root** of a positive number a, write $\sqrt{a}$. To indicate the **negative square root** of a positive number a, write $-\sqrt{a}$. The expression $\pm\sqrt{a}$ indicates both square roots of a. For example, $\sqrt{36} = 6$, $-\sqrt{36} = -6$, and $\pm\sqrt{36} = \pm 6$.

Recall that a *rational number* is a number that can be expressed in the form $\frac{a}{b}$, where a and b are integers and $b \neq 0$. The square of a rational number is a **perfect square.** For example, $\frac{1}{3}$ is a rational number, and $\left(\frac{1}{3}\right)^2 = \frac{1}{9}$, so $\frac{1}{9}$ is a perfect square. Also, 6 is a rational number, and $6^2 = 36$, so 36 is a perfect square. Conversely, the square root of a perfect square is a rational number.

EXAMPLE

Find each square root.

a. $\sqrt{49}$

b. $\sqrt{\frac{25}{64}}$

c. $-\sqrt{49}$

d. $-\sqrt{\frac{25}{64}}$

e. $\pm\sqrt{144}$

f. $\pm\sqrt{\frac{1}{4}}$

SOLUTIONS

a. Since $(7)^2 = 49$, $\sqrt{49} = 7$.

b. Since $\left(\frac{5}{8}\right)^2 = \frac{25}{64}$, $\sqrt{\frac{25}{64}} = \frac{5}{8}$.

c. $-\sqrt{49} = -7$

d. $-\sqrt{\frac{25}{64}} = -\frac{5}{8}$

e. $\pm\sqrt{144} = \pm 12$

f. $\pm\sqrt{\frac{1}{4}} = \pm\frac{1}{2}$

ASSIGNMENT GUIDE

Minimum
1–15 odd, 17–29

Regular
17–37

Maximum
17–39 odd, 41–48

ADDITIONAL ANSWERS

Written Exercises
8. 10, −10

State the square of each number.

1. 3   9   **2.** 7   49   **3.** −4   16   **4.** −1   1   **5.** 6   36   **6.** −8   64

7. 5   25   **8.** 10   100   **9.** 1   1   **10.** −11   121   **11.** −2   4   **12.** 0   0

13. 12   144   **14.** −13   169   **15.** 20   400   **16.** −6   36   **17.** 15   225   **18.** −30   900

Complete.

19. Every ___positive___ real number has two real-number square roots.

20. ___Negative___ real numbers do not have real-number square roots.

21. The real number ___0___ has only one square root.

WRITTEN EXERCISES

A. Name the positive and negative numbers that make each equation true.

  1. $4 = x^2$ 2, −2   **2.** $16 = y^2$ 4, −4   **3.** $36 = z^2$ 6, −6   **4.** $64 = s^2$ 8, −8

  5. $25 = r^2$ 5, −5   **6.** $49 = y^2$ 7, −7   **7.** $81 = t^2$ 9, −9   **8.** $100 = w^2$

Find the indicated square roots.

  9. $\sqrt{1}$ 1   **10.** $\sqrt{0}$ 0   **11.** $-\sqrt{9}$ −3   **12.** $-\sqrt{25}$ −5

13. $\pm\sqrt{64}$ ±8   **14.** $\pm\sqrt{49}$ ±7   **15.** $\sqrt{16}$ 4   **16.** $-\sqrt{36}$ −6

B. 17. $\sqrt{121}$ 11   **18.** $\sqrt{144}$ 12   **19.** $-\sqrt{225}$ −15   **20.** $-\sqrt{169}$ −13

21. $\pm\sqrt{196}$ ±14   **22.** $\pm\sqrt{100}$ ±10   **23.** $\pm\sqrt{400}$ ±20   **24.** $\pm\sqrt{324}$ ±18

25. $\sqrt{900}$ 30   **26.** $-\sqrt{1600}$ −40   **27.** $\pm\sqrt{625}$ ±25   **28.** $-\sqrt{289}$ −17

29. $\sqrt{\dfrac{9}{16}}$ $\frac{3}{4}$ **30.** $\sqrt{\dfrac{36}{49}}$ $\frac{6}{7}$ **31.** $-\sqrt{\dfrac{1}{64}}$ $-\frac{1}{8}$ **32.** $-\sqrt{\dfrac{100}{121}}$ $-\frac{10}{11}$

33. $\pm\sqrt{\dfrac{25}{81}}$ $\pm\frac{5}{9}$ **34.** $\pm\sqrt{\dfrac{169}{400}}$ $\pm\frac{13}{20}$ **35.** $\sqrt{\dfrac{225}{196}}$ $\frac{15}{14}$ **36.** $\sqrt{\dfrac{144}{289}}$ $\frac{12}{17}$

37. $\pm\sqrt{\dfrac{144}{289}}$ $\pm\frac{12}{17}$ **38.** $-\sqrt{\dfrac{49}{324}}$ $-\frac{7}{18}$ **39.** $\sqrt{\dfrac{121}{400}}$ $\frac{11}{20}$ **40.** $\pm\sqrt{\dfrac{225}{169}}$ $\pm\frac{15}{13}$

C. 41. $\sqrt{0.04}$ 0.2   **42.** $\sqrt{0.64}$ 0.8   **43.** $-\sqrt{0.81}$ −0.9   **44.** $\pm\sqrt{1.21}$ ±1.1

Solve the following problems.

45. The lawn area of a square backyard is 900 square feet. What is the length of one side of the lawn?   30 ft

46. A square patch of sidewalk needs to be replaced. What is the length of one side of the patch if its total area is 16 square feet?   4 ft

47. A square deck extends 15 feet from the side of a house. What is the area of the deck in square feet?   225 ft²

48. What is the area in square feet of a square vegetable garden that is enclosed by 48 feet of fencing?   144 ft²

OBJECTIVE

Approximate the square root of a rational number that is not a perfect square, using the *divide-and-average* method.

CLASSROOM EXAMPLES

1. Approximate $\sqrt{17}$ correct to the tenths place.
$16 < 17 < 25$
$\sqrt{16} < \sqrt{17} < \sqrt{25}$
$4 < \sqrt{17} < 5$
$\frac{4 + 5}{2} = 4.5$
$17 \div 4.5 \approx 3.78$
$\frac{4.5 + 3.78}{2} = 4.14$
$17 \div 4.14 \approx 4.106$
$\sqrt{17} \approx 4.1$

2. Approximate $\sqrt{43}$ correct to the hundredths place.
$36 < 43 < 49$
$\sqrt{36} < \sqrt{43} < \sqrt{49}$
$6 < 43 < 7$
$\frac{6 + 7}{2} = 6.5$
$43 \div 6.5 \approx 6.62$
$\frac{6.5 + 6.62}{2} = 6.56$
$43 \div 6.56 \approx 6.555$
$\frac{6.56 + 6.555}{2} = 6.558$
$43 \div 6.558 \approx 6.5569$
$\sqrt{43} \approx 6.56$

MIXED REVIEW

1. $-\sqrt{121}$ -11
2. Simplify $\frac{-30x^3y^2}{-45x^7y}$. $\frac{2y}{3x^4}$

11.2	Approximating Square Roots

Most real numbers are not perfect squares. None of the following numbers are perfect squares.
2 3 5 6 7 8 10 11 12 13 14 15

The square roots of these numbers cannot be expressed as rational numbers. The square roots of these numbers are nonrepeating decimals, or **irrational numbers.**

The number 10 is not a perfect square, so its square root is an irrational number. You can locate 10 between consecutive perfect-square integers.
$9 < 10 < 16$ so $\sqrt{9} < \sqrt{10} < \sqrt{16}$ or $3 < \sqrt{10} < 4$

In other words, $\sqrt{10}$ is between 3 and 4. Notice that between 3 and 4 there are rational numbers whose squares are almost 10.
$(3.1)^2 = 9.61$ $(3.16)^2 = 9.9856$ $(3.162)^2 = 9.998244$

You can approximate irrational square roots. Study the steps of the *divide-and-average method* in the following examples.

EXAMPLES

1 **Approximate $\sqrt{19}$ correct to the tenths place.**

SOLUTION

$16 < 19 < 25$	*Locate the radicand between consecutive perfect-square integers.*
$\sqrt{16} < \sqrt{19} < \sqrt{25}$	*Take the square root of each integer.*
$4 < \sqrt{19} < 5$	*Find the square roots of the perfect squares.*
$\frac{4 + 5}{2} = 4.5$	*Average the square roots of the perfect squares.*
$19 \div 4.5 \approx 4.22$	*Divide the radicand by the average found in the preceding step until the quotient has one more decimal place than the divisor. The quotient is approximately ($\approx$) 4.22.*
$\frac{4.5 + 4.22}{2} = 4.36$	*Average the divisor and the quotient from the preceding step. Always determine the average to the same number of decimal places as the quotient.*
$19 \div 4.36 \approx 4.357$	*Divide the radicand by the average found in the preceding step. Continue the divide-and-average steps until the divisor and the quotient are the same for the decimal places required.*

This time, the divisor and the quotient are the same through the tenths place. Therefore, the square root is *correct to the tenths place.* Thus, $\sqrt{19} \approx 4.3$.

CHECK
Compute $(4.3)^2$.
$(4.3)^2 = 18.49$ *Is this close to 19? Yes.*

In some cases, it may be necessary to average and divide several times before the quotient and the divisor have the same digits in the required decimal places.

| 2 | **Approximate $\sqrt{34}$ correct to the hundredths place.** |

SOLUTION

$25 < 34 < 36$

$\sqrt{25} < \sqrt{34} < \sqrt{36}$

$5 < \sqrt{34} < 6$

$\dfrac{5 + 6}{2} = 5.5$

$34 \div 5.5 \approx 6.18$ *Notice that the quotient has one more decimal place than the divisor.*

$\dfrac{5.5 + 6.18}{2} = 5.84$ *Notice that the average has the same number of decimal places as the quotient.*

$34 \div 5.84 \approx 5.821$ *The quotient again has one more decimal place than the divisor.*

$\dfrac{5.84 + 5.821}{2} = 5.830$ *The average has the same number of decimal places as the quotient.*

$34 \div 5.830 \approx 5.8319$ *The divisor and the quotient are the same through the hundredths place.*

$\sqrt{34} \approx 5.83$

CHECK

Compute $(5.83)^2$.

$(5.83)^2 = 33.9889$ *Is this close to 34? Yes.*

ORAL EXERCISES

Which of the following are perfect squares?

1. 4 yes	**2.** 9 yes	**3.** 3 no	**4.** 4 yes
5. 16 yes	**6.** 50 no	**7.** 49 yes	**8.** 121 yes
9. 20 no	**10.** 169 yes	**11.** 45 no	**12.** 400 yes
13. $\frac{4}{7}$ no	**14.** $\frac{16}{25}$ yes	**15.** $\frac{1}{3}$ no	**16.** $\frac{1}{9}$ yes
17. $\frac{2}{9}$ no	**18.** $\frac{36}{25}$ yes	**19.** $\frac{1}{32}$ no	**20.** $\frac{3}{8}$ no

WRITTEN EXERCISES

A. **Locate each radicand between consecutive prefect-square integers. Then locate the square root between the square roots of the perfect squares.**

1. $\sqrt{3}$	**2.** $\sqrt{5}$	**3.** $\sqrt{12}$	**4.** $\sqrt{31}$
5. $\sqrt{65}$	**6.** $\sqrt{93}$	**7.** $\sqrt{115}$	**8.** $\sqrt{135}$

3. Evaluate $\dfrac{a^2 b}{-b}$ if $a = 3$ and $b = -20$. -9

4. $(-56) - (-135)$ 79

5. Graph $-3 < x < 5$.

TEACHER'S RESOURCE MASTERS

Practice Master 46, Part 1

ASSIGNMENT GUIDE

Minimum
1–15 odd, 25–31

Regular
25–39

Maximum
25–35 odd, 36–44

ADDITIONAL ANSWERS

Written Exercises

1. $1 < 3 < 4$; $1 < \sqrt{3} < 2$
2. $4 < 5 < 9$; $2 < \sqrt{5} < 3$
3. $9 < 12 < 16$; $3 < \sqrt{12} < 4$
4. $25 < 31 < 36$; $5 < \sqrt{31} < 6$
5. $64 < 65 < 81$; $8 < \sqrt{65} < 9$
6. $81 < 93 < 100$; $9 < \sqrt{93} < 10$
7. $100 < 115 < 121$; $10 < \sqrt{115} < 11$
8. $121 < 135 < 144$; $11 < \sqrt{135} < 12$

9. $169 < 172 < 196$;
  $13 < \sqrt{172} < 14$

10. $196 < 198 < 225$;
  $14 < \sqrt{198} < 15$

11. $196 < 205 < 225$;
  $14 < \sqrt{205} < 15$

12. $441 < 453 < 484$;
  $21 < \sqrt{453} < 22$

13. $225 < 228 < 256$;
  $15 < \sqrt{228} < 16$

14. $121 < 134 < 144$;
  $11 < \sqrt{134} < 12$

15. $289 < 320 < 324$;
  $17 < \sqrt{320} < 18$

16. $676 < 725 < 729$;
  $26 < \sqrt{725} < 27$

9. $\sqrt{172}$ 10. $\sqrt{198}$ 11. $\sqrt{205}$ 12. $\sqrt{453}$
13. $\sqrt{228}$ 14. $\sqrt{134}$ 15. $\sqrt{320}$ 16. $\sqrt{725}$

Use the divide-and-average method to approximate each square root correct to the tenths place.

17. $\sqrt{68}$ 8.2   18. $\sqrt{73}$ 8.5   19. $\sqrt{41}$ 6.4   20. $\sqrt{95}$ 9.7
21. $\sqrt{11}$ 3.3   22. $\sqrt{39}$ 6.2   23. $\sqrt{89}$ 9.4   24. $\sqrt{76}$ 8.7

B. Use the divide-and-average method to approximate each square root correct to the hundredths place.

25. $\sqrt{12}$ 3.46   26. $\sqrt{21}$ 4.58   27. $\sqrt{88}$ 9.38   28. $\sqrt{53}$ 7.28
29. $\sqrt{75}$ 8.66   30. $\sqrt{15}$ 3.87   31. $\sqrt{50}$ 7.07   32. $\sqrt{109}$ 10.44
33. $\sqrt{33}$ 5.74   34. $\sqrt{51}$ 7.14   35. $\sqrt{66}$ 8.12   36. $\sqrt{93}$ 9.64
37. $\sqrt{113}$ 10.63   38. $\sqrt{174}$ 13.19   39. $\sqrt{123}$ 11.09   40. $\sqrt{137}$ 11.70

C. Using the divide-and-average method, find each square root correct to the hundredths place. Instead of locating the radicand between perfect-square integers, let the first division be by 2 and proceed to average each divisor and quotient.

41. $\sqrt{17}$ 4.12   42. $\sqrt{18}$ 4.24   43. $\sqrt{16}$ 4   44. $\sqrt{25}$ 5

CALCULATOR

The $\boxed{\sqrt{}}$ key on a calculator is the square-root key. After this key is pressed, the number in the display is replaced by its *principal square root*. When the square root is an irrational number, the calculator shows as many decimal places as possible.

Example 1: Find the square root of 196.

ENTER   DISPLAY
$\boxed{C}$ 196 $\boxed{\sqrt{}}$ $14.$

Example 2: Find the square root of 140.

ENTER   DISPLAY
$\boxed{C}$ 140 $\boxed{\sqrt{}}$ 11.832159

EXERCISES

Use a calculator to find each of the following square roots.

1. $\sqrt{10}$ 3.1622776   2. $\sqrt{23}$ 4.7958315   3. $\sqrt{51}$ 7.1414284
4. $\sqrt{37}$ 6.0827625   5. $\sqrt{73}$ 8.5440037   6. $\sqrt{94}$ 9.6953597
7. $\sqrt{83}$ 9.1104335   8. $\sqrt{99}$ 9.9498743   9. $\sqrt{42}$ 6.4807406
10. $\sqrt{13}$ 3.6055512   11. $\sqrt{123}$ 11.090536   12. $\sqrt{203}$ 14.247806

11.3 | The Pythagorean Theorem

OBJECTIVES

Use the *Table of Squares and Square Roots* to find an approximate value.

Use the Pythagorean theorem to find the length of the hypotenuse of a right triangle.

The **Pythagorean theorem** can be used to find the length of the hypotenuse of a right triangle.

Pythagorean Theorem	**In a right triangle, the square of the length of the hypotenuse is equal to the sum of the squares of the lengths of the legs.**

$$c^2 = a^2 + b^2$$

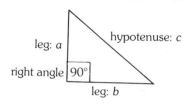

leg: a hypotenuse: c

right angle $90°$

leg: b

TEACHER'S NOTES

See p. T35.

CLASSROOM EXAMPLES

1. $\triangle ABC$ is a right triangle. Show that the square of the length of the hypotenuse is equal to the sum of the squares of the lengths of the legs.

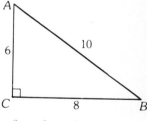

$$c^2 = a^2 + b^2$$
$$10^2 \stackrel{?}{=} 8^2 + 6^2$$
$$100 \stackrel{?}{=} 64 + 36$$
$$100 = 100 \checkmark$$

2. The lengths of the legs of a right triangle are given. Find the length of the hypotenuse.
$$a = 3, b = 4$$
$$c^2 = a^2 + b^2$$
$$c^2 = 3^2 + 4^2$$
$$c^2 = 9 + 16$$
$$c^2 = 25$$
$$c = 5$$
The length of the hypotenuse is 5.

EXAMPLES

1 $\triangle ABC$ **is a right triangle. Show that the square of the length of the hypotenuse is equal to the sum of the squares of the lengths of the legs.**

a.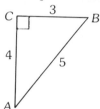

b.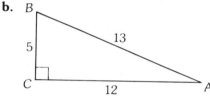

SOLUTIONS

a.
$$c^2 \stackrel{?}{=} a^2 + b^2$$
$$5^2 \stackrel{?}{=} 3^2 + 4^2$$
$$25 \stackrel{?}{=} 9 + 16$$
$$25 = 25 \checkmark$$

b.
$$c^2 \stackrel{?}{=} a^2 + b^2$$
$$13^2 \stackrel{?}{=} 5^2 + 12^2$$
$$169 \stackrel{?}{=} 25 + 144$$
$$169 = 169 \checkmark$$

2 **The lengths of the legs of a right triangle are given. Find the length of the hypotenuse.**

a. $a = 6, b = 8$

b. $a = 1, b = 1$

SOLUTIONS

a.
$$c^2 = a^2 + b^2$$
$$c^2 = 6^2 + 8^2$$
$$c^2 = 36 + 64$$
$$c^2 = 100$$
$$c = 10$$
The length of the hypotenuse is 10.

b.
$$c^2 = a^2 + b^2$$
$$c^2 = 1^2 + 1^2$$
$$c^2 = 1 + 1$$
$$c^2 = 2$$
$$c = \sqrt{2}$$
The length of the hypotenuse is $\sqrt{2}$.

3. Use the *Table of Squares and Square Roots* to find an approximate value for $\sqrt{46}$.

n	n^2	$\sqrt{n}$
46	2116	6.782

$\sqrt{46} \approx 6.782$

MIXED REVIEW

Perform the indicated operation.

1. $(6y + 5)(2y - 8)$
   $12y^2 - 38y - 40$

2. Simplify $5[4 - \left(\frac{12 - 6}{3}\right) \div 2]$.   15

3. Find $f(-3)$ for $f(x) = 2x - 8$. -14

4. Find the slope of the line containing the points $(7, -2)$ and $(5, -6)$.   2

5. Write the equation $3x + y = -6$ in slope-intercept form. $y = -3x - 6$

TEACHER'S RESOURCE MASTERS

Practice Master 46, Part 2

ASSIGNMENT GUIDE

Minimum
4–19

Regular
13–26

Maximum
21–36

ADDITIONAL ANSWERS

Oral Exercises
8. 244

Using the Pythagorean theorem and geometry, you can find the location of $\sqrt{2}$ on the number line.

Place the tip of the compass on the origin and measure the length of the hypotenuse. Use that measure to draw an arc that intersects the number line. The point of intersection is the location of the irrational number.

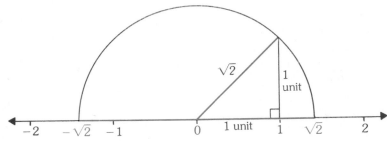

The irrational number $-\sqrt{2}$ is also located on the number line, in the opposite direction.

From the positions on the number line, it appears that $\pm\sqrt{2} \approx \pm 1.4$. Many other irrational numbers can be located on the number line in a similar fashion.

Another way to find an approximation of an irrational number is to use the Table of Squares and Square Roots on page 547.

| 3 |

Use the Table of Squares and Square Roots to find an approximate value for $\sqrt{41}$.

SOLUTION
Find 41 in the n column. Then look to the right to the $\sqrt{n}$ column.

n	n^2	$\sqrt{n}$
41	1681	6.403

$\sqrt{41} \approx 6.403$

ORAL EXERCISES

The lengths of the legs of a right triangle are given. Find the square of the length of the hypotenuse.

1. $a = 4, b = 3$ 25   **2.** $a = 1, b = 2$ 5   **3.** $a = 2, b = 5$ 29   **4.** $a = 2, b = 3$ 13

5. $a = 3, b = 7$ 58   **6.** $a = 9, b = 2$ 85   **7.** $a = 5, b = 6$ 61   **8.** $a = 10, b = 12$

WRITTEN EXERCISES

A. The lengths of the legs of a right triangle are given. Find the length of the hypotenuse.

1. $a = 6, b = 8$ 10   **2.** $a = 12, b = 5$ 13   **3.** $a = 8, b = 15$ 17

4. $a = 9, b = 12$ 15   **5.** $a = 12, b = 16$ 20   **6.** $a = 5, b = 12$ 13

7. $a = 7, b = 9$ $\sqrt{130}$ **8.** $a = 10, b = 11$ $\sqrt{221}$

Use the Table of Squares and Square Roots on page 547 to find each of the following.

9. $\sqrt{5}$ 2.236   **10.** $\sqrt{3}$ 1.732   **11.** $\sqrt{27}$ 5.196   **12.** $\sqrt{50}$ 7.071

13. $\sqrt{59}$ 7.681   **14.** $\sqrt{23}$ 4.796   **15.** $\sqrt{28}$ 5.292   **16.** $\sqrt{82}$ 9.055

17. $\sqrt{96}$ 9.798   **18.** $\sqrt{143}$ 11.958   **19.** $\sqrt{149}$ 12.207   **20.** $\sqrt{128}$ 11.314

B. The lengths of the legs of a right triangle are given. Use the Table of Squares and Square Roots on page 547 to find c, the length of the hypotenuse, to the nearest thousandth.

21. $a = 3, b = 8$ 8.544   **22.** $a = 2, b = 8$ 8.246   **23.** $a = 4, b = 9$ 9.849

24. $a = 4, b = 5$ 6.403   **25.** $a = 6, b = 6$ 8.485   **26.** $a = 10, b = 7$

27. $a = 4, b = 7$ 8.062   **28.** $a = 5, b = 7$ 8.602   **29.** $a = 6, b = 9$ 10.817

30. $a = 8, b = 8$ 11.314   **31.** $a = 5, b = 8$ 9.434   **32.** $a = 10, b = 5$

Written Exercises
26. 12.207
32. 11.180

C. Solve each problem. Use the Table of Squares and Square Roots on page 547.

33.

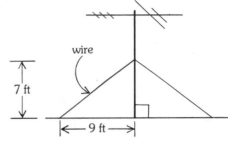

To the nearest tenth of a foot, how long is one of the wires needed to brace a TV antenna as shown? 11.4 ft

34.

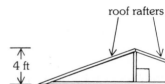

To the nearest tenth of a foot, how long is one roof rafter for the garage roof shown above? 11.7 ft

35.

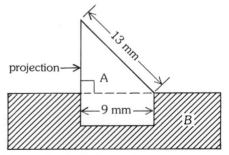

Machine part A fits into part B as shown above. To the nearest thousandth of a millimeter, how much should part A project? 9.381 mm

36.

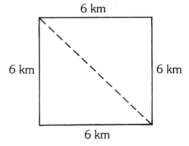

To the nearest tenth of a kilometer, how long is a pipeline that runs diagonally across a square field 6 km on a side?

8.5 km

TEACHER'S NOTES

See p. T35.

CLASSROOM EXAMPLES

1. Find the product of the radicals.

a. $\sqrt{13} \cdot \sqrt{13}$
$\sqrt{13} \cdot \sqrt{13}$
$= \sqrt{13 \cdot 13}$
$= \sqrt{169}$
$= 13$

b. $\sqrt{27} \cdot \sqrt{3}$
$\sqrt{27} \cdot \sqrt{3} = \sqrt{27 \cdot 3}$
$= \sqrt{81}$
$= 9$

c. $\sqrt{2} \cdot \sqrt{3}$
$\sqrt{2} \cdot \sqrt{3} = \sqrt{2 \cdot 3}$
$= \sqrt{6}$

d. $\sqrt{7x} \cdot \sqrt{3y}$
$\sqrt{7x} \cdot \sqrt{3y}$
$= \sqrt{(7x)(3y)}$
$= \sqrt{21xy}$

2. Find the quotient of the radicals.

a. $\dfrac{\sqrt{48}}{\sqrt{3}}$
$\dfrac{\sqrt{48}}{\sqrt{3}} = \sqrt{\dfrac{48}{3}}$
$= \sqrt{16}$
$= 4$

b. $\dfrac{\sqrt{18}}{\sqrt{6}}$
$\dfrac{\sqrt{18}}{\sqrt{6}} = \sqrt{\dfrac{18}{6}}$
$= \sqrt{3}$

c. $\dfrac{\sqrt{42x^2y}}{\sqrt{7xy}}$
$\dfrac{\sqrt{42x^2y}}{\sqrt{7xy}} = \sqrt{\dfrac{42x^2y}{7xy}}$
$= \sqrt{6x}$

11.4 Multiplying and Dividing Radicals

Notice that $\sqrt{4} \cdot \sqrt{9} = 2 \cdot 3 = 6$ and $\sqrt{4 \cdot 9} = \sqrt{36} = 6$. These equations suggest the following property of the multiplication of square roots.

Multiplication of Square Roots	**Let a and b be any nonnegative real numbers. Then** $\sqrt{a} \cdot \sqrt{b} = \sqrt{a \cdot b}.$

EXAMPLES

1 **Find the product of the radicals.**

a. $\sqrt{11} \cdot \sqrt{11}$ b. $\sqrt{50} \cdot \sqrt{2}$ c. $\sqrt{3} \cdot \sqrt{5}$ d. $\sqrt{5x} \cdot \sqrt{6y}$

SOLUTIONS

a. $\sqrt{11} \cdot \sqrt{11} = \sqrt{11 \cdot 11}$
$= \sqrt{121}$
$= 11$

b. $\sqrt{50} \cdot \sqrt{2} = \sqrt{50 \cdot 2}$
$= \sqrt{100}$
$= 10$

c. $\sqrt{3} \cdot \sqrt{5} = \sqrt{3 \cdot 5}$
$= \sqrt{15}$

d. $\sqrt{5x} \cdot \sqrt{6y} = \sqrt{(5x)(6y)}$
$= \sqrt{30xy}$

A radicand cannot be negative because negative real numbers do not have real-number square roots. Therefore, the replacement set for variables is such that every radicand is positive or 0.

Notice that $\dfrac{\sqrt{100}}{\sqrt{4}} = \dfrac{10}{2} = 5$ and $\sqrt{\dfrac{100}{4}} = \sqrt{25} = 5$. These equations suggest the following property of the division of square roots.

Division of Square Roots	**Let a and b be any nonnegative real numbers such that $b \neq 0$.** **Then** $\dfrac{\sqrt{a}}{\sqrt{b}} = \sqrt{\dfrac{a}{b}}.$

2 **Find the quotient of the radicals.**

a. $\dfrac{\sqrt{27}}{\sqrt{3}}$ b. $\dfrac{\sqrt{24}}{\sqrt{8}}$ c. $\dfrac{\sqrt{35x^2y}}{\sqrt{7xy}}$

SOLUTIONS

a. $\dfrac{\sqrt{27}}{\sqrt{3}} = \sqrt{\dfrac{27}{3}}$
$= \sqrt{9}$
$= 3$

b. $\dfrac{\sqrt{24}}{\sqrt{8}} = \sqrt{\dfrac{24}{8}}$
$= \sqrt{3}$

c. $\dfrac{\sqrt{35x^2y}}{\sqrt{7xy}} = \sqrt{\dfrac{35x^2y}{7xy}}$
$= \sqrt{5x}$

Recall that division by 0 is not defined. Therefore, the replacement sets for the variables in a radicand exclude any values that make the denominator 0.

ORAL EXERCISES

Find the product of the radicals.

1. $\sqrt{4} \cdot \sqrt{4}$ 4   **2.** $\sqrt{9} \cdot \sqrt{9}$ 9   **3.** $\sqrt{6} \cdot \sqrt{6}$ 6   **4.** $\sqrt{5} \cdot \sqrt{5}$ 5

5. $\sqrt{7} \cdot \sqrt{3}$ $\sqrt{21}$ **6.** $\sqrt{2} \cdot \sqrt{5}$ $\sqrt{10}$ **7.** $\sqrt{2x} \cdot \sqrt{7y}$ **8.** $\sqrt{6a} \cdot \sqrt{7b}$

Find the quotient of the radicals.

9. $\dfrac{\sqrt{16}}{\sqrt{4}}$ 2   **10.** $\dfrac{\sqrt{100}}{\sqrt{4}}$ 5   **11.** $\dfrac{\sqrt{36}}{\sqrt{12}}$ $\sqrt{3}$ **12.** $\dfrac{\sqrt{16}}{\sqrt{8}}$ $\sqrt{2}$

13. $\dfrac{\sqrt{80}}{\sqrt{8}}$ $\sqrt{10}$ **14.** $\dfrac{\sqrt{28}}{\sqrt{2}}$ $\sqrt{14}$ **15.** $\dfrac{\sqrt{22x}}{\sqrt{11}}$ $\sqrt{2x}$ **16.** $\dfrac{\sqrt{15y}}{\sqrt{5}}$ $\sqrt{3y}$

WRITTEN EXERCISES

A. Find the product or the quotient.

1. $\sqrt{7} \cdot \sqrt{7}$ 7   **2.** $\sqrt{3} \cdot \sqrt{3}$ 3   **3.** $\sqrt{25} \cdot \sqrt{25}$ 25   **4.** $\sqrt{36} \cdot \sqrt{36}$

5. $\sqrt{4} \cdot \sqrt{25}$ 10   **6.** $\sqrt{4} \cdot \sqrt{16}$ 8   **7.** $\dfrac{\sqrt{6}}{\sqrt{6}}$ 1   **8.** $\dfrac{\sqrt{9}}{\sqrt{9}}$ 1

9. $\dfrac{\sqrt{81}}{\sqrt{9}}$ 3   **10.** $\dfrac{\sqrt{64}}{\sqrt{16}}$ 2   **11.** $\dfrac{\sqrt{48}}{\sqrt{3}}$ 4   **12.** $\dfrac{\sqrt{18}}{\sqrt{2}}$ 3

13. $\dfrac{\sqrt{72}}{\sqrt{8}}$ 3   **14.** $\dfrac{\sqrt{80}}{\sqrt{5}}$ 4   **15.** $\dfrac{\sqrt{363}}{\sqrt{3}}$ 11   **16.** $\dfrac{\sqrt{486}}{\sqrt{6}}$ 9

B. 17. $\sqrt{2} \cdot \sqrt{3}$ $\sqrt{6}$ **18.** $\sqrt{5} \cdot \sqrt{7}$ $\sqrt{35}$ **19.** $\sqrt{5x} \cdot \sqrt{3}$ **20.** $\sqrt{13} \cdot \sqrt{2y}$

21. $\sqrt{10x} \cdot \sqrt{11y}$ **22.** $\sqrt{7a} \cdot \sqrt{10b}$ **23.** $\sqrt{\dfrac{1}{2}} \cdot \sqrt{6}$ $\sqrt{3}$ **24.** $\sqrt{\dfrac{1}{3}} \cdot \sqrt{15}$ $\sqrt{5}$

25. $\sqrt{2} \cdot \sqrt{x+3}$ **26.** $\sqrt{5-y} \cdot \sqrt{3}$ **27.** $\dfrac{\sqrt{6}}{\sqrt{3}}$ $\sqrt{2}$ **28.** $\dfrac{\sqrt{15}}{\sqrt{5}}$ $\sqrt{3}$

29. $\dfrac{\sqrt{12x}}{\sqrt{6}}$ $\sqrt{2x}$ **30.** $\dfrac{\sqrt{18x}}{\sqrt{3}}$ $\sqrt{6x}$ **31.** $\dfrac{\sqrt{12x^2}}{\sqrt{4x}}$ $\sqrt{3x}$ **32.** $\dfrac{\sqrt{35y^3}}{\sqrt{7y^2}}$ $\sqrt{5y}$

33. $\dfrac{\sqrt{16m^3n^2}}{\sqrt{8m^2n}}$ $\sqrt{2mn}$ **34.** $\dfrac{\sqrt{25c^5d^7}}{\sqrt{5c^4d^6}}$ $\sqrt{5cd}$ **35.** $\dfrac{\sqrt{36x^2}}{\sqrt{18x}}$ $\sqrt{2x}$ **36.** $\dfrac{\sqrt{36x^8}}{\sqrt{6x^7}}$ $\sqrt{6x}$

37. $\dfrac{\sqrt{42x^7y^2}}{\sqrt{6x^6y}}$ $\sqrt{7xy}$ **38.** $\dfrac{\sqrt{15x^8y^6}}{\sqrt{5x^7y^5}}$ $\sqrt{3xy}$ **39.** $\dfrac{\sqrt{50y^9}}{\sqrt{25y^8}}$ $\sqrt{2y}$ **40.** $\dfrac{\sqrt{98x^{10}y}}{\sqrt{49x^9}}$

C. 41. $9\sqrt{x} \cdot 4\sqrt{x}$ $36x$ **42.** $-4\sqrt{xy} \cdot 3\sqrt{xy}$ $-12xy$ **43.** $t^2\sqrt{s^2t} \cdot 3s\sqrt{s^2t}$

44. $\dfrac{\sqrt{x^3+x^2}}{\sqrt{x^2}}$ $\sqrt{x+1}$ **45.** $\dfrac{\sqrt{3x^2-6x}}{\sqrt{3x}}$ $\sqrt{x-2}$ **46.** $\dfrac{\sqrt{14x^3-7x^2}}{\sqrt{7x^2}}$ $\sqrt{2x-1}$

47. Is it true that $\sqrt{a} + \sqrt{b} = \sqrt{a+b}$?   **48.** Is it true that $\sqrt{a} - \sqrt{b} = \sqrt{a-b}$?

MIXED REVIEW

1. Evaluate $\left(-\dfrac{1}{5}\right)^3$. $-\dfrac{1}{125}$

2. Find the equation of the line if the slope is $-\dfrac{2}{5}$ and the y-intercept is 6.
$y = -\dfrac{2}{5}x + 6$

3. Solve the system of equations. $3x + 4y = 12$ $5x - 4y = 20$
$(4, 0)$

4. Complete $|38|$. 38

5. Factor completely.
$40x^2 - 46x - 42$
$2(5x + 3)(4x - 7)$

TEACHER'S RESOURCE MASTERS

Practice Master 47, Part 1

Quiz 21

ASSIGNMENT GUIDE

Minimum
9–16, 29–37

Regular
17–33

Maximum
17–39 odd, 44–48

ADDITIONAL ANSWERS

Oral Exercises
7. $\sqrt{14xy}$
8. $\sqrt{42ab}$

Written Exercises
4. 36
19. $\sqrt{15x}$
20. $\sqrt{26y}$
21. $\sqrt{110xy}$
22. $\sqrt{70ab}$

Additional Answers
See p. T62.

CALCULATOR

Recall that the ⃞CM , ⃞RM , ⃞M– , and ⃞M+ keys on a calculator are for memory calculations. Pressing ⃞CM *clears* the memory. When you want to *add to* or *subtract from* the memory, press ⃞M+ or ⃞M– . The ⃞M+ and ⃞M– keys also work as the ⃞= key on some calculators. Pressing ⃞RM *recalls* the amount in the memory.

Example 1: The lengths of the legs of a right triangle are 10.8 and 7.3. Use the memory keys on a calculator to find the length of the triangle's hypotenuse to the nearest hundredth. (Use the Pythagorean theorem: $c = \sqrt{a^2 + b^2}$.)

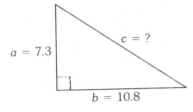

ENTER   DISPLAY
⃞CM 7.3 ⃞× ⃞M+ 10.8 ⃞× ⃞M+ ⃞RM ⃞√   *13.03572*

Therefore, c, the length of the hypotenuse, is approximately 13.04.

Example 2: The length of the hypotenuse of a right triangle is 16.3, and the length of one of its legs is 5.9. Find the length of the other leg of the right triangle to the nearest hundredth. (Use the Pythagorean theorem: $a = \sqrt{c^2 - b^2}$.)

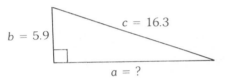

ENTER   DISPLAY
⃞CM 16.3 ⃞× ⃞M+ 5.9 ⃞× ⃞M– ⃞RM ⃞√   *15.194735*

Therefore, a, the length of the other leg, is approximately 15.19.

EXERCISES

The lengths of the legs of a right triangle are given. Find the length of the hypotenuse to the nearest hundredth.

1. $a = 5, b = 7$ 8.60   **2.** $a = 8.1, b = 13.5$ 15.74

3. $a = 15, b = 30.2$ 33.72   **4.** $a = 6.4, b = 8.2$ 10.40

The length of one leg of a right triangle and the length of the hypotenuse are given. Find the length of the other leg to the nearest hundredth.

5. $b = 12.3, c = 17.39$ 12.29   **6.** $b = 14.3, c = 24.67$ 20.10

11.5 | Simplifying Radicals

The multiplication and division properties stated in the previous section can be used in reverse to change the form of radicals.

A radical expression that represents a square root is in **simplest form** when
1. the radicand does not contain a perfect-square factor other than 1.
2. no fraction is under a radical sign.
3. no radical is in a denominator.

TEACHER'S NOTES
See p. T35.

EXAMPLES

1 **Change each radical to simplest form.**

a. $\sqrt{90}$

b. $\sqrt{\dfrac{3}{4}}$

c. $\sqrt{\dfrac{5}{3}}$

SOLUTIONS

a. $\sqrt{90} = \sqrt{9} \cdot \sqrt{10}$
$= 3\sqrt{10}$

b. $\sqrt{\dfrac{3}{4}} = \dfrac{\sqrt{3}}{\sqrt{4}}$
$= \dfrac{\sqrt{3}}{2}$

c. $\sqrt{\dfrac{5}{3}} = \dfrac{\sqrt{5}}{\sqrt{3}}$
$= \dfrac{\sqrt{5}}{\sqrt{3}} \cdot 1$
$= \dfrac{\sqrt{5}}{\sqrt{3}} \cdot \dfrac{\sqrt{3}}{\sqrt{3}}$
$= \dfrac{\sqrt{15}}{3}$

The process of changing a fraction such as $\dfrac{\sqrt{5}}{\sqrt{3}}$ to $\dfrac{\sqrt{15}}{3}$ is called **rationalizing the denominator.** Whenever an irrational number in the form of a radical is in a denominator, rewrite the radical expression so that only rational numbers are in the denominator.

Sometimes there are different approaches possible when you rationalize a denominator.

2 **Change $\dfrac{7}{\sqrt{8}}$ to simplest form.**

SOLUTIONS

a. $\dfrac{7}{\sqrt{8}} = \dfrac{7}{\sqrt{8}} \cdot \dfrac{\sqrt{2}}{\sqrt{2}}$
$= \dfrac{7\sqrt{2}}{\sqrt{16}}$
$= \dfrac{7\sqrt{2}}{4}$

b. $\dfrac{7}{\sqrt{8}} = \dfrac{7}{\sqrt{4 \cdot 2}}$
$= \dfrac{7}{\sqrt{4} \cdot \sqrt{2}}$
$= \dfrac{7}{2\sqrt{2}} \cdot \dfrac{\sqrt{2}}{\sqrt{2}}$
$= \dfrac{7\sqrt{2}}{4}$

CLASSROOM EXAMPLES
1. Change each radical to simplest form.
   a. $\sqrt{80}$
      $\sqrt{80} = \sqrt{16} \cdot \sqrt{5}$
      $= 4\sqrt{5}$
   b. $\sqrt{\dfrac{7}{16}}$
      $\sqrt{\dfrac{7}{16}} = \dfrac{\sqrt{7}}{\sqrt{16}}$
      $= \dfrac{\sqrt{7}}{4}$
   c. $\sqrt{\dfrac{3}{7}}$
      $\sqrt{\dfrac{3}{7}} = \dfrac{\sqrt{3}}{\sqrt{7}}$
      $= \dfrac{\sqrt{3}}{\sqrt{7}} \cdot 1$
      $\dfrac{\sqrt{3}}{\sqrt{7}} \cdot \dfrac{\sqrt{7}}{\sqrt{7}}$
      $= \dfrac{\sqrt{21}}{7}$
2. Change $\dfrac{5}{\sqrt{3}}$ to simplest form.
   $\dfrac{5}{\sqrt{3}} = \dfrac{5}{\sqrt{3}} \cdot \dfrac{\sqrt{3}}{\sqrt{3}}$
   $= \dfrac{5\sqrt{3}}{\sqrt{9}}$
   $= \dfrac{5\sqrt{3}}{3}$
3. Change each radical to simplest form. Assume that negative replacements for the variables are permitted.
   a. $\sqrt{40y^2}$
      $\sqrt{40y^2} = \sqrt{4y^2 \cdot 10}$
      $= \sqrt{4y^2} \cdot \sqrt{10}$
      $= 2|y|\sqrt{10}$
   b. $\sqrt{32y^3}$
      $\sqrt{32y^3} = \sqrt{16y^2 \cdot 2y}$
      $= \sqrt{16y^2} \cdot \sqrt{2y}$
      $= 4y\sqrt{2y}$

c. $\sqrt{\dfrac{a^4}{b^6}}$

$\sqrt{\dfrac{a^4}{b^6}} = \dfrac{\sqrt{a^4}}{\sqrt{b^6}}$

$= \dfrac{a^2}{|b^3|}$

MIXED REVIEW

Perform the indicated operation.

1. $\sqrt{25} \cdot \sqrt{4}$ 10

2. $\dfrac{\sqrt{56x^2y}}{\sqrt{8xy}}$ $\sqrt{7x}$

3. In a right triangle, solve for the hypotenuse if the legs are 7 meters and 11 meters. 13.04 meters

4. Illustrate the associative property of addition. Answers may vary.

5. $(-154) \div (-7)$ 22

TEACHER'S RESOURCE MASTERS

Practice Master 47, Part 2

ASSIGNMENT GUIDE

Minimum
1–23 odd, 41–55 odd

Regular
25–63

Maximum
47–57, 65–73

Consider the expression $\sqrt{x^2}$. If negative numbers are excluded from the replacement set for the variable, then $\sqrt{x^2} = x$. For example, if $x = 3$, then $\sqrt{x^2} = \sqrt{3^2} = \sqrt{9} = 3$.

What if the replacement set for x contains negative numbers? For example, if $x = -3$, what is $\sqrt{(-3)^2}$? According to $\sqrt{x^2} = x$, $\sqrt{(-3)^2}$ should be -3. However, $\sqrt{(-3)^2}$ represents the *principal root* of $(-3)^2$. That is, if $x = -3$, $\sqrt{x^2} = \sqrt{(-3)^2} = \sqrt{9} = 3$.

When a radical expression contains a variable, it is important to use absolute-value symbols in some cases to ensure that the expression represents a positive number.

Definition of a Square Root of a Variable Expression	**For any real number x, $\sqrt{x^2} = |x|$.**

3 **Change each radical to simplest form. Assume that negative replacements for the variables are permitted.**

a. $\sqrt{50x^2}$ **b.** $\sqrt{12x^3}$ **c.** $\sqrt{\dfrac{x^6}{y^4}}$

SOLUTIONS

a. $\sqrt{50x^2} = \sqrt{25x^2 \cdot 2}$ *The value of x can be negative because x^2 is positive.*

$= \sqrt{25x^2} \cdot \sqrt{2}$

$= 5|x|\sqrt{2}$ *Absolute-value symbols ensure that $\sqrt{x^2}$ is positive.*

b. $\sqrt{12x^3} = \sqrt{4x^2 \cdot 3x}$ *The value of x cannot be negative because $\sqrt{12x^3}$ would not*

$= \sqrt{4x^2} \cdot \sqrt{3x}$ *be defined if it were.*

$= 2x\sqrt{3x}$ *Therefore, absolute-value symbols are not needed.*

c. $\sqrt{\dfrac{x^6}{y^4}} = \dfrac{\sqrt{x^6}}{\sqrt{y^4}}$ *The value of either x or y can be negative because x^6 and y^4 are positive.*

$= \dfrac{|x^3|}{y^2}$ *Therefore, absolute-value symbols are needed to ensure that $\sqrt{x^6}$ is positive.*
However, since y^2 is always positive, absolute-value symbols are not needed.

ORAL EXERCISES

Tell why each expression is not in simplest form.

1. $\sqrt{18}$ **2.** $\sqrt{\dfrac{2}{5}}$ **3.** $\sqrt{3y^2}$ **4.** $\dfrac{\sqrt{2}}{\sqrt{3}}$

WRITTEN EXERCISES

A. Change each radical to simplest form.

1. $\sqrt{8}$ $2\sqrt{2}$ **2.** $\sqrt{12}$ $2\sqrt{3}$ **3.** $\sqrt{18}$ $3\sqrt{2}$ **4.** $\sqrt{50}$ $5\sqrt{2}$

5. $\sqrt{24}$ $2\sqrt{6}$ **6.** $\sqrt{54}$ $3\sqrt{6}$ **7.** $\sqrt{45}$ $3\sqrt{5}$ **8.** $\sqrt{27}$ $3\sqrt{3}$

9. $\sqrt{72}$ $6\sqrt{2}$ **10.** $\sqrt{20}$ $2\sqrt{5}$ **11.** $\sqrt{32}$ $4\sqrt{2}$ **12.** $\sqrt{68}$ $2\sqrt{17}$

13. $\sqrt{60}$ $2\sqrt{15}$ 14. $\sqrt{75}$ $5\sqrt{3}$ 15. $\sqrt{192}$ $8\sqrt{3}$ 16. $\sqrt{162}$ $9\sqrt{2}$

17. $\sqrt{88}$ $2\sqrt{22}$ 18. $\sqrt{135}$ $3\sqrt{15}$ 19. $\sqrt{56}$ $2\sqrt{14}$ 20. $\sqrt{147}$ $7\sqrt{3}$

21. $\sqrt{\dfrac{25}{36}}$ $\dfrac{5}{6}$ 22. $\sqrt{\dfrac{49}{81}}$ $\dfrac{7}{9}$ 23. $\sqrt{\dfrac{100}{9}}$ $\dfrac{10}{3}$ 24. $\sqrt{\dfrac{64}{25}}$ $\dfrac{8}{5}$

B. 25. $\sqrt{\dfrac{3}{4}}$ $\dfrac{\sqrt{3}}{2}$ 26. $\sqrt{\dfrac{5}{4}}$ $\dfrac{\sqrt{5}}{2}$ 27. $\sqrt{\dfrac{3}{16}}$ $\dfrac{\sqrt{3}}{4}$ 28. $\sqrt{\dfrac{7}{25}}$ $\dfrac{\sqrt{7}}{5}$

29. $\sqrt{\dfrac{1}{2}}$ $\dfrac{\sqrt{2}}{2}$ 30. $\sqrt{\dfrac{1}{3}}$ $\dfrac{\sqrt{3}}{3}$ 31. $\sqrt{\dfrac{5}{7}}$ $\dfrac{\sqrt{35}}{7}$ 32. $\sqrt{\dfrac{3}{10}}$ $\dfrac{\sqrt{30}}{10}$

33. $\sqrt{\dfrac{4}{3}}$ $\dfrac{2\sqrt{3}}{3}$ 34. $\sqrt{\dfrac{9}{2}}$ $\dfrac{3\sqrt{2}}{2}$ 35. $\sqrt{\dfrac{16}{5}}$ $\dfrac{4\sqrt{5}}{5}$ 36. $\sqrt{\dfrac{49}{3}}$ $\dfrac{7\sqrt{3}}{3}$

37. $\dfrac{2}{\sqrt{12}}$ $\dfrac{\sqrt{3}}{3}$ 38. $\dfrac{5}{\sqrt{8}}$ $\dfrac{5\sqrt{2}}{4}$ 39. $\dfrac{3}{\sqrt{20}}$ $\dfrac{3\sqrt{5}}{10}$ 40. $\dfrac{7}{\sqrt{32}}$ $\dfrac{7\sqrt{2}}{8}$

41. $\dfrac{9}{\sqrt{18}}$ $\dfrac{3\sqrt{2}}{2}$ 42. $\dfrac{8}{\sqrt{24}}$ $\dfrac{2\sqrt{6}}{3}$ 43. $\dfrac{6}{\sqrt{45}}$ $\dfrac{2\sqrt{5}}{5}$ 44. $\dfrac{4}{\sqrt{27}}$ $\dfrac{4\sqrt{3}}{9}$

45. $\sqrt{75x^2}$ $5|x|\sqrt{3}$ 46. $\sqrt{72y^2}$ $6|y|\sqrt{2}$ 47. $\sqrt{48a^3}$ $4a\sqrt{3a}$ 48. $\sqrt{63x^3}$ $3x\sqrt{7x}$

49. $\sqrt{200y^4}$ 50. $\sqrt{300a^4}$ 51. $\sqrt{98b^6}$ $7|b^3|\sqrt{2}$ 52. $\sqrt{128c^6}$

53. $\sqrt{(-6)^2x^5}$ 54. $\sqrt{(-7)^2y^5}$ 55. $\sqrt{a^2b}$ $|a|\sqrt{b}$ 56. $\sqrt{a^4b}$ $a^2\sqrt{b}$

57. $\sqrt{\dfrac{3}{4a^2}}$ $\dfrac{\sqrt{3}}{2|a|}$ 58. $\sqrt{\dfrac{5}{9a^2}}$ $\dfrac{\sqrt{5}}{3|a|}$ 59. $\sqrt{\dfrac{81x^5}{y^6}}$ $\dfrac{9x^2\sqrt{x}}{|y^3|}$ 60. $\sqrt{\dfrac{49x^7}{y^{10}}}$ $\dfrac{7x^3\sqrt{x}}{|y^5|}$

61. $\sqrt{\dfrac{2x^2}{3x^4}}$ $\dfrac{\sqrt{6}}{3|x|}$ 62. $\sqrt{\dfrac{3y^5}{5y}}$ $\dfrac{y^2\sqrt{15}}{5}$ 63. $\sqrt{\dfrac{x^7}{7x^2}}$ $\dfrac{x^2\sqrt{7x}}{7}$ 64. $\sqrt{\dfrac{5y^3}{2y^9}}$ $\dfrac{\sqrt{10}}{2|y^3|}$

C. **Express each product in simplest form.**

65. $\sqrt{5}\cdot\sqrt{10}$ $5\sqrt{2}$ 66. $\sqrt{30}\cdot\sqrt{3}$ $3\sqrt{10}$ 67. $3\sqrt{5}\cdot2\sqrt{15}$ $30\sqrt{3}$

68. $4\sqrt{10}\cdot3\sqrt{6}$ $24\sqrt{15}$ 69. $4\sqrt{2x}\cdot\sqrt{6x}$ $8x\sqrt{3}$ 70. $\sqrt{3a}\cdot3\sqrt{6a}$ $9a\sqrt{2}$

71. $-2\sqrt{2x^2}\cdot\sqrt{10x^6}$ 72. $\sqrt{3x^2}\cdot3\sqrt{3x^4}$ $9|x^3|$ 73. $2\sqrt{6x^4}\cdot-3\sqrt{x^5}$

Written Exercises

49. $10y^2\sqrt{2}$

50. $10a^2\sqrt{3}$

52. $8|c^3|\sqrt{2}$

53. $6x^2\sqrt{x}$

54. $7y^2\sqrt{y}$

71. $-4x^4\sqrt{5}$

73. $-6x^4\sqrt{6x}$

CHALLENGE

Which triangle has the greater area?
The areas of the triangles are equal.

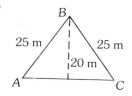

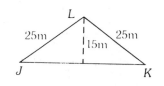

CLASSROOM EXAMPLES

1. Perform the indicated operation.

   a. $3\sqrt{7} + 2\sqrt{7}$

   $3\sqrt{7} + 2\sqrt{7} = (3+2)\sqrt{7}$
   $= 5\sqrt{7}$

   b. $6\sqrt{y} - \sqrt{y}$

   $6\sqrt{y} - \sqrt{y} = (6-1)\sqrt{y}$
   $= 5\sqrt{y}$

2. Perform the indicated operations.

   a. $\sqrt{50} + 3\sqrt{20} - \sqrt{18}$

   $\sqrt{50} + 3\sqrt{20} - \sqrt{18}$
   $= \sqrt{25 \cdot 2} + 3\sqrt{4 \cdot 5}$
   $\quad - \sqrt{9 \cdot 2}$
   $= 5\sqrt{2} + 6\sqrt{5} - 3\sqrt{2}$
   $= (5 - 3)\sqrt{2} + 6\sqrt{5}$
   $= 2\sqrt{2} + 6\sqrt{5}$

   b. $\sqrt{20x^3} + 3x\sqrt{45x}$

   $\sqrt{20x^3} + 3x\sqrt{45x}$
   $= \sqrt{4x^2 \cdot 5x} + 3x\sqrt{9 \cdot 5x}$
   $= 2x\sqrt{5x} + 9x\sqrt{5x}$
   $= (2x + 9x)\sqrt{5x}$
   $= 11x\sqrt{5x}$

   c. $\sqrt{27} - \sqrt{48} + \sqrt{\frac{1}{3}}$

   $\sqrt{27} - \sqrt{48} + \sqrt{\frac{1}{3}}$
   $= \sqrt{9 \cdot 3} - \sqrt{16 \cdot 3} + \frac{\sqrt{1}}{\sqrt{3}}$
   $= 3\sqrt{3} - 4\sqrt{3} + \frac{1}{\sqrt{3}} \cdot \frac{\sqrt{3}}{\sqrt{3}}$
   $= 3\sqrt{3} - 4\sqrt{3} + \frac{1}{3} \cdot \sqrt{3}$
   $= \left(3 - 4 + \frac{1}{3}\right)\sqrt{3}$
   $= -\frac{2}{3}\sqrt{3}$ or $-\frac{2\sqrt{3}}{3}$

11.6 | Adding and Subtracting Radicals

Radical expressions that contain a common radical factor are **like terms**. For example, $2\sqrt{5}$ and $4\sqrt{5}$ are like terms because their radicals are the same. The radical expressions $4\sqrt{3}$ and $4\sqrt{7}$ are **unlike terms** because the radicals are not the same.

You can add or subtract radical expressions that contain a common radical factor by using the *distributive property*.

EXAMPLES

1   **Perform the indicated operation.**

     a. $2\sqrt{5} + 4\sqrt{5}$ **b.** $8\sqrt{x} - \sqrt{x}$

     SOLUTIONS

     a. $2\sqrt{5} + 4\sqrt{5} = (2 + 4)\sqrt{5}$ **b.** $8\sqrt{x} - \sqrt{x} = (8 - 1)\sqrt{x}$
                           $= 6\sqrt{5}$ $= 7\sqrt{x}$

Sometimes it is necessary to first change radical expressions to simplest form.

2   **Perform the indicated operations.**

     a. $\sqrt{32} + 2\sqrt{20} - \sqrt{72}$ **b.** $\sqrt{12x^3} + 2x\sqrt{27x}$ **c.** $\sqrt{18} - \sqrt{8} + \sqrt{\frac{1}{2}}$

     SOLUTIONS

     a. $\sqrt{32} + 2\sqrt{20} - \sqrt{72} = \sqrt{16 \cdot 2} + 2\sqrt{4 \cdot 5} - \sqrt{36 \cdot 2}$
                                        $= 4\sqrt{2} + 4\sqrt{5} - 6\sqrt{2}$
                                        $= (4 - 6)\sqrt{2} + 4\sqrt{5}$
                                        $= -2\sqrt{2} + 4\sqrt{5}$

     b. $\sqrt{12x^3} + 2x\sqrt{27x} = \sqrt{4x^2 \cdot 3x} + 2x\sqrt{9 \cdot 3x}$
                                 $= 2x\sqrt{3x} + 6x\sqrt{3x}$
                                 $= (2x + 6x)\sqrt{3x}$
                                 $= 8x\sqrt{3x}$

     c. $\sqrt{18} - \sqrt{8} + \sqrt{\frac{1}{2}} = \sqrt{9 \cdot 2} - \sqrt{4 \cdot 2} + \frac{\sqrt{1}}{\sqrt{2}}$
                                   $= 3\sqrt{2} - 2\sqrt{2} + \frac{1}{\sqrt{2}} \cdot \frac{\sqrt{2}}{\sqrt{2}}$
                                   $= 3\sqrt{2} - 2\sqrt{2} + \frac{1}{2} \cdot \sqrt{2}$
                                   $= \left(3 - 2 + \frac{1}{2}\right)\sqrt{2}$
                                   $= \frac{3}{2}\sqrt{2}$ or $\frac{3\sqrt{2}}{2}$

Perform the indicated operation.

1. $2\sqrt{3} + \sqrt{3}$ $3\sqrt{3}$
2. $-5\sqrt{6} + 8\sqrt{6}$ $3\sqrt{6}$
3. $4\sqrt{x} - 7\sqrt{x}$ $-3\sqrt{x}$

4. $10\sqrt{y} + 6\sqrt{y}$ $16\sqrt{y}$
5. $-5\sqrt{3} - 7\sqrt{3}$ $-12\sqrt{3}$
6. $-\sqrt{a} + 9\sqrt{a}$ $8\sqrt{a}$

7. $\sqrt{9a} + \sqrt{a}$ $4\sqrt{a}$
8. $\sqrt{4b} + 2\sqrt{b}$ $4\sqrt{b}$
9. $\sqrt{25x} + 2\sqrt{x}$ $7\sqrt{x}$

10. $\sqrt{x} - \sqrt{36x}$ $-5\sqrt{x}$
11. $\sqrt{16x} - 5\sqrt{x}$ $-\sqrt{x}$
12. $\sqrt{81x} - \sqrt{64x}$ $\sqrt{x}$

13. $\sqrt{36y} + 3\sqrt{y}$ $9\sqrt{y}$
14. $\sqrt{200} - 3\sqrt{2}$ $7\sqrt{2}$
15. $\sqrt{12} - \sqrt{3}$ $\sqrt{3}$

WRITTEN EXERCISES

A. Perform the indicated operations.

1. $\sqrt{8} + 3\sqrt{2}$ $5\sqrt{2}$
2. $2\sqrt{2} + \sqrt{18}$ $5\sqrt{2}$
3. $\sqrt{12} - \sqrt{27}$ $-\sqrt{3}$

4. $\sqrt{27} - 2\sqrt{3}$ $\sqrt{3}$
5. $-5\sqrt{a} - 3\sqrt{a}$ $-8\sqrt{a}$
6. $-\sqrt{b} - 9\sqrt{b}$

7. $-3\sqrt{3} + 4\sqrt{3} - 10\sqrt{3}$
8. $5\sqrt{5} + 6\sqrt{5} - 10\sqrt{5}$
9. $-6\sqrt{2} + 5\sqrt{2} + \sqrt{8}$

10. $\sqrt{20} + 2\sqrt{5} - 3\sqrt{5}$
11. $\sqrt{72} + 8\sqrt{2} - 9\sqrt{2}$
12. $5\sqrt{3} - \sqrt{12} - 6\sqrt{3}$

B. 13. $\sqrt{20} + \sqrt{45}$ $5\sqrt{5}$
14. $\sqrt{50} + \sqrt{32}$ $9\sqrt{2}$
15. $\sqrt{12} + \sqrt{48}$ $6\sqrt{3}$

16. $\sqrt{54} + \sqrt{24}$ $5\sqrt{6}$
17. $\sqrt{32} + \sqrt{18}$ $7\sqrt{2}$
18. $\sqrt{75} + \sqrt{27}$ $8\sqrt{3}$

19. $\sqrt{2x} + \sqrt{8x}$ $3\sqrt{2x}$
20. $\sqrt{27y} + \sqrt{3y}$ $4\sqrt{3y}$
21. $\sqrt{8} + \sqrt{18} - 3\sqrt{2}$

22. $\sqrt{12} - 2\sqrt{3} + \sqrt{27}$
23. $2\sqrt{5} - 3\sqrt{80} + \sqrt{125}$
24. $4\sqrt{3} - \sqrt{75} + \sqrt{108}$

25. $\sqrt{72} - \sqrt{98} + \sqrt{8}$
26. $\sqrt{18} - 3\sqrt{8} + \sqrt{50}$
27. $\sqrt{80} - \sqrt{20} + \sqrt{180}$

28. $\sqrt{175} + \sqrt{28} - \sqrt{63}$
29. $\sqrt{360} + \sqrt{90} + \sqrt{250}$
30. $\sqrt{160} + \sqrt{90} + \sqrt{40}$

31. $\sqrt{32} + \sqrt{28} - \sqrt{162}$
32. $\sqrt{96} - \sqrt{54} + \sqrt{12}$
33. $2\sqrt{28} + 3\sqrt{63} - \sqrt{18}$

34. $4\sqrt{48} - \sqrt{12} + 5\sqrt{24}$
35. $\sqrt{12a} + \sqrt{192a}$ $10\sqrt{3a}$
36. $\sqrt{162b} + \sqrt{50b}$

37. $x\sqrt{18x} + \sqrt{8x^3}$ $5x\sqrt{2x}$
38. $y\sqrt{12y} + \sqrt{27y^3}$ $5y\sqrt{3y}$
39. $3y\sqrt{12y} + \sqrt{75y^3}$

40. $2y\sqrt{20y} + \sqrt{80y^3}$
41. $n^2\sqrt{50} + \sqrt{32n^4}$ $9n^2\sqrt{2}$
42. $\sqrt{48x^4} + x^2\sqrt{27}$

43. $\sqrt{8} + \sqrt{\dfrac{1}{2}}$ $\dfrac{5\sqrt{2}}{2}$
44. $\sqrt{12} + \sqrt{\dfrac{1}{3}}$ $\dfrac{7\sqrt{3}}{3}$
45. $\sqrt{24} + \sqrt{6} - \sqrt{\dfrac{3}{2}}$

46. $\sqrt{40} + \sqrt{10} + \sqrt{\dfrac{2}{5}}$
47. $\sqrt{63} + \sqrt{28} - \sqrt{\dfrac{1}{7}}$
48. $\sqrt{54} - \sqrt{\dfrac{1}{6}} + \sqrt{24}$

C. 49. $3\sqrt{2}(\sqrt{6} + 4\sqrt{8})$ $6\sqrt{3} + 48$
50. $4\sqrt{3}(3\sqrt{3} - 2\sqrt{6})$ $36 - 24\sqrt{2}$

51. $\sqrt{\dfrac{x^3}{25}} - \sqrt{\dfrac{x^3}{49}}$ $\dfrac{2x\sqrt{x}}{35}$
52. $\sqrt{\dfrac{y^3}{16}} + \sqrt{\dfrac{y^3}{81}}$ $\dfrac{13y\sqrt{y}}{36}$

53. $\sqrt{\dfrac{x^2}{16}} + \sqrt{\dfrac{x^2}{25}}$ $\dfrac{9|x|}{20}$
54. $\sqrt{\dfrac{a^2}{9}} - \sqrt{\dfrac{a^2}{64}}$ $\dfrac{5|a|}{24}$

55. $\sqrt{x^5} + \sqrt{x^4} + \sqrt{x^3}$ $x^2\sqrt{x} + x^2 + x\sqrt{x}$
56. $\sqrt{x^9} + \sqrt{x^7} - \sqrt{x^5}$

57. $\sqrt{25x^2} + \sqrt{64x^2}$ $13|x|$
58. $\sqrt{49x^3} - \sqrt{16x^4}$ $7x\sqrt{x} - 4x^2$

MIXED REVIEW

Perform the indicated operations.

1. $(-15x^2 + 3xy - 8)$
$- (3x^2 - 4xy + 9)$
$-18x^2 + 7xy - 17$

2. $(-8)\left(-\dfrac{1}{8}\right)$ 1

3. $\dfrac{-6}{0}$ undefined

4. $(18x^2 - 17x - 15) \div$
$(2x - 3)$ $9x + 5$

5. $\sqrt{12} \cdot \sqrt{3}$ 6

TEACHER'S RESOURCE
MASTERS

Practice Master 48, Part 1

ASSIGNMENT GUIDE

Minimum
1–11 odd, 13–26
Regular
25–44
Maximum
34–48, 49–57 odd

ADDITIONAL ANSWERS

Written Exercises

6. $-10\sqrt{b}$

7. $-9\sqrt{3}$

8. $\sqrt{5}$

9. $\sqrt{2}$

10. $\sqrt{5}$

11. $5\sqrt{2}$

12. $-3\sqrt{3}$

21. $2\sqrt{2}$

22. $3\sqrt{3}$

23. $-5\sqrt{5}$

24. $5\sqrt{3}$

Additional Answers
See p. T62.

TEACHER'S NOTES

See p. T35.

CLASSROOM EXAMPLES

1. Multiply $(5 + \sqrt{2})$ and $(6 + 2\sqrt{2})$.
$$(5 + \sqrt{2})(6 + 2\sqrt{2})$$
$$= 5 \cdot 6 + 5 \cdot 2\sqrt{2}$$
$$\quad + 6\sqrt{2} + 2\sqrt{2} \cdot \sqrt{2}$$
$$= 30 + 10\sqrt{2} + 6\sqrt{2}$$
$$\quad + 2 \cdot 2$$
$$= 30 + 16\sqrt{2} + 4$$
$$= 34 + 16\sqrt{2}$$

2. Simplify $(5 + \sqrt{3})^2$.
$$(5 + \sqrt{3})^2$$
$$= 5^2 + 2 \cdot 5\sqrt{3} + (\sqrt{3})^2$$
$$= 25 + 10\sqrt{3} + 3$$
$$= 28 + 10\sqrt{3}$$

3. Simplify $(3 - \sqrt{6})^2$.
$$(3 - \sqrt{6})^2$$
$$= 3^2 - 2 \cdot 3\sqrt{6} + (\sqrt{6})^2$$
$$= 9 - 6\sqrt{6} + 6$$
$$= 15 - 6\sqrt{6}$$

4. Simplify $(3 + 4\sqrt{2})(3 - 4\sqrt{2})$.
$$(3 + 4\sqrt{2})(3 - 4\sqrt{2})$$
$$= 3^2 - (4\sqrt{2})^2$$
$$= 9 - 16 \cdot 2$$
$$= 9 - 32$$
$$= -23$$

5. Multiply $(3 + 2\sqrt{7})(2 + 3\sqrt{5})$.
$$(3 + 2\sqrt{7})(2 + 3\sqrt{5})$$
$$= 3 \cdot 2 + 3 \cdot 3\sqrt{5} + 2\sqrt{7}$$
$$\quad \cdot 2 + 2\sqrt{7} \cdot 3\sqrt{5}$$
$$= 6 + 9\sqrt{5} + 4\sqrt{7} + 6\sqrt{35}$$

11.7 Binomials Containing Radicals

To multiply binomials containing radicals, you can use the same methods you used when you multiplied binomials in Chapter 5.

EXAMPLES

1 **Multiply $(3 + \sqrt{2})$ and $(4 + 2\sqrt{2})$.**

SOLUTION Use the FOIL method.

$$\qquad\qquad\qquad\qquad \overset{F}{} \quad \overset{O}{} \quad \overset{I}{} \quad \overset{L}{}$$
$$(3 + \sqrt{2})(4 + 2\sqrt{2}) = 3 \cdot 4 + 3 \cdot 2\sqrt{2} + 4\sqrt{2} + 2\sqrt{2} \cdot \sqrt{2}$$
$$= 12 + 6\sqrt{2} + 4\sqrt{2} + 2 \cdot 2$$
$$= 12 + 10\sqrt{2} + 4$$
$$= 16 + 10\sqrt{2}$$

2 **Simplify $(8 + \sqrt{3})^2$.**

SOLUTION Use the $(a + b)^2 = a^2 + 2ab + b^2$ pattern.
$$(8 + \sqrt{3})^2 = 8^2 + 2 \cdot 8\sqrt{3} + (\sqrt{3})^2$$
$$= 64 + 16\sqrt{3} + 3$$
$$= 67 + 16\sqrt{3}$$

3 **Simplify $(4 - \sqrt{5})^2$.**

SOLUTION Use the $(a - b)^2 = a^2 - 2ab + b^2$ pattern.
$$(4 - \sqrt{5})^2 = 4^2 - 2 \cdot 4\sqrt{5} + (\sqrt{5})^2$$
$$= 16 - 8\sqrt{5} + 5$$
$$= 21 - 8\sqrt{5}$$

4 **Simplify $(6 + 5\sqrt{2})(6 - 5\sqrt{2})$.**

SOLUTION Use the $(a + b)(a - b) = a^2 - b^2$ pattern.
$$(6 + 5\sqrt{2})(6 - 5\sqrt{2}) = 6^2 - (5\sqrt{2})^2$$
$$= 36 - 25 \cdot 2$$
$$= 36 - 50$$
$$= -14$$

5 **Multiply $(2 + 3\sqrt{7})(1 + 4\sqrt{2})$.**

SOLUTION Use the FOIL method.

$$\qquad\qquad\qquad\qquad \overset{F}{} \quad \overset{O}{} \quad \overset{I}{} \quad \overset{L}{}$$
$$(2 + 3\sqrt{7})(1 + 4\sqrt{2}) = 2 \cdot 1 + 2 \cdot 4\sqrt{2} + 3\sqrt{7} \cdot 1 + 3\sqrt{7} \cdot 4\sqrt{2}$$
$$= 2 + 8\sqrt{2} + 3\sqrt{7} + 12\sqrt{14}$$

Binomials such as $6 + 5\sqrt{2}$ and $6 - 5\sqrt{2}$ are called **conjugates** of each other. The product of two conjugates is a *rational number*. So when you need to rationalize a binomial denominator, use the conjugate of the binomial in the denominator.

6 | **Simplify** $\dfrac{4}{5 - 2\sqrt{3}}$.

SOLUTION $\dfrac{4}{5 - 2\sqrt{3}} = \dfrac{4}{5 - 2\sqrt{3}} \cdot \dfrac{5 + 2\sqrt{3}}{5 + 2\sqrt{3}}$

$$= \dfrac{4(5 + 2\sqrt{3})}{5^2 - (2\sqrt{3})^2}$$

$$= \dfrac{4(5 + 2\sqrt{3})}{25 - 4 \cdot 3}$$

$$= \dfrac{4(5 + 2\sqrt{3})}{25 - 12}$$

$$= \dfrac{20 + 8\sqrt{3}}{13}$$

6. Simplify $\dfrac{3}{5 - 2\sqrt{3}}$.

$\dfrac{3}{5 - 2\sqrt{3}} = \dfrac{3}{5 - 2\sqrt{3}} \cdot \dfrac{5 + 2\sqrt{3}}{5 + 2\sqrt{3}}$

$= \dfrac{3(5 + 2\sqrt{3})}{5^2 - (2\sqrt{3})^2}$

$= \dfrac{3(5 + 2\sqrt{3})}{25 - 4 \cdot 3}$

$= \dfrac{3(5 + 2\sqrt{3})}{25 - 12}$

$= \dfrac{15 + 6\sqrt{3}}{13}$

ORAL EXERCISES

Name the conjugate of each binomial.

1. $7 + 3\sqrt{5}$ $7 - 3\sqrt{5}$ **2.** $4 + 5\sqrt{2}$

3. $9 - 3\sqrt{5}$ **4.** $2 - \sqrt{3}$

5. $8 + 7\sqrt{7}$ $8 - 7\sqrt{7}$ **6.** $6 - \sqrt{13}$

7. $2\sqrt{3} - 7$ **8.** $2\sqrt{5} + 7$

WRITTEN EXERCISES

A. Find each product.

1. $(1 + \sqrt{3})(2 + \sqrt{3})$ $5 + 3\sqrt{3}$

2. $(2 + \sqrt{2})(1 + \sqrt{2})$ $4 + 3\sqrt{2}$

3. $(5 - \sqrt{5})(2 + \sqrt{5})$ $5 + 3\sqrt{5}$

4. $(7 - \sqrt{2})(3 + \sqrt{2})$ $19 + 4\sqrt{2}$

5. $(5 - \sqrt{6})(3 - \sqrt{6})$ $21 - 8\sqrt{6}$

6. $(3 - \sqrt{7})(2 - \sqrt{7})$ $13 - 5\sqrt{7}$

7. $(1 + \sqrt{7})^2$ $8 + 2\sqrt{7}$

8. $(1 + \sqrt{5})^2$ $6 + 2\sqrt{5}$

9. $(4 - \sqrt{7})^2$ $23 - 8\sqrt{7}$

10. $(5 - \sqrt{2})^2$ $27 - 10\sqrt{2}$

11. $(3 + \sqrt{5})(3 - \sqrt{5})$ 4

12. $(2 + \sqrt{3})(2 - \sqrt{3})$ 1

B. 13. $(4 + 2\sqrt{6})(3 + \sqrt{6})$ $24 + 10\sqrt{6}$

14. $(7 + \sqrt{7})(4 + 3\sqrt{7})$ $49 + 25\sqrt{7}$

15. $(9 + \sqrt{5})(3 - 2\sqrt{5})$ $17 - 15\sqrt{5}$

16. $(6 + \sqrt{3})(4 - 3\sqrt{3})$ $15 - 14\sqrt{3}$

17. $(9 - \sqrt{7})(4 - 5\sqrt{7})$ $71 - 49\sqrt{7}$

18. $(8 - \sqrt{5})(4 - 3\sqrt{5})$ $47 - 28\sqrt{5}$

19. $(6 + 3\sqrt{3})^2$ $63 + 36\sqrt{3}$

20. $(2 + 2\sqrt{5})^2$ $24 + 8\sqrt{5}$

21. $(7 - 2\sqrt{11})^2$ $93 - 28\sqrt{11}$

22. $(8 - 3\sqrt{7})^2$ $127 - 48\sqrt{7}$

23. $(4 + 2\sqrt{5})(4 - 2\sqrt{5})$ -4

24. $(3 + 3\sqrt{2})(3 - 3\sqrt{2})$ -9

25. $(4 - 2\sqrt{3})(4 + 2\sqrt{3})$ 4

26. $(6 - 3\sqrt{2})(6 + 3\sqrt{2})$ 18

MIXED REVIEW

1. Find the value of $5(1.3)^2$. 8.45

2. Restate $0.1\overline{34}$ in fractional form. $\frac{133}{990}$

3. Solve $6y + 135 = -3y + 88$. $y = -\frac{47}{9}$

4. Add $5\sqrt{7} + 6\sqrt{7}$. $11\sqrt{7}$

5. $\frac{0}{-4}$ 0

TEACHER'S RESOURCE MASTERS

Practice Master 48, Part 2

ASSIGNMENT GUIDE

Minimum
1–9 odd, 13–32

Regular
13–39 odd, 41–51

Maximum
27–44, 47–53

ADDITIONAL ANSWERS

Oral Exercises
2. $4 - 5\sqrt{2}$
3. $9 + 3\sqrt{5}$
4. $2 + \sqrt{3}$
6. $6 + \sqrt{13}$
7. $2\sqrt{3} + 7$
8. $2\sqrt{5} - 7$

27. $(4 + \sqrt{2})(2 + \sqrt{3})$

28. $(4 + \sqrt{5})(3 + \sqrt{2})$

29. $(3 - \sqrt{3})(2 + \sqrt{5})$

30. $(2 - \sqrt{5})(3 + \sqrt{3})$

31. $(3 - \sqrt{7})(2 - \sqrt{5})$

32. $(4 + \sqrt{5})(6 - \sqrt{2})$

33. $(5 + \sqrt{3})(3 + 3\sqrt{2})$

34. $(4 + \sqrt{2})(2 + 4\sqrt{3})$

35. $(2 + \sqrt{5})(7 - 4\sqrt{3})$

36. $(9 + \sqrt{3})(3 - 2\sqrt{5})$

37. $(9 - \sqrt{7})(2 + 3\sqrt{2})$

38. $(5 + 3\sqrt{5})(7 - \sqrt{3})$

39. $(4 - 3\sqrt{2})(5 + 2\sqrt{3})$

40. $(2 - 4\sqrt{5})(1 + 3\sqrt{2})$

Simplify. (Rationalize the denominator.)

41. $\dfrac{8}{5 + \sqrt{3}}$ $\frac{20 - 4\sqrt{3}}{11}$

42. $\dfrac{7}{6 + \sqrt{5}}$ $\frac{42 - 7\sqrt{5}}{31}$

43. $\dfrac{2}{4 - \sqrt{7}}$ $\frac{8 + 2\sqrt{7}}{9}$

44. $\dfrac{5}{6 - \sqrt{3}}$ $\frac{30 + 5\sqrt{3}}{33}$

45. $\dfrac{\sqrt{5}}{\sqrt{3} - 2}$ $-\sqrt{15} - 2\sqrt{5}$

46. $\dfrac{\sqrt{6}}{\sqrt{5} - 2}$ $\sqrt{30} + 2\sqrt{6}$

C. Find each product.

47. $(4 + \sqrt{3})(\sqrt{6} - \sqrt{2})$ $3\sqrt{6} - \sqrt{2}$

48. $(2\sqrt{3} - 5)(7\sqrt{3} + 2\sqrt{2})$

49. $(\sqrt{5} - 2\sqrt{3})^2$ $17 - 4\sqrt{15}$

50. $(\sqrt{7} + 3\sqrt{5})^2$ $52 + 6\sqrt{35}$

51. $(\sqrt{7} + 2\sqrt{3})(\sqrt{7} - 2\sqrt{3})$ -5

52. $(2\sqrt{3} + 4\sqrt{2})(2\sqrt{3} - 4\sqrt{2})$ -20

Simplify. (Rationalize the denominator.)

53. $\dfrac{4 + 2\sqrt{5}}{5 + 3\sqrt{5}}$ $\frac{5 + \sqrt{5}}{10}$

54. $\dfrac{2 + 3\sqrt{2}}{2\sqrt{6} - \sqrt{2}}$

55. $\dfrac{4 + x\sqrt{y}}{4 - x\sqrt{y}}$

SELF-QUIZ

Find the indicated square roots.

1. $-\sqrt{16}$ -4

2. $\pm\sqrt{121}$ ± 11

3. $\sqrt{\dfrac{81}{16}}$ $\frac{9}{4}$

4. $\sqrt{324}$ 18

The lengths of the legs of a right triangle are given. Find the length of the hypotenuse.

5. $a = 4, b = 3$ 5

6. $a = 6, b = 5$ $\sqrt{61}$

Find the product of the radicals.

7. $\sqrt{2} \cdot \sqrt{7}$ $\sqrt{14}$

8. $\sqrt{2x} \cdot \sqrt{15}$ $\sqrt{30x}$

9. $\sqrt{3a} \cdot \sqrt{7b}$ $\sqrt{21ab}$

Find the quotient of the radicals.

10. $\dfrac{\sqrt{42}}{\sqrt{7}}$ $\sqrt{6}$

11. $\dfrac{\sqrt{34}}{\sqrt{2}}$ $\sqrt{17}$

12. $\dfrac{\sqrt{25y}}{\sqrt{5}}$ $\sqrt{5y}$

Change each radical to simplest form.

13. $\sqrt{52}$ $2\sqrt{13}$

14. $\sqrt{68x^2}$ $2|x|\sqrt{17}$

15. $\sqrt{\dfrac{4}{7}}$ $\frac{2\sqrt{7}}{7}$

11.8 | Radical Equations

A **radical equation** is an equation that has a variable in a radicand. A radical equation can be solved by squaring both sides of the equation.

EXAMPLES

1   **Solve $\sqrt{5x - 4} = 6$.**

SOLUTION

$$\sqrt{5x - 4} = 6$$
$$(\sqrt{5x - 4})^2 = 6^2$$
$$5x - 4 = 36$$
$$5x = 40$$
$$x = 8$$

CHECK   Replace x in the original equation with 8.

$$\sqrt{5x - 4} = 6$$
$$\sqrt{5 \cdot 8 - 4} \stackrel{?}{=} 6$$
$$\sqrt{40 - 4} \stackrel{?}{=} 6$$
$$\sqrt{36} \stackrel{?}{=} 6$$
$$6 = 6 ✔$$

Before squaring both sides of a radical equation, isolate the radical on one side.

2   **Solve $\sqrt{3x - 2} - 5 = 0$.**

SOLUTION

$$\sqrt{3x - 2} - 5 = 0$$
$$\sqrt{3x - 2} = 5$$
$$(\sqrt{3x - 2})^2 = 5^2$$
$$3x - 2 = 25$$
$$3x = 27$$
$$x = 9$$

CHECK   Replace x in the original equation with 9.

$$\sqrt{3x - 2} - 5 = 0$$
$$\sqrt{3 \cdot 9 - 2} - 5 \stackrel{?}{=} 0$$
$$\sqrt{27 - 2} - 5 \stackrel{?}{=} 0$$
$$\sqrt{25} - 5 \stackrel{?}{=} 0$$
$$5 - 5 \stackrel{?}{=} 0$$
$$0 = 0 ✔$$

CLASSROOM EXAMPLES

1. Solve $\sqrt{3x - 5} = 4$.
$$\sqrt{3x - 5} = 4$$
$$(\sqrt{3x - 5})^2 = 4^2$$
$$3x - 5 = 16$$
$$3x = 21$$
$$x = 7$$

2. Solve $\sqrt{5x - 6} - 3 = 0$.
$$\sqrt{5x - 6} - 3 = 0$$
$$\sqrt{5x - 6} = 3$$
$$(\sqrt{5x - 6})^2 = 3^2$$
$$5x - 6 = 9$$
$$5x = 15$$
$$x = 3$$

3. Solve $\sqrt{y + 6} = y + 4$.
$$\sqrt{y + 6} = y + 4$$
$$(\sqrt{y + 6})^2 = (y + 4)^2$$
$$y + 6 = y^2 + 8y + 16$$
$$0 = y^2 + 7y + 10$$
$$0 = (y + 5)(y + 2)$$
$$y + 5 = 0 \quad \text{or} \quad y + 2 = 0$$
$$y = -5 \qquad\qquad y = -2$$
$$\sqrt{y + 6} = y + 4$$
$$\sqrt{-5 + 6} \stackrel{?}{=} -5 + 4$$
$$1 \stackrel{?}{=} -1$$
$$1 \neq -1$$
-5 is an extraneous root.
$$\sqrt{y + 6} = y + 4$$
$$\sqrt{-2 + 6} \stackrel{?}{=} -2 + 4$$
$$\sqrt{4} \stackrel{?}{=} 2$$
$$2 = 2 ✔$$
The solution set is $\{-2\}$.

Sometimes squaring both sides of an equation results in **extraneous roots.** An extraneous root *will not check in the original equation.*

3   **Solve $\sqrt{x + 5} = x + 3$.**

SOLUTION
$$\sqrt{x + 5} = x + 3$$
$$(\sqrt{x + 5})^2 = (x + 3)^2$$
$$x + 5 = x^2 + 6x + 9$$
$$0 = x^2 + 5x + 4$$
$$0 = (x + 4)(x + 1)$$
$$x + 4 = 0 \text{ or } x + 1 = 0$$
$$x = -4 \qquad x = -1$$

CHECK   Replace x in the original equation with -4 and -1.

$$\sqrt{x + 5} = x + 3 \qquad\qquad \sqrt{x + 5} = x + 3$$
$$\sqrt{-4 + 5} \overset{?}{=} -4 + 3 \qquad\qquad \sqrt{-1 + 5} \overset{?}{=} -1 + 3$$
$$\sqrt{1} \overset{?}{=} -1 \qquad\qquad\qquad \sqrt{4} \overset{?}{=} 2$$
$$1 \neq -1 \qquad\qquad\qquad\qquad 2 = 2 ✔$$

-4 is an extraneous root.   The solution set is $\{-1\}$.

ORAL EXERCISES

Tell what equation results from squaring both sides.

1. $\sqrt{x} = 5$ $x = 25$ **2.** $\sqrt{y} = \dfrac{2}{3}$ $y = \dfrac{4}{9}$ **3.** $\sqrt{3x - 2} = 6$

4. $\sqrt{2y} = 8$ $2y = 64$ **5.** $\sqrt{x + 5} = 7$ $x + 5 = 49$ **6.** $\sqrt{4b - 7} = 4$

WRITTEN EXERCISES

A. Solve and check each equation. Watch for extraneous roots.

1. $\sqrt{2y} = 4$ 8   **2.** $\sqrt{3y} = 9$ 27   **3.** $\sqrt{3r} = -3$ ∅   **4.** $\sqrt{5r} = -5$

5. $2\sqrt{x} = 8$ 16   **6.** $3\sqrt{x} = 9$ 9   **7.** $\sqrt{x - 2} = 7$ 51   **8.** $\sqrt{x - 5} = 8$

9. $\sqrt{x + 1} = 5$ **10.** $\sqrt{x + 1} = 6$ **11.** $7 = \sqrt{26 - n}$ **12.** $8 = \sqrt{35 - n}$

13. $\sqrt{\frac{1}{3}x} = 2$ 12   **14.** $\sqrt{\frac{1}{3}x} = 3$ 27   **15.** $\sqrt{5m - 2} = \sqrt{3}$ **16.** $\sqrt{4m} = \sqrt{11}$

B. 17. $\sqrt{n + 3} = 2\sqrt{3}$ 9   **18.** $\sqrt{x + 4} = 3\sqrt{2}$ 14   **19.** $\sqrt{b - 4} = 4\sqrt{5}$ 84

20. $\sqrt{c - 6} = 3\sqrt{6}$ 60   **21.** $\sqrt{3x^2 - 3} = 3$ 2, −2   **22.** $\sqrt{5y^2 + 5} = 5$

23. $\sqrt{5x - 10} - 10 = 0$ 22   **24.** $\sqrt{3y + 3} - 6 = 0$ 11   **25.** $\sqrt{6b - 8} + 7 = 15$

26. $\sqrt{7a + 4} + 11 = 16$ 3   **27.** $\sqrt{x + 6} = x + 4$ −2   **28.** $\sqrt{x + 17} = x + 15$

29. $\sqrt{3x^2 - 11x} = 2$ 4, $-\frac{1}{3}$ **30.** $\sqrt{2x^2 + 3x} = 3$ −3, $\frac{3}{2}$ **31.** $\sqrt{x^2 - 49} = 0$

32. $\sqrt{x^2 - 25} = 0$ 5, −5   **33.** $x = \sqrt{2x + 8}$ 4   **34.** $x = \sqrt{2x + 15}$ 5

35. $\sqrt{2x - 1} = x - 2$ 5   **36.** $\sqrt{3a + 1} = a - 3$ 8   **37.** $1 + \sqrt{y - 1} = y$ 2, 1

38. $\sqrt{x - 2} + 2 = x$ 3, 2   **39.** $\sqrt{n + 3} - 1 = n$ 1   **40.** $2 + \sqrt{7 - 2x} = x$ 3

41. $\sqrt{10 - 6k} + 3 = k$ ∅   **42.** $r - 2\sqrt{5 - 2r} = 4$ ∅   **43.** $\sqrt{2 - t} = \sqrt{t - 2}$ 2

44. $\sqrt{s - 5} = \sqrt{5 - s}$ 5   **45.** $\sqrt{2x^2 - 5x - 3} = 3$ **46.** $\sqrt{6x^2 + 5x} = 2$

C. 47. $\sqrt{6a - 2} - \sqrt{5a + 9} = 0$ 11   **48.** $\sqrt{4b + 5} - \sqrt{7b + 8} = 0$ −1

49. $\sqrt{4t} = \sqrt{t} + 1$ 1   **50.** $\sqrt{x + 2} = \sqrt{x + 12}$ 4

51. $5\sqrt{2x + 2} - 6 = 2\sqrt{2x + 2}$ 1   **52.** $5\sqrt{3y - 1} - 4 = 3\sqrt{3y - 1}$ $\frac{5}{3}$

25. 12

28. −13

31. 7, −7

37. 2, 1

45. $-\frac{3}{2}$, 4

46. $-\frac{4}{3}$, $\frac{1}{2}$

ALGEBRA IN USE

Suppose that you are a passenger in an airplane. When you look out the window, the distance you can see from horizon to horizon is a function of the plane's altitude (height).

If the plane's altitude is given in feet, use
view (in miles) = $\sqrt{\text{altitude}} \times 1.22$.

If the plane's altitude is given in meters, use
view (in kilometers) = $\sqrt{\text{altitude}} \times 3.56$.

Example 1: A plane's altitude is 10,000 feet. What is the distance you can view from this height?

Solution: view = $\sqrt{10,000} \times 1.22$
= 122 miles

Example 2: A plane's altitude is 1500 meters. What is the distance you can view from this height?

Solution: view = $\sqrt{1500} \times 3.56$
≈ 137.9 kilometers

EXERCISES

Find the approximate distance you can view from each given altitude.

1. 1000 feet 38.6 mi   **2.** 25,000 feet 192.9 mi   **3.** 40,000 feet 244 mi

4. 3500 meters 210.6 km   **5.** 6000 meters 275.8 km   **6.** 12 000 meters 390 km

EXPLORATION
Higher-Order Radicals

Higher-order radicals involve cube roots, fourth roots, fifth roots, and so on.

The *cube root* of 64 is 4 because $4^3 = 64$. A *fourth root* of 16 is 2 because $2^4 = 16$. The *fifth root* of 243 is 3 because $3^5 = 243$.

A radical symbol is used with a higher-order radical. An **index** is used to indicate the root. So "the cube root of 64" is written $\sqrt[3]{64}$, "a fourth root of 16" is written $\sqrt[4]{16}$, and "the fifth root of 243" is written $\sqrt[5]{243}$. Notice that -2 is also a fourth root of 16, because $(-2)^4 = 16$.

You can simplify higher-order radicals in a way similar to that used for simplifying square roots.

Example 1: Simplify $-\sqrt[4]{16}$.
Solution: $-\sqrt[4]{16} = -2$

Example 2: Simplify $\sqrt[5]{-32}$.
Solution: $\sqrt[5]{-32} = -2$

Example 3: Simplify $\sqrt[4]{162}$.
Solution: $\sqrt[4]{162} = \sqrt[4]{81 \cdot 2}$
$= \sqrt[4]{81} \cdot \sqrt[4]{2}$
$= 3\sqrt[4]{2}$

Example 4: Simplify $-\sqrt[3]{32}$.
Solution: $-\sqrt[3]{32} = -\sqrt[3]{8 \cdot 4}$
$= -\sqrt[3]{8} \cdot \sqrt[3]{4}$
$= 2\sqrt[3]{4}$

Notice that for a radical expression with an *even* index you find the *principal root*, as with square roots. A negative sign is used to indicate the negative root of a radical expression with an even index.

EXERCISES

Simplify each radical.

1. $\sqrt[4]{48}$ **2.** $\sqrt[3]{24}$ **3.** $\sqrt[5]{-32}$ **4.** $\sqrt[4]{81}$

5. $\sqrt[3]{-192}$ **6.** $-\sqrt[6]{320}$ **7.** $\sqrt[3]{1029}$ **8.** $\sqrt[4]{96}$

Perform the indicated operation.

Example: Find $\sqrt[4]{32} + \sqrt[4]{162}$.
Solution: $\sqrt[4]{32} + \sqrt[4]{162} = \sqrt[4]{16 \cdot 2} + \sqrt[4]{81 \cdot 2}$
$= 2\sqrt[4]{2} + 3\sqrt[4]{2}$
$= 5\sqrt[4]{2}$

9. $\sqrt[3]{16} + \sqrt[3]{54}$ $5\sqrt[3]{2}$ **10.** $\sqrt[3]{-864} + \sqrt[3]{32}$ $-4\sqrt[3]{4}$

11. $\sqrt[5]{96} - \sqrt[5]{729}$ $-\sqrt[5]{3}$ **12.** $\sqrt[4]{324} + \sqrt[4]{64}$ $5\sqrt[4]{4}$

Express each product in simplest form.

Example: Find $\sqrt[3]{20} \cdot \sqrt[3]{100}$.

Solution: $\sqrt[3]{20} \cdot \sqrt[3]{100} = \sqrt[3]{2000}$
$= \sqrt[3]{1000 \cdot 2}$
$= \sqrt[3]{1000} \cdot \sqrt[3]{2}$
$= 10\sqrt[3]{2}$

13. $\sqrt[4]{54} \cdot \sqrt[4]{48}$ $6\sqrt[4]{2}$

14. $3\sqrt[3]{-12} \cdot \sqrt[3]{-4}$ $6\sqrt[3]{6}$

15. $\sqrt[5]{250x^7} \cdot \sqrt[5]{75x^7}$ $5x^2\sqrt[5]{6x^4}$

16. $\sqrt[5]{405x^{11}} \cdot x^3\sqrt[5]{18x^6}$

Rationalize the denominator.

Example: Find $\sqrt[5]{\frac{1}{2}}$.   *Solution:* $\sqrt[5]{\frac{1}{2}} = \frac{\sqrt[5]{1}}{\sqrt[5]{2}} \cdot \frac{\sqrt[5]{16}}{\sqrt[5]{16}}$

$= \frac{\sqrt[5]{16}}{\sqrt[5]{32}}$

$= \frac{\sqrt[5]{16}}{2}$

17. $\sqrt[3]{\frac{1}{3}}$ **18.** $\sqrt[5]{\frac{2}{9}}$ **19.** $\sqrt[6]{\frac{2}{81}}$ **20.** $\sqrt[4]{\frac{3}{125x}}$

16. $3x^6\sqrt[5]{30x^2}$

17. $\frac{\sqrt[3]{9}}{3}$

18. $\frac{\sqrt[5]{54}}{3}$

19. $\frac{\sqrt[6]{18}}{3}$

20. $\frac{\sqrt[4]{15x^3}}{5x}$

ERROR SEARCH

5. $(3x - 5)^2 = 9x^2 - 30x + 25$

6. The slope of the line $x = 4$ is undefined.

ERROR SEARCH

Find the error in each exercise and give the correct answer.

1. $3 - 2x > 7$
$-2x > 4$
$x > -2$ $x < -2$

2. $\{3, 4, 1\} \cap \{2, 3\} = \{1, 2, 3, 4\}$ $\{3\}$

3. $(2^4)(2^3) = 4^7$ 2^7

4. $(-3x^2)^4 = -3x^8$ $81x^8$

5. $(3x - 5)^2 = 9x^2 + 25$

6. The slope of the line $x = 4$ is 0.

7. The greatest common factor of 4 and 12 is 12. 4

8. The slope of the line that passes through the points $(-2, 4)$ and $(3, -5)$ is $-\frac{5}{9}$. $-\frac{9}{5}$

11.9 | The Distance Formula

All points on a horizontal line in the coordinate plane have the same y-coordinate. Point A has the coordinates $(-4, 3)$ and point B has the coordinates $(2, 3)$. The distance between point A and point B, denoted AB, equals the absolute value of the difference of the x-coordinates.

$AB = |-4 - 2| = 6$ or
$AB = |2 - (-4)| = 6$

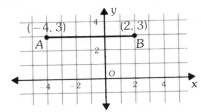

CLASSROOM EXAMPLES

1. Point A has the coordinates $(-4, 2)$, and point B has the coordinates $(6, -8)$. Use the distance formula to find AB.

AB
$= \sqrt{(x_2 - x_1)^2 + (y_2 - y_1)^2}$
$= \sqrt{[6 - (-4)]^2 + (-8 - 2)^2}$
$= \sqrt{10^2 + (-10)^2}$
$= \sqrt{100 + 100}$
$= \sqrt{200}$
$= \sqrt{100 \cdot 2}$
$= 10\sqrt{2}$

The distance AB is $10\sqrt{2}$.

2. The distance between point R with the coordinates $(-6, y)$, and point S, with the coordinates $(3, 6)$, is $\sqrt{82}$. Find all possible values of y.

d
$= \sqrt{(x_2 - x_1)^2 + (y_2 - y_1)^2}$
$\sqrt{82} = \sqrt{(3 + 6)^2 + (6 - y)^2}$
$\sqrt{82} = \sqrt{9^2 + (6 - y)^2}$
$82 = 9^2 + (6 - y)^2$
$82 = 81 + 36 - 12y + y^2$
$0 = 35 - 12y + y^2$
$0 = y^2 - 12y + 35$
$0 = (y - 7)(y - 5)$
$y - 7 = 0$ or $y - 5 = 0$
$y = 7$ $\qquad$ $y = 5$

The values of y are 7 and 5.

All points on a vertical line in the coordinate plane have the same x-coordinate. Point A has the coordinates $(-4, 3)$ and point C has the coordinates $(-4, -5)$. The distance between points A and C equals the absolute value of the difference of the y-coordinates.

$AC = |3 - (-5)| = 8$ or
$AC = |-5 - 3| = 8$

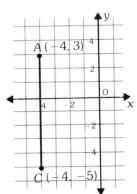

You can find the distance between points B and C by using the Pythagorean theorem. A right triangle is formed when a horizontal line is drawn from point B to point A and when a vertical line is drawn from point C to point A.

$\overline{BC}$ is the hypotenuse of the right triangle ABC.

$(BC)^2 = (AB)^2 + (AC)^2$
$(BC)^2 = 6^2 + 8^2$
$(BC)^2 = 36 + 64$
$(BC)^2 = 100$
$BC = 10$

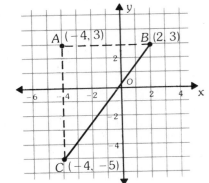

This method can be used to find a formula for the distance between any two points in the coordinate plane. Let point P have the coordinates (x_1, y_1) and point Q have the coordinates (x_2, y_2). Draw a horizontal line and a vertical line to locate point R with the coordinates (x_2, y_1).

$PR = |x_2 - x_1|$ and $QR = |y_2 - y_1|$

$(PQ)^2 = (PR)^2 + (QR)^2$

$(PQ)^2 = |x_2 - x_1|^2 + |y_2 - y_1|^2$

$(PQ)^2 = (x_2 - x_1)^2 + (y_2 - y_1)^2$ *For any real numbers a and b, $|a - b|^2 = (a - b)^2$.*

$PQ = \sqrt{(x_2 - x_1)^2 + (y_2 - y_1)^2}$

Distance Formula	Let P be a point with the coordinates (x_1, y_1) and Q be a point with the coordinates (x_2, y_2). The **distance between points P and Q is** given by the formula $PQ = \sqrt{(x_2 - x_1)^2 + (y_2 - y_1)^2}$.

EXAMPLES

1   Point J has the coordinates $(-2, 1)$, and point K has the coordinates $(3, -4)$. Use the distance formula to find JK.

SOLUTION $JK = \sqrt{(x_2 - x_1)^2 + (y_2 - y_1)^2}$

$= \sqrt{[3 - (-2)]^2 + (-4 - 1)^2}$

$= \sqrt{5^2 + (-5)^2}$

$= \sqrt{25 + 25}$

$= \sqrt{50}$

$= \sqrt{25 \cdot 2}$

$= 5\sqrt{2}$

The distance JK is $5\sqrt{2}$.

2   The distance between point A with the coordinates $(-3, y)$, and point B, with the coordinates $(3, 3)$, is $\sqrt{61}$. Find all possible values of y.

SOLUTION $d = \sqrt{(x_2 - x_1)^2 + (y_2 - y_1)^2}$

$\sqrt{61} = \sqrt{(3 + 3)^2 + (3 - y)^2}$

$\sqrt{61} = \sqrt{6^2 + (3 - y)^2}$

$61 = 6^2 + (3 - y)^2$ *Square both sides.*

$61 = 36 + 9 - 6y + y^2$

$0 = -16 - 6y + y^2$

$0 = y^2 - 6y - 16$

$0 = (y - 8)(y + 2)$ *Factor the quadratic equation.*

$y - 8 = 0$ or $y + 2 = 0$

$y = 8$ $y = -2$

The values of y are 8 and -2.

MIXED REVIEW

1. Determine the LCD of $\frac{1}{x + 5}$ and $\frac{3}{x - 2}$. $(x + 5)(x - 2)$

2. What is 42% of 830? 348.6

3. Multiply $\frac{6a^3}{7b} \cdot \frac{3b^2}{6}$ and simplify. $\frac{3a^3b}{7}$

4. Express in positive exponents. $\frac{x^{-5}}{x^{-9}}$ x^4

5. Solve $\frac{x}{32} = \frac{7}{8}$.   28

TEACHER'S RESOURCE MASTERS

Practice Master 49, Part 2

Quiz 22

ASSIGNMENT GUIDE

Minimum
5-24

Regular
7-26

Maximum
13-32

ORAL EXERCISES

Find the distance on a number line between the two points whose coordinates are given.

1. 7 and 3   4
2. 0 and 6   6
3. 0 and -5 5
4. -3 and 2   5
5. -2 and 5   7
6. -3 and -1 2
7. 2 and 17   15
8. -4 and 2   6

9. Point A has the coordinates $(-3, 6)$, and point B has the coordinates $(2, -5)$. To find the distance between points A and B, use the distance formula $d = \sqrt{(x_2 - x_1)^2 + (y_2 - y_1)^2}$. What is the value of x_1? Of x_2? Of y_1? Of y_2? Explain why it does not matter which set of coordinates is assigned to (x_1, y_1) and which is assigned to (x_2, y_2).

WRITTEN EXERCISES

A. Find the coordinates of point R.

1.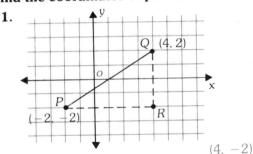

$(4, -2)$

2.

$(3, 2)$

3. **Refer to the graph in exercise 1. Find each distance.**
   a. PR 6
   b. QR 4
   c. PQ $2\sqrt{13}$

4. **Refer to the graph in exercise 2. Find each distance.**
   a. PR 7
   b. QR 6
   c. PQ $\sqrt{85}$

Using the distance formula, find the distance between the two points whose coordinates are given. Express radicals in simplest form.

5. $A(3, 4)$ and $B(0, 0)$ 5
6. $C(0, 0)$ and $D(6, 8)$ 10
7. $S(4, 3)$ and $T(1, 3)$ 3
8. $M(-2, 5)$ and $N(-2, 8)$ 3
9. $J(-1, 4)$ and $K(4, -8)$ 13
10. $X(6, -7)$ and $Y(-2, 8)$ 17

B.
11. $E(1, 5)$ and $F(3, 1)$ $2\sqrt{5}$
12. $G(4, 3)$ and $H(1, 6)$ $3\sqrt{2}$
13. $P(3, 0)$ and $Q(-3, 2)$ $2\sqrt{10}$
14. $R(5, 1)$ and $S(-1, -1)$ $2\sqrt{10}$
15. $A(-2, -8)$ and $B(-7, -3)$ $5\sqrt{2}$
16. $J(-7, -9)$ and $K(-1, -3)$ $6\sqrt{2}$
17. $X(3\sqrt{3}, \sqrt{2})$ and $Y(5\sqrt{3}, 4\sqrt{2})$ $\sqrt{30}$
18. $A(4\sqrt{5}, 3\sqrt{6})$ and $B(2\sqrt{5}, 2\sqrt{6})$
19. $P(\sqrt{7}, -3\sqrt{10})$ and $Q(3\sqrt{7}, \sqrt{10})$
20. $C(-\sqrt{11}, \sqrt{13})$ and $D(\sqrt{11}, 2\sqrt{13})$

The distance between two points is given. Find all possible values for the variable.

21. $(-3, -2)$ and $(x, -5)$; $d = 5$ 1. -7 **22.** $(2, -1)$ and $(x, 3)$; $d = 5$ 5. -1

23. $(3, y)$ and $(9, -6)$; $d = 10$ 2. -14 **24.** $(-4, y)$ and $(2, 2)$; $d = 10$ -6, 10

25. $(8, -4)$ and $(x, 1)$; $d = 13$ -4, 20 **26.** $(7, y)$ and $(-8, 6)$; $d = 17$ -2, 14

27. $(x, 3)$ and $(2, -4)$; $d = \sqrt{74}$ 7. -3 **28.** $(3, 15)$ and $(x, 4)$; $d = \sqrt{202}$ -6, 12

29. $(-3, 4)$ and $(3, y)$; $d = 2\sqrt{13}$ 0. 8   **30.** $(5, 7)$ and $(x, -3)$; $d = 5\sqrt{5}$ 0. 10

C. 31. Can the point with the coordinates $(3, 4)$ be the center of the circle that passes through the points with the coordinates $(-1, 1)$, $(7, 7)$, and $(0, 0)$?   yes

32. Find the perimeter of the triangle whose vertices have the coordinates $(-7, 5)$, $(-7, -7)$, and $(2, -7)$.   36

CAREER
Electrician

Electricians install and maintain electrical systems in homes, factories, offices, and other buildings. Usually they specialize either in new installation or in maintenance and repair work.

Suppose an electrician wants to find the actual range of resistance of an electrical resistor that is rated 500 ohms, plus or minus 3%. What is the range of the resistor?

Suppose an electrician wants to find the voltage needed by a heater that has a resistance of 20 ohms and uses 605 watts. The formula $V = \sqrt{WR}$ can be used. (V is the voltage, W is the power in watts, and R is the resistance in ohms.) What is the voltage?   110 volts

Suppose an electrician wants to find the lost wattage (to the nearest watt) in a circuit that uses 52 amps and has a resistance of 0.04 ohms. The formula $W = I^2R$ can be used. (W is the power in watts, I is the current in amperes, and R is the resistance in ohms.) What is the lost wattage?
108 watts

CAREER
485–515

SKILLS MAINTENANCE

3. all real numbers

For the solutions to exercises 4–6, see Additional Answers, p. T62.

7. $a^2 - a - 6$

9. $4x^2 - 49$

10. $4a^2 - 12ab + 9b^2$

11. $15x^2 + x - 6$

12. $25 - 10x + x^2$

15. $15a^2b - 6a^3$

35. undefined

37. $y = -\frac{4}{3}x + \frac{5}{2}$; $m = -\frac{4}{3}$; $b = \frac{5}{2}$

38. $y = -2$; $m = 0$, $b = -2$

39. $y = \frac{2}{5}x + \frac{1}{5}$; $m = \frac{2}{5}$; $b = \frac{1}{5}$

44. $(1, -2)$

SKILLS MAINTENANCE

Solve each inequality.

1. $3x - 4 \le 14$ $x \le 6$

2. $-6x - 3 \ge 33$ $x \le -6$

3. $3x + 4 > 3x + 1$

Solve. Graph the solution set.

4. $|x| = 7$ 7. -7

5. $|x| < 6$ $-6 < x < 6$

6. $|x + 2| > 6$

Find each product.

7. $(a + 2)(a - 3)$

8. $(x + 8)^2$ $x^2 + 16x + 64$

9. $(2x + 7)(2x - 7)$

10. $(2a - 3b)^2$

11. $(3x + 2)(5x - 3)$

12. $(5 - x)^2$

Simplify.

13. $2x^2 \cdot 3x^3$ $6x^5$

14. $(5x^3y^2)^2$ $25x^6y^4$

15. $3a(5ab - 2a^2)$

16. $\frac{4^5}{4^3}$ 16

17. $\frac{a^3b^8}{a^5b^3}$ $\frac{b^5}{a^2}$

18. $\frac{(2x)^4}{(6x)^2}$ $\frac{4x^2}{9}$

Divide.

19. $(x^2 - 3x - 4) \div (x - 4)$ $x + 1$

20. $(4x^2 + 31x + 21) \div (x + 7)$ $4x + 3$

Factor completely.

21. $16ab^2 - 12a^2b$ $4ab(4b - 3a)$

22. $12x^2 - 27$ $3(2x + 3)(2x - 3)$

23. $16x^2 + 8x + 1$ $(4x + 1)^2$

24. $x^2 + 4x - 21$ $(x + 7)(x - 3)$

25. $2x^2 - x - 15$ $(2x + 5)(x - 3)$

26. $x^4 + 8x^2 + 15$ $(x^2 + 5)(x^2 + 3)$

Solve.

27. $25a^2 - 16 = 0$ $\frac{4}{5}, -\frac{4}{5}$

28. $4x^2 - 20x + 25 = 0$ $\frac{5}{2}$

29. $12x^2 + x = 1$ $-\frac{1}{3}, \frac{1}{4}$

Find each functional value if $h(x) = 2x + 1$.

30. $h(0)$ 1

31. $h(3)$ 7

32. $h(-5)$ -9

33. $h\left(\frac{1}{2}\right)$ 2

Find the slope of the line containing these points.

34. $(2, -3)$ and $(7, 9)$ $\frac{12}{5}$

35. $(2, -8)$ and $(2, 3)$

36. $(3, 4)$ and $(-3, 4)$ 0

Write each equation in slope-intercept form. Then give the slope and the y-intercept.

37. $8x + 6y = 15$

38. $5y + 10 = 0$

39. $-2x + 5y = 1$

For each line write an equation in slope-intercept form.

40. The slope is -5, and the y-intercept is 4. $y = -5x + 4$

41. The coordinates of two points on the line are $(0, 6)$ and $(2, 3)$. $y = -\frac{3}{2}x + 6$

Solve each system.

42. $2x + 3y = -5$
$4x = 8$ $(2, -3)$

43. $x - 2y = -11$
$3x + y = 2$ $(-1, 5)$

44. $4x - 3y = 10$
$3x + 2y = -1$

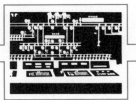

COMPUTER

A set of three positive integers that satisfies the Pythagorean relation is called a Pythagorean triple. Triples such as 3, 4, 5 that have no common factors are called primitive Pythagorean triples. More than 2,000 years ago, the Greek mathematician Euclid proposed the following formula for finding all such triples:

The following conditions must hold for A and B: they must be relatively prime (that is, they can have no common factors); one must be odd and the other even; and A > B.

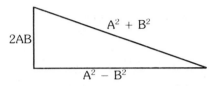

This program asks you to enter values for A and B. It then tests to see if the two values generate a Pythagorean triple.

```
10 PRINT "     2AB        A^2 - B^2        A^2 + B^2"
20 PRINT: PRINT "A MUST BE GREATER THAN B, AND ONE
   MUST BE ODD AND THE OTHER EVEN."
30 PRINT: INPUT "ENTER VALUE FOR A? ";A
40 INPUT "ENTER VALUE FOR B (LESS THAN A)? ";B
50 IF A < = B THEN 20: REM MAKE SURE A IS > THAN B
60 IF (A + B) / 2 = INT ((A + B) / 2) THEN 20: REM MAKE
   SURE ONE IS ODD, OTHER IS EVEN
70 C = INT (2 * A * B)
80 D = INT (A ^ 2 - B ^ 2)
90 E = INT (A ^ 2 + B ^ 2)
100 PRINT: PRINT C;", ";D;", AND ";E;
110 IF (C * C + D * D) / (E * E) = 1 THEN PRINT " IS A
    PYTHAGOREAN": GOTO 130
120 PRINT " IS NOT A PYTHAGOREAN"
130 PRINT "TRIPLE.": PRINT: GOTO 10
```

EXERCISES

1. Try the following values for A and B: 3 and 2, 7 and 6, 8 and 5, and 13 and 12. What are the results?

2. How does the test for odd and even values on line 60 work?

3. This program does not test whether the triple is primitive. Look at the program in Chapter 6, and then modify this program so that it checks in order to see if the three values have any common factors.

ANSWERS

1. 12, 5 and 13; a triple
   84, 13 and 85; a triple
   80, 38 and 39; not a triple
   312, 25 and 313; a triple

2. If A and B are both even or both odd, their sum will be even, so (A + B) / 2 = INT (A + B) / 2.

3. Line 110: after "PYTHAGOREAN", should read as follows:

   :PRINT "TRIPLE.":
   GOSUB 140: GOTO 130

   The following lines are as follows:

   120 PRINT "IS NOT A PYTHAGOREAN": PRINT "TRIPLE."

   130 PRINT: PRINT: GOTO 10

   140 LET X = 2: IF (C / X = INT(C / X) AND D / X = INT (D / X) AND (E / X)) = INT (E / X) THEN PRINT "THIS IS NOT A PRIMITIVE TRIPLE.": GOTO 180

   150 X = X + 1: IF X < SQR (C) THEN 150

   160 PRINT "THIS IS A PRIMITIVE TRIPLE.": RETURN

ENRICHMENT

See Activities 31–32,
p. T49.

ADDITIONAL ANSWERS

4. -10

8. $\pm\frac{3}{5}$

17. $\sqrt{137}$

21. 11.269

24. 6

25. $\sqrt{21x}$

26. $\sqrt{14}$

27. $\sqrt{5x-5}$

28. $\sqrt{2}$

29. 2

30. $\sqrt{17x}$

31. $\sqrt{5xy}$

CHAPTER 11 REVIEW

VOCABULARY

conjugates (11.7)

distance formula (11.9)

divide-and-average method (11.2)

division of square roots (11.4)

extraneous root (11.8)

irrational number (11.2)

like terms (11.6)

multiplication of square roots (11.4)

negative square root (11.1)

perfect square (11.1)

positive square root (11.1)

Pythagorean theorem (11.3)

radical (11.1)

radical equation (11.8)

radical sign (11.1)

radicand (11.1)

rationalizing the denominator (11.5)

simplest form (11.5)

square root (11.1)

square roots of a variable expression (11.5)

unlike terms (11.6)

REVIEW EXERCISES

11.1 **Find the indicated square root.**

   1. $\sqrt{81}$ 9   **2.** $\sqrt{289}$ 17   **3.** $-\sqrt{196}$ -14 **4.** $-\sqrt{100}$

   5. $\sqrt{\frac{64}{49}}$ $\frac{8}{7}$ **6.** $-\sqrt{\frac{169}{36}}$ $-\frac{13}{6}$ **7.** $\pm\sqrt{121}$ ±11 **8.** $\pm\sqrt{\frac{9}{25}}$

11.2 **Use the divide-and-average method to approximate each square root correct to the tenths place.**

   9. $\sqrt{40}$ 6.3   **10.** $\sqrt{11}$ 3.3   **11.** $\sqrt{39}$ 6.2

   Use the divide-and-average method to approximate each square root correct to the hundredths place.

   12. $\sqrt{17}$ 4.12   **13.** $\sqrt{38}$ 6.16   **14.** $\sqrt{62}$ 7.87

11.3 **The lengths of the legs of a right triangle are given. Find the length of the hypotenuse.**

   15. $a=12, b=5$ 13   **16.** $a=4, b=5$ $\sqrt{41}$ **17.** $a=11, b=4$

   Use the Table of Squares and Square Roots on page 547 to find each of the following.

   18. $\sqrt{30}$ 5.477   **19.** $\sqrt{58}$ 7.616   **20.** $\sqrt{98}$ 9.899   **21.** $\sqrt{127}$

   The lengths of the legs of a right triangle are given. Use the Table of Squares and Square Roots on page 547 to find c, the length of the hypotenuse, to the nearest thousandth.

   22. $a=6, b=2$ 6.325   **23.** $a=7, b=8$ 10.630

11.4 **Find the product or the quotient.**

   24. $\sqrt{2}\cdot\sqrt{18}$ **25.** $\sqrt{3x}\cdot\sqrt{7}$ **26.** $\sqrt{2}\cdot\sqrt{7}$ **27.** $\sqrt{5}\cdot\sqrt{x-1}$

   28. $\dfrac{\sqrt{10}}{\sqrt{5}}$ **29.** $\dfrac{\sqrt{52}}{\sqrt{13}}$ **30.** $\dfrac{\sqrt{34x^2}}{\sqrt{2x}}$ **31.** $\dfrac{\sqrt{30x^2y^3}}{\sqrt{6xy^2}}$

11.5 **Change each radical to simplest form.**

32. $\sqrt{48}$ $4\sqrt{3}$

33. $\sqrt{63}$ $3\sqrt{7}$

34. $\sqrt{\dfrac{169}{25}}$ $\dfrac{13}{5}$

35. $\sqrt{\dfrac{9}{289}}$ $\dfrac{3}{17}$

36. $\sqrt{\dfrac{2}{7}}$ $\dfrac{\sqrt{14}}{7}$

37. $\sqrt{\dfrac{5}{6}}$ $\dfrac{\sqrt{30}}{6}$

38. $\dfrac{6}{\sqrt{27}}$ $\dfrac{2\sqrt{3}}{3}$

39. $\dfrac{8}{\sqrt{8}}$ $2\sqrt{2}$

40. $\dfrac{3}{\sqrt{45}}$ $\dfrac{\sqrt{5}}{5}$

41. $\sqrt{x^2y^3}$ $|x|y\sqrt{y}$

42. $\sqrt{a^4b^2}$ $a^2|b|$

43. $\sqrt{\dfrac{3}{25a^2}}$ $\dfrac{\sqrt{3}}{5|a|}$

44. $\sqrt{\dfrac{81a^5}{x^6}}$ $\dfrac{9a^2\sqrt{a}}{|x^3|}$

45. $\sqrt{\dfrac{y^{10}}{2}}$ $\dfrac{|y^5|\sqrt{2}}{2}$

46. $\dfrac{6}{\sqrt{18}}$ $\sqrt{2}$

Express each product in simplest form.

47. $\sqrt{6}\cdot\sqrt{21}$ $3\sqrt{14}$

48. $\sqrt{2}\cdot 3\sqrt{22}$ $6\sqrt{11}$

49. $\sqrt{35}\cdot\sqrt{15}$ $5\sqrt{21}$

50. $\sqrt{14}\cdot\sqrt{28}$ $14\sqrt{2}$

51. $\sqrt{10x^3}\cdot\sqrt{5x^7}$ $5x^5\sqrt{2}$

52. $\sqrt{15}\cdot\sqrt{5x^6}$

53. $\sqrt{6x}\cdot\sqrt{3x}$ $3x\sqrt{2}$

54. $5\sqrt{2x^4}\cdot\sqrt{8x^3}$

55. $-3\sqrt{3x^3}\cdot\sqrt{3x^3}$

11.6 **Perform the indicated operations.**

56. $\sqrt{8}+\sqrt{18}$ $5\sqrt{2}$

57. $\sqrt{3}+\sqrt{27}$ $4\sqrt{3}$

58. $\sqrt{5}+\sqrt{45}$ $4\sqrt{5}$

59. $\sqrt{20x}+\sqrt{45x}$ $5\sqrt{5x}$

60. $\sqrt{32}-\sqrt{98}-\sqrt{18}$

61. $x^2\sqrt{12}+2\sqrt{3x^4}$

62. $\sqrt{40}+\sqrt{360}+\sqrt{810}$

63. $\sqrt{20}+\sqrt{80}-\sqrt{180}$

64. $y\sqrt{7y}+\sqrt{28y^3}$

65. $\sqrt{20}+\sqrt{\dfrac{1}{5}}$ $\dfrac{11\sqrt{5}}{5}$

66. $\sqrt{54}+\sqrt{\dfrac{2}{3}}$ $\dfrac{10\sqrt{6}}{3}$

67. $\sqrt{60}+\sqrt{\dfrac{3}{5}}$ $\dfrac{11\sqrt{15}}{5}$

11.7 **Find each product.**

68. $(1+\sqrt{11})(2-\sqrt{11})$

69. $(2+\sqrt{2})(4+\sqrt{2})$

70. $(5+\sqrt{7})^2$

71. $(6-\sqrt{3})^2$ $39-12\sqrt{3}$

72. $(2-3\sqrt{5})(2+3\sqrt{5})$

73. $(3-\sqrt{2})(3+\sqrt{2})$

74. $(2+3\sqrt{7})(3-4\sqrt{7})$

75. $(4-2\sqrt{3})(5-5\sqrt{3})$

76. $(4-3\sqrt{7})^2$

Simplify. (Rationalize the denominator.)

77. $\dfrac{2}{3-\sqrt{5}}$ $\dfrac{3+\sqrt{5}}{2}$

78. $\dfrac{5}{4+\sqrt{3}}$ $\dfrac{20-5\sqrt{3}}{13}$

79. $\dfrac{\sqrt{3}}{6+\sqrt{2}}$ $\dfrac{6\sqrt{3}-\sqrt{6}}{34}$

11.8 **Solve and check each equation.**

80. $\sqrt{3y}=9$ 27

81. $\sqrt{6y}=-6$ $\varnothing$

82. $\sqrt{x+1}=2$ 3

83. $\sqrt{x+2}=3\sqrt{2}$ 16

84. $x=\sqrt{5x+14}$ 7

85. $\sqrt{x^2-81}=0$

86. $\sqrt{3x-1}=\sqrt{5}$ 2

87. $\sqrt{8y^2-8}=8$ $3,-3$

88. $x=\sqrt{7-x}+1$ 3

89. $\sqrt{12x^2+5x+1}=2$

90. $1+\sqrt{2x+6}=x$ 5

91. $\sqrt{x-7}=\sqrt{7-x}$ 7

11.9 **Using the distance formula, find the distance between the two points whose coordinates are given. Express radicals in simplest form.**

92. $J\,(4, 8)$ and $K\,(1, 5)$ $3\sqrt{2}$

93. $M\,(-2, 3)$ and $R\,(0, -5)$ $2\sqrt{17}$

94. $A\,(-3, 4)$ and $B\,(5, -2)$ 10

95. $X\,(-1, -2)$ and $Y\,(-3, -4)$ $2\sqrt{2}$

52. $5|x^3|\sqrt{3}$
54. $20x\sqrt[3]{x}$
55. $-9x^3$
60. $-6\sqrt{2}$
61. $4x\sqrt[3]{3}$
62. $17\sqrt{10}$
63. 0
64. $3y\sqrt{7y}$
68. $-9+\sqrt{11}$
69. $10+6\sqrt{2}$
70. $32+10\sqrt{7}$
72. -41
73. 7
74. $\sqrt{7}-78$
75. $50-30\sqrt{3}$
76. $79-24\sqrt{7}$
85. $9, -9$
89. $-\dfrac{3}{4}, \dfrac{1}{3}$

TEACHER'S RESOURCE
MASTERS

Chapter 11 Test

Multiple-Choice Test

PROBLEM-SOLVING
HANDBOOK

p. 537

ADDITIONAL ANSWERS

16. $3x\sqrt[3]{14x}$

18. $2y\sqrt{6y}$

20. $10 + 4\sqrt{7}$

27. 3

CHAPTER 11 TEST

Find the indicated square root.

1. $\sqrt{121}$ 11

2. $-\sqrt{196}$ -14

3. $\pm\sqrt{\dfrac{16}{49}}$ $\pm\frac{4}{7}$

Use the divide-and-average method to approximate each square root correct to the given decimal place.

4. $\sqrt{45}$ (to the tenths place)   6.7

5. $\sqrt{34}$ (to the hundredths place)   5.83

The lengths of the legs of a right triangle are given. Find the length of the hypotenuse.

6. $a = 3, b = 4$ 5

7. $a = 6, b = 7$ $\sqrt{85}$

Find the product or the quotient.

8. $\sqrt{7} \cdot \sqrt{10}$ $\sqrt{70}$

9. $\sqrt{5x} \cdot \sqrt{7y}$ $\sqrt{35xy}$

10. $\dfrac{\sqrt{18x^2}}{\sqrt{3x}}$ $\sqrt{6x}$

Change each radical to simplest form.

11. $\sqrt{45}$ $3\sqrt{5}$

12. $\sqrt{\dfrac{5}{7}}$ $\frac{\sqrt{35}}{7}$

13. $\sqrt{\dfrac{24x^4}{y^2}}$ $\frac{2x^2\sqrt{6}}{|y|}$

Express each product in simplest form.

14. $\sqrt{7} \cdot \sqrt{42}$ $7\sqrt{6}$

15. $\sqrt{5} \cdot \sqrt{10x^{10}}$ $5|x^5|\sqrt{2}$

16. $\sqrt{6x^2} \cdot \sqrt{21x^5}$

Perform the indicated operation.

17. $\sqrt{12} + \sqrt{27}$ $5\sqrt{3}$

18. $y\sqrt{150y} - \sqrt{54y^3}$

19. $\sqrt{18} + \sqrt{\dfrac{1}{2}}$ $\frac{7\sqrt{2}}{2}$

Find each product.

20. $(3 + \sqrt{7})(1 + \sqrt{7})$

21. $(2 + \sqrt{6})^2$ $10 + 4\sqrt{6}$

22. $(3 - \sqrt{5})(3 + \sqrt{5})$ 4

Simplify. (Rationalize the denominator.)

23. $\dfrac{3}{2 - \sqrt{6}}$ $\frac{6 + 3\sqrt{6}}{-2}$

24. $\dfrac{\sqrt{6}}{4 + \sqrt{5}}$ $\frac{4\sqrt{6} - \sqrt{30}}{11}$

Solve and check each equation.

25. $\sqrt{5y} = 5$ 5

26. $\sqrt{x + 1} = 7$ 48

27. $x = \sqrt{10 - 3x} + 2$

Using the distance formula, find the distance between the two points whose coordinates are given. Express radicals in simplest form.

28. $A\,(2, 3)$ and $B\,(0, 1)$ $2\sqrt{2}$

29. $C\,(-4, 3)$ and $D\,(-2, 7)$ $2\sqrt{5}$

CUMULATIVE REVIEW
CHAPTERS 8–11

Choose the correct answer.

1. Determine whether the system has one solution, no solution, or an infinite number of solutions. If the system has only one solution, solve by graphing. C

   $x + y = 2$

   $x - y = 4$

   A. none
   B. infinite
   C. one; $(3, -1)$
   D. one; $(-3, 1)$

2. Find the equation that would result from adding the equations in the following system:

   $2x - y = 3$

   $2x + y = -1$ D

   A. $x = 1$
   B. $y = \frac{1}{2}$
   C. $y = -2$
   D. $x = \frac{1}{2}$

3. Find the equation that would result from subtracting the equations in the following system:

   $4x + 3y - 7 = 0$

   $3y = x - 1$ B

   A. $x = 2$
   B. $x = -\frac{8}{5}$
   C. $x = -2$
   D. $x = \frac{6}{5}$

4. Determine which of the given points is a solution of the inequality $3x - 4y < 12$. C

   A. $(4, 0)$
   B. $(0, -3)$
   C. $(0, 3)$
   D. $(4, -4)$

5. What can replace the ? in $\frac{x}{3} = \frac{?}{3x + 12}$ so that the equation is a true sentence? B

   A. $3x + 4$
   B. $x^2 + 4x$
   C. $x + 4$
   D. $3x$

6. Change $\frac{5x - 10}{x^2 - 4x + 4}$ to simplest form. B

   A. $\frac{5(x - 2)}{(x - 2)^2}$
   B. $\frac{5}{(x - 2)}$
   C. $5x - 2$
   D. $\frac{x - 5}{x^2 - 2}$

7. Simplify the expression $(-2y)^{-3}$ by using the properties of integral exponents. A

   A. $-\frac{1}{8y^3}$
   B. $6y^3$
   C. $-\frac{1}{6y^3}$
   D. $-8y^3$

8. Multiply $\frac{2(x^2 - 16)}{3}$ and $\frac{15}{x + 4}$. Express the product in simplest form. C

   A. $10x + 4$
   B. $10(x + 4)$
   C. $10(x - 4)$
   D. $5(x - 4)$

9. Divide $\frac{x - 3}{x}$ by $\frac{x^2 - 3x}{x}$. Express the quotient in simplest form. A

   A. $\frac{1}{x}$
   B. $\frac{(x - 3)^2}{x}$
   C. x
   D. $(x - 3)^2$

10. Find the LCD of rational expressions with denominators of $x^2 - 7x$ and $x^2 + 3x$. C

    A. x
    B. $x^2 - 4x - 21$
    C. $x(x - 7)(x + 3)$
    D. $x(x - 4)$

11. Add $\frac{4}{x+2}$ and $\frac{5}{x+3}$ and express the sum in simplest form.   A

A. $\frac{9x+22}{(x+2)(x+3)}$　　**B.** $\frac{9}{(x+2)(x+3)}$　　**C.** $\frac{9x+5}{(x+2)(x+3)}$　　**D.** $\frac{9}{2x+5}$

12. Subtract $\frac{7x}{x-3}$ from $\frac{5}{x+4}$ and express the difference in simplest form.   B

A. $\frac{5-7x}{2x-7}$　　**B.** $\frac{-7x^2-23x-15}{(x+4)(x-3)}$　　**C.** $\frac{7x^2-23x-15}{(x-4)(x-3)}$　　**D.** $\frac{7x-5}{2x+1}$

13. Solve $\frac{5}{6x-1}=\frac{2}{4x}$.   B

A. $-\frac{1}{2}$　　　　**B.** $-\frac{1}{4}$　　　　**C.** $\frac{1}{2}$　　　　**D.** $\frac{1}{4}$

14. Let y vary directly as x. If $y=10$ when $x=4$, what is x when $y=7$?   B

A. 28　　　　**B.** $2\frac{4}{5}$　　　　**C.** $5\frac{5}{7}$　　　　**D.** 40

15. Solve $\frac{9}{x+3}=\frac{-2}{x-2}$.   C

A. $-\frac{11}{12}$　　　　**B.** 4　　　　**C.** $\frac{12}{11}$　　　　**D.** $3\frac{3}{7}$

16. Which proportion would you use to solve the following: *8 is what percent of 35?*   C

A. $\frac{8}{100}=\frac{x}{35}$　　**B.** $\frac{8}{x}=\frac{35}{100}$　　**C.** $\frac{8}{35}=\frac{x}{100}$　　**D.** $\frac{x}{35}=\frac{100}{8}$

17. Let y vary inversely as x. If $x=2.6$ when $y=5$, what is y when $x=3.25$?   D
A. 1.69　　　　**B.** 6.25　　　　**C.** 42.25　　　　**D.** 4

18. Locate 10 between consecutive perfect-square integers.   A
A. 9 and 16　　**B.** 3 and 4　　**C.** 81 and 121　　**D.** $\sqrt{9}$ and $\sqrt{16}$

19. The lengths of the legs of a right triangle are 7 and 24. Find the length of the hypotenuse.
A. $\sqrt{31}$　　**B.** 625　　**C.** 25　　**D.** 31   C

20. Find the product of $\sqrt{2}$ and $\sqrt{3x}$.   A
A. $\sqrt{6x}$　　**B.** $6x$　　**C.** $\sqrt{5x}$　　**D.** $5x$

21. Find the quotient $\frac{\sqrt{16x^3}}{\sqrt{9x^2}}$.   A

A. $\frac{4\sqrt{x}}{3}$　　**B.** $\frac{4x}{3}$　　**C.** $\frac{4}{3}$　　**D.** $\frac{16x}{9}$

22. Write $\sqrt{\frac{4}{3}}$ in simplest form.   B

A. $\frac{2}{\sqrt{3}}$　　**B.** $\frac{2\sqrt{3}}{3}$　　**C.** $\frac{16}{9}$　　**D.** $\frac{2}{3}$

23. Add $\sqrt{54}$ and $\sqrt{24}$.   D
A. $\sqrt{78}$　　**B.** $13\sqrt{6}$　　**C.** $6\sqrt{6}$　　**D.** $5\sqrt{6}$

24. Find the product of $4+2\sqrt{3}$ and $4-2\sqrt{3}$.   A
A. 4　　**B.** $16-2\sqrt{3}$　　**C.** 28　　**D.** -2

25. Solve $2+\sqrt{7-2x}=x$.   B
A. 3, -1　　**B.** 3　　**C.** -1　　**D.** $-3, 1$

CHAPTER 12

Quadratic Equations

A diver jumps from a 118-foot cliff. Neglecting air resistance, use $118 = 16t^2$ to find the approximate time t (in seconds) of the dive. (Round your answer to the nearest tenth of a second.) 2.7 seconds

OBJECTIVES

Solve a quadratic equation by factoring and using the zero product property.

Given the roots of a quadratic equation, find the equation.

TEACHER'S NOTES

See p. T36.

12.1 Solving Quadratic Equations by Factoring

A **quadratic equation** in one variable is an equation that can be written in the form $ax^2 + bx + c = 0$, where a, b, and c are real numbers and $a \neq 0$. This form is called the **standard form of a quadratic equation.**

If $ax^2 + bx + c$ can be factored, you can use the *zero product property* to solve for x. That is, if $ab = 0$, then either $a = 0$ or $b = 0$ or both are equal to zero.

EXAMPLES

CLASSROOM EXAMPLES

1. Solve $y^2 - 11y + 18 = 0$.

$y^2 - 11y + 18 = 0$

$(y - 9)(y - 2) = 0$

$y - 9 = 0$ or $y - 2 = 0$

$y = 9 \qquad y = 2$

So the solution set is $\{2, 9\}$.

2. Solve $6x^2 + 11x = 10$.

$6x^2 + 11x = 10$

$6x^2 + 11x - 10 = 0$

$(2x + 5)(3x - 2) = 0$

$2x + 5 = 0$ or $3x - 2 = 0$

$x = -\frac{5}{2} \qquad x = \frac{2}{3}$

3. Solve $16m^2 = 49$.

$16m^2 = 49$

$16m^2 - 49 = 0$

$(4m - 7)(4m + 7) = 0$

$4m - 7 = 0$ or $4m + 7 = 0$

$m = \frac{7}{4} \qquad m = -\frac{7}{4}$

4. Solve $9y^2 - 36y + 36 = 0$.

$9y^2 - 36y + 36 = 0$

$(3y - 6)(3y - 6) = 0$

$3y - 6 = 0$ or $3y - 6 = 0$

$y = 2 \qquad y = 2$

1 **Solve $x^2 - 6x + 5 = 0$.**

SOLUTION $x^2 - 6x + 5 = 0$

$(x - 5)(x - 1) = 0$ *Factor.*

$x - 5 = 0$ or $x - 1 = 0$ *Zero product property*

$x = 5 \qquad x = 1$

So the solution set is $\{1, 5\}$.

CHECK $x^2 - 6x + 5 = 0$

$1^2 - 6(1) + 5 \overset{?}{=} 0$

$1 - 6 + 5 \overset{?}{=} 0$

$0 = 0$ ✔

$x^2 - 6x + 5 = 0$

$5^2 - 6(5) + 5 \overset{?}{=} 0$

$25 - 30 + 5 \overset{?}{=} 0$

$0 = 0$ ✔

The solutions of an equation are also called the **roots** of the equation.

2 **Solve $6x^2 + 5x = 4$.**

SOLUTION $6x^2 + 5x = 4$

$6x^2 + 5x - 4 = 0$ *Write the equation in standard form.*

$(2x - 1)(3x + 4) = 0$ *Factor.*

$2x - 1 = 0$ or $3x + 4 = 0$ *Zero product property*

$x = \frac{1}{2} \qquad x = -\frac{4}{3}$

Check these roots.

3 **Solve $9m^2 = 25$.**

SOLUTION $9m^2 = 25$

$9m^2 - 25 = 0$

$(3m - 5)(3m + 5) = 0$

$3m - 5 = 0$ or $3m + 5 = 0$

$m = \frac{5}{3} \qquad m = -\frac{5}{3}$

Check these roots.

4 | **Solve $4y^2 - 20y + 25 = 0$.**

SOLUTION $4y^2 - 20y + 25 = 0$
$$(2y - 5)(2y - 5) = 0$$
$$2y - 5 = 0 \quad \text{or} \quad 2y - 5 = 0$$
$$y = \frac{5}{2} \qquad\qquad y = \frac{5}{2}$$

— same —

The solution $\frac{5}{2}$ is called a **double root**.

Check the root.

ORAL EXERCISES

Express each quadratic equation in standard form.

1. $x^2 = -2x + 8$ $x^2 + 2x - 8 = 0$

2. $-3x^2 + 7 = 4x$ $-3x^2 - 4x + 7 = 0$

3. $3 = -x^2 - 8x$ $x^2 + 8x + 3 = 0$

4. $x^2 = 5x - 9$ $x^2 - 5x + 9 = 0$

Find the roots of each equation.

5. $(x - 1)(x + 7) = 0$ $1, -7$

6. $(2x + 3)(x - 8) = 0$ $-\frac{3}{2}, 8$

7. $(3x - 1)(5x - 6) = 0$ $\frac{1}{3}, \frac{6}{5}$

8. $(2m + 7)(m + 9) = 0$ $-\frac{7}{2}, -9$

9. $(n + 3)(5n - 1) = 0$ $-3, \frac{1}{5}$

10. $(2y + 1)(3y - 8) = 0$ $-\frac{1}{2}, \frac{8}{3}$

WRITTEN EXERCISES

A. Express each quadratic equation in standard form.

1. $x^2 = -3x + 7$ $x^2 + 3x - 7 = 0$

2. $x^2 - 2 = 4x$ $x^2 - 4x - 2 = 0$

3. $36x = x^2 - 2$ $x^2 - 36x - 2 = 0$

4. $15 = x^2 + 6x$ $x^2 + 6x - 15 = 0$

5. $-9 = x^2 - 2x$ $x^2 - 2x + 9 = 0$

6. $24 - x = x^2$ $x^2 + x - 24 = 0$

7. $15 + 2x = -x^2$ $x^2 + 2x + 15 = 0$

8. $7 + 3x^2 = -4x$ $3x^2 + 4x + 7 = 0$

Solve.

9. $x^2 - 4x - 12 = 0$ $6, -2$

10. $x^2 - 5x + 6 = 0$ $3, 2$

11. $y^2 + 6y + 8 = 0$ $-4, -2$

12. $x^2 + x - 30 = 0$ $-6, 5$

13. $m^2 + 12m + 27 = 0$ $-9, -3$

14. $t^2 + 3t - 28 = 0$ $-7, 4$

15. $x^2 - 6x + 9 = 0$ 3

16. $n^2 + 11n + 24 = 0$ $-8, -3$

17. $m^2 - 3m = 88$ $11, -8$

18. $y^2 = 36 - 9y$ $-12, 3$

19. $t^2 = 20t - 96$ $8, 12$

20. $y^2 - 4y = 0$ $4, 0$

B. 21. $2x^2 + 7x - 15 = 0$ $\frac{3}{2}, -5$

22. $12y^2 + 17y - 40 = 0$ $-\frac{8}{3}, \frac{5}{4}$

23. $15t^2 - 35t + 10 = 0$ $2, \frac{1}{3}$

24. $14x^2 + 23x + 3 = 0$ $-\frac{1}{7}, -\frac{3}{2}$

25. $m^2 + 2m - 35 = 0$ $5, -7$

26. $18x^2 + 47x - 56 = 0$ $\frac{8}{9}, -\frac{7}{2}$

MIXED REVIEW

Perform the indicated operation.

1. $3x^2y(-6x^3y + 8y - 2)$
   $-18x^5y^2 + 24x^2y^2$
   $\quad - 6x^2y$

2. $4\sqrt{5} + 3\sqrt{5}$ $7\sqrt{5}$

3. $(2 + \sqrt{3})(2 - \sqrt{3})$ 1

4. 16% of what number is 144?   900

5. $-\frac{14}{16} \div \frac{1}{8}$ -7

TEACHER'S RESOURCE MASTERS

Practice Master 50, Part 1

ASSIGNMENT GUIDE

Minimum
1–29 odd

Regular
21–35

Maximum
27–36, 43–51 odd

27. $3y^2 + 23y + 44 = 0$ $-\frac{11}{3}, -4$

28. $2n^2 = 23n + 105$ $-\frac{7}{2}, 15$

29. $3w^2 + 13w - 56 = 0$ $\frac{8}{3}, -7$

30. $7x^2 - 52x = 32$ $-\frac{4}{7}, 8$

31. $3x^2 = 13x$ $\frac{13}{3}, 0$

32. $20x^2 + 3 = 19x$ $\frac{1}{5}, \frac{3}{4}$

33. $6y^2 = 13y + 63$ $-\frac{7}{3}, \frac{9}{2}$

34. $6m^2 = -m + 77$ $-\frac{11}{3}, \frac{7}{2}$

35. $21x^2 - 4 = 25x$ $-\frac{1}{7}, \frac{4}{3}$

36. $6n^2 + n = 15$ $-\frac{5}{3}, \frac{3}{2}$

Write a quadratic equation in standard form for the given roots.

Example: The roots are -1 and 3.

Then $x - (-1) = 0 \rightarrow x + 1 = 0$ or $x - 3 = 0$.

So $(x + 1)(x - 3) = 0$

$\quad\quad x^2 - 2x - 3 = 0$

37. $0, -2$ $x^2 + 2x = 0$

38. $4, 3$ $x^2 - 7x + 12 = 0$

39. $2, -6$ $x^2 + 4x - 12 = 0$

40. $-3, 7$ $x^2 - 4x - 21 = 0$

41. $-5, -9$ $x^2 + 14x + 45 = 0$

42. $1, 15$ $x^2 - 16x + 15 = 0$

C. Solve.

43. $x^3 + x^2 - 12x = 0$ $0, -4, 3$

44. $2x^3 - 9x^2 - 5x = 0$ $0, -\frac{1}{2}, 5$

45. $4x^3 + 2x^2 - 30x = 0$ $0, \frac{5}{2}, -3$

46. $x(2x - 1)(3x + 2) = 0$ $0, \frac{1}{2}, -\frac{2}{3}$

47. $6x^3 + 19x^2 - 7x = 0$ $0, \frac{1}{3}, -\frac{7}{2}$

48. $(3x - 5)(2x + 4) = 25 - 15x$ $\frac{5}{3}, -\frac{9}{2}$

49. $(5x - 6)(2x - 7) = 2(2x - 7)$ $\frac{8}{5}, \frac{7}{2}$

50. $(2x + 3)(x - 5) + 4x - 20 = 0$

51. $(3x - 2)(2x - 1) = 4x + 2$ $0, \frac{11}{6}$

52. $x(6x - 1)(x - 1) - 4x = 0$ $0, -\frac{1}{3}, \frac{3}{2}$

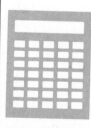

CALCULATOR

The memory key on a calculator can be used to help you check the roots of a quadratic equation. To use this method of checking, you should first write $ax^2 + bx + c = 0$ as $(ax + b)x + c = 0$.

Example: The roots of $2x^2 + 7x - 15 = 0$ are $\frac{3}{2}$ and -5.

Check these roots.

Solution: Check the root $\frac{3}{2}$, or 1.5.

ENTER   DISPLAY

2 $\boxed{\times}$ 1.5 $\boxed{+}$ 7 $\boxed{=}$ $\boxed{\times}$ 1.5 $\boxed{=}$ $\boxed{+}$ 15 $\boxed{+/-}$ $\boxed{=}$ $\mathit{0}$

Check the root -5.

If a root is a repeating decimal, store as much of the decimal form as possible in the calculator's memory. The check may not yield exactly zero but should yield a number very close to zero.

12.2 | The Square-Root Property

The equation $x^2 = 25$ can be solved by factoring. You can also solve this equation by using the **square-root property**.

Square-Root Property	**If $x^2 = a$, then $x = \sqrt{a}$ or $x = -\sqrt{a}$.**

The equation $x^2 = a$, for $a \geq 0$, can be solved by factoring in the same manner as the equation $x^2 = 25$.

$$x^2 = 25 \qquad \text{given} \qquad\qquad x^2 = a$$
$$x^2 = (\sqrt{25})^2 \quad \text{meaning of square root} \qquad x^2 = (\sqrt{a})^2$$
$$x^2 - (\sqrt{25})^2 = 0 \quad \text{Subtract same number from each side.} \qquad x^2 - (\sqrt{a})^2 = 0$$
$$(x + \sqrt{25})(x - \sqrt{25}) = 0 \qquad \text{difference of 2 squares} \qquad (x + \sqrt{a})(x - \sqrt{a}) = 0$$
$$x + 5 = 0 \ \text{ or } \ x - 5 = 0 \qquad \text{Zero product property} \quad x + \sqrt{a} = 0 \ \text{ or } \ x - \sqrt{a} = 0$$
$$x = -5 \qquad x = 5 \qquad \text{solving linear equations} \qquad x = -\sqrt{a} \qquad x = \sqrt{a}$$
$$x = \pm 5 \qquad\qquad\qquad\qquad\qquad\qquad x = \pm\sqrt{a}$$

EXAMPLES

1 | **Solve $3x^2 = 15$.**

SOLUTION
$$3x^2 = 15$$
$$x^2 = 5$$
$$x = \pm\sqrt{5}$$

CHECK

$3x^2 = 15$	$3x^2 = 15$
$3(\sqrt{5})^2 \overset{?}{=} 15$	$3(-\sqrt{5})^2 \overset{?}{=} 15$
$3(5) \overset{?}{=} 15$	$3(5) \overset{?}{=} 15$
$15 = 15$ ✔	$15 = 15$ ✔

2 | **Solve $(x - 3)^2 = 16$.**

SOLUTION
$$(x - 3)^2 = 16$$
$$x - 3 = \pm\sqrt{16}$$
$$x - 3 = 4 \ \text{ or } \ x - 3 = -4 \quad \textit{Write two linear equations.}$$
$$x = 7 \qquad\qquad x = -1$$

Check these roots.

OBJECTIVE

By using the square-root property for equations, solve equations that can be expressed in the form $x^2 = a$ or $(x + y)^2 = a$.

TEACHER'S NOTES

See p. T36.

CLASSROOM EXAMPLES

1. Solve $2x^2 = 14$.
$$2x^2 = 14$$
$$x^2 = 7$$
$$x = \pm\sqrt{7}$$

2. Solve $(x - 5)^2 = 16$.
$$(x - 5)^2 = 16$$
$$x - 5 = \pm\sqrt{16}$$
$$x - 5 = 4 \ \text{ or } \ x - 5 = -4$$
$$x = 9 \qquad x = 1$$

3. Solve $(y - 2)^2 = 13$.
$$(y - 2)^2 = 13$$
$$y - 2 = \pm\sqrt{13}$$
$$y = 2 \pm \sqrt{13}$$

4. Solve $(3x - 3)^2 - 3 = 33$.
$$(3x - 3)^2 - 3 = 33$$
$$(3x - 3)^2 = 36$$
$$3x - 3 = \pm 6$$
$$3x = 9 \ \text{ or } \ 3x = -3$$
$$x = 3 \qquad x = -1$$

MIXED REVIEW

Perform the indicated operation.

1. $\pm\sqrt{\frac{1}{64}}$ $\pm\frac{1}{8}$

2. Approximate $\sqrt{61}$ to the nearest hundredths place.   7.81

3. $\dfrac{\sqrt{75}}{\sqrt{3}}$ 5

4. $16 - (43 + 19)$ -46

5. $\dfrac{30x^2y}{6xy} \div \dfrac{5x^3y^2}{8xy}$ $\dfrac{8}{xy}$

TEACHER'S RESOURCE MASTERS

Practice Master 50, Part 2

ASSIGNMENT GUIDE

Minimum
1–29 odd

Regular
24–38

Maximum
27–41

ADDITIONAL ANSWERS

Oral Exercises

2. $\{-11, 11\}$

4. $\{-12, 12\}$

5. $\{-2\sqrt{3}, 2\sqrt{3}\}$

6. $\{-3, 3\}$

8. $\left\{-\dfrac{11}{7}, \dfrac{11}{7}\right\}$

Written Exercises

4. $\pm 3\sqrt{2}$

8. $\pm 2\sqrt{5}$

9. $\pm\dfrac{3}{2}$

11. $\pm\dfrac{\sqrt{15}}{4}$

12. $\pm\sqrt{3}$

13. $6, -4$

14. $0, -4$

15. $3, -12$

16. $\dfrac{11}{2}, \dfrac{3}{2}$

17. $4, -\dfrac{4}{3}$

18. $\dfrac{11}{4}, -\dfrac{17}{4}$

---

3   **Solve $(x - 1)^2 = 15$.**

SOLUTION

$$(x - 1)^2 = 15$$
$$x - 1 = \pm\sqrt{15}$$
$$x = 1 \pm\sqrt{15}$$

CHECK

$$(x - 1)^2 = 15$$
$$(1 + \sqrt{15} - 1)^2 \overset{?}{=} 15$$
$$(\sqrt{15})^2 \overset{?}{=} 15$$
$$15 = 15 \; \checkmark$$

$$(x - 1)^2 = 15$$
$$(1 - \sqrt{15} - 1)^2 \overset{?}{=} 15$$
$$(-\sqrt{15})^2 \overset{?}{=} 15$$
$$15 = 15 \; \checkmark$$

4   **Solve $(3x - 1)^2 - 1 = 15$.**

SOLUTION

$$(3x - 1)^2 - 1 = 15$$
$$(3x - 1)^2 = 16$$
$$3x - 1 = \pm 4$$
$$3x = 5 \text{ or } 3x = -3$$
$$x = \dfrac{5}{3} \qquad x = -1$$

Check these roots.

ORAL EXERCISES

What is the solution set for each?

1. $x^2 = 36$ $\{-6, 6\}$ **2.** $m^2 = 121$ **3.** $t^2 = 16$ $\{-4, 4\}$ **4.** $y^2 = 144$

5. $x^2 = 12$ **6.** $3y^2 = 27$ **7.** $m^2 = \dfrac{81}{25}$ $\left\{-\dfrac{9}{5}, \dfrac{9}{5}\right\}$ **8.** $n^2 = \dfrac{121}{49}$

WRITTEN EXERCISES

A.   **Solve by using the square-root property.**

1. $x^2 = 4$ ± 2 **2.** $m^2 = 169$ ± 13 **3.** $t^2 = 64$ ± 8 **4.** $y^2 = 18$

5. $n^2 = 32$ $\pm 4\sqrt{2}$ **6.** $3w^2 = 243$ ± 9 **7.** $x^2 + 1 = 10$ ± 3 **8.** $r^2 - 4 = 16$

9. $4x^2 - 1 = 8$ **10.** $9x^2 = 256$ $\pm\dfrac{16}{3}$ **11.** $16y^2 = 15$ **12.** $3m^2 + 4 = 13$

B.   **13.** $(x - 1)^2 = 25$ **14.** $(x + 2)^2 = 4$ **15.** $(2x + 9)^2 = 225$ **16.** $(2x - 7)^2 = 16$

   17. $(3x - 4)^2 = 64$ **18.** $(4m + 3)^2 = 196$ **19.** $(3t - 2)^2 = 289$ **20.** $(4y + 5)^2 = 36$

   21. $3(4n - 3)^2 = 27$ **22.** $\left(x + \dfrac{1}{3}\right)^2 - \dfrac{4}{9} = \dfrac{12}{9}$ **23.** $(x - \sqrt{6})^2 = 24$

   24. $\left(n + \dfrac{1}{2}\right)^2 = \dfrac{9}{4}$ **25.** $(t - \sqrt{7})^2 = 28$ **26.** $(3x - 5.4)^2 = 0.81$

27. $(4m - 3.6)^2 = 0.64$ **28.** $2(3r + 4)^2 = 0.98$ **29.** $(5x + 6)^2 + 4 = 20$

30. $(3x - 8)^2 - 3 = 15$ **31.** $(3m + 5)^2 - 6 = 30$ **32.** $4(2x - 1)^2 = 20$

33. $5(x - 3)^2 = 30$ **34.** $\frac{4}{9}(2x - 1)^2 = \frac{16}{81}$ **35.** $\frac{3}{5}(3x - 1)^2 = \frac{27}{125}$

C. **HINT: Write each equation in the form $(ax + b)^2 = c$. Then solve.**

36. $x^2 - 6x + 9 = 25$ **37.** $9x^2 - 24x + 16 = 121$ **38.** $9x^2 + 12x + 4 = 64$

39. $25x^2 - 20x + 4 = 144$ **40.** $4x^2 + 28x + 49 = 169$ **41.** $4x^2 - 4x + 1 = 36$

42. $9y^2 + 48y + 64 = \frac{16}{25}$ **43.** $16m^2 - 8m + 1 = \frac{169}{25}$ **44.** $4v^2 - 4v + 1 = \frac{121}{9}$

45. $9y^2 + 12y + 4 = 1.44$ **46.** $9w^2 + 42w + 49 = 0.36$

19. $\frac{19}{3}, -5$
20. $\frac{1}{4}, -\frac{11}{4}$
21. $\frac{3}{2}, 0$
22. $1, -\frac{5}{8}$
23. $3\sqrt{6}, -\sqrt{6}$
24. $1, -2$
25. $3\sqrt{7}, -\sqrt{7}$
26. $2.1, 1.5$
27. $1.1, 0.7$
28. $-1.1, -1.5\overline{6}$
29. $-\frac{2}{5}, -2$
30. $\frac{8 \pm 3\sqrt{2}}{3}$
31. $\frac{1}{3}, -\frac{11}{3}$
32. $\frac{1 \pm \sqrt{5}}{2}$
33. $3 \pm \sqrt{6}$
34. $\frac{5}{6}, \frac{1}{6}$
35. $\frac{8}{15}, \frac{2}{15}$
36. $8, -2$
37. $5, -\frac{7}{3}$
38. $2, -\frac{10}{3}$
39. $\frac{14}{5}, -2$
40. $3, -10$
41. $\frac{7}{2}, -\frac{5}{2}$
42. $-\frac{12}{5}, -\frac{44}{15}$
43. $\frac{9}{10}, -\frac{2}{5}$
44. $\frac{7}{3}, -\frac{4}{3}$
45. $-0.2\overline{6}, -1.0\overline{6}$
46. $-2.1\overline{3}, -2.5\overline{3}$

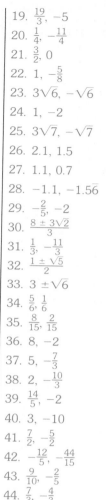

IN OTHER FIELDS
Mathematics and Poetry

There are few areas in art and literature that allow for more creativity than poetry. There are few disciplines in science more rigid and more structured than mathematics. Yet the influence of mathematics is apparent in poetry.

The term *meter*, used to refer to a unit of measure in mathematics, is used in poetics to refer to a regular rhythmic pattern. Another term that represents a unit of measure in mathematics is *foot*. In poetry, a foot is a metrical unit of two or more syllables. A metrical line of poetry is called a *verse* and is named according to the number of feet it contains.

dimeter: two feet   *tetrameter:* four feet
trimeter: three feet   *pentameter:* five feet

To describe the meter of a verse, indicate both the kind of foot that predominates in it and the number of feet it contains. Each of the following lines from Keats's *Endymion* contains 5 two-syllable feet. A two-syllable foot in which the second syllable has more stress than the first is called an *iamb*. The meter of this poem is based on a pattern of five iambs per line. Thus, the poem is said to be written in *iambic pentameter*.

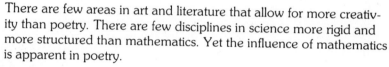

A thing of beauty is a joy forever:

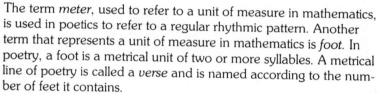

Its loveliness increases; it will never
Pass into nothingness; but still will keep
A bower quiet for us, and a sleep

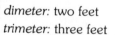

Full of sweet dreams, and health, and quiet breathing.

1. Solve $y^2 + 14y + 30 = 0$.

$$y^2 + 14y + 30 = 0$$
$$y^2 + 14y = -30$$
$$y^2 + 14y + 49 = -30 + 49$$
$$(y + 7)^2 = 19$$
$$y + 7 = \pm\sqrt{19}$$
$$y = -7 \pm \sqrt{19}$$

2. Solve $y^2 - 3y - 1 = 0$.

$$y^2 - 3y - 1 = 0$$
$$y^2 - 3y = 1$$
$$y^2 - 3y + \left(-\tfrac{3}{2}\right)^2 = 1 + \left(-\tfrac{3}{2}\right)^2$$
$$\left(y - \tfrac{3}{2}\right)^2 = \tfrac{13}{4}$$
$$y - \tfrac{3}{2} = \pm\tfrac{\sqrt{13}}{2}$$
$$y = \tfrac{3}{2} + \tfrac{\sqrt{13}}{2} \text{ or } y = \tfrac{3}{2} - \tfrac{\sqrt{13}}{2}$$
$$y = \tfrac{3 + \sqrt{13}}{2} \qquad y = \tfrac{3 - \sqrt{13}}{2}$$

3. Solve $3x^2 - 7x + 1 = 0$.

$$3x^2 - 7x + 1 = 0$$
$$x^2 - \tfrac{7}{3}x + \tfrac{1}{3} = 0$$
$$x^2 - \tfrac{7}{3}x = -\tfrac{1}{3}$$
$$x^2 - \tfrac{7}{3}x + \left(-\tfrac{7}{6}\right)^2 = -\tfrac{1}{3} + \left(-\tfrac{7}{6}\right)^2$$
$$\left(x - \tfrac{7}{6}\right)^2 = -\tfrac{1}{3} + \tfrac{49}{36}$$
$$\left(x - \tfrac{7}{6}\right)^2 = \tfrac{37}{36}$$
$$x - \tfrac{7}{6} = \pm\tfrac{\sqrt{37}}{6}$$
$$x = \tfrac{7 + \sqrt{37}}{6} \text{ or } x = \tfrac{7 - \sqrt{37}}{6}$$

1. Change $\dfrac{x^2 + 11x + 18}{x^2 - 81}$ to simplest form. $\dfrac{x + 2}{x - 9}$

12.3 | Completing the Square

Some quadratics cannot be factored over the real numbers. Nor is it always easy to use the square-root property. In such cases, however, by adding a real number to each side of the equation, you can make one side of the equation a perfect-square trinomial. Then you can use the square-root property to solve the equation.

EXAMPLES

1 **Solve $x^2 + 6x + 7 = 0$.**

SOLUTION

$$x^2 + 6x + 7 = 0$$
$$x^2 + 6x = -7 \qquad \textit{Rewrite the equation in the form } ax^2 + bx = -c.$$
$$x^2 + 6x + 9 = -7 + 9 \qquad \textit{Add a number to each side to make a}$$
$$\textit{perfect-square trinomial on the left.}$$
$$(x + 3)^2 = 2 \qquad \textit{Factor the trinomial and simplify the right-hand side.}$$
$$x + 3 = \pm\sqrt{2} \qquad \textit{Use the square-root property.}$$
$$x = -3 \pm \sqrt{2} \qquad \textit{Solve for x.}$$

CHECK $\qquad x^2 + 6x + 7 = 0 \qquad\qquad\qquad\qquad x^2 + 6x + 7 = 0$

$(-3 + \sqrt{2})^2 + 6(-3 + \sqrt{2}) + 7 \stackrel{?}{=} 0 \qquad (-3 - \sqrt{2})^2 + 6(-3 - \sqrt{2}) + 7 \stackrel{?}{=} 0$

$9 - 6\sqrt{2} + 2 - 18 + 6\sqrt{2} + 7 \stackrel{?}{=} 0 \qquad 9 + 6\sqrt{2} + 2 - 18 - 6\sqrt{2} + 7 \stackrel{?}{=} 0$

$0 = 0 \qquad\qquad\qquad\qquad\qquad\qquad 0 = 0$

The method used in Example 1 is called **completing the square.** Look at the following:

$$(x + 4)^2 = (x + 4)(x + 4) \qquad\qquad (x - 7)^2 = (x - 7)(x - 7)$$
$$= x^2 + 2(4x) + 16 \qquad\qquad\qquad = x^2 - 2(7x) + 49$$
$$= x^2 + 8x + 16 \qquad\qquad\qquad\qquad = x^2 - 14x + 49$$

Notice that the constant term of the trinomial can be found by taking half of the coefficient of the x term and then squaring this number. (Remember that the coefficient of x^2 is 1.)

2 **Solve $x^2 + 3x - 1 = 0$.**

SOLUTION $\quad x^2 + 3x - 1 = 0$

$$x^2 + 3x = 1$$
$$x^2 + 3x + \left(\tfrac{3}{2}\right)^2 = 1 + \left(\tfrac{3}{2}\right)^2 \qquad \textit{Take half the coefficient of the x term.}$$
$$\left(x + \tfrac{3}{2}\right)^2 = \tfrac{13}{4}$$
$$x + \tfrac{3}{2} = \pm\tfrac{\sqrt{13}}{2}$$
$$x = -\tfrac{3}{2} + \tfrac{\sqrt{13}}{2} \text{ or } x = -\tfrac{3}{2} - \tfrac{\sqrt{13}}{2}$$
$$x = \tfrac{-3 + \sqrt{13}}{2} \qquad x = \tfrac{-3 - \sqrt{13}}{2}$$

Check these roots.

3 | **Solve $2x^2 - 9x + 2 = 0$.**

SOLUTION

$$2x^2 - 9x + 2 = 0$$

The coefficient of x^2 is not 1. Divide both sides of the equation by 2 so that the coefficient of x^2 is 1.

$$x^2 - \frac{9}{2}x + 1 = 0$$

$$x^2 - \frac{9}{2}x = -1$$

Rewrite the equation in the form $ax^2 + bx = -c$.

$$x^2 - \frac{9}{2}x + \left(\frac{9}{4}\right)^2 = -1 + \left(\frac{9}{4}\right)^2$$

$$\left(x - \frac{9}{4}\right)^2 = -1 + \frac{81}{16}$$

$$\left(x - \frac{9}{4}\right)^2 = \frac{65}{16}$$

$$x - \frac{9}{4} = \pm\frac{\sqrt{65}}{4}$$

$$x = \frac{9 + \sqrt{65}}{4} \quad \text{or} \quad x = \frac{9 - \sqrt{65}}{4}$$

Check these roots.

ORAL EXERCISES

What number will make the polynomial a perfect-square trinomial?

1. $x^2 + 8x + \underline{\ 16\ }$ **2.** $x^2 - 14x + \underline{\ 49\ }$ **3.** $n^2 + 24n + \underline{\ 144\ }$

4. $m^2 - 16m + \underline{\ 64\ }$ **5.** $x^2 - x + \underline{\frac{1}{4}}$ **6.** $t^2 + 5t + \underline{\frac{25}{4}}$

7. $x^2 + \frac{3}{4}x + \underline{\frac{9}{64}}$ **8.** $t^2 - \frac{5}{3}t + \underline{\frac{25}{36}}$ **9.** $y^2 + \frac{7}{8}y + \underline{\frac{49}{256}}$

WRITTEN EXERCISES

A. What number is to be added to each side of the equation to complete the square?

1. $x^2 + 6x = 4$ $\quad 3^2$ **2.** $x^2 - 8x = 14$ $\quad 4^2$

3. $x^2 - 9x = -3$ $\quad \left(\frac{9}{2}\right)^2$ **4.** $y^2 - 2y = 1$ $\quad 1^2$

5. $t^2 - \frac{7}{2}t = \frac{1}{16}$ $\quad \left(\frac{7}{4}\right)^2$ **6.** $m^2 + \frac{1}{3}m = \frac{1}{8}$ $\quad \left(\frac{1}{6}\right)^2$

7. $w^2 + \frac{5}{2}w = \frac{3}{16}$ $\quad \left(\frac{5}{4}\right)^2$ **8.** $n^2 - \frac{2}{5}n = \frac{3}{10}$ $\quad \left(\frac{1}{5}\right)^2$

9. $y^2 + \frac{7}{8}y = \frac{5}{16}$ $\quad \left(\frac{7}{16}\right)^2$ **10.** $v^2 - \frac{2}{3}v = -\frac{1}{18}$ $\quad \left(\frac{1}{3}\right)^2$

B. Solve by completing the square.

11. $x^2 + 6x = 16$ **12.** $y^2 - 8y = 9$ **13.** $t^2 + 14t = -13$

14. $w^2 - 18w = 63$ **15.** $m^2 - 12m = -20$ **16.** $n^2 + 16n = -55$

2. Add $\sqrt{60x^2} + \sqrt{28x^2}$. $\quad 2|x|\sqrt{15} + 2|x|\sqrt{7}$

3. Multiply $(5 + 3\sqrt{7})(6 + 2\sqrt{7})$. $\quad 72 + 28\sqrt{7}$

4. Solve $\sqrt{2x - 3} = 5$. $\quad 14$

5. Solve $\frac{y}{52} = \frac{15}{260}$. $\quad 3$

TEACHER'S RESOURCE MASTERS

Practice Master 51, Part 1

ASSIGNMENT GUIDE

Minimum
1–9 odd, 14–31

Regular
11–33

Maximum
17–34, 41–49 odd

ADDITIONAL ANSWERS

Written Exercises

11. $2, -8$

12. $9, -1$

13. $-1, -13$

14. $21, -3$

15. $10, 2$

16. $-5, -11$

17. $\frac{3 + \sqrt{12}}{2}, \frac{3 - \sqrt{13}}{2}$

18. $\frac{-5 + \sqrt{29}}{2}, \frac{-5 - \sqrt{29}}{2}$

19. $\frac{-1 + \sqrt{13}}{2}, \frac{-1 - \sqrt{13}}{2}$

20. $\frac{-7 + \sqrt{85}}{2}, \frac{-7 - \sqrt{85}}{2}$

21. $\frac{5 + \sqrt{41}}{2}, \frac{5 - \sqrt{41}}{2}$

22. $0, -12$

23. $\frac{9}{2} + 2\sqrt{5}, \frac{9}{2} - 2\sqrt{5}$

24. $6, -1$

25. $4, -3$

26. $\frac{2}{3}, -2$

27. $2, -\frac{3}{2}$

28. $\frac{3}{2}, -\frac{9}{2}$

29. $\frac{1}{2}, -3$

30. $\frac{7 + \sqrt{73}}{12}, \frac{7 - \sqrt{73}}{12}$

31. $\frac{9}{4}, -\frac{3}{4}$

32. $3 + 2\sqrt{2}, 3 - 2\sqrt{2}$

33. $\frac{1}{5}, -\frac{3}{2}$

34. $\frac{3}{7}, -4$

35. $2 + \frac{3\sqrt{6}}{4}, 2 - \frac{3\sqrt{6}}{4}$

36. $\frac{2}{5}, \frac{1}{3}$

37. $\frac{3}{4}, -\frac{2}{3}$

38. $\frac{-1 + \sqrt{97}}{8}, \frac{-1 - \sqrt{97}}{8}$

39. $\frac{1 + \sqrt{385}}{24}, \frac{1 - \sqrt{385}}{24}$

40. $\frac{1 + \sqrt{46}}{15}, \frac{1 - \sqrt{46}}{15}$

41. $\frac{5 + \sqrt{13}}{2}, \frac{5 - \sqrt{13}}{2}$

42. $\frac{-7 + \sqrt{97}}{12}, \frac{-7 - \sqrt{97}}{12}$

43. $0, -8$

44. $2 \pm \sqrt{3}$

45. $\frac{41}{3}, 4$

46. $2, -\frac{41}{3}$

47. $\frac{8}{5}, -1$

48. -2

49. $\frac{-b + \sqrt{b^2 - 4c}}{2}$

50. $\frac{-b + \sqrt{b^2 - 4ac}}{2a}$

---

17. $x^2 - 3x = 1$

18. $v^2 + 5v - 1 = 0$

19. $y^2 + y - 3 = 0$

20. $w^2 + 7w = 9$

21. $m^2 - 5m - 4 = 0$

22. $t^2 + 12t = 0$

23. $y^2 - 9y + \frac{1}{4} = 0$

24. $m^2 - 6 = 5m$

25. $r^2 = r + 12$

26. $v^2 + \frac{4}{3}v = \frac{4}{3}$

27. $2n^2 - n - 6 = 0$

28. $4x^2 + 12x = 27$

29. $2m^2 + 5m = 3$

30. $6q^2 - 7q = 1$

31. $4y^2 - 6y = \frac{27}{4}$

32. $v^2 = 6v - 1$

33. $10n^2 + 13n = 3$

34. $25q = 12 - 7q^2$

35. $8w^2 = 32w - 5$

36. $15x^2 - 11x = -2$

37. $12s^2 = s + 6$

38. $2y^2 + \frac{1}{2}y - 3 = 0$

39. $3x^2 - \frac{1}{4}x - 2 = 0$

40. $5m^2 - \frac{2}{3}m - 1 = 0$

C. **Write each equation in the form $x^2 + bx = -c$. Then solve by completing the square.**

41. $(2x - 3)^2 - x(x + 3) = 0$

42. $(3y - 4)(2y + 3) + (6y + 10) = 0$

43. $(m + 2)^2 + 4(m + 2) = 12$

44. $\frac{y^2 - 3y}{y - 4} = \frac{y - 1}{y - 4}$

45. $\frac{2x + 1}{x - 7} + \frac{3x - 1}{x - 3} = 8$

46. $\frac{x - 3}{x + 2} - \frac{x + 1}{x - 5} = \frac{3}{4}$

47. $\frac{3m - 1}{m - 2} + \frac{2m + 3}{m - 1} = \frac{5}{6}$

48. $\frac{3t + 2}{2t - 1} - \frac{2t + 1}{t - 3} = \frac{1}{5}$

49. $x^2 + bx + c = 0$

50. $ax^2 + bx + c = 0, a \neq 0$

EXPLORATION
Conic Sections

The circle, the ellipse, and the hyperbola are examples of quadratic relations. These three, together with the parabola, are called **conic sections.** A conic section is a curve formed when a plane is passed through a right circular cone.

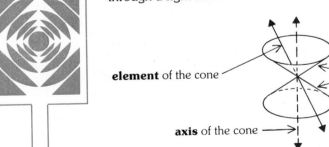

element of the cone

Notice that the cone has two parts, called **nappes.**

axis of the cone

If the plane is parallel to an element of the cone, the curve formed is a **parabola.** As with straight lines, the equation of a parabola can be written in more than one way. In the following equations, h, k, and p are constants.

1. $(x - h)^2 = 4p(y - k)$
2. $(x - h)^2 = -4p(y - k)$
3. $(y - k)^2 = 4p(x - h)$
4. $(y - k)^2 = -4p(x - h)$

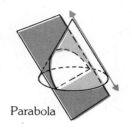

Parabola

If the plane is perpendicular to the axis of the cone, the curve formed is a **circle.** The general equation of a circle is

5. $\dfrac{(x - h)^2}{a^2} + \dfrac{(y - k)^2}{a^2} = 1, a \neq 0$

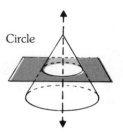

Circle

If the plane is not perpendicular to or parallel to the axis of the cone and is not parallel to an element of the cone, the curve formed is an **ellipse.** In the general equation of an ellipse, h, k, a, and b are constants.

6. $\dfrac{(x - h)^2}{a^2} + \dfrac{(y - k)^2}{b^2} = 1$ or

7. $\dfrac{(y - k)^2}{a^2} + \dfrac{(x - h)^2}{b^2} = 1, a > b$

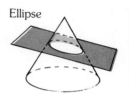

Ellipse

If the plane is parallel to the axis and passes through both nappes, the curve formed is a **hyperbola.** The general equation of a hyperbola is

8. $\dfrac{(x - h)^2}{a^2} - \dfrac{(y - k)^2}{b^2} = 1$ or

9. $\dfrac{(y - k)^2}{a^2} - \dfrac{(x - h)^2}{b^2} = 1$

(a does not have to be greater than b.)

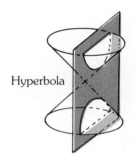

Hyperbola

EXERCISES

Tell if each equation is the equation of a parabola, a circle, an ellipse, or a hyperbola.

1. $\dfrac{(x - 3)^2}{9} + \dfrac{(y + 2)^2}{4} = 1$

2. $\dfrac{(x + 1)^2}{9} + \dfrac{(y - 3)^2}{9} = 1$

3. $\dfrac{(y - 3)^2}{16} - \dfrac{(x - 2)^2}{4} = 1$

4. $\dfrac{(x + 5)^2}{16} + \dfrac{(y + 4)^2}{16} = 1$

5. $(y + 2)^2 = -8(x - 7)$

6. $(x - 3)^2 = 8(y + 1)$

7. $(x - 2)^2 = -24(y + 6)$

8. $(y - 3)^2 = 12(x + 5)$

EXPLORATION

Exercises
1. ellipse
2. circle
3. hyperbola
4. circle
5. parabola
6. parabola
7. parabola
8. parabola

TEACHER'S NOTES

See p. T37.

CLASSROOM EXAMPLES

1. Solve $6x^2 + 11x - 10 = 0$.

$a = 6 \quad b = 11 \quad c = -10$

$x = \dfrac{-b \pm \sqrt{b^2 - 4ac}}{2a}$

$x = \dfrac{-11 \pm \sqrt{11^2 - 4(6)(-10)}}{2(6)}$

$\quad = \dfrac{-11 \pm \sqrt{361}}{12}$

$\quad = \dfrac{-11 \pm 19}{12}$

So $x = \frac{2}{3}$ or $x = -\frac{5}{2}$.

2. Solve $4x^2 = 10x - 6$.

$4x^2 - 10x + 6 = 0$

$a = 4 \quad b = -10 \quad c = 6$

$x = \dfrac{-b \pm \sqrt{b^2 - 4ac}}{2a}$

$x =$

$\dfrac{-(-10) \pm \sqrt{(-10)^2 - 4(4)(6)}}{2(4)}$

$\quad = \dfrac{10 \pm \sqrt{4}}{8}$

So $x = \frac{3}{2}$ or $x = 1$.

3. Solve $7x^2 + x - 5 = 0$. Express the roots as decimals.

$x = \dfrac{-b + \sqrt{b^2 - 4ac}}{2a}$

$x = \dfrac{-1 + \sqrt{1^2 - 4(7)(-5)}}{2(7)}$

$\quad = \dfrac{-1 + \sqrt{141}}{14}$

$\quad \dfrac{-1 \pm 11.874}{14}$

So $x \approx 0.777$ or $x \approx -0.920$.

MIXED REVIEW

1. $A = \frac{1}{2}bh$, solve for h.

$h = \frac{2A}{b}$

12.4 | The Quadratic Formula

If you look at the standard form of a quadratic equation, you can develop a formula that can be used to find the real-number roots of any quadratic equation.

$ax^2 + bx + c = 0$	*standard form*
$x^2 + \dfrac{b}{a}x + \dfrac{c}{a} = 0$	*Divide each side by a so that the coefficient of x^2 is 1.*
$x^2 + \dfrac{b}{a}x = -\dfrac{c}{a}$	*Add $-\dfrac{c}{a}$ to each side.*
$x^2 + \dfrac{b}{a}x + \left(\dfrac{b}{2a}\right)^2 = -\dfrac{c}{a} + \left(\dfrac{b}{2a}\right)^2$	*Complete the square.*
$\left(x + \dfrac{b}{2a}\right)^2 = -\dfrac{c}{a} + \dfrac{b^2}{4a^2}$	*Factor the left side and simplify the right side.*
$\left(x + \dfrac{b}{2a}\right)^2 = -\dfrac{c}{a}\left(\dfrac{4a}{4a}\right) + \dfrac{b^2}{4a^2}$	
$\left(x + \dfrac{b}{2a}\right)^2 = \dfrac{-4ac}{4a^2} + \dfrac{b^2}{4a^2}$	
$\left(x + \dfrac{b}{2a}\right)^2 = \dfrac{b^2 - 4ac}{4a^2}$	*Add the fractions on the right side.*
$x + \dfrac{b}{2a} = \pm\sqrt{\dfrac{b^2 - 4ac}{4a^2}}$	*Square-root property*
$x + \dfrac{b}{2a} = \pm\dfrac{\sqrt{b^2 - 4ac}}{2a}$	*Simplify the radical.*
$x = -\dfrac{b}{2a} \pm \dfrac{\sqrt{b^2 - 4ac}}{2a}$	*Add $-\dfrac{b}{2a}$ to each side.*
$x = \dfrac{-b \pm \sqrt{b^2 - 4ac}}{2a}$	*Simplify the right side.*

The last equation above is known as the **quadratic formula.**

The Quadratic Formula	**For any quadratic equation in standard form, $ax^2 + bx + c = 0$, the roots are $x = \dfrac{-b \pm \sqrt{b^2 - 4ac}}{2a}$, for $b^2 - 4ac \geq 0$.**

EXAMPLES

1 **Solve $3x^2 - 2x - 1 = 0$.**

SOLUTION The equation is in standard form. $a = 3 \quad b = -2 \quad c = -1$

$x = \dfrac{-b \pm \sqrt{b^2 - 4ac}}{2a}$

$x = \dfrac{-(-2) \pm \sqrt{(-2)^2 - 4(3)(-1)}}{2(3)}$

$\quad = \dfrac{2 \pm \sqrt{16}}{6}$

$\quad = \dfrac{2 \pm 4}{6}$

So $x = 1$ or $x = -\frac{1}{3}$.

CHECK

$$3x^2 - 2x - 1 = 0$$
$$3(1)^2 - 2(1) - 1 \stackrel{?}{=} 0$$
$$3 - 2 - 1 \stackrel{?}{=} 0$$
$$0 = 0 \ ✔$$

$$3x^2 - 2x - 1 = 0$$
$$3\left(-\frac{1}{3}\right)^2 - 2\left(-\frac{1}{3}\right) - 1 \stackrel{?}{=} 0$$
$$\frac{1}{3} + \frac{2}{3} - 1 \stackrel{?}{=} 0$$
$$0 = 0 \ ✔$$

| 2 | **Solve $2x^2 = 5x - 3$.** |

SOLUTION Write the equation in standard form. $2x^2 - 5x + 3 = 0$

$$a = 2 \qquad b = -5 \qquad c = 3$$
$$x = \frac{-b \pm \sqrt{b^2 - 4ac}}{2a}$$
$$x = \frac{-(-5) \pm \sqrt{(-5)^2 - 4(2)(3)}}{2(2)}$$
$$= \frac{5 \pm \sqrt{1}}{4}$$

So $x = \frac{3}{2}$ or $x = 1$.

Check these roots.

When the roots have radicals in them, you can use the table of square roots on page 547 or your calculator to find decimal approximations for the roots.

| 3 | **Solve $5x^2 + x - 3 = 0$. Express the roots as decimals.** |

SOLUTION $x = \dfrac{-b \pm \sqrt{b^2 - 4ac}}{2a}$

$$x = \frac{-1 \pm \sqrt{1^2 - 4(5)(-3)}}{2(5)}$$
$$= \frac{-1 \pm \sqrt{61}}{10}$$
$$\approx \frac{-1 \pm 7.810}{10}$$

So $x \approx 0.681$ or $x \approx -0.881$.

Check these roots.

ORAL EXERCISES

When each equation is in standard form, what is the value of a, b, and c?

1. $2x^2 - x - 15 = 0$ $2, -1, -15$
2. $-x^2 - x + 30 = 0$ $-1, -1, 30$
3. $4x^2 - 17x + 18 = 0$
4. $8x^2 - 4x - 1 = 0$ $8, -4, -1$
5. $15x^2 = x + 2$ $15, -1, -2$
6. $9x^2 = 12x + 1$ $9, -12, -1$
7. $49x^2 - 70x + 23 = 0$ $49, -70, 23$
8. $x + 14 = 30x^2$ $-30, 1, 14$
9. $7x^2 + 9 = 24x$ $7, -24, 9$
10. $4x^2 - 8x + 3 = 0$ $4, -8, 3$
11. $5x^2 - 6x - 8 = 0$ $5, -6, -8$
12. $3x^2 - 6x = 0$ $3, -6, 0$

2. $P = 2l + 2w$, solve for w.
$w = \frac{P - 2l}{2}$
3. 30 is what percent of 600? 5%
4. Restate $0.\overline{53}$ in fractional form. $\frac{53}{99}$
5. Find the product of $\frac{4}{5}$ and $-\frac{5}{8}$. $-\frac{1}{2}$

TEACHER'S RESOURCE MASTERS

Practice Master 51, Part 2

ASSIGNMENT GUIDE

Minimum
1–12, 13–35 odd

Regular
13–36

Maximum
19–36, 37–47 odd

ADDITIONAL ANSWERS

Oral Exercises
3. 4, −17, 18

Written Exercises
1. 3, $-\frac{5}{2}$
2. −6, 5
3. $\frac{9}{4}$, 2
4. $\frac{1 \pm \sqrt{3}}{4}$
5. $\frac{2}{5}$, $-\frac{1}{3}$
6. $\frac{2 \pm \sqrt{5}}{3}$
7. $\frac{5 \pm \sqrt{2}}{7}$
8. $\frac{7}{10}$, $-\frac{2}{3}$
9. 3, $\frac{3}{7}$
10. $\frac{3}{2}$, $\frac{1}{2}$
11. 2, $-\frac{4}{5}$
12. 2, 0

WRITTEN EXERCISES

A. 1–12. Solve each exercise in Oral Exercises by using the quadratic formula. Express radicals in simplest form.

B. 13. $40x^2 = 2x + 3$ **14.** $y^2 + y + 8 = 0$ **15.** $m^2 + 6m + 6 = 0$

16. $r^2 - 4r + 1 = 0$ **17.** $v^2 - 6v + 2 = 0$ **18.** $3x^2 = 5x$

19. $y^2 - 3y - 2 = 0$ **20.** $25x^2 - 130x + 167 = 0$ **21.** $2t^2 + 6t = 3$

22. $x^2 = 7x - 2$ **23.** $v^2 + 4v = 1$ **24.** $-y^2 + 7y + 2 = 0$

25. $m^2 + 11m + 8 = 0$ **26.** $5z^2 + 10z + 1 = 0$ **27.** $2q^2 + 4q = 3$

28. $x^2 = 9x - 20$ **29.** $4n^2 - 4n + 1 = 0$ **30.** $15t^2 = 23t + 28$

Solve by using the quadratic formula. When necessary, use the table of square roots on page 547 to write answers in decimal form.

31. $63r^2 + 17r = 10$ **32.** $9x^2 = 6x + 1$ **33.** $n^2 - 16n - 665 = 0$

34. $t^2 - 61t + 798 = 0$ **35.** $y^2 + 29y + 210 = 0$ **36.** $y^2 = 5y + 104$

C. Solve.

37. $x^2 + 2\sqrt{3}x + 3 = 0$ **38.** $\sqrt{2}x^2 + 2x - 2\sqrt{2} = 0$

39. $x^2 - 2\sqrt{5}x + 5 = 0$ **40.** $x^2 - 2\sqrt{2}x - 1 = 0$

41. $\sqrt{3}x^2 + 12x - 15\sqrt{3} = 0$ **42.** $\sqrt{5}x^2 + 25x - 30\sqrt{5} = 0$

43. $-\dfrac{1}{x + 1} = \dfrac{3}{x} + 2$ **44.** $\dfrac{1}{x - 2} = \dfrac{2}{x} + 1$ **45.** $-\dfrac{3}{2x + 1} = \dfrac{5}{x} + 3$

Solve.

46. The base of a triangle is 6 centimeters more than the altitude. Find the altitude and the base if the area of the triangle is 80 cm².   10 cm, 16 cm

47. The length of a rectangle is three times the width. Find the width to the nearest tenth if the area of the rectangle is 50 m².   4.1 m

SELF-QUIZ

Solve by factoring.

1. $6x^2 - 7x - 3 = 0$ $-\frac{1}{3}, \frac{3}{2}$ **2.** $9x^2 + 25 = 30x$ $\frac{5}{3}$

Solve by using the square-root property.

3. $x^2 = 81$ ± 9 **4.** $(x + 3)^2 = 121$ 8, −14

Solve by completing the square.

5. $x^2 - 8x + 2 = 0$ $4 \pm \sqrt{14}$ **6.** $3x^2 + 6x - 9 = 0$ −3, 1

Solve by using the quadratic formula.

7. $x^2 - 5x + 6 = 0$ 3, 2   **8.** $2x^2 - 11x + 5 = 0$ 5, $\frac{1}{2}$

12.5 | The Discriminant

In the quadratic formula, the expression $b^2 - 4ac$ is called the **discriminant**. You can determine certain information about the solutions of a quadratic equation by looking at the value of its discriminant.

OBJECTIVE

Find the value of the discriminant of a quadratic equation. Then tell if the roots are real and equal, if the roots are rational and not equal, if they are irrational and unequal, or if there are no real-number roots.

EXAMPLES

If the value of the discriminant is negative, there are no real-number roots.

1 **Describe the roots of $x^2 + x + 1 = 0$.**

    SOLUTION $b^2 - 4ac = 1^2 - 4(1)(1)$
$$= -3$$

    There are no real-number roots. $\sqrt{-3}$ is not a real number.

If the value of the discriminant is 0, the roots are rational numbers and they are equal.

2 **Describe the roots of $4x^2 + 4x + 1 = 0$.**

    SOLUTION $b^2 - 4ac = 4^2 - 4(4)(1)$
$$= 0$$

    There are two real, equal roots. Since $\sqrt{0} = 0$, the roots are $-\frac{1}{2}$ and $-\frac{1}{2}$. That is, $x = \frac{-4 \pm \sqrt{0}}{2(4)} = -\frac{1}{2}$.

If the value of the discriminant is positive and is a perfect square, and if a, b, and c are rational numbers, the roots are rational and are not equal.

3 **Describe the roots of $2x^2 - 11x + 5 = 0$.**

    SOLUTION $b^2 - 4ac = (-11)^2 - 4(2)(5)$
$$= 81$$

    There are two real, unequal roots. Since 81 is a perfect square, the roots are rational numbers. That is, $x = \frac{-(-11) \pm \sqrt{81}}{2(2)}$, so $x = 5$ or $x = \frac{1}{2}$.

If the value of the discriminant is positive and is not a perfect square, and if a, b, and c are rational numbers, the roots are unequal and irrational.

4 **Describe the roots of $4x^2 + 6x + 1 = 0$.**

    SOLUTION $b^2 - 4ac = 6^2 - 4(4)(1)$
$$= 20$$

    There are two real, unequal roots. Since 20 is not a perfect square, the roots are irrational numbers. That is, $x = \frac{-6 \pm \sqrt{20}}{2(4)}$, so $x = \frac{-3 + \sqrt{5}}{4}$ or $x = \frac{-3 - \sqrt{5}}{4}$.

TEACHER'S NOTES

See p. T37.

CLASSROOM EXAMPLES

1. Describe the roots of $x^2 + x + 3 = 0$.
$$b^2 - 4ac = 1^2 - 4(1)(3)$$
$$= -11$$
There are no real-number roots. $\sqrt{-11}$ is not a real number.

2. Describe the roots of $3y^2 - 6y + 3 = 0$.
$$b^2 - 4ac = (-6)^2 - 4(3)(3)$$
$$= 0$$
There are two real, equal roots. Since $\sqrt{0} = 0$, the roots are 1 and 1. That is, $y = \frac{6 \pm \sqrt{0}}{2(3)} = 1$.

3. Describe the roots of $4x^2 - 22x + 10 = 0$.
$$b^2 - 4ac = (-22)^2 - 4(4)(10)$$
$$= 324$$
There are two real, unequal roots. Since 324 is a perfect square, the roots are rational numbers. That is, $x = \frac{-(-22) \pm \sqrt{324}}{2(4)}$, so $x = 5$ or $x = \frac{1}{2}$.

4. Describe the roots of $8x^2 + 12x + 2 = 0$.

$b^2 - 4ac = 12^2 - 4(8)(2)$
$= 80$

There are two real, un-equal roots. Since 80 is not a perfect square, the roots are irrational numbers. That is,

$x = \frac{-12 \pm \sqrt{80}}{2(8)}$, so

$x = \frac{-3 \pm \sqrt{5}}{4}$

or $x = \frac{-3 - \sqrt{5}}{4}$.

MIXED REVIEW

1. Illustrate the distributive property of multiplication over addition. Answers may vary.

2. Factor completely. $12r^2 - 3s^2$ $3(2r - s)(2r + s)$

3. Solve $\frac{x}{5} = -18$. -90

4. Find the value of $(-1.6)^2$. 2.56

5. Complete $|-30|$. 30

TEACHER'S RESOURCE MASTERS

Practice Master 52, Part 1

Quiz 23

ASSIGNMENT GUIDE

Minimum
1–11 odd, 13–25 odd

Regular
13–25

Maximum
22–26, 29–36

ORAL EXERCISES

1. What is the name given to the expression $b^2 - 4ac$? the discriminant

Describe the roots of a quadratic equation if the discriminant has the given value (real roots or no real roots, equal or unequal roots, rational or irrational roots).

2. 23   **3.** −9   **4.** 25   **5.** 82   **6.** 0

7. 196   **8.** 13   **9.** −64   **10.** 12   **11.** 36

WRITTEN EXERCISES

A. Find the value of the discriminant for each.

1. $x^2 - 3x + 2 = 0$ 1
2. $y^2 - 6y + 9 = 0$ 0
3. $t^2 + t - 1 = 0$ 5
4. $v^2 + 7v + 19 = 0$ −27
5. $4m^2 - 4m + 1 = 0$ 0
6. $2q^2 + 6q - 1 = 0$ 44
7. $5r^2 + 3r - 2 = 0$ 49
8. $2s^2 + 5s - 3 = 0$ 49
9. $n^2 - 10n + 25 = 0$ 0
10. $18s^2 + 9s - 2 = 0$
11. $49n^2 - 56n + 16 = 0$
12. $5x^2 + 2x + 1 = 0$

B. Find the value of the discriminant. Then describe the roots of the quadratic equation (real roots or no real roots, equal or unequal roots, rational or irrational roots).

13. $3y^2 - 4y + 2 = 0$
14. $4m^2 + 6m - 1 = 0$
15. $25v^2 + 70v + 49 = 0$
16. $14x^2 + 3x = 5$
17. $27y^2 = 6y + 16$
18. $4n^2 + 1 = 9n$
19. $-5q^2 + q + 1 = 0$
20. $4 = 3x^2 + 11x$
21. $2 = 5t^2 + 9t$
22. $-7r^2 + r + 1 = 0$
23. $\frac{3}{4}y^2 + \frac{1}{4} = 0$
24. $\frac{2}{3}m^2 = 0$
25. $4y^2 + 9 = 12y$
26. $3x^2 + 6x + 4 = 0$

C. Solve each equation. Use the table of square roots on page 547 or your calculator to approximate answers where necessary.

27. $x^2 + 2\sqrt{6}x + 4 = 0$
28. $y^2 + 4\sqrt{11}y + 32 = 0$
29. $\sqrt{3}m - 2m^2 - 3 = 0$
30. $\sqrt{7}x^2 + 2x = \sqrt{63}$
31. $\frac{3}{2r} - r + \sqrt{6} = 0$
32. $t^2 + \sqrt{15}t + 3 = 0$

Describe the roots of $ax^2 + bx + c = 0$ in each case. a, b, and c are real numbers.

33. $a \neq 0$, $b \neq 0$, $c = 0$
34. $b^2 = 4ac$
35. $b = 0$; a and c are both positive or both negative
36. $b = 0$; a is positive and c is negative, or vice versa

12.6 | Problem Solving

You have solved problems of similar content before. This time, the problems will result in quadratic equations.

EXAMPLES

1 The product of two consecutive odd integers is 255. What are the integers?

Understand: *Given:* two consecutive odd integers whose product is 255

To find: the integers

Plan: Let x = the first odd integer. Then $x + 2$ = the next odd integer. Solve the equation $x(x + 2) = 255$.

Solve:
$$x(x + 2) = 255$$
$$x^2 + 2x - 255 = 0$$
$$(x + 17)(x - 15) = 0$$
$$x = -17 \quad \text{or} \quad x = 15$$

Answer: There are two pairs of odd integers: -17 and -15, or 15 and 17.

Review: $-17(-15) = 255$ ✔
$15(17) = 255$ ✔

2 A rectangular vegetable garden has a length three feet more than the width. If the area of the garden is 180 square feet, what is the length and what is the width of the garden?

Understand: *Given:* The length of a rectangle with an area of 180 ft^2 is 3 ft more than the width.

To find: the length and width

Plan: Draw a picture. Using one variable, write and solve an equation for the area.

Solve: Let w = width.
Then $w + 3$ = length.
$$180 = (w + 3)w$$
$$0 = w^2 + 3w - 180$$
$$0 = (w - 12)(w + 15)$$
$$w = 12 \quad \text{or} \quad w = -15$$

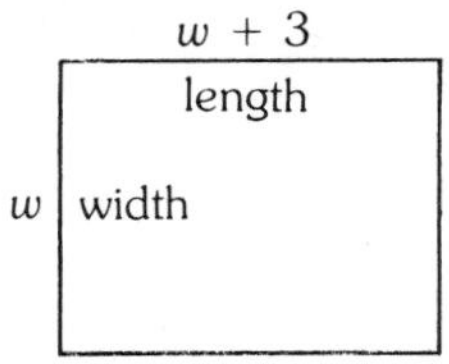

(diagram: rectangle labeled with $w + 3$ and "length" along the top, w and "width" along the side)

Answer: Width cannot be negative. Therefore, the width is 12 feet. The length is $12 + 3$, or 15, feet.

Review: $12(15) = 180$ ✔

CLASSROOM EXAMPLES

1. The product of two consecutive odd integers is 483. What are the integers?

Let x = the first odd integer. Then $x + 2$ = the next odd integer.
$$x(x + 2) = 483$$
$$x^2 + 2x - 483 = 0$$
$$(x + 23)(x - 21) = 0$$
$$x = -23 \quad \text{or} \quad x = 21$$
There are two pairs of odd integers: -23 and -21, or 21 and 23.

2. Susan's rectangular garden has a length five feet more than the width. If the area of the garden is 150 square feet, what is the length and what is the width of the garden?

Let w = width. Then $w + 5$ = length.
$$150 = (w + 5)w$$
$$0 = w^2 + 5w - 150$$
$$0 = (w - 10)(w + 15)$$
$$w = 10 \quad \text{or} \quad w = -15$$
Width cannot be negative. Therefore, the width is 10 feet. The length is $10 + 5$, or 15 feet.

3. Tamara's boat can travel 8 kilometers per hour in still water. She traveled upstream for 48 kilometers in 3 more hours than she traveled downstream for 64 kilometers. What is the speed of the current of the river?

Let c = the speed of the current.

Let t = time traveled downstream.

	Distance	Rate	Time
Upstream	48	$8 - c$	$t + 3$
Downstream	64	$8 + c$	t

Upstream $\frac{48}{8 - c} = t + 3$ or $\frac{48}{8 - c} - 3 = t$

Downstream $\frac{64}{8 + c} = t$

$\frac{48}{8 - c} - 3 = \frac{64}{8 + c}$

$3c^2 + 112c - 320 = 0$

$(3c - 8)(c + 40) = 0$

$3c - 8 = 0$

$\quad c = \frac{8}{3}$ or

$c + 40 = 0$

$\quad c = -40$

The current cannot flow at a negative speed. So the speed is $\frac{8}{3}$, or $2\frac{2}{3}$, km/h.

4. Nance, working alone, could finish painting a house in five hours less than Peter could if he worked alone. Working together, they can paint the house in six hours. How long would it take Nance to paint the house by herself?

If x = time if Nance works alone, then $\frac{1}{x}$ = her hourly rate.

---

3 Jennifer's boat can travel 5 miles per hour in still water. She traveled upstream for 36 miles in 2 more hours than she traveled downstream for 42 miles. What is the speed of the current of the river?

Understand: *Given:* A boat travels 5 mi/h. It takes 2 hr more to travel 36 mi upstream than 42 mi downstream.

To find: the speed of the current

Plan: Use the formula $d = rt$ to write an equation. Use a table to help organize the information.

Solve: Let c = the speed of the current. Let t = time traveled downstream.

	Distance	Rate	Time
Upstream	36	$5 - c$	$t + 2$
Downstream	42	$5 + c$	t

Write two equations:

Upstream

$\frac{36}{5 - c} = t + 2$, or $\frac{36}{5 - c} - 2 = t$

Downstream

$\frac{42}{5 + c} = t$

$\frac{36}{5 - c} - 2 = \frac{42}{5 + c}$ Substitute $\frac{42}{5 + c}$ for t in the first equation.

$c^2 + 39c - 40 = 0$

$(c + 40)(c - 1) = 0$

$c = -40$ or $c = 1$

Answer: The current cannot flow at a negative speed. So the speed is 1 mi/h.

Review: For $c = 1$, find the time traveled downstream.

$(5 + 1)t = 42$

$\quad t = 7$

Using $c = 1$ and $t = 7$, check the upstream equation.

$(5 - 1)(7 + 2) \overset{?}{=} 36$

$\quad 4(9) = 36$ ✔

4 Ann, working alone, could finish painting a room in three hours less than her father could if he worked alone. Working together, they can paint the room in two hours. How long would it take Ann to paint the room by herself?

Understand: *Given:* Ann and her father can paint a room in 2 hr. Ann could paint the room alone in 3 hr less than her father.

To find: the time it would take Ann to paint the room alone

Plan: Write and solve an equation. Use a table to help organize information. If x = time if Ann works alone, then $\frac{1}{x}$ = her hourly rate.

Solve:

	Rate of work	Time	Work completed
Ann	$\frac{1}{x}$	2	$\frac{2}{x}$
Father	$\frac{1}{x + 3}$	2	$\frac{2}{x + 3}$

$$\frac{2}{x} + \frac{2}{x+3} = 1$$
$$x^2 - x - 6 = 0$$
$$(x-3)(x+2) = 0$$
$$x = 3 \quad \text{or} \quad x = -2$$

The sum of the work done by each person equals 1 job done.

Answer: Ann could paint the room by herself in three hours.

Review: $\frac{2}{3} + \frac{2}{6} = \frac{4}{6} + \frac{2}{6} = 1$ ✔

	Rate of work	Time	Work completed
Nance	$\frac{1}{x}$	6	$\frac{6}{x}$
Peter	$\frac{1}{x+5}$	6	$\frac{6}{x+5}$

$$\frac{6}{x} + \frac{6}{x+5} = 1$$
$$x^2 - 7x - 30 = 0$$
$$(x-10)(x+3) = 0$$
$$x = 10 \quad \text{or} \quad x = -3$$

Nance could paint the house by herself in ten hours.

ORAL EXERCISES

With two printing presses, the morning edition of the *Times* can be printed in 3 hours. The faster of the two presses can print an edition in 8 hours less than the slower press. How long would it take the slower press alone? Let x represent the number of hours it would take the faster press alone.

1. What would $\frac{1}{x}$ represent?

2. What would represent the rate of the slower press?

3. What would the sum of the work completed by each press equal?

4. If the equation factors into $(x+6)(x-4) = 0$, what is the solution to this problem?

5. What equation would you use to check your solution to this problem?

MIXED REVIEW

Perform the indicated operation.

1. $(9)\left(-\frac{1}{9}\right)$ -1

2. $-0.62 + (-1.15)$ -1.77

3. $-9k^2(8k^3m - 5m)$ $-72k^5m + 45k^2m$

4. $53 - (-19)$ 72

5. $-5.4 \div 0.06$ -90

TEACHER'S RESOURCE MASTERS

Practice Master 52, Part 2

ASSIGNMENT GUIDE

Minimum
1–6

Regular
5–10

Maximum
7–12

ADDITIONAL ANSWERS
Oral Exercises
1. the rate of work of the faster press
(continued on next page)

WRITTEN EXERCISES

A. 1. The product of two consecutive integers is 240. What are the integers?

2. Find two numbers whose product is 64 and whose difference is 12.

3. The length of a rectangle is 2 meters less than twice the width. If the area of the rectangle is 112 square meters, what is the width? 8 m

4. Four times the area of a square is 64 square feet. Find the length of each side. 4 feet

B. 5. The product of two positive rational numbers is $\frac{36}{5}$. If one number is $\frac{4}{5}$ of the other, what are the two numbers? 3, $\frac{12}{5}$

6. A river is flowing at a rate of 5 miles per hour. A boat travels 12 miles upstream and 36 miles downstream in a total of 9 hours. What is the speed of the boat in still water? 17 mi/h

7. The length of a rectangular garden is 3 feet more than the width. If the length were decreased by 2 feet and the width increased by 2 feet, the garden would have an area of 182 square feet. What are the length and the width of the garden? $l = 15$ ft; $w = 12$ ft

8. One pipe, working alone, can fill a vat in 6 fewer hours than a second pipe can. If both pipes, working together, can fill the vat in 4 hours, how long would it take the faster pipe to do the job alone? 6 hours

C.

9. The sum of a number and the number's reciprocal is $2\frac{1}{12}$. What are the number and the reciprocal? $\frac{3}{4}, \frac{4}{3}$

10. John can paint a house in 3 days less than Lee. When they work together, they can paint a house in $5\frac{1}{7}$ days. How long would it take each if they worked alone?

11. The outside dimensions of a picture frame are 12 inches by 15 inches. How wide is the picture frame if the picture has an area of 88 square inches?

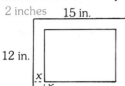

2 inches   15 in.

12 in.

x

x

12. One pipe can fill a tank in x hours. A smaller pipe is used to empty the tank after the tank is completely full, and takes 3 hours longer to empty it than it takes the first pipe to fill it. When both pipes were accidentally left open at the same time, the tank filled in 60 hours. How long does it take the first pipe to fill the tank when the second pipe is shut off?   12 hours

MATH HERITAGE/Witch or Angel?

Maria Gaetana Agnesi (1718–1799) was one of the most extraordinary woman scholars of all time. Born in Italy at a time when there was strong opposition to any form of higher education for women, Maria had the advantage of being raised by parents who carefully planned her education. When her father refused to allow her to enter a convent, Agnesi spent the next ten years writing two large volumes on differential and integral calculus. One of the most important mathematical publications produced by a woman, it was essentially a compendium of the works of various mathematicians, including Newton and Leibniz.

In her *Analytical Institutions,* Maria discussed the versed sine curve. The original Italian word for "versed" was mistranslated into English as "witch." From that time on, the curve discussed by Maria has been known as the Witch of Agnesi. Over the years, Maria received much recognition from the academic world for her work in mathematics.

After her father's death in 1752, Maria devoted her life to charitable works until her death at the age of 81. She was buried in a common grave with 15 of the old people for whom she had cared.

At the home for the ill and infirm where Maria worked, she was called "an angel of consolation to the sick and dying." It appears that "the witch" was actually the work of an angel.

12.7 | Quadratic Functions

The equation $y = ax^2 + bx + c$ defines a **quadratic function,** where a, b, and c are real numbers, and $a \neq 0$.

Each of the following is a quadratic function:

$$y = -2x^2 \qquad y = x^2 + 7 \qquad y = -x^2 + 3x - 1$$

You can graph a quadratic function by finding several ordered pairs that satisfy the equation.

EXAMPLES

1 **Graph $y = x^2 - 8x + 12$.**

SOLUTION

x	y
1	5
2	0
3	-3
4	-4
5	-3
6	0
7	5

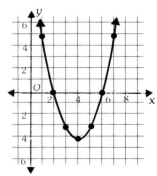

Notice that the graph of a quadratic function is not a straight line. The graph of a quadratic function is called a **parabola.** The parabola can open upward or downward, depending on whether the coefficient of x^2 in $y = ax^2 + bx + c$ is positive or negative. The coefficient of x^2 in Example 1 is positive. The parabola opens upward.

2 **Graph $y = -2x^2 + 3$.**

SOLUTION

x	y
-2	-5
-1	1
0	3
1	1
2	-5

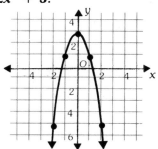

The coefficient of x^2 is negative. The parabola opens downward. Notice that the parabola in Example 1 has a point that is lowest on the graph, a **minimum point.** The parabola in Example 2 has a point on the graph that is highest on the graph, a **maximum point.** Each of these points is called the **turning point** of the parabola, or the **vertex.**

OBJECTIVES

Tell whether or not an equation describes a quadratic function.

Graph a quadratic function.

TEACHER'S NOTES

See p. T37.

CLASSROOM EXAMPLES

1. Graph $y = x^2 - 4x + 6$.

x	y
0	6
1	3
2	2
3	3
4	6

2. Graph $y = -2x^2 + 2$.

x	y
-2	-6
-1	0
0	2
1	0
2	-6

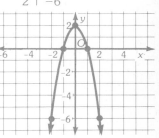

3. Find the vertex for $y = -2x^2 + 4x + 1$.

(continued on next page)

$x = \frac{-b}{2a}$

$x = \frac{-4}{2(-2)} = \frac{-4}{-4} = 1$

$y = -2x^2 + 4x + 1$

$\quad = -2(1)^2 + 4(1) + 1$

$\quad = 3$

The vertex is $(1, 3)$.

4. Find the x-intercept of $y = x^2 - x - 12$.

$y = x^2 - x - 12$

$0 = x^2 - x - 12$

$\quad = (x - 4)(x + 3)$

$x = 4$ or $x = -3$

So the x-intercepts are 4 and -3.

5. Tell how many x-intercepts there are for the graph of $y = x^2 + x + 2$.

$b^2 - 4ac = 1 - 8 = -7$

The discriminant is negative, so there are no real-number solutions (roots) of the quadratic equation. So there are no x-intercepts for the parabola.

MIXED REVIEW

Solve.

1. $(y - 5)^2 = 16$ 9, 1

2. $16y^2 = 49$ $\frac{7}{4}, -\frac{7}{4}$

3. $-3y = y + 9$ $-\frac{9}{4}$

4. $\frac{8c}{2} + 5 = 19$ $\frac{7}{2}$

5. $\frac{35}{y} = \frac{105}{63}$ 21

TEACHER'S RESOURCE MASTERS

Practice Master 53, Part 1

COMPUTER SOFTWARE

Graphing Quadratic Equations

Through the vertex is a vertical line, called the **axis of symmetry.** The axis of symmetry is halfway between any two points on the parabola that have the same y-coordinate. That is, if the parabola were folded in half along the axis of symmetry, the two parts of the parabola would coincide.

The equation of the axis of symmetry in Example 1 is $x = 4$ and in Example 2 it is $x = 0$. In general, the equation of the axis of symmetry for the graph of any quadratic function $y = ax^2 + bx + c$ can be found by the formula $x = \frac{-b}{2a}$.

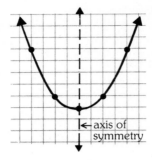
← axis of symmetry

Since this is also the x-coordinate of the vertex, you can use the formula to find the coordinates of the vertex.

3   **Find the vertex for $y = -3x^2 + 6x + 1$.**

SOLUTION

$x = \frac{-b}{2a}$ *Use the formula to find x.*

$x = \frac{-6}{2(-3)} = \frac{-6}{-6} = 1$

$y = -3x^2 + 6x + 1$

$\quad = -3(1)^2 + 6(1) + 1$ *Substitute the x-coordinate into the quadratic function.*

$\quad = 4$

The vertex is $(1, 4)$.

You can also make use of the **x-intercepts** when you graph a parabola. The y-coordinate of an x-intercept is 0, so substitute 0 for y.

4   **Find the x-intercept of $y = x^2 - x - 30$.**

SOLUTION

$y = x^2 - x - 30$

$0 = x^2 - x - 30$

$\quad = (x - 6)(x + 5)$

$x = 6$ or $x = -5$

So the x-intercepts are 6 and -5.

Notice that the x-intercepts are the roots of the quadratic equation $0 = x^2 - x - 30$. A quadratic equation like $0 = x^2 - x - 30$ can be solved by graphing the corresponding quadratic function $y = x^2 - x - 30$.

5   **Tell how many x-intercepts there are for the graph of $y = x^2 + x + 1$.**

SOLUTION

$b^2 - 4ac = 1 - 4 = -3$ *Find the discriminant of $x^2 + x + 1 = 0$.*

The discriminant is negative, so there are no real-number solutions (roots) of the quadratic equation. So there are no x-intercepts for the parabola.

Recall that the value of the discriminant can be positive, negative, or zero.

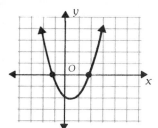

The discriminant is positive.
There are two x-intercepts.

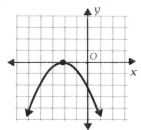

The discriminant is 0.
There is one x-intercept.

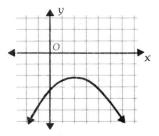

The discriminant is negative.
There is no x-intercept.

ASSIGNMENT GUIDE

Minimum
1–7 odd, 13–29 odd, 30

Regular
17–30

Maximum
11–27 odd, 31–39 odd

ADDITIONAL ANSWERS

Oral Exercises

8. downward

9. upward

Written Exercises

For the odd-numbered solutions, see *Answers to Selected Exercises*, p. 593.

2.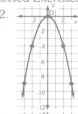

4.

6.

8.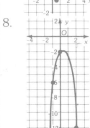

(continued on next page)

ORAL EXERCISES

1. The graph of a quadratic function is called a ___parabola___.
2. The minimum point or maximum point of a parabola is called the ___turning___ point or the ___vertex___.
3. The vertical line passing through the vertex of a parabola is called the ___axis of symmetry___.

Will each of these parabolas open upward or downward?

4. $y = \frac{1}{2}x^2$ upward

5. $y = -2x^2$ downward

6. $y = 7x^2 - 3x$ upward

7. $y = -3x^2 - 4x$ downward

8. $y = -\frac{1}{2}x^2 - 2x + 7$

9. $y = 5x^2 - 2x + 8$

WRITTEN EXERCISES

A. Graph each quadratic function.

1. $y = x^2$

2. $y = -x^2$

3. $y = x^2 + 4$

4. $y = x^2 - 4$

5. $y = -x^2 + x$

6. $y = x^2 - x$

7. $y = 2x^2 + x + 4$

8. $y = -3x^2 + x - 2$

B. Find the equation of the axis of symmetry for each parabola.

9. $y = -2x^2 + 5x - 3$

10. $y = \frac{1}{2}x^2 + 3x - 1$

11. $y = x^2 - 3x + 4$

12. $y = -x^2 + 6x + 3$

13. $y = -3x^2 + 2x - 8$

14. $y = 2x^2 - 3x + 4$

Find the vertex of each parabola, and tell if the parabola opens upward or downward.

15. $y = x^2 + 4$

16. $y = -2x^2 + 5x - 1$

17. $y = x^2 + 8x$

18. $y = -x^2 + 2x$

19. $y = -x^2 + 4x + 1$

20. $y = 3x^2 - 2x + 1$

Use the discriminant to determine how many x-intercepts each quadratic function would have if graphed.

21. $y = x^2 + 4x + 4$

22. $y = x^2 - 3x + 2$

23. $y = x^2 + x + 1$

24. $y = 2x^2 - 3x + 4$

25. $y = 2x^2 + x - 8$

26. $y = -x^2 + 3x + 1$

Find the x-intercepts, if any.

27. $y = x^2 - 5x + 6$

28. $y = 2x^2 + 9x - 5$

29. $y = x^2 + 2x - 15$

30. $y = -3x^2 + 6x$

C. Graph each quadratic function after finding the following: (a) the axis of symmetry; (b) the vertex; (c) the x-intercepts, if any; (d) the y-intercept. (HINT: What is the value of x for the y-intercept?) You may have to approximate a radical to the nearest tenth in order to graph the parabola.

31. $y = x^2 - 8x + 3$

32. $y = 2x^2 + 16x + 4$

33. $y = -x^2 + 6x - 9$

34. $y = -3x^2 - x - 4$

35. $y = x^2 + 2x + 3$

36. $y = -x^2 + x - 2$

Graph each quadratic function and determine the roots of the corresponding quadratic equation.

37. $y = x^2 + 4x + 4$ -2

38. $y = x^2 + 2x + 1$ -1

39. $y = x^2 + 2x - 3$ $-3, 1$

40. $y = x^2 + 4x + 3$ $-3, -1$

CHALLENGE

Summer heat caused a 2-kilometer-long bridge to expand 1 meter and bulge upward. If the highest point of the bridge was in the middle of the bridge, how high above its normal position was it? Express your answer to the nearest tenth of a meter.

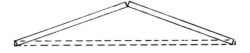

Problem Solving With Quadratic Functions

You can use quadratic functions to solve certain problems.

OBJECTIVES

Find the real-number roots, if any, for a quadratic equation by graphing.

Solve maximum-minimum problems by graphing quadratic functions.

EXAMPLES

1 A rock is thrown straight up from the ground at a velocity of 80 feet per second. The formula $h = -16t^2 + 80t$ gives the rock's height (in feet) after t seconds. After how many seconds will the rock be 96 feet above the ground?

Understand: *Given:* A rock is thrown straight up from the ground at a velocity of 80 feet per second. The formula $h = -16t^2 + 80t$ gives the rock's height after t seconds.

To find: the number of seconds after which the rock will be 96 feet above the ground

Plan: Substitute 96 for h in the formula and solve for t.

Solve:
$$h = -16t^2 + 80t$$
$$96 = -16t^2 + 80t$$
$$0 = -16t^2 + 80t - 96$$
$$0 = -16(t^2 - 5t + 6)$$
$$0 = t^2 - 5t + 6$$
$$0 = (t - 2)(t - 3)$$
$$t = 2 \text{ or } t = 3$$

Answer: Both "2 seconds" and "3 seconds" can be accepted as answers. From the graph, notice that at 2 seconds, the rock has reached a height of 96 feet. At 3 seconds, the rock is falling back to the ground and is again at a height of 96 feet.

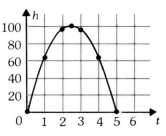

Review: Using the formula, check each solution for t.

2 Nicole wants to build a rectangular pen for her dog. She can use the back of her house for one side of the pen. If she has 120 feet of fencing, what dimensions for the pen will give the maximum area? What is the maximum area?

Understand: *Given:* 120 feet of fencing for a rectangular pen, one side of which does not need fencing

To find: the dimensions of the pen with the maximum area and the maximum area

TEACHER'S NOTES

See p. T37.

CLASSROOM EXAMPLES

1. A rocket is launched straight up from the ground at a velocity of 144 feet per second. The formula $h = -16t^2 + 144t$ gives the rocket's height (in feet) after t seconds. After how many seconds will the rocket be 320 feet above the ground?

   Substitute 320 for h in the formula and solve for t.
   $$h = -16t^2 + 144t$$
   $$320 = -16t^2 + 144t$$
   $$0 = -16t^2 + 144t - 320$$
   $$0 = -16(t^2 - 9t + 20)$$
   $$0 = t^2 - 9t + 20$$
   $$0 = (t - 4)(t - 5)$$
   $$t = 4 \text{ or } t = 5$$
   Both "4 seconds" and "5 seconds" can be accepted as answers.

2. Ellen wants to fence a rectangular area for a garden. She can use the side of her garage for one side of the garden. If she has 200 feet of fencing, what dimensions for the garden will give the maximum area? What is the maximum area?

(continued on next page)

garage

$A = x(200 - 2x)$

$A = 200x - 2x^2$

$x = \frac{-b}{2a} = \frac{-200}{2(-2)} = 50$

x	A
20	3200
30	4200
40	4800
50	5000
60	4800
70	4200
80	3200

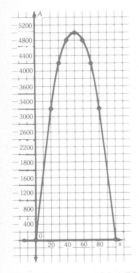

The width should be 50 feet and the length should be 100 feet. The maximum area is 5000 square feet, as shown on the graph.

MIXED REVIEW

1. Solve $y^2 = 49$.   7, −7

Plan: Draw a picture. Write a quadratic function representing the area A. Then graph the function and determine the point where the area is a maximum.

Solve: $A = x(120 - 2x)$

$A = 120x - 2x^2$

$x = \frac{-b}{2a} = \frac{-120}{2(-2)} = 30$

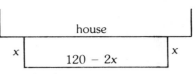

x	A
0	0
10	1000
20	1600
30	1800
40	1600
50	1000
60	0

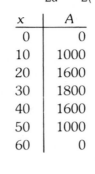

Answer: The width should be 30 feet and the length should be 60 feet. The maximum area is 1800 square feet, as shown on the graph.

Review: Some other possible dimensions and areas of the pen are given.

Width	Length	Area
45	30	1350
40	40	1600
35	50	1750
30	60	1800
25	70	1750
20	80	1600
15	90	1350

Does it seem reasonable that 1800 square feet is the maximum possible area?

ORAL EXERCISES

1. In Example 2, why is the length represented by $120 - 2x$?

2. In Example 2, how were the answers "length = 60 feet" and "area = 1800 square feet" arrived at?   by graphing

3. In Example 1, what does h represent? What does t represent?   height; time

4. In Example 1, what is the number of seconds needed for the rock to reach its greatest height above the ground? $2\frac{1}{2}$ seconds

WRITTEN EXERCISES

A. Solve.

If a ball is thrown upward vertically at a starting speed of 64 feet per second, the height h (in feet) that it will reach at the end of t seconds is given by the quadratic function $h = -16t^2 + 64t$ graphed below. Use the graph for exercises 1–4.

t	h
0	0
1	48
2	64
3	48
4	0

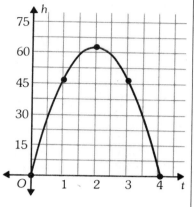

1. What is the maximum height h reached by the ball?
2. After how many seconds is the maximum height reached? 2 sec
3. What is the height h after 1 second? After 3 seconds? 48 ft; 48 ft
4. At what times is the ball at the starting height? 0 sec and 4 sec

B. A ball is thrown straight up from the ground at a velocity of 96 feet per second. Use $h = -16t^2 + 96t$ for exercises 5–8.

5. How high will the ball be after 2 seconds? 128 ft

6. How many seconds will it take the ball to reach its maximum height? 3 seconds

7. What is the maximum height? 144 ft

8. How many seconds will it take the ball to return to the ground? 6 seconds

9. A business finds that if it sells x items, its revenue (amount brought in from sales) in dollars is given by $R(x) = 200x - x^2 - 300$. How many items should be sold for the business to achieve its maximum revenue? What is the maximum revenue?

10. A rectangular yard at a lake cottage is to be fenced in on three sides, with the lake as the fourth side. What are the dimensions of the fenced-in region with the maximum area if 400 feet of fencing are available? 100 ft by 200 ft

C.
11. The power W (in watts) that can be produced in a circuit through which a current I (in amperes) is flowing is given by $W = -RI^2 + EI$. R represents the resistance of the circuit (in ohms) and E represents the voltage (in volts). Find the maximum power that can be produced with a voltage of 110 volts in a circuit that has a resistance of 5 ohms.

12. Jason has 1200 meters of fencing. He wants to build a rectangular pen, then divide the pen into two smaller pens by placing a fence in the middle, parallel to the two shorter sides. With what dimensions should he build the pen to enclose the maximum area?

Each problem consists of two quantities, one in Column I and one in Column II.

Compare the two quantities and answer
A if the quantity in Column I is greater,
B if the quantity in Column II is greater,
C if the two quantities are equal,
D if the relationship cannot be determined from the information given.

	COLUMN I	COLUMN II	
		It takes x persons a days to do a job. It takes y persons $a + 3$ days to do the same job.	
1.	x	y	A
2.	$\sqrt{16.9}$	1.3	A
		$x = y$	
3.	$x(x - y)$	1	B
		$y = 2x - 15$ $x + y = 0$	
4.	x	$3y$	A
		$a > b$	
5.	a^2	b^2	D
		$x^2 = 16$ and $y = 4$	
6.	x	y	D
7.	$\sqrt{0.25}$	$\dfrac{1}{3}$	A

$$x^2 = xy$$

8.	x	y	C
9.	$\sqrt{0.04}$	$(0.2)^2$	A
10.	$(\sqrt{18})(2\sqrt{8})$	$3 \cdot 2^3$	C
11.	The distance between point $J(-1, 2)$ and point $K(3, 5)$	5	C
12.	Cecelia's rate if she walks 8 miles in 2 hr	Nora's rate if she walks 5 miles in $1\frac{1}{2}$ hr	A

$$0 < x < y$$

13.	$\dfrac{1}{y}$	$\dfrac{1}{x}$	D

$$x^2 = 4 \text{ and}$$
$$y^2 = 9$$

14.	x	y	D
15.	Matt is 5 times as old as Nick. Pat is $\frac{1}{6}$ of Matt's age.		
	Nick's age	Pat's age	A
16.	$\sqrt{\dfrac{1}{9}} + \sqrt{\dfrac{1}{16}}$	$\sqrt{\dfrac{1}{9} + \dfrac{1}{16}}$	A

$$x^2 = xy$$

17.	x	$-y$	D

$$a = 2$$
$$b = 3$$
$$c = 0$$

18.	$4a + 2b - 6abc$	12	A
19.	$\sqrt{0.36}$	$(0.2)^3$	A
20.	The time for an auto to cover 1 mile traveling 50 miles per hour	72 seconds	C

SKILLS MAINTENANCE

Let $a = -3$, $b = 5$, $c = -2$, $d = 4$, and $e = 6$. Evaluate each polynomial.

1. $a^2 - 4a + 12$ 33   **2.** $b^2 + 7b - 13$ 47   **3.** $4d^2e + 2de^2$ 672

4. $ab + bd - de$ -19 **5.** $\frac{1}{2}ab + dec$ $-55\frac{1}{2}$ **6.** $\frac{1}{2}a^2 + c^2 - \frac{1}{4}e^2$ $-\frac{1}{2}$

Simplify.

7. $-18 + 23 + 148$ 153   **8.** $[58 - (-15)] - 42$ 31   **9.** $-13(-15)$ 195

10. $-5(0)(9)(-73)$ 0   **11.** $-1472 \div (-64)$ 23   **12.** $2394 \div (-42)$ -57

Solve each equation. The replacement set is the set of integers.

13. $x + 3x = 20$ 5   **14.** $9x - 5x = 40$ 10   **15.** $-x + 13x = -60$

16. $8x = -136$ -17 **17.** $1.2x = 24$ 20   **18.** $\frac{3}{4}x = -6$ -8

Solve.

19. $5(-3x + 4) = -10x + 5$ 3   **20.** $4(-2x + 3) = -5x + 3$ 3

21. $3x = 9x - (3x - 18)$ -6 **22.** $7 - (5x + 5) = -x$ $\frac{1}{2}$

Solve each inequality.

23. $x + (-256) < 182$ $x < 438$ **24.** $-1.94 + x > -1.07$ $x > 0.87$

25. $-25.7 + x > -14.8$ $x > 10.9$ **26.** $x - 48 < 25.6$ $x < 73.6$

Factor completely.

27. $x^2 + 4x + 3$ $(x + 3)(x + 1)$ **28.** $x^2 + 7x + 6$ $(x + 6)(x + 1)$

29. $x^2 - 11x + 18$ $(x - 9)(x - 2)$ **30.** $x^2 - x - 6$ $(x - 3)(x + 2)$

31. $x^2 - 9x + 14$ $(x - 7)(x - 2)$ **32.** $x^2 - 14x - 15$ $(x - 15)(x + 1)$

Find each product and express it in simplest form.

33. $\frac{2x}{x} \cdot \frac{x^2}{4x}$ $\frac{x}{2}$ **34.** $\frac{x + 2}{3} \cdot \frac{2}{x + 2}$ $\frac{2}{3}$ **35.** $\frac{x - 5}{5} \cdot \frac{x}{x - 5}$ $\frac{x}{5}$

36. $\frac{6x^3y}{5x^2} \cdot \frac{10y}{3x^2}$ $\frac{4y^2}{x}$ **37.** $\frac{16x^2y^3}{6x} \cdot \frac{9xy^2}{4y^3}$ $6x^2y^2$ **38.** $\frac{12x^4y}{8x^2} \cdot \frac{5y^2}{3xy}$ $\frac{5xy^2}{2}$

Add or subtract and express each answer in simplest form.

39. $\frac{x}{y} + \frac{2y}{3x}$ $\frac{3x^2 + 2y^2}{3xy}$ **40.** $\frac{m + 2}{3} + \frac{m - 1}{6}$ $\frac{m + 1}{2}$ **41.** $\frac{x - 3}{6} - \frac{x - 1}{10}$ $\frac{x - 6}{15}$

42. $\frac{5}{t - 1} - \frac{5}{t^2 - t}$ $\frac{5}{t}$ **43.** $\frac{3}{m^2 + m} + \frac{3}{m + 1}$ $\frac{3}{m}$ **44.** $\frac{y + 1}{y - 5} + \frac{y}{2y - 10}$

Solve each proportion.

45. $\frac{4}{5} = \frac{x}{30}$ 24   **46.** $\frac{3}{2} = \frac{5}{x}$ $\frac{10}{3}$ **47.** $\frac{1}{11} = \frac{-3}{b}$ -33 **48.** $\frac{12}{3x} = \frac{10}{3}$ $\frac{6}{5}$

49. $\frac{4}{x + 1} = \frac{2}{1}$ 1   **50.** $\frac{x + 2}{3} = \frac{2x}{4}$ 4   **51.** $\frac{x + 3}{5} = \frac{2x}{7}$ 7   **52.** $\frac{8}{3x} = \frac{16}{3}$ $\frac{1}{2}$

SKILLS MAINTENANCE

15. -5

44. $\frac{3y + 2}{2(y - 5)}$

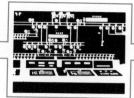

COMPUTER

TEACHER'S RESOURCE MASTERS

Computer Master 12

Do you know the square root of 136,161, which is a perfect square? Without having a computer or a calculator, how would you go about finding the square root? One method of finding a square root involves estimating and trial and error. For example, if you do not know the square root of 625 but do know that the square of 20 is 400 and the square of 30 is 900, then the square root of 625 must be somewhere in between. Some trial-and-error computations will lead you to 25. With a number like 136,161, however, such a method is laborious, if not impractical.

Do not enter the following program, but study it.

```
10 PRINT: INPUT "ENTER ANY NUMBER: ";N
20 X = 1: T = 0: S = N
30 IF N = 0 THEN 100
40 IF N < 0 THEN 110
50 PRINT "STEP ";T + 1;"     ";N;" - ";X;" = ";:
   N = N - X: PRINT N
60 X = X + 2: T = T + 1
70 GOTO 30
100 PRINT "THE SQUARE ROOT OF ";S;" IS ";T;".":
    GOTO 10
110 PRINT S;" IS NOT A WHOLE NUMBER PERFECT": PRINT
    "SQUARE.": GOTO 10
```

EXERCISES

1. Regardless of what the perfect square is, what is the relationship between the square root and the number of steps it takes the computer to find the square root?

2. Enter the program and RUN it. What do the PRINT output statements on line 50 do?

3. As it is, the program with large numbers seems very slow. What can you do to the program to speed it up?

ANSWERS

1. If N is a perfect square, the computer will run in N complete steps.

2. The PRINT statements subtract such numbers from N so that after the Tth step, T^2 has been subtracted from the original number N.

3. A possible program variant: Change the following lines:

    30 IF N < = 0 THEN 50

    40 N = N − X : X = X + 2 : T = T + 1 : GOTO 30

    50 IF N = 0 THEN PRINT "THE SQUARE ROOT OF ;S; "IS";T;".": GOTO 10

    60 PRINT S;" IS NOT A WHOLE NUMBER PERFECT": PRINT "SQUARE.": GOTO 10

and delete lines 70–110.

ENRICHMENT

See Activities 33–34,
p. T50.

ADDITIONAL ANSWERS

20. $-3 \pm 2\sqrt{6}$

22. $\frac{3 \pm \sqrt{13}}{2}$

29. $\frac{2 \pm \sqrt{10}}{6}$

30. $\frac{-8 \pm \sqrt{74}}{5}$

33. 0; real, equal, rational

34. 361; real; unequal; rational

CHAPTER 12 REVIEW

VOCABULARY

axis of symmetry (12.7)

completing the square (12.3)

discriminant (12.5)

double root (12.1)

maximum point (12.7)

minimum point (12.7)

parabola (12.7)

quadratic equation (12.1)

quadratic formula (12.4)

quadratic function (12.7)

root (12.1)

square-root property (12.2)

standard form of a quadratic
equation (12.1)

turning point (12.7)

vertex (12.7)

x-intercept (12.7)

REVIEW EXERCISES

12.1 **Solve by factoring.**

1. $x^2 - 11x + 24 = 0$ 8, 3

2. $2x^2 - 15x - 27 = 0$ $-\frac{3}{2}$, 9

3. $3x^2 + 23x + 40 = 0$ $-\frac{8}{3}$, -5

4. $10x^2 + 33x = 7$ $\frac{1}{5}$, $-\frac{7}{2}$

5. $8x^2 + 34x = 9$ $\frac{1}{4}$, $-\frac{9}{2}$

6. $14x^2 = x + 4$ $\frac{4}{7}$, $-\frac{1}{2}$

7. $x^2 + 2x - 15 = 0$ 3, -5

8. $16x^2 - 24x + 9 = 0$ $\frac{3}{4}$

12.2 **Solve by using the square-root property.**

9. $x^2 = 144$ ± 12

10. $(m - 1)^2 = 16$ 5, -3

11. $(y + 3)^2 = 8$ $-3 \pm 2\sqrt{2}$

12. $(3x - 1)^2 = 25$ 2, $-\frac{4}{3}$

13. $(2n + 5)^2 = 16$ $-\frac{1}{2}$, $-\frac{9}{2}$

14. $(5v + 1)^2 = 18$ $\frac{-1 + 3\sqrt{2}}{5}$

15. $12 = y^2 - 16y + 64$ $8 \pm 2\sqrt{3}$

16. $8 = x^2 - 18x + 81$ $9 \pm 2\sqrt{2}$

12.3 **Solve by completing the square.**

17. $x^2 - 10x + 9 = 0$ 9, 1

18. $x^2 + 7x - 1 = 0$ $\frac{-7 \pm \sqrt{53}}{2}$

19. $y^2 - 3y - 4 = 0$ 4, -1

20. $2m^2 + 12m - 30 = 0$

21. $3v^2 - 7v - 6 = 0$ 3, $-\frac{2}{3}$

22. $-5t^2 + 15t + 5 = 0$

23. $3x^2 - 8 = 2x$ 2, $-\frac{4}{3}$

24. $4s^2 + 12s = 27$ $\frac{3}{2}$, $-\frac{9}{2}$

12.4 **Solve by using the quadratic formula.**

25. $x^2 - 5x + 6 = 0$ 3, 2

26. $y^2 - 4y + 1 = 0$ $2 \pm \sqrt{3}$

27. $2m^2 + 4m + 1 = 0$ $\frac{-2 \pm \sqrt{2}}{2}$

28. $3t^2 + 6t - 1 = 0$ $\frac{-3 \pm 2\sqrt{3}}{3}$

29. $6v^2 = 4v + 1$

30. $5n^2 + 16n = 2$

31. $2r^2 = 5r + 7$ $\frac{7}{2}$, -1

32. $2s^2 = s + 10$ $\frac{5}{2}$, -2

12.5 **Find the value of the discriminant. Then describe the roots of the quadratic equation (real roots or no real roots, equal or unequal roots, rational or irrational roots).**

33. $4m^2 - 20m + 25 = 0$

34. $14t^2 + 5t - 6 = 0$

35. $16x^2 - 16x + 1 = 0$

36. $2y^2 + y + 8 = 0$

37. $5x^2 + 6x = 11$

38. $25r^2 + 20r + 4 = 0$

12.6 Solve.

39. The sum of two numbers is 29. Their product is 210. What are the numbers?

40. The length of a rectangle is 5 inches more than three times the width. Find the length and the width if the rectangle has an area of 182 square inches.

41. A rectangle is 5 centimeters longer than it is wide. Its area is 66 square centimeters. Find its length and its width.   11 cm; 6 cm

42. The width of a rectangle is 7 meters less than its length. Its area is 44 m². Find its length and its width.   11 m; 4 m

12.7 Graph each quadratic function.

43. $y = 2x^2 + 3x + 1$

44. $y = -x^2 + 5x + 2$

45. $y = x^2 - 4x + 3$

46. $y = 2x^2 - 3x + 1$

Find the equation of the axis of symmetry.

47. $y = x^2 + 6x - 5$

48. $y = -x^2 + 3x + 1$

49. $y = x^2 - 2x + 3$

50. $y = x^2 - 2x + 2$

Find the coordinates of the vertex.

51. $y = 2x^2 + 6x + 1$

52. $y = -3x^2 + 5x + 4$

Find the x-intercepts, if any.

53. $y = x^2 + 2x - 15$

54. $y = -2x^2 - 3x + 5$

55. $y = x^2 - 5x + 6$

56. $y = x^2 - 4x + 3$

12.8

57. A rectangular pen is to be built with 100 meters of fencing. What dimensions for the pen will give the maximum area? What is the maximum area?   25 m by 25 m; 625 m²

58. If a dolphin jumps straight out of the water at a starting speed of 32 feet per second, the height h (in feet above the water) that it will reach in t seconds is given by $h = -16t^2 + 32t$. Find the maximum height h and the number of seconds it takes the dolphin to return to the water.   16 ft; 2 sec

35. 192; real, unequal, irrational

36. −63; no real roots

37. 256; real, unequal, rational

38. 0; real, equal, rational

39. 14 and 15

40. 7 in. by 26 in.

For the solutions to exercises 43 and 45, see *Answers to Selected Exercises*, p. 594.

44.
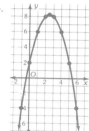

46.

47. $x = -3$

48. $x = \frac{3}{2}$

49. $x = 1$

50. $x = 1$

51. $\left(-\frac{3}{2}, -\frac{7}{2}\right)$

52. $\left(\frac{5}{6}, \frac{73}{12}\right)$

53. −5, 3

54. $-\frac{5}{2}$, 1

55. 3, 2

56. 3, 1

TEACHER'S RESOURCE
MASTERS

Chapter 12 Test

Multiple-Choice Test

PROBLEM–SOLVING
HANDBOOK
p. 538

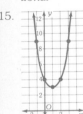
CHAPTER 12 TEST

Solve by factoring.

1. $2x^2 + 7x = 15$ $\quad \frac{3}{2}, -5$ **2.** $6x^2 - 12x = 0$ $\quad 0, 2$ **3.** $2n^2 + n = 3$ $\quad 1, -\frac{3}{2}$

Solve by using the square-root property.

4. $(x - 5)^2 = 25$ $\quad 10, 0$ **5.** $(2m - 1)^2 = 49$ $\quad 4, -3$ **6.** $(x + 1)^2 = 81$

Solve by completing the square.

7. $y^2 - 12y + 35 = 0$ $\quad 5, 7$ **8.** $x^2 + 6x + 8 = 0$ $\quad -4, -2$ **9.** $x^2 - 2x - 8 = 0$

Solve by using the quadratic formula.

10. $2v^2 - 4v - 3 = 0$ **11.** $6a^2 + 13a + 6 = 0$ **12.** $x^2 + 3x + 1 = 0$

Find the value of the discriminant. Then describe the roots of the quadratic equation (real roots or no real roots, equal or unequal roots, rational or irrational roots).

13. $4x^2 - 28x + 49 = 0$ **14.** $3m^2 - 9m + 5 = 0$

15. Graph $y = x^2 - 2x + 4$.

16. Find the equation of the axis of symmetry of $y = -x^2 + 7x + 1$.

17. Find the coordinates of the vertex of $y = 2x^2 - 7x + 2$.

18. Find the x-intercepts of $y = x^2 - 11x + 18$.

Solve.

19. The sum of two numbers is 13 and their product is 40. Find the numbers. 5, 8

20. The product of two consecutive even integers is 48. Find the integers.

21. The area of a rectangle is 45 square centimeters. The length is 1 centimeter less than twice the width. Find the dimensions of the rectangle. 5 cm by 9 cm

22. One leg of a right triangle is 3 units longer than the other leg. The hypotenuse is 15 units long. How long is each leg? one leg 9 units, other 12 units

23. Ralph can complete a repair job in 2 hours more than one third of the time it would take Dan to complete the repair job. Working together, they can complete the repair job in 4 hours. How long would it take Dan, working alone, to complete the repair job?

24. A rock is thrown straight up from the ground at a velocity of 160 feet per second. Use $h = -16t^2 + 160t$ to find the maximum height the rock will reach and the number of seconds until it reaches this height. 400 ft; 5 sec

CHAPTER 13

Statistics

Make a stem-and-leaf display for these
times (in seconds) for running 400 meters.
62 68 78 84 82 66 87 72
77 68 82 64 82

6   2, 4, 6, 8, 8
7   2, 7, 8
8   2, 2, 2, 4, 7

431

1. Make a stem-and-leaf display for the following data: 46   23   51   36   50   27   34   29   56

   2 | 3, 7, 9
   3 | 4, 6
   4 | 6
   5 | 0, 1, 6

2. Make a stem-and-leaf display for the following data, using two-digit stems: 253   246   241   260   259   250   240

   24 | 0, 1, 6
   25 | 0, 3, 9
   26 | 0

3. Make a two-sided stem-and-leaf display for the two sets of scores. Then answer the following questions:

   a. What is the greatest score for Class 1? for Class 2?

   b. Which class has more of the greater scores?

   c. How many scores from both classes were from 70 through 79?

   Class 1:   63   58   75   69   73   70   80   95   92

   Class 2:   58   63   73   70   67   93   90   85   97

13.1 | Stem-and-Leaf Displays

Statistics involves collecting, organizing, studying, and interpreting numbers and facts. These numbers and facts are called **data.**

Raw data usually mean very little at just a glance. After the data are collected, they are organized so that they might be studied more easily. A **stem-and-leaf display** is one way to organize raw data.

Look through the raw data to find the smallest number and the largest number. You can decide from these numbers what the *stems* should be. After you determine the stems, you can organize the *leaves.*

EXAMPLES

1   **Make a stem-and-leaf display for the following data:**

28 56 87 32 47 29 59 68 79 75 42 38 29 74 86 72 75 38 64 53 94 26 67 59 23

SOLUTION

The smallest number is 23. The largest number is 94. The stems can be the tens digits. List the stems in a column, from smallest to largest. After each stem, list the ones digits. These are the leaves. Separate the stems from the leaves by using a vertical line.

2 | 8, 9, 9, 6, 3   *2|8 represents the number 28.*
3 | 2, 8, 8
4 | 7, 2
5 | 6, 9, 3, 9
6 | 8, 4, 7
7 | 9, 5, 4, 2, 5
8 | 7, 6
9 | 4

Then arrange the leaves for each stem in increasing order.

2 | 3, 6, 8, 9, 9
3 | 2, 8, 8
4 | 2, 7
5 | 3, 6, 9, 9
6 | 4, 7, 8
7 | 2, 4, 5, 5, 9
8 | 6, 7
9 | 4

The stems or the leaves can have more than one digit.

2 **Make a stem-and-leaf display for the following data, using two-digit stems for this problem:**

256 259 247 249 238 231 263 257 277 274 236 291 298 250 239
246 275 272 251 240

SOLUTION

The smallest number is 231. The largest number is 298. The stems are to be two-digit stems. First list the numbers from 23 through 29. Then arrange the leaves for each stem.

23	1, 6, 8, 9
24	0, 6, 7, 9
25	0, 1, 6, 7, 9
26	3
27	2, 4, 5, 7
28	*The stem 28 has no leaves.*
29	1, 8

You can use a **two-sided stem-and-leaf display** to compare two sets of data.

3 **The same test was given to two algebra classes. Make a two-sided stem-and-leaf display for the two sets of scores. Then answer the following questions:**

a. What is the greatest score for Class 1? For Class 2?
b. Which class has more of the greater scores?
c. How many scores from both classes were from 80 through 89?

Class 1: 56 92 76 83 64 79 75 84 55 72 96 68 74 99 69 73 78 80 72 75

Class 2: 63 79 93 94 80 82 92 72 91 69 75 78 90 93 68 75 83 90 82 89 93

SOLUTIONS

Class 1		Class 2
6, 5	5	
9, 8, 4	6	3, 8, 9
9, 8, 6, 5, 5, 4, 3, 2, 2	7	2, 5, 5, 8, 9
4, 3, 0	8	0, 2, 2, 3, 9
9, 6, 2	9	0, 0, 1, 2, 3, 3, 3, 4

Notice that the scores for Class 1 are read from right to left.

a. The greatest score for Class 1 is 99. The greatest score for Class 2 is 94.
b. Class 2 has more of the greater scores.
c. Eight scores from both classes were from 80 through 89.

	Class 1		Class 2
	8	5	8
	9, 3	6	3, 7
	5, 3, 0	7	0, 3
	0	8	5
	5, 2	9	0, 3, 7

a. The greatest score for Class 1 is 95. The greatest score for Class 2 is 97.

b. Class 2 has more of the greater scores.

c. Five scores from both classes were from 70 through 79.

MIXED REVIEW

1. Rewrite $y = -5x + 8$ in standard form. $5x + y = 8$

2. State the domain and the range of {(8, 3), (5, 7), (6, 9)}. domain = {8, 5, 6} range = {3, 7, 9}

3. Find the y-intercept of the line for $y = -7x + 9$. 9

4. Write as an algebraic expression: The sum of two fifths of a number and three times the number. $\frac{2}{5}x + 3x$

5. Restate 0.147 in fractional form. $\frac{49}{333}$

TEACHER'S RESOURCE MASTERS

Practice Master 54, Part 1

ASSIGNMENT GUIDE

Minimum
1–4, 10–13

Regular
8–14

Maximum
10–15

ADDITIONAL ANSWERS

Oral Exercises

7. 46, 52, 73, 89

8. 86, 87, 92, 95, 97

Written Exercises

1. 2 | 5, 5, 7, 8
   3 | 2, 6, 9
   4 | 1, 4
   5 | 2, 9
   6 |
   7 | 1, 3, 4

2. 5 | 7, 9
   6 | 1, 2, 3, 9, 9
   7 | 3, 5
   8 | 4, 9, 9, 9
   9 | 2, 7, 9

3. 3 | 2, 8
   4 | 3, 5, 7
   5 | 2, 6, 8, 9
   6 | 3, 3, 7, 8
   7 | 4, 8
   8 | 2, 5, 7, 9, 9
   9 | 0, 0, 3, 8

4. 1 | 5, 7, 8
   2 | 3, 7
   3 | 2
   4 | 6, 7, 9
   5 | 1, 2, 7, 9
   6 | 3, 5, 7
   7 | 4
   8 | 2
   9 | 1, 1, 5, 7, 7, 8, 9

ORAL EXERCISES

Complete.

1. ___Statistics___ involves collecting, organizing, studying, and interpreting numbers and facts.

2. The numbers and facts are called ___data___.

3. One way to organize raw data is with a ___stem-and-leaf display___.

4. A ___two-sided stem-and-leaf display___ can be used to compare two sets of data.

Use the stem-and-leaf display below to answer exercises 5–10.

1 | 46, 52, 73, 89
2 | 29, 34
3 | 86, 87, 92, 95, 97
4 | 03, 91
5 | 07

5. Name the stems. 1, 2, 3, 4, 5

6. Name the leaves for stem 4. 03, 91

7. Name the leaves for stem 1.

8. Name the leaves for stem 3.

9. Name the smallest number. 146

10. Name the largest number. 507

WRITTEN EXERCISES

A. Make a stem-and-leaf display for each.

1. 25 25 27 28 32 36 39 41 44 52 59 71 73 74

2. 57 59 61 62 63 69 69 73 75 84 89 89 89 92 97 99

3. 32 38 43 45 47 52 56 58 59 63 63 67 68 74 78 82 85 87 89 89 90 90 93 98

4. 15 17 18 23 27 32 46 47 49 51 52 57 59 63 65 67 74 82 91 91 95 97 97 98 99

B. 5. 16 92 27 82 87 93 54 48 57 73 84 17 59 64 52 75 79 83 85 96 24 43 47 25 80 68

6. 29 38 74 29 52 86 34 76 92 47 53 86 93 37 48 76 72 89 82 39 32 26 87 89 94 99 74 58 37

Use two-digit stems in exercises 7–8.

7. 146 179 172 163 158 159 143 147 152 167 176 152 173 158 169 175 177 162 153 140 161 173 178 150

8. 2001 2397 2456 2152 2134 2252 2307 2051 2193 2471 2252 2241 2307 2496 2068 2175 2192

Make a two-sided stem-and-leaf display for each.

9. *Group 1:* 15 26 19 37 42 21 25 19 23 32 31 27 45 46 18
   Group 2: 26 18 13 47 51 37 43 19 29 23 36 32 37 47 56 11 15 27

10. *Group 1:* 62 79 58 92 75 64 59 83 69 72 75 73 68 91 94 87 82 81
   74 85 93 52 65
   Group 2: 93 58 92 64 93 76 85 92 78 52 99 73 98 61

Use the two-sided stem-and-leaf display for exercises 11–14.

Group 1		Group 2
7, 2	4	3, 7
7, 5, 2, 1	5	2, 6, 9
7, 5, 0	6	3, 6, 9
9, 9, 8	7	2, 3, 5, 9, 9

11. How many scores are there for Group 1? 12

12. How many scores are there for Group 2? 13

13. What is the lowest score for Group 1? 42

14. What is the highest score for Group 2? 79

C. When the number of data becomes very large, you can spread out the data by using a dot in the stem column to continue the leaves for that stem on the next line.

1	0, 0, 1, 3, 3, 3,
·	4, 4, 4, 7, 8, 9
2	1, 1, 1, 3, 4,
·	5, 5, 6, 8, 9
3	2, 2, 2, 2, 2,
·	3, 5, 7, 7, 7, 8, 9

Make a stem-and-leaf display for each set of data. Spread the data out so that the leaves for each stem are divided into two roughly equal lines.

15. 27 19 24 56 18 23 42 67 89 26 13 47 52 51 19 26 73 75 82 91 35 42
   48 93 87 73 56 52 14 23 26 38 31 30 40 26 93 12 40 47 52 64 73 76
   81 90 70 56 57 44 49 69 62 67 83 88 98 15 24 27 32 38 47 53 54 67
   76 81 90 34 87 88

16. 22 27 28 46 92 37 48 64 69 74 72 51 71 88 92 47 53 26 51 57 62 64
   75 77 89 88 98 94 47 50 27 28 29 64 53 42 41 39 76 71 70 37 30 42
   47 56 63 80 85 92 97 89 80 46 42 47 52 47 86 67 92 72 77 89 90 14
   13 11 12 14 21 17 93 87 12 75 72

5.
1	6, 7
2	4, 5, 7
3	
4	3, 7, 8
5	2, 4, 7, 9
6	4, 8
7	3, 5, 9
8	0, 2, 3, 4, 5, 7
9	2, 3, 6

6.
2	6, 9, 9
3	2, 4, 7, 7, 8, 9
4	7, 8
5	2, 3, 8
6	
7	2, 4, 4, 6, 6
8	2, 6, 6, 7, 9, 9
9	2, 3, 4, 9

7.
14	0, 3, 6, 7
15	0, 2, 2, 3, 8, 8, 9
16	1, 2, 3, 7, 9
17	2, 3, 3, 5, 6, 7, 8, 9

8.
20	01, 51, 68
21	34, 52, 75, 92, 93
22	41, 52, 52
23	07, 07, 97
24	56, 71, 96

9.
Group 1		Group 2
9, 9, 8, 5	1	1, 3, 5, 8, 9
7, 6, 5, 3, 1	2	3, 6, 7, 9
7, 2, 1	3	2, 6, 7, 7
6, 5, 2	4	3, 7, 7
	5	1, 6

10.
Group 1		Group 2
9, 8, 2	5	2, 8
9, 8, 5, 4, 2	6	1, 4
9, 5, 5, 4, 3, 2	7	3, 6, 8
7, 5, 3, 2, 1	8	5
4, 3, 2, 1	9	2, 2, 3, 3, 8, 9

Additional Answers
See p. T63.

CLASSROOM EXAMPLES

1. Make a frequency distribution for the following quiz scores: 8 3 5 9 2 10 6 4 8 2 3 0 3

Score	Tally	Frequency
0	I	1
1		0
2	I I	2
3	I I I	3
4	I	1
5	I	1
6	I	1
7		0
8	I I	2
9	I	1
10	I	1
	Total	13

3. Use the intervals 0–99, 100–199, 200–299, and 300–399 to make a grouped frequency distribution for the following data: 84 156 236 165 93 109 308

Interval	Tally	Frequency
0–99	I I	2
100–199	I I I	3
200–299	I	1
300–399	I	1
	Total	7

MIXED REVIEW

1. Evaluate $\frac{x + y + z}{z^2}$ if x = −1, y = 5, and z = −2. $\frac{1}{2}$

13.2 | Frequency Distributions

In Section 13.1 you used stem-and-leaf displays to organize raw data. A table called a **frequency distribution** is another way to organize raw data.

EXAMPLES

1 **Make a frequency distribution for the following quiz scores:**

10 8 2 6 0 7 8 9 10 9 1 5 10 8 8 8 7 7 7 7 5 9 8 8 3 3 5 6 6 8

SOLUTION

Score	Tally	Frequency
0	I	1
1	I	1
2	I	1
3	II	2
4		0
5	III	3
6	III	3
7	卌	5
8	卌 III	8
9	III	3
10	III	3
	Total	30

List the scores from smallest to largest.

Tally a score each time it occurs.

When there are a large number of raw data or when there is a great difference between the largest value and the smallest value, a **grouped frequency distribution** is useful. The data are grouped according to certain intervals.

2 **Use the intervals 100–199, 200–299, 300–399, 400–499, 500–599, and 600–699 to make a grouped frequency distribution for the following data:**

146 207 116 379 647 503 529 469 288 682 263 109 214 192 684 509 233 318 647 471 289 311 243 219

SOLUTION

Interval	Tally	Frequency
100–199	IIII	4
200–299	卌 III	8
300–399	III	3
400–499	II	2
500–599	III	3
600–699	IIII	4
	Total	24

Complete.

1. A _____ frequency distribution _____ is a way to organize raw data.

2. A _____ grouped frequency distribution _____ can be used when there are a large number of data or when the difference between the largest and the smallest value is great.

Complete the frequency distribution.

	Score	Tally	Frequency
3.	10	IIII	? 4
4.	20	卌 II	? 7
5.	30	卌 卌 II	? 12
6.	40	卌 I	? 6
7.	50	卌 卌 III	? 13
8.	60	卌	? 5
9.		Total	? 47

A. **Make a frequency distribution for each set of data. Use an appropriate title for the first column, such as *Score, Day of the week,* or *Color*.**

1. 4 4 4 4 4 5 5 5 5 6 6 6 6 6 6 7 7 8 8 8 8 8 8 8 8 9 9 9
   10 10 10 10 10

2. 23 23 23 23 24 25 25 26 26 27 27 27 27 30 31 31 33 33 36 36 36 36
   36 36 45 45

3. Monday Monday Monday Monday Tuesday Tuesday Tuesday Tuesday Tuesday
   Tuesday Tuesday Tuesday Wednesday Wednesday Wednesday Thursday Thursday
   Friday Friday Friday Friday Friday Friday Friday Friday Friday Friday Friday
   Saturday Saturday

4. 2 3 7 4 5 8 10 10 9 7 7 5 8 9 7 7 6 7 8 4

B. 5. 70 90 110 70 80 60 100 110 70 90 80 80 80 100 90 90 80 80 70 90
   110 120 70 80

6. red green white blue red yellow green blue blue blue blue green red white green
   blue blue yellow yellow blue blue green white white blue blue

7. 59 61 60 59 64 65 68 63 59 66 67 67 62 65 66 69 70 59 62 68 67

8. $5\frac{1}{2}$ 7 $7\frac{1}{2}$ 6 6 $6\frac{1}{2}$ 6 $6\frac{1}{2}$ $7\frac{1}{2}$ 9 $8\frac{1}{2}$ $9\frac{1}{2}$ 8 7 5 $5\frac{1}{2}$ $7\frac{1}{2}$ 9 $9\frac{1}{2}$ 6 6 6 $6\frac{1}{2}$ $7\frac{1}{2}$

2. Evaluate $\frac{14x}{y+z}$ if $x = -1$, $y = 5$, and $z = -2$ $-\frac{14}{3}$

3. Find $f(-2)$ for $f(x) = \frac{1}{2}x + 12$.   11

4. Rewrite $4x + 3y = -10$ in slope-intercept form.
   $y = -\frac{4}{3}x - \frac{10}{3}$

5. Solve the system of equations: $2x - 5y = 6$
   $y = 4x + 6$
   $(-2, -2)$

TEACHER'S RESOURCE MASTERS

Practice Master 54, Part 2

Quiz 25

ASSIGNMENT GUIDE

Minimum
1–9 odd

Regular
9–13

Maximum
11–15

ADDITIONAL ANSWERS

Written Exercises

1. | Score | Frequency |
   |---|---|
   | 4 | 5 |
   | 5 | 4 |
   | 6 | 6 |
   | 7 | 2 |
   | 8 | 10 |
   | 9 | 3 |
   | 10 | 5 |
   | Total | 35 |

2. | Score | Frequency |
|---|---|
| 23 | 4 |
| 24 | 1 |
| 25 | 2 |
| 26 | 2 |
| 27 | 4 |
| 30 | 1 |
| 31 | 2 |
| 33 | 2 |
| 36 | 6 |
| 45 | 2 |
| Total | 26 |

3. | Day of the week | Frequency |
|---|---|
| Monday | 4 |
| Tuesday | 8 |
| Wednesday | 3 |
| Thursday | 2 |
| Friday | 11 |
| Saturday | 2 |
| Total | 30 |

4. | Score | Frequency |
|---|---|
| 2 | 1 |
| 3 | 1 |
| 4 | 2 |
| 5 | 2 |
| 6 | 1 |
| 7 | 6 |
| 8 | 3 |
| 9 | 2 |
| 10 | 2 |
| Total | 20 |

5. | Score | Frequency |
|---|---|
| 60 | 1 |
| 70 | 5 |
| 80 | 7 |
| 90 | 5 |
| 100 | 2 |
| 110 | 3 |
| 120 | 1 |
| Total | 24 |

Additional Answers
See p. T63.

Use the given intervals to make a grouped frequency distribution for each set of data.

9. **1–10, 11–20, 21–30, 31–40, 41–50, 51–60**

   9 17 25 56 60 50 32 16 5 43 36 28 29 57 59 60 42 37 39 26 18 12 15 2 36 41 50 56

10. **0.6–1.0, 1.1–1.5, 1.6–2.0, 2.1–2.5, 2.6–3.0, 3.1–3.5**

    0.6 3.2 0.8 2.9 2.6 1.6 1.9 1.8 1.4 2.3 3.4 0.6 1.1 0.9 1.0 1.1 2.0 2.7 2.9 3.0 2.4 2.5 3.0 1.0 0.6 0.7 1.2 2.3

11. **101–110, 111–120, 121–130, 131–140, 141–150, 151–160, 161–170**

    162 139 118 142 169 132 127 118 121 140 146 163 170 164 160 102 112 163 147 136 129 104 113 126 141 168 133 147

12. **11–20, 21–30, 31–40, 41–50, 51–60, 61–70**

    15 32 29 14 57 62 39 18 47 58 64 30 28 29 11 52 17 59 60 61 69 17 25 38

C. A **cumulative frequency** column is often included with a frequency distribution or a grouped frequency distribution. This column is used to record the total number of data that are less than or equal to a given number. For Example 2, the cumulative grouped frequency distribution would be:

Interval	Frequency	Cumulative frequency	
100–199	4	4	4
200–299	8	12	4 + 8
300–399	3	15	12 + 3
400–499	2	17	15 + 2
500–599	3	20	17 + 3
600–699	4	24	20 + 4

Make a cumulative frequency distribution for each of the following:

13. 25 13 12 14 20 25 12 14 13 25 18 25 14 13 13 18 25 13 12 12 12 14 12 12

14. 50 70 50 60 50 60 50 80 90 100 60 70 70 50 90 100 50 70 70 70 70 80 90 50

Using the given intervals, make a cumulative grouped frequency distribution for each of the following:

15. **1–5, 6–10, 11–15, 16–20, 21–25, 26–30**

    4 2 15 18 29 22 26 23 11 17 22 19 14 12 13 4 12 7 3 12 16 24 29 30 15 17 3 9 12 26 28 21 16 18 9 8 4 2 29 17

16. **101–200, 201–300, 301–400, 401–500, 501–600, 601–700**

    204 371 492 683 348 129 187 162 318 426 501 399 207 568 493 307 118 235 386 529 637 204 658 293 306 642 536 428 203 476 532 679 583 298 638 347 523 124 438

<table>
<tr><td>13.3</td><td>Using Graphs to Describe Data</td></tr>
</table>

OBJECTIVE

Use a bar chart, histogram, or frequency polygon to describe data.

TEACHER'S NOTES

See p. T38.

Stem-and-leaf displays and frequency distributions are ways to organize data. Sometimes graphs are used to present data in an even more understandable way. A picture makes it easy to see the information that is in the display or table.

A **bar chart** is often used when the data being graphed are not numbers. The bars on the graph are all the same width. The height of each bar represents the frequency for a category.

EXAMPLES

1   **Use the bar chart below to answer the following questions:**

   a. How many people said white was their favorite color?

   b. What color was chosen by the smallest number of people?

   c. What color was chosen by the greatest number of people?

   d. Which two colors were chosen by the same number of people?

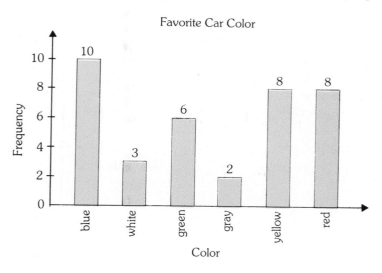

Favorite Car Color

SOLUTIONS

   a. Three people chose white.

   b. Gray was chosen by the smallest number of people.

   c. Blue was chosen by the greatest number of people.

   d. Yellow and red were chosen by the same number of people.

A **histogram** is similar to a bar chart. It is used when the data are numbers, especially when the numbers are organized into a grouped frequency distribution.

CLASSROOM EXAMPLES

1. Use the bar chart below to answer the following questions:

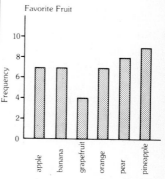

Favorite Fruit

  a. How many people said pear was their favorite fruit? Eight people chose pear.

  b. What fruit was chosen by the smallest number of people? Grapefruit was chosen by the smallest number of people.

  c. What fruit was chosen by the greatest number of people? Pineapple was chosen by the greatest number of people.

  d. Which three fruits were chosen by the same number of people? Apple, banana, and orange were chosen by the same number of people.

2. Use the histogram in Example 2 to answer the following questions:

a. Which age group has the highest average yearly income?   45–54

b. Which age group has the lowest average yearly income?   65 and over

c. Which age group has the higher average yearly income, 15–44 or 45 and over?   45 and over

MIXED REVIEW

1. Find the average of 14.2, 20.7, 26.1, 28.2, 23.5, and 12.6.   20.883

2. Find the midpoint of each of the following intervals.

a. 15–34   24.5
b. 35–54   44.5
c. 25–44   34.5
d. 45–64   54.5
e. 15–44   29.5

3. Solve the quadratic equation $9x^2 + 3x - 6 = 0$.
$\frac{2}{3}, -1$

4. Solve the quadratic equation $3x^2 + 9x + 8 = 0$.
$\emptyset$

5. Simplify $\frac{6 - \sqrt{6}}{2 - \sqrt{6}}$.
$-2\sqrt{6}$

TEACHER'S RESOURCE MASTERS

Practice Master 55, Part 1

2 | **Use the histogram below to describe the general trend of the income of the head of the house as his or her age increases.**

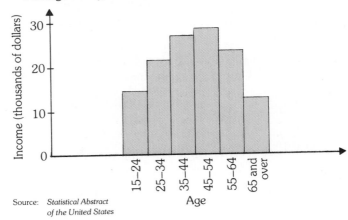

Average Yearly Income for Head of House in a Recent Year

Source: *Statistical Abstract of the United States*

SOLUTION   The income increases until the person is about 55 years old, then decreases.

A **frequency polygon** is a type of line graph. The horizontal axis represents the different groups of data, and the vertical axis represents the frequency for each.

If the frequency polygon is made from a grouped frequency distribution, the *midpoint* of each interval is often used to represent the interval on the horizontal axis. The midpoint of an interval is found by adding the smallest number of the interval and the largest number of the interval, then dividing by 2.

A frequency polygon for the histogram in Example 2 is

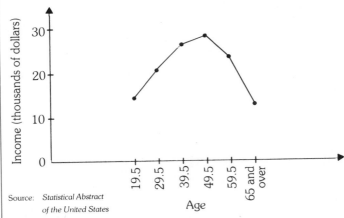

Average Yearly Income for Head of House in a Recent Year

Source: *Statistical Abstract of the United States*

NOTE: The interval "65 and over" does not have a midpoint. Why not?

1. What kind of graph can be used with data that are not numbers? bar chart
2. What kind of graph is similar to a bar chart but can be used when the data are numbers?
3. One kind of line graph is a ___frequency polygon___.
4. What is the midpoint of the interval 6–18? 12

WRITTEN EXERCISES

A. Use the bar chart below to answer exercises 1–4.

1. How many students have green eyes?
2. How many students have green or blue eyes? 13
3. What color eyes do the greatest number of students have? brown
4. How many students are there in first-hour algebra? 29

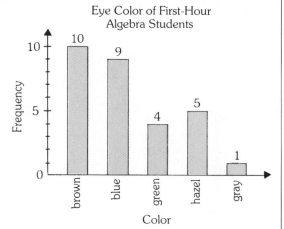

Eye Color of First-Hour Algebra Students

B. Use the histogram below to answer exercises 5–7.

5. How many hours of work were needed in 1952 to harvest 100 bushels of corn? 36
6. How many hours were needed in 1956? 20
7. What seems to be the trend over the years? Why do you think this might be?

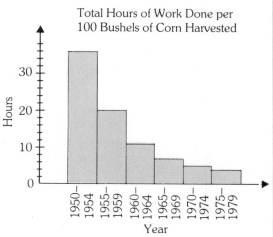

Total Hours of Work Done per 100 Bushels of Corn Harvested

Source: *Statistical Abstract of the United States*

ASSIGNMENT GUIDE
Minimum
1–6
Regular
5–10
Maximum
7–12

ADDITIONAL ANSWERS
Oral Exercises
2. histogram
Written Exercises
1. 4
7. Fewer hours are needed. Typical answer: Better farm machinery is being used.

11.

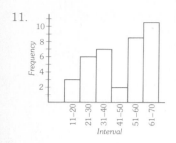

12.

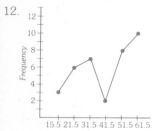

Use the frequency polygon below to answer exercises 8–10.

8. How many people wrote a report of 3 or 4 pages? 5

9. How many people wrote at least 5 pages? 13

10. How many people wrote reports? 22

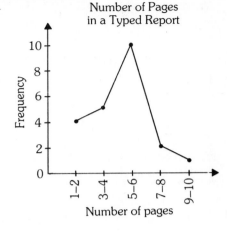

Number of Pages in a Typed Report

C. **Use the table below for exercises 11–12.**

Interval	Frequency
11–20	3
21–30	6
31–40	7
41–50	2
51–60	8
61–70	10

11. Make a histogram.

12. Make a frequency polygon.

SELF-QUIZ

1. Make a stem-and-leaf display for the following data, using two-digit stems:
   254 263 259 273 289 280 272 271 250 254 253 267 269 260 273 278 288 283 282 256 257 264 272 274 283 280 256 277

2. Make a frequency distribution for the following data:
   10 90 20 10 80 70 60 100 10 20 100 30 40 70 90 50 80 90 100 10 50 70 80 20

3. Use the histogram to determine the year that the profits for Jamie's Place were the greatest and the year that they were the least.

Profits for Jamie's Place

ALGEBRA IN USE

Sometimes a graphic representation of data can be misleading. The information is correct, but the graph is designed in such a way that the impression it makes is more dramatic than it should be.

One type of graph that can be misleading is a bar chart or a histogram in which the labels on one axis have been eliminated.

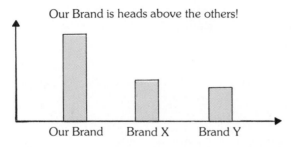

Our Brand is heads above the others!

Our Brand   Brand X   Brand Y

Without the labels, you don't know the units being used for the comparison. The difference might be very great, or it might be insignificant.

Another type of graph that can be misleading is the **pictograph.**

A company makes the following *true* claim: "Our Product has twice as many essential ingredients!" The company uses the following pictograph to accompany the claim:

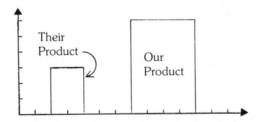

Their Product

Our Product

In the graph, the height of Our Product is twice that of Their Product, but so is the width. The words of the claim say "twice as much," comparing units of ingredients. But when you look at the graph, you are seeing a comparison of the areas of the two rectangles. And the area of the rectangle representing Our Product is actually 2×2, or 4, times as great as that of the rectangle representing Their Product.

EXERCISE

Find graphs that could be misleading in a newspaper or magazine. Bring them to class and discuss them with your classmates.

CLASSROOM EXAMPLES

1. Find the mode of the following data: 3 5 5 7 8 9 9 9 11 12 13 13 14
   The mode is 9.

2. Find the median of the following data: 30 17 25 35 6 18 32
   Arrange the numbers in order.

   6 17 18   25   30 32 35
   ⎵⎵⎵⎵⎵⎵⎵ | ⎵⎵⎵⎵⎵⎵⎵
   3 numbers | 3 numbers
              median

3. Find the mean of the following data: 30 26 43 27 32 40 32 29
   30 + 26 + 43 + 27 + 32 + 40 + 32 + 29 = 259
   $\frac{259}{8}$ = 32.375

4. Find the mode, the median, and the mean from the stem-and-leaf display below.

   1 | 6, 7, 8
   2 | 1, 2, 2, 2, 5
   3 | 0, 3, 4, 4, 5
   4 | 2, 2, 2, 4, 5, 6
   5 | 1, 2, 2, 3, 4, 5

13.4 | Measures of Central Tendency

One measure is often used to represent an entire set of data. That measure is usually the **mode,** the **median,** or the **mean.** The mode, the median, and the mean are **measures of central tendency.** Each one is an **average** and can give an overall picture of what the data are. These measures are often used when comparing two different sets of data.

The *mode* (if one exists) is the item or items that occur with the greatest frequency. If no item occurs more often than the rest, there is no mode.

EXAMPLES

1   **Find the mode of the following data:**
2 3 5 5 6 8 8 9 12 15 15 16 18 20

SOLUTION
The modes are 5, 8, and 15. These numbers occur twice, and the other numbers occur only once.

NOTE: A mode can be found for data that are not numbers.

The *median* is the middle number when the numbers are arranged from smallest to largest or from largest to smallest. If there are two middle numbers, the median is found by adding the two middle numbers, then dividing by 2.

2   **Find the median of the following data:**
15 29 18 38 42 43 16 12 204

SOLUTION
Arrange the numbers in order.

12 15 16 18   29   38 42 43 204
⎵⎵⎵⎵⎵⎵⎵⎵⎵⎵   ↑   ⎵⎵⎵⎵⎵⎵⎵⎵⎵⎵
4 numbers | 4 numbers
              median

NOTE: The median is not affected by **extreme values,** such as 204 in Example 2.

The *mean* is found by adding all of the numbers, then dividing by the number of data.

3   **Find the mean of the following data:**
29 15 33 17 15 13 25 26 35 19 20 18 17 20 19 12 35 28 14 23

SOLUTION
29 + 15 + 33 + 17 + 15 + 13 + 25 + 26 + 35 + 19 + 20 + 18 + 17 + 20 + 19 + 12 + 35 + 28 + 14 + 23 = 433

$\frac{433}{20}$ = 21.65

NOTE: The mean is what many people think of when they see the word "average." The mean is affected by every number, since all data are added.

The mean is often represented by the following formula:

$$\overline{x} = \frac{x_1 + x_2 + x_3 + \cdots + x_n}{n} \quad (\overline{x} \text{ is read "x-bar."})$$

In the formula, $\overline{x}$ represents the mean, x_1 through x_n represent the individual data, and n represents the number of data.

The mode, the median, and the mean can be found from a stem-and-leaf display or from a frequency distribution.

4 **Find the mode, the median, and the mean from the stem-and-leaf display below.**

2	0, 3, 3, 5
3	2, 5, 5, 7, 7, 7
4	1, 3, 8
5	2, 8, 9
6	0, 4, 7

SOLUTION

The mode is 37. This number occurs three times; the other numbers occur only one or two times.

There are 19 numbers, so the median is the 10th number, or 37.

The mean is 41.89, rounded to the nearest hundredth. The sum of the numbers is 796. $796 \div 19 \approx 41.89$.

5 **Find the mode and the median from the frequency distribution below.**

Number	Frequency
2	4
5	4
8	7
12	15
15	6
Total	36

SOLUTION

The mode is 12, since 12 has the greatest frequency.

The total number of data is even. So there are two middle numbers, the 18th and the 19th. To find the median, add these two numbers and then divide by 2.

18th score = 12
19th score = 12
          24

$\frac{24}{2} = 12$

The modes are 22 and 42. These numbers occur three times; the other numbers occur only one or two times. There are 25 numbers, so the median is the 13th number, or 35. The mean is 36.28. The sum of the numbers is 907. $907 \div 25 = 36.28$.

5. Find the mode and the median from the frequency distribution below.

Number	Frequency
3	4
4	5
9	3
14	8
15	2
Total	22

The mode is 14, since 14 has the greatest frequency.

11th score = 9
12th score = 9
          18

$\frac{18}{2} = 9$

6. Find the mean from the frequency distribution below.

Number	Frequency
2	3
3	5
4	2
5	4
Total	14

$\overline{x} = \frac{2(3) + 3(5) + 4(2) + 5(4)}{14}$
$= 3.5$

MIXED REVIEW

Factor completely.

1. $12x^2 - 12y^2$ $12(x - y)(x + y)$

2. $6x^2 + 35x + 36$ $(2x + 9)(3x + 4)$

3. $a^2 + b^2$ prime

4. $64a^2 - 49b^2$ $(8a - 7b)(8a + 7b)$

5. $3a(x + y) + 5b(x + y)$ $(3a + 5b)(x + y)$

TEACHER'S RESOURCE MASTERS

Practice Master 55, Part 2

ASSIGNMENT GUIDE

Minimum
1–15 odd

Regular
8–15

Maximum
12–16, 19–21

ADDITIONAL ANSWERS

Written Exercises

2. (*a*) 65 and 69
   (*b*) 69   (*c*) 76

4. (*a*) 42 and 52
   (*b*) 49.5   (*c*) 53

You can use a formula to find a mean from a frequency distribution.

$$\bar{x} = \frac{x_1 f_1 + x_2 f_2 + \cdots + x_k f_k}{n}$$

x_1 represents the first number and f_1 represents the frequency of the first number. Each number and its frequency are multiplied, then all the products are added. Again, n represents the total number of data.

6   **Find the mean from the frequency distribution below.**

Number	Frequency
2	4
5	4
8	7
12	15
15	6
Total	36

SOLUTION $\bar{x} = \dfrac{2(4) + 5(4) + 8(7) + 12(15) + 15(6)}{36}$

$= 9.8\bar{3}$, or 9.8 when rounded to the nearest tenth

ORAL EXERCISES

1. What are the three measures of central tendency?   mode, median, mean

2. Which measure of central tendency can be found for data that are not numbers?   mode

3. Which measure of central tendency can be used when extreme values are not an important consideration?   median

4. Which measure of central tendency is the one people usually think of when they see the word "average"?   mean

WRITTEN EXERCISES

A. **For each exercise, find (*a*) the mode, (*b*) the median, and (*c*) the mean. When necessary, round the mean to the nearest hundredth.**

1. 2 2 5 5 7 9 11 11 11   11; 7; 7

2. 63 64 65 65 65 69 69 69 73 84 85 87 89 95 98

3. 1.5 1.7 2.3 2.4 2.5 2.7 2.9 3.1 3.4 3.6   no mode; 2.6; 2.61

4. 23 24 27 31 37 39 41 42 42 47 52 52 63 65 69 71 74 82 85 94

B. 5. 123 204 118 149 306 277 289   no mode; 204; 209.43

6. 26 18 39 14 49 51 36 39 26   26 and 39; 36; 33.11

7. 18.3 24.6 13.7 29.8 17.4 16.5 18.3 23.1 26.7 13.1 10.7 21.3 18.3 20.4 15.6   18.3; 18.3; 19.19

8. 5 7 3 2 6 1 4 5 7 5 7 2 7 7 5 6 5 3 8 9 9 2 7 6 5 7 4 7 8 7 9 3 7
5 4 7   7; 6; 5.58

9. 18 20 10 26 16 26 16 10 18 20   no mode; 18; 18

10. 15.2 18.3 14.6 20.7 18.1 14.6 26.1 23.4 12.9 18.1 14.7 20.1

11. 130 210 380 175 240 395 280 195 230 240 185 205 380 190 410 405

12. 3 7 8 9 9 3 9 7 2 9 9 4 5 9 2 9 1 9 9 6 8 9 4 2

13.

0	5, 5, 5
1	0, 0, 0, 0, 0, 5, 5
2	7, 8, 8, 8, 9
3	0, 0, 1, 5, 7 10; 21; 19.9

14.

1	2, 2, 2, 8, 8, 8, 8, 8
2	1, 4, 4, 4, 4, 4, 5, 5
3	6

18 and 24; 21; 20.76

15.

Number	Frequency
20	3
30	12
40	5
50	16
60	2
70	4
80	3
Total	45 50; 50; 45.78

16.

Number	Frequency
8	1
10	2
13	4
15	4
16	4
18	3
20	2
Total	20

17.

Number	Frequency
180	3
200	3
210	3
220	3
250	3
270	3
Total	18 no mode; 215; 221.67

18.

Number	Frequency
25	10
50	3
75	4
100	2
125	7
150	4
Total	30 25; 75; 79.17

C. **An independent testing firm conducted a gasoline mileage test on three different cars. The test was repeated five times for each car, with the following results (in miles per gallon):**

car 1:   26.6 26.7 26.8 26.9 27.0

car 2:   20.6 25.3 27.1 27.2 27.3

car 3:   24.2 24.3 24.5 24.5 31.5

Each manufacturer would like to claim that its car has the best "average" number of miles per gallon of the three cars. Each will use a different average when comparing its car to the other two.

19. Which average would the manufacturer of car 1 use to claim that car 1 is the best?

20. Which average would the manufacturer of car 2 use to claim that car 2 is the best?

21. The manufacturer of car 3 had to use a fourth measure of central tendency, called the **midrange** (the mean of the smallest and the largest score). Show that by using the midrange, the manufacturer of car 3 could claim that car 3 is the best.

10. (a) 14.6 and 18.1
(b) 18.1   (c) 18.07

11. (a) 240 and 380
(b) 235   (c) 265.625

12. (a) 9   (b) 7.5   (c) 6.33

16. (a) 13, 15, and 16
(b) 15   (c) 14.9

19. mean

20. median

21. car 1: 26.8; car 2: 23.95;
car 3: 27.85; car 3 has
the greatest midrange.

EXPLORATION
The Mean From a Grouped Frequency Distribution

When data are given in a grouped frequency distribution, you do not know the exact value of all the numbers within each interval. You can still calculate an approximate value for the mean.

Interval	Frequency
1–3	3
4–6	6
7–9	2
10–12	8
13–15	12
16–18	3
19–21	6
Total	40

In the interval 1–3, you do not know if the numbers are all ones, two ones and a two, and so on. You can use the midpoint of the interval, 2, to represent all three numbers. Do the same for each interval. Then

$$\bar{x} = \frac{2(3) + 5(6) + 8(2) + 11(8) + 14(12) + 17(3) + 20(6)}{40}$$

$$= \frac{479}{40} = 11.975$$

EXERCISES

Find the mean for each grouped frequency distribution. Round each answer to the nearest hundredth.

1.

Interval	Frequency
9–15	3
16–22	15
23–29	8
30–36	2
37–43	12
44–50	9
Total	49 30.57

2.

Interval	Frequency
0.1–0.9	2
1.0–1.8	7
1.9–2.7	3
2.8–3.6	2
3.7–4.5	4
4.6–5.4	5
Total	23 2.85

3.

Interval	Frequency
2–6	3
7–11	7
12–16	4
17–21	2
22–26	5
27–31	7
Total	28 17.57

4.

Interval	Frequency
110–116	4
117–123	3
124–130	8
131–137	3
138–144	7
145–151	11
Total	36 134.58

CALCULATOR

You may find using a calculator helpful when finding a mean from a frequency distribution.

Example: Find the mean from the following frequency distribution:

Number	Frequency
10	3
15	4
20	7
25	2
30	8
Total	24

Solution:

ENTER   DISPLAY

10 ⊠ 3 [M+] 15 ⊠ 4 [M+] 20 ⊠ 7 [M+] 25
⊠ 2 [M+] 30 ⊠ 8 [M+] [RM] ⊡ 24 [=]   *21.666666*

EXERCISES

Check your answers to exercises 15–18 in Section 13.4.

CHALLENGE

```
  FORTY
    TEN
+   TEN
 SIXTY
```

Can you solve this addition problem? Each letter represents one of the ten digits. If a letter is used more than once, it represents the same digit each time. A meaningful (true) addition problem must result. What is the addition problem?

CHALLENGE
```
  29786
    850
+   850
  31486
```

OBJECTIVES

Find the range of a set of data.

Find the variance and the standard deviation of a set of data.

CLASSROOM EXAMPLES

1. Find the range for Class 1 scores and for Class 2 scores.

   Class 1: 63 93 85 72 90 58 78

   Class 2: 85 62 93 95 81 73 84

   The range for Class 1 is 93 − 58 = 35.

   The range for Class 2 is 95 − 62 = 33.

2. Find the mean of the deviation scores for the following data: 6 3 9 4 2 5 8 7

   $\bar{x} = \dfrac{6 + 3 + 9 + 4 + 2 + 5 + 8 + 7}{8}$

   $= 5.5$

x	$x - \bar{x}$
6	0.5
3	−2.5
9	3.5
4	−1.5
2	−3.5
5	−0.5
8	2.5
7	1.5
	0

13.5 | The Range and the Standard Deviation

In an algebra class of 25 students, Test Form A was given to 13 students, and Test Form B was given to 12 students. The results of the tests were as follows:

Test Form A:

86 85 84 83 83 82 82 82 82 81 79 79 78

Test Form B:

100 99 98 97 96 82 82 81 80 79 60 30

The mode, the median, and the mean of the scores for each test form are all 82. But the scores for the test forms seem to be different in nature. The scores for Test Form A are very close to 82, but the scores for Test Form B seem to vary quite a bit from 82. (Consider the lowest score, 30!)

People who use statistics need **measures of variation** in addition to measures of central tendency to help them describe a set of data. Measures of variation help to describe how all the data of a set compare to the measure of central tendency used to represent the data. A measure of central tendency does not always give the best picture of what all the data are. A measure of variation can indicate this.

One measure of variation is the **range.** The range of a set of data is found by subtracting the smallest value from the largest value.

EXAMPLES

1 **Find the range for Test Form A and for Test Form B.**

SOLUTION

Subtract the lowest score from the highest score.

The range for Test Form A is 86 − 78 = 8.

The range for Test Form B is 100 − 30 = 70.

The next measure of variation uses the mean as the measure of central tendency for a set of data. For this measure of variation, the mean is subtracted from each value in the set of data—that is, $x_1 - \bar{x}, \ldots, x_n - \bar{x}$.

These differences are called **deviation scores.** Notice that some of the deviation scores will be positive and some will be negative. If you add all these deviation scores, the sum is 0.

2 **Find the mean of the deviation scores for the following data:**

3 7 2 5 10 12 6 4 15 11

SOLUTION

$$\bar{x} = \frac{3 + 7 + 2 + 5 + 10 + 12 + 6 + 4 + 15 + 11}{10} = 7.5$$

x	$x - \bar{x}$
3	-4.5
7	-0.5
2	-5.5
5	-2.5
10	2.5
12	4.5
6	-1.5
4	-3.5
15	7.5
11	3.5
	0 *sum*

$$\frac{0}{10} = 0$$

If each of the differences $x - \bar{x}$ is squared, then each number will be positive. Their sum will not be zero, so the mean of the squares of the deviation scores will not be zero. This value is called the **variance.** Its symbol is S^2.

> **3** **Find the variance for Example 2.**

SOLUTION

$\bar{x} = 7.5$

x	$x - \bar{x}$	$(x - \bar{x})^2$
3	-4.5	20.25
7	-0.5	0.25
2	-5.5	30.25
5	-2.5	6.25
10	2.5	6.25
12	4.5	20.25
6	-1.5	2.25
4	-3.5	12.25
15	7.5	56.25
11	3.5	12.25
		166.5 *sum*

$$S^2 = \frac{166.5}{10} = 16.65$$

You can use the following formula to find the variance:

$$S^2 = \frac{(x_1 - \bar{x})^2 + (x_2 - \bar{x})^2 + \cdots + (x_n - \bar{x})^2}{n}$$

Each of the differences $x - \bar{x}$ was squared in finding the variance. To find the **standard deviation** for a set of data, take the square root of the variance. If the standard deviation is close to zero, then the data were all close to the mean. The standard deviation becomes greater as the data become farther away from the mean.

3. Find the variance for Classroom Example 2.

$\bar{x} = 5.5$

x	$x - \bar{x}$	$(x - \bar{x})^2$
6	0.5	0.25
3	-2.5	6.25
9	3.5	12.25
4	-1.5	2.25
2	-3.5	12.25
5	-0.5	0.25
8	2.5	6.25
7	1.5	2.25
		42.0

$S^2 = \frac{42}{8} = 5.25$

4. Find the standard deviation for Classroom Example 3.

$S^2 = 5.25$

$S = \sqrt{5.25} \approx 2.29$

MIXED REVIEW

1. 15 is 40% of what number?   37.5

2. $A = \pi r^2$, solve for r.
$r = \frac{\sqrt{\pi A}}{\pi}$

3. Solve $\frac{15}{40} = \frac{3}{y}$.   8

4. Find the LCD of $\frac{3x}{2x - 6}$ and $\frac{2}{x - 3}$. $2(x - 3)$

5. Restate 0.32 in fractional form. $\frac{8}{25}$

TEACHER'S RESOURCE MASTERS

Practice Master 56, Part 1

ASSIGNMENT GUIDE

Minimum
1–15 odd

Regular
12–19

Maximum
14–21

ADDITIONAL ANSWERS

Oral Exercises

1. range

2. deviation scores

3. variance

| 4 | **Find the standard deviation for Example 3.** |

SOLUTION

$$S^2 = 16.65$$
$$S = \sqrt{16.65} \approx 4.08$$

You can use the following formula to find the standard deviation:

$$S = \sqrt{\frac{(x_1 - \bar{x})^2 + (x_2 - \bar{x})^2 + \cdots + (x_n - \bar{x})^2}{n}}$$

ORAL EXERCISES

1. Which measure of variation is found by subtracting the smallest value from the largest value?

2. Which measure of variation is found by subtracting the mean from each value?

3. Which measure of variation is the mean of the squares of all the differences $x - \bar{x}$?

4. Which measure of variation is the square root of the variance? standard deviation

WRITTEN EXERCISES

A. Find the range.

1. 2 7 9 15 26 34 37 35

2. 1.5 2.3 8.6 9.1 9.1 10.7 9.2

3. 12 15 29 36 49 52 57 63 69 57

4. $1\frac{1}{4}$ $1\frac{1}{4}$ $1\frac{1}{2}$ $1\frac{2}{3}$ $2\frac{1}{10}$ $2\frac{2}{3}$ $3\frac{1}{8}$ $3\frac{1}{4}$ $3\frac{1}{2}$ $2\frac{1}{4}$

5.	2	5, 5, 6
	4	0, 3, 3, 5, 6, 9
	5	1, 1, 4, 6, 7
	6	0, 0, 8
	7	9
	8	0 55

6.	*Number*	*Frequency*
	19	26
	21	20
	24	10
	26	11
	28	12
	Total	79 9

B. 7. 27 52 63 35 19 83 4 26 79

8. 14 102 37 115 93 26 29 17 101

9. 26 92 43 3 2 29 18 104 102

10. 14.3 12.6 8.9 7.5 15.9 16.3 8.1 5.4 10.9

Find (*a*) the variance and (*b*) the standard deviation for each exercise. Round each answer to the nearest hundredth.

11. 3 5 7 9 12 15 16 21   32.75; 5.72

12. 4 6 9 12 15 17 19 23 26 29   63.8; 7.99

13. 10 15 15 20 20 20 25 30 35 50   124; 11.14

14. 231 114 109 269 99 78 206 198   4446.5; 66.68

15. 15 15 31 15 29 46 12 15 20   111.78; 10.57

16. 1.6 2.8 3.2 1.3 4.2 1.2 5.7 1.6   2.27; 1.51

17. 2.3 5.9 1.3 4.6 6.1 1.2 8.3 1.1   6.64; 2.58

18. 8 7 5 4 9 3 8 5 6 8 7 9   3.58; 1.89

C. 19.

1	3, 5, 6
2	4, 4, 7, 7
3	2, 6, 8
4	7, 9 128.5; 11.34

20.

10	6, 7, 7
11	2, 4, 5, 6, 8
12	3, 9
	48.81; 6.99

21. Find the standard deviations of the scores for Test Form A and Test Form B of Example 1. Which test results have the smaller standard deviation?   2.25; 19.35; Test Form A

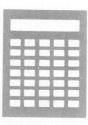

CALCULATOR

A calculator can be used when you are finding the standard deviation of a set of data.

Example: Find the standard deviation of the following data:

18 15 16 21 13 26 17 14

Solution: $\bar{x} = 17.5$

ENTER   DISPLAY

18 $-$ 17.5 $\times$ $\boxed{M+}$ 15 $-$ 17.5 $\times$ $\boxed{M+}$ 16 $-$ 17.5 $\times$ $\boxed{M+}$

21 $-$ 17.5 $\times$ $\boxed{M+}$ 13 $-$ 17.5 $\times$ $\boxed{M+}$ 26 $-$ 17.5 $\times$

$\boxed{M+}$ 17 $-$ 17.5 $\times$ $\boxed{M+}$ 14 $-$ 17.5 $\times$ $\boxed{M+}$

$\boxed{RM}$ $\div$ 8 $=$ $\sqrt{}$ 3.9686269

In the sequence 18 $-$ 17.5 $\times$ $\boxed{M+}$, 18 $-$ 17.5 is $x - \bar{x}$. The $\times$ key squares the difference, and $\boxed{M+}$ stores this result.

Remember that on some calculators, $=$ may have to be pressed before the $\times$ key or the $\boxed{M+}$ key.

EXERCISES

Check your answers to exercises 11–18 in Section 13.5.

IN OTHER FIELDS
Mathematics and Social Sciences

Social sciences include many areas of study, such as history, political science, economics, sociology, and law.

An important part of the social sciences is studying and classifying human behavior. Statistics is often used, since this branch of mathematics deals specifically with organizing, studying, and interpreting data.

Some people consider education to be one of the social sciences. Statistics is very useful in studying educational results. The **normal curve** is often used in education. The normal curve is shaped like a bell. The horizontal axis usually contains test results. The vertical axis shows the frequency of the scores.

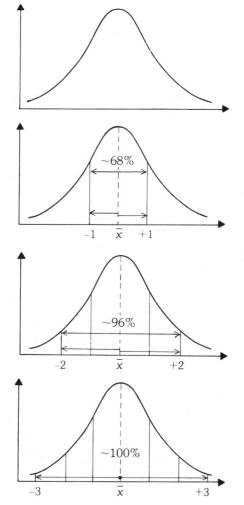

Standard deviations are used with a normal curve. If the frequency of the test results of a population is normal, then about 68% of all the test scores are within 1 standard deviation of the mean (either greater than or less than the mean).

About 96% of all the test scores are within 2 standard deviations of the mean.

Almost 100% of all the scores are within 3 standard deviations of the mean.

13.6 | Quartiles

Quartiles are associated with the median. There are three quartiles, represented by Q_1, Q_2, and Q_3. The three quartiles divide the data into four equal groups when the data are listed from smallest to largest.

75% of numbers less than or equal to	Q_3
50% of numbers less than or equal to	Q_2
25% of numbers less than or equal to	Q_1

Q_3	25% of numbers greater than or equal to
Q_2	50% of numbers greater than or equal to
Q_1	75% of numbers greater than or equal to

Q_2 is the median of the data. You already know how to find Q_2.

To find Q_1 and Q_3, find the median of the first half of the data and the median of the second half of the data.

EXAMPLES

1   **Find Q_1, Q_2, and Q_3 for the following data:**

23 27 34 36 42 49 56 58 59 60 63 64 69 72 75 77 82 87 92 95

SOLUTION

There are 20 numbers. The numbers are listed in order. To find Q_2, add the 10th and 11th numbers, then divide by 2.

$$Q_2 = \frac{60 + 63}{2} = 61.5$$

There are 10 numbers less than the median, Q_2. Do not count Q_2 when Q_2 is the average of two numbers. So the median of these numbers is found by adding the 5th and 6th numbers, then dividing by 2.

$$Q_1 = \frac{42 + 49}{2} = 45.5$$

There are 10 numbers greater than the median, Q_2. Again, do not count Q_2. So the median of these data is found by adding the 5th and 6th numbers of these 10 numbers, then dividing by 2.

$$Q_3 = \frac{75 + 77}{2} = 76$$

OBJECTIVES

Find the quartiles for a set of data.

Find the interquartile range and the semi-interquartile range for a set of data.

Make and use box-and-whisker plots.

TEACHER'S NOTES

See p. T38.

CLASSROOM EXAMPLES

1. Find Q_1, Q_2, and Q_3 for the following
   data: 25   26
   28   30   32   34   35   38
   39   40
   $Q_2 = \frac{32 + 34}{2} = 33$
   $Q_1 = 28$
   $Q_3 = 38$

2. Find Q_1, Q_2, and Q_3 for the following data: 6, 8, 10, 11, 12, 15, 17, 18, 19, 21, 22, 25, 27, 29, 30
   $Q_2 = 18$
   $Q_1 = \frac{11 + 12}{2} = 11.5$
   $Q_3 = \frac{22 + 25}{2} = 23.5$

3. Find the semi-interquartile range for the data in Classroom Example 2.
   $Q_3 = 23.5$ $Q_1 = 11.5$
   $\frac{Q_3 - Q_1}{2} = \frac{23.5 - 11.5}{2}$
   $= 6$

4. Use the information in Classroom Example 1 to make a box-and-whisker plot.

The extreme values are 25 and 40.

$Q_1 = 28$, $Q_2 = 33$, and $Q_3 = 38$.

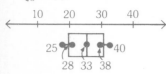

5. At a gymnastics contest, judges were asked to rate the performances of two gymnasts, using a scale from 0 to 10. Use the results for each gymnast to answer these questions:

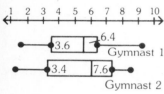

a. Which gymnast received the higher rating?
Gymnast 1 had the higher rating.

b. Which gymnast had the smaller interquartile range? Do you think the ratings for this gymnast were probably more consistent in representing judges' ratings, or more diverse?
Gymnast 1 had the smaller interquartile range. The judges' ratings were probably more consistent; the range for 50% of the judges was 2.8 for Gymnast 1 and 4.2 for Gymnast 2.

---

2   **Find Q_1, Q_2, and Q_3 for the following data:**

8 12 13 17 21 23 24 29 32 33 35 42 48 53 62

SOLUTION

There are 15 numbers. The numbers are listed in order. Q_2 is the 8th number.

$Q_2 = 29$

There are 8 numbers less than or equal to the median, Q_2. Count Q_2 when Q_2 is one of the data. So the median of these numbers is found by adding the 4th and 5th numbers, then dividing by 2.

$$Q_1 = \frac{17 + 21}{2} = 19$$

There are 8 numbers greater than or equal to the median, Q_2. Again, count Q_2. So the median of these numbers is found by adding the 4th and 5th numbers of this group, then dividing by 2.

$$Q_3 = \frac{35 + 42}{2} = 38.5$$

The **interquartile range** is a measure of variation found by subtracting Q_1 from Q_3: $Q_3 - Q_1$.

The **semi-interquartile range** (sometimes called the *quartile deviation*) is half this amount: $\frac{Q_3 - Q_1}{2}$.

3   **Find the semi-interquartile range for the data in Example 1.**

SOLUTION

$Q_3 = 76$ $Q_1 = 45.5$

$$\frac{Q_3 - Q_1}{2} = \frac{76 - 45.5}{2} = 15.25$$

NOTE: The range depends on the extreme values of a set of data. The semi-interquartile range depends on the center 50% of the data.

You can make a **box-and-whisker plot** by using the quartiles and the extreme values of a set of data. A box-and-whisker plot can be used to display information about a set of data, much as graphs were used in Section 13.3.

4   **Use the information in Example 1 to make a box-and-whisker plot.**

SOLUTION

The extreme values are 23 and 95.

$Q_1 = 45.5$, $Q_2 = 61.5$, and $Q_3 = 76$.

Mark these values *below* a number line.

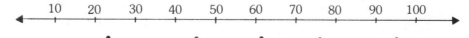

Draw a box, using Q_1 and Q_3 as the vertical sides. Draw in horizontal sides to complete a box. Draw a vertical line segment through Q_2 to the horizontal sides. Draw line segments from Q_1 to the smallest value and from Q_3 to the largest value.

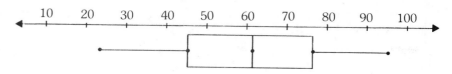

You can use box-and-whisker plots to compare sets of data.

5   **At a high-school dance, students were asked to rate two records, using a scale from 0 to 100. Use the results for each record to answer these questions:**

a. Which record received the higher rating?

b. Which record had the smaller interquartile range? Do you think the ratings for this record were probably more consistent in representing students' reactions, or more diverse?

c. For which record was Q_3 larger?

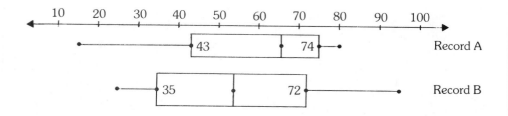

SOLUTIONS

a. Record B had the higher rating.

b. Record A had the smaller interquartile range. The students' ratings were probably more consistent; the range for 50% of the students was 31 for Record A and 37 for Record B.

c. Record A had the larger value for Q_3.

ORAL EXERCISES

1. How many quartiles are there for a set of data?   3

c. For which gymnast was Q_3 larger?   Gymnast 2 had the larger value for Q_3.

MIXED REVIEW

Perform the indicated operation.

1. $(3y + 8)(6y - 3)$ $18y^2 + 39y - 24$

2. $(5x^2 + 3xy - y^2) - (3y^2 + 6x^2 + 5xy)$ $-x^2 - 2xy - 4y^2$

3. Use positive exponents.
$\dfrac{y^{-8}}{y^{-2}}$ $\dfrac{1}{y^6}$

4. $\dfrac{12x^2y^3}{5xy} \div \dfrac{30xy}{10x^4y^3}$ $\dfrac{4}{5}x^4y^4$ or $\dfrac{4}{5}x^4y^4$

5. $-5rt(-8r^3t^2 + 6r^2t)$
$40r^4t^3 - 30r^3t^2$

TEACHER'S RESOURCE MASTERS

Practice Master 56, Part 2

Quiz 26

ASSIGNMENT GUIDE

Minimum
3–19 odd, 27

Regular
13–20, 24, 26

Maximum
16–21, 28, 36–38

2. Q_2 is also known as the ___median___.

3. Find the interquartile range if $Q_1 = 26$ and $Q_3 = 52$.   26

4. Find the semi-interquartile range if $Q_1 = 19$ and $Q_3 = 84$.   32.5

5. You can use a ___box-and-whisker plot___ to show the relationship between the quartiles and the extreme values of a set of data.

WRITTEN EXERCISES

A. Find the interquartile range and the semi-interquartile range for each.

    1. $Q_1 = 9, Q_3 = 15$ 6; 3   **2.** $Q_1 = 21, Q_3 = 85$ 64; 32

    3. $Q_1 = 9, Q_3 = 73$ 64; 32   **4.** $Q_1 = 12, Q_3 = 92$ 80; 40

    5. $Q_1 = 15, Q_3 = 35$ 20; 10   **6.** $Q_1 = 103, Q_3 = 247$ 144; 72

B. **7.** $Q_1 = 5, Q_3 = 18$ 13; 6.5   **8.** $Q_1 = 53, Q_3 = 84$ 31; 15.5

    9. $Q_1 = 17.5, Q_3 = 24$ 6.5; 3.25   **10.** $Q_1 = 19, Q_3 = 26.5$ 7.5; 3.75

    11. $Q_1 = 14\frac{1}{2}, Q_3 = 26\frac{1}{4}$ $11\frac{3}{4}; 5\frac{7}{8}$ **12.** $Q_1 = 8\frac{1}{3}, Q_3 = 10\frac{2}{3}$ $2\frac{1}{3}; 1\frac{1}{6}$

Find Q_1, Q_2, and Q_3.

13. 5 6 7 10 12 15 18 21 24 25 26 30   8.5; 16.5; 24.5

14. 18 20 26 35 39 42 53 67 69 72 75 78 87   35; 53; 72

15. 20 20 20 30 40 40 40 40 50 50 60 70 70 70 80 90

16. 15 18 20 21 24 25 27 30 32 35 38 39 40 42 45 46 51 52 54 58

17. 4 13 18 20 21 22 27 36 39 40 42 47 51 57 58 61 63 65 68 74 82 87 89 95   24.5; 49; 66.5

18. 13 17 22 25 29 32 37 42 47 52 59 63 64 67 71 73 76 81 85 92 97   32; 59; 73

19. | Number | Frequency |
|:---:|:---:|
| 10 | 2 |
| 15 | 3 |
| 20 | 5 |
| 25 | 1 |
| 30 | 6 |
| Total | 17 |

15; 20; 30

20. | Number | Frequency |
|:---:|:---:|
| 50 | 8 |
| 60 | 3 |
| 70 | 10 |
| 80 | 5 |
| 90 | 6 |
| Total | 32 |

55; 70; 80

21. | 1 | 3, 4, 4, 9 |
|:---:|:---|
| 2 | 5, 8, 8, 9 |
| 3 | 0, 4, 7, 8 |

16.5; 28; 32

22. | 4 | 0, 0, 3 |
|:---:|:---|
| 5 | 1 |
| 6 | 2, 7, 9, 9 |

41.5; 56.5; 68

Make a box-and-whisker plot for each.

23. For exercise 13. **24.** For exercise 14.

25. For exercise 15. **26.** For exercise 16.

27. For exercise 17. **28.** For exercise 18.

Use the box-and-whisker plots to answer each question.

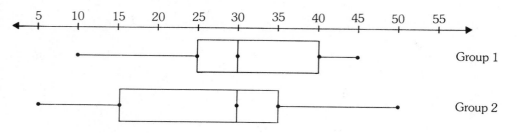

Group 1

Group 2

29. Which group has the lower score? Group 2

30. For which group is Q_3 higher? Group 1

31. Which group has the smaller interquartile range? Group 1

32. How does Q_2 compare for the two groups? same

C. **Find the interquartile range and the semi-interquartile range for each.**

33. 8 10 12 12 15 18 21 27 32 40   15; 7.5

34. 32 35 36 38 40 41 45 49 53 63 68 71 73 80 87

35. 18 29 15 52 37 84 39 26 15 17 24 32 56 63 72   33; 16.5

36. 3.0 4.9 5.1 6.2 7.4 8.3 9.2 8.4 3.6 2.4 5.6 8.9 9.3   3.5; 1.75

37.

Number	Frequency
75	1
80	3
85	5
90	1
95	3
100	7
Total	20 15; 7.5

38.

Number	Frequency
5.5	3
5.6	7
5.7	1
5.8	4
5.9	3
6.0	3
Total	21 0.3; 0.15

39.

3	0, 0, 4, 4, 5, 7, 9
4	2, 2, 2, 3, 6, 6, 8
5	1, 4
6	2, 5, 6, 6, 7, 8, 9
7	0, 1, 3 27; 13.5

40.

2	4, 4, 5, 5, 5, 6
3	0, 0, 1
4	3, 4, 4, 7, 7, 7, 9
5	2, 8, 9
6	0, 6, 6, 6, 7, 9, 9, 9 33; 16.5

23.

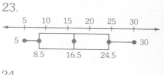

24.

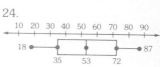

25.

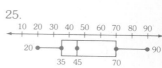

26.

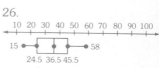

27.

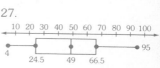

28.

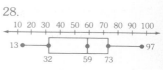

34. 30.5; 15.25

SKILLS MAINTENANCE

Simplify.

1. $3[7(8 \div 2) + 13 - 8 \div 2]$ 111

2. $14\{[39 \div (4 + 9) + 12] - 5\}$ 140

Perform the indicated operation.

3. $803 - (-113)$ 916

4. $-1374.6 + 1564.72$ 190.12

5. $3\frac{2}{3}\left(-4\frac{1}{2}\right)$ $-16\frac{1}{2}$

6. $-10{,}971 \div (-207)$ 53

Solve.

7. $3x + 8 = 29$ 7

8. $5(y + 3) = 7(y - 7)$ 32

9. $3v + 6 \le 12$ $v \le 2$

10. $2m - 3 > 7m + 12$ $m < -3$

11. $|2b + 1| = 3$ $1, -2$

12. $|3c| > 27$ $c > 9 \text{ or } c < -9$

Factor.

13. $x^2 - 3x + 2$ $(x - 2)(x - 1)$

14. $t^2 - 4$ $(t + 2)(t - 2)$

15. $5b^2c + 10bc^4$ $5bc(b + 2c^3)$

16. $w^2 + 6w + 9$ $(w + 3)^2$

17. $2r^2 + 5r - 3$ $(2r - 1)(r + 3)$

18. $12z^2 + 17z + 6$ $(3z + 2)(4z + 3)$

Perform the indicated operation.

19. $(a^2 + 3a + 4) + (3a^2 - a + 9)$

20. $(3v^2 - 8v + 7) - (2v^2 + v - 11)$

21. $(2w + 3)(3w + 4)$ $6w^2 + 17w + 12$

22. $(2m^2 - m - 21) \div (m + 3)$ $2m - 7$

Solve each system of equations.

23. $3x - y = -8$
$x + y = -4$ $(-3, -1)$

24. $4x - y = 1$
$2x + 3y = 25$ $(2, 7)$

25. $x + 3y = 11$
$2x - y = -6$ $(-1, 4)$

26. $3x + y = 1$
$2x + 3y = -11$ $(2, -5)$

Perform the indicated operation.

27. $\dfrac{1}{a + 2} + \dfrac{3}{a - 1}$ $\dfrac{4a + 5}{(a + 2)(a - 1)}$

28. $\dfrac{2}{b - 3} - \dfrac{1}{b + 4}$ $\dfrac{b + 11}{(b + 4)(b - 3)}$

29. $\dfrac{3xy}{x + 4} \cdot \dfrac{x^2 - 16}{9y}$ $\dfrac{x(x - 4)}{3}$

30. $\dfrac{x + 1}{x^2 + 5x + 6} \div \dfrac{x}{x + 2}$ $\dfrac{x + 1}{x(x + 3)}$

Simplify.

31. $\sqrt{24} + 2\sqrt{6}$ $4\sqrt{6}$

32. $3\sqrt{8} - (-2\sqrt{32})$ $14\sqrt{2}$

33. $(3\sqrt{5})(2\sqrt{15})$ $30\sqrt{3}$

34. $\sqrt{\dfrac{4}{3}}$ $\dfrac{2\sqrt{3}}{3}$

Find the roots of each quadratic equation.

35. $2x^2 - x - 3 = 0$ $\frac{3}{2}, -1$

36. $2m^2 + 7m = 4$ $\frac{1}{2}, -4$

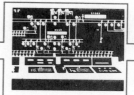

COMPUTER

Computers are very helpful for measuring sets of data in statistical work. The program below generates a set of 27 random values between 1 and 100, and then calculates the median and mode(s).

```
10 DIM DT(26),SR(27),MD(100): PRINT "GENERATING RANDOM
   DATA"
20 FOR I = 1 TO 27: SR(I) = 100: NEXT I
30 FOR J = 0 TO 26: DT(J) = INT (100 * RND (1) + 1)
40 X = DT(J): MD(X) = MD(X) + 1: IF CNT < MD(X) THEN
   CNT = MD(X)
50 PRINT DT(J),: NEXT J: PRINT
60 REM FIRST CALCULATE MEAN
90 REM NEXT, CALCULATE MEDIAN
100 FOR L = 1 TO 27
110 FOR M = 0 TO 26
120 IF DT(M) > SR(L - 1) AND DT(M) < SR(L) THEN SR(L) =
    DT(M)
130 NEXT M: NEXT L
140 PRINT "THE MEDIAN IS ";SR(14)
150 REM FINALLY, PRINT MODE(S)
160 PRINT "THE MODE(S): ";
170 IF CNT = 1 THEN PRINT "NONE": GOTO 230
180 FOR I = 1 TO 100: IF CNT = MD(I) THEN PRINT I;"   ";:
    NM = NM + 1
200 NEXT I
210 REM NOW PRINT RANGE
230 END
```

EXERCISES

1. Enter the program and RUN it. Add the necessary lines so that the computer calculates the mean and the range also. (HINT: For calculating the range, note the variable NM on line 180.)

2. What is happening on lines 100 to 140? What does the array SR do?

3. What is happening on lines 160 to 200?

4. What changes would have to be made so that the program analyzes a larger set of data?

ANSWERS

1. Add the following lines:
   - 37 L = DT(J): if L < LOW THEN LOW = L
   - 38 U = DT(J): IF U > UPP THEN UPP = U
   - 60 FOR K = 0 TO 26: TTAL = TTAL + DT(K): NEXT K
   - 70 MEAN = TTAL / 27
   - 80 PRINT "THE MEAN IS"; MEAN
   - 220 PRINT: PRINT "RANGE IS FROM" ;LOW;" TO ";UPP

   Also, at end of line 10 add the following:
   :LOW = 100

2. The program sorts the data (in the DT array) in a new array, SR, in increasing order.

3. The program prints the data value(s) that appeared most frequently and counts the number of modes as NM.

4. The dimensions on DT and SR would increase, as would the size of the FOR loops.

ENRICHMENT

See Activities 35–36,
p. T51.

ADDITIONAL ANSWERS

```
1. 1 | 7
   2 | 6, 6, 7, 9
   3 | 1, 2, 2, 4, 8
   4 | 2, 6, 9
   5 | 3, 3, 3, 6
   6 | 7
   7 | 2, 3, 4, 5, 5, 8, 9
   8 | 2, 4, 5, 9
   9 | 3
```

```
2. 1 | 3
   2 | 6, 9
   3 | 6, 7, 8
   5 | 0, 4, 7, 8, 8
   6 | 3, 5, 8
   7 | 0, 1, 3, 3, 4, 6, 8
   8 | 2, 2, 3, 5, 7
   9 | 2, 5, 6, 8
```

```
3. 1 | 4, 8
   2 | 4, 5, 6, 6, 7
   3 | 2, 2, 2, 3, 6, 6, 9
   4 | 3, 6, 8
   5 | 1, 2
```

4.

Group 1		Group 2
9	2	
7, 2, 2	3	8
6	4	7, 7, 9
9, 4	5	
8, 4, 0	6	2, 5
9, 5, 5, 2	7	4, 6, 9
7, 6, 5, 4	8	2, 6, 8, 9, 9
6, 6, 4, 1	9	0, 1, 7

CHAPTER 13 REVIEW

VOCABULARY

average (13.4)

bar chart (13.3)

box-and-whisker plot (13.6)

cumulative frequency (13.2)

data (13.1)

deviation score (13.5)

extreme value (13.4)

frequency distribution (13.2)

frequency polygon (13.3)

grouped frequency distribution (13.2)

histogram (13.3)

interquartile range (13.6)

mean (13.4)

measure of central tendency (13.4)

measure of variation (13.5)

median (13.4)

midrange (13.4)

mode (13.4)

quartile (13.6)

range (13.5)

semi-interquartile range (13.6)

standard deviation (13.5)

statistics (13.1)

stem-and-leaf display (13.1)

two-sided stem-and-leaf display (13.1)

variance (13.5)

REVIEW EXERCISES

13.1 **Make a stem-and-leaf display for each.**

1. 27 89 34 79 72 46 53 67 74 38 29 32 56 73 84 85 93 42 53 26 17 32 49 31 26 75 78 53 75 82

2. 98 73 26 13 54 63 37 95 57 65 74 68 73 78 82 58 29 96 87 85 83 76 71 50 36 58 70 92 38 82

3. 14 39 26 32 18 24 46 51 52 43 36 36 32 48 32 33 25 26 27

4. Make a two-sided stem-and-leaf display for the following data:

   Group 1: 29 54 87 64 32 46 75 86 91 37 59 60 68 75 94 32 96 84 72 79 85 96

   Group 2: 47 38 91 47 65 86 76 79 82 89 90 49 62 74 88 89 97

13.2 **Make a frequency distribution for each.**

5. 100 120 130 100 110 120 140 120 110 100 140 110 110 110 100 120 110 100 110 110 140 130 140 120 100 110

6. 60 70 50 60 40 60 70 50 60 30 40 50 40 60 80 70 90 70 60 60 30 60 70 60

7. Use the intervals 0–2, 3–5, 6–8, and 9–11 to make a grouped frequency distribution for the following data:
   5 7 9 11 0 2 7 1 2 3 4 9 10 8 7 1 4 7 8 9 11 0 10 5 6 7 7 4 3 0 2 8 9 8 11 6

13.3 **Use the bar chart to answer exercises 8–11.**

   8. Who had the most votes? Page

   9. Who had the fewest votes? Roth

   10. Which two candidates received almost the same number of votes?

   11. How many votes were cast in all? 271

Votes Cast for Four Candidates

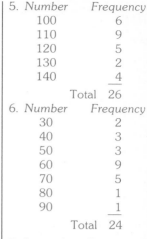

13.4, **Use the following data for exercises 12–19:**
13.5,
13.6 10 27 13 15 19 28 23 17 19

   12. Find the mode. 19

   13. Find the median. 19

   14. Find the mean. 19

   15. Find the range. 18

   16. Find the variance to the nearest hundredth. 33.11

   17. Find the standard deviation to the nearest hundredth. 5.75

   18. Find Q_1, Q_2, and Q_3. 15; 19; 23

   19. Find the semi-interquartile range.

Use the following data for exercises 20–27:
28 53 40 27 56 39 43 29 56 39

   20. Find the mode. 39 and 56

   21. Find the median. 39.5

   22. Find the mean. 41

   23. Find the range. 29

   24. Find the variance. 111.6

   25. Find the standard deviation to the nearest hundredth.

   26. Find Q_1, Q_2, and Q_3. 29; 39.5; 53

   27. Find the semi-interquartile range.

   28. Make a box-and-whisker plot for the following data:
   30 32 38 40 43 47 49 49 52 56 60

Use the box-and-whisker plots to answer exercises 29–31.

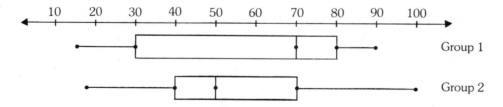

   29. Which group has the higher score? Group 2
   30. For which group is Q_2 larger? Group 1
   31. Which group has the smaller semi-interquartile range? Group 2

5. Number	Frequency
100	6
110	9
120	5
130	2
140	4
Total	26

6. Number	Frequency
30	2
40	3
50	3
60	9
70	5
80	1
90	1
Total	24

7. Interval	Frequency
0–2	8
3–5	7
6–8	12
9–11	9
Total	36

10. Boyenga and Page

19. 4

25. 10.56

27. 12

28.

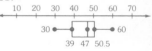

TEACHER'S RESOURCE
MASTERS

Chapter 13 Test

Multiple–Choice Test

PROBLEM-SOLVING
HANDBOOK

p. 538

ADDITIONAL ANSWERS

1.
$$
\begin{array}{c|l}
2 & 9 \\
2 & 0, 7, 8 \\
4 & 2 \\
5 & 0, 3, 6, 6, 9 \\
6 & 2, 3, 4, 8 \\
7 & 1, 2 \\
8 & 2, 4, 7, 9 \\
\end{array}
$$

2.
Group 1		Group 2
9, 4	6	7
8, 5, 3,	7	2, 2, 5,
3, 2		5, 8
8, 7, 4,	8	1, 3, 6,
4, 3		7
6, 3, 1	9	1, 3, 9

3.
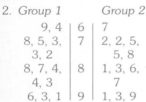

Interval	Frequency
11–15	5
16–20	5
21–25	3
26–30	9
31–35	3
36–40	5
Total	30

13.

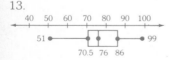

CHAPTER 13 TEST

1. Make a stem-and-leaf display for the following data:
   37 56 38 29 53 84 64 72 87 63 59 42 68 71 82 56 30 89 50 62

2. Make a two-sided stem-and-leaf display for the following data:
   Group 1: 73 64 78 69 83 96 84 91 75 72 73 84 88 87 93
   Group 2: 67 72 87 75 93 99 75 78 81 83 86 72 91

3. Use the intervals 11–15, 16–20, 21–25, 26–30, 31–35, and 36–40 to make a grouped frequency distribution for the following data:
   17 29 38 37 26 24 25 19 27 36 32 40 14 29 23 15 19 26 37 14 29 32 27
   13 19 17 26 28 31 11

4. Use the frequency polygon to determine how many students had from 6 to 8 correct answers. 2

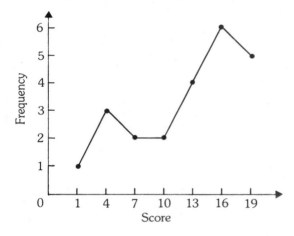

Number of Correct Answers out of 20 Questions

Use the following data for exercises 5–12:
   5 7 11 8 4 2 9 9 8

5. Find the mode. 8 and 9

6. Find the median. 8

7. Find the mean. 7

8. Find the range. 9

9. Find the variance to the nearest hundredth. 7.11

10. Find the standard deviation to the nearest hundredth. 2.67

11. Find Q_1, Q_2, and Q_3. 5; 8; 9

12. Find the semi-interquartile range. 2

13. Make a box-and-whisker plot for the following data:
    83 89 76 51 98 99 74 72 81 65 69

CHAPTER 14

Probability

In how many ways can you arrange the
first six barrels in a row? 720 ways

Determine the sample space of a given situation by making a list, a table, or a tree diagram.

Use the fundamental counting principle to determine how many outcomes are possible for a given situation.

TEACHER'S NOTES

See p. T39.

CLASSROOM EXAMPLES

1. What are the possible outcomes in the sample space when a penny is tossed?
   The possible outcomes in the sample space are heads and tails.

2. What are the possible outcomes when two pennies are tossed? A table shows the possible outcomes.

   The ordered pairs are (first penny, second penny).

		Second penny	
		H	T
First	H	(H, H)	(H, T)
penny	T	(T, H)	(T, T)

3. Sue has three sweaters and two skirts. The sweaters are black, brown, and maroon. The skirts are plaid and striped. How many ways can she create an outfit, using one sweater and one skirt? Draw a tree diagram.

14.1 | Sample Spaces and the Fundamental Counting Principle

Before you can learn about probability, you need to know what **outcomes** are possible for a given situation. A **sample space** is the set of all possible outcomes for the situation. You can determine what outcomes are possible by making a list, a table, or a tree diagram.

EXAMPLES

1 **What are the possible outcomes in the sample space when a die is rolled?**

SOLUTION The possible outcomes in the sample space are 1, 2, 3, 4, 5, and 6 dots.

2 **What are the possible outcomes when two dice are rolled?**

SOLUTION A table shows the possible outcomes. The ordered pairs are (first die, second die).

	Second die					
First die	1	2	3	4	5	6
1	(1, 1)	(1, 2)	(1, 3)	(1, 4)	(1, 5)	(1, 6)
2	(2, 1)	(2, 2)	(2, 3)	(2, 4)	(2, 5)	(2, 6)
3	(3, 1)	(3, 2)	(3, 3)	(3, 4)	(3, 5)	(3, 6)
4	(4, 1)	(4, 2)	(4, 3)	(4, 4)	(4, 5)	(4, 6)
5	(5, 1)	(5, 2)	(5, 3)	(5, 4)	(5, 5)	(5, 6)
6	(6, 1)	(6, 2)	(6, 3)	(6, 4)	(6, 5)	(6, 6)

} Sample Space

3 **A book designer has three colors available for a book cover: red, blue, and green. Four photographs are available for the cover: A, B, C, and D. How many covers can the book designer design, using one color and one photo?**

SOLUTION Draw a tree diagram.

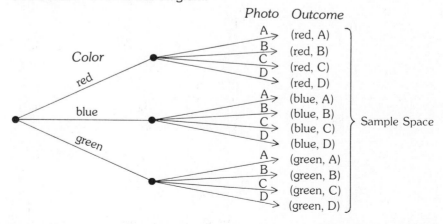

Each "branch" represents a different cover. There are 12 different covers.

Notice that the number of colors (3) times the number of photos (4) equals the number of covers (12).

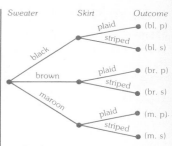

Sweater	Skirt	Outcome
black	plaid	(bl. p)
	striped	(bl. s)
brown	plaid	(br. p)
	striped	(br. s)
maroon	plaid	(m. p)
	striped	(m. s)

Each "branch" represents a different outfit. There are 6 different outfits.

Fundamental Counting Principle	If Task A can be completed in a ways and Task B can be completed in b ways, then Task A followed by Task B can be completed in $a \cdot b$ ways.

The fundamental counting principle can be extended to more than two tasks.

4 An experiment consists of tossing a coin, then rolling a die, and then drawing a card from a deck of five cards. How many outcomes are possible in the sample space?

SOLUTION

Task A		Task B		Task C		
2	·	6	·	5	=	60
ways a coin can land (H or T)		ways a die can land (1, 2, 3, 4, 5, 6)		number of cards to choose from		number of possible outcomes

4. An experiment consists of tossing a coin, then rolling a die, and then drawing a card from a deck of 7 cards. How many outcomes are possible in the sample space?

Task A	Task B	Task C	
2 ·	6 ·	7	= 84

ORAL EXERCISES

Choose the correct word.

1. Example 1 used a (<u>list</u>, table, tree diagram) to show all possible outcomes.

2. Example 2 used a (list, <u>table</u>, tree diagram) to show all possible outcomes.

3. Example 3 used a (list, table, <u>tree diagram</u>) to show all possible outcomes.

4. In the fundamental counting principle, you (add, subtract, <u>multiply</u>, divide) the number of ways Task A can be completed and the number of ways Task B can be completed.

WRITTEN EXERCISES

A. Refer to Examples 2 and 3 to answer exercises 1–8.

1. How many outcomes are in the sample space for rolling two dice? 36

2. In how many outcomes do both dice show the same number? 6

3. How many outcomes consist of one odd number and one even number (in either order)? 18

4. How many outcomes consist of numbers that total 7? 6

MIXED REVIEW

Perform the indicated operation.

1. $(6x^2 - 8x + 9) - (3x^2 + 5x - 7)$ $3x^2 - 13x + 16$

2. $-6rs^2(-8r^3s^3 + 4s^2t)$ $48r^4s^5 - 24rs^4t$

3. $\frac{9}{15} = \frac{y}{43}$ $25\frac{4}{5}$

4. 15% of 436   65.4

5. $\frac{10a^2b}{4ab} \cdot \frac{12a^3b}{6ab}$ $5a^3$

TEACHER'S RESOURCE MASTERS

Practice Master 57, Part 1

ASSIGNMENT GUIDE

Minimum
1–17 odd

Regular
9–18

Maximum
15–24

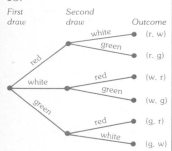
5. In how many outcomes does photo A occur? 3

6. In how many outcomes is the cover blue? 4

7. In how many outcomes would photo B or C be used? 6

8. How many outcomes include a blue cover or photo A? 6

B. Give the sample space for exercises 9–14 by making a list.

9. tossing two coins at the same time

10. dialing a one-digit phone number

11. selecting an even number from {1, 2, 3, 5, 7, 9, 12, 18}

12. selecting an odd number from {1, 2, 3, 5, 7, 9, 12, 18}

13. selecting two different symbols from {△, ○, *} (The order in which the symbols are picked does not matter.)

14. tossing three coins at the same time
HHH, HHT, HTH, THH, TTH, THT, HTT, TTT

Draw a tree diagram to show the sample space for exercises 15–16.

15. selecting two marbles from a bag that contains one red, one white, and one green marble (Do not replace the first marble.)

16. selecting two numbers from {1, 2, 3, 4} (The order of selection *does* matter. You may not use a number twice.)

Make a table to show the sample space for exercises 17–18.

17. a coin is tossed and a die is rolled

18. two four-sided dice are rolled

Use the number on the bottom as the outcome.

Use the fundamental counting principle to find the number of outcomes in the sample space for exercises 19–20.

19. the number of license plates that have two letters followed by two numbers (You *may* repeat letters and numbers used.) 67,600

20. the number of license plates that have two letters followed by two numbers (You may *not* repeat letters and numbers used.) 58,500

C. 21. Find the number of possible chairs that can be made if the manufacturer has six types of wood, four types of fabric, and four styles to choose from. 96

22. Find the number of possible seven-digit phone numbers if the first digit cannot be 0 or 1. 8,000,000

23. Three books are chosen from five books on a shelf. If the books are labeled A, B, C, D, and E, list the outcomes for the sample space. (The order of selection does *not* matter.)

24. A bag contains six table-tennis balls, numbered 1 through 6. Three balls are chosen. List the outcomes for the sample space. (The order of selection does *not* matter.)

Permutations and **combinations** are two more ways to count how many outcomes there are in a sample space.

OBJECTIVES

Find factorials.

Find a permutation of k objects chosen from a set of n objects.

Find a combination of k objects chosen from a set of n objects.

EXAMPLES

1   **In how many ways can Tom, Judy, Liz, Jenny, and Emilio be seated in a straight row of five chairs?**

SOLUTION

$$\underline{\quad 5 \quad} \quad \underline{\quad 4 \quad} \quad \underline{\quad 3 \quad} \quad \underline{\quad 2 \quad} \quad \underline{\quad 1 \quad} \qquad \text{\textit{number of people to choose from}}$$
$$\text{1st} \qquad \text{2nd} \qquad \text{3rd} \qquad \text{4th} \qquad \text{5th} \qquad \text{\textit{for each seat}}$$
$$\text{seat} \qquad \text{seat} \qquad \text{seat} \qquad \text{seat} \qquad \text{seat}$$

There are five people to choose from for the first seat. Since the same person can't sit in two seats, there are only four left to choose from for the second seat, and so on.
$$5 \cdot 4 \cdot 3 \cdot 2 \cdot 1 = 120$$
The five people can be seated in 120 ways.

Example 1 is a special case of the fundamental counting principle. Once an object has been used, it cannot be used again.

When you multiply numbers in the form $n \cdot (n - 1) \cdot (n - 2) \cdot \ldots \cdot 3 \cdot 2 \cdot 1$ (n consecutive numbers, ending with 1), you can use the symbol $n!$ (read **"n factorial"**).
So, $5! = 5 \cdot 4 \cdot 3 \cdot 2 \cdot 1 = 120$.

A *permutation* is an ordered arrangement of objects of a set. The object cannot be repeated. Example 1 is a permutation of all five objects of a set of five objects.

2   **How many three-letter "words," real or imaginary, can be made from the set {m, a, g, n, e, t}? A letter cannot be used twice.**

SOLUTION

$$\underline{\quad 6 \quad} \cdot \underline{\quad 5 \quad} \cdot \underline{\quad 4 \quad} = 120 \quad \text{\textit{a permutation of 3 objects chosen from a set of 6}}$$
$$\text{1st} \qquad \text{2nd} \qquad \text{3rd}$$
$$\text{letter} \qquad \text{letter} \qquad \text{letter}$$

There are 120 "words" that can be formed.

You can use factorial symbols for a permutation even when all n objects are not being arranged. A permutation of k objects from a set of n objects is
$$\underbrace{n \cdot (n - 1) \cdot (n - 2) \cdot \ldots \cdot (n - k + 1)}_{k \text{ factors}}.$$

This can be written as $\dfrac{n \cdot (n - 1) \cdot (n - 2) \cdot \ldots \cdot (n - k + 1) \cdot (n - k) \cdot \ldots \cdot 3 \cdot 2 \cdot 1}{(n - k) \cdot \ldots \cdot 3 \cdot 2 \cdot 1}$

$= \dfrac{n!}{(n - k)!}$ *a permutation of k objects chosen from a set of n objects*

TEACHER'S NOTES

See p. T39.

CLASSROOM EXAMPLES

1. In how many ways can six students arrange themselves in a straight row of six chairs?

$$\underline{6} \;\; \underline{5} \;\; \underline{4} \;\; \underline{3} \;\; \underline{2} \;\; \underline{1}$$
$$\text{1st} \;\; \text{2nd} \;\; \text{3rd} \;\; \text{4th} \;\; \text{5th} \;\; \text{6th}$$
$$\text{chair chair chair chair chair chair}$$

$6 \cdot 5 \cdot 4 \cdot 3 \cdot 2 \cdot 1 = 720$

The six students can arrange themselves in 720 ways.

2. How many three-letter "words," real or imaginary, can be made from the set {m, a, t, h}? A letter cannot be used twice.

$$\underline{\;4\;} \cdot \underline{\;3\;} \cdot \underline{\;2\;} = 24$$
$$\text{1st} \quad \text{2nd} \quad \text{3rd}$$
$$\text{letter} \quad \text{letter} \quad \text{letter}$$

There are 24 "words" that can be formed.

3. How many permutations are there if you have eight different magazines and want to arrange three of them for a display?

$\dfrac{n!}{(n - k)!}$

$= \dfrac{8!}{(8 - 3)!}$

$= \dfrac{8 \cdot 7 \cdot 6 \cdot 5 \cdot 4 \cdot 3 \cdot 2 \cdot 1}{5 \cdot 4 \cdot 3 \cdot 2 \cdot 1}$

$= 336$ permutations

4. Seven people were selected for a committee. In how many ways can a subcommittee of three be chosen from the committee?

$$\frac{7!}{3!(7-3)!}$$
$$= \frac{7!}{3!(4!)}$$
$$= \frac{7 \cdot 6 \cdot 5 \cdot 4 \cdot 3 \cdot 2 \cdot 1}{3 \cdot 2 \cdot 1 \cdot 4 \cdot 3 \cdot 2 \cdot 1}$$
$$= 35$$

There are 35 possible subcommittees of three people.

5. How many committees of five can be formed from five people?

$$\frac{5!}{5!(5-5)!} = \frac{5!}{5!(0!)}$$
$$= \frac{1}{0!}$$
$$= 1$$

Since there are five people available and all five must be chosen, there is only 1 committee possible.

MIXED REVIEW

1. Rewrite $0.0\overline{23}$ in fractional form. $\frac{23}{990}$

2. Solve. $3y + 8 + 2y = 19 - 5y$ $\frac{11}{10}$

3. Complete. $-|-37|$ -37

4. Evaluate $4^2(z^2)$ if $z = -3$. 144

5. Find $f(4)$ for $f(x) = \frac{1}{3}x - 8$. $-6\frac{2}{3}$

TEACHER'S RESOURCE MASTERS

Practice Master 57, Part 2

Quiz 27

---

3 **How many permutations are there if you have seven different books and want to arrange four of them for a display?**

SOLUTION
$$\frac{n!}{(n-k)!} = \frac{7!}{(7-4)!}$$
$$= \frac{7 \cdot 6 \cdot 5 \cdot 4 \cdot 3 \cdot 2 \cdot 1}{3 \cdot 2 \cdot 1}$$
$$= 840 \text{ permutations}$$

As with permutations, objects cannot be repeated when finding *combinations*. But with combinations, the order of arrangement does not matter, just which objects are chosen.

4 **A committee of two people is to be chosen from the following five people: Mary, Rafael, Karl, Elizabeth, and Matt. In how many ways can a committee of two be chosen?**

SOLUTION The order in which the two people are chosen to serve on a committee is not important. What is important is whether a person is chosen or not. So, "Mary, Rafael" is the same committee as "Rafael, Mary." The different committees are

Mary, Rafael   Mary, Karl   Mary, Elizabeth
Mary, Matt   Rafael, Karl   Rafael, Elizabeth
Rafael, Matt   Karl, Elizabeth   Karl, Matt
Elizabeth, Matt

There are 10 possible committees of two people.

Notice that this is
$$\frac{5!}{2!(5-2)!} = \frac{5!}{2!(3!)}$$
$$= \frac{5 \cdot 4 \cdot 3 \cdot 2 \cdot 1}{2 \cdot 1 \cdot 3 \cdot 2 \cdot 1}$$
$$= 10$$

A combination of k objects chosen from a set of n objects is $\frac{n!}{k!(n-k)!}$.

5 **How many committees of four can be formed from four people?**

SOLUTION The order in which one is chosen to serve on a committee does not matter. So this is a combination of four objects chosen from a set of four.

$$\frac{4!}{4!(4-4)!} = \frac{4!}{4!(0!)}$$
$$= \frac{1}{0!}$$
$$= ?$$

Since there are four people available and all four must be chosen, there is only 1 committee possible.

So, $\frac{1}{0!} = 1$.

$$1 = 1 \cdot 0!$$
$$0! = 1 \quad \textit{Zero factorial}$$

ASSIGNMENT GUIDE

Minimum
1–7 odd, 9–14

Regular
9–18

Maximum
13–22

ADDITIONAL ANSWERS

Written Exercises
10. 120

ORAL EXERCISES

Choose the correct answer.

1. In a permutation, the order in which the objects are chosen (<u>does</u>, does not) matter.

2. In a combination, the order in which the objects are chosen (does, <u>does not</u>) matter.

Evaluate.

3. $3!$ 6 | 4. $4!$ 24 | 5. $1!$ 1 | 6. $2!$ 2

7. $\frac{3!}{2!}$ 3 | 8. $\frac{7!}{4!}$ 210 | 9. $\frac{6!}{3!(3!)}$ 20 | 10. $\frac{8!}{5!(3!)}$ 56

WRITTEN EXERCISES

A. Evaluate.

   1. $0!$ 1   **2.** $6!$ 720   **3.** $7!$ 5040   **4.** $8!$ 40,320

   5. $\frac{9!}{5!}$ 3024   **6.** $\frac{10!}{3!}$ 604,800   **7.** $\frac{12!}{3!(9!)}$ 220   **8.** $\frac{11!}{5!(6!)}$ 462

   9. In how many ways can you arrange four books on a shelf? 24

   10. Liza wants to take three travel books with her when she goes on vacation. In how many ways can she do this if she has ten travel books to choose from?

B. 11. A play has been written that requires a cast of three men. Seven men try out for the three roles. How many different casts are possible? (The roles are Mr. Atkins, Tom, and Officer Flannigan.) 210

   12. Another play requires a cast of four women. How many casts are possible if ten women try out for the roles? (The roles are Susie, Miss Wellman, Mrs. Boyenga, and Dr. Justis.) 5040

   13. From a class of 25 students, three are to be chosen to serve on the Homecoming Committee. In how many ways can this be done? 2300

   14. How many four-letter words (real or imaginary) can be formed from the letters of the word *ANSWER*? 360

   15. In how many ways can you draw five cards from a standard deck of cards? (Order does not matter.) 2,598,960

   16. In how many ways can you draw two queens from a standard deck of cards? (Order does not matter.) 6

C. A bag contains 8 marbles: 2 red, 3 green, 1 white, and 2 yellow.

   17. In how many ways can you draw 2 marbles? 28

   18. In how many ways can you draw 2 green marbles? 3

   19. In how many ways can you draw 2 yellow marbles? 1

   20. In how many ways can you draw 1 red marble and 1 green marble? 6

   21. In how many ways can you draw 2 green marbles and 1 yellow marble? 6

   22. In how many ways can you draw 2 white marbles? 0

OBJECTIVE

Find the experimental probability of an event, and express
it as a fraction, a decimal, or
a percent.

CLASSROOM EXAMPLE

Suppose a coin is tossed 100
times. The results are
recorded in a table. What is
the ratio of the number of
heads to the total number of
outcomes?

Outcome   Frequency
heads   58
tails   42
total trials   100
The ratio is $\frac{58}{100}$, or $\frac{29}{50}$.

MIXED REVIEW

Compute.

1. 60% of what number is
   24? 40

2. $(-36 + 58) \div (0 \div 5)$
   undefined

3. Find the slope of the line
   containing the points
   $(9, -2)$ and $(6, -4)$. $\frac{2}{3}$

4. Multiply $(8x + 9)(3x - 4)$.
   $24x^2 - 5x - 36$

5. Simplify and use positive
   exponents. $\frac{5y^{-3}}{10y^{-8}}$ $\frac{y^5}{2}$

TEACHER'S RESOURCE
MASTERS

Practice Master 58, Part 1

14.3 | Experimental Probability

When you toss a coin, you expect about half of the outcomes to be heads and about half of the
outcomes to be tails. "Heads" and "tails" are **events**. An event is a subset of a sample space.
An event can be one outcome or can consist of more than one outcome of the sample space.

EXAMPLE

**Suppose a coin is tossed 120 times. The results are recorded in a table.
What is the ratio of the number of heads to the total number of outcomes?**

Outcome   Frequency
heads   72
tails   48
total trials   120

SOLUTION   The ratio is $\frac{72}{120}$, or $\frac{3}{5}$.

The ratio $\frac{3}{5}$ is called the **experimental probability** of the event "heads."

In an experiment with chance, the *experimental probability* of an event is $\frac{s}{n}$, where s is the
number of outcomes that make up the event and n is the total number of times that the experiment is performed.

The experimental probability of "heads," written $ex\ p$ (heads), can be expressed as $\frac{3}{5}$, 0.6,
or 60%.

ORAL EXERCISES

**A student tossed a die 50 times to obtain the table below. Find the experimental
probability of getting each result.**

Outcome	1	2	3	4	5	6
Frequency	5	7	12	10	7	9

1. 2 $\frac{7}{50}$ **2.** 5 $\frac{7}{50}$ **3.** 3 $\frac{6}{25}$ **4.** 6 $\frac{9}{50}$

5. 1 $\frac{1}{10}$ **6.** 4 $\frac{1}{5}$ **7.** 8 0   **8.** 0 0

9. an odd number $\frac{12}{25}$ **10.** a number less than 7 1

WRITTEN EXERCISES

**A. Turn to a page in a telephone book. Select at random 20 telephone numbers.
Record the last digit of each telephone number in a table that contains the digits
0 through 9.** Answers will vary.

1. Find $ex\ p$ (1).   **2.** Find $ex\ p$ (5).

3. Find $ex\ p$ (a digit greater than 5).   **4.** Find $ex\ p$ (a digit less than 4).

B. Toss a penny and a dime 40 times, recording the results in a table like the following: Answers will vary.

Outcome		Frequency
(penny)	(dime)	
H	H	
H	T	
T	H	
T	T	

5. What is *ex p* (two heads)?

6. What is *ex p* (one head, one tail)?

7. Would you expect two heads to occur the same number of times as one head and one tail? Why or why not?

8. What is *ex p* (two tails)?

9. Is it possible for two tails to occur all 40 times? Does it seem likely to happen?

10. Find *ex p* (two heads) + *ex p* (two tails).

C. A letter of the alphabet will occur with about the same frequency in different samples of writing if the samples are large. For exercises 11–12, choose a page of a newspaper, a magazine, or a book. Begin with any paragraph and count a sample of 500 letters. Answers will vary.

11. The letter *e* usually occurs with the greatest frequency, with *e*'s making up about $13\frac{1}{2}\%$ of all the letters in a writing sample. Count the number of *e*'s in your sample. What percent of the 500 letters do *e*'s make up?

12. Usually, about 9% of the letters in a writing sample are *t*'s. Count the number of *t*'s in your sample. What percent of the 500 letters do *t*'s make up?

ASSIGNMENT GUIDE

Minimum
1–8

Regular
3–10

Maximum
5–12

SELF-QUIZ

1. List the sample space for selecting two numbers from {1, 2, 3, 8, 9}. (The order of selection does not matter.)

2. Find the number of possible license plates that have two letters followed by four numbers. (You may repeat letters and numbers.) 6,760,000

Evaluate.

3. 3! 6

4. $\frac{5!}{2!}$ 60

5. 0! 1

6. In how many ways can four people be arranged in a straight row for a photograph? 24

7. In how many ways can a committee of three be chosen from 7 people? 35

8. A coin was tossed 50 times. The coin landed tails 28 times. What is *ex p* (T)? $\frac{14}{25}$

OBJECTIVES

Find the theoretical probability of an event.

Find the probability of an
event certain to happen or
certain not to happen.

Find the probability of the
complement of an event.

Make predictions, using
probability.

TEACHER'S NOTES

See p. T39.

CLASSROOM EXAMPLES

1. One die is rolled. What is
   p (an odd number)?

   Three outcomes are odd
   numbers.

   p (an odd number) $= \frac{3}{6}$
   $= \frac{1}{2}$

2. Two dice are rolled. What
   is the probability that the
   sum of the number of dots
   on the dice is 7?

   There are $6 \cdot 6 = 36$ total
   outcomes. If the ordered
   pairs are listed as (first die,
   second die), the ways to
   get a sum of 7 are (1, 6),
   (2, 5), (3, 4), (4, 3), (5, 2),
   (6, 1).

   p (a sum of 7) $= \frac{6}{36} = \frac{1}{6}$

3. Two coins are tossed.
   What is the probability that
   the outcome will be two
   heads?

   There are $2 \cdot 2 = 4$ possible outcomes. {HH, HT,
   TH, TT}

   p (HH) $= \frac{1}{4}$

14.4 | Theoretical Probability

Suppose you are playing a board game in which you roll a die to see how many spaces you can move. It is your turn to roll the die. If you roll a three, you will win the game. What is the probability of rolling a three?

When you find the probability of an event *before* an experiment is performed, you are finding the **theoretical probability** (or mathematical probability).

Suppose a sample space consists of n **equally likely outcomes;** that is, each outcome has the same probability of occurring. Then the probability of event A is the ratio of the number of outcomes that make up event A to the total number of outcomes.

$$p(A) = \frac{s}{n}$$

So, the probability of rolling a three is $\frac{1}{6}$.

Hereafter, the word *probability* will be understood to be theoretical probability (unless stated otherwise).

EXAMPLES

1 **One die is rolled. What is p (an even number)?**

SOLUTION Three outcomes are even numbers.

$$p \text{ (an even number)} = \frac{3}{6} = \frac{1}{2}$$

2 **Two dice are rolled. What is the probability that the sum of the number of dots on the dice is 5?**

SOLUTION There are $6 \cdot 6 = 36$ total outcomes. (See the table on page 466.) If the ordered pairs are listed as (first die, second die), the ways to get a sum of 5 are (1, 4), (2, 3), (3, 2), (4, 1).

$$p \text{ (a sum of 5)} = \frac{4}{36} = \frac{1}{9}$$

3 **Two coins are tossed. What is the probability that the outcome will be two tails?**

SOLUTION There are $2 \cdot 2 = 4$ possible outcomes. {HH, HT, TH, TT}

$$p \text{ (TT)} = \frac{1}{4}$$

4 **One card is drawn at random from a well-shuffled standard deck of cards. What is the probability of drawing a heart?**

SOLUTION $p \text{ (a heart)} = \frac{13}{52} = \frac{1}{4}$

The probability of an event that is certain to happen is 1.

| 5 | **A die is rolled. What is the probability that the outcome will be a number greater than 0?** |

SOLUTION

p (a number greater than 0) $= \frac{6}{6} = 1$

The probability of an event that is certain *not* to happen is 0.

| 6 | **A die is rolled. What is the probability of rolling a 7?** |

SOLUTION

$p(7) = \frac{0}{6} = 0$

The event {not a 3} is the **complement** of the event {3}.

| 7 | **What is the probability of *not* rolling a 3 when a die is rolled?** |

SOLUTION

p (not a 3) $= \frac{5}{6}$

Notice that this is $1 - p(3)$.

The symbol for the complement of an event is A'. So, $p(A') = 1 - p(A)$.

| 8 | **One card is drawn from a standard deck of cards. What is the probability that it is a queen *and* a red card?** |

SOLUTION

p (a queen and a red card) $= \frac{2}{52} = \frac{1}{26}$ *There are 2 red queens.*

| 9 | **A box contains 6 red marbles and 2 white marbles, all the same size. One marble is taken from the box, then another marble is taken without replacing the first. What is the probability that both marbles are red?** |

SOLUTION

Since the marbles are drawn without replacement (no repetition) and the order in which the red marbles are drawn doesn't matter, you can use combinations to solve this problem.

p (2 red marbles) $= \dfrac{\frac{6!}{2!(4!)}}{\frac{8!}{2!(6!)}}$ *number of ways you can draw 2 of the 6 red marbles*
number of ways you can draw 2 of the 8 marbles

$= \dfrac{\frac{6 \cdot 5}{2}}{\frac{8 \cdot 7}{2}}$

$= \dfrac{15}{28}$

4. One card is drawn at random from a well-shuffled standard deck of cards. What is the probability of drawing a club?
   p (a club) $= \frac{13}{52} = \frac{1}{4}$

5. A die is rolled. What is the probability that the outcome will be a number greater than 4?
   p (a number greater than 4) $= \frac{2}{6} = \frac{1}{3}$

6. A die is rolled. What is the probability of rolling a ten?
   $p(10) = \frac{0}{6} = 0$

7. What is the probability of *not* rolling a 5 when a die is rolled?
   p (not a 5) $= \frac{5}{6}$

8. One card is drawn from a standard deck of cards. What is the probability that it is a king *and* a red card?
   p (a king and a red card) $= \frac{2}{52} = \frac{1}{26}$

9. A can contains 5 blue marbles and 3 yellow marbles, all the same size. One marble is taken from the can, then another marble is taken without replacing the first. What is the probability that both marbles are blue?
   p (2 blue marbles)
   $= \dfrac{\frac{5!}{2!(3!)}}{\frac{8!}{2!(6!)}}$
   $= \dfrac{\frac{5 \cdot 4}{2}}{\frac{8 \cdot 7}{2}}$
   $= \dfrac{5}{14}$

10. A die is to be rolled 852 times. Predict how many times a 5 should occur.
$p(5) = \frac{1}{6}$
So $\frac{1}{6}$ of the rolls should result in a 5.
$\frac{1}{6} \cdot 852 = 142$
A 5 should occur 142 times.

MIXED REVIEW

1. Solve the system of equations.
$4x + 8y = 32$
$-2x + 6y = 14$ (2, 3)

2. Factor $x^2 - 7x - 18$.
$(x + 2)(x - 9)$

3. Simplify $\sqrt{24} \cdot \sqrt{6}$.   12

4. Solve $x^2 - x = 12$.   4, -3

5. Simplify $(5\sqrt{6})(4\sqrt{3})$.
$60\sqrt{2}$

TEACHER'S RESOURCE MASTERS

Practice Master 58, Part 2

ASSIGNMENT GUIDE

Minimum
7–19 odd, 21–24

Regular
18–28

Maximum
22–32

ADDITIONAL ANSWERS

Oral Exercises

4. {a card other than a diamond is drawn}

You can use probability to make **predictions**.

| 10 | **A die is to be rolled 624 times. Predict how many times a 3 should occur.** |

SOLUTION $p(3) = \frac{1}{6}$

So $\frac{1}{6}$ of the rolls should result in a 3.

$\frac{1}{6} \cdot 624 = 104$

A 3 should occur 104 times.

ORAL EXERCISES

1. If there are 12 possible outcomes and event A can happen in 3 ways, what is $p(A)$? $\frac{1}{4}$

2. What is the probability of an event that is certain to happen? 1

3. What is the probability of an event that is certain not to happen? 0

4. If event A is {a diamond is drawn}, what is the complementary event?

5. If $p(A) = \frac{2}{9}$, what is $p(A')$? $\frac{7}{9}$

6. A coin is to be tossed 800 times. Predict how many times a head should occur.

WRITTEN EXERCISES

A. Refer to the table on page 466 for exercises 1–6. Find each probability.

1. rolling a sum of 2 $\frac{1}{36}$

2. rolling a sum of 7 $\frac{1}{6}$

3. rolling a sum of 11 $\frac{1}{18}$

4. rolling a sum that is less than 9 $\frac{13}{18}$

5. rolling a sum that is greater than 2 $\frac{35}{36}$

6. rolling a sum that is less than 13 and greater than 5 $\frac{13}{18}$

B.
7. The probability of Tom being selected for the team is 0.8. What is the probability that Tom will not be selected?

8. There is a 30% probability of rain today. What is the probability that it won't rain today? 70%

9. A box contains 92 good light bulbs and 8 defective light bulbs. One bulb is chosen at random from the box. What is the probability that the light bulb is defective? $\frac{2}{25}$

10. A box contains eight 60-watt light bulbs, ten 75-watt light bulbs, and thirty-two 100-watt light bulbs. One bulb is chosen at random. What is the probability that it is not a 100-watt bulb? $\frac{9}{25}$

One card is drawn at random from a standard deck. What is the probability that it is

11. an ace? $\frac{1}{13}$

12. a three and a black card? $\frac{1}{26}$

13. a club? $\frac{1}{4}$

14. a red card? $\frac{1}{2}$

The possible outcomes for the sexes of children in a three-child family (where B stands for boy and G stands for girl) are {BBB, BBG, BGB, GBB, BGG, GBG, GGB, GGG}. Find the probability that

6. 400

Written Exercises

7. 0.2

32. $\frac{3}{5}$

15. the first child is a girl. $\frac{1}{2}$

16. there are exactly two boys. $\frac{3}{8}$

17. there is at least one girl. $\frac{7}{8}$

18. the children are all girls or all boys. $\frac{1}{4}$

19. the last two children are boys. $\frac{1}{4}$

20. there are at least two girls. $\frac{1}{2}$

21. A die is to be tossed 300 times. Predict how many times a number less than 5 should occur. 200 times

22. A die is to be tossed 450 times. Predict how many times an odd number should occur. 225 times

23. There are 20 true-false questions on a test. If you guess at every answer, how many questions should you answer correctly? 10

24. There are 30 multiple-choice questions on a test, with 3 choices for each question. If you guess at every answer, how many questions should you answer correctly? 10

C. 25. A coin is tossed 5 times. What is the probability of getting 5 tails? $\frac{1}{32}$

26. Two cards are drawn at the same time from a standard deck. What is the probability that both are aces? $\frac{1}{221}$

27. Three cards are drawn at the same time from a standard deck. What is the probability that all three are black cards? $\frac{2}{17}$

28. A box of 100 light bulbs contains 5 light bulbs that are defective. If a person randomly inspects three of the light bulbs, what is the probability that all three are good? $\frac{27683}{32340}$

***Odds* are defined in probability as the following ratio:**

$$\frac{\text{probability that the event will occur}}{\text{probability that the event will not occur}}$$

Example: The probability that Tim will win the race is $\frac{1}{10}$. Find the odds in favor of Tim's winning the race.

Solution:

$$\text{odds} = \frac{\frac{1}{10}}{1 - \frac{1}{10}}$$

$$= \frac{\frac{1}{10}}{\frac{9}{10}}$$

$$= \frac{1}{9}$$

$\frac{1}{9}$ can also be written as *1:9* or *1 to 9*.

29. Find the odds in favor of rolling a 6 on a die. $\frac{1}{5}$

30. Find the odds in favor of rolling an even number on a die. $\frac{1}{1}$

31. Find the odds in favor of *not* rolling a 6 on a die. $\frac{5}{1}$

32. Find the probability of winning a race if the odds in favor of winning are 3 to 2.

ALGEBRA IN USE

In many businesses or industries, sales or production can vary by a great amount. People in these fields can use an **expected value** to make decisions that are based on probabilities. An expected value is a type of average that is based on certain outcomes and the probabilities that these outcomes will occur.

Example: A ski-resort manager knows from past experience that if the winter season is good, she can make a profit of $500,000. If the winter season is bad, however, she can lose $75,000. There is a 65% chance that the winter season will be good this year. What is the ski-resort manager's expected profit?

Solution: Let E represent the expected profit.

$$E = \left(\begin{array}{c}\text{expected profit}\\\text{for a good}\\\text{season}\end{array}\right) \cdot \left(\begin{array}{c}\text{probability}\\\text{of a good}\\\text{season}\end{array}\right) + \left(\begin{array}{c}\text{expected profit}\\\text{for a bad}\\\text{season}\end{array}\right) \cdot \left(\begin{array}{c}\text{probability}\\\text{of a bad}\\\text{season}\end{array}\right)$$

$= \$500,000(0.65) + (-\$75,000)(0.35)$ *Change the percent to a decimal.*

$= \$325,000 + (-\$26,250)$ *p (bad season) = 1 − p (good season).*

$= \$298,750$ *The $75,000 is negative because it is a loss.*

EXERCISES

1. The profits for an outdoor peanut vendor can depend on the weather. On a sunny day, the vendor's profits are usually $75. On a cloudy day, the profits are usually $30. One morning, the weather forecaster predicted a 70% chance of a sunny day. What are the expected profits of the day? $61.50

2. A construction company can show a $120,000 profit after a good year or a $50,000 loss after a bad year. The chance of a good year is 80% for the next year. Find the construction company's expected profits for the next year.

ALGEBRA IN USE

Exercises

2. $86,000

14.5 | Addition of Probabilities

One way to find the probability of event A *or* event B happening is to look at a sample space.

EXAMPLES

1 A paper bag contains 8 red, 3 yellow, 4 orange, and 5 green marbles, all the same size and weight. One marble is drawn at random. What is the probability of drawing a red or an orange marble?

SOLUTION There are 12 marbles that are either red or orange.

$$p \text{ (a red or an orange marble)} = \frac{12}{20} = \frac{3}{5}$$

Notice in Example 1 that the probability of a red or an orange marble is equal to p (a red marble) + p (an orange marble). This is because the two events, $A = $ {a red marble} and $B = $ {an orange marble}, are **mutually exclusive events.** Two events are mutually exclusive if they have no element in common. That is, $A \cap B = \varnothing$. So for mutually exclusive events, you can use the following rule to find the probability of A or B:

Addition Rule for "A or B," A and B Mutually Exclusive	Given any two mutually exclusive events, **A** and **B**, $p\,(A \cup B) = p\,(A) + p\,(B).$

This rule can be extended to more than two events.

2 One card is drawn from a standard deck. What is the probability that the card is an ace or a two?

SOLUTION $p \text{ (an ace or a two)} = \frac{4}{52} + \frac{4}{52} = \frac{8}{52} = \frac{2}{13}$

3 Two dice are rolled. What is the probability of rolling a sum of 3 or 4?

SOLUTION $p \text{ (a sum of 3 or 4)} = \frac{2}{36} + \frac{3}{36} = \frac{5}{36}$

4 A die is rolled. What is the probability of an odd or an even number?

SOLUTION $p \text{ (an odd or an even)} = \frac{1}{2} + \frac{1}{2} = 1$

You can use the following formula to find the probability of A or B when A and B are not mutually exclusive (A and B do have at least one element in common):

Addition Rule for Events Not Mutually Exclusive	$p\,(A \cup B) = p\,(A) + p\,(B) - p\,(A \cap B)$

OBJECTIVE

Find the probability of "A or B" for A and B mutually exclusive and not mutually exclusive.

TEACHER'S NOTES

See p. T39.

CLASSROOM EXAMPLES

1. A can contains 4 orange, 3 green, 8 blue, and 5 yellow marbles, all the same size and weight. One marble is drawn at random. What is the probability of drawing a green or a blue marble?

   There are 11 marbles that are either green or blue.

   p (a green or a blue marble) $= \frac{11}{20}$

2. One card is drawn from a standard deck. What is the probability that the card is a king or an eight?

   p (a king or an eight) $= \frac{4}{52}$ $+ \frac{4}{52} = \frac{8}{52} = \frac{2}{13}$

3. Two dice are rolled. What is the probability of rolling a sum of 4 or 5?

   p (a sum of 4 or 5) $= \frac{3}{36}$ $+ \frac{4}{36} = \frac{7}{36}$

4. A coin is tossed. What is the probability of a head or a tail?

   p (a head or a tail) $= \frac{1}{2}$ $+ \frac{1}{2} = 1$

5. A card is picked at random from a standard deck. What is the probability that it is a seven or a club?

p (a seven or a club) $= \frac{4}{52} + \frac{13}{52} - \frac{1}{52} = \frac{4}{13}$

MIXED REVIEW

1. Simplify $\sqrt{30} \cdot \sqrt{9}$. $3\sqrt{30}$

2. Simplify $\frac{x-9}{x^2-81}$. $\frac{1}{x+9}$

3. Divide $\frac{32x^2y}{5xy} \div \frac{16x^3y^2}{20xy}$. $\frac{8}{xy}$

4. Find the y-intercept of the line for $y = \frac{4}{5}x - 7$. -7

5. Write $y = 5x - 8$ in standard form. $5x - y = 8$

TEACHER'S RESOURCE MASTERS

Practice Master 59, Part 1

ASSIGNMENT GUIDE

Minimum
1–5 odd, 7–14

Regular
9–19

Maximum
12–22

ADDITIONAL ANSWERS

Oral Exercises

8. no

Written Exercises

2. $\frac{2}{3}$

| 5 | A card is picked at random from a standard deck. What is the probability that it is an ace or a heart? |

SOLUTION p (an ace or a heart) $= \frac{4}{52} + \frac{13}{52} - \frac{1}{52} = \frac{4}{13}$

p (an ace) p (a heart) p (the ace of hearts)

ORAL EXERCISES

Two coins are tossed. The sample space is {HH, HT, TH, TT}.

$A = \{$**first coin is H**$\}$ $B = \{$**second coin is H**$\}$

1. What is p (A)? $\frac{1}{2}$

2. What is p (B)? $\frac{1}{2}$

3. What is p (A ∩ B)? $\frac{1}{4}$

4. What is p (A ∪ B)? $\frac{3}{4}$

Tell if each two events are mutually exclusive or not.

5. The first coin shows heads and the second coin shows tails.   no

6. A sum of the dots on two dice is six or eight.   yes

7. A card drawn is a seven or a queen.   yes

8. A card drawn is a king or a diamond.

9. A die shows a three or a four.   yes

10. A die shows an even number or a number less than three.   no

WRITTEN EXERCISES

A. A die is rolled. Find each probability.

1. The die shows a three or a five. $\frac{1}{3}$

2. The die shows a four or an odd number.

3. The die shows a six or a number less than three. $\frac{1}{2}$

4. The die shows a four or an even number. $\frac{1}{2}$

A marble is drawn at random from a bag containing 3 red, 4 yellow, and 2 green marbles.

5. What is the probability that the marble is red or yellow? $\frac{7}{9}$

6. What is the probability that the marble is yellow or green? $\frac{2}{3}$

B. Two dice are rolled. Consider the following five events:

$A = \{$**the sum is 2**$\}$ $B = \{$**the first die shows a 1**$\}$

$C = \{$**the sum is 10**$\}$ $D = \{$**the second die shows a 4**$\}$

$E = \{$**the same number shows on both dice**$\}$

Find each probability. Refer to the 36 outcomes on page 466.

7. p (A ∪ E) $\frac{1}{6}$

8. p (B ∪ C) $\frac{1}{4}$

9. p (A ∪ C) $\frac{1}{9}$

10. $p(D \cup E)$ $\frac{11}{36}$ **11.** $p(C \cup E)$ $\frac{2}{9}$ **12.** $p(A \cup D)$ $\frac{7}{36}$

13. In a three-child family, what is the probability that there are exactly 2 boys or exactly 2 girls? $\frac{3}{4}$

14. A team has a probability of 0.6 of winning the game and a probability of 0.3 of losing the game. What is the team's probability of a tie?   0.1

15. A coin is tossed twice. What is the probability that heads will appear at least once? $\frac{3}{4}$

16. A class of 25 students has 12 females and 13 males. Eight of the females are in the band and 5 of the males are in the band. If a student is chosen at random, what is the probability that the student is in the band or is a male? $\frac{21}{25}$

C. 17. In a class of 30 students, 16 are females and 14 are males. Ten of the females are in the chorus and 5 of the males are in the chorus. If a student is picked at random, what is the probability that the student is female or is not in the chorus? $\frac{5}{6}$

18. In a class of 31 students, eight are studying Spanish. Twenty-two students are studying French. Of the twenty-two students, seventeen are also studying math. One of the students studying Spanish is also studying math. If a student is chosen at random, what is the probability that he or she is studying French or Spanish, but not math? $\frac{12}{31}$

One card is drawn from a standard deck. Find the probability that it is

19. an ace or a red card. $\frac{7}{13}$

20. a number less than 4 or a black card. (Do not count the ace as a number less than 4.) $\frac{15}{26}$

21. a red card or a king, a queen, or a jack. $\frac{8}{13}$

22. a black card or an ace, a two, a three, or a four. $\frac{17}{26}$

CHALLENGE

Careless Carl wrote out checks to pay 4 bills, but he put some of the checks in the wrong preaddressed envelopes. Did he put exactly 3 of them in the right envelopes, put exactly 2 of them in the right envelopes, or put exactly 1 of them in the wrong envelope?

Actuaries design insurance plans. For life insurance, actuaries gather statistics into a Mortality Table. Then, using this table, they calculate the probability of death at any given age. This information is a major factor in determining premiums for life insurance.

CAREER
Actuary

Commissioners 1980 Standard Ordinary Mortality Table

	MALE		FEMALE			MALE		FEMALE	
Age	Deaths per 1000	Expectation of Life (Years)	Deaths per 1000	Expectation of Life (Years)	Age	Deaths per 1000	Expectation of Life (Years)	Deaths per 1000	Expectation of Life (Years)
0	4.18	70.83	2.89	75.83	50	6.71	25.36,	4.96	29.53
1	1.07	70.13	.87	75.04	51	7.30	24.52	5.31	28.67
2	.99	69.20	.81	74.11	52	7.96	23.70	5.70	27.82
3	.98	68.27	.79	73.17	53	8.71	22.89	6.15	26.98
4	.95	67.34	.77	72.23	54	9.56	22.08	6.61	26.14
5	.90	66.40	.76	71.28	55	10.47	21.29	7.09	25.31
6	.86	65.46	.73	70.34	56	11.46	20.51	7.57	24.49
7	.80	64.52	.72	69.39	57	12.49	19.74	8.03	23.67
8	.76	63.57	.70	68.44	58	13.59	18.99	8.47	22.86
9	.74	62.62	.69	67.48	59	14.77	18.24	8.94	22.05
10	.73	61.66	.68	66.53	60	16.08	17.51	9.47	21.25
11	.77	60.71	.69	65.58	61	17.54	16.79	10.13	20.44
12	.85	59.75	.72	64.62	62	19.19	16.08	10.96	19.65
13	.99	58.80	.75	63.67	63	21.06	15.38	12.02	18.86
14	1.15	57.86	.80	62.71	64	23.14	14.70	13.25	18.08
15	1.33	56.93	.85	61.76	65	25.42	14.04	14.59	17.32
16	1.51	56.00	.90	60.82	66	27.85	13.39	16.00	16.57
17	1.67	55.09	.95	59.87	67	30.44	12.76	17.43	15.83
18	1.78	54.18	.98	58.93	68	33.19	12.14	18.84	15.10
19	1.86	53.27	1.02	57.98	69	36.17	11.54	20.36	14.38
20	1.90	52.37	1.05	57.04	70	39.51	10.96	22.11	13.67
21	1.91	51.47	1.07	56.10	71	43.30	10.39	24.23	12.97
22	1.89	50.57	1.09	55.16	72	47.65	9.84	26.87	12.28
23	1.86	49.66	1.11	54.22	73	52.64	9.30	30.11	11.60
24	1.82	48.75	1.14	53.28	74	58.19	8.79	33.93	10.95
25	1.77	47.84	1.16	52.34	75	64.19	8.31	38.24	10.32
26	1.73	46.93	1.19	51.40	76	70.53	7.84	42.97	9.71
27	1.71	46.01	1.22	50.46	77	77.12	7.40	48.04	9.12
28	1.70	45.09	1.26	49.52	78	83.90	6.97	53.45	8.55
29	1.71	44.16	1.30	48.59	79	91.05	6.57	59.35	8.01
30	1.73	43.24	1.35	47.65	80	98.84	6.18	65.99	7.48
31	1.78	42.31	1.40	46.71	81	107.48	5.80	73.60	6.98
32	1.83	41.38	1.45	45.78	82	117.25	5.44	82.40	6.49
33	1.91	40.46	1.50	44.84	83	128.26	5.09	92.53	6.03
34	2.00	39.54	1.58	43.91	84	140.25	4.77	103.81	5.59
35	2.11	38.61	1.65	42.98	85	152.95	4.46	116.10	5.18
36	2.24	37.69	1.76	42.05	86	166.09	4.18	129.29	4.80
37	2.40	36.78	1.89	41.12	87	179.55	3.91	143.32	4.43
38	2.58	35.87	2.04	40.20	88	193.27	3.66	158.18	4.09
39	2.79	34.96	2.22	39.28	89	207.29	3.41	173.94	3.77
40	3.02	34.05	2.42	38.36	90	221.77	3.18	190.75	3.45
41	3.29	33.16	2.64	37.46	91	236.98	2.94	208.87	3.15
42	3.56	32.26	2.87	36.55	92	253.45	2.70	228.81	2.85
43	3.87	31.38	3.09	35.66	93	272.11	2.44	251.51	2.55
44	4.19	30.50	3.32	34.77	94	295.90	2.17	279.31	2.24
45	4.55	29.62	3.56	33.88	95	329.96	1.87	317.32	1.91
46	4.92	28.76	3.80	33.00	96	384.55	1.54	375.74	1.56
47	5.32	27.90	4.05	32.12	97	480.20	1.20	474.97	1.21
48	5.74	27.04	4.33	31.25	98	657.98	.84	655.85	.84
49	6.21	26.20	4.63	30.39	99	1,000.00	.50	1,000.00	.50

1. At what age is a male's probability of death at least 1%?
2. At what age is a female's probability of death at least 1%?

CAREER

14.6 | Multiplication of Probabilities

OBJECTIVE

Find the probability of successive events, for A and B independent events or dependent events.

When one event is followed by a successive event, you multiply to find the probability that *both* events will happen. But first you need to know if the events are **independent events** or **dependent events**.

When two events are *independent*, the probability of one event's happening has no influence on the probability of the other event's happening. The events {a coin shows heads} and {a die shows a 1} are independent events.

TEACHER'S NOTES

See p. T39.

Multiplication Rule	**If A and B are successive, independent events,** $p(A \cap B) = p(A) \cdot p(B)$.

EXAMPLES

1 **You toss a coin and roll a die. What is the probability that the coin shows tails and the die shows a number less than 3?**

SOLUTION Let $A = \{$coin shows tails$\}$, $B = \{$die shows a number less than 3$\}$.

Then $p(A \cap B) = p(A) \cdot p(B)$
$$= \frac{1}{2} \cdot \frac{1}{3}$$
$$= \frac{1}{6}$$

2 **You draw one card from a standard deck of cards, replace the card, then draw another card. What is the probability that each card drawn is a diamond?**

SOLUTION $A = \{$first card is a diamond$\}$ $B = \{$second card is a diamond$\}$

$p(A \cap B) = \dfrac{13}{52} \cdot \dfrac{13}{52}$
$$= \frac{1}{16}$$

If two successive events are not independent, they are *dependent*. That is, the probability of the second event depends on the probability of the first event. You still multiply to find the probability that both events will happen.

3 **You draw one card from a standard deck of cards, then draw another card *without replacing* the first card drawn. What is the probability that each card drawn is a diamond?**

SOLUTION $A = \{$first card is a diamond$\}$ $B = \{$second card is a diamond$\}$

$p(A \cap B) = \dfrac{13}{52} \cdot \dfrac{12}{51}$ *only 12 diamonds left*
                                  only 51 cards left
$$= \frac{1}{17}$$

CLASSROOM EXAMPLES

1. You toss a coin and roll a die. What is the probability that the coin shows heads and the die shows a number greater than 4?

   Let $A = \{$coin shows heads$\}$, $B = \{$die shows a number greater than 4$\}$.

   Then $p(AB) = p(A) \cdot p(B)$
   $= \frac{1}{2} \cdot \frac{1}{3}$
   $= \frac{1}{6}$

2. You draw one card from a standard deck of cards, replace the card, then draw another card. What is the probability that each card drawn is a heart?

   $A = \{$first card is a heart$\}$
   $B = \{$second card is a heart$\}$
   $p(AB) = \frac{13}{52} \cdot \frac{13}{52}$
   $= \frac{1}{16}$

3. You draw one card from a standard deck of cards, then draw another card *without replacing* the first card drawn. What is the probability that each card drawn is a heart?

(continued on next page)

ORAL EXERCISES

Describe each of the two successive events as independent or dependent.

1. picking a card that is red and then picking a card that is a 2

2. picking a black card and then picking a card that is a 3

3. rolling an even number on a die and then a number less than 4

4. rolling an odd number on a die and then a number less than 7

WRITTEN EXERCISES

A. Use the drawing below to answer exercises 1–8. A marble is picked at random, it is replaced, and a second marble is picked. Find the probability that

1. the first is a 5 and the second is a 1. $\frac{1}{100}$

2. both are white. $\frac{9}{25}$

3. the first is white and the second is an 8. $\frac{3}{50}$

4. the first is a 4 and the second is a 4. $\frac{1}{100}$

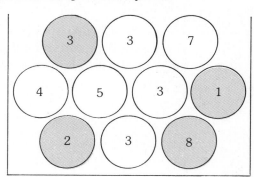

B. A marble is picked at random. A second marble is picked without replacing the first. Find the probability that

5. the first is a 5 and the second is a 1. $\frac{1}{90}$

6. both are white. $\frac{1}{3}$

7. the first is white and the second is an 8. $\frac{1}{15}$

8. the first is a 4 and the second is a 4.   0

A red die and a green die are rolled. Find the probability that

9. the red die shows a 1 and the green die shows a 6. $\frac{1}{36}$

10. the green die shows a number less than 4 and the red die shows an odd number.

11. the green die shows an even number and the red die shows a number greater than 4. $\frac{1}{6}$

12. both show a 5. $\frac{1}{36}$

C. You pick a card from a standard deck, then pick another card without replacing the first. Find the probability that

13. each card is red. $\frac{25}{102}$

14. each card is a 9. $\frac{1}{221}$

15. the first card is an ace and the second card is a king. $\frac{4}{663}$

16. the first card is a red ace and the second card is a club. $\frac{1}{102}$

EXPLORATION
Conditional Probability

In **conditional probability,** you are to find the probability of an event, *given* that another event has already happened.

Example: A new family has moved into your neighborhood. The family has three children. Find the probability that the family has exactly two girls if you know that the oldest child is a girl.

Solution:

Let A = {oldest child of the three children is a girl}.

Let B = {exactly two of the three children are girls}.

The conditional probability is written as $p(B|A)$ and is read as "the probability of event B, *given that* event A has happened."

Event A changes the original sample space by eliminating some of the original outcomes.

Sample space for a three-child family:

BBB	BBG	BGB	GBB
GGB	GBG	BGG	GGG

You are given that event A has happened. So the sample space is reduced to only those outcomes where the first child is a girl:

GBB	GGB	GBG	GGG

Now find the probability of event B.

p {exactly two of the three children are girls} $= \dfrac{2}{4} = \dfrac{1}{2}$

EXERCISES

Find each conditional probability. Use the sample space for the three-child family.

1. at least two boys, given that the youngest is a boy $\frac{3}{4}$

2. at most one boy, given that the middle child is a girl $\frac{3}{4}$

3. exactly one girl, given that the middle child is a girl $\frac{1}{4}$

4. all girls, given that there are at least two girls $\frac{1}{4}$

5. all girls, given that there is at least one girl $\frac{1}{7}$

6. all boys, given that there is at least one girl 0

Solve.

1. $12x - 3 = 7x + 12$ 3

2. $3(2m - 9) = 2(5m - 17)$ $1\frac{3}{4}$

3. $3y - 5 \le 2y + 8$ $y \le 13$

4. $3t + 6 > 7t - 6$ $t < 3$

5. $|r - 3| \ge 8$ $r \ge 11$ or $r \le -5$

6. $|2y + 1| < 5$ $-3 < y < 2$

Factor.

7. $x^2 + 5x - 14$ $(x - 2)(x + 7)$

8. $y^2 + 10y + 24$ $(y + 4)(y + 6)$

9. $2v^2 + 5v - 3$ $(2v - 1)(v + 3)$

10. $6w^2 + w - 2$ $(3w + 2)(2w - 1)$

Solve.

11. $x^2 - x - 12 = 0$ $4, -3$

12. $6y^2 - 11y + 3 = 0$ $\frac{1}{3}, 1\frac{1}{2}$

13. $3v^2 - 7v + 4 = 0$ $1, 1\frac{1}{3}$

14. $q^2 - 11q + 28 = 0$ $4, 7$

Solve each system of equations.

15. $2x + 4y = 16$
$-x + 3y = 7$ $(2, 3)$

16. $2x + 3y = 15$
$3x + 2y = 5$ $(-3, 7)$

17. $2x - 3y = 23$
$5x + 2y = 10$ $(4, -5)$

18. $-2x + y = 0$
$3x - 2y = 3$ $(-3, -6)$

Perform the indicated operation.

19. $\dfrac{3x + 1}{x + 2} + \dfrac{4}{x - 1}$ $\dfrac{3x^2 + 2x + 7}{(x + 2)(x - 1)}$

20. $\dfrac{-1}{x + 4} + \dfrac{1}{x - 5}$ $\dfrac{9}{(x + 4)(x - 5)}$

21. $\dfrac{5}{y + 2} - \dfrac{3}{y + 5}$ $\dfrac{2y + 19}{(y + 2)(y + 5)}$

22. $\dfrac{2m - 1}{m + 2} - \dfrac{m + 7}{m - 2}$ $\dfrac{m^2 - 14m - 12}{(m + 2)(m - 2)}$

23. $\dfrac{3w + 9}{w - 2} \cdot \dfrac{5}{w + 3}$ $\dfrac{15}{w - 2}$

24. $\dfrac{2t^2 + 3t + 1}{t^2 + 5t + 4} \cdot \dfrac{2t^2 + 11t + 12}{2t^2 - 5t - 3}$ $\dfrac{2t + 3}{t - 3}$

25. $\dfrac{5b - 10}{b + 4} \div \dfrac{10}{b + 4}$ $\dfrac{b - 2}{2}$

26. $\dfrac{z^2 + 2z - 3}{z^2 + 5z + 6} \div \dfrac{z^2 + z - 12}{z^2 - z - 6}$ $\dfrac{z - 1}{z + 4}$

Write the equation of each line in slope-intercept form.

27. The line has slope $-\frac{2}{3}$ and y-intercept 6. $y = -\frac{2}{3}x + 6$

28. The line has slope 5 and passes through the point (2, 5). $y = 5x - 5$

29. The line passes through the points (2, 1) and (6, 8). $y = \frac{7}{4}x - \frac{5}{2}$

30. The line is parallel to $y = 3x + 8$ and passes through (1, 1). $y = 3x - 2$

Simplify.

31. $\sqrt{24}$ $2\sqrt{6}$

32. $\sqrt{\dfrac{5x^3}{2}}$ $\frac{x}{2}\sqrt{10x}$

33. $3\sqrt{5} + 8\sqrt{5}$ $11\sqrt{5}$

34. $(3\sqrt{6})(2\sqrt{3})$ $18\sqrt{2}$

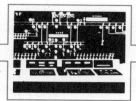

COMPUTER

TEACHER'S RESOURCE MASTERS

Computer Master 14

You are negotiating a new weekly allowance with your parents. You have asked for $6 per week, but your parents think you should get only $4. After discussing the problem with each other, your parents suggest a possible solution.

They will place a ten-dollar bill in a paper bag, along with five one-dollar bills. You will reach into the bag and draw two of the bills, drawing either a total of $2 or $11. The probability that you will draw two one-dollar bills is greater. Is this a fair solution? Should you go along with it?

Problem: Write a program to determine the long-term yearly average allowance.

Program

```
10 REM ALLOWANCE PROBLEM
20 REM SIMULATE RANDOM WEEKLY DRAWING
30 YTTAL = 0: REM YOUR YEARLY TOTAL
40 FOR I = 1 TO 52: REM 52 WEEKS PER YEAR
50 FIRST = INT (6 * RND(1) + 1): REM ONE OF SIX BILLS
60 IF FIRST = 1 THEN 100
70 SECND = INT (5 * RND(1) + 1)
80 IF SECND = 1 THEN 100
90 YTTAL = YTTAL + 2: GOTO 110: REM TWO ONES DRAWN
100 YTTAL = YTTAL + 11: REM A TEN DRAWN
110 NEXT I
120 PRINT "YEARLY TOTAL = ";YTTAL
130 PRINT "AVERAGE IN 52 WEEKS = ";YTTAL / 52
140 END
```

EXERCISES

1. RUN the program several times. Did you expect to see the results it produced?

2. What effect would removing one of the one-dollar bills have on the average? What effect would adding another one-dollar bill have? Modify the program to test these questions.

ANSWERS

1. Answers will vary; the averages have a value close to 5.0.

2. Program modifications: Removing a one-dollar bill: in lines 50, replace 6 by 5; in line 70, replace 5 by 4.

   Adding a one-dollar bill: replace 6 by 7 in line 50, and replace 5 by 6 in line 70.

   Results: With a dollar bill added, averages are roughly 4.60; with a dollar removed, the average = 5.65.

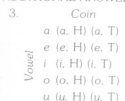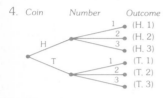
CHAPTER 14 REVIEW

VOCABULARY

addition rule (14.5)

combination (14.2)

complement (14.4)

dependent events (14.6)

equally likely outcomes (14.4)

event (14.3)

experimental probability (14.3)

fundamental counting principle (14.1)

independent events (14.6)

multiplication rule (14.6)

mutually exclusive events (14.5)

n factorial (14.2)

outcome (14.1)

permutation (14.2)

prediction (14.4)

sample space (14.1)

theoretical probability (14.4)

REVIEW EXERCISES

14.1
1. How many two-digit numbers can be formed from the digits 1, 2, and 3 if repetition of digits is allowed?   9

2. List the sample space for selecting two symbols from {~, %, ×, √ }.
~, %   ~, ×   ~, √   %, ×
%, √   ×, √

3. Make a table to show the sample space if a coin is tossed and a vowel (*a, e, i, o,* or *u*) is chosen.

4. Make a tree diagram showing the sample space for tossing a coin and choosing a number from {1, 2, 3}.

14.2   Evaluate.

5. 8!   40,320

6. $\frac{6!}{4!}$ 30

7. $\frac{7!}{5!(2!)}$ 21

8. $\frac{5!}{0!(5!)}$ 1

9. In how many ways can you arrange six people in a row for a photo?   720

10. In how many ways can you choose three people from six people to serve on a committee?   20

11. How many three-letter words, real or imaginary, can you make from the letters of the word *MUSIC*?

12. In how many ways can you choose two varieties of houseplants from fifteen available varieties?

14.3   **The table below shows the results a student had when she rolled a die 50 times. Find each probability.**

Outcome	1	2	3	4	5	6
Frequency	4	7	10	8	12	9

13. *ex p* (2) $\frac{7}{50}$

14. *ex p* (6) $\frac{9}{50}$

15. *ex p* (4) $\frac{4}{25}$

16. *ex p* (1) $\frac{2}{25}$

14.4
17. A die is rolled. What is *p* (a number greater than 5)? $\frac{1}{6}$

18. Two dice are rolled. What is *p* (a sum of 13)?   0

19. The probability of snow tomorrow is 25%. What is the probability of no snow tomorrow?   75%

20. There are 20 multiple-choice questions on a test, with four choices for each question. If you guess at every answer, how many questions should you answer correctly?   5

14.5 **21.** On a die, what is the probability of rolling a number less than 3 or an even number? $\frac{2}{3}$

22. Two coins are tossed. What is the probability of getting two heads or two tails? $\frac{1}{2}$

23. A card is drawn from a standard deck. What is the probability it is a seven or a ten? $\frac{2}{13}$

24. A card is drawn from a standard deck. What is the probability it is a seven or a diamond? $\frac{4}{13}$

14.6 **25.** Two dice are rolled. What is the probability of rolling a number less than three on the first die and an even number on the second die? $\frac{1}{6}$

26. Two coins are tossed. What is the probability that the first coin shows heads and the second coin shows tails? $\frac{1}{4}$

27. One card is drawn from a standard deck, it is replaced, and then another card is drawn. What is the probability that the first card is a seven and the second card is red? $\frac{1}{26}$

28. One card is drawn from a standard deck, then a second card is drawn without replacing the first. What is the probability that the first card is a diamond and the second card is a heart? $\frac{13}{204}$

ERROR SEARCH

Find the error in each exercise and give the correct answer.

1. $3(2x + 7) = 5x + 8$
$6x + 7 = 5x + 8$
$x = 1$ -13

2. $-3x + 4 \le x - 4$
$-2x \le -8$
$x \le 4$ $x \ge 2$

3. $(2x + y)^2 = 4x^2 + y^2$ $4x^2 + 4xy + y^2$

4. $\frac{3}{2x} + \frac{5}{4x} = \frac{8}{4x}$
$= \frac{2}{x}$ $\frac{11}{4x}$

TEACHER'S RESOURCE
MASTERS

Chapter 14 Test

Multiple-Choice Test

PROBLEM–SOLVING
HANDBOOK

p. 539

ADDITIONAL ANSWERS

1.

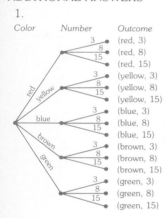

13. $\frac{1}{4}$

14. $\frac{1}{13}$

CHAPTER 14 TEST

1. Show the sample space of possible outcomes by using a tree diagram: One color is to be chosen from {red, yellow, blue, brown, green} and one number is to be chosen from {3, 8, 15}.

2. How many four-digit numbers can be formed from the digits {0, 1, 2, 3, 4, 5} if the first digit cannot be 0 and repetition of digits is allowed?   1080

Evaluate.

3. 6!   720

4. $\frac{8!}{3!}$ 6720

5. $\frac{9!}{5!(4!)}$ 126

6. In how many ways can a president, a vice-president, and a secretary be chosen from five available people?   60

7. In how many ways can a committee of three be chosen from five available people?   10

8. In how many ways can you arrange five trophies on a shelf?   120

9. In how many ways can you select three records to purchase from six available records?   20

10. Use the table to find *ex p* (green). $\frac{1}{2}$

Color	red	green	blue	yellow
Frequency	10	15	3	2

11. Two dice are rolled. What is *p* (a sum of 11)? $\frac{1}{18}$

12. What is the probability of rolling an 8 on a die?   0

13. What is the probability of drawing a diamond from a standard deck of cards?

14. What is the probability of drawing a six from a standard deck of cards?

15. Two coins are tossed. The probability that both coins show tails is 0.25. What is the probability that both coins do not show tails?   0.75

16. In a survey, $\frac{2}{5}$ of those asked were in favor of passing a new law. Predict how many of 500 people would be in favor of passing the new law.   200

17. A card is drawn from a standard deck. What is the probability that it is red or a king? $\frac{7}{13}$

18. Two dice are rolled. What is the probability that the sum is 2 or 3? $\frac{1}{12}$

19. A die is rolled and a coin is tossed. What is the probability that the die shows a 5 and the coin shows heads? $\frac{1}{12}$

20. A card is picked from a standard deck, then another card is picked without replacing the first. Find the probability that each card is a king. $\frac{1}{221}$

CHAPTER 15

Right-Triangle Trigonometry

The angle of depression from a lighthouse on shore to a boat at sea is 30°. If the lighthouse is 140 feet above sea level, about how far is the boat from the lighthouse?   about 242.5 feet

OBJECTIVES

Find the measure of the complement of an acute angle.

Find the measure of the supplement of an angle.

Find the measure of the third angle of a triangle, given the measures of the other two angles.

TEACHER'S NOTES

See p. T39.

CLASSROOM EXAMPLES

1. Find the measure of the complement of $\angle B$ if m$\angle B$ = 53.

   Let x represent the measure of the complement of $\angle B$.

   m$\angle B + x = 90$

   $53 + x = 90$

   $x = 37$

   The measure of the complement of $\angle B$ is 37.

2. Find the measure of the supplement of $\angle B$ if m$\angle B$ = 146.

   Let x represent the measure of the supplement of $\angle B$.

   m$\angle B + x = 180$

   $146 + x = 180$

   $x = 34$

   The measure of the supplement of $\angle B$ is 34.

3. In $\triangle XYZ$, m$\angle X = 50$ and m$\angle Y = 62$.
   Find m$\angle Z$.

| 15.1 | Angles and Triangles |

A **ray** is a set of collinear points that extends without end in one direction from an *endpoint*. For example, ray RT, denoted by $\overrightarrow{RT}$, is the set of collinear points that contains the endpoint R, the point T, and every point on the same side of R as T.

An **angle** is the union of two noncollinear rays that have the same endpoint. For example, $\angle SRT$ (read "angle SRT") is the union of $\overrightarrow{RT}$ and $\overrightarrow{RS}$. The rays are the **sides of the angle,** and the common endpoint R is the **vertex of the angle.** Other names for $\angle SRT$ are $\angle TRS$ and $\angle R$.

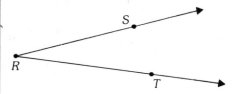

Angles are measured in degrees (°) and are classified according to their measurements.

An **acute angle** is an angle whose measurement is less than 90°.

A **right angle** is an angle whose measurement is 90°.

An **obtuse angle** is an angle whose measurement is between 90° and 180°.

Two angles are **complementary** if the sum of their measurements is 90°. Each angle is the **complement** of the other.

Two angles are **supplementary** if the sum of their measurements is 180°. Each angle is the **supplement** of the other.

The symbol for the measure of angle A is m$\angle A$. It is understood that the measure of angle A, or m$\angle A$, refers to the *number* of degrees in angle A. Therefore, it is not necessary to include the degree symbol when referring to the measure of an angle.

EXAMPLES

| 1 | **Find the measure of the complement of $\angle A$ if m$\angle A$ = 49.** |

SOLUTION Let x represent the measure of the complement of $\angle A$.

m$\angle A + x = 90$

$49 + x = 90$

$x = 41$

The measure of the complement of $\angle A$ is 41.

CHECK The sum of the measures of complementary angles is 90.

$49 + 41 \stackrel{?}{=} 90$

$90 = 90$ ✔

<table>
<tr><td>

2 **Find the measure of the supplement of ∠A if m∠A = 123.**

SOLUTION   Let x represent the measure of the supplement of ∠A.

$$m\angle A + x = 180$$
$$123 + x = 180$$
$$x = 57$$

The measure of the supplement of ∠A is 57.

CHECK   The sum of the measures of supplementary angles is 180.

$$123 + 57 \stackrel{?}{=} 180$$
$$180 = 180 \;\; ✔$$

</td></tr>
</table>

A triangle has three angles. Triangles can be classified according to the measurements of their angles.

An **acute triangle** is a triangle with *three acute angles.*

A **right triangle** is a triangle with *one right angle.*

An **obtuse triangle** is a triangle with *one obtuse angle.*

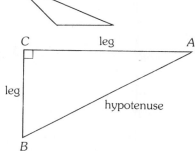

Triangles are named by their **vertices** (plural of *vertex*). For example, △ABC (read "triangle ABC") is a right triangle.

Recall that in any right triangle, the side opposite the right angle is the **hypotenuse.** The other two sides are **legs.** Each leg is opposite one acute angle and adjacent to the other acute angle. The leg opposite ∠B and adjacent to ∠A is the **line segment** that has endpoints A and C. The symbol for this line segment is $\overline{AC}$. The leg opposite ∠A and adjacent to ∠B is $\overline{BC}$. The lengths of $\overline{AB}$, $\overline{BC}$, and $\overline{AC}$ can be represented by AB, BC, and AC. You will use the terms *opposite* and *adjacent* as you study right-triangle trigonometry in this chapter.

The length of a side of a triangle is usually represented by the lowercase version of the letter that names the vertex of the angle opposite that side. For example, in △ABC, the length of the side opposite ∠A is symbolized by a, the length of the side opposite ∠B is symbolized by b, and the length of the side opposite ∠C is symbolized by c.

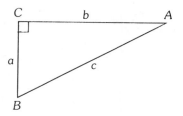

In any triangle, the sum of the measures of the three angles is 180.

Let z represent the measure of ∠Z.

$$m\angle X + m\angle Y + z = 180$$
$$50 + 62 + z = 180$$
$$112 + z = 180$$
$$z = 68$$
$$m\angle Z = 68$$

4. In △KLM, the measure of ∠K is three times the measure of ∠L. The measure of ∠M is 20 less than the measure of ∠L. Find the measure of each angle.

Let x = m∠L. Then 3x = m∠K and x − 20 = m∠M.

$$m\angle L + m\angle K + m\angle M = 180$$
$$x + 3x + (x - 20) = 180$$
$$5x - 20 = 180$$
$$5x = 200$$
$$x = 40$$
$$m\angle L = 40, \; m\angle K = 120,$$
and m∠M = 20

MIXED REVIEW

Solve.

1. $16y = 43 - 3y$ $\frac{43}{19}$
2. $\frac{63}{83} = \frac{104}{y}$ approximately 137.02
3. If $I = prt$, solve for r. $r = \frac{I}{pt}$
4. What percent of 82 is 14?   approximately 17%
5. 50 is what percent of 25?   200%

TEACHER'S RESOURCE MASTERS

Practice Master 60, Part 1

3   **In △ABC, m∠A = 40 and m∠B = 57. Find m∠C.**

SOLUTION

Let x represent the measure of $\angle C$.

$$m\angle A + m\angle B + x = 180$$
$$40 + 57 + x = 180$$
$$97 + x = 180$$
$$x = 83$$

$m\angle C = 83$

CHECK

The sum of the measures of the three angles of any triangle is 180.

$$40 + 57 + 83 \overset{?}{=} 180$$
$$180 = 180 \ \checkmark$$

4   **In △JKL, the measure of ∠J is two times the measure of ∠K. The measure of ∠L is 20 less than the measure of ∠K. Find the measure of each angle.**

SOLUTION

Let $x = m\angle K$.

Then $2x = m\angle J$ and $x - 20 = m\angle L$.

$$m\angle K + m\angle J + m\angle L = 180$$
$$x + 2x + (x - 20) = 180$$
$$4x - 20 = 180$$
$$4x = 200$$
$$x = 50$$

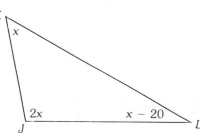

$m\angle K = 50$, $m\angle J = 100$, and $m\angle L = 30$.

CHECK

The sum of the measures of the three angles of any triangle is 180.

$$50 + 100 + 30 \overset{?}{=} 180$$
$$180 = 180 \ \checkmark$$

ORAL EXERCISES

Give three names for each angle. $\angle SRQ, \angle QRS, \angle R$

1. $\angle JKL, \angle LKJ, \angle K$ **2.**   **3.**   **4.**

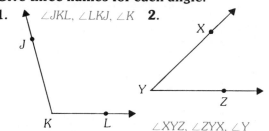

$\angle XYZ, \angle ZYX, \angle Y$

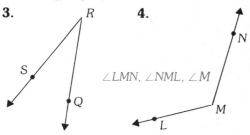

$\angle LMN, \angle NML, \angle M$

Classify an angle with the given measurement as acute, right, or obtuse.

5. 90° right   **6.** 28° acute   **7.** 16° acute   **8.** 130° obtuse   **9.** 179° obtuse

State whether angles with the given measurements are (a) complementary or (b) supplementary.

10. 68°, 22° a   **11.** 5°, 85° a   **12.** 149°, 31° b   **13.** 95°, 85° b

Name the hypotenuse and the legs of each right triangle.

14.  $\overline{AB}$; $\overline{BC}$, $\overline{AC}$

15. 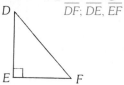 $\overline{DF}$; $\overline{DE}$, $\overline{EF}$

16. 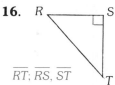 $\overline{RT}$; $\overline{RS}$, $\overline{ST}$

Classify each triangle on the basis of its angle measurements.

17. acute   **18.** obtuse   **19.** right

WRITTEN EXERCISES

A. Fill in the blank.

1. A right triangle has one _____right_____ angle.

2. The sum of the angle measures in any triangle is _____180_____.

3. In a right triangle the side opposite the right angle is called the _____hypotenuse_____.

Use △JKL for exercises 4–10.

4. What line segment is the hypotenuse? ___$\overline{JL}$___

5. Name the line segments that are legs. ___$\overline{LK}$___ ___$\overline{JK}$___

6. What letter commonly represents the length of the side opposite ∠J? ___j___ The side opposite ∠K? ___k___ The side opposite ∠L? ___ℓ___

7. Name the leg adjacent to ∠J. ___$\overline{JK}$___

8. Name the leg adjacent to ∠L. ___$\overline{LK}$___

9. Name the leg opposite ∠L. ___$\overline{JK}$___

10. Name the leg opposite ∠J. ___$\overline{LK}$___

B. Give the measurement of the complement of an angle with the given measurement.

11. 45° 45°   **12.** 85° 5°   **13.** 16° 74°   **14.** 70° 20°

15. $x°$ $(90 - x)°$ **16.** $(3x)°$ $(90 - 3x)°$ **17.** $(x + 25)°$ **18.** $(x - 5)°$

ASSIGNMENT GUIDE

Minimum
1–9 odd, 24–38

Regular
11–14, 19–22, 27–38

Maximum
22–41

ADDITIONAL ANSWERS

Written Exercises
17. $(65 - x)°$
18. $(95 - x)°$

25. $(155 - x)°$
26. $(185 - x)°$

Give the measurement of the supplement of an angle with the given measurement.

19. $45°$ $135°$ **20.** $85°$ $95°$ **21.** $16°$ $164°$ **22.** $70°$ $110°$

23. $x°$ $(180 - x)°$ **24.** $(3x)°$ $(180 - 3x)°$ **25.** $(x + 25)°$ **26.** $(x - 5)°$

The measurements of two angles of a triangle are given. Find the measurement of the third angle.

27. $80°, 63°$ $37°$ **28.** $90°, 30°$ $60°$ **29.** $45°, 37°$ $98°$ **30.** $72°, 90°$ $18°$

31. $46°, 90°$ $44°$ **32.** $85°, 45°$ $50°$ **33.** $25°, 37°$ $118°$ **34.** $39°, 60°$ $81°$

Find the measure of each angle of the given triangle.

35. In $\triangle ABC$, the measure of $\angle A$ is one-half the measure of $\angle B$. The measure of $\angle C$ is 25 more than the measure of $\angle B$. $m\angle A = 31, m\angle B = 62, m\angle C = 87$

36. In $\triangle PQR$, the measure of $\angle Q$ is three times the measure of $\angle R$. The measure of $\angle P$ is equal to the measure of $\angle R$. $m\angle P = 36, m\angle Q = 108, m\angle R = 36$

37. In $\triangle LMN$, the measure of $\angle M$ is twice the measure of $\angle L$. The measure of $\angle N$ is three times the measure of $\angle M$. $m\angle L = 20, m\angle M = 40, m\angle N = 120$

38. In $\triangle XYZ$, the measure of $\angle X$ is one-half the measure of $\angle Y$. The measure of $\angle Z$ is three times the measure of $\angle X$. $m\angle X = 30, m\angle Y = 60, m\angle Z = 90$

C. Use the Pythagorean theorem to determine whether the given numbers could represent the lengths of the sides of a right triangle.

39. $9, 12, 15$ yes **40.** $5, 13, 12$ yes **41.** $10, 15, 18$ no

ERROR SEARCH

Find the error in each exercise and give the correct answer.

1. $5 - 2(12 + 6 \div 2 \times 3) = 3(18 \div 6)$
$= 3(3)$
$= 9$ -37

2. $-\dfrac{5}{4}x + \dfrac{3}{4}x > 8$
$-\dfrac{2}{4}x > 8$
$-\dfrac{1}{2}x > 8$
$x > -16$ $x < -16$

3. $(2x + 5)^2 = 4x^2 + 25$ $4x^2 + 20x + 25$

4. $\sqrt{10} \cdot \sqrt{5} = 2\sqrt{5}$ $5\sqrt{2}$

5. $\dfrac{2}{b + 3} + \dfrac{1}{b + 3} = \dfrac{1}{b}$ $\dfrac{3}{b + 3}$

6. The equation of a line with slope 2 and y-intercept -3 is $y = 2m + 3$.

ERROR SEARCH
6. $y = 2x - 3$

15.2	Similar Triangles

The two triangles below have the same shape but not the same size. If you measured the angles, you would find that the angles in △ABC have the same measures as those in △DEF.

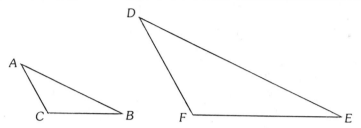

Angles that have equal measures are called **congruent angles.** Two triangles having three pairs of congruent angles are called **similar triangles.** So △ABC and △DEF are similar triangles. The expression △ABC ~ △DEF is read "Triangle ABC is similar to triangle DEF."

If two triangles are similar, the angles in each pair of congruent angles are called **corresponding angles.** The sequence of the letters in the expression △ABC ~ △DEF identifies the corresponding angles.

Corresponding angles

∠A and ∠D
∠B and ∠E
∠C and ∠F

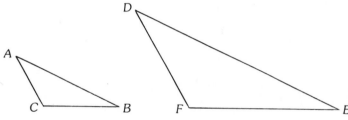

The sides of similar triangles also correspond. **Corresponding sides** are sides opposite corresponding angles.

Corresponding sides

$\overline{BC}$ and $\overline{EF}$
$\overline{AC}$ and $\overline{DF}$
$\overline{AB}$ and $\overline{DE}$

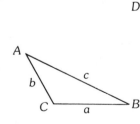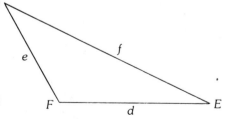

The lengths of the corresponding sides of similar triangles are proportional.

$$\frac{a}{d} = \frac{b}{e} = \frac{c}{f}$$

For example, if △ABC ~ △DEF, then $\frac{4}{8} = \frac{3}{6} = \frac{6}{12}$.

Here, the ratio of any pair of corresponding sides is $\frac{1}{2}$.

OBJECTIVE

Solve proportions involving similar triangles.

TEACHER'S NOTES

See p. T39.

CLASSROOM EXAMPLE

△RST ~ △VWX. r = 7, t = 8, s = 5, and v = 9. Find the lengths of the other sides.

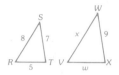

$\frac{x}{8} = \frac{9}{7}$ $\frac{w}{5} = \frac{9}{7}$

$7x = 8 \cdot 9$ $7w = 5 \cdot 9$

$7x = 72$ $7w = 45$

$x = 10\frac{2}{7}$ $w = 6\frac{3}{7}$

MIXED REVIEW

1. Compute $\frac{7!}{2!}$.   2520

2. $c^2 = a^2 + b^2$, find b if c = 14 and a = 9.   approximately 10.72

3. Find the quotient $-\frac{14}{18} \div \frac{1}{3}$. $-\frac{7}{3}$

4. Simplify $\frac{18 - 2}{8}$ + 3(7 + 9).   50

5. Simplify 5 · (−9 − 2).   −55

TEACHER'S RESOURCE MASTERS

Practice Master 60, Part 2

Quiz 29

$\triangle ABC \sim \triangle DEF$. $a = 7$, $b = 6$, $c = 5$, and $e = 9$. **Find the lengths of the other sides.**

SOLUTION Sketch the triangles and label the known lengths and the lengths to be determined.

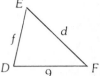

Set up a proportion for each missing length, using the lengths of corresponding sides. Solve each proportion.

$$\frac{f}{5} = \frac{9}{6}$$
$$6f = 5 \cdot 9$$
$$6f = 45$$
$$f = 7\frac{1}{2}$$

$$\frac{d}{7} = \frac{9}{6}$$
$$6d = 7 \cdot 9$$
$$6d = 63$$
$$d = 10\frac{1}{2}$$

CHECK $\frac{f}{5} = \frac{9}{6}$

$\frac{7\frac{1}{2}}{5} \overset{?}{=} \frac{9}{6}$

$45 = 45$ ✔

$\frac{d}{7} = \frac{9}{6}$

$\frac{10\frac{1}{2}}{7} \overset{?}{=} \frac{9}{6}$

$63 = 63$ ✔

ORAL EXERCISES

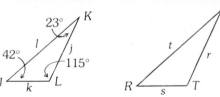

For exercises 1–15, $\triangle JKL \sim \triangle RST$. Find the measure of each angle.

1. $m\angle R = \underline{42}$
2. $m\angle S = \underline{23}$
3. $m\angle T = \underline{115}$

Name the side opposite each angle.

4. $\angle R$ $\overline{ST}$
5. $\angle K$ $\overline{JL}$
6. $\angle T$ $\overline{RS}$
7. $\angle J$ $\overline{KL}$
8. $\angle S$ $\overline{RT}$
9. $\angle L$ $\overline{JK}$

Complete each pair of corresponding sides.

10. $\overline{KL}$ and $\underline{\overline{ST}}$
11. $\overline{RS}$ and $\underline{\overline{JK}}$
12. $\overline{JL}$ and $\underline{\overline{RT}}$

Complete the following.

13. $\frac{j}{r} = \frac{k}{?}$ s
14. $\frac{s}{k} = \frac{?}{l}$ t
15. $\frac{t}{l} = \frac{?}{j}$ r

ASSIGNMENT GUIDE

Minimum
1–9 odd, 11–19

Regular
9–22

Maximum
11–24

A. For exercises 1–10, $\triangle XYZ \sim \triangle PQR$. Name the angle opposite each side.

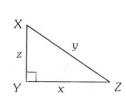
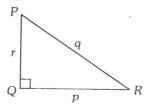

$\triangle XYZ \sim \triangle PQR$

1. $\overline{XZ}$ $\angle Y$

2. $\overline{XY}$ $\angle Z$

3. $\overline{YZ}$ $\angle X$

4. Name the pairs of corresponding angles. $\angle X$ and $\angle P$, $\angle Y$ and $\angle Q$, $\angle Z$ and $\angle R$

5. Name the pairs of corresponding sides. $\overline{XY}$ and $\overline{PQ}$, $\overline{XZ}$ and $\overline{PR}$, $\overline{YZ}$ and $\overline{QR}$

Complete the following proportions. Remember that x stands for the length of the side opposite $\angle X$ and so on.

6. $\dfrac{x}{p} = \dfrac{?}{q} = \dfrac{z}{?}$ y, r

7. $\dfrac{q}{y} = \dfrac{r}{?} = \dfrac{?}{?}$ z, p, x

Fill in the blanks.

8. If $m\angle X = 53$, then $m\angle P = \underline{\;53\;}$.

9. If $m\angle R = 37$, then $m\angle\,\underline{\;Z\;} = 37$.

10. If $m\angle Y = 90$, then $m\angle\,\underline{\;Q\;} = \underline{\;90\;}$.

B. For each pair of similar triangles, complete the given proportions.

11. $\dfrac{4.5}{3} = \dfrac{7.5}{?}$ 5

$\dfrac{7.5}{5} = \dfrac{?}{4}$ 6

$\dfrac{6}{?} = \dfrac{4.5}{3}$ 4

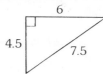

12. $\dfrac{8}{2} = \dfrac{?}{2.5}$ 10

$\dfrac{1.5}{?} = \dfrac{2}{8}$ 6

$\dfrac{10}{2.5} = \dfrac{6}{?}$ 1.5

13. $\dfrac{4.9}{?} = \dfrac{5}{2.5}$ 2.45

$\dfrac{7}{3.5} = \dfrac{?}{2.45}$ 4.9

$\dfrac{?}{2.5} = \dfrac{7}{3.5}$ 5

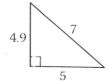

14. $\dfrac{8.85}{17.70} = \dfrac{6}{?}$ 12

$\dfrac{6.5}{?} = \dfrac{8.85}{17.70}$ 13

$\dfrac{?}{12} = \dfrac{6.5}{13}$ 6

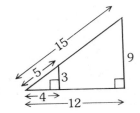

15. $\dfrac{3}{?} = \dfrac{5}{15}$ 9

$\dfrac{4}{12} = \dfrac{?}{9}$ 3

$\dfrac{5}{15} = \dfrac{4}{?}$ 12

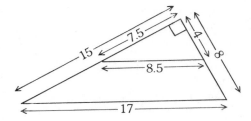

16. $\dfrac{15}{7.5} = \dfrac{8}{?}$ 4

$\dfrac{?}{8.5} = \dfrac{8}{4}$ 17

$\dfrac{4}{8.5} = \dfrac{?}{17}$ 8

$\triangle ABC \sim \triangle DEF$. **For each set of measures, find the lengths of the other sides.**

17. $a = 36, b = 44, c = 52, d = 54$

18. $a = 25, d = 15, e = 12, f = 21$

19. $b = 15, d = 4, e = 6, f = 8$

20. $c = 7, d = 23, e = 19, f = 14$

21. $a = 5, b = 2.5, c = 4, e = 4$

22. $d = 4.8, e = 3, f = 7.5, b = 2$

C. The triangles in each pair are similar. Find the missing lengths.

23. $j = 2.5, t = 7.5$

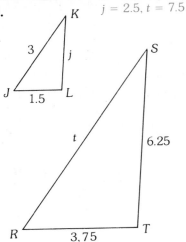

24. $b = 15, a = 14, y = 42,$ $x = 18$

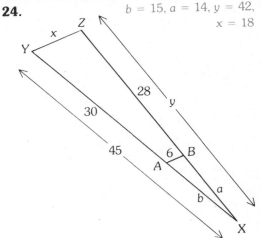

500 Chapter 15 • Right-Triangle Trigonometry

15.3 | Trigonometric Ratios

The lengths of the sides of any *right* triangle can be used to determine the **trigonometric ratios** of the *acute angles* of the triangle. Below are three ratios for $\angle A$ of right triangle ABC.

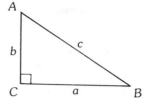

Name	Abbreviation	Meaning
sine of $\angle A$	$\sin A$	$\dfrac{\text{length of side opposite } \angle A}{\text{length of hypotenuse}} = \dfrac{a}{c}$
cosine of $\angle A$	$\cos A$	$\dfrac{\text{length of side adjacent to } \angle A}{\text{length of hypotenuse}} = \dfrac{b}{c}$
tangent of $\angle A$	$\tan A$	$\dfrac{\text{length of side opposite } \angle A}{\text{length of side adjacent to } \angle A} = \dfrac{a}{b}$

EXAMPLES

1 $\triangle ABC$ **is a right triangle. Find the sine, the cosine, and the tangent of** $\angle A$ **and** $\angle B$**.**

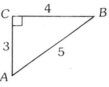

SOLUTIONS

$\sin A = \dfrac{4}{5}$ $\sin B = \dfrac{3}{5}$

$\cos A = \dfrac{3}{5}$ $\cos B = \dfrac{4}{5}$

$\tan A = \dfrac{4}{3}$ $\tan B = \dfrac{3}{4}$

2 $\triangle DEF$ **is a right triangle. m$\angle F = 90$, $e = 1$, and $d = 2$. Find the sine, the cosine, and the tangent of** $\angle D$ **and** $\angle E$**.**

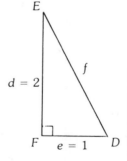

SOLUTION   First use the Pythagorean theorem to find f.

$f^2 = e^2 + d^2$

$f^2 = 1^2 + 2^2$

$f^2 = 1 + 4$

$f^2 = 5$

$f = \sqrt{5}$

Find the three trigonometric ratios of the acute angles. Remember to express radicals in *simplest form*.

$\sin D = \dfrac{2}{\sqrt{5}} = \dfrac{2 \cdot \sqrt{5}}{\sqrt{5} \cdot \sqrt{5}} = \dfrac{2\sqrt{5}}{5}$ $\sin E = \dfrac{1}{\sqrt{5}} = \dfrac{1 \cdot \sqrt{5}}{\sqrt{5} \cdot \sqrt{5}} = \dfrac{\sqrt{5}}{5}$

$\cos D = \dfrac{1}{\sqrt{5}} = \dfrac{1 \cdot \sqrt{5}}{\sqrt{5} \cdot \sqrt{5}} = \dfrac{\sqrt{5}}{5}$ $\cos E = \dfrac{2}{\sqrt{5}} = \dfrac{2 \cdot \sqrt{5}}{\sqrt{5} \cdot \sqrt{5}} = \dfrac{2\sqrt{5}}{5}$

$\tan D = \dfrac{2}{1} = 2$ $\tan E = \dfrac{1}{2}$

OBJECTIVE

Find the sine, cosine, and tangent of the acute angles of a right triangle.

TEACHER'S NOTES

See p. T40.

CLASSROOM EXAMPLES

1. $\triangle DEF$ is a right triangle. Find the sine, the cosine, and the tangent of $\angle D$ and $\angle E$.

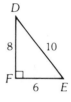

$\sin D = \frac{3}{5}$ $\sin E = \frac{4}{5}$

$\cos D = \frac{4}{5}$ $\cos E = \frac{3}{5}$

$\tan D = \frac{3}{4}$ $\tan E = \frac{4}{3}$

2. $\triangle JKM$ is a right triangle. m$\angle J = 90$, $k = 2$ and $m = 3$. Find the sine, the cosine, and the tangent of $\angle K$ and $\angle M$.

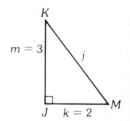

$j^2 = m^2 + k^2$

$j^2 = 3^2 + 2^2$

$j^2 = 9 + 4$

$j^2 = 13$

$j = \sqrt{13}$

(continued on next page)

$\sin K = \frac{2}{\sqrt{13}} = \frac{2 \cdot \sqrt{13}}{\sqrt{13} \cdot \sqrt{13}}$
$= \frac{2\sqrt{13}}{13}$
$\cos K = \frac{3}{\sqrt{13}} = \frac{3 \cdot \sqrt{13}}{\sqrt{13} \cdot \sqrt{13}}$
$= \frac{3\sqrt{13}}{13}$
$\tan K = \frac{2}{3}$
$\sin M = \frac{3}{\sqrt{13}} = \frac{3 \cdot \sqrt{13}}{\sqrt{13} \cdot \sqrt{13}}$
$= \frac{3\sqrt{13}}{13}$
$\cos M = \frac{2}{\sqrt{13}} = \frac{2 \cdot \sqrt{13}}{\sqrt{13} \cdot \sqrt{13}}$
$= \frac{2\sqrt{13}}{13}$
$\tan M = \frac{3}{2}$

MIXED REVIEW

1. Write $6x - 5y = -20$ in slope-intercept form.
   $y = \frac{6}{5}x + 4$

2. Simplify $\frac{8}{\sqrt{12}}$. $\frac{4\sqrt{3}}{3}$

3. Factor completely $x^2 + 2xy + y^2$. $(x + y)^2$

4. Evaluate $\left(-\frac{3}{8}\right)^2$. $\frac{9}{64}$

5. Multiply $-6k^3(-15k^2m)$.
   $90\ k^5m$

TEACHER'S RESOURCE MASTERS

Practice Master 61, Part 1

ASSIGNMENT GUIDE

Minimum
3–10, 13–20

Regular
7–22

Maximum
13–28

ADDITIONAL ANSWERS
13. $\sin D = \frac{40}{41}$; $\sin E = \frac{9}{41}$;
   $\cos D = \frac{9}{41}$; $\cos E = \frac{40}{41}$;
   $\tan D = \frac{40}{9}$; $\tan E = \frac{9}{40}$

ORAL EXERCISES

$\triangle JKL$ **is a right triangle. Find the value of each trigonometric ratio.**

1. $\sin J$ $\frac{12}{13}$

2. $\sin K$ $\frac{5}{13}$

3. $\cos J$ $\frac{5}{13}$

4. $\cos K$ $\frac{12}{13}$

5. $\tan J$ $\frac{12}{5}$

6. $\tan K$ $\frac{5}{12}$

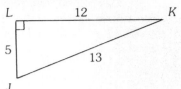

WRITTEN EXERCISES

A. $\triangle ABC$ **is a right triangle. Find the trigonometric ratios of the acute angles.**

1. $\sin A$ $\frac{8}{17}$

2. $\sin B$ $\frac{15}{17}$

3. $\cos A$ $\frac{15}{17}$

4. $\cos B$ $\frac{8}{17}$

5. $\tan A$ $\frac{8}{15}$

6. $\tan B$ $\frac{15}{8}$

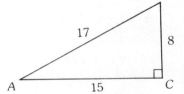

$\triangle RST$ **is a right triangle. Find the trigonometric ratios of the acute angles. Remember to express radicals in simplest form.**

7. $\sin R$ $\frac{2\sqrt{2}}{3}$

8. $\sin S$ $\frac{1}{3}$

9. $\cos R$ $\frac{1}{3}$

10. $\cos S$ $\frac{2\sqrt{2}}{3}$

11. $\tan R$ $2\sqrt{2}$

12. $\tan S$ $\frac{\sqrt{2}}{4}$

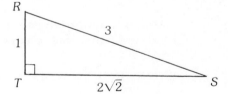

B. For each right triangle, find the sine, the cosine, and the tangent of each acute angle. (For exercises 15–24, first use the Pythagorean theorem to find the length of the third side of each right triangle.) Express radicals in simplest form.

13.

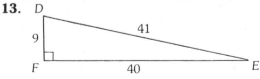

14.

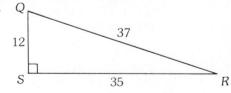

15.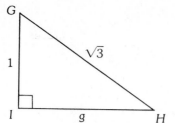

16.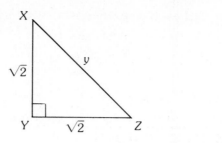

17.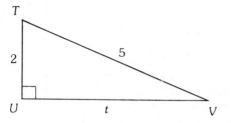

18.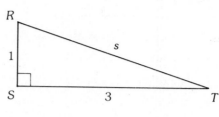

19.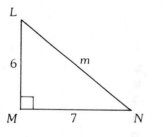

20.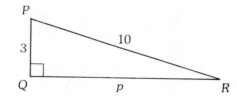

21.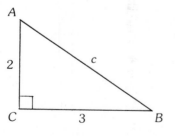

22.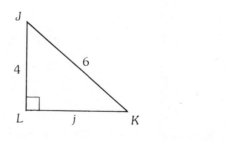

23.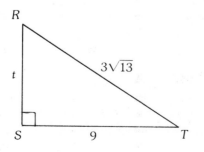

24.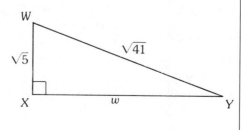

14. $\sin Q = \frac{35}{37}$; $\sin R = \frac{12}{37}$;
   $\cos Q = \frac{12}{37}$; $\cos R = \frac{35}{37}$;
   $\tan Q = \frac{35}{12}$; $\tan R = \frac{12}{35}$

15. $g = \sqrt{2}$
   $\sin G = \frac{\sqrt{6}}{3}$; $\sin H = \frac{\sqrt{3}}{3}$;
   $\cos G = \frac{\sqrt{3}}{3}$; $\cos H = \frac{\sqrt{6}}{3}$;
   $\tan G = \sqrt{2}$; $\tan H = \frac{\sqrt{2}}{2}$

16. $y = 2$
   $\sin X = \frac{\sqrt{2}}{2}$; $\sin Z = \frac{\sqrt{2}}{2}$;
   $\cos X = \frac{\sqrt{2}}{2}$; $\cos Z = \frac{\sqrt{2}}{2}$;
   $\tan X = 1$; $\tan Z = 1$

17. $t = \sqrt{21}$
   $\sin T = \frac{\sqrt{21}}{5}$; $\sin V = \frac{2}{5}$;
   $\cos T = \frac{2}{5}$; $\cos V = \frac{\sqrt{21}}{5}$;
   $\tan T = \frac{\sqrt{21}}{2}$; $\tan V = \frac{2\sqrt{21}}{21}$

18. $s = \sqrt{10}$
   $\sin R = \frac{3\sqrt{10}}{10}$; $\sin T = \frac{\sqrt{10}}{10}$;
   $\cos R = \frac{\sqrt{10}}{10}$; $\cos T = \frac{3\sqrt{10}}{10}$;
   $\tan R = 3$; $\tan T = \frac{1}{3}$

19. $m = \sqrt{85}$
   $\sin L = \frac{7\sqrt{85}}{85}$; $\sin N = \frac{6\sqrt{85}}{85}$;
   $\cos L = \frac{6\sqrt{85}}{85}$; $\cos N = \frac{7\sqrt{85}}{85}$;
   $\tan L = \frac{7}{6}$; $\tan N = \frac{6}{7}$

20. $p = \sqrt{91}$
   $\sin P = \frac{\sqrt{91}}{10}$; $\sin R = \frac{3}{10}$;
   $\cos P = \frac{3}{10}$; $\cos R = \frac{\sqrt{91}}{10}$;
   $\tan P = \frac{\sqrt{91}}{3}$; $\tan R = \frac{3\sqrt{91}}{91}$

21. $c = \sqrt{13}$
   $\sin A = \frac{3\sqrt{13}}{13}$; $\sin B = \frac{2\sqrt{13}}{13}$;
   $\cos A = \frac{2\sqrt{13}}{13}$; $\cos B = \frac{3\sqrt{13}}{13}$;
   $\tan A = \frac{3}{2}$; $\tan B = \frac{2}{3}$

(continued on next page)

22. $j = 2\sqrt{5}$

$\sin J = \frac{2\sqrt{5}}{6}$; $\sin K = \frac{2}{3}$;

$\cos J = \frac{2}{3}$; $\cos K = \frac{2\sqrt{5}}{6}$;

$\tan J = \frac{\sqrt{5}}{2}$; $\tan K = \frac{2\sqrt{5}}{5}$

23. $t = 6$

$\sin R = \frac{3\sqrt{13}}{13}$; $\sin T$

$= \frac{2\sqrt{13}}{13}$;

$\cos R = \frac{2\sqrt{13}}{13}$; $\cos T$

$= \frac{3\sqrt{13}}{13}$;

$\tan R = \frac{3}{2}$; $\tan T = \frac{2}{3}$

24. $w = 6$

$\sin W = \frac{6\sqrt{41}}{41}$; $\sin Y$

$= \frac{\sqrt{205}}{41}$;

$\cos W = \frac{\sqrt{205}}{41}$; $\cos Y$

$= \frac{6\sqrt{41}}{41}$;

$\tan W = \frac{6\sqrt{5}}{5}$; $\tan Y = \frac{\sqrt{5}}{6}$

C. **Find each trigonometric ratio.**

25. If $\sin A = \frac{21}{29}$, what is $\cos A$? $\frac{20}{29}$

26. If $\sin B = \frac{9}{41}$, what is $\tan B$? $\frac{9}{40}$

27. If $\tan E = \frac{12}{35}$, what is $\sin E$? $\frac{12}{37}$

28. If $\cos D = \frac{5}{6}$, what is $\tan D$? $\frac{\sqrt{11}}{5}$

SELF-QUIZ

$\triangle ABC$ **is a right triangle. Use** $\triangle ABC$ **for exercises 1–3.**

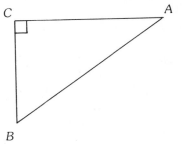

1. Name the side adjacent to $\angle A$. $\overline{AC}$

2. Name the side opposite $\angle B$. $\overline{AC}$

3. Name the hypotenuse of $\triangle ABC$. $\overline{AB}$

4. Give the measurement of the complement of an angle whose measurement is 60°.   30°

5. The measurements of two angles of a triangle are 46° and 85°. Find the measurement of the third angle of the triangle.   49°

6. $\triangle DEF \sim \triangle GHI$. Find the missing lengths. $d = 5$; $h = 9$

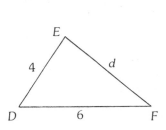

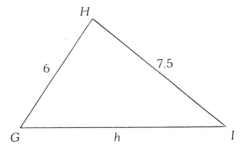

$\triangle XYZ$ **is a right triangle. Find each of the following trigonometric ratios.**

7. $\sin X$ $\frac{4}{5}$

8. $\sin Y$ $\frac{3}{5}$

9. $\cos X$ $\frac{3}{5}$

10. $\cos Y$ $\frac{4}{5}$

11. $\tan X$ $\frac{4}{3}$

12. $\tan Y$ $\frac{3}{4}$

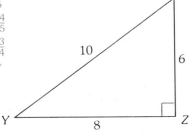

<table>
<tr><td>15.4</td><td colspan="2"><h1>Trigonometric Tables</h1></td></tr>
</table>

A trigonometric ratio depends only on the measure of the acute angle in a right triangle. The size of the right triangle is irrelevant. For example, in the triangle below, $\angle A$ and $\angle X$ have the same measurements. You can see that the trigonometric ratios of $\angle A$ and $\angle X$ are the same.

TEACHER'S NOTES

See p. T40.

CLASSROOM EXAMPLES

1. Find the sine, the cosine, and the tangent of a 52° angle.

   $\sin 52° \approx 0.7880$

   $\cos 52° \approx 0.6157$

   $\tan 52° \approx 1.2799$

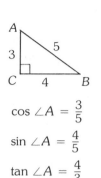

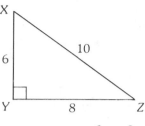

$\cos \angle A = \dfrac{3}{5}$

$\sin \angle A = \dfrac{4}{5}$

$\tan \angle A = \dfrac{4}{3}$

$\cos \angle X = \dfrac{6}{10} = \dfrac{3}{5}$

$\sin \angle X = \dfrac{8}{10} = \dfrac{4}{5}$

$\tan \angle X = \dfrac{8}{6} = \dfrac{4}{3}$

2. Find the measurement of an angle B whose cosine is 0.8290.

   $\cos 34° = 0.8290$

   The measurement of $\angle B$ is 34°.

A table of angle measures and *decimal approximations* of the corresponding trigonometric ratios is on page 548. This table lists decimal approximations of the ratios for angles with measurements from 1° to 89°.

3. Find the measurement of an angle C whose sine is 0.6597.

   $\sin 41° = 0.6561$ and $\sin 42° = 0.6691$.

   Therefore, the measurement of $\angle C$ is between 41° and 42°.

   Since 0.6597 is closer to 0.6561 than it is to 0.6691, the measurement of $\angle C$ is 41°, to the nearest degree.

EXAMPLES

1   **Find the sine, the cosine, and the tangent of a 49° angle.**

SOLUTION

$\sin 49° \approx 0.7547$

$\cos 49° \approx 0.6561$

$\tan 49° \approx 1.1504$

Angle	Sine	Cosine	Tangent
46°	.7193	.6947	1.0355
47°	.7314	.6820	1.0724
48°	.7431	.6691	1.1106
49°	.7547	.6561	1.1504
50°	.7660	.6428	1.1918
51°	.7771	.6293	1.2349

It is customary to use $=$ instead of $\approx$ when writing trigonometric expressions and their corresponding approximations.

2   **Find the measurement of an angle A whose cosine is 0.8829.**

SOLUTION

$\cos 28° = 0.8829$

The measurement of $\angle A$ is 28°.

Angle	Sine	Cosine	Tangent
26°	.4384	.8988	.4877
27°	.4540	.8910	.5095
28°	.4695	.8829	.5317
29°	.4848	.8746	.5543

MIXED REVIEW

1. Factor completely $144a^2 - 64b^2$. $16(3a + 2b)(3a - 2b)$

2. Factor completely $r^2 - s^2$. $(r - s)(r + s)$

3. Solve $y - 8 = -16 + 3y$.   4

4. Complete $-\left|-\frac{3}{8}\right|$. $-\frac{3}{8}$

5. Evaluate $\frac{y^3}{x^3}$ if $y = -2$ and $x = -1$.   8

TEACHER'S RESOURCE MASTERS

Practice Master 61, Part 2

ASSIGNMENT GUIDE

Minimum
1–12, 25–30, 43–51, 58–66

Regular
12–24, 31–36, 40–54, 67, 68

Maximum
25–33, 40–62, 66–69

ADDITIONAL ANSWERS

Oral Exercises

1. 0.2588; 0.9659; 0.2679

2. 0.9659; 0.2588; 3.7321

3. 0.8387; 0.5446; 1.5399

4. 0.7071; 0.7071; 1.0000

5. 0.1219; 0.9925; 0.1228

6. 0.4848; 0.8746; 0.5543

| 3 |

Find the measurement of an angle A whose sine is 0.6.

SOLUTION

According to the table, $\sin 36° = 0.5878$ and $\sin 37° = 0.6018$.

Therefore, the measurement of $\angle A$ is between 36° and 37°.

Angle	Sine	Cosine	Tangent
36°	.5878	.8090	.7265
37°	.6018	.7986	.7536

Since 0.6 is closer to 0.6018 than it is to 0.5878, the measurement of $\angle A$ is 37°, to the nearest degree.

ORAL EXERCISES

Use the table on page 548 to find the sine, the cosine, and the tangent of angles with the following measurements.

1. 15°   **2.** 75°   **3.** 57°   **4.** 45°   **5.** 7°   **6.** 29°

WRITTEN EXERCISES

A. Use the table on page 548 to find each of the following trigonometric ratios.

1. $\sin 31°$ 0.5150   **2.** $\tan 58°$ 1.6003   **3.** $\cos 48°$ 0.6691

4. $\cos 51°$ 0.6293   **5.** $\sin 39°$ 0.6293   **6.** $\tan 72°$ 3.0777

7. $\tan 80°$ 5.6713   **8.** $\cos 65°$ 0.4226   **9.** $\sin 41°$ 0.6561

10. $\sin 62°$ 0.8829   **11.** $\cos 10°$ 0.9848   **12.** $\tan 55°$ 1.4281

13. $\cos 21°$ 0.9336   **14.** $\sin 75°$ 0.9659   **15.** $\tan 5°$ 0.0875

16. $\tan 18°$ 0.3249   **17.** $\cos 28°$ 0.8829   **18.** $\sin 16°$ 0.2756

19. $\cos 77°$ 0.2250   **20.** $\sin 12°$ 0.2079   **21.** $\tan 63°$ 1.9626

22. $\sin 74°$ 0.9613   **23.** $\tan 89°$ 57.2900   **24.** $\cos 9°$ 0.9877

Use the table on page 548 to find the measurement of angle A.

25. $\sin A = 0.9962$ 85°   **26.** $\cos A = 0.5878$ 54°   **27.** $\tan A = 0.2309$ 13°

28. $\cos A = 0.7880$ 38°   **29.** $\tan A = 1.1106$ 48°   **30.** $\sin A = 0.7071$ 45°

31. $\tan A = 5.6713$ 80°   **32.** $\cos A = 0.8572$ 31°   **33.** $\sin A = 0.5736$ 35°

34. $\sin A = 0.7314$ 47°   **35.** $\tan A = 0.6494$ 33°   **36.** $\cos A = 0.8660$ 30°

B. Use the table on page 548 to find the measurement of angle A to the nearest degree.

37. $\sin A = 0.8572$ 59°   **38.** $\cos A = 0.6947$ 46°   **39.** $\tan A = 0.1054$ 6°

40. $\sin A = 0.1739$ 10°   **41.** $\cos A = 0.4219$ 65°   **42.** $\tan A = 0.6012$ 31°

43. $\sin A = 0.9278$ 68°   **44.** $\cos A = 0.1732$ 80°   **45.** $\tan A = 2.4751$ 68°

46. $\sin A = 0.0542$ 3°   **47.** $\cos A = 0.9959$ 5°   **48.** $\tan A = 0.4251$ 23°

49. $\sin A = 0.5745$ 35°   **50.** $\cos A = 0.5001$ 60°   **51.** $\tan A = 11.4301$ 85°

52. $\sin A = 0.9751$ 77° **53.** $\cos A = 0.6402$ 50° **54.** $\tan A = 3$ 72°

55. $\sin A = 0.4702$ 28° **56.** $\cos A = 0.0531$ 87° **57.** $\tan A = 1.5$ 56°

58. $\sin A = 0.6038$ 37° **59.** $\cos A = 0.1551$ 81° **60.** $\tan A = 0.21$ 12°

61. $\sin A = 0.4223$ 25° **62.** $\cos A = 0.9965$ 5° **63.** $\tan A = 0.3642$ 20°

64. $\sin A = 0.9850$ 80° **65.** $\cos A = 0.4065$ 66° **66.** $\tan A = 9.516$ 84°

C. 67. What is the measurement of the angle whose sine and cosine are the same? 45°

68. What is the tangent of an angle that has the same sine and cosine? 1

69. What is the relationship between the sine of an acute angle and the cosine of its complement? They are the same.

CALCULATOR

The ⌐sin⌐ ⌐cos⌐ and ⌐tan⌐ keys on a calculator can be used to find the sine, the cosine, and the tangent of any acute angle. First enter the measure of the angle. Then press the appropriate trig-function key on the calculator. The calculator will display as many decimal places as possible.

Example 1: Find the sine of an angle whose measurement is 43°.

ENTER DISPLAY
Ⓒ 43 ⌐sin⌐ *0.681994*

Example 2: Find the cosine of an angle whose measurement is 38°.

ENTER DISPLAY
Ⓒ 38 ⌐cos⌐ *0.7880108*

Example 3: Find the tangent of an angle whose measurement is 17°.

ENTER DISPLAY
Ⓒ 17 ⌐tan⌐ *0.3057307*

EXERCISES

Use a calculator to find each of the following trigonometric ratios.

1. $\sin 50°$	**2.** $\cos 32°$	**3.** $\tan 16°$
4. $\sin 75°$	**5.** $\cos 15°$	**6.** $\tan 23°$
7. $\sin 18°$	**8.** $\cos 47°$	**9.** $\tan 34°$
10. $\sin 5°$	**11.** $\cos 56°$	**12.** $\tan 16°$
13. $\sin 67°$	**14.** $\cos 78°$	**15.** $\tan 88°$

Calculator
1. 0.766044443
2. 0.848048096
3. 0.286745385
4. 0.965925826
5. 0.965925826
6. 0.424474816
7. 0.309016994
8. 0.68199836
9. 0.674508516
10. 0.087155742
11. 0.559192903
12. 0.286745385
13. 0.920504853
14. 0.20791169
15. 28.63625328

CLASSROOM EXAMPLES

1. Given that $\triangle XYZ$ is a right triangle and that $m\angle Y$ = 44, $m\angle X$ = 90, and z = 8, find y to the nearest tenth.

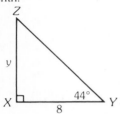

$\tan Y = \frac{\text{length of side opposite}}{\text{length of side adjacent}}$

$\tan 44° = \frac{y}{8}$

$0.9657 = \frac{y}{8}$

$8(0.9657) = y$

$7.7 = y$

2. Given that $\triangle FGK$ is a right triangle and that $m\angle G$ = 90, f = 4, and g = 12, find $m\angle F$.

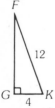

$\sin F = \frac{\text{length of side opposite}}{\text{length of hypotenuse}}$

$\sin F = \frac{4}{12} = \frac{1}{3}$

$\sin F = 0.3333$

$\sin 19° = 0.3256$ and

$\sin 20° = 0.3420$

$m\angle F = 19$

15.5 | Solving Right Triangles

You can use the Table of Trigonometric Ratios to **solve a right triangle.** Solving a right triangle consists of finding the measure of each side and each angle that is not given.

EXAMPLES

1 | **Given that $\triangle ABC$ is a right triangle and that $m\angle B = 41$, $m\angle C = 90$, and $a = 7$, find b to the nearest tenth.**

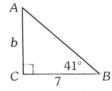

SOLUTION

$\tan B = \frac{\text{length of side opposite}}{\text{length of side adjacent}}$ *Decide which trigonometric ratio of $\angle B$ involves a given measurement and the measurement to be found.*

$\tan 41° = \frac{b}{7}$ *Write the ratio.*

$0.8693 = \frac{b}{7}$ *Use the table to determine the decimal approximation.*

$7(0.8693) = b$ *Solve for b.*

$6.1 = b$ *Round b to the nearest tenth.*

2 | **Given that $\triangle ABC$ is a right triangle and that $m\angle C = 90$, $a = 5$, and $c = 13$, find $m\angle A$.**

SOLUTION

$\sin A = \frac{\text{length of side opposite}}{\text{length of hypotenuse}}$ *Decide which trigonometric ratio of $\angle A$ involves the given measurements.*

$\sin A = \frac{5}{13}$ *Write the ratio.*

$\sin A = 0.3846$ *Write the ratio as a decimal approximation.*

$\sin 22° = 0.3746$ and $\sin 23° = 0.3907$ *Use the Table of Trigonometric Ratios to locate*

$m\angle A = 23$ *the angle whose sine is nearest to 0.3846.*

3 | **$\triangle ABC$ is a right triangle, $m\angle C = 90$, $a = 24$, and $c = 40$. Solve the triangle by finding the length of the third side and the measures of $\angle A$ and $\angle B$.**

SOLUTION   Sketch the triangle and label the given measurements and the measurements to be determined.

$a^2 + b^2 = c^2$ *Use the Pythagorean theorem to find b.*

$24^2 + b^2 = 40^2$

$576 + b^2 = 1600$

$\quad b^2 = 1024$

$\quad b = 32$

$$\tan \angle A = \frac{\text{length of side opposite}}{\text{length of side adjacent}} \qquad \textit{Choose a trigonometric ratio of } \angle A.$$

$$\tan \angle A = \frac{24}{32} \qquad\qquad\qquad \textit{Write the ratio.}$$

$$\tan \angle A = 0.75 \qquad\qquad\quad \textit{Write the ratio as a decimal.}$$

$$\tan 37° = 0.75 \qquad\qquad\quad \textit{Find the angle whose tangent is nearest to 0.75.}$$

$$\text{m}\angle A = 37$$

$$\text{m}\angle A + \text{m}\angle B + \text{m}\angle C = 180 \quad \textit{Find the measure of } \angle B.$$

$$37 + \text{m}\angle B + 90 = 180$$

$$\text{m}\angle B = 53$$

ORAL EXERCISES

State which trigonometric ratio you would use to find the indicated length in each triangle.

1. 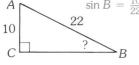 $\sin 25° = \frac{16}{c}$

2. 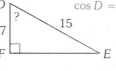 $\tan 60° = \frac{18}{a}$

3. 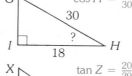 $\cos 43° = \frac{b}{20}$

4. 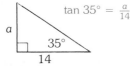 $\tan 35° = \frac{a}{14}$

5. 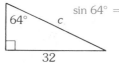 $\sin 64° = \frac{32}{c}$

6. 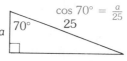 $\cos 70° = \frac{a}{25}$

State which trigonometric ratio you would use to find the indicated angle measurement in each triangle.

7. 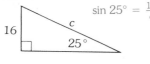 $\sin B = \frac{10}{22}$

8. 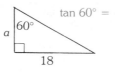 $\cos D = \frac{7}{15}$

9. 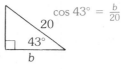 $\cos H = \frac{18}{30}$

10. 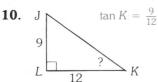 $\tan K = \frac{9}{12}$

11. 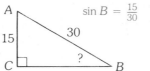 $\sin B = \frac{15}{30}$

12. 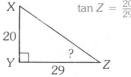 $\tan Z = \frac{20}{29}$

WRITTEN EXERCISES

A. 1–6. Find the indicated length to the nearest tenth in each triangle in Oral Exercises 1–6. **1.** 37.9 **2.** 10.4 **3.** 14.6 **4.** 9.8 **5.** 35.6 **6.** 8.6

7–12. Find the indicated angle measurement to the nearest degree in each triangle in Oral Exercises 7–12. **7.** 27° **8.** 62° **9.** 53° **10.** 37° **11.** 30° **12.** 35°

---

3. $\triangle ABC$ is a right triangle, $\text{m}\angle C = 90$, $b = 15$, and $c = 25$. Solve the triangle by finding the length of the third side and the measures of $\angle A$ and $\angle B$.

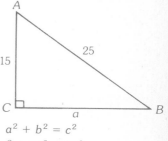

$$a^2 + b^2 = c^2$$
$$a^2 + 15^2 = 25^2$$
$$a^2 + 225 = 625$$
$$a^2 = 400$$
$$a = 20$$

$$\tan \angle A = \frac{\text{length of side opposite}}{\text{length of side adjacent}}$$
$$\tan \angle A = \frac{20}{15}$$
$$\tan \angle A = 1.33$$
$$\tan 53° = 1.33$$
$$\text{m}\angle A = 53$$
$$\text{m}\angle A + \text{m}\angle B + \text{m}\angle C = 180$$
$$53 + \text{m}\angle B + 90 = 180$$
$$\text{m}\angle B = 37$$

MIXED REVIEW

1. Find the equation of the line if the slope is -4 and the y-intercept is 9. $y = -4x + 9$

2. Find $f(-3)$ for $f(x) = \frac{2}{3}x + 5$.   3

3. Rewrite $0.\overline{171}$ in fractional form. $\frac{19}{111}$

4. Multiply $(3y + 9)(2y - 12)$. $6y^2 - 18y - 108$

5. Subtract $6x^3 - 4x^2 + 5$ from $9x^3 + 5x^2 - 10$. $3x^3 + 9x^2 - 15$

ASSIGNMENT GUIDE

Minimum
4–8, 15–24

Regular
13–27

Maximum
16–30

ADDITIONAL ANSWERS

Written Exercises

13. $c = 10$; $m\angle A = 37$;
$m\angle B = 53$

14. $b = 15$; $m\angle A = 28$;
$m\angle B = 62$

15. $a = 12$; $m\angle A = 67$;
$m\angle B = 23$

16. $c = 37$; $m\angle A = 19$;
$m\angle B = 71$

17. $b = 7$; $m\angle A = 74$;
$m\angle B = 16$

18. $a = 70$; $m\angle A = 71$;
$m\angle B = 19$

19. $c = 41$; $m\angle A = 13$;
$m\angle B = 77$

20. $b = 4.5$; $m\angle A = 42$;
$m\angle B = 48$

21. $a = 5$; $m\angle A = 45$;
$m\angle B = 45$

22. $c = 3.6$; $m\angle A = 34$;
$m\angle B = 56$

23. $c = 11.4$; $m\angle A = 52$;
$m\angle B = 38$

24. $c = 12.2$; $m\angle A = 55$;
$m\angle B = 35$

B. $\triangle ABC$ is a right triangle and $m\angle C = 90$. The lengths of two sides are given. Solve the triangle. Express the length of the third side in simplest radical form. Find the measures of $\angle A$ and $\angle B$ to the nearest degree.

13. $a = 6$, $b = 8$ **14.** $a = 8$, $c = 17$ **15.** $b = 5$, $c = 13$

16. $a = 12$, $b = 35$ **17.** $a = 24$, $c = 25$ **18.** $b = 24$, $c = 74$

19. $a = 9$, $b = 40$ **20.** $a = 4$, $c = 6$ **21.** $b = 5$, $c = 5\sqrt{2}$

22. $a = 2$, $b = 3$ **23.** $a = 9$, $b = 7$ **24.** $a = 10$, $b = 7$

C. Solve each triangle. Find lengths to the nearest tenth and measures of angles to the nearest degree.

25.
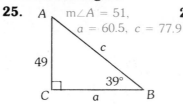
$m\angle A = 51$,
$a = 60.5$, $c = 77.9$

26.
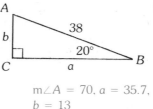
$m\angle A = 70$, $a = 35.7$,
$b = 13$

27.
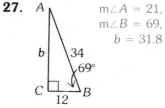
$m\angle A = 21$,
$m\angle B = 69$,
$b = 31.8$

28.
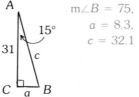
$m\angle B = 75$,
$a = 8.3$,
$c = 32.1$

29.

$m\angle A = 25$, $b = 38.6$,
$c = 42.6$

30.
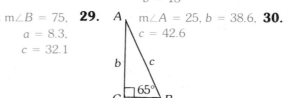
$m\angle A = 41$,
$a = 16.4$,
$b = 18.9$

CHALLENGE

A plane leaves the runway and flies at an angle of 30° until it reaches an altitude of 10 000 meters. How far does the plane fly before it reaches this height?   20 000 meters

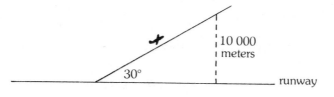

ALGEBRA IN USE

The inclined plane is one of the six fundamental tools. (The others are the lever, the pulley, the screw, the wedge, and the wheel and axle.)

An inclined plane is a flat surface that inclines from a horizontal surface.

An object is to be pushed up an inclined plane. Let the object weigh W pounds. A force F is to be applied to the object to move it up the inclined plane. If this force F will act at an angle A to the inclined plane, then the formula

$$F = \frac{W \cdot \sin B}{\cos A}$$

tells you the least number of pounds of force that will be needed to move the object up the inclined plane, whose angle of incline is represented by B.

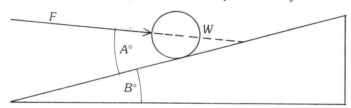

Example: A barrel weighing 800 pounds is being pushed up a 15° inclined plane. What force is needed if the force is applied at a 20° angle to the plane? (Ignore the friction involved in pushing the barrel up the inclined plane.)

Solution:

$$F = \frac{800 \times \sin 15°}{\cos 20°}$$

$$F = \frac{800 \times 0.2588}{0.9397}$$

$$F \approx 220 \text{ pounds}$$

EXERCISES

Find the force needed to push the object up a 10° inclined plane.

1. $W = 300$ pounds; $m\angle A = 12$ 53 pounds

2. $W = 200$ pounds; $m\angle A = 30$ 40 pounds

3. $W = 500$ pounds; $m\angle A = 30$ 100 pounds

4. $W = 600$ pounds, $m\angle A = 25$ 115 pounds

CLASSROOM EXAMPLES

1. A support wire is attached to the top of a tent pole and to the ground at a point 30 feet from the base of the pole. The wire makes a 62° angle with the ground. How long is the wire to the nearest foot?

Let x = the length of the wire.

$$\cos 62° = \frac{30}{x}$$
$$0.4695 = \frac{30}{x}$$
$$0.4695x = 30$$
$$x = \frac{30}{0.4695}$$
$$x = 63.9$$

The length of the wire is about 64 feet.

2. A bird is perched on a tree 68 feet above the base of the tree. The angle of depression from the bird to the birdbath is 30°. What is the distance along the ground from a point beneath the bird to the birdbath?

15.6 | Problem Solving

Trigonometry is used to solve problems involving the indirect determination of measurements.

EXAMPLES

1 A cable is attached to the top of a utility pole and to the ground at a point 25 feet from the base of the pole. The cable makes a 54° angle with the ground. How long is the cable to the nearest foot?

Understand: *Given:* A cable is attached to the top of a utility pole and to the ground at a point 25 feet from the base of the pole. The cable makes a 54° angle with the ground.

To find: the length of the cable to the nearest foot

Plan: Let x = the length of the cable. Sketch the triangle and label the given measurements and the measurements to be found. Decide which trigonometric ratio involves the 54° angle, the adjacent side with a length of 25 feet, and the hypotenuse x.

$$\cos 54° = \frac{25}{x}$$

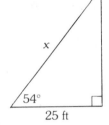

Solve:
$$\cos 54° = \frac{25}{x}$$
$$0.5878 = \frac{25}{x}$$
$$0.5878x = 25$$
$$x = \frac{25}{0.5878}$$
$$x \approx 42.5$$

Answer: The length of the cable is about 43 feet.

Review: Does it seem reasonable that the cable is about 43 feet long if it makes a 54° angle with the ground and is attached to the ground at a point 25 feet from the base of the pole?

Often the terms **angle of elevation** and **angle of depression** are used. Each of these angles is formed by the *horizontal line of sight* and the *line of sight*.

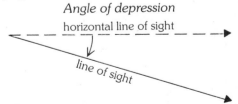

2

A hot-air balloon is 750 feet above level ground. The angle of depression from the balloon to the landing area is 25°. What is the distance along the ground from a point beneath the balloon to the landing area?

Understand: *Given:* A hot-air balloon is 750 feet above level ground. The angle of depression from the balloon to the landing area is 25°.

To find: the distance along the ground from a point beneath the balloon to the landing area

Plan: Let x = the distance along the ground. Sketch the triangle and label the given measurements and the measurement to be found.

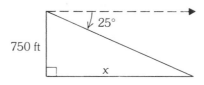

Find the complement of the 25° angle of depression.
$90 - 25 = 65$
Decide which trigonometric ratio involves the 65° angle, the adjacent side with a length of 750 feet, and the opposite side x.

$$\tan 65° = \frac{x}{750}$$

Solve:
$$2.1445 = \frac{x}{750}$$
$$750(2.1445) = x$$
$$1608.4 \approx x$$

Answer: It is about 1608 feet along the ground from a point beneath the balloon to the landing area.

Review: Does it seem reasonable that a point beneath the balloon is 1608 feet from the landing area if the balloon is 750 feet above ground?

Let x = the distance along the ground.

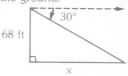

$90 - 30 = 60$
$\tan 60° = \frac{x}{68}$
$1.7321 = \frac{x}{68}$
$68(1.7321) = x$
$117.8 \approx x$

It is about 118 feet along the ground from a point beneath the bird to the birdbath.

MIXED REVIEW

1. What is 12 percent of 500?   60

2. Divide $\frac{-16xy^4}{64xy^2} \div \frac{8x^3y}{4x^2y^4}$. $-\frac{y^5}{8x}$

3. Simplify $\frac{z^{-7}}{z^{-4}}$ using positive exponents. $\frac{1}{z^3}$

4. Find the LCD of $\frac{3x}{x-7}$ and $\frac{2x}{x-5}$. $(x-7)(x-5)$

5. Solve $\frac{y}{510} = \frac{46}{300}$.   78.2

TEACHER'S RESOURCE MASTERS

Practice Master 62, Part 2

Quiz 30

ORAL EXERCISES

For each triangle below, state the trigonometric ratio you would use to find x.

1.

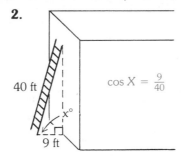

12 ft $\tan 70° = \frac{x}{12}$

2.

40 ft $\cos X = \frac{9}{40}$ 9 ft

3. $\cos 50° = \frac{x}{20}$

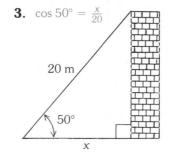

20 m   50° x

4. $\sin 6° = \frac{x}{1000}$

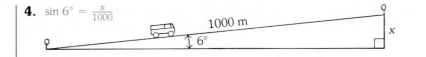

1000 m

6°

x

5.

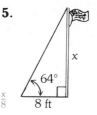

x

64°

$\tan 64° = \frac{x}{8}$

8 ft

6.

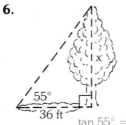

x

55°

36 ft

$\tan 55° = \frac{x}{36}$

7. $\sin X = \frac{30}{600}$

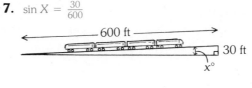

600 ft

30 ft

$x°$

8.

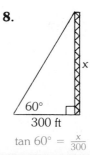

x

60°

300 ft

$\tan 60° = \frac{x}{300}$

WRITTEN EXERCISES

A. 1–8. Find x in each triangle in Oral Exercises 1–8. Find lengths to the nearest whole number and measures of angles to the nearest degree.

B. Solve. Find lengths to the nearest whole number and measurements of angles to the nearest degree.

9. A kite's string is 75 yards long and forms an angle of 40° with the ground. How high is the kite above the ground? 48 yards

10. Radar had detected a plane at a horizontal distance of 22 miles from the control tower. The angle of elevation from the tower to the plane is 10°. How high is the plane above the ground? 4 miles

11. A 25-foot aluminum ladder rests against the side of a house. The bottom of the ladder is about 6 feet from the wall. Find the angle the ladder forms with the ground. 76°

12. A 72-foot-long escalator rises 21 feet from the first floor to the second. Find the angle that the escalator forms with the first floor. 17°

13. A television transmitting tower is 200 feet high. Each support cable forms an angle of 58° with the ground. How long is each support cable? 236 feet

14. A point on the ground is 35 feet from the base of a tree. The angle of elevation from that point to the top of the tree is 42°. Find the height of the tree.

15. The length of the shadow cast by a flagpole is 16 meters. The angle of elevation from the end of the shadow to the top of the flagpole is 42°. Find the height of the flagpole. 14 meters

16. While standing at a certain place near the base of the 555-foot-high Washington Monument, tourists can view the top of the monument at a 60° angle of elevation. How far away are they from the base of the monument? 320 feet

17. A wheelchair ramp forms a 4° angle with level ground. If the ramp is 20 meters long, how high above the ground is the top of the ramp?   1 meter

18. A straight section of railroad track is 250 feet long and forms a 3° angle with level ground. How much higher than the level ground is the train after traveling along that section of track?   13 feet

19. The angle of depression from the balcony of an apartment to the edge of a swimming pool is 60°. The balcony is 75 feet above the ground. How far from the building is the edge of the pool?   43 feet

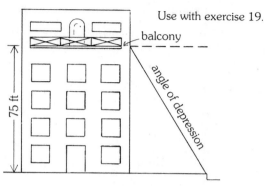

Use with exercise 19.

20. A plane is flying at an altitude of 37,000 feet. The airport is 100 miles ahead. What will the plane's angle of descent be as it approaches the airport if the pilot starts a steady descent at that point?   4°

C. 21. The angle of depression from a lighthouse on shore to a boat at sea is 18°. If the lighthouse is 300 feet above sea level, how far is the boat from the shore?   923 feet

22. A forest ranger sights a small fire from the top of a fire tower that is 148 feet high. If the measure of the angle of depression is 16°, how far is the fire from the base of the tower?   516 feet

---

CAREER

Surveyor

Surveyors measure land areas. They may be involved in resolving boundary conflicts, subdividing construction areas, or interpreting land descriptions prior to transfers of property. Surveyors use a *transit* to measure angles. This tool is a small telescope set upon a tripod.

Suppose a surveyor uses a transit to measure the angle of elevation from the transit to the top of a building. The distance from the transit to the building is 100 feet, the angle measures 35°, and the height of the transit is 5.5 feet. How high is the building?   75.52 ft

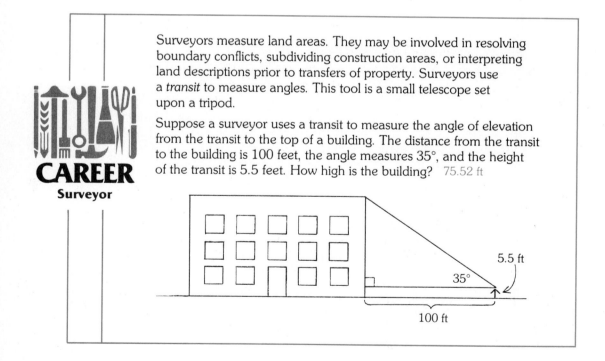

SKILLS MAINTENANCE

Write an algebraic expression for each phrase.

1. three less than a number a $a - 3$

2. the sum of two numbers a and b $a + b$

3. four more than five times a number b

4. a number x decreased by 20 $x - 20$

Rename each rational number as a terminating or a repeating decimal.

5. $\frac{3}{11}$ $0.\overline{27}$

6. $\frac{5}{6}$ $0.8\overline{3}$

7. $\frac{5}{4}$ 1.25

8. $\frac{2}{5}$ 0.4

Change each percent to a decimal.

9. 9% 0.09

10. 12% 0.12

11. 2.3% 0.023

12. 80% 0.8

Solve.

13. A real-estate agent received a 7% commission for selling a house. The commission was $6440. What was the selling price of the house? $92,000

14. The interest on a car loan from one year is $715. If $6500 is the amount borrowed, what is the interest rate?   11%

Write the conjunction without using the word *and*.

15. $x < -2$ and $x < 4$ $x < -2$

16. $7 > a$ and $a > -2$ $-2 < a < 7$

Determine whether each system is (*a*) consistent, (*b*) consistent and dependent, or (*c*) inconsistent.

17. $y = -2x$
$3y = 1 - 6x$ c

18. $2x + 3y = 8$
$x - 2y = -3$ a

19. $2x + 3y = 6$
$4x + 6y = 12$ b

Solve each of the following by using a proportion.

20. What number is 30% of 60?   18

21. 90 is 36% of what number?   250

Change each radical to simplest form.

22. $\sqrt{88}$ $2\sqrt{22}$

23. $\sqrt{\frac{5}{13}}$ $\frac{\sqrt{65}}{13}$

24. $\sqrt{500a^2}$ $10|a|\sqrt{5}$

Simplify. (Rationalize the denominator).

25. $\frac{7}{2 - \sqrt{3}}$ $14 + 7\sqrt{3}$

26. $\frac{\sqrt{2}}{\sqrt{5} - 1}$ $\frac{\sqrt{10} + \sqrt{2}}{4}$

Solve.

27. The units digit of a two-digit number is 1 less than the tens digit. What is the number if it equals one more than 6 times the sum of its digits.   43

28. The sum of the digits of a two-digit number is 8. If the digits are reversed, the new number formed is 18 less than the original number. Find the original number.   53

Solve by using the quadratic formula.

29. $6x^2 - 5x - 4 = 0$ $-\frac{1}{2}, \frac{4}{3}$

30. $2x^2 - 9x + 1 = 0$ $\frac{9 \pm \sqrt{73}}{4}$

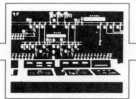

COMPUTER

BASIC has trigonometric functions to determine the sine, cosine, and tangent of an angle—important functions for any work dealing with right triangles. Shapes other than right triangles, however, also use these functions. What would happen if one corner of a triangle were kept in a fixed position on the screen, if the length of the hypotenuse remained constant, and if a loop were used to change the triangle's inner angles? Study the program below.

```
 10 HGR: REM GENERATE A SERIES OF TRIANGLES
 20 HOME: VTAB 22: PRINT "ENTER RADIUS AND AMOUNT TO
    INCREASE": PI = 3.14159
 30 INPUT "ANGLE (R,S): ";R,S
 40 HGR: FOR ANGLE = 0 TO 2 * PI STEP S * PI / 180
 50 X = SIN (ANGLE) * R: Y = COS (ANGLE) * R
 60 X = X + 140: Y = Y + 85: REM CENTER THE DRAWING
 70 HCOLOR= 3
 80 HPLOT 140,85 TO X,Y: REM HYPOTENUSE
 90 HPLOT X,Y TO X,85: REM OPPOSITE
100 HPLOT X,85 TO 140,85: REM ADJACENT
110 NEXT ANGLE
120 GOTO 20
```

EXERCISES

1. If you have access to an Apple II computer, enter the program and RUN it. (If the computer is not an Apple, see the Computer Handbook on pages 541–546 for Applesoft commands that must be modified for other computers.) Try entering decimal values, as well as integers, for S. What happens?

2. Which lines should you remove to draw just the hypotenuse? What effect would that have?

3. What would you change to draw just the outer circle?

4. You may have noticed that the circle is not perfect because the pixels, or individual points on the screen, are not perfectly square. Can you multiply x by some number so that the circle will appear round?

ANSWERS

1. The program prints a set of triangles of hypotenuse R, centered with one angle at the origin, and spaced S degrees apart.

2. Remove lines 90 and 100; the new picture resembles a star or asterisk with $\frac{360}{S}$ lines.

3. Change line 80 to

   80 HPLOT X,Y: REM PLOT POINT

   and delete 90 and 100.

4. Multiplying X by 1.1 in line 50 makes the circle rounder.

ENRICHMENT

See Activities 39–41,
p. T52.

CHAPTER 15 REVIEW

VOCABULARY

acute angle (15.1)

acute triangle (15.1)

angle (15.1)

angle of depression (15.6)

angle of elevation (15.6)

complement (15.1)

complementary angles (15.1)

congruent angles (15.2)

corresponding angles (15.2)

corresponding sides (15.2)

cosine (15.3)

hypotenuse (15.1)

legs (15.1)

line segment (15.1)

obtuse angle (15.1)

obtuse triangle (15.1)

ray (15.1)

right angle (15.1)

right triangle (15.1)

sides of an angle (15.1)

similar triangles (15.2)

sine (15.3)

solve a right triangle (15.5)

supplement (15.1)

supplementary angles (15.1)

tangent (15.3)

trigonometric ratio (15.3)

vertex of an angle (15.1)

vertices (15.1)

REVIEW EXERCISES

15.1 **Classify an angle with the given measurement as acute, obtuse, or right.**

1. 90° right

2. 75° acute

3. 101° obtuse

Give the measurement of the complement of each angle.

4. 29° 61°

5. 47° 43°

6. 85° 5°

Give the measurement of the supplement of each angle.

7. 16° 164°

8. 75° 105°

9. 149° 31°

The measurements of two angles of a triangle are given. Find the measurement of the third angle.

10. 16°, 15° 149°

11. 30°, 105° 45°

12. 90°, 45° 45°

13. In △ABC, the measure of ∠C is 65 more than the measure of ∠A, and the measure of ∠B is three times the measure of ∠A. Find the measure of each angle.

m∠A = 23, m∠B = 69, m∠C = 88

△PQR is a right triangle.

14. What is the hypotenuse? $\overline{PR}$

15. What are the legs? $\overline{PQ}$ and $\overline{QR}$

16. What leg is opposite ∠P? $\overline{QR}$

17. What leg is adjacent to ∠R?
$\overline{QR}$

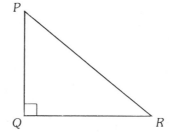

15.2 For exercises 18–23, △*RST*   △*CDE*. Complete each pair of corresponding sides.

18. $\overline{ST}$ and $\underline{\quad DE \quad}$ **19.** $\overline{CD}$ and $\underline{\quad RS \quad}$ **20.** $\overline{RT}$ and $\underline{\quad CE \quad}$

Complete each pair of corresponding angles.

21. $\angle S$ and $\underline{\quad \angle D \quad}$ **22.** $\angle E$ and $\underline{\quad \angle T \quad}$ **23.** $\angle C$ and $\underline{\quad \angle R \quad}$

△*ABC* ~ △*DEF*. For each set of measures, find the lengths of the other sides.

24. $a = 4$, $b = 7$, $c = 5$, $d = 6$ **25.** $d = 6$, $c = 12$, $f = 15$, $b = 8$

15.3 △*XYZ* is a right triangle. Find the trigonometric ratios of the acute angles. Remember to express radicals in simplest form.

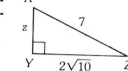

26. $\sin X$ $\frac{2\sqrt{10}}{7}$ **27.** $\sin Z$ $\frac{3}{7}$

28. $\cos X$ $\frac{3}{7}$ **29.** $\cos Z$ $\frac{2\sqrt{10}}{7}$

30. $\tan X$ $\frac{2\sqrt{10}}{3}$ **31.** $\tan Z$ $\frac{3\sqrt{10}}{20}$

15.4 Use the table on page 548 to find each of the following ratios.

32. $\sin 49°$ 0.7547 **33.** $\cos 23°$ 0.9205 **34.** $\tan 64°$ 2.0503

Use the table on page 548 to find the measurement of angle *A*.

35. $\cos A = 0.8746$ $29°$ **36.** $\sin A = 0.9877$ $81°$

37. $\tan A = 9.5144$ $84°$ **38.** $\cos A = 0.5592$ $56°$

Use the table on page 548 to find the measurement of angle *A* to the nearest degree.

39. $\sin A = 0.3589$ $21°$ **40.** $\cos A = 0.3914$ $67°$

41. $\tan A = 0.3444$ $19°$ **42.** $\sin A = 0.3427$ $20°$

15.5 △*ABC* is a right triangle and m$\angle C = 90$. The lengths of two sides are given. Solve the triangle. Express the length of the third side in simplest radical form. Find the measures of $\angle A$ and $\angle B$ to the nearest degree.

43. $a = 5$, $b = 6$ **44.** $a = 3$, $c = 7$ **45.** $b = 4$, $c = 2\sqrt{13}$

15.6 Solve. Find lengths to the nearest whole number and measurements of angles to the nearest degree.

46. A 16-foot ladder rests against a wall. The ladder forms a 70° angle with the ground. How far from the ground does the top of the ladder rest? 15 ft

47. Find the angle of elevation from a takeoff point to a jet that is 55 miles high and 170 miles from the takeoff point. 19°

TEACHER'S RESOURCE
MASTERS

Chapter 15 Test

Multiple-Choice Test

PROBLEM–SOLVING
HANDBOOK

p. 540

CHAPTER 15 TEST

1. Find the measurement of the complement of an angle whose measurement is 72°. 18°

2. Find the measurement of the supplement of an angle whose measurement is 85°. 95°

3. The measurements of two angles of a triangle are 62° and 34°. Find the measurement of the third angle. 84°

4. In $\triangle ABC$, the measure of $\angle A$ is 24 more than the measure of $\angle B$, and the measure of $\angle C$ is two times the measure of $\angle B$. Find the measure of each angle.

$\triangle JKL \sim \triangle PQR$. For each set of measures, find the lengths of the other sides. Express answers to the nearest tenth.

5. $j = 8$, $k = 6$, $\ell = 13$, $q = 8$

6. $j = 8\frac{1}{4}$, $\ell = 3$, $r = 6$, $q = 11$

For each right triangle, find the sine, the cosine, and the tangent of each acute angle. Remember to express radicals in simplest form.

7.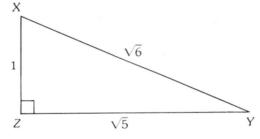

8.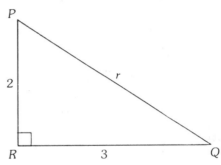

Use the table on page 548 to find each of the following trigonometric ratios.

9. $\sin 19°$ 0.3256

10. $\cos 80°$ 0.1736

11. $\tan 24°$ 0.4452

Use the table on page 548 to find the measurement of angle A to the nearest degree.

12. $\cos A = 0.6550$

13. $\sin A = 0.4400$

14. $\tan A = 1.2375$

$\triangle ABC$ is a right triangle and $m\angle C = 90$. The lengths of two sides are given. Solve the triangle. Express the length of the third side in simplest radical form. Find the measures of $\angle A$ and $\angle B$ to the nearest degree.

15. $a = 5$, $b = 7$

16. $a = 6$, $c = 10$

17. A 36-foot-high pole is supported by a wire attached from the top of the pole to the ground 16 feet from the base of the pole. What is the measure of the angle (to the nearest 1°) formed by the support wire and the ground? 66°

CUMULATIVE REVIEW: CHAPTERS 8–15

Choose the correct answer.

1. How would you describe the following system: $2x + 3y = 1$
$$2x + 4y = 3 \quad \text{A}$$

  A. consistent   **B.** consistent and dependent

  C. inconsistent   **D.** inconsistent and dependent

2. Solve the following system for y: $3x - 2y = 7$
$$4x - 3y = 1 \quad \text{A}$$

  A. $y = 25$ **B.** $y = -25$ **C.** $y = 19$ **D.** $y = -19$

3. Graph $y - x < 2$.   B

  A.   **B.**   **C.**   **D.**

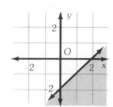 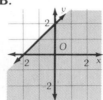 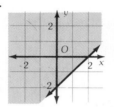 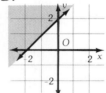

4. The sum of two numbers is 16. The larger number is one more than twice the smaller number. What is the smaller number?   C

  A. 11   **B.** -11 **C.** 5   **D.** -5

5. Change $\dfrac{x^2 + 5x + 6}{x^2 - x - 6}$ to simplest form.   A

  A. $\dfrac{x + 3}{x - 3}$ **B.** $-\dfrac{5x + 6}{x + 6}$ **C.** -1 **D.** -5

6. Simplify $(-6a)^{-3}$.   C

  A. $-\dfrac{1}{18a^3}$ **B.** $\dfrac{1}{18a^3}$ **C.** $-\dfrac{1}{216a^3}$ **D.** $\dfrac{1}{216a^3}$

7. Find the quotient $\dfrac{x^2 + 6x + 9}{x^2 + x - 6} \div \dfrac{x^2 - 9}{3 - x}$ and express it in simplest form.   D

  A. $-\dfrac{(x + 3)^2}{x - 2}$ **B.** $\dfrac{1}{x - 2}$ **C.** $\dfrac{3 - x}{(x - 2)(x - 3)}$ **D.** None of these

8. Find the LCD of fractions with the following denominators: $x^2 + 2x$ and $x^2 - 3x - 10$.   B

  A. $(x + 2)(x - 5)$ **B.** $x(x + 2)(x - 5)$ **C.** $x(x + 2)^2(x - 5)$ **D.** $(x + 2)$

9. Express the difference $\dfrac{3b}{2b - 8} - \dfrac{b + 2}{b - 4}$ in simplest form.   A

  A. $\dfrac{1}{2}$ **B.** $\dfrac{b + 4}{2(b - 4)}$ **C.** $\dfrac{5b + 4}{2(b - 4)}$ **D.** $\dfrac{2(b - 1)}{b - 4}$

10. Solve $\dfrac{5}{x+2} = \dfrac{3}{x-1}$.   C

A. 0 　　　　　　**B.** $\dfrac{1}{2}$ 　　　　　　**C.** $\dfrac{11}{2}$ 　　　　　　**D.** $\varnothing$

11. Solve $A = \dfrac{d_1 \cdot d_2}{2}$ for d_1.   A

A. $d_1 = \dfrac{2A}{d_2}$ 　　**B.** $d_1 = \dfrac{Ad_2}{2}$ 　　**C.** $d_1 = 2A - d_2$ 　　**D.** $d_1 = \dfrac{A}{2} - d_2$

12. Give the direct-variation equation for the following: *The total cost c of work completed at $15 an hour varies directly as the time t in hours.*   D

A. $t = 15c$ 　　**B.** $ct = 15$ 　　**C.** $c = \dfrac{1}{15t}$ 　　**D.** $c = 15t$

13. What proportion would you use to solve the following problem: *36 is 90% of what number?*   A

A. $\dfrac{36}{x} = \dfrac{90}{100}$ 　　**B.** $\dfrac{x}{36} = \dfrac{90}{100}$ 　　**C.** $\dfrac{90}{36} = \dfrac{x}{100}$ 　　**D.** $\dfrac{36}{90} = \dfrac{100}{x}$

14. If y varies inversely as x and $x = 3$ when $y = 6$, what is x when $y = 9$?   B

A. $\dfrac{9}{2}$ 　　**B.** 2 　　**C.** 18 　　**D.** None of these

15. If y varies directly as x and $x = 5$ when $y = 2$, what is the constant of variation k?   A

A. $\dfrac{2}{5}$ 　　**B.** $\dfrac{5}{2}$ 　　**C.** 2 　　**D.** 5

16. Which of the following equations describes an inverse variation?   D

A. $\dfrac{y}{x} = 5$ 　　**B.** $y = 2x$ 　　**C.** $8 = \dfrac{y}{4x}$ 　　**D.** $xy = \dfrac{2}{3}$

17. What proportion would you use to solve the following problem: *The length b of the base of a triangle with a given area varies inversely as the triangle's altitude h. If $b = 3$ cm when $h = 6$ cm, what is b when $h = 9$ cm?*   C

A. $\dfrac{6}{3} = \dfrac{9}{b}$ 　　**B.** $\dfrac{3}{b} = \dfrac{6}{9}$ 　　**C.** $\dfrac{3}{b} = \dfrac{9}{6}$ 　　**D.** $\dfrac{3}{9} = \dfrac{6}{b}$

18. Find the product $\sqrt{5} \cdot \sqrt{2}$.   B

A. 10 　　**B.** $\sqrt{10}$ 　　**C.** $\sqrt{7}$ 　　**D.** 7

19. Change $\dfrac{3}{\sqrt{12}}$ to simplest form.   D

A. $\dfrac{3}{2\sqrt{3}}$ 　　**B.** $\dfrac{1}{4}$ 　　**C.** $\dfrac{1}{2}$ 　　**D.** $\dfrac{\sqrt{3}}{2}$

20. Find $\sqrt{12} + \sqrt{192}$.   C

A. $\sqrt{204}$ 　　**B.** $3\sqrt{10}$ 　　**C.** $10\sqrt{3}$ 　　**D.** $2\sqrt{51}$

21. Find $(3 - \sqrt{5})^2$.   D

A. 4 　　**B.** 14 　　**C.** $14 + 6\sqrt{5}$ 　　**D.** $14 - 6\sqrt{5}$

22. Find the distance between $(-2, 3)$ and $(4, -1)$.   B

A. $4\sqrt{5}$ 　　**B.** $2\sqrt{13}$ 　　**C.** 10 　　**D.** $13\sqrt{2}$

23. Solve $2x^2 - x - 6 = 0$.   C

A. $-\dfrac{3}{2}$ 　　**B.** 2 　　**C.** $-\dfrac{3}{2}, 2$ 　　**D.** $-\dfrac{3}{2}, 0, 2$

24. Solve $3m^2 + 1 = 13$. B

    A. ± 4 **B.** ± 2 **C.** 2   **D.** 4

25. What number would you add to both sides of $x^2 + 4x + 8 = 0$ to complete the square?

    A. 4   **B.** -2 **C.** 2   **D.** -4 D

26. What is the value of the discriminant of $2x^2 + 3x - 1 = 0$? C

    A. $\dfrac{\sqrt{17}}{4}$ **B.** $\dfrac{\sqrt{17}}{2}$ **C.** 17   **D.** $\sqrt{17}$

27. Find the vertex of the following parabola: $y = 2x^2 - x + 1$.   A

    A. $\left(\dfrac{1}{4}, \dfrac{7}{8}\right)$ **B.** $\left(\dfrac{7}{8}, \dfrac{1}{4}\right)$ **C.** $(1, 2)$ **D.** $(2, 1)$

28. How many x-intercepts does the parabola $y = 3x^2 - 2x + 1$ have?   C

    A. two   **B.** one   **C.** none   **D.** three

29. Find the mode of the following data: 4 6 7 4 2 7 8 7   B

    A. 5   **B.** 7   **C.** $\dfrac{13}{2}$ **D.** $\dfrac{45}{2}$

30. Find the median of the following data: 1 7 8 1 3 2 10   C

    A. 1   **B.** $\dfrac{32}{7}$ **C.** 3   **D.** 9

31. Find the mean of the following data: 12 13 6 3 5 14 3   B

    A. 3   **B.** 8   **C.** 6   **D.** 11

32. Find the range of the following data: 23 2 8 21 17 14 2 2 5   D

    A. 2   **B.** $\dfrac{94}{9}$ **C.** 8   **D.** 21

33. If $Q_1 = 28$, $Q_2 = 37$, and $Q_3 = 41$, what is the semi-interquartile range?   C

    A. 13   **B.** 4   **C.** 6.5   **D.** 2

34. Use the stem-and-leaf display at the right. What are the stems?   A

    A. 1, 2, 3, 4   **B.** 4, 5, 6

    C. 0, 1, 2, 4, 5   **D.** 460

1	40, 52
2	41, 55
3	44
4	52, 60

35. How many three-digit numbers can be formed from the digits 6, 5, 3, and 2 if you may repeat digits?   B

    A. 24   **B.** 64   **C.** 16   **D.** 180

36. Evaluate 7!.   C

    A. 720   **B.** 28   **C.** 5040   **D.** None of these

37. In how many ways can you choose 3 people from 5 people to serve on a committee?   B

    A. 6   **B.** 10   **C.** 60   **D.** 120

38. How many different arrangements can you make if you have 6 pictures and want to display 3 of them on a wall? D

A. 20 **B.** 6 **C.** 720 **D.** 120

39. If one card is drawn at random from a well-shuffled standard deck of cards, what is the probability that it is a queen? B

A. 1 **B.** $\frac{1}{13}$ **C.** 0 **D.** $\frac{1}{4}$

40. What is the probability of *not* drawing a heart from a well-shuffled standard deck of cards? B

A. $\frac{1}{4}$ **B.** $\frac{3}{4}$ **C.** $\frac{1}{52}$ **D.** $\frac{51}{52}$

41. You pick a card from a standard deck and replace it. Then you pick another card. What is the probability that the first card is a queen and the second card is red? A

A. $\frac{1}{26}$ **B.** $\frac{1}{52}$ **C.** $\frac{17}{52}$ **D.** $\frac{4}{13}$

42. What is the measurement of the supplement of an angle whose measurement is 35°? D

A. 10° **B.** 55° **C.** 35° **D.** 145°

43. Refer to △ABC. What is sin A? B

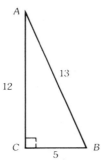

A. $\frac{12}{13}$ **B.** $\frac{5}{13}$ **C.** $\frac{13}{12}$ **D.** $\frac{13}{b}$

44. Which trigonometric ratio would you use to find the measurement of ∠A? A

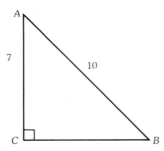

A. $\cos A = \frac{7}{10}$ **B.** $\cos A = \frac{10}{7}$ **C.** $\sin A = \frac{7}{10}$ **D.** $\sin A = \frac{10}{7}$

PROBLEM-SOLVING HANDBOOK

Make a Table
A blue sweater is missing.

Draw a Diagram
Six different pairings are possible.

The following list of strategies is useful in solving a great variety of problems:

- Make a table.
- Draw a diagram.
- Use a formula.
- Look for a pattern.
- Write and solve an equation.
- Use a model.
- Make a guess and then check the answer.
- Work backwards.
- Solve a simpler but related problem.
- Use logical reasoning.
- Use estimation.

It is important for you to realize that more than one strategy is often used in solving a given problem. It is entirely possible that you might solve a problem by using a different set of strategies than someone else.

To help you understand these problem-solving strategies, a brief description of each one is given, as well as a problem that might be solved by using the given strategy. A hint is given as to how you might solve each problem, but the work is left to you.

Make a Table

This strategy is useful in organizing the given information into a more understandable form that makes it easier to identify missing or superfluous information or to recognize a pattern.

Example:

A window decorator has the following sweaters and vests for a display: a red long-sleeved sweater, a white vest, a black vest, a black long-sleeved sweater, a blue vest, a white long-sleeved sweater, and a red vest. The decorator wants to have one long-sleeved sweater and one vest of each of the four colors (red, white, black, and blue). Which colors of sweaters or vests are missing?

HINT: Make a table as follows:

	Red	White	Black	Blue
Sweater	X	X	X	
Vest	X	X	X	X

Draw a Diagram

Often it is helpful to draw a sketch, a geometric figure, a number line, or any other diagram so that the relationships can be visualized more easily and a method for solving the problem will become more apparent.

Examples:

Four people, Lou, Marian, Pete, and Rich, each want to play one game of tennis with each of the other people. How many different pairings are possible?

HINT: One way to solve this problem is to draw a point to stand for each person and then connect the points in as many ways as possible to determine the possible number of pairings. Let L stand for Lou, M for Marian, P for Pete, and R for Rich.

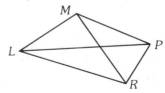

Use a Formula

This strategy is useful in situations in which a standard mathematical formula might apply.

Use a Formula
Its area is 128 ft^2.

Look for a Pattern
The next number in the sequence is 37.

Write and Solve an Equation
She is 20 years old now.

Use a Model

Sometimes the formula is stated, but often it is not. Some commonly used formulas are $d = rt$, (distance = rate × time), $I = prt$ (interest = principal × rate × time), and $E = IR$ (voltage = current × resistance). Other useful formulas are the area and volume formulas for geometric figures.

Example:

A roof section is shaped like a trapezoid. What is its area?

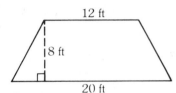

HINT: The formula for the area of a trapezoid is $A = \frac{1}{2}h(b_1 + b_2)$, where h = height, and b_1 and b_2 are bases.

Look for a Pattern

A sequence of numbers, geometric figures, ordered pairs, or other data may form a pattern that can be used to solve a problem.

Example:

What is the next number in the sequence? 2, 5, 10, 17, 26, . . .
HINT: $1^2 = 1, 2^2 = 4$, etc.

Write and Solve an Equation

This strategy is often used in solving algebraic problems. Problems that might be difficult to solve become easy to solve by using this strategy. (NOTE: Sometimes this strategy is extended to include inequalities.)
CAUTION: Be sure that the equation you write states the conditions of the problem. Otherwise, you might solve the equation correctly, but not solve the problem.

Example:

In 10 years Harriet will be 3 times as old as she was 10 years ago. How old is she now?

HINT: Let x = Harriet's present age. How old will she be in 10 years? How old was she 10 years ago? What equation represents the conditions of the problem?

Use a Model

A model is any concrete representation of the problem that uses objects or people to make the problem concrete.

Example:

How could you arrange these four shapes to form a rectangle?

HINT: Trace these shapes and cut out the four pieces. Rearrange them to form a rectangle.

Make a Guess and Then Check the Answer

This strategy can be very useful if no other strategy seems appropriate. You make a reasonable guess and then check it against the conditions of the problem. The process is repeated until the correct answer is found or until a method for solving the problem is recognized.

Example:

Place one of the following numbers in each of the small squares in the larger square below so that the sum of the numbers in each row, in each column, and in each diagonal is 30: 2, 4, 6, 8, 10, 12, 16, 18

12	2	16
14	10	6
4	18	8

HINT: Place 10 in the middle square.

Work Backwards

In using this strategy, you start with the end result and work backwards to the initial conditions. (The end result might be given in the problem, or it might be a guess.)

Example:

Paige has $1 left at the end of a shopping trip. She told a friend, "Each time I made a purchase, I had half as much money left as I had before I made the purchase. I made 5 purchases." How much money did Paige have before she started shopping?

HINT: If Paige had $1 left, how much was her last purchase? How much money did she have before her last purchase? How much was her next-to-last purchase? Continue working backwards to answer the problem.

Solve a Simpler but Related Problem

Often it is easier to solve a simpler problem that is less complex in terms of the magnitude or type of numbers, the number of possible cases, or the number of steps.

Example:

How many squares are in the figure below?

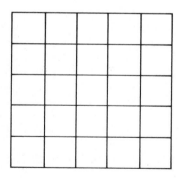

HINT: How many 1 × 1 squares are in the figure? How many 2 × 2 squares are in the figure? How many 3 × 3 squares? Continue the process. Notice that by breaking the problem into a number of simpler problems, you can solve the problem more easily.

Use Logical Reasoning

You use this strategy any time you ask yourself questions such as "If this, then what?" Sometimes this type of reasoning is called deductive reasoning.

Example:

Don had 24 blue socks and 24 black socks in a drawer. If the light was poor and he could not tell a black sock from a blue sock, how many socks would he have had to pull out of the drawer to be sure to get a matching pair?

HINT: If you pull out 2 socks, are you sure of having a matched pair? Does it matter if the matched pair is blue or black?

Use Estimation

This strategy is particularly useful when you don't need an exact answer or when it is impossible to obtain an exact answer.

Example:

Estimate in square centimeters the area of the following figure.

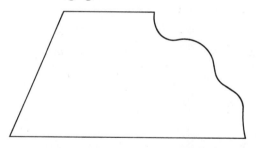

HINT: Trace the figure on a centimeter grid. Then count the number of squares. You will have to estimate the fractional parts.

Problem Solving—Chapter 1

1. The first eight numbers in the Fibonacci sequence are 1, 1, 2, 3, 5, 8, 13, 21. Find the next three numbers in the sequence. 34, 55, 89

2. A rectangle has two diagonals, a pentagon has five, and a hexagon has nine. How many diagonals does an octagon have? 20

3. Madonna decided to save a penny on January 1 and to double the amount in her bank account each day. How much did she have in her account on January 15? $163.84

4. Mr. and Mrs. Jones had one son. The son had three children. Each of these three children had three children. This pattern continued. How many direct descendants were in the Jones family in the sixth generation? 81

5. Goldie Goldfinger won $1,000,000 in a lottery. She gave away half the money the first year and gave away half that amount the second year. If she continues to give away money in this fashion, how much will she have left after ten years? $976.57

6. What is the sum of the first 9 prime numbers? 100

7. Find two square numbers whose sum is 194. 25 and 169

8. Find a square number that is also a cube number. typical answer: 64

9. Joe and Mike started a bicycle trip from the same point, traveling in opposite directions. Joe travels at a speed that is twice as fast as Mike's speed. After 2 hours they are 84 miles apart. What is Joe's speed? 28 mi/h

10. A car is available in four colors: red, green, black, and blue. The convertible tops are available in white, black, or tan. How many color combinations are possible? 12

11. Nine girls from Central High School are very good friends. Each girl talks to each of the other girls on the telephone once a week. How many phone calls between these girls take place each week? 36

12. A recipe requires $\frac{1}{2}$ teaspoon of baking powder for every $\frac{3}{4}$ cup of flour. If the recipe is increased and now requires 6 cups of flour, how many teaspoons of baking powder are needed? 4 tsp

13. Find two consecutive even integers whose product is 80. 8, 10

14. If you double the length of each side of a square whose perimeter is 12 in., what is the area of the new square?

15. On a blueprint for a house, $\frac{1}{8}$ inch represents 1 foot of real length. If a house has the dimensions 40 ft by 120 ft, what is the smallest size paper you can use to draw the blueprint? 5 in. x 15 in.

16. If it takes 22.44 gallons of water to fill the aquarium pictured below to the top with water, how much water is needed to fill the aquarium to 3 inches from the top? 18.7 gal

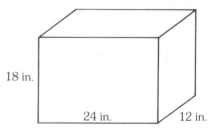

18 in.   24 in.   12 in.

Problem Solving—Chapter 2

1. Jamie had $3 in nickels and dimes. He had three fewer dimes than nickels. How many nickels and dimes did he have? 22 nickels, 19 dimes

2. When Kelli and Beth swam in a swim-a-thon, they swam a total of 123 laps. Kelli swam twice as many laps as

Beth, however. How many laps did each girl swim? Beth, 41; Kelli, 82

3. Name the next number in the sequence. 0, 7, 26, 63, 124, . . . 215

4. In a two-digit number the tens digit is five more than the units digit. The sum of the digits is 11. Find the number. 83

5. **a.** Mr. Jackson has a backyard that measures 42 feet by 96 feet. If he wants to fence in the yard, placing the fence posts 3 feet apart, how many fence posts does he need? 92

   b. Suppose Mr. Jackson wants to fence in only three sides, as shown. How many fence posts are needed? 79

   ```
       96 ft
   _____
                    |
                    |  42 ft
                    |
   _____
       96 ft
   ```

6. Complete the pattern:
   $$100 = 10^2$$
   $$1{,}000 = 10^3$$
   $$10{,}000{,}000 = 10^? \quad 10^7$$

7. A total of 522 people attended 3 hearings on pollution in Smogsville. At each hearing there were 3 people more than at the hearing before. How many people attended each hearing? 171, 174, 177

8. The sum of the digits of a 2-digit number is 11. If the digits are interchanged, the new number is 27 greater than the original number. What is the original number? 47

9. Place the following numbers in a magic square so that the sum of each row, each column, and each diagonal is the same: $\frac{1}{3}, \frac{7}{24}, \frac{1}{6}, \frac{3}{8}, \frac{1}{12}, \frac{5}{24}, \frac{1}{4}$,

$\frac{1}{8}$, and $\frac{1}{24}$. (Use each number only once.)

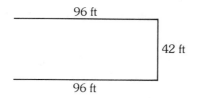

$\frac{1}{4}$	$\frac{1}{24}$	$\frac{1}{3}$
$\frac{7}{24}$	$\frac{5}{24}$	$\frac{1}{8}$
$\frac{1}{12}$	$\frac{3}{8}$	$\frac{1}{6}$

10. Two hamburgers and a milk shake cost $3.40. Three hamburgers and two milk shakes cost $5.60. How much does a hamburger cost? A milk shake?

11. Complete the pattern. Note that $2^{-1} = \frac{1}{2^1}$, etc.
   $$2^1 + 2^{-1} = 2\tfrac{1}{2}$$
   $$2^2 + 2^{-2} = 4\tfrac{1}{4}$$
   $$2^3 + 2^{-3} = 8\tfrac{1}{8}$$
   $$2^6 + 2^{-6} = ? \quad 64\tfrac{1}{64}$$

12. A merry-go-round makes a full turn every 30 seconds. If Tanya is riding a horse placed 14 ft from the center of the merry-go-round, what is her speed in ft/min? 176 ft/min

13. Tanya's friend, Maria, is riding a horse 7 ft from the center of the merry-go-round. How fast is she going? 88 ft/min

14. Tom and Ray are playing catch. They start out by standing 12 feet apart and increase the distance between them by one half after each throw. What is the total distance the ball has traveled after five throws? $158\tfrac{1}{4}$ ft

15. Five canaries are sitting in a row. Using the following clues, figure out the order in which they are seated.
   Clyde is the same distance from Alvin as he is from Benny.
   Ed is seated between Donald and Alvin.
   Benny is sitting next to Ed.
   Ed is not seated between Benny and Donald. no correct solution

16. In the drawing, figures *A, B, C, D, E, F, G, H,* and *I* are squares. If the area of square *C* is 64 and the area of square *D* is 81, can you figure out the areas of the other squares? $I = 1, H = 49,$ $F = 100, G = 16, B = 225, E = 196,$ $A = 324$

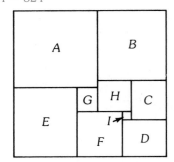

Problem Solving—Chapter 3

1. A rectangular yard is 2 meters long and 2.5 meters wide. How many meters of fence are needed to enclose the yard? 9 m

2. At 3:00 P.M. a train leaves Grand Central Station and heads south at 180 km/h. At the same time a second train leaves, heading north at 160 km/h. When will they be 1 700 km apart?

3. Kevin's scores on 4 tests were 86, 72, 94, and 77. He wants his average on 5 tests to be 85. What is the lowest score he can get on the fifth test? 96

4. If the length of a rectangle is 3 times the width and the perimeter is 24 m, then what is the width? 3 m

5. A square slab of concrete for the foundation of a building is 17.2 meters long on each side. Find the area. Use $A = bh$ or $A = s^2$. 295.84 m²

6. The distance from Jill's house to school is 1.5 miles. If Jill's mother drives her to school at a rate of 25 mi/h, how long will it take her to get to school? Use $d = rt$. 0.06 of an hour, or 3 min 36 sec

7. A shopper bought a pair of gloves at a "15% off" sale. The price of the gloves was reduced by $2.40. Find the original price of the gloves. $16.00

8. The Concorde SST flies at an average speed of 1550 miles per hour. How far can a Concorde fly in 5 hours?

9. If a box is 2 feet high, 3 feet wide, and 4 feet long, what is its volume? Use $V = lwh$. 24 ft³

10. The interest on Sam's loan amounts to $196.80. What is the principal if the rate is 12% and he pays it back in 2 years? Use $I = prt$. $820

11. The sales tax in Joe's state is 4%. He paid a sales tax of $5.50 on an overcoat. Find the price of the coat to the nearest dollar. $138

12. Three less than twice the sum of some number and 7 is 41. Find the number.

13. Two planes leave an airport at 2 P.M., one flying south at 675 mi/h, the other flying north at 450 mi/h. In how long will they be 3600 miles apart?

14. The baseball team ordered new uniforms at a total cost of $949.50. There are 18 players on the team. Find the cost of one uniform. Use $C = np$.

15. When 3.8 is added to twice some number, the result is 12. Find the number.

16. The height of a triangle is 7 mm more than the base. The area of the triangle is 30 mm². Find the height and base. Use $A = \frac{1}{2}bh$. $b = 5, h = 12$

Problem Solving—Chapter 4

1. Marty can make a down payment of $1500 on a new car and pay the remainder of the cost in 48 equal monthly payments. What is the most he can pay each month if he plans to spend less than $5820? $89.99

2. Mrs. Blanco is paid $18,000 a year plus a 5% commission on her sales. What range of sales does she need in order to receive an annual income between $20,000 and $24,000?

3. Bill estimates that a sweater costs $15 less than a certain jacket. He plans to buy both items for less than $50. Find the greatest amount he can spend for the jacket. $32.49

4. Two people share an apartment. They estimate that the amount spent each month for rent should be twice the amount spent for food. The amount they can pay each month for food and rent must be less than $630. What is the greatest amount they can pay each month for food? $209.99

5. Jenny's scores for three games in bowling were 76, 103, and 121. In order to have an average greater than 100 for four games, what is the lowest score she can bowl in the next game? 101

6. The perimeter of a rectangular yard is 64 meters, and the length is 2 meters more than the width. Find the area of yard. 255 m²

7. A hot dog costs $1.25 and a glass of milk costs $0.70. If you want to buy two hot dogs, how many glasses of milk can you buy and still spend less than $5.00? 3

8. If 13 is subtracted from a number and that difference is divided by 2, then the quotient is more than 45. What numbers are possible? $x > 103$

9. Mr. Smith knows that he can write checks totaling an amount less than $250 and still maintain the required minimum balance in his checking account. If he writes a check for $137, how much money will be available in the account? $x < 113$

10. If 21 is added to a number and that sum is multiplied by 3, then the product is more than 89. What numbers are possible? Round to the nearest whole number. $x \geq 9$

11. A parking lot charges $1.50 for the first hour and $0.85 for each additional hour or part of an hour. For how many hours can a person park a car and spend less than $5.00? 5 hours or less

12. The width of a rectangular building is three times its length. If the perimeter is between 24 meters and 40 meters, what are the possible values of the width? 9 m to 15 m

13. During the month of June, Annie wants her average golf score to be less than 76. She has already shot rounds of 78, 81, 73, and 76. Find the highest score she can shoot on her fifth round of golf.

14. David is 3 times as old as Art, minus 5 years. David is 25. How old is Art? 10

15. Out of 120 students in a school band, 24 play woodwind instruments. What percent of the students play woodwind instruments? 20%

16. A ticket taker at a show earns $3 an hour for working part-time. How many full hours must she work to earn at least $25 a week? 9

Problem Solving—Chapter 5

1. At noon an airplane leaves an airport and flies due east at 540 km/h. At 1:00 P.M. a second airplane leaves the airport, also flying east but at 720 km/h. When does the second plane overtake the first? 4:00 P.M.

2. Lois and Norma live 800 km from each other. If Lois drives 65 km/h toward Norma's house and Norma drives 86 km/h toward Lois's, in how many hours will they meet? $5\frac{1}{3}$ hr

3. Matt rode his bike a certain distance at 2 mi/h. Steve rode his bike the same distance at 4 mi/h, but Steve left 30 minutes after Matt. How long did it take Steve to catch up to Matt? $\frac{1}{2}$ hr

4. Aaron walks and jogs to school each day. He averages 5 km/h walking and 9 km/h jogging. The distance from home to school is 8 km, and he makes the trip in 1 hour. How far does he jog in a trip?

5. A private airplane leaves an airport and flies due south at 192 km/h. Two hours later a jet leaves the same airport and flies due south at 960 km/h. When will the jet overtake the private plane?

6. A train leaves Chicago and travels east at 35 mi/h. An hour later another train leaves Chicago on a parallel track at 40 mi/h. How far from Chicago will the trains meet?   280 miles

7. Two cars passed each other, going in opposite directions. The eastbound car was traveling 15 km/h faster than the westbound car. In 3 hours, they were 345 km apart. How fast was each car traveling?   50 km/h and 65 km/h

8. A car leaves Boston and travels north at 56 km/h. Another car leaves Boston one hour later, traveling north at 84 km/h. How far from Boston will the second car overtake the first?   168 km

9. John gets a ride in his parents' car to school. The car travels 20 mi/h. John must walk home from school and does so, along the same route, at a rate of 4 mi/h. If he walks $\frac{1}{2}$ hour longer than he rides, how long does the whole trip take?   45 min

10. A new stereo system costs $875.00 plus sales tax of $61.25. What is the sales-tax rate?   7%

11. Puerto is 25 km downriver from Haven. At noon a tugboat leaves Haven and travels upstream at 15 km/h. At 3 P.M. a barge leaves Puerto also traveling upstream, but at 50 km/h. At what time does the barge pass the tugboat?   5 P.M.

12. At noon a plane left an airport and flew due west at 525 km/h. At 2:00 P.M. a second plane left the same airport and flew due east at 625 km/h. At what time were they 4500 km apart?   5:00 P.M.

13. If you fly a plane from Newfoundland to Ireland (a distance of 2026 miles) in 7 hours, what is your average speed in miles per hour?   289.43 mi/h

14. A softball player got a hit 30% of 40 times at bat. How many hits did the player get?   12

15. Mr. and Mrs. Charbonneau borrow $15,000 to start a new business. The yearly interest rate on the loan is 11%. How much interest is due every 3 months? $412.50

16. A family plans to buy a television set and a video recorder. They estimate that the video recorder will cost $300 more than the TV set. They want to spend no more than $1400 in all. What is the greatest amount they can spend on the TV set? $550

Problem Solving–Chapter 6

1. A photograph is 10 inches long and 8 inches wide. It is surrounded by a border of uniform width. If the border and photo together occupy an area of 168 inches^2, how wide is the border?   2 in.

2. The sum of 5 and some unknown number, multiplied by that same unknown number, is 24. Find the possibilities for the unknown number. -8, 3

3. The length of a rectangle is twice the width. The length is decreased by 3 m, and the width is increased by 2 m. The area of the resulting rectangle is 30 m². Find the dimensions of the original rectangle.   4 m by 8 m

4. Nine more than the square of a number equals six times that number. Find the number.   3

5. The area of a rectangular garden is 200 square meters. The perimeter is 60 meters. Find the dimensions of the garden.   10 m by 20 m

6. Boat A takes 45 minutes longer than Boat B to travel between two harbors. The boats leave at the same time and travel toward each other. Boat A travels 24 mi/h and Boat B travels 40 mi/h. When will they meet? $1\frac{1}{8}$ hr

7. The square of a number plus seven times the number is 120. Find the number. -15 or 8

8. The length of a rectangle is 4 m greater than the width. The area of the rectangle is 96 m². Find the length and the width. $w = 8, l = 12$

9. The length of one side of a square is decreased by 1 mm and that of an adjacent side is increased by 2 mm in order to fit into a rectangular opening. If the area of the rectangle is 180 mm², find the length of a side of the original square.   13 mm

10. The sum of some number squared and six times that number is 27. Find the number. -9 or 3

11. A swimming pool 25 m long and 12 m wide is surrounded by a deck that is the same width all around the pool. If the pool and deck together occupy an area of 464 m², how wide is the deck?   2 m

12. The difference of some number and 7, multiplied by that number, equals -6. Find that number.   6 or 1

13. The area of a rectangle is 84 cm². The perimeter is 40 cm. Find the dimensions.   14 cm by 6 cm

14. Eight more than the square of a number is six times the number. Find the number.   4 or 2

15. The sides of a square are extended to form a rectangle. One side of the square is extended 5 cm and the other side is extended 2 cm. The area of the new rectangle is 130 cm². Find the length of a side of the square.   8 cm

16. The square of a number minus five times the number is 84. Find the number.   12 or -7

Problem Solving—Chapter 7

1. Dan sells albums. The first hour he sold three albums. After that, each hour he sold two more albums than he did the hour before. How many had he sold at the end of eight hours?   80 albums

2. In a triangle the longest side is twice the shortest side, and the third side is 5 centimeters less than the longest side. Find the three sides if the perimeter is 45 centimeters.   10 cm, 15 cm, 20 cm

3. Gail's bowling scores were 117, 129, and 132. What must she score in her next game to keep her average of 128?

4. Two cars start from the same town at the same time and travel in opposite directions. One car averages 40 mi/h and the other car averages 50 mi/h. In how many hours will they be 450 miles apart?   5 hours

5. The square of a number is 20 more than 8 times the number. Find the number.   10 or -2

6. 75 grams of water at 60°C is added to 100 grams of water at 40°C. What is the temperature of the mixture?

7. 250 grams of water at 80°C is added to 50 grams of water at 40°C. What is the temperature of the mixture?

8. 125 grams of water at 55°C is added to 200 grams of water at 30°C. What is the temperature of the mixture?

9. 150 grams of water at 70°C is added to 50 grams of water at 20°C. What is the temperature of the mixture? 57.5°C

10. 175 grams of water at 50°C is added to 30 grams of water at 25°C. What is the temperature of the mixture? about 46°C

11. A car's velocity is 13 meters per second at 1 second and 25 meters per second at 5 seconds. What is the car's velocity at 10 seconds? 40 m/sec

12. A car's velocity is 12 meters per second at 0 seconds and 24 meters per second at 4 seconds. What is the car's velocity at 8 seconds? 36 m/sec

13. A van's velocity is 50 meters per second at 2 seconds and 30 meters per second at 6 seconds. What is the van's velocity at 8 seconds? 20 m/sec

14. A car's velocity is 14 meters per second at 0 seconds and 30 meters per second at 4 seconds. What is the car's velocity at 7 seconds? 42 m/sec

15. A truck's velocity is 36 meters per second at 1 second and 12 meters per second at 5 seconds. What is the truck's velocity at 7 seconds? 0 m/sec

16. A car's velocity is 45 meters per second at 2 seconds and 30 meters per second at 5 seconds. What is the car's velocity at 9 seconds? 10 m/sec

Problem Solving—Chapter 8

1. Kathy has 2 quarters, 4 dimes, and 6 nickels. If she had 6 quarters, 4 dimes, and 2 nickels, how much more money would she have? $0.80

2. Frank spent $7.15 plus 6% sales tax on food items at the grocery store. He also spent $12.29 plus 7% sales tax on non-food items. What was his total bill at the store? $20.73

3. A doll manufacturer prices its dolls at 2 times the manufacturing cost plus $3.25 per doll. If the company wants to make a doll that sells for $34.99 at the most, what must the manufacturing cost of the doll be? less than or equal to $15.87

4. The length of a rectangle is 4 times the width. The area is 9 square centimeters. Find the length and the width of the rectangle. $1\frac{1}{2}$ cm, 6 cm

5. The owner of a fabric store spent $750 on 5000 patterns and bobbins. The patterns cost $0.48 each and the bobbins cost $0.08 each. How many of each did the owner buy?

6. A right angle is divided into two angles so that the larger angle is 3° less than twice the smaller angle. Find the measurement of each angle. 31° and 59°

7. Tickets for a play cost $1.50 for each adult and $0.75 for each child. If 275 tickets were sold for a total of $348.75, how many tickets of each kind were sold?

8. The length of a rectangle is 7 inches more than the width. The perimeter is 34 inches. Find the length and the width. 12 in., 5 in.

9. A sum of money amounting to $3.90 consists of dimes and quarters. If there are 27 coins in all, how many quarters are there? 8

10. The sum of the digits of a two-digit number is 11. The number itself is 7 more than twice the number that results from interchanging the digits. Find the number. 83

11. The board of directors of a corporation granted a bonus of $6,000 to be divided between two employees, with the senior of the two receiving $2,800 more than the junior. How much did each person receive? $4400 and $1600

12. Two women started a business, one investing more than the other. The first year's profit is $12,000. The bigger investor will get $800 more than her partner. How much will each woman receive? $6400 and $5600

13. The sum of the digits of a two-digit number is 13. If the digits are interchanged, the new number is 27 greater than the original number. Find the original number. 58

14. A supermarket stocks pretzels that sell for $0.80 per pound and peanuts that sell for $1.04 per pound. How many pounds of each should be used in 24 pounds of a mixture that sells for $0.90 a pound? 14 lbs pretzels, 10 lbs peanuts

15. A plane flew 96 miles with the wind in 36 minutes and returned against the wind in 48 minutes. How fast would the plane have flown in still air, and what was the speed of the wind? 140 mi/h, 20 mi/h

Problem Solving—Chapter 9

1. The number 18 can be written as the sum of three whole-number addends such that adding 3 to the first addend yields the second addend, and multiplying the first addend by 3 yields the third addend. What are the three addends?

2. Two cars traveling in opposite directions meet on a highway. Car A averages 45 mi/h and Car B averages 30 mi/h. In how many hours will they be 150 miles apart? 2 hr

3. Jill plans to spend no more than $25.00 on gas and oil. She got 15 gallons of gas at $1.46 per gallon. How much can she spend on oil? less than or equal to $3.10

4. Tillie and John started from the same point at the same time and drove in opposite directions. Tillie drove 5 mi/h faster than John. After 3 hours, they were 177 miles apart. Find the rate of each. John, 27 mi/h; Tillie, 32 mi/h

5. If one side of a square was increased by 5 ft and another side was decreased by 2 ft, the new area would be 44 square feet. Find a side of the square. 6 ft

6. Jay can mow a lawn in 4 hours and Neil can mow the same lawn in 3 hours. How long will the job take if they work together? $1\frac{5}{7}$ hours

7. The sum of the digits of a two-digit number is 7. If the digits are interchanged, a new number is formed that is 27 less than the original number. Find the original number. 52

8. A man made a deposit of $154 in his account. If his deposit consisted of 62 bills, some of which were one-dollar bills and the rest five-dollar bills, how many bills of each kind did he have? 39 one-dollar bills and 23 five-dollar bills

9. An airplane cruises at 160 mi/h in still air. At that speed, the airplane flew 500 miles with the wind in the same amount of time it took to fly 350 miles back against the wind. Assuming that the wind speed is constant, what is the wind speed? 28.2 mi/h

10. A swimming pool has 2 inlet pipes. One of them can fill the pool in 3 hours, and the other pipe can fill it in 2 hours. How long will it take to fill the pool if both pipes are used? $1\frac{1}{5}$ hours

Chapter 9
1. 3, 6, 9
3. less than or equal to $3.10

11. A bank teller counts a certain amount of money in 16 minutes, but if another teller helps, they can count the money in 10 minutes. How long will it take the second teller to count the money alone?

12. Laurie can wallpaper a room in 8 hours. She and Mila can paper the room in 6 hours if they work together. How long will it take Mila alone? 24 hr

13. On a fishing trip Tom and Dan traveled 20 miles downstream in the same amount of time it took to return 16 miles upstream. The speed of the boat at full throttle in still water is 40 mi/h. What is the speed of the current?

14. It takes a roofer 36 hours to do a new roof alone, and another roofer takes 24 hrs. How long will it take them to do it together? 14.4 hr

15. The hot-water faucet fills a tub in 30 minutes and the cold-water faucet in 20 minutes. The tub can be drained in 15 minutes. If both faucets are on and the drain is open, how soon will the tub be full? 60 min

16. A farmer has 2 tractors. With his new one, he can plow a field in 15 hours, 3 hours faster than with his old one. How long will it take to plow the field using both tractors? 8.18 hr

Problem Solving—Chapter 10

1. Martin borrowed $15,000 from a bank to open a health club. He paid the loan back in 2 years, and the interest amounted to $3600. What annual rate of interest did the bank charge Martin?

2. Jay plans to rent a car for 3 days. He must pay $36 per day and $0.18 per mile. He estimates that the total cost will be at least $140 and no more than $160. How many miles does he plan to drive the car? $178 \le x \le 289$

3. An eastbound jet leaves an airport and travels 300 miles per hour. At the same time a westbound jet departs and travels at 650 miles per hour. In how many hours will the planes be 5700 miles apart? 6 hr

4. The product of two consecutive odd integers is 143. Find the two numbers.

5. A car's velocity at 2 seconds is 40 meters per second, and at 6 seconds it is 20 meters per second. What is the car's velocity at 8 seconds? 10 m/sec

6. One van, heading east, leaves a campground. Two hours later a second van, heading west, leaves the same campground. The second van is traveling 15 mi/h faster than the first. Six hours after the second van leaves, the two vans are 580 miles apart. Find the rate at which each van is traveling.

7. John can pour a concrete patio in 48 minutes. He and Pat can pour it in 30 minutes. How long will it take Pat alone? 80 min

8. The cost for a lawn-care service is directly proportional to the lawn's size. The cost for 25,000 ft^2 is $30. What is the cost for 32,000 ft^2? $38.40

9. The cost for a team of professional movers is directly proportional to the time it takes for the team to load and unload the moving van. If it took $4\frac{1}{2}$ hours for one job and the cost was $250, how long would it take to do a job costing $375? 6.75 hr

10. If it takes 20 minutes to walk a certain distance at 2 mi/h, how long would it take to travel the same distance at 3 mi/h? The time needed varies inversely as the rate of travel. 13.3 min

11. Chris went to the beauty shop and left a 15% tip for the beautician. If the amount of the tip was determined by the total price, which was $56, how much was the tip that Chris left? $8.40

12. Donny earned $18,150 a year. After he received a promotion, his annual salary was $21,235.50. This reflected what percent of increase? 17%

13. The weight of an object on the moon varies directly as its weight on the earth. A person who weighs 160 lbs on the earth weighs 28 lbs on the moon. How much would Helen weigh on earth if she weighed 21 lbs on the moon?

14. The weight of an object on the moon varies directly as its weight on the earth. A person who weighs 225 lbs on earth weighs 38 lbs on the moon. If Lisa weighs 85 lbs on earth, how much would she weigh on the moon?

15. When the tension on a wire is kept constant, the number of vibrations per second varies inversely as the length of the wire. A wire 500 centimeters long vibrates 140 times per second. What will the number of vibrations per second be for a wire 240 centimeters long?

16. The distance required for a vehicle to come to a complete stop varies directly as the square of the speed of the vehicle. If the stopping distance for a vehicle traveling 12 kilometers per hour is 6 meters, what is the stopping distance for a vehicle traveling 55 kilometers per hour? 126.0 meters

Problem Solving—Chapter 11

1. The area of a square garden is 225 square feet. What is the length of one side of the garden? 15 ft

2. What is the area of a square dog pen that is enclosed by 12 feet of fencing?

3. A checkerboard consisting of 64 squares has a total area of 256 square inches. Find the length of the side of each square. 2 in.

4. The area of a square picture, including the frame, is 100 square inches. If the area of the frame is 25 square inches, find the length of each side of the picture in inches to the nearest tenth.

5. To the nearest tenth, find the length of the diagonal of a rectangle whose sides are 8 m and 12 m. 14.4 m

6. The diagonal of a square is 14 cm. Find the length of each side. 9.9 cm

7. The area of a square backyard is 625 square feet. If three sides of the yard are to be fenced, how much fencing is needed? 75 ft

8. Robert hiked 10 miles due south and then 8 miles due west. How far is he from his starting point? 12.8 mi

9. Two telephone poles, 22 feet and 28 feet high, are 30 feet apart. How long is the wire stretched from the top of one pole to the top of the other? 30.6 ft

10. The length of a rectangle is three times its width. The area of the rectangle is 147 square units. Find the dimensions to the nearest tenth. 7 and 21 units

11. The square root of the product of 16 and a number is 12. Find the number.

12. Four less than the square root of twice a number is 0. Find the number. 8

13. Twice the square root of a number increased by 5 is 15. Find the number.

14. Three times a number is decreased by 6. The square root of the resulting number equals 6. Find the number. 14

15. The quotient of twice the square root of a number and 3 is 10. Find the number. 225

16. The square root of the product of 2 and a number is decreased by 3. The result is 5. Find the number. 32

Problem Solving—Chapter 12

1. The length of a rectangle is three times its width. Find the length of the rectangle if the area of the rectangle is 48 m^2.

2. The altitude of a triangle is 3 cm more than the base. Find the base of the triangle if the area of the triangle is 44 cm^2. 8 cm

3. The product of two consecutive even integers is 168. Find the integers.

4. The square of a number is ten more than three times the number. Find the number. 5 or −2

5. In a theater, the number of seats in each row is eight fewer than the number of rows. The theater seats 560 persons. How many seats are there in each row? 20

6. Together, John and Sue can paint a room in 5 hours. Alone, John can paint the room in 3 hours less than Sue can do it alone. How many hours will it take each to do the job? John 8.7, Sue 11.7

7. If a number is increased by nine times its reciprocal, the result is six. Find the number. 3

8. Find two numbers whose product is 84 and whose difference is 5.

9. Hose A and Hose B together can fill a pool in 4 hours. Hose A can fill the pool 6 hours faster than Hose B. How long would it take Hose B to fill the pool alone? 12 hr

10. A rectangular pool is 10 feet wide and 18 feet long. A uniform deck is built around the pool such that the area of the pool and the deck combined is 384 square feet. How wide is the deck?

11. Find two numbers whose product is 52 and whose sum is 17. 13 and 4

12. The sum of a number and its reciprocal is $2\frac{1}{6}$. Find the number and its reciprocal. $\frac{2}{3}$ and $\frac{3}{2}$

13. A rectangle has a perimeter of 30 inches. Its area is 54 square inches. Find its dimensions. 6 in. x 9 in.

14. One number exceeds another number by four. The sum of the squares of the numbers is 58. Find the two numbers.

15. If a playground that measures 40 meters by 60 meters is to be doubled in area by extending each side an equal amount, how much should each side be extended? 20 meters

16. A rectangular backyard is to be enclosed by using the house as one side and 20 yards of fencing for the other three sides. What is the greatest area that can be enclosed? 50 yd^2

Problem Solving—Chapter 13

1. The amount of gain or loss in the price of a stock for each of five days was $-\frac{5}{8}$, $\frac{3}{4}$, $\frac{1}{8}$, $-\frac{3}{8}$, and $\frac{1}{2}$. Find the mean price change. $+\frac{3}{40}$

2. The temperatures for five days were 98°, 101°, 99°, 97°, and 102°. Find the mean temperature. 99.4°

3. On six science tests, Sam had the following scores: 38, 52, 45, 38, 35, and 42. What is the mode? 38

4. Attendance for five games was 34,823; 33,502; 34,025; 36,227; and 34,673. What is the median attendance?

5. Six gymnasts have the following heights: 5′2″, 5′6″, 5′0″, 5′1″, 5′7″, and 5′4″. What is the median height?   5′3″

6. Jane can complete her paper route in a mean time of 2 hours. It took her 1.75 hours on Monday, 2 hours on Tuesday, 2.25 hours on Wednesday, and 2.5 hours on Thursday. How long did it take her on Friday?   1.5 hours

7. John bought a stock at $32.00 per share. Over the next four days, the gain or loss in the price of the stock was $-2\frac{1}{4}$, $-1\frac{1}{2}$, $\frac{3}{8}$, and $-\frac{1}{4}$. If John sold it on the sixth day at the median price for the first five days, how much money did he gain or lose?   He lost $3.375 per share.

8. Ryan's mathematics quiz scores are as follows: 33, 41, 33, 35, 38, and 36. What will he have to score on the next quiz to raise his average by 2 points?

9. In a geometry class of 12 students, Test Form A was given. Find the range for the test if the scores were 79, 86, 82, 95, 91, 72, 87, 91, 79, 80, 75, and 93.

10. The range in age for a group of 8 people is 17 years. Seven of the people are the following ages: 12, 26, 15, 18, 17, 23, and 14. How old is the eighth person if the youngest person in the group of people is 12?   29

11. A sample of 20 families were surveyed to determine the number of cars owned by each household. Following are the results:

Number of cars	Number of households
0	4
1	7
2	5
3	3
4	1

Find the mean number of cars per family.   1.5

12. In a city block, the number of persons living in each house was tabulated as follows: 2, 4, 5, 3, 4, 3, 1, 2, 6, 7, 3, 3, 2, 5, 4, 6. Determine the mean, the median, and the mode.   3.75, 3.5, 3

13. Bob earned the following amounts for selling magazines on 8 different days: $8, $5, $11, $6, $4, $7, $6, and $9. Find the

mean   7
median   6.5
mode   6
range   7
variance   4.5
standard deviation   2.12
interquartile range   3

Problem Solving—Chapter 14

1. Find the number of men's suits that can be made if the manufacturer has five types of fabric, four colors of fabric, and three styles to choose from.   60

2. In how many ways can four students be seated in a row?   24

3. How many 7-digit telephone numbers can be formed from 1, 2, 3, 4, 5, 6, 7, 8, 9, 0?   10,000,000

4. In how many different ways can nine people be assigned positions to form distinct baseball teams?   362,880

5. From a group of twelve people a committee of five is to be chosen. In how many different ways can this committee be chosen?   792

6. A play has been written that requires a cast of three women. Six women try out for the three roles. How many different casts are possible?   20 casts

7. If the name of one of the fifty states is selected at random, what is the probability that the name of the state begins with *I*? $\frac{2}{25}$

Chapter 13
8. 50
9. 23

8. You draw one card from a standard deck of cards, replace the card, then draw another card. What is the probability that the first card is a king and the second card is a queen? $\frac{1}{169}$

9. You draw one card from a standard deck of cards, then draw another card without replacing the first card drawn. What is the probability that each card drawn is a spade? $\frac{1}{17}$

10. What is the probability that one card drawn from a deck of 52 cards will be a heart or a king? $\frac{4}{13}$

11. A bag contains four red marbles and ten black marbles. If two marbles are drawn in succession, and if the first is not replaced, what is the probability that the first is red and the second is black? $\frac{20}{91}$

12. A red die and a white die are thrown. What is the probability that the sum of the numbers thrown is seven? $\frac{1}{6}$

13. A box contains five books, three are science books and two are mathematics books. All books are the same size. A book is drawn at random and replaced in the box, and then a second book is drawn. What is the probability that both books drawn are science books? $\frac{9}{25}$

14. A die is thrown and a card is drawn from a 52-card deck. What is the probability that the die shows 2 or 6 and the card is a club? $\frac{1}{12}$

Problem Solving—Chapter 15

Find lengths to the nearest whole number and measurements of angles to the nearest degree.

1. One of two complementary angles is ten more than three times the other. Find the measurement of each. 20° and 70°

2. One of two supplementary angles is five less than four times the other. Find the measurement of each. 37° and 143°

3. The measurement of the supplement of an angle is 60 degrees less than three times the measurement of the complement of the angle. Find the measurement of the angle. 15°

4. The sum of an angle and four times its complement is 30 degrees more than the supplement of the angle. Find the measurement of the angle. 75°

5. The measurement of one of the angles of a right triangle is four times that of a second angle of the triangle. What are the measurements of the three angles?

6. Sarah left home and walked 5 blocks east and 12 blocks south. If she decides to go straight home from her destination, how far must she walk? 13 blocks

7. The top of a vertical tree broken by the wind hits the ground 30 feet from the foot of the tree. If the upper portion makes an angle of 40° with the horizontal ground, what was the original height of the tree? 64 ft

8. One end of a guy wire 28 meters long is attached to the top of a flagpole and the other end of the wire is attached to the ground. The wire makes an angle of 35° with the ground. Find the height of the flagpole. 16 m

9. A 90-foot ladder, leaning against a building, makes an angle of 75° with the ground. Find the distance of the base of the ladder from the building.

10. An aircraft takes off and climbs steadily at 400 miles per hour along a straight path making an angle of 20° with the ground. How high is the airplane after 15 minutes? 34 miles

COMPUTER HANDBOOK

Working With Computers and Their Languages

Computers are always ready to do your bidding, provided that you instruct them in a language they understand.

There are many computer languages, some of which are FORTRAN, PASCAL, C, BASIC, PL/1 and COBOL. All of these, however, provide for essentially the same operations.

All computer languages have statements for receiving and reporting about data. These statements are called Input/Output statements, or I/O statements for short.

There are also statements that operate on data once it is inside the machine. These statements are used to add, multiply, rearrange, regroup, or in a word, manipulate data. Finally, there is a group of statements which control program flow, that is, what to do next. Each language has its own way of communicating these operations to the computer. There are even differences between one BASIC and another. Most of these occur in the I/O statements, especially the graphic ones. The BASIC used throughout this book is APPLESOFT BASIC. If you are using a different type, be sure to check the last section of this handbook.

Working in BASIC

Statements are entered in a BASIC program with line numbers preceding them. It does not matter in which order you type the line numbers. BASIC will place them in sequential order. It is good practice to number your lines by tens, therefore making it easy to insert additional lines later on.

To change a statement, just retype the line number and the statement associated with it, and it will be replaced.

To erase a line, just type in the line number followed by RETURN.

BASIC will accept more than one statement on a line as long as the statements are separated by colons. The following is a valid line in BASIC:

10 X = X + 1: PRINT: GOTO 10

BE CAREFUL—If you do not save a file before changing disks or shutting off the computer, *you will lose your program* and will have to start over! Using SAVE, you can always come back to your file later.

If the Program Doesn't Work

The first thing to do is to check to see if you typed it in correctly. If you have a syntax error and you are working on an APPLE, the problem will most likely be a typing error.

If you are working on another type of computer, be sure you checked that computer's BASIC manual for the correct syntax. Some of the things to look for are the following:

1. Raising to a power might require ! instead of ^.
2. VTAB, HTAB, and all of the graphic statements are very APPLE specific. Be sure to substitute the correct ones from your BASIC.
3. Some BASICs do not have string arrays. These also would not have the MID$ statement.

For your own programs, once you are sure of all the syntax, try using the TRACE command to follow the program's flow. Something else to try is to stop the program at critical points with either an END statement or by typing control-C and printing out the current values of the variables. Stopping a program does not cause it to change, so you can examine it at any time.

Dictionary of Computer Terms

The following list of computer commands and computer terminology will be useful for you to refer to when you perform the computer activities throughout this book.
NOTE: All items marked by an asterisk (*) are commands or functions that are unique to the Applesoft version of the BASIC language. These commands all relate to screen-formatting and graphics-formatting commands.
The programs in the computer activities in this book may be modified to be used on computers other than the Apple II series computers. Consult the reference guide to your computer.
Brackets [ ] are used in this handbook to indicate optional elements of commands, statements, and functions.
Whenever parentheses ( ) are used in the examples of correct format, they are part of the command, statement, or function.

ABS( )
The ABS function returns the absolute value of a positive or a negative variable or constant.

ASC( )
The ASC function returns the ASCII equivalent of a character in a string or string variable. ASC("A") will result in the value 65. ASC("1") will result in the value 49.

ASCII
The standard code for converting characters to numbers that a computer can understand and converting numbers back to characters is called ASCII, an acronym for American Standard Code for Information Interchange.

CHR$( )
The CHR$ function returns the character equivalent of an ASCII code (between 0 and 255). CHR$(65) will result in the letter "A", and CHR$(49) will result in the number "1".

COS( )
The trigonometric COS function returns the cosine of the value within parentheses.

DATA
A DATA statement creates a list of numeric or string values to be assigned by READ statements. The correct format is

    DATA numeric or string constant
    [, numeric or string constant,
    . . .]

DIM
The DIM command is used to set the maximum dimensions (matrix) of a string or numeric array. DIM A(5) sets one-dimensional array A as having 5 elements. DIM A(5,5) sets array A as having a matrix of 5 × 5 elements.

END
The END command ends execution program and returns control back to the user.

FOR/NEXT
The FOR command works together with the NEXT command to create a loop in which one or more commands will be repeated a specified number of times. The correct format is

    FOR numeric variable = starting value
    TO ending value [STEP step value]
    NEXT numeric variable

When the computer encounters a FOR/NEXT loop, it assigns the numeric variable to the starting value, and performs any commands it finds before the first NEXT command encountered. Then it increases or decreases the numeric variable, depending on the STEP value specified (the default is + 1). If the new value is in the specified range (including the ending value), the loop repeats. If not, control goes to the following line.

GOSUB

The GOSUB command followed by a line number functions almost exactly like the GOTO command, with the exception that the computer "remembers" the line number that told it to make the branch to the specified subroutine. The RETURN instruction, which is necessary to end the subroutine, restores execution of the program to the command following the GOSUB.

GOTO

The GOTO command followed by a line number instructs the computer to branch to a specified line in the program and to continue execution of the program from that point.

*HCOLOR

The Applesoft BASIC command HCOLOR sets the plotting color for all consecutive HPLOT commands to the hires (high-resolution) graphic screen. The correct format is

HCOLOR = numeric value or variable

In the above statement, the variable must be between 0 and 255.

*HGR

The Applesoft BASIC command HGR sets up graphics screen page one for hires (high-resolution) graphic plotting.

*HOME

The Applesoft BASIC command HOME instructs the computer to clear the display screen and position the cursor at the upper left-hand corner.

*HPLOT

The Applesoft BASIC command HPLOT either plots a point or connects a series of points on the hires graphics screen in the color specified by the most recent HCOLOR command. The correct format is

HPLOT x1,y1 TO x2,y2 [TO
x3,y3 ...]

In the above statement, x1 and y1

represent the horizontal and vertical coordinates, respectively, of point 1; x2 and y2 represent the coordinates of point 2. In high resolution, horizontal values are within the 0 to 279 range, and vertical values are within the 0 to 191 range.

*HTAB

The Applesoft BASIC command HTAB positions the cursor at a specified column (1 to 40) prior to a PRINT command.

IF/THEN

The IF and THEN commands test or compare one or more sets of values and instruct the computer to act depending on the outcome of the test. The correct format is

IF variable = [or >=, <=, <>, <, or
>] second variable THEN instruction

If the comparison results in a "true" evaluation, such as IF 5 = 5 , , , or IF 4 < > 5, , , , the commands following THEN will be executed. If the comparison is "false," the program will continue on the next program line. Multiple comparisons using the Boolean operators AND, NOT, and OR may be combined in one IF/THEN statement.

INPUT

The INPUT command instructs the computer to accept a value from the keyboard or another open channel or device. The correct format is

INPUT variable name

If the variable name is of the numeric type, such as X, the computer will evaluate the numeric entry before assigning it to the stated variable. If the variable name is of the string type, such as X$, the computer will accept any entry and will not evaluate it before assigning it to that string variable.

INT( )

The INT function gives the integer value of a floating-point (decimal) value or numeric variable. INT(5.15) will give the value 5.

INTEGER (%) VARIABLES

Numeric variables followed by a % symbol are regarded as integer variables. Thus any decimal or floating point value will be truncated. In the statement

    LET A% = 3.14159

the integer variable A% will hold the value 3.

LEFT$( )

The LEFT$ command returns a specified number of characters from the leftmost portion of a specified string. The correct format is

    LEFT$ (string or string-variable
    name , number of characters)

In both of the following cases,
LEFT$(A$,3) and
LEFT$("string",3), the result will be a 3-character-long portion of the string specified.

LEN( )

The LEN command returns the character length of a string variable. The correct format is

    LEN (string or string-variable name)

These are two examples of the LEN command: LEN(A$), LEN("string").

LET

The LET command assigns a value to a numeric or string variable. The correct format is

    LET variable name = statement

If the variable is of the string type, the statement must be enclosed in quotation marks. If the variable is of the numeric type, the statement may be any numeric value or valid operation, and must be entered without quotation marks.

LIST

The LIST command instructs the computer to display a list of the current program in memory.

*LOAD

The LOAD command instructs the computer to load a specified BASIC program into memory from disk. The correct format is

    LOAD filename

Any program currently in memory when a LOAD is executed will be wiped out.

MID$( )

The MID$ command returns a specified number of characters from the middle of a string. The correct format is

    MID$ (string or string-variable name ,
    start , number of characters)

In the following case, MID$(A$,3,5), the result will be a 5-character-long portion of A$ beginning with the third character in A$.

ON GOTO/ON GOSUB

The ON command, used with either the GOTO or the GOSUB command, instructs the computer to transfer program execution to a specified line or subroutine, depending on the value of the variable given in the statement. If the variable = 1, then program execution will transfer to the first line number listed. If the variable = 2, then GOTO or GOSUB will transfer execution to the second line number given, etc. If the variable is zero or greater than the number of lines listed, the GOTO or GOSUB will not be executed and program execution will continue with the next line. A negative variable value causes an error condition. The correct format is

    ON variable GOTO/GOSUB line number,
    [, line number , line number , . . .]

OPERATIONS SYMBOLS +, -, /, * and ^

The following symbols are used in BASIC to perform mathematical operations:

    + addition; 5 + 5 (10)
    - subtraction; 5 - 3 (2)
    * multiplication; 5 * 5 (25)
    / division; 25 / 5 (5)
    ^ power; 5 ^ 2 (25)

PRINT

The PRINT command instructs the computer to display various types of information to the screen or to another output device. The correct format is

> PRINT statement

The statement following the PRINT command may or may not be enclosed in quotation marks. If the statement to be printed is enclosed in quotation marks, the computer will print the statement. If the statement is not enclosed in quotation marks, it will be evaluated by the computer prior to printing the result of the evaluation. Following a PRINT command, the cursor normally drops to the first column of the following row. If a *semicolon* follows the statement, the cursor will remain at the position immediately after the previously displayed information. A *comma* will position it at the next active tab stop (column).

READ

The READ command assigns values to numeric or string variables from DATA statements within the program. The correct format is

> READ variable [, variable , variable , . . .]

REM

The REM command allows the programmer to place a remark on a program line that is ignored when the program is RUN. Other commands that are to be executed may not follow a REM command on the same line.

RETURN

The RETURN command ends a subroutine, and restores execution of the program to the command following the GOSUB. Any commands following RETURN on a program line will be ignored.

RIGHT$( )

The RIGHT$ command returns a specified number of characters from the rightmost portion of a string. The correct format is

> RIGHT$ (string or string-variable name , number of characters)

In both of the following cases, RIGHT$(A$,3) and RIGHT$ ("string",3), the result will be a 3-character-long portion of the string specified.

RND( )

The RND function returns a random decimal value between 0 and 1. The outcome of the returned value may be multiplied by a factor to extend the limits on this value. INT(10 * RND(1)) will return a random integer value between 0 and 9, inclusive.

RUN

The RUN command, used in direct (immediate) mode, instructs the computer to execute any BASIC program currently in memory, starting from the lowest line number in the program.

*SAVE

The SAVE command saves the current program in memory to disk. The correct format is

> SAVE filename

CAUTION: Any previous editions saved under this filename will be wiped out! See LOAD.

SGN( )

The SGN function determines whether a number is positive, negative, or zero. The correct format is

> SGN (numeric constant or variable)

The result of the SGN function will either be 1, 0, or −1 for positive, zero, and negative constants or variables, respectively.

SIN( )

The trigonometric SIN function returns the sine of the value within parentheses.

SQR( )

The SQR function returns the square root of the value or numeric variable within the parentheses. SQR(4) will result in a value of 2.

STR$( )

The STR$ function creates a string containing the digits in a numeric variable. STR$(123) will return the string "123".

VAL( )

The VAL function returns the numeric value of a string variable. VAL("123") will result in a value of 123, and VAL ("ABC123") will result in a value of 0, since the letters A, B, and C are nonnumeric characters.

*VTAB

The Applesoft BASIC command VTAB is used to position the cursor on a specified row (1 to 24) prior to a PRINT command.

TABLES—Squares and Square Roots

n	n^2	$\sqrt{n}$	n	n^2	$\sqrt{n}$	n	n^2	$\sqrt{n}$
1	1	1.000	51	2,601	7.141	101	10,201	10.050
2	4	1.414	52	2,704	7.211	102	10,404	10.100
3	9	1.732	53	2,809	7.280	103	10,609	10.149
4	16	2.000	54	2,916	7.348	104	10,816	10.198
5	25	2.236	55	3,025	7.416	105	11,025	10.247
6	36	2.449	56	3,136	7.483	106	11,236	10.296
7	49	2.646	57	3,249	7.550	107	11,449	10.344
8	64	2.828	58	3,364	7.616	108	11,664	10.392
9	81	3.000	59	3,481	7.681	109	11,881	10.440
10	100	3.162	60	3,600	7.746	110	12,100	10.488
11	121	3.317	61	3,721	7.810	111	12,321	10.536
12	144	3.464	62	3,844	7.874	112	12,544	10.583
13	169	3.606	63	3,969	7.937	113	12,769	10.630
14	196	3.742	64	4,096	8.000	114	12,996	10.677
15	225	3.873	65	4,225	8.062	115	13,225	10.724
16	256	4.000	66	4,356	8.124	116	13,456	10.770
17	289	4.123	67	4,489	8.185	117	13,689	10.817
18	324	4.243	68	4,624	8.246	118	13,924	10.863
19	361	4.359	69	4,761	8.307	119	14,161	10.909
20	400	4.472	70	4,900	8.367	120	14,400	10.954
21	441	4.583	71	5,041	8.426	121	14,641	11.000
22	484	4.690	72	5,184	8.485	122	14,884	11.045
23	529	4.796	73	5,329	8.544	123	15,129	11.091
24	576	4.899	74	5,476	8.602	124	15,376	11.136
25	625	5.000	75	5,625	8.660	125	15,625	11.180
26	676	5.099	76	5,776	8.718	126	15,876	11.225
27	729	5.196	77	5,929	8.775	127	16,129	11.269
28	784	5.292	78	6,084	8.832	128	16,384	11.314
29	841	5.385	79	6,241	8.888	129	16,641	11.358
30	900	5.477	80	6,400	8.944	130	16,900	11.402
31	961	5.568	81	6,561	9.000	131	17,161	11.446
32	1,024	5.657	82	6,724	9.055	132	17,424	11.489
33	1,089	5.745	83	6,889	9.110	133	17,689	11.533
34	1,156	5.831	84	7,056	9.165	134	17,956	11.576
35	1,225	5.916	85	7,225	9.220	135	18,225	11.619
36	1,296	6.000	86	7,396	9.274	136	18,496	11.662
37	1,369	6.083	87	7,569	9.327	137	18,769	11.705
38	1,444	6.164	88	7,744	9.381	138	19,044	11.747
39	1,521	6.245	89	7,921	9.434	139	19,321	11.790
40	1,600	6.325	90	8,100	9.487	140	19,600	11.832
41	1,681	6.403	91	8,281	9.539	141	19,881	11.874
42	1,764	6.481	92	8,464	9.592	142	20,164	11.916
43	1,849	6.557	93	8,649	9.644	143	20,449	11.958
44	1,936	6.633	94	8,836	9.695	144	20,736	12.000
45	2,025	6.708	95	9,025	9.747	145	21,025	12.042
46	2,116	6.782	96	9,216	9.798	146	21,316	12.083
47	2,209	6.856	97	9,409	9.849	147	21,609	12.124
48	2,304	6.928	98	9,604	9.899	148	21,904	12.166
49	2,401	7.000	99	9,801	9.950	149	22,201	12.207
50	2,500	7.071	100	10,000	10.000	150	22,500	12.247

TABLES—Sines, Cosines, and Tangents

Angle	Sin	Cos	Tan	Angle	Sin	Cos	Tan
0°	.0000	1.0000	.0000	45°	.7071	.7071	1.0000
1	.0175	.9998	.0175	46	.7193	.6947	1.0355
2	.0349	.9994	.0349	47	.7314	.6820	1.0724
3	.0523	.9986	.0524	48	.7431	.6691	1.1106
4	.0698	.9976	.0699	49	.7547	.6561	1.1504
5	.0872	.9962	.0875	50	.7660	.6428	1.1918
6	.1045	.9945	.1051	51	.7771	.6293	1.2349
7	.1219	.9925	.1228	52	.7880	.6157	1.2799
8	.1392	.9903	.1405	53	.7986	.6018	1.3270
9	.1564	.9877	.1584	54	.8090	.5878	1.3764
10	.1736	.9848	.1763	55	.8192	.5736	1.4281
11	.1908	.9816	.1944	56	.8290	.5592	1.4826
12	.2079	.9781	.2126	57	.8387	.5446	1.5399
13	.2250	.9744	.2309	58	.8480	.5299	1.6003
14	.2419	.9703	.2493	59	.8572	.5150	1.6643
15	.2588	.9659	.2679	60	.8660	.5000	1.7321
16	.2756	.9613	.2867	61	.8746	.4848	1.8040
17	.2924	.9563	.3057	62	.8829	.4695	1.8807
18	.3090	.9511	.3249	63	.8910	.4540	1.9626
19	.3256	.9455	.3443	64	.8988	.4384	2.0503
20	.3420	.9397	.3640	65	.9063	.4226	2.1445
21	.3584	.9336	.3839	66	.9135	.4067	2.2460
22	.3746	.9272	.4040	67	.9205	.3907	2.3559
23	.3907	.9205	.4245	68	.9272	.3746	2.4751
24	.4067	.9135	.4452	69	.9336	.3584	2.6051
25	.4226	.9063	.4663	70	.9397	.3420	2.7475
26	.4384	.8988	.4877	71	.9455	.3256	2.9042
27	.4540	.8910	.5095	72	.9511	.3090	3.0777
28	.4695	.8829	.5317	73	.9563	.2924	3.2709
29	.4848	.8746	.5543	74	.9613	.2756	3.4874
30	.5000	.8660	.5774	75	.9659	.2588	3.7321
31	.5150	.8572	.6009	76	.9703	.2419	4.0108
32	.5299	.8480	.6249	77	.9744	.2250	4.3315
33	.5446	.8387	.6494	78	.9781	.2079	4.7046
34	.5592	.8290	.6745	79	.9816	.1908	5.1446
35	.5736	.8192	.7002	80	.9848	.1736	5.6713
36	.5878	.8090	.7265	81	.9877	.1564	6.3138
37	.6018	.7986	.7536	82	.9903	.1392	7.1154
38	.6157	.7880	.7813	83	.9925	.1219	8.1443
39	.6293	.7771	.8098	84	.9945	.1045	9.5144
40	.6428	.7660	.8391	85	.9962	.0872	11.4301
41	.6561	.7547	.8693	86	.9976	.0698	14.3007
42	.6691	.7431	.9004	87	.9986	.0523	19.0811
43	.6820	.7314	.9325	88	.9994	.0349	28.6363
44	.6947	.7193	.9657	89	.9998	.0175	57.2900
45	.7071	.7071	1.0000	90	1.0000	.0000	

Glossary

A

Abscissa The first number in an ordered pair. Also called the x-coordinate. (p. 210)

Absolute value The distance of any real number x from 0 on the number line. Represented by $|x|$. (p. 34)

Acceleration The rate of increase of velocity per unit of time. (p. 240)

Acute angle An angle whose measurement is less than 90°. (p. 492)

Acute triangle A triangle with three acute angles. (p. 493)

Addition property of equality If a, b, and c are any real numbers and $a = b$, then $a + c = b + c$. (p. 71)

Addition property of inequality Let a, b, and c be any real numbers.
If $a < b$, then $a + c < b + c$.
If $a > b$, then $a + c > b + c$. (p. 109)

Additive inverse property For any real number x, $x + (-x) = 0$. (p. 41)

Additive inverses Two numbers that are the same distance, in opposite directions, from 0 on the number line. The sum of two additive inverses is 0. (p. 41)

Algebraic expression An expression containing at least one variable. (p. 2)

Angle The union of two noncollinear rays that have the same endpoint. The rays are called the angle's sides, and the endpoint is called its vertex. (p. 492)

Associative properties Let a, b, and c be real numbers.
Addition: $(a + b) + c = a + (b + c)$.
Multiplication: $(ab)c = a(bc)$. (p. 11)

Axiom A statement assumed to be true. (p. 57)

Axis of symmetry A line that intersects a parabola at its vertex and divides the parabola into two congruent parts. (p. 418)

B

Bar chart A type of graph especially useful for displaying data that are not numbers. The lengths of the bars represent the frequencies for the various categories of data. (p. 439)

Base The repeated factor in a power. In a^4, the base is a. (p. 8)

Binomial A polynomial consisting of two terms. (p. 18)

Boundary line A line separating a plane into two half planes. (p. 280)

Box-and-whisker plot A diagram displaying the relationship between the quartiles and the extreme values of a set of data. (p. 456)

C

Closure properties Let a, b, and c be any real numbers.
Addition: $a + b$ is a real number.
Multiplication: ab is a real number. (p. 57)

Coefficient A number by which a variable or a product of variables is multiplied. (p. 8)

Combination An arrangement of elements of a set, in which elements cannot be repeated and the order of their arrangement does not matter. (p. 470)

Commutative properties Let a and b be real numbers.
Addition: $a + b = b + a$.
Multiplication: $ab = ba$. (p. 11)

Complementary angles Two angles the sum of whose measurements is 90°. (p. 492)

Conditional probability A probability of an event's occurrence when it is given that another event has already occurred. (p. 485)

Congruent angles Angles whose measures are equal. (p. 497)

Conic section A curve formed by the intersection of a plane with a right circular cone. (p. 406)

Conjecture A statement that has not been proved true or false. (p. 222)

Conjugates A pair of binomials of the form $a + \sqrt{b}$ and $a - \sqrt{b}$. (p. 379)

Conjunction A sentence formed by combining two sentences with the word *and*. (p. 123)

Consistent and dependent system A system of equations that has an infinite number of solutions. (p. 255)

Consistent system A system of equations that has one solution. (p. 255)

Constant A monomial that contains no variables. (p. 18)

Constant function A linear function in which *every* element in the domain is paired with the same element in the range. (p. 224)

Constant of variation The constant k in a direct variation of the form $y = kx$. Also called the constant of proportionality. (p. 336)

Coordinate plane The plane determined by the x-axis and the y-axis. (p. 210)

Coordinates (of a point) The numbers in the ordered pair that locates the point on the coordinate plane. (p. 210)

Corresponding angles A pair of congruent angles of similar triangles. (p. 497)

Corresponding sides Sides that are opposite corresponding angles of similar triangles. (p. 497)

Cosine A trigonometric ratio associated with an acute angle, determined by dividing the measure of the side adjacent to the angle in a right triangle by the measure of the hypotenuse. (p. 501)

Counting numbers The numbers in the set $\{1, 2, 3, 4, 5, \ldots\}$. (p. 30)

D

Data The numbers and facts dealt with in statistics. (p. 432)

Degree (of a monomial) The sum of the exponents of the variable factors. (p. 18)

Degree (of a polynomial) The degree of the term of greatest degree. (p. 138)

Dependent events A pair of events in which the probability of the second depends on the probability of the first. (p. 483)

Deviation score A value obtained by subtracting the mean of a set of numerical data from an element of the set. (p. 450)

Difference of two squares A binomial of the form $a^2 - b^2$. (p. 181)

Direct variation A linear function defined by an equation of the form $y = kx$, where $k \neq 0$. (p. 336)

Discriminant The expression $b^2 - 4ac$ in the quadratic formula. (p. 411)

Disjunction A sentence formed by combining two sentences with the word *or*. (p. 123)

Distance formula The formula
$$PQ = \sqrt{(x_2 - x_1)^2 + (y_2 - y_1)^2},$$
used for determining the distance between a point P with coordinates (x_1, y_1) and a point Q with coordinates (x_2, y_2). (p. 387)

Distributive property of multiplication over addition If a, b, and c are real numbers, then $a(b + c) = ab + ac$ and $(b + c)a = ba + ca$. (p. 11)

Divide-and-average method A method for approximating the square root of a number. (p. 364)

Division property of equality If a, b, and c are any real numbers and $a = b$ and $c \neq 0$, then $\frac{a}{c} = \frac{b}{c}$. (p. 75)

Domain The set of first elements of the ordered pairs in a relation. (p. 218)

E

Element (of a set) Any of the members of the set. (p. 30)

Empty set   A set that contains no elements. (p. 31)

Equation   An algebraic sentence in which two expressions are connected by the symbol $=$. (p. 68)

Equivalent rational expressions   Rational expressions that have the same value for all values of the variable(s). (p. 294)

Equivalent sentences   Open sentences that have the same solution set. (p. 68)

Evaluate   To replace each variable in an expression with a value and simplify the result. (p. 2)

Event   A subset of a sample space. (p. 472)

Experimental probability   A probability determined empirically—equivalent to the ratio $\frac{s}{n}$, where s is the number of times that the relevant outcome occurred and n is the total number of times that the experiment was performed. (p. 472)

Exponent   A number that tells how many times a base is used as a factor. In 3^4, the exponent is 4. (p. 8)

Extraneous root   A root, found in solving an equation, that does not satisfy the equation and is not a member of the solution set. (p. 320)

Extremes   The first and last elements in a proportion. In the proportion $\frac{y_1}{x_1} = \frac{y_2}{x_2}$, y_1 and x_2 are the extremes.

F

Factorial   The product of the consecutive counting numbers from 1 to any positive integer n. Represented by $n!$ (read "n-factorial"). (p. 469)

Factors   The numbers multiplied in a multiplication expression. (p. 8)

Finite set   A set in which the count of the elements has an end. (p. 30)

FOIL method   A shortcut for finding the product of two binomials, in which the first terms, the outside terms, the inside terms, and the last terms of the binomials are respectively multiplied and the resulting products are added. (p. 151)

Frequency distribution   A table used to organize raw numerical data so that the frequency of each datum is readily apparent. (p. 436)

Frequency polygon   A type of line graph used to organize data. The data are represented along a horizontal axis, and their frequencies are indicated by distances along a vertical axis. (p. 440)

Function   A relation in which each element in the domain is paired with exactly one element in the range. (p. 218)

Fundamental counting principle   The principle that the number of possible outcomes of a set of tasks is the product of the numbers of possible outcomes of the individual tasks. (p. 467)

G

Graph (of an ordered pair)   The point on the coordinate plane that corresponds to the ordered pair. (p. 210)

Graph (of a number)   The point on the number line that corresponds to a number. (p. 33)

Greatest common factor   The largest integer that is a factor of each of two or more integers. (p. 175)

Grouped frequency distribution   A table used to organize a large number of raw data or data in which there is a great difference between the largest value and the smallest value. The scores are grouped according to certain intervals. (p. 436)

Grouping symbols   Symbols used to indicate the order of operations in an expression. Examples are parentheses, brackets, and the fraction bar. (p. 3)

H

Half plane   One of the two regions into which a boundary line divides a plane. (p. 280)

Higher-order radicals   Radicals that involve cube roots, fourth roots, fifth roots, and so on. (p. 384)

Histogram   A graph, similar to a bar chart, used to display numerical data. (p. 439)

Hypotenuse   The side opposite the right angle in a right triangle. (p. 493)

I

Identity property   Let a be a real number. Addition: $a + 0 = 0 + a = a$. Multiplication: $a \cdot 1 = 1 \cdot a = a$. (p. 11)

Inconsistent system   A system of equations that has no solution. (p. 255)

Independent events   A pair of events in which the probability of the second does not depend on the probability of the first. (p. 483)

Index   A number used to indicate the root in a higher-order radical. (p. 384)

Inequality   A mathematical sentence containing the symbol $<$, $>$, $\leq$, $\geq$ or $\neq$. (p. 106)

Infinite set   A set in which the count of the elements is endless. (p. 30)

Integers   The numbers in the set $\{ \ldots, -3, -2, -1, 0, 1, 2, 3, \ldots \}$. (p. 30)

Intersection (of two sets)   A set consisting of the elements that are common to both sets. (p. 120)

Inverse variation   A function defined by an equation of the form $xy = k$ or $y = \frac{k}{x}$, where $x \neq 0$ and k is a nonzero real-number constant. (p. 345)

Irrational number   A real number that cannot be expressed in the form $\frac{a}{b}$, where a and b are integers and $b \neq 0$. (p. 31)

L

Least common denominator   The least common multiple of the denominators of two or more fractions. (p. 310)

Leg (of a right triangle)   Either of the sides adjacent to the right angle. Each leg is opposite an acute angle. (p. 493)

Like terms   Terms that differ only in their coefficients. (p. 18)

Linear equation in two variables   An equation whose graph in the coordinate plane is a line. (p. 215)

Linear function   A set of ordered pairs that is the solution set of a linear equation in two variables. (p. 224)

Linear programming   A method for solving problems that involve finding a maximum or minimum value of a function. (p. 282)

Linear term   A term of degree one. (p. 188)

M

Mean   A measure of central tendency obtained by dividing the sum of the numerical data in a set by the number of data. (p. 444)

Means   The middle elements in a proportion. In the proportion $\frac{y_1}{x_1} = \frac{y_2}{x_2}$, x_1 and y_2 are the means. (p. 339)

Measures of central tendency   The mode, the median, and the mean. Each is an average and gives an overall picture of the data. (p. 444)

Measures of variation   Values that indicate how all the data in a set compare to the measures of central tendency of the set. (p. 450)

Median   The middle number, or the mean of the two middle numbers, of a set of numerical data when the numbers in the set are arranged from smallest to the largest. (p. 444)

Mixed expression   The sum or difference of a polynomial and a rational expression. (p. 166)

Mode   The item or items that occur with the greatest frequency in a set. (p. 444)

Monomial   A term that is a number (called a constant), a variable or product of variables, or a product of a number and one or more variables. (p. 18)

Multiplication property of equality If a, b, and c are any real numbers and $a = b$, then $ca = cb$. (p. 74)

Multiplication property of inequality Let a, b, and c be any real numbers.
If $a < b$ and $c > 0$, then $ac < bc$.
If $a > b$ and $c > 0$, then $ac > bc$.
If $a < b$ and $c < 0$, then $ac > bc$.
If $a > b$ and $c < 0$, then $ac < bc$. (p. 112)

Multiplication property of -1 For every real number a, $-a = -1(a)$. (p. 49)

Multiplication property of 0 For every real number a, $0 \cdot a = 0$. (p. 57)

Multiplicative inverse A unique real number of the form $\frac{1}{a}$ that exists for any nonzero real number a such that $a(\frac{1}{a}) = \frac{1}{a}(a) = 1$. Also called a reciprocal. (p. 52)

Mutually exclusive events Two events that have no element in common. (p. 479)

N

Numerical expression An expression that names a number. (p. 2)

O

Obtuse angle An angle whose measurement is between 90° and 180°. (p. 492)

Obtuse triangle A triangle with one obtuse angle. (p. 493)

Odds A ratio obtained by dividing the probability that an event will occur by the probability that it will not occur. (p. 477)

Open sentence An equation or inequality that contains one or more variables. (p. 68)

Opposite (of a polynomial) A polynomial whose terms are the opposites of the terms of the given polynomial. (p. 141)

Opposites Numbers corresponding to points that are the same distance, in opposite directions, from the 0 point on the number line. (p. 34)

Ordered pair A pair of numbers in a specified order. (p. 210)

Ordinate The second number in an ordered pair. Also called the y-coordinate. (p. 210)

Origin The 0 point on both the horizontal and the vertical number line of the coordinate plane. (p. 210)

P

Parabola A conic section formed by the intersection of a right circular cone with a plane parallel to an element of the cone. The graph of a quadratic function is a parabola. (p. 407)

Parallel lines Coplanar lines that do not intersect. (p. 233)

Percent A hundredth part of a whole. For example, $\frac{3}{100} = 3\%$. (p. 342)

Perfect square The square of a rational number. (p. 362)

Perfect-square trinomial A trinomial of the form $a^2 + 2ab + b^2$ or $a^2 - 2ab + b^2$. (p. 184)

Permutation An ordered arrangement of elements of a set, in which elements cannot be repeated. (p. 469)

Perpendicular lines Lines that intersect at right angles. (p. 235)

Polynomial A monomial or the sum or difference of monomials. (p. 18)

Power An expression of repeated multiplication by the same factor. For example, the fourth power of 3 is $3^4 = 3 \cdot 3 \cdot 3 \cdot 3$. (p. 8)

Power function A function defined by an equation of the form $y = kx^2$, where k is a nonzero constant. (p. 355)

Prime number Any integer greater than 1 that has only two positive integral factors, 1 and itself. (p. 174)

Prime polynomial A polynomial from whose terms no common variable factors and no common integral factors except 1 and -1 can be removed. (p. 178)

Principal square root The positive square root of a positive real number a. Represented by $\sqrt{a}$. (p. 362)

Proof The chain of reasoning by which a theorem is shown to be true. (p. 57)

Proportion An equation that states that two ratios are equal. (p. 339)

Pythagorean theorem The principle that in a right triangle the square of the length of the hypotenuse is equal to the sum of the squares of the lengths of the legs. (p. 367)

Q

Quadrant One of the four regions formed by the axes of the coordinate plane. (p. 211)

Quadratic equation An equation that can be written in the form $ax^2 + bx + c = 0$, where a, b, and c are real numbers and $a \neq 0$. (p. 398)

Quadratic formula The formula $x = \frac{-b \pm \sqrt{b^2 - 4ac}}{2a}$, which yields the roots of any quadratic equation in standard form, $ax^2 + bx + c = 0$. (p. 408)

Quadratic function A function defined by an equation of the form $y = ax^2 + bx + c$, where a, b, and c are real numbers and $a \neq 0$. (p. 417)

Quartiles Measures of variation associated with the median. The three quartiles divide the data into four equal groups when the data are listed from smallest to largest. (p. 455)

R

Radical An expression of the form $\sqrt{x}$. (p. 362)

Radical equation An equation that has a variable in a radicand. (p. 381)

Radical sign The symbol $\sqrt{}$, used to indicate a square root. (p. 362)

Radicand The number under the radical sign in a radical. (p. 362)

Range (measure of variation) The difference between the largest number and the smallest number of a set. (p. 450)

Range (of a relation) The set of second elements of the ordered pairs in a relation. (p. 218)

Ratio A comparison of two numbers by division. (p. 339)

Rational expression An expression that can be written in the form $\frac{N}{D}$, where N and D are polynomials and $D \neq 0$. (p. 294)

Rationalizing the denominator Rewriting a fraction so that only rational numbers are in the denominator. (p. 373)

Rational numbers Numbers that can be expressed in the form $\frac{a}{b}$, where a and b are integers and $b \neq 0$. (p. 31)

Ray A set of collinear points that extends without end in one direction from an endpoint. (p. 492)

Real numbers The union of the set of rational numbers and the set of irrational numbers. (p. 31)

Reflexive property For every real number a, $a = a$. (p. 60)

Relation Any set of ordered pairs. (p. 218)

Repeating decimal A decimal in which a digit or group of digits repeats without end. (p. 77)

Replacement set The set of numbers from which the replacements for a variable are chosen. (p. 68)

Right angle An angle whose measurement is 90°. (p. 492)

Root (of an equation) A solution of an equation. (p. 398)

S

Sample space The set of all possible outcomes for a situation. (p. 466)

Scientific notation A system in which a number is expressed as the product of some power of 10 and a number n, where $1 \leq n < 10$. (p. 302)

Set A collection of objects. (p. 30)

Similar triangles Two triangles that have three pairs of congruent angles. (p. 497)

Simplest form (of a radical expression) A form of radical expression in which the radicand does not contain a perfect-square factor other than 1, no fraction is under a radical sign, and no radical sign is in a denominator. (p. 373)

Simplest form (of a rational expression) A form of rational expression in which the numerator and the denominator have no common factors other than 1. (p. 296)

Simplify To replace an expression with the simplest or most common name for its value. (p. 2)

Sine A trigonometric ratio associated with an acute angle, determined by dividing the measure of the side opposite the angle in a right triangle by the measure of the hypotenuse. (p. 501)

Slope The ratio of the vertical change to the horizontal change between two points on a line, provided that the horizontal change is not 0. (p. 227)

Slope-intercept form A form of linear equation, $y = mx + b$, in which m is the slope of the equation's graph and b is its y-intercept. (p. 232)

Solution set the set of numbers from the replacement set that makes an open sentence true. (p. 68)

Solve (a right triangle) To find the measure of each side and each angle that is not given. (p. 508)

Square root One of a pair of equal factors of a number. If $x^2 = y$, then x is a square root of y. (p. 362)

Square-root property If $x^2 = a$, then $x = \sqrt{a}$ or $x = -\sqrt{a}$. (p. 401)

Standard deviation The square root of a variance. (p. 451)

Standard form (of a linear equation) A form of linear equation, $ax + by = c$, in which a, b, and c are real numbers, a and b are not both zero, and x and y are variables. (p. 215)

Standard form (of a rational number) A form of rational number, $\frac{a}{b}$ or $-\frac{a}{b}$, in which a and b are positive integers. (p. 51)

Statistics The collection, organization,

study, and interpretation of numbers and facts. (p. 432)

Stem-and-leaf display A tabular organization of raw numerical data, in which certain digits are used as stems and the remaining digits are used as leaves. For example, the data 28, 29, 31, 33, 41, 42, 44, and 49 might be represented as follows:

2	8, 9
3	1, 3
4	1, 2, 4, 9 (p. 432)

Subset A set each of whose elements is an element of another set. (p. 30)

Substitution method An algebraic method for solving a system of equations, in which one equation is solved for a variable and the solution is substituted for that variable in the other equation(s). (p. 258)

Substitution property If $a = b$, then a may be substituted for b. (p. 11)

Subtraction property of equality If a, b, and c are any real numbers and $a = b$, then $a - c = b - c$. (p. 72)

Subtraction property of inequality Let a, b, and c be any real numbers.
If $a < b$, then $a - c < b - c$.
If $a > b$, then $a - c > b - c$. (p. 109)

Supplementary angles Two angles the sum of whose measurements is 180°. (p. 492)

Symmetric property For all real numbers a and b, if $a = b$, then $b = a$. (p. 60)

System of equations Two or more linear equations in the same two variables. (p. 252)

T

Tangent A trigonometric ratio associated with an acute angle, determined by dividing the measure of the side opposite the angle in a right triangle by the measure of the side adjacent to the angle. (p. 501)

Term A number, a variable, or an indicated product or quotient. (p. 2)

Terminating decimal A decimal in which the only repeating digit is 0. (p. 77)

Theorem A statement that is shown to be true by using definitions, axioms, theorems that have already been proved, and logical reasoning. (p. 57)

Theoretical probability A probability that is determined without performing an experiment. (p. 474)

Transitive property For all real numbers a, b, and c, if $a = b$ and $b = c$, then $a = c$. (p. 60)

Trigonometric ratio A ratio of a pair of sides of a right triangle, associated with an acute angle of the triangle. (p. 501)

Trinomial A polynomial consisting of three terms. (p. 18)

U

Union (of two sets) A set consisting of all elements that belong to either set or to both sets. (p. 120)

Unique factoring property The prime factorization of any composite positive integer into a product of primes is unique except for the order of factors. (p. 174)

V

Value The number named by an expression. (p. 2)

Variable A letter that represents an unknown value. (p. 2)

Variance The mean of the squares of the deviation scores for a set of data. (p. 451)

Velocity The speed of a moving object. Described by the linear equation $y = mx + b$, where x represents the time (in some unit), y represents the velocity (distance per unit of time), and the slope m represents the acceleration. (p. 240)

Vertex (of a parabola) The minimum point or maximum point of the parabola. (p. 417)

W

Whole numbers The set of all counting numbers and zero. (p. 30)

X

x-axis The horizontal number line in a coordinate plane. (p. 210)

x-coordinate The first number in an ordered pair. Also called the abscissa. (p. 210)

x-intercept The x-coordinate of a point where a graph crosses the x-axis. (p. 418)

Y

y-axis The vertical number line in a coordinate plane. (p. 210)

y-coordinate The second number in an ordered pair. Also called the ordinate. (p. 210)

y-intercept The y-coordinate of the point where a line intersects the y-axis. (p. 232)

Z

Zero exponent An exponent with a value of zero. If x is any nonzero real number, then $x^0 = 1$. (p. 299)

Zero product property If a and b are real numbers and $ab = 0$, then $a = 0$ or $b = 0$ or both a and b are 0. (p. 198)

INDEX

A

Abscissa, 210
Absolute value, 34, 127, 374
in radical expression, 374
sentences involving, 127–128
Absolute-value equations, graphing, 286
Acceleration, 240
Addition
inverse operation of, 58
on number line, 37–38
of polynomials, 138
of probabilities, 479–480
properties of, 11, 41, 57
of radicals, 376
of rational expressions, 310, 314–315
of real numbers, 37–38, 40–41
using absolute value, 40–41
Addition property
of equality, 71
of inequality, 109
Additive inverse, 41, 141, 262
Age problems, 56, 202, 276, 413
Algebraic expression, 2–3
"Algebra in Use," 43, 146, 270, 322, 383, 443, 478, 511
Angle(s)
acute, 492–493, 501
complementary, 492
congruent, 497
corresponding, 497
of depression, 512
of elevation, 512
measure of, 492–493, 497, 507–508
obtuse, 492–493
right, 492–493
sides of, 492
supplementary, 268, 492
trigonometric ratios of, 505
vertex of, 492–493
Area
of circle, 90

of rectangle, 89–90, 201, 345
perimeter options for, using computer, 357
of triangle, 90
Area problems, 20, 89–91, 95, 201–202, 421
Artificial intelligence in computers, 243
Associative property
of addition, 11, 57
of multiplication, 11, 57
Averages, 444–445
Axiom, 57–60
Axis (axes)
of cone, 406–407
in coordinate plane, 210–211
of symmetry, 418

B

Bar chart, 439
Base of a power, 8
Binary number system, 153
Binomial factor, common, 179
Binomial(s), 18
containing radicals, 378–379
division by, 166
FOIL method of multiplying, 151
product of, 151
square of a difference, 151
square of a sum, 151
Boolean algebra, 126
Boundary line of half plane, 280
Box-and-whisker plot, 456–457
Break-even analysis, 270

C

"Calculator," 6, 17, 39, 148, 177, 287, 318, 344, 366, 372, 400, 449, 453, 507
"Career"
actuary, 482

civil engineer, 239
electrician, 389
landscape architect, 95
photographer, 203
real-estate agent, 278
surveyor, 515
veterinarian, 355
Central tendency, measure of, 444–446, 450
"Challenge," 20, 50, 53, 73, 111, 140, 180, 200, 242, 257, 261, 264, 279, 309, 329, 350, 375, 420, 449, 481, 510
Circle
area of, 90
circumference of, 90
equation of, 407
Clock arithmetic, 60–61
Closure property
of addition, 57
of multiplication, 57
Coefficients, 8
Coin problems, 269, 472, 474
Combinations, 469–470
Combined variation, 350
Commutative property
of addition, 11, 57
of multiplication, 11, 57
Complementary angles, 492
Complement of an event, 475
Completing the square, 187, 404–405
Complex fractions, 326
Composite numbers, 174
Compound sentences, 123–124
"Computer"
addition and subtraction, 63
area of rectangle, 357
artificial intelligence, 243
graphing inequalities, 133
magic square, 169
prime factorization with, 205
probability, simulation with, 487
problem solving
digit problems, 25

real, 31, 33, 210, 362, 364
square, 143
square of, 362
triangular, 24, 143
whole, 30–31, 33–34
Number theory, elementary,
222

O

Odds, 477
Open sentences, 68, 214, 218
Opposite angle, 493
Opposites, 34, 38, 41
Order
of numbers, 106
of operations, 14–17
Ordered pairs, 210–211, 218,
224, 252, 259
Ordinate, 210
Origin, 210
Outcome, 466, 474
Output value, 223

P

Parabola, 406–407, 417–418
Parallel lines, 233, 255, 259
Pentagonal numbers, 24, 143
Percent, 96–97, 342
Perfect numbers, 222
Perfect square, 362, 364
Perfect-square trinomial,
184–185, 404
Perimeter, 4, 89–90
Permutations, 469–470
Perpendicular lines, 235
Pi, 70
Pictograph, 443
Plane
coordinate, 210–211, 280
half, 280–281, 284
Point
coordinate(s) of
on number line, 33
in plane, 210
maximum, 417
minimum, 417
turning, 417
Point-slope form, 238
Polygonal numbers, 24, 143
Polynomial(s), 18
addition of, 138–140

additive inverse of, 141
classifying, 18
degree of, 138
division of, 164, 166–167
factoring, 178–179, 195, 201
multiplication of, 147–149
prime, 178
simplest form of, 138
simplifying, 18, 138
solving equations involving,
154
subtraction of, 141
Positive numbers, 33, 37, 362
Power function, 355
Power(s), 8, 148
division of, 162, 299
multiplication of, 12, 144
of a power, 144, 148
of a product, 144
product of, 144
of a quotient, 162–163
quotient of, 162–163
Predictions, 476
**"Preparing for College En-
trance Exams,"** 44,
160–161, 312–313,
424–425
Prime factorization, 174–175
using computer, 205
Prime numbers, 174, 222
Prime polynomials, 178
Principal root, 374, 384
Principal square root, 362,
366
Probabilities
addition of, 479–480
multiplication of, 483–484
Probability
computer simulation with, 487
conditional, 485
experimental, 472
mathematical, 474
theoretical, 474–477
Problem solving
age, 56, 202, 276, 413
area, 20, 89–91, 95, 201–
202, 421
coin, 269, 472, 474
cost, 89, 91, 94, 130–131,
146, 268, 270
digit, 55, 276–277
using computer, 25
direct variation, 336, 339,
344, 352–353, 355
distance formula, 387

distance/rate/time, 89, 91, 93,
156–158, 269, 272–
273, 324, 414
factoring polynomials, 178,
183, 190, 193–194,
196–197, 201
inequalities, 46, 109–110,
118–119, 124–125,
130–131
integers, 23–24, 45–46, 54–
55, 88, 130, 174–175,
177, 413
interest, 89, 91, 132, 276–
277
inverse variation, 352–353
linear programming, 282
maximum-minimum, 420–
422
mixture, 242, 273–274
percent, 96–98, 132, 274,
342
using computer, 331
perimeter, 56, 89–91, 95,
132, 202, 269
proportion, 339–340, 342,
345, 348, 352–353
puzzle, 276–277
Pythagorean theorem, 367–
368, 372, 386
quadratic functions, 421–422
system of equations, 253–
260, 262–263, 265–
266, 268, 276–277
trigonometry, 511–513, 515
uniform motion, 156–158,
273
velocity, 240–241, 421
volume, 89–90, 168
work, 323, 337, 345, 348,
414–415

Problem-solving strategy
draw diagram, 22–23, 93,
156–158
guess-and-check, 22, 54, 276
look for pattern, 22–23, 55
make table, 22, 55, 156–158,
272–274, 323, 414
solve simpler problem, 22, 55
"top-down" (computer), 289
use estimation, 22
use formula, 22, 89–91, 93,
156–159, 272, 323–
324, 414
use logical reasoning, 22, 54
use model, 22

work backwards, 22
write equation, 22, 92–93, 96, 156–158, 201, 413–414

Product
of binomials, 151
of conjugates, 379
power of, 144
of powers, 144
of rational expressions, 303
of real numbers, 48–49
of square roots, 370
of the sum and difference of two numbers, 151

Profit, expected, 478
Projective geometry, 197
Proof, 57–58
Proportionality, constant of, 336, 345
Proportion problems, 339–340, 342, 345, 348, 352–353
Puzzle problems, 276–277
Pythagorean theorem, 36, 367–368, 386
Pythagorean triple, generated by computer, 391

Q

Quadrant, 211
Quadratic equations, 398, 404, 408, 411, 413, 418
solving
completing square, 404–405, 408
factoring, 398–399, 401, 404, 408
graphing, 418–419, 422
using quadratic formula, 408–409, 411
using square-root property, 401–402, 404–405
standard form of, 398–408
Quadratic formula, 408–409
Quadratic functions, 417–419, 421–422
graphing, 417–419, 422
problem solving with, 421–422
Quadratic term, 188
Quartile, 455–457
Quartile deviation, 456
Quotient, 51

power of, 162–163
of powers, 162–163
of square roots, 370

R

Radical(s), 362, 373, 376
addition of, 376
binomial containing, 378–379
conjugate, 379
division of, 370, 373
equation, 381–382
expression, 373–374, 376, 384
factor, 376
higher-order, 384
index of, 384
multiplication of, 370, 373
simplifying, 373–374, 376, 384
subtraction of, 376
symbol, 362, 384
Radicand, 362, 370, 373
Range
interquartile, 456–457
of relation, 218
semi-interquartile, 456–457
of variation, 450–452, 456
Range value, 223
Ratio, 339–340
Rational expressions
addition of, 310, 314–315
division of, 307
in equation, 319–320
equivalent, 294, 310
multiplication of, 303–304
rationalizing denominator of, 373, 379
simplifying, 296–297
subtraction of, 310, 314–315
Rational numbers, 31, 77, 294
approximating square root by, 364
decimal renaming, 77–78
using computer, 99
equivalent, 294
graphing, 33
perfect square, 362
product of, 303
product of conjugates, 379
standard form of, 51
Ray, 492
Real number, 31

Reciprocal, 52
Rectangle
area of, 89–90, 201, 345
perimeter of, 4, 89–90
Rectangular solid, volume of, 90
Reflexive property, 60
Relation, 218–219, 406
Repeating decimal, 77–79
Replacement set, 68
Riemannian geometry, 197
Right angle, 492–493
Right triangle, 386, 501, 505
legs of, 367, 493
Pythagorean theorem, 36, 367–368, 386
solving, 508–509
trigonometric ratios, 501–502, 505
Root
double, 399
extraneous, 320, 382
higher-order, 384
negative, 384
principal, 374, 384
of quadratic equation, 398–400, 408–409, 411, 418
square, 362, 364–368, 370, 374, 427

S

Sample space, 466–467, 472, 479
Scientific notation, 302
Score
deviation, 450
extreme, 444
"Self-Quiz," 13, 46, 82, 119, 153, 187, 226, 285, 306, 344, 380, 410, 442, 473, 504
Semi-interquartile range, 456–457
Sentence
compound, 123–124
open, 68, 214, 218
Set-builder notation, 30
Set(s), 21, 30–31, 68–69
complete listing of, 30
element of, 30
empty, 31
finite, 30
infinite, 30
intersection of, 120–121, 123

ANSWERS TO SELECTED EXERCISES

Pages 3–5   Section 1.1   WRITTEN EXERCISES
1. $a + b$ **3.** $\frac{r}{s}$ **5.** $6x + y$ **7.** $a(5)$ **9.** 6 **11.** 60 **13.** 36 **15.** 2.1 **17.** $\frac{1}{8}$ **19.** 90 **21.** 6.4
23. 33.6 **25.** 1.2 **27.** 40 **29.** 1 **31.** $\frac{33}{2}$ **33.** 56 **35.** $y - x$ **37.** $y + 2$ **39.** $xy - 1$
41. $P = 66$ mm **43.** $\frac{a}{60}$ mi/per min **45.** $(y + 5)$ years **47.** $(c + 2c + k)$ cal **49.** $8 \cdot (2 - 2) = 0$
51. $15 - (5 - 3) = 13$ **53.** $3 \cdot (8 \div 4) = 6$ or $(3 \cdot 8) \div 4 = 6$ **55.** $(13 + 8) \div 3 = 7$

Pages 9–10   Section 1.2   WRITTEN EXERCISES
1. 5^3 **3.** $(5x)^2$ **5.** $3b^3$ **7.** 25 **9.** 32 **11.** 49 **13.** 100 **15.** 10,000 **17.** 1,000,000 **19.** 12
21. 32 **23.** 36 **25.** 48 **27.** 256 **29.** 32 **31.** 64 **33.** 1296 **35.** 50 **37.** 200 **39.** 50
41. 32 **43.** 225 **45.** 24 **47.** 12 **49.** $\frac{3}{125}$ **51.** 0.008 **53.** $\frac{1}{27}$ **55.** 1 **57.** $\frac{1}{81}$ **59.** 0.004096
61. 0.375 **63.** 80.613 cm^3 **65.** 177.4728 cm^3 **67.** x

Page 13   Section 1.3   WRITTEN EXERCISES
1. 3000 **3.** 57 **5.** 120 **7.** $26a$ **9.** $42a$ **11.** $3ab$ **13.** $10a^5$ **15.** $8x^4$ **17.** $30x^5y^3$
19. $6x^4$ **21.** $6.5a^3b^3c$ **23.** yes **25.** $2n^2$ **27.** $0.7r^2s^3$
29. $3x + 6x = (3 + 6)x$, Dist. prop.; $(3 + 6)x = 9x$, Substitution prop. **31.** x^2y^2 **33.** $2x^{n+2}y_n$

Pages 16–17   Section 1.4   WRITTEN EXERCISES
1. 9 **3.** 36 **5.** 17 **7.** $\frac{9}{8}$ **9.** 6 **11.** 9 **13.** $\frac{27}{7}$ **15.** 4 **17.** 131 **19.** 1.4 **21.** 5.2 **23.** 11
25. 14 **27.** 29 **29.** 18 **31.** 5 **33.** 6 **35.** 0.5 **37.** 6 **39.** 30 **41.** $\frac{3}{10}$ **43.** 42 **45.** 20
47. 76 **49.** 634 **51.** $\frac{11}{20}$ **53.** $\frac{15}{2}$ **55.** 1 **57.** 23 **59.** 0 **61.** $12 + 4^2 \cdot [(24 - 18) \div 3] = 44$
63. $(24 + 2)^2 - (3 - 2) \cdot 6 = 670$ **65.** $(3 + 4)^2 - (6 + 1) \cdot (8 - 3) = 14$ **67.** yes **69.** yes

Pages 19–20   Section 1.5   WRITTEN EXERCISES
1. binomial **3.** monomial **5.** binomial **7.** yes **9.** no **11.** yes **13.** yes **15.** no
17. any number but 0 **19.** 3; 5 **21.** any number but 0 **23.** $21g$ **25.** $20g$ **27.** $10y^2$ **29.** $25s^4$
31. $32a^2b + 16ab$ **33.** $16x$ **35.** $21x^2y$ **37.** $5x^2$ **39.** 2700 **41.** Answers will vary.

Pages 23–24   Section 1.6   WRITTEN EXERCISES
1. 14 **3.** 100 **5.** 55 **7.** 56 **9.** 225 cars **11.** 30,720 cells **13.** 21 handshakes **15.** 1080°

Pages 26–27   CHAPTER 1   REVIEW
1. 110 **3.** 3 **5.** 24 **7.** 18 **9.** 2 **11.** 48 **13.** $x - 2$ **15.** mx **17.** 16 **19.** 9.61 **21.** 13.824
23. 16.8 **25.** 38.44 **27.** 158.76 **29.** 8.82 **31.** 16 **33.** a^5 **35.** $3m^2n$ **37.** $3r^3s^4$ **39.** $16a^{14}$
41. $6r^3s^5$ **43.** $\frac{1}{3}n^{12}$ **45.** $2s^8$ **47.** 6 **49.** 2 **51.** 4.83 **53.** 7 **55.** 10 **57.** 24 **59.** 11
61. $13a$ **63.** $17x^2y$ **65.** $10m^2 + 12m$ **67.** $5x^2y + 6xy^2$ **69.** 13

Pages 31–32   Section 2.1   WRITTEN EXERCISES
1. $\in$ **3.** $\subset$ **5.** $\not\subset$ **7.** $\notin$ **9.** $\subset$ **11.** $\in$ **13.** A, E **15.** C, F **17.** B, D **19.** A, B, D, E
21. $\{0, 1, 2, 3, 4, 5, 6, 7, 8, 9, 10, 11, 12, 13, 14\}$, $\{0, 1, 2, \ldots, 14\}$
23. $\{-4, -3, -2, -1, 0, 1, 2, 3, 4\}$, $\{x \mid x$ is an integer from -4 through 4$\}$

25. {1, 3, 5, 7, 9, 11, 13, 15, 17, 19}, {$x|x$ is an odd whole number less than 20}
27. finite **29.** finite **31.** finite **33.** finite **35.** {0, 1, 2, 3, 4, 5, 6} **37.** {1, 3, 5}
39. {10, 20, 30, 40, 50, 60, 70, 80, 90} **41.** {0, 1, 2, 3, . . .} **43.** { . . . , 0, 1, 2}
45. {9, 10, 11, 12, . . .} **47.** real, rational, integer, whole **49.** real, rational **51.** real
53. real, rational, integer, whole, counting **55.** real, rational **57.** real, rational
59. real, rational **61.** real, rational

Page 35   Section 2.2   WRITTEN EXERCISES

1. > **3.** < **5.** > **7.** = **9.** the number itself

11.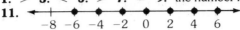

13.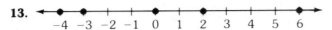

15.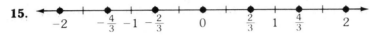

17. 5 **19.** 5 **21.** 0 **23.** 5.76 **25.** −7 **27.** −6 **29.** −3 **31.** 4 **33.** 2.7 **35.** −5

Page 39   Section 2.3   WRITTEN EXERCISES

1. 6 **3.** −6 **5.** 2 **7.** −6 **9.** 5 **11.** −4 **13.** 0 **15.** 0 **17.** 0 **19.** 3 **21.** −1 **23.** −6
25. 3 **27.** 1.5 **29.** 1.36 **31.** 0.06 **33.** 0.13 **35.** 0.25 **37.** $\frac{2}{7}$ **39.** −1 **41.** 5.81
43. −1.169 **45.** 4.55 **47.** $\frac{11}{20}$ **49.** $-\frac{31}{72}$

Pages 41–43   Section 2.4   WRITTEN EXERCISES

1. Add. fact **3.** Add. inverse prop. **5.** Add. fact **7.** Assoc. prop. of add. **9.** Ident. prop. of add.
11. Add. rule II **13.** Subst. prop. or Add. fact **15.** Assoc. prop. of add. **17.** Ident. prop. of add.
19. Subst. prop. or Add. fact **21.** Assoc. prop. of add. **23.** Ident. prop. of add. **25.** −6
27. −9 **29.** −56 **31.** 185 **33.** 426 **35.** −888 **37.** 124 **39.** −523 **41.** −1.52
43. 8.3 **45.** −5.83 **47.** $-\frac{5}{7}$ **49.** $\frac{1}{12}$ **51.** $-\frac{1}{3}$ **53.** c **55.** b **57.** d **59.** b **61.** −27
63. 36 **65.** 9 **67.** −306 **69.** $-\frac{19}{24}$

Pages 45–46   Section 2.5   WRITTEN EXERCISES

1. 11 **3.** −21 **5.** 79 **7.** −14 **9.** 56 **11.** −66 **13.** 14 **15.** 14 **17.** 56 **19.** −56
21. −14 **23.** 29 **25.** −22 **27.** 10 **29.** −51 **31.** −87 **33.** 1.43 **35.** 0.052 **37.** $\frac{8}{7}$
39. $\frac{9}{35}$ **41.** $\frac{5}{9}$ **43.** $\frac{17}{60}$ **45.** no **47.** $w - (-12)$ **49.** $c - 0.25c$ **51.** −1.3 **53.** 915
55. −130

Pages 49–50   Section 2.6   WRITTEN EXERCISES

1. 155 **3.** −60 **5.** −2408 **7.** 752 **9.** 120 **11.** −170 **13.** 1 **15.** 1 **17.** 48 **19.** 1
21. 1 **23.** −1332 **25.** 768 **27.** $\frac{32}{15}$ **29.** $\frac{32}{15}$ **31.** −2912 **33.** −2912 **35.** 0 **37.** −112
39. −4620 **41.** −192 **43.** −280 **45.** −2752.8 **47.** −30,705 **49.** $-\frac{6}{35}$ **51.** $-\frac{8}{49}$
53. −1.456 **55.** −0.966 **57.** 0.0256 **59.** 16.38 **61.** −1.69 **63.** $n(-4.6)$
65. $n(n + 1)$, where n is an integer **67.** 35 **69.** 642 **71.** 192 **73.** 50 **75.** −5120

Pages 52–53   Section 2.7   WRITTEN EXERCISES

1. $\frac{5}{2}$ **3.** $-\frac{7}{4}$ **5.** $-\frac{3}{10}$ **7.** −36 **9.** 36 **11.** 69 **13.** −69 **15.** 45 **17.** −45 **19.** −5
21. −0.9 **23.** −7 **25.** 40 **27.** −0.9 **29.** −300 **31.** $\frac{6}{5}$ **33.** $\frac{8}{49}$ **35.** $-\frac{10}{7}$ **37.** $\frac{1}{15}$
39. $-\frac{4}{3}$ **41.** 12 **43.** −60 **45.** 23 **47.** −3 **49.** $-\frac{2}{3}$ **52.** b **53.** a

Pages 55–56   Section 2.8   WRITTEN EXERCISES

1. $\frac{19}{12}$ **3.** 3 years **5.** 6 trees **7.** 4, 8, 3 **9.** 2849 **11.** Column B
13. Typical answer: any fraction with a positive numerator and a negative denominator and an equivalent fraction with a negative numerator and a positive denominator

Pages 59–60   Section 2.9   WRITTEN EXERCISES

1. Dist. prop. of mult. over add. **3.** Ident. prop. of mult. **5.** Inv. prop. of add.
7. Comm. prop. of mult. **9.** Ident. prop. of add. **11.** Assoc. prop. of add.
13. Def. of mult.; Thm. from Example 3 **15.** Ident. prop. of mult. **17.** Assoc. prop. of add.
19. Mult. prop. of -1 **21.** Mult. prop. of -1 **23.** Dist. prop. of mult. over add.
25. Assoc. prop. of mult. **27.** Subt. prop. from exer. 9–12
29. $a - c = a - c$, Reflexive prop.; $a = b$, Given; $a - c = b - c$, Subst. prop.

Pages 64–65   CHAPTER 2   REVIEW

1. $\subset$ **3.** $\in$ **5.** $\subset$ **7.** $\in$ **9.** $=$ **11.** $<$ **13.** $>$ **15.** $=$ **17.** 6 **19.** 4 **21.** 1.6 **23.** $\frac{5}{6}$
25. -4 **27.** 0 **29.** -2 **31.** -5 **33.** 16 **35.** -13 **37.** -17 **39.** -19 **41.** 9.11
43. -3.1 **45.** $\frac{4}{3}$ **47.** $-\frac{17}{15}$ **49.** 29 **51.** 1 **53.** -67 **55.** -22 **57.** 2.77 **59.** 11.3 **61.** $\frac{5}{4}$
63. $-\frac{7}{6}$ **65.** $\frac{77}{12}$ **67.** 760 **69.** -442 **71.** 20.64 **73.** -48 **75.** $\frac{4}{7}$ **77.** $\frac{3}{5}$ **79.** -648
81. 4 **83.** 4 **85.** -18 **87.** 3 **89.** $\frac{2}{11}$ **91.** $\frac{3}{4}$ **93.** 6.3 **95.** -5 **97.** -11 points
99. Mult. prop. of -1

Pages 69–70   Section 3.1   WRITTEN EXERCISES

1. {6} **3.** {2} **5.** {12} **7.** {14} **9.** {14} **11.** {-3} **13.** {1} **15.** {5} **17.** {-10} **19.** {5}
21. {-10} **23.** {25} **25.** {15} **27.** {15} **29.** {5} **31.** {2} **33.** {4} **35.** {2} **37.** { }
39. {$-12, 12$} **41.** {-10} **43.** {$-13, 13$}

Page 73   Section 3.2   WRITTEN EXERCISES

1. 3 **3.** 0 **5.** 14 **7.** 1 **9.** 11 **11.** 7 **13.** 5 **15.** -29 **17.** 56 **19.** 22 **21.** 17.6 **23.** 16
25. 231 **27.** -2.16 **29.** -1.44 **31.** 25.1 **33.** -6.7 **35.** $\frac{1}{2}$ **37.** $\frac{2}{3}$ **39.** $\frac{1}{8}$ **41.** $\frac{7}{12}$ **43.** 11
45. -2 **47.** 13.54 **49.** -5.5 **51.** $\frac{5}{4}$ **53.** $-\frac{7}{12}$

Page 76   Section 3.3   WRITTEN EXERCISES

1. 4 **3.** 6 **5.** 6 **7.** 18 **9.** 27 **11.** -12 **13.** 7 **15.** -103 **17.** 12 **19.** -12 **21.** 20
23. -0.8 **25.** 5 **27.** 2 **29.** -8 **31.** -18 **33.** 36 **35.** -16 **37.** 90 **39.** $\frac{2}{15}$ **41.** 4
43. 6 **45.** $-2\frac{1}{2}$ **47.** $1\frac{2}{3}$ **49.** $-24\frac{1}{2}$ **51.** 24 **53.** -18 **55.** \$0.32 **57.** \$0.23 **59.** 100

Page 79   Section 3.4   WRITTEN EXERCISES

1. $0.\overline{6}$ **3.** -0.6 **5.** 0.9 **7.** -0.27 **9.** $6.\overline{6}$ **11.** 0.5 **13.** $0.\overline{4}$ **15.** $0.\overline{18}$ **17.** $3.\overline{6}$ **19.** $2.\overline{1}$
21. 0.84375 **23.** $0.\overline{142857}$ **25.** $\frac{3}{10}$ **27.** $\frac{3}{8}$ **29.** $\frac{2}{9}$ **31.** $\frac{2}{11}$ **33.** $4\frac{5}{6}$ **35.** $\frac{62}{333}$ **37.** $\frac{8}{27}$
39. $-5\frac{2}{15}$ **41.** $-1\frac{25}{66}$ **43.** $\frac{373}{450}$ **45.** $\frac{13}{60}$ **47.** $\frac{1}{7}$

Page 81   Section 3.5   WRITTEN EXERCISES

1. 2 **3.** 3 **5.** 2 **7.** 8 **9.** 3 **11.** 4 **13.** 3 **15.** 4 **17.** 9 **19.** 4 **21.** 0.2 **23.** 1 **25.** 3
27. 6 **29.** 40 **31.** 18 **33.** 5 **35.** -6 **37.** 6 **39.** 1 **41.** $-1\frac{19}{23}$ **43.** -15 **45.** 4
47. -0.2 **49.** $x = \frac{b}{a}$ **51.** $x = \frac{d}{a-c}$

Pages 84–85   Section 3.6   WRITTEN EXERCISES

1. Subt. $2x$; Subt. 3; Div. by 4. **3.** Subt. $2a$; Subt. 4; Div. by -5.

5. Subt. 5x; Add 6; Div. by 3. **7.** Add a; Subt. 10; Div. by -1. **9.** Add s; Add 9; Div. by 7.
11. Add 2x; Subt. 9; Div. by 3. **13.** 4 **15.** 1 **17.** -2 **19.** $\frac{3}{5}$ **21.** 2 **23.** 16 **25.** -2
27. -0.4 **29.** -7 **31.** -11 **33.** 1 **35.** 9 **37.** -4 **39.** 9 **41.** $\frac{3}{4}$ **43.** -2 **45.** 3 **47.** 5
49. -1 **51.** 6 **53.** 30 **55.** -16 **57.** $-1\frac{1}{6}$ **59.** $2\frac{1}{2}$ **61.** $-\frac{16}{21}$ **63.** $x = c - a$
65. $x = \frac{d - b}{a - c}$ **67.** Lake Michigan: 22,300 mi²; Lake Erie: 9910 mi²; Lake Superior: 31,700 mi²

Pages 87–88   Section 3.7   WRITTEN EXERCISES
1. 5 **3.** 9 **5.** -8 **7.** 2 **9.** 2 **11.** 3 **13.** 10 **15.** -5 **17.** -24 **19.** 5 **21.** -14 **23.** 18
25. 2 **27.** $\frac{1}{2}$ **29.** -5 **31.** 3 **33.** -9 **35.** $\frac{1}{2}$ **37.** -9 **39.** -2 **41.** 32 **43.** 3
45. $3\frac{1}{2}$ **47.** $x = \frac{c}{a} - b$ **49.** $x = \frac{cd - ab}{a - c}$ **51.** 24 and 25 **53.** 180

Pages 90–91   Section 3.8   WRITTEN EXERCISES
1. 40 ft **3.** 62.8 ft **5.** 37 in. **7.** 200.96 cm² **9.** 1130.4 ft³ **11.** $d = rt$; 15 mi/h
13. $A = \frac{1}{2}bh$; 48 ft² **15.** $I = prt$; $660 **17.** $A = \frac{1}{2}bh$; 20 in. **19.** $C = np$; $8.95 **21.** 6
23. 6 **25.** 60 mi

Pages 94–95   Section 3.9   WRITTEN EXERCISES
1. b; 5 and 11 **3.** c; 20 feet **5.** $19 **7.** $147.50 **9.** 15 years **11.** 10 games **13.** 24 minutes
15. 5 feet, 13 feet **17.** one-engine: 176 mi/h; two-engine: 266 mi/h; four-engine: 352 mi/h

Pages 97–98   Section 3.10   WRITTEN EXERCISES
1. $8.00 **3.** $1200; $300 **5.** $85,000 **7.** 80% **9.** $150 **11.** $95,000 **13.** 7% **15.** $8.10
17. $0.105 **19.** 40% **21.** $39; 10%

Pages 100–101   CHAPTER 3   REVIEW
1. 7 **3.** 8 **5.** 6 **7.** 10 **9.** 17 **11.** $1\frac{7}{12}$ **13.** -12 **15.** 0.16 **17.** 32 **19.** 0.45 **21.** $0.1\overline{6}$
23. $\frac{4}{5}$ **25.** $\frac{3}{11}$ **27.** 8 **29.** -9 **31.** 48 **33.** 6 **35.** -5 **37.** $\frac{2}{3}$ **39.** 8 **41.** 6 **43.** 0.5
45. 16% **47.** $175

Page 107   Section 4.1   WRITTEN EXERCISES

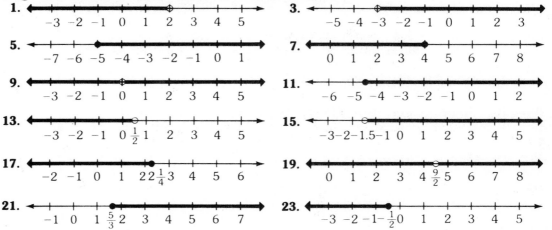

25.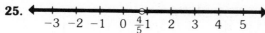

27.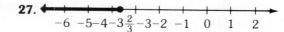

29.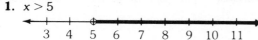

31. "is not greater than"

33. "is not less than or equal to"   **35.** b   **37.** c

Pages 110–111   Section 4.2   WRITTEN EXERCISES

1. $x > 5$

3. $z < -1$

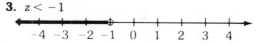

5. $q \geq -7$

7. $m < 16$

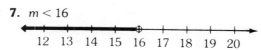

9. $t < -4$

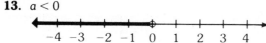

11. $z \leq -3$

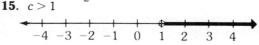

13. $n < 4.7$ **15.** $x \leq 3$ **17.** $t > 10\frac{1}{3}$ **19.** $z > 17.2$ **21.** $q \geq 8.9$ **23.** $y > -0.7$ **25.** $w \leq -2.6$
27. $x < 12\frac{5}{6}$ **29.** $q \geq 0.803$ **31.** $b > 7\frac{1}{12}$ **33.** $r < -11\frac{13}{20}$ **35.** $g \geq -12.365$ **37.** $i \leq 14\frac{5}{6}$
39. $n > 9.8067$ **41.** $t \leq -4.3$ **43.** $m > 0.9$ **45.** $y > -2$ **47.** $x < -12$ **49.** $t > 5$

Page 114   Section 4.3   WRITTEN EXERCISES

1. $x < -4$ **3.** $z < -6$ **5.** $t > 6$ **7.** $n \geq -1$ **9.** $v \leq 6$ **11.** $z \geq \frac{5}{2}$
13. $a < 0$

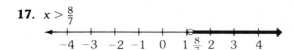

15. $c > 1$

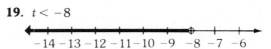

17. $x > \frac{8}{7}$

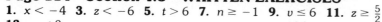

19. $t < -8$

21. $x > 22$

23. $s < -0.5$

25. $c < 0$ **27.** $c < 0$ **29.** $c > 0$ **31.** $c > 0$

Pages 116–117   Section 4.4   WRITTEN EXERCISES

1. $t > -2$ **3.** $s > \frac{21}{2}$ **5.** $y < \frac{1}{5}$ **7.** $m > \frac{2}{5}$ **9.** $x < \frac{11}{6}$ **11.** $m < -9$ **13.** $x < 0$ **15.** $m < \frac{3}{11}$
17. $m < 4$ **19.** $p > 22$ **21.** $q > -16$ **23.** $r < -35$ **25.** all real numbers   **27.** $\varnothing$
29. $r > -0.4$ **31.** $z < -\frac{1}{3}$ **33.** $r < -z$

Pages 118–119   Section 4.5   WRITTEN EXERCISES

1. $3m > 12$ **3.** $3v < v + 12$ **5.** $z \leq 7$ **7.** $4t \leq \frac{2}{3}$ **9.** $2n - 7 > n + 3$ **11.** $m + 12 < 3m$
13. $d - 20 \geq 48$ **15.** $6t + 8 \geq 50$ **17.** $s \geq 30$ **19.** $r \leq 378$ **21.** $r \geq 3.35$ **23.** $a \leq 146$
25. $c \geq 18$ **27.** $c > 3d$

Pages 121–122 Section 4.6 WRITTEN EXERCISES

1. $\{12\}$; $\{3, 4, 6, 8, 9, 12, 16\}$ **3.** $\{-2, 0\}$; $\{-4, -2, 0, 2\}$ **5.** $\{-1, 0, 1\}$; $\{-2, -1, 0, 1, 2\}$
7. $\{3, 5, 7\}$; $\{1, 2, 3, 5, 7, 9, 11\}$ **9.** $\{2, 4, 6, \ldots\}$; $\{1, 2, 3, \ldots\}$ **11.** $\varnothing$; $\{1, 2, 3, \ldots\}$
13. $\{-8, -4\}$ **15.** $\{4, 8\}$ **17.** $\{-8, -4, 4, 6, 8\}$ **19.** $\{-8, -6, -4, 4, 8\}$ **21.** $\{-6, 4, 6, 8\}$
23. $\{-8, -6, -4, 4, 6, 8\}$ **25.** F **27.** G **29.** $\{-7, -5\}$ **31.** H **33.** I **35.** G **37.** E **39.** I
41. all real numbers

43. $-3 < x \le 5$

45. all real numbers

47. J

49. $-3 < x \le 5$

Page 125 Section 4.7 WRITTEN EXERCISES

1. $x < 3$ **3.** $-3 < s < 5$ **5.** $-1 < t < 5$ **7.** $0 < m < 8$

9.

11.

13.

15.

17.

19.

21. $3\frac{1}{2} < x < 5$

23. $3 < z < 5$

25. $a < -0.5$ or $a > 0.5$

27. all real numbers

29. $c < 3$

31. $e \le -2$

33. $n \ne 1$

35. $x \le -\frac{2}{3}$

Pages 128–129 Section 4.8 WRITTEN EXERCISES

1. $x = 4$ or $x = -4$

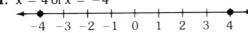

3. $-5 < s < 5$ [number line from -8 to 8]

5. $m > 7$ or $m < -7$ [number line from -8 to 8]

7. $p \geq 4$ or $p \leq -4$ [number line from -8 to 8]

9. $-4 \leq v \leq 4$ [number line from -4 to 4]

11. $z > 3$ or $z < -3$ [number line from -4 to 4]

13. $r = 7$ or $r = -7$ [number line from -8 to 8]

15. $m \geq 2$ or $m \leq -2$ [number line from -4 to 4]

17. $y \geq 7$ or $y \leq -7$ [number line from -8 to 8]

19. $x = 5$ or $x = 1$ [number line from -1 to 7]

21. $-10 < m < -4$ [number line from -12 to 4]

23. $x > -2$ or $x < -4$ [number line from -6 to 2]

25. $n = 17$ or $n = -1$ **27.** $m = 3.4$ or $m = -3.4$ **29.** $f = 3.2$ or $f = -3.2$
31. $c > 2$ or $c < -8$ **33.** $3 < x < 7$ **35.** $-5.6 < n < 9.6$ **37.** $-3 < m < 3$
39. $-32.4 \leq w \leq 32.4$ **41.** $-3.1 < v < 3.1$ **43.** $-3 < y < 3$ **45.** $m \geq 10$ or $m \leq -10$
47. $b > 30$ or $b < -30$ **49.** $e > \frac{2}{3}$ or $e < -2$ **51.** $-1 < r < \frac{2}{3}$ **53.** $w = 11.3$ or $w = 6.5$
55. $-3 < w < 6$ **57.** $t = \frac{12}{5}$ or $t = -2$ **59.** $b > 3$ or $b < -4$ **61.** $v \geq \frac{8}{5}$ or $v \leq -2$
63. $-\frac{7}{2} \leq v \leq \frac{5}{2}$ **65.** $-\frac{5}{2} < h < 2$ **67.** $-1 < t < \frac{4}{3}$ **69.** $-\frac{1}{3} < p < \frac{13}{3}$
71. $-3 \leq d \leq 11$ **73.** $x \neq 0$

Page 132   Section 4.9   WRITTEN EXERCISES
1. less than 113 miles   **3.** more than 40 bushels   **5.** no more than 5 rolls of film   **7.** 6 weeks
9. no more than 3 hamburgers   **11.** at least 72 additional copies   **13.** at least 8 full hours
15. between 1.67 m and 3.67 m   **17.** between \$11,200 and \$15,200

Pages 134–135   CHAPTER 4   REVIEW
1. [number line from -2 to 6]   **3.** [number line from -4 to 4]

5. [number line from -1 to 7]   **7.** $m \leq -1$ **9.** $z \geq -2$

11. $a \geq \frac{1}{2}$ **13.** $c \leq -3$ **15.** $\varnothing$ **17.** $3m \leq 11$ **19.** $y - 6 \leq 18$

21. $\{0, 10\}$; $\{0, 5, 10, 15, 20\}$ **23.** $\varnothing$; $\{3, 7, -8\}$ **25.** $\{0\}$; $\{-3, -2, -1, 0, 1, 2, 3\}$
27. $\{-2, -1, 0, 1, 2\}$ **29.** $\{-1, 1\}$ **31.** $\{-1, 1\}$ **33.** $\{-3, -2, -1, 0, 1, 2, 3\}$ **35.** $5 < t < 12$
37. $b > 5$

39.  **41**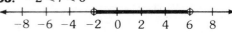

43. $m > 4$ **45.** all real numbers **47.** $2 \leq b \leq 10$ **49.** $g \geq 3$
51. $-7 < w < 7$ 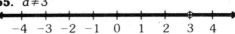 **53.** $-2 < r < 6$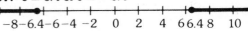

55. $d \neq 3$ 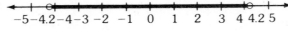 **57.** $c \geq 6.4$ or $c \leq -6.4$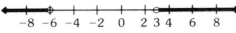

59. $-4.2 < f < 4.2$

61. $d > 3$ or $d < -6$

63. $-\frac{1}{6} < g < \frac{1}{2}$

65. no more than \$788 **67.** at least 146

Pages 139–140 Section 5.1 WRITTEN EXERCISES

1. $x^3 - 3x^2 + x$ **3.** $t^3 + 10t^2 + 8t$ **5.** $2x^3 + x^2 - 2x - 5$ **7.** $-7t^3 + 8t^2 + 4t + 9$
9. $8m^4 + 2m^3 - m^2 - 7m$ **11.** $5x - 5$ **13.** $11y - 2$ **15.** $7a + 1$ **17.** $21x - 3$ **19.** $5y - 1$
21. $2x^2 - 9x + 10$ **23.** $7x - 8y - 9z$ **25.** $r^2 + 3rs + s^2 + 4$ **27.** $4x^2 - 9x + 10$
29. $18p + 3q + 13r$ **31.** $9x^2 - 2xy - y^2$ **33.** $11a + 2b - 5c$ **35.** $-3p + 3r$
37. $7a - b - 2c$ **39.** $vw + 3vw^2 - 16vw^3$ **41.** $11m - 12p$ **43.** $-4a^2 + 3ab - 5b^2$
45. $5x^2 - 6xy$ **47.** $-4a + 4b$ **49.** $-6m^2 - m$ **51.** $11u$ **53.** $2ab^2$
55. $-14xy^3 + 16xy^2 + 5xy$ **57.** $5xy^2 + 5xy$ **59.** $2st^3 + 6st^2$ **61.** $5r^2 - 8rs + 3s^2$
63. $3c^3d + 9c^2d + 14c^2d^2 + 8cd + 7cd^2 + 3cd^3$

Pages 142–143 Section 5.2 WRITTEN EXERCISES

1. $-5r - 13$ **3.** $-6t - 11$ **5.** $-10m - 3$ **7.** $-3x - 11$ **9.** $-5s + 5$ **11.** $2r$ **13.** $5b - 0.3$
15. $15c + 12.8$ **17.** $x - 2 - y$ **19.** $7y - z + 1$ **21.** $-5a - b + 3$ **23.** $a + ab - 4b$
25. $12x - xy + y$ **27.** $3x^2 + 12x$ **29.** $-10x + 14$ **31.** $-9x - 7$ **33.** $-4x^2 - 16x + 9$
35. $5x^2 - 15x + 5$ **37.** $4x^2y^2 + 11xy$ **39.** $8x^2 - 11x + 14$ **41.** $18p^2 - 6$
43. $-6n^2 + 30n + 3$ **45.** $-6x^2t^2 - 10xt + 23$ **47.** -4 **49.** $2x^2 - 7x + 16$ **51.** $-x^2$
53. $-2x^2 - 10y^2$

Pages 145–146 Section 5.3 WRITTEN EXERCISES

1. $-7n$ **3.** $4ab$ **5.** $15ab$ **7.** $6.3m^2$ **9.** $21t^5$ **11.** x^5 **13.** a^6 **15.** $144x^2$ **17.** $8z^3$ **19.** $49x^8$
21. $98s^6t^5$ **23.** $-7m^7$ **25.** $-12n^5s^3$ **27.** $-1.5r^3s^2$ **29.** $-8s^3$ **31.** $729x^9$ **33.** x^3y^7 **35.** a^5d
37. w^6t^6 **39.** $2000b^7$ **41.** s^{12} **43.** $-y^{14}$ **45.** $x^5y^5z^5$ **47.** $256s^6$ **49.** $-2x^4y^8$ **51.** 3^{3x+4}

Page 148 Section 5.4 WRITTEN EXERCISES

1. $14x^2y^2 + 56xy$ **3.** $18rs - 12s^2$ **5.** $15x^3 - 10x^2 + 15x$ **7.** $24m^3n^3 + 20m^2n^2$
9. $12x^3 - 18x^2 + 12x$ **11.** $2c^2$ **13.** $-15a^2 - 40$ **15.** $8b^4 - 16b^2$ **17.** $-8d^7 - 22d^6$

19. $6a^3b + 14a^2b^2 - 12ab^3$ **21.** $-33t^3 - 18t^2w - 36tw^2$ **23.** $-x^6 + x^5 - x^4 + 2x^3$
25. $-4xy - 5txy - 6x^2y$ **27.** $3st^3$ **29.** $6c^3 - 10c^2 - 3c$ **31.** $a^{x+3} + a^{y+2}$ **33.** $x^{2a+1} + x^{a+2}$

Page 150   Section 5.5   WRITTEN EXERCISES
1. $x^2 + 7x + 12$ **3.** $s^2 + 5s - 14$ **5.** $3c^2 + 4c - 15$ **7.** $4n^2 - 33n + 35$
9. $x^3 - 4x^2 + 3x - 12$ **11.** $2x^3 + 19x^2 + 37x + 14$ **13.** $2a^3 + 11a^2 + 24a + 18$
15. $9t^3 + 15t^2 + 7t + 1$ **17.** $4a^3 - 39a^2 + 90a + 25$ **19.** $8x^3 - 28x^2 + 30x - 9$
21. $3x^2 - 6xy + 3y^2 - 7x + 7y + 4$ **23.** $3b^{2a} - 5b^a - 2$ **25.** $y^{2c} - 9$

Pages 152–153   Section 5.6   WRITTEN EXERCISES
1. $x^2 + 5x + 6$ **3.** $z^2 + 10z + 24$ **5.** $2s^2 - 13s + 21$ **7.** $m^2 - 25$ **9.** $r^2 - 2r + 1$
11. $y^2 + 14y + 49$ **13.** $6t^2 + 16st + 8s^2$ **15.** $35x^2 - 74x + 35$ **17.** $12x^2y^2 + xy - 20$
19. $40t^2 + 21t - 27$ **21.** $28y^2 - 33y - 28$ **23.** $x^2 - 12x + 36$ **25.** $64s^2 + 144s + 81$
27. $b^2 - 225$ **29.** $d^2 - 14d + 49$ **31.** $9p^5 + 24p^4 + 16p^3$ **33.** $4x^2 - 12xy + 9y^2$
35. $2x^{2a} - 3x^a - 2$ **37.** $3y^{2b} - 14y^b + 8$ **39.** $y^{4a} - 4$ **41.** $s^{2m} + 2s^m t^n + t^{2n}$ **43.** $y^{2a} - z^{2b}$

Page 155   Section 5.7   WRITTEN EXERCISES
1. -7 **3.** -16 **5.** 11 **7.** 1 **9.** 1 **11.** 1 **13.** $-\frac{1}{3}$ **15.** -4 **17.** $-\frac{25}{6}$ **19.** 2 **21.** 1
23. -13 **25.** $-\frac{4}{3}$ **27.** all real numbers **29.** n **31.** $3a + 2$

Page 159   Section 5.8   WRITTEN EXERCISES
1. 96 km/h, 120 km/h **3.** 3 hours **5.** $\frac{1}{2}$ hour **7.** $2\frac{1}{2}$ hours **9.** 1:45 P.M.

Page 163   Section 5.9   WRITTEN EXERCISES
1. 1000 **3.** $\frac{1}{4}$ **5.** 1 **7.** $\frac{1}{8}$ **9.** $\frac{-r^7}{w^7}$ **11.** -125 **13.** 0.16 **15.** a^2b^2 **17.** r^4s^7
19. $\frac{1}{m^4n^2}$ **21.** $\frac{x^4}{y^4}$ **23.** $16p^4$ **25.** $\frac{8x^3}{27y^3}$ **27.** $-b$ **29.** $-6mn$ **31.** y **33.** $x^{a-b}y^2$
35. $a^{m-4n}b$ **37.** $\frac{-3(x - y)}{x^2}$ **39.** $x^{2d}y^e z^f$

Page 165   Section 5.10   WRITTEN EXERCISES
1. $12x^3$ **3.** $-\frac{1}{3t^3}$ **5.** $\frac{8}{5}x$ **7.** $13y - 11$ **9.** $1 - 2b$ **11.** $4x + 2$ **13.** $3y$ **15.** -0.4 **17.** $\frac{3}{z^2}$
19. $4xy$ **21.** $-5vw$ **23.** $4x^2 + 6x - 2$ **25.** $6x^2 + 2x - 5$ **27.** $2t^2 - 3t - \frac{9}{11}$ **29.** $-x + 2$
31. $6r^2 - 4r$ **33.** $x^2 + 7x - 3 + \frac{2}{x}$ **35.** $2ab - 3$ **37.** $2z^2 + 3z - 1$ **39.** $2st$ **41.** $\frac{9}{2ab}$
43. $-\frac{3}{2}x^2 + \frac{7}{8}x - 17$ **45.** $-4y^2 - 3y + 2$ **47.** $a^2b - 2ac^2 + \frac{1}{4}b^2c^3$ **49.** 3 **51.** $-\frac{3}{4y^c}$
53. $-\frac{3}{z^{2a}}$

Pages 167–168   Section 5.11   WRITTEN EXERCISES
1. $x + 1$ **3.** $z + 3$ **5.** $x + 2$ **7.** $x - 3$ **9.** $5x - 7$ **11.** $4a - 5$ **13.** $2x^2 + 3x + 7 + \frac{12}{2x - 3}$
15. $3y - 2 + \frac{4}{9y - 2}$ **17.** $4m + 1 + \frac{8}{12m - 1}$ **19.** $x^2 - 6x + 1 + \frac{3}{6x + 1}$
21. $2x^2 + 3x - 4 + \frac{3}{x + 3}$ **23.** $-5t - 6 - \frac{3}{-4t + 9}$ **25.** $5w + 4 - \frac{30}{2w + 3}$ **27.** $x^2 + 2x + 1$
29. $2x^2 + 3x + 1$ **31.** $(x + 2)(x^2 - 2x + 4)$ **33.** $(x - 1)(x^2 + x + 1)$
35. $(2x + 1)(4x^2 - 2x + 1)$ **37.** $(x^2 - 2)(x^2 - 3)$ **39.** $2x$ ft

Pages 170–171   CHAPTER 5   REVIEW
1. $7x - 5$ **3.** $6a^2 + 5a - 15$ **5.** $-4x - 13$ **7.** $-2x + 5y$ **9.** $8xy$ **11.** $-12x^3y^5$

13. $12m^2 - 21m$ **15.** $2y^3z - 3yz^2$ **17.** $a^2 + 7a + 10$ **19.** $12x^2y^2 + xy - 20$ **21.** $m^2 - 1$
23. $y^2 + 7y + 12$ **25.** 8 **27.** 3 **29.** 40 mi/h, 55 mi/h **31.** x^4 **33.** a^4b^4 **35.** $8a^2$ **37.** $3a$
39. $2x - 2$ **41.** $3x - 4$

Page 176   Section 6.1   WRITTEN EXERCISES
1. 2^3 **3.** $2^2 \cdot 3$ **5.** $2 \cdot 3^2$ **7.** $2^2 \cdot 3^2$ **9.** $-1 \cdot 2^5$ **11.** $2^3 \cdot 3$ **13.** $3 \cdot 5^2$ **15.** 5^3 **17.** $2^4 \cdot 3$
19. $2 \cdot 3 \cdot 7$ **21.** $2^3 \cdot 3^2$ **23.** $-1 \cdot 2^4 \cdot 3^2$ **25.** $2 \cdot 5^3$ **27.** $2 \cdot 3 \cdot 5 \cdot 7$ **29.** $2^5 \cdot 7$ **31.** 5^4
33. 4 **35.** 9 **37.** 27 **39.** 8 **41.** 9 **43.** 12 **45.** 30 **47.** 25 **49.** 24 **51.** 169 **53.** 40
55. 270 **57.** 96 **59.** 168 **61.** 315 **63.** 300 **65.** 3600 **67.** 363 **69.** 37,800 **71.** 2431
73. 72 inches **75.** A and C sharp

Pages 179–180   Section 6.2   WRITTEN EXERCISES
1. 3 **3.** m, n **5.** $3x$ **7.** n **9.** 6 **11.** 4 **13.** 9 **15.** 5 **17.** 3 **19.** $8y$ **21.** $4(x + 2)$
23. $6(a + 4)$ **25.** $3(x + 4)$ **27.** $2(a - 5b)$ **29.** $9(s + 8)$ **31.** $x(6x + 7)$ **33.** $3(x - 5y)$
35. $b^2(a + 3)$ **37.** $y(xy + 1)$ **39.** $2a^2(4a^2 - 2a + 1)$ **41.** $5b(b^2 + 2b + 3)$
43. $8xy(4x^2 - 3x + 1)$ **45.** $3mn(3m^2 + m + 2)$ **47.** $(m + n)(x + y)$ **49.** $(b - c)(a + d)$
51. $(a + b)(2 - c)$ **53.** $(a + c)(b + d)$ **55.** $(n - p)(m + r)$ **57.** $(x + n)(m + y)$
59. $(4 - 5a)(2x - 3)$

Pages 182–183   Section 6.3   WRITTEN EXERCISES
1. $(a + b)(a - b)$ **3.** $(3 + m)(3 - m)$ **5.** $(4a + 3)(4a - 3)$ **7.** $4(y + 2z)(y - 2z)$
9. $(6m + 7n)(6m - 7n)$ **11.** $(4ab + 9)(4ab - 9)$ **13.** $(m + n); m^2 - n^2$ **15.** $(7 + a); 49 - a^2$
17. $(2x + 7); 4x^2 - 49$ **19.** $(4a - 9b); 16a^2 - 81b^2$ **21.** $(a^2 - 3); a^4 - 9$ **23.** $(9 + x)(9 - x)$
25. $(a + 4b)(a - 4b)$ **27.** $(x + y)(x - y)$ **29.** $(8 + 7a)(8 - 7a)$ **31.** $(9x + 5y)(9x - 5y)$
33. $4(1 + b)(1 - b)$ **35.** $4(y + 3)(y - 3)$ **37.** $7(mn + 1)(mn - 1)$ **39.** $11(ab + 3)(ab - 3)$
41. $5(1 + 3xy)(1 - 3xy)$ **43.** $2(a + 3b)(a - 3b)$ **45.** $a^2(1 + b)(1 - b)$
47. $6m^2(n + 3p)(n - 3p)$ **49.** 80 **51.** 5000 **53.** 440 **55.** 520 **57.** 16 **59.** -15
61. $(x + y + m + n)(x + y - m - n)$ **63.** $(m - n + x + y)(m - n - x - y)$
65. $(a^2 + b^2 + 4)(a^2 - b^2 - 2)$ **67.** $(x^2 + y^2 + a^2 + b^2)(x^2 + y^2 - a^2 - b^2)$
69. $(x^2 + y^2)(x + y)(x - y)$ **71.** $(m^2 + 9n^2)(m + 3n)(m - 3n)$

Pages 185–187   Section 6.4   WRITTEN EXERCISES
1. $x^2 + 6x + 9$ **3.** $a^2 - 10a + 25$ **5.** $4x^2 + 12x + 9$ **7.** $16m^2 - 48m + 36$
9. $4x^2 + 12xy + 9y^2$ **11.** $16m^2 + 64mn + 64n^2$ **13.** $x^2y^2 - 6xy + 9$ **15.** $y^4 - 10y^2 + 25$
17. $(x + 1)^2$ **19.** no **21.** $(n + 3)^2$ **23.** $(x - 9)^2$ **25.** no **27.** $(x - y)^2$ **29.** no
31. $(6a + b)^2$ **33.** $(5x - 3y)^2$ **35.** $(4a - b)^2$ **37.** no **39.** $(a + 10)^2$ **41.** $(xy - 2)^2$ **43.** no
45. $(5 - 2m)^2$ **47.** no **49.** $(1 - 7m)^2$ **51.** $(1 - 6n)^2$ **53.** $(5x - 6y)^2$ **55.** $(a + 3)(a - 3)$
57. $(3x + 2)^2$ **59.** $2(a^2 + 8a + 2)$ **61.** $(4y + 9)(4y - 9)$ **63.** $5(a^2 + a + 6)$
65. $4(n + 3)(n - 3)$ **67.** $(8a - 1)^2$ **69.** $4^2; (a + 4)^2$ **71.** $5^2; (y - 5)^2$ **73.** $6^2; (m - 6)^2$
75. $b^2; (4a + b)^2$ **77.** $(4n)^2; (5m - 4n)^2$ **79.** $(2b)^2; (5a + 2b)^2$ **81.** $24xb; (4x + 3b)^2$
83. $(3x)^2; (3x - 5y)^2$ **85.** $\left(x + \frac{1}{4}\right)^2$ **87.** $\left(\frac{1}{2}a + \frac{2}{3}\right)^2$ **89.** $(x + 0.7)^2$ **91.** $(0.2a + 0.3)^2$
93. $(0.4c + 0.3d)^2$ **95.** $3s - 2$

Page 190   Section 6.5   WRITTEN EXERCISES
1. $(a + 2)(a + 4)$ **3.** $(y + 3)(y + 4)$ **5.** $(m + 3)(m + 7)$ **7.** $(a + 5)(a - 2)$ **9.** $(x + 4)(x - 2)$
11. $(m + 7)(m - 6)$ **13.** $(a + 5)(a + 1)$ **15.** $(x - 7)(x - 2)$ **17.** $(m - 5)(m - 1)$
19. $(a - 6)(a - 3)$ **21.** $(x - 4)(x + 2)$ **23.** $(m - 9)(m + 8)$ **25.** $(a + 8)(a - 4)$
27. $(x + 5)(x + 4)$ **29.** $(m - 4)(m - 2)$ **31.** $(a - 5)(a - 3)$ **33.** $(x + 8)(x + 2)$
35. $(m - 11)(m - 2)$ **37.** $(x + 6y)(x + 2y)$ **39.** $(m - 5n)(m - 2n)$ **41.** $(x + 3y)(x - 4y)$
43. $(a - 8b)(a - 6b)$ **45.** $(x + 15z)(x - 3z)$ **47.** $(s + 10t)(s - 7t)$ **49.** $(a^2 + 8b)(a^2 - 8b)$
51. $(m^2 - 2)(m + 3)(m - 3)$ **53.** $(m - n + 4)(m - n + 3)$

55. $(4x - y - 5)(4x - y + 2)$ **57.** $5(x + 3)(x + 1)$ **59.** $5(s + 8)(s - 6)$
61. $3(x - 6y)(x - 5y)$

Pages 193–194   Section 6.6   WRITTEN EXERCISES

1. $(3b + 2)(b + 1)$ **3.** $(5b - 1)(b + 2)$ **5.** $(5y + 7)(y - 1)$ **7.** $(3b + 1)(b + 1)$
9. $(2b + 3)(b + 1)$ **11.** $(2n - 5)(n - 1)$ **13.** $(3b - 5)(b - 1)$ **15.** $(2b + 5)(b + 2)$
17. $(3a + 1)(a - 4)$ **19.** $(3x + 5)(x + 2)$ **21.** $(3x - 7)(x - 1)$ **23.** $(2n - 5)(n - 2)$
25. $(2a - 3)(a - 2)$ **27.** $(4x + 1)(2x - 1)$ **29.** $(2m - 5)(2m - 1)$ **31.** $(3a + 2)(3a - 1)$
33. $(3x + 4)(3x - 1)$ **35.** $(3a - 4)(2a + 3)$ **37.** $(2x - 3)(7x + 4)$ **39.** $(3a - 4)(2a - 3)$
41. $(3m - 2)(3m + 4)$ **43.** $(4a - 7b)(3a - 2b)$ **45.** $(7m + 3n)(2m - 9n)$ **47.** $(4a + 7b)^2$
49. $9(b - 2)^2$ **51.** $4(x + 2)^2$ **53.** $x^2(2x + 5)(2x - 5)$ **55.** $6(n - 2)(n - 1)$

Pages 196–197   Section 6.7   WRITTEN EXERCISES

1. $3(2a + 1)(a - 4)$ **3.** $2(n + 4)(n + 1)$ **5.** $5(n - 2)(n + 6)$ **7.** $(8a + 1)(8a - 1)$ **9.** $(b - 1)^2$
11. $3n(n - 1)$ **13.** $(x - 6)(x + 3)$ **15.** $3y(2y - 5)(y + 2)$ **17.** $2a(4a - 3)(a + 1)$
19. $3(a + 4)(a - 2)$ **21.** $4(y - 5)(y - 1)$ **23.** $3m(m - 7)(m - 4)$ **25.** $2(n + 3)(n + 4)$
27. $(m - 5)(m - 9)$ **29.** $3(x + 2)^2(x - 2)^2$ **31.** $(b - 3)^2$ **33.** $(y + 4)(y - 4)(y + 1)(y - 1)$
35. $(3a - 2)(a + 1)$ **37.** $(m^2 + 9)(m + 1)(m - 1)$ **39.** $(y - 14)(y + 2)$ **41.** $(b^2 - 8)(b^2 + 2)$
43. $y(y + 1)(y - 1)$ **45.** $(1 + 3n)(1 - 3n)$ **47.** $(b + 2)(a + 10)(a - 10)$
49. $(n + p)(m + 4)(m - 4)$ **51.** $\frac{1}{2}(x - 2)^2$ **53.** $(a - 5 + b)(a - 5 - b)$ **55.** $\frac{1}{2}(y + 4)(y + 1)$
57. $-1(m + 3)(m - 1)(m^2 - 2m + 3)$ **59.** $4ab$ **61.** $(d + 2)(d - 2)(c^2 + b^2)$
63. $(x - y + 3)(x - y - 3)$ **65.** $(x + 3)(x - 3)(x + 1)(x - 1)$

Pages 199–200   Section 6.8   WRITTEN EXERCISES

1. $2, 3$ **3.** $-10, 10$ **5.** $-1, 6$ **7.** $-2, 5$ **9.** $-7, 0$ **11.** $-1, 9$ **13.** $-6, 6$ **15.** $-5, 5$
17. $-2, 6$ **19.** $-5, -2$ **21.** $-5, 5$ **23.** $0, 4$ **25.** $-3, -1$ **27.** $0, 7$ **29.** 3
31. $-4, 3$ **33.** $-4, -3$ **35.** $-12, 0$ **37.** $-3, 1$ **39.** 4 **41.** $-4, 6$ **43.** $1, 3\frac{2}{3}$
45. $-1\frac{1}{3}, -\frac{1}{2}$ **47.** $-1\frac{2}{3}, 1\frac{1}{2}$ **49.** $\frac{1}{2}, \frac{3}{5}$ **51.** $-\frac{4}{5}, 1\frac{2}{3}$ **53.** $-3, 4$ **55.** $-6, 1$ **57.** $-1, 0, \frac{1}{3}$
59. $-3, 0, 3$ **61.** $-3, 3$ **63.** all real numbers

Page 202   Section 6.9   WRITTEN EXERCISES

1. 12 ft, 10 ft **3.** smaller **5.** yes

Pages 206–207   CHAPTER 6   REVIEW

1. $2^2 \cdot 3^3$ **3.** $3^2 \cdot 5^2$ **5.** 14 **7.** 80 **9.** 105 **11.** $2x$ **13.** $(x + y)$ **15.** $2(3a^2 + 1)$
17. $2a^2(2a - 3)$ **19.** $(3a + 4)(3a - 4)$ **21.** $(6s + 7t)(6s - 7t)$ **23.** $(c + 3d)^2$ **25.** $(4s + 5t)^2$
27. $(y + 3)(y + 2)$ **29.** $(c - 8)(c + 2)$ **31.** $(5d - 2)(d + 1)$ **33.** $(2x - 5)(4x + 3)$
35. $b(a - 4)(a + 1)$ **37.** $8(b + 2)(b - 2)$ **39.** $2(z - 2)^2$ **41.** -6 **43.** $-1, 6$ **45.** $-\frac{2}{5}, 1$
47. $1\frac{1}{2}$ inches

Pages 212–213   Section 7.1   WRITTEN EXERCISES

1. A **3.** C **5.** G **7.** K **9.** O **11.** J **13.** $(2, 3)$ **15.** $(-6, 0)$ **17.** $(-2, 2)$ **19.** $(-6, 5)$
21. A **23.** F, G **25.** O, C **27.** O
29. 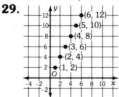   **31.** 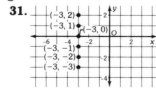   **33.**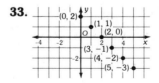

35.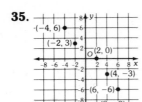

37.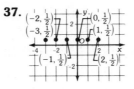

39.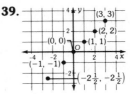

41. 0

43.

45.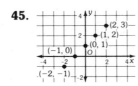

47.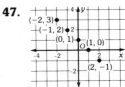

49.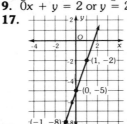

51.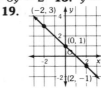

53.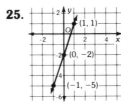

55. The points form a straight line.

Page 217   Section 7.2   WRITTEN EXERCISES

1. $-3(-2) + 4 = 10$; $-3(0) + 4 = 4$; $-3(2) + 4 = -2$

3. $\frac{1}{2}(-2) + 1 = 0$; $\frac{1}{2}(0) + 1 = 1$; $\frac{1}{2}(2) + 1 = 2$ **5.** $3x + 2y = 8$ **7.** $x - y = 4$

9. $0x + y = 2$ or $y = 2$ **11.** $4x + 5y = 2$ **13.** $y = 16$ **15.** $y = 12$

17.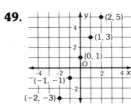

19.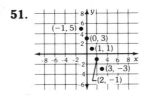

21.

23.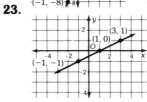

25.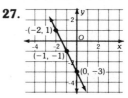

27.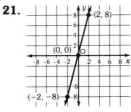

29.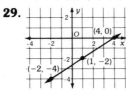

31.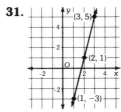

33.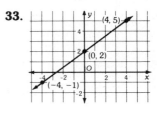

35.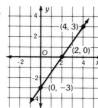

37.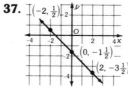

39.

41.

43.

45.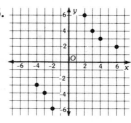

Pages 219–221   Section 7.3   WRITTEN EXERCISES

1. domain = {3, −3, 1, 2}; range = {0, 2, 6}   **3.** domain = {0.8, 1.2, 1.5, 2.3, 2.8}; range = {2, 3, 6, 9}
5. domain = {1, −1, 2, −2, 3, −3, 4, −4}; range = {1, 2, 3, 4}   **7.** yes   **9.** yes   **11.** no

13. (*a*) {(2, 3), (8, 9), (16, 17), (64, 65),
(128, 129)}   (*b*)   *D*   *R*; yes
2 ———→3
8 ———→9
16 ——→17
64 ——→65
128 —→129

15. (*a*) {(4, 7), (4, 8), (4, 9), (5, 2), (5, 3)}
(*b*) *D*   *R*; no
4 ⟶ 7
5 ⟶ 8
⟶ 9
⟶ 2
⟶ 3

17. (*a*) {(1, 2), (2, 4), (3, 6), (4, 8), (5, 10),
(6, 12)}   (*b*) *D*   *R*; yes
1 ——→2
2 ——→4
3 ——→6
4 ——→8
5 ——→10
6 ——→12

19. (*a*) {(0, 1), (0, 2), (1, 1), (1, 3), (3, 6),
(4, 7)}   (*b*) *D*   *R*; no
0 ⟶ 1
1 ⟶ 2
3 ⟶ 3
4 ⟶ 6
⟶ 7

21. (*a*) {(3, 5), (4, 5), (6, 6), (7, 8), (8, 7), (5, 1)}
(*b*) *D*   *R*; yes
3 ——→5
4 ⟶ 6
6 ⟶ 8
7 ⟶ 7
8 ⟶ 1
5

23. yes   **25.** no

   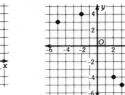

27. yes

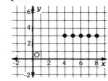

29. (0, 0), (1, 5), (2, 10), (3, 15), (4, 20); yes

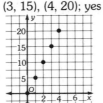

31. (0, 0), $\left(1, \frac{1}{2}\right)$, (2, 1), $\left(3, \frac{1}{2}\right)$, (4, 2); yes

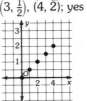

33. (0, 1), (1, 0), (2, 1), (3, 2), (4, 3); yes

35. (0, 1), (1, −1), (2, −3), (3, −5), (4, −7); yes

37. (0, 0), (1, 1), (2, 4), (3, 9), (4, 16); yes

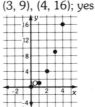

39. (0, 0), (1, 1), (2, 2), (3, 3), (4, 4); yes

41. $n = 2$ **43.** $n = \frac{7}{4}$ **45.** $n = -\frac{40}{7}$ **47.** $n = -2$ **49.** $n = \frac{9}{2}$

Pages 225–226   Section 7.4   WRITTEN EXERCISES

1. $y = 3x + 4$ **3.** $y = -2x + 1$ **5.** $y = x + 1$ **7.** $f(x) = -\frac{1}{7}x + 4$ **9.** $g(x) = 5x - \frac{3}{4}$
11. $f(x) = \frac{1}{2}x + \frac{1}{4}$ **13.** −5 **15.** −14 **17.** −4 **19.** 6 **21.** 2 **23.** 6
25. yes; $m = -\frac{4}{5}$, $b = 4$ **27.** yes; $m = 0$, $b = 3$ **29.** not a linear function
31. yes; $m = -2$, $b = 4$ **33.** yes; $m = -3$, $b = 12$ **35.** not a linear function
37. yes; $m = -2$, $b = -1$ **39.** 27, 34 **41.** $\frac{1}{2}x + \frac{1}{2}h - 5$ **43.** $x^2 + 2xh + h^2$
45. $x^2 + 2xh + h^2 + x + h$ **47.** $x^2 + 2xh + h^2 + 3x + 3h - 4$
49. $x^2 + 2xh + h^2 - 3x - 3h + 2$

Pages 230–231   Section 7.5   WRITTEN EXERCISES

1. 2 **3.** −1 **5.** undefined **7.** undefined **9.** 6 **11.** −5
13.

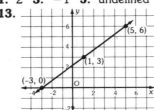

15.

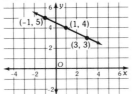

17.

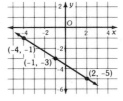

19.

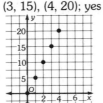

21.

23. yes **25.** no **27.** yes

29. $m\,\overline{AB} = \frac{5}{3}$; $m\,\overline{BC} = \frac{2}{5}$; $m\,\overline{CD} = 5$; $m\,\overline{DA} = -\frac{3}{5}$ **31.** $m\,\overline{AB} = \frac{3}{5}$; $m\,\overline{BC} = -\frac{1}{2}$; $m\,\overline{CD} = -4$; $m\,\overline{DE} = \frac{5}{2}$; $m\,\overline{EF} = 0$; $m\,\overline{FA} = -4$ **33.** 5 **35.** 14 **37.** $\frac{21}{2}$

Pages 234–235   Section 7.6   WRITTEN EXERCISES

1. $m = 4, b = 7$ **3.** $m = \frac{5}{2}, b = -11$ **5.** $m = 11, b = 17$ **7.** $m = 1, b = -3$

9. $m = -\frac{11}{5}, b = 0$ **11.** $y = \frac{1}{3}x - \frac{5}{3}; m = \frac{1}{3}, b = -\frac{5}{3}$ **13.** $y = -4x + 5; m = -4, b = 5$

15. $y = \frac{3}{2}x - \frac{7}{2}; m = \frac{3}{2}, b = -\frac{7}{2}$ **17.** $y = -2; m = 0, b = -2$

19. 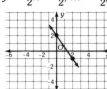   **21.**   **23.**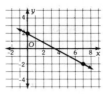

25. yes   **27.** no   **29.** no   **31.**   **33.**

35. parallel   **37.** perpendicular   **39.** perpendicular

Pages 237–238   Section 7.7   WRITTEN EXERCISES

1. $y = 4x + 2$ **3.** $y = -x + 3$ **5.** $y = -6$ **7.** $y = \frac{1}{2}x - \frac{2}{3}$ **9.** $y = 2x + 1$ **11.** $y = \frac{1}{2}x + 6$

13. $y = -3x + 4$ **15.** $y = -\frac{1}{4}x + \frac{3}{2}$ **17.** $y = -\frac{4}{3}x + \frac{25}{3}$ **19.** $y = \frac{5}{2}x + \frac{3}{2}$

21. $y = -\frac{4}{3}x + \frac{31}{3}$ **23.** $y = 2$ **25.** $2x - y = -3$ **27.** $x - 4y = 5$ **29.** $8x - 5y = -8$

31. $4x + y = 35$ **33.** $y = 2x + 1$ **35.** $y = -4x + 5$ **37.** $y = 6x - \frac{8}{3}$ **39.** $y = \frac{1}{2}x - \frac{3}{4}$

41. $\overline{AB}: y = \frac{1}{9}x + \frac{40}{9}; \overline{BC}: y = \frac{7}{2}x - \frac{25}{2}; \overline{CA}: y = -\frac{6}{7}x + \frac{4}{7}$

Pages 241–242   Section 7.8   WRITTEN EXERCISES

1. $y = 5x + 10$ **3.** $y = 5x + 10$ **5.** $y = -5x + 30$ **7.** 30 meters per second

9. 45 meters per second   **11.** 55°C   **13.** about 32°C

Pages 244–245   CHAPTER 7   REVIEW

1. 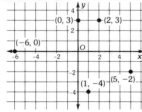   **3.** 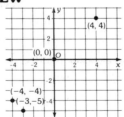   **5.** y-axis

7. II   **9.**   **11.**

13. domain = $\{3, 5, 0\}$; range = $\{2, 5, -1, 0\}$; no

15. $(-3, -14), (-1, -10), (0, -8), (1, -6), (3, -2)$

17. $(-3, -2), \left(-1, -\frac{4}{3}\right), (0, -1), \left(1, -\frac{2}{3}\right), (3, 0)$ **19.** 6 **21.** yes **23.** yes **25.** 3

27. 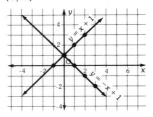 **29.** $y = -\frac{3}{4}x + \frac{5}{2}$; $m = -\frac{3}{4}$, $b = \frac{5}{2}$ **31.** $y = -\frac{8}{5}x + \frac{33}{5}$

33. $y = \frac{10}{7}x + 4$ **35.** $y = 5x + 12$

Pages 253–254   Section 8.1   WRITTEN EXERCISES

1. false **3.** true **5.** (0,0) **7.** (0, 1)

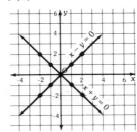

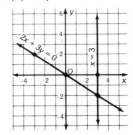

9. $(3, -2)$ **11.** $(3, 5)$ **13.** $(3, -2)$

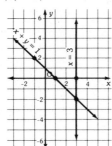

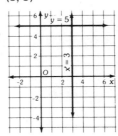

15. $(-4, 3)$ **17.** $(5, -4)$ **19.** $(-2, 4)$

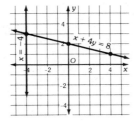

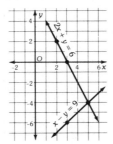

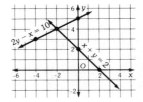

21. $(3, -4)$

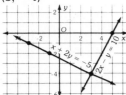

23. $(-1, 3)$

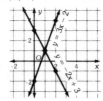

25. $(1, 1)$

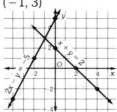

27. $(1, 2)$

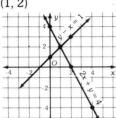

29. $(3, -2)$

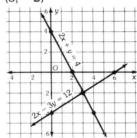

31. $\left(-\frac{1}{4}, \frac{1}{2}\right)$

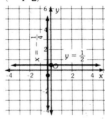

33. $(1, 2)$

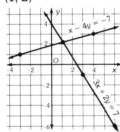

35. $(2, 0)$

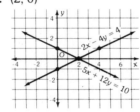

37. $(-2, 0)$

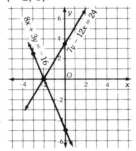

39. $\left(\frac{3}{2}, -\frac{3}{2}\right)$

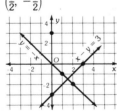

41. 4

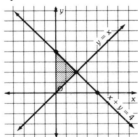

43. 27

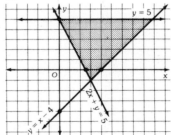

45. $\left(\frac{7}{8}, \frac{2}{5}\right)$

47. $(4, 2)$

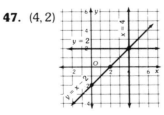

49. $(4, 2)$

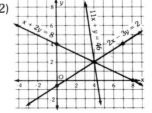

1. one; $(-1, 3)$

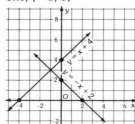

3. one; $(2, -4)$

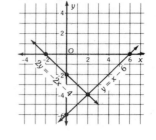

5. infinite **7.** none **9.** infinite

11. one; $(3, 1)$

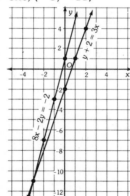

13. infinite **15.** none

17. one; $(-3, -11)$

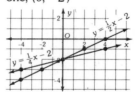

19. one; $(0, -2)$

21. none

23. one; $(-2, 3)$

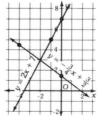

25. none

27. infinite **29.** one; (12, 7)

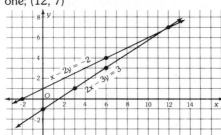

31. one; (2, 6)

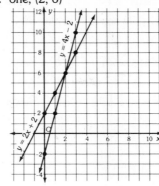

33. one; (−4, 3)

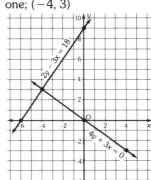

35. $-\frac{1}{2}$ **37.** 4 **39.** $\frac{3}{4}$ **41.** 5

43. $\frac{A}{D} = \frac{1}{2}$; $\frac{B}{E} = \frac{1}{2}$; $\frac{C}{F} = -\frac{5}{2}$; $\frac{A}{D} = \frac{B}{E} \neq \frac{C}{F}$; inconsistent

45. $\frac{A}{D} = 1$; $\frac{B}{E} = 1$; $\frac{C}{F} = 1$; $\frac{A}{D} = \frac{B}{E} = \frac{C}{F}$; consistent and dependent

47. $\frac{A}{D} = 1$; $\frac{B}{E} = 1$; $\frac{C}{F} = 1$; $\frac{A}{D} = \frac{B}{E} = \frac{C}{F}$; consistent and dependent

Page 260 Section 8.3 WRITTEN EXERCISES
1. (3, 0) **3.** (2, 12) **5.** (2, 1) **7.** (1, 0) **9.** (6, 2) **11.** (2, −2) **13.** (−4, 3) **15.** (1, 1)
17. infinite **19.** (3, −2) **21.** (20, 10) **23.** $\left(\frac{1}{3}, \frac{1}{3}\right)$ **25.** (8, 2, 4) **27.** (7, 5, 3) **29.** (3, 2, 4)

Pages 263–264 Section 8.4 WRITTEN EXERCISES
1. (2, −1) **3.** (0, 2) **5.** (3, −6) **7.** (−14, −9) **9.** (1, −1) **11.** $\left(0, \frac{7}{3}\right)$ **13.** (3, 2)
15. (5, −1) **17.** $\left(\frac{1}{2}, -2\right)$ **19.** (2, 5) **21.** (2, 3) **23.** (6, 8) **25.** none **27.** infinite
29. (2, 6) **31.** (3.2, 4) **33.** $\left(-\frac{7}{5}, \frac{4}{25}\right)$ **35.** (−0.5, 2)

Page 266 Section 8.5 WRITTEN EXERCISES
1. (4, 0) **3.** (6, 0) **5.** (−6, 13) **7.** (5, 1) **9.** infinite **11.** (2, −6) **13.** (2, 1) **15.** (2, −2)
17. $\left(\frac{4}{3}, \frac{1}{3}\right)$ **19.** (8, −2) **21.** $\left(\frac{21}{19}, \frac{5}{19}\right)$ **23.** (1.5625, −3.75) **25.** (2.75, 1.5) **27.** (−3, 4)
29. (−6, −18)

Page 269 Section 8.6 WRITTEN EXERCISES
1. 135 ft, 45 ft **3.** 6 people, 34 people **5.** 54, 126 **7.** 6 cm long, 1 cm wide
9. 11 field goals, 12 free throws **11.** 120 singles, 16 fives **13.** 45 km/h, 55 km/h

Page 275   Section 8.7   WRITTEN EXERCISES

1. 135 km/h, 15 km/h   **3.** 3 km/h, 1 km/h   **5.** 17.5 km/h, 2.5 km/h   **7.** $1\frac{2}{5}$ lb, $\frac{3}{5}$ lb
9. $3\frac{9}{17}$ gal, $4\frac{8}{17}$ gal   **11.** 16.67 g, 83.33 g

Pages 277–278   Section 8.8   WRITTEN EXERCISES

1. 8 and 4   **3.** 73   **5.** 11 and 16   **7.** 19 and 14   **9.** 24   **11.** 36   **13.** 0.36

Pages 281–282   Section 8.9   WRITTEN EXERCISES

1. 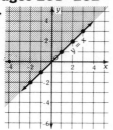   **3.** 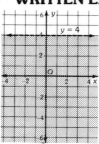   **5.**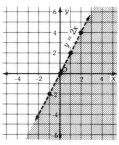

7. 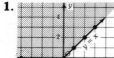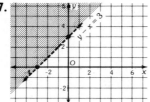   **9.** 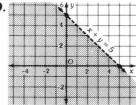   **11.**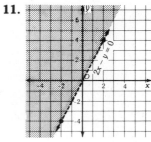

13. 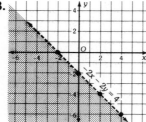   **15.**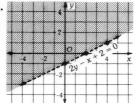

17. $y \geq -x + 1$

19. (4, 1), (5, 1), (3, 1), (2, 1), (1, 1), (1, 2), (2, 2)

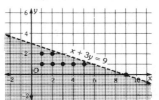

Page 285   Section 8.10   WRITTEN EXERCISES

1.

3.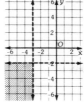

5.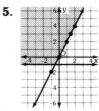

7.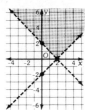

9.

11.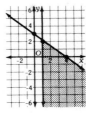

13.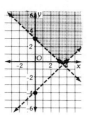

15.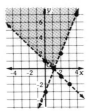

17.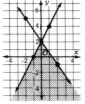

19.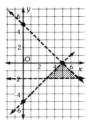

21.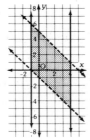

Page 287   Section 8.11   WRITTEN EXERCISES

1.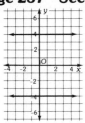

3.

5.

7.

9.

11.

13.

15.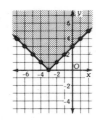

17. Translate the graph of $y = |x|$ one unit up.

Pages 290–291 CHAPTER 8 REVIEW

1. (1, 2)

3. (−4, 3)

5. (3, −2)

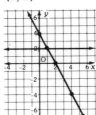

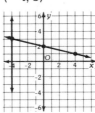

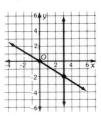

7. b **9.** c **11.** c **13.** (3, 0) **15.** (−1, 2) **17.** (4, 1) **19.** (1, 1) **21.** (5, 7) **23.** (5, 0)
25. (5, 2) **27.** (9, 4) **29.** (−6, 13) **31.** 85 m, 255 m **33.** 55 mi/h, 5 mi/h **35.** 18 yr, 14 yr
37.   **39.**

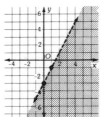

41.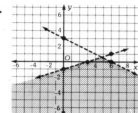

43.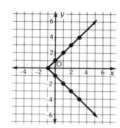

Page 295   Section 9.1   WRITTEN EXERCISES

1. $\frac{35}{42}$ **3.** $\frac{12}{4x}$ **5.** $\frac{-6n}{-21}$ **7.** $\frac{n^2 + 3n}{3n + 9}$ **9.** $\frac{x^2 + 5x + 6}{x^2 + x - 2}$ **11.** 24 **13.** 15 **15.** 36 **17.** $4x$

19. $-a$ **21.** mn **23.** $a^2 + 3a$ **25.** $x^2 + 5x + 4$ **27.** 0 **29.** 1 **31.** 0, 1 **33.** 1, -3 **35.** 1, 5

Page 298   Section 9.2   WRITTEN EXERCISES

1. $\frac{2}{3}$ **3.** $\frac{n}{3}$ **5.** $\frac{4y^2}{xz}$ **7.** $\frac{2q^2m^2}{7n^3}$ **9.** $\frac{x - y}{x + y}$ **11.** $\frac{b}{3}$ **13.** $\frac{3}{x - 5}$ **15.** $\frac{a + 5}{a - 4}$ **17.** $\frac{1}{y - 2}$ **19.** $\frac{3x}{2(x + 1)}$

21. $\frac{1}{n - 4}$ **23.** -1 **25.** -2 **37.** $\frac{v}{v + 1}$ **29.** m **31.** $\frac{6}{n + 3}$ **33.** $-a$ **35.** $\frac{5}{n - 2}$ **37.** $-\frac{x - 1}{x + 1}$

39. $\frac{x - 2}{x + 2}$ **41.** $\frac{x - 4}{x - 2}$ **43.** $\frac{a + 1}{a + 6}$ **45.** $\frac{x - 1}{x - 2}$ **47.** $\frac{2k + 1}{k - 1}$ **49.** $\frac{m + 4}{m}$ **51.** $\frac{4}{w + y}$ **53.** $\frac{s - 1}{s + 4}$

55. -1 **57.** $\frac{m + 1}{m - 2}$ **59.** $\frac{3d - 2}{2d + 3}$ **61.** $\frac{3(n + 3)}{n - 6}$ **63.** $\frac{3(a + 4)}{a + 3}$ **65.** $-\frac{x - 1}{2(x - 3)}$ **67.** $\frac{n + 4}{n - 7}$

69. $\frac{4x + 3}{4x - 3}$ **71.** $a + b - 1$ **73.** $\frac{6(4x + 7)}{5(2x + 1)}$

Page 301   Section 9.3   WRITTEN EXERCISES

1. 1 **3.** $\frac{1}{16}$ **5.** 1 **7.** $\frac{1}{9}$ **9.** 1 **11.** $\frac{b^2}{a^2}$ **13.** 1 **15.** 27 **17.** $-\frac{1}{4}$ **19.** $-\frac{1}{8}$ **21.** $\frac{1}{243}$ **23.** $\frac{1}{12}$

25. 3 **27.** a **29.** $\frac{4}{3}$ **31.** $\frac{7}{8}$ **33.** $-\frac{1}{5}$ **35.** $-\frac{1}{a}$ **37.** -9 **39.** $-b$ **41.** $-\frac{3}{2}$ **43.** $\frac{1}{64}$

45. $\frac{1}{a^3}$ **47.** $\frac{1}{b^4}$ **49.** y^3 **51.** $\frac{1}{16b^2}$ **53.** $-\frac{1}{8n^3}$ **55.** $\frac{1}{a^{11}b^{11}}$ **57.** $\frac{27}{8y^3}$ **59.** $\frac{1}{64x^3y^3}$ **61.** 1

63. 20,000 **65.** 40,000 **67.** $-13x^2y^6$ **69.** $\frac{2s^8}{5t^8}$

Pages 304–306   Section 9.4   WRITTEN EXERCISES

1. x **3.** $\frac{a - 1}{a + 1}$ **5.** $\frac{4b}{a}$ **7.** $\frac{ns}{3t}$ **9.** $\frac{z}{y}$ **11.** $\frac{1}{x - 4}$ **13.** $\frac{3y}{2}$ **15.** $6m^2n^2$ **17.** $\frac{9st^2}{4}$ **19.** 2

21. $2(x - 3)$ **23.** $\frac{6xy}{x + y}$ **25.** $-\frac{5}{9a}$ **27.** 3 **29.** $\frac{8}{x - 1}$ **31.** $\frac{1}{3}$ **33.** $\frac{y^2}{9x}$ **35.** $\frac{x - 4}{2(x + 4)}$

37. $-(a - 5)$ **39.** $\frac{5(n + 1)}{n - 1}$ **41.** $\frac{3(m - 6)}{(m - 2)(m - 5)}$ **43.** $(a + 2)(a + 1)$ **45.** $x + 2$ **47.** $\frac{m - 3}{m}$

49. $\frac{b + 4}{b}$ **51.** $\frac{m + n}{m(m + 1)}$ **53.** -1 **55.** $\frac{e + 5}{e + 1}$ **57.** $\frac{4y - 1}{y}$ **59.** $\frac{(z - 4)(z + 1)}{z^2}$ **61.** $\frac{v - 7}{3(v + 2)}$

63. $a + b$ **65.** $\frac{2n + 3}{2n - 1}$ **67.** $\frac{2x - 1}{2x - 5}$ **69.** $\frac{(m - n)(n - 4)}{m + n}$ **71.** 1

Pages 308–309   Section 9.5   WRITTEN EXERCISES

1. 5 **3.** $\frac{y}{x}$ **5.** $\frac{m}{5}$ **7.** $\frac{5}{x}$ **9.** $\frac{d}{c}$ **11.** $\frac{m}{n^2}$ **13.** $\frac{n}{m}$ **15.** $\frac{1}{6x}$ **17.** $\frac{a - 3}{a + 1}$ **19.** $n - 3$ **21.** $\frac{x + 3}{x + 4}$

23. $\frac{1}{n}$ **25.** $\frac{3m}{4t}$ **27.** $-\frac{1}{2}$ **29.** $\frac{4}{9x}$ **31.** $\frac{3}{8a}$ **33.** $\frac{a - 3}{a + 3}$ **35.** $\frac{y + 3}{3(y - 3)}$ **37.** 1 **39.** $\frac{m}{5(m + 5)}$

41. $\frac{x + 4}{x - 2}$ **43.** $\frac{2y - 3}{3y + 1}$ **45.** $\frac{b(a + b)}{a(a - b)}$ **47.** $\frac{ns^2(n - s - m)}{m^2(n - s)}$ **49.** $\frac{x}{y}$ **51.** m **53.** $\frac{5(a - 2)}{a - 4}$ **55.** 1

Page 311   Section 9.6   WRITTEN EXERCISES
1. 60 **3.** 216 **5.** $18b$ **7.** $3x^2$ **9.** $4(a - 3b)$ **11.** $15(2a^2 - 3)$ **13.** $(x + 3)^2(x - 3)$
15. $(y + 6)^2(y - 3)$ **17.** $(x - 2)(x + 1)(x + 2)$ **19.** $-4(a - b)$ **21.** $-6(m + 3)(m - 3)$
23. $(y + 2)(y - 2)(y - 3)$ **25.** $3(x + 5y)(x - 5y)$ **27.** $(3n - 1)(n - 4)(2n + 3)$

Pages 316–317   Section 9.7   WRITTEN EXERCISES
1. $\frac{1}{2}$ **3.** $\frac{7}{a}$ **5.** $\frac{a}{2}$ **7.** 0 **9.** $\frac{2x + 12}{3x}$ **11.** $\frac{11a + 3b - 5}{4}$ **13.** $\frac{10y + 2}{3}$ **15.** $\frac{8x}{10x^2}, \frac{3}{10x^2}$

17. $\frac{5x - 10}{(x + 1)(x - 2)}, \frac{3x + 3}{(x + 1)(x - 2)}$ **19.** $\frac{15x - 9}{(2x + 1)(5x - 3)}, \frac{8x + 4}{(2x + 1)(5x - 3)}$ **21.** $\frac{3x + 15}{7x(x + 5)}, \frac{7x^2}{7x(x + 5)}$

23. $\frac{2}{m - 3}, -\frac{m}{m - 3}$ **25.** $\frac{4x^2 + 8x + 3}{(x - 4)(2x + 1)}, \frac{x^3 - 7x + 12}{(x - 4)(2x + 1)}$ **27.** $\frac{8x^2}{15}$ **29.** $\frac{4x^2y + 3xy^2}{12}$

31. $\frac{1}{15a}$ **33.** $\frac{n + 5}{2n}$ **35.** $\frac{5a - 6}{3a}$ **37.** $\frac{a - 4}{6}$ **39.** $\frac{n - 6}{15}$ **41.** $\frac{b + 6}{(b - 3)^2}$ **43.** $\frac{2}{x - 4}$ **45.** $\frac{3(y + 2)}{(y + 3)^2}$

47. $\frac{3a - 5}{(a - 4)^2}$ **49.** $\frac{3m - 2n}{6(m + n)}$ **51.** $\frac{2x + y}{3x - y}$ **53.** $\frac{3n - 13}{n - 5}$ **55.** $\frac{3a - 1}{(a + 3)(a + 5)}$ **57.** $\frac{x(x - 5)}{x - 2}$

59. $\frac{5ab}{(2b - 3)(3b - 2)}$ **61.** $\frac{1}{2(a + 3)}$ **63.** $\frac{3a^2 - ab + 2b^2}{(a + b)(a - b)}$ **65.** $\frac{8x + 1}{3(x + 2)(x - 1)}$ **67.** $\frac{m - 4}{1 - 2m}$

69. $\frac{4z + 1}{(3z + 1)(3z - 1)}$ **71.** $\frac{v + 19}{2(v - 1)^2}$ **73.** $\frac{9}{(r - 2)(r + 1)^2}$ **75.** $\frac{2}{(y - 3)(y + 1)}$ **77.** $\frac{13ab - 11ac + 7ab}{abc}$

79. $\frac{1}{y - 2}$ **81.** $\frac{2}{b - 1}$ **83.** $\frac{-15n^2 + 7n + 10}{6(n + 1)(n - 1)}$ **85.** $-\frac{(m + 4)(m - 3)}{(m - 1)^2(m + 1)}$

Page 321   Section 9.8   WRITTEN EXERCISES
1. 5 **3.** 24 **5.** $\frac{1}{2}$ **7.** -6 **9.** 2 **11.** -15 **13.** $\varnothing$ **15.** $\frac{1}{2}$ **17.** -5 **19.** 2 **21.** $5\frac{1}{2}$
23. 0 **25.** $\varnothing$ **27.** $2\frac{1}{2}$ **29.** -14 **31.** 5 **33.** $-\frac{1}{2}$ **35.** -3 **37.** $\frac{6}{7}$ **39.** 3

Page 325   Section 9.9   WRITTEN EXERCISES
1. $1\frac{1}{5}$ h **3.** 20 mi/h **5.** 180 km/h **7.** $11\frac{1}{4}$ h **9.** $19\frac{1}{5}$ min

Pages 328–329   Section 9.10   WRITTEN EXERCISES
1. $\frac{5y}{4y - 3}$ **3.** $\frac{4y}{3(20y - 3)}$ **5.** $\frac{4y}{3(y - 1)}$ **7.** $\frac{5x + 18}{2(x - 3)}$ **9.** $\frac{9x}{4(15x - 1)}$ **11.** $\frac{3x}{4x - 5}$ **13.** $\frac{7x + 4}{4 - 3x}$ **15.** $\frac{5x}{7x + 3}$
17. $\frac{2A}{b}$ **19.** $\frac{2S - na}{n}$ **21.** $\frac{p - 2\ell}{2}$ **23.** $\frac{I}{Pr}$ **25.** $\frac{9C + 160}{5}$ **27.** $\frac{3V}{B}$ **29.** $\frac{RD^2}{K}$ **31.** $\frac{80H}{d^3}$ **33.** $\frac{Fgr}{v^2}$
35. $\frac{24c}{R(n + 1)}$ **37.** $\frac{1.732}{I - S}$ **39.** $\frac{1000kw}{E}$ **41.** $\frac{4Cc}{\pi b^2}$ **43.** 100 pounds **45.** 2000 pounds

Pages 332–333   CHAPTER 9   REVIEW
1. 35 **3.** $3x + 6$ **5.** $3b + 12$ **7.** 0 **9.** 6 **11.** 1, 6 **13.** $\frac{3}{8}$ **15.** $\frac{x - 4}{x + 7}$ **17.** $\frac{2s + 3}{s + 5}$ **19.** 64
21. $\frac{b^2}{a^2}$ **23.** m^4 **25.** $rsxy^3$ **27.** $\frac{x + y}{4}$ **29.** $\frac{(x - 4)(x - 1)}{(x - 5)(x - 2)}$ **31.** $\frac{b - 9}{b + 6}$ **33.** $\frac{3}{xy}$ **35.** $\frac{m + 2}{m - 1}$
37. $n - 5$ **39.** $\frac{t}{t + 2}$ **41.** $54a$ **43.** $4x(x - 2)$ **45.** $\frac{1}{x}$ **47.** $\frac{3(b - 1)}{b - 2}$ **49.** $-\frac{4y - 3}{y - 2}$ **51.** $\frac{11}{2(x + 2)}$
53. -1 **55.** -7 **57.** 3 **59.** $3\frac{3}{7}$ h **61.** $\frac{3y - 10}{y + 2}$ **63.** $v - gt$ **65.** $\frac{v}{\ell h}$

Pages 337–338   Section 10.1   WRITTEN EXERCISES

1. $\frac{3}{7}$ **3.** -2 **5.** $\frac{1}{6}$ **7.** 15 **9.** 15 **11.** -6 **13.** $c = 12t$ **15.** $n = 60t$ **17.** \$96
19. 45 minutes **21.** \$712.50 **23.** \$1800 **25.** \$276.25 **27.** \$87.50
29. 150 miles **31.** 720 grains

Pages 340–341   Section 10.2   WRITTEN EXERCISES

1. 68 **3.** 95 **5.** 432 **7.** 6.75 **9.** 12 **11.** -12 **13.** $\frac{27}{4}$ **15.** 4 **17.** 15 **19.** 126
21. $\frac{6}{5}$ **23.** 1 **25.** 2 **27.** 7 **29.** 3 **31.** $\frac{34}{11}$ **33.** \$170 **35.** 258 km **37.** 24 oz
39. 256 m **41.** 2.36 m **43.** -1 **45.** 4

Page 343   Section 10.3   WRITTEN EXERCISES

1. 9 **3.** 60 **5.** 36 **7.** 40% **9.** 80% **11.** \$194.25 **13.** 2% **15.** \$3350 **17.** 78%
19. 72 students

Pages 346–347   Section 10.4   WRITTEN EXERCISES

1. 8 **3.** 108 **5.** $\frac{3}{2}$ **7.** $1\frac{9}{16}$ **9.** 4 **11.** 6 **13.** 2.1 **15.** 0.625 **17.** 2.4 hours **19.** 6 feet
21. 12 inches **23.** 32 kilograms **25.** 40 chairs **27.** 12.5 centimeters **29.** 5 lumens

Pages 349–350   Section 10.5   WRITTEN EXERCISES

1. 9 **3.** 12 **5.** 6 **7.** 8 **9.** $\frac{3}{4}$ **11.** 4 **13.** 180 strides **15.** 4 days **17.** 300 tiles
19. 100 plants **21.** 6 **23.** 0.07 **25.** $\frac{1}{2}$

Pages 353–355   Section 10.6   WRITTEN EXERCISES

1. 23 pounds **3.** \$203 **5.** 6 persons **7.** 3 feet **9.** \$36 **11.** 20 amps **13.** 8.25 meters
15. 20% **17.** 63 meters

Pages 358–359   CHAPTER 10   REVIEW

1. $\frac{4}{9}$ **3.** -2 **5.** 18 **7.** 54 **9.** 30 gallons **11.** 8 **13.** 3 **15.** -16 **17.** 7 **19.** $-\frac{39}{11}$
21. 75% **23.** 70 **25.** 25 **27.** \$552.50 **29.** \$225 **31.** direct **33.** inverse **35.** inverse
37. 25 **39.** 3.1 **41.** 4 **43.** 11 **45.** 8 meters

Page 363   Section 11.1   WRITTEN EXERCISES

1. 2, -2 **3.** 6, -6 **5.** 5, -5 **7.** 9, -9 **9.** 1 **11.** -3 **13.** ± 8 **15.** 4 **17.** 11 **19.** -15
21. ± 14 **23.** ± 20 **25.** 30 **27.** ± 25 **29.** $\frac{3}{4}$ **31.** $-\frac{1}{8}$ **33.** $\pm\frac{5}{9}$ **35.** $\frac{15}{14}$ **37.** $\pm\frac{12}{17}$ **39.** $\frac{11}{20}$
41. 0.2 **43.** -0.9 **45.** 30 ft **47.** 225 ft^2

Pages 365–366   Section 11.2   WRITTEN EXERCISES

1. $1 < 3 < 4$; $1 < \sqrt{3} < 2$ **3.** $9 < 12 < 16$; $3 < \sqrt{12} < 4$ **5.** $64 < 65 < 81$; $8 < \sqrt{65} < 9$
7. $100 < 115 < 121$; $10 < \sqrt{115} < 11$ **9.** $169 < 172 < 196$; $13 < \sqrt{172} < 14$
11. $196 < 205 < 225$; $14 < \sqrt{205} < 15$ **13.** $225 < 228 < 256$; $15 < \sqrt{228} < 16$
15. $289 < 320 < 324$; $17 < \sqrt{320} < 18$ **17.** 8.2 **19.** 6.4 **21.** 3.3 **23.** 9.4 **25.** 3.46
27. 9.38 **29.** 8.66 **31.** 7.07 **33.** 5.74 **35.** 8.12 **37.** 10.63 **39.** 11.09 **41.** 4.12 **43.** 4

Pages 368–369   Section 11.3   WRITTEN EXERCISES

1. 10 **3.** 17 **5.** 20 **7.** $\sqrt{130}$ **9.** 2.236 **11.** 5.196 **13.** 7.681 **15.** 5.292 **17.** 9.798
19. 12.207 **21.** 8.544 **23.** 9.849 **25.** 8.485 **27.** 8.062 **29.** 10.817 **31.** 9.434 **33.** 11.4 ft
35. 9.381 mm

Page 371   Section 11.4   WRITTEN EXERCISES

1. 7 **3.** 25 **5.** 10 **7.** 1 **9.** 3 **11.** 4 **13.** 3 **15.** 11 **17.** $\sqrt{6}$

19. $\sqrt{15x}$ **21.** $\sqrt{110xy}$ **23.** $\sqrt{3}$ **25.** $\sqrt{2x+6}$ **27.** $\sqrt{2}$ **29.** $\sqrt{2x}$ **31.** $\sqrt{3x}$ **33.** $\sqrt{2mn}$
35. $\sqrt{2x}$ **37.** $\sqrt{7xy}$ **39.** $\sqrt{2y}$ **41.** $36x$ **43.** $3s^3t^3$ **45.** $\sqrt{x-2}$ **47.** no

Pages 374–375　Section 11.5　WRITTEN EXERCISES
1. $2\sqrt{2}$ **3.** $3\sqrt{2}$ **5.** $2\sqrt{6}$ **7.** $3\sqrt{5}$ **9.** $6\sqrt{2}$ **11.** $4\sqrt{2}$ **13.** $2\sqrt{15}$ **15.** $8\sqrt{3}$ **17.** $2\sqrt{22}$
19. $2\sqrt{14}$ **21.** $\frac{5}{6}$ **23.** $\frac{10}{3}$ **25.** $\frac{\sqrt{3}}{2}$ **27.** $\frac{\sqrt{3}}{4}$ **29.** $\frac{\sqrt{2}}{2}$ **31.** $\frac{\sqrt{35}}{7}$ **33.** $\frac{2\sqrt{3}}{3}$ **35.** $\frac{4\sqrt{5}}{5}$
37. $\frac{\sqrt{3}}{3}$ **39.** $\frac{3\sqrt{5}}{10}$ **41.** $\frac{3\sqrt{2}}{2}$ **43.** $\frac{2\sqrt{5}}{5}$ **45.** $5|x|\sqrt{3}$ **47.** $4a\sqrt{3a}$ **49.** $10y^3\sqrt{2}$
51. $7|b^3|\sqrt{2}$ **53.** $6x^2\sqrt{x}$ **55.** $|a|\sqrt{b}$ **57.** $\frac{\sqrt{3}}{2|a|}$ **59.** $\frac{9x^2\sqrt{x}}{|y^3|}$ **61.** $\frac{\sqrt{6}}{3|x|}$ **63.** $\frac{x^2\sqrt{7x}}{7}$ **65.** $5\sqrt{2}$
67. $30\sqrt{3}$ **69.** $8|x|\sqrt{3}$ **71.** $-4x^4\sqrt{5}$ **73.** $-6x^4\sqrt{6x}$

Page 377　Section 11.6　WRITTEN EXERCISES
1. $5\sqrt{2}$ **3.** $-\sqrt{3}$ **5.** $-8\sqrt{a}$ **7.** $-9\sqrt{3}$ **9.** $\sqrt{2}$ **11.** $5\sqrt{2}$ **13.** $5\sqrt{5}$ **15.** $6\sqrt{3}$ **17.** $7\sqrt{2}$
19. $3\sqrt{2x}$ **21.** $2\sqrt{2}$ **23.** $-5\sqrt{5}$ **25.** $\sqrt{2}$ **27.** $8\sqrt{5}$ **29.** $14\sqrt{10}$ **31.** $2\sqrt{7}-5\sqrt{2}$
33. $13\sqrt{7}-3\sqrt{2}$ **35.** $10\sqrt{3a}$ **37.** $5x\sqrt{2x}$ **39.** $11y\sqrt{3y}$ **41.** $9n^2\sqrt{2}$ **43.** $\frac{5\sqrt{2}}{2}$ **45.** $\frac{5\sqrt{6}}{2}$
47. $\frac{34\sqrt{7}}{7}$ **49.** $6\sqrt{3}+48$ **51.** $\frac{2x\sqrt{x}}{35}$ **53.** $\frac{9|x|}{20}$ **55.** $x^2\sqrt{x}+x^2+x\sqrt{x}$ **57.** $13|x|$

Pages 379–380　Section 11.7　WRITTEN EXERCISES
1. $5+3\sqrt{3}$ **3.** $5+3\sqrt{5}$ **5.** $21-8\sqrt{6}$ **7.** $8+2\sqrt{7}$ **9.** $23-8\sqrt{7}$ **11.** 4 **13.** $24+10\sqrt{6}$
15. $17-15\sqrt{5}$ **17.** $71-49\sqrt{7}$ **19.** $63+36\sqrt{3}$ **21.** $93-28\sqrt{11}$ **23.** -4 **25.** 4
37. $8+4\sqrt{3}+2\sqrt{2}+\sqrt{6}$ **29.** $6+3\sqrt{5}-2\sqrt{3}-\sqrt{15}$ **31.** $6-3\sqrt{5}-2\sqrt{7}+\sqrt{35}$
33. $15+15\sqrt{2}+3\sqrt{3}+3\sqrt{6}$ **35.** $14-8\sqrt{3}+7\sqrt{5}-4\sqrt{15}$
37. $18+27\sqrt{2}-3\sqrt{14}-2\sqrt{7}$ **39.** $20-15\sqrt{2}+8\sqrt{3}-6\sqrt{6}$ **41.** $\frac{20-4\sqrt{3}}{11}$ **43.** $\frac{8+2\sqrt{7}}{9}$
45. $-\sqrt{15}-2\sqrt{5}$ **47.** $3\sqrt{6}-\sqrt{2}$ **49.** $17-4\sqrt{15}$ **51.** -5 **53.** $\frac{5+\sqrt{5}}{10}$
55. $\frac{16+8x\sqrt{y}+x^2y}{16-x^2y}$

Pages 382–383　Section 11.8　WRITTEN EXERCISES
1. 8 **3.** $\varnothing$ **5.** 16 **7.** 51 **9.** 24 **11.** -23 **13.** 12 **15.** 1 **17.** 9 **19.** 84 **21.** $-2,2$
23. 22 **25.** 12 **27.** -2 **29.** $-\frac{1}{3}$ **31.** $-7,7$ **33.** 4 **35.** 5 **37.** $1,2$ **39.** 1 **41.** $\varnothing$
43. 2 **45.** $-\frac{3}{2},4$ **47.** 11 **49.** 1 **51.** 1

Pages 388–389　Section 11.9　WRITTEN EXERCISES
1. $(4,-2)$ **3. a.** 6 **b.** 4 **c.** $2\sqrt{13}$ **5.** 5 **7.** 3 **9.** 13 **11.** $2\sqrt{5}$ **13.** $2\sqrt{10}$ **15.** $5\sqrt{2}$
17. $\sqrt{30}$ **19.** $2\sqrt{47}$ **21.** $-7,1$ **23.** $-14,2$ **25.** $-4,20$ **27.** $-3,7$ **29.** $0,8$ **31.** yes

Pages 392–393　CHAPTER 11　REVIEW
1. 9 **3.** -14 **5.** $\frac{8}{7}$ **7.** ±11 **9.** 6.3 **11.** 6.2 **13.** 6.16 **15.** 13 **17.** $\sqrt{137}$ **19.** 7.616
21. 11.269 **23.** 10.630 **25.** $\sqrt{21x}$ **27.** $\sqrt{5x-5}$ **29.** 2 **31.** $\sqrt{5xy}$ **33.** $3\sqrt{7}$ **35.** $\frac{3}{17}$
37. $\frac{\sqrt{30}}{6}$ **39.** $2\sqrt{2}$ **41.** $|x|y\sqrt{y}$ **43.** $\frac{\sqrt{3}}{5|a|}$ **45.** $\frac{|y^5|\sqrt{2}}{2}$ **47.** $3\sqrt{14}$ **49.** $5\sqrt{21}$ **51.** $5x^5\sqrt{2}$
53. $3x\sqrt{2}$ **55.** $-9x^3$ **57.** $4\sqrt{3}$ **59.** $5\sqrt{5x}$ **61.** $4x^3\sqrt{3}$ **63.** 0 **65.** $\frac{11\sqrt{5}}{5}$ **67.** $\frac{11\sqrt{15}}{5}$
69. $10+6\sqrt{2}$ **71.** $39-12\sqrt{3}$ **73.** 7 **75.** $50-30\sqrt{3}$ **77.** $\frac{3+\sqrt{5}}{2}$ **79.** $\frac{6\sqrt{3}-\sqrt{6}}{34}$
81. $\varnothing$ **83.** 16 **85.** $-9,9$ **87.** $-3,3$ **89.** $-\frac{3}{4},\frac{1}{3}$ **91.** 7 **93.** $2\sqrt{17}$ **95.** $2\sqrt{2}$

Pages 399–400　Section 12.1　WRITTEN EXERCISES
1. $x^2+3x-7=0$ **3.** $x^2-36x-2=0$ **5.** $x^2-2x+9=0$ **7.** $x^2+2x+15=0$

9. 6, -2 **11.** $-4, -2$ **13.** $-9, -3$ **15.** 3 **17.** 11, -8 **19.** 8, 12 **21.** $\frac{3}{2}, -5$ **23.** $\frac{1}{3}, 2$
25. $-7, 5$ **27.** $-\frac{11}{3}, -4$ **29.** $\frac{8}{3}, -7$ **31.** 0, $\frac{13}{3}$ **33.** $-\frac{7}{3}, \frac{9}{2}$ **35.** $-\frac{1}{7}, \frac{4}{3}$ **37.** $x^2 + 2x = 0$
39. $x^2 + 4x - 12 = 0$ **41.** $x^2 + 14x + 45 = 0$ **43.** $-4, 3$ **45.** $\frac{5}{2}, -3$ **47.** $\frac{1}{3}, -\frac{7}{2}$
49. $\frac{8}{5}, \frac{7}{2}$ **51.** 0, $\frac{11}{6}$

Pages 402–403 Section 12.2 WRITTEN EXERCISES

1. ± 2 **3.** ± 8 **5.** $\pm 4\sqrt{2}$ **7.** ± 3 **9.** $\pm \frac{3}{2}$ **11.** $\pm \frac{\sqrt{15}}{4}$ **13.** 6, -4 **15.** 3, -12
17. 4, $-\frac{4}{3}$ **19.** $\frac{19}{3}, -5$ **21.** $\frac{3}{2}, 0$ **23.** $3\sqrt{6}, -\sqrt{6}$ **25.** $3\sqrt{7}, -\sqrt{7}$ **27.** 1.1, 0.7
29. $-\frac{2}{5}, -2$ **31.** $\frac{1}{3}, -\frac{11}{3}$ **33.** $3 \pm \sqrt{6}$ **35.** $\frac{8}{15}, \frac{2}{15}$ **37.** 5, $-\frac{7}{3}$ **39.** $\frac{14}{5}, -2$
41. $\frac{7}{2}, -\frac{5}{2}$ **43.** $\frac{9}{10}, -\frac{2}{5}$ **45.** $-0.2\overline{6}, -1.0\overline{6}$

Pages 405–406 Section 12.3 WRITTEN EXERCISES

1. 3^2 **3.** $\left(\frac{9}{2}\right)^2$ **5.** $\left(\frac{7}{4}\right)^2$ **7.** $\left(\frac{5}{4}\right)^2$ **9.** $\left(\frac{7}{16}\right)^2$ **11.** 2, -8 **13.** $-1, -13$ **15.** 10, 2 **17.** $\frac{3 \pm \sqrt{13}}{2}$
19. $\frac{-1 \pm \sqrt{13}}{2}$ **21.** $\frac{5 \pm \sqrt{41}}{2}$ **23.** $\frac{9}{2} \pm 2\sqrt{5}$ **25.** 4, -3 **27.** 2, $-\frac{3}{2}$ **29.** $\frac{1}{2}, -3$ **31.** $\frac{9}{4}, -\frac{3}{4}$
33. $\frac{1}{5}, -\frac{3}{2}$ **35.** $2 \pm \frac{3\sqrt{6}}{4}$ **37.** $\frac{3}{4}, -\frac{2}{3}$ **39.** $\frac{1 \pm \sqrt{385}}{24}$ **41.** $\frac{5 \pm \sqrt{13}}{2}$ **43.** 0, -8 **45.** $\frac{41}{3}, 4$
47. $\frac{8}{5}, -1$ **49.** $\frac{-b \pm \sqrt{b^2 - 4c}}{2}$

Page 410 Section 12.4 WRITTEN EXERCISES

1. 3, $-\frac{5}{2}$ **3.** $\frac{9}{4}, 2$ **5.** $\frac{2}{5}, -\frac{1}{3}$ **7.** $\frac{5 \pm \sqrt{2}}{7}$ **9.** 3, $\frac{3}{7}$ **11.** 2, $-\frac{4}{5}$ **13.** $\frac{3}{10}, -\frac{1}{4}$ **15.** $-3 \pm \sqrt{3}$
17. $3 \pm \sqrt{7}$ **19.** $\frac{3 \pm \sqrt{17}}{2}$ **21.** $\frac{-3 \pm \sqrt{15}}{2}$ **23.** $-2 \pm \sqrt{5}$ **25.** $\frac{-11 \pm \sqrt{89}}{2}$ **27.** $\frac{-2 \pm \sqrt{10}}{2}$
29. $\frac{1}{2}$ **31.** $\frac{2}{7}, -\frac{5}{9}$ **33.** 35, -19 **35.** $-14, -15$ **37.** $-\sqrt{3}$ **39.** $\sqrt{5}$ **41.** $\sqrt{3}, -5\sqrt{3}$
43. $\frac{-3 \pm \sqrt{3}}{2}$ **45.** $\frac{-8 \pm \sqrt{34}}{6}$ **47.** 4.1 m

Page 412 Section 12.5 WRITTEN EXERCISES

1. 1 **3.** 5 **5.** 0 **7.** 49 **9.** 0 **11.** 0 **13.** -8, no real roots **15.** 0, real, equal, rational
17. 1764, real, unequal, rational **19.** 21, real, unequal, irrational **21.** 121, real, unequal, rational
23. $-\frac{3}{4}$, no real roots **25.** 0, real, equal, rational **27.** -1.035 or -3.863 **29.** no real roots
31. 2.9565 or -0.5075 **33.** real, unequal, may be rational or irrational, depending on the value of b
35. no real roots

Pages 415–416 Section 12.6 WRITTEN EXERCISES

1. 15 and 16 or -16 and -15 **3.** 8 m **5.** 3 and $\frac{12}{5}$ **7.** width, 12 ft; length, 15 ft
9. $\frac{4}{3}$ and $\frac{3}{4}$ **11.** 2 inches

Pages 419–420 Section 12.7 WRITTEN EXERCISES

1. **3.** 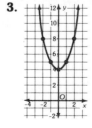 **5.** **7.**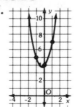

9. $x = \frac{5}{4}$ **11.** $x = \frac{3}{2}$ **13.** $x = \frac{1}{3}$ **15.** $(0, 4)$, upward **17.** $(-4, -16)$, upward **19.** $(2, 5)$, downward **21.** one **23.** none **25.** two **27.** $3, 2$ **29.** $-5, 3$
31. (a) $x = 4$ (b) $(4, -13)$ **33.** (a) $x = 3$ (b) $(3, 0)$ **35.** (a) $x = 1$ (b) $(-1, 2)$
(c) 7.6 or 0.4 (d) 3 (c) 3 (d) -9 (c) no x-intercepts (d) 3

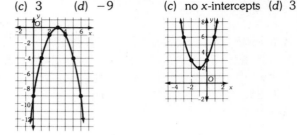

37. -2 **39.** $-3, 1$

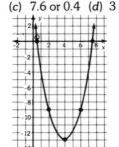
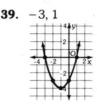

Page 423   Section 12.8   WRITTEN EXERCISES
1. 64 ft **3.** 48 ft, 48 ft **5.** 128 ft **7.** 144 ft **9.** $9700 **11.** 605 watts

Pages 428–429   CHAPTER 12   REVIEW
1. $8, 3$ **3.** $-\frac{8}{3}, -5$ **5.** $\frac{1}{4}, -\frac{9}{2}$ **7.** $-5, 3$ **9.** ± 12 **11.** $-3 \pm 2\sqrt{2}$ **13.** $-\frac{1}{2}, -\frac{9}{2}$
15. $8 \pm 2\sqrt{3}$ **17.** $9, 1$ **19.** $4, -1$ **21.** $3, -\frac{2}{3}$ **23.** $2, -\frac{4}{3}$ **25.** $3, 2$ **27.** $\frac{-2 \pm \sqrt{2}}{2}$
29. $\frac{2 \pm \sqrt{10}}{6}$ **31.** $\frac{7}{2}, -1$ **33.** 0, real, equal, rational **35.** 192, real, unequal, irrational
37. 256, real, unequal, rational **39.** $14, 15$ **41.** 11 cm long, 6 cm wide
43. **45.** **47.** $x = \frac{3}{2}$ **49.** $x = 1$ **51.** $\left(-\frac{3}{2}, -\frac{7}{2}\right)$

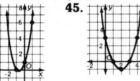

53. $-5, 3$ **55.** $3, 1$ **57.** 25 m by 25 m

Pages 434–435   Section 13.1   WRITTEN EXERCISES

1.
2	5, 5, 7, 8
3	2, 6, 9
4	1, 4
5	2, 9
7	1, 3, 4

3.
3	2, 8
4	3, 5, 7
5	2, 6, 8, 9
6	3, 3, 7, 8
7	4, 8
8	2, 5, 7, 9, 9
9	0, 0, 3, 8

5.
1	6, 7
2	4, 5, 7
4	3, 7, 8
5	2, 4, 7, 9
6	4, 8
7	3, 5, 9
8	0, 2, 3, 4, 5, 7
9	2, 3, 6

7.
14	0, 3, 6, 7
15	0, 2, 2, 3, 8, 8, 9
16	1, 2, 3, 7, 9
17	2, 3, 3, 5, 6, 7, 8, 9

9.

Group 1		Group 2
9, 9, 8, 5	1	1, 3, 5, 8, 9
7, 6, 5, 3, 1	2	3, 6, 7, 9
7, 2, 1	3	2, 6, 7, 7
6, 5, 2	4	3, 7, 7
	5	1, 6

11. 12 **13.** 42

15.
1	2, 3, 4, 5, 8, 9, 9
2	3, 3, 4, 4, 6, 6, 6, 6, 7, 7
3	0, 1, 2, 4, 5, 8, 8
4	0, 0, 2, 2, 4, 7, 7, 7, 8, 9
5	1, 2, 2, 2, 3, 4, 6, 6, 6, 7
6	2, 4, 7, 7, 7, 9
7	0, 3, 3, 3, 5, 6, 6
8	1, 1, 2, 3, 7, 7, 8, 8, 9
9	0, 0, 1, 3, 3, 8

Pages 437–438   Section 13.2   WRITTEN EXERCISES

1.
Score	Frequency
4	5
5	4
6	6
7	2
8	10
9	3
10	5
Total	35

3.
Day of the week	Frequency
Monday	4
Tuesday	8
Wednesday	3
Thursday	2
Friday	11
Saturday	2
Total	30

5.
Score	Frequency
60	1
70	5
80	7
90	2
100	2
110	3
120	1
Total	24

7.
Score	Frequency
59	4
60	1
61	1
62	2
63	1
64	1
65	2
66	2
67	3
68	2
69	1
70	1
Total	21

9.
Interval	Frequency
1–10	3
11–20	5
21–30	4
31–40	5
41–50	5
51–60	6
Total	28

11.
Interval	Frequency
101–110	2
111–120	4
121–130	4
131–140	5
141–150	5
151–160	1
161–170	7
Total	28

13.
Number	Frequency	Cumulative frequency
12	7	7
13	5	12
14	4	16
18	2	18
20	1	19
25	5	24

15.
Interval	Frequency	Cumulative frequency
1–5	7	7
6–10	4	11
11–15	9	20
16–20	8	28
21–25	5	33
26–30	7	40

Pages 441–442   Section 13.3   WRITTEN EXERCISES

1. 4 **3.** brown **5.** 36

7. Fewer hours are needed. Typical answer: Better farm machinery is being used. **9.** 13

11.

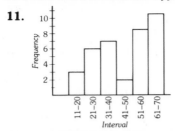

Pages 446–447   Section 13.4   WRITTEN EXERCISES

1. (a) 11
(b) 7
(c) 7

3. (a) no mode
(b) 2.6
(c) 2.61

5. (a) no mode
(b) 204
(c) 209.43

7. (a) 18.3
(b) 18.3
(c) 19.19

9. (a) no mode
(b) 18
(c) 18

11. (a) 240 and 380
(b) 235
(c) 265.625

13. (a) 10
(b) 21
(c) 19.9

15. (a) 50
(b) 50
(c) 45.78

17. (a) no mode
(b) 215
(c) 221.67

19. mean   **21.** *car 1*: 26.8; *car 2*: 23.95; *car 3*: 27.85

Pages 452–453   Section 13.5   WRITTEN EXERCISES

1. 35 **3.** 57 **5.** 55 **7.** 79 **9.** 102

11. (a) 32.75
(b) 5.72

13. (a) 124
(b) 11.14

15. (a) 111.78
(b) 10.57

17. (a) 6.64
(b) 2.58

19. (a) 128.5
(b) 11.34

21. 2.25; 19.35; Test Form A

Pages 458–459   Section 13.6   WRITTEN EXERCISES

1. 6; 3 **3.** 64; 32 **5.** 20; 10 **7.** 13; 6.5 **9.** 6.5; 3.25 **11.** $11\frac{3}{4}$; $5\frac{7}{8}$ **13.** 8.5; 16.5; 24.5

15. 35; 45; 70 **17.** 24.5; 49; 66.5 **19.** 15; 20; 30 **21.** 16.5; 28; 32

23.

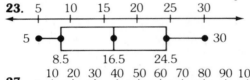

25.

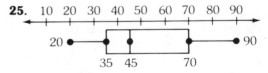

27.

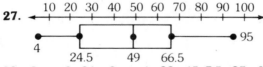

29. Group 2 **31.** Group 1 **33.** 15; 7.5 **35.** 33; 16.5 **37.** 15; 7.5 **39.** 27; 13.5

Pages 462–463   CHAPTER 13   REVIEW

1.

1	7
2	6, 6, 7, 9
3	1, 2, 2, 4, 8
4	2, 6, 9
5	3, 3, 3, 6
6	7
7	2, 3, 4, 5, 5, 8, 9
8	2, 4, 5, 9
9	3

3.

1	4, 8
2	4, 5, 6, 6, 7
3	2, 2, 2, 3, 6, 6, 9
4	3, 6, 8
5	1, 2

5.

Number	Frequency
100	6
110	9
120	5
130	2
140	4
Total	26

7.

Interval	Frequency
0–2	8
3–5	7
6–8	12
9–11	9
Total	36

9. Roth **11.** 271 **13.** 19 **15.** 18 **17.** 5.75 **19.** 4

21. 39.5 **23.** 29 **25.** 10.56 **27.** 12 **29.** Group 2 **31.** Group 2

Pages 467–468   Section 14.1   WRITTEN EXERCISES

1. 36 **3.** 18 **5.** 3 **7.** 6 **9.** HH, HT, TH, TT **11.** 2, 12, 18 **13.** △°, △*, °*

15.

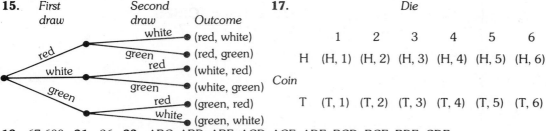

First draw, Second draw, Outcome:
red → white (red, white); red → green (red, green); white → red (white, red); white → green (white, green); green → red (green, red); green → white (green, white)

17.

	Die					
	1	2	3	4	5	6
Coin H	(H, 1)	(H, 2)	(H, 3)	(H, 4)	(H, 5)	(H, 6)
T	(T, 1)	(T, 2)	(T, 3)	(T, 4)	(T, 5)	(T, 6)

19. 67,600 **21.** 96 **23.** ABC, ABD, ABE, ACD, ACE, ADE, BCD, BCE, BDE, CDE

Page 471   Section 14.2   WRITTEN EXERCISES

1. 1 **3.** 5040 **5.** 3024 **7.** 220 **9.** 24 **11.** 210 **13.** 2300 **15.** 2,598,960 **17.** 28 **19.** 1
21. 6

Pages 472–473   Section 14.3   WRITTEN EXERCISES

1. Answers will vary. **3.** Answers will vary. **5.** Answers will vary.
7. No. One head and one tail can occur two different ways—a head on the penny and a tail on the dime or a head on the dime and a tail on the penny. Two heads can occur only one way.
9. yes; no **11.** Answers will vary.

Pages 476–477   Section 14.4   WRITTEN EXERCISES

1. $\frac{1}{36}$ **3.** $\frac{1}{18}$ **5.** $\frac{35}{36}$ **7.** 0.2 **9.** $\frac{2}{25}$ **11.** $\frac{1}{13}$ **13.** $\frac{1}{4}$ **15.** $\frac{1}{2}$ **17.** $\frac{7}{8}$ **19.** $\frac{1}{4}$ **21.** 200 times
23. 10 **25.** $\frac{1}{32}$ **27.** $\frac{2}{17}$ **29.** $\frac{1}{5}$ **31.** $\frac{5}{1}$

Pages 480–481   Section 14.5   WRITTEN EXERCISES

1. $\frac{1}{3}$ **3.** $\frac{1}{2}$ **5.** $\frac{7}{9}$ **7.** $\frac{1}{6}$ **9.** $\frac{1}{9}$ **11.** $\frac{2}{9}$ **13.** $\frac{3}{4}$ **15.** $\frac{3}{4}$ **17.** $\frac{5}{6}$ **19.** $\frac{7}{13}$ **21.** $\frac{8}{13}$

Page 484   Section 14.6   WRITTEN EXERCISES

1. $\frac{1}{100}$ **3.** $\frac{3}{50}$ **5.** $\frac{1}{90}$ **7.** $\frac{1}{15}$ **9.** $\frac{1}{36}$ **11.** $\frac{1}{6}$ **13.** $\frac{25}{102}$ **15.** $\frac{4}{663}$

Pages 488–489   CHAPTER 14   REVIEW

1. 9 **3.**

	Vowel				
	a	e	i	o	u
Coin H	(H, a)	(H, e)	(H, i)	(H, o)	(H, u)
T	(T, a)	(T, e)	(T, i)	(T, o)	(T, u)

5. 40,320 **7.** 21 **9.** 720

11. 60 **13.** $\frac{7}{50}$ **15.** $\frac{4}{25}$ **17.** $\frac{1}{6}$ **19.** 75% **21.** $\frac{2}{3}$ **23.** $\frac{2}{13}$ **25.** $\frac{1}{6}$ **27.** $\frac{1}{26}$

Pages 495–496   Section 15.1   WRITTEN EXERCISES
1. right **3.** hypotenuse **5.** $\overline{LK}, \overline{JK}$ **7.** $\overline{JK}$ **9.** $\overline{JK}$ **11.** 45° **13.** 74° **15.** $(90 - x)°$
17. $(65 - x)°$ **19.** 135° **21.** 164° **23.** $(180 - x)°$ **25.** $(155 - x)°$ **27.** 37° **29.** 98° **31.** 44°
33. 118° **35.** $m\angle A = 31, m\angle B = 62, m\angle C = 87$ **37.** $m\angle L = 20, m\angle M = 40, m\angle N = 120$
39. yes **41.** no

Pages 499–500   Section 15.2   WRITTEN EXERCISES
1. $\angle Y$ **3.** $\angle X$ **5.** $\overline{XY}$ and $\overline{PQ}, \overline{XZ}$ and $\overline{PR}, \overline{YZ}$ and $\overline{QR}$ **7.** z, p, x **9.** Z **11.** 5, 6, 4
13. 2.45, 4.9, 5 **15.** 9, 3, 12 **17.** $e = 78, f = 66$ **19.** $a = 7.5, c = 11.25$
21. $d = 5, f = 2.5$ **23.** $j = 2.5, t = 7.5$

Pages 502–504   Section 15.3   WRITTEN EXERCISES
1. $\frac{8}{17}$ **3.** $\frac{15}{17}$ **5.** $\frac{8}{15}$ **7.** $\frac{2\sqrt{2}}{3}$ **9.** $\frac{1}{3}$ **11.** $2\sqrt{2}$
13. $\sin D = \frac{40}{41}, \sin E = \frac{9}{41}, \cos D = \frac{9}{41}, \cos E = \frac{40}{41}, \tan D = \frac{40}{9}, \tan E = \frac{9}{40}$
15. $\sin G = \frac{\sqrt{6}}{3}, \sin H = \frac{\sqrt{3}}{3}, \cos G = \frac{\sqrt{3}}{3}, \cos H = \frac{\sqrt{6}}{3}, \tan G = \sqrt{2}, \tan H = \frac{\sqrt{2}}{2}$
17. $\sin T = \frac{\sqrt{21}}{5}, \sin V = \frac{2}{5}, \cos T = \frac{2}{5}, \cos V = \frac{\sqrt{21}}{5}, \tan T = \frac{\sqrt{21}}{2}, \tan V = \frac{2\sqrt{21}}{21}$
19. $\sin L = \frac{7\sqrt{85}}{85}, \sin N = \frac{6\sqrt{85}}{85}, \cos L = \frac{6\sqrt{85}}{85}, \cos N = \frac{7\sqrt{85}}{85}, \tan L = \frac{7}{6}, \tan N = \frac{6}{7}$
21. $\sin A = \frac{3\sqrt{13}}{13}, \sin B = \frac{2\sqrt{13}}{13}, \cos A = \frac{2\sqrt{13}}{13}, \cos B = \frac{3\sqrt{13}}{13}, \tan A = \frac{3}{2}, \tan B = \frac{2}{3}$
23. $\sin R = \frac{3\sqrt{13}}{13}, \sin T = \frac{2\sqrt{13}}{13}, \cos R = \frac{2\sqrt{13}}{13}, \cos T = \frac{3\sqrt{13}}{13}, \tan R = \frac{3}{2}, \tan T = \frac{2}{3}$ **25.** $\frac{20}{29}$ **27.** $\frac{12}{37}$

Pages 506–507   Section 15.4   WRITTEN EXERCISES
1. 0.5150 **3.** 0.6691 **5.** 0.6293 **7.** 5.6713 **9.** 0.6561 **11.** 0.9848 **13.** 0.9336 **15.** 0.0875
17. 0.8829 **19.** 0.2250 **21.** 1.9626 **23.** 57.2900 **25.** 85° **27.** 13° **29.** 48° **31.** 80°
33. 35° **35.** 33° **37.** 59° **39.** 6° **41.** 65° **43.** 68° **45.** 68° **47.** 5° **49.** 35° **51.** 85°
53. 50° **55.** 28° **57.** 56° **59.** 81° **61.** 25° **63.** 20° **65.** 66° **57.** 45°
69. They are the same.

Pages 509–510   Section 15.5   WRITTEN EXERCISES
1. 37.9 **3.** 14.6 **5.** 35.6 **7.** 27° **9.** 53° **11.** 30° **13.** $c = 10, m\angle A = 37, m\angle B = 53$
15. $a = 12, m\angle A = 67, m\angle B = 23$ **17.** $b = 7, m\angle A = 74, m\angle B = 16$
19. $c = 41, m\angle A = 77, m\angle B = 13$ **21.** $a = 5, m\angle A = 45, m\angle B = 45$
23. $c = 11.4, m\angle A = 52, m\angle B = 38$ **25.** $m\angle A = 51, a = 60.5, c = 77.9$
27. $m\angle A = 21, m\angle B = 69, b = 31.8$ **29.** $m\angle A = 25, b = 38.6, c = 42.6$

Pages 514–515   Section 15.6   WRITTEN EXERCISES
1. 33 **3.** 13 **5.** 16 **7.** 3 **9.** 48 yards **11.** 76° **13.** 236 feet **15.** 14 meters **17.** 1 meter
19. 43 feet **21.** 923 feet

Pages 518–519   CHAPTER 15   REVIEW
1. right **3.** obtuse **5.** 43° **7.** 164° **9.** 31° **11.** 45° **13.** $m\angle A = 23, m\angle B = 69, m\angle C = 88$
15. $\overline{PQ}$ and $\overline{QR}$ **17.** $\overline{QR}$ **19.** $\overline{RS}$ **21.** $\angle D$ **23.** $\angle R$ **25.** $a = 4.8, e = 10$ **27.** $\frac{3}{7}$ **29.** $\frac{2\sqrt{10}}{7}$
31. $\frac{3\sqrt{10}}{20}$ **33.** 0.9205 **35.** 29° **37.** 84° **39.** 21° **41.** 19°
43. $c = \sqrt{61}, m\angle A = 40, m\angle B = 50$ **45.** $a = 6, m\angle A = 76, m\angle B = 14$ **47.** 19°